Dear West Customer:

West Academic Publishing has changed the look of its American Casebook Series®.

In keeping with our efforts to promote sustainability, we have replaced our former covers with book covers that are more environmentally friendly. Our casebooks will now be covered in a 100% renewable natural fiber. In addition, we have migrated to an ink supplier that favors vegetable-based materials, such as soy.

Using soy inks and natural fibers to print our textbooks reduces VOC emissions. Moreover, our primary paper supplier is certified by the Forest Stewardship Council, which is testament to our commitment to conservation and responsible business management.

The new cover design has migrated from the long-standing brown cover to a contemporary charcoal fabric cover with silver-stamped lettering and black accents. Please know that inside the cover, our books continue to provide the same trusted content that you've come to expect from West.

We've retained the ample margins that you have told us you appreciate in our texts while moving to a new, larger font, improving readability. We hope that you will find these books a pleasing addition to your bookshelf.

Another visible change is that you will no longer see the brand name Thomson West on our print products. With the recent merger of Thomson and Reuters, I am pleased to announce that books published under the West Academic Publishing imprint will once again display the West brand.

It will likely be several years before all of our casebooks are published with the new cover and interior design. We ask for your patience as the new covers are rolled out on new and revised books knowing that behind both the new and old covers, you will find the finest in legal education materials for teaching and learning.

Thank you for your continued patronage of the West brand, which is both rooted in history and forward looking towards future innovations in legal education. We invite you to be a part of our next evolution.

Best regards,

Louis H. Higgins
Editor in Chief, West Academic Publishing

COMPUTER CRIME LAW

Second Edition

. . .

By

Orin S. Kerr

Professor
George Washington University Law School

AMERICAN CASEBOOK SERIES®

WEST®
A Thomson Reuters business

Mat #40807477

To my father, the original Professor Kerr

PREFACE

This book is designed to fill a gap in the modern law school curriculum. Traditional course offerings in criminal law and procedure largely ignore computer crimes. This was understandable a few years ago, when computer crime law was an esoteric specialty. Today, however, computer crime law is emerging as an important area of criminal law practice. A growing number of prosecutors and defense attorneys find themselves working with legal questions unique to digital crimes. The existing curriculum does not cover these topics, except perhaps for brief mention in a "cyberlaw" survey course. This book attempts to correct that situation by offering comprehensive coverage of the new field, assembled together in one place for the first time.

The materials are organized around three questions. First, what conduct involving a computer is prohibited by the criminal law? Second, what legal rules govern the collection of digital evidence in criminal investigations? Third, what powers do state, national, and foreign government shave to investigate and prosecute computer crimes? The first question looks at the substantive law of computer crimes, and is addressed in Chapters 2, 3, and 4. The second question examines the law of criminal procedure for digital evidence, and is covered in Chapters 5 and 6. The third question considers the role of jurisdiction and sovereignty in a world of global online crime, and is addressed in Chapters 7 and 8.

Although the materials are intended primarily for classroom use, my hope is that they will reach a broader audience. First, the materials should be helpful to criminal law practitioners. Computer crime law lacks a treatise that summarizes the field and explains how the pieces fit together. In light of that, I have made special efforts to explain basic doctrine in a way that practitioners should find useful. The law remains complex and sometimes uncertain, and this book makes no effort to pretend otherwise. At the same time, I hope these materials will serve as a reference work for prosecutors and defense attorneys in need of a primer on existing law.

The book also should be a useful resource for scholars. Computer crime law is new and evolving, and many issues remain open. Surprisingly little has been written about the major issues in the field. My hope is that the framework introduced in this book will help encourage and direct future scholarly efforts. To that end, the extensive commentary in these materials attempts both to review existing scholarship and to ask important questions for scholars to answer.

The materials in this book are best suited for classroom use in a one-semester course offered to upper-level law students, either as a three-credit class or a two-credit seminar. I assume that readers have some experience with basic criminal law, such as a first-year law school survey course. On the other hand, I do not assume that readers are familiar with the law of criminal procedure. In addition, I assume that readers have no special background with computers. Students with advanced knowledge of computers or criminal procedure will have a slight advantage understanding a few concepts, but the advantages on the whole are modest. In any event, no such background is assumed or required.

This project began with materials assembled for a computer crime seminar in the Fall 2000 semester, and I have many people to thank for their help during the road to publication. Mark Eckenwiler, Erica Hashimoto, Mike Levy, Paul Ohm, Rick Salgado, and Peter Winn provided feedback on drafts and chapters. GW Law students Noah Falk '05, Kemp Brinson '04, and Tejbir Singh '03 collected materials during in the early stages of the project. Melissa Colangelo helped prepare the 1st edition, and Amy Ramsey helped with the preparation of the second edition. Dean Fred Lawrence provided resources and welcome encouragement. Finally, I am particularly grateful to my former colleagues at the Computer Crime and Intellectual Property Section (CCIPS) of the United States Department of Justice. This book covers issues I first encountered as an attorney at CCIPS from 1998 to 2001, and I could not have written it without the benefit of many illuminating discussions at CCIPS during that period. I am especially indebted to my friend Mark Eckenwiler, who patiently answered countless questions when I was new to the field.

To improve the readability of the materials, I have taken the liberty of removing citations, deleting unrelated portions of opinions, and otherwise streamlining the cases without necessarily indicating that the original material has been altered. Readers in need of greater precision should always consult the original sources.

ORIN S. KERR
WASHINGTON, D.C.

October 2009

ACKNOWLEDGMENTS

Excerpts from the following books and articles appear with the kind of permission of the copyright holders.

Bellia, Patricia L., Defending Cyberproperty, 79 N.Y.U. L. Rev. 2164 (2004). Copyright © 2004 by New York University Law Review. Reprinted by permission.

Berg, Terrence, WWW.WILDWEST.GOV: The Impact of the Internet on State Power to Enforce the Law, B.Y.U. L. Rev. 1305 (2000). Copyright © 2000 Brigham Young University Law Review. Reprinted by permission.

Brenner, Susan W., Need for Reciprocal Enforcement of Warrants and Subpoenas in Cybercrime Cases, 37 Prosecutor 29 (2003). Copyright © 2003 by the author. Reprinted by permission.

Brenner, Susan W. and Frederiksen, Barbara A., Computer Searches And Seizures: Some Unresolved Issues, 8 Mich. Telecomm. & Tech. L. Rev. 39 (2001–2002). Copyright © 2002 by Michigan Telecommunications and Technology Law Review. Reprinted with permission.

Demetriou, Christina; Silke, Andrew; A Criminological Internet "Sting": Experimental Evidence of Illegal and Deviant Visits to a Website Trap, 43 Brit. J. Criminology 213 (2003). Copyright © 2003 by Oxford University Press. Reprinted by permission.

Howell, Beryl A., Real World Problems of Virtual Crime, 7 Yale J. L. & Tech. 103 (2004–2005). Copyright © 2005 by the author. Reprinted by permission.

Ingraham, Donald G., On Charging Computer Crime, 2 Computer/L.J. 429 (1980). Copyright © 1980 by John Marshall Journal of Computer & Information Law. Reprinted by permission.

Katyal, Neal Kumar, Criminal Law In Cyberspace, 149 U. Penn. L. Rev. 1003 (2001). Copyright © 2001 by University of Pennsylvania Law Review. Reprinted by permission.

Kerr, Orin, Cybercrime's Scope: Interpreting "Access" and "Authorization" in Computer Misuse Statutes, 79 N.Y.U. L. Rev. 1596 (2003). Copyright © 2003 by New York University Law Review.

Olivenbaum, Joseph M., Ctrl–Alt–Delete: Rethinking Federal Computer Crime Legislation, 27 Seton Hall L. Rev. 574 (1997).

Rasch, Mark, Ashcroft's Global Internet Power–Grab, available at http://online.securityfocus.com/Columnists/39 (Nov. 25, 2001). Copyright © 2001 by the author. Reprinted by permission.

Robinson, Paul H. and Darley, John M., The Role of Deterrence in the Formulation of Criminal Law Rules: At Its Worst When Doing Its Best, 91 Geo. L.J. 949 (2003). Copyright © 2003 by Georgetown Law Journal. Reprinted by permission of the publisher, Georgetown Law Journal (2003).

Rychlak, Ronald J., Legal Problems with On–Line Gambling, Engage: The Journal of the Federalist Society's Practice Groups Volume 6, Issue 1 (2005). Copyright © 2005 by the Federalist Society. Reprinted by permission from The Federalist Society.

Smith, Bruce, Hacking, Poaching, and Counterattacking: Digital Counterstrikes and the Contours of Self–Help, 1 J.L. Econ. & Pol'y 171 (2005). Copyright © 2005 by the Journal of Law, Economics and Policy. Reprinted by permission.

Solove, Daniel J., Reconstructing Electronic Surveillance Law, 72 Geo. Wash. L. Rev. 1264 (2004). Copyright © 2004 by The George Washington Law Review. Reprinted by permission.

Stevenson, Dru, Entrapment by Numbers, 16 U. Fla. J. L. & Pub. Pol'y 1 (2005). Copyright © 2005 by University of Florida Journal of Law and Public Policy. Reprinted by permission.

Sussmann, Michael A., The Critical Challenges From International High–Tech and Computer–Related Crime at the Millennium, 9 Duke J. Comp. & Int'l L. 451 (1999). Copyright © 1999 by the author. Reprinted by permission.

Winick, Raphael, Searches and Seizures of Computers and Computer Data, 8 Harv. J.L. & Tech. 75 (1994). Copyright © 1994 by the Harvard Journal of Law & Technology. Reprinted by permission.

Summary of Contents

TABLE OF CONTENTS

TABLE OF CASES

The principal cases are in bold type. Cases cited or discussed in the text are in roman type. References are to pages. Cases cited in principal cases and within other quoted materials are not included.

TABLE OF STATUTES

TABLE OF AUTHORITIES

References are to Pages

COMPUTER CRIME LAW
Second Edition

CHAPTER 1

INTRODUCTION

■ ■ ■

What is a computer crime? What topics are covered in a course on computer crime law? And what makes computer crimes different from other types of crimes?

These are three good questions, and this short introductory chapter will provide a few answers. The chapter begins with a brief overview of the field of computer crime law, as well as the coverage of this book. It then offers a hypothetical that introduces the basic differences between the law of traditional physical crimes and the law of modern computer crimes.

A. OVERVIEW OF COMPUTER CRIME LAW

There are two reasons to label criminal conduct a computer crime. First, an individual might use a computer to engage in criminal activity. Second, the evidence needed to prove a criminal case might be stored in computerized form. The law governing use of a computer to commit a crime is *substantive* computer crime law, because it concerns the scope of substantive conduct that has been criminalized. The law governing the collection of computerized evidence is *procedural* computer crime law, because it concerns the legal procedures investigators can use to collect digital evidence in criminal investigations.

Substantive computer crime law divides into two basic categories: computer misuse crimes and traditional crimes. Computer misuse crimes are a new type of criminal offense involving intentional interference with the proper functioning of computers. Examples include hacking offenses, virus crimes, and denial-of-service attacks. These offenses punish interference with the intended operation of computers, either by exceeding a user's privileges (as in the case of a hacking crime) or by denying privileges to others (as in the case of a denial-of-service attack).

As the label implies, traditional crimes are traditional criminal offenses facilitated by computers. These are information crimes with obvious physical-world counterparts. Examples include Internet fraud schemes, online threats, distributing digital images of child pornography, and theft of trade secrets over the Internet.

1

Much like substantive computer crime law, procedural computer crime law consists of two relatively discrete topics. The first topic is the Fourth Amendment, which prohibits unreasonable searches and seizures. In the physical world, the Fourth Amendment creates constitutional limits on where the police can go and what evidence the police can collect in criminal investigations. Procedural computer crime law considers how the Fourth Amendment applies in the case of digital evidence collection. For example, when is retrieving evidence from a computer a "search"? When is it a "seizure"? When is the search or seizure "reasonable"?

The second area of procedural computer crime law is statutory privacy law. Traditional criminal procedure is primarily constitutional law, but much of the law regulating digital evidence collection derives from three privacy statutes: the Wiretap Act, the Pen Register statute, and the Stored Communications Act. As a practical matter, the divide between statutory and constitutional law often tracks the divide between evidence collection from stand-alone computers and computer networks. The law governing computer network surveillance is primarily statutory, and the law regulating retrieval of evidence from stand-alone computers is predominantly constitutional.

Jurisdictional disputes provide the third area of inquiry in computer crime cases. Traditional crimes usually are local. The defendant, the victim, and the evidence often are in the same place, and the charges tend to be brought under state criminal codes wherever the offense occurred. Computer crimes present a very different dynamic. A defendant in one place may connect to a computer in a second place and launch an attack against a computer located in a third place. The victim, the defendant, and the evidence are located in different places—maybe different states, or even different countries. As a result, the law must define for each sovereign what kinds of conduct outside its borders can and should be criminalized, as well as what procedures regulate extraterritorial evidence collection. The global nature of Internet surveillance and terrorism investigations also creates jurisdictional friction between two competing legal regimes, the law of criminal investigations and the law of national security investigations.

The organization of this book tracks these three basic questions. Chapters 2, 3, and 4 address the substantive law of computer crimes; Chapters 5 and 6 cover procedural law; and Chapters 7 and 8 explore jurisdictional issues. In an investigation, the three questions typically present themselves in the reverse order from their order in the book. After a crime has occurred, the first issues are jurisdictional: What agency has jurisdiction over the offense, as well as the ability to collect evidence to prove it in court? The next issues are procedural: What rules must law enforcement officials follow to collect evidence and identify the suspect? The final questions are substantive: What crimes have been committed that the government can charge in court and try to prove beyond a reasonable doubt?

The three questions of computer crime law are really variations on a single theme, and that theme explains why it makes sense to study computer crime law in a separate course. Criminal law and procedure are both highly sensitive to facts, and the facts of computer crimes tend to be different from the facts of equivalent physical crimes. The shift from physical crimes to digital crimes changes the facts of how and where crimes are committed as well as how and where evidence is collected. When the facts change, the law must change with it. Old laws must adapt and new laws must emerge to restore the function of preexisting law.

Of course, the broad policy goals of criminal law and procedure are timeless. Criminal law identifies public conduct that is harmful and culpable, and criminal procedure articulates reasonable limits on police powers. So in a broad sense, nothing is new. But implementing those policy goals with legal rules depends on the facts, and the facts of digital crimes consistently challenge the assumptions of existing substantive, procedural, and jurisdictional laws. We can begin with the old legal rules, but after a while it becomes clear that some of the old rules need to bend and others need replacement. Computer crime law is the search for and study of new answers to timeless questions of criminal law when the facts switch from a physical environment to a digital environment.

B. COMPARING PHYSICAL CRIMES AND COMPUTER CRIMES

Consider the following two hypotheticals. The first is a traditional physical crime; the second is a roughly analogous computer crime. What if anything changes when we switch from the first example to the second example?

Physical Crime

Fred Felony is a resident of Phoenix, Arizona. Fred finds himself low on cash one day, and he decides to rob a jewelry store in downtown Phoenix. Fred drives to the store and parks his car on the street in front of the store. He walks in to the store and browses for a few minutes until the other customers depart.

After the customers leave, Fred pulls out a gun and runs over to the clerk working at the store that day. "This is a stick-up!" he yells to the clerk. "Give me some gold and no one will get hurt!" The clerk is extremely frightened that she will be shot, and she nervously opens one of the cabinets and hands Fred a collection of gold jewelry. Fred grabs the jewelry and stuffs it into a bag he is carrying. He runs out of the store, jumps into his getaway car, and speeds away.

After Fred leaves, the clerk immediately calls the store manager. She reports that the robber took jewelry with a retail value of about $5,000. The clerk is shaken up by the robbery, as well. Over the next month, she takes two weeks of sick leave to recuperate from her traumatic experience. She also has occasional nightmares of being victimized again.

Fred returns home with the loot and hides the jewelry in a closet for safekeeping. After a week, he visits a local Phoenix pawn shop and sells the jewelry for $800 in cash.

Computer Crime

This time, Fred Felony decides to commit his crime using a computer. Fred decides that he will steal credit cards remotely instead of stealing gold jewelry in person. His new target: An e-commerce company located in Los Angeles, California.

Fred logs on to the Internet from his home in Phoenix using an account he holds with a large Internet service provider (ISP) located in Virginia. Although Fred's ultimate goal is to hack into the e-commerce site in Los Angeles, he first loops his attack through an intermediary computer to disguise his tracks. Starting from his Virginia ISP, Fred hacks into a computer in Ottawa, Canada, run by the Canadian tourism bureau. With access to the Canadian computer established, Fred targets the server of the e-commerce site in Los Angeles.

After several tries, Fred eventually guesses the master password correctly and logs in to the server hosted by the Los Angeles e-commerce site. He locates a file containing five hundred credit card numbers and downloads it to his computer at home. Later that day, Fred visits an Internet relay chat room occasionally used to arrange the sale of stolen credit card numbers. He sells the numbers for $800 to a user who goes by the handle "Boris11." Boris11 wires the $800 directly to an online bank account Fred controls. Fred does not know where Boris11 is located, but Boris11's English is quite poor. Fred suspects that Boris11 lives somewhere in Eastern Europe.

The next morning, an employee at the e-commerce site in Los Angeles realizes that the company has been victimized and that the credit card file has been accessed. The company spends $50,000 upgrading its computer security to ensure that no such attacks are successful again. It then notifies its customers and their banks that the breach occurred. Although the banks put a hold on all five hundred accounts, they are too late. By the time the accounts are frozen, an unknown individual in Moscow runs up a tab of $40,000 on several of the stolen accounts.

NOTES AND QUESTIONS

1. *Substantive law.* Compare the physical crime and the computer crime from the standpoint of substantive law. What crimes did Fred commit when he entered the jewelry store with a gun and ordered the store clerk to hand over the jewelry? How serious are those crimes? What harms did Fred cause? Why should the law deter such activity, and why was it morally culpable?

Now turn to the computer crime. How was Fred's conduct different in the second hypothetical? What harms did Fred cause when he committed the computer crime? Why should the law deter such activity, and why was it morally culpable? Did Fred actually "steal" anything, and does it matter? Is the computer crime fundamentally the same as the physical crime, or is it different?

Does punishing the computer crime require new laws, or are the traditional laws applicable in the case of the physical crime also sufficient to punish the computer crime? Which offense should be punished more severely: the physical crime or the computer crime? What punishment is appropriate for each?

2.   *Procedural law*. Now compare the two crimes from the perspective of investigatory procedure. Imagine that you are a police officer in Phoenix, Arizona, and you are called to the jewelry store to investigate the crime just hours after it occurred. You want to collect evidence, identify a suspect, and prove your case beyond a reasonable doubt in court. What evidence can you collect, and how do you collect it? Who do you interview? What questions do you ask? What kind of evidence are you likely to find? How would you plan to investigate the case and prove it beyond a reasonable doubt in court?

Again, switch to the computer crime. Now imagine that you are a Los Angeles police officer called by the e-commerce company after they discover that they have been hacked and the file accessed without permission. What evidence do you collect, and how do you collect it? Who do you interview? What questions do you ask? What kind of evidence are you likely to find? How might you plan to investigate the case and trace the crime back to the wrongdoer?

What legal rules should regulate the steps you would take to investigate the physical crime? What rules should regulate the steps needed to investigate the computer crime? Are they the same or are they different?

3.   As you ponder these questions, it may help to know a little bit about how computer intrusion investigations generally work. Most investigations follow two basic steps: tracing communications over the Internet back to their source, and then recovering and analyzing the computer used in the offense.

Investigators attempt to track communications to their source by collecting network logs. Computer networks normally are run by a system administrator, or "sysadmin" for short, who is responsible for keeping the computer running and for troubleshooting difficulties. System administrators ordinarily set their computers to generate records known as logs that record how the network was used. For example, a server might be configured to record the incoming Internet Protocol (IP) addresses and times of every attempt to log in to an account on the server. (IP addresses are numerical addresses that are akin to Internet phone numbers. Every user connected to the Internet is assigned an IP address, and the address is used to send information to the user.) In the case of an e-commerce site, it's a good bet that the network system administrator will have configured the network to generate access logs that recorded the time, IP address, and any other relevant information about each login into the network.

To trace back the crime, the investigators normally must go step by step, hop by hop, tracing the chain of communications from server to server. This is true because the IP addresses stored in a log only record the most immediate hop back in the chain of communications. If the e-commerce site in Los Angeles kept logs of the intrusion, those logs will show the attack coming from the Canadian tourism bureau in Ottawa, not Fred in Phoenix. At each stage investigators must try to collect evidence of the prior hop until they trace the attack back to the wrongdoer.

Most computer hacking investigations end with the seizure and subsequent search of the suspect's personal computer. The reason is simple: Because there are no eyewitnesses to most computer crimes, proving a case beyond a reasonable doubt usually requires direct evidence. The discovery of stolen files or other evidence on a suspect's personal computer can provide powerful evidence that the computer owner was responsible for the offense (and if no such evidence exists, can help exonerate the suspect). Personal computers often keep very detailed records of how and when they have been used, and those records can provide very powerful evidence in court.

What legal rules should regulate these steps of computer crime investigations? Should investigators need a search warrant or other authorization to collect logs from system administrators? Should they need a warrant or other authorization to search the suspect's computer for evidence? What rules should govern the search of the computer?

4. *Jurisdictional issues.* Finally, let's compare the physical crime and the computer crime from the standpoint of jurisdiction. What agency should investigate the jewelry store robbery? Where is the evidence of the crime located? If Fred is caught and prosecuted, what court will bring charges? Is the physical crime a case for state or federal investigators?

Now consider the computer crime. You are a Los Angeles police officer called to investigate the crime, and the system administrator tells you that his logs indicate the attack came from Ottawa, Canada. Does the Los Angeles Police Department have any powers to collect evidence in Canada? For that matter, if you can trace the attack back to the ISP in Virginia, do you have authority to collect evidence in Virginia? Imagine you decide to pass up the case to the Federal Bureau of Investigation field office in Los Angeles. Can they collect evidence in Canada? How can they obtain the records needed to trace the crime?

Imagine the FBI successfully traces the attack through the Canadian site and the Virginia ISP back to Fred Felony's home in Arizona. Can Fred Felony be charged with a violation of California law? Arizona law? Federal law? Should he be prosecuted in Phoenix? Los Angeles? What if the Canadian authorities want to bring Fred Felony to Ottawa to face charges for hacking into the Canadian tourism bureau site. Can Fred be extradited to Canada? If the Canadian authorities request the FBI's assistance in gathering evidence to charge Fred Felony in Canada, does the FBI have an obligation to provide that assistance?

5. *The road ahead.* Keep these questions in mind as you study the chapters ahead. The materials will start with substantive law, turn next to procedural law, and finish with jurisdictional issues. By the end of the book, you will be able to answer all of these questions for any computer-related crime.

CHAPTER 2

COMPUTER MISUSE CRIMES

■ ■ ■

Computer misuse crimes are offenses involving interference with the proper functioning of computers. Every computer is programmed to perform a particular set of functions for a particular set of users. Interfering with those functions can be a culpable act that causes significant harm.

Computer misuse can occur in two distinct ways. First, a user might exceed his privileges on a computer. For example, a person might hack into a remote network and view confidential files he is not supposed to see. Second, a person might deny others their privileges to use a computer. For example, a person might launch a denial-of-service attack that incapacitates a target network. Legitimate users will try to use the network but find that they cannot. These two types of computer misuse are distinct, but represent two sides of the same coin. In the first, the user exceeds his own privileges; in the second, the user denies privileges to others.

This chapter explores the law of computer misuse. It begins with a policy question: Should computer misuse be a crime, and if so, when? The materials then consider whether traditional criminal laws can address computer misuse, or whether new statutes are needed. The remaining parts of the chapter study the three most common types of computer misuse statutes: unauthorized access statutes, computer fraud statutes, and computer damage statutes.

A. WHY PUNISH COMPUTER MISUSE?

Every first-year law student learns that there are two major reasons why wrongful acts are punished. The first reason is utilitarian. Utilitarians believe that punishment should be imposed because it can decrease the amount of crime in the future. For example, criminal punishment can deter harmful conduct: the prospect of punishment can encourage a person not to commit a criminal act. Punishment also can prevent crime by incapacitating or rehabilitating a defendant. *See generally* Herbert L. Packer, The Limits of the Criminal Sanction 39–61 (1968).

The second goal of criminal punishment is retribution. Retributivists believe that punishment should be imposed to ensure that individuals receive their just deserts. Some retributivists believe that punishment reflects society's revenge against the wrongdoer; from this perspective, punishment is an "eye for an eye." Others contend that punishment restores the moral order by denying the wrongdoer's claim to superiority. The common theme of retributive approaches to punishment is that they look back at the wrongfulness of the defendant's act rather than look forward at the effect punishment will have on future criminal activity.

Do these theories justify punishment for computer misuse? Consider the following two problems.

PROBLEM 1

Bryan Smith is a 17 year-old high school senior living in Lincoln, Nebraska. His father is a small businessman, and his mother teaches second grade at a local public school. Bryan gets good grades, especially in math and science, and he hopes to attend college next fall at either Georgia Tech or MIT to study computer science. Bryan also has a strong interest in computer programming. He learned the rudiments of the UNIX operating system, and he often visits chat rooms devoted to computer programming and Internet security.

In the last year, Bryan's interests in programming led him to experiment with computer hacking. Using the hacker pseudonym "KillerBee," Bryan started using prepared programs known as "scripts" to test the security of different sites on the Internet. He would usually test the site for obvious security flaws, and if the site had such a flaw, he would try to gain access to its central server. Once inside the network, he would take a quick look around, and then send a message from KillerBee to the network's system administrator explaining that he had broken in to the network using a widely known vulnerability and that the system administrator needed to pay better attention to network security. On occasion, in an effort to impress his girlfriend, Bryan would try to replace the site's web page with a large picture of a skull and a message saying "This Site Has Been Hacked by Killerbee! Sarah Is #1!" So far, Bryan has successfully placed this message on about a half-dozen websites, including those of a community college in Bangor, Maine; the Alabama Public Service Commission; and a small e-commerce company based in Miami, Florida.

Although Bryan realizes that the site owners probably don't appreciate his activities, Bryan believes that his hacking is justifiable. Bryan reasons that his harmless pranks will encourage negligent system administrators to spend the time and money they will need to defend their sites against more malicious attacks. In less altruistic moments, Bryan will also admit that "KillerBee" thinks hacking is lots of fun: acting the part of a fearless online adventurer provides a much-needed escape from the tedium and stress of high school. Bryan also expects that as his hacking skills advance, he may someday be able to obtain work as an Internet security consultant. He figures that hacking today will develop the computer skills he will need in the future to help make the Internet safer (and to be paid handsomely for it).

Unsurprisingly, the network system administrators who are responsible for maintaining security at the computers targeted by KillerBee have a different take on Bryan's conduct. From their perspective, KillerBee's hacking is a nuisance, and an expensive nuisance at that. For example, in response to his activities, the e-commerce company hired security consultants who charged the company $100,000 just to review the contents of the company's servers, confirm that KillerBee had not done any other damage, and patch the vulnerability that had allowed KillerBee to break in. The company also suffered from lost business when the site was down for a few hours, and took a public relations hit among their vendors from being offline. Several of KillerBee's targets also concluded that they had to spend thousands of dollars to improve their security: two of them invested over $80,000 each in security products and testing to thwart hackers in the future.

PROBLEM 2

Sarah Jones works as a network system administrator at a community hospital in Washington, D.C. Sarah's job, which she has held for two years, is to maintain the hospital's computer network. The hospital relies heavily on the network, using it to store and process patient medical records, employee records, supply records, and all of the hospital's financial records. As the system administrator, Sarah has "root" access to the network. This means that Sarah has a master account that allows her to access and modify any file within the network.

One afternoon while at work, Sarah decides to help out her friend Beth. Beth recently started a company that provides direct advertising for pharmaceutical companies. Beth's company targets individual patients in need of medical care and sends them advertisements for pharmaceutical products that relate to their medical problems. Sarah figures that she can help Beth by acquiring the names and mailing addresses of some of the hospital's patients, along with a short description of their medical conditions, and sending them on to Beth.

Sarah logs on to the network by entering her username, "sjones," and her password, "freekevin." She then bypasses the usual warning banner that appears on her monitor. The banner states: "WARNING: This network is authorized for official use only." Sarah accesses the portion of the computer where patient medical records are stored. Sarah starts scanning through the records for names and addresses. When she realizes that it will take several hours to obtain the names and addresses manually, she creates an automated program that scans the network's servers and looks for key words that signal patient medical records. Sarah designs the program to collect the records automatically and e-mail the file directly to Beth. Sarah also installs a surveillance tool called a "sniffer" that will read any new medical record as it is entered into the network and automatically e-mail it to Beth.

Beth is quite surprised when she accesses her e-mail the next day and finds a file from Sarah containing thousands of patient records. The records include patient names, addresses, and medical diagnoses along with lists of currently prescribed medications. Uncertain of the ethics and legality of using the list, Beth calls Sarah and asks her not to send any additional records.

Sarah apologizes, and explains that she was only trying to help Beth with her new company. Beth decides to keep her copy of the list just in case she needs it, although she feels confident that she will never use or share it.

NOTES AND QUESTIONS

1. Should Bryan Smith's conduct be a crime? Should Sarah Jones's conduct be a crime? What punishment is appropriate for Bryan Smith? For Sarah Jones?

2. *The Hacker Ethic.* In the early days of computers in the late 1950s and early 1960s, a culture developed among some users that encouraged creative experimentation. In his book *Hackers*, Steven Levy focuses on the members of a student club at the Massachusetts Institute of Technology called the Tech Model Railroad Club. Members spent a great deal of time working on an early computer called the TX–0, and developed a number of principles that later coalesced into the "Hacker Ethic."

The Hacker Ethic reflects an open and free approach to using and exploring computers. One principle is that "access to computers—and anything which might teach you something about the way the world works—should be unlimited and total." Another related principle teaches that "all information should be free." The basic idea is that any computer user should have a right to tinker with and improve any computer, and that rules governing access should not be followed. *See* Steven Levy, Hackers 24–28 (1984). The term "hackers" was originally used in this sense to refer to skilled and enthusiastic computer programmers with a deep understanding of how computers work. Over time, however, the term has become synonymous with those who commit acts of unauthorized access to computers. *See* Pekka Himanen, The Hacker Ethic, at vii–ix (2001).

Does the hacker ethic help answer when computer misuse should be criminalized? Consider the argument that misuse consistent with the hacker ethic can help improve security. Hackers can identify security flaws and create patches, or inform others that the flaws exist. In addition, a teenager who becomes skilled at exploiting today's computers may become tomorrow's computer security professional tasked with protecting important networks. If hackers need to explore computers to improve them, should the law ensure that such exploration is possible? Is the notion that hacking is a form of "misuse" itself misguided?

Alternatively, is the hacker ethic a juvenile mythology that simply attempts to excuse harmful activity? Consider the teaching that "information should be free." Do you think that the medical records viewed by Sarah Jones should be free? Should we approve of her effort to share the records with her friend Beth as an attempt to "free" the medical records? Can the hacker ethic coexist with widely-held beliefs in the value of privacy?

3. *Responsibility for the consequences of poor computer security.* Every computer network is run by a system administrator who is tasked with keeping the network operating smoothly, responding to problems, setting up new accounts, and performing other routine network maintenance tasks. System administrators are usually the first to notice and respond to network

intrusions. Consider this imaginary (but representative) exchange of views between a hacker and a system administrator:

Hacker: System administrators should blame themselves if their networks are vulnerable. Many system administrators pay little or no attention to security, and their negligence is the true cause of most of the financial losses that result from so-called "computer crime." Hackers raise the level of network security by testing networks, offering solutions to existing vulnerabilities, and making sure that security remains a priority. Taking steps to understand a network shouldn't be a crime. Instead, it should be recognized as a public service.

System Administrator: Your argument blames the victim for being victimized. We don't blame homeowners when their houses are burglarized just because they left weak locks on their front doors; instead, we blame the burglars. Also, it's hard to see why we should thank hackers for forcing us to spend money on network security, given that it is the hackers themselves we are trying to keep out. Here's an analogy: people who live in high-crime neighborhoods may have several locks on their doors and steel bars on their windows, but they don't thank the local burglars for encouraging them to raise the level of security in their homes. All hacking without the target's consent should be criminalized.

Hacker: You're missing the point. Unlike homes, computers are inherently open. Any computer attached to the Internet can be accessed by millions of people around the world at any moment. The question is not *whether* a computer will be compromised, but rather *when* and *how*. In this environment, network operators should be responsible for network security, and should recognize that hackers play a vital role in helping system administrators secure their networks against the *real* criminals.

System Administrator: No, you're the one who is missing the point. This is my network, and you don't have a right to break in to it. If you want to help me by exposing my network's vulnerabilities, you can just ask me for permission. If I think you can help me, I will let you try to hack in. But that's for me to decide, not you.

Hacker: You are mired in the old way of thinking. Computers are different, and the law needs to recognize that.

Who has the stronger argument? If you think the hacker's argument is stronger, does it follow that "state and federal governments should immediately decriminalize all forms of non-malicious hacking?" Michael Lee, et. al., Comment, *Electronic Commerce, Hackers, and the Search for Legitimacy: A Regulatory Proposal*, 14 Berkeley Tech. L.J. 839, 882 (1999). If so, how would you articulate the difference between malicious hacking and non-malicious hacking?

4. *Financial loss from computer misuse.* Estimates of the losses caused by computer crime suggest that they are quite high. One FBI estimate put the cost of computer crimes in 2004 at about $400 billion. *See* McAfee Virtual Technology Report 5 (2005). Even individual computer misuse crimes can be quite costly. For example, the "I Love You" virus that spread around the world in 2000 has been estimated to have caused as much as $10 billion in

loss. *See* Patricia L. Bellia, *Chasing Bits Across Borders*, 2001 U. Chi. Legal F. 35, 36. In 2005, 700 computer security practitioners responding to a joint CSI/FBI survey collectively reported about $130 million in losses arising from computer misuse crimes in the previous year. *See* 2005 CSI/FBI Computer Crime and Security Survey (2005).

The figures are impressive. But are they accurate? Most estimates of loss tend to be fairly rough, as they are derived primarily from anecdotal evidence and extrapolation. Further, the estimates generally rely on businesses and companies to self-report how much loss they suffered from a computer crime. Skeptics of high loss figures point to the institutional incentives of those who make such estimates. For example, some estimates are produced by consulting firms that offer a range of products and services to potential victims of computer misuse. Other estimates are produced by law enforcement agencies that may then use these figures to argue for larger budgets to address computer-related crime. *See* Elinor Abreu, *Net Crime Does Pay—For Cops*, The Industry Standard, Feb. 21, 2000. In light of these concerns, do you trust the loss figures reported in such studies?

If you were tasked with designing a survey to estimate the losses caused by computer crime, how would you do it? Is it possible to measure accurately the loss caused by computer crimes?

5. *Culpability and intent to profit.* Some hackers abide by the hacker ethic, and hack for the intellectual excitement or the thrill. Others hack for profit. Some attempt to hack into e-commerce sites to collect credit card numbers that can be sold later in anonymous Internet chat rooms. Others gain unauthorized access to distribute spam anonymously for a fee, or to look for an advantage over business competitors. According to some reports, Russian organized crime groups are actively involved in computer hacking. The Russian mafia hires hackers both to steal credit card numbers and to break into victim sites and demand expensive "consulting fees" in exchange for not doing significant damage. Others are hired to break into computers and find trade secrets that can be sold to competitors or outsiders. *See, e.g.,* Laura Lorek, *Russian Mafia Net Threat*, Eweek.com, July 16, 2001.

Does computer misuse deserve greater punishment when undertaken for profit? On one hand, perhaps computer misuse combined with a profit motive is likely to be more harmful because intent to profit generally suggests a lack of concern for other possible harms or the likelihood the conduct will be repeated. On the other hand, some of the harms caused by computer misuse are unintentional byproducts of otherwise intentional activity. The harm may have no direct link to the intent to profit. For example, imagine a person hacks into a computer for profit, and accidentally causes a great deal of damage to the server. Is that hacking really more culpable by virtue of the intent to profit?

6. *Insiders vs. outsiders.* Should "insiders" to a computer system (that is, those with accounts and certain access rights) be treated differently than "outsiders" to the system (who have no access rights, or only very limited access rights)? Compare the conduct of Bryan Smith from Problem 1 with that of Sarah Jones from Problem 2. Did Sarah Jones really misuse the hospital's computers? Unlike Smith, Jones did not have to "break in" to the

network: her account gave her root access, which entitled her to look at any file in the system. Is Sarah Jones's interference with the hospital computer different from Bryan Smith's interference with the computer he hacked? In what way? Does it matter that Smith broke in to the computer while Jones did not?

Consider the effect of the hospital policy stating that the network was "authorized for official use only." Is using a network for unauthorized purposes as culpable as breaking in to that network? Does it matter whether the restriction on network use is reasonable or unreasonable? Imagine that an ISP's Terms of Service state that subscribers are not authorized to access the ISP to engage in conduct that "may be considered offensive." A user accesses the ISP and uses the ISP to send an offensive e-mail. Has that user engaged in computer misuse? Should the user be held criminally liable for violating the ISP's Terms of Service?

B.   PROPERTY CRIMES AS A RESPONSE TO COMPUTER MISUSE

Assuming computer misuse should be criminalized, at least in some circumstances, the next question becomes *how* to criminalize it. Does the problem of computer misuse require new criminal laws? Or can traditional criminal laws handle these new crimes? This section considers whether traditional property crime laws can address the problem of computer misuse, or, alternatively, whether computer misuse requires the passage of new laws.

The enormous potential harms of computer misuse first became apparent in the early 1970s.[1] At that time, no legislature had enacted a computer crime statute. When prosecutors considered bringing criminal charges for computer misuse, they naturally turned to existing property crime laws, such as laws prohibiting trespass, burglary, and theft. The fit proved a poor one, however. In the case of trespass and burglary, the scope of existing laws plainly did not extend to computer misuse. In the case of theft, the law could be stretched to apply, but required judicial sleight of hand and resort to an unpredictable legal fiction.

Consider the crimes of trespass and burglary, both predominantly state offenses. Trespass crimes generally punish knowing entrance or presence on another person's property despite notice that the property owner forbids it. At common law, burglary prohibited "breaking and entering" into a building without authorization and with the intent to commit a crime therein. Modern statutes tend to focus more on entering a building or occupied structure without license or privilege, combined with intent to commit a crime inside. Like trespass crimes, burglary focuses on the entry onto property without permission. Unlike trespass, however, burglary requires the intent to commit a crime, and usually carries relatively stiff criminal penalties.

---

1.   This material is adapted from Orin S. Kerr, *Cybercrime's Scope: Interpreting "Access" and "Authorization" in Computer Misuse Statutes*, 78 N.Y.U. L. Rev. 1596, 1605–10 (2003).

At first blush, trespass and burglary law may appear to provide a logical starting point for applying property crimes to punish and deter computer misuse. It has been noted widely that many acts of computer misuse resemble trespasses. A user can exceed her privileges on a computer much like a trespasser can exceed her privileges on physical land. Computer hacking, for example, is akin to a trespass in cyberspace. Similarly, a hacker may break into a computer with intent to do mischief much like a burglar might break into a house with the same intent.

Despite the common principles, it seems that criminal trespass and burglary statutes have never been used to prosecute computer misuse. The primary reason is that both trespass and burglary statutes remain closely tied to the physical world rather than a virtual one. For example, trespass statutes generally require that part of the defendant's person pass the line of the threshold of the property trespassed. The same goes for burglary offenses. Criminal trespass and burglary statutes focus narrowly on presence of a human body on physical land, not interference with property rights more generally. This limited scope makes it difficult to apply trespass or burglary statutes to computer misuse; because the user does not physically enter the target computer, the existing statutes do not apply. Indeed, it appears that no criminal prosecution has ever used burglary or general criminal trespass statutes to prosecute computer misuse.

In contrast with burglary and trespass, the crime of theft has been used often to prosecute computer misuse. Theft crimes consist of a family of related offenses, including larceny, embezzlement, conversion, fraud, and false pretenses. Today, most states have consolidated these various crimes into a single theft statute, which prohibits larceny, embezzlement, and false pretenses together. Federal theft crimes are more limited in scope, reflecting the constitutional limits of federal criminal law. The mail fraud and wire fraud statutes are the broadest federal theft offenses; they prohibit many interstate fraudulent schemes to obtain property. These statutes make it illegal to send an interstate wire, radio, or television communication, or to place a stolen item in the U.S. mail or with an interstate mail carrier, to help further a fraudulent scheme designed to obtain money or property.

Efforts to prosecute computer misuse as theft crimes generally follow a fairly simple rationale. By upsetting intended privileges relating to a computer, the thinking goes, the defendant committed a theft—the taking of property belonging to another. This rationale may seem plausible at first blush, but it creates serious difficulties defining a property interest and then identifying when that property has been taken. Theft statutes presume the existence of an identifiable piece of property, some clearly-defined "thing," that when taken deprives the owner of its bounty. We can understand this easily in the case of tangible property. For example, if someone steals my bicycle, it is easy to identify the property stolen (the bicycle) and to tell whether or not I have been deprived of it (either I have the bicycle or I don't).

In the case of computer misuse, however, identifying a property interest and then concluding that it was taken can require considerable creativity.

UNITED STATES v. SEIDLITZ

United States Court of Appeals for the Fourth Circuit, 1978.
589 F.2d 152.

Field, Senior Circuit Judge.

Bertram Seidlitz appeals from his conviction on two counts of fraud by wire in violation of 18 U.S.C. § 1343.[1] As grounds for reversal, he urges that * * * the prosecution failed to establish certain material elements of the crime. Although advanced in a somewhat novel factual context, we find appellant's contentions to be without merit.

On January 1, 1975, defendant Seidlitz assumed the position of Deputy Project Director for Optimum Systems, Inc. (OSI), a computer service company which was under contract to install, maintain, and operate a computer facility at Rockville, Maryland, for use by the Federal Energy Administration (FEA). Under the arrangement between OSI and FEA, persons working for FEA in various parts of the country could use key boards at communications terminals in their offices to send instructions over telephone circuits to the large computers in Rockville, and the computers' responses would be returned and reflected on a CRT (cathode ray tube) terminal which is a typewriter-like device with a keyboard and display screen similar to a television screen upon which the information is displayed as it is sent and received.[2] Mr. Seidlitz helped to prepare the software which was installed at the Rockville facility as part of the project, and he was also responsible for the security of the central computer system. During his tenure, he had full access to the computers and to a software system known as "WYLBUR" which resided within them. In June, 1975, Seidlitz resigned this job and returned to work at his own computer firm in Alexandria, Virginia.

William Coakley, a computer specialist employed by FEA, was assigned temporarily to the OSI facility. On December 30, 1975, in an

---

1. The federal wire fraud statute, 18 U.S.C. § 1343, provides:

Whoever, having devised or intending to devise any scheme or artifice to defraud, or for obtaining money or property by means of false or fraudulent pretenses, representations, or promises, transmits or causes to be transmitted by means of wire, radio, or television communication in interstate or foreign commerce, any writings, signs, signals, pictures, or sounds for the purpose of executing such scheme or artifice, shall be fined not more than $1,000 or imprisoned not more than five years, or both.

2. A remote user would dial on an ordinary telephone one of the several unpublished telephone numbers to which OSI subscribed and which were assigned to the computers. He would then connect the telephone to his terminal so that messages could be relayed between the terminal and the computers in the form of signals traveling over the telephone line. Because any of a number of commercially available terminal units could accomplish such a link to the computers, the user, as a security precaution, had to enter on his terminal keyboard a special access code before he would be permitted full use of the system. The code contained, among other things, the user's personal initials, which were to be invalidated when he left OSI or FEA. This "access code" would be communicated to the central computers which, if they recognized the code as belonging to an authorized user, would proceed to perform the work the individual sent along.

attempt to locate a friend who might be using the OSI system, he had the computer display the initials of everyone who was then using the WYL-BUR software. Among the initials displayed by the computer were those of his supervisor, who was standing nearby and who was not using the computer. Suspicious that an unauthorized "intruder" might be using these initials in order to gain access to the system, Coakley asked Mr. Ewing, an OSI employee, if Ewing could determine what was happening. He also asked Mr. Wack, an OSI supervisor, if he (Wack) could determine whether the mysterious user was at a remote terminal or at one of the terminals within the OSI complex which were directly wired to the computer and did not employ telephone circuits. Ewing instructed the computer to display for him the data it was about to transmit to the possible intruder, and it proved to be a portion of the "source code" of the WYLBUR software system. Using other data provided by the computer, Wack concluded that the connection was by telephone from outside the complex. At his request, the telephone company manually traced the call to the Alexandria office of the defendant.[7] Wack was told that the trace was successful, but the telephone company informed him that it could not divulge the results of the trace except in response to a legal subpoena.

The following day, OSI activated a special feature of the WYLBUR system known as the "Milten Spy Function," which automatically record-ed, after they had been received by the machinery at Rockville, any requests made of the computer by the intruder. The "spy" also recorded, before they were sent out to the intruder over the telephone lines, the computer's responses to such requests. Mr. Wack again asked the tele-phone company to trace the line when it was suspected that the unautho-rized person, employing the same initials, was using the computer to receive portions of the WYLBUR source code. This manual trace on December 31 led once more to the defendant's office in Virginia, although OSI was not so informed.

Advised by OSI of the events of December 30 and 31, the FBI on January 3, 1976, secured, but did not then execute, a warrant to search the defendant's Alexandria office. At the FBI's suggestion, the telephone company conducted two additional manual traces when alerted to incom-ing calls by OSI, but in each instance the calls were terminated before the traces had progressed beyond the telephone company's office in Lanham, Maryland, which served 10,000 subscribers. The phone company then installed "originating accounting identification equipment" in the Lan-ham office, the function of which was to automatically and quickly ascertain, without intercepting the contents of any communication, the telephone number of any of the 10,000 area telephones from which any subsequent calls to the OSI computers originated. Two such calls were made on the morning of January 9, and the equipment attributed both of them to a phone at the defendant's Lanham residence. That afternoon,

---

7. A manual trace is accomplished without listening in on the line or breaking into the conversation. It entails a physical tracing of the telephone circuitry backward through the various switching points from the equipment which receives the call.

the FBI executed the warrant to search Seidlitz' Alexandria office, seizing, among other items, a copy of the user's guide to the OSI system and some 40 rolls of computer paper upon which were printed the WYLBUR source code. A warrant was then issued to search the Seidlitz residence in Lanham, where officers found a portable communications terminal which contained a teleprinter for receiving written messages from the computer, as well as a notebook containing information relating to access codes previously assigned to authorized users of the OSI computers.

The indictment handed down on February 3, 1976, charged that the defendant had, on December 30 and 31, transmitted telephone calls in interstate commerce as part of a scheme to defraud OSI of property consisting of information from the computer system. A motion to suppress the evidence seized from the office and the residence was considered at a hearing on April 30, after which the district judge rendered an oral opinion rejecting the defendant's argument that the searches were invalidated by the use of illegal electronic surveillance to obtain the information contained in the affidavits supporting the warrants.

Over defense objection, much of the challenged evidence was admitted at trial, and the telephone traces, as well as the operation of the "Milten Spy," were described to the jury. In the face of this evidence, the defendant conceded that he had retrieved the information from the computers, but claimed to have acted only out of concern for the security of the OSI system. In negation of fraudulent intent, Seidlitz testified that he acquired the data with the sole intention of presenting the printouts to OSI officials to prove to them that the steps taken to prevent unauthorized use of the computers were inadequate. Additionally, it was his position at trial that the WYLBUR software was not a trade secret or other property interest of OSI sufficient to qualify as "property" within the meaning of the wire fraud statute. On appeal he * * * argues that the evidence before the jury was insufficient to establish either his fraudulent intent or that WYLBUR constituted "property."

Viewed in the light most favorable to the government, there was sufficient evidence from which the jury could find that the WYLBUR system was "property" as defined in the instruction given by the trial judge which is not contested on appeal. Even though software systems similar to OSI's WYLBUR were in use at non-OSI facilities, the evidence that OSI invested substantial sums to modify the system to suit its peculiar needs, that OSI enjoyed a multi-million dollar competitive advantage because of WYLBUR, and that OSI took steps to prevent persons other than clients and employees from using the system permitted a finding that the pilfered data was the property of OSI and not, as the defendant contends, property in the public domain subject to appropriation by persons such as himself. In a similar vein, the defendant disputes the sufficiency of the evidence to establish fraudulent intent, but in essence his argument is only that he feels the jury should not have discredited his own explanation of the purpose for which he acquired the WYLBUR data. It is of no consequence that Seidlitz was not shown by the government to have used the data retrieved from the OSI computers in his own business or to have attempted to sell it to others, and the circumstantial evidence in this case is ample to support a finding of the requisite intent.

NOTES AND QUESTIONS

1. WYLBUR was a text-editing program that allowed users to direct computers to perform particular tasks. In what sense was the WYLBUR software "property?" Scholars and judges have struggled to agree upon a simple definition of property. Consider the following definitions:

A. "That is property to which the following label can be attached. To the world: Keep off X unless you have my permission, which I may grant or withhold. Signed: private citizen. Endorsed: the state." Felix S. Cohen, *Dialogue on Private Property*, 9 Rutgers L. Rev. 357, 374 (1954).

B. "Give someone the right to exclude others from a valued resource, i.e., a resource that is scarce relative to the human demand for it, and you give them property. Deny someone the exclusion right and they do not have property." Thomas W. Merrill, Essay, *Property and the Right to Exclude*, 77 Neb. L. Rev. 730, 730 (1998).

C. "[Property] consists in the free use, enjoyment, and disposal of all his acquisitions, without any control or diminution, save only by the laws of the land." 1 William Blackstone, Commentaries on the Laws of England *138.

D. "[Property is] a euphonious collection of letters which serves as a general term for the miscellany of equities that persons hold in the commonwealth." Walter Hamilton, 11 Encyclopedia of the Social Sciences 528 (1937).

Under which of these definitions is the WYLBUR software property?

2. In Carpenter v. United States, 484 U.S. 19 (1987), an influential Wall Street Journal columnist conspired with others to buy and sell stocks in anticipation of the effect his newspaper column "Heard on the Street" would have on the stock prices of companies he discussed. The government charged the columnist and his co-conspirators with mail fraud and wire fraud on the theory that the conspiracy had defrauded the Wall Street Journal of its property. According to the government, the "property" was the confidential information scheduled to appear in the newspaper. The Supreme Court agreed and affirmed the convictions:

Here, the object of the scheme was to take the Journal's confidential business information–the publication schedule and contents of the "Heard" column–and its intangible nature does not make it any less "property" protected by the mail and wire fraud statutes. * * *

Both courts below expressly referred to the Journal's interest in the confidentiality of the contents and timing of the "Heard" column as a property right, and we agree with that conclusion. Confidential business information has long been recognized as property. Confidential information acquired or compiled by a corporation in the course and conduct of its business is a species of property to which the corporation has the exclusive right and benefit, and which a court of equity will protect through the injunctive process or other appropriate remedy. The Journal had a property right in keeping confidential and making exclusive use, prior to publication, of the schedule and contents of the "Heard" column.

Id. at 25–26.

Why should confidential business information be considered property for the purposes of criminal fraud statutes? Does the information's market value automatically mean that it should be treated as property? Should confidential information that has no market value also be treated as property? What about publicly-known information? Is all information property?

For an argument that *Carpenter* reflects an overly broad conception of property that permits theft prosecutions for an improperly wide range of conduct, see John C. Coffee, Jr., Hush!: *The Criminal Status of Confidential Information After* McNally *and* Carpenter *and the Enduring Problem of Overcriminalization*, 26 Am. Crim. L. Rev. 121, 130–40 (1988).

3. Whatever conceptual problems may be raised by labeling information as property for the purpose of property crime statutes, courts have done so in a wide range of cases involving computers. Courts have concluded that computer usage was property, *see* United States v. Collins, 56 F.3d 1416, 1420 (D.C. Cir. 1995), that the data stored in a computer counted as property, *see* United States v. Girard, 601 F.2d 69, 71 (2d Cir. 1979), and even that the password that controlled access to a computer account was property, *see* People v. Johnson, 560 N.Y.S.2d 238, 241, 243–44 (Crim. Ct. 1990).

4. Conviction under the federal wire fraud statute requires intent to defraud, which requires knowing conduct together with intent to deceive. *See* United States v. Keller, 14 F.3d 1051, 1056 (5th Cir. 1994). Who did Seidlitz deceive when he logged on to the OSI computer and instructed the computer to send him data? One answer might be the OSI computer itself: Seidlitz identified himself to the computer as William Coakley's supervisor, tricking the computer into giving him access. But is it possible to deceive a machine? Imagine that a car thief picks the lock on a car door, and then steals the car. Would the thief be guilty of fraud, on the theory that he tricked the car lock into opening by convincing the lock that he was the car's rightful owner?

STATE v. McGRAW

Supreme Court of Indiana, 1985.
480 N.E.2d 552.

PRENTICE, JUSTICE.

Defendant was charged with nine counts of theft under Ind. Code § 35–43–4–2, by information alleging that he knowingly exerted "unauthorized control over the property of the City of Indianapolis, Indiana, to-wit: the use of computers and computer services with intent to deprive the City of Indianapolis." He was convicted upon two counts, following a trial by jury. The trial court, thereafter, granted his renewed motion to dismiss, citing, among other grounds, the insufficiency of the evidence. The Court of Appeals reversed the trial court and ordered the verdicts reinstated.

Defendant was employed by the City of Indianapolis, as a computer operator. The City leased computer services on a fixed charge or flat rate basis, hence the expense to it was not varied by the extent to which it was used. Defendant was provided with a terminal at his desk and was assigned a portion of the computer's information storage capacity, called a "private library," for his utilization in performing his duties. No other employees were authorized to use his terminal or his library.

Defendant became involved in a private sales venture and began soliciting his co-workers and using a small portion of his assigned library to maintain records associated with the venture. He was reprimanded several times for selling his products in the office and on "office time," and he was eventually discharged for unsatisfactory job performance and for continuing his personal business activities during office hours.

Defendant, at the time of his being hired by the City, received a handbook, as do all new employees, which discloses the general prohibition against the unauthorized use of city property. Other city employees sometimes used the computer for personal convenience or entertainment; and although Defendant's supervisor knew or suspected that Defendant was using the computer for his business records, he never investigated the matter or reprimanded Defendant in this regard, and such use of the computer was not cited as a basis for his discharge.

Defendant, following his discharge, applied for and received unemployment compensation benefits, over the protest of the City. He requested a former fellow employee to obtain a "print-out" of his business data and then to erase it from what had been his library. Instead, the "print-out" was turned over to Defendant's former supervisor and became the basis for the criminal charges.

Assuming that Defendant's use of the computer was unauthorized and that such use is a "property" under the theft statute, there remains an element of the offense missing under the evidence. The act provides: "A person who knowingly or intentionally exerts unauthorized control over property of another person with *intent* to deprive the other of any part of its value or use, commits theft, a class D felony." Ind. Code § 35–43–4–2. It is immediately apparent that the *res* of the statute, the harm sought to be prevented, is a deprivation to one of his property or its use— not a benefit to one which, although a windfall to him, harmed nobody.

The Court of Appeals focused upon Defendant's unauthorized use of the computer for monetary gain and upon the definition of "property" as used in the statute and as defined by Ind. Code § 35–41–1–2, which we may assume, arguendo, includes the "use" of a computer, although we think that it would be more accurate to say that the *information* derived by use of a computer is *property*. Having determined that Defendant's use was property, was unauthorized and was for his monetary benefit, it concluded that he committed a theft. Our question is, "Who was deprived of what?"

Not only was there no evidence that the City was ever deprived of any part of the value or the use of the computer by reason of Defendant's conduct, the uncontradicted evidence was to the contrary. The computer was utilized for City business by means of terminals assigned to various employee-operators, including Defendant. The computer processed the data from the various terminals simultaneously, and the limit of its capacity was never reached or likely to have been. The computer service was leased to the City at a fixed charge, and the tapes or discs upon which the imparted data was stored were erasable and reusable. Defendant's unauthorized use cost the City nothing and did not interfere with its use by others. He extracted from the system only such information as he had previously put into it. He did not, for his own benefit, withdraw City data intended for its exclusive use or for sale.

Thus, Defendant did not deprive the City of the "use of computers and computer services" as the information alleged that he intended to do. We find no distinction between Defendant's use of the City's computer and the use, by a mechanic, of the employer's hammer or a stenographer's use of the employer's typewriter, for other than the employer's purposes. Under traditional concepts, the transgression is in the nature of a trespass, a civil matter–and a de minimis one, at that. Defendant has likened his conduct to the use of an employer's vacant bookshelf, for the temporary storage of one's personal items, and to the use of an employer's telephone facilities for toll-free calls. The analogies appear to us to be appropriate.

We have written innumerable times, that intent is a mental function and, absent an admission, it must be determined by courts and juries from a consideration of the conduct and natural and usual consequences of such conduct. It follows that when the natural and usual consequences of the conduct charged and proved are not such as would effect the wrong which the statute seeks to prevent, the intent to effect that wrong is not so inferable. No deprivation to the City resulted from Defendant's use of the computer, and a deprivation to it was not a result to be expected from such use, hence not a natural and usual consequence. There was no evidence presented from which the intent to deprive, an essential element of the crime, could be inferred.

PIVARNIK, JUSTICE, dissenting.

I must dissent from the majority opinion wherein the majority finds that Defendant did not take property of the City "with intent to deprive the owner of said property." In the first place, intent is clearly shown in that Defendant used the City computer system for his personal business, well knowing that he was doing so and well knowing that it was unauthorized. I think the Court of Appeals properly focused upon Defendant's unauthorized use of the computer for monetary gain and upon the definition of property as used in the statute and as defined by Ind. Code § 35–41–1–2. Time and use are at the very core of the value of a computer system. To say that only the information stored in the computer plus the tapes and discs and perhaps the machinery involved in the computer system, are the only elements that can be measured as the value or property feature of that system, is incorrect.

I think it is irrelevant that the computer processed the data from various terminals simultaneously and the limit of its capacity was never reached by any or all of the stations, including the defendant's. It is also irrelevant that the computer service was leased to the City at a fixed charge and that the tapes or discs upon which the imparted data was stored were erasable and reusable. The fact is the City owned the computer system of all the stations including the defendant's. The time and use of that equipment at that station belonged to the City. Thus, when the defendant used the computer system, putting on data from his private business and taking it out on printouts, he was taking that which was property of the City and converting it to his own use, thereby depriving the City of its use and value. The majority says: "Thus, Defendant did not deprive the City of the 'use of computers and computer services' as the information alleged that he intended to do." I disagree. I feel that is exactly what he did and I think the Court of Appeals properly found so.

NOTES AND QUESTIONS

1. The majority argues that McGraw's conduct did not deprive the City of its property. But did McGraw infringe upon the City's right to exclude others from using its valuable resources? If the City's computer resembles a limitless fountain of property, as the majority's opinion suggests, doesn't the City have a right to control who should receive its bounty?

On the other hand, do you think an employee should be prosecuted criminally for using his employer's computer for personal reasons when that use does not interfere with the employer's interests? Do you think this question influenced the court in *McGraw*?

2. In the case of physical property, depriving the owner of property transfers that property from its owner to the defendant. The victim's loss is the same as the defendant's gain, namely the property taken. In *McGraw*, by contrast, the defendant received a benefit but the victim did not suffer a loss. The owner retained the property allegedly "taken."

This also occurred in the *Seidlitz* case. Seidlitz obtained a copy of the WYLBUR software, which potentially harmed OSI by allowing Seidlitz or others to compete against OSI on a more equal footing. But OSI's loss did not equal Seidlitz's gain: OSI was not deprived of WYLBUR, but rather of the economic benefits flowing from the exclusive use of WYLBUR. *Seidlitz* held that the WYLBUR program was property, which seems plausible. But did Seidlitz have intent to deprive OSI of that property? Should it matter?

3. *Conversion*. The doctrine of conversion might be used to prosecute an employee's computer misuse when the employee does not intend to deprive others of the use of the computer. Unlike theft, conversion does not generally require an intent to deprive the owner of the property.

This approach was tried in United States v. Collins, 56 F.3d 1416 (D.C. Cir. 1995). Collins, an employee of the Defense Intelligence Agency, used a highly classified government computer network to store hundreds of personal documents relating to his interest in ballroom dancing. He was charged with converting government property in violation of 18 U.S.C. § 641. The D.C. Circuit rejected the government's theory that Collins had converted government property by using the classified computer network for personal purposes:

> The cornerstone of conversion is the unauthorized exercise of control over property in such a manner that *serious interference* with ownership rights occurs. Section 228 of the Restatement (Second) of Torts states "[o]ne who is authorized to make a particular use of a chattel, and uses it in a manner exceeding the authorization, is subject to liability for conversion to another whose right to control the use of the chattel is thereby *seriously violated*." *Id.* (emphasis added). The interference is of such a magnitude that the converter must pay the rightful owner the full value of the property converted. Restatement (Second) of Torts § 222A.

> The court's decision in *United States v. Wilson*, 636 F.2d 225 (8th Cir. 1980), is illuminating on this point. Appellant was found guilty by a jury of converting government property in violation of section 641. Specifically, appellant was charged with converting secretarial time by using a government secretary to type documents for his personal business. No evidence existed, however, that the work interfered with the secretary's official duties. The district court granted a motion for judgment of acquittal, and the appellate court affirmed this judgment. The court held there was no evidence that appellant's conduct seriously interfered with the rights of the government. The court focused on the fact that appellant and his secretary had little or no assigned work during the period in question. Consequently, appellant could not have seriously interfered with the government's ownership rights because the government was never deprived of the use or possession of its property. Thus, while appellant may have engaged in a breach of fiduciary duty, his conduct was not criminal.

> Similarly, the government did not provide a shred of evidence in the case at bar that appellant seriously interfered with the government's ownership rights in its computer system. While appellant concedes he typed in data and stored information on the computer regarding his personal activities, no evidence exists that such conduct prevented him or others from performing their official duties on the computer. The government did not even attempt to show that appellant's use of the computer prevented agency personnel from accessing the computer or storing information. Thus, appellant's use of the government computer in no way seriously interfered with the government's ownership rights.

Id. at 1420–21.

Compare *Collins* with United States v. Girard, 601 F.2d 69 (2d Cir. 1979). In *Girard,* a corrupt Drug Enforcement Administration (DEA) agent used the DEA's computer to access and download files identifying undercover DEA agents that he then planned to sell to drug dealers. The defendant was charged with converting government property in violation of 18 U.S.C. § 641. The Second Circuit affirmed the conviction, announcing in a conclusory fashion that the defendant had converted the government's property.

How do you reconcile *Collins* and *Girard*? Is the difference that *Girard* had at best thwarted DEA investigations and at worst risked the lives of DEA undercover agents, but *Collins* had not caused any harm to his government employer?

Imagine that you are a defense attorney in a future § 641 case that involves less harm than the facts of *Girard* but more harm than the facts of *Collins*. How can you persuade the court that your case is more like *Collins* than *Girard*?

4. Does the law of theft provide a useful way of prohibiting computer misuse? Here is a critical perspective:

> When computer misuse caused harm to a victim in some way, courts [applying theft law to computer misuse] generally concluded that property had in fact been taken and held the defendants liable. When no appreciable harm resulted, courts tended to find that no property was taken and hold that the defendants had committed no crime. To the extent that it was made explicit, the reasoning seemed to go something like this: When a person is harmed, the person loses something of value; when a person loses something of value, they are deprived of property. Therefore the infliction of harm triggers a theft. This reasoning allowed courts to reach reasonable results in particular cases, but followed no deeper principle than the courts' ex post assessments of whether particular instances of computer misuse had caused substantial harm.

Orin S. Kerr, *Cybercrime's Scope: Interpreting "Access" and "Authorization" in Computer Misuse Statutes,* 78 N.Y.U. L. Rev. 1596, 1611 (2003). If the use of theft law to punish computer misuse was result-oriented, is that a good thing or a bad thing?

5. *Arguments for and against computer crime statutes.* Starting in the late 1970s, dissatisfaction with the cases applying theft law to computer misuse led to a movement to adopt new computer misuse statutes. State computer crime prosecutor Donald Ingraham offered one rationale for such statutes in an early article. *See* Donald G. Ingraham, *On Charging Computer Crime,* 2 Computer/L.J. 429 (1980). Ingraham reasoned that computer crime statutes were needed for the same reason criminal codes prohibit burglary and trespass. It would be possible to repeal burglary and trespass laws and simply prosecute every property crime as a theft, Ingraham noted. But such an approach would be quite awkward:

> For example, attempted commercial burglary could be regarded as a usurpation of store floor space, and treated as a theft of the property interest in occupancy. Under such a statute, the victim would necessarily be compelled to calculate the value of the property invaded and the duration of the invasion. The prosecution would be for the theft of those values, and not for the intrusion as a crime complete in itself. It is precisely that absurdity—the requirement that the victim prepare evi-

dence of an injury other than that with which he is really concerned—which the so-called computer crime bills have recognized and sought to redress.

Id. at 429–30.

More recently, some commentators have questioned whether the specific computer crime statutes are necessary. Consider this argument that traditional property laws are sufficient to deter and punish computer misuse:

> Legislators and others apprehensive about the misuse of technology too often have perceived a need to enact statutes to counteract "computer crimes" that are in fact already existing crimes accomplished with new techniques. To the extent that such statutes merely prohibit conduct that is already criminal, they are simply redundant. To the extent that they are drafted in "technology-specific" language, the pace of technological change and the ingenuity of computer-literate criminals guarantee that those statutes will be obsolete almost as soon as they are enacted. To the extent that they focus on technological means, rather than on the harm caused by a defendant's conduct, those statutes tend towards overbreadth by sweeping within their ambit anyone who uses the means regardless of result. To the extent that computer-specific statutes are enacted by legislators unfamiliar or uncomfortable with technology, such statutes tend to reflect a lack of clarity or understanding or, sometimes, simply fear. Thus, a "computer-specific" approach results, too often, in criminal statutes that are unnecessary, imprecise, clumsy, over-inclusive, or ineffective.

Joseph M. Olivenbaum, *Ctrl–Alt–Delete: Rethinking Federal Computer Crime Legislation*, 27 Seton Hall L. Rev. 574, 575–76 (1997).

In an article on the differences between physical crime and virtual crime, Professor Susan W. Brenner has also expressed some skepticism about the need for new laws. "[T]he principles we have traditionally used to impose liability for crimes," Brenner argues, "can be extrapolated to encompass many, if not all, of the activities characterized as cybercrimes." Brenner contends that this approach is preferable to "trying to devise new principles of criminal liability, a new law of cybercrimes, to address anti-social behavior occurring within or committed via cyberspace." Brenner acknowledges that "there may be reasons for devising a new law of cybercrimes, such as the greater harms that can be inflicted by cybercriminals and the advantages they enjoy in avoiding detection and prosecution." However, she cautions against taking "hasty action" because we should "wait to see how crime in cyberspace evolves before committing ourselves to the adoption of cybercrime laws." Susan W. Brenner, *Is There Such a Thing as "Virtual Crime?"* 4 Cal. Crim. L. Rev. 1, ¶ 129 (2001).

In contrast, Beryl Howell, former Chief Counsel to the Senate Judiciary Committee under Senator Patrick Leahy, has defended the computer-specific approach to prohibiting computer misuse against such criticisms:

> Specific laws directed to specific problems are important for two main reasons. First, they serve to guide law enforcement as to how investigations may be conducted with appropriate respect for civil liberties and

privacy. Second, specific laws make clear to people the boundary of legally permissible conduct.

Does this require endless effort to update the laws to keep pace with technology? Yes, but Congress returns every year with the job of making new laws. Will the pace of legal changes always be behind technological developments? Yes, but in my view the correct pace is a slow one. By the time a proposal has gone through the legislative process, the problem it seeks to address will have become more defined. Policy-makers are better able to craft a narrow and circumscribed law to address a clearly defined problem, and thus, minimize the risk of an overly expansive law that could chill innovation and technological development.

Beryl A. Howell, *Real World Problems of Virtual Crime*, 7 Yale J. L. & Tech. 103, 104–105 (2004–2005).

When evaluating the need for computer crime statutes, it is worth noting that criminal codes contain many technology-specific statutes. For example, the United States Code includes statutes criminalizing the destruction of aircraft (18 U.S.C. § 32), use of aircraft or motor vehicles to hunt protected wild horses (18 U.S.C. § 47), sending a threatening communication through the postal mail (18 U.S.C. § 876), using a radio or television station to broadcast information about an unauthorized lottery (18 U.S.C. § 1304), broadcasting obscene language by radio (18 U.S.C. § 1464), carjacking (18 U.S.C. § 2119), transporting stolen vehicles (18 U.S.C. § 2312), selling or receiving stolen vehicles (18 U.S.C. § 2313), and engaging in telemarketing fraud (18 U.S.C. § 2326). In light of this list, do you think that a statute prohibiting computer misuse is really out of place? Are technology-specific criminal statutes the exception or the rule?

C.   UNAUTHORIZED ACCESS STATUTES

1. INTRODUCTION TO UNAUTHORIZED ACCESS STATUTES

The perceived deficiencies of prosecuting computer misuse using theft laws led the federal government and all fifty states to enact statutes specifically prohibiting computer misuse. Florida passed the first state statute in 1978; the final state to enact a statute was Vermont in 1999. Congress enacted the first federal computer crime law in 1984, broadened it considerably in 1986, and then updated it in various ways in 1990, 1994, 1996, and 2001. No two of these statutory schemes are exactly alike, and many of the laws enumerate several distinct crimes in response to different types of misuse. *See generally* Susan W. Brenner, *State Cybercrime Legislation in the United States of America: A Survey*, 7 Rich. J.L. & Tech. 28 (2001). For a comprehensive review of all of the statutes, see A. Hugh Scott, Computer and Intellectual Property Crime: Federal and State Law (2001).

Despite the differences among the federal and state statutes, the statutory schemes share a number of basic features. The most important is the common building block of unauthorized access to a computer. Every state and the federal government has an unauthorized access statute. This basic offense is usually supplemented by other elements to create additional criminal prohibitions, such as statutes prohibiting computer fraud and computer damage.

To understand modern computer crime law, it is essential to understand the meaning of the basic prohibition on unauthorized access to a computer. The most helpful way to learn about unauthorized access statutes is to focus primarily on the influential federal statute, 18 U.S.C. § 1030.

Overview of 18 U.S.C. § 1030

18 U.S.C. § 1030 is the federal computer misuse statute, sometimes referred to as the Computer Fraud and Abuse Act or CFAA. Section 1030(a) lists seven distinct crimes, most of which are keyed to the basic unauthorized access prohibition. Oddly, the first of the seven crimes is the least important in practice: § 1030(a)(1) is an extremely narrow statute that prohibits accessing a computer without authorization or exceeding authorized access to obtain classified information to injure the United State or aid a foreign power. Although it is the first in the list of § 1030(a) crimes, it appears never to have been used.

In contrast, § 1030(a)(2) is the most frequently charged § 1030 crime. Section 1030(a)(2) prohibits accessing a computer without authorization or exceeding authorized access and obtaining information. Section 1030(a)(3) is only rarely used, and applies specifically to United States government computers. The statute prohibits accessing a United States government computer without authorization. Section 1030(a)(4) is the federal computer fraud statute: it combines the unauthorized access prohibition of § 1030(a)(2) with the basic workings of the wire fraud statute. Section 1030(a)(5) is the federal computer damage statute. It prohibits both unauthorized damage to a computer and also unauthorized access that results in damage. Section 1030(a)(6) prohibits computer password trafficking, and is based heavily on the federal credit card fraud statute, 18 U.S.C. § 1029. Finally, § 1030(a)(7) is an extortion statute, based largely on the federal interstate threat statute, 18 U.S.C. § 875. Section 1030(a)(7) prohibits extorting money or other property using threats to cause damage to computers.

The remaining sections of 18 U.S.C. § 1030 supplement the basic seven crimes in 18 U.S.C. § 1030(a). Section 1030(b) makes clear that attempts are covered by the statute; any attempt to engage in conduct that would be a violation of § 1030(a) if successful is considered a violation of § 1030(b). Section 1030(c) contains the statutory maximum punishments for all of the different §§ 1030(a) and (b) offenses. Section 1030(c) is quite detailed, as Congress chose to treat some § 1030 offenses as misdemeanors, others as felonies with 5–year maximum punishments, and others as more serious felonies. This subsection effectively adds elements to the different § 1030 crimes to trigger felony liability in some circumstances.

Sections 1030(d), 1030(f), and 1030(h) are mostly unimportant for our purposes. They concern jurisdiction, oversight, and create an exception for government investigations in some cases. In contrast, § 1030(e) and § 1030(g) are noteworthy. Section 1030(e) is critical from a doctrinal perspective because it contains statutory definitions of all of the key terms used elsewhere. Section 1030(g) is important at a conceptual level because it explains much of the shape of existing law. Section 1030(g) provides a civil remedy for some kinds of violations, permitting victims of computer misuse to sue in federal court. Thanks to § 1030(g), most of the published cases interpreting § 1030 arise in the civil context rather than the criminal context.

18 U.S.C. § 1030(a)(2)

The two provisions in § 1030 that embody the basic unauthorized access prohibition are 18 U.S.C. §§ 1030(a)(2) and (a)(3). Section 1030(a)(2) states that it is a crime if a person:

> intentionally accesses a computer without authorization or exceeds authorized access, and thereby obtains—

> (A) information contained in a financial record of a financial institution, or of a card issuer as defined in section 1602(n) of title 15, or contained in a file of a consumer reporting agency on a consumer, as such terms are defined in the Fair Credit Reporting Act (15 U.S.C. 1681 et seq.);

> (B) information from any department or agency of the United States; or

> (C) information from any protected computer.

The requirement that the defendant must obtain information required under (a)(2)(A), (B), or (C) may sound significant at first, but proves a surprisingly low hurdle. The Senate Report that accompanied the passage of § 1030(a)(2) contains the following discussion:

> The Department of Justice has expressed concerns that the term "obtains information" in 18 U.S.C. 1030(a)(2) makes that subsection more than an unauthorized access offense, i.e., that it might require the prosecution to prove asportation of the data in question. Because the premise of this subsection is privacy protection, the Committee wishes to make clear that "obtaining information" in this context includes mere observation of the data. Actual asportation, in the sense of physically removing the data from its original location or transcribing the data, need not be proved in order to establish a violation of this subsection.

S. Rep. No. 99–432 (1986), *reprinted in* 1986 U.S.C.C.A.N. 2479, 2484. It is unclear whether § 1030(a)(2) requires actual observation of the data, or whether merely coming into possession of the data is sufficient. In any event, the fact that most computer intruders will see information inside the victim network means that most computer hacking will end up violating 18 U.S.C. § 1030(a)(2).

The broad scope of § 1030(a)(2) is due largely to § 1030(a)(2)(C). Sections 1030(a)(2)(A) and (a)(2)(B) are comparatively narrow; the former covers financial records as defined in § 1030(e)(4)–(5), and the latter covers only information obtained from United States government computers as defined in § 1030(e)(7). In contrast, § 1030(a)(2)(C) has vast scope, because the definition of "protected computer" is extremely broad. Section 1030(e)(2) provides that the term "protected computer" means a computer:

> (A) exclusively for the use of a financial institution or the United States Government, or, in the case of a computer not exclusively for such use, used by or for a financial institution or the United States Government and the conduct constituting the offense affects that use by or for the financial institution or the Government; or

> (B) which is used in or affecting interstate or foreign commerce or communication, including a computer located outside the United States that is used in a manner that affects interstate or foreign commerce or communication of the United States.

Under this definition, most computers are protected computers.* As a result, "obtaining information" from a "protected computer" in § 1030(a)(2) covers a vast range of activity.

The mens rea required under § 1030(a)(2) is intent. The Senate Report that accompanied a change of the mens rea from "knowingly" to "intentionally" in 1986 offered the following explanation for the change:

> First, intentional acts of unauthorized access—rather than mistaken, inadvertent, or careless ones—are precisely what the Committee intends to proscribe. Second, the Committee is concerned that the "knowingly" standard in the existing statute might be inappropriate for cases involving computer technology. The Senate's Report on the Criminal Code states that a person is said to act knowingly if he is aware "that the result is practically certain to follow from his conduct, whatever his desire may be as to that result."

> While appropriate to many criminal statutes, this standard might not be sufficient to preclude liability on the part of those who inadvertently "stumble into" someone else's computer file or computer data. This is particularly true in those cases where an individual is authorized to sign onto and use a particular computer, but subsequently exceeds his authorized access by mistakenly entering another computer file or data that happens to be accessible from the same terminal. Because the user had "knowingly" signed onto that terminal in the first place, the danger exists that he might incur liability for his mistaken access to another file. This is so because, while he may not have desired that

---

* For a discussion of the scope of "protected computer," see page 561.

result, i.e., the access of another file, it is possible that a trier of fact will infer that the user was "practically certain" such mistaken access could result from his initial decision to access the computer. The substitution of an "intentional" standard is designed to focus Federal criminal prosecutions on those whose conduct evinces a clear intent to enter, without proper authorization, computer files or data belonging to another. Again, this will comport with the Senate Report on the Criminal Code, which states that "intentional" means more than that one voluntarily engaged in conduct or caused a result. Such conduct or the causing of the result must have been the person's conscious objective.

S. Rep. No. 99–432, *reprinted in* 1986 U.S.C.C.A.N. 2479, 2483–84.

Federal law classifies crimes into felonies and misdemeanors. Misdemeanors are less serious offenses, and felonies are more serious offenses. Federal law classifies misdemeanors as crimes punishable by one year or less of prison time. Felonies are crimes that allow the possibility of a sentence of more than one year of prison. *See* 18 U.S.C. § 3559(a). As a result, it is possible to classify federal crimes as felonies or misdemeanors based on the maximum statutory punishment the offense allows.

Violations of 18 U.S.C. § 1030(a)(2) ordinarily are misdemeanors. *See* 18 U.S.C. § 1030(c)(2)(A). However, the government can charge violations of § 1030(a)(2) as felonies with a five-year statutory maximum if it alleges any one of three additional provisions:

(i) the offense was committed for purposes of commercial advantage or private financial gain;

(ii) the offense was committed in furtherance of any criminal or tortious act in violation of the Constitution or laws of the United States or of any State; or

(iii) the value of the information obtained exceeds $5,000.

18 U.S.C. § 1030(c)(2)(B). If the government charges a felony violation of § 1030(a)(2) and alleges one of these three provisions, it must prove the existence of the provision as an extra element of the offense beyond a reasonable doubt. If the government cannot prove the felony element, the government can obtain a misdemeanor conviction under § 1030(a)(2), as the misdemeanor violation is a lesser-included offense of the felony charge.

18 U.S.C. § 1030(a)(2) offenses can also be felonies in the unlikely event that a defendant has a previous conviction under § 1030. In that case, a violation of § 1030(a)(2) is a felony with a maximum punishment of 10 years in prison. *See* 18 U.S.C. § 1030(c)(2)(C).

18 U.S.C. § 1030(a)(3)

Section 1030(a)(3) states that it is a crime if a person:

intentionally, without authorization to access any nonpublic computer of a department or agency of the United States, accesses such a computer of that department or agency that is exclusively for the use of the Government of the United States or, in the case of a computer not exclusively for such use, is used by or for the Government of the United States and such conduct affects that use by or for the Government of the United States.

Violations of § 1030(a)(3) are misdemeanors unless the defendant has a prior conviction under § 1030. If the defendant has a prior conviction, the crime is a felony punishable by up to ten years in prison. See 18 U.S.C. § 1030(c)(2)(C).

Section 1030(a)(3) is different from § 1030(a)(2) in a number of ways. First, § 1030(a)(3) applies only to access into United States government computers. Second, it is a simple trespass statute; there is no requirement that any information be obtained by the defendant. Third, the basic prohibition is limited to "access without authorization," whereas § 1030(a)(2) includes both a defendant who "accessed without authorization" and a defendant who "exceeds authorized access." As we will see, the precise distinction between access without authorization and exceeding authorized access is quite difficult to follow, and it's not clear that a robust distinction exists. But the limitation of § (a)(3) reflects a design for the statute to reach only a limited class of cases.

The Senate Report that accompanied the enactment of the modern version of 18 U.S.C. § 1030(a)(3) included the following discussion of its scope:

> * * * [I]t applies to acts of simple trespass against computers belonging to, or being used by or for, the Federal Government. The Department of Justice and others have expressed concerns about whether the present subsection covers acts of mere trespass, i.e., unauthorized access, or whether it requires a further showing that the information perused was "used, modified, destroyed, or disclosed." To alleviate those concerns, the Committee wants to make clear that the new subsection will be a simple trespass offense, applicable to persons without authorized access to Federal computers.

S.Rep. 99–432 (1986), reprinted in 1986 U.S.C.C.A.N. 2479, 2484.

2. WHAT IS "ACCESS"?

Now that we have seen the basic framework of two unauthorized access statutes, let's look in depth at the meaning of "access." The prohibition on unauthorized access can be understood at a very general level as a sort of computer trespass crime. The statute focuses on the defendant's rights at the time he accesses the computer. Liability does not hinge on whether we can artificially define some kind of property interest, or whether the computer owner was deprived of some kind of right. Instead, the law monitors the defendant's "access" to the victim computer and then asks whether that access was authorized. But what is "access" to a computer? Consider the following discussion:

Obviously a computer user does not access a computer by physically getting inside the computer. Some other principle must govern. But what principle should that be? One approach would look at computers from the standpoint of virtual reality, and try to draw analogies between using a computer and entering real property. We could say that access hinges on whether the user has made a virtual entrance into the computer. For example, imagine a user tries to use a password-protected computer network and is confronted by a screen that requires a valid username and password to proceed. We might say that this screen is akin to a lock on a front door, and that entering a username and password is like using a key to open the lock. This approach suggests that a user who enters a valid username and password has accessed the computer, but a user who inputs an incorrect name or password has been denied access.

Similarly, we could say that visiting a publicly accessible website is something like visiting an open store in the physical world. Determining whether access has occurred then depends on whether visiting an open store can be deemed "entering" in the physical world. The correct answer is not obvious: Visiting a website could be seen as equivalent to viewing a shop window from a public street rather than actually entering the store. But at a conceptual level, the analogy to virtual space provides one heuristic to understand what it means to "access" a computer.

The virtual analogy does not provide the only tool, however. We can also look at the question of access from the standpoint of physical reality, in which we recognize that computers are simply machines that communicate with each other by sending and receiving information. For example, when a user visits a website, the user's computer sends requests to the computer that hosts the website asking the computer to send back computer files; when the files are returned to the user, the user's computer reassembles the files and presents them in the form of a website. If we focus on how computers operate, we can interpret access by looking to whether a user has sent communications that have physically entered the computer. For example, one standard could be that a user accesses a computer when she sends a command to that computer instructing the computer to perform a task, and the computer performs the request as instructed. Another standard could be that a user accesses a computer when the user sends a command requesting information in return and the computer responds by sending back information to the user. In this sense, accessing a computer is no different from simply using a computer.

Notably, physical-world standards and virtual-world standards can produce different outcomes. Imagine a user wishes to log on to a password-protected computer, and sends a request to the computer asking it to send back the page that prompts the user to enter a username and password. The computer complies, sending the page back to the user. This would not access the computer from a virtual perspective, as it would be something like walking up to a locked door but not yet trying the key. From a physical-world perspective, however, the request would be an access; the user sent a command to the computer and received the desired response. Similarly, consider whether sending an e-mail accesses the computers of the recipient's Internet service provider. From a virtual perspective, the answer would seem to be no; a user who sends an e-mail to the ISP does not understand herself to have "entered" the ISP. From a physical perspective, however, the answer seems to be yes; the user has in fact sent a communication to the ISP that its servers received and processed.

Which standard governs? The statutes themselves offer little guidance. Most computer crime statutes (including the federal statute) do not define access, and most statutes that do include a definition shed little light on these questions.

Orin S. Kerr, *Cybercrime's Scope: Interpreting "Access" and "Authorization" in Computer Misuse Statutes,* 78 N.Y.U. L. Rev. 1596, 1619–21 (2003). Consider these questions as you read the following case construing "access" in the context of a state unauthorized access statute.

STATE v. RILEY

Supreme Court of Washington, 1993.
846 P.2d 1365.

GUY, JUSTICE.

Northwest Telco Corporation is a company that provides long distance telephone service. Telco's customers dial a publicly available general access number, then enter an individualized 6–digit access code and the long distance number they wish to call. A computer at Telco's central location then places the call and charges it to the account corresponding to the entered 6–digit code.

On January 9, 1990, Cal Edwards, Director of Engineering at Telco, observed that Telco's general access number was being dialed at regular intervals of approximately 40 seconds. After each dialing, a different 6–digit number was entered, followed by a certain long distance number. Edwards observed similar activity on January 10, between 10 p.m. and 6 a.m. From his past experience, Edwards recognized this activity as characteristic of that of a "computer hacker" attempting to obtain the individualized 6–digit access codes of Telco's customers. Edwards surmised that the hacker was using a computer and modem to dial Telco's general access number, a randomly selected 6–digit number, and a long distance number. Then, by recording which 6–digit numbers enabled the long distance call to be put through successfully, the hacker was able to obtain the valid individual access codes of Telco's customers. The hacker could then use those codes fraudulently to make long distance calls that would be charged improperly to Telco's paying customers.

On January 11, Edwards contacted Toni Ames, a U.S. West security investigator, and requested her assistance in exposing the hacker. In response, Ames established a line trap, which is a device that traces telephone calls to their source. By 3 p.m., Ames had traced the repeated dialing to the home of Joseph Riley in Silverdale, Washington. The dialing continued until 6 a.m. on January 12.

Ames contacted the Kitsap County Prosecutor's Office on January 12, 1990, and was directed to Investigator Richard Kitchen. Kitchen filed an affidavit for a search warrant after interviewing both Ames and Edwards.

On January 16, Kitchen arrived at Riley's house with the search warrant. Prior to executing the search, Kitchen informed Riley of his rights, although Riley was not arrested. Kitchen then questioned Riley about the occupancy of the house to ascertain which occupant was responsible for the hacking. Riley then admitted having attempted to obtain Telco customer access codes. Riley told Kitchen that he had tried to obtain the access codes for 3 days in the past week, but that he was not certain of the specific dates.

Evidence discovered during the subsequent search included four stolen access codes, a computer program that conducted the rapid repeated dialing and entry of random 6–digit numbers, handwritten notes detailing Riley's hacking activity, and a how-to-hack manual.

Riley was later charged with and convicted of two counts of computer trespass against Telco.

Riley contends that his convictions of computer trespass against Telco must be reversed because his conduct—repeatedly dialing Telco's general access number and entering random 6–digit numbers in an attempt to discover access codes belonging to others—does not satisfy the statutory definition of computer trespass. We disagree.

RCW 9A.52.110 provides in relevant part that "a person is guilty of computer trespass in the first degree if the person, without authorization, intentionally gains access to a computer system or electronic data base of another."

Riley contends the telephone company's long distance switch is not a "computer" under RCW 9A.52.110. We reject this contention. The trial court explicitly found that the switch is a computer. This finding was based on unrebutted expert testimony. A trial court's findings of fact will not be disturbed on appeal when they are supported by undisputed evidence.

Riley also argues that acts accomplished by simply dialing the telephone are not encompassed within the statutorily defined crime of computer trespass, and are merely the equivalent of placing a telephone call. He contends he is not guilty of computer trespass because he did not enter, read, insert, or copy data from the telephone system's computer switch.

Riley's acts were not equivalent to placing a telephone call. He used his home computer to dial Telco's general access number and enter random 6–digit numbers representing customer access codes every 40 seconds for several hours at a time. Moreover, RCW 9A.52.110 criminalizes the unauthorized, intentional "access" of a computer system. The term "access" is defined under RCW 9A.52.010(6) as "to approach . . . or otherwise make use of any resources of a computer, directly or by electronic means." Riley's repeated attempts to discover access codes by sequentially entering random 6–digit numbers constitute "approach[ing]" or "otherwise mak[ing] use of any resources of a computer". The switch is a computer. Long distance calls are processed through the switch. Riley was approaching the switch each time he entered the general access number, followed by a random 6–digit number representing a customer access code, and a destination number. Therefore, Riley's conduct satisfied the statutory definition of "access" and so was properly treated as computer trespass.[5]

NOTES AND QUESTIONS

1. Compare *Riley* to State v. Allen, 917 P.2d 848 (1996), which had facts similar to those of *Riley*. Allen used his computer to dial up access numbers of Southwestern Bell, and he then faced the prompts that asked him for a password that would enable him to make free long-distance telephone calls. The access numbers were only supposed to be known to Southwestern Bell employees. There was no direct evidence that Allen had responded to the password prompt. The Kansas Supreme Court held that Allen had not accessed Southwestern Bell's computers:

> Webster's defines "access" as "freedom or ability to obtain or make use of." Webster's New Collegiate Dictionary, p. 7 (1977). This is similar to the construction used by the trial court to find that no evidence showed that Allen had gained access to Southwestern Bell's computers. Until Allen proceeded beyond the initial banner and entered appropriate passwords, he could not be said to have had the ability to make use of Southwestern Bell's computers or obtain anything. Therefore, he cannot be said to have gained access to Southwestern Bell's computer systems as gaining access is commonly understood.

Id. at 114. *Allen* suggests that a person accesses a computer only when she goes beyond the initial prompt and gains the ability to make use of the computer. Put another way, *Allen* requires actually getting "inside" the computer. Merely "knocking on the door" is not enough. This appears to be a virtual reality approach to access, in which access requires a kind of virtual entrance to the machine.

Are *Riley* and *Allen* consistent? If not, which is better, the physical approach applied in *Riley* or the virtual approach applied in *Allen*?

---

5. This interpretation of the statute does not criminalize repeated dialing of a busy telephone number because a computer trespass conviction requires an "intent to commit another crime". RCW 9A.52.110(1)(a). It is not disputed that Riley had such an intent.

2.   The statutory definition of "access" used by the Washington statute at issue in *Riley* was influenced by an early bill introduced in Congress in 1977, the Federal Computer Systems Protection Act introduced by Senator Ribicoff. S. 1766, 95th Cong. (1977). *See generally* Michael M. Krieger, *Current and Proposed Computer Crime Legislation*, 2 Computer/L.J. 721, 723 (1980) (compiling legislation). Senator Ribicoff's bill was never enacted by Congress, but it did influence a number of state computer crime statutes. Notably, Congress opted not to define "access" when it enacted 18 U.S.C. § 1030. Do you think it is wise for legislatures to try to define access, or should they leave it up to the courts to decide on a case-by-case basis?

3.   *Does sending an e-mail message "access" a computer?* In America Online v. National Health Care Discount, Inc., 121 F. Supp.2d 1255 (N.D. Iowa 2000), the Internet service provider America Online ("AOL") brought a civil case under 18 U.S.C. § 1030(g) against National Health Care Discount ("NHCD"), a company that sells discount health care plans, for hiring a spammer to send bulk e-mails about NHCD to AOL customers. AOL reasoned that by harvesting e-mail addresses and sending e-mail to AOL customers in violation of AOL's policies, the spammers had accessed AOL's computers without authorization. AOL moved for summary judgment, prompting the court to consider whether a computer user "accesses" another computer when he sends e-mail to that computer. The court answered in the affirmative, offering this expansive interpretation of "access":

> The CFAA does not define "access," but the general definition of the word, as a transitive verb, is to "gain access to." Merriam–Webster's Collegiate Dictionary 6 (10th ed. 1994). As a noun, "access," in this context, means to exercise the "freedom or ability to . . . make use of" something. The question here, therefore, is whether NHCD's e-mailers, by harvesting e-mail addresses of AOL members and then sending the members UBE messages, exercised the freedom or ability to make use of AOL's computers. The court finds they did. For purposes of the CFAA, when someone sends an e-mail message from his or her own computer, and the message then is transmitted through a number of other computers until it reaches its destination, the sender is making use of all of those computers, and is therefore "accessing" them. This is precisely what NHCD's e-mailers did with respect to AOL's computers.

Id. at 1272–1273.

4.   *Do port scans "access" scanned computers?* Both computer hackers and security professionals regularly evaluate the security of networks by performing a series of well-known tests on the networks. One common test is a "port scan," which checks the targeted computer for open ports. Every computer connected to the Internet has 65,535 ports, which are akin to access doors by which a remote user can log into the computer. A port scan checks each port and reports back as to whether the port is open and listening, or whether it is closed. Port scanning is a common surveillance tool that often gives intruders important insights into how they can exploit weaknesses in a network. In a civil dispute between two computer security firms, a federal court concluded that port scans do not "access" the targeted computer under

18 U.S.C. § 1030. *See* Moulton v. VC3, No. 1:00CV434–TWT, 2000 WL 33310901, at *7 (N.D. Ga. 2000).

> 5. *What is a "computer"?* 18 U.S.C. § 1030(e)(1) defines "computer" as:
>
> an electronic, magnetic, optical, electrochemical, or other high speed data processing device performing logical, arithmetic, or storage functions, and includes any data storage facility or communications facility directly related to or operating in conjunction with such device, but such term does not include an automated typewriter or typesetter, a portable hand held calculator, or other similar device.

Does this definition include a cellular telephone? A Blackberry? A thumb drive? As a policy matter, should such devices be included in the statutory definition?

United States v. Mitra, 405 F.3d 492 (7th Cir. 2005), may shed some light on these questions. Mitra, a student at the University of Wisconsin, had figured out how to commandeer the radio system used by police, fire, ambulance, and other emergency workers in Madison, Wisconsin. The radio system was a Motorola Smartnet II, a sophisticated system that used a computer to host many different communications on a small number of radio frequencies. Mitra had learned how to control the system using a radio transmitter, and he used his transmitter to block the radio system to stop receiving signals. Mitra's conduct effectively blocked Madison emergency workers from being able to use their radio system and to coordinate emergency responses to incidents in the city.

Mitra was charged and convicted of violating 18 U.S.C. § 1030(a)(5), and appealed his conviction on the ground that the Madison radio system was not a "computer" covered by § 1030. In an opinion by Judge Easterbrook, the Seventh Circuit disagreed and affirmed the conviction:

> Every cell phone and cell tower is a "computer" under this statute's definition; so is every iPod, every wireless base station in the corner coffee shop, and many another gadget. Reading § 1030 to cover all of these, and police radio too, would give the statute wide coverage, which by Mitra's lights means that Congress cannot have contemplated such breadth.
>
> Well of course Congress did not contemplate or intend this particular application of the statute. * * * But although legislators may not know about [it], they *do* know that complexity is endemic in the modern world and that each passing year sees new developments. That's why they write general statutes rather than enacting a list of particular forbidden acts. And it is the statutes they enacted—not the thoughts they did or didn't have—that courts must apply.
>
> Section 1030 is general. Exclusions show just *how* general. Subsection (e)(1) carves out automatic typewriters, typesetters, and handheld calculators; this shows that other devices with embedded processors and software are covered. As more devices come to have built-in intelligence, the effective scope of the statute grows. This might prompt Congress to amend the statute but does not authorize the judiciary to give the existing version less coverage than its language portends.

Id. at 495.

6. In a world of computer networks, concepts of access have to consider not just one computer, but many. For example, imagine you are at home and you access the Internet from your home computer via your Internet service provider. You spend a few minutes surfing the web, and then you intentionally distribute a computer virus as an attachment to an e-mail. Did you "access" your home computer? Your ISP's server? Routers and mailservers that may have transferred your communications in the course of delivery? The webserver that stored the files you retrieved when you were surfing the web? The ISP of the person who received your e-mail? The ISPs of other people who eventually received the virus?

7. Which is better, a virtual approach to access or a physical approach to access? Should access require a virtual entrance, or should the key question be whether communications physically enter the machine? Scholars have disagreed on the question. The author of these materials has argued in favor of a physical approach to access:

> The problem with a narrow construction of access is that individual users interact with computers in countless ways for countless reasons, and it is difficult to carve out a type of interaction that should be exempted entirely from computer misuse laws. A typical computer user might log on to a network using a password, open files stored on a server, surf the web, and send e-mail. If any one of these activities does not constitute an access, then that entire category of activity may be exempted from laws that are designed broadly to prohibit exceeding privileges on a computer.

> Further, the distinctions between different types of use are sufficiently fluid, and the technology of the Internet changes so rapidly, that such distinctions would prove highly unstable and ultimately arbitrary. While a narrow meaning for access may have made sense in the 1970s, today's technologies cannot support it. * * *

> In light of the difficulty of drawing robust and sensible lines between different types of interactions with computers and limiting access to just some of them, the better approach is to allow access to refer broadly to any successful interaction with a computer, no matter how minor. The functional effect of this broad construction is to eliminate access as a limit on the scope of unauthorized access statutes, and to place major weight on the meaning of authorization.

Orin S. Kerr, *Cybercrime's Scope: Interpreting "Access" and "Authorization" in Computer Misuse Statutes,* 78 N.Y.U. L. Rev. 1596, 1647–48 (2003). In contrast, Patricia Bellia has argued in favor of a virtual reality approach to access, at least in the context of the federal unauthorized access statute:

> The narrower reading of "access" is in fact the more natural one. The provisions [of 18 U.S.C. § 1030] clearly contemplate conduct that involves obtaining information not generally available to the public, including national security information and financial and other records, or conduct that involves access to computers that are nonpublic. Since the information is not available to the public, it is necessarily segregated by code–

whether by a password or other technical measure, or by being placed on a system not generally accessible to the public.

Patricia L. Bellia, *Defending Cyberproperty*, 79 N.Y.U. L. Rev. 2164, 2254 (2004).

8. Do you think the meaning of "access" was a difficult issue in the 1980s, when the Computer Fraud and Abuse Act was passed? Is the problem that computer technologies are very different today as compared to what they were in the 1980s?

9. *How much does the meaning of "access" matter if access must also be "without authorization"?* Liability under an unauthorized access statute requires more than just access: that access must also be "without authorization" or, in some cases, must exceed authorization. The fact that the prohibition on access never stands alone raises the question of how much the definition of access actually matters in practice.

In particular, consider those cases in which a broad physical interpretation of access leads to the conclusion that the computer was accessed, but a narrow virtual interpretation leads to the conclusion that it was not. From a virtual perspective, the computer will not have been accessed because the virtual user was not let "inside." That is, there was no password gate or other barrier that demarcated the entry into the computer. But this same concept can be restated from a physical perspective using concepts of authorization. From a physical perspective, the computer will have been accessed, but there will be no liability because any such access will have been authorized. Any access that is not blocked by a password gate or other barrier is authorized access.

If this is correct, then the definition of access is not very important. The real work must be done through the meaning of authorization.

3. WHAT IS AUTHORIZATION? THE CASE OF CODE–BASED RESTRICTIONS

Perhaps the most complex issues raised by computer misuse statutes concern authorization. Most computer misuse statutes criminalize unauthorized access to a computer, and some prohibit exceeding authorized access. In contrast, authorized access remains legal. This raises obvious questions. When is access unauthorized? Who can grant the authority to access a computer, and in what circumstances? Given that millions of computer users access millions of computers every day, finding the line between authorized and unauthorized access obviously is quite important. Specifically, deciding when an access is "without authorization" or "in excess of authorization" often determines the line between an act that is criminal and one that is not. But what exactly it means for access to be "without authorization" or "exceeding authorized access" turns out to be far from clear.

Imagine that a college student tasked with writing a research paper on the Ku Klux Klan decides to conduct her research using the Internet.[3] She logs on to her AOL account, which is governed by a Terms of Service agreement containing the following clause: "You may not use your AOL account to post, transmit, or promote any unlawful, harmful, threatening, abusive, harassing, defamatory, vulgar, hateful, racially, ethnically or otherwise objectionable content." Once connected to the Internet, she finds a web site hosted by a KKK chapter. The main page contains a click-through agreement: "Only white supremacists are authorized to access this site," the agreement states. "Access by people who are not white supremacists is unauthorized. By clicking 'I agree,' you agree that you are a white supremacist." Although she is not a white supremacist, she clicks "I Agree" and examines the site. The site contains links to other Klan-related sites, and when she clicks on one of the links, she is connected to a university-hosted site about the history of the Klan that asks her to enter a username and password. Although she does not have an account with the university, she guesses a username and password correctly, and the site grants her access to its contents. She then copies some of the information contained in the site, and e-mails it to her best friend, who previously has told her to stop e-mailing her information about her KKK research project.

Assuming that our student has "accessed" all four of the computers used in this example, which of these acts of access were "without authorization?" Did the student access AOL's computers without authorization because she used AOL to "transmit . . . hateful . . . or otherwise objectionable content" in violation of AOL's Terms of Service? Did she access the Klan's computers without authorization because she was not a white supremacist? Did she access the university's computer without authorization by guessing the username and password and then entering disguised as a legitimate user? Finally, did she access her friend's computer without authorization by sending her friend the e-mail after her friend had told her not to send it?

More broadly, who and what determines whether access is authorized, and under what circumstances? Can a computer owner set the scope of authorization by contractual language? Or do these standards derive from the social norms of Internet users? The statutes are silent on these questions. The phrase "without authorization" generally is left undefined.

To answer some of these questions, it may be useful to identify three basic ways in which access might be unauthorized. Every computer is configured to permit its users to enjoy a set of privileges, and there are three basic ways to set those privileges: by code, by contract, or by social norms. This means that a computer user can engage in computer misuse in three possible ways: by circumventing code-based restrictions, by breaching contract-based restrictions, or by breaching social norms on computer access.

---

3. This material is taken from Orin S. Kerr, *Cybercrime's Scope: Interpreting "Access" and "Authorization" in Computer Misuse Statutes,* 78 N.Y.U. L. Rev. 1596, 1622–24 (2003).

When an owner regulates privileges by code, the owner or her agent designs and programs the computer's hardware and software so that the code limits each users' privileges. Perhaps every user must have an account, and access to that account is protected by a password. This regulates privileges by code because it limits the ability of others to access a particular person's account. For a user to exceed privileges imposed by code, the user must somehow "trick" the computer into giving the user greater privileges. The code creates a barrier designed to limit privileges.

Alternatively, a computer owner or operator may regulate computer privileges by contract. Access to the computer can be conditioned on the user's promise to abide by a set of terms such as Terms of Service for an e-mail account or Terms of Use for a website. Regulation by contract offers a significantly weaker form of regulation than regulation by code. Regulation by code enforces limits on privileges by actually blocking the user from performing the proscribed act, at least absent circumvention. In contrast, regulation by contract works by conditioning access based on a promise. To borrow a physical-world analogy, the difference between regulation by code and regulation by contract resembles the difference between trying to keep a stranger out by locking the front door, on one hand, and trying to keep a stranger out by putting a sign in front of the open door announcing that strangers may not enter.

Both types of regulatory approaches are familiar to every computer user. For example, imagine that you sign up for Internet service with a local Internet service provider and that the service comes with an e-mail account. Signing up for the service requires you to agree to the ISP's Terms of Service, and also requires you to select a username and password. If you use the account in a way that violates the Terms of Service, you will be breaching a contract-based restriction. You agreed to comply with the ISP's Terms of Service, but you accessed the ISP while violating that agreement. Now imagine that your friend Fred wants to read your e-mail, and successfully guesses your username and password and accesses your account without your permission. In that case, Fred has circumvented a code-based restriction. He has bypassed the password gate that was created to limit access to your account.

Third, computer use might be unauthorized if it violates a social norm on computer use. Social norms are widely shared attitudes that specify what behaviors an actor ought to exhibit. In the context of computer misuse, access might violate a social norm if most computer users would understand that you're not supposed to access the computer in that particular way even if it does not circumvent a code-based restriction or breach an explicit contract-based restriction. For example, perhaps it is understood that a user is not supposed to use an automated software program to send thousands of web queries in a short period of time to a particular web server, causing the server to slow down considerably. In such a case, social norms may set up an implicit contractual restriction; by accessing the computer in a way contrary to the expectations of most users, the access may be implicitly unauthorized. (This is arguably just a version of regulation by contract, but for our purposes it helps to treat it separately.)

Should circumvention of a code-based restriction make an access "without authorization" or in excess of authorization? How about breach of a contract-based restriction? How about breach of a social norm? The following materials consider these questions, beginning with the relatively straightforward case of code-based restrictions.

UNITED STATES v. MORRIS

United States Court of Appeals for the Second Circuit, 1991.
928 F.2d 504.

JON O. NEWMAN, CIRCUIT JUDGE.

This appeal presents two narrow issues of statutory construction concerning a provision Congress recently adopted to strengthen protection against computer crimes. Section 2(d) of the Computer Fraud and Abuse Act of 1986, 18 U.S.C. § 1030(a)(5)(A) (1988), punishes anyone who intentionally accesses without authorization a category of computers known as "federal interest computers" and damages or prevents authorized use of information in such computers, causing loss of $1,000 or more. The issues raised are * * * what satisfies the statutory requirement of "access without authorization."

These questions are raised on an appeal by Robert Tappan Morris from the May 16, 1990, judgment of the District Court for the Northern District of New York convicting him, after a jury trial, of violating 18 U.S.C. § 1030(a)(5)(A). Morris released into INTERNET, a national computer network, a computer program known as a "worm"[2] that spread and multiplied, eventually causing computers at various educational institutions and military sites to "crash" or cease functioning.

We conclude * * * that there was sufficient evidence for the jury to conclude that Morris acted "without authorization" within the meaning of section 1030(a)(5)(A). We therefore affirm.

Facts

In the fall of 1988, Morris was a first-year graduate student in Cornell University's computer science Ph.D. program. Through undergraduate work at Harvard and in various jobs he had acquired significant computer experience and expertise. When Morris entered Cornell, he was given an account on the computer at the Computer Science Division. This account gave him explicit authorization to use computers at Cornell. Morris engaged in various discussions with fellow graduate students about the security of computer networks and his ability to penetrate it.

---

2. In the colorful argot of computers, a "worm" is a program that travels from one computer to another but does not attach itself to the operating system of the computer it "infects." It differs from a "virus," which is also a migrating program, but one that attaches itself to the operating system of any computer it enters and can infect any other computer that uses files from the infected computer.

In October 1988, Morris began work on a computer program, later known as the INTERNET "worm" or "virus." The goal of this program was to demonstrate the inadequacies of current security measures on computer networks by exploiting the security defects that Morris had discovered. The tactic he selected was release of a worm into network computers. Morris designed the program to spread across a national network of computers after being inserted at one computer location connected to the network. Morris released the worm into INTERNET, which is a group of national networks that connect university, governmental, and military computers around the country. The network permits communication and transfer of information between computers on the network.

Morris sought to program the INTERNET worm to spread widely without drawing attention to itself. The worm was supposed to occupy little computer operation time, and thus not interfere with normal use of the computers. Morris programmed the worm to make it difficult to detect and read, so that other programmers would not be able to "kill" the worm easily.

Morris also wanted to ensure that the worm did not copy itself onto a computer that already had a copy. Multiple copies of the worm on a computer would make the worm easier to detect and would bog down the system and ultimately cause the computer to crash. Therefore, Morris designed the worm to "ask" each computer whether it already had a copy of the worm. If it responded "no," then the worm would copy onto the computer; if it responded "yes," the worm would not duplicate. However, Morris was concerned that other programmers could kill the worm by programming their own computers to falsely respond "yes" to the question. To circumvent this protection, Morris programmed the worm to duplicate itself every seventh time it received a "yes" response. As it turned out, Morris underestimated the number of times a computer would be asked the question, and his one-out-of-seven ratio resulted in far more copying than he had anticipated. The worm was also designed so that it would be killed when a computer was shut down, an event that typically occurs once every week or two. This would have prevented the worm from accumulating on one computer, had Morris correctly estimated the likely rate of reinfection.

Morris identified four ways in which the worm could break into computers on the network:

(1) through a "hole" or "bug" (an error) in SEND MAIL, a computer program that transfers and receives electronic mail on a computer;

(2) through a bug in the "finger demon" program, a program that permits a person to obtain limited information about the users of another computer;

(3) through the "trusted hosts" feature, which permits a user with certain privileges on one computer to have equivalent privileges on another computer without using a password; and

(4) through a program of password guessing, whereby various combinations of letters are tried out in rapid sequence in the hope that one will be an authorized user's password, which is entered to permit whatever level of activity that user is authorized to perform.

On November 2, 1988, Morris released the worm from a computer at the Massachusetts Institute of Technology. MIT was selected to disguise the fact that the worm came from Morris at Cornell. Morris soon discovered that the worm was replicating and reinfecting machines at a much faster rate than he had anticipated. Ultimately, many machines at locations around the country either crashed or became "catatonic." When Morris realized what was happening, he contacted a friend at Harvard to discuss a solution. Eventually, they sent an anonymous message from Harvard over the network, instructing programmers how to kill the worm and prevent reinfection. However, because the network route was clogged, this message did not get through until it was too late. Computers were affected at numerous installations, including leading universities, military sites, and medical research facilities. The estimated cost of dealing with the worm at each installation ranged from $200 to more than $53,000.

Morris was found guilty, following a jury trial, of violating 18 U.S.C. § 1030(a)(5)(A). He was sentenced to three years of probation, 400 hours of community service, a fine of $10,050, and the costs of his supervision.

Discussion

Section 1030(a)(5)(A) penalizes the conduct of an individual who "intentionally accesses a Federal interest computer without authorization." Morris contends that his conduct constituted, at most, "exceeding authorized access" rather than the "unauthorized access" that the subsection punishes. Morris argues that there was insufficient evidence to convict him of "unauthorized access," and that even if the evidence sufficed, he was entitled to have the jury instructed on his "theory of defense."

We assess the sufficiency of the evidence under the traditional standard. Morris was authorized to use computers at Cornell, Harvard, and Berkeley, all of which were on INTERNET. As a result, Morris was authorized to communicate with other computers on the network to send electronic mail (SEND MAIL), and to find out certain information about the users of other computers (finger demon). The question is whether Morris's transmission of his worm constituted exceeding authorized access or accessing without authorization.

The Senate Report stated that section 1030(a)(5)(A), like the new section 1030(a)(3), would "be aimed at 'outsiders,' *i.e.,* those lacking authorization to access any Federal interest computer." Senate Report at 10, U.S. Code Cong. & Admin. News at 2488. But the Report also stated, in concluding its discussion on the scope of section 1030(a)(3), that it applies "where the offender is completely outside the Government, ... *or where the offender's act of trespass is interdepartmental in nature." Id.* at 8, U.S. Code Cong. & Admin. News at 2486 (emphasis added).

Morris relies on the first quoted portion to argue that his actions can be characterized only as exceeding authorized access, since he had authorized access to a federal interest computer. However, the second quoted portion reveals that Congress was not drawing a bright line between those who have some access to any federal interest computer and those who have none. Congress contemplated that individuals with access to some federal interest computers would be subject to liability under the computer fraud provisions for gaining unauthorized access to other federal interest computers. *See, e.g., id.* (stating that a Labor Department employee who uses Labor's computers to access without authorization an FBI computer can be criminally prosecuted).

The evidence permitted the jury to conclude that Morris's use of the SEND MAIL and finger demon features constituted access without authorization. While a case might arise where the use of SEND MAIL or finger demon falls within a nebulous area in which the line between accessing without authorization and exceeding authorized access may not be clear, Morris's conduct here falls well within the area of unauthorized access. Morris did not use either of those features in any way related to their intended function. He did not send or read mail nor discover information about other users; instead he found holes in both programs that permitted him a special and unauthorized access route into other computers.

Moreover, the jury verdict need not be upheld solely on Morris's use of SEND MAIL and finger demon. As the District Court noted, in denying Morris' motion for acquittal,

> Although the evidence may have shown that defendant's initial insertion of the worm simply exceeded his authorized access, the evidence also demonstrated that the worm was designed to spread to other computers at which he had no account and no authority, express or implied, to unleash the worm program. Moreover, there was also evidence that the worm was designed to gain access to computers at which he had no account by guessing their passwords. Accordingly, the evidence did support the jury's conclusion that defendant accessed without authority as opposed to merely exceeding the scope of his authority.

In light of the reasonable conclusions that the jury could draw from Morris's use of SEND MAIL and finger demon, and from his use of the trusted hosts feature and password guessing, his challenge to the sufficiency of the evidence fails.

Morris endeavors to bolster his sufficiency argument by contending that his conduct was not punishable under subsection (a)(5) but was punishable under subsection (a)(3). That concession belies the validity of his claim that he only exceeded authorization rather than made unauthorized access. Neither subsection (a)(3) nor (a)(5) punishes conduct that exceeds authorization. Both punish a person who "accesses" "without authorization" certain computers. Subsection (a)(3) covers the computers of a department or agency of the United States; subsection (a)(5) more broadly covers any federal interest computers, defined to include, among other computers, those used exclusively by the United States, 18 U.S.C. § 1030(e)(2)(A), and adds the element of causing damage or loss of use of a value of $1,000 or more. If Morris violated subsection (a)(3), as he concedes, then his conduct in inserting the worm into the INTERNET must have constituted "unauthorized access" under subsection (a)(5) to the computers of the federal departments the worm reached, for example, those of NASA and military bases.

To extricate himself from the consequence of conceding that he made "unauthorized access" within the meaning of subsection (a)(3), Morris subtly shifts his argument and contends that he is not within the reach of subsection (a)(5) at all. He argues that subsection (a)(5) covers only those who, unlike himself, lack access to *any* federal interest computer. It is true that a primary concern of Congress in drafting subsection (a)(5) was to reach those unauthorized to access any federal interest computer. The Senate Report stated, "This subsection (a)(5) will be aimed at 'outsiders,' *i.e.*, those lacking authorization to access any Federal interest computer." Senate Report at 10, U.S. Code Cong. & Admin. News at 2488. But the fact that the subsection is "aimed" at such "outsiders" does not mean that its coverage is limited to them.

Congress understandably thought that the group most likely to damage federal interest computers would be those who lack authorization to use any of them. But it surely did not mean to insulate from liability the person authorized to use computers at the State Department who causes damage to computers at the Defense Department. Congress created the misdemeanor offense of subsection (a)(3) to punish intentional trespasses into computers for which one lacks authorized access; it added the felony offense of subsection (a)(5) to punish such a trespasser who also causes damage or loss in excess of $1,000, not only to computers of the United States but to any computer within the definition of federal interest computers. With both provisions, Congress was punishing those, like Morris, who, with access to some computers that enable them to communicate on a network linking other computers, gain access to other computers to which they lack authorization and either trespass, in violation of subsection (a)(3), or cause damage or loss of $1,000 or more, in violation of subsection (a)(5).

Morris also contends that the District Court should have instructed the jury on his theory that he was only exceeding authorized access. The District Court decided that it was unnecessary to provide the jury with a definition of "authorization." We agree. Since the word is of common usage, without any technical or ambiguous meaning, the Court was not obliged to instruct the jury on its meaning.

An instruction on "exceeding authorized access" would have risked misleading the jury into thinking that Morris could not be convicted if some of his conduct could be viewed as falling within this description. Yet, even if that phrase might have applied to some of his conduct, he could nonetheless be found liable for doing what the statute prohibited, gaining access where he was unauthorized and causing loss.

Additionally, the District Court properly refused to charge the jury with Morris's proposed jury instruction on access without authorization. That instruction stated, "To establish the element of lack of authorization, the government must prove beyond a reasonable doubt that Mr. Morris was an 'outsider,' that is, that he was not authorized to access any Federal interest computer in any manner." As the analysis of the legislative history reveals, Congress did not intend an individual's authorized access to one federal interest computer to protect him from prosecution, no matter what other federal interest computers he accesses.

NOTES AND QUESTIONS

1. The *Morris* opinion suggests two ways in which access to a computer can be "without authorization." The first is the "intended function" test. According to the court, Morris accessed federal interest computers without authorization because he did not use SENDMAIL and finger demon "in any way related to their intended function." Although the *Morris* court does not provide an elaborate explanation of the intended function test, it appears to derive largely from a sense of social norms in the community of computer users. Under these norms, software designers design programs to perform certain tasks, and network providers enable the programs to allow users to perform those tasks. Providers implicitly authorize users to use their computers to perform the intended functions, but implicitly do not authorize users to exploit weaknesses in the programs that allow them to perform unintended functions. When a user exploits weaknesses in a program and uses a function in an unintended way to access a computer, that access is "without authorization."

How can a court determine the "intended function" of a computer program or command? Should the court seek out its primary author and ask him what function he had in mind when he created it? How should a court determine the purpose of a computer command that is an open source project, such as the finger demon command at issue in *Morris*, and that has no one author?

What level of generality should a court apply to determine the intended function of a computer command? The meaning of the intended function test hinges on this question. For example, is the intended function of e-mail software to send communications generally? Or is its intended function to send communications in the form of e-mail messages, or to send communications in a way that complies with the network provider's Terms of Service? As the intended function of a command or program is described in increasingly specific ways, the scope of criminality that the intended function test creates will expand. Conversely, the more general the function, the narrower the scope of conduct that the intended function test prohibits.

2.   The *Morris* opinion suggests that gaining access to a computer by correctly guessing or using a stolen password also can constitute access "without authorization." Another court has made a similar suggestion. *See* Sherman & Co. v. Salton Maxim Housewares, Inc., 94 F. Supp.2d 817, 821 (E.D. Mich. 2000). This makes sense: Guessing a password is something like picking a physical lock, and using a stolen password is something like making a copy of the key and using it without the owner's permission. Indeed, bypassing password gates using stolen or guessed passwords is a common way to "hack" into a computer.

At the same time, the addition of a third party raises interesting legal questions about when access to a computer using another person's password is "without authorization." In the case of access to a locked physical space using a lock pick or a stolen key, determining whether access was "without authorization" is easy in most cases. Only the legitimate keyholder who lives in or controls the place to be accessed can determine the scope of authorization; either the legitimate keyholder gave the defendant permission to access or he did not. Computer passwords are a bit different, at least in most cases. Usually there are two parties that have plausible claims to set authorization: the owner/operator of the computer, and the legitimate computer account holder. Which determines the scope of the defendant's authorization?

As an example, imagine that an ISP's Terms of Service state that subscribers are not permitted to distribute their passwords to other people, and that only access by the subscriber is permitted. Joe, a new subscriber, gives his password to Mary so Mary can check Joe's account for him while he is on a camping trip. Is Mary's access to the computer "without authorization?" It is authorized by Joe but not by the ISP. Which governs? Note that if you believe the ISP's Terms of Service should govern it does not necessarily mean that Mary's act of accessing Joe's account would violate an unauthorized access statute. Most unauthorized access statutes require that the mental state concerning lack of authorization must be intentional. If Mary accesses Joe's account and thinks that his permission is sufficient, Mary will not have intentionally accessed Joe's account without authorization.

3.   *Outsiders and insiders.* The *Morris* opinion refers extensively to the legislative history of § 1030, and in particular to its discussion of liability for "insiders" and "outsiders." In the 1980s, drawing a line between the liability for "insiders" and "outsiders" made sense for several reasons. First, most computer network users used terminals to access a mainframe computer; access to the mainframe computer generally required an account or privileges at another computer that was a trusted host. Second, the scope of § 1030 was very narrow. From 1986 until 1996, § 1030 applied only to "federal interest" computers, which were defined as a) computers used by financial institutions or the United States government in whole or in part or b) computers that were part of an interstate network if the offense was committed using computers in multiple states. In that environment, it made at least some sense to distinguish between users that had access privileges on some federal interest computers and those that did not.

The distinction is harder to understand today. Section 1030 now applies to "protected computers," and the definition is broad enough that every computer connected to the Internet is a protected computer. Anyone can sign up for an Internet account, and software applications such as the Web routinely grant access privileges to the public. In light of these changes, it is difficult (if not impossible) to classify computer users as "insiders" or "outsiders" in the abstract. A user may be an "insider" with respect to a group of machines and an "outsider" with respect to another group. Or, a user may be an "insider" with respect to some information stored on a server but an "outsider" with respect to other information.

A more profitable way to approach such questions is by asking whether the user circumvented a code-based restriction or breached a contract-based or norms-based restriction. A rough equivalence exists between the two sets of concepts. Those who circumvent code-based restrictions will often be considered outsiders, and those who merely breach contract-based or norms-based restrictions will often be considered insiders. At the same time, focusing on the means of gaining access to particular information provides a more precise and reliable tool for purposes of distinguishing among different types of authorization than the status-based distinction between outsiders and insiders.

4.   Consider the following hypothetical criticism:

> The concept of unauthorized access to a computer is nonsensical. Access to a computer is always authorized. A user can access a computer only if the computer authorizes the user to access it. In fact, what we call computer hacking is really the art of convincing a computer to authorize you to access the computer. When you hack in to a computer, you gain the computer's authorization to access it. Accordingly, all access is authorized.

What does this assume about how authorization to access a computer is granted or denied? What does it assume about *who* has the authority to grant authorized access to a computer?

The High Court of Australia's opinion in Kennison v. Daire, 160 C.L.R. 129 (1986), may help you answer these questions. In *Daire*, a man withdrew $200 (AU) from an offline Automatic Teller Machine (ATM) using an expired card from a closed account. Bank employees had programmed their computers to dispense money whenever a person used an ATM card from that bank using a proper password. When the ATMs were offline, however, the machines were programmed to dispense money without checking whether there was money in the relevant account, or even if the account was still open. The defendant in *Daire* intentionally exploited this defect, took $200, and was charged and convicted of larceny. On appeal, he argued that he had not committed larceny because the bank, through the ATM, had consented to his taking the money. The High Court of Australia rejected the argument:

> The fact that the bank programmed the machine in a way that facilitated the commission of a fraud by a person holding a card did not mean that the bank consented to the withdrawal of money by a person who had no account with the bank. It is not suggested that any person, having the authority of the bank to consent to the particular transaction, did so. The

machine could not give the bank's consent in fact and there is no principle of law that requires it to be treated as though it were a person with authority to decide and consent. The proper inference to be drawn from the facts is that the bank consented to the withdrawal of up to $200 by a card holder who presented his card and supplied his personal identification number, only if the card holder had an account which was current. It would be quite unreal to infer that the bank consented to the withdrawal by a card holder whose account had been closed.

Id. at 130. Do you agree? How do you know what "the bank" wanted? Who is "the bank," anyway? The person who programmed the bank's computer? The local branch manager? The bank's CEO?

4. WHAT IS AUTHORIZATION? THE CASE OF CONTRACT–BASED RESTRICTIONS

Does breaching an explicit condition on access to a computer make the access without authorization or in excess of authorization? Computer users encounter such conditions often in the form of Terms of Use and Terms of Service on Internet services, software, and websites. Employers routinely place restrictions on their employees, as well. Such restrictions can be clear or vague, broad or narrow. Should violating such restrictions be a crime?

UNITED STATES v. DREW

United States District Court for the Central District of California, 2009.
___ F.R.D. ___, 2009 WL 2872855.

GEORGE H. WU, DISTRICT JUDGE.

This case raises the issue of whether (and/or when will) violations of an Internet website's terms of service constitute a crime under the Computer Fraud and Abuse Act, 18 U.S.C. § 1030.

I. *BACKGROUND*

A. *Indictment*

The Indictment included, *inter alia,* the following allegations (not all of which were established by the evidence at trial). Drew, a resident of O'Fallon, Missouri, entered into a conspiracy in which its members agreed to intentionally access a computer used in interstate commerce without (and/or in excess of) authorization in order to obtain information for the purpose of committing the tortious act of intentional infliction of emotional distress upon "M.T.M.," subsequently identified as Megan Meier.

Megan was a 13 year old girl living in O'Fallon who had been a classmate of Drew's daughter Sarah. Pursuant to the conspiracy, on or about September 20, 2006, the conspirators registered and set up a profile for a fictitious 16 year old male juvenile named "Josh Evans" on the www. MySpace.com website, and posted a photograph of a boy without that boy's knowledge or consent. Such conduct violated My Space's terms of service.

The conspirators contacted Megan through the MySpace network (on which she had her own profile) using the Josh Evans pseudonym and began to flirt with her over a number of days. On or about October 7, 2006, the conspirators had "Josh" inform Megan that he was moving away. On or about October 16, 2006, the conspirators had "Josh" tell Megan that he no longer liked her and that "the world would be a better place without her in it." Later on that same day, after learning that Megan had killed herself, Drew caused the Josh Evans MySpace account to be deleted.

B. *MySpace.com*

MySpace is a social networking website where members can create profiles and interact with other members. In 2006, to become a member, one had to go to the sign-up section of the MySpace website and register by filling in personal information (such as name, email address, date of birth, country/state/postal code, and gender) and creating a password. In addition, the individual had to check on the box indicating that "You agree to the MySpace Terms of Service and Privacy Policy." As used in its website, "terms of service" refers to the "MySpace.com Terms of Use Agreement" ("MSTOS"). The MSTOS in 2006 stated, *inter alia*:

> This Terms of Use Agreement ("Agreement") sets forth the legally binding terms for your use of the Services. You are only authorized to use the Services (regardless of whether your access or use is intended) if you agree to abide by all applicable laws and to this Agreement.

> By using the Services, you represent and warrant that (a) all registration information you submit is truthful and accurate; (b) you will maintain the accuracy of such information; (c) you are 14 years of age or older; and (d) your use of the Services does not violate any applicable law or regulation.

The MSTOS prohibited the posting of a wide range of content on the website including (but not limited to) material that: "provides information that you know is false or misleading or promotes illegal activities or conduct that is abusive, threatening, obscene, defamatory or libelous"; "includes a photograph of another person that you have posted without that person's consent"; [or] "involves commercial activities and/or sales without our prior written consent." Further, My Space was allowed to unilaterally modify the terms of service, with such modifications taking effect upon the posting of notice on its website.

At one point, MySpace was receiving an estimated 230,000 new accounts per day and eventually the number of profiles exceeded 400 million with over 100 million unique visitors worldwide. Generally speaking, MySpace would not monitor new accounts to determine if they complied with the terms of service except on a limited basis, mostly in regards to photographic content.

II. *DISCUSSION*

A. *The Misdemeanor 18 U.S.C. § 1030(a)(2)(C) Crime Based on Violation of a Website's Terms of Service*

The only basis for finding that Drew intentionally accessed MySpace's computer/servers without authorization and/or in excess of authorization was her and/or her co-conspirator's violations of the MSTOS by deliberately creating the false Josh Evans profile, posting a photograph of a juvenile without his permission and pretending to be a sixteen year old O'Fallon resident for the purpose of communicating with Megan. Therefore, if conscious violations of the My Space terms of service were not sufficient to satisfy the first element of the CFAA misdemeanor violation as per 18 U.S.C. §§ 1030(a)(2)(C) and 1030(b)(2)(A), Drew's Rule 29(c) motion would have to be granted on that basis alone. However, this Court concludes that an intentional breach of the MSTOS can potentially constitute accessing the MySpace computer/server without authorization and/or in excess of authorization under the statute.

There is nothing in the way that the undefined words "authorization" and "authorized" are used in the CFAA (or from the CFAA's legislative history) which indicates that Congress intended for them to have specialized meanings. As delineated in *Webster's New World Dictionary* at 92, to "authorize" ordinarily means "to give official approval to or permission for." It cannot be considered a stretch of the law to hold that the owner of an Internet website has the right to establish the extent to (and the conditions under) which members of the public will be allowed access to information, services and/or applications which are available on the website. Nor can it be doubted that the owner can relay and impose those limitations/restrictions/conditions by means of written notice such as terms of service or use provisions placed on the home page of the website.

While issues might be raised in particular cases as to the sufficiency of the notice and/or sufficiency of the user's assent to the terms, and while public policy considerations might in turn limit enforcement of particular restrictions, the vast majority of the courts (that have considered the issue) have held that a website's terms of service/use can define what is (and/or is not) authorized access vis-a-vis that website. Clearly, the MSTOS was capable of defining the scope of authorized access of visitors, members and/or users to the website.

B. *Contravention of the Void-for-Vagueness Doctrine*

In *Kolender v. Lawson*, 461 U.S. 352, 357–58 (1983), the Court explained that:

> As generally stated, the void-for-vagueness doctrine requires that a penal statute define the criminal offense with sufficient definiteness that ordinary people can understand what conduct is prohibited and in a manner that does not encourage arbitrary and discriminatory enforcement. Although the doctrine focuses both on actual notice to citizens and arbitrary enforcement, we have recognized recently that

the more important aspect of the vagueness doctrine is not actual notice, but the other principal element of the doctrine—the requirement that a legislature establish minimal guidelines to govern law enforcement. Where the legislature fails to provide such minimal guidelines, a criminal statute may permit a standardless sweep that allows policemen, prosecutors, and juries to pursue their personal predilections.

The pivotal issue herein is whether basing a CFAA misdemeanor violation as per 18 U.S.C. §§ 1030(a)(2)(C) and 1030(c)(2)(A) upon the conscious violation of a website's terms of service runs afoul of the void-for-vagueness doctrine. This Court concludes that it does primarily because of the absence of minimal guidelines to govern law enforcement, but also because of actual notice deficiencies.

Definitional/Actual Notice Deficiencies

Terms of service which are incorporated into a browsewrap or clickwrap agreement can, like any other type of contract, define the limits of authorized access as to a website and its concomitant computer/server(s). However, the question is whether individuals of "common intelligence" are on notice that a breach of a terms of service contract can become a crime under the CFAA. Arguably, they are not.

First, an initial inquiry is whether the statute, as it is written, provides sufficient notice. Here, the language of § 1030(a)(2)(C) does not explicitly state (nor does it implicitly suggest) that the CFAA has "criminalized breaches of contract" in the context of website terms of service. Normally, breaches of contract are not the subject of criminal prosecution. Thus, while "ordinary people" might expect to be exposed to civil liabilities for violating a contractual provision, they would not expect criminal penalties.

Second, if a website's terms of service controls what is "authorized" and what is "exceeding authorization"—which in turn governs whether an individual's accessing information or services on the website is criminal or not—§ 1030(a)(2)(C) would be unacceptably vague because it is unclear whether any or all violations of terms of service will render the access unauthorized, or whether only certain ones will. If *any* violation of *any* term of service is held to make the access unauthorized, that strategy would probably resolve this particular vagueness issue; but it would, in turn, render the statute incredibly overbroad and contravene the second prong of the void-for-vagueness doctrine as to setting guidelines to govern law enforcement.

Third, by utilizing violations of the terms of service as the basis for the § 1030(a)(2)(C) crime, that approach makes the website owner—in essence—the party who ultimately defines the criminal conduct. This will lead to further vagueness problems. The owner's description of a term of service might itself be so vague as to make the visitor or member reasonably unsure of what the term of service covers. Moreover, website owners can establish terms where either the scope or the application of the provision are to be decided by them *ad hoc* and/or pursuant to undelineated standards.

The Absence of Minimal Guidelines to Govern Law Enforcement

Treating a violation of a website's terms of service, without more, to be sufficient to constitute "intentionally access[ing] a computer without authorization or exceed[ing] authorized access" would result in transforming § 1030(a)(2)(C) into an overwhelmingly overbroad enactment that would convert a multitude of otherwise innocent Internet users into misdemeanant criminals.

One need only look to the MSTOS terms of service to see the expansive and elaborate scope of such provisions whose breach engenders the potential for criminal prosecution. Obvious examples of such breadth would include: 1) the lonely-heart who submits intentionally inaccurate data about his or her age, height and/or physical appearance, which contravenes the MSTOS prohibition against providing "information that you know is false or misleading"; 2) the student who posts candid photographs of classmates without their permission, which breaches the MSTOS provision covering "a photograph of another person that you have posted without that person's consent"; and/or 3) the exasperated parent who sends out a group message to neighborhood friends entreating them to purchase his or her daughter's girl scout cookies, which transgresses the MSTOS rule against "advertising to, or solicitation of, any Member to buy or sell any products or services through the Services."

However, one need not consider hypotheticals to demonstrate the problem. In this case, Megan (who was then 13 years old) had her own profile on MySpace, which was in clear violation of the MSTOS which requires that users be "14 years of age or older." No one would seriously suggest that Megan's conduct was criminal or should be subject to criminal prosecution.

If every such breach [of the MSTOS] does qualify, then there is absolutely no limitation or criteria as to which of the breaches should merit criminal prosecution. All manner of situations will be covered from the more serious (*e.g.* posting child pornography) to the more trivial (*e.g.* posting a picture of friends without their permission). All can be prosecuted.[31]

In sum, if any conscious breach of a website's terms of service is held to be sufficient by itself to constitute intentionally accessing a computer without authorization or in excess of authorization, the result will be that § 1030(a)(2)(C) becomes a law that affords too much discretion to the police and too little notice to citizens who wish to use the Internet.

---

31. In comparison, the felony violation of 18 U.S.C. § 1030(a)(2)(C) contains effective scienter elements because it not only requires the intentional accessing of a computer without authorization or in excess of authorization, but also the prerequisite that such access must be "in furtherance" of a crime or tortious act which, in turn, will normally contain additional scienter and/or wrongful intent conditions.

For the reasons stated above, the Defendant's motion is granted.

NOTES AND QUESTIONS

1. The question raised by the *Drew* case is whether Drew's access to the MySpace.com computers was "without authorization" or "exceeded authorized access" merely because it violated the MySpace Terms of Service. Judge Wu held that such a legal interpretation would render the statute unconstitutional, and therefore he dismissed the charges. But does that mean that a contractual restriction on computer use can never render computer use in breach of contractual terms "without authorization"? Or does it only mean that such a theory cannot be pursued in this particular case given the resulting constitutional vagueness concerns?

Put another way, how do you reconcile Part II.A. of the *Drew* opinion, in which Judge Wu seems to say that a contractual breach can render access unauthorized, with Part II.B. of the opinion, in which Judge Wu seems to say that such a theory would render the statute unconstitutional? When, if ever, can breach of a contract render access "without authorization" or in excess of authorization? Is use of a computer in breach of a contract "without authorization" in the same way that a use of a computer by hacking into someone else's account is without authorization?

2. *Misuse of sensitive computers by government employees.* A number of criminal cases have held that violating a term of use violates unauthorized access statutes for government employees who misused sensitive government computers. In these cases, the apparent test for whether the defendant had violated an unauthorized access statute was whether the defendant had violated explicit workplace policies on computer access.

A. In United States v. Czubinski, 106 F.3d 1069 (1st Cir. 1997), an IRS employee browsed through an IRS database containing tax returns, and viewed the tax returns of various personal friends and enemies. IRS regulations made clear that employees "may not use any Service computer system for other than official purposes." Although the First Circuit reversed his convictions, the court did note in passing that Czubinski's conduct "unquestionably exceeded authorized access" to the IRS computer.

B. In Commonwealth v. McFadden, 850 A.2d 1290 (Pa. Super. Ct. 2004), a police officer sent a message over the police computer system from her squad car pretending to be a terrorist who had taken control of the car and was planning a terrorist attack. The officer was authorized to use the police computer system for official purposes only, and she was charged with and convicted of having accessed the police computer system "without authorization." The appellate court affirmed the conviction, reasoning that the defendant accessed the computer system "for purposes of typing a false threat message" rather than for official purposes.

C. In State v. Olson, 735 P.2d 1362 (Wash. Ct. App. 1987), a police officer used the police computer database to access and print out the driver's license photographs of female college students who attended a nearby university. The officer was charged and convicted at trial of having accessed the police computer database "without authorization." After carefully reviewing the workplace policies at the police department, the appellate court reversed the conviction. The workplace policies prohibited use of information obtained from the police computers, but not did not limit access to the computers conditioned on those uses. Because the defendant's access did not violate an explicit policy, it was not without authorization and the defendant was not liable.

Do you agree with these cases? If so, do you agree with them because you fear the consequences of government employee abuse of sensitive databases and computer systems? Or do you agree because you think that computer owners should have an absolute right to determine the scope of authorized access to their computers?

3. In State v. Schwartz, 21 P.3d 1128 (Or. Ct. App. 2001), an employee was convicted under Oregon's computer crime statute for using his employer's computer network in several ways that the employer had explicitly informed him were not authorized. The employee was charged with "unlawfully, knowingly and without authorization alter[ing] a computer and computer network" in violation of ORS 164.377(3). On appeal following conviction, the defendant argued that the line between authorized and unauthorized access was so unclear that it was unconstitutionally vague. The court summarized the arguments for and against as follows:

> Defendant also contends that the phrase "without authorization" in ORS 164.377(3) is unconstitutionally vague. According to defendant, because that phrase does not identify what sort of authorization is required, or from what source it must come, it is vague. Defendant further suggests that ORS 164.377(3), as written, requires that any alteration be authorized and that such a construction is so broad as to allow ad hoc enforcement. The state responds that only substantial certainty is required. The state observes that ORS 164.377(3) criminalizes alteration of a computer only when a person *knows* that he or she is without authorization. The state further argues that we should read ORS 164.377(3) as a whole; as such, it is sufficiently clear that the source of the authorization must be the person in control of the computer.

Schwartz, 21 P.3d at 1133. The Court then rejected the defendant's argument:

> "Without authorization" in ORS 164.377(3) provides sufficiently definite notice of the prohibited conduct. In this case, defendant himself acknowledged that installing gate programs (computer programs that allow users to obtain remote access to a computer network) was against company policy. He did not argue that, despite company policy, he had obtained permission to install a gate program. Confronted with the phrase "without authorization," a potential violator of ORS 164.377(3) would be reasonably certain that he or she would run afoul of that prohibition by doing something to a computer in violation of the policy of the company that owned the computer without having sought permission for an exception to the policy.

Id. at 1135. In rejecting the defendant's vagueness claim, has the court provided a useful definition of the phrase "without authorization?" If so, how do we determine who the "owner" of a computer is, or what the owner's "policy" is?

4.   Consider the policy implications of a rule that violating a contractual restriction on computer access renders that access without authorization or in excess of authorization. The cases involving government employee misuse of sensitive databases are at one end of the spectrum, as the information typically is sensitive and the public interest in the contractual restriction generally is clear. But most contractual restrictions arise in very different contexts. Anyone can own a computer, and computer owners can place an infinite range of different contractual restrictions on access. Should unauthorized access statutes permit all computer owners to rely on the criminal law to enforce all types of contractual restrictions on access? Or should the law protect only some types of computer owners, some types of sensitive data, and some types of reasonable restrictions?

Computer network users frequently agree to be bound to contracts that condition their use of a computer network on certain restrictions. For example, law students have access to free Westlaw and Lexis accounts, but may use the accounts only for specific reasons. Similarly, the Terms of Service (TOS) of many Internet service providers impose many conditions: for example, some TOS state that the user may not use the account to view offensive material. If a person uses the network in a way that violates those conditions, should access to the network be considered without authorization or in excess of authorization? If a law student uses Westlaw to read an article on a baseball game or research old newspaper stories about his favorite musician, is the student guilty of committing a federal crime? Does that depend on the precise wording of Westlaw's TOS? Should it?

5.   Is criminal liability for breaching contract-based restrictions consistent with the theories of punishment? Is breaching a contractual restriction on access always or often a morally culpable act that demands punishment from a retributive perspective? Is it always or often a harmful act that the law should attempt to deter? Or does that depend on the nature of the restriction?

When you consider these questions, note that contract law generally is civil law. Breaching a contract ordinarily leads to liability to pay damages, but not criminal punishment. Does a contract-based approach to unauthorized access effectively criminalize contract law online? Moreover, does it do so in an environment in which users are unlikely to be aware of the contracts that they are entering into? If a computer owner can issue any arbitrary set of rules over how its network must be used, and those rules are backed by the sanction of criminal law, the criminal law will end up subjecting Internet users to a range of more or less arbitrary restrictions on their conduct. Is this desirable?

6.   *Analogies to consent in criminal law.* One way of evaluating the merits of criminalizing the breach of contract-based restrictions on computer access is to draw analogies to how the criminal law deals with similar problems elsewhere. The prohibition on access without authorization and exceeding authorized access arguably resembles traditional prohibitions on conduct without the victim's consent found in doctrines such as trespass (entering or staying on a person's property without their consent) and rape

(sexual intercourse without a person's consent). In both contexts, a body of law exists to determine whether trickery or fraud vitiates consent.

For example, a person might pose as a traveling salesman and gain access to a home when in fact he plans to commit a burglary inside. Does the trickery render the entrance to the home "without consent," such that entering the home is a trespass? In the context of rape law, a man posing as a doctor might invent a story that he must have sexual intercourse with a woman to cure her of a terrible disease. If the woman believes him and agrees, does the man's deception render the act of sexual intercourse "without consent" and therefore a sexual assault? *See* Boro v. People, 210 Cal. Rptr. 122 (Ct. App. 1985).

Although the comparison may seem odd at first, we might look at the legal consequences of code-based or contract-based restrictions on computer access as raising similar questions. For example, computer misuse laws prohibit access to a computer without authorization, whereas trespass laws prohibit entrance or continued presence in a home without permission. Speaking anthropomorphically for a moment, the computer is "tricked" into authorizing the defendant to access the computer in a way conceptually similar to how a homeowner might be tricked into allowing a person into their home. The question is, when does the trickery vitiate the computer's consent, such that access allowed by the computer is without authorization or in excess of authorization?

The traditional approach is to distinguish between "fraud in the factum" and "fraud in the inducement." *See generally* Rollin M. Perkins & Ronald N. Boyce, Criminal Law 1075–84 (3d ed. 1982). The overall question is, did the victim actually consent to the act that occurred, regardless of whether the victim consented in reliance on representations concerning collateral matters? If the answer is yes, then the trickery is only fraud in the inducement and the consent is valid. If the answer is no, and the victim was tricked as to the nature of the consent given, then the fraud is fraud in the factum and the consent is not valid. Of course, this framework does not answer everything: it requires courts to identify the nature of the act and distinguish it from mere collateral matters. At the same time, it provides a traditional doctrinal framework for understanding the scope of access without authorization and exceeding authorized access.

Judge Kozinski suggested that this approach might be the proper way to interpret unauthorized access statutes in Theofel v. Farey–Jones, 359 F.3d 1066 (9th Cir. 2004), a case arising under 18 U.S.C. § 2701. Section 2701 is part of the Stored Communications Act, a law explored in depth in Chapter Six. Section 2701 is an unauthorized access statute that applies specifically to Internet service providers, and prohibits both intentionally accessing an ISP's computer without authorization and intentionally exceeding an authorization to do so. In a civil case concerning an invalid subpoena served on a company that led to the disclosure of private information, Judge Kozinski offered the following framework for interpreting authorization in the context of § 2701, *id.* at 1073–74:

> We interpret federal statutes in light of the common law. Especially relevant here is the common law of trespass. Like the tort of trespass, the

Stored Communications Act protects individuals' privacy and proprietary interests. The Act reflects Congress's judgment that users have a legitimate interest in the confidentiality of communications in electronic storage at a communications facility. Just as trespass protects those who rent space from a commercial storage facility to hold sensitive documents, *cf.* Prosser and Keeton on the Law of Torts § 13, at 78 (W. Page Keeton ed., 5th ed.1984), the Act protects users whose electronic communications are in electronic storage with an ISP or other electronic communications facility.

A defendant is not liable for trespass if the plaintiff authorized his entry. *See* Prosser & Keeton § 13, at 70. But "an overt manifestation of assent or willingness would not be effective if the defendant knew, or probably if he ought to have known in the exercise of reasonable care, that the plaintiff was mistaken as to the nature and quality of the invasion intended." Id. § 18, at 119. Thus, the busybody who gets permission to come inside by posing as a meter reader is a trespasser. So too is the police officer who, invited into a home, conceals a recording device for the media.

Not all deceit vitiates consent. "The mistake must extend to the essential character of the act itself, which is to say that which makes it harmful or offensive, rather than to some collateral matter which merely operates as an inducement." Prosser & Keeton § 18, at 120. In other words, it must be a "substantial mistake concerning the nature of the invasion or the extent of the harm." Restatement (Second) of Torts § 892B(2) cmt. g. Unlike the phony meter reader, the restaurant critic who poses as an ordinary customer is not liable for trespass, nor, unlike the wired cop, is the invitee who conceals only an intent to repeat what he hears. These results hold even if admission would have been refused had all the facts been known.

These are fine and sometimes incoherent distinctions. But the theory is that some invited mistakes go to the essential nature of the invasion while others are merely collateral. Classification depends on the extent to which the intrusion trenches on the specific interests that the tort of trespass seeks to protect.

Assuming the framework is a valid one, does the law of trespass necessarily provide the right comparison to understand the scope of authorization in computer misuse statutes? Trespass is usually a civil offense, not a crime, and when it is a crime it tends to be a violation or at most a misdemeanor. Further, in order to protect the home, courts have been unusually willing to find that misrepresentation or bad faith triggers a trespass. *See, e.g.,* People v. Peeples, 616 N.E.2d 294 (Ill. 1993) (holding that the defendant's criminal actions undertaken inside another person's house vitiated the homeowner's consent to enter the house, rendering him guilty of trespass). Are computers different? Although a homeowner has a tremendous interest in protecting the privacy of his home, computers connected to computer networks generally are designed to be open. Networks can be used by thousands of people at the same time in countless different ways. A person can be in only one home at a time, while computer users can access dozens of computers at a time and thousands of computers in a day. Unauthorized access statutes are primarily criminal statutes, and often impose serious felony liability.

Given these differences, is trespass law a helpful standard? Is gaining entrance to a home by pretending to be a meter reader akin to visiting a website by pretending to be someone who will comply with the Terms of Use? Consider that in *Theofel*, Judge Kozinski reached the rather remarkable conclusion that serving an invalid subpoena on an ISP constituted an unauthorized access to that ISP in violation of 18 U.S.C. § 2701. According to Judge Kozinski, the fact that the subpoena was overly broad made the effort to obtain information unauthorized; serving the court order was deemed the legal equivalent of hacking into the computer. *See Theofel*, 359 F.3d at 1074. Do you agree? A narrower application of the same traditional principles of criminal law would reach very different outcomes. For example, if you define the purpose of access restrictions as confirming that the person accessing the computer is the particular individual who is authorized to use it, then the traditional approach would prohibit circumventing code-based restrictions but not breaching contract-based restrictions.

5. WHAT IS AUTHORIZATION? THE CASE OF NORMS–BASED RESTRICTIONS

Should misuse of a computer render access to that computer unauthorized even if it neither circumvents a code-based restriction nor breaches an explicit contractual restriction? Are there some types of computer use that are simply understood as sufficiently out of bounds or contrary to the computer owner's interests that such access should be deemed "without authorization" or in excess of authorization? If so, it might be considered a norms-based approach to authorization. Access that violates generally understood social norms on normal or reasonable computer access might render that access without authorization or in excess of authorization.

For example, what if an employee uses an employer's computer in a way contrary to the employer's interests? Does using the employer's computer in a way contrary to its interests constitute an access without authorization or in excess of authorization?

UNITED STATES v. NOSAL

United States District Court for the Northern District of California, 2009.
2009 WL 981336.

MARILYN HALL PATEL, DISTRICT JUDGE.

Nosal was a high level executive at an international executive search firm, Korn/Ferry International ("KFI"), from approximately April 1996 to October 2004. KFI was one of the leading providers of executive recruitment services, engaging in searches to fill executive, board-of-director, and similar high level positions, for businesses in the United States. Nosal terminated his employment with KFI in October 2004, with plans to start a competing executive search firm.

Upon his departure, Nosal voluntarily entered into a separation agreement and agreed to serve as an independent contractor to KFI from November 1, 2004 through October 15, 2005. Under the terms of that Separation and General Release Agreement and an Independent Contractor Agreement (collectively, "the Nosal–KFI Agreements"), Nosal agreed to cooperate with KFI on certain ongoing search assignments and agreed not to compete with KFI by not performing executive search, executive placement, management assessment, or management audit services on behalf of any other entity than KFI during the period the Nosal–KFI Agreements were in place. In exchange for his services, Nosal was to receive $25,000 per month during that year, as well as two lump-sum payments on July 31st and October 15, 2005.

Becky Christian was an employee of KFI from approximately September 1999 through January 2005. The individual identified in the Superceding Indictment as "J.F." was employed by KFI from approximately December 1997 to August 2005. J.F. was Nosal's executive assistant prior to Nosal's departure from KFI.

According to the Superceding Indictment, both individuals helped Nosal set up his new executive search firm and assisted Nosal in obtaining trade secrets and other things of value from KFI's computer system, prior to and upon termination of their employment with KFI by using their own KFI password-protected user accounts. Specifically, the Superceding Indictment alleges that J.F. and Christian assisted Nosal in obtaining source lists and other custom reports of names and contact information from the KFI "Searcher" database, a highly confidential and proprietary database of executives and companies.

On April 10, 2008, Nosal and co-defendant Becky Christian were charged by indictment with federal statutory violations relating to their alleged involvement in stealing confidential and proprietary information from KFI for the purpose of assisting Nosal in his own executive search activities.

[Nosal was charged with several offenses, including accessing a computer without authorization or in excess of authorization to further a scheme to defraud in violation of 18 U.S.C. § 1030(a)(4). Nosal moved to dismiss the charges on the ground that the facts alleged in the indictment failed to state an offense.]

Nosal contends that the terms "without authorization" and "to exceed authorized access" should be read narrowly to exclude the misuse or misappropriation of information obtained with permission.

The Superceding Indictment alleges that two KFI employees, defendant Christian and J.F., used their employee user accounts and passwords to access a protected computer belonging to KFI, and, without authorization and by exceeding authorized access, downloaded, copied and duplicated source lists and other contact information from KFI's proprietary "Searcher" database, and gave that information to Nosal. These actions were allegedly performed for Nosal's benefit and for the purpose of retaining clients and placing candidates as part of non-KFI executive search activities. The government contends these actions were performed conspiratorially, in violation of the Nosal–KFI Agreements and knowingly and with the intent to defraud KFI, in violation of the CFAA. Nosal's position is that the CFAA was aimed primarily at computer hackers and that the statute does not cover employees who misappropriate information or who violate contractual confidentiality agreements by using employer-owned information in a manner inconsistent with those agreements.

Here too, Nosal acknowledges that the law in this area is somewhat unsettled. The Ninth Circuit has not yet ruled on the issue, and courts in other jurisdictions have split views on the question of whether an employee with an improper purpose may be held liable for accessing computer information that s/he is otherwise permitted to access within the scope of his or her employment. Under the CFAA, the term "exceeds authorized access" means "to access a computer with authorization and to use such access to obtain or alter information in the computer that the accesser is not entitled so to obtain or alter." 18 U.S.C.A. § 1030(e)(6). The term "authorization" is not defined by statute. The issue for the court to decide is whether an employee may act "without authorization" or "in excess of authorized access" when he accesses confidential and proprietary business information from his employer's computer that he has permission to access, but then uses that information in a manner inconsistent with the employer's interests or in violation of other contractual obligations, and where the employee intended to use the information in that manner at the time of access.

The parties note the two lines of diverging case law on this issue. Some courts, including two courts of appeal, have broadly construed the CFAA to hold an employee acting to access an employer's computer to obtain business information with intent to defraud, i.e., for their own personal benefit or the benefit of a competitor, act "without authorization" or "exceed authorization" in violation of the statute. *See, e.g., Int'l Airport Ctrs., L.L.C. v. Citrin,* 440 F.3d 418, 420–21 (7th Cir. 2006); *EF Cultural Travel BV v. Explorica, Inc.,* 274 F.3d 577, 582–84 (1st Cir. 2001); *Shurgard Storage Ctrs., Inc. v. Safeguard Self Storage, Inc.,* 119 F. Supp.2d 1121, 1125 (W.D. Wash. 2000); *ViChip Corp. v. Lee,* 438 F. Supp.2d 1087, 1100 (N.D. Cal. 2006) (Hamilton, J.); *Hanger Prosthetics & Orthotics, Inc. v. Capstone Orthopedic, Inc.,* 556 F. Supp.2d 1122, 1131 (E.D. Cal. 2008); *Pac. Aerospace & Elec., Inc. v. Taylor,* 295 F. Supp.2d 1188, 1195–97 (E.D. Wash. 2003); *Calyon v. Mizuho Sec. USA, Inc.,* 2007 WL 2618658, *1 (S.D.N.Y. 2007); *Condux Intern., Inc. v. Haugum,* 2008 WL 5244818, *4, n3 (D. Minn. 2008) (collecting cases). These courts have generally held that authorized access to a company computer terminated once an employee acted with adverse or nefarious interests and against the duty of loyalty imposed on an employee in an agency relationship with his or her employer or former employer.

Other courts have refused to hold employees with access and nefarious interests within the statute, concluding that a violation for accessing a protected computer "without authorization" or in "excess of authorized access" occurs only when initial access or the access of certain information is not permitted in the first instance. *See, e.g., Black & Decker (US), Inc. v. Smith,* 568 F. Supp.2d 929, 933 (W.D. Tenn. 2008); *Diamond Power Intern., Inc. v. Davidson,* 540 F. Supp.2d 1322, 1341–43 (N.D. Ga. 2007); *B & B Microscopes v. Armogida,* 532 F. Supp.2d 744, 758 (W.D. Pa. 2007); *Brett Senior & Assocs., P.C. v. Fitzgerald,* 2007 WL 2043377, *2–4 (E.D. Pa. 2007); *Lockheed Martin Corp. v. Speed,* 2006 WL 2683058, *5 (M.D. Fla. 2006); *Int'l Ass'n of Machinists and Aerospace Workers v. Werner– Masuda,* 390 F. Supp.2d 479, 495 (D. Md. 2005); *Bridal Expo, Inc. v. van Florestein,* 2009 WL 255862, *10 (S.D. Tex. 2009) (collecting cases). Those courts have generally reasoned that the CFAA is intended to punish computer hackers, electronic trespassers and other "outsiders" but not employees who abuse computer access privileges to misuse information derived from their employment.

Nosal argues that reasoning should be followed and the broader "misappropriation" theory of the CFAA should be rejected, because the CFAA was intended to cover "classic" hacking activities over violations of agency or fiduciary duties principles, the plain language targets the unauthorized procurement of information over its wrongful use, and the rule of lenity compels a narrower reading.

The court is not persuaded by Nosal's arguments or by the narrower view of "authorization" embraced in the latter line of cases. As noted by the Third Circuit, "the scope of the CFAA's reach has been expanded over the last two decades." *P.C. Yonkers, Inc. v. Celebrations the Party and Seasonal Superstore, LLC.,* 428 F.3d 504, 510 (3d Cir. 2005). Employers are increasingly taking advantage of the CFAA's civil remedies to sue former employees and their new companies who seek a competitive edge through wrongful use of information from the former employer's computer system. There is no reason why this expansion should be limited to civil challenges of the unauthorized access of information from a company's computer database by an employee to further a fraud.

Here, the government has alleged that the employees' acts of accessing KFI's information were not only purposeful, but also with the intent to defraud, and that confidential and proprietary information was both taken and used to further the intended fraud, i.e., to advance Nosal's own executive search activities, to the detriment of KFI. Christian and J.F. were not authorized to initially access the KFI computer with the intent to defraud KFI. That they accessed the information at issue with nefarious intent rendered the access "without authorization" or "in excess of authorized access."

The First Circuit relied on this definition of "exceeds authorized access" to find the necessary elements for a successful CFAA charge in the employer-employee context in *EF Cultural Travel,* 274 F.3d at 583–84. In so doing, the First Circuit affirmed that an employee of a tour company acted outside the scope of his confidentiality agreement by providing proprietary information to a competitor tour company employee. *Id.* The same logic applies with increased force here, not only because Christian and J.F. were bound by confidentiality agreements at the time of the alleged acts, but also because the Nosal–KFI agreements created a continued quasi-employment relationship between Nosal and KFI with additional and ongoing duties of confidentiality and non-competition.

Finally, Nosal's argument concerning the rule of lenity in criminal cases is unavailing because it is only appropriate when there is statutory ambiguity. The court finds no ambiguity in the statute here. Although no court has heretofore addressed § 1030(a)(4) in the criminal context, ample authority exists to permit criminal actions to proceed based on violations of this section by employees, as interpreted by civil cases, and there is simply no statutory basis to suggest otherwise.

NOTES AND QUESTIONS

1.   Can you identify exactly what rendered the access to a computer in *Nosal* either without authorization or in excess of authorization? Was it the breach of the confidentiality agreement? Or was it the "nefarious" intent? If it was the latter, why should nefarious intent turn an authorized access into access without authorization or in excess of authorization? And what exactly makes an intent "nefarious"?

2.   In Fugarino v. State, 531 S.E.2d 187 (Ga. Ct. App. 2000), a system administrator became upset when his employer hired an additional system administrator. He announced to his boss that the company's network was "his product, that no one else was going to work on his code, that nobody was going to take his place and he was 'going to take his code with him.'" *Id.* at 188. He then deleted several important sections of code from the employer's computer. On appeal following his conviction, a Georgia state appellate court concluded that the defendant's accessing his employer's computer to delete the code was "without authority" because "[t]he owner of the company * * * did not give Fugarino authority or permission to delete portions of the company's program." *Id.* at 189.

Are all employee uses of an employer's computer unauthorized until they are explicitly permitted? How should an employee know what uses are permitted and what uses are illegal?

3.   In State v. Wolf, 2009 WL 1152185 (Ohio App. 2009), the defendant was an employee of a city wastewater treatment plant who spent some of his time at work surfing the Internet for pornography using the treatment plant's computer network. While at work, the defendant also spent time trying to set up sexual encounters with various women using an adult dating site. The defendant was charged with violating Ohio's unauthorized access statute, R.C. § 2913.04(B), which provides in relevant part that "no person ... shall knowingly gain access ... to any computer, ... without the consent of, or beyond the scope of the express or implied consent of, the owner of the computer." The jury convicted the defendant of having violated the statute, and an Ohio appellate court affirmed the conviction:

> Having found that the State presented evidence Appellant used his computer to upload nude pictures of himself onto adult dating sites and to access certain pornographic websites to support the charge of solicitation, in addition to using his computer to engage in the criminal act of solicitation, we find such conduct was "beyond the scope of the express or implied consent" and the charge of "unauthorized use of a computer" was based upon sufficient evidence.

Id. at *6.

4. As Judge Patel's opinion in *United States v. Nosal* suggests, a large body of civil caselaw considers whether it constitutes an unauthorized access for an employee to use an employer's computer in a way contrary to the employer's interests. Most of the civil cases involve an employee using the employer's computer to help or help plan a competitor business. Lower courts are presently divided on the question.

An early example rejecting this theory of liability is Sherman & Co. v. Salton Maxim Housewares, 94 F. Supp.2d 817 (E.D. Mich. 2000), a case interpreting 18 U.S.C. § 2701, an unauthorized access statute that appears in the Stored Communications Act. The court reasoned, *id.* at 821:

> [Section 2701's] prohibition on intentional exceeding of authorized access anticipates that a person with authorization to a computer database or certain public portions of a database is not thereby authorized to visit "private" zones of data in the system. *See* Raphael Winick, *Searches and Seizures of Computers and Computer Data*, 8 Harv. J.L. & Tech. 75, 98 (1994). Yet, for "intentional" access in excess of authorization to be a crime and actionable civilly, the offender must have obtained the access to private files without authorization (e.g., using a computer he was not to use, or obtaining and using someone else's password or code without authorization). At a minimum, there must be a clearer and more explicit restriction on the authorized access. * * * Here [the] access * * * was in no way restricted by technical means or by any express limitation. Because § 2701 of the ECPA prohibits only unauthorized access and not the misappropriation or disclosure of information, there is no violation of § 2701 for a person with authorized access to the database no matter how malicious or larcenous his intended use of that access. Section 2701 outlaws illegal entry, not larceny.

In contrast, the court in Shurgard Storage Centers, Inc. v. Safeguard Self Storage, Inc., 119 F. Supp.2d 1121 (W.D. Wash. 2000), held that such access does render the access "without authorization." The court interpreted the phrase "without authorization" in 18 U.S.C. § 1030 by looking to agency principles embodied in section 112 of the Restatement (Second) of Agency (1958). That section states that "[u]nless otherwise agreed, the authority of an agent terminates if, without knowledge of the principal, he acquires adverse interests or if he is otherwise guilty of a serious breach of loyalty to the principal." Applying the Restatement to employees who accessed their employer's computer to help a future employer, the court held that the purpose to aid the future employer made the access without authorization:

> Under this rule, the authority of the plaintiff's former employees ended when they allegedly became agents of the defendant. Therefore, for the

purposes of this 12(b)(6) motion, they lost their authorization and were "without authorization" when they allegedly obtained and sent the proprietary information to the defendant via e-mail. The plaintiff has stated a claim under 18 U.S.C. § 1030(a)(2)(c).

Id. at 1125. *See also* International Airport Centers v. Citrin, 440 F.3d 418, 421 (7th Cir. 2006) (Posner, J.) (adopting the *Shurgard* approach in dicta).

Which approach makes more sense? Consider the fact that most employees use their employer's computers for personal reasons at least on occasion. If an employee accesses his network account at work in order to send a personal e-mail, has the employee committed an illegal unauthorized access to the employer's computer? What if the employee surfs the web in a search for a better job when he is on his lunch break? Does 18 U.S.C. § 1030 create an nationwide employee loyalty test, such that every time an employee accesses his employer's network for reasons not aligned with his employer's interest, the employee is committing a federal crime?

5. Many cases interpreting 18 U.S.C. § 1030 arise in a civil context, and this may have a significant effect on the law interpreting the prohibition on access without authorization and exceeding authorized access. The vague language of § 1030 and the civil remedy of § 1030(g) provide a tempting tool for businesses seeking to litigate against competitors. Because computers are integral to most businesses, a business can file a civil suit in federal court under § 1030(g) whenever there is a claim of potential foul play by a competitor. The theory will be that the foul play somehow involved accessing a computer, and it rendered the access without authorization or in excess of authorization. Judges faced with such claims in the civil context may be unaware that 18 U.S.C. § 1030 is primarily a criminal statute, and may adopt broad interpretations of authorization that make sense for injunctions sought in business disputes but make little sense in the context of a criminal prosecution against an individual. A sensible standard for stopping a company from using a particular business practice may be much broader than the standard to put a person in jail.

This dynamic may explain cases such as Register.com v. Verio, Inc., 126 F. Supp.2d 238 (S.D.N.Y. 2000). In *Verio*, the defendant company used an automated program to send queries to a database maintained by a business competitor, the plaintiff. The search robot gathered contact information about the plaintiff's customers, and the defendant's employees would then contact them and invite them to switch service providers from the plaintiff to the defendant. The plaintiff sued, and moved for a preliminary injunction against the use of the search robots on the ground (among others) that the defendant's use of the search robot constituted an unauthorized access to its database in violation of 18 U.S.C. § 1030. The district court agreed, holding that uses of the search robot "represent an unauthorized access" because the plaintiff "objects to [the defendant]'s use of search robots." In effect, the fact that the computer owner had at some point decided to object to the defendant's use of its computer made any prior accesses to the computer "without authorization."

Can you imagine a court adopting *Verio*'s theory of authorization in a criminal case? If not, should courts in criminal cases decline to follow broad interpretations of 18 U.S.C. § 1030 from civil cases? Courts generally use civil and criminal interpretations of federal statutes interchangeably absent an indication that Congress intended a contrary approach.

6.   In EF Cultural Travel BV v. Zefer Corp, 318 F.3d 58 (1st Cir. 2003), the First Circuit considered whether use of a "scraper" program to make thousands of queries of a website exceeded authorized access on the ground that it was understood that such use of a website was beyond the reasonable expectations of the site's owner. Zefer had designed the scraper to be used to query the website of EF Cultural Travel, a travel company, so as to help EF's competitor, Explorica, undercut EF's prices. The First Circuit concluded that use of the scraper did not exceed authorized access in the absence of an explicit ban on the use of scrapers in the website Terms of Service or elsewhere. In particular, the First Circuit rejected the idea that the use of the scraper was without authorization or exceeded authorization merely because the use of the scraper was beyond the reasonable expectations of website use:

> However useful a reasonable expectations test might be in other contexts where there may be a common understanding underpinning the notion, its use in this context is neither prescribed by the statute nor prudentially sound.

> Our basis for this view is not, as some have urged, that there is a presumption of open access to Internet information. The CFAA, after all, is primarily a statute imposing limits on access and enhancing control by information providers. Instead, we think that the public website provider can easily spell out explicitly what is forbidden and, consonantly, that nothing justifies putting users at the mercy of a highly imprecise, litigation-spawning standard like "reasonable expectations." If EF wants to ban scrapers, let it say so on the webpage or a link clearly marked as containing restrictions.

> This case itself illustrates the flaws in the "reasonable expectations" standard. Why should the copyright symbol, which arguably does not protect the substantive information anyway, or the provision of page-by-page access for that matter, be taken to suggest that downloading information at higher speed is forbidden. EF could easily include—indeed, by now probably has included—a sentence on its home page or in its terms of use stating that "no scrapers may be used," giving fair warning and avoiding time-consuming litigation about its private, albeit "reasonable," intentions.

> Needless to say, Zefer can have been in no doubt that EF would dislike the use of the scraper to construct a database for Explorica to undercut EF's prices; but EF would equally have disliked the compilation of such a database manually without the use of a scraper tool. EF did not purport to exclude competitors from looking at its website and any such limitation would raise serious public policy concerns.

7.   The Michigan legislature has tried to clarify the line between authorized and unauthorized access to a computer by enacting the following "rebuttable presumption" in the Michigan computer crime statute:

> It is a rebuttable presumption in a prosecution for [unauthorized access to computers] that the person did not have authorization from the owner, system operator, or other person who has authority from the owner or system operator to grant permission to access the computer program, computer, computer system, or computer network or has exceeded authorization unless 1 or more of the following circumstances existed at the time of access:
>
> (a) Written or oral permission was granted by the owner, system operator, or other person who has authority from the owner or system operator to grant permission of the accessed computer program, computer, computer system, or computer network.
>
> (b) The accessed computer program, computer, computer system, or computer network had a pre-programmed access procedure that would display a bulletin, command, or other message before access was achieved that a reasonable person would believe identified the computer program, computer, computer system, or computer network as within the public domain.
>
> (c) Access was achieved without the use of a set of instructions, code, or computer program that bypasses, defrauds, or otherwise circumvents the pre-programmed access procedure for the computer program, computer, computer system, or computer network.

M.C.L.A. 752.797(6) (West 2001). Is this a useful solution to the problem of distinguishing authorized from unauthorized access? Note that the presumed lack of authorization may raise constitutional problems. *See* Sandstrom v. Montana, 442 U.S. 510, 524 (1979) (holding that a "presumption which, although not conclusive, had the effect of shifting the burden of persuasion to the defendant" in a criminal case violates the Due Process Clause).

8. *"Access without authorization" versus "exceeds authorized access."* What is the difference between "access without authorization" and conduct that "exceeds authorized access"? Some statutes, such as 18 U.S.C. § 1030(a)(3), prohibit only the former, while other statutes, such as 18 U.S.C. § 1030(a)(2), prohibit both. What does the former prohibit that the latter does not? Section 1030 does not define "without authorization," but it does define "exceeds authorized access" in 18 U.S.C. § 1030(e)(6):

> the term "exceeds authorized access" means to access a computer with authorization and to use such access to obtain or alter information in the computer that the accesser is not entitled so to obtain or alter.

This isn't a particularly helpful definition, as it begs the question of how we measure what a user is "entitled" to do. In light of this ambiguity, several different schools of thought have emerged on the different meaning of "access without authorization" and "exceeds authorized access."

The first school of thought contends that the prohibition on "access without authorization" is limited to the circumvention of code-based restrictions, such as the facts of *Morris*. In contrast, the prohibition on exceeding authorized access extends beyond the circumvention of code-based restrictions, covering at least some kinds of contract-based and norms-based breaches. As the imprecise vernacular would put it, "without authorization" applies to outsiders but not insiders, while "exceeds authorized access" includes insiders. The legislative history cited in the *Morris* case suggests such a distinction, as does a Senate Report that accompanied 1996 amendments to Section 1030. *See* S. Rep. No. 104–357 (1996).

Perhaps the strongest statutory case for this understanding is the language Congress used in the first version of § 1030 enacted in 1984. In the 1984 version of § 1030, 18 U.S.C. §§ 1030(a)(1) and (a)(2) covered both whoever accessed a federal interest computer without authorization and also one who "having accessed a computer with authorization, uses the opportunity such access provides for purposes to which such authorization does not extend." The Computer Fraud and Abuse Act of 1986 amended this language, creating the phrase "exceeds authorized access" and defining that phrase in § 1030(e)(6). The accompanying Senate Report suggests that the change was designed only to simplify the "cumbersome phrase" in the 1984 version, not to change its meaning. S. Rep. 99–432, at 9 (1986), *reprinted in* 1986 U.S.C.C.A.N. 2479, 2486. The 1984 language arguably suggests a clearer distinction between access without authorization and exceeding authorized access: the former is focused on gaining access, which may suggest bypassing a code-based restriction, and the latter is focused on using access for inappropriate purposes, which may suggest breaching contract-based or code-based restrictions. *Cf.* Briggs v. State, 704 A.2d 904 (Md. Ct. App. 1998) (concluding that a system administrator who misused his employer's computer had not gained access without authorization, but suggesting that he may have exceeded his authorized access).

A second school of thought suggests that the only difference is whether the user has some preexisting relationship with the computer, and that the actual prohibited acts are the same under the two standards. The arguments for this position are as follows. First, despite the possible statutory clues discussed in the preceding paragraph, courts in fact often use the terms "access without authorization" and "exceeding authorized access" interchangeably. A number of courts have held that circumvention of contract-based or norms-based restrictions made the access "without authorization," and the existence of these cases makes it difficult to adopt a clear line between the two phrases. Second, under a broad construction of access it is hard to see how the definition of "exceeds authorized access" differs from the meaning of "access without authorization." The definition of "exceeds authorized access" is textually meaningless; it states that a person exceeds authorized access when she does what she is not entitled to do, which simply restates the test for when access is without authorization. Third, readings of "exceeding authorized access" as broadly prohibiting contract and norms-based breaches may raise constitutional problems, counseling against such an interpretation.

Judge Posner suggested a third approach in dicta found in International Airport Centers v. Citrin, 440 F.3d 418 (7th Cir. 2006). Ruminating about 18 U.S.C. § 1030, Judge Posner contended that "[t]he difference between 'without authorization' and 'exceeding authorized access' is paper thin, but not quite invisible." According to Judge Posner, EF Cultural Travel BV v. Explorica, Inc., 274 F.3d 577 (1st Cir. 2001), involved only exceeding authorized access:

> [T]he former employee of a travel agent, in violation of his confidentiality agreement with his former employer, used confidential information that he had obtained as an employee to create a program that enabled his new travel company to obtain information from his former employer's website that he could not have obtained as efficiently without the use of that confidential information. The website was open to the public, so he was authorized to use it, but he exceeded his authorization by using confidential information to obtain better access than other members of the public.

440 F.3d at 420. In contrast, Posner suggested, the facts of *Citrin* satisfied the "access without authorization" standard. Citrin had been assigned a laptop by his company, and he decided to leave the company and start a competitor business. Citrin allegedly deleted the files on the laptop so his employer could not benefit from them when he returned the laptop. According to Judge Posner, "Citrin's breach of his duty of loyalty terminated his agency relationship (more precisely, terminated any rights he might have claimed as IAC's agent—he could not by unilaterally terminating any duties he owed his principal gain an advantage!) and with it his authority to access the laptop, because the only basis of his authority had been that relationship." *Id.* at 420–21.

Which of these approaches is the most persuasive?

D.   COMPUTER FRAUD STATUTES

Computer fraud statutes are hybrids between unauthorized access statutes and fraud statutes. The federal computer fraud statute is 18 U.S.C. § 1030(a)(4). It punishes whoever:

> knowingly and with intent to defraud, accesses a protected computer without authorization, or exceeds authorized access, and by means of such conduct furthers the intended fraud and obtains anything of value, unless the object of the fraud and the thing obtained consists only of the use of the computer and the value of such use is not more than $5,000 in any one-year period.

All § 1030(a)(4) crimes are felonies; the maximum punishment is 5 years for the first offense, and 10 years if the defendant has a prior § 1030 conviction. *See* 18 U.S.C. § 1030(c)(3).

The hybrid status of § 1030(a)(4) is readily apparent from its text. On one hand, it clearly is closely related to § 1030(a)(2). The basic prohibition on accessing a protected computer without authorization or exceeding authorized access is shared between the two. On the other hand, the prohibition is also similar to the wire fraud statute, 18 U.S.C. § 1343. The wire fraud statute punishes whoever,

> having devised or intending to devise any scheme or artifice to defraud, or for obtaining money or property by means of false or fraudulent pretenses, representations, or promises, transmits or causes to be transmitted by means of wire, radio, or television communication in interstate or foreign commerce, any writings, signs,

signals, pictures, or sounds for the purpose of executing such scheme or artifice.

Section 1030(a)(4) puts the two basic concepts together. It combines the intent to defraud and obtaining of anything of value from the wire fraud statute and matches it with the *actus reus* of accessing a protected computer without authorization or exceeding authorized access from § 1030(a)(2). The hybrid status raises interesting questions about why § 1030(a)(4) exists. Just what does it punish that the combination of § 1030(a)(2) and the wire fraud statute does not?

The difference between unauthorized access statutes, wire fraud statutes, and computer fraud statutes was explored in the Senate Report that accompanied the enactment of § 1030(a)(4):

> The new subsection 1030(a)(4) to be created by this bill is designed to penalize thefts of property via computer that occur as part of a scheme to defraud. It will require a showing that the use of the computer or computers in question was integral to the intended fraud and was not merely incidental. It has been suggested that the Committee approach all computer fraud in a manner that directly tracks the existing mail fraud and wire fraud statutes. However, the Committee was concerned that such an approach might permit prosecution under this subsection of acts that do not deserve classification as "computer fraud."

> The Committee was concerned that computer usage that is wholly extraneous to an intended fraud might nevertheless be covered by this subsection if the subsection were patterned directly after the current mail fraud and wire fraud laws. If it were so patterned, the subsection might be construed as covering an individual who had devised a scheme or artifice to defraud solely because he used a computer to keep records or to add up his potential "take" from the crime. The Committee does not believe that a scheme or artifice to defraud should fall under the ambit of subsection (a)(4) merely because the offender signed onto a computer at some point near to the commission or execution of the fraud. While such a tenuous link might be covered under current law where the instrumentality used is the mails or the wires, the Committee does not consider that link sufficient with respect to computers. To be prosecuted under this subsection, the use of the computer must be more directly linked to the intended fraud. That is, it must be used by an offender without authorization or in excess of his authorization to obtain property of another, which property furthers the intended fraud. Likewise, this subsection may be triggered by conduct that can be shown to constitute an attempted offense.

> This approach is designed, in part, to help distinguish between acts of theft via computer and acts of computer trespass. In intentionally trespassing into someone else's computer files, the offender obtains at the very least information as to how to break into that computer

system. If that is all he obtains, the offense should properly be treated as a simple trespass. But because the offender has obtained the small bit of information needed to get into the computer system, the danger exists that his and every other computer trespass could be treated as a theft, punishable as a felony under this subsection. * * *

The Committee remains convinced that there must be a clear distinction between computer theft, punishable as a felony, and computer trespass, punishable in the first instance as a misdemeanor. The element in the new paragraph (a)(4), requiring a showing of an intent to defraud, is meant to preserve that distinction, as is the requirement that the property wrongfully obtained via computer furthers the intended fraud.

S. Rep. No. 99–432, at 10 (1986), *reprinted in* 1986 U.S.C.C.A.N. 2479, 2488.

UNITED STATES v. CZUBINSKI

United States Court of Appeals for the First Circuit, 1997.
106 F.3d 1069.

TORRUELLA, CHIEF JUDGE.

Defendant-appellant Richard Czubinski appeals his jury conviction on nine counts of wire fraud, and four counts of computer fraud, 18 U.S.C. § 1030(a)(4). The wire fraud and computer fraud prosecution that led to the conviction survived serious challenges put forward by Czubinski in various pre-trial motions. Given the broad scope of the federal fraud statutes, motions charging insufficient pleadings or selective prosecution generally deserve careful consideration. We need not scrutinize the lower court's rejection of the defendant's arguments in favor of dismissing the indictment, however, because we reverse the conviction on the clearer ground that the trial evidence mustered by the government was insufficient to support a guilty verdict, and hold that the defendant's motion for judgment of acquittal should have been granted on all counts. Unauthorized browsing of taxpayer files, although certainly inappropriate conduct, cannot, without more, sustain this federal felony conviction.

Background

For all periods relevant to the acts giving rise to his conviction, the defendant Czubinski was employed as a Contact Representative in the Boston office of the Taxpayer Services Division of the Internal Revenue Service. To perform his official duties, which mainly involved answering questions from taxpayers regarding their returns, Czubinski routinely accessed information from one of the IRS's computer systems known as the Integrated Data Retrieval System ("IDRS"). Using a valid password given to Contact Representatives, certain search codes, and taxpayer social security numbers, Czubinski was able to retrieve, to his terminal screen in Boston, income tax return information regarding virtually any taxpayer—information that is permanently stored in the IDRS "master file" located in Martinsburg, West Virginia. In the period of Czubinski's employ, IRS rules plainly stated that employees with passwords and access codes were not permitted to access files on IDRS outside of the course of their official duties.[1]

In 1992, Czubinski carried out numerous unauthorized searches of IDRS files. He knowingly disregarded IRS rules by looking at confidential information obtained by performing computer searches that were outside of the scope of his duties as a Contact Representative, including, but not limited to, the searches listed in the indictment. Audit trails performed by internal IRS auditors establish that Czubinski frequently made unauthorized accesses on IDRS in 1992. For example, Czubinski accessed information regarding: the tax returns of two individuals involved in the David Duke presidential campaign; the joint tax return of an assistant district attorney (who had been prosecuting Czubinski's father on an unrelated felony offense) and his wife; the tax return of Boston City Counselor Jim Kelly's Campaign Committee (Kelly had defeated Czubinski in the previous election for the Counselor seat for District 2); the tax return of one of his brothers' instructors; the joint tax return of a Boston Housing Authority police officer, who was involved in a community organization with one of Czubinski's brothers, and the officer's wife; and the tax return of a woman Czubinski had dated a few times. Czubinski also accessed the files of various other social acquaintances by performing unauthorized searches.

Nothing in the record indicates that Czubinski did anything more than knowingly disregard IRS rules by observing the confidential information he accessed. No evidence suggests, nor does the government contend, that Czubinski disclosed the confidential information he accessed to any third parties. The government's only evidence demonstrating any intent to use the confidential information for nefarious ends was the trial testimony of William A. Murray, an acquaintance of Czubinski who briefly participated in Czubinski's local Invisible Knights of the Ku Klux Klan chapter and worked with him on the David Duke campaign. Murray testified that Czubinski had once stated at a social gathering in "early 1992" that "he intended to use some of that information to build dossiers on people" involved in "the white supremacist movement." There is, however, no evidence that Czubinski created dossiers, took steps toward making dossiers (such as by printing out or recording the information he browsed), or shared any of the information he accessed in the years following the single comment to Murray. No other witness testified to having any knowledge of Czubinski's alleged intent to create "dossiers" on KKK members.

---

1. In 1987 Czubinski signed an acknowledgment of receipt of the IRS Rules of Conduct, which contained the following rule: Employees must make every effort to assure security and prevent unauthorized disclosure of protected information data in the use of Government owned or leased computers. In addition, employees may not use any Service computer system for other than official purposes.

In addition, Czubinski received separate rules regarding use of the IDRS, one of which states: Access only those accounts required to accomplish your official duties.

The record shows that Czubinski did not perform any unauthorized searches after 1992. He continued to be employed as a Contact Representative until June 1995, when a grand jury returned an indictment against him on ten counts of federal wire fraud under 18 U.S.C. §§ 1343, 1346, and four counts of federal interest computer fraud under 18 U.S.C. § 1030(a)(4).

The portion of the indictment alleging wire fraud states that Czubinski defrauded the IRS of confidential property * * * by using his valid password to acquire confidential taxpayer information as part of a scheme to: 1) build "dossiers" on associates in the KKK; 2) seek information regarding an assistant district attorney who was then prosecuting Czubinski's father on an unrelated criminal charge; and 3) perform opposition research by inspecting the records of a political opponent in the race for a Boston City Councilor seat. The wire fraud indictment, therefore, articulated particular personal ends to which the unauthorized access to confidential information through interstate wires was allegedly a means.

The portion of the indictment setting forth the computer fraud charges stated that Czubinski obtained something of value, beyond the mere unauthorized use of a federal interest computer, by performing certain searches—searches representing a subset of those making up the mail fraud counts.

Discussion

I. The Wire Fraud Counts

To support a conviction for wire fraud, the government must prove two elements beyond a reasonable doubt: (1) the defendant's knowing and willing participation in a scheme or artifice to defraud with the specific intent to defraud, and (2) the use of interstate wire communications in furtherance of the scheme. Although defendant's motion for judgment of acquittal places emphasis on shortcomings in proof with regard to the second element, by arguing that the wire transmissions at issue were not proved to be interstate, we find the first element dispositive and hold that the government failed to prove beyond a reasonable doubt that the defendant willfully participated in a scheme to defraud within the meaning of the wire fraud statute.

The government correctly notes that confidential information may constitute intangible "property" and that its unauthorized dissemination or other use may deprive the owner of its property rights. *See Carpenter v. United States*, 484 U.S. 19, 26 (1987). Where such deprivation is effected through dishonest or deceitful means, a "scheme to defraud," within the meaning of the wire fraud statute, is shown. Thus, a necessary step toward satisfying the "scheme to defraud" element in this context is showing that the defendant intended to "deprive" another of their protected right.

The government, however, provides no case in support of its contention here that merely accessing confidential information, without doing, or clearly intending to do, more, is tantamount to a deprivation of IRS property under the wire fraud statute. In *Carpenter*, for example, the confidential information regarding the contents of a newspaper column was converted to the defendants's use to their substantial benefit. *See id.* at 27 (defendants participated in "ongoing scheme to share profit from trading in anticipation" of newspaper column). We do not think that Czubinski's unauthorized browsing, even if done with the intent to deceive the IRS into thinking he was performing only authorized searches, constitutes a "deprivation" within the meaning of the federal fraud statutes.

Binding precedents, and good sense, support the conclusion that to "deprive" a person of their intangible property interest in confidential information under section 1343, either some articulable harm must befall the holder of the information as a result of the defendant's activities, or some gainful use must be intended by the person accessing the information, whether or not this use is profitable in the economic sense. Here, neither the taking of the IRS' right to "exclusive use" of the confidential information, nor Czubinski's gain from access to the information, can be shown absent evidence of his "use" of the information. Accordingly, without evidence that Czubinski used or intended to use the taxpayer information (beyond mere browsing), an intent to deprive cannot be proven, and, a fortiori, a scheme to defraud, is not shown.

All of the cases cited by the government in support of their contention that the confidentiality breached by Czubinski's search in itself constitutes a deprivation of property in fact support our holding today, for they all involve, at a minimum, a finding of a further intended use of the confidential information accessed by the defendants. The government's best support comes from *United States v. Seidlitz*, 589 F.2d 152, 160 (4th Cir. 1978), in which a former employee of a computer systems firm secretly accessed its files, but never was shown to have sold or used the data he accessed, and was nevertheless convicted of wire fraud. The affirming Fourth Circuit held, however, that a jury could have reasonably found that, at the time the defendant raided a competitor's computer system, he intended to retrieve information that would be helpful for his own start-up, competing computer firm. In the instant case, Czubinski did indeed access confidential information through fraudulent pretenses—he appeared to be performing his duties when in fact he used IRS passwords to perform unauthorized searches. Nevertheless, it was not proven that he intended to deprive the IRS of their property interest through either disclosure or use of that information.

The resolution of the instant case is complex because it is well-established that to be convicted of mail or wire fraud, the defendant need not successfully carry out an intended scheme to defraud. The government does not contend either that Czubinski actually created dossiers or that he accomplished some other end through use of the information. It need not do so. All that the government was required to prove was the intent to follow through with a deprivation of the IRS's property and the use or foreseeable use of interstate wire transmissions pursuant to the accomplishment of the scheme to defraud. In the case at bar, the government failed to make even this showing.

The fatal flaw in the government's case is that it has not shown beyond a reasonable doubt that Czubinski intended to carry out a scheme to deprive the IRS of its property interest in confidential information. Had there been sufficient proof that Czubinski intended either to create dossiers for the sake of advancing personal causes or to disseminate confidential information to third parties, then his actions in searching files could arguably be said to be a step in furtherance of a scheme to deprive the IRS of its property interest in confidential information.

Mere browsing of the records of people about whom one might have a particular interest, although reprehensible, is not enough to sustain a wire fraud conviction on a "deprivation of intangible property" theory. Curiosity on the part of an IRS officer may lead to dismissal, but curiosity alone will not sustain a finding of participation in a felonious criminal scheme to deprive the IRS of its property.

II.   The Computer Fraud Counts

Czubinski was convicted on all four of the computer fraud counts on which he was indicted; these counts arise out of unauthorized searches that also formed the basis of four of the ten wire fraud counts in the indictment. Specifically, he was convicted of violating 18 U.S.C. § 1030(a)(4), a provision enacted in the Computer Fraud and Abuse Act of 1986. Section 1030(a)(4) applies to:

> whoever ... knowingly and with intent to defraud, accesses a Federal interest computer without authorization, or exceeds authorized access, and by means of such conduct furthers the intended fraud and obtains anything of value, unless the object of the fraud and the thing obtained consists only of the use of the computer.

We have never before addressed section 1030(a)(4). Czubinski unquestionably exceeded authorized access to a Federal interest computer. On appeal he argues that he did not obtain "anything of value." We agree, finding that his searches of taxpayer return information did not satisfy the statutory requirement that he obtain "anything of value." The value of information is relative to one's needs and objectives; here, the government had to show that the information was valuable to Czubinski in light of a fraudulent scheme. The government failed, however, to prove that Czubinski intended anything more than to satisfy idle curiosity.

The plain language of section 1030(a)(4) emphasizes that more than mere unauthorized use is required: the "thing obtained" may not merely be the unauthorized use. It is the showing of some additional end—to which the unauthorized access is a means—that is lacking here. The evidence did not show that Czubinski's end was anything more than to satisfy his curiosity by viewing information about friends, acquaintances, and political rivals. No evidence suggests that he printed out, recorded, or used the information he browsed. No rational jury could conclude beyond a reasonable doubt that Czubinski intended to use or disclose that information, and merely viewing information cannot be deemed the same as obtaining something of value for the purposes of this statute.[15]

The legislative history further supports our reading of the term "anything of value." In the game of statutory interpretation, statutory language is the ultimate trump card, and the remarks of sponsors of legislation are authoritative only to the extent that they are compatible with the plain language of section 1030(a)(4). Here, a Senate co-sponsor's comments suggest that Congress intended section 1030(a)(4) to punish attempts to steal valuable data, and did not wish to punish mere unauthorized access:

> The acts of fraud we are addressing in proposed section 1030(a)(4) are essentially thefts in which someone uses a federal interest computer to wrongly obtain something of value from another.... Proposed section 1030(a)(4) is intended to reflect the distinction between the theft of information, a felony, and mere unauthorized access, a misdemeanor.

132 Cong. Rec. 7128, 7129, 99th Cong., 2d. Sess. (1986). The Senate Committee Report further underscores the fact that this section should apply to those who steal information through unauthorized access as part of an illegal scheme:

> The Committee remains convinced that there must be a clear distinction between computer theft, punishable as a felony [under section 1030(a)(4)], and computer trespass, punishable in the first instance as a misdemeanor [under a different provision]. The element in the new paragraph (a)(4), requiring a showing of an intent to defraud, is meant to preserve that distinction, as is the requirement that the property wrongfully obtained via computer furthers the intended fraud.

S. Rep. No. 432, 99th Cong., 2d Sess., *reprinted in* 1986 U.S.C.C.A.N. 2479, 2488. For the same reasons we deemed the trial evidence could not support a finding that Czubinski deprived the IRS of its property, *see* discussion of wire fraud under section 1343 *supra,* we find that Czubinski has not obtained valuable information in furtherance of a fraudulent scheme for the purposes of section 1030(a)(4).

Conclusion

We add a cautionary note. The broad language of the mail and wire fraud statutes are both their blessing and their curse. They can address

---

15. The district court, in denying a motion to dismiss the computer fraud counts in the indictment, found that the indictment sufficiently alleged that the confidential taxpayer information was itself a "thing of value" to Czubinski, given his ends. The indictment, of course, alleged specific uses for the information, such as creating dossiers on KKK members, that were not proven at trial. In light of the trial evidence—which, as we have said, indicates that there was no recording, disclosure or further use of the confidential information—we find that Czubinski did not obtain "anything of value" through his unauthorized searches.

new forms of serious crime that fail to fall within more specific legislation. On the other hand, they might be used to prosecute kinds of behavior that, albeit offensive to the morals or aesthetics of federal prosecutors, cannot reasonably be expected by the instigators to form the basis of a federal felony. The case at bar falls within the latter category. Also discomforting is the prosecution's insistence, before trial, on the admission of inflammatory evidence regarding the defendant's membership in white supremacist groups purportedly as a means to prove a scheme to defraud, when, on appeal, it argues that unauthorized access in itself is a sufficient ground for conviction on all counts. Finally, we caution that the wire fraud statute must not serve as a vehicle for prosecuting only those citizens whose views run against the tide, no matter how incorrect or uncivilized such views are.

NOTES AND QUESTIONS

1. *Comparing § 1030(a)(4) and § 1030(a)(2).* Consider the key differences between computer fraud and basic unauthorized access. *Czubinski* and the legislative history of § 1030 instruct that the most basic difference is that the unauthorized access and retrieval of information in a case of computer fraud is part of a broader scheme that harms the victim in an appreciable way. Absent such a broader scheme to harm the victim, the crime is mere trespass, a misdemeanor unauthorized access violation under § 1030(a)(2). Was Czubinski guilty of violating 18 U.S.C. § 1030(a)(2)(B)? If he was, why did the government charge Czubinski under § 1030(a)(4) instead?

Other slight differences exist between § 1030(a)(4) and § 1030(a)(2). For example, the mens rea of computer fraud is knowledge and intent to defraud, while the mens rea of unauthorized access is intentionally accessing without authorization. In addition, violations of § 1030(a)(2) typically require that the conduct involve a communication that traveled across state lines, while violations of § 1030(a)(4) do not.

With that said, the felony provisions of § 1030(a)(2) create a great deal of overlap with § 1030(a)(4). Felony liability under § 1030(a)(2) is triggered if the offense was committed "for purposes of commercial advantage or private financial gain," the offense was committed "in furtherance of any criminal or tortious act in violation of the Constitution or laws of the United States or of any State," or the value of the information obtained exceeds $5,000. 18 U.S.C. § 1030(c)(2). How different is this from *Czubinski*'s requirement of a broader scheme to harm the victim? To the extent there is a difference, which is a better approach?

2. *Comparing § 1030(a)(4) and § 1343.* Note the basic differences between the computer fraud statute and the wire fraud statute. The actus reus of computer fraud is accessing a computer without authorization or exceeding authorized access, while the actus reus of wire fraud is transmitting a wire, radio, or television communication across state or national boundaries. The computer fraud statute requires that the actus reus must further the fraud, while the wire fraud statute does not. Further, the computer fraud statute specifies that "use of the computer" cannot be the object of value fraudulently

obtained if "the value of such use is not more than $5,000 in any one-year period," while the wire fraud statute contains no analogous limitation.

The limitation on use of a computer as an object obtained under the computer fraud statute is largely a leftover from the economics of computer usage in the 1980s. At that time, computers were rare and computer usage often had considerable economic value. Unauthorized access to a computer per se could impose costs on the computer's owner. The legislative history of § 1030(a)(4) suggests that the limitation on computer use as an object of value was designed to distinguish computer fraud from unauthorized access:

> [T]he mere use of a computer or computer service has a value all its own. Mere trespasses onto someone else's computer system can cost the system provider a "port" or access channel that he might otherwise be making available for a fee to an authorized user. At the same time, the Committee believes it is important to distinguish clearly between acts of fraud under (a)(4), punishable as felonies, and acts of simple trespass, punishable in the first instance as misdemeanors. That distinction would be wiped out were the Committee to treat every trespass as an attempt to defraud a service provider of computer time. One simply cannot trespass into another's computer without occupying a portion of the time that that computer service is available. Thus, that suggested approach would treat every act of unauthorized entry to a Federal interest computer—no matter how brief—as an act of fraud, punishable at the felony level. The Committee does not believe this is a proper approach to this problem. For that reason, the Committee has excluded from coverage under this subsection those instances where "the object of the fraud and the thing obtained consists only of the use of the computer."

S. Rep. No. 99–432, at 10 (1986), *reprinted in* 1986 U.S.C.C.A.N. 2479, 2488.

E. COMPUTER DAMAGE STATUTES

Computer damage statutes are the third and final type of basic computer misuse statute. Computer damage statutes focus on the harm inflicted on the computer owner and attempt to impose criminal liability for conduct that caused a particular amount of harm. Computer damage statutes can be divided into two types. Some computer damage statutes are focused on conduct that exceeds privileges to use a computer. These statutes typically combine the basic prohibition on unauthorized access with an additional requirement that the conduct caused a particular amount of damage or harm.

Other statutes focus on conduct that denies privileges to other users. Such provisions do not require unauthorized access, but instead look to unauthorized acts of deleting, damaging, altering, or rendering inaccessible a set of files or programs on the victim computer. The line between the two types of computer damage statutes can be slippery in practice, in part because a user may exceed his privileges in the course of engaging in conduct that ultimately denies privileges to others. Indeed, many state statutes combine the two types into a single prohibition.

The federal computer damage statute is found at 18 U.S.C. § 1030(a)(5). Section 1030(a)(5) has been substantially rewritten several times, most recently by Title II of the Former Vice President Protection Act, Pub. L. 110–326, enacted on September 26, 2008. Under the Ex Post Facto clause, the government will generally charge the version of the statute in effect at the time the crime was committed. As a result, students should be aware that the applicable law for a particular offense depends on when it was committed.

In its current form, as amended by Pub. L. 110–326, enacted on September 26, 2008, 18 U.S.C. § 1030(a)(5) prohibits three different offenses. It punishes whoever

(A) knowingly causes the transmission of a program, information, code, or command, and as a result of such conduct, intentionally causes damage without authorization, to a protected computer;

(B) intentionally accesses a protected computer without authorization, and as a result of such conduct, recklessly causes damage; or

(C) intentionally accesses a protected computer without authorization, and as a result of such conduct, causes damage and loss.

There is considerable overlap among the three prohibitions of 18 U.S.C. § 1030(a)(5). The first prohibition targets conduct that denies privileges to other users, such as sending out computer viruses and launching denial-of-service attacks. 18 U.S.C. § 1030(a)(5)(A) prohibits "knowingly caus[ing] the transmission of a program, information, code, or command, and as a result of such conduct, intentionally caus[ing] damage without authorization, to a protected computer." Note that the absence of authorization does not refer to the access, but rather to causing damage. Damage is defined in 18 U.S.C. § 1030(e)(8) as "any impairment to the integrity or availability of data, a program, a system, or information." While it may seem odd that the statute would require that the damage be unauthorized, authorized damage is possible. For example, an employee may be authorized to encrypt information belonging to an employer; the act of encrypting data constitutes damage because it impairs the availability of the encrypted information.

The second and third prohibitions in § 1030(a)(5) are variations on unauthorized access statutes. 18 U.S.C. § 1030(a)(5)(B) prohibits "intentionally access[ing] a protected computer without authorization, and as a result of such conduct, recklessly caus[ing] damage." Note that the authorization requirement extends only to access "without authorization," and does not include exceeding authorized access. Here the conduct element is accessing a protected computer without authorization, and the result element that must be caused by the access is "damage," that is, "any impairment to the integrity or availability of data, a program, a system, or information."

The third prohibition, 18 U.S.C. § 1030(a)(5)(C), is very similar to the second prohibition, 18 U.S.C. § 1030(a)(5)(B). There are only two differences. The first difference is that a violation of 18 U.S.C. § 1030(a)(5)(C) must cause both damage *and* some amount of loss, while a violation of 18 U.S.C. § 1030(a)(5)(B) need only cause damage. The second difference is the mens rea with respect to causing an impairment to the integrity or availability of data or information. The second prohibition requires that the defendant must be reckless with respect to causing that impairment; the third prohibition imposes strict liability with respect to causing the impairment. The Senate Report that accompanied the enactment of these provisions explained Congress's decision to punish even entirely accidental damage:

> Although those who intentionally damage a system, without authority, should be punished regardless of whether they are authorized users, it is equally clear that anyone who knowingly invades a system without authority and causes significant loss to the victim should be punished as well, even when the damage caused is not intentional. In such cases, it is the intentional act of trespass that makes the conduct criminal. To provide otherwise is to openly invite hackers to break into computer systems, safe in the knowledge that no matter how much damage they cause, it is no crime unless that damage was either intentional or reckless. Rather than send such a dangerous message (and deny victims any relief), it is better to ensure that section 1030(a)(5) criminalizes all computer trespass, as well as intentional damage by insiders, albeit at different levels of severity.

S. Rep. 104–357, at 11 (1996).

So far, § 1030(a)(5) seems relatively simple, if perhaps a bit redundant. But the key to understanding § 1030(a)(5) is that it works in conjunction with the sentencing provisions of § 1030(c)(4). Violations of § 1030(a)(5) can be misdemeanors or felonies, and the enhancements that make the offenses felonies end up adding what are effectively additional elements of § 1030(a)(5), albeit hidden away inside the surprisingly complex provisions of § 1030(c)(4). To understand the federal computer damage statute, we need to see how it interacts with § 1030(c)(4).

If there are no enhancements, violations of § 1030(a)(5) are misdemeanors. *See* 18 U.S.C. § 1030(c)(4)(G)(i). Indeed, violations of § 1030(a)(5)(C) are ordinarily misdemeanors. They can become felonies only in the unlikely event that the defendant has been convicted previously of violating § 1030. *See* 18 U.S.C. § 1030(c)(4)(D)(i) (imposing a 10–year statutory maximum punishment in such cases).

In contrast, violations of § 1030(a)(5)(A) and § 1030(a)(5)(B) can become felonies for first offenses if one of the following six harms was caused by the defendant's conduct:

> (I) loss to 1 or more persons during any 1–year period (and, for purposes of an investigation, prosecution, or other proceeding brought by the United States only, loss resulting from a related course of conduct affecting 1 or more other protected computers) aggregating at least $5,000 in value;

(II) the modification or impairment, or potential modification or impairment, of the medical examination, diagnosis, treatment, or care of 1 or more individuals;

(III) physical injury to any person;

(IV) a threat to public health or safety;

(V) damage affecting a computer used by or for an entity of the United States Government in furtherance of the administration of justice, national defense, or national security; or

(VI) damage affecting 10 or more protected computers during any 1–year period.

18 U.S.C. § 1030(c)(4)(A)(i) (imposing a 5–year statutory maximum punishment when such harms result with § 1030(a)(5)(B) offenses). *See also* 18 U.S.C. § 1030(c)(4)(B)(i) (imposing a 10–year statutory maximum punishment when such harms result with § 1030(a)(5)(A) offenses).

This list of six harms is very important to fully understand § 1030(a)(5) violations. In most cases, the list effectively creates the line between mere misdemeanor violations and more serious felony violations. Most of the provisions are efforts to identify particularly sensitive types of computers, computer data, and resulting harms.

The most commonly relevant form of harm is the first. This provision addresses monetary loss. It requires:

loss to 1 or more persons during any 1–year period (and, for purposes of an investigation, prosecution, or other proceeding brought by the United States only, loss resulting from a related course of conduct affecting 1 or more other protected computers) aggregating at least $5,000 in value.

Under this provision, a felony conviction under § 1030(a)(5) can be obtained if there is at least $5,000 in loss. The parenthetical concerning cases brought by the United States is designed to limit § 1030(a)(5) civil claims in class action lawsuits while allowing aggregation of losses from a course of conduct in criminal cases. Thus, in criminal cases, the loss is calculated by adding up the losses from the defendant's "course of conduct" over any 1–year period.

Violations of 18 U.S.C. § 1030(a)(5) can become felonies in other ways beyond the six harms listed above. Violations of § 1030(a)(5)(A) and § 1030(a)(5)(B) can become felonies in the unlikely event that a defendant has a previous § 1030 conviction. *See* 18 U.S.C. § 1030(c)(4)(C)(i) (imposing a 20 year statutory maximum punishment). Violations of § 1030(a)(5)(A) can be particularly serious felonies if the conduct involves the causation of bodily injury or death. If the defendant "attempts to cause or knowingly or recklessly causes serious bodily injury from conduct in violation of subsection (a)(5)(A)," the offense is a felony with a 20–year maximum punishment. 18 U.S.C. § 1030(c)(4)(E). If the defendant "attempts to cause or knowingly or recklessly causes death from conduct in violation of subsection (a)(5)(A)," the offense is a felony with a maximum punishment of life in prison. 18 U.S.C. § 1030(c)(4)(F).

———————

Prosecutions brought under § 1030(a)(5) generally raise two questions. First, what is the methodology for calculating $5,000 of loss, which turns out to be the most common way of establishing a felony violation? And second, what mens rea applies with respect to each of the result elements? The following cases consider these questions in turn. It is worth noting that both cases interpret earlier generations of § 1030(a)(5), and therefore use slightly different terminology and interpret slightly different text. It turns out that the cases remain highly relevant, however: In two of the three cases, the current text of § 1030(a)(5) was written in part to codify their holdings.

UNITED STATES v. MIDDLETON

United States Court of Appeals for the Ninth Circuit, 2000.
231 F.3d 1207.

GRABER, CIRCUIT JUDGE.

Defendant Nicholas Middleton challenges his conviction for intentionally causing damage to a "protected computer" without authorization, in violation of 18 U.S.C. § 1030(a)(5)(A). Defendant * * * argues that the trial court incorrectly instructed the jury on the "damage" element of the offense and that the government presented insufficient evidence of the requisite amount of damage. We disagree with each of Defendant's contentions and, therefore, affirm the conviction.

Factual and Procedural Background

Defendant worked as the personal computer administrator for Slip. net, an Internet service provider. His responsibilities included installing software and hardware on the company's computers and providing technical support to its employees. He had extensive knowledge of Slip.net's internal systems, including employee and computer program passwords. Dissatisfied with his job, Defendant quit. He then began to write threatening e-mails to his former employer.

Slip.net had allowed Defendant to retain an e-mail account as a paying customer after he left the company's employ. Defendant used this account to commit his first unauthorized act. After logging in to Slip.net's system, Defendant used a computer program called "Switch User" to switch his account to that of a Slip.net receptionist, Valerie Wilson. This subterfuge allowed Defendant to take advantage of the benefits and privileges associated with that employee's account, such as creating and deleting accounts and adding features to existing accounts.

Ted Glenwright, Slip.net's president, discovered this unauthorized action while looking through a "Switch User log," which records all attempts to use the Switch User program. Glenwright cross-checked the information with the company's "Radius Log," which records an outside user's attempt to dial in to the company's modem banks. The information established that Defendant had connected to Slip.net.'s computers and had then switched to Wilson's account. Glenwright immediately terminated Defendant's e-mail account.

Nevertheless, Defendant was able to continue his activities. Three days later, he obtained access to Slip.net's computers by logging in to a computer that contained a test account and then using that test account to gain access to the company's main computers. Once in Slip.net's main system, Defendant accessed the account of a sales representative and created two new accounts, which he called "TERPID" and "SANTOS." Defendant used TERPID and SANTOS to obtain access to a different computer that the company had named "Lemming." Slip.net used Lemming to perform internal administrative functions and to host customers' websites. Lemming also contained the software for a new billing system. After gaining access to the Lemming computer, Defendant changed all the administrative passwords, altered the computer's registry, deleted the entire billing system (including programs that ran the billing software), and deleted two internal databases.

Glenwright discovered the damage the next morning. He immediately contacted the company's system administrator, Bruno Connelly. Glenwright and Connelly spent an entire weekend repairing the damage that Defendant had caused to Slip.net's computers, including restoring access to the computer system, assigning new passwords, reloading the billing software, and recreating the deleted databases. They also spent many hours investigating the source and the extent of the damage. Glenwright estimated that he spent 93 hours repairing the damage; Connelly estimated that he spent 28 hours; and other employees estimated that they spent a total of 33 hours. Additionally, Slip.net bought new software to replace software that Defendant had deleted, and the company hired an outside consultant for technical support.

Defendant was arrested and charged with a violation of 18 U.S.C. § 1030(a)(5)(A). He moved to dismiss the indictment, arguing that Slip.net was not an "individual" within the meaning of the statute. The district court denied the motion, holding that "the statute encompasses damage sustained by a business entity as well as by a natural person." *United States v. Middleton*, 35 F. Supp.2d 1189, 1192 (N. D. Cal. 1999).

The case was then tried to a jury. Defendant filed motions for acquittal, arguing that the government had failed to prove that Slip.net suffered at least $5,000 in damage. The district court denied the motions. Defendant requested a jury instruction on the meaning of "damage." This request, too, was denied, and the court gave a different instruction.

The jury convicted Defendant. The district court sentenced him to three years' probation, subject to the condition that he serve 180 days in community confinement. The court also ordered Defendant to pay $9,147 in restitution. This timely appeal ensued.

Discussion

Congress originally enacted the Computer Fraud and Abuse Act in 1984. The 1990 version of § 1030(a)(5)(A) prohibited conduct that damages a "Federal interest computer" and "causes loss to one or more others of a value aggregating $1,000 or more." A "Federal interest computer" was defined as a computer owned or used by the United States Government or a financial institution, or "one of two or more computers used in committing the offense, not all of which are located in the same State." 18 U.S.C. § 1030(e)(2)(A) & (B) (1990). In 1994, Congress replaced the term "Federal interest computer" with the phrase "computer used in interstate commerce or communication" and changed the damage provision to read, "causes loss or damage to one or more other persons of value aggregating $1,000 or more." 18 U.S.C. § 1030(a)(5)(A)(ii)(II)(aa) (1995). Before the 1994 amendment, a hacker could escape the statute's prohibitions by containing activities within a single state. Congress' 1994 amendment attempted to broaden the statute's reach. Congress' 1994 amendments also added a private cause of action for victims of computer crime. 18 U.S.C. § 1030(g).

In 1996, Congress amended § 1030(a)(5) to its current form, using the term "protected computer" and concomitantly expanding the number of computers that the statute "protected." 18 U.S.C. § 1030(a)(5) & (e)(2). The 1996 amendments also altered the definition of damage to read, "loss aggregating at least $5,000 in value during any 1–year period to one or more individuals." 18 U.S.C. § 1030(e)(8)(A). We have found no explanation for this change. We do not believe, however, that this change evidences an intent to limit the statute's reach.

To the contrary, Congress has consciously broadened the statute consistently since its original enactment. The Senate Report on the 1996 amendments notes:

> As intended when the law was originally enacted, the Computer Fraud and Abuse statute facilitates addressing in a single statute the problem of computer crime. . . . *As computers continue to proliferate in businesses and homes, and new forms of computer crimes emerge, Congress must remain vigilant to ensure that the Computer Fraud and Abuse statute is up-to-date and provides law enforcement with the necessary legal framework to fight computer crime.*

S.Rep. No. 104–357, pt. II (emphasis added). The report instructs that "the definition of 'damage' is amended to be sufficiently broad to encompass the types of harm against which people should be protected." The report notes that the interaction between § 1030(a)(5)(A) (the provision that prohibits conduct causing damage) and § 1030(e)(8) (the provision that defines damage) will prohibit a hacker from stealing passwords from an existing log-on program, when this conduct requires "all system users to change their passwords, and requires the system administrator to devote resources to resecuring the system.... If the loss to the victim meets the required monetary threshold, the conduct should be criminal, and the victim should be entitled to relief." * * *

Defendant * * * argues that the district court instructed the jury improperly on the definition of "damage." Defendant requested this instruction: "Damage does not include expenses relating to creating a better or making a more secure system than the one in existence prior to the impairment." The court refused the request and gave a different instruction. The court explained to the jury that "damage" is an impairment to Slip.net's computer system that caused a loss of at least $5,000. The court continued:

> The term "loss" means any monetary loss that Slip.net sustained as a result of any damage to Slip.net's computer data, program, system or information that you find occurred.

> And in considering whether the damage caused a loss less than or greater than $5,000, you may consider any loss that you find was a natural and foreseeable result of any damage that you find occurred.

> In determining the amount of losses, you may consider what measures were reasonably necessary to restore the data, program, system, or information that you find was damaged or what measures were reasonably necessary to resecure the data, program, system, or information from further damage.

In reviewing jury instructions, the relevant inquiry is whether the instructions as a whole are misleading or inadequate to guide the jury's deliberation. In this case, the district court's instructions on "damage" and "loss" correctly stated the applicable law. Defendant concedes that "damage" includes any loss that was a foreseeable consequence of his criminal conduct, including those costs necessary to "resecure" Slip.net's computers. He does not argue, therefore, that the court misstated the law.

Defendant contends instead that the court's instruction might have led the jury to believe that it could consider the cost of creating a better or more secure system and that his proposed additional instruction was needed to avoid that possibility. The district court's instruction, when read in its entirety, adequately presented Defendant's theory. The court instructed the jury that it could consider only those costs that were a "natural and foreseeable result" of Defendant's conduct, only those costs that were "reasonably necessary," and only those costs that would "resecure" the computer to avoid "further damage." That instruction logically excludes any costs that the jury believed were excessive, as well as any costs that would merely create an improved computer system unrelated to preventing further damage resulting from Defendant's conduct. In particular, the term "resecure" implies making the system as secure as it was before, not making it more secure than it was before. We presume that the jury followed the court's instructions.

Because the district court's instructions fairly and adequately covered the elements of the offense, we review the instruction's 'precise formulation' for an abuse of discretion. The district court in this case did not abuse its discretion in rejecting Defendant's "precise formulation" of the definition of "damage."

Defendant's final argument is that the government presented insufficient evidence of the requisite $5,000 in damage. The government computed the amount of damage that occurred by multiplying the number of hours that each employee spent in fixing the computer problems by their respective hourly rates (calculated using their annual salaries), then adding the cost of the consultant and the new software. The government estimated the total amount of damage to be $10,092. Defendant and the government agree that the cost of Glenwright's time made up the bulk of that total.

Defendant observes that Slip.net paid Glenwright a fixed salary and that Slip.net did not pay Glenwright anything extra to fix the problems caused by Defendant's conduct. There also is no evidence, says Defendant, that Glenwright was diverted from his other responsibilities or that such a diversion caused Slip.net a financial loss. Defendant argues that, unless Slip.net paid its salaried employees an extra $5,000 for the time spent fixing the computer system, or unless the company was prevented from making $5,000 that it otherwise would have made because of the employees' diversion, Slip.net has not suffered "damage" as defined in the statute. We disagree.

In *United States v. Sablan,* 92 F.3d 865, 869 (9th Cir. 1996), this court held that, under the Sentencing Guidelines for computer fraud, it was permissible for the district court to compute "loss" based on the hourly wage of the victim bank's employees. The court reasoned, in part, that the bank would have had to pay a similar amount had it hired an outside contractor to repair the damage. Analogous reasoning applies here. There is no basis to believe that Congress intended the element of "damage" to depend on a victim's choice whether to use hourly employees, outside contractors, or salaried employees to repair the same level of harm to a protected computer. Rather, whether the amount of time spent by the employees and their imputed hourly rates were reasonable for the repair tasks that they performed are questions to be answered by the trier of fact.

Our review of the record identifies sufficient evidence from which a rational trier of fact could have found that Slip.net suffered $5,000 or more in damage. Glenwright testified that he spent approximately 93 hours investigating and repairing the damage caused by Defendant. That total included 24 hours investigating the break-in, determining how to fix it, and taking temporary measures to prevent future break-ins. Glenwright testified that he spent 21 hours recreating deleted databases and 16 hours reloading and configuring the billing software and its related applications. Glenwright estimated that his time was worth $90 per hour, based on his salary of $180,000 per year. He also testified, among other things, that he did not hire an outside contractor to repair the damage because he believed that he, as a computer expert with a pre-existing knowledge of the customized features of his company's computers, could fix the problems more efficiently. It is worth noting that, because the jury had to find only $5,000 worth of damage, it could have discounted Glenwright's number of hours or his hourly rate considerably and still have found the requisite amount of damage.

Other Slip.net employees testified to the hours that they spent fixing the damage caused by Defendant, and to their respective salaries. The government then presented expert testimony from which a jury could determine that the time spent by the employees was reasonable. Defendant cross-examined the government's witnesses on these issues vigorously, and he presented contrary expert testimony. By the verdict, the jury found the government witnesses' testimony to be more credible, a finding that was within its power to make. We hold, on this record, that the conviction was not based on insufficient evidence.

NOTES AND QUESTIONS

1. The Uniting and Strengthening America by Providing Appropriate Tools Required to Intercept and Obstruct Terrorism Act of 2001, Pub. L. No. 107–56 (2001), generally known as the Patriot Act, restructured 18 U.S.C. § 1030(a)(5) and codified the holding of the *Middleton* case. Before the Patriot Act, the section prohibited causing damage, and defined damage as impairment to the availability or integrity of information causing at least $5,000 in loss. Under the Patriot Act, damage has been redefined without the loss requirement and "loss" has been defined in 18 U.S.C. § 1030(e)(11) to mean:

> any reasonable cost to any victim, including the cost of responding to an offense, conducting a damage assessment, and restoring the data, program, system, or information to its condition prior to the offense, and any revenue lost, cost incurred, or other consequential damages incurred because of interruption of service.

The Justice Department issued a Field Guide to the Patriot Act in late 2001 explaining that this amendment was designed to "codify the appropriately broad definition of loss adopted in Middleton." *See* Computer Crime and Intellectual Property Section (CCIPS), *Field Guidance on New Authorities that Relate to Computer Crime and Electronic Evidence Enacted in the USA Patriot Act of 2001, at* www.cybercrime.gov/PatriotAct.htm (last updated Nov. 5, 2001).

2. *Types of costs included in the loss definition.* The definition of loss in § 1030(e)(11) is quite broad. It refers to "any" reasonable cost, and includes what appears to be a non-exclusive list of costs taken largely from the *Middleton* case. What categories of costs can you imagine that are not expressly included in the list? A computer intrusion can incur monetary losses for the victim in a number of different ways. Imagine that an intruder gains unauthorized access to the servers of XYZ Corporation, an e-commerce

company, and publicizes the intrusion. The following occurs as a consequence of the intrusion:

A.   The company hires a security consultant to assess the damage and patch the vulnerability.

B.   The company calls a meeting of the board of directors to discuss possible responses, and the meeting lasts a full day. An expensive lunch is served.

C.   The company hires a very skillful public relations specialist to deal with press attention relating to the intrusion.

D.   The company loses a stream of future business when the public hears that XYZ has poor computer security.

E.   Rumors that XYZ has poor security pushes its publicly-traded stock down one dollar per share.

F.   The company loses revenue when it has to take its website offline for one day.

G.   The company loses a stream of future business when a client becomes so frustrated the website is down that he decides he will never work with XYZ again.

All of these events are associated with monetary losses, either directly or by occupying XYZ employees for a number of hours. Which of these losses are covered by 18 U.S.C. § 1030(e)(11)?

3.   In United States v. Millot, 433 F.3d 1057 (8th Cir. 2006), a former employee of Aventis Pharmaceuticals hacked in to the Aventis network and deleted the account belonging to another employee. Aventis had outsourced its security functions to International Business Machines (IBM), and two IBM employees spent a total of 407 hours reconstructing the deleted account, investigating the intrusion, and performing a security audit to verify that all existing access accounts belonged to current employees. The contract between Aventis and IBM required both IBM employees to work full-time on Aventis security matters, although IBM normally billed its staff's services at $50 per hour. The government calculated damages at $20,350 ($50 per hour x 407 hours). The Eighth Circuit affirmed the conviction, rejecting the defendant's argument that the hours spent by the employees did not count because their costs were absorbed by the contract: "This argument neglects the fact that the hours spent ... addressing the issues caused by Millot's unauthorized intrusion could have been spent on other duties under the contract." *Id.* at 1061.

4.   In Nexans Wires S.A v. Sark–USA, Inc., 319 F. Supp.2d 468 (S.D.N.Y. 2004), the plaintiff was a German company that kept the pricing schedules and manufacturing information for its line of advanced copper and optical fiber products in a password-protected area of a client's computer server in New York. According to the complaint, employees of the client company accessed that information and used it to start a competitor company to compete against the plaintiff company. The plaintiff company sued the competitor company, claiming that the defendants' unauthorized access to the plaintiff's data had triggered at least a $5,000 "loss" in two ways. First, the

plaintiff had paid for its senior executives to take two trips from Germany to the client's headquarters in New York to discuss "the activities of [their] faithless employees" with the executives of the client. Second, it claimed it had lost two business opportunities taken by the defendant, which was now competing with the plaintiff.

The district court rejected the plaintiff's arguments that either could be considered losses under § 1030. The international trips could not be counted as losses because they were not related to computers, the court concluded:

> Nothing in either case law or legislative history suggests that something as far removed from a computer as the travel expenses of senior executives constitutes "loss." Therefore, the international travel expenses that plaintiffs' senior executives incurred to attend a meeting with their customer's senior executive, in which no computers are said to have been examined, and no computer consultant [is] said to have been present cannot satisfy the $5,000 "loss" requirement of the statute.

Id. at 477. The court also rejected the plaintiff's argument that they had suffered "loss" when they had lost business to the competitor company given its use of the allegedly stolen data:

> [T]he "revenue lost" which constitutes "loss" under § 1030(e)(11) appears from the plain language of the statute to be revenue lost "because of [an] interruption of service." § 1030(e)(11). Therefore, if [the plaintiffs] had lost revenue because the computer systems of [the client] were down, that would seem to be the type of lost revenue contemplated by the statute. However, plaintiffs are not claiming to have lost money because the computers of [the client] were inoperable, but rather because of the way the information was later used by defendants.

Id. According to the court, this was insufficient: "revenue lost because the information was used by the defendant to unfairly compete after extraction from a computer does not appear to be the type of 'loss' contemplated by the statute." *See also* Civic Center Motors, Ltd. v. Mason Street Import Cars, Ltd., 387 F. Supp.2d 378, 382 (S.D.N.Y. 2005) (same).

Is this reading of 18 U.S.C. § 1030(e)(11) persuasive? Do you think the phrase "because of interruption of service" is designed to modify only "other consequential damages," or is it also designed to modify "revenue lost" and "cost incurred?" District courts have divided on these questions owing to the statutory ambiguity in § 1030(e)(11).

5. In B&B Microscopes v. Armogida, 532 F. Supp.2d 744 (W.D. Pa. 2007), an employee named Armogida developed a valuable computer program known as the KPICS System for his employer B&B Microscopes. At some point, Armogida decided that the program belonged to him rather than his employer, and he quit the company and deleted the program from the laptop computer his employer had provided him for his work. When asked, Armogida refused to provide B&B Microscopes with a copy of the KPICS System. Instead, Armogida represented to purchasers that the software belonged to him, and he sold a copy of the software to the State of Utah for a profit of $10,000.

B&B Microscopes sued Armogida under § 1030 and claimed $51,400 in loss. The alleged loss consisted of $1,400 for a computer forensic analysis to attempt to recover the KPICS software from the laptop, and $50,000 in expected lost profits for the sale of the KPICS program over the course of one year. The District Court recognized $11,400 in loss but rejected the larger claim as too speculative:

> B&B sustained a loss of $1,400 relating to the costs incurred in performing a damage assessment. I find such costs to be reasonable under the circumstances.

> Additionally, B&B sustained a loss of $10,000 relating to lost revenue because of an "interruption of service." B&B was deprived of the opportunity to sell the KPICS System when the data related to the KPICS System was deleted from Armogida's laptop. B&B had no other access to the underlying algorithm necessary to reproduce the KPICS System. Accordingly, the loss of the data from Armogida's laptop constituted an interruption of service within the meaning of 18 U.S.C. § 1030(e)(11).

> I reject, as too speculative, B&B's contention that it lost $50,000.00 in revenue from the first year of sales of the KPICS System. Instead, I find that B&B lost $10,000 in profit from the sale Armogida made of the KPICS System to the State of Utah.

Id. at 758–59.

6. *The reasonableness requirement*. The definition of loss that codifies the holding of *Middleton* requires that the relevant costs must be "reasonable." 18 U.S.C. § 1030(e)(11). As a textual matter, the definition does not make clear whether the enumerated examples are categories of loss that Congress deems reasonable per se, or whether costs involving those enumerated examples must be scrutinized for reasonableness. The *Middleton* opinion suggests the latter, as it approvingly noted that the jury instruction used at trial in that case "logically excludes any costs that the jury believed were excessive." Thus it seems likely that all costs must be scrutinized for reasonableness to count as "loss" for the purposes of getting to $5,000.

Does that make sense? The legal question is whether the conduct prohibited in § 1030(a)(5)(A) "caused" the loss. Principles of causation in criminal law ordinarily do not ask whether the victim's suffering was reasonable. The question is only whether the conduct was the 'but for' and 'proximate' cause of the result. Under this approach, the defendant ordinarily must take the victim as he finds him. For example, if a man assaults an elderly lady, and the elderly lady dies from the shock to her frail system, a defendant cannot escape liability for the homicide on the ground that a younger woman would have been able to survive the assault. *See, e.g.*, People v. Brackett, 510 N.E.2d 877 (Ill. 1987). The victim's condition is relevant only if the victim engages in unforeseeable conduct that breaks the chain of causation, severing the link of culpability between the conduct and the result.

Is the reasonableness requirement in § 1030(e)(11) consistent with this principle? Under the existing definition, a hacker can raise the hypothetical question of whether a more careful victim would have suffered the specified harm (that is, the $5,000 loss). Whether the victim reasonably suffered $5,000 in loss becomes a question of fact for the jury, in effect putting the victim on trial.

Is this a sensible approach? The *Middleton* court seemed concerned that a victim should not be able to use a minor event as an excuse to upgrade its computer security, thus triggering $5,000 in loss and suddenly making the minor event a major felony. If a victim uses a minor event as an excuse to spend money on security, however, isn't the problem that the minor event did not actually *cause* the loss, rather than that the loss wasn't *reasonable*? Does the reasonableness requirement in § 1030(e)(11) erroneously incorporate questions of causation into the definition of loss?

7.   Does *Middleton* turn 18 U.S.C. § 1030(a)(5) prosecutions into battles between dueling expert witnesses? The defense expert witness will testify that a reasonable victim would have been able to respond to the unauthorized activity by suffering less than $5,000 in loss, and the government expert witness will testify that a reasonable victim would have suffered more than $5,000 in loss. Does it make sense for computer hacking trials to be focused on the loss suffered by this hypothetical reasonable victim? How well do you think jurors can tell which expert witness is correct?

8.   When a computer is restored following a hack, it is standard for the restorer to "patch" the security flaw (that is, correct the programming error or bug) that allowed the hacker to gain unauthorized access to the network. Can the costs of patching the system be included in the loss? Doesn't patching the security flaw go beyond restoring the computer to its prior condition, and actually result in a more secure computer than existed previously? Or should a court assume that before the unauthorized activity the computer was secure, and that any costs that go towards bringing the computer back to the level of security that the computer network was believed to have is part of the reasonable loss?

9.   In State v. Allen, 917 P.2d 848 (Kan. 1996), Allen used his modem to dial up the computers of Southwestern Bell in an apparent effort to place unauthorized free long distance phone calls. Although Southwestern Bell could not establish that Allen had "accessed" their computers, Allen's conduct led Southwestern Bell to decide to invest $23,796 towards enhancing its computer security. The Supreme Court of Kansas rejected the prosecution's argument that Allen had "damaged" Southwestern Bell under the Kansas computer crime statute. According to the Court, "the State is essentially saying that a person looking at a no trespassing sign on a gate causes damage to the owner of the gate if the owner decides as a result to add a new lock." *Id.* at 853.

10.   *Additional means of proving felony violations of § 1030(a)(5).* Establishing $5,000 of loss is the most common way that the government triggers the felony provision of § 1030(a)(5). However, 18 U.S.C. § 1030(c)(4)(A)(i) lists six ways of triggering felony liability, and proving $5,000 of loss is only the first of the six ways. Recall the other five harms that, if caused, trigger felony liability:

(II) the modification or impairment, or potential modification or impairment, of the medical examination, diagnosis, treatment, or care of 1 or more individuals;

(III) physical injury to any person;

(IV) a threat to public health or safety;

(V) damage affecting a computer used by or for an entity of the United States Government in furtherance of the administration of justice, national defense, or national security; or

(VI) damage affecting 10 or more protected computers during any 1–year period.

18 U.S.C. § 1030(c)(4)(A)(i). Let's take a look at the other five provisions in the order that they appear, which also happens to be the chronological order in which they were added by Congress.

The first provision, the one involving medical diagnosis and treatment, traces back to the original version of § 1030(a)(5) enacted in 1986. In the 1986 statute, there were two just types of harms that could establish a § 1030(a)(5) violation: establishing pecuniary loss (then just $1,000, later changed to $5,000), and impairing medical diagnosis or treatment. According to the Senate Report accompanying the 1986 legislation, the concern with medical diagnoses and treatment was largely a response to a 1983 episode that received significant press attention:

> A group of adolescents known as the '414 Gang' broke into the computer system at Memorial Sloan–Kettering Cancer Center in New York. In so doing, they gained access to the radiation treatment records of 6,000 past and present cancer patients and had at their fingertips the ability to alter the radiation treatment levels that each patient received. No financial losses were at stake in this case, but the potentially life-threatening nature of such mischief is a source of serious concern to the Committee.

> The Sloan–Kettering case * * * is but one example of computer crimes directed at altering medical treatment records. Where such conduct impairs or potentially impairs an individual's medical care, the Committee does not believe a showing of * * * financial losses is necessary. Tampering with computerized medical treatment records, especially given the potentially life-threatening nature of such conduct, is serious enough to warrant punishment without a showing of pecuniary loss to the victim or victims. The Committee also wishes to make clear that convictions are attainable under this subsection without a showing that the victim was actually given an incorrect or harmful treatment, or otherwise suffered as a result of the changed medical record. That his examination, diagnosis, treatment, or care was potentially changed or impaired is sufficient to warrant prosecution under this subsection.

S. Rep. 99–432 (1986), at *2–3, 12.

The next two of these provisions, those involving physical injury and threats to public health and safety, were added in 1996 as part of a general expansion of the scope of 18 U.S.C. § 1030. At the time, Congress saw that computer networks and the Internet were beginning to assume a larger role in American life. The Senate Report accompanying the legislation expanded the types of covered harms to recognize the new ways that computers could be used to harm the public:

As the [National Information Infrastructure] and other network infra-structures continue to grow, computers will increasingly be used for access to critical services such as emergency response systems and air traffic control, and will be critical to other systems which we cannot yet anticipate. Thus, the definition of "damage" is amended to be sufficiently broad to encompass the types of harm against which people should be protected.

S. Rep. 104–357 (1996), at *11.

The next provision, involving government computers used in furtherance of the administration of justice, national defense, or national security, was added in 2001 as part of the USA Patriot Act. The Justice Department Field Guide to the Patriot Act offered the following argument in its favor:

Section 1030 previously had no special provision that would enhance punishment for hackers who damage computers used in furtherance of the administration of justice, national defense, or national security. Thus, federal investigators and prosecutors did not have jurisdiction over efforts to damage criminal justice and military computers where the attack did not cause over $5,000 loss (or meet one of the other special require-ments). Yet these systems serve critical functions and merit felony prosecutions even where the damage is relatively slight. Indeed, attacks on computers used in the national defense that occur during periods of active military engagement are particularly serious—even if they do not cause extensive damage or disrupt the war-fighting capabilities of the military—because they divert time and attention away from the military's proper objectives. Similarly, disruption of court computer systems and data could seriously impair the integrity of the criminal justice system.

Computer Crime and Intellectual Property Section (CCIPS), *Field Guidance on New Authorities that Relate to Computer Crime and Electronic Evidence Enacted in the USA Patriot Act of 2001, at* www.cybercrime.gov/PatriotAct. htm (last updated Nov. 5, 2001). This provision was addressed in United States v. Mitra, 405 F.3d 492 (7th Cir. 2005), which involved interference with a radio system used by local police, fire, ambulance, and other emergency workers in Madison, Wisconsin. The court noted with apparent approval the government's argument that interfering with messages sent over the system implicated this language because the defendant had "hacked into a govern-mental safety-related communications system." *Id.* at 495.

The final provision, involving damage that affects 10 or more protected computers during any 1–year period, was added in 2008 in response to the increasingly widespread practice of compromising large numbers of computers and then controlling them remotely. The computers that are compromised are generally known as "zombies," and are then used as "bots" (short for "robots") by the wrongdoer who controls them. The wrongdoer can then use the botnet (that is, the collection of bots) to send out spam, launch a distributed denial-of-service attack, or for other purposes. Under this provi-sion, an individual who compromises ten or more computers as part of the creation of a botnet will trigger felony liability under § 1030(a)(5).

11. *The transmission requirement.* 18 U.S.C. § 1030(a)(5)(A) requires "knowingly caus[ing] the transmission of a program, information, code, or command." What exactly does this mean?

In International Airport Centers v. Citrin, 440 F.3d 418 (7th Cir. 2006), an employee of a real estate business decided to leave his company and go into business himself. The employee, Citrin, had been provided a laptop computer by his employer, IAC. The computer contained data Citrin had collected for IAC about potential real estate acquisitions. To ensure that IAC would be unable to access those files, Citrin obtained a "secure erase" software program that could permanently delete computer files from the laptop. Before returning the computer to IAC, Citrin deleted the files from the laptop.

IAC brought a civil suit against Citrin, claiming that he had violated 18 U.S.C. § 1030(a)(5)(A)(i). In an opinion by Judge Posner, the Seventh Circuit concluded that these facts were sufficient to establish "the transmission of a program, information, code, or command":

> Citrin argues that merely erasing a file from a computer is not a "transmission." Pressing a delete or erase key in fact transmits a command, but it might be stretching the statute too far (especially since it provides criminal as well as civil sanctions for its violation) to consider any typing on a computer keyboard to be a form of "transmission" just because it transmits a command to the computer.

> There is more here, however: the transmission of the secure-erasure program to the computer. We do not know whether the program was downloaded from the Internet or copied from a floppy disk (or the equivalent of a floppy disk, such as a CD) inserted into a disk drive that was either inside the computer or attached to it by a wire. Oddly, the complaint doesn't say; maybe IAC doesn't know–maybe all it knows is that when it got the computer back, the files in it had been erased. But we don't see what difference the precise mode of transmission can make. In either the Internet download or the disk insertion, a program intended to cause damage (not to the physical computer, of course, but to its files— but "damage" includes "any impairment to the integrity or availability of data, a program, a system, or information," 18 U.S.C. § 1030(e)(8)) is transmitted to the computer electronically. The only difference, so far as the mechanics of transmission are concerned, is that the disk is inserted manually before the program on it is transmitted electronically to the computer. The difference vanishes if the disk drive into which the disk is inserted is an external drive, connected to the computer by a wire, just as the computer is connected to the Internet by a telephone cable or a broadband cable or wirelessly.

> There is the following contextual difference between the two modes of transmission, however: transmission via disk requires that the malefactor have physical access to the computer. By using the Internet, Citrin might have erased the laptop's files from afar by transmitting a virus. Such long-distance attacks can be more difficult to detect and thus to deter or punish than ones that can have been made only by someone with physical access, usually an employee. The inside attack, however, while easier to detect may also be easier to accomplish. Congress was concerned with

both types of attack: attacks by virus and worm writers, on the one hand, which come mainly from the outside, and attacks by disgruntled programmers who decide to trash the employer's data system on the way out (or threaten to do so in order to extort payments), on the other. If the statute is to reach the disgruntled programmer, which Congress intended by providing that whoever "*intentionally* accesses a protected computer without authorization, and as a result of such conduct, recklessly causes damage" violates the Act, 18 U.S.C. § 1030(a)(5)(A)(ii) (emphasis added), it can't make any difference that the destructive program comes on a physical medium, such as a floppy disk or CD.

Id. at 419–20.

Does transmission include off-line transmission? In North Texas Preventive Imaging v. Eisenberg, No. SA CV 96–71AHS(EEX), 1996 WL 1359212 (C.D. Cal. 1996), the plaintiffs purchased a computer system from the defendants to perform advanced medical diagnostics. The plaintiffs became unsatisfied with the system and informed the defendants that they wished to cancel the purchase and have some of their money returned. The defendants then sent a floppy disk to the plaintiffs, apparently through the postal mail, that the defendants claimed would "update" the computer system. In fact, the floppy disk contained a program that at a future date would disable the software so the plaintiffs could no longer use it.

The plaintiffs installed the "update" not realizing that it would insert code that would eventually disable the network. After realizing that the "update" was a so-called "time bomb," the plaintiffs brought a civil action alleging that the defendants' conduct violated 18 U.S.C. § 1030(a)(5). Specifically, they claimed that sending the floppy disk that contained the harmful code constituted a "transmission of a program, information, code, or command." The district court agreed:

> By casting the net broadly to include many different "transmission" techniques, the 1994 amendment shifted the CFAA's focus from the act of unauthorized access to the intent of the defendant. The transmission of a disabling code by floppy computer disk may fall within the new language, if accompanied by the intent to cause harm.

Id. at *6.

The final set of questions concerning 18 U.S.C. § 1030(a)(5) address the required mens rea with respect to each element of the offense. The materials begin with the mens rea with respect to the elements that appear in § 1030(a)(5) itself, and then turn to the mens rea for the felony enhancements such as the causing of $5,000 in damage.

UNITED STATES v. CARLSON

United States Court of Appeals for the Third Circuit, 2006.
209 Fed. Appx. 181.

IRENAS, SENIOR DISTRICT JUDGE.

On July 14, 2005, the District Court for the Eastern District of Pennsylvania imposed upon Appellant Allan Eric Carlson a sentence of 48 months imprisonment, a term of supervised release of three years, restitution of $14,970.63, and a special assessment of $7,900.00 after a jury found him guilty of computer and identification fraud in violation of 18 U.S.C. § 1030(a)(5).[1] Carlson appeals the order denying his Fed. R. Crim. P. 29 motion for judgment of acquittal. The basis for his motion was insufficiency of the evidence brought against him under the Computer Fraud and Information Act. We will affirm.

I.

Prior to his arrest and conviction, Carlson was an avid Philadelphia Phillies fan living in California. He became savvy with Internet use and technology in 1999, and in 2000 began posting messages on online bulletin boards devoted to the Philadelphia Phillies as a way to communicate with other Phillies fans.

Beginning in 2001, Carlson engaged in two types of e-mail activities that caused damage to other internet users: "direct attack" e-mailing, in which Carlson sent thousands of e-mails to one particular e-mail address,[3] and "indirect attack" e-mailing, where he sent one e-mail to many e-mail addresses.[4]

In employing the direct attack method, Carlson sent thousands of e-mails mainly to a few e-mail addresses at the Philadelphia Phillies. Although the 'from' field indicated that the e-mails were sent from various e-mail addresses not his own, such as the FBI and the Philadelphia Phillies, they were not sent from those individuals and entities, but rather by Carlson using the Internet Protocol ("IP") addresses of other computers. Carlson claims that he sent these e-mails in an attempt to inform journalists and Phillies management about issues with the management of the Phillies that he considered problematic, and to start conversations among other internet users concerning such problems. The evidence produced at trial showed that while some e-mails concerned the Phillies, others did not.

Examples of Carlson's direct attacks are as follows. On November 7, 2001, Carlson sent 1,168 e-mails entitled "The Mariner's Didn't Trade A–Rod" from "*Special Prosecutor@fbi.gov,*" an e-mail address belonging to a Canadian internet user, to six writers at Philadelphia Newspapers, Inc. ("PNI"). On November 11, 2001, Carlson sent over 5,000 e-mails entitled "Sign JASON GIAMBI" to one address at the Phillies. On March 12,

---

1. Specifically, the jury convicted Carlson of 26 counts of intentionally causing damage to a protected computer [and] 26 counts of knowingly making unauthorized access to a protected computer and thereby recklessly causing damage.

3. The Government referred to such tactics as "direct attacks" on individual e-mail users, as the user's e-mail inbox would immediately flood with e-mails sent by Carlson through a third party's IP address.

4. The Government referred to this as an "indirect attack," in that it did not flood any one e-mail user's account immediately, but rather would flood the sender's e-mail address when e-mails sent to invalid addresses were bounced back to the sender. Because Carlson sent e-mails from addresses of other internet users, e-mails would be bounced back to those inboxes, rather than the inbox of Carlson.

Carlson sent 1,800 e-mails to one address at the Phillies, and another 1,800 e-mails to another Phillies' address. On March 14, 2002, Carlson sent an e-mail entitled "The Color of Crime" about raced-based crimes to 5,514 employees of PNI. The e-mails appeared to be from either Lillian Swanson, Ombudsman of the Philadelphia Inquirer, or Walker Lundy, an editor of the Inquirer.

When employing the indirect attack method, Carlson would send spam e-mails from spoofed accounts to thousands of people whose addresses he collected primarily by using computer software. For example, On November 16, 2001, Carlson used the e-mail address of Greg Dubrow, a man with whom he had disagreements in conversations on an internet bulletin board. Carlson sent over 5,000 e-mails from Dubrow's address to a Phillies address, as well as thousands of e-mails to other addresses, from which Dubrow received 6,000 returned e-mails. On November 19, 2001, Carlson spoofed the e-mail address of Paul Hagen, a sports writer at the Philadelphia Daily News, which caused 6,638 copies of this e-mail to be returned to Paul Hagen's e-mail inbox. On April 9, 2002, Carlson sent thousands of e-mails from an address of a man who he claimed "stalked" him on the internet, 7,000 of which were returned as undeliverable to the alleged stalker's inbox.

At trial, Carlson admitted to engaging in these activities, but denied that he knew that each time he employed the "indirect attack" method of e-mailing, it would result in a spoofed e-mailer's receipt of hundreds of returned e-mails.[7] He also denied intending to cause damage by sending thousands of e-mails to one e-mail address, which would clog the address, result in delays, and at times require the purging of all e-mails, causing valuable business-related e-mails to be permanently lost.[8]

The present appeal centers around whether the jury's conviction of Mr. Carlson based upon the finding that he intended to cause damage when he sent e-mails, using both direct and indirect attacks, was supported by the evidence.

II

The Computer Fraud and Abuse Act requires proof that a criminal defendant:

> knowingly cause[d] the transmission of a program, information, code, or command, and as a result of such conduct, *intentionally* cause[d] damage without authorization, to a protected computer.

---

7. Carlson obtained many e-mail addresses from the unsecured networks of high school and college alumni websites. Because the e-mail addresses of students typically become invalid after they graduate, such websites contain a large number of invalid addresses. Carlson claims he did not consider this result.

8. For example, on August 4, 2002, Carlson sent thousands of e-mails from the e-mail address of the vice president of public relations at Knight–Ridder, PNI's parent company, which resulted in the return of 12,000 e-mail messages. Carlson engaged in a similar activity on August 14, 2002. However on this occasion the e-mails were sent from the address of Knight–Ridder's president. The number of returned e-mails was so large that the company had to shut down its server and rid it of all pending e-mails.

Section 1030(e)(8) defines "damage" as "any impairment to the integrity or availability of data, a program, a system, or information." Although the statute itself does not define "intentionally," this Court has defined it in the criminal context as performing an act deliberately and not by accident. Accordingly, the Government was required to prove at trial that Carlson deliberately caused an impairment to the integrity or availability of data, a program, a system, or information.

The jury, after being properly charged as to both the elements of the crime and the definitions of relevant terms used therein, found that Carlson knowingly accessed a computer without authorization and intentionally caused damage thereto. Significantly, the District Court defined the meaning of intent as follows:

> A person acts intentionally when what happens was the defendant's conscious objective. To act intentionally means to do an act deliberately and not by accident. The ultimate fact of intent, though subjective, may be established by circumstantial evidence based upon a person's outward manifestations, his words, his conduct, his acts and all the surrounding circumstances disclosed by the evidence and the rational and logical inferences that may be drawn from them. To find the defendant guilty of Counts 1 through 26, you must find beyond a reasonable doubt that he intended to cause damage to the protected computer.

At trial, Carlson admitted that in using the direct e-mailing method and sending thousands of e-mails to one inbox, the targeted inbox would flood with e-mails and thus impair the user's ability to access his other "good" e-mails. Carlson argued, however, that he only believed the targeted e-mail user's ability to access his email would be impaired for a few minutes.

Carlson contended that, in employing the indirect e-mailing method, although he intentionally spoofed e-mail addresses from which he sent thousands of e-mails at a time, he did not intend that the consequence of this would be to flood the spoofed sender's mailboxes with mail that was returned to sender and with replies requesting that the sender not e-mail the recipient in the future.

The testimony reflected, however, that Carlson was a sophisticated internet and email user. Carlson himself admitted to extensive knowledge of use of the internet and software, including knowledge of how to harvest e-mail addresses from websites, to send mass mailings, to use proxy servers, and to spoof e-mail addresses. It is clear from the evidence that Carlson's level of internet savvy, combined with his actions, could rationally be used as circumstantial evidence to conclude that Carlson intended the consequences of his actions.

We hold that sufficient evidence was presented at trial such that a reasonable juror could have found that Carlson, who intentionally accessed a computer without authorization, also intended the resultant damage. The Judgment of Conviction is affirmed.

NOTES AND QUESTIONS

1. *General overview of mental states (mens rea).* In criminal law, a mens rea is the mental state required with respect to each element of the offense to establish criminal liability. Although federal law does not follow the Model Penal Code generally, the legislative history of § 1030 suggests that its drafters wished to incorporate the MPC's mens rea provisions. *See, e.g.*, S. Rep. 101–544, at 9 (1990 amendments) ("The standard for recklessness used in the bill is taken from the Model Penal Code."); S. Rep. No. 99–432, *reprinted in* 1986 U.S.C.C.A.N. 2479, 2483–84 (1986 amendments) (discussing intent using the key phrases of the MPC). Under this framework, the primary mental states are intent, knowledge, and recklessness. *See* Model Penal Code § 2.02 (Official Draft 1962). The precise meaning of each mental state can vary depending on whether the element is a conduct element (describing the defendant's actions), a result element (describing a fact caused by the defendant's actions), or an attendant circumstances element (describing the state of the world surrounding the defendant's actions).

Specifically, a person acts intentionally when it is his conscious object to engage in conduct of that nature or to cause such a result; in the case of attendant circumstances, a person acts intentionally with respect to that element if he is aware of the element's existence, or he hopes or believes it will occur. *See* § 2.02(2)(a). A person acts knowingly if he is aware that his conduct is of that nature or that such circumstances exist; in the case of result elements, he acts knowingly if he is practically certain his conduct will cause such a result. *See* M.P.C. § 2.02(2)(b). Finally, a person acts recklessly if he consciously disregards a substantial and unjustifiable risk that the element exists or will result, and the disregard of the risk involves a gross deviation from the standard of a law-abiding person in the actor's situation considering the nature and purpose of the actor's conduct and the circumstances known to him. *See* M.P.C. § 2.02(2)(c).

2. *The mental states of 18 U.S.C. § 1030(a)(5).* Now consider the prohibition of § 1030(a)(5)(A), which punishes "knowingly caus[ing] the transmission of a program, information, code, or command, and as a result of such conduct, intentionally caus[ing] damage without authorization, to a protected computer." Under this provision, the transmission must be knowing, and both the causing of damage and the lack of authorization must be intentional. (Note that this standard does not require knowledge of or intent to satisfy the legal standards of damage or lack of authorization. Rather, it requires intent to impair the integrity or availability of data without authorization.)

In contrast, § 1030(a)(5)(B) prohibits "intentionally access[ing] a protected computer without authorization, and as a result of such conduct, recklessly caus[ing] damage." Here, the access and lack of authorization must be intentional, and the causing of damage must be reckless. The only somewhat ambiguous element in this provision is the attendant circumstance element "protected computer." It is not entirely clear from the text of the statute whether it requires intent that the computer is a protected computer, which in this case would mean awareness that the computer is a government computer or a computer used in or affecting interstate or foreign commerce or communication. The general rule is that there is no mens rea required for jurisdictional elements in federal criminal law, which suggest that in all likelihood this is a strict liability element. Either way, the definition of protected computer is sufficiently broad that this question seems unlikely to arise often.

Finally, § 1030(a)(5)(B) prohibits "intentionally access[ing] a protected computer without authorization, and as a result of such conduct, caus[ing] damage and loss." The access and lack of authorization must be intentional. Further, the unauthorized access must cause both damage and at least some amount of loss. However, the offense is strict liability as to damage and loss: No mental state is required.

3. *The meaning of "damage" and of "impairment to the integrity or availability of data."* 18 U.S.C. § 1030(e)(8) defines "damage" as "any impairment to the integrity or availability of data, a program, a system, or information." This is an important phrase, in part because the mental states are tied to it: The statute requires intent, recklessness, or strict liability as to damage, which raises the important question of exactly what "damage" means.

The meaning of the phrase "impairment to the integrity or availability of data, a program, a system, or information" is found in technical authorities rather than legal ones, as the terms "integrity" and "availability" are well known in the field of computer security. Computer security specialists generally refer to the three foundational goals of computer security as protecting the confidentiality, integrity, and availability of data or information. *See, e.g.,* Matt Bishop, Introduction to Computer Security (2004).

Congress presumably intended availability and integrity to have the same meaning in § 1030 that they have in the computer security field. It seems likely that the third basic concept, confidentiality, was excluded from the damage definition because confidentiality is about exposure of information, a matter dealt with in § 1030(a)(2) rather than § 1030(a)(5).

Of the two concepts Congress did use, the availability of data or information is easier to understand. A denial-of-service attack impairs the availability of data or information, as does encrypting it, as does as any conduct that causes the computer be taken off-line for repairs. Conduct that interferes with the proper functioning of computers by denying other users their privileges impairs the availability of data, a program, a system, or information.

Impairing the "integrity" of information is somewhat more difficult to understand. As one treatise on computer security explains:

Integrity refers to the trustworthiness of data or resources, and it is usually phrased in terms of preventing improper or unauthorized change. Integrity includes data integrity (the content of the information) and origin integrity (the source of the data, often called authentication). The source of the information may bear on its accuracy and credibility and on the trust that people place in the information. . . .

Example: A newspaper may print information obtained from a leak at the White House but attribute it to the wrong source. The information is printed as received (preserving data integrity), but its source is incorrect (corrupting origin integrity).

Matt Bishop, Introduction to Computer Security 3 (2004).

This definition suggests that conduct impairs the integrity of information when it diminishes the trustworthiness of either the information's content or authenticity. Because "any" impairment of integrity constitutes damage, it seems that most or even all cases of unauthorized access trigger damage. The facts of the unauthorized access often leave unclear whether the data accessed has been changed or altered in some way. *Compare* Shurgard Storage Centers, Inc. v. Safeguard Self Storage, Inc., 119 F. Supp.2d 1121 (W.D. Wash. 2000) (finding than an unauthorized access impaired the integrity of the computer accessed) *with* Moulton v. VC3, No. 1:00CV434–TWT, 2000 WL 33310901 (N.D. Ga. 2000) (finding no impairment to integrity when "[d]efendant's network security was never actually compromised"). *See also* United States v. Mitra, 405 F.3d 492, 494 (7th Cir. 2005) (suggesting that a defendant who had hacked into a government computer and added a message to the end of every government communication had impaired the integrity of the communications).

4. *Mens rea of the felony enhancements.* The mental states that attach to the elements of § 1030(a)(5) are mostly clear from the face of the statute. However, felony violations of § 1030(a)(5) will generally be based on the conduct having caused one of the felony enhancements of 18 U.S.C. § 1030(c)(4)(A)(i). What mental state should apply to these felony enhancements? The following case considers that question, based on an early version of the statute which incorporated the felony enhancement directly into the text of § 1030(a)(5) rather than placing them in § 1030(c)(4)(A)(i).

UNITED STATES v. SABLAN

United States Court of Appeals for the Ninth Circuit, 1996.
92 F.3d 865.

HUG, CHIEF JUDGE.

Bernadette H. Sablan appeals her conviction for computer fraud under 18 U.S.C. § 1030(a)(5) following a conditional guilty plea. Sablan argues that the district court wrongly interpreted the elements of the crime and, alternatively, that the statute is unconstitutional. We affirm Sablan's conviction and her sentence.

Facts

In the early hours of August 15, 1992, Sablan, a former employee of the Bank of Hawaii's Agana, Guam branch, left a bar where she had been drinking with a friend. Sablan had recently been fired from the bank for circumventing security procedures in retrieving files. That morning, Sablan left the bar and entered the closed bank through an unlocked loading dock door. She went to her former work site (using a key she had kept) and used an old password to log into the bank's mainframe. Sablan contends that she then called up several computer files and logged off. The

Government asserts that Sablan changed several of the files and deleted others. Under either version, Sablan's conduct severely damaged several bank files.

Sablan was charged with computer fraud in violation of 18 U.S.C. § 1030(a)(5). In a pretrial motion to dismiss, Sablan attacked the statute for its failure to require a *mens rea* for each of the essential elements of the offense. In the alternative, Sablan requested a jury instruction that required the Government to prove intent as to all elements of the crime. In particular, Sablan wanted the jury to be instructed that the Government needed to prove that she had the intent to damage bank files. The district court denied the motion and ruled that, as used in the computer fraud statute, the word "intentionally" applied only to the access element of the crime. Sablan then entered into a conditional plea agreement that preserved her right to appellate review of the issue raised in her motion.

Discussion

Sablan contends on appeal that the computer fraud statute must have a *mens rea* requirement for all elements of the crime. She asserts that the indictment was defective because it did not allege the appropriate *mens rea* required by the statute. In the alternative, Sablan asserts that a jury instruction was required to inform the jurors that the state had to prove intent for every element of the crime.

Sablan was convicted under the version of the computer fraud statute in effect from 1986 to 1994. That statute stated:

> (a) Whoever-(5) intentionally accesses a Federal interest computer without authorization, and by means of one or more instances of such conduct alters, damages, or destroys information in any such Federal interest computer ... and thereby-(A) causes loss to one or more others of a value aggregating $1,000 or more during any one year period; shall be punished as provided.

18 U.S.C. § 1030 (amended by Pub.L. No. 103–354). In order to have violated the statute, a defendant must have (1) accessed (2) a federal interest computer (3) without authorization and (4) have altered, damaged, or destroyed information (5) resulting in the loss to one or more others (6) of at least one thousand dollars. The district court held that the statute's *mens rea* requirement, "intentionally," applied only to the access element of the crime.

A.

We begin our analysis by noting that the statute is ambiguous as to its *mens rea* requirement. Although the statute explains that one must "intentionally access a Federal interest computer without authorization, and destroy information in any such Federal interest computer," punctuation sets the "accesses" phrase off from the subsequent "damages" phrase. With some statutes, punctuation has been used to indicate that a phrase set off by commas is independent of the language that followed.

However, punctuation is not always decisive in construing statutes. In *Liparota v. United States,* 471 U.S. 419 (1985), and *United States v. X–Citement Video,* 513 U.S. 64 (1994), for example, the Supreme Court applied the mental state adjacent to initial words to later clauses without regard to intervening punctuation. In both cases, the Supreme Court resorted to legislative history to clarify the ambiguous language.

We conclude that the comma after "authorization" does not resolve the ambiguity. Allowing the *mens rea* requirement to reach subsequent elements of the crime would comport with general linguistic rules. Similarly, it is proper to read the statute without extending "intentionally" to the other clauses of the sentence. Therefore, we look to the statute's legislative history to clear up the textual ambiguity.

In *United States v. Morris,* 928 F.2d 504 (2d Cir. 1991), the Second Circuit examined the legislative history of the computer fraud statute and concluded that the "intentionally" standard applied only to the "accesses" element of the crime. The court focused on the fact that the original version of the statute, passed in 1984, punished anyone who

> *knowingly* accesses a computer without authorization, or having accessed a computer with authorization, uses the opportunity such access provides for purposes to which such authorization does not extend, and by means of such conduct *knowingly* uses, modifies, destroys, or discloses information in, or prevents authorized use of, such computer, if such computer is operated for or on behalf of the Government of United States and such conduct affects such operation.

Pub.L. No. 98–473, subsection (a)(3) (amended latest by Pub.L. No. 103–354) (emphasis added). When the statute was amended in 1986, the scienter requirement was changed from knowingly to intentionally and the second *mens rea* reference was eliminated. By contrast, other subsections of section 1030 retained the "dual-intent" language by placing the *mens rea* requirement at the beginning of both the "accesses" phrase and the "damages" phrase. *See, e.g.,* 18 U.S.C. § 1030(a)(1). The court concluded that the decision of Congress not to repeat the scienter requirement within this statute evidenced an intent not to require the Government to prove a defendant's intent to cause damage.

Sablan urges this court to reject the holding in *Morris,* contending that the 1986 bill was intended only to apply to those who intentionally damage computer data. She points to one line in a Senate report that evidenced a desire to retain the dual intent language: "The new subsection 1030(a)(5) to be created by the bill is designed to penalize those who intentionally alter, damage, or destroy certain computerized data belonging to another." 1986 U.S.C.C.A.N. at 2488. Thus, Sablan argues, the computer fraud statute has a *mens rea* requirement for the damages clause of the bill. We disagree.

As the *Morris* court concluded:

Despite some isolated language in the legislative history that arguably suggests a scienter component for the "damages" phrase of section 1030(a)(5)(A), the wording, structure, and purpose of the subsection, examined in comparison with its departure from the format of its predecessor provision persuade us that the "intentionally" standard applies only to the "accesses" phrase of section 1030(a)(5)(A), and not to its "damages" phrase.

We adopt the reasoning of the *Morris* court and hold that the computer fraud statute does not require the Government to prove that the defendant intentionally damaged computer files.

B.

Sablan contends that if the computer fraud statute does not have a *mens rea* requirement for the damages element of the offense, the statute is unconstitutional. Relying on the Supreme Court's decision in *X–Citement Video,* Sablan states that a *mens rea* must be applied to all elements of an offense or due process standards are violated. We review *de novo* the district court's determination of federal constitutional law.

The Supreme Court has never ruled that *mens rea* is a constitutional requirement. However, in *X–Citement Video,* the Supreme Court stated that a statute without any scienter requirements "would raise serious constitutional doubts." Sablan contends that lack of a scienter requirement for the damages element of the offense renders the statute constitutionally infirm. In *X–Citement Video,* the Court construed the "knowingly" scienter requirement beyond the most proximate clause of 18 U.S.C. § 2252 to clarify that one charged with trafficking in child pornography must know that the material involves the use of a minor.

After reviewing the cases interpreting criminal statutes to include broadly applicable scienter requirements the Court held that the "presumption in favor of a scienter requirement should apply to each of the statutory elements which criminalize otherwise innocent conduct." However, the computer fraud statute does not criminalize otherwise innocent conduct. Under the statute, the Government must prove that the defendant intentionally accessed a federal interest computer without authorization. Thus, Sablan must have had a wrongful intent in accessing the computer in order to be convicted under the statute. This case does not present the prospect of a defendant being convicted without any wrongful intent as was the situation in *X–Citement Video.* Therefore, we hold that the computer fraud statute's *mens rea* requirement is sufficient to meet constitutional standards.

NOTES AND QUESTIONS

1. Although Sablan involves an earlier generation of § 1030(a)(5), one critical aspect of it appears to survive into the current version of the statute: The felony enhancements found in § 1030(c)(4)(A)(i) are strict liability. That is, it does not matter whether a defendant intended to cause $5,000 in loss, or

intended to cause physical injury, or intended to cause damage affecting 10 or more computers: All that matters is that the defendant *did in fact do so*. The resulting harm can be a freakish accident, and will nonetheless raise the level of liability from a misdemeanor under § 1030(c)(4)(A)(i).

2. Is strict liability for the felony enhancements found in § 1030(c)(4)(A)(i) consistent with the theories of punishment? Does a defendant whose conduct accidentally or through freakish circumstances leads to greater harm deserve greater punishment? Should the law seek to deter such unlucky defendants? Or is the point that by punishing unlucky defendants, the law can deter other defendants from engaging in inherently risky conduct? To what extent should the difficulty of proving mens rea enter into the equation? How can the government prove intent to damage, or intent to cause a particular amount of damage?

Your answer to these questions may be guided by your sense of whether computer intrusions are inherently risky and harmful or usually innocent and sometimes even helpful. If you believe that hacking is inherently dangerous and likely to cause harm, then you may find it appropriate to punish those whose intrusions lead to additional harm. On the other hand, if you see most intrusions as generally harmless, you may conclude that the mens rea requirements of § 1030(a)(5) are far too broad. Consider the latter argument from a student author:

> Few outside hackers intend to cause damage. In fact, most hackers break into systems to learn or to challenge themselves. Strict hacker ethics prohibit hackers from damaging the accessed systems. These types of hackers * * * should be punished less than those with the intent to damage. However, the 1996 Act includes not only hackers who truly intend to cause damage, but even the outsiders who accidentally cause damage. By punishing hackers who lack criminal intent in the same manner as those who possess criminal intent, Congress has overlooked the goal of retribution.

Haeji Hong, Note, *Hacking Through the Computer Fraud and Abuse Act*, 31 U.C. Davis L. Rev. 283, 303 (1997). Do you agree?

3. Consider the following hypothetical cases. Which of the two defendants deserves a greater punishment? What kinds of criminal liability are they likely to face under 18 U.S.C. § 1030?

A. *Discovered Versus Undiscovered Attacks*. On Monday, Hacker Bob hacks into the servers of the XYZ corporation and snoops around. On Tuesday, Hacker Joe hacks into the servers of the same company and also snoops around. On Wednesday, the system administrator at XYZ corporation finds evidence of Joe's attack and spends 50 hours over the next week (at a rate of $125 per hour) responding to the attack, conducting a damage assessment, and resecuring the server. The system administrator never notices Bob's attack.

B. *Differing Intents*. Two friends, Kate and Jane, don't like a large Internet service provider called Burns Online. Kate decides that she wants to destroy Burns Online by inflicting as much loss as she can upon it. Jane decides that she wants to cause only an infinitesimal amount of harm to Burns Online. Both Kate and Jane download a program that purports to allow the user to launch a denial-of-service attack. Jane configures the program so that it will disable Burns Online for only 1 second; Kate configures the program so that it will disable Burns Online indefinitely. At the second that Jane launches her one-second attack, a doctor who is a subscriber to Burns Online attempts to send an e-mail to one of his patients urging his patient to exercise more and maintain a balanced diet. Due to the one-second attack, he cannot send it, and decides to log off. Kate's attack takes Burns Online offline for ten minutes, until the system administrator at Burns Online comes up with a defense against it.

4. *Due process and the meaning of authorization.* The *Sablan* court concludes that requiring the government to prove intentional access without authorization is sufficient to satisfy any constitutional requirements of mens rea; the remaining elements can be strict liability elements without violating the Due Process clause. Although the Supreme Court has never expressly held that mens rea is a constitutional requirement, it has tended to read a mens rea requirement into criminal statutes when the conduct otherwise prohibited is innocent conduct. *See generally* Staples v. United States, 511 U.S. 600 (1994). The *Sablan* court concludes that no such construction of § 1030(a)(5) is needed because the Section "does not criminalize otherwise innocent conduct."

> Under the statute, the Government must prove that the defendant intentionally accessed a federal interest computer without authorization. Thus, [the defendant] must have had a wrongful intent in accessing the computer in order to be convicted under the statute.

Sablan, 92 F.3d at 869. Does this analysis hinge on a narrow definition of "without authorization"? If you adopt a broad contract-based or norms-based view of authorization, is § 1030(a)(5) unconstitutional?

5. *Offensive "self-help," a.k.a. hacking back.* Computer intrusions and denial-of-service attacks can cause a significant amount of economic and other damage to their victims. Should an owner/operator of a victim computer have a right to "hack back" against an intruder? If *A* launches an attack at *B* in violation of 18 U.S.C. § 1030(a)(5), can *B* launch a counterattack at *A* designed to stop *A*'s attack? Does the counterattack violate § 1030 as well, or is it excused under principles of cyber-self-defense?

A number of scholars have advocated such a cyber-self-defense doctrine. For example, Michael O'Neill has argued that "just as settlers in the American West could not reliably count on the local sheriff to protect them, and instead kept a weapon handy to stymie potential aggressors, Internet users may need to protect themselves." Michael E. O'Neill, *Old Crimes in New Bottles: Sanctioning Cybercrime*, 9 Geo. Mason. L. Rev. 237, 277 (2000). According to Professor O'Neill, the threat of a counterstrike will deter attacks. "Just as a homeowner may defend his house, . . . computer companies ought to not only be permitted, but encouraged, to unleash their considerable talents to launch countermeasures against cyber-criminals." *Id.* at 280. Bruce Smith has also suggested that the law should recognize a hack-back defense. *See* Bruce Smith, *Hacking, Poaching, and Counterattacking:*

Digital Counterstrikes and the Contours of Self–Help, 1 J.L. Econ. & Pol'y 171, 191 (2005):

> A reasonably strong case can be made that counterstrikes against "hackers"—at least when such measures are proportionate to the threat posed—should be privileged. * * * Section 77 of the *Restatement (Second) of Torts* authorizes persons to use "reasonable force" to protect their property in instances where the intrusion is not "privileged," the property owner "reasonably believes that the intrusion can be prevented or terminated only by the force used," and the property owner "reasonably believes that a request will be useless or that substantial harm will be done before it can be made." And Section 84 permits the use of "devices" to accomplish these ends—merely adding the requirement that "the device [be] one customarily used for such a purpose, or reasonable care [be] taken to make its use known to probable intruders." Although it might well be the case that a party that "hacked back" against a network intruder might fall within the language of [18 U.S.C. § 1030] or other statutes, the party would seem to possess a colorable claim—at least under traditional tort principles—that a proportionate counterstrike against a hacker should not expose the counterattacker to either criminal or civil liability.

Other commentators have disagreed, noting that it is very easy to disguise your tracks online. As a result, victims often are unable to tell who exactly is attacking them, and often will accidentally launch counterattacks at innocent third-parties. Those innocent third-parties will in turn believe they are under attack, and will launch counterattacks as well. The result may be more computer misuse, not less. *See, e.g.,* Orin S. Kerr, *Virtual Crime, Virtual Deterrence: A Skeptical View of Self–Help, Architecture, and Civil Liability,* 1 J.L. Econ. & Pol'y 197, 204–06 (2005). Richard Epstein has noted that the high chances of error in a cyber-counterattack raises a number of difficult legal questions:

> What should be done if the program picks up the wrong target and wrecks the computer of an innocent party? What should be done if the attacked target is a zombie computer that has unwittingly transferred the offending material across cyberspace? Are there any limits of proportionality that are associated with these attacks? Should the self-help remedy be denied on the grounds that some form of civil liability could be imposed?

Richard Epstein, *The Theory and Practice of Self–Help,* 1 J.L. Econ. & Pol'y 1, 31 (2005). No defendant in a computer hacking case has attempted to invoke such a defense. State laws on the defense-of-property justification vary state-to-state, and federal law has recognized such a defense only intermittently. Do you think courts should recognize a right to cyber-self-defense right? And if so, what should it look like?

6.   Are existing computer misuse statutes an effective response to the problem of computer misuse? Should we look for other answers? A number of scholars have suggested that the most effective methods for deterring computer misuse crimes look beyond criminal law. For example, some scholars have suggested imposing civil liability on ISPs for the criminal acts of their

subscribers. The idea is that this will encourage ISPs to monitor and disable wrongdoers before significant harms occur. *See, e.g.,* Doug Lichtman & Eric Posner, *Holding Internet Service Providers Accountable*, in The Law and Economics of Cybersecurity (Mark Grady & Francesco Parisi eds., 2005). Others have suggested that computer owners should be subject to negligence suits if their poor computer security facilitates computer misuse offenses. *See, e.g.,* Stephen E. Henderson & Matthew E. Yarborough, *Suing the Insecure?: A Duty of Care in Cyberspace,* 32 N.M. L. Rev. 11 (2002).

Some scholars have looked to social norms instead of civil liability. Neal Katyal has suggested that computer crime can be deterred by redesigning the architecture of the on-line experience in a way that will encourage community monitoring and discourage vandalism. *See* Neal Kumar Katyal, Essay, *Digital Architecture as Crime Control,* 112 Yale L.J. 2261 (2003). In a similar vein, Brent Wible has argued that official "hack-in" contests for hackers challenging them to attack dummy networks can channel the urge to engage in unauthorized conduct and generate a respect for law that will deter computer crime. *See* Brent Wible, Note, *A Site Where Hackers Are Welcome: Using Hack-in Contests to Shape Preferences and Deter Computer Crime,* 112 Yale L.J. 1577 (2003).

Are these proposals realistic? Do they complement the need for computer misuse laws such as 18 U.S.C. § 1030, or could they replace such statutes? More broadly, what is the purpose of computer misuse laws? Is their purpose to punish culpable individuals? To deter criminal activity? To improve computer security? What kinds of laws beyond unauthorized access, computer fraud, and computer damage statutes are needed to address computer misuse crimes?

7. The scope of criminal liability for computer misuse is very broad. A critic of existing law might say that the legislature's basic approach is to criminalize everything and then rely on prosecutorial discretion to select appropriate cases for criminal punishment.

Is this criticism accurate? And if it is, do you think the legislature has acted wisely? Computer technologies and social practices change rapidly, and it may be difficult for the law to keep up. Is it sensible for legislatures to impose broad criminal liability ex ante, so that prosecutors are rarely or never in a position of being unable to charge a worthy case? Or should the legislature only impose liability narrowly, so that new computer technologies can evolve without the threat of criminal punishment? Do you trust prosecutors to charge only appropriate cases? Does the threat of criminal punishment have a significant chilling effect on legitimate computer use?

CHAPTER 3

TRADITIONAL CRIMES

■ ■ ■

There are many types of computer crimes beyond computer misuse offenses. Of course, not all crimes are relevant to a course in computer crime law. Computers are tools that transmit and store information, which means that crimes with no necessary link to transmitting information are not likely to arise often in computer-related cases. At the same time, a number of traditional crimes do involve transmitting and storing information. These information-based crimes often find a natural home in the world of computers and the Internet. In some cases, the computer's ability to process and transmit information quickly and with relative anonymity has led entire subcultures of criminal activity to migrate from the physical world to a digital environment.

The purpose of this chapter is to study traditional crimes committed using computers. As with the previous chapter, the materials will focus primarily on federal law with some coverage of state law. The chapter begins with laws concerning economic crimes, such as theft and copyright infringement, that exist primarily to protect economic interests. The materials turn next to crimes against persons, such as threats and harassment. The next subjects are vice crimes, such as Internet gambling and obscenity-related offenses. The chapter concludes with laws regarding child exploitation crimes such as offenses involving images of child pornography.

As you read these materials, consider whether criminal conduct changes when it shifts from the physical world to computer networks. Many of these crimes raise the issue of "old wine in new bottles," and ask us to adjust concepts and statutory language from an old set of facts to a new one. Should it matter whether a crime is committed using computer networks and the Internet? Does anything change when a traditional crime is committed using computers?

A. ECONOMIC CRIMES

Control of information can have considerable economic value. A file stored on a server may contain valuable secrets about a new product to go on the market. Alternatively, the file may be an expensive piece of software or a sought-after movie or sound recording. Whatever the source of the file's value, that value depends on information control. The more widely available information becomes, the less valuable it tends to be. You might pay for a stock tip from a private investment manager, but you won't pay if you can read the same stock tip in the newspaper for free. You might have exclusive rights to control access to a new piece of software, but fewer people are likely to purchase those rights if they can obtain illegal copies easily for free.

How should criminal law regulate control of information to protect these economic interests? Federal criminal law includes four types of information control statutes: general property crimes, such as theft and possession of stolen property; specific information-based crimes such as the Economic Espionage Act of 1996; statutes that govern authentication devices; and intellectual property laws such as the copyright statutes.

1. PROPERTY CRIMES

Property crimes were originally designed to protect interests in physical property. The basic idea is that physical property has an owner who enjoys the right to exclude others from accessing or using that property. Taking property away from the owner without the owner's consent constitutes theft. Retaining the property, knowing it has been taken from its owner, constitutes possession of stolen property.

Can these principles be used to protect rights in information? Does information have an "owner"? What does it mean for information to be "stolen"? What does it mean to "possess" information?

PEOPLE v. JOHNSON

Criminal Court for the City of New York, 1990.
560 N.Y.S.2d 238.

CHARLES J. HEFFERNAN, JR., JUDGE.

This is another in a series of nearly identical fact patterns prosecuted in this jurisdiction with increasing frequency: a charge that use of an illegally possessed AT&T credit card number was unlawfully offered, for a fee, to travelers at the Port Authority terminal in Manhattan. Here, as in other cases, the People assert that the "service" was offered by a form of huckstering—in this case, that defendant's words were "you can call the whole world for $8.00." Such cases have engaged various legal issues, determined by the crimes charged in the respective prosecutions.

This case * * * [considers whether] charging criminal possession of stolen property in the fifth degree (P.L. § 165.40), should be dismissed for facial insufficiency on the ground that a telephone credit card number is not "property" under P.L. § 155.00(1).

The Facts

Deponent [a police officer who saw the alleged crime occur] states that he observed defendant at the above location saying to passersby "you can call the whole world for $8.00" and that deponent approached an unapprehended individual who said he was from Poland, and deponent then observed defendant pull a small scrap of paper from defendant's pocket and start dialing a number from the paper onto a phone.

Deponent further states that when defendant saw deponent approach, deponent observed defendant tear said scrap of paper and throw it to the ground.

Deponent states that he is informed by Tony Largo, of AT&T security that the number on said piece of paper had been used to make approximately 240 calls during the 2 hours before the defendant was arrested, and informant is the custodian of the phone computer code system and the credit card number and states that defendant had no permission or authority to access or attempt to access the phone computer code systems or to possess or use the said credit card number.

Deponent further states that defendant was apprehended in an area which had signs posted that said the area was for "Ticketed Passengers Only" and that deponent observed defendant had no bus ticket.

The Stolen Property Count

Defendant * * * moves to dismiss the third count of the information, charging the crime of criminal possession of stolen property in the fifth degree (P.L. § 165.40), also on the ground of facial insufficiency. Defendant rests his argument on the opinion in *People v. Molina,* 145 Misc.2d 612 (Crim. Ct. Queens Co. 1989), where the court granted an identical motion on essentially identical facts. In both cases theallegation was that defendant possessed telephone credit card numbers belonging to AT&T, such numbers being written on a piece of paper that defendant possessed.

The court noted that:

> the potentially unique 14 digit pattern and sequence of these numbers could support the People's assertion that they are unique AT&T credit card numbers. The identity of the nature of the numbers is not mere speculation. Adequate support for the conclusion that they are AT&T card numbers was provided by a representative of New York Telephone. It is also worth noting that defendant possessed three different patterns of numbers, and all were identified as having the necessary unique AT&T pattern. Any claims by defendant that these numbers had an independent significance goes towards challenging findings made by a trier of fact. This aspect of the complaint is sufficient.

Molina, supra, at 614, 615.

What troubled the *Molina* court, however, was the "property" element of the crime, the court finding that the defendant was not accused of holding the actual AT&T credit cards from which the numbers were presumably obtained. The court noted that the paper on which the numbers were written is the tangible personal property of the defendant, not of the credit card holders—a fact that would seemingly be undisputed. Nor would a reasonable person likely gainsay the *Molina* court's view that the credit card holders have no possessory interest in that paper.

The final step in the *Molina* analysis, however, is the point at which this court takes respectful departure from that holding: *i.e.,* that "the numbers in and of themselves are not tangible property." *Molina, supra,* at 615. It was the belief of that court that a more expansive reading would violate the rule that criminal statutes are to be strictly and narrowly construed.

Strict construction, however, need not ignore the clear import of facts and circumstances attending a criminal allegation implicating a technically-oriented charge. To do so would be unmindful of the ever-changing nature of American technology and its components.

P.L. § 155.00(1) defines "property" as meaning "any money, personal property, real property, computer data, computer program, thing in action, evidence of debt or contract, or any article, substance or thing of value, including any gas, steam, water or electricity, which is provided for a charge or compensation."

To rest the distinction between culpability and inculpability upon the type of physical material on which the credit card number is listed—or upon the absence of such material—would be to defeat the purpose underlying the statute at issue. The generic crime of criminal possession of stolen property is meant to proscribe knowing possession of property wrongfully taken from a lawful holder. On the facts before this court, there is little, if any, relevance to the form in which the telephone credit card number is possessed. Under the *Molina* rationale, a person who steals a telephone credit card would be criminally liable if he or she is found in possession of the card. The thief would escape liability, however, by either recording the card number on a piece of paper owned by the wrongdoer and then destroying the card, or by committing the number to memory after destroying the card. The lack of logic in that thesis is evidenced by the following question: is the number with the card of any more value to a person intent on placing phone calls without charge than is the number without the card? The number itself is what is crucial, and not who has the superior possessory interest in the paper on which the number is recorded, or whether the number is written as opposed to being memorized.

Such a number clearly has inherent value, apart from the card onto which the numbers are embossed. Most other credit cards require either that the card be presented for use or, as a pre-condition to its acceptance for use by telephone, that some verifying data as to the card or the party to whom it was issued be tendered. The use of a telephone credit card, on the other hand, is not encumbered by such constraints. Rather, a person in possession of a validly issued telephone credit card number can place a local, national or international call without immediate scrutiny simply by inputting the credit card number by dialing or pushing a button on the telephone instrument. Lawful bearers of that number will incur later cost for that service. Those who come into possession of those numbers without authorization, however, can place calls at no cost; the bill for those calls will, in due course, be sent to the lawful holder of the credit cards. It is, therefore, beyond quarrel that a telephone credit card number qualifies as a "thing of value."

More, however, is required in this analysis. While a telephone credit card number is a "thing of value," care must be taken to be sure that the number in question is indeed such a number. A court must be satisfied that the number possessed is not some innocuous number, innocently had by a defendant. Such a judgment can be made, of course, only in the context of attending circumstances. In the context of a motion to dismiss a count of an information for facial insufficiency, a court must look to the information itself.

The information before the court contains several factual assertions that are helpful in deciding whether the number in question was an AT&T credit card, as opposed to something else: (1) a security representative of AT&T, Tony Largo, states that he is the custodian of the phone computer system and the credit card number; (2) Mr. Largo also states that defendant had no permission to possess that number; (3) Detective Joseph Rullo of the Port Authority Police Department states that he saw defendant saying to passersby "you can call the whole world for $8.00"; (4) Detective Rullo further states that he saw defendant approach a person who said that he was from Poland, that defendant pulled a scrap of paper from defendant's pocket and began to dial a number from that paper onto a telephone; (5) Detective Rullo states that when defendant saw Detective Rullo approaching, defendant tore the scrap of paper and threw it to the ground; (6) Mr. Largo states that the number on the paper had been used to make approximately 240 calls during the 2 hours before defendant's apprehension.

The confluence of those factors persuades this court that the number that defendant is charged with possessing is, indeed, an AT&T credit card number, a "thing of value." That is, however, not the end of the inquiry on the question whether the telephone credit card number is "property" under P.L. § 155.00(1).

The statute couples "thing of value" with the modifying clause "which is provided for a charge or compensation." On the facts pled herein, there is no indication that the card was provided to the lawful owner in exchange for immediate charge or compensation. Nor need there be such an assertion. For the charge attaching to the credit card number is, of course, a subsequent charge, for calls that are placed by using that number. This is sufficient to meet the compensation or charge requirement of P.L. § 155.00(1).

Accordingly, this court does not concur with the sole challenge made by defendant to the facial sufficiency of the pleading of the count charging Criminal Possession of Stolen Property in the Fifth Degree: *i.e.,* that the number on the slip of paper in question is not "property" within the statutory definition. On the facts at bar, the AT&T telephone credit card number qualifies for inclusion within the statutory definition of "property."

NOTES AND QUESTIONS

1. The defendant in *Johnson* wrongfully obtained a calling card number that enabled him to place long-distance phone calls for free. The number was an access code—a password, a sort of intangible key—and its market value derived from the value of the service that could be accessed using the number.

Individuals use access codes every day. E-mail passwords and ATM PIN numbers are common examples. You can probably think of less high-tech examples as well. In high school, you probably had a locker that you protected with a combination lock. In grade school, you may have conditioned access to your neighborhood clubhouse on an entrant's knowledge of the "secret password." The combination for the lock and the secret password are both access codes. In the past, did you think of these access codes as your property? Does the fact that an access code can be used to obtain property mean that the access code is itself property? Why wasn't Johnson charged with fraud for placing the illegal calls, instead of possession of stolen property for knowing the card number?

2. What does it mean to "possess" a number? The legal concept of possession generally requires two elements: knowledge of the property and control over it. If you put a piece of paper in your wallet, you possess that paper because you know the paper exists and you control the contents of your pocket. Does it make sense to say that you also possess the intangible writing on the piece of paper, such as a number written on it? Can you control a number in the same way that you can control a physical object?

Arguably, the *Johnson* court evades this difficulty by simply eliminating the control requirement of possession and equating possession with knowledge. The court reasons that Johnson would be liable for possessing stolen property if he had merely seen the calling card numbers and then memorized them. Does that make sense?

Imagine a robber holds up a victim at gun point, demands that the victim tell him something valuable, and that the victim, afraid for his life, tells the robber his credit card number. If the robber memorizes the number, *Johnson* suggests, he would be guilty of possessing stolen property. What if the robber takes out an advertisement in the local newspaper that says, "Memorize this stolen credit card number!" and includes the number? Would anyone who reads the advertisement carefully be guilty of possessing stolen property, even if they have no intent to use the number fraudulently? What if the robber simply forgets the credit card number? Does he no longer possess the stolen property?

3. Every Anglo–American crime must include a guilty act (in Latin, an *actus reus*). *See* Wayne R. LaFave, Criminal Law 206 (3d ed. 2000). According to this doctrine, the government cannot punish merely having a state of mind. If possession can be satisfied by knowledge alone, does the crime of possessing stolen property violate this principle? If you were the defense attorney in *Johnson*, what argument would you make on appeal to persuade a higher

court that the trial court's construction is inconsistent with the *actus reus* requirement?

4. If information can be property, what does it take for information to become "stolen" property? Physical property becomes stolen when someone intentionally takes it away from its owner. The same concept can apply to data: if Joe steals Jane's iPod, the data files stored in the iPod are stolen in exactly the same way as the physical iPod itself. But what if the information is divorced from physical storage media? If Joe copies Jane's computer data and Jane retains her copy, is that data stolen?

The facts of *Johnson* are instructive. AT&T issued a calling card to a legitimate customer, and Johnson found out the number and used it to place calls billed to that customer's account. Try to identify exactly what (if anything) made that number stolen. Was it stolen simply because Johnson possessed the number and was not an authorized account holder? This seems somewhat unlikely. Was the number stolen because Johnson did not have a legitimate business reason to possess the number? Was it stolen because Johnson had an intent to use the number to place calls but not pay for them?

Another possibility is that the word "stolen" expresses a result, not a legal status. Was the number stolen because Johnson deserves punishment for using AT&T's services without their permission?

5. Under the New York law at issue in *Johnson*, property includes any "thing of value." Whether data has value is contextual, of course. Go back to the hypothetical in which a robber holds up a victim at gun point and demands that the victim tell him something valuable. The victim, afraid for his life, advises the robber to buy stock in General Motors. Is that advice a "thing of value"? Does it depend on whether General Motors' stock later goes up or down?

As these questions suggest, attempts to value a number generally measure the benefit of the use of that number in a specific context, rather than the value of the number as an abstract matter. Thus in *Johnson*, the court looked to the specific context in which Johnson had the number to determine whether he would use the number to obtain valuable services. The number was a thing of value because Johnson was using the number to obtain valuable services for free; in the court's terms, the number was not merely "some innocuous number, innocently had by a defendant."

Is this a helpful way to determine the value of information? What is the court really measuring?

UNITED STATES v. FARRAJ

United States District Court for the Southern District of New York, 2001.
142 F. Supp.2d 484.

MARRERO, DISTRICT JUDGE.

Defendants Said Farraj ("Said") and Yeazid Farraj ("Yeazid") are charged in a three-count indictment with * * * interstate transportation of stolen property in violation of 18 U.S.C. § 2314. Said now moves * * * to dismiss * * * on the ground that the allegedly stolen property does not fall within the scope of § 2314.

For the reasons discussed below, the motions are denied.

Background

In summer of 2000, Said Farraj was a paralegal with the law firm of Orrick, Harrington & Sutcliffe LLP. At the time, Orrick represented plaintiffs in a class action tobacco case: *Falise v. American Tobacco Co.,* No. CV 99–7392(JBW) (E.D.N.Y.). In preparation for the *Falise* trial, the attorneys and paralegals at Orrick created a trial plan exceeding 400 pages and including, among other things, trial strategy, deposition excerpts and summaries, and references to anticipated trial exhibits. Only Orrick employees assigned to *Falise* were permitted access to the Trial Plan. The Indictment does not reveal whether Said was included among such employees.

The Government charges that Said, using the moniker "FlyGuyNYt," e-mailed an 80–page excerpt of the Trial Plan to the *Falise* defendants' attorneys and offered to sell them the entire Plan. An FBI agent posing as one of the *Falise* defendants' attorneys negotiated with Said via e-mail and ultimately agreed to purchase the Trial Plan for $2 million. On July 21, 2000, Yeazid, Said's brother, met with a second undercover FBI agent at a McDonald's restaurant in lower Manhattan to receive payment. Yeazid was arrested then and gave a statement to the FBI implicating his brother in the conspiracy charged in the Indictment.

Discussion

The Government charges in count two that by e-mailing the Trial Plan excerpt across state lines, Said violated 18 U.S.C. § 2314, which provides, in relevant part, that "whoever transports, transmits, or transfers in interstate or foreign commerce any goods, wares, merchandise, securities, or money, of the value of $5,000 or more, knowing the same to have been stolen, converted, or taken by fraud ... shall be fined under this title or imprisoned." Said moves to dismiss, arguing that § 2314 applies only to the physical asportation of tangible goods or currency, not to "information" stored and transmitted electronically, such as the Trial Plan excerpt e-mailed here. Neither the Supreme Court nor the Second Circuit has addressed this question directly, and this appears to be an issue of first impression in this District.

The Second Circuit has held that the phrase "goods, wares, or merchandise" is "a general and comprehensive designation of such personal property or chattels as are ordinarily a subject of commerce." *In re Vericker,* 446 F.2d 244, 248 (2d Cir. 1971) (Friendly, J.). Said, relying on *Vericker,* argues that the Second Circuit has at times determined that documents fall outside the scope of § 2314. At other times, however, the Second Circuit and other courts have held that documents may be considered "goods, wares, or merchandise" under § 2314. *See, e.g., United States v. Greenwald,* 479 F.2d 320 (6th Cir. 1973) (documents containing secret chemical formulae); *United States v. Bottone,* 365 F.2d 389 (2d Cir. 1966) (drug manufacturing processes); *United States v. Caparros,* No. 85 Cr. 990, 1987 WL 8653 (S.D.N.Y. March 25, 1987) (secret business plans).

The FBI documents at issue in *Vericker* detailed the criminal activity of certain individuals. Judge Friendly reasoned that the FBI documents were not "goods, wares, or merchandise" within the meaning of the statute because the substance contained in the documents was not ordinarily the subject of commerce. The Trial Plan at issue here, however, as is true for trial plans generally, was the work product of a business relationship between client and attorney, and may thus be viewed as an ordinary subject of commerce, created for a commercial purpose and carrying inherent commercial value at least as to the persons directly interested in the matter.

Said argues that even if trial plans generally may be viewed as goods under § 2314, he is accused of transmitting an "intangible," an electronic form of the document, and therefore that it was not a good, but merely "information."

The text of § 2314 makes no distinction between tangible and intangible property, or between electronic and other manner of transfer across state lines. Indeed, in 1988, Congress amended § 2314 to include the term "transmits" to reflect its agreement with the Second Circuit and other courts which had held that § 2314 applied to money wire transfers, where the only interstate transportation took place electronically and where there was no transportation of any physical item. In *United States v. Gilboe,* 684 F.2d 235 (2d Cir. 1982), the Second Circuit addressed the issue of electronic transfer for the first time and recognized that

> the manner in which funds were moved does not affect the ability to obtain tangible paper dollars or a bank check from the receiving account. Indeed, we suspect that actual dollars rarely move between banks, particularly in international transactions. The primary element of this offense, transportation, does not require proof that any specific means of transporting were used.

684 F.2d at 238.

The Second Circuit has also held that § 2314 was violated when the defendants stole documents containing some drug manufacturing process, copied and returned them, and then sent the copies abroad. *See Bottone,* 365 F.2d at 391–92. The court noted that it did not matter that the item stolen was not the same as that transported. Rather, as observed by Judge Friendly,

> where the physical form of the stolen goods is secondary in every respect to the matter recorded in them, the transformation of the information in the stolen papers into a tangible object never possessed by the original owner should be deemed immaterial. It would offend common sense to hold that these defendants fall outside the statute simply because, in efforts to avoid detection, their confederates were

at pains to restore the original papers to the employer and transport only copies or notes.

Id. at 394.

Relying in part on the Second Circuit's decisions in *Gilboe* and *Bottone,* the court in *United States v. Riggs,* 739 F. Supp. 414 (N.D. Ill. 1990) held that the defendant violated § 2314 when he downloaded a text file containing propriety information onto a home computer, transferred it over a computer network to his co-defendant in another state, who then uploaded it onto a computer bulletin board. The court reasoned that just because the defendant stored the information on a computer, rather than printing it on paper, his acts were not removed from the purview of the statute:

> In the instant case, if the information in Bell South's E911 text file had been affixed to a floppy disk, or printed out on a computer printer, then the defendant's transfer of that information across state lines would clearly constitute the transfer of "goods, wares, or merchandise" within the meaning of § 2314. This court sees no reason to hold differently simply because the defendant stored the information inside a computer instead of printing it out on paper. In either case, the information is in a transferrable, accessible, even salable form.

Id. at 421. The court noted that "reading a tangibility requirement into the definition of 'goods, wares, or merchandise' might unduly restrict the scope of § 2314, especially in this modern technological age," and recognized that although not tangible in a conventional sense, the stolen property was physically stored on a computer hard drive and could be viewed and printed out with the push of a button. "The accessibility of the information in readable form from a particular storage place also makes the information tangible, transferable, salable, and in this court's opinion, brings it within the definition of 'goods, wares, or merchandise' under § 2314."

The Supreme Court's decision in *Dowling v. United States,* 473 U.S. 207 (1985), relied on here by Said, was appropriately distinguished by the *Riggs* court. In *Dowling,* the Supreme Court held that where the victim holds only a copyright, distinct from the possessory interest of the owner of a simple good, and the only act charged involves an unauthorized infringement of that copyright, there is no violation of § 2314. The *Dowling* Court remarked that § 2314 contemplates "a physical identity between the items unlawfully obtained and those eventually transported." Said reads this statement to mean that the electronic transfer of a document falls without the statute.

The Tenth Circuit, relying on *Dowling,* has also taken the view that § 2314 requires the transfer of physical goods, wares, or merchandise. *See United States v. Brown,* 925 F.2d 1301, 1308 (10th Cir. 1991). The defendant in *Brown* crossed state lines with stolen computer code stored on a computer disk. The district court dismissed the indictment, stating that the material contained in the notebooks and on the hard drive was "not the type of property which is contemplated within the language of the statute, goods, wares or merchandise." The Tenth Circuit affirmed the dismissal, observing that "§ 2314 applies only to physical 'goods, wares or merchandise.' Purely intellectual property is not within this category. It can be represented physically, such as through writing on a page, but the underlying, intellectual property itself remains intangible." In this Court's view, the reasoning in *Brown* does not square with the Second Circuit's *Bottone* decision, and may be based on a misapplication of *Dowling.*

Lastly, Said turns to *United States v. Stafford,* 136 F.3d 1109 (7th Cir. 1998). In *Stafford,* the objects of the questioned transfers were "Comdata codes"—a sequence of numbers truckers use to acquire cash while on the road. The driver receives the code from his employer, writes them down on a "comcheck" and then cashes it like a check. The Seventh Circuit held that the codes were not "goods" but merely "information", and that therefore stealing them did not violate § 2314. Importantly, the Seventh Circuit does not reveal how the codes were transferred (presumably they were communicated over the telephone), and the court specifically declined to address whether § 2314 would be implicated if the perpetrator had written down the codes on a piece of paper and transported them across state lines. Consequently, the reasoning in *Stafford* sheds little light on the statute's application to the conduct charged against Said.

Weighing the scant authority at hand, the Court is persuaded that the view most closely analogous to Second Circuit doctrine is that which holds that the transfer of electronic documents via the Internet across state lines does fall within the purview of § 2314. The indictment is therefore upheld and the motion to dismiss count two is denied.

NOTES AND QUESTIONS

1. Farraj had access to the valuable Trial Plan in New York, and he e-mailed an excerpt from it to opposing counsel. Imagine other ways Farraj could have provided the excerpt to opposing counsel:

A. He could have stolen a paper version of the Trial Plan and shipped it via postal mail to opposing counsel.

B. He could have obtained a paper version of the Trial Plan, photocopied it, returned the original, and shipped the photocopied version to opposing counsel.

C. He could have saved an electronic copy of the Trial Plan onto a floppy diskette, put the diskette in an envelope, and shipped the envelope to opposing counsel.

D. He could have memorized the Trial Plan, traveled to the office of opposing counsel, and then written out a copy of the Trial Plan from memory.

Scenario A is a classic violation of 18 U.S.C. § 2314. But what about Scenarios B, C, and D? If you agree that Farraj violates § 2314 in Scenario B, must the same conclusion follow for Scenarios C and D? Note that Scenario B is the first to separate the physical item from the information it contains. Scenario C puts the data in electronic form, but transported via a physical storage device. The facts of *Farraj* put the data in electronic form, but transported electronically. Finally, the facts of Scenario D put the data in the neural networks of the human brain, transported by physically moving that brain (and the person below it, naturally) across state lines. Can you distinguish among these cases, or do they all involve basically the same thing?

In United States v. Bottone, 365 F.2d 389 (2d Cir. 1966), Judge Henry Friendly offered a rationale to distinguish Scenario B from Scenario D. *Bottone* raised the basic facts of Scenario B: the defendants had stolen papers that contained the victim company's secret manufacturing processes, photocopied the papers, returned the originals, and sent the photocopies. As the *Farraj* court notes, Judge Friendly agreed with the government that the photocopies were 'goods' which had been 'stolen, converted or taken by fraud' pursuant to 18 U.S.C. § 2314. In a part of the opinion not discussed in *Farraj*, Judge Friendly distinguished this set of facts from those akin to Scenario D in the following way:

> To be sure, where no tangible objects were ever taken or transported, a court would be hard pressed to conclude that 'goods' had been stolen and transported within the meaning of 2314; the statute would presumably not extend to the case where a carefully guarded secret formula was memorized, carried away in the recesses of a thievish mind and placed in writing only after a boundary had been crossed. The situation, however, is quite different where tangible goods are stolen and transported and the only obstacle to condemnation is a clever intermediate transcription or use of a photocopy machine.

Bottone, 365 F.2d at 393. Are you convinced? How would Judge Friendly resolve the *Farraj* case? Is there a difference between memorizing information and crossing a state line and e-mailing that information across a state line?

2. *Does sending an electronic signal "transport" property?* When property is tangible, it is possible to track its motion to establish that it has been transported across state lines. If property is merely electronic data, however, the only property being transported are the electrons that constitute the bits and bytes of the data. Does setting up a circuit that sends electrons across state lines "transport" property? In United States v. Gilboe, 684 F.2d 235 (2d Cir. 1982), discussed in *Farraj*, a defendant wired an electronic funds transfer to the Bahamas. The defendant argued that he did not actually "transport" any property to the Bahamas. In an opinion by Judge Feinberg, the Second Circuit disagreed:

> Electronic signals in this context are the means by which funds are transported. The beginning of the transaction is money in one account and the ending is money in another. The manner in which the funds were moved does not affect the ability to obtain tangible paper dollars or a bank check from the receiving account. Indeed, we suspect that actual dollars rarely move between banks, particularly in international transactions. If anything, the means of transfer here were essential to the success of the fraudulent scheme. Defendant depended heavily on his ability to move funds rapidly out of reach of disgruntled shipowners who

were to receive payment within days of loading the grain. And it was not until the funds, through a series of bank transfers, came to rest in the Bahamas that defendant's scheme was complete.

Id. at 238. Is the court right to focus not on the details of how the technology works, but rather on the net effect of the transaction?

3. *Property crimes and information misuse.* Cases such as *Johnson* and *Farraj* try to rework traditional property crimes to address information misuse. The cases assume that information is property that has an owner who sets the rules for its proper usage. When a wrongdoer obtains a copy of that information and misuses it in violation of those rules, the misuse renders that copy stolen property. Retaining the information constitutes possession of stolen property (*Johnson*), and sending that information can be considered transporting it (*Farraj*). Taken together, such cases create a theoretical framework for punishing misuse of information using general property crimes.

Is the effort a successful one? Both *Johnson* and *Farraj* involve individuals who deserved punishment for their harmful acts. *Johnson* obtained valuable services without paying, and *Farraj* attempted to sell a confidential litigation document so it could be used against his law firm's client. From a standpoint of criminal law theory, both men committed acts that deserve punishment and that the law should try to deter. But how close is the nexus between the defendants' wrongful acts and the theory of criminal liability applied by the courts? Is a general crime of information misuse derived from property law appropriate?

How similar is the crime of information misuse to the concepts of computer misuse described in Chapter Two? Both regimes imagine a proper usage of computers and/or information, and both punish deviations from that proper usage. In the case of computer misuse crimes, access at some point becomes unauthorized; in the case of information misuse crimes, information at some point becomes stolen. Does either regime feature a clear way to distinguish proper from improper conduct? Is the law here premised mostly on an intuition that at some point conduct becomes harmful enough that it should trigger criminal sanctions? If so, do some principles explain that intuition, or is it simply a moral judgment made on a case-by-case basis? From an ethical perspective, is it appropriate for prosecutors to make aggressive arguments about the scope of traditional criminal laws, or should they focus on prosecuting conduct that is clearly proscribed by existing statutes? Why am I asking so many questions? (Heh, just kidding.)

2. THE ECONOMIC ESPIONAGE ACT

One alternative to charging information misuse under general property crimes is for the legislature to enact new criminal statutes that punish information misuse in specific contexts. An example of this approach is the Economic Espionage Act of 1996 (EEA), Pub. L. No. 104–294, codified at 18 U.S.C. §§ 1831–39. The EEA was designed to punish and deter the theft of a specific type of information, namely trade secrets.

UNITED STATES v. GENOVESE

United States District Court for the Southern District of New York, 2005.
409 F. Supp.2d 253.

PAULEY, J.

By Indictment dated January 3, 2005, the Government charged the defendant, William P. Genovese, Jr., with one count of unlawfully downloading and selling a trade secret in violation of 18 U.S.C. § 1832(a)(2). Genovese moves to dismiss the Indictment pursuant to Rule 12(b)(3)(B) of the Federal Rules of Criminal Procedure. Genovese contends that the statute criminalizing trade secret theft is facially overbroad in violation of the First Amendment and unconstitutionally vague as applied to him. For the reasons set forth below, Genovese's motion to dismiss the Indictment is denied.

Background

In February 2004, portions of Microsoft Corporation's source code for two of its computer operating systems, Windows NT 4.0 and Windows 2000, appeared on the Internet.

The Indictment charges Genovese with downloading, copying, selling and attempting to sell Microsoft source code without authorization. Specifically, the Government contends that on February 12, 2004, Genovese posted a message on his website offering the code for sale: "win2000 source code jacked ... and illmob.org got a copy of it ... im sure if you look hard you can find it or if you wanna buy it ill give you a password to my ftp."

According to the Complaint, an investigator retained by Microsoft responded to the message later that month by sending Genovese an email that offered twenty dollars for the code. After Genovese accepted the offer, the investigator transferred twenty dollars to Genovese through an online payment service. Genovese then provided access to the source code through his FTP server. Microsoft alerted the FBI. In July 2004, an undercover Government agent contacted Genovese and purchased the Microsoft source code. Genovese was arrested and charged with violating 18 U.S.C. § 1832(a)(2).

Discussion

Section 1832 was enacted as part of the Economic Espionage Act of 1996. In relevant part, the statute applies to anyone who,

> with intent to convert a trade secret, that is related to or included in a product that is produced for or placed in interstate or foreign commerce, to the economic benefit of anyone other than the owner thereof, and intending or knowing that the offense will, injure any owner of that trade secret, knowingly ... without authorization copies, duplicates, sketches, draws, photographs, downloads, uploads,

alters, destroys, photocopies, replicates, transmits, delivers, sends, mails, communicates, or conveys such information.

18 U.S.C. § 1832(a)(2). "Trade secret," in turn, is defined to encompass

all forms and types of financial, business, scientific, technical, economic, or engineering information, including patterns, plans, compilations, program devices, formulas, designs, prototypes, methods, techniques, processes, procedures, programs, or codes, whether tangible or intangible, and whether or how stored, compiled, or memorialized physically, electronically, graphically, photographically, or in writing if (A) the owner thereof has taken reasonable measures to keep such information secret; and (B) the information derives independent economic value, actual or potential, from not being generally known to, and not being readily ascertainable through proper means by, the public.

18 U.S.C. § 1839(3). The statute carries a ten-year maximum term of imprisonment. 18 U.S.C. § 1832(a).

Genovese argues that § 1832 violates the First Amendment because it restricts protected speech and sweeps more broadly than necessary. A statute is unconstitutionally overbroad if there exists "a substantial risk that application of the provision will lead to the suppression of speech." *Nat'l Endowment for the Arts v. Finley,* 524 U.S. 569, 580 (1998). When a litigant challenges a statute on its face as overly broad, the prudential limitations against third party standing are relaxed, and the litigant may assert the rights of individuals whose interests might be affected by the statute but who are not before the court.

While the First Amendment protects the formulation of source code and other types of trade secrets encompassed by the EEA, *see Universal City Studios, Inc. v. Corley*, 273 F.3d 429, 445–46 (2d Cir. 2001), the statute criminalizes their unauthorized copying, duplicating, downloading and uploading. 18 U.S.C. § 1832(a)(2). Moreover, the EEA limits its reach to such conduct that is done "with intent to convert a trade secret . . . to the economic benefit of anyone other than the owner thereof." 18 U.S.C. § 1832(a)(2). Such conduct is not protected speech. *See United States v. Thompson*, 76 F.3d 442, 452 (2d Cir. 1996) ("A prohibition against corrupt acts is clearly limited to constitutionally unprotected and purportedly illicit activity."). Because § 1832 is specifically targeted toward illegal activity and does not reach protected speech, the statute is not unconstitutionally overbroad.

The void-for-vagueness doctrine requires that a statute define the criminal offense with sufficient precision "that ordinary people can understand what conduct is prohibited." *Kolender v. Lawson,* 461 U.S. 352, 357 (1983). Courts must also consider whether the law provides explicit standards for those who apply it. Vagueness challenges to statutes which do not involve First Amendment freedoms must be examined in the light of the facts of the case at hand.

Genovese does not contend that § 1832(a)(2) imprecisely describes the prohibited act (*i.e.*, that an individual is guilty if he "copies, duplicates, sketches, draws, photographs, downloads, uploads, alters, destroys, photocopies, replicates, transmits, delivers, sends, mails, communicates, or conveys" a trade secret). Rather, he maintains that Section 1839(3)'s definition of "trade secret" is unconstitutionally vague as applied to the facts of this case and does not afford due process. Specifically, Genovese argues that having found the source code on the Internet after it had been released to the general public by a third-party, he could not have known that it was "not . . . generally known to . . . the public" and that Microsoft had taken "reasonable measures" to safeguard it.

1. *"Not . . . generally known to . . . the public"*

Genovese maintains that "he had every reason to believe the code had become publicly available" when he found it on the Internet. However, a trade secret does not lose its protection under the EEA if it is temporarily, accidentally or illicitly released to the public, provided it does not become "generally known" or "readily ascertainable through proper means." 18 U.S.C. § 1839(3)(B). Genovese merges these two standards and, in so doing, elevates the standard for trade secret status to one of absolute secrecy. This formulation impermissibly writes the critical modifier "generally" out of the statutory definition and attempts to inject a vagueness otherwise absent from the facts of this case.

Indeed, a reasonable inference from Genovese's website posting is that he knew that the source code derived independent value because it was not "generally known." The Government alleges that he described the code as "jacked" and indicated that others would have to "look hard" to find it elsewhere. As such, Genovese was on notice that Microsoft had not publicly released the code and recognized its public scarcity. Moreover, because Genovese offered the code for sale and successfully sold it, he was on notice that it derived value from its relative obscurity, notwithstanding that it was available from other sources. *See United States v. Hsu,* 40 F. Supp.2d 623, 630–31 (E.D. Pa. 1999) (rejecting a similar challenge to the definition of "trade secret" where the evidence showed that the defendant "knew (or at a minimum believed) that the information he was seeking to acquire was not generally known to or readily ascertainable through proper means by the public").

A statute may also be unconstitutionally vague if it "authorizes and even encourages arbitrary and discriminatory enforcement." *City of Chicago v. Morales,* 527 U.S. 41, 56 (1999). In this regard, Genovese argues that the statute provided no guidance to law enforcement officials to determine whether the source code constituted a trade secret. However, just as Genovese's announcement and conduct reflect his belief that the "jacked" source code was valuable because it was not generally known, it provided the FBI reason to believe that Genovese was trafficking in Microsoft's trade secret.

2. *"Reasonable measures"*

With respect to the "reasonable measures" element of the EEA's "trade secret" definition, Genovese contends that he "was in no position to make a determination about whether Microsoft took any measures to protect the secrecy of its source code, let alone whether those measures were 'reasonable.'"

Once again, Genovese's website posting belies any claim that he was a casual Internet browser who happened upon the source code without knowledge of its owner or the manner in which the code entered the public domain. As discussed above, the posting reveals that Genovese knew that a third-party had "jacked" the source code from Microsoft. Having acknowledged both that the source code was proprietary to Microsoft and that someone else penetrated whatever safeguards Microsoft enlisted to protect it, Genovese cannot now argue that the statute was insufficient to put him on notice that the source code constituted a trade secret under the EEA. For Section 1839(3)'s "trade secret" definition to survive a vague-as-applied challenge, a "defendant need not have been aware of the particular security measures taken by" the trade secret's owner, as long as the "defendant knew the information was proprietary." *United States v. Krumrei,* 258 F.3d 535, 539 (6th Cir. 2001) (noting that the defendant "was aware that he was selling confidential information to which he had no claim"). In this case, one can infer that Genovese knew not only that the source code was proprietary, but that any protective measures by Microsoft had been circumvented. At a later stage in this proceeding, Genovese may choose to argue to this Court or to a jury that Microsoft's measures were not "reasonable," or that Genovese could not have known what, if any, measures Microsoft maintained. For purposes of his vagueness challenge, however, Genovese's knowledge that the source code belonged to Microsoft and that others had stolen it was sufficient for him to "reasonably understand" that the conduct alleged in the Indictment was proscribed by Section 1832(a)(2).

As such, Section 1839(3) defines "trade secret" with "sufficient definiteness" so that an ordinary person in Genovese's position could understand that trafficking in the Windows source code was prohibited by law. As applied to the facts of this case, the statute is not so vague that it violates the defendant's due process.

Notes and Questions

1. Assuming the court is correct that prosecuting Genovese does not raise constitutional difficulties, do you think Genovese violated the Economic Espionage Act? Assume that Genovese found a copy of the source code online, copied it, and uploaded it to his ftp server. Assume from the facts that he knew the source code had been stolen from Microsoft and that Microsoft did not want the code to be available to the public. To be liable, Genovese must have "intent to convert a trade secret," "to the economic benefit of anyone other than the owner thereof," "intending or knowing that the offense will,

injure any owner of that trade secret," and must upload, download or copy it "knowingly ... without authorization." Has Genovese done so? Does it matter if the source code is widely available online? Did Genovese know that his conduct would injure Microsoft? Given that he found the copy online, is his conduct clearly "without authorization"? The legislative history of the EEA indicates that "authorization is the permission, approval, consent or sanction of the owner" to obtain, destroy or convey the trade secret. 142 Cong. Rec. S12202, S12212 (daily ed. Oct. 2, 1996).

2. How much narrower is the EEA compared to the general property approach seen in *Johnson* and *Farraj*? Which approach do you prefer?

3. Consider how the EEA handles the problem of identifying when information such as a trade secret becomes "stolen." The EEA punishes one who:

> (1) steals, or without authorization appropriates, takes, carries away, or conceals, or by fraud, artifice, or deception obtains such information;

> (2) without authorization copies, duplicates, sketches, draws, photographs, downloads, uploads, alters, destroys, photocopies, replicates, transmits, delivers, sends, mails, communicates, or conveys such information;

> (3) receives, buys, or possesses such information, knowing the same to have been stolen or appropriated, obtained, or converted without authorization[.]

18 U.S.C. §§ 1831(a), 1832(a). Does this answer the question? Note that the definition of a trade secret may make it easier to determine when a trade secret is "stolen" or copied "without authorization." A trade secret exists only if it has an identifiable owner who has exercised his right to exclude others from his property by taking reasonable measures to keep it a secret. Reasonable measures generally include the imposition of clear rules governing when the secret can be copied, transmitted, and conveyed. In that context, then, copying or distributing the trade secret in violation of the rules needed to ensure that the secret remains a secret constitutes a copying or distributing "without authorization."

Does this shed light on the broader problem of identifying when information is "stolen"? Does it provide a reason to limit information misuse crimes to trade secrets?

4. Professor Geraldine Moohr has argued that the EEA probably does more harm than good in light of preexisting civil laws protecting trade secrets. *See* Geraldine Szott Moohr, *The Problematic Role of Criminal Law in Regulating Use of Information: The Case of the Economic Espionage Act*, 80 N.C. L. Rev. 853, 919 (2002).

According to Professor Moohr, the criminal provisions of the EEA are likely to have three negative consequences. First, the threat of criminal prosecution may scare some employees into staying at their companies instead of leaving for better jobs or starting new businesses. Moohr argues that employees with access to trade secrets at work may fear that legitimate efforts to start competitor businesses will lead to criminal prosecution for allegedly stealing trade secrets. Second, the combination of criminal punishments and the difficulty of identifying exactly what is a trade secret may overdeter competitors from using information in the public domain. Businesses will be extra careful, and decline to use information that can lead to better products out of a misplaced fear that they will end up being prosecuted under the EEA. Third, the EEA may overdeter individuals from disclosing trade secrets even when that disclosure would serve the public interest by placing ideas into the public domain.

Professor Moohr contends that civil remedies are likely to be a more effective way to regulate information misuse than criminal remedies:

> [C]ivil remedies appear to motivate adequately the creation of new products, while not over-compensating in a way that inhibits long-term innovation and economic growth. Civil remedies more effectively address the real harm that results when an information product is taken: the loss of value to its holder. * * * On the whole, civil law is more likely to produce a nuanced solution that takes into account the rights of others and the public policy of promoting efficient use of knowledge and information.

Id. at 919. Do you agree? What if the defendant is judgment-proof or the harm is irreversible? Do you think Microsoft could recover civil damages from Genovese that would "precisely account" for Microsoft's loss? Imagine a college student obtains the secret formula for Coca–Cola and posts it on the Web. Is a lawsuit against the student a viable option?

Another issue implicated by civil versus criminal remedies is the likelihood of legal action. Companies do not need anyone's permission to file a lawsuit against a business competitor; unsurprisingly, civil trade secret litigation between competitors is fairly common. In contrast, criminal prosecutions brought by federal prosecutors under the EEA remain quite rare. If civil trade secret lawsuits are common, but criminal trade secret prosecutions are rare, which is more likely to have the negative consequences that Professor Moohr predicts?

5. For a review of state criminal laws that address theft of trade secrets, see Eli Lederman, *Criminal Liability for Breach of Confidential Commercial Information*, 38 Emory L.J. 921, 947–65 (1989). For a discussion of the First Amendment implications of trade secret laws, see Eugene Volokh, *Freedom of Speech and Intellectual Property: Some Thoughts after* Eldred, 44 Liquormart, *and* Bartnicki, 40 Hous. L. Rev. 697, 739–48 (2003).

3. IDENTITY THEFT AND ACCESS DEVICE FRAUD

The federal criminal code contains two information misuse statutes that deal specifically with misuse of authentication and access device methods. 18 U.S.C. § 1028 is the federal identity theft statute, and prohibits fraud and misuse of identification documents such as driver's licenses and passports. 18 U.S.C. § 1029 is the federal access device fraud statute, and prohibits fraud and misuse of credit card numbers, computer passwords, and other information that controls account access. The basic thinking behind both statutes is the same: Access to information, property, and other rights may hinge on documents or data that are designed to authenticate individuals. The use of false or fraudulently obtained authentication methods can cause tremendous harms. Both § 1028 and § 1029 try to deter that use by prohibiting possessing, buying, selling, and making documents or data that provide false authentication. Both statutes attempt to punish and deter the harms associated with false identification by punishing misuse of identification information even if no access rights are fraudulently obtained.

UNITED STATES v. CABRERA

United States Court of Appeals for the First Circuit, 2000.
208 F.3d 309.

STAHL, CIRCUIT JUDGE.

Defendant-appellant Vladimir Cabrera appeals his conviction for possession of a document-making implement under 18 U.S.C. § 1028. Specifically, he asserts that under a proper interpretation of § 1028, the prosecution presented insufficient evidence upon which to ground a conviction. * * * We affirm.

Background

In early 1998, Cabrera and an accomplice, Joseph Medeiros, engaged in a scheme to produce counterfeit identification documents, including Massachusetts and Rhode Island driver's licenses, Massachusetts and Rhode Island state employee identification cards, Rhode Island and Puerto Rico birth certificates, U.S. Department of Health and Human Services Social Security cards, and U.S. Department of Justice Immigration and Naturalization Service Resident Alien cards. The government's evidence supported the conclusions that Cabrera employed a computer, a document scanner, a printer, and commercial software that together could be used to scan, alter, and reproduce documents. When used in conjunction with this hardware and software, computer files containing previously scanned official documents stripped of all identifying material served as digitized "templates" from which forgeries could easily be fabricated. First, using the aforementioned equipment, Cabrera scanned genuine documents into his computer, saved the images on his computer hard drive and on floppy disks, removed or altered the identifying information and photographs on the documents, and then printed the documents on photographic paper. Medeiros then inserted new identifying information onto the documents, trimmed the counterfeits, and laminated them as appropriate. Cabrera kept the computer equipment at his home, while the equipment Medeiros used was stored in a suitcase that the two owned jointly.

On June 10, 1998, U.S. Secret Service Agents searched Cabrera's apartment pursuant to a warrant. They found Cabrera's computer equipment, a board used for measuring and trimming documents, Microsoft's "Picture It!" software, which Cabrera apparently had used to create the counterfeit materials, the digitized templates, and sundry fake documents in various stages of completion.

Subsequently, on January 20, 1999, a federal grand jury in the District of Rhode Island returned a two-count indictment, charging, inter alia, that Cabrera possessed document-making implements with the intent that such implements be used in the production of false identification documents, in violation of 18 U.S.C. § 1028(a)(5). At the relevant time period, the statute defined "document-making implement" to mean "any implement or impression specially designed or primarily used for making an identification document, a false identification document, or another document-making implement." Count One—the only count relevant to this appeal—was based on Cabrera's possession of the computer, printer, and scanner.

During Cabrera's trial, Secret Service Agent James Mooney testified for the government regarding the templates found on Cabrera's hard drive and on the diskettes. Agent Mooney also described the software installed on Cabrera's computer and how it could be used for scanning, altering and reproducing documents. On cross-examination, Agent Mooney acknowledged that computers were available to the public and that they had uses aside from those of which Cabrera stood accused. But when Cabrera's counsel then attempted to further examine him regarding the general uses to which anyone could put computer equipment, the court intervened, and the following sidebar exchange regarding the meaning of § 1028's "primarily used" prong ensued:

> THE COURT: Congress might have been a little bit more precise in their definition, but as I read that definition in the context of this statute, I read it as referring to the possession and the intent of the possessor in putting it to use. So I think that the general use that anyone might put a computer to . . . is not relevant.
>
> MR. McCORMICK [Cabrera's Counsel]: I wanted to ask generally if computer equipment was primarily used for the making of—
>
> THE COURT: No, because that primarily refers to the possession of this individual, not the general public.

At the trial's close, the district court instructed the jury only that: "as used in these instructions, the term 'document making implement' means any implement or impression specially designed or primarily used for making an identification document, a false identification document or another document making implement."

The instructions did not specify any particular meaning for the terms "specially designed" or "primarily used." Although Cabrera's counsel did not object to these instructions, the government did object, stating that they did not adequately specify that the statute referred to Cabrera's primary use of the equipment rather than the general uses to which any computer user primarily would put such equipment.

Meanwhile, Cabrera had moved for judgment of acquittal on both counts, arguing that "on the evidence presented, it had not been shown that the computer, printer and scanner referred to in the indictment were document making implements." The district judge reserved judgment on the motion. On May 21, 1999, the jury convicted Cabrera on Count One, and the district judge denied his motion for a judgment of acquittal on that count. Cabrera appeals.

Discussion

Cabrera argues first that his computer system was not proven to constitute a document-making implement within the meaning of the statute, because "there was no proof, either directly [sic] or by inference, that it was specially designed or generally used to produce identification documents, false identification documents or other document making implements." To determine the sufficiency of the evidence, we canvass the evidence (direct and circumstantial) in the light most agreeable to the prosecution and decide whether that evidence, including all plausible inferences extractable therefrom, enables a rational factfinder to conclude beyond a reasonable doubt that the defendant committed the charged crime.

A. *"Specially Designed"*

We first find that Cabrera's computer system was "specially designed" for the production of identification documents. As an initial matter, we hold that the statute's text is unambiguous. It does not exclude from its reach implements that could have legitimate other uses if not altered by the perpetrator's modifications. Cabrera suggests that the "specially designed" prong refers not to a defendant's specific implements, but to implements that as a class are uniquely configured to fabricate false identification documents. His interpretation is not tenable. Neither the statute nor Cabrera provides any basis upon which a court could determine the proper level of generality at which to define the class. Should we look to the class of "computers fitted with scanners, printers, document-altering software and digitized templates"? The class of all "computers"? All "electronic implements"? All "implements" of any sort? Nothing in § 1028 requires such arbitrary classification. Rather, the statute unambiguously asks the fact-finder to consider whether the item that the defendant is charged with possessing was "specially designed" for producing forgeries.

Asserting that the statute is ambiguous, Cabrera notes that courts may look to a statute's legislative history when its language itself is not conclusive and clear. But even if § 1028 were unclear (and we believe it is not) Cabrera's resort to its legislative history would be unavailing. The House Judiciary Committee's report on the False Identification Crime Control Act of 1982—in which the disputed "specially designed" language was first introduced—stated that "the committee intended to exclude implements such as office photocopying machines, which are designed for more general and legitimate purposes." H.R. Rep. No. 97–802, at 11 (1982), reprinted in 1982 U.S.C.C.A.N. 3519, 3530. This language might support an argument that standard computer equipment, bereft of any special-purpose hardware or software, would fall beyond the statute's reach. Perhaps an offender could, it would seem, have used an ordinary word processor and an ordinary printer with ordinary paper to produce false documents, just as an offender could have used an office photocopier to do so, without having violated former § 1028. But Cabrera's computer arrangement, unlike a standard office photocopier, was specifically designed to facilitate counterfeiting. A modern computer is not analogous to an "office photocopying machine" circa 1982, which in Congress's view likely could not be altered or specialized, but rather to a modern photocopier fitted with software and hardware that render it uniquely suited to produce illicit materials. We have no reason to believe that such a device would escape § 1028's reach simply because both it and its 1982 analogue were called "photocopiers." A photocopier configured with special-purpose hardware or software may be "specially designed" for the fabrication of identifying documents, and so may a similarly configured computer.

In fact, the more relevant portion of the legislative history is that which precedes the language quoted above. The House committee report noted that the term "document-making implement" would include "text in a distinctive type face and layout that when reproduced [is] part of an identification document." Id. This statement, of course, accurately describes the templates, which were merely computer files containing digital images of "text in a distinctive type face and layout." Alone, each template formed "part of an identification document" and together with the inserted data, each would constitute a complete document.

Cabrera contends that his system was not specially designed for the fabrication of false identification documents, emphasizing that the hardware at issue—namely, the computer, printer, and scanner—were not uniquely suited to such activity. However, the evidence adduced at trial permitted a jury to conclude that Cabrera's system also included software, such as the "Picture It!" program, which testimony indicated "could be used to accept scanned images and also to place those images onto computer-produced documents." Most tellingly, the system also included digitized templates of various official identification documents stored on Cabrera's hard drive and floppy disks. A jury viewing this paraphernalia as a whole could reasonably have deemed the system specially designed for making a false identification document.

B. "Primarily Used"

Cabrera urges that the "primarily used" prong of the "document-making implement" definition refers to an item's "general usage" rather than the particular use to which a defendant put it. The government acknowledges that if it was required to prove that as a general matter, computers, scanners, and printers are primarily used for making identification documents or false identification documents, Cabrera's conviction must be overturned because the court was presented with no evidence supporting that conclusion. The government contends, however, that the relevant inquiry focuses not on the uses of some hypothetical user, but on Cabrera's own primary use of the computer system. We share the government's view, and find that a jury reasonably could have found that Cabrera's equipment was "primarily used" for the fabrication of documents as that term is set forth in former § 1028.

First, as the government notes, Congress could have used a word such as "generally" in lieu of "primarily" if it intended the meaning that Cabrera proposes. Congress's choice not to use that term suggests that it did not intend the inquiry to focus on an item's typical use within society. Relatedly, the section's legislative history suggests that Congress fully expected § 1028 to cover implements that were "generally" used for purposes other than the fabrication of documents. The House Judiciary Committee report noted that "specialized paper or ink" could constitute document-making implements under the "primarily used" prong. H.R.Rep. No. 97–802, at 11, reprinted in 1982 U.S.C.C.A.N. at 3530. Paper and ink–even "specialized" paper and ink–are not "generally" used for the production of false identification documents, but could, in a given case, be "primarily used" in the service of such ends by a particular defendant. The committee's remarks, then, lend credence to the government's case-specific interpretation of the "primarily used" prong.

Moreover, the treatment which former § 1028 has been accorded by the courts suggests that "primarily used" refers to the defendant's primary use of the item in question. While no court appears to have analyzed the meaning of this prong, it has been found to encompass an assortment of paraphernalia not "generally" used for illicit purposes, including laminating machines, plastic laminating pouches, packets of rub-on letters, erasers, tape, scissors, and small photographs.

The evidence showed that Cabrera repeatedly used his computer, scanner, printer, software, and digitized templates to create false identification documents. This system was used in conjunction with laminates, Exacto blades, a supply of photographic-quality paper, and genuine identification documents. There was no evidence to demonstrate that Cabrera used his system for any other purpose. The jury thus reasonably could have found that this equipment was "primarily used" for Cabrera's document production.

NOTES AND QUESTIONS

1. The current language of 18 U.S.C. § 1028(d)(2) makes the statutory question in *Cabrera* somewhat different today, as it defines "document-making implement" as follows:

> any implement, impression, template, computer file, computer disc, electronic device, or computer hardware or software, that is specifically configured or primarily used for making an identification document, a false identification document, or another document-making implement.

What does it mean for a computer to be "specifically configured" to make an identification document? What software, hardware, or file does that require, and how (if at all) is that computer different from a typical personal computer purchased and loaded with standard software programs? 18 U.S.C. § 1028(a)(5) punishes one who knowingly possesses a document-making implement with intent that it will be used to make false identification documents. Does that just mean possessing a computer with intent to use it to make a false ID is a crime?

2. 18 U.S.C. § 1029 punishes a wide range of access device frauds, and is most often used to punish credit card fraud. An "access device" is broadly defined as:

> any card, plate, code, account number, electronic serial number, mobile identification number, personal identification number, or other telecommunications service, equipment, or instrument identifier, or other means of account access that can be used, alone or in conjunction with another access device, to obtain money, goods, services, or any other thing of value, or that can be used to initiate a transfer of funds (other than a transfer originated solely by paper instrument).

18 U.S.C. § 1029(e)(1). The statute also defines an "unauthorized access device" as "any access device that is lost, stolen, expired, revoked, canceled, or obtained with intent to defraud." 18 U.S.C. § 1029(e)(3). Among the acts prohibited by this statute are trafficking in and possessing unauthorized access devices with intent to defraud. *See* § 1029(a)(2)–(3).

Recall the facts of People v. Johnson, 560 N.Y.S.2d 238 (Crim. Ct. N.Y. 1990), from the beginning of this Chapter. Johnson possessed an AT&T credit card number on a slip of paper. The number was stolen and was being used by Johnson without the consent of the account holder. At the federal level, Johnson's criminal liability is clear. 18 U.S.C. § 1029(a)(6) punishes whoever, "without the authorization of the issuer of the access device, knowingly and with intent to defraud solicits a person for the purpose of ... offering an access device ... or selling information regarding ... an access device." Isn't this exactly what Johnson did? Does it make more sense for Johnson to be punished under a specific access device fraud statute or a general property crime statute?

3. In Flores–Figueroa v. United States, ___ U.S. ___, 129 S.Ct. 1886 (2009), the defendant was a citizen of Mexico who resided in the United States. To secure employment, the defendant gave his employer a fake name and a counterfeit Social Security number and alien registration card. The defendant was charged with committing the crime of aggravated identity theft under 18 U.S.C. § 1028A(a)(1), which prohibits committing a predicate offense while "knowingly" using a means of identification "of another person." The defendant claimed that he did not actually know that the Social Security number he had provided belonged to another person: He knew it was not his own number, but he did not know if the number had been assigned.

The Supreme Court held that as a matter of textual interpretation, the Government must prove knowledge that the number belonged to another person. The Court rejected the prosecution's argument that this interpretation would create practical problems because the government normally would not know whether an illegal immigrant knew that the number belonged to another:

> [I]n the classic case of identity theft, intent is generally not difficult to prove. For example, where a defendant has used another person's identification information to get access to that person's bank account, the Government can prove knowledge with little difficulty. The same is true when the defendant has gone through someone else's trash to find discarded credit card and bank statements, or pretends to be from the victim's bank and requests personal identifying information. Indeed, the examples of identity theft in the legislative history (dumpster diving, computer hacking, and the like) are all examples of the types of classic identity theft where intent should be relatively easy to prove, and there will be no practical enforcement problem.... [T]o the extent that Congress may have been concerned about criminalizing the conduct of a broader class of individuals, the concerns about practical enforceability are insufficient to outweigh the clarity of the text.

Id. at *7.

4. COPYRIGHT LAW

Copyright law is designed to provide economic incentives for authors to create new and original works such as stories, books, music, and movies. Digital technologies and the Internet have begun to revolutionize how such original works are made and distributed, raising a number of vital questions about the future of copyright law. At the same time, copyright law is overwhelmingly an area of civil law, not criminal law. The rights granted under the copyright laws generally are enforced by civil lawsuits brought by copyright owners, not criminal indictments obtained by federal prosecutors. The role of criminal law in the enforcement of copyright law traditionally has been much narrower than the role of civil law. As a result, few criminal copyright cases have been brought.

Should computer-facilitated copyright infringement change that traditional role? The Internet facilitates copyright infringement on a grand scale; it is now far easier and cheaper than ever before to copy and distribute copyrighted works in a relatively anonymous environment. Should criminal copyright laws be enforced to deter the digital reproduction and distribution of copyrighted materials? Can criminal prosecutions limit infringement in a way that civil penalties cannot? Or are criminal prosecutions too heavy-handed given that technology and social practice is in considerable flux?

A) Introduction

DAVID GOLDSTONE—PROSECUTING INTELLECTUAL PROPERTY CRIMES

Computer Crime and Intellectual Property Section.
United States Department of Justice (2001).

The central precept of copyright law is:

For a limited time, an original work in fixed form may not be copied (or otherwise infringed) without permission.

Copyright law is intended to protect the creators of original expressive works. Copyright law protects the original expression of an idea or concept in tangible form (be it a novel, a song, a carpet design, or computer source code), but does not extend to protection of the idea or concept itself. Thus, copyright law protects interests distinct from those protected by the patent laws, which provide exclusive rights to inventors of new methods or processes, and the trademark laws, which protect the exclusive use of certain names and slogans in connection with certain goods or services.

A rich body of law has developed to give greater content to this edict, supported by an administrative scheme established and refined by Congress. For federal prosecutors, however, the critical aspects of copyright law can be distilled to a few basic questions: What is the legal basis for creating a property right in original intellectual property, such as a book, a movie, or computer software? What are the major developments in federal copyright protection? How does intellectual property become protected by copyright law? Does it need to be registered? How long does that protection last? What counts as "infringement" of a copy? Is infringement really a crime, and, if so, why? What if the infringer was not making any money?

What is the legal basis for creating a "property right" in original intellectual property, such as a book, a movie, or computer software? Since 1790, Congress has enacted numerous statutes developing and fine-tuning the copyright law, which is now codified primarily in Title 17 of the United States Code. The Constitution grants Congress both general authority to regulate interstate commerce, U.S. Const. art. I, § 8, cl. 3, and specific authority "to Promote the Progress of Science and Useful Arts, by securing for Limited Times to Authors and Inventors the exclusive Right to their respective Writings and Discoveries." U.S. Const. art. I, § 8, cl. 8.

What are the major developments in federal copyright protection? Since 1790, Congress has enacted and repeatedly amended copyright laws, with a trend of continually increased coverage and increased remedies. Beginning in 1909, Congress also imposed criminal penalties for certain types of copyright infringement. The major revision in 1976 was a watershed moment in copyright law; it revolutionized copyright law by establishing federal pre-emption over state law. *See* 17 U.S.C. § 301. Other significant recent legislative developments include: (1) the Computer Software Copyright Act of 1980 (codified at 17 U.S.C. §§ 101, 117), which clarified that computer software is entitled to copyright protection; (2) expansion of criminal penalties for certain works in 1982 and for all works in 1992; *see* 17 U.S.C. § 506 and 18 U.S.C. § 2319; (3) the creation of an exclusive right pertaining to digital audio transmission of sound recordings by the Digital Performance Right in Sound Recordings Act of 1995 (1995); (4) the criminalization of large-scale copying even in the absence of economic motivation by the No Electronic Theft (NET) Act (1997); (5) the 1998 extension of the term of copyrights; *see* Sonny Bono Copyright Term Extension Act (1998); and (6) the Digital Millennium Copyright Act (codified at 17 U.S.C. §§ 1201–1205).

How does intellectual property become protected by copyright law? Does it need to have been registered with the Copyright Office? Congress has provided copyright protection to all "original works of authorship fixed in any tangible medium of expression, now known or later developed, from which they can be perceived, reproduced, or otherwise communicated, either directly or with the aid of a machine or device." 17 U.S.C. § 102(a). This definition has two components, originality and fixation, which set the outer limits of federal copyright protection. While copyright protection exists from the time of the creation of a work, civil infringement actions may be brought only with respect to those works that have been registered with the Register of Copyrights. Similarly, criminal prosecutions should be sought only after the infringed works have been registered.

How long does copyright protection last? The term of copyright protection for works created in 1978 or later is life of the author plus seventy years. Pre–1978 works are protected for ninety-five years from the date of creation. Corporate copyrights are treated similarly.

What constitutes "infringement" of a copyrighted work? Generally, infringement is the violation of one of five exclusive rights granted to a copyright owner by federal law. The five exclusive rights are: (1) reproduction, (2) distribution, (3) public display, or (4) public performance of the copyrighted work, as well as (5) preparation of derivative works based upon the original copyrighted work. *See* 17 U.S.C. § 106(1)–(5). An unlicensed use of the copyright is not an infringement unless it conflicts with one of these specific exclusive rights conferred by the copyright statute.

What makes copyright infringement a crime? Is it a felony? Copyright infringement is a crime where it is done willfully and either: (1) for commercial advantage or private financial gain, 17 U.S.C. § 506(a)(1); or (2) by reproduction or distribution on a large scale (i.e., copying works with a total retail value of over $1,000), 17 U.S.C. § 506(a)(2). Felony punishment is provided only for reproduction or distribution of at least 10 copies during any 180 days of copyrighted works worth more than $2,500. 18 U.S.C. § 2319(b)–(c). The reason that copyright infringement is a crime is to punish and deter the misappropriation of intellectual property that an author—who may have no means to prevent copying—invested time, energy and money to create.

What other criminal laws protect copyrighted material besides 17 U.S.C. § 506(a) and 18 U.S.C. § 2319? A number of other federal laws specifically protect copyrighted works. 18 U.S.C. § 2318 prohibits the counterfeit labeling of copyrighted works. Further, in 1994, Congress created 18 U.S.C. § 2319A, which expressly covers the unauthorized "fixation" of and trafficking in recordings and musical videos of live musical performances. Systems of copyright management are protected by 17 U.S.C. § 1201 and § 1202. 17 U.S.C. § 506 also provides lesser criminal sanctions for conduct which does not constitute copyright infringement but which nonetheless undermines the integrity of the copyright system, such as for false representations in copyright applications.

There are four essential elements to a charge of felony copyright infringement. In order to obtain a felony conviction under 17 U.S.C. § 506(a) and 18 U.S.C. § 2319, the government must demonstrate that:

1. A copyright exists,

2. It was infringed by the defendant by reproduction or distribution of the copyrighted work,

3. The defendant acted willfully, and

4. The defendant infringed at least 10 copies of one or more copyrighted works with a total retail value of more than $2,500 within a 180–day period.

See 17 U.S.C. § 506(a)(2); 18 U.S.C. § 2319(a), (c)(1). The maximum punishment for this crime is 3 years imprisonment and $250,000.

Another element, if proven, enhances the maximum penalty: That the defendant acted "for purposes of commercial advantage or private financial gain." If it is proven, the statutory maximum prison sentence can rise to 5 years. *See* 17 U.S.C. § 506(a)(1); 18 U.S.C. § 2319(a), (b)(1) * * * * Moreover, a commercial motivation case will usually have better jury appeal than a case without commercial motivation. Indeed, if commercial motivation is not alleged, defendants may be more inclined to raise the affirmative defense of fair use, codified at 17 U.S.C. § 107, since fair use defenses are more plausible when defendants do not profit financially by their acts of infringement.

NOTES AND QUESTIONS

1. Many of the statutory elements of copyright liability are relatively clear-cut. Consider, for example, the requirement that the defendant's conduct infringed an existing copyright via reproduction or distribution. Downloading a copyrighted computer file constitutes reproducing it, and sending it to another counts as distribution. The primary legal issues raised in criminal copyright cases tend to be the willfulness requirement, fair use, and (if needed) the requirement of an intent to profit.

2. *Fair use.* Copying or distributing copyrighted works does not constitute infringement if it falls within the statutory fair use exception:

[T]he fair use of a copyrighted work * * * for purposes such as criticism, comment, news reporting, teaching (including multiple copies for classroom use), scholarship, or research, is not an infringement of copyright. In determining whether the use made of a work in any particular case is a fair use the factors to be considered shall include—

(1) the purpose and character of the use, including whether such use is of a commercial nature or is for nonprofit educational purposes;

(2) the nature of the copyrighted work;

(3) the amount and substantiality of the portion used in relation to the copyrighted work as a whole; and

(4) the effect of the use upon the potential market for or value of the copyrighted work.

17 U.S.C. § 107. The fair use doctrine requires applying this multi-factor test in light of the specific facts of the case.

The fair use defense arose in a civil case brought for downloading music over a peer-to-peer network in BMG Music v. Gonzalez, 430 F.3d 888 (7th Cir. 2005). The defendant, Cecilia Gonzalez, downloaded copyrighted music using the KaZaA file-sharing network. Judge Easterbrook held that the fair use defense did not apply to her conduct:

A "fair use" of copyrighted material is not infringement. Gonzalez insists that she was engaged in fair use under the terms of 17 U.S.C. § 107—or at least that a material dispute entitles her to a trial. It is undisputed, however, that she downloaded more than 1,370 copyrighted songs during a few weeks and kept them on her computer until she was caught. Her position is that she was just sampling music to determine what she liked enough to buy at retail. Because this suit was resolved on summary judgment, we must assume that Gonzalez is telling the truth when she says that she owned compact discs containing some of the songs before she downloaded them and that she purchased others later. She concedes, however, that she has never owned legitimate copies of 30 songs that she downloaded. (How many of the remainder she owned is disputed.)

Instead of erasing songs that she decided not to buy, she retained them. It is these 30 songs about which there is no dispute concerning ownership that formed the basis of the damages award. This is not a form of time-shifting, along the lines of *Sony Corp. of America v. Universal City Studios*, Inc., 464 U.S. 417 (1984) (*Betamax*). A copy downloaded, played, and retained on one's hard drive for future use is a direct substitute for a purchased copy—and without the benefit of the license fee paid to the broadcaster. The premise of *Betamax* is that the broadcast was licensed for one transmission and thus one viewing. *Betamax* held that shifting the time of this single viewing is fair use. The files that Gonzalez obtained, by contrast, were posted in violation of copyright law; there was no license covering a single transmission or hearing—and, to repeat, Gonzalez kept the copies. Time-shifting by an authorized recipient this is not. See William M. Landes & Richard A. Posner, *The Economic Structure of Intellectual Property Law* 117–22 (2003).

Section 107 provides that when considering a defense of fair use the court must take into account "(1) the purpose and character of the use, including whether such use is of a commercial nature or is for nonprofit educational purposes; (2) the nature of the copyrighted work; (3) the amount and substantiality of the portion used in relation to the copyrighted work as a whole; and (4) the effect of the use upon the potential market for or value of the copyrighted work." Gonzalez was not engaged in a nonprofit use; she downloaded (and kept) whole copyrighted songs (for which, as with poetry, copying of more than a couplet or two is deemed excessive); and she did this despite the fact that these works often are sold per song as well as per album. This leads her to concentrate on the fourth consideration: "the effect of the use upon the potential market for or value of the copyrighted work."

As she tells the tale, downloading on a try-before-you-buy basis is good advertising for copyright proprietors, expanding the value of their inventory. The Supreme Court thought otherwise in *Grokster*, with considerable empirical support. As file sharing has increased over the last four years, the sales of recorded music have dropped by approximately 30%. Perhaps other economic factors contributed, but the events likely are related. Music downloaded for free from the Internet is a close substitute for purchased music; many people are bound to keep the downloaded files without buying originals. That is exactly what Gonzalez did for at least 30 songs. It is no surprise, therefore, that the only appellate decision on point has held that downloading copyrighted songs cannot be defended as fair use, whether or not the recipient plans to buy songs she likes well enough to spring for. *See A & M Records, Inc. v. Napster, Inc.*, 239 F.3d 1004, 1014–19 (9th Cir. 2001).

Id. at 889–90.

For scholarly discussions of how the fair use doctrine does–and should– apply to copyright infringement online, *see* Ann Bartow, *Electrifying Copyright Norms and Making Cyberspace More Like a Book,* 48 Vill. L. Rev. 13 (2003); Niva Elkin–Koren, *Cyberlaw and Social Change: A Democratic Approach to Copyright Law in Cyberspace,* 14 Cardozo Arts & Ent. L.J. 215 (1996); Glynn S. Lunney, Jr., *The Death of Copyright: Digital Technology, Private Copying, and the Digital Millennium Copyright Act,* 87 Va. L. Rev. 813 (2001); Ruth Okediji, *Givers, Takers, and Other Kinds of Users: A Fair Use Doctrine for Cyberspace,* 53 Fla. L. Rev. 107 (2001).

B) The Willfulness Requirement

The willfulness requirement provides the most important line distinguishing civil from criminal copyright liability. Under current law, infringement cannot be a crime unless it is "willful." What does it mean to infringe a copyright willfully?

UNITED STATES v. MORAN

United States District Court for the District of Nebraska, 1991.
757 F.Supp. 1046.

RICHARD G. KOPF, UNITED STATES MAGISTRATE JUDGE.

The parties have consented to try this misdemeanor case before me. Trial was held on January 15, 1991, and briefs were received on January 23, 1991. I now find that the defendant is not guilty of the alleged willful infringement of a copyrighted video cassette in violation of 17 U.S.C. § 506(a).

Facts

Dennis Moran, the defendant, is a full-time Omaha, Nebraska, police officer and the owner of a "mom-and-pop" movie rental business which rents video cassettes of copyrighted motion pictures to the public. On April 14, 1989, agents of the Federal Bureau of Investigation executed a court-ordered search warrant on the premises of Moran's business. The FBI seized various video cassettes appearing to be unauthorized copies of copyrighted motion pictures, including "Bat 21," "Big," "Crocodile Dundee II," "The Fourth Protocol," "Hell–Bound: Hellraiser II," and "Mystic Pizza." The parties have stipulated that these six motion pictures are validly copyrighted motion pictures. The parties have further stipulated that each of the six motion pictures was distributed to Moran, with the permission of the copyright holder, between February 1, 1989, and April 14, 1989. The parties have further stipulated that at least one of the movies identified was reproduced by Moran onto a video cassette, without the authorization of the copyright holder, placed into inventory for rental, and subsequently rented.

At the time the FBI executed the search warrant, Moran was fully cooperative. He told the FBI agents he put the "duped" copies out for rental and held the "originals" back because he feared the "original" motion pictures would be stolen or damaged. Moran told the FBI agents at the time they executed the warrant that he believed this practice was legal as long as he had purchased and was in possession of the "original" motion picture. Moran further advised the FBI agents that he would affix to the "duped" copies title labels for the copyrighted motion pictures and a copy of the FBI copyright warning label commonly found on video cassette tapes. Moran advised the FBI agents that he put the title labels and FBI warning on the tapes to stop customers from stealing or duplicating the tapes.

Moran testified at trial. He indicated that he had been employed as an Omaha, Nebraska, police officer for approximately twenty-two-and-a-half years, including service as a narcotics investigator and as a bodyguard to the mayor of the City of Omaha. Moran has a reputation for honesty among his associates.

Moran testified that he began to "insure" copyrighted video cassettes, meaning that he duplicated copyrighted video cassettes which he had validly purchased from distributors, when he realized copyrighted tapes were being vandalized. Moran testified he was under the impression that "insuring" tapes was legal whereas "pirating" tapes was not. For practical purposes, Moran defined "insuring" versus "pirating" as meaning that he could duplicate a copyrighted tape provided he had purchased the copyrighted tape and did not endeavor to rent both the copyrighted tape and the duplicate he had made. Moran testified that he formulated his belief about "insuring" versus "pirating" when talking with various colleagues in the business and from reading trade publications. However, Moran was not able to specifically identify the source of his information.

There was no persuasive evidence that Moran made multiple copies of each authorized version of the copyrighted material. The evidence indicates that Moran purchased more than one copyrighted tape of the same movie, but the persuasive evidence also reveals that Moran made only one copy of each copyrighted tape he purchased. There was no persuasive evidence that Moran endeavored to rent both the copyrighted tape and the duplicate. When Moran made the unauthorized copy, he put the unauthorized copy in a package made to resemble as closely as possible the package containing the original copyrighted motion picture Moran had purchased from an authorized distributor.

Law

Moran makes two arguments. First, Moran argues that the government must prove that he had the specific intent to violate the law, that is, he knew that what he was doing was illegal and he committed the act nevertheless. Secondly, Moran argues that he did not have the specific intent to violate the law and, as a consequence, should be found not guilty.

In pertinent part 17 U.S.C. § 506(a) punishes as a criminal any "person who infringes a copyright willfully and for purposes of commercial advantage or private financial gain." Pursuant to 17 U.S.C. § 106(3), the owner of a copyright has the exclusive right to "distribute copies . . . of the copyrighted work to the public by sale or other transfer of ownership, or by rental, lease, or lending." The "exclusive right" of the owner of a copyright is subject to a variety of exceptions. *See* 17 U.S.C. §§ 107–118.

A.

It must first be determined whether the word "willfully," as used in 17 U.S.C. § 506(a), requires a showing of "bad purpose" or "evil motive" in the sense that there was an "intentional violation of a known legal duty." Adopting the research of the Motion Picture Association of America, the government argues that the term "willful" means only "an intent to copy and not to infringe." On the other hand, Moran argues that the use of the word "willful" implies the kind of specific intent required to be proven in federal tax cases, which is to say, a voluntary, intentional violation of a known legal duty.

The general rule is, of course, that ignorance of the law or mistake of the law is no defense to a criminal prosecution. However, when the term "willfully" is used in complex statutory schemes, such as federal criminal tax statutes, the term "willful" means a "voluntary, intentional violation of a known legal duty." *Cheek v. United States,* 498 U.S. 192 (1991) (holding in a criminal tax prosecution that a good faith misunderstanding of the law or a good faith belief that one is not violating the law negates willfulness, whether or not the claimed belief or misunderstanding is objectively reasonable). As the Court recognized in *Cheek,* in *United States v. Murdock,* 290 U.S. 389, 396 (1933), the Supreme Court said that:

> Congress did not intend that a person, by reason of a bona fide misunderstanding as to his liability for the tax, as to his duty to make a return, or as to the adequacy of the records he maintained, should become a criminal by his mere failure to measure up to the prescribed standard of conduct.

This was evidently so because "the proliferation of statutes and regulations has sometimes made it difficult for the average citizen to know and comprehend the extent of the duties and obligations imposed by the tax law."

Apparently no case has compared and analyzed the competing arguments, i.e., whether the word "willfully" requires either a showing of specific intent, as suggested by Moran, or the more generalized intent suggested by the government. Indeed, a leading text writer acknowledges that there are two divergent lines of cases, one of which requires specific intent and another which does not. 3 M. Nimmer & D. Nimmer, *Nimmer on Copyright,* § 15.01 at 15–5 n. 13 (1990) (hereinafter *Nimmer*). As pointed out by the government, some courts have suggested that "willful" only means an intent to copy, not to infringe. On the other hand, as suggested by Moran, other courts have seemingly required evidence of specific intent. At least two courts have specifically approved jury instructions essentially stating that an act of infringement done "willfully" means an act voluntarily and purposely done with specific intent to do that which the law forbids, that is to say, with bad purpose either to disobey or disregard the law. None of the cases recognize that there are divergent lines of cases on this point, and none of the cases endeavor to explain why one line of cases is more compelling than the other.

I am persuaded that under 17 U.S.C. § 506(a) "willfully" means that in order to be criminal the infringement must have been a "voluntary, intentional violation of a known legal duty." *Cheek,* 111 S.Ct. at 610. I am so persuaded because I believe that in using the word "willful" Congress intended to soften the impact of the common-law presumption that ignorance of the law or mistake of the law is no defense to a criminal prosecution by making specific intent to violate the law an element of federal criminal copyright offenses. I came to this conclusion after examining the use of the word "willful" in the civil copyright infringement context and applying that use to the criminal statute.

In the civil context there is "strict liability" for infringement, even where the infringement was "innocent." In this connection, a plaintiff in a civil case need not prove actual damages, but rather may seek what are called statutory damages. The term "willful" is used in the context of statutory damages, and it is instructive to compare the definition of the term "willful," as used in the civil context regarding statutory damages, with the definition of the term "willful" used in the criminal context.

In the statutory damage context, a civil plaintiff is generally entitled to recover no less than $250.00 nor more than $10,000.00 per act of infringement. 17 U.S.C. § 504(c)(1). But where the infringement is committed "willfully," the court in its discretion may increase the award of statutory damages up to a maximum of $50,000.00 per act of infringement. 17 U.S.C. § 504(c)(2). On the other hand, in the case of "innocent infringement," if the defendant sustains the burden of proving he/she was not aware, and had no reason to believe, that his/her acts constituted an infringement of the copyright, and the court so finds, the court may in its discretion reduce the applicable minimum to $100.00 per act of infringement. 17 U.S.C. § 504(c)(2).

As noted text writers have concluded, the meaning of the term "willful," used in 17 U.S.C. § 504, must mean that the infringement was with knowledge that the defendant's conduct constituted copyright infringement. *Nimmer, supra*, § 14.04[B][3] at 14–40.3–14–40.4 (citations omitted). Otherwise, there would be no point in providing specially for the reduction of awards to the $100.00 level in the case of "innocent" infringement since any infringement which was nonwillful would necessarily be innocent.

The circuit courts of appeal which have considered the issue have all adopted *Nimmer's* formulation with regard to the meaning of the word "willful" for purposes of 17 U.S.C. § 504(c)(2) and statutory civil damages. In other words, the term "willful," when used in the civil statutory damage statute, has consistently been interpreted to mean that the infringement must be "with knowledge that the defendant's conduct constitutes copyright infringement." *Nimmer, supra*, § 14.04[B][3] at 14–40.3–14–40.4.

There is nothing in the text of the criminal copyright statute, the overall scheme of the copyright laws, or the legislative history to suggest that Congress intended the word "willful," when used in the criminal statute, to mean simply, as the government suggests, an intent to copy. Rather, since Congress used "willful" in the civil damage copyright context to mean that the infringement must take place with the defendant being knowledgeable that his/her conduct constituted copyright infringement, there is no compelling reason to adopt a less stringent requirement in the criminal copyright context. Accordingly, I find that "willfully," when used in 17 U.S.C. § 506(a), means a "voluntary, intentional violation of a known legal duty."

B.

Having determined that the standard enunciated by the Supreme Court in *Cheek* applies, it is important to recognize that the rule does not require that a defendant's belief that his conduct is lawful be judged by an objective standard. Rather, the test is whether Moran truly believed that the copyright laws did not prohibit him from making one copy of a video cassette he had purchased in order to "insure" against vandalism. In other words, the test is not whether Moran's view was objectively reasonable, but rather, whether Moran truly believed that the law did not proscribe his conduct. Of course, the more unreasonable the asserted belief or misunderstanding, the more likely it is that the finder of fact will consider the asserted belief or misunderstanding to be nothing more than simple disagreement with known legal duties imposed by the law, and will find that the government has carried its burden of proving knowledge.

Most of the government's argument that it proved beyond a reasonable doubt that Moran violated the criminal copyright statute, even if the word "willfully" is defined as Moran suggests, is based upon the assumption that Moran's beliefs must be "objectively" reasonable. As indicated above, Moran's beliefs need not have been objectively reasonable; rather, if Moran truly believed that he was not subject to the copyright laws, then his subjective belief would defeat a finding that he "willfully" violated the statute.

First, I note that I had an opportunity to observe Moran when he testified. Moran struck me as an honest, albeit naive, person. I was left with the definite impression that Moran was befuddled and bewildered by the criminal prosecution.

Second, although Moran is a local police officer of long standing, there is nothing in his background to suggest any particular sophistication about business matters, and there is no evidence to suggest that he has any particular knowledge about the intricacies of the copyright laws. When confronted by FBI agents upon the execution of the search warrant, Moran was entirely cooperative. On the day the search warrant was executed, he told his story in the same way he now tells his story.

Third, Moran said he had heard from others and read in various publications that it was legally appropriate to engage in the practice he called "insuring." Moran could not cite the specific source of his information. In this regard, I note that the copyright laws permit libraries and archives to replace a copyrighted article that is damaged, deteriorated, lost, or stolen, if the library or archives have, after reasonable effort, determined that an unused replacement cannot be obtained at a fair price. 17 U.S.C. § 108(c). While Moran obviously did not operate his business as a library or archives, the government's assertion that the practice of "insuring" is patently unreasonable is belied by the recognition that under certain circumstances certain users of copyrighted materials may lawfully engage in copying activity which is similar to Moran's conduct.

Fourth, Moran testified that he made only one copy of the original motion picture purchased from the authorized distributor. The government doubts his testimony, but offers no persuasive evidence to contradict it. Moreover, Moran testified that he never rented both the original copyrighted version of the video cassette purchased from the authorized distributor and the copy he made. Instead, he testified that he always held back the original motion picture. Once again, the government doubts this testimony in its brief, but offers no persuasive evidence to the contrary. Furthermore, the evidence indicates that Moran purchased more than one authorized cassette of a particular motion picture, but made only one duplicate for each authorized cassette purchased.

This evidence suggests that Moran was not acting with a willful intention to violate the copyright laws because if he had such an intention it would make absolutely no sense to purchase multiple authorized video cassettes and then make only one duplicate of each authorized cassette. It would have been far simpler, and certainly more lucrative, for Moran to purchase one authorized cassette of a particular motion picture and make multiple copies from the authorized version. In this way Moran would have had to pay only one fee. The fact that Moran seems to have consistently followed the practice of buying an authorized version, but making only one copy of it, suggests that he was acting in accordance with his belief that to duplicate an authorized version in order to "insure it" was lawful so long as only one copy was made and the authorized version and copy were not both rented.

Fifth, the government argues that Moran must have known that what he was doing constituted a copyright infringement because he had before him the FBI warning label and in fact affixed such labels to the unauthorized copies he made. In pertinent part, the FBI warning states, "Federal law provides severe civil and criminal penalties for the *unauthorized* reproduction, distribution or exhibition of copyrighted motion pictures and video tapes" (emphasis added). Moran explained that he thought these warning labels applied to the renting public, not to him. The use of the word "unauthorized" on the warning label suggested to Moran that vendors who had purchased an authorized version were not subject to the legal restrictions expressed in the warning to the extent that the practice of "insuring" was legal. As Moran suggests, the FBI warning label does not specifically address the claim of legality professed by Moran. Accordingly, Moran's failure to heed the warning label is not determinative.

Sixth, the government further argues that Moran's effort to place the unauthorized copy into a video cassette package displaying a label on its spine and an FBI warning label suggests a sinister motivation. I disagree. Moran's testimony, as I understood it, indicated that when he made a copy he endeavored to make the duplicate look like the original in all respects. After all, the whole purpose of the practice of "insuring" was to use the unauthorized copy in lieu of the original when renting to the public. It was perfectly consistent with Moran's view of the law to make the unauthorized copy look as nearly as possible like the authorized version.

In summary, when Moran's actions were viewed from the totality of the circumstances, the government failed to convince me beyond a reasonable doubt that Moran acted willfully. Moran is a long-time street cop who was fully cooperative with law enforcement authorities. He is obviously not sophisticated and, at least from the record, his business operation of renting movies to the public was not large or sophisticated. Rather, Moran's business appears to have been of the "mom-and-pop" variety. Moran's practice of "insuring," while obviously shifting the risk of loss from Moran to the copyright holder, was conducted in such a way as not to maximize profits, which one assumes would have been his purpose if he had acted willfully. For example, Moran purchased multiple authorized copies of the same movie, but he made only one unauthorized copy for each authorized version purchased. This suggests that Moran truly believed that what he was doing was in fact legal. I therefore find Moran not guilty.

NOTES AND QUESTIONS

1.   Compare *Moran* to United States v. Draper, 2005 WL 2746665 (W.D. Va. 2005). The defendant, Don Draper (yes, "Mad Men" fans, this was his real name), was selling pirated copies of the copyrighted DVD *Passion of the Christ* at a time that the movie was still in theaters. Postal inspectors learned of Draper's conduct when a package directed to him broke open during shipping, revealing 100 pirated DVDs. An investigation revealed that Draper had previously sold a copy of the DVD to another postal employee. Postal inspectors resealed the package and then delivered it to Draper: When Draper accepted the package, he was arrested and charged with copyright infringement. The District Court held a bench trial, and the central question at trial was whether Draper's copyright violations were "willful." Draper testified in his own defense, and he told the judge that a stranger had sent him the package and that he did not know what the package contained or that the DVD he sold was unauthorized.

The Court ruled that the violations were willful and that Draper was guilty. The judge summarized the evidence supporting his conclusion as follows:

Before his arrest, Draper told the Postal Inspector that he was aware that others were selling illegal DVDs in the area and that he had seen *Barber Shop II* and *Passion of the Christ* for sale on Fayette Street. Postmaster Corbett testified that he witnessed Draper offering to sell a DVD of the *Passion of the Christ* at the post office, and that in connection with such efforts, Draper said that it was a "good copy" from New York. Corbett testified that he told Draper that the movie was then number one in theater box offices and that he could not sell such contraband on postal service property. Thus, Draper was clearly aware that selling such DVDs was illegal, and his efforts to sell the pirated video were neither mistaken nor inadvertent.

Katherine Baugus, a postal worker, testified that she bought a copy of the *Passion of the Christ,* in March, 2004 from Draper for $15. Baugus stated that shortly thereafter, the Postal Inspector called Corbett about the package containing one hundred (100) pirated copies of the movie. Baugus became concerned that the video was not legitimate and returned it to Draper, telling him that she did not want it if there was something wrong with it. Draper accepted the DVD back, and although he was not asked for a refund, Draper did not give Baugus her money back. Thereafter, the package with the one hundred (100) pirated DVDs was delivered to Draper. Both this incident and his earlier attempt to sell the DVD to postal employees clearly establishes that Draper was put on notice that his conduct was improper.

Furthermore, Draper's testimony was not credible. Draper stated that he had been given one copy of the *Passion of the Christ* DVD by a stranger who also showed Draper a number of other items he was peddling, including designer clothes. Draper stated that he gave this stranger his address and was told to expect a package, but Draper claimed that he had no idea what was going to be in the package. Of course, when the package arrived, it contained one hundred (100) unauthorized copies of the movie. Draper testified that he offered to sell the DVD to Baugus that day because this stranger had given him a copy, he had no way to play the movie, and he happened to have it in his possession at the post office. Draper said that he knows nothing of movies, release dates of DVDs, or the copyright laws. While Draper testified that he had only a ninth grade education and had some years ago suffered a head injury due to a gunshot wound, his own admissions to the agents indicate that he was aware that the sale of such movies was illegal, and the evidence made plain the willful nature of his actions.

Id. at 2.

2. The willfulness requirement is designed to ensure that defendants are not held criminally liable when the law is murky. It is an exception to the usual rule that "ignorance of the law is no excuse." When Congress uses the willfulness standard, ignorance of the law *is* an excuse. Criminal liability is reserved for cases in which a defendant knew he acted wrongfully.

Does the willfulness requirement create a sensible line between civil and criminal copyright liability? A defendant can have an entirely unreasonable belief that his conduct was lawful. Under the willfulness standard as construed in *Cheek* and applied in *Moran*, however, no crime has occurred so long as the defendant actually believes that he has acted legally. How does a defendant know whether his conduct is illegal if there are so few cases addressing the scope of copyright liability online?

3. Despite the clear holding of *Moran*, the exact meaning of willfulness in criminal copyright law is not necessarily settled. *See* Lydia Pallas Loren, *Digitization, Commodification, Criminalization: The Evolution of Criminal Copyright Infringement and the Importance of the Willfulness Requirement*, 77 Wash. U. L.Q. 835, 872 (1999). The differences in the various interpretations are generally minor ones, however. A majority of modern courts have adopted the *Cheek* approach applied in *Moran*. At least one court has suggested a different test: a decision by the Seventh Circuit concludes that a defendant acts willfully when he realizes "a high likelihood of being held by a court of

competent jurisdiction to be [in] violation of a criminal statute." United States v. Heilman, 614 F.2d 1133, 1138 (7th Cir. 1980). It's worth wondering how different these standards are: What is the difference between knowing that you are violating the law and realizing a high likelihood of being held in violation of a criminal statute? *Cf.* Model Penal Code § 2.02(2)(b)(ii) (defining "knowingly" in the case of a conduct element as being "aware that it is practically certain that his conduct will cause such a result").

4. *Willfulness and the Digital Millennium Copyright Act.* The Digital Millennium Copyright Act (DMCA), Pub. L. No. 105–304 (1998), is an effort to maintain the effectiveness of technological restrictions that copyright owners may place on access to their copyrighted works to prevent unauthorized copying and distribution. In response to the tendency of digital technologies and the Internet to facilitate copyright infringement, some copyright owners have placed technological controls on their copyrighted works. Instead of hoping that users will follow the rules of copyright law, these copyright owners have used computer code to place the digital equivalent of "locks" around their copyrighted works to prevent unauthorized copying and distribution. Unsurprisingly, the presence of digital locks around copyrighted works has generated new digital lockpicking tools—computer programs that can be used to circumvent the technological restrictions on access and copying of copyrighted works.

The DMCA prohibits possession and distribution of digital lock-picking tools designed to circumvent technological restrictions on access to copyrighted works. By restricting access to digital lockpicking tools, the thinking goes, the DMCA will result in fewer picked locks. Fewer picked locks will mean more enforceable restrictions on copying and distributing copyrighted works, counterbalancing the Internet's ability to facilitate copyright infringement. Criminal liability under the DMCA resembles criminal liability for copyright law: it also contains a requirement that the infringement must be "willful." 17 U.S.C. § 1204(a).

The meaning of willfulness played an important role in the first criminal prosecution brought under the anticircumvention provisions of the DMCA. A Russian software company, ElcomSoft, created a program called the "Advanced eBook Processor" that cracked the protections on Adobe Systems' eBooks. The FBI arrested ElcomSoft employee Dmitry Sklyarov for his role in creating the Advanced eBook Processor, and Sklyarov eventually agreed to testify for the government against ElcomSoft. The two-week trial focused on ElcomSoft's state of mind in creating and distributing their product. Sklyarov and ElcomSoft President Alexander Katalov testified that they did not believe their software was illegal and had no intent for it to be used for illegal purposes.

The jury rendered a verdict of not guilty. According to press accounts, the jury acquitted because they did not believe the company acted willfully:

> Jury foreman Dennis Strader said the jurors agreed ElcomSoft's product was illegal but acquitted the company because they believed the company didn't mean to violate the law.

> "We didn't understand why a million-dollar company would put on their Web page an illegal thing that would ruin their whole business if they

were caught," he said in an interview after the verdict. Strader added that the panel found the DMCA itself confusing, making it easy for jurors to believe that executives from Russia might not fully understand it.

Lisa M. Bowman, *Elcomsoft Verdict: Not Guilty*, CNET News.com, Dec. 17, 2002, http://news.com.com/2100–1023–978176.html.

C) Total Retail Value

Criminal liability under the copyright laws can depend on the total retail value of the works copied. The next case considers what "total retail value" means and how it can be established.

UNITED STATES v. ARMSTEAD

United States Court of Appeals for the Fourth Circuit, 2008.
524 F.3d 442.

NIEMEYER, CIRCUIT JUDGE:

After selling 100 "bootleg" DVDs of unreleased movies to an undercover federal agent on June 11, 2003, and then selling 200 more to the same agent on January 13, 2004, David Armstead was indicted and convicted on two felony counts of willful copyright infringement for private financial gain by distributing at least 10 unauthorized DVDs on each occasion, having "a total retail value of more than $2,500," in violation of 17 U.S.C. § 506(a)(1) and 18 U.S.C. § 2319(b)(1). At trial, Armstead contested only the total retail value of the DVDs sold and urged that he be convicted of only misdemeanors for selling DVDs with a total retail value of $2,500 or less. *See* 18 U.S.C. § 2319(b)(3). The jury, however, convicted Armstead of the felony charges, and he was sentenced to six months' home detention.

On appeal, Armstead focuses on the fact that he sold the DVDs in the first transaction for a total of $500 and in the second transaction for a total of $1,000, and that the government offered no adequate alternative value to prove that the "total retail value" of the DVDs sold in each transaction was more than $2,500, as required for felony convictions. He requests that we vacate the felony convictions and enter judgments for misdemeanor offenses, remanding the case for resentencing accordingly.

As a matter of first impression, we hold that "retail value" as used in 18 U.S.C. § 2319(b)(1) refers to the value of copies of the copyrighted material at the time the defendant committed the violation and sold the copies and that the retail value is determined by taking the highest of the "face value," "par value," or "market value" of copies of the copyrighted material in a retail context. *See* 18 U.S.C. § 2311. Because the evidence of retail value, so construed, supported felony convictions, we affirm.

I

On June 11, 2003, Armstead sold 100 illicit movies in DVD format for $500 ($5 per DVD) to an undercover agent of the Bureau of Immigration and Customs Enforcement ("ICE") at the parking lot of the Springfield

Mall in northern Virginia. The 100 bootleg DVDs included 25 copies of "2 Fast 2 Furious"; 25 copies of "The Matrix Reloaded"; 25 copies of "Finding Nemo"; 15 copies of "The Italian Job"; and 10 copies of "Wrong Turn." Again on January 13, 2004, Armstead sold the same agent more illicit movies in DVD format, this time 200 DVDs for $1,000 (again $5 per DVD). The 200 bootleg DVDs included 75 copies of "Lord of the Rings: The Return of the King"; 75 copies of "Paycheck"; 25 copies of "Bad Santa"; 15 copies of "My Baby's Daddy"; and 10 copies of "Gang of Roses."

The copies sold on both occasions were, for the most part, made by using a hand-held camcorder to record the films as they played in movie theaters and were, with a few exceptions, of poor quality. At the time, however, better copies of the DVD movies sold to the undercover agent were not available, as the movies were only in the "theatrical release" stage and authorized DVDs were not yet available. According to the undercover agent, legitimate DVDs would not be available until three to six months after the movie was released to theaters.

Armstead was indicted in two felony counts, one for each occasion on which he sold DVDs to the undercover agent.

At trial, Armstead conceded all elements of the offenses against him except the "total retail value" of the DVDs, claiming that their total value on each date was far less than $2,500, the threshold amount for felony liability under 18 U.S.C. § 2319(b)(1). He contended that with the proper finding of retail value, he could be convicted of only misdemeanors. He grounded his retail value assertions on the fact that the only hard evidence of retail value was the price of the DVDs in the "thieves' market," which priced the DVDs at $500 on the first occasion and $1,000 on the second.

Although the jury was instructed that if it found every element of the crime other than a retail value of over $2,500, it could return only misdemeanor convictions, it returned felony convictions on both counts. The district court sentenced Armstead to six months' home detention, five years' probation, and ordered him to pay $1,500 in restitution.

On appeal, Armstead presents the single issue of retail value and argues that "retail value," as used in § 2319(b)(1), refers to "the price a willing buyer would pay a willing seller at the time and in the market in which the infringing DVDs are sold—the thieves' market." With that definition of "retail value," Armstead contends that the evidence at trial was insufficient to support felony convictions.

II

The Copyright Act, in relevant part, provides that "[a]ny person who willfully infringes a copyright shall be punished as provided under section 2319 of title 18, if the infringement was committed—(A) for purposes of commercial advantage or private financial gain." 17 U.S.C. § 506(a)(1)(A). Section 2319 of Title 18, in turn, provides in relevant part:

> Any person who commits an offense under section 506(a)(1)(A) of title 17—shall be imprisoned not more than 5 years, or fined in the amount set forth in this title, or both, if the offense consists of the reproduction or distribution, including by electronic means, during any 180–day period, of at least 10 copies or phonorecords, of 1 or more copyrighted works, *which have a total retail value of more than $2,500.*

18 U.S.C. § 2319(b)(1) (emphasis added). Section 2319 also provides that if the $2,500–retail-value element is not satisfied, the defendant is to be punished for a misdemeanor. *See id.* § 2319(b)(3).

Armstead's argument that the government failed to produce sufficient evidence that the DVDs he sold to the undercover agent had an aggregate retail value of more than $2,500 hinges on the meaning of "retail value" as used in § 2319(b)(1). He asserts that retail value, as used in the statute, means "the price a willing buyer would pay a willing seller at the time and in the market in which it is sold—the thieves' market." With this definition of "retail value," he argues that what a willing buyer would pay a willing seller at the time was evidenced by what the undercover agent paid him and therefore that the retail value amount was insufficient to satisfy the felony threshold amount of $2,500.

The government contends that "retail value" refers to the higher value of what a willing buyer would pay a willing seller for a *legitimate* copy of the infringed item, such as an authentic, authorized DVD of the same movie. The government states that retail value as used in the statute is not the " 'bootleg value' the defendant received on the black market." It argues, "if the Congress had meant to use the 'bootleg value' or 'wholesale value' of counterfeit products, it certainly would have used that or similar language; instead, the Congress used the phrase 'total retail value' of the copyright works." Both parties seem to be arguing about a "market value," debating whether the relevant "market" from which to draw this market value refers to the market for bootleg products or the market for legitimate products. But their debate fails to account for the statutory language, which produces a broader formulation of "retail value."

"Retail value," as a phrase, is not defined in the statute, but "value" is. Section 2311, which provides definitions for chapter 113 of Title 18 (addressing "Stolen Property") defines "value" for the entire chapter (in which § 2319 is included) as "the face, par, or market value, *whichever is the greatest.*" 18 U.S.C. § 2311 (emphasis added). Thus, "value" is measured not only by actual transactions that define a market, but also by face or par values assigned to commodities or goods before reaching the market, and the statute instructs that the greatest of those "values" be used. "Retail," which is not defined at all, refers, in its ordinary meaning, to sales transactions of commodities or goods in small quantities to ultimate consumers. *See, e.g.,* Webster's Third New International Dictionary 1938 (1993). As distinct from "retail," "wholesale" refers to sales transactions of goods and commodities in quantity for resale. It follows, accordingly, that retail prices are higher than wholesale prices.

Thus considering "retail" and "value" as component terms that are individually defined by common understanding and by § 2311, respectively, we conclude that "retail value" refers to the greatest of any face value, par value, or market value of commodities or goods in reference to actual or potential sales to ultimate consumers. Thus, while market value—a value determined by the price that a willing buyer would pay a willing seller—is included in the class of values defined as "retail value," it is not the exclusive determinant. It follows that if a manufacturer of DVDs sells its DVDs at wholesale with a suggested retail price of $29 and the retailer actually sells the DVDs to the consumer at the discounted price of $19, the "retail value" as used in § 2319(b)(1) refers to the greater of the two numbers, or $29 per DVD. Of course, if the prices paid in actual retail transactions were the *only* evidence presented to support a prosecution under § 2319(b)(1), those prices could be considered as evidence of an actual "market value," which would be a permissible value for consideration as the "retail value."

In this case, while the parties agree that a "market value" may be determined by the price that a willing buyer would pay a willing seller, they disagree on whether that market value may be determined by sales in a "thieves' market." The government provides no authority to support the position that prices paid in a "thieves' market" cannot be a market value. Indeed, its only definition—the price of a movie "if it were sold to a member of the public"—would seem to include any market, except for the fact that the government argues for a value determined only by a market of "legitimate" copies. The government's assertion that the market for illicit goods is not determinative of "retail value" may be correct, but only if there is other evidence of a higher "value." *See* 18 U.S.C. § 2311. Otherwise, a black market for illegitimate goods undoubtedly may provide evidence of a "market value." And § 2311 directs that the criterion for satisfying the threshold amount for a felony conviction be the "greatest" of the permissible values in evidence.

It remains undisputed by the parties that whatever value is used, it must be a value applicable at the time the violations occurred and the transactions in question took place—in this case, June 2003 and January 2004.

Accordingly, retail value, as used in § 2319(b)(1), refers to prices assigned to commodities and goods for sale at the retail level at the time of sales at issue, representing face value or par value, *or* prices of commodities and goods determined by actual transactions between willing buyers and willing sellers at the retail level—*whichever is the greatest*. This understanding of "retail value," which is derived from §§ 2311 and 2319, is confirmed by the House Committee Report that accompanied enactment of § 2319. That Report provided:

The term "retail value" is deliberately undefined, since in most cases it will represent the price at which the work is sold through normal retail channels. At the same time, *the Committee recognizes that copyrighted works are frequently infringed before a retail value has been established,* and that in some cases, copyrighted works are not marketed through normal retail channels. Examples include motion pictures prints distributed only for theatrical release, and beta-test versions of computer programs. *In such cases, the courts may look to the suggested retail price, the wholesale price, the replacement cost of the item, or financial injury caused to the copyright owner.*

H.R.Rep. No. 102–997, at 6–7 (1992), *as reprinted in* 1992 U.S.C.C.A.N. 3569, 3574–75.

III

In this case, Armstead sold the illicit DVDs to an undercover agent when the movies recorded on them had only been distributed for theatrical release (and perhaps for hotel and airline release) but certainly before they had been released on DVDs to the public. Thus, at the time of the illicit transactions, there was no legitimate retail market for the sale of DVDs except as evidenced by the occasional and sporadic illicit transactions of the kind represented in this case. As noted, prices paid in those illicit transactions might be evidence of a market value. But in this case, the "thieves' market" prices were not the only evidence. The government presented evidence of other kinds of value that related to retail value during the theatrical release stage of the movies when the illegal transactions occurred.

First, the government offered the testimony of two different witnesses who indicated that, based on information from the Motion Picture Association of America, a single copy of a motion picture sold during the prerelease stage to hotels and airlines carries a price of at least $1,000 per copy, and, depending on the movie, up to $50,000 per copy. As one ICE agent explained, this was so because "at the time that these films are released in theaters, there is no legitimate market for the public to get DVDs. And the only people who can get a licensed copy of this film while it's in theaters is a hotel chain or an airline." The witness explained further that $1,000 was the price for the low-end films, and the more popular films could cost anywhere from $25,000 to $50,000 a copy. A piracy investigator for the Motion Picture Association of America then gave his opinion that there was "a good argument" to be made that the actual bootleg copies sold by Armstead "had a retail value of $1,000 a copy, as much as $50,000 a copy," even though he acknowledged that the number might be reduced somewhat to accommodate deficiencies in quality.

The government also presented testimony that after a movie was released to the public through DVDs—when prices for DVDs are much lower than prerelease values—the average retail price of the 10 DVD movies involved in this case would be "in every instance higher than $19" per DVD.

Finally, the government proffered evidence that the "suggested retail price" of each of the DVDs sold by Armstead was between $25 and $30 per copy, but the district court excluded that evidence precisely because it was only suggested, and not actual. This was error, however, because the suggested retail price was relevant to determine a "face value" or "par value" that would be especially relevant to determining prerelease retail value. Indeed, the House Report that accompanied the bill for § 2319 explicitly noted that for unreleased movies, courts could look at suggested retail prices. H.R.Rep. No. 102–997, at 6–7. And since there would be evidence of both face value (had the court properly allowed it) and market value, the higher would be applicable in determining the threshold amount for a felony conviction under § 2319(b)(1).

Based on our reading of the statute, the government's evidence of the prerelease values of copies of movies, the actual selling prices of legitimate copies of movies in the postrelease period, as well as the suggested retail prices (which were erroneously excluded by the trial court), were all appropriate evidence for a jury to consider in determining total retail value of the illicit transactions. Likewise, the evidence relied on by Armstead of the actual transaction prices in the wholesale "thieves' market" was appropriate evidence for a jury to consider. But in considering whether the evidence supports a conviction, we of course take the evidence actually presented to the jury and consider it in a view most favorable to the Government.

While the government's evidence about the wholesale cost of a single copy of a movie sold to hotels before DVDs were released to the public was not directly on point, it was a benchmark from which the jury could rationally have concluded that DVDs sold during that period had a retail value that exceeded $25 per copy. The minimum $1,000 per copy for a movie sold to hotels was a wholesale price that included payment for a license to show the movie to hotel customers. But the jury could conclude that, if there were a market for the retail sale of such DVDs, it would be higher than the wholesale price. And even though hotels did not resell the copies they bought, they nonetheless recovered their costs and profits from multiple retail rentals in hotel rooms. In this manner, the jury could readily reason from the $1,000 threshold level to conclude that the retail value of a single DVD *before general release of the movie as a DVD* exceeded $25. This conclusion would be buttressed by the fact that the average postrelease price of DVDs in the legitimate market would be greater than $19 per copy, indicating a much greater price for such DVDs prerelease.

The fact that Armstead actually sold his DVDs in bulk for $5 per copy was also evidence that the jury could have considered. But this evidence would not be evidence of the *greatest* value; rather, it provided evidence of the lowest value that could be assigned to the DVDs. Indeed, the $5–per–

copy price was a wholesale price, suggesting a "retail" value somewhat greater than $5 per copy.

Armstead makes much of the fact that the DVDs he sold were of poor quality, since most of them were recorded with camcorders in theaters. While he may be correct that the quality of the infringing copy might bear on retail value, this was something that he was able to, and did, argue to the jury, and the jury was fully able to take that into account in determining the retail value of the DVDs. But it could have recognized, for example, that at this prerelease stage, advance knowledge of the plot of a movie, the action, and how the movie ends might be far more significant to retail value than reproduction quality.

At bottom, the jury had sufficient evidence from which to conclude that each copy of the DVDs sold by Armstead to undercover agents during the period before the films' release to the public on authorized DVDs had a retail value exceeding $25 per copy and therefore that each transaction exceeded the threshold amount for a felony conviction. Moreover, with respect to the second transaction, which involved the sale of 200 DVDs, even the $19 per copy ($3,800 in total), testified to by government witnesses as a retail value for the postrelease market, exceeded the $2,500 threshold amount.

The judgment of the district court is affirmed.

NOTES AND QUESTIONS

1. Why does 18 U.S.C. § 2319 require proof that the defendant "infringed at least 10 copies of one or more copyrighted works with a total retail value of more than $2,500 within a 180–day period"? The House Report that accompanied the passage of this language contains the following explanation:

> The requirement that a requisite number of infringing copies or phonorecords be reproduced or distributed within a 180 day period serves a number of important purposes. First, it excludes from felony prosecution children making copies for friends as well as other incidental copying of copyrighted works having a relatively low retail value. Second, the requirement of reproducing or distributing at least 10 copies within a 180 day period removes the possibility that the increased penalties under the bill for computer program infringement can be used as a tool of harassment in business disputes over reverse engineering. Assuming arguendo that infringement due to unauthorized reverse engineering is established, and that the infringement was done with the requisite mens rea (which, as noted above, is unlikely), no felony liability should arise, since the Committee has been informed that reverse engineering does not require the reproduction of more than a handful of copies.

H.R. Rep. No. 102–997, at 6 (1992), *reprinted in* 1992 U.S.C.C.A.N. 3569, 3574. The Report continues:

> The phrase "of one or more copyrighted works" is intended to permit aggregation of different works of authorship to meet the required number of copies and retail value. For example, a defendant's reproduction of 5

copies of a copyrighted word processing computer program having a retail value of $1,300 and the reproduction of 5 copies of a copyrighted spreadsheet computer program also having a retail value of $1,300 would satisfy the requirement of reproducing 10 copies having a retail value of at least $2,500, if done within a 180 day period.

Id. at 3574–75.

D) Intent to Profit

Should copyright law require an intent to profit or achieve private financial gain before attaching criminal penalties? It did before 1997. In 1997, however, Congress passed the No Electronic Theft (NET) Act, Pub. L. No. 105–147 (1997), which eliminated the requirement. Under current law, intent to achieve commercial advantage or private financial gain is important for sentencing purposes but not liability. The NET Act is generally understood as a response to changing technology, and especially computers and the Internet. Was it a wise move? To evaluate this question, consider the facts from a fairly typical criminal copyright case from the early 1980s.

UNITED STATES v. SHABAZZ

United States Court of Appeals for the Eleventh Circuit, 1984.
724 F.2d 1536.

JONES, SENIOR CIRCUIT JUDGE.

The appellant was engaged in the business of reproducing and distributing pirated eight track and cassette tapes. "Bootleg" or pirated tapes are the results of the illegal and unauthorized duplication of a sound recording without the permission of the copyright owners. Pirated tapes reproduce the sound but do not reproduce the tape cover or packaging of the legitimate tapes. The creation of a copyrighted tape begins with the studio master recording in the studio. One of the first duplicates of the studio master recording accompanies the copyright application. Another is sent to the Federal Bureau of Investigation for use in copyright infringement cases. A third duplicate is used for the production of legitimate copyrighted records and tapes.

The appellant purchased sophisticated audio equipment which was used for reproduction of audio tapes. He also purchased large quantities of unrecorded eight track and cassette tapes. He ordered eight track and cassette tape labels to be printed which listed the musicians and songs. He hired three employees to reproduce eight track and cassette tapes of copyrighted sound recordings of popular music. His employees, working in his home, would review work orders and reproduce selected music tapes by use of a high speed duplicator. The employees checked the tapes to insure music selection and sound quality. The tapes were individually wrapped in cellophane, placed in boxes and then sold.

An investigation lead to the issuance of a search warrant for the appellant's home and automobile. Federal agents seized blank and legitimate copyrighted tapes, duplicating equipment, blank and preprinted eight track and cassette labels, and various business records and materials. Ten legitimate copyrighted tapes and ten pirated copies were seized. The appellant was arrested for violating United States copyright laws under Title 17, §§ 106(1) and 506(a).

At the trial the government introduced ten copyright registrations, one for each tape alleged to be an infringement. Copyright owner representatives testified to the ownership of copyrights of the music recordings and to the absence of authorization for appellant to reproduce the legitimate copyrighted tapes. They also testified that it was a regular practice to send duplicates of such copyrighted recordings to the FBI for use in criminal copyright infringement cases. However, none of the copyright owner representatives had compared the duplicate sent to the FBI with either the studio master recording or the duplicate which accompanied the application to the United States copyright office.

Two FBI agents testified to examining the tapes seized from appellant's home. One agent testified that he listened to the seized legitimate copyrighted tapes and pirated copies to make sure the music listed on the tape label or box was contained on that particular tape. The second agent, an experienced aural examiner, was qualified by the district court as an expert witness. He acknowledged that the FBI received copyright owners' duplicates to compare legitimate copyrighted tapes with pirated tapes. The expert compared the copyright owners' duplicates with the legitimate copyrighted tapes and the pirated tapes seized from appellant's home and determined that the music on all three tapes had been produced from the same original source. The expert also testified that during the course of his examination of the pirated tapes, he listened to the entire tape and found that the tape labels and boxes accurately reflected the musical contents. The expert did not compare the copyright owners duplicates or the pirated tapes with the studio master recording or the duplicate which accompanied the application to the United States Copyright Office. There was no evidence that the copyright owner duplicates were tampered with or altered in any way or contained anything other than the music indicated on the tape label or box. A jury returned a verdict of guilty to ten counts of copyright infringement.

The appellant asserts that the government failed to prove that any of the tapes introduced in evidence were made for commercial profit as required by the Statute. An employee identified specific tapes made in bulk under appellant's direction as reproduced for local and out of state sale. The appellant sold pirated tapes, solicited wholesale customers, and shipped large quantities of tapes out of state. This evidence is sufficient to show that the tapes produced were made with the intention to make a profit. It is not necessary that he actually made a profit. The only requirement is that he engaged in business "to hopefully or possibly make a profit."

NOTES AND QUESTIONS

1. Consider the economics of the operation in *Shabazz*. Shabazz created a considerable business enterprise to copy and distribute copyrighted materials. He had to purchase sophisticated equipment and pay several employees. The case for prohibiting conduct such as the operation in *Shabazz* is easy to make: Shabazz had created his own business that competed against the operations of the legitimate copyright owners. He was trying to line his pockets with money that should have gone to the copyright holders. Further, note the direct correlation between the scope of the operation and the intent to profit. Each bootleg cassette was costly for Shabazz to produce, and it seems unlikely that he would have been willing to engage in such widespread bootlegging without an economic incentive. In that environment, the statutory requirement of intent to profit makes sense. The requirement distinguishes a case like *Shabazz* from a case of small scale or personal copying.

Next consider how the picture changes when we shift to digital reproduction and distribution of copyrighted materials. Digital technologies bring the cost of copying and distributing files close to zero. A person can set up a server, connect it to the Internet, and make copyrighted files available to thousands of people at little or no cost to himself. How should the law respond, if at all?

2. *United States v. LaMacchia and the NET Act*. The traditional rationale of the intent-to-profit requirement caught up to the new facts of the Internet with the case of David LaMacchia. In 1994, LaMacchia was a 21 year-old college student at the Massachusetts Institute of Technology. LaMacchia set up an electronic bulletin board and encouraged visitors to share popular copyrighted software such as Excel and WordPerfect. Users could both upload software they possessed and download software they wanted, all for free and without the permission of the copyright holders. LaMacchia did not have an intent to profit from his efforts, which meant that he could not be prosecuted under the then-existing criminal copyright laws.

Prosecutors instead tried to prosecute LaMacchia under the wire fraud statute, 18 U.S.C. § 1343. Judge Stearns dismissed the indictment on the ground that trying to prosecute a copyright offense using the wire fraud statute ran afoul of Dowling v. United States, 473 U.S. 207 (1985). *See* United States v. LaMacchia, 871 F.Supp. 535 (D. Mass. 1994). In *Dowling*, prosecutors charged a defendant who had manufactured "bootleg" Elvis Presley records and distributed them in interstate commerce under the Interstate Transportation of Stolen Property Act, codified at 18 U.S.C. § 2314. In an opinion by Justice Blackmun, the Court held that the government could not use the ITSP Act to punish what amounted to a scheme of copyright infringement. Doing so would allow the government to circumvent Congress's design to have only narrow criminal liability for copyright infringement.

In the *LaMacchia* case, Judge Stearns held that the same rationale blocked the government from prosecuting LaMacchia under the wire fraud statute:

While the government's objective is a laudable one, particularly when the facts alleged in this case are considered, its interpretation of the wire fraud statute would serve to criminalize the conduct of not only persons like LaMacchia, but also the myriad of home computer users who succumb to the temptation to copy even a single software program for private use. It is not clear that making criminals of a large number of consumers of computer software is a result that even the software industry would consider desirable.

Accordingly, I rule that the decision of the Supreme Court in *Dowling v. United States* precludes LaMacchia's prosecution for criminal copyright infringement under the wire fraud statute.

This is not, of course, to suggest that there is anything edifying about what LaMacchia is alleged to have done. If the indictment is to be believed, one might at best describe his actions as heedlessly irresponsible, and at worst as nihilistic, self-indulgent, and lacking in any fundamental sense of values. Criminal as well as civil penalties should probably attach to willful, multiple infringements of copyrighted software even absent a commercial motive on the part of the infringer. One can envision ways that the copyright law could be modified to permit such prosecution. But, it is the legislature, not the Court which is to define a crime, and ordain its punishment.

LaMacchia, 871 F.Supp. at 544.

Congress responded by passing the NET Act in 1997 to "reverse the practical consequences of United States v. LaMacchia." H.R. Rep. No. 105–339, at 3 (1997). Under the NET Act, individuals can receive criminal punishments for copyright infringement even if they do not have commercial motives. Any person who commits willful copyright infringement can be:

> imprisoned not more than 3 years, or fined in the amount set forth in this title, or both, if the offense consists of the reproduction or distribution of 10 or more copies or phonorecords of 1 or more copyrighted works, which have a total retail value of $2,500 or more;

18 U.S.C. § 2319(c)(1). If the government can show that the infringement took place "for purposes of commercial advantage or private financial gain," 17 U.S.C. § 506(a)(1), the maximum penalty is raised from three years to five years. *See* 18 U.S.C. § 2319(b)(1). The NET Act also redefined the term "financial gain" so that it now "includes receipt, or expectation of receipt, of anything of value, including the receipt of other copyrighted works." 17 U.S.C. § 101.

3.   Is the NET Act too broad? *See generally* Lydia Pallas Loren, *Digitization, Commodification, Criminalization: The Evolution of Criminal Copyright Infringement and the Importance of the Willfulness Requirement*, 77 Wash. U. L.Q. 835, 871 (1999) ("Even if comfort is found in relying on prosecutorial discretion to curb the possible over-breadth of the NET Act, the mere threat of criminal prosecution will deter at least some lawful uses of copyrighted works. Unfortunately some of these lawful uses are precisely the types of conduct that the policies underlying copyright law seek to encourage, not discourage.").

4. The NET Act expands the scope of criminal liability to counter the effect of technological developments. But do those same technological developments alter the potential harms that follow from copyright infringement, and if so, what effect should that have on the scope of criminal liability?

> Technological change * * * suggests it is time to revisit [the need for criminal copyright law]. It may no longer be necessary to rely so heavily on law to provide an incentive to create. The tools of digitization, broadband capacity, and the Internet make low-cost distribution a reality that may stimulate creation. Although in its infant stages, Internet commerce allows authors, musicians, and others to sell their work directly to consumers. Avoiding the added costs imposed by distribution companies may decrease costs to consumers.

Geraldine Szott Moohr, *The Crime Of Copyright Infringement: An Inquiry Based On Morality, Harm, And Criminal Theory*, 83 B.U. L. Rev. 731, 758 (2003).

5. *Private financial gain and the DMCA.* It is interesting to note, in light of *LaMacchia* and the NET Act, that the criminal provisions of the Digital Millennium Copyright Act apply only to willful conduct committed "for purposes of commercial advantage or private financial gain." 17 U.S.C. § 1204(a). In addition, the criminal prohibitions cannot apply to any "nonprofit library, archives, educational institution, or public broadcasting entity." 17 U.S.C. § 1204(b). Why did Congress use a narrower criminal prohibition for the DMCA than for copyright law?

E) Prosecutorial Discretion

The broad scope of criminal copyright liability places a premium on prosecutorial discretion. The law permits prosecutors to charge a large number of infringers. Should they? Who should be targeted?

UNITED STATES DEPARTMENT OF JUSTICE— ILLEGAL "WAREZ" ORGANIZATIONS AND INTERNET PIRACY

http://www.cybercrime.gov/ob/OBorg&pr.htm.

In the early 1990s, groups of individuals working in underground networks organized themselves into competitive gangs that obtained software, "cracked," or "ripped" it (i.e. removed various forms of copy protections) and posted it on the Internet for other members of the group. This network of individuals and groups, numbering in the thousands, evolved into what is today loosely called the "warez scene" or community.

At the top of the warez scene are a handful of "release" groups that specialize in being the first to obtain, crack (i.e., remove or circumvent copyright protections), and distribute or release the latest software, games, movies, or music to the warez scene. Frequently, these new "releases" reach the Internet days or weeks before the product is commercially available. Release groups compete against each other to attain a reputation as the fastest providers of the highest quality, free pirated software, including utility and application software, computer and console games, and movies.

As technology has advanced, the top warez groups have become more technologically sophisticated and security conscious to avoid detection by law enforcement. Many of the elite groups communicate about warez business only through private e-mail servers, sometimes using encryption, and in closed, invite-only IRC channels. Additionally, most members disguise their true IP addresses (and thus their true locations) when communicating in IRC by routing their communications through "virtual hosts" or bounce boxes. Finally, many warez groups protect their large FTP archive sites—which can contain tens of thousands of copies of software, games, music, and music for free downloading—through a combination of security measures that include bounce sites, automated programs for IP address and user password verification, and the use of non-standard ports for FTP traffic.

The specific reasons that an individual becomes and remains involved in the top warez "release" or "courier" organizations may vary. However, it is almost always the case that a primary motivator is the desire to gain access to a virtually unlimited amount of free software, game, movie, and/or music titles available on the huge file storage and transfer sites (FTP sites) maintained by, or offering user privileges to, these elite warez groups. These computer sites not only offer a tremendous variety of quality copyrighted works, but they also generally have extremely fast Internet connections for rapid, efficient download and uploading. Other possible motivators or enticements for warez group members may include: (1) the thrill and social comraderie they obtain through clandestine participation in illegal activity; (2) the improved personal reputation or fame in the warez scene that comes with membership in the "top" groups, and in helping to keep those groups on top; and (3) financial profit, as some involved in the larger warez organizations take the pirated products and sell them for commercial gain.

Today it is estimated that approximately 8–10 of the largest warez "release" groups in the world are responsible for the majority of the pirated software, games, and movies available on the Internet. These highly organized "release" groups specialize in being the first to release new pirated software, games, and movies to the warez community for unauthorized reproduction and further distribution worldwide. Individual groups generally specialize in "releasing" only certain types of copyrighted works; for instance, two of the oldest groups, DrinkOrDie and Razor1911, specialize in releasing application software and PC or console games, respectively. In addition to their release work, these warez groups also maintain large FTP archive (or "leech") sites for the benefit of their members and others engaged in Internet software piracy. An average FTP archive site may contain between 10,000 to 25,000 individual titles of software, games, movies, and music, all of which is made available for free downloading ("leeching") by group members and valued warez associates or contributors to the site.

The top-level release groups are highly structured organizations with defined roles and leadership hierarchy. These organizations generally have a Leader, who oversees and directs all aspects of the group; three Council members or Senior Staff, who direct and manage the day-to-day operations of the group; 10 to 15 Staff, who frequently are the most active and skilled contributors to the group's day to day "release" work; and finally, the general membership, whose functions and involvement in the group vary. Members generally only interact via the Internet and know each other only by their screen nicknames, such as "bandido," "hackrat," "erupt," or "doodad."

A pirated version of a software application, game or movie is frequently available worldwide even before it is made commercially available to the public. In many instances, warez groups illegally obtain advanced copies of copyrighted products from company or industry insiders, then crack the copyright protections before distributing the pirated versions on the Internet to an ever-expanding web of FTP sites worldwide. Within hours of first being posted on the Internet, a pirated version of a copyrighted product can be found on thousands of Internet sites worldwide. Eventually, these pirated versions find their way onto pay-for-access websites from China to the U.S., where users are charged monthly or per-purchase fees for downloading the unauthorized copies.

Additionally, these warez "releases" provide an unending supply of new product to counterfeit hard goods criminal organizations. For instance, almost every new PC and console game is "cracked" and available on warez sites either before or within 24 hours of their commercial release ("0–Day" releases). Hard good pirate syndicates in Asia and Russia (for example) will download a "warez" 0–Day game release and mass produce it at optical disc manufacturing facilities. These counterfeit hard goods are then illegally sold in foreign markets often weeks before the manufacturer ships the authentic goods for the official release date in those particular markets. This can cripple the market for the legitimate products.

The "Release" Process:

Speed and efficiency are essential to the process for preparing and packaging new pirated software for release and distribution to the warez community. The process generally has four stages and can occur within a matter of hours:

SUPPLY: First, a group member known as a supplier will post an original digital copy of new computer software to the group's Internet drop site, which is a computer where software is posted for retrieval by members of the group. Frequently, warez suppliers are company insiders who have access to final versions of the company's new software products before their public release date.

CRACK: Once the new supply is posted to the drop site, another group member, known as a cracker, retrieves the software and removes or circumvents all embedded copyright protection controls (e.g., serial numbers, tags, duplication controls, dongle protections, security locks).

TESTING and PACKING: Following a successful crack, the software must be tested to ensure that it is still fully operational. Following testing, the software is then "packed," or broken into file packets that are more easily distributed by other group members.

PRE–RELEASE/COURIER: After the software has been cracked, tested and packed, it is returned to the drop site, where individuals who will transfer or distribute the pirated copy across the Internet are waiting for new arrivals. Once picked up by the "preers," the illegal product is distributed to warez locations around the world in a matter of minutes. In each instance, the new "release" will include an information file (aka ".nfo file") which, among other things, proclaims and attributes credit for the release to the originating warez group. These messages allow groups and their members to get the credit they crave and develop not only their own reputations within the scene, but also that of the group.

NOTES AND QUESTIONS

1. Should members of warez groups be prosecuted? Would such prosecutions advance the goals of deterrence, retribution, or incapacitation? When picking which cases to bring, prosecutors of intellectual property crimes generally consider factors such as the amount of loss, the blatancy of the piracy, and the adequacy of civil remedies. See Kent Walker, *Federal Criminal Remedies for the Theft of Intellectual Property,* 16 Hastings Comm. & Ent. L.J. 681, 689 (1994). How should these factors play out in warez cases?

2. *Copyright, criminal punishment, and the separation of powers.* Criminal copyright liability is broad in theory, but very few prosecutions are brought. Cases that are prosecuted tend to involve egregious facts far from the thresholds of liability.

The gap between the law and its enforcement owes largely to the different roles of legislators and prosecutors. Prosecutors tend to pick cases in which the defendant is morally culpable and societal losses are clear. The social norms surrounding copyright are unclear, however. Some people analogize infringement to theft, but others analogize it to sharing. In this environment, few prosecutors will be interested in prosecuting copyright cases. Indeed, the federal government has not brought *any* criminal prosecutions against individuals for using the Internet to obtain copyrighted materials without permission for their personal use. Copyright owners have brought civil lawsuits against users, and prosecutors have charged warez group members, but prosecutors have not charged mere users.

The legislative picture is quite different. Legislators decide what is a crime and what is not a crime. Legislators give prosecutors the tools to bring prosecutions when prosecutors wish to do so. When Congress wants to encourage more prosecutions, however, its options are limited. Members of Congress cannot order prosecutors to indict particular kinds of cases. Congress can fund task forces and provide money to hire prosecutors in particular areas, but even then it cannot determine what cases are brought. Legislators are also influenced by powerful lobbying groups, including those of copyright owners and their representatives. If Congress wants to "do something" to address copyright infringement, its primary option in the context of criminal law is to broaden the scope of criminality. Congress can expand the scope of what is criminal even if few if any prosecutors want to bring the cases that Congress has permitted them to bring.

This dynamic may explain the basic contour of criminal copyright law. The law is tremendously broad on paper, and penalties are harsh. But the law is actually used only very rarely. If you could design a regime of enforcing copyrights from scratch, would you propose something like the current system? Or would you favor less draconian laws combined with more enforcement?

3. *Peer-to-peer filesharing and criminal copyright infringement.* Starting in the late 1990s, peer-to-peer technologies such as Napster began to transform how individuals obtain copies of copyrighted works online. Peer-to-peer technologies have generated civil lawsuits against the owners and creators of the technologies. *See, e.g.,* A & M Records, Inc. v. Napster, Inc., 239 F.3d 1004 (9th Cir. 2001). These technologies have not led to criminal indictments, however. Why not? Is the barrier the willfulness requirement? Or is the reason that copyright owners can bring civil suits, and law enforcement intervention may not be necessary?

The design of different peer-to-peer technologies may also influence the role of criminal law. Napster's file-sharing technology was centralized. The Napster company ran centralized servers, providing a clear target for civil or criminal legal action. The next generation of file-sharing technologies is distributed. Programs such as Gnutella and Freenet allow users to make their own files available to others, as well as to access the files of others who use the software. No centralized database exists.

Do distributed file-sharing programs make it impossible for the government to enforce copyright laws? One option would be for prosecutors to use techniques modeled on the enforcement of speeding laws over the "distributed network" of public highways. Every state has laws that regulate the speed of cars driven on public roads. These laws are difficult to enforce, however, as the roads are decentralized and a single police officer can at most monitor one location on one road at any given time. However, the possibility (however low) that a driver will be ticketed for speeding does appear to impact the speed at which most people drive. Although most drivers speed, they presumably speed less often and less egregiously than they would if they knew that the government was not policing the roads. Should the government mirror this strategy to enforce copyright laws on the Internet? If so, how?

B. CRIMES AGAINST PERSONS

There are two major types of computer crimes that can be categorized as crimes against persons. The first type covers threats and harassment, and the second covers invasion of privacy crimes such as wiretapping. These crimes address harms to individuals that violate their sense of privacy and safety. They raise a difficult question: What kinds of online conduct violate an individual's sense of privacy and safety enough that it should be declared a crime? How can we draw lines between criminal and non-criminal conduct in light of the contingent and rapidly evolving norms of computer usage? Most of the materials focus on threats and harassment law. Invasion of privacy crimes will be covered briefly in this section, and a detailed discussion appears in Chapter 6.

1. THREATS AND HARASSMENT

Criminal laws that prohibit threats and harassment attempt to balance two policy concerns. On one hand, the laws try to deter and punish the social harms associated with threats and harassment. Those harms include both inducing fear that threats will be carried out and the harms that follow if they actually are. On the other hand, the First Amendment's protection of free speech sharply restricts the government's ability to punish threats and harassment. Threats can be a form of speech, and the Supreme Court has held that governments can only punish threats that amount to "true threats." In light of this balance, understanding threat and harassment law requires understanding two sources of law: the statutory laws that create the prohibitions and the constitutional doctrines that limit their application.

Three federal statutes address online threats and harassment. The most important is 18 U.S.C. § 875, and specifically 18 U.S.C. § 875(c). This section broadly prohibits interstate threats to harm a person:

> Whoever transmits in interstate or foreign commerce any communication containing any threat to kidnap any person or any threat to injure the person of another, shall be fined under this title or imprisoned not more than five years, or both.

Section 875(d) also covers extortionate threats to harm property, and is supplemented by the computer-specific extortionate threat prohibition found in 18 U.S.C. § 1030(a)(7).

A second statute that prohibits both threats and harassment is 47 U.S.C. § 223. Section 223 was originally enacted as a telephone misuse and harassment statute passed as part of the federal Communications Act of 1934. Over time, its scope has expanded from telephones to other communications devices. The statute in its current form is complex and quite long, and some of the sections are dormant due to obvious First Amendment difficulties. (The Supreme Court's decision in Reno v. ACLU, 521 U.S. 844 (1997), invalidated parts of § 223 that were amended by a part of the Telecommunications Act of 1996 known as the Communications Decency Act.) Two provisions in § 223 are occasionally used to prosecute Internet threats and harassment. These two provisions, 47 U.S.C. § 223(a)(1)(C) and § 223(a)(1)(E), punish whoever:

> (c) makes a telephone call or utilizes a telecommunications device, whether or not conversation or communication ensues, without disclosing his identity and with intent to annoy, abuse, threaten, or harass any person at the called number or who receives the communications; * * * or

(E) makes repeated telephone calls or repeatedly initiates communication with a telecommunications device, during which conversation or communication ensues, solely to harass any person at the called number or who receives the communication[.]

The third federal statute relevant here is the federal stalking statute first enacted in 1996 codified at 18 U.S.C. § 2261A. The statute was expanded in 2000 specifically to address "cyberstalking," the use of computers and the Internet to engage in stalking activity. The most important part of the statute for our purposes is § 2261A(2)(B), which punishes one who,

> with the intent * * * to place a person in another State or tribal jurisdiction, or within the special maritime and territorial jurisdiction of the United States, in reasonable fear of the death of, or serious bodily injury to—
>
> (i) that person;
>
> (ii) a member of the immediate family (as defined in section 115) of that person; or
>
> (iii) a spouse or intimate partner of that person,
>
> uses the mail or any facility of interstate or foreign commerce to engage in a course of conduct that places that person in reasonable fear of the death of, or serious bodily injury to, any of the persons described in clauses (i) through (iii).

Taken together, these three statutes offer relatively broad coverage of threats and harassing conduct that can occur via computers and the Internet. Of course, the fact that the statutes are relatively broad does not mean that they are limitless—or that the meaning of the various terms in the statutes are always clear. The following case considers one such limit, focusing on the meaning of the phrase "containing any threat" in 18 U.S.C. § 875(c).

UNITED STATES v. ALKHABAZ

United States Court of Appeals for the Sixth Circuit, 1997.
104 F.3d 1492.

BOYCE F. MARTIN, JR., CHIEF JUDGE.

Claiming that the district court erred in determining that certain electronic mail messages between Abraham Jacob Alkhabaz, a.k.a. Jake Baker, and Arthur Gonda did not constitute "true threats," the government appeals the dismissal of the indictment charging Baker with violations of 18 U.S.C. § 875(c).

From November 1994 until approximately January 1995, Baker and Gonda exchanged e-mail messages over the Internet, the content of which expressed a sexual interest in violence against women and girls. Baker sent and received messages through a computer in Ann Arbor, Michigan, while Gonda—whose true identity and whereabouts are still unknown—used a computer in Ontario, Canada.

Prior to this time, Baker had posted a number of fictional stories to "alt.sex.stories," a popular interactive Usenet news group. Using such shorthand references as "B & D," "snuff," "pedo," "mf," and "nc," Baker's fictional stories generally involved the abduction, rape, torture, mutilation, and murder of women and young girls. On January 9, Baker posted a story describing the torture, rape, and murder of a young woman who shared the name of one of Baker's classmates at the University of Michigan.

On February 9, Baker was arrested and appeared before a United States Magistrate Judge on a criminal complaint alleging violations of 18 U.S.C. § 875(c), which prohibits interstate communications containing threats to kidnap or injure another person. The government made the complaint based on an FBI agent's affidavit, which cited language from the story involving Baker's classmate. The Magistrate Judge ordered Baker detained as a danger to the community and a United States District Court affirmed his detention. Upon Baker's motion to be released on bond, this Court ordered a psychological evaluation. When the evaluation concluded that Baker posed no threat to the community, this Court ordered Baker's release.

On February 14, a federal grand jury returned a one-count indictment charging Baker with a violation of 18 U.S.C. § 875(c). On March 15, 1995, citing several e-mail messages between Gonda and Baker, a federal grand jury returned a superseding indictment, charging Baker and Gonda with five counts of violations of 18 U.S.C. § 875(c). The e-mail messages supporting the superseding indictment were not available in any publicly accessible portion of the Internet.

On April 15, Baker filed a Motion to Quash Indictment with the district court. In *United States v. Baker,* 890 F. Supp. 1375, 1381 (E.D. Mich. 1995), the district court dismissed the indictment against Baker, reasoning that the e-mail messages sent and received by Baker and Gonda did not constitute "true threats" under the First Amendment and, as such, were protected speech. The government argues that the district court erred in dismissing the indictment because the communications between Gonda and Baker do constitute "true threats" and, as such, do not implicate First Amendment free speech protections. In response, Baker urges this Court to adopt the reasoning of the district court and affirm the dismissal of the indictment against him.

Neither the district court's opinion, nor the parties' briefs contain any discussion regarding whether Baker's e-mail messages initially satisfy the requirements of Section 875(c). For the reasons stated below, we conclude that the indictment failed, as a matter of law, to allege violations of Section 875(c). Accordingly, we decline to address the First Amendment issues raised by the parties.

An indictment is sufficient if it sets forth the offense in the words of the statute itself, as long as those words fully, directly, and expressly set forth all the elements necessary to constitute the offense *intended* to be punished. Accordingly, in determining the sufficiency of the indictment against Baker, we must consider the elements of the offense that Congress intended to prohibit when it created Section 875(c). Because Congress's intent is essentially a question of statutory interpretation, we review the district court's decision *de novo.*

Title 18, United States Code, Section 875(c) states:

Whoever transmits in interstate or foreign commerce any communication containing any threat to kidnap any person or any threat to injure the person of another, shall be fined under this title or imprisoned not more than five years, or both.

The government must allege and prove three elements to support a conviction under Section 875(c): (1) a transmission in interstate or foreign commerce; (2) a communication containing a threat; and (3) the threat must be a threat to injure or kidnap the person of another. In this case, the first and third elements cannot be seriously challenged by the defendant. However, the second element raises several issues that this Court must address. As this Court has recognized, it is one of the most fundamental postulates of our criminal justice system that conviction can result only from a violation of clearly defined standards of conduct. Indeed, our law does not punish bad purpose standing alone, however; instead we require that mens rea accompany the actus reus specifically proscribed by statute. As the Supreme Court has recognized, William Shakespeare's lines here illustrate sound legal doctrine.

His acts did not o'ertake his bad intent; And must be buried but as an intent That perish'd by the way: thoughts are no subjects, Intents but merely thoughts.

United States v. Apfelbaum, 445 U.S. 115, 131 n. 13 (1980) (quoting William Shakespeare's Measure for Measure, Act V, Scene 1; G. Williams, Criminal Law, The General Part 1 (2d ed. 1961)).

Although its language does not specifically contain a mens rea element, this Court has interpreted Section 875(c) as requiring only general intent. Accordingly, Section 875(c) requires proof that a reasonable person would have taken the defendant's statement as "a serious expression of an intention to inflict bodily harm."

Additionally, Section 875(c) does not clearly define an actus reus. The language of Section 875(c) prohibits the transmission of "any communication containing any threat to kidnap any person or any threat to injure the person of another." However, in *United States v. Bellrichard,* 779 F. Supp. 454, 459 (D. Minn. 1991), *aff'd,* 994 F.2d 1318 (8th Cir. 1993), a Minnesota district court recognized the absurdity of a literal interpretation of this language in the context of Section 876, the companion statute of Section 875(c).

The statute should not be interpreted to cover every letter which, apart from its context, seems to threaten a person other than the addressee or letter recipient, as the government argues. For example, if a prosecutor mailed defendant's letters to another government official for analysis or review, that conduct could be covered by the statute—mailing a threat to injure the person of another. Similarly, if the court mails this opinion to West Publishing Company, having quoted verbatim the language used by defendant which is alleged to be threatening, that conduct could be covered by the statute. Also covered would be conduct of a member of the general public, who, attending this trial of widespread interest, took notes of defendant's statements and mailed them to a family member, law professor, or newspaper for their information.

The *Bellrichard* court concluded that such contingencies could be avoided by requiring that proscribable threats be communicated either to the threatened individual, or to a third party with "some connection" to the threatened individual.

We agree with the district court in *Bellrichard* that a literal interpretation of Section 875(c) would lead to absurd results not intended by Congress. However, instead of applying a test that requires "some connection," the unintended results noted in *Bellrichard* may be avoided simply by considering the type of offense that Congress intended to prohibit when it enacted Section 875(c).

To determine what type of action Congress intended to prohibit, it is necessary to consider the nature of a threat. At their core, threats are tools that are employed when one wishes to have some effect, or achieve some goal, through intimidation. This is true regardless of whether the goal is highly reprehensible or seemingly innocuous.

For example, the goal may be extortionate or coercive. In *United States v. Cox,* 957 F.2d 264 (6th Cir. 1992), a bank repossessed the defendant's vehicle, including several personal items. The defendant then telephoned the bank and threatened to "hurt people" at the bank, unless the bank returned his property. Similarly, in *United States v. Schroeder,* 902 F.2d 1469 (10th Cir. 1990), the defendant informed an Assistant United States Attorney that "people would get hurt" if the government did not give him money. In both cases, the defendant used a threat in an attempt to extort property from the threatened party.

Additionally, the goal, although not rising to the level of extortion, may be the furtherance of a political objective. For example, in *United States v. Kelner,* 534 F.2d 1020 (2d Cir. 1976), the defendant threatened to assassinate Yasser Arafat, leader of the Palestine Liberation Organization, during a news conference. Kelner claimed that his sole purpose in issuing the threat was to inform the PLO that "we (as Jews) would defend ourselves and protect ourselves." Although Kelner's threat was not extortionate, he apparently sought to further the political objectives of his organization by intimidating the PLO with warnings of violence.

Finally, a threat may be communicated for a seemingly innocuous purpose. For example, one may communicate a bomb threat, even if the bomb does not exist, for the sole purpose of creating a prank. However, such a communication would still constitute a threat because the threatening party is attempting to create levity (at least in his or her own mind) through the use of intimidation.

The above examples illustrate threats because they demonstrate a combination of the mens rea with the actus reus. Although it may offend our sensibilities, a communication objectively indicating a serious expression of an intention to inflict bodily harm cannot constitute a threat unless the communication also is conveyed for the purpose of furthering some goal through the use of intimidation.

Accordingly, to achieve the intent of Congress, we hold that, to constitute "a communication containing a threat" under Section 875(c), a communication must be such that a reasonable person (1) would take the statement as a serious expression of an intention to inflict bodily harm (the mens rea), and (2) would perceive such expression as being communicated to effect some change or achieve some goal through intimidation (the actus reus).

The dissent argues that Congress did not intend to include as an element of the crime the furthering of some goal through the use of intimidation. Emphasizing the term "any" in the language of the statute, the dissent maintains that Congress did not limit the scope of communications that constitutes criminal threats. While we agree that Congress chose inclusive language to identify the types of threats that it intended to prohibit, we cannot ignore the fact that Congress intended to forbid only those communications that in fact constitute a "threat." The conclusion that we reach here is one that the term "threat" necessarily implies. To emphasize the use of the term "any" without acknowledging the limitations imposed by the term "threat" ignores the intent of Congress and results in the absurd conclusions identified in *Bellrichard,* 779 F. Supp. at 459.

It is important to note that we are not expressing a subjective standard. This Court has held that the mens rea element of a Section 875(c) violation must be determined objectively. The rationale for applying an objective standard to establish the mens rea element of a Section 875(c) violation is equally as compelling with regard to establishing the actus reus element. Accordingly, * * * the actus reus element of a Section 875(c) violation must be determined objectively, from the perspective of the receiver.

Our interpretation of the actus reus requirement of Section 875(c) conforms not only to the nature of a threat, but also to the purpose of prohibiting threats. Several other circuits have recognized that statutes prohibiting threats are designed to protect the recipient's sense of personal safety and well being. If an otherwise threatening communication is not, from an objective standpoint, transmitted for the purpose of intimidation, then it is unlikely that the recipient will be intimidated or that the recipient's peace of mind will be disturbed.

For example, under a hypothetical expressed in *Bellrichard,* "if the court mails this opinion to West Publishing Company, having quoted verbatim the language used by defendant which is alleged to be threatening," it is unlikely that any reader's sense of personal safety and well being would be jeopardized. Likewise, if "a member of the general public, who, attending this trial of widespread interest, took notes of defendant's statements and mailed them to a family member, law professor, or newspaper for their information," such communication would not, from an objective standpoint, compromise the recipient's sense of personal safety. In both cases, the recipient's sense of well-being is not endangered because, from an objective standpoint, the sender has no desire to intimidate.

Applying our interpretation of the statute to the facts before us, we conclude that the communications between Baker and Gonda do not constitute "communications containing a threat" under Section 875(c). Even if a reasonable person would take the communications between Baker and Gonda as serious expressions of an intention to inflict bodily harm, no reasonable person would perceive such communications as being conveyed to effect some change or achieve some goal through intimidation. Quite the opposite, Baker and Gonda apparently sent e-mail messages to each other in an attempt to foster a friendship based on shared sexual fantasies.

Ultimately, the indictment against Baker fails to set forth all the elements necessary to constitute the offense intended to be punished and must be dismissed as a matter of law. We agree with the district court, that whatever Baker's faults, and he is to be faulted, he did not violate 18 U.S.C. § 875(c)

KRUPANSKY, CIRCUIT JUDGE, dissenting.

The words in section 875(c) are simple, clear, concise, and unambiguous. The plain, expressed statutory language commands only that the alleged communication must contain *any threat* to kidnap or physically injure *any person,* made for *any reason* or no reason. Section 875(c) by its terms does *not* confine the scope of criminalized communications to those directed to identified individuals and intended to effect some particular change or goal.

The panel majority attempts to justify its improper fusion of an extra-legislative element re the "intent to intimidate some change or goal" upon section 875(c) by embracing an artificially narrow legal definition of the term "threat." The panel majority posits, "at their core, threats are tools that are employed when one wishes to have some effect, or achieve some goal, through intimidation." However, this interpretation does not comprise the *exclusive* ordinary or legal meaning of the word "threat." Undeniably, a simple, credible declaration of an intention to cause injury to some person, made for any reason, or for no reason whatsoever, may *also* constitute a "threat."

Although some reported threat convictions have embraced a form or degree of intimidation, this circuit has not previously adopted that element as an essential component of a prosecution under 18 U.S.C. § 875(c). To the contrary, controlling precedents clearly reflect the principle that a message is a "threat" *if a reasonable recipient would tend to believe that the originator of the message was serious about his words and intended to effect the violence or other harm forewarned,* regardless of the speaker's actual motive for issuing the communication.

The plain language of 18 U.S.C. § 875(c), together with its interpretive precedents, compels the conclusion that "threats" within the scope of the statute in controversy include all reasonably credible communications which express the speaker's objective intent to kidnap or physically injure another person. Whether the originator of the message intended to intimidate or coerce anyone thereby is irrelevant. Rather, the pertinent inquiry is whether a jury could find that a reasonable recipient of the communication would objectively tend to believe that the speaker was serious about his stated intention. There can be no doubt that a rational jury could find that some or all of the minacious communications charged in the superseding indictment against Baker constituted threats by the defendant to harm a female human being, which a reasonable objective recipient of the transmissions could find credible.

NOTES AND QUESTIONS

1.   The *Alkhabaz* case received a tremendous amount of attention as an early "cyberlaw" case. The investigation began when Alkhabaz (using the pseudonym Jake Baker) posted a story on USENET, a public forum for posting messages on the Internet. The FBI began investigating the case, and investigators obtained the contents of Alkhabaz's e-mails with Gonda. The government's initial theory was that Alkhabaz and Gonda planned to act on their stories, and that a prosecution was needed to protect the young woman described in the stories. Somewhat oddly, however, the government based its case entirely on Alkhabaz's private e-mails with Gonda rather than his publicly posted messages; instead of claiming that Baker and Gonda had entered into a conspiracy to harm the young woman, the government argued that the communications themselves amounted to "threats." As a matter of law, isn't the *Alkhabaz* case an easy case for the defense?

2.   If a defendant posts a threat online, should courts assume that victims will find them? Is the real harm that third parties will act on what they see posted online, or that the victim will find out about the threat and fear it will be carried out?

In People v. Munn, 688 N.Y.S.2d 384 (Crim. Ct. 1999), the defendant posted a message on an Internet newsgroup stating: "Please kill Police Lt. Steven Biegel, all other NYPD cops, and all of their adult relatives and friends...." The defendant was charged with violating New York state harassment law, which prohibits sending a communication by mechanical or electronic means with intent to harass, annoy, threaten or alarm another person. The court held that the law covered the defendant's conduct, and concluded:

> Furthermore, the message was one directed at the complainant. The defendant's alleged posting of his message on an Internet "newsgroup" with the complainant's name included then transformed the communication to one not only intended for the general public, but specially generated to be communicated to the complainant. Indeed in this case, the complainant himself read the message on the computer screen, and became annoyed and alarmed.

Id. at 386.

3. While threats and harassment can be sent directly to their victims, the Internet also facilitates less direct forms of harassment. Consider the facts of People v. Kochanowski, 719 N.Y.S.2d 461, 462–63 (App. Term 2000):

> In late November 1998, defendant approached a younger co-worker who was more familiar with computers and asked if they could create an anonymous web site. Defendant's stated purpose was to negatively depict complainant, a woman with whom he had shared a prior relationship. Defendant said that complainant was falsely accusing and harassing him, that she had had him arrested and that he just wanted to strike back at her. The co-worker, who would later testify for the People at trial, agreed to set up the site. Defendant furnished suggestive photographs of complainant which the co-worker put on the Internet while trying to leave no trail. During the creation of the web site, the two chatted on AOL through a real time chat program. The co-worker typed in express references to intimate body parts and attributed to complainant an infatuation with sex. At one or two points within the web page, defendant asked him to include statements that complainant would drive out to meet people and that they should contact her. Defendant supplied complainant's address and telephone numbers for the web page, so that she could be reached at home, where she lived with her parents and younger sisters, or at her place of employment. Defendant subsequently asked the co-worker to create another anonymous E-mail account so that they could read what people were saying about the web site. In addition, defendant mentioned making the web site [known] to another witness who knew him and complainant.

> The evidence also includes the testimony of complainant concerning her receipt of two calls at work in December 1998 and her reactions of crying and being frightened. She asked the first caller to send her the offensive material and she subsequently received copies of the three pages in the mail. The second caller gave her the address of the web site, and complainant, with the help of a friend's husband, obtained a print-out from a computer.

Should Kochanowski be any more or less liable for his conduct because he used the Internet? Would you feel differently about his conduct if he had placed an advertisement in the local newspaper instead of creating a website?

What if he had placed a full-page advertisement in the *New York Times* and the *USA Today*?

4. In a report on the problem of "cyberstalking," the Justice Department has argued that stalking via the Internet differs from offline stalking in three ways:

- Offline stalking generally requires the perpetrator and the victim to be located in the same geographic area; cyberstalkers may be located across the street or across the country.

- Electronic communications technologies make it much easier for a cyberstalker to encourage third parties to harass and/or threaten a victim (e.g., impersonating the victim and posting inflammatory messages to bulletin boards and in chat rooms, causing viewers of that message to send threatening messages back to the victim "author.")

- Electronic communications technologies also lower the barriers to harassment and threats; a cyberstalker does need to physically confront the victim.

Cyberstalking: A New Challenge for Law Enforcement and Industry, A Report from the Attorney General to the Vice President (1999). Do you agree? Is "cyberstalking" something new, or is it merely another form of harassment via a new communications medium?

––––––––––––

Although many criminal laws prohibit threats and harassment, they all must comply with the First Amendment and its "true threat" doctrine. The "true threat" doctrine teaches that the government cannot punish threats that in context are mere advocacy or political hyperbole, as these are protected speech under the First Amendment. The government can punish only "true threats."

The Supreme Court has never answered exactly how to measure whether a threat is a "true" threat. The lower courts have offered somewhat differing views. Some courts have held that a threat is a true threat when "a reasonable person would foresee that the statement would be interpreted by those to whom the maker communicates the statement as a serious expression of intent to harm or assault." United States v. Orozco–Santillan, 903 F.2d 1262, 1265 (9th Cir. 1990). Other courts have said that the critical question is whether an "ordinary, reasonable recipient who is familiar with the context of the [statement] would interpret it as a threat of injury." United States v. Maisonet, 484 F.2d 1356, 1358 (4th Cir. 1973). How should the true threat doctrine apply to threats that occur online? How can courts develop the context needed to identify true threats online?

The following case applies the true threat doctrine to a website operated by a defendant charged in a drug case. The government moved for a protective order that would have required the defendant to take down the website, and the district court considered whether the website was protected speech under the First Amendment's true threat doctrine.

UNITED STATES v. CARMICHAEL

United States District Court for the Middle District of Alabama, 2004.
326 F. Supp.2d 1267.

MYRON H. THOMPSON, DISTRICT JUDGE.

Carmichael was arrested in November 2003 in Montgomery, Alabama, after Gary Wayne George and Robert Patrick Denton—themselves under arrest for marijuana distribution—informed Drug Enforcement Administration (DEA) Task Force Agent R. David DeJohn that Carmichael had employed them to assist in his marijuana-distribution activities. On the day of his arrest, Denton told Agent DeJohn that Carmichael had been expecting a shipment of several hundred pounds of marijuana the previous day and that Carmichael had told him to assist Freddie Williams with re-packaging the marijuana. Denton's information led to a search of Williams's residence later that day; the search turned up eleven duffle bags filled with marijuana. Carmichael was arrested the same day by DEA Agent Thomas Halasz.

As stated, Carmichael is charged with one count of conspiracy to possess marijuana with the intent to distribute, and one count of conspiracy to commit money laundering. The conspiracy count alleges that, since 1993, Carmichael and others have conspired to possess with the intent to distribute 1000 kilograms or more of marijuana. Williams, Carmichael's co-defendant, is also named in the conspiracy count.

The Website

The Internet website at issue in this case is www.carmichaelcase.com. * * * The website first appeared in December 2003 and first came to the attention of law enforcement in January 2004. The site has gone through roughly three versions. The original version contained a picture of the Montgomery federal courthouse, and it stated that the media had misrepresented the case. The site allowed users to post comments about the case, and it contained links to articles about the case, including an article from a local weekly newspaper that identified Denton by name and listed his home address. The site also included a statement to the effect that Denton had been charged with six felonies.

Sometime in February 2004, the website was changed. The second version showed a picture of the scales of justice on the left side of the page below the words "we are under construction." On the right side of the page, the site displayed the statement, "Look for a new look at this very important case. We will have photos and information on all of the courtroom participants: Defendant, Defense Attorneys, U.S. Attorneys, DEA Agents, Informants." At some point prior to the end of February, this version of the site was amended to include a picture of Carmichael and the statement, "Only public records will be published on this site. This includes all participants, in this case, including their names, pictures, and statements."

Sometime around the beginning of April 2004, the website was changed to its current format. At the top of the site is the word "Wanted" in large, red letters, beneath which are the words "Information on these Informants and Agents." Underneath this header are eight boxes, each containing the name of a witness or agent involved in the case and, in parentheses, the word "Agent" or "Informant." The four "informants" listed are Denton, George, Sherry D. Pettis, and Walace Salery. The four "agents" listed are DeJohn, Halasz, Devin Whittle, and Robert Greenwood. As the site appeared on April 27, 2004, three of the eight boxes contained pictures of the named individuals; the individuals pictured were Denton, Pettis, and George. Currently, a fourth "informant"—Salery—is pictured as well. In the boxes without pictures, the words "Picture Coming" appear in parentheses.

Beneath the eight boxes, this statement appears: "If you have any information about these informants and agents, regardless of how insignificant you may feel it is, Please contact"; the statement is followed by a list of Carmichael's attorneys and their telephone numbers. At one point, only one of Carmichael's attorneys was listed. Currently, four of his attorneys are listed.

This latest version of the site was modified in the middle of April to include, at the bottom of the page, the following language:

"This website, or any posters and advertisements concerning the Carmichael Case, is definitely not an attempt to intimidate or harass any informants or agents, but is simply an attempt to seek information. The Carmichael Case will not be a 'closed door' case.

"Pictures (when available), names and testimonies of informants, agents and witnesses will be on television, on the web site, on the radio and published in newspapers. Carmichael maintains his innocence, and wants the public to know all the facts as well as the participants in this case."

This disclaimer was removed around the end of April. The current version of the website, however, now contains a similarly worded disclaimer.

Carmichael argues that the protective order sought by the government would infringe his free-speech rights under the First Amendment. The first question is whether Carmichael's website is protected speech. Because threats are not protected by the First Amendment, the court can issue a protective order shutting the site down or otherwise restricting it if the site is a 'true threat.' If the site is protected by the First Amendment, the court can issue the protective order sought by the government only if the government satisfies the constitutional rules for imposing prior restraints on the speech of trial participants.

As stated, true threats are not protected by the First Amendment. *Virginia v. Black*, 538 U.S. 343, 359 (2003); *Watts v. United States*, 394 U.S. 705, 707 (1969) (per curiam). True threats encompass those statements where the speaker means to communicate a serious expression of an intent to commit an act of unlawful violence to a particular individual or group of individuals. The prohibition on true threats protects individuals from the fear of violence and from the disruption that fear engenders, in addition to protecting people from the possibility that the threatened violence will occur.

Watts is the origin of the true threat doctrine. In *Watts*, the petitioner appealed his conviction for violating 18 U.S.C. § 871, which prohibits any person from knowingly and willfully making any threat to take the life of or to inflict bodily harm upon the President of the United States. The basis of petitioner's conviction was a statement he made during a 1966 anti-Vietnam War rally on the mall in Washington: "They always holler at us to get an education. And now I have already received my draft classification as 1–A and I have got to report for my physical this Monday coming. I am not going. If they ever make me carry a rifle the first man I want to get in my sights is L.B.J."

The Supreme Court, per curiam, reversed on the ground that petitioner's speech was not a threat. After noting that the government's valid, "even overwhelming," interest in the life of the President, the Court wrote: "Nevertheless, a statute such as this one, which makes criminal a form of pure speech, must be interpreted with the commands of the First Amendment clearly in mind. What is a threat must be distinguished from what is constitutionally protected speech."

"Against the background of a profound national commitment to the principle that debate on public issues should be uninhibited, robust, and wide open, and that it may well include vehement, caustic, and sometimes unpleasantly sharp attacks on government and public officials," the Court interpreted § 871 not to reach "the kind of political hyperbole indulged in by petitioner." The Court held that the petitioner's speech was not a true threat and was thus protected by the First Amendment.

The Supreme Court has not settled on a definition of a true threat, but the United States Court of Appeals for the Eleventh Circuit has:

> "A communication is a threat when in its context it would have a reasonable tendency to create apprehension that its originator will act according to its tenor. In other words, the inquiry is whether there was sufficient evidence to prove beyond a reasonable doubt that the defendant intentionally made the statement under such circumstances that a reasonable person would construe them as a serious expression of an intention to inflict bodily harm. Thus, the offending remarks must be measured by an objective standard."

United States v. Alaboud, 347 F.3d 1293, 1296–97 (11th Cir. 2003). The Eleventh Circuit's objective approach accords with that taken by the majority of the United States Courts of Appeals.

A number of factors are relevant to determine whether speech is a threat proscribable under the First Amendment. First, the court must consider the language itself. Second, the court must look at the context in which the communication was made to determine if it would cause a reasonable person to construe it as a serious intention to inflict bodily harm. Third, testimony by the recipient of the communication is relevant to determining whether it is a threat or an act of intimidation.

a. The Website Itself

The language of Carmichael's website does not make out a threat. There is no explicit threat on the site, and neither the request for information nor the list of Carmichael's attorneys is threatening or intimidating. The statement that "Mr. Carmichael maintains his innocence and wants the public to know all the facts as well as all the participants in this case" is similarly unmenacing. Furthermore, the site actually disclaims any intent to threaten; the site includes the following statement at the bottom of the page: "This web site, or any posters, and advertisements concerning the Carmichael Case, is definitely not an attempt to intimidate or harass any informants or agents, but is simply an attempt to seek information." Indeed, these elements make the site appear to be just what Carmichael maintains it is: another way of gathering information to prepare his defense.

b. Context

The court must also consider the context in which the website operates in order to determine whether the reasonable viewer would see it as a threat. The importance of context is vividly illustrated by * * * cases arising under the Freedom of Access to Clinics Entrances Act (FACE), 18 U.S.C. § 248. FACE provides criminal penalties for

> "whoever by force or threat of force or by physical obstruction, intentionally injures, intimidates or interferes with or attempts to injure, intimidate or interfere with any person because that person is or has been, or in order to intimidate such person or any other person or any class of persons from, obtaining or providing reproductive health services."

18 U.S.C. § 248(a)(1). FACE also provides for a private right of action for "any person aggrieved by reason of the conduct prohibited by subsection (a)." 18 U.S.C. § 248(c)(1)(A). These * * * cases are helpful because they involve statements which surely lie at the outside edge of the definition of 'true threats.'

In *Planned Parenthood of the Columbia/Willamette, Inc. v. American Coalition of Life Activists*, 290 F.3d 1058 (9th Cir. 2002) (en banc), four doctors who provide abortions—Drs. Hern, Crist, Elizabeth Newhall, and James Newhall—and two abortion clinics brought a lawsuit under FACE's private cause-of-action provision against the American Coalition of Life Activists, Advocates of Life Ministries, and a number of individuals associated with these two groups. The plaintiffs' claim was that two posters and an Internet website produced by the defendants constituted "threats of force" under FACE. A jury found for the plaintiffs and awarded them substantial damages, including nearly $80 million in punitive damages. The trial court also permanently enjoined the defendants from publishing or distributing its posters and from providing material to the website. On appeal, the defendants argued that the posters and website were not 'true threats' and were thus protected by the First Amendment.

Like the www.carmichaelcase.com website, neither the posters nor the website in *Planned Parenthood* expressly threatened the plaintiffs. The first poster, published in January 1995, was captioned "GUILTY," beneath which were the words "OF CRIMES AGAINST HUMANITY." Under the heading "THE DEADLY DOZEN," the poster identified 13 doctors, including three of the plaintiffs, and listed their home addresses. At the bottom, the poster bore the legend "ABORTIONIST" in large, bold typeface. The second poster, released in August 1995, identified one of the plaintiff doctors and bore the word "GUILTY" in large bold letters at the top followed by the words "OF CRIMES AGAINST HUMANITY." The poster gave the doctor's home and work address, and it also bore the legend "ABORTIONIST" in large bold type at the bottom.

The website at issue was put up on the Internet in January 1997. It was called the "Nuremberg Files" in reference to the location of the post-World War II Nazi war crimes trial, and it listed information on abortion-providers, judges and politicians, and prominent abortion-rights supporters. The website listed the names of approximately 400 individuals and provided the following legend to interpret the font in which each name was listed: "Black font (working); Greyed-out Name (wounded); Strikethrough (fatality)." The names of three abortion providers who had been murdered between March 1993 and July 1994—Drs. Gunn, Patterson, and Britton—were struck through.

Applying roughly the same standard for determining when speech is a threat that the Eleventh Circuit applies, the United States Court of Appeals for the Ninth Circuit, sitting en banc, held that the two posters and the "Nuremberg Files" website constituted 'true threats' and affirmed the jury's verdict in favor of the plaintiffs. The court's reasoning was based on the history of violence directed against abortion-providers prior to the defendants' creation of the posters and the website. The court described how in the two years prior to January 1995, when the defendants produced the first poster, three abortion providers—Drs. Gunn, Patterson, and Britton—were killed after they appeared on similar posters which gave information about them and bore headings like "WANTED" and "unWANTED." The court described its reasoning this way:

> It is use of the 'wanted'-type format in the context of the poster pattern—poster followed by murder—that constitutes the threat. Because of the pattern, a 'wanted'-type poster naming a specific doctor who provides abortions was perceived by physicians, who are providers of reproductive health services, as a serious threat of death or

bodily harm. After a 'WANTED' poster on Dr. David Gunn appeared, he was shot and killed. After a 'WANTED' poster on Dr. George Patterson appeared, he was shot and killed. After a 'WANTED' poster on Dr. John Britton appeared, he was shot and killed. None of these 'WANTED' posters contained threatening language, either. Neither did they identify who would pull the trigger. But knowing this pattern, knowing that unlawful action had followed 'WANTED' posters on Gunn, Patterson and Britton, and knowing that 'wanted'-type posters were intimidating and caused fear of serious harm to those named on them, ACLA published a 'GUILTY' poster in essentially the same format on Dr. Crist and a Deadly Dozen 'GUILTY' poster in similar format naming Dr. Hern, Dr. Elizabeth Newhall and Dr. James Newhall because they perform abortions. Physicians could well believe that ACLA would make good on the threat. One of the other doctors on the Deadly Dozen poster had in fact been shot before the poster was published. In the context of the poster pattern, the posters were precise in their meaning to those in the relevant community of reproductive health service providers. They were a true threat.

Thus, even though the defendants were responsible neither for the earlier 'wanted posters' nor the earlier killings, the context created by those posters and killings gave the defendants' posters and website a threatening meaning.

The present case is obviously different because Carmichael's website was not put up in the context of a recent string of murders linked to similar publications. The crucial circumstance for the court in *Planned Parenthood* was the pattern of posters followed by murders that pre-dated the defendants' publication of their posters. The analogous situation in this case would be if there were a history of witnesses or government agents being threatened or killed after the release of 'wanted-style' posters on which they were pictured. Such a pattern does not exist here, so the case that www.carmichaelcase.com is a threat is not in any way as strong as that in *Planned Parenthood*.

This case is not totally dissimilar from *Planned Parenthood*, however. Just as the court in *Planned Parenthood* considered the history of violence against abortion providers, this court considers the history of violence committed against informants in drug-distribution cases generally. A brief search of recent reported decisions in the Federal Reporter reveals numerous cases involving the murder of informants in drug-conspiracy cases. This is the broad context in which Carmichael's site exists.

The facts of the present case are similar to those in the cases cited above. Carmichael is accused of heading a far-flung, long-running drug-distribution conspiracy. Denton and George—two of the 'informants' pictured on the site—have admitted to involvement in such a drug conspiracy, and marijuana and firearms have already been seized in this case.

Viewed in light of the general history of informants being killed in drug conspiracy cases and the evidence of a drug-conspiracy and other criminal activity in this case, www.carmichaelcase.com looks more like a threat. Indeed it may be that it is only this context that gives the site a threatening meaning. To illustrate how much of the website's threatening meaning is derived from the factual context of this case, imagine the same website put up by a defendant in a securities-fraud case. In the context of a white-collar crime prosecution, the same site might be an annoyance, but, absent other circumstances, it would be nearly impossible to conclude that it is a threat.

Nevertheless, it is important to recall that the inquiry here is whether a reasonable person would view Carmichael's website as "a serious expression of an intention to inflict bodily harm," *Alaboud*, 347 F.3d 1297, not whether the site calls to mind other cases in which harm has come to government informants, not whether it would be reasonable to think that Carmichael would threaten an informant, and not whether Carmichael himself is somehow threatening. Context can help explain the website's meaning, but it is the website that is the focus of the court's inquiry. Although the broad social context makes the case closer, the background facts described above are too general to make the Carmichael case site a 'true threat.'

The government's strongest argument based on context may not be that the Carmichael site is a direct threat that he will inflict harm on the 'informants' and 'agents,' but that the website is meant to encourage others to inflict harm on them. Agent Borland of the DEA suggested this interpretation when he testified that the website looked to him like a solicitation for others to inflict harm on the witnesses and agents.

The problem with this argument is that implicates the Supreme Court's stringent 'incitement' doctrine. *Brandenburg v. Ohio*, 395 U.S. 444, 447 (1969). *Brandenburg* stands for the proposition that, as a general rule, "the constitutional guarantees of free speech and free press do not permit a State to forbid or proscribe advocacy of the use of force or of law violation." To fall outside the First Amendment's protection, advocacy of violence must be "directed to inciting or producing imminent lawless action and [be] likely to incite or produce such action." There is no evidence that Carmichael's site meets the imminency requirement of *Brandenburg*. Indeed, in *Planned Parenthood*, Judge Kozinski in dissent noted that there was so little chance of proving that the posters and website in that case met the imminency requirement in *Brandenburg* that the plaintiffs did not even raise the argument. 290 F.3d at 1092 n. 5 (Kozinski, J., dissenting). Thus, the court cannot proscribe Carmichael's site as constitutionally unprotected advocacy of violence.

A final piece of 'context' evidence relevant to determining if the www.carmichaelcase.com website is a threat is the very fact that it is a website posted on the Internet. Courts and commentators have noted the unique features of the Internet, *see, e.g. Reno v. American Civil Liberties Union*,

521 U.S. 844, 851 (1997); Scott Hammack, *The Internet Loophole: Why Threatening Speech On–Line Requires a Modification of the Courts' Approach to True Threats and Incitement*, 36 Colum. J.L. & Soc. Probs. 65, 81–86 (2002), and a number of commentators have argued that these features make content posted on the Internet more likely to be threatening, *see, e.g.*, Hammack, *supra*; Jennifer L. Brenner, *True Threats—A More Appropriate Standard for Analyzing First Amendment Protection and Free Speech When Violence is Perpetrated Over the Internet*, 78 N.D. L. Rev. 753, 763–64 (2002). In fact, DEA Agent Borland testified at this court's hearing that one of his concerns about Carmichael's 'wanted poster' is that it is posted on the world-wide web.

That Carmichael's 'wanted poster' is on the Internet, however, is not enough to transform it into a true threat. First, notwithstanding the commentary cited above, the Supreme Court has held that speech on the Internet is subject to no greater or lesser constitutional protection than speech in more traditional media. Second, the general rule in the case law is that speech that is broadcast to a broad audience is less likely to be a true threat, not more. Thus, to the extent that the government's concern is that Carmichael's website will be seen by a lot of people, that fact makes the site look less like a true threat, not more.

Based on all of the above factors and the evidence presented, the court holds that Carmichael's website is not a true threat and is thus protected by the First Amendment.

NOTES AND QUESTIONS

1. The Eleventh Circuit uses an objective test to identify true threats. The question is whether a reasonable observer would construe the statements as a serious expression of an intent to inflict bodily harm. How does a reasonable observer determine whether a statement posted on a website is a serious expression of an intent to inflict bodily harm? Does it depend on the appearance of the page, which can vary depending on the browser used? Does it depend on the URL? On the other sites that link to the statement? On how much traffic the site receives? Is a reasonable observer a savvy Internet user or an Internet novice?

2. *The case of the anonymous blog.* Chris Langdell receives an anonymous e-mail one afternoon recommending that he take a look at http:// langdellwilldie.blogspot.com. Langdell clicks on the link, and it takes him to an anonymous blog titled "CHRIS LANGDELL WILL DIE!!!" The blog has four posts, each of which claims that the anonymous author is planning to murder Chris Langdell. One post includes some personal details of Chris's life and states the following:

LANGDELL'S DAYS ARE NUMBERED:

[Posted by Anon. July 10, 2009 at 8:49pm] 0 Trackbacks

Chris, we know where you live. You live at 129 Main Street. You drive a silver Honda, too. Do you feel unsafe yet?

Langdell is terribly worried, and calls the police.

Is the blog a "true threat"? Why or why not? Does it matter how easy it is to set up such a blog? Does it matter how much it costs? Does it matter whether it is common to set up anonymous blogs? Does it matter how easy it is to trace the account and find out who set up the anonymous blog?

3. How can a court determine the immediacy of a threat posted on the Internet? In People v. Neuman, 2002 WL 800516 (Cal. App. 2002), a man was convicted of making criminal threats in violation of California state law for posting a webpage about a police officer who had given the defendant several traffic tickets and had impounded the defendant's car. The defendant added the page to his personal website that described his views about the illegitimacy of the government. The page stated:

> WANTED! Dead or Alive! (Reward) For Grand Theft Auto on 12/23/1998[.] J. Giles; Badge #233 VENTURA POLICE DEPARTMENT Height 6'3″, Weight; approx. 280 lbs. Race: Aff. Amer. Last seen 12/29/1998 under HWY 101 Bridge/Johnston Rd. exit on a motorcycle. This Rogue Police Officer has been indicted and found guilty of Grand theft Auto. But has yet to be captured and brought to justice. THIS MAN IS ARMED AND DANGEROUS! USE EXTREME PREJUDICE IN APPREHENDING!

On appeal following his conviction, the defendant argued that the fact that he had posted this message on his website meant that it lacked the immediacy of a threat. According to the defendant, the message was "buried in an obscure web page, undelivered," and was therefore "too attenuated to convey a gravity of purpose and an immediate prospect of execution of the threat." *Id.* at *4. The state appellate court disagreed:

> We cannot agree that the "WANTED" notice was "buried" when it was prominently posted on a Web site accessible to millions of Internet users. The prosecution's computer expert testified that appellant's Web site had been indexed on three Internet search engines that would allow users to find it if they typed in key words such as "freedom" and "liberty."

Id. Doesn't this description apply to most things posted on the Web? Does this mean that every threat posted online is an immediate threat? What test would you devise for distinguishing immediate from non-immediate threats posted online?

4. *Brandenburg v. Ohio.* As the *Carmichael* court notes, the First Amendment framework that applies to incitement of illegal conduct—speech that encourages others to take action, rather than suggests an intent for the speaker to act—generally is governed by Brandenburg v. Ohio, 395 U.S. 444, 447 (1969) (per curiam). *Brandenburg* involved a KKK rally held by twelve hooded members of the Klan, in which one member of the Klan delivered a speech about the KKK that included the following warning:

> We're not a revengent organization, but if our President, our Congress, our Supreme Court, continues to suppress the white, Caucasian race, it's possible that there might have to be some revengeance taken.

The Supreme Court held that this warning of possible "revengeance" could not be punished under an Ohio law that punished advocating violence to achieve political goals. According to the Court, "the constitutional guarantees of free speech and free press do not permit a State to forbid or proscribe advocacy of the use of force or of law violation except where such advocacy is directed to inciting or producing imminent lawless action and is likely to incite or produce such action." *Id.* at 447–48.

A speech delivered in person may be likely to produce "imminent lawless action." Is an equivalent speech that appears posted on a website likely to do so? Will any efforts to use the Internet to urge others to engage in violence be likely to produce "imminent lawless action"? How does the imminence requirement apply to speech posted on a website? Who is the relevant audience, and how can a court measure when that audience is likely to be inspired into action?

5. Several commentators have argued that the First Amendment rules that apply to threats and incitement should be rethought for threats and incitement over the Internet. They reason that the basic facts of Internet threats and solicitations change when the architecture is shifted from the physical world to the Internet, and that the tests should change along with the changing architecture. Consider two such proposals:

- "A person makes a 'true threat' when the person makes a statement that, in context, a reasonable listener would interpret as communicating a serious expression of an intent to inflict or cause serious harm on or to the listener (objective); and the speaker intended that the statement be taken as a threat that would serve to place the listener in fear for his or her personal safety, regardless of whether the speaker actually intended to carry out the threat (subjective)." Scott Hammack, *The Internet Loophole: Why Threatening Speech On–Line Requires A Modification of the Courts' Approach to True Threats and Incitement*, 36 Colum. J.L. & Soc. Probs. 65, 97 (2002) (quoting Planned Parenthood of the Columbia/Willamette, Inc. v. American Coalition of Life Activists, 41 F. Supp.2d 1130, 1155 n.1 (D. Or. 1999)).

- "The Internet incitement standard should consider four primary factors: (1) imminence from the perspective of the listener; (2) content of the message; (3) likely audience; and (4) nature of the issue involved." John P. Cronan, *The Next Challenge for the First Amendment: The Framework for an Internet Incitement Standard,* 51 Cath. U. L. Rev. 425, 455 (2002).

What test would you devise to determine when an online threat can be punished consistently with the First Amendment?

2.   INVASION OF PRIVACY CRIMES

Congress has enacted three federal crimes to deter and punish personal invasions of privacy involving computers and the Internet. The offenses criminalize invasions of privacy involving a person's data online. The most important statute is the felony criminal prohibition found in the Wiretap Act, 18 U.S.C. § 2511, and the remaining two statutes are the misdemeanor criminal prohibitions found in the Stored Communications Act, 18 U.S.C. § 2701, and the Pen Register statute, 18 U.S.C. § 3121.

The Wiretap Act, Stored Communications Act, and Pen Register statute are complex surveillance statutes that were enacted to create a statutory form of the Fourth Amendment applicable to computer networks. The criminal prohibitions contained in these three statutes are best (and perhaps only) understood in the context of a broader study of surveillance law. Each of the statutes sets up both a regime of criminal procedure and a related criminal prohibition, and it helps to study the former to understand the latter. Chapter Six explores all three statutes in considerable detail, so a complete study of the three criminal offenses must await those materials.

For now, however, it is helpful to get just a flavor. The most important provision is the criminal prohibition contained in the Wiretap Act, codified at 18 U.S.C. § 2511. Section 2511(1)(a) penalizes one who "intentionally intercepts, endeavors to intercept, or procures any other person to intercept or endeavor to intercept, any wire, oral, or electronic communication." The statute defines "intercept" as "the aural or other acquisition of the contents of any wire, electronic, or oral communication through the use of any electronic, mechanical, or other device." 18 U.S.C. § 2510(4). The basic idea is that it is a crime to intentionally wiretap a private person's telephone or Internet communications. For example, a person who installs a "sniffer" Internet surveillance tool that reads an Internet user's e-mail in "real time" generally violates the Wiretap Act. If the person installs the sniffer intending to intercept a person's communications, he can be charged with criminal wiretapping. The Wiretap Act also contains criminal prohibitions against using and disclosing intercepted communications in a number of circumstances, but they are less often charged and also can raise First Amendment problems. *See* 18 U.S.C. § 2511(b)–(e); Bartnicki v. Vopper, 532 U.S. 514 (2001).

The prohibition contained in the Pen Register statute resembles that of the Wiretap Act. There are two key differences. First, violations of the Pen Register statute are only misdemeanors, *see* 18 U.S.C. § 3121(d), and are only very rarely prosecuted. Second, while violations of the Wiretap Act involve interception of the contents of information such as telephone calls and e-mail, the Pen Register statute is violated when a person obtains in real time the dialing, routing, addressing, and signaling information relating to an individual's telephone calls or Internet communications. The Pen Register statute's criminal prohibition appears in 18 U.S.C. § 3121(a) and (d), and states that one who knowingly "install[s] or use[s] a pen register or a trap and trace device without first obtaining a court order" can be prosecuted. The statute defines both pen registers and trap and trace devices in 18 U.S.C. § 3127(3)–(4), and defines those terms as devices that obtain dialing, routing, addressing, and signaling information relating to telephone and Internet communications. Put together, the statute prohibits knowingly using a device to obtain in real-time the dialing, routing, addressing, or signaling information relating to Internet communications of another person.

The criminal prohibition contained in the Stored Communications Act was discussed briefly in Chapter 2. The prohibition is a specific type of unauthorized access law, punishing one who "intentionally accesses without authorization a facility through which an electronic communication service is provided, [or] intentionally exceeds an authorization to access that facility; and thereby obtains, alters, or prevents authorized access to a wire or electronic communication while it is in electronic storage in such system." 18 U.S.C. § 2701(a). This prohibition is a close cousin of § 1030(a)(2). To be a bit imprecise, it is an unauthorized access law that applies specifically to Internet service providers. The statute is largely redundant in light of the broad scope of 18 U.S.C. § 1030(a)(2)(C).

C. VICE CRIMES

Offenses involving pornography, narcotics, prostitution, and gambling are sometimes labeled "vice crimes." As a historical matter, such crimes exist because they are believed by many to relate to moral vices. Vice crimes can be controversial, as one person's upholding the moral fabric is another person's interfering with private affairs. As a general matter, however, vice crimes involve consensual transactions. The law seeks to block the defendant from engaging in a consensual transaction or conduct that a majority of the public finds harmful.

Computers often alter the ways in which vice crimes are committed. Traditionally, a person wishing to commit a vice crime needed to meet face-to-face with the person providing the sought-after goods or services. Some transactions could occur via postal mail (such as purchasing obscene books), and others could occur via the telephone (such as placing bets), but most vice crimes tended to occur face-to-face. Computers and the Internet change that. The transaction is no longer person-to-person; it is now person-to-computer. An individual sits at her computer, often in the comfort and privacy of her own home, and interacts with machines located hundreds or thousands of miles away.

The shift to digital vice crimes raises two difficult policy questions. The first is whether the new factual environment changes basic assumptions of the legal doctrine. Vice prohibition is often justified by its effect on the local physical environment. For example, a local prohibition on gambling may be a way to protect a neighborhood from illegal activities sometimes associated with gambling, such as organized crime and prostitution. The Internet brings new facts, and it is worth considering whether the new facts justify new law.

Second, the Internet may make it more difficult to enforce vice crime laws effectively. The enforcement of person-to-person vice crimes in the physical world focuses on particular places, which can help law enforcement allocate resources. Prostitutes may be known to walk a particular neighborhood or street; a particular park may be known for its narcotics market; an organized crime gang may run an illegal casino in a basement apartment. To commit a physical vice crime, a person must ordinarily go to a particular place in the physical world. The police can concentrate their enforcement efforts on those physical places.

In contrast, vice crimes online simply require a server, an Internet connection, and a user. The user and the server can be anywhere in the world. To investigate the offense, the police will have to conduct surveillance of the user or the server. Is this possible? Imagine that a defendant in Kansas likes to gamble online using a website that hosts its servers in the Cayman Islands. If you are a Kansas police officer, how can you gather sufficient evidence to charge the defendant in a Kansas court? Given your limited resources, are you likely to focus your efforts on investigating illegal online gambling happening in your state? Is it a coincidence that in the case of both Internet gambling and obscenity law, the legal prohibitions are broad but prosecutions remain quite rare?

1. INTERNET GAMBLING

RONALD J. RYCHLAK—LEGAL PROBLEMS WITH ON–LINE GAMBLING

Engage, May 2005, at 36.

Introduction

Not long ago, Nevada and Atlantic City, New Jersey stood out from the rest of the nation as jurisdictions where one could bet legally. With the emergence of Indian gaming, state lotteries, riverboat gambling, and other forms of legal wagering, today two states (Utah and Hawaii) stand alone as the only jurisdictions without some form of legalized gaming. In fact, today anyone with a computer and Internet access can go to a "virtual casino" and gamble on almost any casino-style game or place bets on professional and collegiate sporting events.

Online gaming is emerging as a major enterprise for the Internet, and a serious concern for lawmakers. There are presently more than 1,400 gambling sites on the web. With about 14.5 million patrons, it is estimated that global revenues for Internet gaming were about $4.2 billion in 2003. Many observers believe that Internet gaming is well on its way to becoming a $100 billion-a-year industry.

Despite its prevalence, Internet gambling is illegal in all fifty states. Several foreign nations, however, either sanction Internet gaming or do not enforce laws against it. Since web pages do not recognize international borders, a gaming site operated in any nation can attract gamblers from every other nation. Most Internet gamblers are from the United States, and that is a serious concern for American lawmakers.

Gambling, of course, has traditionally been seen as a vice, and in the United States it has a history associated with organized crime. As states have moved toward legalization, they have also instituted strict regulatory schemes designed to keep the games fair and the ownership honest. With Internet gaming, however, this may be impossible. One of the most heavily regulated industries in the world has crashed with full force into one of the most unregulated, and inherently unregulatable, phenomenon of modern times.

Several different concerns lead to the call for regulation or prohibition of Internet gambling:

- Concern about underage gamblers. Obviously, it is harder to verify age over the Internet than in person.

- Concern about fraud by Internet casino operators. Internet casino operators have already avoided paying their customers either by refusing to pay or by moving their website to another address and changing the name.

- Concern that video gambling (whose addictive nature has been compared to crack cocaine) from the privacy of one's own home will lead to an increase in gambling addiction.

- Concern that Internet casinos will negatively affect state tax revenues by taking business away from brick-and-mortar casinos that pay taxes.

These reasons for wanting to control Internet gaming, however, do not translate easily into action. When it comes to regulation or prohibition, there are two basic lines of thought. One line holds that Internet gambling cannot be entirely stopped, so it has to be regulated. The opposing argument is that it cannot be regulated, so it must be prohibited. Unfortunately, both groups are partially correct: Internet gaming is very difficult to regulate or to prohibit.

Since many of the Internet gaming web pages are sanctioned by some foreign government, one possibility would be simply to rely upon the regulatory authority provided by that nation. An obvious problem with that solution is that regulation in another nation is unlikely to protect American gamblers. More importantly, many (but not all) of the sanctioned virtual casinos are located in small, island nations that provide virtually no actual regulation; they just charge a fee. Consider:

> In Nevada and New Jersey the applicant for an unrestricted gaming license can expect the process to take one to two years. The applicant has the burden of proving to the licensing authorities that it is legitimate and has the necessary skills available to operate a casino in compliance with the law. The applicant must pay the costs of the independent investigation undertaken to test the accuracy and complete truthfulness of its responses to the myriad questions answered in filling out the application. These costs routinely amount to between $500,000 and $1,000,000. There are public hearings to delve into personal and business transgressions admitted in the application or turned up in the investigation. These amounts do not take into consideration the legal fees that each applicant incurs in getting help and advice in connection with the process.

In contrast, most of the off-shore nations that license Internet casinos charge between $8,000 and $20,000, and the time to obtain the license is between one and five weeks. Obviously, these other nations do not devote as much time and effort to gaming regulation as is expected in the United States. As such, reliance on the laws of other nations will not meet the needs of American lawmakers.

Since gambling has traditionally been a matter of state concern, some individual states have taken action to try to stop Internet gambling. In 2001, for instance, New Jersey's Attorney General filed civil suits against three offshore casinos. This is in line with similar actions taken by officials in New York, Minnesota, and Missouri. In Florida, the Attorney General distributed "cease and desist" letters to at least ten media companies providing publishing or broadcasting advertisements for off-shore computer gambling sites.

The Attorney Generals of Indiana, Minnesota, and Texas have all issued opinions specifically declaring Internet gambling illegal under the laws of their respective states, and other states are putting new legislation in place. Legal actions, however, are very difficult to bring. The Internet casino operations are usually located beyond the state's jurisdictional limits, and even if the necessary evidence could be uncovered, prosecutors are unlikely to go after individual gamblers. As such, states have been unable to significantly impact online betting.

Conclusion

In 2002, the United States General Accounting Office performed a survey of Internet gambling web sites. The findings showed that current federal statutes are not effective in controlling Internet gambling. Recent legislative proposals that have focused on ISPs or financial institutions also have difficulties. Must, then, American lawmakers resign themselves to permanent, unregulated Internet casinos? Maybe not.

Since Internet casinos cannot be stopped as long as they are legal in other nations, American lawmakers should focus on a certification process for online casinos. Those casinos that are already operating traditional gambling establishments within the United States could be given the opportunity to develop online casinos which would be accessible through a regulatory gateway page. These online casinos would face competition from unregulated virtual casinos, which might be able to operate at a lower cost than the regulated web pages. Gamblers wanting assurance of fair games, however, would presumably be interested in using the regulat-ed pages, particularly when they are linked to well-established casino brand names. Regulators (and tax authorities) would have substantial control over these online casinos, because of the brick-and-mortar casinos over which they also have control. As such, reasonable regulations could be put in place to assure fair games, verify the age of gamblers, collect taxes, and minimize the risk to problem gamblers (to the extent that is possible). Unregulated online gaming would still exist, but if this regula-tion were done correctly, these officially sanctioned web pages should be able to capture a significant portion of the market. Consumers would have the choice of betting with casinos that are regulated and fair, or they could take their risks with other entities that are less secure but might offer better odds. In the end, the market could play a significant role in bringing online gaming under control.

NOTES AND QUESTIONS

1. Consider some of the ways Internet gambling is different from traditional forms of gambling. If you visit a casino, you first have to travel to it. You will subject yourself to the legal rules applicable in the jurisdiction where the casino is located; the casino will be a known business with physical assets and employees that can be audited and taxed; and the presence of the casino is likely to have spillover effects (whether negative or positive) on the physical neighborhood surrounding the casino. When you log on to a gambling website, however, you do not need to travel. You may not know what legal regime regulates the gambling transaction or where the company is located; you may not know anything about the gambling site; and the site will not have spillover effects in any physical neighborhood. Do these differences justify regulating Internet gambling differently than traditional forms of gambling?

2. The difficulty of enforcing gambling prohibitions over the Internet led Congress to enact the Unlawful Internet Gambling Enforcement Act, Pub.L. No. 109–347 (2006) ("UIGEA"). The UIGEA states in relevant part:

> No person engaged in the business of betting or wagering may knowingly accept, in connection with the participation of another person in unlawful Internet gambling—
>
> (1) credit, or the proceeds of credit, extended to or on behalf of such other person (including credit extended through the use of a credit card);
>
> (2) an electronic fund transfer, or funds transmitted by or through a money transmitting business, or the proceeds of an electronic fund transfer or money transmitting service, from or on behalf of such other person; [or]
>
> (3) any check, draft, or similar instrument which is drawn by or on behalf of such other person and is drawn on or payable at or through any financial institution.

31 U.S.C. § 5363. The statute also requires the Board of Governors of the Federal Reserve System and the Secretary of the Department of the Treasury acting jointly to enact regulations

> requiring each designated payment system, and all participants therein, to identify and block or otherwise prevent or prohibit restricted transactions through the establishment of policies and procedures reasonably designed to identify and block or otherwise prevent or prohibit the acceptance of restricted transactions in any of the following ways:
>
> (1) The establishment of policies and procedures that—

(A) allow the payment system and any person involved in the payment system to identify restricted transactions by means of codes in authorization messages or by other means; and (B) block restricted transactions identified as a result of the policies and procedures developed pursuant to subparagraph (A).

(2) The establishment of policies and procedures that prevent or prohibit the acceptance of the products or services of the payment system in connection with a restricted transaction.

31 U.S.C. § 5364(a). The regulations appear at 12 C.F.R. § 233.1–233.7, and they contain fairly detailed rules on what designated payment systems can and cannot do.

The basic idea behind the UIGEA is to make it more difficult for individual bettors to finance their bets. Credit card companies will not accept purchases of credits at Internet betting sites, and the betting sites cannot accept the transactions on their end, either. Put another way, the idea is to deter criminal conduct by making it more difficult to commit the crime rather than through the threat of criminal punishment. Is this a more promising way to deter Internet gambling than through criminal prosecutions?

3.   If the federal government and state and local governments cannot enact an effective ban on Internet gambling, what should they do? Is there value to having a law on the books even if many violate that law? If state gambling laws are ineffective, why do all fifty states prohibit Internet gambling?

The following case involves one of the few prosecutions for operating an Internet gambling operation.

UNITED STATES v. COHEN

United States Court of Appeals for the Second Circuit, 2001.
260 F.3d 68.

KEENAN, DISTRICT JUDGE.

In 1996, the Defendant, Jay Cohen was young, bright, and enjoyed a lucrative position at Group One, a San Francisco firm that traded in options and derivatives. That was not all to last, for by 1996 the Internet revolution was in the speed lane. Inspired by the new technology and its potential, Cohen decided to pursue the dream of owning his own e-business. By year's end he had left his job at Group One, moved to the Caribbean island of Antigua, and had become a bookmaker.

Cohen, as President, and his partners, all American citizens, dubbed their new venture the World Sports Exchange ("WSE"). WSE's sole business involved bookmaking on American sports events, and was purportedly patterned after New York's Off–Track Betting Corporation. WSE targeted customers in the United States, advertising its business throughout America by radio, newspaper, and television. Its advertisements invited customers to bet with WSE either by toll-free telephone or by Internet.

WSE operated an "account-wagering" system. It required that its new customers first open an account with WSE and wire at least $300 into that account in Antigua. A customer seeking to bet would then contact WSE either by telephone or Internet to request a particular bet. WSE would issue an immediate, automatic acceptance and confirmation of that bet, and would maintain the bet from that customer's account.

In one fifteen-month period, WSE collected approximately $5.3 million in funds wired from customers in the United States. In addition, WSE would typically retain a "vig" or commission of 10% on each bet. Cohen boasted that in its first year of operation, WSE had already attracted nearly 1,600 customers. By November 1998, WSE had received 60,000 phone calls from customers in the United States, including over 6,100 from New York.

In the course of an FBI investigation of offshore bookmakers, FBI agents in New York contacted WSE by telephone and Internet numerous times between October 1997 and March 1998 to open accounts and place bets. Cohen was arrested in March 1998 under an eight-count indictment charging him with conspiracy and substantive offenses in violation of 18 U.S.C. § 1084. That statute reads as follows:

> (a) Whoever being engaged in the business of betting or wagering knowingly uses a wire communication facility for the transmission in interstate or foreign commerce of bets or wagers or information assisting in the placing of bets or wagers on any sporting event or contest, or for the transmission of a wire communication which entitles the recipient to receive money or credit as a result of bets or wagers, or for information assisting in the placing of bets or wagers, shall be fined under this title or imprisoned not more than two years, or both.

> (b) Nothing in this section shall be construed to prevent the transmission in interstate or foreign commerce of information for use in news reporting of sporting events or contests, or for the transmission of information assisting in the placing of bets or wagers on a sporting event or contest from a State or foreign country where betting on that sporting event or contest is legal into a State or foreign country in which such betting is legal.

See § 1084(a)–(b). In the conspiracy count (Count One) and in five of the seven substantive counts (Counts Three through Six, and Eight), Cohen was charged with violating all three prohibitive clauses of § 1084(a)(1) transmission in interstate or foreign commerce of bets or wagers, (2) transmission of a wire communication which entitles the recipient to receive money or credit as a result of bets or wagers, (3) information assisting in the placement of bets or wagers). In two counts, Counts Two and Seven, he was charged only with transmitting "information assisting in the placing of bets or wagers."

Cohen was convicted on all eight counts on February 28, 2000 after a ten-day jury trial before Judge Thomas P. Griesa. The jury found in special interrogatories that Cohen had violated all three prohibitive clauses of § 1084(a) with respect to the five counts in which those violations were charged. Judge Griesa sentenced Cohen on August 10, 2000 to a term of twenty-one months' imprisonment. He has remained on bail pending the outcome of this appeal.

Cohen appeals the district court for instructing the jury to disregard the safe-harbor provision contained in § 1084(b). That subsection provides a safe harbor for transmissions that occur under both of the following two conditions: (1) betting is legal in both the place of origin and the destination of the transmission; and (2) the transmission is limited to mere information that assists in the placing of bets, as opposed to including the bets themselves. *See* § 1084(b).

The district court ruled as a matter of law that the safe-harbor provision did not apply because neither of the two conditions existed in the case of WSE's transmissions. Cohen disputes that ruling and argues that both conditions did, in fact, exist. He argues that betting is not only legal in Antigua, it is also "legal" in New York for the purposes of § 1084. He also argues that all of WSE's transmissions were limited to mere information assisting in the placing of bets. We agree with the district court's rulings on both issues.

A.   "Legal" Betting

There can be no dispute that betting is illegal in New York. New York has expressly prohibited betting in both its Constitution, *see* N.Y. Const. art. I, § 9 ("no ... bookmaking, or any other kind of gambling [with certain exceptions pertaining to lotteries and horseracing] shall hereafter be authorized or allowed within this state"), and its General Obligations Law, *see* N.Y. Gen. Oblig. L. § 5–401 ("All wagers, bets or stakes, made to depend on any race, or upon any gaming by lot or chance, or upon any lot, chance, casualty, or unknown or contingent event whatever, shall be unlawful"). Nevertheless, Cohen argues that Congress intended for the safe-harbor provision in § 1084(b) to exclude only those transmissions sent to or from jurisdictions in which betting was a crime. Cohen concludes that because the placing of bets is not a crime in New York, it is "legal" for the purposes of § 1084(b).

By its plain terms, the safe-harbor provision requires that betting be "legal," *i.e.,* permitted by law, in both jurisdictions. *See* § 1084(b); *see also* Black's Law Dictionary 902 (7th ed. 1999); Webster's 3d New Int'l Dictionary 1290 (1993). The plain meaning of a statute should be conclusive, except in the rare cases in which the literal application of a statute will produce a result demonstrably at odds with the intentions of its drafters. This is not the rare case.

Although, as Cohen notes, the First Circuit has stated that Congress "did not intend for § 1084 to criminalize acts that neither the affected states nor Congress itself deemed criminal in nature," it did not do so in the context of a § 1084 prosecution. *See Sterling Suffolk Racecourse Ltd. P'ship v. Burrillville Racing Ass'n,* 989 F.2d 1266, 1273 (1st Cir. 1993). Instead, that case involved a private bid for an injunction under RICO and the Interstate Horseracing Act ("IHA"). It does not stand for the proposition that § 1084 permits betting that is illegal as long as it is not criminal.

In *Sterling,* the defendant was an OTB office in Rhode Island that accepted bets on horse races from distant tracks and broadcasted the races. The office typically obtained the various consents required under the IHA, *i.e.,* from the host track, the host racing commission, and its own racing commission. However, it would often neglect to secure the consent of the plaintiff, a live horse-racing track located within the statutory sixty-mile radius from the OTB office. The plaintiff sought an injunction against the OTB office under RICO, alleging that it was engaged in a pattern of racketeering activity by violating § 1084 through its noncompliance with the IHA.

The *Sterling* court affirmed the district court's denial of the RICO injunction. It noted first that because the OTB office's business was legitimate under all applicable state laws, it fell under the safe-harbor provision in § 1084(b). Furthermore, the court held that in enacting the IHA, Congress had only created a private right of action for damages on the part of certain parties; it did not intend for any Government enforcement of the IHA. Consequently, the plaintiff could not use the IHA together with § 1084 to transform an otherwise legal OTB business into a criminal racketeering enterprise.

Neither *Sterling* nor the legislative history behind § 1084 demonstrates that Congress intended for § 1084(b) to mean anything other than what it says. Betting is illegal in New York, and thus the safe-harbor provision in § 1084(b) cannot not apply in Cohen's case as a matter of law. As a result, the district court was not in error when it instructed the jury to disregard that provision.

B.   Transmission of a Bet, Per Se

Cohen appeals the district court's instructions to the jury regarding what constitutes a bet *per se.* Cohen argues that under WSE's account-wagering system, the transmissions between WSE and its customers contained only information that enabled WSE itself to place bets entirely from customer accounts located in Antigua. He argues that this fact was precluded by the district court's instructions. We find no error in those instructions.

Judge Griesa repeatedly charged the jury as follows:

If there was a telephone call or an Internet transmission between New York and [WSE] in Antigua, and if a person in New York said or signaled that he or she wanted to place a specified bet, and if a person on an Internet device or a telephone said or signaled that the bet was accepted, this was the transmission of a bet within the meaning of Section 1084. Congress clearly did not intend to have this statute be made inapplicable because the party in a foreign gambling business deemed or construed the transmission as only starting with an employee in an Internet mechanism located on the premises in the foreign country.

Jury instructions are not improper simply because they resemble the conduct alleged to have occurred in a given case; nor were they improper in this case. It was the Government's burden in this case to prove that someone in New York signaled an offer to place a particular bet and that someone at WSE signaled an acceptance of that offer. The jury concluded that the Government had carried that burden.

Most of the cases that Cohen cites in support of the proposition that WSE did not transmit any bets involved problems pertaining either to proof of the acceptance of transmitted bets, or to proof of the locus of a betting business for taxation purposes.

No such problems existed in this case. This case was never about taxation, and there can be no dispute regarding WSE's acceptance of customers' bet requests. For example, a March 18, 1998 conversation between Spencer Hanson, a WSE employee, and a New York-based under-cover FBI agent occurred as follows:

Agent: Can I place a bet right now?

Hanson: You can place a bet right now.

Agent: Alright, can you give me the line on the um Penn State/Georgia Tech game, it's the NIT Third Round game tonight.

Hanson: It's Georgia Tech minus 7 1/2, total is 147.

Agent: Georgia Tech minus 7 1/2, umm I wanna take Georgia Tech. Can I take 'em for 50?

Hanson: Sure.

WSE could only book the bets that its customers requested and authorized it to book. By making those requests and having them accepted, WSE's customers were placing bets. So long as the customers' accounts were in good standing, WSE accepted those bets as a matter of course.

Moreover, the issue is immaterial in light of the fact that betting is illegal in New York. Section 1084(a) prohibits the transmission of information assisting in the placing of bets as well as the transmission of bets themselves. This issue, therefore, pertains only to the applicability of § 1084(b)'s safe-harbor provision. As we have noted, that safe harbor excludes not only the transmission of bets, but also the transmission of betting information to or from a jurisdiction in which betting is illegal. As a result, that provision is inapplicable here even if WSE had only ever transmitted betting information.

NOTES AND QUESTIONS

1. *The scope of the Wire Act.* Does the Wire Act forbid nonsports-related gambling such as online casinos, or does it only apply to sports-related gambling? The text of the Wire Act is ambiguous: it covers "bets or wagers or

information assisting in the placing of bets or wagers on any sporting event or contest, or . . . the transmission of a wire communication which entitles the recipient to receive money or credit as a result of bets or wagers, or . . . information assisting in the placing of bets or wagers" 18 U.S.C. § 1084(a). Should the limitation "on any sporting event or contest" be read to apply to all of the clauses above, or only the first clause?

In a civil case brought by gamblers against credit card companies for facilitating their Internet gambling practices, the Fifth Circuit concluded that as a textual matter, the Wire Act only applies to gambling activity "related to a sporting event or contest" and does not prohibit the use of Internet casinos. In re MasterCard Int'l, 313 F.3d 257, 262 n.20 (5th Cir. 2002). As a result, online gambling that does not relate to sports does not currently violate federal law, at least in the Fifth Circuit (although it may violate state laws).

Is there a reason that federal law should address sports gambling but not other types of gambling?

2. The Wire Act applies only to those "engaged in the business of betting or wagering." What does that mean? Case law indicates that the phrase is designed to refer to bookmakers, also known as "bookies." *See, e.g.,* United States v. Tomeo, 459 F.2d 445, 447 (10th Cir. 1972). It can also refer to those who have a business relationship with bookmakers. For example, in United States v. Scavo, 593 F.2d 837 (8th Cir. 1979), the defendant established a working relationship with Dwight Mezo, who operated a substantial bookmaking business in the Minneapolis area. The defendant, Scavo, then a resident of Las Vegas, Nevada, provided Mezo with "line" information. Line information refers to the odds or point spread established for various sporting events. The Eighth Circuit concluded that this was sufficient to make Scavo one who was "engaged in the business of betting or wagering":

> [The Wire Act] is not limited to persons who are exclusively engaged in the business of betting or wagering and the statute does not distinguish between persons engaged in such business on their own behalf and those engaged in the business on behalf of others.
>
> Although we reject appellant's blanket assertion that suppliers of line information are outside the scope of § 1084(a), we must nevertheless determine whether the government introduced evidence sufficient to show that appellant was "engaged in the business of betting and wagering." At trial, the government proceeded on the theory that appellant was part of Mezo's bookmaking business and on this aspect of the case the authorities relied upon by appellant are relevant to a prosecution under § 1084(a). They are not controlling, however, because the evidence adduced showed more than a mere occasional exchange of line information between appellant and Mezo.
>
> Viewed in the light most favorable to the government, the evidence showed that appellant furnished line information to Mezo on a regular basis; that Mezo relied on this information; that some sort of financial arrangement existed between appellant and Mezo; that appellant was fully aware of Mezo's bookmaking operation; and that accurate and up-to-date line information is of critical importance to any bookmaking operation.

Id. at 841–42.

3.   The Wire Act is not the only federal criminal law that regulates gambling. In United States v. Gotti, 459 F.3d 296 (2d Cir. 2006), a defendant named Bondi was charged with gambling offenses under 18 U.S.C. § 1955 for running a set of computer poker machines. 18 U.S.C. § 1955 provides for criminal punishment of "whoever conducts, finances, manages, supervises, directs, or owns all or part of an illegal gambling business." The question in *Gotti* was whether the poker machines constituted an illegal gambling business. New York law prohibited gambling, and defined gambling in relevant part as the staking or risking of "something of value upon the outcome of a contest of chance." N.Y. Penal Law § 225.00(2). A "contest of chance" was in turn defined as a game "in which the outcome depends in a material degree upon an element of chance, notwithstanding that the skill of the contestants may also be a factor therein." N.Y. Penal Law § 225.00(1). Bondi argued that the poker machines were not illegal because poker is a game of skill rather than a contest of chance. The Second Circuit disagreed:

> As to Bondi's argument that the games were games of skill rather than chance, he fails to recognize that a "contest of chance" encompasses games in which the skill of the contestants may play a role, as long as the outcome depends in a material degree on chance. Bondi concedes that the games in question had the theme of poker, and he has not contended in his brief that chance does not play a material role in the outcome of a poker game.

Id. at 342.

2.   OBSCENITY

State and federal law has long punished the distribution and display of obscene materials with the goal of maintaining moral order. To over-simplify a very complex history, the thinking has been that there are some types of pornography and other types of displays and images that have no redeeming social value but that can corrupt and coarsen the moral fabric of society. To protect that social order and express society's disgust for the corrupting materials, the law prohibits the display and distribution of obscene materials.

Does obscenity law have a place in the Internet age? And if so, what should that place be? To understand the current state of the law, it is necessary to look at the Supreme Court decisions that have cut back on the definition of obscenity and the government's power to prosecute obscenity-related crimes. The starting point is Roth v. United States, 354 U.S. 476 (1957), an opinion by Justice Brennan that held that obscenity is categorically beyond First Amendment protection. Under *Roth*, the key question is defining the scope of what can be labeled "obscene" under the First Amendment. The definition of obscenity becomes a constitutional question for the Supreme Court; if an item falls within the definition of obscenity, the First Amendment does not apply. Over time, the Supreme Court has used a variety of different definitions to describe obscene materials. The present definition was announced in the following case.

MILLER v. CALIFORNIA

Supreme Court of the United States, 1973.
413 U.S. 15.

MR. CHIEF JUSTICE BURGER delivered the opinion of the Court.

This is one of a group of 'obscenity-pornography' cases being reviewed by the Court in a re-examination of standards enunciated in earlier cases involving what Mr. Justice Harlan called 'the intractable obscenity problem.'

Appellant conducted a mass mailing campaign to advertise the sale of illustrated books, euphemistically called 'adult' material. After a jury trial, he was convicted of violating California Penal Code § 311.2(a), a misdemeanor, by knowingly distributing obscene matter, and the Appellate Department, Superior Court of California, County of Orange, summarily affirmed the judgment without opinion. Appellant's conviction was specifically based on his conduct in causing five unsolicited advertising brochures to be sent through the mail in an envelope addressed to a restaurant in Newport Beach, California. The envelope was opened by the manager of the restaurant and his mother. They had not requested the brochures; they complained to the police.

The brochures advertise four books entitled 'Intercourse,' 'Man–Woman,' 'Sex Orgies Illustrated,' and 'An Illustrated History of Pornography,' and a film entitled 'Marital Intercourse.' While the brochures contain some descriptive printed material, primarily they consist of pictures and drawings very explicitly depicting men and women in groups of two or more engaging in a variety of sexual activities, with genitals often prominently displayed.

I

This case involves the application of a State's criminal obscenity statute to a situation in which sexually explicit materials have been thrust by aggressive sales action upon unwilling recipients who had in no way indicated any desire to receive such materials. This Court has recognized that the States have a legitimate interest in prohibiting dissemination or exhibition of obscene material when the mode of dissemination carries with it a significant danger of offending the sensibilities of unwilling recipients or of exposure to juveniles. It is in this context that we are called on to define the standards which must be used to identify obscene material that a State may regulate without infringing on the First Amendment as applicable to the States through the Fourteenth Amendment.

Since the Court now undertakes to formulate standards more concrete than those in the past, it is useful for us to focus on two of the landmark cases in the somewhat tortured history of the Court's obscenity decisions. In *Roth v. United States*, 354 U.S. 476 (1957), the Court sustained a conviction under a federal statute punishing the mailing of 'obscene, lewd, lascivious or filthy' materials. The key to that holding was the Court's rejection of the claim that obscene materials were protected by the First Amendment. Five Justices joined in the opinion stating:

> 'All ideas having even the slightest redeeming social importance—unorthodox ideas, controversial ideas, even ideas hateful to the prevailing climate of opinion—have the full protection of the (First Amendment) guaranties, unless excludable because they encroach upon the limited area of more important interests. But implicit in the history of the First Amendment is the rejection of obscenity as utterly without redeeming social importance.... This is the same judgment expressed by this Court in Chaplinsky v. New Hampshire, 315 U.S. 568, 571–572:

> '... There are certain well-defined and narrowly limited classes of speech, the prevention and punishment of which have never been thought to raise any Constitutional problem. These include the lewd and obscene. *It has been well observed that such utterances are no essential part of any exposition of ideas, and are of such slight social value as a step to truth that any benefit that may be derived from them is clearly outweighed by the social interest in order and morality. ...*' (Emphasis by Court in *Roth* opinion.)

> 'We hold that obscenity is not within the area of constitutionally protected speech or press.'

Nine years later, in *Memoirs v. Massachusetts*, 383 U.S. 413 (1966), the Court veered sharply away from the *Roth* concept and, with only three Justices in the plurality opinion, articulated a new test of obscenity. The plurality held that under the *Roth* definition

> 'as elaborated in subsequent cases, three elements must coalesce: it must be established that (a) the dominant theme of the material taken as a whole appeals to a prurient interest in sex; (b) the material is patently offensive because if affronts contemporary community standards relating to the description or representation of sexual matters; and (c) the material is utterly without redeeming social value.'

While *Roth* presumed 'obscenity' to be 'utterly without redeeming social importance,' *Memoirs* required that to prove obscenity it must be affirmatively established that the material is 'utterly without redeeming social value.' Thus, even as they repeated the words of *Roth*, the *Memoirs* plurality produced a drastically altered test that called on the prosecution to prove a negative, i.e., that the material was 'utterly without redeeming social value'—a burden virtually impossible to discharge under our criminal standards of proof. Such considerations caused Mr. Justice Harlan to wonder if the 'utterly without redeeming social value' test had any meaning at all.

Apart from the initial formulation in the *Roth* case, no majority of the Court has at any given time been able to agree on a standard to determine what constitutes obscene, pornographic material subject to regulation under the States' police power. This is not remarkable, for in the area of freedom of speech and press the courts must always remain sensitive to any infringement on genuinely serious literary, artistic, political, or scientific expression. This is an area in which there are few eternal verities.

II

This much has been categorically settled by the Court, that obscene material is unprotected by the First Amendment. * * * We acknowledge, however, the inherent dangers of undertaking to regulate any form of expression. State statutes designed to regulate obscene materials must be carefully limited. As a result, we now confine the permissible scope of such regulation to works which depict or describe sexual conduct. That conduct must be specifically defined by the applicable state law, as written or authoritatively construed. A state offense must also be limited to works which, taken as a whole, appeal to the prurient interest in sex, which portray sexual conduct in a patently offensive way, and which, taken as a whole, do not have serious literary, artistic, political, or scientific value.

The basic guidelines for the trier of fact must be: (a) whether 'the average person, applying contemporary community standards' would find that the work, taken as a whole, appeals to the prurient interest; (b) whether the work depicts or describes, in a patently offensive way, sexual conduct specifically defined by the applicable state law; and (c) whether the work, taken as a whole, lacks serious literary, artistic, political, or scientific value. We do not adopt as a constitutional standard the 'utterly without redeeming social value' test of *Memoirs v. Massachusetts*, 383 U.S. at 419; that concept has never commanded the adherence of more than three Justices at one time. If a state law that regulates obscene material is thus limited, as written or construed, the First Amendment values applicable to the States through the Fourteenth Amendment are adequately protected by the ultimate power of appellate courts to conduct an independent review of constitutional claims when necessary.

We emphasize that it is not our function to propose regulatory schemes for the States. That must await their concrete legislative efforts. It is possible, however, to give a few plain examples of what a state statute could define for regulation under part (b) of the standard announced in this opinion, supra:

(a) Patently offensive representations or descriptions of ultimate sexual acts, normal or perverted, actual or simulated.

(b) Patently offensive representation or descriptions of masturbation, excretory functions, and lewd exhibition of the genitals.

Sex and nudity may not be exploited without limit by films or pictures exhibited or sold in places of public accommodation any more than live sex and nudity can be exhibited or sold without limit in such public places. At a minimum, prurient, patently offensive depiction or description of sexual conduct must have serious literary, artistic, political, or scientific value to merit First Amendment protection. For example, medical books for the education of physicians and related personnel necessarily use graphic illustrations and descriptions of human anatomy. In resolving the inevitably sensitive questions of fact and law, we must continue to rely on the jury system, accompanied by the safeguards that judges, rules of evidence, presumption of innocence, and other protective features provide, as we do with rape, murder, and a host of other offenses against society and its individual members.

Under the holdings announced today, no one will be subject to prosecution for the sale or exposure of obscene materials unless these materials depict or describe patently offensive 'hard core' sexual conduct specifically defined by the regulating state law, as written or construed. We are satisfied that these specific prerequisites will provide fair notice to a dealer in such materials that his public and commercial activities may bring prosecution. If the inability to define regulated materials with ultimate, god-like precision altogether removes the power of the States or the Congress to regulate, then 'hard core' pornography may be exposed without limit to the juvenile, the passerby, and the consenting adult alike, as, indeed, Mr. Justice Douglas contends. * * * In this belief, however, Mr. Justice Douglas now stands alone.

III

Under a National Constitution, fundamental First Amendment limitations on the powers of the States do not vary from community to community, but this does not mean that there are, or should or can be, fixed, uniform national standards of precisely what appeals to the 'prurient interest' or is 'patently offensive.' These are essentially questions of fact, and our Nation is simply too big and too diverse for this Court to reasonably expect that such standards could be articulated for all 50 States in a single formulation, even assuming the prerequisite consensus exists. When triers of fact are asked to decide whether 'the average person, applying contemporary community standards' would consider certain materials 'prurient,' it would be unrealistic to require that the answer be based on some abstract formulation. The adversary system, with lay jurors as the usual ultimate factfinders in criminal prosecutions, has historically permitted triers of fact to draw on the standards of their community, guided always by limiting instructions on the law. To require a State to structure obscenity proceedings around evidence of a national 'community standard' would be an exercise in futility.

As noted before, this case was tried on the theory that the California obscenity statute sought to incorporate the tripartite test of *Memoirs*. This, a 'national' standard of First Amendment protection enumerated by a plurality of this Court, was correctly regarded at the time of trial as limiting state prosecution under the controlling case law. The jury, however, was explicitly instructed that, in determining whether the 'dominant theme of the material as a whole . . . appeals to the prurient interest' and in determining whether the material 'goes substantially beyond customary limits of candor and affronts contemporary community standards of decency,' it was to apply 'contemporary community standards of the State of California.'

We conclude that neither the State's alleged failure to offer evidence of 'national standards,' nor the trial court's charge that the jury consider state community standards, were constitutional errors. Nothing in the First Amendment requires that a jury must consider hypothetical and unascertainable 'national standards' when attempting to determine whether certain materials are obscene as a matter of fact.

* * * It is neither realistic nor constitutionally sound to read the First Amendment as requiring that the people of Maine or Mississippi accept public depiction of conduct found tolerable in Las Vegas, or New York City. People in different States vary in their tastes and attitudes, and this diversity is not to be strangled by the absolutism of imposed uniformity. * * * [T]he primary concern with requiring a jury to apply the standard of 'the average person, applying contemporary community standards' is to be certain that, so far as material is not aimed at a deviant group, it will be judged by its impact on an average person, rather than a particularly susceptible or sensitive person—or indeed a totally insensitive one. We hold that the requirement that the jury evaluate the materials with reference to 'contemporary standards of the State of California' serves this protective purpose and is constitutionally adequate.

IV

The dissenting Justices sound the alarm of repression. But, in our view, to equate the free and robust exchange of ideas and political debate with commercial exploitation of obscene material demeans the grand conception of the First Amendment and its high purposes in the historic struggle for freedom. It is a misuse of the great guarantees of free speech and free press. The First Amendment protects works which, taken as a whole, have serious literary, artistic, political, or scientific value, regardless of whether the government or a majority of the people approve of the ideas these works represent. The protection given speech and press was fashioned to assure unfettered interchange of ideas for the bringing about of political and social changes desired by the people, but the public portrayal of hard-core sexual conduct for its own sake, and for the ensuing commercial gain, is a different matter.

MR. JUSTICE DOUGLAS, dissenting.

Today we leave open the way for California to send a man to prison for distributing brochures that advertise books and a movie under freshly written standards defining obscenity which until today's decision were never the part of any law.

Today the Court retreats from the earlier formulations of the constitutional test and undertakes to make new definitions. This effort, like the earlier ones, is earnest and well intentioned. The difficulty is that we do not deal with constitutional terms, since 'obscenity' is not mentioned in the Constitution or Bill of Rights. And the First Amendment makes no such exception from 'the press' which it undertakes to protect nor, as I have said on other occasions, is an exception necessarily implied, for there was no recognized exception to the free press at the time the Bill of Rights was adopted which treated 'obscene' publications differently from other types of papers, magazines, and books. So there are no constitutional guidelines for deciding what is and what is not 'obscene.' The Court is at large because we deal with tastes and standards of literature. What shocks me may be sustenance for my neighbor. What causes one person to boil up in rage over one pamphlet or movie may reflect only his neurosis, not shared by others. We deal here with a regime of censorship which, if adopted, should be done by constitutional amendment after full debate by the people.

While the right to know is the corollary of the right to speak or publish, no one can be forced by government to listen to disclosure that he finds offensive. * * * No one is being compelled to look or to listen. Those who enter newsstands or bookstalls may be offended by what they see. But they are not compelled by the State to frequent those places; and it is only state or governmental action against which the First Amendment, applicable to the States by virtue of the Fourteenth, raises a ban.

The idea that the First Amendment permits government to ban publications that are 'offensive' to some people puts an ominous gloss on freedom of the press. That test would make it possible to ban any paper or any journal or magazine in some benighted place. The First Amendment was designed to invite dispute, to induce a condition of unrest, to create dissatisfaction with conditions as they are, and even to stir people to anger. The idea that the First Amendment permits punishment for ideas that are 'offensive' to the particular judge or jury sitting in judgment is astounding. No greater leveler of speech or literature has ever been designed. To give the power to the censor, as we do today, is to make a sharp and radical break with the traditions of a free society.

NOTES AND QUESTIONS

1. Should the Supreme Court revisit *Miller v. California*? At the time *Miller* was decided, an adult could purchase pornography by buying a copy of *Playboy* at a local magazine store, but access to more hard-core pornography was often more difficult. The *Miller* test seems to target hard-core pornography that was relatively rare and difficult to find at the time. Today, however, anyone can access hard-core pornography via the Internet. Does the *Miller* test work in a world in which hard core pornography is readily available over the Internet? Has the Internet rendered *Miller* obsolete? Alternatively, does the ready availability of materials that would seem to be prohibited under the *Miller* test make obscenity prosecutions more important, not less?

2. The *Miller* obscenity standard assumes the existence of distinct local community standards. Residents of New York City will have one standard,

residents of Utah will have another, and residents of Boston will have a third. The local standard test used in *Miller* is designed to ensure that persons in New York are not judged by the standards of Utah. Is this assumption sensible in an age when many individuals derive their standards from peers and the Internet? What effect has the Internet had on "community" standards? Has the global Internet reduced the local variation in community standards? And how could this be measured?

In a concurring opinion in Ashcroft v. American Civil Liberties Union, 535 U.S. 564, 590–91 (2002), Justice Breyer argued that Congress's use of the phrase "community standards" in the context of the Child Online Protection Act should be read to mean a national standard rather than a community standard. He offered the following argument in support of his approach:

> [T]his view of the statute avoids the need to examine the serious First Amendment problem that would otherwise exist. To read the statute as adopting the community standards of every locality in the United States would provide the most puritan of communities with a heckler's Internet veto affecting the rest of the Nation. The technical difficulties associated with efforts to confine Internet material to particular geographic areas make the problem particularly serious. And these special difficulties also potentially weaken the authority of prior cases in which they were not present. A nationally uniform adult-based standard * * * significantly alleviates any special need for First Amendment protection. Of course some regional variation may remain, but any such variations are inherent in a system that draws jurors from a local geographic area and they are not, from the perspective of the First Amendment, problematic.

Does a "community standard" based on the concept of a physical-world community make sense if allegedly obscene images are obtained and distributed online?

3. *Stanley v. Georgia.* The Supreme Court held that the government cannot criminalize mere private possession of obscenity in a pre-*Miller* case, Stanley v. Georgia, 394 U.S. 557 (1969). *Stanley* reasoned that the state had no legitimate interest in controlling what people read in the confines of their own homes. Consider this excerpt from the Court's opinion:

> Whatever may be the justifications for other statutes regulating obscenity, we do not think they reach into the privacy of one's own home. If the First Amendment means anything, it means that a State has no business telling a man, sitting alone in his own house, what books he may read or what films he may watch. Our whole constitutional heritage rebels at the thought of giving government the power to control men's minds.

> And yet, in the face of these traditional notions of individual liberty, Georgia asserts the right to protect the individual's mind from the effects of obscenity. We are not certain that this argument amounts to anything more than the assertion that the State has the right to control the moral content of a person's thoughts. To some, this may be a noble purpose, but it is wholly inconsistent with the philosophy of the First Amendment. * * * Nor is it relevant that obscene materials in general, or the particular films before the Court, are arguably devoid of any ideological content. The line between the transmission of ideas and mere entertainment is

much too elusive for this Court to draw, if indeed such a line can be drawn at all. Whatever the power of the state to control public dissemination of ideas inimical to the public morality, it cannot constitutionally premise legislation on the desirability of controlling a person's private thoughts.

Perhaps recognizing this, Georgia asserts that exposure to obscene materials may lead to deviant sexual behavior or crimes of sexual violence. There appears to be little empirical basis for that assertion. But more important, if the State is only concerned about printed or filmed materials inducing antisocial conduct, we believe that in the context of private consumption of ideas and information we should adhere to the view that 'among free men, the deterrents ordinarily to be applied to prevent crime are education and punishment for violations of the law * * *.' Given the present state of knowledge, the State may no more prohibit mere possession of obscene matter on the ground that it may lead to antisocial conduct than it may prohibit possession of chemistry books on the ground that they may lead to the manufacture of homemade spirits.

Finally, we are faced with the argument that prohibition of possession of obscene materials is a necessary incident to statutory schemes prohibiting distribution. That argument is based on alleged difficulties of proving an intent to distribute or in producing evidence of actual distribution. We are not convinced that such difficulties exist, but even if they did we do not think that they would justify infringement of the individual's right to read or observe what he pleases. Because that right is so fundamental to our scheme of individual liberty, its restriction may not be justified by the need to ease the administration of otherwise valid criminal laws.

Id. at 565–67. The Supreme Court has taken a very different path in the context of criminal laws that prohibit the *distribution* of obscene materials. In United States v. Reidel, 402 U.S. 351 (1971), decided soon after *Stanley*, the Court reaffirmed pre-*Stanley* law that the government could criminalize distributing obscene materials. The Court distinguished *Stanley* in the following way:

The right *Stanley* asserted was "the right to read or observe what he pleases—the right to satisfy his intellectual and emotional needs in the privacy of his own home." The Court's response was that "a State has no business telling a man, sitting alone in his own house, what books he may read or what films he may watch. Our whole constitutional heritage rebels at the thought of giving government the power to control men's minds." The focus of this language was on freedom of mind and thought and on the privacy of one's home. It does not require that we fashion or recognize a constitutional right in people like Reidel to distribute or sell obscene materials. The personal constitutional rights of those like Stanley to possess and read obscenity in their homes and their freedom of mind and thought do not depend on whether the materials are obscene or whether obscenity is constitutionally protected. Their rights to have and view that material in private are independently saved by the Constitution.

> Reidel is in a wholly different position. He has no complaints about governmental violations of his private thoughts or fantasies, but stands squarely on a claimed First Amendment right to do business in obscenity and use the mails in the process. But Roth v. United States, 354 U.S. 476 (1957), has squarely placed obscenity and its distribution outside the reach of the First Amendment and they remain there today. *Stanley* did not overrule *Roth* and we decline to do so now.

402 U.S. at 355–56.

Is this rationale persuasive? Does it make sense for distribution to be a crime if the possession that follows from the distribution is constitutionally protected? One possible explanation for this otherwise puzzling result is that it channels law enforcement efforts by allowing the government to prosecute distributors but not users. Is that a desirable result?

4. *The impact of Lawrence v. Texas.* In Lawrence v. Texas, 539 U.S. 558 (2003), the Supreme Court invalidated a Texas statute that criminalized consensual sodomy on the ground that it was inconsistent with the Due Process clause. In its briefs to the Court, Texas had attempted to justify the statute under rational basis scrutiny as an effort to advance and recognize societal mores relating to sexuality and decency. In ruling against Texas, Justice Kennedy's opinion for the Court agreed with Justice Stevens' dissenting position in Bowers v. Hardwick, 478 U.S. 186 (1986), that "the fact that the governing majority in a State has traditionally viewed a particular practice as immoral is not a sufficient reason for upholding a law prohibiting the practice." Writing in dissent in *Lawrence*, Justice Scalia argued that the Court's decision implicitly signaled that other legislation premised on "majoritarian sexual morality," including laws against obscenity, might also be unconstitutional:

> The Texas statute undeniably seeks to further the belief of its citizens that certain forms of sexual behavior are "immoral and unacceptable,"— the same interest furthered by criminal laws against fornication, bigamy, adultery, adult incest, bestiality, and obscenity. *Bowers* held that this *was* a legitimate state interest. The Court today reaches the opposite conclusion. The Texas statute, it says, "furthers *no legitimate state interest* which can justify its intrusion into the personal and private life of the individual." The Court embraces instead Justice Stevens' declaration in his *Bowers* dissent, that "the fact that the governing majority in a State has traditionally viewed a particular practice as immoral is not a sufficient reason for upholding a law prohibiting the practice." This effectively decrees the end of all morals legislation. If, as the Court asserts, the promotion of majoritarian sexual morality is not even a *legitimate* state interest, none of the above-mentioned laws can survive rational-basis review.

Id. at 559 (Scalia, J., dissenting).

Does *Lawrence* compel the invalidation of obscenity laws, effectively overruling United States v. Reidel, 402 U.S. 351 (1971)? In United States v. Extreme Assocs., Inc, 352 F. Supp.2d 578 (W.D. Pa. 2005), a district court concluded that it did:

It cannot be seriously disputed that, historically, the government's purpose in completely banning the distribution of sexually explicit obscene material, including to consenting adults, was to uphold the community sense of morality. That is, to prevent, to the extent possible, individuals from entertaining lewd or lustful thoughts stimulated by viewing material that appeals to one's prurient interests. Harboring such thoughts, the government deems, is immoral conduct even when done by consenting adults in private.

After *Lawrence,* however, upholding the public sense of morality is not even a legitimate state interest that can justify infringing one's liberty interest to engage in consensual sexual conduct in private. Therefore, this historically asserted state interest certainly cannot rise to the level of a compelling interest, as is required under the strict scrutiny test.

Id. at 592–93.

The Third Circuit reversed, however, on the ground that the district had overstepped its bounds. Under established Supreme Court precedent, it is up to the Supreme Court to overturn its decisions; a lower court cannot rule that an older Supreme Court decision on the books is no longer in effect because it is inconsistent with the reasoning of more recent Supreme Court decisions. As a result, *Reidel* is still good law unless or until the U.S. Supreme Court overturns it. *See* United States v. Extreme Assocs., Inc., 431 F.3d 150 (3d Cir. 2005).

The Third Circuit also rejected the argument that the facts of the Internet compelled a different approach to obscenity:

Extreme Associates argues that the relevant cases are distinguishable because they were all decided before the advent of the Internet, suggesting that the commercial transportation of obscenity considered by the Court in those cases was of a more public variety than the Internet commerce at issue here. As such, the concern for community decency and order that arose in the other obscenity cases is irrelevant to this prosecution.

We decline to join appellees in that analytical leap. The mere fact, without more, that the instant prosecution involves Internet transmissions is not enough to render an entire line of Supreme Court decisions inapplicable given their analytical and other factual similarities to this case.

* * * [T]he [Supreme] Court thus far has not suggested that obscenity law does not apply to the Internet or even that a new analytical path is necessary in Internet cases. If the Supreme Court wishes to treat all Internet obscenity cases as *sui generis* for purposes of federal obscenity law analysis, it has not yet said so, "tacitly" or otherwise.

The Internet is a channel of commerce covered by the federal statutes regulating the distribution of obscenity. Extreme Associates was indicted for engaging in commercial transactions that its own brief on appeal describes as "Internet commerce." This case cannot be meaningfully distinguished merely because it involves the Internet.

Id. at 160–61.

––––––––––

The federal obscenity statutes are codified at 18 U.S.C. §§ 1460–70. The statutes prohibit a range of offenses, ranging from selling obscene materials on federal land, 18 U.S.C. § 1460, to using a means of interstate commerce to transfer obscene materials to a minor, 18 U.S.C. § 1470. Owing to their pre-*Miller* heritage, the language of these statutes is quite archaic, and much broader than the modern first Amendment would allow. For example, many of the statutes refer to material that is not merely "obscene," but also "lewd, lascivious, or filthy." Only obscene materials can be prohibited under the First Amendment, however, so the statutes can be read as effectively being limited to obscene materials.

In the context of Internet-related crimes, the two key federal obscenity provisions are 18 U.S.C. § 1462 and 18 U.S.C. § 1465. Both sections prohibit a range of activities involving obscene materials that include using an "interactive computer service" to carry, receive, or transport obscene materials in interstate commerce. The phrase "interactive computer service" is defined in 47 U.S.C. § 230(f)(2):

> The term "interactive computer service" means any information service, system, or access software provider that provides or enables computer access by multiple users to a computer server, including specifically a service or system that provides access to the Internet and such systems operated or services offered by libraries or educational institutions.

This broad definition encompasses essentially all use of computer networks and the Internet. *See* Carafano v. Metrosplash.com, Inc., 339 F.3d 1119, 1123 (9th Cir. 2003).

UNITED STATES v. EXTREME ASSOCIATES, INC.

United States District Court for the Western District Of Pennsylvania, 2009.
2009 WL 113767.

GARY L. LANCASTER, DISTRICT JUDGE.

This is a criminal prosecution in which the United States has charged defendants with distribution of obscene material via the mails and the Internet. Defendants have filed a motion asking the court to issue a pretrial ruling regarding how the "as a whole" and "community standards" elements of the *Miller* test will be applied in this case.

Defendants have been charged with ten counts of violating the federal obscenity statutes. In particular, defendants have been charged with mailing three video tapes to an undercover United States postal inspector in Pittsburgh and delivering six digital video clips over the Internet to that same undercover postal inspector. The Inspector ordered the video tapes through Extreme Associates' publicly available website and accessed the video clips after purchasing a monthly membership to the members-only section of Extreme Associates' website.

The Supreme Court has established a three part test to be used when determining whether material is legally obscene. Under this test, referred to as "the *Miller* test," material is obscene if:

1. The average person, applying contemporary community standards, would find that the work, taken as a whole, appeals to the prurient interest;

2. The average person, applying contemporary community standards, would find that the work depicts or describes sexual conduct in a patently offensive way; and

3. A reasonable person would find, taking the work as a whole, that it lacks serious literary, artistic, political, or scientific value.

Miller v. California, 413 U.S. 15, 24–25 (1973).

A. *As a Whole*

Defendants allege that the "as a whole" element of the *Miller* test as applied to the digital video clip charges should be the "entire Extreme Associates Website," including all web pages to which it is linked. Defendants' only support for this position is a concurring opinion authored by Justice Kennedy in the first case challenging the Child Online Protection Act. *Ashcroft v. American Civil Liberties Union,* 535 U.S. 564, 593 (2002). Justice Kennedy's concurrence is not controlling law, nor does it address the exact issue raised in this case.

Instead, we must apply existing obscenity case law regarding the "as a whole" element to these digital video clips. Although this may be unchartered territory, our task is not as difficult as it may appear to be. The "as a whole" element was established in *Roth v. United States,* 354 U.S. 476 (1957), in which the Supreme Court rejected the previously accepted proposition that obscenity could be judged on the basis of an isolated, detached, or separate excerpt from a larger work because it was unconstitutionally restrictive of the freedoms of speech and press.

The Supreme Court more recently reiterated the notion that individual scenes cannot be judged in isolation under the "as a whole" test if they are presented in conjunction with, or as part of, a larger work. *Ashcroft v. Free Speech Coalition,* 535 U.S. 234, 248 (2002) (stating that "where the scene is part of the narrative, the work itself does not for this reason become obscene, even though the scene in isolation might be offensive"). On the other hand, where a person removes passages from other works, and combines them into a new, free-standing compilation, that compilation becomes the new work "as a whole."

Under these standards, we must view the context and manner in which the material has been created, packaged, and presented by the author to the intended audience in order to decide what the work "as a whole" is for purposes of the *Miller* test.

As the government demonstrated at the December 2008 hearing, the digital video clips are presented to the audience as independent videos, complete in and of themselves, and unrelated in content to any other material around them. The charged clips are found on individual fetish web pages within the members-only website. These fetish pages are comprised of numerous individual still pictures, arranged in rows and columns, with a text title below each picture. The text title acts as a link to the digital video clip represented by the still picture appearing above the title. In order to view any particular video clip on the page, the user must click on the title associated with the clip. The clips are related to each other only by general fetish subject matter, and are not presented by defendants as being interconnected to each other, or to any other section of the Extreme Associates website. Nor do defendants indicate to their audience that the clips are part of another, larger work.

As such, regardless of whether the digital video clips are scenes from longer films, given the manner in which the defendants excerpted and posted the clips we find that they are themselves free standing, independent works. Therefore, the work "as a whole" will be each individual digital video clip referenced in the indictment.

B. *Community Standards*

Defendants contend that the applicable community for determining community standards for purposes of this case should be "the World Wide Web," or at least the entire United States. Defendants explicitly acknowledged at oral argument that defining the community in this way would be an "expansion" of existing law, but argued that such an expansion was warranted because "times have changed" due to the advent of the Internet. The Court of Appeals for the Third Circuit has already rejected this exact argument in this case. In its opinion reversing our order dismissing the indictment, the Court of Appeals stated that "the Supreme Court has not suggested that obscenity law does not apply to the Internet or even that a new analytical path is necessary in Internet cases." *United States v. Extreme Associates, Inc., et al.,* 431 F.3d 150, 160–61 (3d Cir. 2005). Under the explicit direction of the Court of Appeals, we decline defendants' invitation to expand existing Supreme Court precedent simply because this case involves the Internet.

However, even were we to entertain defendants' arguments in support of creating new law in this case, we would not find them persuasive under the facts of this case. At its core, defendants' argument is that the Internet is different than any other method of delivering sexually explicit materials because material available on the Internet can be viewed from anywhere in the world, without the publisher knowing where the viewer is located. Defendants contend that it is unconstitutional to hold Internet publishers to differing community standards when they have no control over, or knowledge of, from where their material is being viewed. Thus, defendants advocate the creation of a new World Wide Web, or at least national, community standard for any content provided over the Internet. Alternatively, defendants argue that the place of publication should be used to determine the community standard for Internet content providers because that is the only place that the publisher has knowingly conducted business.

The flaw in defendants' argument is that the government has not charged defendants with violating the obscenity statutes by displaying materials on their publicly available website. Instead, for the video tape counts, the materials were delivered through the mail to a Pittsburgh address. For the digital video clip counts the material was provided to a user who had previously purchased access to the members-only section of the Extreme Associates website, by, among other things, providing defendants with a credit card and a Pittsburgh address. Thus, in both instances, defendants knew where their audience was located, and the basic premise of their argument fails.

Instead, this case falls within the parameters of existing Supreme Court precedent that has rejected the need to create a national community standard for speakers who choose to send their material into many communities, each with differing community standards. As such, as in those cases, the standards of the community from which the jurors are drawn will be used in this case. Therefore, the relevant community for both the video tape charges and the digital video clip charges will be those areas within the jurisdiction of the Pittsburgh Division of the United States District Court for the Western District of Pennsylvania.

NOTES AND QUESTIONS

1. Under the law as articulated in *Extreme Associates*, courts must continue to apply the traditional obscenity test from *Miller v. California* to cases involving Internet obscenity. If the defendants are convicted, they can then argue on appeal there was insufficient evidence to support the verdict under the *Miller* standard. *See, e.g.,* Varkonyi v. State, 276 S.W.3d 27 (Tex. App. El Paso 2008) (denying such a motion). If such arguments are unsuccessful, they can then ask the Supreme Court to review the conviction and reconsider whether the traditional *Miller* test should apply to the Internet. So far, however, the Supreme Court has not taken up the invitation. Should it?

2. *Venue in obscenity cases.* Given the role of community standards in obscenity law, the venue of the trial has obvious importance. The "venue" of the trial refers to the federal district in which the prosecution is brought. Venue in federal criminal cases is ordinarily governed by 18 U.S.C. § 3237(a):

> Except as otherwise expressly provided by enactment of Congress, any offense against the United States begun in one district and completed in another, or committed in more than one district, may be inquired of and prosecuted in any district in which such offense was begun, continued, or completed.

> Any offense involving the use of the mails, transportation in interstate or foreign commerce, or the importation of an object or person into the United States is a continuing offense and, except as otherwise expressly provided by enactment of Congress, may be inquired of and prosecuted in

any district from, through, or into which such commerce, mail matter, or imported object or person moves.

This rule allows the government to set up an undercover investigation in the district of its choice; have the defendant send potentially obscene materials into that district; and then bring the prosecution in that district. *See e.g.,* United States v. Thomas, 74 F.3d 701, 711–12 (6th Cir. 1996).

Is that a fair approach? Does it depend on whether the defendant knew that the item passed through that district? Imagine a person in New York e-mails a pornographic image to another person in San Francisco, and the e-mail just happens to be routed through a server in Utah. No person in Utah ever sees the image. Does § 3237(a) allow an obscenity prosecution in Utah under the community standards of Utah?

3. *Challenging venue through vindictive prosecution claims.* In United States v. Harb, 2009 WL 499467 (D. Utah 2009), a Department of Justice obscenity task force in Washington, DC, was investigating individuals in Ohio who sold pornographic materials. The task force selected Utah as the site of the undercover location and purchased materials that were then sent to Utah for delivery. The defendants were charged with obscenity offenses in Utah, and they moved to dismiss the indictment on grounds of vindictive prosecution. According to the defendants, the government had picked Utah because Utah is known for its strict community standards: The purpose of the investigation was therefore to deprive the defendants of their First Amendment rights. The district court disagreed:

> Defendants' main argument is that the choice to order the material into this district and to thereafter prosecute this district shows overreaching and a likelihood of vindictiveness simply because Defendants argue that this district has more restrictive community standards. The Court finds that the Defendants do not establish either actual or likely vindictiveness by arguing or establishing that there are more restrictive community standards in this district than the district where they operate their business. There is no requirement that the government be able to show a parity in the community standards between the district from which and the district into which the material moved in order to avoid a presumption of vindictiveness. Otherwise, the provision of § 3237(a) allowing these types of continuing offenses to be prosecuted in any district into which the material allegedly moves would be rendered null. It has been long established that the fact that distributors of allegedly obscene materials may be subjected to varying community standards in the various federal judicial districts into which they transmit the materials does not render a federal statute unconstitutional because of the failure of application of uniform national standards of obscenity. This rule cannot be avoided by imposing a parity of community standards limitation on the prosecution's exercise of its prerogative to seek indictments in districts as permitted by § 3237(a).

Id. at *3–*4.

4. Can obscenity prosecutions change the availability of obscene materials given that obscene materials are available from outside the United States over the Internet? Is the effect of obscenity prosecutions merely to push such

businesses outside the United States? If so, does that justify such prosecutions?

5. *Online obscenity and Internet gambling compared.* In some ways, the regulation of Internet gambling and the regulation of online obscenity raise similar issues. The law has traditionally regulated a transaction that in the past occurred person-to-person, whether by meeting in person, through the mail, or by telephone. Computers and the Internet replace that with a person-to-computer transaction, and the computer need not be in the United States. In some ways, the relevance of the switch in fact patterns is similar. For example, policy arguments for preexisting law rooted in the community impact of the conduct regulated may be less powerful, and policy arguments rooted in the effects of the conduct on the individual in isolation may be strengthened. The law seems harder to enforce, and prosecutions are rare. Given these similarities, do you think the future of the law of Internet gambling and obscenity law will or should be the same? Or do the two present different problems?

6. Can mere words constitute obscenity? Courts have held that the answer is "yes." *See* United States v. Whorley, 550 F.3d 326, 335 (4th Cir. 2008); Kaplan v. California, 413 U.S. 115, 199 (1973) ("Obscenity can, of course, manifest itself in conduct, in the pictorial representation of conduct, or in the written and oral description of conduct. The Court has applied similarly conceived First Amendment standards to moving pictures, to photographs, and to words in books."). Obscenity prosecutions for mere text are very rare, but they have occurred. *See, e.g.,* Paula Reed Ward, *Afraid of Public Trial, Author to Plead Guilty in Online Obscenity Case,* Pittsburgh Post–Gazette, May 17, 2008 (discussing charges and guilty plea of defendant charged with distributing obscene materials for hosting website that collected written stories of sexual abuse of children). Should the First Amendment be interpreted to allow such prosecutions? Is there a constitutional difference between verbal descriptions and pictures?

7. *Minors, pornography, and the Internet.* One significant argument in favor of obscenity laws is that it allows legislatures to shield hard-core pornography from children. In the last decade, Congress has made several efforts to protect children online by enacting criminal laws that go beyond traditional obscenity laws. For example, the Communications Decency Act (CDA), Pub. L. No. 104–104, § 502 (1996), tried to limit the exposure of children to indecent materials online. The Supreme Court invalidated the CDA in Reno v. American Civil Liberties Union, 521 U.S. 844 (1997), on the ground that the law was not narrowly tailored to its compelling state interest of protecting children.

Congress then tried again in the form of the Child Online Protection Act (COPA), Pub. L. No. 105–277, §§ 1401–06 (1998), codified at 47 U.S.C. § 231. COPA is considerably narrower than the CDA, but it has been ruled unconstitutional, as well. *See* American Civil Liberties Union v. Mukasey, 534 F.3d 181 (3d Cir. 2008), *cert. denied,* ___ U.S. ___, 129 S.Ct. 1032 (2009). Do you think Congress should be able to regulate how minors can access non-obscene pornography and other indecent materials via the Internet? Or does attempting to regulate when minors can access pornography inevitably place an impermissible burden on the rights of adults to access non-obscene pornography?

D. CHILD EXPLOITATION CRIMES

Tragically, child exploitation crimes are among the most common types of computer crimes. Such crimes fall into two basic categories. The first consists of offenses involving images of child pornography. These cases involve use of a computer to send, receive, and/or possess images of minors engaged in explicit sexual activity. The second category consists of offenses involving actual or attempted sexual contact with minors by adults. In these cases, the computer's role is facilitating the attempted or actual contact. The materials in this section begin with child pornography crimes and then turn to offenses involving attempted sexual contacts.

1. CHILD PORNOGRAPHY

A) Introduction

Child pornography is a term generally used to describe images of persons under the age of 18 engaged in sexually explicit conduct. Before the 1960s, such images were banned under the obscenity laws. Following *Miller v. California*, however, at least some images of child pornography fell outside the definition of obscenity. In the mid-to-late 1970s, many people believed that the loosening of obscenity standards both in the United States and in Europe had gone too far. They feared that the growing availability of sexualized images of minors facilitated widespread exploitation and abuse. *See generally* Philip Jenkins, Beyond Tolerance: Child Pornography on the Internet, 30–37 (2001); Amy Adler, *The Perverse Law of Child Pornography*, 101 Colum. L. Rev. 209 (2001). Legislatures responded by enacting laws specifically addressing child pornography. By 1982, the federal government and twenty states had enacted child pornography laws, although they varied in scope considerably. *See* New York v. Ferber, 458 U.S. 747, 749 (1982). Today, the federal government and every state has a child pornography law.

Child pornography laws generally address both the creation of child pornography and then its subsequent distribution, receipt, and possession. Punishments for the creation of child pornography are severe. The federal statute that prohibits the creation of child pornography is found at 18 U.S.C. § 2251, and it provides for a mandatory minimum prison term of 15 years in prison for a first offense. If the conduct results in the death of the minor, the death penalty is an available punishment. If the death penalty is not imposed, the statute provides for a mandatory minimum prison term of 30 years. *See* 18 U.S.C. § 2251(e). The materials in this section will not focus on the law governing the creation of child pornography. Instead, it will address the computer-related crimes that occur after the images are created: specifically, the distribution, receipt, and possession of the images.

Although child pornography and obscenity both involve sexual imagery of some kind, the distribution, receipt, and possession of such materials are prohibited for very different reasons. The distribution, receipt, and possession of child pornography is prohibited to protect children from sexual molestation and abuse. As the Supreme Court explained in *Ferber*, prohibiting child pornography can deter its creation. The creation of child pornography often involves sexual abuse, and distribution of the images inflicts a continuing harm on the child victim. Prohibiting the distribution, receipt, and possession of child pornography also can help "dry up the market" for such images, lowering demand for their creation. *See id.* at 757–61. In Osborne v. Ohio, 495 U.S. 103 (1990), the Supreme Court identified two more reasons for banning possession of child pornography images. First, a ban on possession can encourage those who possess such images to destroy them. Second, pedophiles use images of child pornography to show to potential victims to present child sexual activity as normal, a process sometimes referred to as 'grooming.' *See id.* at 111.

B) The Proxy Rationale

Another possible rationale for child pornography offenses—albeit a rationale not used to justify their constitutionality—is the perceived correlation between possession of images and acts of child molestation. This is a difficult argument to evaluate, in large part because little reliable empirical work exists on how strong the correlation may be. *See generally* Julian Sher & Benedict Carey, *Debate on Child Pornography's Link to Molesting*, New York Times, July 19, 2007.

Consider two competing perspectives. On one hand, some people believe that those who collect images of child pornography are likely to engage in actual acts of molestation. They reason that knowing possession of such images signals sexual attraction to children. Given the serious criminal liability that attaches to mere possession of the images, those who collect the images are also likely to attempt actual sexual contact with children. Possession thus indicates future dangerousness. On the other hand, some people look at the problem very differently. They reason that interest in viewing images of child pornography is different from engaging in actual sexual contact. An interest in viewing violent movies is very different from engaging in actual acts of violence, they note, and the same distinction can be made in the context of child pornography.

There have been two notable studies that have tried to measure the link between child pornography possession and acts of molestation. In one study, a group of researchers attempted to identify and analyze all of the arrests for child sex crimes that in any way involved child pornography possession that occurred in the United States in the one-year period starting July 1, 2000. *See* Janis Wolak, David Finkelhor, & Kimberly J. Mitchell, Child Pornography Possessors Arrested in Internet–Related Crimes: Findings from the National Juvenile Online Victimization Study (2005). The researchers identified 1,713 such arrests, and they studied the characteristics of the crimes and of the individuals arrested. The study concluded that within the group of individuals charged with sex crimes that included child pornography, 40% were known to have victimized a child at some point. Another 15% were known to have attempted to do so. *Id.* at 16. Among the cases that began as investigations only into child pornography possession, one in six led to discoveries that resulted in concurrent charges for actual or attempted child molestation. *Id.* at 17.

A second empirical study is an unpublished study by Dr. Andres Hernandez, director of the Sex Offender Treatment Program at the Federal Bureau of Prisons in Butner, North Carolina. *See* Andres E. Hernandez, *Self–Reported Contact Sexual Crimes of Federal Inmates Convicted of Child Pornography Crimes*, presented at the 19th Annual Research and Treatment Conference of the Association for the Treatment of Sexual Abusers (November 2000). This study involved 54 adult males in a voluntary sex offender treatment program at a medium-security federal prison. All of the participants were serving prison time for possessing or distributing child pornography. The sex offender treatment program encouraged participants to divulge their past sexual contacts with children as part of an intensive therapy program. The study then compared the total number of reported sexual contacts with the number of known sexual contacts at the time the defendants were sentenced for child pornography offenses.

Just over 50% of the participants in the study—29 out of 54—had no known sexual contacts with minors at the time of their sentencing. The remaining group, consisting of 25 participants, had been known to have contacted a collective total of 53 victims. Following therapy in the sex offender treatment program, however, the participants self-reported quite different histories. Participants in the program self-reported an average of 26.37 past victims each. Among the 29 participants with no known past sexual contacts with minors, 11 continued to report no past contacts. However, 18 of the 29 who had no known past contacts disclosed past contacts. This group self-reported an average of more than 12 victims each. Altogether, the percentage of participants with known past sexual contacts with minors went from 46% to 80%, and the known number of victims jumped from 53 to 1,371.

Do these studies make a persuasive case for a link between possession of child pornography and actual acts of child molestation? Is the sample size sufficient to make a judgment? Do you think the results of a self-supported study are likely to be accurate? Are inmates who volunteered for treatment likely to be representative?

C) 18 U.S.C. § 2252

The primary federal statute prohibiting child pornography distribution, receipt, and possession appears in 18 U.S.C. § 2252. It was originally enacted as part of the Protection of Children Against Sexual Exploitation Act, Pub. L. No. 95–225 (1978). In its present form, it contains four distinct offenses in §§ 2252(a)(1)–(a)(4). The first, found at § 2252(a)(1), prohibits knowingly transporting or shipping in interstate or foreign commerce a visual depiction of a minor engaging in sexually explicit conduct. The second, § 2252(a)(2), prohibits receiving or distributing such depictions that have been sent in interstate or foreign commerce, or which contain materials which have been transported in interstate commerce, or reproducing such materials for distribution in interstate or foreign commerce.

The third and fourth prohibitions, §§ 2252(a)(3) and (a)(4), deal with possession-related crimes. Section 2252(a)(3) concerns selling or having possession with intent to sell, and § 2252(a)(4) concerns mere possession of such materials. Section 2252(a)(4) also permits defendants to raise an affirmative defense, albeit one that is invoked only rarely. If a defendant possesses only one or two "matters" containing child pornography, they can avoid criminal liability if they "promptly and in good faith, and without retaining or allowing any person, other than a law enforcement agency, to access any visual depiction or copy thereof . . . took reasonable steps to destroy each such visual depiction; or . . . reported the matter to a law enforcement agency and afforded that agency access to each such visual depiction." 18 U.S.C. § 2252(c).

Violations of §§ 2252(a)(1), (a)(2), or (a)(3) trigger a five-year mandatory minimum punishment, and can lead to higher punishments as well. *See* 18 U.S.C. § 2252(b)(1). Violations of § 2252(a)(4), the possession provision, do not trigger a mandatory minimum sentence, but permit a maximum punishment of up to ten years. *See* 18 U.S.C. § 2252(b)(2). In both cases, prior convictions will trigger higher punishments.

D) 18 U.S.C. § 2252A and 18 U.S.C. § 2256

Congress passed the Child Pornography Prevention Act, Pub. L. No. 104–208 (1996), in response to concerns that computer technologies were rendering existing child pornography laws out of date. Specifically, Congress was concerned that pedophiles could use computer software to create computer-generated child pornography, either by "morphing" a digital image of a real child's face to a computer-generated image of a child's body or by generating a life-like image entirely by computer. The CPPA was designed to expand the then-existing child pornography laws to encompass these new forms of child pornography.

Instead of amending 18 U.S.C. § 2252, Congress opted to create a new child pornography statute, 18 U.S.C. § 2252A and 18 U.S.C. § 2256. The decision to draft a new statute rather than amend the existing one was based largely on concerns that the new statute might be struck down in whole or in part under the First Amendment. If a court struck down the new statute and found that it was not severable from the preexisting language, the court's decision would leave no law on the books until Congress could act again. By creating a new statute, Congress preserved § 2252 and created new ground in 18 U.S.C. § 2252A and § 2256.

The text of 18 U.S.C. § 2252A is a modernized and expanded version of § 2252, with definitions of key terms appearing in 18 U.S.C. § 2256.

Sections 2252A(a)(1), (a)(2), and (a)(3)(A) largely recreate the prohibitions in § 2252(a)(1) and (2). Sections 2252A(a)(4) and (a)(5) largely mirror § 2252(a)(3) and (a)(4); Section 2252A(d) mirrors the affirmative defense of § 2252(c). Sections 2252A(a)(3)(B) and 2252A(a)(6) are expansions beyond the traditional scope of child pornography laws; the former is addressed at advertising and soliciting images, and the latter at luring minors. Section 2256 provides definitions for key terms used in 2252A, most notably a definition of child pornography that goes beyond images of actual children to include morphed images of child pornography and virtual images of child pornography that are indistinguishable from real images. 18 U.S.C. § 2256(8) (2003).

E) Statutory Elements of 18 U.S.C. §§ 2252 and 2252A

When § 2252 was first enacted in 1978, materials containing images of child pornography typically appeared as physical books, magazines, and photographs. Existing law still reflects that assumption in some ways. The law prohibits conduct such as transporting, shipping, receiving, and possessing images, all conduct that is readily understood in the context of physical items. But what does it mean to "distribute" or "possess" data?

UNITED STATES v. SHAFFER

United States Court of Appeals for the Tenth Circuit, 2007.
472 F.3d 1219.

GORSUCH, CIRCUIT JUDGE.

Aaron Shaffer challenges his conviction for distribution and possession of child pornography. Mr. Shaffer claims that he did not, as a matter of law or fact, "distribute" child pornography when he downloaded images and videos from a peer-to-peer computer network and stored them in a shared folder on his computer accessible by other users of the network.

I.

Kazaa is a peer-to-peer computer application that allows users to trade computer files through the Internet. It is hardly a unique service; at any one time today, there are apparently in excess of four to five million people online sharing over 100 million files.

Users begin at Kazaa's website. There, they obtain the software necessary for file trading by clicking an installation "wizard" that walks them through a step-by-step setup process. Before installation, the wizard requires users to acknowledge and accede to Kazaa's licensing agreement. Users then identify a destination on their computers where they want the Kazaa file sharing software located, and Kazaa creates a "shortcut" icon on the user's desktop.

Upon installation, Kazaa's software walks users through certain steps to create a folder called "My Shared Folder" (hereinafter, "shared folder") on their computer's hard drive. Here, Kazaa users store the files they download from the shared folders of other Kazaa users. At the same time, anything one has in one's own Kazaa shared folder may be accessed and downloaded by other Kazaa users. Kazaa's software also shows the user in real time exactly how many of his or her files are being accessed and copied by other Kazaa users. A user can, however, select an option that precludes other users from downloading materials from his or her computer.

To download an item from another computer's shared folder, a Kazaa user simply double clicks on that file, and it is then transferred to the shared folder on the recipient user's computer. There are only two ways for items to be placed in a user's shared folder. First, one must go online, search for an item, and download the material into the shared folder. Second, one may take files already existing on his or her computer and move them into the shared folder. Either way, the placement of items in one's shared folder involves a conscious effort. A user can of course move items out of the shared folder to other folders on his or her computer, and doing so precludes other Kazaa users from accessing and downloading such material.

This case arose when Ken Rochford, an Arizona-based special agent from the United States Department of Homeland Security's Bureau of Immigration and Customs Enforcement ("ICE"), noticed that a certain Kazaa account user with the screen name shaf@Kazaa had in his shared folder accessible to other Kazaa users a large number of files containing images and videos of child pornography. Special Agent Rochford sought to download some of those images from shaf@Kazaa' s computer onto his own and had no difficulty doing so.

Authorities later learned that the user associated with shaf@Kazaa was Mr. Shaffer, then a 27–year-old college student living with his mother and stepfather in Topeka, Kansas. David Zimmer, a Kansas-based ICE special agent, obtained and executed a search warrant on Mr. Shaffer's residence and computer. ICE special agents ultimately found within Mr. Shaffer's Kazaa shared folder approximately 19 image files and 25 videos containing child pornography, along with text documents describing stories of adults engaging in sex with children.

During the course of the search of his home and computer, Mr. Shaffer consented to an interview with Special Agent Zimmer. During that interview, according to Special Agent Zimmer's testimony at trial, Mr. Shaffer admitted to being the sole user of the computer in his home; employing the screen name shaf@Kazaa; and knowingly downloading through Kazaa 100 movies and 20 still photos involving child pornography, which he estimated occupied a total of approximately 10 gigabytes.

Mr. Shaffer further admitted that he stored images of child pornography in his Kazaa shared folder. He explained that he did so because, among other things, Kazaa gave him "user points" and various incentive rewards corresponding to how many images other users downloaded from his computer. Mr. Shaffer indicated he knew that other people had downloaded child pornography from him. And he stated that it takes up to

100 hours to download certain files using Kazaa, so sometimes when he went to work he would leave his computer on in order to make his images and videos available for download by other users.

Mr. Shaffer also testified at trial. He did not dispute that he gave an interview to Special Agent Zimmer or much of Special Agent Zimmer's description of that interview. Mr. Shaffer did testify, however, that he could not recall telling Special Agent Zimmer that he knew other Kazaa users had downloaded child pornography from his computer. After a four-day trial, a jury returned guilty verdicts against Mr. Shaffer for both possession and distribution of child pornography. The District Court subsequently sentenced him to 60 months of incarceration.

II.

Mr. Shaffer contends there was insufficient evidence presented at trial to sustain his conviction for distribution of child pornography. Under Section 2252A(a)(2), it is unlawful for a person knowingly to distribute child pornography by any means, including by computer.[6] Mr. Shaffer frankly concedes that he allowed, or caused, distribution by leaving files on his computer that other Kazaa users could access. He also now concedes that a rational jury could infer that he did so knowingly (and even intentionally): [His brief acknowledges that] "a reasonable jury could conclude from this evidence that Mr. Shaffer intended to allow others to take the material from his computer."

But, Mr. Shaffer argues, to "distribute" something, a person must actively transfer possession to another, such as by mail, e-mail, or handing it to another person. And here, Mr. Shaffer contends, he was only a passive participant in the process; there is no evidence that he personally completed any such transaction.

The relevant statute does not itself define the term "distribute," so we look to how the term is understood as a matter of plain meaning. Black's offers this definition: "1. To apportion; to divide among several. 2. To arrange by class or order. 3. To deliver. 4. To spread out; to disperse." Black's Law Dictionary 508 (8th ed. 2005). Webster's adds this understanding: "to divide among several or many ... deal out ... apportion esp. to members of a group or over a period of time ... allot ... dispense ... to give out or deliver." Webster's Third New Int'l Dictionary Unabridged 660 (2002). The instruction offered by the District Court to the jury captured much the same sentiment: "To distribute something simply means to deliver or transfer possession of it to someone else."

We have little difficulty in concluding that Mr. Shaffer distributed child pornography in the sense of having delivered, transferred, dispersed, or dispensed it to others. He may not have actively pushed pornography on Kazaa users, but he freely allowed them access to his computerized

---

6. Though it could have done so, the government did not charge Mr. Shaffer with the knowing *receipt* of child pornography under this statutory provision.

stash of images and videos and openly invited them to take, or download, those items.

It is something akin to the owner of a self-serve gas station. The owner may not be present at the station, and there may be no attendant present at all. And neither the owner nor his or her agents may ever pump gas. But the owner has a roadside sign letting all passersby know that, if they choose, they can stop and fill their cars for themselves, paying at the pump by credit card. Just because the operation is self-serve, or in Mr. Shaffer's parlance, passive, we do not doubt for a moment that the gas station owner is in the business of distributing, delivering, transferring or dispersing gasoline; the *raison d'etre* of owning a gas station is to do just that. So, too, a reasonable jury could find that Mr. Shaffer welcomed people to his computer and was quite happy to let them take child pornography from it.

Indeed, Mr. Shaffer admitted that he had downloaded child pornography from other users' Kazaa shared folders and understood that file sharing was the very purpose of Kazaa. He admitted that he had child pornography stored in his computer's Kazaa shared folder. Mr. Shaffer could have, but did not, save the illicit images and videos in a computer folder not susceptible to file sharing. Likewise, he could have, but did not, activate the feature on Kazaa that would have precluded others from taking materials from his shared folder. Quite the opposite. According to Special Agent Zimmer, Mr. Shaffer acknowledged that he *knew* other people had downloaded child pornography from his shared folder. Mr. Shaffer cannot recall making this particular admission, but we are obliged to view the facts in the light most favorable to the government, and the jury was free to credit Special Agent Zimmer's testimony and discredit Mr. Shaffer's.

The District Court's judgment is affirmed.

NOTES AND QUESTIONS

1. Imagine Shaffer had placed the files on his computer intending that other Kazaa users could access them, but that no users had actually done so. Is Shaffer still liable?

2. The punishment for knowingly distributing images of child pornography is the same as the punishment for knowingly receiving those images. If *A* possesses an image of child pornography, *B* asks for it, and *A* gives the image to *B*, then *A* and *B* are punished equally by the same statute. Does that make sense as a matter of policy? Does your answer depend on whether the image is a physical photograph or an electronic file? Note that if the image is a physical photograph, *A* can only distribute the image once. After *A* has given the image to *B*, *A* will no longer have a copy to distribute. In contrast, if the image is a computer file, *A* can distribute the image many times. Should that make a difference? Does your answer depend on whether distributing a single image multiple times is treated by the law as a single crime of distributing many images or as many distinct crimes of distributing a single image?

3. *The receipt/possession distinction.* The receipt of child pornography is almost always accompanied by its possession. However, the penalties for receipt under § 2252(a)(2) are considerably more severe than the punishment for possession under § 2252(a)(4). If the conduct usually is the same, why did Congress impose two different levels of punishment?

In United States v. Richardson, 238 F.3d 837 (7th Cir. 2001), Judge Posner speculated about one possible reason:

> The explanation may be that receivers increase the market for child pornography and hence the demand for children to pose as models for pornographic photographs; possessors, at least qua possessors, as distinct from receivers, though most of them are that too, do not. The possessor who creates his own pornography strictly for his personal use is not part of the interstate and international traffic in child pornography, a traffic that not only increases the demand for the production of such pornography but, by virtue of its far-flung scope, makes it extremely difficult to locate, let alone protect, the children exploited by it. Concern with the welfare of the children who are used to create pornography is part of the public concern over child pornography, and this makes the receiver a greater malefactor than the possessor.

Id. at 839.

The role of prosecutorial discretion may offer a more persuasive explanation. The statutory definition of child pornography arguably is quite broad, and it encompasses a number of different kinds of cases. The statutory overlap between receipt and possession crimes permits prosecutors to charge more severe cases differently than less severe cases. A prosecutor can inquire as to the nature of the images in the case and can choose whether to charge the defendant with the lesser offense of possession or the greater offense of receipt. The receipt/possession distinction may also give prosecutors an extra tool to pressure defendants to plead guilty. If the government's case is weak, a prosecutor may offer the defendant a choice between pleading guilty to possession or going to trial on more severe receipt charges.

Do any of these explanations justify the different treatment of receipt and possession?

4. Is the existing definition of child pornography too broad? Consider State v. Senters, 699 N.W.2d 810 (Neb. 2005). The defendant was a 28 year-old high school teacher who had a consensual sexual relationship with a 17 year-old student. The two decided to videotape themselves having intercourse, and the defendant kept the videotape in his apartment. The defendant's roommate later discovered the videotape and contacted the high school where he taught. Representatives of the school then contacted the police. The age of consent in Nebraska is sixteen, which meant that statutory rape charges could not be brought. Instead, state prosecutors charged the defendant with manufacturing child pornography. He was convicted and sentenced to two years of probation. The Nebraska Supreme Court affirmed the conviction, rejecting the defendant's claim that prosecuting him violated the Due Process and Equal Protection clauses. *See id.* at 817–18.

5. In United States v. X–Citement Video, Inc., 513 U.S. 64 (1994), the Supreme Court considered the mens rea that applies to the statutory element of the age of the person visually depicted contained in 18 U.S.C. §§ 2252(a)(1) and (a)(2). In an opinion by Chief Justice Rehnquist, the Court held that the "knowing" mens rea applied to the person's age. It is not enough that a defendant transported or received images that happen to contain child pornography; rather, the government must prove the defendant's knowledge that the person depicted in the image was under the age of eighteen. The Court justified this holding on a number of factors, including the odd results that would follow from a contrary approach:

> If the term "knowingly" applies only to the relevant verbs in § 2252— transporting, shipping, receiving, distributing and reproducing—we would have to conclude that Congress wished to distinguish between someone who knowingly transported a particular package of film whose contents were unknown to him, and someone who unknowingly transported that package. It would seem odd, to say the least, that Congress distinguished between someone who inadvertently dropped an item into the mail without realizing it, and someone who consciously placed the same item in the mail, but was nonetheless unconcerned about whether the person had any knowledge of the prohibited contents of the package.

> Some applications of respondents' position would produce results that were not merely odd, but positively absurd. If we were to conclude that "knowingly" only modifies the relevant verbs in § 2252, we would sweep within the ambit of the statute actors who had no idea that they were even dealing with sexually explicit material. For instance, a retail druggist who returns an uninspected roll of developed film to a customer "knowingly distributes" a visual depiction and would be criminally liable if it were later discovered that the visual depiction contained images of children engaged in sexually explicit conduct. Or, a new resident of an apartment might receive mail for the prior resident and store the mail unopened. If the prior tenant had requested delivery of materials covered by § 2252, his residential successor could be prosecuted for "knowing receipt" of such materials. Similarly, a Federal Express courier who delivers a box in which the shipper has declared the contents to be "film" "knowingly transports" such film. We do not assume that Congress, in passing laws, intended such results.

Id. at 69.

6. According to a comprehensive study of the child pornography under-world, images of child pornography generally are distributed in ways that are different from ways of distributing obscenity. *See* Philip Jenkins, Beyond Tolerance (2001). Professor Jenkins explains that individuals interested in obtaining child pornography often mask their identity using proxy servers and anonymous accounts with foreign computers. The images themselves generally are not posted on public websites with fixed addresses. Such sites are discovered quickly, and the system administrators then contact law enforcement.

According to Professor Jenkins, individuals use bulletin board services, e-groups, and other relatively anonymous services to distribute information and materials. For example, an individual wanting to share images might open a free account with a website that permits users to post files anonymously, and then will upload encrypted images of child pornography from his collection. He will then post a message on one of several international bulletin boards informing readers that the images are posted to that site. In the hours before the site system administrator realizes that the site is hosting child pornography and shuts it down, hundreds of anonymous users will download the encrypted files. The individual then will send another message to the bulletin board posting the key to decrypt the files, permitting them to be viewed. For a more detailed account, see Jenkins, Ch. 3.

BARTON v. STATE

Court of Appeals of Georgia, 2007.
648 S.E.2d 660.

MILLER, JUDGE.

On appeal from the trial court's denial of his motion for a new trial, Barton asserts that the State failed to prove his knowing possession of child pornography. Finding that the State failed to prove knowing possession of child pornography, as charged in the indictment, we reverse.

The evidence shows that, after the Walker County Sheriff's Department began investigating allegations of child molestation against Barton, his wife provided authorities with Barton's laptop computer. Upon conducting a forensic examination of that computer, law enforcement retrieved 156 images they believed met the definition of child pornography stored on the computer's hard drive. Barton was indicted for sexual exploitation of children with respect to 106 of those images. Specifically, Barton was charged with "knowingly possessing" child pornography in violation of OCGA § 16–12–100(b)(8), which makes it unlawful "for any person knowingly to possess or control any material which depicts a minor or a portion of a minor's body engaged in any sexually explicit conduct."

At trial, the State sought to prove Barton's knowing possession of child pornography via the testimony of Special Agent Ben Murray of the United States Secret Service, a forensic computer analyst. Murray testified that all computers will store pictures or other information viewed over the internet on the computer's hard drive, in temporary internet file folders. There is nothing that such a user can do to prevent the computer from storing such items. Murray also explained that not everything stored in a computer's temporary internet file folders results from the affirmative conduct of a computer user. Rather, even those images which "pop-up" on a computer screen, even though neither sought nor desired by the computer user, are stored on the computer's hard drive. Furthermore, despite the fact that they are stored on the hard drive, Murray testified that no one using the computer can retrieve information stored in the temporary internet file folders without special forensic software. No such software was present on Barton's computer.

Murray testified that each of the pornographic images on Barton's computer was stored on the hard drive of his computer, in temporary internet file folders. This meant that Barton had viewed the pictures over the internet, but had taken no affirmative action to save them on his computer. Barton could not access or alter the pictures found stored on his computer's hard drive. Murray further testified that Barton had viewed all of the images within two separate time periods, totaling slightly less than four hours, on December 2 and 3, 2003. He offered no testimony as to whether the images resulted from some affirmative action by Barton, represented "pop-ups" which appeared on Barton's computer, or both. Although Murray could not tell how long Barton had spent viewing each individual image, or how long he had kept those images open on his computer, he could say that Barton had never opened any image more than once.

Barton argues that this testimony was insufficient to establish his knowing possession of child pornography because: (1) he took no affirmative action to store the images on his computer; (2) he was unaware that the computer had automatically saved those images to the hard drive; and (3) he had no ability to retrieve or access those images. Reluctantly, we must agree.

In beginning our analysis, we emphasize that the question before us is not whether the viewing of child pornography over the Internet represents the same evil sought to be eradicated by the statute prohibiting the possession of child pornography. Nor is the issue whether the legislature has the power to punish the accessing or viewing of pornographic materials over the Internet. Rather, the question is whether that conduct is punishable as "knowing possession" of child pornography, as charged in the indictment—i.e., does the mere accessing and viewing of pornographic materials over the internet, which results in those materials being stored on a computer's hard drive, constitute the knowing possession of those materials?

While this question is one of first impression in Georgia, it has been addressed by a number of state and federal courts. Each of those courts has found that possession in this context can result only where the defendant exercises "dominion and control" over the child pornography. *See United States v. Kuchinski,* 469 F.3d 853, 863 (9th Cir. 2006); *United States v. Romm,* 455 F.3d 990, 998 (9th Cir. 2006); *United States v. Bass,* 411 F.3d 1198, 1201–1202 (10th Cir. 2005); *United States v. Tucker,* 305 F.3d 1193, 1204 (10th Cir. 2002).

These decisions differ as to whether possession requires that a defendant take some affirmative action to download or save internet images onto his computer. None of those decisions, however, found that a defendant may be convicted of possessing child pornography stored in his computer's temporary internet file folders, also known as cache files,[4] absent some evidence that the defendant was aware those files existed. Several of those courts specifically found that there can be no possession where the defendant is unaware that the images have been saved in the cache files, reasoning that such ignorance precludes a finding that the defendant could exercise dominion or control over those images. As one federal court has explained: "Where a defendant lacks knowledge about the cache file, and concomitantly lacks access to and control over those files, it is not proper to charge him with possession of the child pornography images located in those files, without some other indication of dominion and control over the images." *Kuchinski,* supra, 469 F.3d at 863.

Georgia law requires that we reach a similar conclusion. Under Georgia law, a person who knowingly has direct physical control over a thing at a given time is in actual possession of it. A person who, though not in actual possession, knowingly has both the power and the intention at a given time to exercise dominion or control over a thing is then in constructive possession of it. In any criminal prosecution for possession, therefore, the State must prove that the defendant was *aware* he possessed the contraband at issue. Thus, in this case, the State was required to show that Barton had knowledge of the images stored in his computer's cache files.

Here, the State's brief fails to address the issue of Barton's knowledge, and we find that at trial the State failed to meet its burden on this issue. The sole witness on this issue—Agent Murray—testified that Barton took no affirmative action to save these images to his computer, a conclusion supported by the fact that all of the pictures were stored on the cache drive as "thumbnails." Murray offered no testimony indicating that Barton was aware that the computer was storing these images, but instead established only that these files were stored automatically, without Barton having to do anything. Murray also testified that Barton would have been unable to view or access these images without using software that was not present on Barton's computer. Thus, there was no way that Barton could have learned of the cache files in the normal course of using his computer. Nor did the State present any circumstantial evidence that would have allowed the jury to infer Barton's knowledge of these files-i.e., they did not show that Barton was an experienced or sophisticated computer user who would have been aware of this automatic storage process. In short, the State presented *no* evidence that Barton was aware of the existence of the files at issue, and in doing so, they failed to prove that Barton knowingly possessed these images.

For the reasons set forth above, we find that the mere existence of pornographic images in the cache files of an individual's computer is insufficient to constitute knowing possession of those materials absent proof that the individual either: (1) took some affirmative action to save or

---

4. Temporary internet files are stored in the cache, "a storage mechanism designed to speed up the loading of internet displays." 19 Berkeley Tech L.J. 1227, 1229 (Fall 2004). The courts deciding the cases cited above, therefore, refer to the temporary internet files as the cache files.

download those images to his computer; or (2) had knowledge that the computer automatically saved those files. We are therefore compelled to conclude that the evidence was insufficient to sustain Barton's conviction for knowing possession of child pornography under OCGA § 16–12–100(b)(8), and we reverse the same.

NOTES AND QUESTIONS

1. Although *Barton* is a state case, the state statute at issue resembles the federal child pornography possession statute. Does it make sense that liability for possession should hinge on whether the individual understands how computers work? Does computer expertise make the conduct more culpable, or more deserving of greater punishment?

2. Is the issue in *Barton* whether Barton possessed the images stored in the cache? Or is the issue whether the stored images in the cache provide sufficient evidence of prior possession based on the initial downloading that would be sufficient to uphold the jury verdict?

3. In Commonwealth v. Simone, 2003 WL 22994245 (Va. Cir. Ct. 2003), the defendant used an Internet search engine to locate and view images of child pornography. The search terms he used included "lolitas," "pre-teens," and "pedophelia." Three images of child pornography were found in the cache of viewed images on his computer. However, there was no evidence that the defendant realized that the images he viewed had been saved to the cache. The court nonetheless found that there was sufficient evidence that the defendant had possessed the images. According to the court, the test for whether a defendant possessed contraband computer data should be whether he "reached out and controlled the images at issue." The court reasoned that this test best captured how the concept of possession applies in the physical world:

> If a person walks down the street and notices an item (such as child pornography or an illegal narcotic) whose possession is prohibited, has that person committed a criminal offense if they look at the item for a sufficient amount of time to know what it is and then walks away? The obvious answer seems to be "no." However, if the person looks at the item long enough to know what it is, then reaches out and picks it up, holding and viewing it and taking it with them to their home, that person has moved from merely viewing the item to knowingly possessing the item by reaching out for it and controlling it.

Id. at *7. Do you agree? Is searching for and viewing child pornography "in essence" the same as taking it home, or is it more like walking down the street, searching for contraband, and then looking at it when you find it? Does the court's approach redraft a statute that punishes knowingly possessing child pornography so that it prohibits intentionally viewing child pornography?

4. In United States v. Romm, 455 F.3d 990 (9th Cir. 2006), the defendant used an Internet connection from a hotel room in Las Vegas to search for images of child pornography. Romm later told federal agents that when he visited a site that contained such images, he would "save" the pictures for a

few minutes and then "delete" them. A subsequent search of Romm's computer revealed 42 images of child pornography stored in the browser cache. However, government investigators did not find images outside the browser cache. A government expert witness testified at trial that it was possible for a user to access the cache and control the images stored there. However, no evidence was presented that Romm knew how to access the cache.

On appeal, the Ninth Circuit rejected Romm's claim that that there was insufficient evidence he had knowingly possessed the images. The court stated that "to possess the images in the cache, the defendant must, at a minimum, know that the unlawful images are stored on a disk or other tangible material in his possession." *Id*. at 1000. The court concluded that Romm's conduct established sufficient control over the images:

> Romm exercised control over the cached images while they were contemporaneously saved to his cache and displayed on his screen. At that moment, as the expert testimony here established, Romm could print the images, enlarge them, copy them, or email them to others. No doubt, images could be saved to the cache when a defendant accidentally views the images, as through the occurrence of a "pop-up," for instance. But that is not the case here.

> By his own admission to [federal agents], Romm repeatedly sought out child pornography over the internet. When he found images he "liked," he would "view them, save them to his computer, look at them for about five minutes and then delete them." * * * He described his activities as the "saving" and "downloading" of the images. While the images were displayed on screen and simultaneously stored to his cache, Romm could print them, email them, or save them as copies elsewhere. Romm could destroy the copy of the images that his browser stored to his cache. And according to [the government's expert witness], Romm did just that, either manually, or by instructing his browser to do so. Forensic evidence showed that Romm had enlarged several thumbnail images for better viewing. In short, given the indicia that Romm exercised control over the images in his cache, there was sufficient evidence for the jury to find that Romm committed the act of knowing possession.

> * * * [A]s the record here indicates, Romm had access to, and control over, the images that were displayed on his screen and saved to his cache. He could copy the images, print them or email them to others, and did, in fact, enlarge several of the images. This control clearly differentiates Romm's conduct from that of a visitor to the Louvre who gazes on the Mona Lisa, even if we put aside the stringent museum rules against photographing or copying without museum permission.

> In short, * * * given Romm's ability to control the images while they were displayed on screen, and the forensic and other evidence that he actually exercised this control over them, there was sufficient evidence to support the jury's finding that Romm possessed three or more images of child pornography. Coupled with Romm's conceded knowledge that the images were saved to his disk, the prosecution produced sufficient evi-

dence to establish every element of knowingly possessing child pornography under 18 U.S.C. § 2252A.

Id. at 1000–01. Is this analysis persuasive? Does it depend on what Romm meant when he told the federal agents that he "saved" the images and later "deleted" them? Or does it depend on whether Romm knew how to access the browser cache?

5. *The difference between knowing possession and knowing receipt.* Imagine a computer user is searching for child pornography, and he views some images of child pornography that are then stored, without his knowledge, in his computer's browser cache. If the individual does not know how computers work, and he is unaware the images are stored on his computer, he may not be guilty of knowing possession. But is he guilty of knowing receipt of the images?

This issue arose in State v. Jensen, 173 P.3d 1046 (Ariz. App. 2008). Jensen went online and searched for child pornography, and he then viewed the images online. He was charged with sexual exploitation of a minor in violation of Arizona law, A.R.S. § 13–3553(A)(2), which prohibits knowingly receiving or knowingly possessing images of child pornography. On appeal, Jensen argued that based on his lack of knowledge of how computers work, he did not "possess" the images that he had viewed. The court concluded that whether he had possessed the images was irrelevant, because there was sufficient evidence that he had knowingly received them:

> Whether the computer automatically downloaded the images without Jensen's knowledge is irrelevant to whether Jensen knowingly "received" the images. A.R.S. § 13–3553(A)(2) criminalizes not only knowing possession, but also knowing receipt of images of child pornography.

> There is no question Jensen knowingly received such images because he actively searched for those types of images on the computer over an extended period of time, resulting in nearly 25,000 hits for websites containing certain key phrases and combinations of words often associated with child pornography and exploitation of minors.

> Jensen's knowledge of receipt of illegal pornography is implicit in his intentional searches for child pornography. Contrary to Jensen's contention, the act of intentionally searching for and accessing a website for child pornography is not the equivalent of merely looking at a picture in a museum. Detective Core explained that in accessing a website, the computer loads a copy of the digital information available at the website into the computer's random access memory or RAM. In other words, the operator actually obtains a copy of whatever is viewed on the monitor, in this case the three images of child pornography, by the act of accessing the website. The fact that the images were contemporaneously saved automatically on the hard drive without further action by the operator is irrelevant because it does not diminish the nature and fact of the receipt of the images.

Id. at 1051–52.

In *Jensen*, the defendant argued that searching for and viewing images of child pornography was like going to a museum and looking at pictures. The court rejected the analogy on the ground that it does not accurately describe how computers work. But what if a person genuinely believes that this is how computers work? Imagine that a person goes online, searches for child pornography, and then views it, but he believes that the computer is a magic box that brings him to the images rather than the images to him. Is he guilty of knowing receipt?

6. *Liability for accidental receipt and possession.* Imagine a computer user surfs the web and innocently clicks on a link that happens to bring up an image of child pornography. Clicking on the link causes the image of child pornography to travel across the network and store itself automatically in the user's browser cache. Is the user criminally liable, either for receipt or possession?

Consider the Seventh Circuit's answer in United States v. Watzman, 486 F.3d 1004, 1019 (7th Cir. 2007):

> To be convicted of receiving, the defendant must have known the materi-al he was receiving depicted minors engaged in sexually explicit conduct. Accordingly, a person who receives child pornography by accident (for example, if he sought adult pornography but was sent child pornography instead) is not guilty of knowingly receiving it, though he is guilty of possessing it if he retains it.

To understand why a person could be guilty of possession if he retains it, think about the meaning of possession. A person knowingly possesses contra-band when he has knowledge and control over the contraband, regardless of whether he initially wanted to have that control when he first came into possession of the substance. For example, imagine *A* hands *B* a jar of leafy substance with the label "oregano." *B* believes the leafy substance is oregano. When he gets home, however, he opens the jar and realizes that the substance is marijuana. Under traditional principles of criminal law, *B* will be guilty of knowing possession as soon as he realizes that the substance is marijuana but does not take immediate steps to dispossess himself of the marijuana. Trans-ferring that concept to digital images, a defendant has knowing possession of an accidentally downloaded image of child pornography when he realizes that the image contains child pornography and is stored in his computer but does not take immediate steps to dispossess himself of the image.

This dynamic may help explain why the safety valve clauses of 18 U.S.C. § 2252(c) and 18 U.S.C. § 2252A(d) are limited to possession and do not cover distribution or receipt. A person who accidentally comes into possession of child pornography cannot be guilty of knowingly transporting or receiving child pornography, but he may be guilty of knowing possession. The affirma-tive defenses in § 2252(c) and § 2252A(d) are quite narrow, however. First, they only apply if a defendant possesses one or two "matters" containing child pornography, which presumably means one or two images. Second, the defendant must "promptly and in good faith, and without retaining or allowing any person, other than a law enforcement agency, to access any visual depiction or copy thereof," either take "reasonable steps to destroy each such visual depiction" or "report[] the matter to a law enforcement agency and afford[] that agency access to each such visual depiction."

7. For a useful discussion of how a person could unintentionally obtain a contraband digital image, see Matthew James Zappen, Comment, *How Well Do You Know Your Computer? The Level of Scienter in 18 U.S.C. § 1462*, 66 Alb. L. Rev. 1161, 1165–76 (2003). For more on the legal issues raised by prosecutions for possessing child pornography based on evidence found in the browser cache, see Ty E. Howard, *Don't Cache Out Your Case: Prosecuting Child Pornography Possession Laws Based on Images Located in Temporary Internet Files*, 19 Berkeley Tech. L.J. 1227 (2004).

8. Does copying a computer file containing images of child pornography constitute a separate crime beyond possession? Should it?

In People v. Hill, 715 N.W.2d 301 (Mich. Ct. App. 2006), a defendant downloaded images of child pornography from the Internet and then saved the images on a CD. Michigan law prohibits making, possessing, and distributing child pornography, but does not prohibit receiving it. The government charged the defendant with making child pornography (a 20–year felony) instead of merely possessing child pornography (a 4–year felony) on the theory that copying the digital images onto the CD literally "made" child pornography. The defendant argued that "making" child pornography referred only to recording actual acts of child molestation, not copying digital files. A Michigan intermediate appellate court agreed with the government:

> The CD–Rs, as compiled by defendant, were defendant's own creations; he made child-pornography CD–Rs. The term "make" is defined as follows: "to bring into existence by shaping, changing, or combining material." Random House Webster's College Dictionary (2001). Defendant acquired child sexually abusive material via the Internet, and he shaped, formed, and combined the material through placement of various selected pictures, videos, and images onto specific CD–Rs, bringing into existence something that had not previously existed, i.e., distinctly created and compiled child-pornography CD–Rs.

> Given the intricacies of computer and Internet technology, we think it helpful to present an analogy, viewing a simpler scenario in which an individual obtains a magazine containing photographs of children engaging in sexual acts from another person or source. Receipt and retention of the magazine would merely reflect evidence of possession, which would give rise to a four-year felony under MCL 750.145c(4). In this scenario, the amount of child pornography in our society is not increased by the act of transferring the magazine to another and the purchaser's mere possession of the magazine. If, however, the person in possession of the magazine makes copies and reproductions of the pornographic material, he has increased the amount of existing child pornography, or stated differently, he has engaged in acts leading to the proliferation of child pornography in our society. Under such circumstances, he would be guilty of a 20–year felony under the plain language of MCL 750.145c(2) as discussed above. This is essentially what occurred here, except it was accomplished through the use of a computer and CD–Rs.

Id. at 309–10. The Supreme Court of Michigan declined to review the decision over the dissent of Justice Markman, who argued that that the common meaning of the word "make" pointed in a different direction:

Does a person who downloads a pirated movie "make" such a movie and would the person be subject to the same penalty as the person who originally pirated the movie? Does a person who downloads a pirated song "make" such a song and would the person be subject to the same penalty as the person who originally made available the song? Does a person who downloads a defamatory article from the Internet "make" such an article and would the person be subject to the same penalty as the original publisher of the defamation?

People v. Hill, 722 N.W.2d 665, 666 (Mich. 2006) (Markman, J., dissenting).

Under the approach of the appeals court in *Hill*, doesn't every effort to possess child pornography also involve "making" child pornography? Or is there a legal difference between a browser's making a temporary copy as a step toward permitting the user to view a file and a user's making a permanent copy by burning a CD? As a policy matter, should burning a CD of child pornography be a distinct crime beyond mere possession? Or does the prohibition against distributing images address this concern?

9. *Law enforcement possession of contraband.* The child pornography statutes do not have an explicit exception for law enforcement receipt, distribution, and possession of contraband images in the course of a criminal investigation. This presents a potential problem. If a government investigator or prosecutor must seize child pornography and must possess it in the course of a criminal investigation and prosecution, isn't it a crime to investigate or prosecute child pornography? Aren't the police and prosecutors guilty of the same offense as the defendants?

The answer is "no," thanks to an implied exception that courts have traditionally read into criminal statutes: Criminal statutes do not apply to law enforcement acting in the course of their official duties if it would lead to absurd results. This rule is sometimes referred to as the *Nardone* doctrine after its discussion in Nardone v. United States, 302 U.S. 379 (1937).

One of the cases cited in *Nardone*, State v. Gorham, 188 P. 457 (1920), provides an illustration. In *Gorham*, a sheriff on a motorcycle chased after a man who had stolen a car. In order to catch the stolen car, the sheriff had to break the speed limit. Remarkably, however, the sheriff was himself pulled over for speeding by another state police officer. The sheriff was then charged with speeding on the theory that he had been exceeding the speed limit and the statute had no express exclusion for police officers. The Washington Supreme Court overturned the conviction:

That the enforcement of statutory or ordinance provisions limiting the speed at which a motor-propelled vehicle shall be driven over a public highway against a peace officer would have a tendency to hamper him in the performance of his official duties can hardly be doubted. The case in hand affords an illustration. Here the felon was fleeing with a stolen automobile. Naturally he would pay but little regard to the minor offense of exceeding the speed limit. And, if the sheriff must confine himself to that limit, pursuit in the manner adopted would have been useless, since the felon could not have been overtaken. The rule contended for would also hinder the public peace officer in enforcing the statutes regulating traffic upon the state highways. The statutes contain somewhat stringent regulations as to the speed a motor-propelled vehicle may be driven over them, and contain no exception in favor of the peace officers whose duty it is made to enforce them. If these officers may not pursue and overtake one violating the regulations without themselves becoming amenable to the penalties imposed by them, the old remedy of hue and cry is not available in such instances, and many offenders who are now brought to answer will escape.

Under this doctrine, law enforcement can knowingly receive, possess, and distribute child pornography in the course of their official duties investigating and prosecuting such crimes.

10. *Defense counsel possession of contraband and the requirements of the Adam Walsh Act.* Imagine you are a lawyer for a defendant charged in a child pornography case. The government alleges that it has analyzed your client's computer and found hundreds of images of child pornography stored in it. Your client informs you that the child pornography does not belong to him: He thinks his roommate put it there, or perhaps the computer had been compromised and the images were placed there by a hacker. You want to challenge the government's case by obtaining a copy of the computer and having a professional forensic expert analyze the computer and determine who placed the images on the computer.

Should the law allow you to receive a copy of the computer that contains child pornography? Or is that a prohibited act of knowingly receiving child pornography? Should the *Nardone* doctrine apply to defense attorneys? What if a criminal defendant is representing himself? How can an innocent defendant defend himself at trial if he cannot obtain a copy of the computer and hire an expert to analyze it to show the weakness of the government's case?

In 2006, Congress passed the Adam Walsh Child Protection and Safety Act, Pub. L. 109–248, in part to limit defense access to child pornography. One provision of the Act sharply limits defense access to child pornography in the course of pre-trial preparation:

(1) In any criminal proceeding, any property or material that constitutes child pornography (as defined by section 2256 of this title) shall remain in the care, custody, and control of either the Government or the court.

(2)(A) Notwithstanding Rule 16 of the Federal Rules of Criminal Procedure, a court shall deny, in any criminal proceeding, any request by the defendant to copy, photograph, duplicate, or otherwise reproduce any property or material that constitutes child pornography (as defined by section 2256 of this title), so long as the Government makes the property or material reasonably available to the defendant.

(B) For the purposes of subparagraph (A), property or material shall be deemed to be reasonably available to the defendant if the Government provides ample opportunity for inspection, viewing, and examination at a Government facility of the property or material by the defendant, his or her attorney, and any individual the defendant may seek to qualify to furnish expert testimony at trial.

18 U.S.C. § 3509(m).

Is this provision constitutional, or does it violate a defendant's constitutional right to a fair trial? Courts have attempted to resolve the constitutional difficulties by interpreting "ample opportunity" relatively broadly:

> An ample opportunity to forensically examine seized computer items means an examination whereby the government can supply reasonably up-to-date tools (hardware and software) and facilities such that a defendant can construct a reasonable, available forensic defense, if one is available at all, and whereby the analysis will not be impeached because it was not supported by the proper hardware or software. An ample opportunity will permit a defense expert to utilize his or her hardware or software. An ample opportunity also requires that the analysis be performed in a situation where attorney-client privilege and work product will not be easily, accidently exposed to the government, and in a facility which is open to the defense at its request during normal working hours, and to the extent feasible, during non-working hours.

United States v. Flinn, 521 F. Supp.2d 1097 (E.D. Cal. 2007). Courts have concluded that this standard satisfies the constitutional requirement of a fair trial:

> An 'ample opportunity for inspection, viewing, and examination' is akin to the due process requirement that a criminal defendant be afforded fair opportunity to defend against the State's accusations and be free from arbitrary and disproportionate restrictions on his right to confront witnesses and present evidence. The plain meaning of the statutory language thus appears to be consistent with the requirements of due process.

United States v. O'Rourke, 470 F. Supp.2d 1049, 1056 (D.Ariz. 2007).

11. The first section of this Chapter explored how property crimes involving the possession and transportation of stolen property could be applied to economic crimes involving computers. One of the major questions was how the courts could apply concepts such as "transporting" and "possessing" stolen property to cases involving unauthorized uses of data. How do the child pornography laws approach these types of questions? Do the child pornography laws shed light on the use of stolen property laws to punish unauthorized uses of data, or vice versa?

F) Constitutional Issues

Child pornography laws raise a number of important First Amendment issues. The Constitution permits the government to criminalize possession of child pornography. Osborne v. Ohio, 495 U.S. 103 (1990). At the same time, the First Amendment places constitutional limits on the definition of child pornography much like Miller v. California, 413 U.S. 15 (1973), places limits on the definition of obscenity. Those limits were explored in the following case, which considered a constitutional challenge to aspects of the Child Pornography Prevention Act of 1996 that broadly regulated "virtual" child pornography.

ASHCROFT v. FREE SPEECH COALITION

Supreme Court of the United States, 2002.
535 U.S. 234.

JUSTICE KENNEDY delivered the opinion of the Court.

We consider in this case whether the Child Pornography Prevention Act of 1996 (CPPA), 18 U.S.C. § 2251 *et seq.*, abridges the freedom of speech. The CPPA extends the federal prohibition against child pornography to sexually explicit images that appear to depict minors but were produced without using any real children. The statute prohibits, in specific circumstances, possessing or distributing these images, which may be created by using adults who look like minors or by using computer imaging. The new technology, according to Congress, makes it possible to create realistic images of children who do not exist.

By prohibiting child pornography that does not depict an actual child, the statute goes beyond *New York v. Ferber,* 458 U.S. 747 (1982), which distinguished child pornography from other sexually explicit speech because of the State's interest in protecting the children exploited by the production process. As a general rule, pornography can be banned only if obscene, but under *Ferber,* pornography showing minors can be proscribed whether or not the images are obscene under the definition set forth in *Miller v. California,* 413 U.S. 15 (1973). *Ferber* recognized that the *Miller* standard, like all general definitions of what may be banned as obscene, does not reflect the State's particular and more compelling interest in prosecuting those who promote the sexual exploitation of children.

While we have not had occasion to consider the question, we may assume that the apparent age of persons engaged in sexual conduct is relevant to whether a depiction offends community standards. Pictures of young children engaged in certain acts might be obscene where similar depictions of adults, or perhaps even older adolescents, would not. The CPPA, however, is not directed at speech that is obscene; Congress has proscribed those materials through a separate statute. 18 U.S.C. §§ 1460–1466. Like the law in *Ferber,* the CPPA seeks to reach beyond obscenity, and it makes no attempt to conform to the *Miller* standard. For instance, the statute would reach visual depictions, such as movies, even if they have redeeming social value.

The principal question to be resolved, then, is whether the CPPA is constitutional where it proscribes a significant universe of speech that is neither obscene under *Miller* nor child pornography under *Ferber.*

I

Before 1996, Congress defined child pornography as the type of depictions at issue in *Ferber,* images made using actual minors. 18 U.S.C. § 2252 (1994 ed.). The CPPA retains that prohibition at 18 U.S.C. § 2256(8)(A) and adds three other prohibited categories of speech, of which the first, § 2256(8)(B), and the third, § 2256(8)(D), are at issue in this case. Section 2256(8)(B) prohibits "any visual depiction, including any photograph, film, video, picture, or computer or computer-generated image or picture" that "is, or appears to be, of a minor engaging in sexually explicit conduct." The prohibition on "any visual depiction" does not depend at all on how the image is produced. The section captures a range of depictions, sometimes called "virtual child pornography," which include computer-generated images, as well as images produced by more tradition-al means. For instance, the literal terms of the statute embrace a Renais-sance painting depicting a scene from classical mythology, a "picture" that "appears to be, of a minor engaging in sexually explicit conduct." The statute also prohibits Hollywood movies, filmed without any child actors, if a jury believes an actor "appears to be" a minor engaging in "actual or simulated . . . sexual intercourse." § 2256(2).

These images do not involve, let alone harm, any children in the production process; but Congress decided the materials threaten children in other, less direct, ways. Pedophiles might use the materials to encour-age children to participate in sexual activity. "A child who is reluctant to engage in sexual activity with an adult, or to pose for sexually explicit photographs, can sometimes be convinced by viewing depictions of other children 'having fun' participating in such activity." Congressional Find-ing note (3), notes following § 2251. Furthermore, pedophiles might "whet their own sexual appetites" with the pornographic images, "there-by increasing the creation and distribution of child pornography and the sexual abuse and exploitation of actual children." *Id.*, Findings (4), (10)(B). Under these rationales, harm flows from the content of the images, not from the means of their production. In addition, Congress identified another problem created by computer-generated images: Their existence can make it harder to prosecute pornographers who do use real minors. See *id.*, Finding (6)(A). As imaging technology improves, Congress found, it becomes more difficult to prove that a particular picture was produced using actual children. To ensure that defendants possessing child pornography using real minors cannot evade prosecution, Congress extended the ban to virtual child pornography.

Section 2256(8)(C) prohibits a more common and lower tech means of creating virtual images, known as computer morphing. Rather than creat-ing original images, pornographers can alter innocent pictures of real children so that the children appear to be engaged in sexual activity. Although morphed images may fall within the definition of virtual child pornography, they implicate the interests of real children and are in that sense closer to the images in *Ferber*. Respondents do not challenge this provision, and we do not consider it.

Respondents do challenge § 2256(8)(D). Like the text of the "appears to be" provision, the sweep of this provision is quite broad. Section 2256(8)(D) defines child pornography to include any sexually explicit image that was "advertised, promoted, presented, described, or distributed in such a manner that conveys the impression" it depicts "a minor engaging in sexually explicit conduct." One Committee Report identified the provision as directed at sexually explicit images pandered as child pornography. *See* S.Rep. No. 104–358, p. 22 (1996) ("This provision prevents child pornographers and pedophiles from exploiting prurient interests in child sexuality and sexual activity through the production or distribution of pornographic material which is intentionally pandered as child pornography"). The statute is not so limited in its reach, however, as it punishes even those possessors who took no part in pandering. Once a work has been described as child pornography, the taint remains on the speech in the hands of subsequent possessors, making possession unlawful even though the content otherwise would not be objectionable.

II

Congress may pass valid laws to protect children from abuse, and it has. *E.g.,* 18 U.S.C. §§ 2241, 2251. The prospect of crime, however, by itself does not justify laws suppressing protected speech. It is also well established that speech may not be prohibited because it concerns subjects offending our sensibilities.

As a general principle, the First Amendment bars the government from dictating what we see or read or speak or hear. The freedom of speech has its limits; it does not embrace certain categories of speech, including defamation, incitement, obscenity, and pornography produced with real children. While these categories may be prohibited without violating the First Amendment, none of them includes the speech prohibited by the CPPA. In his dissent from the opinion of the Court of Appeals, Judge Ferguson recognized this to be the law and proposed that virtual child pornography should be regarded as an additional category of unprotected speech. It would be necessary for us to take this step to uphold the statute.

The Government * * * argu[es] that speech prohibited by the CPPA is virtually indistinguishable from child pornography, which may be banned without regard to whether it depicts works of value. Where the images are themselves the product of child sexual abuse, *Ferber* recognized that the State had an interest in stamping it out without regard to any judgment about its content. The production of the work, not its content, was the target of the statute. The fact that a work contained serious literary, artistic, or other value did not excuse the harm it caused to its child participants. It was simply "unrealistic to equate a community's toleration for sexually oriented materials with the permissible scope of legislation aimed at protecting children from sexual exploitation."

Ferber upheld a prohibition on the distribution and sale of child pornography, as well as its production, because these acts were "intrinsically related" to the sexual abuse of children in two ways. First, as a permanent record of a child's abuse, the continued circulation itself would harm the child who had participated. Like a defamatory statement, each new publication of the speech would cause new injury to the child's reputation and emotional well-being. Second, because the traffic in child pornography was an economic motive for its production, the State had an interest in closing the distribution network. "The most expeditious if not the only practical method of law enforcement may be to dry up the market for this material by imposing severe criminal penalties on persons selling, advertising, or otherwise promoting the product." Under either rationale, the speech had what the Court in effect held was a proximate link to the crime from which it came.

Later, in *Osborne v. Ohio,* 495 U.S. 103 (1990), the Court ruled that these same interests justified a ban on the possession of pornography produced by using children. "Given the importance of the State's interest in protecting the victims of child pornography," the State was justified in "attempting to stamp out this vice at all levels in the distribution chain." *Osborne* also noted the State's interest in preventing child pornography from being used as an aid in the solicitation of minors. The Court, however, anchored its holding in the concern for the participants, those whom it called the "victims of child pornography." It did not suggest that, absent this concern, other governmental interests would suffice.

In contrast to the speech in *Ferber,* speech that itself is the record of sexual abuse, the CPPA prohibits speech that records no crime and creates no victims by its production. Virtual child pornography is not "intrinsically related" to the sexual abuse of children, as were the materials in *Ferber.* While the Government asserts that the images can lead to actual instances of child abuse, the causal link is contingent and indirect. The harm does not necessarily follow from the speech, but depends upon some unquantified potential for subsequent criminal acts.

The Government says these indirect harms are sufficient because, as *Ferber* acknowledged, child pornography rarely can be valuable speech. This argument, however, suffers from two flaws. First, *Ferber's* judgment about child pornography was based upon how it was made, not on what it communicated. The case reaffirmed that where the speech is neither obscene nor the product of sexual abuse, it does not fall outside the protection of the First Amendment.

The second flaw in the Government's position is that *Ferber* did not hold that child pornography is by definition without value. On the contrary, the Court recognized some works in this category might have significant value, but relied on virtual images—the very images prohibited by the CPPA—as an alternative and permissible means of expression: If it were necessary for literary or artistic value, a person over the statutory age who perhaps looked younger could be utilized. Simulation outside of the prohibition of the statute could provide another alternative. *Ferber,* then, not only referred to the distinction between actual and virtual child pornography, it relied on it as a reason supporting its holding. *Ferber* provides no support for a statute that eliminates the distinction and makes the alternative mode criminal as well.

III

Finally, the Government says that the possibility of producing images by using computer imaging makes it very difficult for it to prosecute those who produce pornography by using real children. Experts, we are told, may have difficulty in saying whether the pictures were made by using real children or by using computer imaging. The necessary solution, the argument runs, is to prohibit both kinds of images. The argument, in essence, is that protected speech may be banned as a means to ban unprotected speech. This analysis turns the First Amendment upside down.

The Government may not suppress lawful speech as the means to suppress unlawful speech. Protected speech does not become unprotected merely because it resembles the latter. The Constitution requires the reverse. The possible harm to society in permitting some unprotected speech to go unpunished is outweighed by the possibility that protected speech of others may be muted. The overbreadth doctrine prohibits the Government from banning unprotected speech if a substantial amount of protected speech is prohibited or chilled in the process.

In sum, § 2256(8)(B) covers materials beyond the categories recognized in *Ferber* and *Miller*, and the reasons the Government offers in support of limiting the freedom of speech have no justification in our precedents or in the law of the First Amendment. The provision abridges the freedom to engage in a substantial amount of lawful speech. For this reason, it is overbroad and unconstitutional.

JUSTICE THOMAS, concurring in the judgment.

In my view, the Government's most persuasive asserted interest in support of the Child Pornography Prevention Act of 1996 is the prosecution rationale—that persons who possess and disseminate pornographic images of real children may escape conviction by claiming that the images are computer generated, thereby raising a reasonable doubt as to their guilt. At this time, however, the Government asserts only that defendants *raise* such defenses, not that they have done so successfully. In fact, the Government points to no case in which a defendant has been acquitted based on a "computer-generated images" defense. While this speculative interest cannot support the broad reach of the CPPA, technology may evolve to the point where it becomes impossible to enforce actual child pornography laws because the Government cannot prove that certain pornographic images are of real children. In the event this occurs, the Government should not be foreclosed from enacting a regulation of virtual child pornography that contains an appropriate affirmative defense or some other narrowly drawn restriction.

The Court suggests that the Government's interest in enforcing prohibitions against real child pornography cannot justify prohibitions on virtual child pornography, because "this analysis turns the First Amendment upside down. The Government may not suppress lawful speech as the means to suppress unlawful speech." But if technological advances thwart prosecution of "unlawful speech," the Government may well have a compelling interest in barring or otherwise regulating some narrow category of "lawful speech" in order to enforce effectively laws against pornography made through the abuse of real children. The Court does leave open the possibility that a more complete affirmative defense could save a statute's constitutionality, implicitly accepting that some regulation of virtual child pornography might be constitutional. I would not prejudge, however, whether a more complete affirmative defense is the only way to narrowly tailor a criminal statute that prohibits the possession and dissemination of virtual child pornography. Thus, I concur in the judgment of the Court.

NOTES AND QUESTIONS

1. *Free Speech Coalition* holds that the government may not prohibit the possession of "virtual" child pornography, and that such images are protected by the First Amendment unless they fall within the definition of obscenity from *Miller v. California*. This leaves open the possibility that virtual child pornography can be prosecuted as obscenity if it meets the standard of *Miller*. As a result, one effect of *Free Speech Coalition* is a likely increase in the frequency of obscenity prosecutions. Is this a positive development?

2. Congress passed the PROTECT Act, Pub. L. No. 108–21 (2003), a year after the *Free Speech Coalition* decision. Section 502(a) of the PROTECT Act reworked the definition of 18 U.S.C. § 2256(8) so that it now defines "child pornography" for use in § 2252A as follows:

> any visual depiction, including any photograph, film, video, picture, or computer or computer-generated image or picture, whether made or produced by electronic, mechanical, or other means, of sexually explicit conduct, where—
>
> (a) the production of such visual depiction involves the use of a minor engaging in sexually explicit conduct;
>
> (b) such visual depiction is a digital image, computer image, or computer-generated image that is, or is indistinguishable from, that of a minor engaging in sexually explicit conduct; or
>
> (c) such visual depiction has been created, adapted, or modified to appear that an identifiable minor is engaging in sexually explicit conduct.

Note that § 2256(8)(a), involving actual minors, and § 2256(8)(c), which involves so-called "morphed" images, both remain unchanged from the original 1996 Act. Section 2256(8)(d), struck down in *Free Speech Coalition*, has been repealed. Section 2256(8)(b), also invalidated in *Free Speech Coalition*, has been replaced with a much narrower version that applies only to virtual images "indistinguishable from" actual minors. Do you think that the PROTECT Act's narrow definition of virtual child pornography used in § 2256(8)(b) is constitutional?

3. In United States v. Bach, 400 F.3d 622 (8th Cir. 2005), the Eighth Circuit considered a constitutional challenge to punishment for receiving a "morphed" image of child pornography. The image in *Bach* was a morphed

picture combining a headshot of a known and identifiable boy, referred to in the opinion as "AC," inserted onto a preexisting photograph of an unidentified nude boy. The effect was to create the impression that the image was a nude picture of AC. The Eighth Circuit concluded that punishing the receipt of this image did not violate the First Amendment:

> Although there is no contention that the nude body actually is that of AC or that he was involved in the production of the image, a lasting record has been created of AC, an identifiable minor child, seemingly engaged in sexually explicit activity. He is thus victimized every time the picture is displayed. Unlike the virtual pornography or the pornography using youthful looking adults which could be prosecuted under subsections (B) and (D), as discussed in *Free Speech Coalition*, this image created an identifiable child victim of sexual exploitation. In *Free Speech Coalition* the Supreme Court continued to recognize the government's compelling interest in protecting a minor's physical and psychological well being, building on its decision in *Ferber*, pointing out the harm arising from pornography which is "intrinsically related" to the sexual abuse of children.

> Although there may well be instances in which the application of § 2256(8)(c) violates the First Amendment, this is not such a case. The interests of real children are implicated in the image received by Bach showing a boy with the identifiable face of AC in a lascivious pose. This image involves the type of harm which can constitutionally be prosecuted under *Free Speech Coalition* and *Ferber*.

Id. at 632. Do you agree? Would you reach the same result if the real headshot of a known child had been inserted in a realistic way onto the body of an 18 year-old? What if the headshot of a known 18 year-old had been inserted in a realistic way onto the body of a child? What if the headshot had been inserted in a realistic way onto a computer-generated image of a child?

4. In *United States v. Williams*, ___ U.S. ___, 128 S.Ct. 1830 (2008), the Supreme Court rejected a First Amendment challenge to 18 U.S.C. § 2252A(a)(3)(B), the so-called "pandering" statute. The statute prohibits presenting, promoting, or advertising materials in a way that leaves the impression that they are images of child pornography, even if the images are virtual child pornography or something else. The Court held that the statute was distinguishable from *Free Speech Coalition* and did not violate the First Amendment:

> Offers to engage in illegal transactions are categorically excluded from First Amendment protection. * * * Offers to provide or requests to obtain unlawful material, whether as part of a commercial exchange or not, are similarly undeserving of First Amendment protection. It would be an odd constitutional principle that permitted the government to prohibit offers to sell illegal drugs, but not offers to give them away for free.

> To be sure, there remains an important distinction between a proposal to engage in illegal activity and the abstract advocacy of illegality. The Act before us does not prohibit advocacy of child pornography, but only offers to provide or requests to obtain it. There is no doubt that this prohibition

falls well within constitutional bounds. The constitutional defect we found in the pandering provision at issue in *Free Speech Coalition* was that it went *beyond* pandering to prohibit possession of material that could not otherwise be proscribed.

In sum, we hold that offers to provide or requests to obtain child pornography are categorically excluded from the First Amendment.

Id. at 1841–42.

5. *As-applied First Amendment exceptions?* During oral argument in the *United States v. Williams* case discussed in the note above, several Justices and the Solicitor General appeared to agree that there may be as-applied First Amendment defenses to charges for mere possession of child pornography beyond those in the narrow statutory "safety valve" exception. The issue arose in the context of understanding the relationship between possession offenses and the pandering offenses challenged in that case. Consider the following exchange between the Justices and Solicitor General Paul Clement:

JUSTICE KENNEDY: There are some terrible practices in the child-trafficking area where children are held in brothels for the most debased of acts. There are abuses in prisons, abuses in schools. If there are videotapes showing those things, it seems to me that the statute is—that they're clearly covered by the statute, and maybe even a killing of a little girl in public might be sadistic. Assume that that's covered by the statute. Is there anything in the "presents" and the "promotes" language in the scienter component of the statute that gives some protection to these materials? Is it just [something raised in an] as-applied [constitutional challenge]? Is that what we have to do?

GENERAL CLEMENT: Here is how I would try to analyze it, Justice Kennedy, which is I would say that there would be an as-applied challenge there because the basic prohibition on child pornography that would apply to the underlying materials, there would be an as-applied exception to that.

JUSTICE KENNEDY: So we want the public to see this to show them how bad it is, and that is permitted under the statute, because it is not "presenting"?

GENERAL CLEMENT: I mean there would be another way to try to get at that.... Because it would be clear that, although I was presenting it as visual depictions of children who had that happen to them, I was presenting it exclusively for its scientific, artistic, literary value.

JUSTICE SCALIA: Of course, you have a problem not just with the presenting, not just with the pandering of it. You have a problem with the mere possession of it. You have to find some exception for that anyway. You have to find some as-applied challenge exception for the mere possession of it, even if you don't pander it.

GENERAL CLEMENT: Well, Justice Scalia, that's exactly right. And that's why I would think the logical way to proceed would be you would find an as-applied exception to the basic prohibition. And then, naturally, that would apply to the pandering provision.

How broad should the as-applied exception to liability for possession be? During the *Williams* argument, Justice Souter suggested that it may apply to cases of accidental possession; Justice Stevens suggested that it may apply when the image is of a person 17 years old. What should the test be?

6. Perhaps the most important practical impact of *Free Speech Coalition* arises when it is combined with United States v. X–Citement Video, Inc., 513 U.S. 64 (1994). *X–Citement Video* construed the mens rea requirement of 18 U.S.C. §§ 2252(a)(1) and (a)(2) to require proof that the defendant knew the images were of a minor. Knowledge that an image is of a minor arguably presupposes knowledge that the image is of an actual child. A defendant with a good faith belief that an image is "virtual" child pornography presumably cannot act knowingly with respect to the factual element that the image is actual child pornography. Putting *Free Speech Coalition* and *X–Citement Video* together suggests that the government must not only prove that an image was of an actual child, but that the defendant *knew* the image was of an actual child. How can the government satisfy this burden? The following case explores these issues.

UNITED STATES v. MARCHAND

United States District Court for the District of New Jersey, 2004.
308 F. Supp.2d 498.

HOCHBERG, DISTRICT JUDGE.

The Defendant, Anthony Marchand, is accused of possessing Child Pornography, in violation of the Child Pornography Prevention Act, 18 U.S.C. § 2252A(a)(5)(B). The Defendant knowingly and voluntarily waived his right to a jury trial. Therefore, this Court is responsible for both findings of fact and conclusions of law. The issues for this Court are: 1) whether the images that the Defendant possessed depicted real minors and 2) whether the Defendant knew that the images he possessed depicted real minors.

I. Findings of Fact

A. *Background*

Dr. Anthony Marchand was employed by Atlantic Health Systems ("AHS") as director of the pathology lab at Overlook Hospital in Summit, New Jersey. In October or November of 2000, the hospital experienced substantial problems with its computer network. During an investigation into the cause of these problems, a network engineer for the hospital noticed that Dr. Marchand's computer was accessing and downloading imagery from the Internet, resulting in massive re-transmissions on the network. These re-transmissions would cause the network to crash. In April 2001, new firewall software was installed, due to the problems the hospital had experienced with the network. In addition, AHS installed a sniffer to monitor traffic through the AHS firewall in an effort to identify Internet use that violated AHS' policy.

Dr. Marchand used a computer designated OBE, with the password "amarchand" in his office at Overlook. Between April and August 2001, the OBE computer generated sniffer alerts several times a week while being operated by Dr. Marchand. AHS then assigned a static IP address to Computer OBE to make it easier for the sniffer to trace information to and from Computer OBE and the Internet. Monitoring of the sniffer revealed that Dr. Marchand accessed a variety of web sites that appeared to display child pornography. For example, the sniffer program indicated that the web sites accessed by the OBE computer contained information such as "free illegal site," "free illegal kds," "illegal ki()s porno video," "illegally shocking 3–11y.o," and "_real_illegal_lolitas archive."

AHS contacted the Federal Bureau of Investigation, and on March 14, 2002, pursuant to a search warrant, the Government conducted a search of Dr. Marchand's office and office computer. When Dr. Marchand was informed that a search warrant for child pornography was being executed in his office, he accompanied the FBI agents and hospital staff to another office where he answered questions. He also handed several computer disks to Special Agent William DeSa ("Agent DeSa"). Later in the interview, Agent DeSa stated that his use of the term child pornography referred to "actual kids engaging in sexual activity, either with children or with adults." During the interview at the hospital, Dr. Marchand stated that he had additional images at home, and that he thought he had approximately 500 images of child pornography. Dr. Marchand then accompanied Agent DeSa and Special Agent Tanya Lamb DeSa ("Agent Lamb") to his home, where he turned over several additional CDs and a computer. In total, the agents retrieved six CDs from Dr. Marchand's office and home as well as the central processing unit from Dr. Marchand's home computer. Dr. Marchand told Agent Lamb that collecting these images "was a hobby, that he didn't realize that it was illegal or improper for him to have for personal enjoyment." Dr. Marchand also explained to Agent Lamb "that some of the images on the CDs were images that he had morphed."

B. The Images

The Government introduced into evidence 35 images from the total number seized. The evidence depicts prepubescent children engaged in sexually explicit conduct. * * *

The children in each of the 35 images look real to the viewer. There is no indication in any of the pictures to alert the viewer that the image was created other than with the use of real children. The lighting in the images appears as it would in a photograph. The children's physical characteristics and their often highly expressive facial features are visible in great detail. A staple is visible in one of the images, indicating that the picture was taken from a compilation of multiple pages, such as a centerfold from a magazine. Some of the children are the subjects of a series of pictures. In each of the pictures within one series, the child depicted has the same appearance, and other details of the images do not vary.

The children in the images range in age from three to fifteen. The Government's expert, Dr. Robert Johnson, estimated the age of the children by comparing the level of development of the children depicted in the images with the stages of sexual maturation designed by John Tanner ("the Tanner Scale"). The Tanner Scale shows pubic hair at specific stages and the age at which it is most likely to occur and the breast development in females and the genitalia, penis, and testicle development in males.

Eleven of the images introduced were earlier published as photographs in child pornography magazines that were printed prior to 1986, a date when computer technology to create realistic virtual images of human beings did not exist. Eight of the images introduced depict actual identified and named children from the United States, England, and Brazil, who had been the subject of investigations by law enforcement into the sexual abuse they suffered. Six of the images were part of two different series of photographs. Each of the images had a file name, and Dr. Marchand organized them into folders. He named the subdirectory containing these folders, "child."

C.   Technology for Virtual Images

Defense Counsel maintained a thorough, creative, and vigorous defense, attacking the Government's case. The main thrust of the Defense was to show that technology exists to create realistic virtual images of child pornography that are indistinguishable from real images of child pornography, and that nothing in the bit structure of the digitized computer image would inform a diligent observer that the image was real rather than virtual. This defense was presented in order to rebut the Government's proofs that the images possessed by the Defendant were of real human children and to create reasonable doubt as to whether Dr. Marchand knew that the images were real rather than virtual from information available to him at the time he possessed the images.

Computer software such as POSER was presented by the Defense. POSER is a tool for artists to use in creating virtual images of people. Although the Defense did not submit any images that had been created using POSER, the Government introduced a limited number of virtual images of clothed adults as examples of what POSER can do. Two of these images were part of a recent contest held by POSER. No nude adults or children were adduced nor were any virtual images of sexually aroused body parts.

The degree to which the images created with POSER appear real and the accuracy of the details depend on the skill of the artist. For example, the software does not create details such as hair growth or vein visibility through skin, although POSER will adjust the size of each body part to be in proportion with the size of the overall human figure. Unlike images that are created by manipulating and "cutting and pasting" pre-existing images, images created with POSER will not contain internal inconsistencies in the background, known as artifacts, which indicate that the pictures are not real. However, when backgrounds other than those created by POSER are imported into the images, POSER will not automatically create proper lighting effects, leaving it to the artist to ensure that the lighting effects, such as shadows cast by one body upon an adjacent figure or upon the ground, appear realistic. The pictures that the Defendant's expert characterized as indicative of pictures created with POSER do not appear at all realistic to the viewer.

II.　Application of the Facts to the Law

A.　*The Charges Against the Defendant*

Dr. Marchand is charged with violating 18 U.S.C. § 2252A(a)(5)(B) by knowingly and willfully possessing six computer disks which contained at least three images of child pornography as defined in 18 U.S.C. § 2256(8)(A), which images were shipped and transported in interstate and foreign commerce and which were produced using materials that had been shipped and transported in interstate and foreign commerce.

B.　*The Elements of the Crime of Possession of Child Pornography under the CPPA*

The Government must prove: 1) that the Defendant possessed at least one image of a real minor engaged in sexually explicit conduct; and 2) that the Defendant knew that at least one of the images contained a picture of a real minor engaged in sexually explicit conduct.

[handwritten margin note: Requirement of Possession]

To prosecute a defendant under this section, the Government first must prove beyond a reasonable doubt that the image depicts a real child. Prior to the U.S. Supreme Court's decision in *Free Speech Coalition et al. v. Ashcroft,* 535 U.S. 234 (2002), the definition of child pornography included a visual depiction which appeared to be a minor engaging in sexually explicit conduct. 18 U.S.C. § 2256(8)(B). To the extent that this definition encompassed images that were generated entirely by computer, without the use of any actual minors, the Supreme Court held in *Free Speech Coalition* that, absent an obscenity charge, such material was protected by the First Amendment. Thus, the possession of virtual images of minors engaged in sexually explicit conduct is not a crime under the statute charged in this case.

The Government must also prove beyond a reasonable doubt that the Defendant knew that the images he possessed depicted real minors engaged in sexually explicit conduct. *United States v. X–Citement Video, Inc.,* 513 U.S. 64, 78 (1994). In *X–Citement Video,* the Court held that the term "knowingly" refers to the minority age of the persons depicted and the sexually explicit nature of the material. Thus, *Free Speech Coalition* and *X–Citement Video,* read together, require the Government to prove that the defendant knew the images he possessed depicted real children engaged in sexually explicit conduct.

C. Proofs That the Images Depicted Real Minors

The Government presented evidence that: 1) eleven of the images were taken from magazines created prior to the invention of computer technology that might make it possible to digitally create such images; 2) law enforcement agents from the U.S., England, and Brazil could positively identify by name the children in eight of the pictures as children whom they had met in person at a time not distant from the age that the child was when he or she was photographed; and 3) an opinion, from a qualified expert who reliably studied the images, that the physical development of the children depicted in the 35 images corresponds to the Tanner scale designed to show the level of physical development that children reach at different ages.

The Government linked the pre–1986 magazine photographs to the images that the Defendant downloaded from the Internet. The Government's computer expert testified that one of the ways to determine whether an image depicts real children is to compare the image to those in the FBI's Child Exploitation and Obscenity Reference File ("Reference File"). The Reference File contains approximately 10,000 images of scanned child pornography that were taken when computer technology was so primitive that a sound inference could be drawn that an image found in the Reference File depicts a real child. Eleven images possessed by Dr. Marchand matched the images in the Reference File and are found to be images of real minors engaged in sexually explicit conduct.

The Government also adduced proof in the form of direct witness identification of real children in eight of the images in evidence. These witnesses identified the children who appeared in the pictures, having met the children during law enforcement investigations into the abuse that these children had suffered.

Officer James Feehan of the Police Department in Peoria, Illinois positively identified the child in G122 as Melissa, who was between nine and ten years old when her father took pornographic pictures of her and distributed them over the Internet. During his investigation, Officer Feehan met Melissa when she was fifteen years old. He testified that Melissa looked nearly the same at that age as she had looked five or six years earlier when the pornographic pictures were taken. [Other children were identified through similar means.]

* * *

This evidence leaves no reasonable doubt that the images depict real children. Through direct identification of children, both by law enforcement and by comparison with the FBI Reference File, and through evidence of the appropriate level of development of each of the children depicted, the Government has proven beyond reasonable doubt that the files Dr. Marchand possessed contain pictures of real children.

D.   The Defendant's State of Knowledge

The Court has reviewed evidence regarding: 1) the appearance of the images; 2) the number of images; 3) the number and identity of web sites the Defendant accessed; 4) the language used in the web sites; 5) the mode and manner by which the Defendant viewed and stored the images; 6) the Defendant's state of mind; and 7) the available computer technology and manual skill required to create realistic virtual images, including a small sample of such images posted on the Internet and created with the software most frequently discussed by the Defense. From this evidence, this Court must determine whether there is sufficient evidence from which an inference can be drawn beyond a reasonable doubt that the Defendant knew that the images he possessed were of real children engaged in sexually explicit conduct.

The knowledge element can be proven through direct and/or circumstantial evidence of actual knowledge and through a finding of willful blindness. A Defendant acts knowingly if the fact finder finds beyond reasonable doubt that the Defendant acted with deliberate disregard of the truth. The Government may prove that a person acted knowingly by proving beyond a reasonable doubt that that person deliberately closed his eyes to what otherwise would have been obvious to him. One cannot avoid responsibility for an offense by deliberately ignoring what is obvious. To find knowledge based on willful blindness, it is not enough that a reasonable person would have been aware of the high probability of the truth. The Defendant himself must have been aware of the high probability that the images depicted real children. The Defendant's stupidity or negligence in not knowing is not sufficient to support a finding of knowledge based on willful blindness.

* * * The crux of the issue in this case is whether the Government's evidence proved beyond a reasonable doubt that the Defendant knew that the pictures were of real children. Among other evidence, the Court considers: the details of each image, the staple that appeared in one of the images, a file name that includes the age of the child, the large number of images and the substantial number of separate web sites from which the pictures were downloaded, the fact that certain images showed the same child over and over again as part of a series, the very real facial expressions of the children (sometimes multiple children in the same image), the extremely detailed close-up * * * [of various sexual acts], and the background in the photographs depicting highly detailed furniture, rumpled bedding, general household clutter, and extremely realistic lighting effects.

The circumstantial evidence from which an inference of knowledge may be drawn includes the appearance and number of images which were proven to depict real children. *United States v. Pabon–Cruz,* 255 F. Supp.2d 200, 207 (S.D.N.Y. 2003) (holding that jurors could determine from the appearance and number of images possessed that the defendant could not have believed they were all produced using digital technology rather than real children). The Government presented this Court with fewer images than it presented to the jury in *Pabon–Cruz*. However, *Pabon–Cruz* is still instructive regarding the type of evidence from which an inference of knowledge may be drawn. The appearance of the images and the number of them, once they are proven to depict real children, is appropriate circumstantial evidence that this Court may use to draw an inference of knowledge, including whether or not there is reasonable doubt that Dr. Marchand knew that at least one of the 35 images in evidence depicted a real child engaged in sexually explicit conduct.

This Court has viewed the images itself in considering whether reasonable doubt exists as to Dr. Marchand's knowledge that the children depicted in the images were real. All of the children in the 35 images look utterly real. The level of detail of the children's features in all of the images contrasts startlingly with the sample of POSER virtual images adduced as evidence of the best examples of what virtual-image technology can do. * * *

The multiplicity of images and the fact that the Defendant download-ed them from different web sites also supports a finding that Dr. Mar-chand knew that at least one of the images depicted a real child. The Court considers all of the evidence, including logical inferences therefrom, based on human experience. Could the Defendant have thought that each of the 35 images, downloaded from many unrelated web sites, was each digitally created by an artist who was skillful enough to complete the task so extraordinarily realistically? It is not as though Dr. Marchand confined himself to one web site which he believed was dedicated to virtual images. Is there reasonable doubt that this Defendant knew that in surfing the web for diverse child pornography sites, he would find at least one picture of a real child engaged in sexually explicit conduct?

In addition to the 35 images themselves, the Government also pre-sented direct evidence regarding the Defendant's state of mind. Dr. Marchand defended himself in his interview with Agent Lamb by saying, *inter alia,* that he did not know it was illegal to possess the images and that some of the images were morphed (digitally manipulated using parts of different real children) on the CDs that he created. By distinguishing between pictures that were morphed and those that were not, the Defen-dant certainly implied that he believed that the "un-morphed" images depicted real children. Dr. Marchand attempted to exculpate his conduct by claiming that some images were morphed, but his effort at exculpation never claimed that some of the images were virtual. Moreover, the FBI agents told Dr. Marchand that they were interested in pictures of "actual kids engaging in sexual activity, either with children or with adults," and Dr. Marchand responded by saying that he had about 500 images of child pornography. This also sheds light on his state of mind. The Defendant's characterization of 500 of his images as child pornography, especially in light of his effort to distinguish between those that were morphed and those that were not, supports a strong inference that he knew that at least one depicted a real child.

In an effort to rebut the Government's proof as to the Defendant's state of mind, the Defendant points to evidence that he had labeled some of the disks that were seized "Yoda." Defendant argues that this indicates that he believed the children in the images were not real, just as Yoda, a fictional character from the movie Star Wars, is not a real person. This label does not shed light on Defendant's knowledge of the content of the pictures he downloaded, because Yoda was his pet name for the very large computer play station that he used to view the images, and bears no relationship to the images themselves.

The Defense did prove that software like POSER exists and can be used to create virtual images. In order to be persuaded by the Defendant's argument that the existence of POSER creates reasonable doubt, the fact finder must consider whether the Defendant believed that this virtual software was so widely used in 2002, with such consistent skill, that 35 different realistic action images of nude children and adults, including several in a single image, would appear on a wide range of child pornographic web sites. The Government introduced proof that POSER-created images do not look even remotely realistic. No POSER-created image was adduced of a single realistic-looking human, even fully clothed. No evidence of virtual, nude, sexually-aroused adults or virtual, nude, prepubescent children was adduced. No virtual action image was introduced. When asked whether the POSER images introduced into evidence were typical of the type of images that could be created using POSER, the Defendant's computer and Internet technology expert testified that the images were indicative, though not necessarily typical, of the kind of images that could be created using POSER. Not one looked like a real person. Yet, every picture that the Defendant possessed appears absolutely real. Even the lighting and the shadows in each of the pictures is perfectly consistent with the various backgrounds contained in the images, a highly difficult feat to accomplish virtually. Even the Defendant's computer expert, when asked to point out those images that did not look like real photographs, could only point to one image, G121, and no others. Moreover, the expert conceded that when he looked at the pictures, he thought they were real.

Conclusion

The Government has proved beyond a reasonable doubt each element of the crime of possession of child pornography by Dr. Marchand. While *Free Speech Coalition* now imposes a heavy burden on the Government in its proofs, in this case, that burden has been satisfied.

NOTES AND QUESTIONS

1. Proving that a defendant possessed at least one image that depicted a real child is not difficult for the government in most child pornography cases. Many images of child pornography are from collections that are well known to collectors of child pornography as well as to law enforcement. Some images are known to have been created in a period before computer animation was

well-established, often in the 1970s. *See* Philip Jenkins, Beyond Tolerance 80–83 (2001). Others involve known victims. In a case involving a collection of many images of child pornography, the government can search the defendant's computer and select a subset of the images known to involve a real child.

2. Proving a defendant knew that an image involved a real child presents a more difficult task. Imagine that a collector of child pornography reads *Marchand* and takes defensive action based on its teachings. He labels the real child pornography he receives "virtual1," "virtual2," "virtual3," etc.; adds the prefix "virtual" to everything he says or writes regarding pornography; and buys a book on computer-generated images and places it next to his computer. Imagine that the defendant is later arrested and he asserts his Fifth Amendment privilege. If you are the defense attorney, what are your chances of creating reasonable doubt that your client didn't know the images depicted real children? Alternatively, if you are the prosecutor, how might you try to prove beyond a reasonable doubt that the "virtual" defense is a sham?

Marchand offers a number of suggestions for prosecutors. To prove the elements of the offense, the government must present proof beyond a reasonable doubt that the defendant knew at least one of the images was of a real child. To do this, the government can base its case on a group of images that are particularly real-looking. The government may be able to retrieve information from the defendant's computer indicating the source of the images, and it may be able to show that the images saved as "virtual1" and "virtual2" were not retrieved with such filenames. Further, the government may be able to find evidence that the defendant planned a sham virtual defense. As with any such effort, an unintended inconsistency may expose the defendant's scheme.

Finally, imagine a person is interested in collecting only virtual child pornography. He makes an earnest attempt to collect only virtual images, all of which are protected under the First Amendment. Within the collection of mostly virtual images, however, the person ends up with a handful of images that (unbeknownst to him) depict real children. Assume that a prosecutor wrongly concludes that this is a "sham" virtual pornography case, and the prosecutor believes that the virtual collector has knowledge that the images depicted real children. He indicts the collector, and you are appointed to defend him against the charges. What is your trial strategy to show the jury that your client lacks the required mens rea?

3. Imagine that the government searches a suspect's computer hard drive and discovers 500 images of child pornography. The government selects twenty particularly real looking images and another twenty known images to offer as evidence of possession. Assume that there is some overlap between the two groups; some of the known images also look particularly real. Is it sufficient that the government can prove beyond a reasonable doubt that at least one of the images in the group was real and that the defendant believed one of the images in the group was real? Or must the government prove beyond a reasonable doubt that at least one of the images was both real and believed to be real? If you are a defense attorney in such a case, do you want the trier of fact to be a judge or a jury?

4. As modified by the PROTECT Act of 2003, federal law prohibits the possession, receipt, and distribution of virtual child pornography if it is "indistinguishable" from images of actual children. *See* 18 U.S.C. §§ 2252A, 2256(8)(b) (2003). Assuming this law is constitutional, what must the government prove to establish a violation for possessing, distributing, or receiving virtual child pornography? Must the government prove that the image looks real, and that the defendant actually believed it was real? Or is it sufficient for the government to prove that the image looks real, and the defendant knew that it looked real? As a matter of statutory interpretation, does the combination of 18 U.S.C. §§ 2252A and 2256(8)(b) require proof of knowledge that the image involves a real child, or is the statute satisfied by knowledge that the image is virtual but indistinguishable from an image of a real child? If the latter, what exactly does it mean to know that a virtual image is indistinguishable from an image of a minor?

5. *The role of the jury.* If it is difficult for a juror to know whether an image is real or computer-generated, does that difficulty render child pornography laws unconstitutionally vague? In United States v. Boehman, 2009 WL 1210989 (W.D. Ky. 2009), the district court held that the answer is "no." Whether the image is real or computer-generated is a factual issue for the jury, the court concluded, and does not render the statute vague. Note that courts have also concluded that expert testimony is not required to assist the jury: Although either side may wish to put on an expert to testify as to whether the images are real, no experts are required. *See, e.g.,* United States v. Salcido, 506 F.3d 729, 734 (9th Cir. 2007).

6. At present, realistic computer generated images are very rare. That is changing rapidly, however: Technological advances are leading to more realistic images every year. Assume this trend continues, and imagine the year is 2050. It is now easy to use a computer to generate a picture that looks real. There is no way to distinguish real photographs from computer-generated ones, and all photographs are presumed to be fake. In fact, one popular software program permits a user to scan in a set of photographs of a person, and the computer can then use those images to construct a computer-generated composite. The computer can output an endless series of entirely realistic images of that person, at any age, performing a wide range of acts as directed by the user.

If this future becomes reality, what will happen to child pornography laws?

2. TRAVELER CASES AND ENTRAPMENT

A second type of child exploitation offense involves so-called "traveler" cases. Traveler cases trace their lineage back to the White Slave Traffic Act, Pub. L. No. 61–277 (1910). This law is often referred to as the Mann Act, after its chief sponsor, Illinois Congressman James Mann.

The Mann Act was passed during a period of tremendous public concern that young girls, many of them recent immigrants, were being kidnapped and forced into lives of prostitution. Given the limits of federal court jurisdiction, especially at the time, Congress responded by passing a law that focused liability on the crossing of state lines with the purpose of engaging in illegal sexual activities. For example, the key provisions of the Act prohibited transporting women across interstate lines and enticing women and younger girls to cross state lines with the intent of having them engage in "prostitution or debauchery, or for any other immoral purpose."

The modern version of the Mann Act appears at 18 U.S.C. § 2421 *et seq.*, and contains a number of prohibitions that are often used in child exploitation cases involving the Internet. The statutes harness state law, and particular state statutory rape law, which generally prohibits sexual contact with a person under the age of consent as determined in that state. For example, 18 U.S.C. § 2422(b) prohibits using "the mail or any facility or means of interstate or foreign commerce" to entice a minor to engage in illegal sexual activity. The Internet obviously is such a means, which permits § 2422(b) to be used widely in cases involving the luring of children online. Similarly, 18 U.S.C. § 2423(a) prohibits enticing a minor to travel in interstate commerce to engage in "any sexual activity for which any person can be charged with a criminal offense," and § 2423(b) prohibits traveling in interstate commerce with the purpose of engaging in such an activity. This means that if an adult uses the Internet to contact a young girl, and then either travels across state lines to meet her or has her travel to meet him, the traveling or enticing violates § 2423.

The federal government prosecutes several hundred traveler cases every year. Many of the cases arise from undercover operations which begin with law enforcement officers posing as minors in Internet chat rooms. In many cases, the defendant contacts the undercover agent and asks to meet to engage in a sexual act. He then travels across state lines with the intent to meet the young victim. Upon crossing state lines, the defendant is arrested. In such cases, the elements of the offense are usually easy for the government to prove and difficult for a defense attorney to challenge. The traveling in interstate commerce is easy to show, and the government's case tends to focus on proving the defendant's intent to engage in sexual activity with a minor. Proving intent is straightforward in most cases. The combination of the chat room logs and items in the defendant's possession at the time of his arrest normally will establish the defendant's intent beyond a reasonable doubt.

The primary legal issue raised by traveler cases involves the defense of entrapment. Entrapment is not a constitutional defense, which means that federal and state standards for entrapment can and do vary. *See* Kevin A. Smith, *Psychology, Factfinding, and Entrapment*, 103 Mich. L. Rev. 759 (2005). There are generally two different aspects to entrapment law. The first aspect is inducement, which occurs when a government agent pressures or encourages a suspect to commit a crime. It is not enough for the agent to merely provide the suspect with an opportunity to commit the crime. Rather, the government must actively encourage or promote the offense. United States v. Gendron, 18 F.3d 955, 961 (1st Cir. 1994).

The second aspect of entrapment is predisposition, which looks at whether facts known about the suspect suggest that he was unusually likely to have agreed to commit the offense absent the inducement. Predisposition might be established by past criminal convictions; if a defendant has committed the same offense in the past, it will often show a predisposition to commit the same offense again. Predisposition might also be established by statements or acts by the defendant establishing his interest in the offense before any inducement occurred.

Exactly how the two aspects of entrapment relate to each other can vary based on the jurisdiction. Some jurisdictions focus entirely on inducement. Others look to both inducement and predisposition. Under federal law, the defendant must put forward evidence of inducement and lack of predisposition before being entitled to an instruction on entrapment. If some evidence is put forward by the defendant, then the government bears the burden of proving beyond a reasonable doubt that the defendant either was not induced to commit the crime or was predisposed to commit the offense.

STATE v. DAVIES

Court of Appeals of Arizona, 2008.
2008 WL 4965306.

SWANN, JUDGE.

Russell Paul Davies appeals his conviction for Luring a Minor for Sexual Exploitation because the trial court refused to instruct the jury regarding the affirmative defense of entrapment. We agree that the jury should have been so instructed. We, therefore, reverse his conviction and remand for a new trial.

Facts

On July 31, 2006, the State of Arizona charged Defendant with one count of Luring a Minor for Sexual Exploitation, a class three felony and a dangerous crime against children. The charge stemmed from events occurring on July 27, 2006, when Defendant engaged in an Internet chat with a Phoenix detective, who was posing as a fourteen-year-old girl. The chat became sexual in nature, and Defendant was taken into custody when he arrived to meet the fictitious girl in an apartment complex parking lot.

Defendant entered a plea of not guilty and the matter proceeded to its first trial in the Maricopa County Superior Court on March 20, 2007. There, the trial court included an instruction on the entrapment defense. The jury was unable to reach a verdict and a mistrial was declared.

The case proceeded to trial for a second time before a different judge on August 23, 2007. As in the first trial, the evidence presented by the State included a transcript of the Internet chat and a videotaped interview of Defendant conducted by police the night he was taken into custody.

Also, as in the first trial, the evidence included the testimony of the detective who had posed as the minor.

Before the cross examination of the detective in the second trial, Defendant requested that the trial court instruct the jury on the entrapment defense. Defendant argued that the transcript of the Internet chat presented by the State could be interpreted in a manner that would constitute sufficient evidence of entrapment to entitle him to the jury instruction. The State conceded that "as far as predisposition goes, we don't believe that there's been any evidence that he had a predisposition to this type of crime," but argued that there was, nonetheless, no entrapment because the idea to commit the offense did not originate with the detective and because the detective did not urge or induce Defendant to commit the offense.

The trial court denied the request and refused to include the entrapment instruction.

The defendant exercised his right against self-incrimination and did not testify. The court did not reconsider the request for the entrapment instruction.

On August 29, 2007, the jury found Defendant guilty of the charged offense. He was subsequently sentenced to ten years of probation, with conditions including five months of jail time, sex offender registration, and GPS monitoring.

Discussion

On appeal, Defendant contends that the trial court abused its discretion in refusing to instruct the jury on entrapment. The State disagrees. The State also argues that even if there was error, it was harmless error, and therefore Defendant is not entitled to a reversal of his conviction.

The issue whether a defendant asserting entrapment has met his burden as to the elements of the affirmative defense is normally an issue of fact for the jury to decide. It is an abuse of discretion for the trial court to decide the issue, unless there is no evidence to support the defense of entrapment or there is uncontradicted evidence of entrapment.

In Arizona, a defendant is entitled to a jury instruction on any theory of defense recognized by law, so long as that theory is reasonably supported by the evidence. This is not a demanding standard—while a Defendant must show more than a mere scintilla of evidence, an instruction *must* be given if there is evidence upon which the jury could rationally sustain the defense. If the standard is satisfied, but the trial court refuses to give the instruction, then there is reversible error.

Under A.R.S. § 13–206, to prevail on an entrapment defense, the defendant must prove the following elements by clear and convincing evidence:

1. The idea of committing the offense started with law enforcement officers or their agents rather than with the person.

2. The law enforcement officers or their agents urged and induced the person to commit the offense.

3. The person was not predisposed to commit the type of offense charged before the law enforcement officers or their agents urged and induced the person to commit the offense.

The record reveals that there was not an absence of evidence supporting entrapment; rather, there was some evidence reasonably supporting the defense. Therefore, the issue of whether Defendant was entrapped was for the jury to decide, and the trial court abused its discretion by deciding the issue based upon its own evaluation of the facts.

The transcript[4] of the Internet chat could reasonably be interpreted as supporting the elements of the entrapment defense. The exchanges recorded between Defendant and the fictitious minor are not unambiguous, and a reasonable juror could conclude that the idea of sexualizing the conversation originated with the detective rather than Defendant.[5] Specifically, a reasonable juror could conclude that Defendant was not asking about sex (much less sex with a minor) when he asked: "Russell D: you have a bf or too young? Lol."

There is evidence from which a reasonable juror could also find that when Defendant asked about dates with an ex-boyfriend, he was not asking about sex. The juror could then find that the detective was therefore the first to bring up the topic of sex when he used the phrases "bf and gf stuff" and "kiss and stuff," phrases that at trial he acknowledged as referring to sex:

Russell D: where'd you and your bf go on dates to?

sweetgirlinaz2006: movies the mall stuff like that

sweetgirlinaz2006: he come over here sometimes

sweetgirlinaz2006: when mom not home

Russell D: why when mom not home?

Russell D: she not like him?

sweetgirlinaz2006: not alot

Russell D: what would you do over there?

sweetgirlinaz2006: hang out

Russell D: cool

Russell D: kinda boring jk lol

sweetgirlinaz2006: lol

sweetgirlinaz2006: we would do bf and gf stuff

---

4. Portions of the transcript are reproduced below. The screen name "Russell D" is Defendant and "sweetgirlinaz2006" is the detective. Original spelling, punctuation, acronyms, and abbreviations are preserved to avoid confusion.

5. The conversation took place in a chat room that was neither explicitly sexual by nature nor suggestive of the presence of minors.

Russell D: at 14 what do bfs and gf's do? lol

sweetgirlinaz2006: kiss and stuff

A juror could also find that the idea of meeting originated with the detective rather than Defendant. The juror could find that Defendant spoke in jest when he brought up the topic of meeting because he used acronyms such as "lol" for "laughing out loud" and "jk" for "just kidding." The juror could find that it was the detective who first addressed the topic seriously and who asked whether Defendant wanted to meet:

Russell D: your mom would be really mad if I showed up at your place LoL

sweetgirlinaz2006: yea

sweetgirlinaz2006: lol

sweetgirlinaz2006: shes not here

sweetgirlinaz2006: shes at work then goin out with bf

Russell D: so you inviting me over? jk haha

sweetgirlinaz2006: lol

sweetgirlinaz2006: u leeve

Russell D: no I'm still here lol

sweetgirlinaz2006: k

Russell D: you still here? jk lol

sweetgirlinaz2006: yep

Russell D: YaY

Russell D: thought may of scared you away lol

sweetgirlinaz2006: no why

Russell D: I don't know

Russell D: saying if you were inviting me over LoL that was kinda weird

sweetgirlinaz2006: oh

sweetgirlinaz2006: u want ot come over

Moreover, there is evidence on the record from which a reasonable juror could find that the idea of engaging in illegal sexual conduct originated with the detective rather than Defendant, and also that the detective urged and induced Defendant to commit the offense. The juror could find that Defendant initially only wanted to "hang out" and kiss, and it was only after the detective urged and induced Defendant that he offered to engage in sexual conduct. Kissing is not proscribed by the statute under which Defendant was charged. A.R.S. §§ 13–3554 (defining the offense of Luring a Minor for Sexual Exploitation as the solicitation or offering of "sexual conduct" with a minor),–3551(9) (2001) (omitting "kissing" as a type of "sexual conduct").

sweetgirlinaz2006: what all we gonna do

Russell D: we can kiss and go from there. whatever you are comfortable with

sweetgirlinaz2006: tell me so i know what ur thinkin is all russell

sweetgirlinaz2006: just want to knwo what ur thinkin is all

sweetgirlinaz2006: what we gonna do

Russell D: hang out

sweetgirlinaz2006: and do what

Russell D: watch tv or something

sweetgirlinaz2006: nevermind russell ur not bein straight with me

sweetgirlinaz2006: take it easy

Russell D: what do you mean?

sweetgirlinaz2006: bye russell

Russell D: what don't go

Russell D: I want to meet you

Russell D: if we hit it off we can kiss

sweetgirlinaz2006: k

Russell D: is that ok?

sweetgirlinaz2006: what else I just wnat to know what im gettin in to is all

Russell D: I think we should just kiss for now

sweetgirlinaz2006: k

Russell D: are you ok with that?

sweetgirlinaz2006: i think ur lyin about what we gonna do

sweetgirlinaz2006: i just dont wnat to get into somthin without knowin before is all

Russell D: I didn't want to say anything specific cause if I go and you decide we don't hit it off and don't want to kiss me then I don't want you to feel bad

sweetgirlinaz2006: but what would u wanna do

Russell D: thats something we'd have to decide together at the moment

Russell D: at a minimum I want to meet you

Russell D: we can talk for a little bit and if you like me we can start to kiss

sweetgirlinaz2006: k

sweetgirlinaz2006: what else

Russell D: for now thats all I want to do

sweetgirlinaz2006: tonite thats all

Russell D: yeah

Russell D: then if we get together well e can meet up again

Russell D: is that okay with you?

sweetgirlinaz2006: no i dont want to risk u coming over just for that

sweetgirlinaz2006: thx for bein honest

sweetgirlinaz2006: russell

Russell D: what more would you like to do?

sweetgirlinaz2006: i appreciate it

Russell D: I really don't know what else you're looking for

Russell D: I don't want to scare you away

Russell D: How is that risking it just for that?

Russell D: I could do more if you are willing

sweetgirlinaz2006: like what

Russell D: are you willing

Russell D: ?

sweetgirlinaz2006: to do what

Russell D: we could touch each other

sweetgirlinaz2006: where

Russell D: inbetween legs

A reasonable juror could also find (as the State conceded at trial) that Defendant met his burden to show that he was not predisposed to commit the offense. This possibility is bolstered by the State's admission at trial that there was no evidence of predisposition. A reasonable juror could find that the detective's testimony at trial about the common characteristics of online sexual predators that were lacking in Defendant, combined with a cumulative reading of the chat transcript, show that Defendant was not predisposed.

Although it is undoubtedly true that a reasonable juror could review the transcript and other evidence and come to the conclusion that Defendant failed to carry his burden on the defense of entrapment, the record confirms the existence of "some evidence" reasonably supporting the defense and the requested instruction. There is some evidence that the idea to commit the offense originated with the detective, that the detective urged and induced Defendant, and that Defendant was not predisposed.

The trial court therefore erred in refusing to instruct the jury regarding the entrapment defense.

We review a trial court's error in refusing to give a jury instruction for harmless error. Harmless error exists when we can conclude beyond a reasonable doubt that [the error] did not influence the verdict.

In this case, there were two trials. In the first trial, the jury, considering essentially the same evidence as the jury in the second trial, was given the entrapment instruction and was unable to agree on a verdict. It is possible that this jury was unable to agree because it had been given the entrapment instruction, which was the core of the defense. Accordingly, we cannot conclude beyond a reasonable doubt that the trial court's error in refusing to give the instruction in the second trial, in which Defendant was convicted, did not influence the verdict.

Therefore, the error was not harmless and we must reverse Defendant's conviction.

NOTES AND QUESTIONS

1. Do you think Davies was entrapped? Did the undercover agent induce Davies into committing the crime?

2. Footnote 5 of Davies states that "[t]he conversation [between Davies and the undercover officer] took place in a chat room that was neither explicitly sexual by nature nor suggestive of the presence of minors." Imagine the chatroom conversation had instead been initiated between "Russell D" and "sweetgirlinaz2006" from a chatroom called "oldermenwholikegirls." Would these facts make a difference? Would the nature of the chatroom show predisposition?

3. You are a lawyer in the Office of the General Counsel at the Federal Bureau of Investigation. What guidelines would you put in place to regulate FBI online undercover operations to avoid entrapment issues in future prosecutions for child exploitation crimes? For example, would you permit your agents to place advertisements in online publications posing as young children? Would you permit them to post an undercover profile on myspace.com? To enter an Internet chatroom called "britneyspears" while using the screenname "sarah13"? How about an Internet chatroom called "oldermforyoungf"? If you permit agents to visit chatrooms posing as minors, would you let them contact individuals in the chatrooms, or would you require them to wait to be contacted by others?

4. Do the dynamics of online interactions indicate a need for changes in entrapment doctrine? Consider Dru Stevenson, *Entrapment by Numbers*, 16 U. Fla. J.L. & Pub. Pol'y 1, 69–70 (2005):

> There is less accountability for government where the enforcement method is cheap and relatively invisible when orchestrated. Traditional stings typically require a host of armed "backup" agents nearby in case the primary undercover operative encounters trouble. Catching pedophiles can be done mostly from a cubicle in an office. In addition, the Internet enables a single officer to entrap multiple individuals at once, as through on-line bulletin board postings. This feature of on-line entrapment may not be undesirable from a policy perspective, but it is a significant change from the traditional arrangement that the entrapment defense contemplated. Third, the inexpensive, relatively invisible nature of such operations also permits private entrapment to become rampant, which is not

the case in off-line settings or with other crimes. On-line vigilantism against pedophiles, in fact, has taken on unexpected proportions.

Do you agree that there is less police accountability online? If an agent turns on a logging function so that every word in a chat room or IM exchange is recorded, isn't there greater accountability online rather than less? Won't agents turn on that function to collect evidence against the defendant? And if there is more private entrapment online, is that a good thing or a bad one?

For other perspectives on Internet entrapment, see Jennifer Gregg, Note, *Caught In The Web: Entrapment In Cyberspace*, 19 Hastings Comm. & Ent. L.J. 157 (1996); Jarrod S. Hanson, Comment, *Entrapment In Cyberspace: A Renewed Call For Reasonable Suspicion*, 1996 U. Chi. Legal F. 535 (1996).

5. *Private entrapment.* There is no defense of private entrapment. The legal defense of entrapment can only be raised if the inducement was made by a government actor or a private person acting as an agent of the government. Is this sound as a matter of policy?

6. In United States v. Poehlman, 217 F.3d 692 (9th Cir. 2000), the Ninth Circuit overturned the conviction of a man who answered an online advertisment looking for a relationship that had been placed by an undercover agent. The man, Poehlman, admitted up front that he was a crossdresser and foot-fetishist. Poehlman received a response from "Sharon," who purported to be a widower with three young daughters in need of guidance. Poehlman communicated via e-mail with Sharon, and eventually Sharon indicated to Poehlman that she wanted Poehlman to engage in a sexual relationship with her daughters. Poehlmann was initially reluctant, as he only wanted a relationship with Sharon, but Sharon conditioned a relationship with her on Poehlman also having a relationship with her daughters. Poehlman eventually overcame his reluctance and agreed to meet Sharon and her daughters to engage in sexual relations with her daughters. When Poehlman entered the room to meet the daughters, he was arrested.

In an opinion by Judge Kozinski, the Ninth Circuit overturned the conviction on the ground that no reasonable juror could have failed to conclude that Poehlman was entrapped. There was little evidence of predisposition, the court held, and the government's conduct plainly amounted to inducement:

> [T]here is no doubt that the government induced Poehlman to commit the crime here. Had Sharon merely responded enthusiastically to a hint from Poehlman that he wanted to serve as her daughters' sexual mentor, there certainly would have been no inducement. But Sharon did much more. Throughout the correspondence with Poehlman, Sharon made it clear that she had made a firm decision about her children's sexual education, and that she believed that having Poehlman serve as their sexual mentor would be in their best interest.

> It is clear, moreover, that Poehlman continued to long for an adult relationship with Sharon, as well as a father-like relationship with the girls. He offered marriage; talked about quitting his job and moving to California; discussed traveling with Sharon and the girls; even offered his military health insurance benefits as an inducement. While refusing to

give Poehlman hope of a sexual relationship with her, Sharon encouraged these fantasies; she went so far as to check out Poehlman's job prospects in California. The government thus played on Poehlman's obvious need for an adult relationship, for acceptance of his sexual proclivities and for a family, to draw him ever deeper into a sexual fantasy world involving these imaginary girls.

[T]he record is clear that it was the Government's insistence and artful manipulation of appellant that finally drew him into the web skillfully spun by the detective. Through its aggressive intervention, the government materially affected the normal balance between risks and rewards from the commission of the crime, and thereby induced Poehlman to commit the offense.

When the Government's quest for convictions leads to the apprehension of an otherwise law-abiding citizen who, if left to his own devices, likely would have never run afoul of the law, the courts should intervene. So far as this record discloses, Poehlman is such a citizen. Prior to his unfortunate encounter with Sharon, he was on a quest for an adult relationship with a woman who would understand and accept his proclivities, which did not include sex with children. There is surely enough real crime in our society that it is unnecessary for our law enforcement officials to spend months luring an obviously lonely and confused individual to cross the line between fantasy and criminality.

Id. at 702–03, 705.

7. Prosecutions under 18 U.S.C. § 2422 and § 2423(a) normally require a violation or attempted violation of state law. The statutes prohibit traveling or enticing with intent to engage in sexual activity "for which any person can be charged with a criminal offense," which generally requires an analysis of state sexual assault law. State sexual assault laws can vary, however, which may create issues as to whether particular conduct is prohibited by state law in that jurisdiction.

Consider the facts of United States v. Patten, 397 F.3d 1100 (8th Cir. 2005). A police officer in West Fargo, North Dakota, posed in an Internet chat room as a 16 year-old girl. The defendant, 26 year-old Casey Patten, visited the chat room from his home in nearby Moorhead, Minnesota. The officer persuaded Patten to come to a grocery store in West Fargo, where the defendant was arrested. The law of North Dakota and Minnesota differ in a critical respect: in Minnesota, consensual sexual conduct between a 26 year-old man and a 16 year-old girl is legal, whereas the same conduct is illegal in North Dakota.

The defendant argued that there was insufficient evidence that he had intended to engage in sexual activity in North Dakota, and therefore that he had not violated the federal statute. According to the defendant, he had planned to engage in the activity in Minnesota, where it would have been legal. The Eighth Circuit affirmed the conviction, ruling that there was sufficient evidence from the facts of the case for a reasonable juror to conclude that the defendant intended to persuade the girl to engage in sexual activity in North Dakota. *See id*. at 1103–04.

8. *The impossibility defense.* Defendants in Internet undercover cases sometimes try to raise the impossibility defense. They argue that although they did try to meet a child to engage in sexual activity, they cannot be prosecuted because no actual child was involved. The offense was "impossible," the argument runs, because the child was actually an adult officer. Such defenses have been universally rejected, consistent with the modern trend away from recognizing an impossibility defense in other contexts. Courts have reasoned that the presence of a child is irrelevant because the liability is for attempt rather the substantive crime of engaging in sexual activities with a minor. *See, e.g.*, People v. Thousand, 631 N.W.2d 694 (Mich. 2001) (en banc).

CHAPTER 4

SENTENCING

■ ■ ■

When a defendant is convicted, a court must next impose a sentence. The law of criminal sentencing tends to focus on two issues. The first issue is whether to impose a prison term, and the length of any prison term imposed. The second issue is the conditions of any period of probation or post-incarceration supervised release.

The materials in this chapter consider sentencing law for computer crimes. The first part considers as a policy matter whether sentences for computer-related crimes should be different from sentences for equivalent physical crimes. The second part introduces the reader to the United States Sentencing Guidelines, and explores how the guidelines apply in child pornography cases. The third part considers how the Sentencing Guidelines apply in cases brought under 18 U.S.C. § 1030. The fourth section covers restrictions on computer use imposed in federal court as a condition of probation or supervised release.

A. ARE COMPUTER CRIMES DIFFERENT?

NEAL KUMAR KATYAL—CRIMINAL LAW IN CYBERSPACE

149 U. Pa. L. Rev. 1003, 1042–47, 1071–75 (2001).

Before computers, a criminal typically needed to work with other individuals to conduct serious criminal activity. Group crime arose for obvious reasons, from economies of scale to specialization of the labor pool. For example, it is nearly impossible for one person to rob a bank successfully. Several individuals are needed to carry weapons and provide firepower (economies of scale); someone needs to plan the operation (a form of specialization of labor); another must serve as a lookout (specialization again); and many people are needed to carry the money. Working together with others, whether in the criminal or corporate world, creates obvious efficiencies, as Ronald Coase explains in his pathbreaking article about why firms develop.

But computers change all this, and undermine the need for criminal conspiracy. * * * [A] cyberthief can, by herself, design a program to steal money from an electronic bank account or data from the Defense Department, rather than enlist a team to do so. A fraud artist can, by herself, send thousands of e-mails to unsuspecting recipients to create a Ponzi scheme. A child pornographer can create, store, and distribute images, and receive royalties or access fees without assistance. In these situations, a computer enables a single individual to launch a crime: No individual in realspace could break and enter a physical premise, and remove and steal the classified material without detection, perpetrate all the aspects of a Ponzi scheme, or run a child pornography ring. Cyberspace, however, is different. The electronic walls that secure money and data are pierced, not by additional thugs, but, rather, by additional computer power. In addition, cyberspace avoids the physical constraints of realspace (a burglar can only carry away a certain amount of loot and be in one place at a time).

If [the goal of criminal punishment is to deter harm], then it makes sense to punish the use of a computer to carry out a crime as if the computer were a quasi-conspirator. Doing so will deter the greater damage computer crime can incur per unit of investment in the enterprise. * * *

In sum, the law might develop penalties for using computers to aid a criminal offense. The case for criminalization proceeds from the fact that computers and co-conspirators are substitutes for each other. The solution proposed would not necessarily require treating computers as full co-conspirators, but it would require eliminating the law's current conceptualization of a computer as simply a method of crime, not a type of (or substitute for) a participant in crime.

A separate form of reduced costs to the criminal in cyberspace is the ease of escape. Because computer crime can be perpetrated by anyone, even someone who has never set foot near the target, the range of potential suspects is huge. This is unlike traditional crime, in which there is a high likelihood that a crime is committed by someone known to or seen by either the victim or the community in which the crime took place. A criminal in realspace has to be physically present to rob a bank, but a cybercriminal can be across the globe. This makes the crime easier to carry out, easier to conceal, and tougher to prosecute.

Despite some indications of the government's ability to trace criminal suspects online, the truth is that tracing is very difficult. A criminal may leave behind a trail of electronic footprints, but the footprints often end with a pseudonymous e-mail address from an ISP that possesses no subscriber information. Moreover, finding the footprints is often very difficult. Criminals can be sophisticated at weaving their footprints through computers based in several countries, which makes getting permission for real-time tracing very difficult. Unlike a criminal who needs to escape down a particular road, a criminal in cyberspace could be on any road, and these roads are not linked together in any meaningful fashion. The internet works by sending packets of data through whatever electronic pathway it finds most efficient at a given time. The protocol moves these packets a step closer to their destination, an electronic hop, without trying to map out a particular course for the next node to use when the packet arrives. Each hop ends in a host or router, which in turn sends the information on to the next host. What's more, sometimes large packets divide into smaller packets to be reassembled by the end-user when all the packets show up. Sometimes packets never arrive, due to network congestion and mistakes.

The upshot is that it is very difficult for law enforcement to find a criminal after an attack, particularly when the criminal can be on any road and evidence of her crime can be split into numerous subparcels, each of which is not itself incriminating. Even in those cases in which law enforcement has the technology and permission under applicable law to trace an attack, the investigators must be skilled at carrying out such a trace in order for it to be successful, and they must have knowledge about how to preserve the data trails in such a way that they will be admissible evidence in a criminal trial. Regular and frequent training of law enforcement is a necessity, as is up-to-date technological equipment. Government prosecutors and police must also be trained in the application of constitutional and statutory liberties in the internet context. Furthermore, the contraband and materials can be physically stored anywhere on the planet, making such evidence difficult to find and difficult to introduce in a court. Incriminating files of a criminal organization, such as the profits made from drug dealing, may be stored thousands of miles away. Alternatively, the evidence could reside in the United States but be moved abroad literally with a keystroke—whenever a person or an entity comes under criminal suspicion. Computers could also make it easier for criminals to disrupt law enforcement by spying on informants and sabotaging networks.

Because these factors lower the probability of successful enforcement, it may be appropriate to offset this lowered probability by increasing the magnitude of the criminal sanction.

NOTES AND QUESTIONS

1.   Every technological tool has the capacity to facilitate criminal activity. When should using a tool to commit a crime lead to greater punishment? Imagine a man robs a bank while wearing a ski mask (to avoid being identified) and while carrying a gun (to encourage compliance with his demands). Should the defendant receive a higher punishment because he wore the ski mask? Should he receive a higher punishment because he carried the gun? Are the gun and ski mask "quasi-conspirators" in the bank robbery? What general principle explains our intuitions about when use of a tool to facilitate a crime should change the appropriate punishment? How do computers fit in to that picture?

2.   Professor Katyal argues that higher punishments are needed for computer crimes to offset the ways computers facilitate crime. The thinking is that defendants will know they are facing greater punishments for computer crimes, and the fear of greater punishment will deter criminal behavior. Is this view of deterrence realistic?

3.   Sentencing schemes usually factor in the amount of loss or damage caused by a particular criminal offense. If a crime causes greater damage, it leads to greater punishment regardless of how the crime was committed. This means that if computers help wrongdoers commit crimes on a broader scale than before, computer crimes will trigger higher punishment even without special rules for computer-related offenses. Does this make it unnecessary to have new rules for punishing computer crimes?

4.   *Retribution and computer crime.* Deterrence is one goal of criminal punishment; retribution is another. What kinds of punishment are appropriate for computer crimes from a retributive perspective?

Retributivists might argue that a person who consciously confronts the wrongfulness of his conduct but continues with the offense is more culpable than one who does not fully appreciate the wrongfulness of his behavior. Computer-related crimes may seem more virtual, less harmful, and less real than their offline equivalents. From a retributive perspective, is someone who commits a computer-related crime likely to be *less* deserving of punishment than someone who commits an otherwise equivalent physical crime?

Imagine John breaks into a closed store at night and snoops around. That same night, Jane goes online and hacks into a server at an e-commerce site and looks through various files. It takes John two days to plan the physical crime and three hours to commit it; it takes Jane thirty minutes to plan and commit the digital version of the offense. To John, the offense is very real; to Jane, it feels like a computer game. Should Jane receive a higher sentence than John because computer crimes are easier to commit and harder to detect? Or should John receive a higher sentence because he fully appreciated the wrongfulness of his conduct?

If deterrence theory points in the direction of greater punishments for cybercrimes, and retributive theory points in the opposite direction, which theory should win out? Should we call it a tie?

5.   It is widely believed that the relative anonymity of the Internet encourages unlawful behavior. But is it true? Researchers tried to answer this question using a decoy website. The goal was to determine how often Internet users searching for innocent material online would try to copy stolen software, obtain stolen passwords, and view hard-core pornography if given the chance. *See* Christina Demetriou & Andrew Silke, *A Criminological Internet "Sting": Experimental Evidence of Illegal and Deviant Visits to a Website Trap,* 43 Brit. J. Criminology 213 (2003).

The designers of the study set up a decoy website called "Cyber Magpie," and turned on logging functions that recorded every visit to the site. They advertised the site on newsgroups, promoting it as a legal source of "excellent freeware and shareware games." Upon entering the site, however, visitors were offered a choice of both legal and illegal materials. The site was configured to show visitors seven links: 1) a legal disclaimer, 2) shareware and freeware, 3) games (both free and hacked), 4) illegally obtained commercial software, 5) soft-core pornography, 6) hard-core pornography, and 7) stolen passwords that could be used to access pornographic sites. (The site did not actually distribute such materials; users who attempted to access them would encounter a message that the materials were unavailable.)

The Cyber Magpie site was available for 88 days, and during that time it logged 803 visitors. The researchers determined that 93% of the visitors initially accessed the site looking for legal shareware or freeware games. However, the most popular link turned out to be hard-core pornography: 60% of visitors to Cyber Magpie clicked on the link to try to view it. Further, 45% of users accessed the portion of the site that hosted soft-core pornography; 41% attempted to access the part of the site containing illegal copyrighted commercial software; and 38% accessed the portion of the site that claimed to have illegally hacked games. Roughly similar numbers accessed the parts of the website that featured the shareware and freeware games and other legally accessible software. Only 2% of visitors viewed the legal disclaimer.

Are you surprised by these results? The authors of the study comment, *id.* at 220:

> The acts observed in this study * * * occurred in a situation of perceived anonymity for the perpetrators, and there were immediate personal rewards for the visitors to do what they did. Such a combination of factors creates a situation where deviant behavior is not simply common, it actually becomes the norm. Only a minority of visitors to Cyber Magpie avoided the illegal or pornographic sections. Such findings have disturbing implications with regard to how we think about–and respond to–crime and deviancy in cyberspace. As more and more people access and use the Internet on an increasingly regular basis, we can expect more people to become aware of, and exposed to, a range of opportunities to commit various illegal and socially questionable behaviours. Worryingly, this research suggests that a majority of Internet users will not resist temptation. The implications of this loom large for those charged with policing the Internet and with developing policy on how it should and can be governed.

Are the authors' concerns valid? Are Internet users who choose to visit a freeware site called "Cyber Magpie" representative of Internet users as a whole? On the other hand, if the authors are correct that "the majority of Internet users will not resist temptation" to engage in criminal activity online, how should the law respond?

6.   In federal court, criminal sentences are imposed under the complex structure of the United States Sentencing Guidelines. Materials later in this chapter consider in detail how the Sentencing Guidelines apply to computer crimes. For now, however, it is worth noting that Congress and the Sentencing Commission have treated computer crimes differently from analogous physical crimes in a number of ways.

For example, provisions of the Sentencing Guidelines applicable to child pornography offenses provide for an enhanced sentence "[i]f the offense involved the use of a computer or an interactive computer service for the possession, transmission, receipt, or distribution of the material." U.S.S.G. § 2G2.2(b)(6). This enhancement was first enacted in 1995. The House Report accompanying the legislation that led to this enhancement explained the rationale:

> Distributing child pornography through computers is particularly harmful because it can reach an almost limitless audience. Because of its wide

dissemination and instantaneous transmission, computer-assisted trafficking is also more difficult for law enforcement officials to investigate and prosecute. Additionally, the increasing use of computers to transmit child pornography substantially increases the likelihood that this material will be viewed by, and thus harm, children. Finally, the Committee notes with particular concern the fact that pedophiles may use a child's fascination with computer technology as a lure to drag children into sexual relationships. In light of these significant harms, it is essential that those who are caught and convicted for this conduct be punished severely.

H.R. Rep. No. 104–90, at 3–4 (1995), *reprinted in* 1995 U.S.C.C.A.N. 759, 760–61. Do you agree? Most child pornography offenses prosecuted today involve computers. Does this make the case for an enhancement stronger or weaker today than in 1995, when Congress first enacted the enhancement?

7. *Use of a special skill.* The Sentencing Guidelines allow sentencing judges to increase the punishment when a defendant uses a special skill to facilitate the commission of an offense. The use of a special skill leads to an increase in the defendant's offense level, which, as we will see, corresponds to a higher sentence. The section, U.S.S.G. § 3B1.3, applies broadly across federal crimes:

> If the defendant abused a position of public or private trust, or used a special skill, in a manner that significantly facilitated the commission or concealment of the offense, increase by 2 levels. This adjustment may not be employed if an abuse of trust or skill is included in the base offense level or specific offense characteristic[.] * * *

Application Note 3 then explains that special skills "refers to a skill not possessed by members of the general public and usually requiring substantial education, training or licensing. Examples would include pilots, lawyers, doctors, accountants, chemists, and demolition experts."

When is using a computer in a crime "use of a special skill"? Are computer skills "special"? If a defendant commits a computer crime, does he necessarily deserve greater punishment?

UNITED STATES v. LEE

United States Court of Appeals for the Ninth Circuit, 2002.
296 F.3d 792.

KLEINFELD, CIRCUIT JUDGE.

This case involves application of the special skills sentencing adjustment to the use of a computer.

Facts

The Honolulu Marathon Association has a web site at "www.honolulu-marathon.org." During the relevant time, U.S. residents could use the site to register for the Honolulu Marathon and pay the registration fee online. Although many Japanese enter the race, the site did not permit online registration from Japan, but told Japanese entrants to register through an office in Japan.

The appellant, Kent Aoki Lee, lived in Honolulu, where he owned a video rental store. Lee came up with a scheme to sell marathon services to the marathon's Japanese market. Lee owned a computer server, which he kept on the premises of an internet service provider with whom he had a dial-up internet account. He registered the domain name "www.honolulu-marathon.com" and created a site almost identical to the official Honolulu Marathon site by copying its files onto his server. While the official site did not permit online registration from Japan, Lee's site contained an online registration form written in Japanese on which runners could enter personal information and credit card information. While the official registration fee was $65, Lee's site charged $165. The extra $100 over the registration fee covered a package including transportation to the race site, a meal, and a tour. Of course, none of this was legitimate, since Lee's web site and registration package were not authorized by the Honolulu Marathon Association. Seventeen people tried to register through Lee's site.

Lee's scheme was uncovered and he pleaded guilty to one count of wire fraud and one unrelated count of selling Viagra without a prescription. The main issue at sentencing was whether the district court could impose the special skills adjustment based on Lee's use of computer skills in creating his phony site.

Lee created his phony site by copying the legitimate site's files onto his computer server. Web sites consist of multiple web pages, which consist of individual computer files written in "hypertext markup language," or "HTML." The HTML files constituting a web site are located through a directory on a computer server. A computer directory is like a card in an old-fashioned library catalog, that tells where to find a book on a shelf. However a site's HTML files are referenced, they are linked together in the directory to create the whole web site. These links reflect the specific location of individual files within the server's structure of directories and subdirectories. The graphics on a web page are actually individual computer files to which that page's HTML file links, causing them to appear when the web page is displayed. An individual graphic file may be in the same directory as the HTML file to which it's linked, or in a subdirectory, or on another computer server altogether, and the link reflects that specific location. To copy a web site onto another computer server, it's not enough to copy the HTML file and the graphics for each web page. The copier must also recreate the directory structure of the original site or edit the links in the HTML files to reflect the different directory structure.

The creator of the genuine Honolulu Marathon site testified that Lee could have copied most of the site without knowing much about its directory structure, by using off-the-shelf software such as Microsoft's *FrontPage 98,* aided by a general circulation book such as *FrontPage 98 for Dummies.* She also testified that a program like *FrontPage* would have written a line of code into the fake site's HTML files, indicating that it had been used. There weren't any such lines of code in the HTML files on

Lee's site, suggesting that he didn't use this easy approach to copying the site. The creator of the authorized web site also testified that Lee could have pirated the site, much more slowly and laboriously, by using a text editor to copy it page by page (there were 130 individual web pages) and recreating the original site's directory structure so that each web page would properly display graphics and link to the other pages on the site. The legitimate site had two features, databases containing entrants' registration information and a list of past race results, that Lee could not copy onto his phony site, so he linked to those features on the genuine site so that they would appear to be part of his fake web site.

Lee's phony site contained one feature that was not on the genuine site, the online entry form that allowed residents of Japan to sign up for the marathon and provide a credit card account number to be billed for payment of the entry fee. The information entered on this form was processed using a "script," which is a program written in "common gateway interface," or "CGI," a programming language. The CGI script used by Lee's phony site didn't directly charge credit cards. It just stored the credit card data in a file on Lee's server, so that Lee could manually charge the cards later. (This database file was password protected, which the government's witness testified would require some knowledge of the server's operating system.) An excerpt of *FrontPage 98 for Dummies* that was read into the record told readers that to do CGI scripts, they should get help from someone experienced with computer programming. The official site's creator testified that writing a CGI form-handling script from scratch would have required significant programming expertise, but that modifying an existing script would have been much easier. She also testified that CGI scripts could be downloaded from the internet, and that web sites could be found that advised how to modify scripts to suit particular online forms.

The district court did not make a finding as to whether Lee copied the web site the easy way, such as by using *FrontPage 98* and *FrontPage 98 for Dummies* (and perhaps deleting the software's identifying code using a text editor), or the hard way, using a text editor to copy the web site's HTML files page by page and figuring out the original site's directory structure. Nor did the court make a finding as to whether Lee downloaded the CGI script for his online form from the internet or made it himself from scratch, and if so, whether he had any expert assistance. Nor did the court make a finding as to whether Lee or his internet service provider maintained his server. The district court found that Lee "was skilled at accessing and manipulating computer systems" and imposed the special skills enhancement. The adjustment raised the guideline sentencing range from six to twelve months to ten to sixteen months. This increase deprived the district court of the sentencing option of imposing no imprisonment.

Although Lee pleaded guilty, he reserved his right to appeal if the district court imposed the two-level special skill adjustment under U.S.S.G. § 3B1.3. Serving of the sentence awaits disposition of this appeal.

Analysis

The special skill adjustment provides for a two-level increase "[i]f the defendant abused a position of public or private trust, or used a special skill, in a manner that significantly facilitated the commission or concealment of the offense." The abuse of a position of trust part of the adjustment applies to positions "characterized by professional or managerial discretion," such as an attorney serving as a guardian who embezzles the client's money, a bank executive's fraudulent loan scheme, or a physician who sexually abuses a patient under the guise of an examination, but not to embezzlement by a bank teller or hotel clerk. The application note defining "special skill" says that it is "a skill not possessed by members of the general public and usually requiring substantial education, training, or licensing. Examples would include pilots, lawyers, doctors, accountants, chemists, and demolition experts."

The district court based its imposition of the adjustment on our decision in *United States v. Petersen,* 98 F.3d 502 (9th Cir. 1996). The issue in the case at bar is whether Lee was more like the defendant in *Petersen,* or more like the defendant in another of our special skills cases, going the other way, *United States v. Green,* 962 F.2d 938 (9th Cir. 1992). We conclude that the scope of discretion was not broad enough, in view of the limited findings, to treat this case like *Petersen,* and that it has to be put in the same class as *Green,* where we held that it was an abuse of discretion to impose the special skills adjustment. This conclusion keeps our circuit's law consistent with that of the Sixth Circuit, which held in *United States v. Godman,* 223 F.3d 320 (6th Cir. 2000), that a level of computer expertise like Lee's did not justify imposition of the adjustment.

The defendant in *United States v. Petersen,* which upheld the adjustment, was an expert hacker. He hacked into a national credit reporting agency's computer system and stole personal information that he used to order fraudulent credit cards. Then he hacked into a telephone company's computers, seized control of the telephone lines to a radio station, and arranged for himself and his confederates to be the callers who "won" two Porsches, $40,000, and two trips to Hawaii in a radio call-in contest. Then he hacked into a national commercial lender's computer and got it to wire $150,000 to him through two other banks. This goes far beyond the computer skills of a clever high school youth or even many people who earn their livings as computer technicians and software engineers. The district court found that Petersen had "extraordinary knowledge of how computers work and how information is stored, how information is retrieved, and how the security of those systems can be preserved or invaded" and imposed the special skill adjustment. We affirmed, holding that "despite Petersen's lack of formal training or licensing, his sophisticated computer skills reasonably can be equated to the skills possessed by pilots, lawyers, chemists, and demolition experts" for purposes of the special skills adjustment.

In a footnote, we went out of our way in *Petersen* to caution against routine application of the special skills enhancement to people with computer skills:

> We do not intend to suggest that the ability to use or access computers would support a special skill adjustment under all circumstances. Computer skills cover a wide spectrum of ability. Only where a defendant's computer skills are particularly sophisticated do they correspond to the Sentencing Commission's examples of special skills—lawyer, doctor, pilot, etc. Courts should be particularly cautious in imposing special skills adjustments where substantial education, training, or licensing is not involved.

This footnote distinguishes *Petersen* from the case at bar, because Lee's skills are not "particularly sophisticated" like Petersen's, and unlike Petersen's, don't correspond to the Sentencing Commission's examples of special skills—lawyer, doctor, pilot, etc. As we said in *Petersen,* where substantial education, training or licensing is not involved, district courts must be especially cautious about imposing the adjustment.

Petersen distinguished *United States v. Green,* where we reversed a special skills adjustment. Green took graphic design classes, learned from an instructor about paper that could be used for currency and about how it could be properly cut, ordered the special paper from a paper company (which tipped off the Secret Service), and took numerous photographs of currency, in the course of his counterfeiting scheme. We held that the printing and photographic skills were not so special as to permit the district court to impose the adjustment, saying it's not enough that "the offense was difficult to commit or required a special skill to complete."

In *United States v. Godman,* the Sixth Circuit considered *Petersen* and quoted and followed our limiting footnote that we quote above. Like Green, Godman was a counterfeiter, but Godman used an off-the-shelf professional page publishing program, Adobe PageMaker, with a scanner and a color inkjet printer. He'd learned PageMaker in a week, and had specialized computer experience preparing and repeatedly updating a color catalog. Godman held that the special skills adjustment could not properly be imposed, because Godman's level of computer skills was not analogous to the level of skill possessed by the lawyers, doctors, pilots, etc. listed in the application note. The Sixth Circuit held that the district court erred by stressing "overmuch" that Godman's skills were not shared by the general public: "As the Application Note's reference to the substantial training of such professionals as doctors and accountants suggests, emphasis is better placed on the difficulty with which a particular skill is acquired." The Sixth Circuit emphasized that "such skills are acquired through months (or years) of training, or the equivalent in self-tutelage."

Our own cases have suggested factors that might make a skill "special" for purposes of this sentencing adjustment, including a "public trust" rationale, the level of sophistication, and special educational or licensing requirements. But this adjustment becomes open-ended to the point of meaninglessness if the phrase "special skill" is taken out of its context. There probably isn't an occupation on earth that doesn't involve some special skill not possessed by people outside it, and few of us who sit as judges would know how to do the work of most of the people who appear before us. So asking whether a skill is "special," in the sense of not being common among the adult population, like driving a car, doesn't get us very far toward deciding any cases.

And focusing much on the "specialness" of a skill is also hard to reconcile with our precedents. In *United States v. Harper,* 33 F.3d 1143 (9th Cir. 1994), the defendant's skills were very special indeed. The robber had worked for both a bank and an ATM service company, and used the knowledge gained in both occupations to come up with a unique scheme to rob an ATM. At just the right time for the last service call of the day, when the ATM service office would empty out while the robbery was going on, she made a withdrawal from an ATM but didn't take the money. She knew that leaving the cash would cause the ATM to shut itself down and generate a service call, which would put technicians on the site, and that they would open the machine so that she and her confederates could rob it. As skills go, Harper's were quite special, but we reversed the sentence because they weren't like those of pilots, lawyers, doctors, accountants, chemists and demolition experts.

Our cases are best reconciled, and this sentencing guideline is best read, as a two-part test. The test is not just whether the skill is "not possessed by members of the general public," but also, as a *sine qua non,* whether it is a skill "usually requiring substantial education, training, or licensing." The application note's reference to "pilots, lawyers, doctors, accountants, chemists, and demolition experts" requires reasoning by analogy, not just reference to dictionary definitions of "special" and "skill." The special skill adjustment falls within the same guideline as an adjustment for people who abuse a "position of public or private trust, or used a special skill." The application notes limit the position of trust adjustment to people with "professional or managerial discretion," analo-gous to attorneys who hold their clients' money in trust, physicians who treat patients, and "executives" (but not tellers) who manage a bank's loans. The application note for special skills parallels the application note for positions of trust in its reference to people trained or employed at a high level.

Lee was a video rental store operator who copied a web site. The findings don't establish whether he used off-the-shelf software or had to know more about programming, but it doesn't matter because either way, his level of sophistication was nothing like Petersen's. His skills were more like Green's or Godman's than Petersen's, and not in the class of "pilots, lawyers, doctors, accountants, chemists, and demolition experts." Thus, under our precedents and the guideline's application notes, the district court's imposition of the special skills adjustment was not sup-ported by the findings. We therefore reverse and remand for resentencing.

Notes and Questions

1. In United States v. Mainard, 5 F.3d 404, 406 (9th Cir. 1993), the Ninth Circuit contended that the purpose of the special skills enhancement is "to add to the punishment of those who turn legitimate special skills to the perpetration of evil deeds":

> In a sense, abuse of a special skill is a special kind of abuse of trust. It is a breach of the trust that society reposes in a person when it enables him to acquire and have a skill that other members of society do not possess. That special societal investment and encouragement allows a person to acquire skills that are then held in a kind of trust for all of us. When the person turns those skills to evil deeds, a special wrong is perpetrated upon society, just as other abuses of trust perpetrate a special wrong upon their victims.

Do you find this retributive rationale persuasive? How does it apply to computer skills?

2. What kinds of computer skills should count as special skills? In 1985, was reasonable proficiency in the use of a personal computer a special skill? How about today? Does the answer depend on the defendant's age? For example, an average set of computer skills among 18 year-olds might be exceptional among 75 year-olds. What standard should govern? Is the best answer a "reasonable person" standard at the time of the offense? Or should computer skills be categorically exempt from the special skills enhancement?

3. Technical skills may be needed to commit a particular crime. Can those skills also constitute "special skills" that justify a higher sentence following conviction?

In United States v. Young, 932 F.2d 1510 (D.C. Cir. 1991), the defendant was convicted of conspiring to manufacture and distribute 100 grams or more of pure phencyclidine ("PCP"). Manufacturing PCP requires following a complex chemical process, and the defendant had set up a laboratory to manufacture the drug. The government argued that the understanding of chemistry needed to manufacture PCP amounted to special skills justifying an enhancement. The D.C. Circuit disagreed, ruling that the defendant did not deserve the enhancement because he was not a trained chemist. Understanding chemistry just enough to commit the offense was insufficient:

> Section 3B1.3 provides a two-level enhancement if the defendant used a special skill, in a manner that significantly facilitated the commission or concealment of the offense. The use of the word "facilitate"—which means "to make easier," see Webster's New Collegiate Dictionary (1977)—is important in this context. It indicates to us that the Sentencing Commission assumed that the defendant knows how to commit the offense in the first place and that he uses a special skill to make it easier to commit the crime. Thus, the special skill necessary to justify a § 3B1.3 enhancement must be more than the mere ability to commit the offense; it must constitute an additional, pre-existing skill that the defendant uses to facilitate the commission or concealment of the offense.

* * * Nothing in the commentary suggests that § 3B1.3 applies to a criminal who, like appellant, bones up on the tricks of his trade and becomes adept at committing a crime that the general public does not know how to commit. To the contrary, the commentary indicates that § 3B1.3 was intended to punish those who abuse their special skills by using them to facilitate criminal activity rather than legal, socially beneficial activity.

Id. at 1512–13.

How should this apply to computer crimes? Does it matter that most Americans have some computer skills, and that given the broad scope of 18 U.S.C. § 1030, most Americans are also capable of accessing a computer without authorization or exceeding authorized access? Does applying the special skills enhancement to a computer crime amount to double-counting?

4. Imagine that *A* is a skilled programmer who creates a new and dangerous computer virus. *B* is *A*'s friend and a novice computer user. *A* shares the virus with *B*, and both *A* and *B*, acting individually, send out the virus in a series of e-mails. Is *A* more culpable than *B*, assuming that they have the same intent to cause damage? Would *A* receive the special skills enhancement under prevailing law?

B. SENTENCING IN CHILD PORNOGRAPHY CASES

Criminal sentences imposed for federal crimes are determined under a framework set up by the United States Sentencing Guidelines. The Sentencing Guidelines are complicated, and studying how they apply in every detail would require a course of its own. For our purposes, however, we can quickly and profitably appreciate the basics of the Guidelines that arise in federal computer crime cases. This will let us see how courts determine the length of prison terms in most cases, even if it glosses over some of the details.

The Sentencing Guidelines are very important because substantive criminal law typically leaves open a wide range of criminal punishments that a court can impose following conviction. Every crime has a statutory maximum punishment, such as five years imprisonment or twenty years imprisonment. A small number of crimes also have mandatory minimum punishments that courts must impose regardless of the circumstances. In most cases, however, substantive statutory law leaves trial judges a great deal of sentencing discretion. For example, if a defendant is convicted of violating a crime with a ten-year statutory maximum punishment and no mandatory minimum punishment, the sentencing judge can in theory impose any prison sentence from zero days up to ten years.

The Sentencing Guidelines were enacted to limit this discretion and to ensure more uniform sentences. The basic idea is that factors relevant to sentencing are considered explicitly by the Guidelines, and this consideration leads sentencing judges to a very specific range of sentences that can be imposed in that particular case. For each case, the judge calculates the "offense level" for the case, calculates the defendant's criminal history category, and then matches up the offense level and criminal history category with a set range of prison time as measured in months. Under the Supreme Court's decision in United States v. Booker, 543 U.S. 220 (2005), Guidelines determinations are not binding on sentencing judges. Post–*Booker*, however, the Guidelines continue to be the primary authority used to determine the length of federal sentences.

Applying the Guidelines generally involves six steps:

1) Select the offense guideline.

The first step is to select the proper offense conduct guideline for the specific criminal offenses that the defendant violated. Chapter Two of the Guidelines contains the offense conduct guidelines that are applicable in different types of criminal offenses. Each offense conduct guideline explains how to calculate the offense level for that type of offense. For example, U.S.S.G. § 2A1.1 is the offense conduct guideline for first-degree murder cases, U.S.S.G. § 2A1.2 is for second-degree murder cases, and U.S.S.G. § 2A1.3 is for manslaughter cases. An appendix associated with the Guidelines contains a chart connecting most federal criminal statutes to their relevant offense conduct guidelines.

The Chapter Two offense guidelines that are most important in computer crime cases are U.S.S.G. § 2G2.2, applicable in child pornography offenses, and U.S.S.G. § 2B1.1, applicable in most economic crime cases including most computer misuse offenses. Because these are the two most important offense guidelines, the remainder of the material in this chapter will focus on their application.

2) Determine the offense level for the crime.

The next step is to determine the offense level for the crime by applying the relevant offense guideline from Chapter Two. To calculate this, start with the base offense level and then adjust that number by applying the special offense characteristics. This excerpt from § 2G2.2 provides the key guidance used to calculate sentences in most child pornography offenses:

(a) Base Offense Level:

    (1) 18, if the defendant is convicted of ... § 2252(a)(4), or § 2252A(a)(5).

    (2) 22, otherwise.

(b) Specific Offense Characteristics

    (1) If (A) subsection (a)(2) applies; (B) the defendant's conduct was limited to the receipt or solicitation of material involving the sexual exploitation of a minor; and (C) the defendant did not intend to traffic in, or distribute, such material, decrease by 2 levels.

(2) If the material involved a prepubescent minor or a minor who had not attained the age of 12 years, increase by 2 levels.

(3) (Apply the greatest) If the offense involved:

    (A) Distribution for pecuniary gain, increase by the number of levels from the table in § 2B1.1 (Theft, Property Destruction, and Fraud) corresponding to the retail value of the material, but by not less than 5 levels.

    (B) Distribution for the receipt, or expectation of receipt, of a thing of value, but not for pecuniary gain, increase by 5 levels.

    (C) Distribution to a minor, increase by 5 levels.

    (D) Distribution to a minor that was intended to persuade, induce, entice, or coerce the minor to engage in any illegal activity, other than illegal activity covered under subdivision (E), increase by 6 levels.

    (E) Distribution to a minor that was intended to persuade, induce, entice, coerce, or facilitate the travel of, the minor to engage in prohibited sexual conduct, increase by 7 levels.

    (F) Distribution other than distribution described in subdivisions (A) through (E), increase by 2 levels.

(4) If the offense involved material that portrays sadistic or masochistic conduct or other depictions of violence, increase by 4 levels.

(5) If the defendant engaged in a pattern of activity involving the sexual abuse or exploitation of a minor, increase by 5 levels.

(6) If the offense involved the use of a computer or an interactive computer service for the possession, transmission, receipt, or distribution of the material, increase by 2 levels.

(7) If the offense involved—

    (A) at least 10 images, but fewer than 150, increase by 2 levels;

    (B) at least 150 images, but fewer than 300, increase by 3 levels;

    (C) at least 300 images, but fewer than 600, increase by 4 levels; and

    (D) 600 or more images, increase by 5 levels.

Notably, the Sentencing Guidelines direct the sentencing court to include all "relevant conduct" in the court's calculations, even if that conduct was not charged in the indictment, admitted in a guilty plea, or proved at trial. *See* U.S.S.G. § 1B1.3. As a result, when considering what conduct the offense "involved," you should include all of the defendant's acts that relate to the crime, not just the specific facts that led to the conviction.

An example will help illustrate how these rules work in practice. Imagine an undercover agent is in an Internet chat room posing as a collector of child pornography, and that a suspect sends the agent one image of child pornography. The agent obtains the suspect's Internet records, finds out where he lives, and then searches his home to seize his computer. A search of the suspect's home computer reveals 200 images of child pornography. The suspect then pleads guilty to possessing child pornography. What offense level should be reached in the case? Begin with a base offense level of 18 under § 2G.2.2(a)(1) because the defendant pled guilty to possession instead of receipt or distribution. Second, increase two levels under § 2G2.2(b)(3)(F) because the relevant conduct included distributing the image to an undercover police officer. Next, increase two levels under § 2G.2.2(b)(6) because the crime involved a computer. Finally, increase another three levels under § 2G.2.2(b)(7)(B) because of the quantity of images. The resulting offense level should be 25.

3) Apply upward or downward adjustments.

Chapter Three of the Sentencing Guidelines contains adjustments to the offense level that a court can make to reflect the specific circumstances of the crime, the defendant, and the victim. These adjustments apply to all crimes, not just crimes covered in a specific offense conduct guideline. For example, a defendant who had a major role in a conspiracy can receive an increase in the offense level, *see* U.S.S.G. § 3B1.1, while a defendant who played only a minor role in a conspiracy can receive a decrease in the offense level, *see* U.S.S.G. § 3B1.2. As noted earlier, a defendant who used special skills in the commission of an offense can receive an increase in the offense level pursuant to U.S.S.G. § 3B1.3.

One downward adjustment that is applied in a majority of cases is the adjustment for acceptance of responsibility, U.S.S.G. § 3E1.1. This adjustment usually applies when a defendant elects to plead guilty rather than go to trial:

(a) If the defendant clearly demonstrates acceptance of responsibility for his offense, decrease the offense level by 2 levels.

(b) If the defendant qualifies for a decrease under subsection (a), the offense level determined prior to the operation of subsection (a) is level 16 or greater, and the defendant has assisted authorities in the investigation or prosecution of his own misconduct by taking one or more of the following steps: (1) timely providing complete information to the government concerning his own involvement in the offense; or (2) timely notifying authorities of his intention to enter a plea of guilty, thereby permitting the government to avoid preparing for trial and permitting the court to allocate its resources efficiently, decrease the offense level by 1 additional level.

Application Note 2 to this provision explains that "[t]his adjustment is not intended to apply to a defendant who puts the government to its burden of proof at trial by denying the essential factual elements of guilt, is convicted, and only then admits guilt and expresses remorse."

The Guidelines also include rules on grouping offenses when a defendant is convicted of multiple offenses. Such rules are necessary because a defendant may be convicted of multiple crimes, some of which are related to each other and others of which are not, and each crime will lead to its own offense level. The grouping rules appear in Chapter Three, Part D of the Guidelines, and explain how the different crimes and offense levels should be resolved to create a single offense level. The rules are quite complicated when considered in detail, but here is the basic approach:

(1) When the conduct involves fungible items, e.g., separate drug transactions or thefts of money, the amounts are added and the guidelines apply to the total amount.

(2) When nonfungible harms are involved, the offense level for the most serious count is increased (according to a somewhat diminishing scale) to reflect the existence of other counts of conviction.

United States Sentencing Commission, Guidelines Manual 6–7 (2005).

4) Determine the defendant's criminal history category.

Chapter Four of the Guidelines contains the rules for calculating a defendant's criminal history category. Criminal history categories range from I to VI, and are based on the number of criminal history "points" revealed by the defendant's record of past convictions. Criminal history is a very important part of criminal sentencing: If two defendants are convicted of the same crime, the defendant with a significant criminal history normally will receive a greater prison sentence than the defendant without such a history.

The general rule is that a defendant receives three points of criminal history for every past conviction that led to a sentence of greater than one year in prison; two points of criminal history for every past conviction that led to a sentence between sixty days and a year of prison; and one point for every other criminal conviction up to four points. *See* U.S.S.G. § 4A1.1. A defendant with zero or one criminal history points will have a criminal history category of I; a defendant with two or three points will have a criminal history category of II; four, five, or six points will be category III; and so forth.

5) Find the sentencing range from the sentencing table.

Chapter Five of the Guidelines contains a sentencing table that assigns a presumptive sentencing range based on the defendant's offense level and criminal history category. The table indicates the range of recommended sentences in months:

Sentencing Table

(in months of imprisonment)

	Offense Level	Criminal History Category (Criminal History Points)					
		I (0 or 1)	II (2 or 3)	III (4, 5, 6)	IV (7, 8, 9)	V (10, 11, 12)	VI (13 or more)
Zone A	1	0–6	0–6	0–6	0–6	0–6	0–6
	2	0–6	0–6	0–6	0–6	0–6	1–7
	3	0–6	0–6	0–6	0–6	2–8	3–9
	4	0–6	0–6	0–6	2–8	4–10	6–12
	5	0–6	0–6	1–7	4–10	6–12	9–15
	6	0–6	1–7	2–8	6–12	9–15	12–18
	7	0–6	2–8	4–10	8–14	12–18	15–21
	8	0–6	4–10	6–12	10–16	15–21	18–24
Zone B	9	4–10	6–12	8–14	12–18	18–24	21–27
Zone C	10	6–12	8–14	10–16	15–21	21–27	24–30
	11	8–14	10–16	12–18	18–24	24–30	27–33
	12	10–16	12–18	15–21	21–27	27–33	30–37
Zone D	13	12–18	15–21	18–24	24–30	30–37	33–41
	14	15–21	18–24	21–27	27–33	33–41	37–46
	15	18–24	21–27	24–30	30–37	37–46	41–51
	16	21–27	24–30	27–33	33–41	41–51	46–57
	17	24–30	27–33	30–37	37–46	46–57	51–63
	18	27–33	30–37	33–41	41–51	51–63	57–71
	19	30–37	33–41	37–46	46–57	57–71	63–78
	20	33–41	37–46	41–51	51–63	63–78	70–87
	21	37–46	41–51	46–57	57–71	70–87	77–96
	22	41–51	46–57	51–63	63–78	77–96	84–105
	23	46–57	51–63	57–71	70–87	84–105	92–115
	24	51–63	57–71	63–78	77–96	92–115	100–125
	25	57–71	63–78	70–87	84–105	100–125	110–137
	26	63–78	70–87	78–97	92–115	110–137	120–150
	27	70–87	78–97	87–108	100–125	120–150	130–162
	28	78–97	87–108	97–121	110–137	130–162	140–175
	29	87–108	97–121	108–135	121–151	140–175	151–188
	30	97–121	108–135	121–151	135–168	151–188	168–210
	31	108–135	121–151	135–168	151–188	168–210	188–235
	32	121–151	135–168	151–188	168–210	188–235	210–262
	33	135–168	151–188	168–210	188–235	210–262	235–293
	34	151–188	168–210	188–235	210–262	235–293	262–327
	35	168–210	188–235	210–262	235–293	262–327	292–365
	36	188–235	210–262	235–293	262–327	292–365	324–405
	37	210–262	235–293	262–327	292–365	324–405	360–life
	38	235–293	262–327	292–365	324–405	360–life	360–life
	39	262–327	292–365	324–405	360–life	360–life	
	40	292–365	324–405	360–life	360–life	360–life	
	41	324–405	360–life	360–life	360–life	360–life	
	42	360–life	360–life	360–life	360–life	360–life	
	43	life	life	life	life	life	

6) Consider whether a non-guidelines sentence is appropriate.

The last step is to consider whether a non-guidelines sentence is appropriate. Chapter Five of the Guidelines contains provisions that permit a judge to depart from the Guidelines range in special circumstances. For example, a defendant who provided substantial assistance to the prosecution can receive a downward departure under U.S.S.G. § 5K1.1. More broadly, the Supreme Court's decision in United States v. Booker, 543 U.S. 220 (2005), permits sentencing judges to sentence defendants to prison terms outside the relevant Guidelines range so long as the departures from the Guidelines range are "reasonable." *Id.* at 261–62.

Notes and Questions

1.   The Sentencing Guidelines rely on the concept of a "heartland," a typical violation of a particular criminal offense. For example, in United States v. DeBeir, 186 F.3d 561 (4th Cir. 1999), the defendant was caught in an online undercover sting and charged with traveling in interstate commerce with the intent to engage in a sexual act with a minor in violation of 18 U.S.C. § 2423(b). The district judge sentenced the defendant to probation after departing downward under the "catch-all" provision of U.S.S.G. § 5K2.0, which permits judges to award sentences outside the Guidelines range of the facts of the case bring it outside the heartland of typical cases. The district court judge relied on a number of factors, including that the crime was "victimless" because it involved an Internet sting rather than an actual child. The Fourth Circuit reversed:

> The crux of the district court's * * * finding seems to be its conclusion that DeBeir is not the type of offender that the guideline is really aimed at targeting. We cannot agree. In fact, offenses of this nature are increasingly committed with the help of the internet, and in such cases the offender must necessarily have had access to and the skills to use a computer. Thus we find nothing extraordinary about the particular factual landscape of this case—*i.e.,* that DeBeir is an intelligent and well-educated adult, has a strong employment history, had no prior exposure to life in prison, is neither a chronic offender nor a pedophile, was caught in a sting operation, received coverage in the media, later attempted counseling, and experienced remorse—that brings it outside the heartland of cases sentenced under this guideline.

DeBeir, 186 F.3d at 573.

2.   What are the practical consequences of an extra offense level in terms of the jail time a defendant receives? The answer depends on whether the offense level is at the high end of the Guidelines or the low end, as well as the defendant's criminal record. Assuming a defendant has no criminal record, each added offense level generally translates to about two months of extra jail time at the low end of the Guidelines, but an extra seven or eight months at the high end. If the defendant has a significant criminal history, the impact of an extra offense level is substantially greater.

3. Do you agree with the policy choices embodied in U.S.S.G. § 2G2.2? Under § 2G2.2, the length of the prison term depends on factors such as the types of images, the number of images, and what the defendant did with the images. For example, under § 2G2.2(b)(7), a defendant who possessed fifty images of child pornography will generally face a prison term about ten months longer than a defendant who possessed five images (that is, two extra levels); a defendant who possesses 200 images will face about five more months in prison than one who possessed fifty images (one extra level); and a defendant who possessed 1,000 images will face about ten more months in prison than the defendant who possessed 200 images (two extra levels).

Do these numbers make sense? Are the punishments imposed by the Guidelines in child pornography cases too light, too heavy, or about right? Keep in mind that several child pornography offenses contain mandatory minimum punishments. If the Guidelines range is less than the statutory minimum, the statutory minimum trumps the guidelines range.

C. SENTENCING IN COMPUTER MISUSE CASES

The offense conduct guideline that applies in most computer misuse cases is U.S.S.G. § 2B1.1. This provision is known as the "economic crimes" guideline because it is broadly applicable in economic crime cases involving theft or fraud. *See generally* Frank O. Bowman, III, *The 2001 Federal Economic Crime Sentencing Reforms: An Analysis and Legislative History*, 35 Ind. L. Rev. 5 (2001).

The fact that computer misuse crimes are sentenced along with other economic crimes provides the answer to one basic question about how the Guidelines might apply. For the most part, computer misuse offenses are sentenced just like any other economic crime. At the same time, U.S.S.G. § 2B1.1 contains a number of special wrinkles that apply only in computer misuse cases.

Section 2B1.1 offenses start with a base offense level of 6. The loss chart contained in § 2B1.1(b)(1) adds to the base offense level depending on the dollar amount of the loss involved:

If the loss exceeded $5,000, increase the offense level as follows:

	Loss (apply the greatest)	Increase in level
(A)	$5,000 or less	no increase
(B)	More than $5,000	add 2
(C)	More than $10,000	add 4
(D)	More than $30,000	add 6
(E)	More than $70,000	add 8
(F)	More than $120,000	add 10
(G)	More than $200,000	add 12
(H)	More than $400,000	add 14
(I)	More than $1,000,000	add 16
(J)	More than $2,500,000	add 18
(K)	More than $7,000,000	add 20
(L)	More than $20,000,000	add 22

Loss (apply the greatest)	Increase in level
(M) More than $50,000,000 .... add 24	
(N) More than $100,000,000 .... add 26	
(O) More than $200,000,000 .... add 28	
(P) More than $400,000,000 .... add 30	

As the loss chart suggests, the dollar value of loss is a critical factor used to determine the sentence in a computer misuse case. Application Note 3(a) to U.S.S.G. § 2B1.1 provides specific guidance on calculating loss, including a special rule for § 1030 cases. According to the application note, "loss is the greater of actual loss or intended loss." Actual loss and intended loss are defined as follows:

(i) Actual Loss.—"Actual loss" means the reasonably foreseeable pecuniary harm that resulted from the offense.

(ii) Intended Loss.—"Intended loss" (I) means the pecuniary harm that was intended to result from the offense; and (II) includes intended pecuniary harm that would have been impossible or unlikely to occur (e.g., as in a government sting operation, or an insurance fraud in which the claim exceeded the insured value).

(iii) Pecuniary Harm.—"Pecuniary harm" means harm that is monetary or that otherwise is readily measurable in money. Accordingly, pecuniary harm does not include emotional distress, harm to reputation, or other non-economic harm.

(iv) Reasonably Foreseeable Pecuniary Harm.—For purposes of this guideline, "reasonably foreseeable pecuniary harm" means pecuniary harm that the defendant knew or, under the circumstances, reasonably should have known, was a potential result of the offense.

(v) Rules of Construction in Certain Cases.—In the cases described in subdivisions (I) through (III), reasonably foreseeable pecuniary harm shall be considered to include the pecuniary harm specified for those cases as follows:

* * *

(III) Offenses Under 18 U.S.C. § 1030.—In the case of an offense under 18 U.S.C. § 1030, actual loss includes the following pecuniary harm, regardless of whether such pecuniary harm was reasonably foreseeable: Any reasonable cost to any victim, including the cost of responding to an offense, conducting a damage assessment, and restoring the data, program, system, or information to its condition prior to the offense, and any revenue lost, cost incurred, or other damages incurred because of interruption of service.

Note that the special rule of construction for offenses under 18 U.S.C. § 1030 defines "actual loss" using the statutory definition of loss from 18 U.S.C. § 1030(e)(11), which itself attempted to codify United States v. Middleton, 231 F.3d 1207 (9th Cir. 2000). As a result, the methodology used to measure the statutory $5,000 loss requirement for 18 U.S.C. § 1030(a)(5) cases is also used to calculate loss at sentencing, and is used even if the case was not charged under § 1030(a)(5). The loss need not have been reasonably foreseeable, unlike the loss used for other types of cases.

U.S.S.G. § 2B1.1(b)(14) also contains a special rule for enhancements in some types of § 1030 offenses:

(A) (Apply the greatest) If the defendant was convicted of an offense under:

(i) 18 U.S.C. § 1030, and the offense involved (I) a computer system used to maintain or operate a critical infrastructure, or used by or for a government entity in furtherance of the administration of justice, national defense, or national security; or (II) an intent to obtain personal information, increase by 2 levels.

(ii) 18 U.S.C. § 1030(a)(5)(A)(I), increase by 4 levels.

(iii) 18 U.S.C. § 1030, and the offense caused a substantial disruption of a critical infrastructure, increase by 6 levels.

(B) If subdivision (A)(iii) applies, and the offense level is less than level 24, increase to level 24.

Application Note 13(A) to U.S.S.G. § 2B1.1 then provides more specific guidance on several of the terms used:

"Critical infrastructure" means systems and assets vital to national defense, national security, economic security, public health or safety, or any combination of those matters. A critical infrastructure may be publicly or privately owned. Examples of critical infrastructures include gas and oil production, storage, and delivery systems, water supply systems, telecommunications networks, electrical power delivery systems, financing and banking systems, emergency services (including medical, police, fire, and rescue services), transportation systems and services (including highways, mass transit, airlines, and airports), and government operations that provide essential services to the public.

"Government entity" has the meaning given that term in 18 U.S.C. § 1030(e)(9).

"Personal information" means sensitive or private information (including such information in the possession of a third party), including (i) medical records; (ii) wills; (iii) diaries; (iv) private correspondence, including e-mail; (v) financial records; (vi) photographs of a sensitive or private nature; or (vii) similar information.

In general, the most important practical effect of U.S.S.G. § 2B1.1(b)(14) is that it increases the penalties when a defendant is convicted of 18 U.S.C. § 1030(a)(5)(A)(I). Under § 2B1.1(b)(14)(A)(ii), a conviction under 18 U.S.C. § 1030(a)(5)(A)(I) raises the offense level by four points, which on average will generally translate into an 8–12 month increase in the length of a prison term.

Finally, Application Note 19 to § 2B1.1 provides special guidance on when an upward departure may be needed to account for non-monetary harms. The guidance is general, but some of it relates specifically to 18 U.S.C. § 1030 offenses:

> There may be cases in which the offense level determined under this guideline substantially understates the seriousness of the offense.

> In such cases, an upward departure may be warranted. The following is a nonexhaustive list of factors that the court may consider in determining whether an upward departure is warranted:

> * * *

> (ii) The offense caused or risked substantial non-monetary harm. For example, the offense caused physical harm, psychological harm, or severe emotional trauma, or resulted in a substantial invasion of a privacy interest (through, for example, the theft of personal information such as medical, educational, or financial records). An upward departure would be warranted, for example, in an 18 U.S.C. § 1030 offense involving damage to a protected computer, if, as a result of that offense, death resulted. * * *

> (v) In a case involving stolen information from a "protected computer", as defined in 18 U.S.C. § 1030(e)(2), the defendant sought the stolen information to further a broader criminal purpose.

This application note gives courts relatively wide discretion to fashion appropriate sentences to account for privacy harms in computer misuse cases.

NOTES AND QUESTIONS

1. Are sentences for federal computer misuse crimes too low, too high, or about right? How do sentences for typical 18 U.S.C. § 1030 offenses compare with sentences for typical child pornography offenses?

2. Why do you think the sentencing guidelines have special rules for calculating "actual loss" in 18 U.S.C. § 1030 cases? Why should unforeseeable pecuniary harms be included in § 1030 cases but not for any other type of criminal offense? Is the idea that any loss resulting from a § 1030 offense is actually foreseeable? If so, is it fair for a defendant to have his sentence increased under § 2B1.1 if he commits a § 1030 offense that leads to truly unforeseeable harms? Is the defendant more culpable in such cases? Is a defendant more responsible for unforeseeable harms in § 1030 cases than in other cases? Or is the idea to punish those who commit computer misuse crimes more harshly than those who commit other crimes because computer misuse crimes are more dangerous?

3. Are losses suffered in computer misuse cases similar to losses suffered in other economic crime cases? Consider the example of a garden-variety

fraud case. For the most part, the victim's loss will equal the defendant's gain. If *A* defrauds *B* out of $50,000, *B* has lost the money and *A* has gained it. In all likelihood, *A* will have controlled the extent of the loss, and will benefit more and more as the losses increase.

In a computer misuse case, however, the victim's loss generally will not equal the defendant's gain. If *A* hacks into *B*'s server, and *B* takes its computers offline and suffers $50,000 in loss from the interruption of service, *A* does not gain anything from *B*'s $50,000 loss. In all likelihood, *A* will have little to no control over the extent of the loss, and will not benefit as the losses mount.

The guidelines do not distinguish between these two types of cases. The victim's loss in the former example is treated for sentencing purposes the same as the victim's loss in the latter example. Does that make sense?

4. *Problem.* Imagine that the Smith family has three brothers: Larry, Moe, and Curly. All three brothers are skilled computer hackers. One day, each of the three brothers hacks into a server operated by a different local e-commerce company. Assume that all three intrusions are essentially the same, but that the responses of the system administrators in charge of the three victim networks are very different. The system administrator at the company targeted by Larry notices the attack but decides to ignore it. The system administrator at the company that Moe attacks takes the intrusion seriously, and his response to the offense racks up $50,000 in loss. The system administrator at the company that Curly hacks into also takes the intrusion extremely seriously, and responding to the offense racks up $250,000 in loss.

Assume that Larry, Moe, and Curly are all charged and convicted of violating § 1030. Based on the loss chart of § 2B1.1(b)(1), Moe's offense level will be six points higher than Larry's, and Curly's will be six offense levels higher than Moe's. This works out on average to about an extra year in prison for Moe, and an extra two years in prison for Curly, all based on the response of the system administrator. Is this a sensible result?

5. *Calculating loss in virus and worm cases.* How should courts calculate "actual loss" in cases involving computer viruses and worms? In such cases, the losses may be distributed among thousands or even tens of thousands of victims. It is presumably impractical to measure the losses from each individual victim. Application Note 3(c) to U.S.S.G. § 2B1.1 states that "[t]he court need only make a reasonable estimate of the loss. The sentencing judge is in a unique position to assess the evidence and estimate the loss based upon that evidence. For this reason, the court's loss determination is entitled to appropriate deference." The Application Note also states that the court may estimate the loss by considering "[t]he approximate number of victims multiplied by the average loss to each victim." *Id.* cmt. n.3(c)(iii).

What guidance does this provide in computer worm or virus cases? How can the court estimate the number of victims, and how can it determine the average loss to each victim? Do victims outside the United States count, or are only losses suffered inside the United States relevant?

The fact that the loss chart contained in U.S.S.G. § 2B1.1(b)(1) contemplates losses higher than $400 million dollars may be attributable to the particular needs of computer virus cases. In March 1999, David Smith launched the "Melissa" virus, a computer virus that spread as an e-mail attachment. The virus spread quickly, and shut down computers around the globe. At the time, the loss chart for U.S.S.G. § 2B1.1 maxed out when losses exceeded $80 million. The losses caused by the global Melissa virus were widely believed to dwarf this figure. Because the loss amounts exceeded $80 million by a wide margin, the guilty plea agreement between the government and the United States stipulated that the damage had been more than $80 million and gave Smith the full enhancement based on loss amount. *See Plea Agreement of David Smith* (Dec. 8, 1999), *available at* http://www.usdoj.gov/criminal/cybercrime/meliplea.htm.

6.   Jennifer S. Granick, *Faking It: Calculating Loss in Computer Crime Sentencing*, 2 I/S: J. L. & Pol'y for Info. Soc'y 207, 229 (2006):

> I believe sentencing computer crimes based mainly on economic loss is a mistake. These types of crimes are characterized by intangible harms which are difficult to measure economically. Fields of economics are devoted to measuring harm from security incidents, the value of privacy, and other intangibles. But these academic endeavors are too speculative, malleable, and theoretical to be the basis for prison terms.

What are the alternatives? Can you devise a better way to determine sentences for computer misuse offenses?

D.   SUPERVISED RELEASE AND PROBATION RESTRICTIONS

The federal court system generally uses three different forms of punishment: prison time, fines, and probation or supervised release. Probation and supervised release are similar: each permit a defendant to avoid prison time, contingent upon the defendant's compliance with terms of probation or supervised release. The difference between probation and supervised release primarily relates to timing: probation is in lieu of jail time, whereas supervised release follows jail time. For example, a defendant may be sentenced to a period of probation, or may be sentenced to a prison term followed by a period of supervised release. If a defendant violates the terms of probation or supervised release, the defendant may at the discretion of the trial judge be sent to prison to serve out the remaining period of the sentence.

Supervised release and probation raise a very interesting computer-related question: What kinds of restrictions on computer and Internet use can a court impose as a condition of probation or supervised release?

UNITED STATES v. PAUL

United States Court of Appeals for the Fifth Circuit, 2001.
274 F.3d 155.

KING, CHIEF JUDGE:

After pleading guilty to a charge of knowingly possessing child pornography in violation of 18 U.S.C. § 2252A, Defendant–Appellant Ronald

Scott Paul was sentenced to five years of imprisonment and three years of supervised release pursuant to section 2G2.2 of the United States Sentencing Guidelines. Paul appeals to this court, challenging * * * the conditions of his supervised release * * *. For the following reasons, we affirm Paul's conviction and his sentencing determination, including the conditions of supervised release.

Factual and Procedural Background

On May 8, 2000, Defendant–Appellant Ronald Scott Paul took his personal computer to Electronic Services and Repair, a small computer repair business in Port Isabel, Texas. While working on the computer, a technician discovered child pornography on the hard drive and contacted the Federal Bureau of Investigations. The FBI's background check on Paul revealed a 1986 offense involving child pornography. After Paul had retrieved his computer from the repair technician, FBI agents searched Paul's residence pursuant to a valid warrant. The agents seized the computer, which contained a large number of files with images of child pornography that had been downloaded from the Internet. The agents also seized assorted photographs of children, magazines with nude photographs of children and adults, books with pictures of nude prepubescent boys, videotapes of random children filmed in public settings, a large bag of children's clothes, and several children's swimsuits covered with sand.

Additionally, the agents seized a medical bag containing basic medical supplies and Spanish-language flyers advertising lice removal for children. In the flyers, Paul informed parents that he would spray their children with a product that kills lice. The flyers also stated that Paul would conduct a complete physical examination on each child for "overall health," which necessarily required the child to completely undress. The agents also found between ten and twenty personal cameras in Paul's residence.

Further review of Paul's computer revealed electronic mail communications discussing sources of child pornography, including websites, chat rooms, and newsgroups that allowed both receiving and sending of pornographic images. In one of these e-mails, Paul discussed how easy it was to find "young friends" by scouting single, dysfunctional parents through Alcoholics Anonymous or local welfare offices and winning their friendship, thereby securing access to their young sons.

On July 17, 2000, Paul pled guilty to one charge of knowingly possessing a computer hard drive with three or more images of child pornography that traveled through interstate commerce, in violation of the Child Pornography Prevention Act. *See* 18 U.S.C. § 2252A(a)(5)(B). The government offered four images as samples of the child pornography that Paul possessed. Paul admitted that these exhibits were images he received from the Internet and stored on his computer hard drive.

After Paul pled guilty to possession of child pornography and was rearraigned, the court ordered the probation office to prepare a presentence report ("PSR"). Applying section 2G2.2 of the Sentencing Guidelines, the PSR determined that Paul's total offense level was 35. *See* U.S. Sentencing Guidelines Manual § 2G2.2 (1998). The PSR then factored in Paul's criminal history category (category I), which resulted in an imprisonment range of 121 to 151 months. However, the PSR noted that the statutory maximum penalty was 60 months.

The district court imposed a number of special conditions on Paul's supervised release term. He must "undergo a complete psychological evaluation and/or participate in a sex offender/mental health program as deemed necessary and approved by the probation officer." Paul is also directed to avoid "direct and indirect contact with minors," as well as "places, establishments, and areas frequented by minors," and is prohibited from "engaging in any paid occupation or volunteer service which exposes him either directly or indirectly to minors." The conditions further provide that Paul "shall not have, possess or have access to computers, the Internet, photographic equipment, audio/video equipment, or any item capable of producing a visual image." Finally, Paul is instructed to "register with the sex offender registration in any state where he resides, is employed, carries on a vocation, or is a student, as directed by the probation officer and as required by law."

The Special Conditions of Supervised Release

A district court has wide discretion in imposing terms and conditions of supervised release. However, this discretion is limited by 18 U.S.C. § 3583(d), which provides that a court may impose special conditions of supervised release only when the conditions meet certain criteria. First, special conditions of supervised release must be reasonably related to the factors set forth in § 3553(a)(1), (a)(2)(B), (a)(2)(C), and (a)(2)(D). *See* 18 U.S.C. § 3583(d). These factors include: (1) "the nature and circumstances of the offense and the history and characteristics of the defendant," (2) the need "to afford adequate deterrence to criminal conduct," (3) the need "to protect the public from further crimes of the defendant," and (4) the need "to provide the defendant with needed [training], medical care, or other correctional treatment in the most effective manner." 18 U.S.C. § 3553(a)(1)–(2). In addition, supervised release conditions cannot involve a greater deprivation of liberty than is reasonably necessary to achieve the latter three statutory goals. *See* 18 U.S.C. § 3583(d). We review the district court's determination of supervised release conditions for abuse of discretion.

Paul contends that a blanket prohibition on computer or Internet use is excessively broad and cannot be justified based solely on the fact that his offense involved a computer and the Internet. He points out that computers and Internet access have become indispensable communication tools in the modern world and that the restriction imposed by the district court would prohibit him from accessing computers and the Internet for legitimate purposes, such as word processing and research.

The government responds that the order prohibiting Paul from using a computer or the Internet is rationally related to his offense and that such an order is an appropriate public protection measure. The government points out that Paul's computer contained over 1200 images of child pornography and contained evidence that Paul had used the Internet to access child pornography chat rooms, bulletin boards, and newsgroups. According to the government, Paul also used his e-mail to advise fellow consumers of child pornography how to "scout" single, dysfunctional parents and gain access to their children and to solicit the participation of like-minded individuals in trips to "visit" children in Mexico. Under these circumstances, the government argues, restricting Paul's access to computers and the Internet is reasonably tailored to his offense and conviction and serves the dual purpose of deterrence and public protection.

The government correctly points out that a number of courts have upheld Internet and computer-use prohibitions as conditions of supervised release. *See, e.g., United States v. Crandon,* 173 F.3d 122, 127–28 (3d Cir. 1999) (upholding an Internet restriction as a condition of supervised release for a child pornography offender); *United States v. Mitnick,* 145 F.3d 1342 (unpublished table decision), *available at* 1998 WL 255343 (9th Cir. 1998) (determining that the district court did not abuse its discretion in prohibiting a defendant convicted of offenses related to computer "hacking" from accessing "computers, computer-related equipment, and certain telecommunications devices" during his probationary period without prior approval of his probation officer).

Most factually analogous to the instant case is *Crandon,* wherein a defendant convicted of receiving child pornography challenged the district court's imposition of a supervised release condition dictating that he could not "possess, procure, purchase, or otherwise obtain access to any form of computer network, bulletin board, Internet or exchange format involving computers unless specifically approved by the U.S. Probation Office." 173 F.3d at 125. The district court found that this restriction on the defendant's Internet access was "reasonably related to his criminal activities, to the goal of deterring him from engaging in further criminal conduct, and to protecting the public," in light of the fact that the defendant had once used the Internet as a means to develop an illegal sexual relationship with a young girl. The court was unpersuaded by the defendant's argument that the Internet prohibition was overly broad and would unnecessarily restrict his career opportunities and his freedoms of speech and expression. Noting that supervised release conditions restricting employment and First Amendment freedoms are permissible if the statutory tailoring requirements are satisfied, the court ultimately concluded that the restriction on the defendant was not overly broad despite its effects on his business opportunities and expressive activities.

As in *Crandon,* the supervised release condition at issue in the instant case is reasonably related to Paul's offense and to the need to prevent recidivism and protect the public. The record reveals that Paul has in the past used the Internet to encourage exploitation of children by seeking out fellow "boy lovers" and providing them with advice on how to find and obtain access to "young friends." Restricting his access to this communication medium clearly serves the dual statutory goals of protecting the public and preventing future criminal activity. While the condition at issue in the instant case is broader than the restriction at issue in *Crandon* because it prohibits access to both computers and the Internet and it contains no proviso permitting Paul to use these resources with the approval of his probation office, we cannot say that the district court abused its discretion in determining that an absolute ban on computer and Internet use was reasonably necessary to protect the public and to prevent recidivism.

In arguing that the district court's computer and Internet prohibition was an abuse of discretion, Paul points to the Tenth Circuit's decision in *United States v. White,* 244 F.3d 1199 (10th Cir. 2001). In *White,* the court of appeals remanded to the sentencing court a special condition of supervised release that was substantially similar to Paul's condition. While the Tenth Circuit was unclear about the scope of the restriction at issue in that case, it indicated that if the condition were read to absolutely ban all Internet and computer use, it would be "greater than necessary" to serve the goals of supervised release outlined in 18 U.S.C. § 3583(d). The Tenth Circuit reasoned that *Crandon* did not dictate a different result. While acknowledging that the Third Circuit did uphold an Internet restriction in *Crandon,* the *White* court noted that the *Crandon* court did not impose an absolute *ban* on computer or Internet access, despite the fact that the defendant in *Crandon* (unlike the defendant in *White*) had clearly used the Internet to "initiate and facilitate a pattern of criminal conduct and victimization that produced an immediate consequence and directly injured the victim" in that case.

We find the Tenth Circuit's reasoning in *White* unpersuasive. Initially, we note that there is some evidence that Paul did in fact use the Internet to "initiate and facilitate a pattern of criminal conduct and victimization," and thus that *White* can be distinguished on these grounds. More importantly, we reject the *White* court's implication that an absolute prohibition on accessing computers or the Internet is *per se* an unacceptable condition of supervised release, simply because such a prohibition might prevent a defendant from using a computer at the library to "get a weather forecast" or to "read a newspaper online" during the supervised release term. We find that such a supervised release condition can be acceptable if it is reasonably necessary to serve the statutory goals outlined in 18 U.S.C. § 3583(d). In the instant case, the district court had strong evidentiary support for its determination that a strict ban on computer and Internet use was reasonably necessary. Moreover, Paul has articulated no specific objections to the computer and Internet ban suggesting how his occupational affairs or his expressive activities will be adversely impacted by the fact that he will be unable to "use a computer or the Internet at a library, cybercafe or an airport" during the term of his supervised release. We conclude that the district court did not abuse its discretion in imposing this condition of supervised release.

UNITED STATES v. SOFSKY

United States Court of Appeals for the Second Circuit, 2002.
287 F.3d 122.

Jᴏɴ O. Nᴇᴡᴍᴀɴ, Cɪʀᴄᴜɪᴛ Jᴜᴅɢᴇ.

This opinion concerns only a challenge to a condition of supervised release included as part of the sentence of ten years and one month imposed on Gregory Sofsky by the District Court for the Eastern District of New York after Sofsky pled guilty to receiving child pornography in violation of 18 U.S.C. § 2252A(a)(2)(A). The condition prohibits Sofsky from using a computer or the Internet without the approval of his probation officer. We conclude that the condition exceeds even the broad discretion of the sentencing judge with respect to conditions of supervised release, and must be substantially modified.

Prior to the entry of a guilty plea on the third day of trial, the Government presented overwhelming evidence that Sofsky had received on his home computer via the Internet more than 1,000 images of child pornography in the form of both still and moving pictures. Some of the images had been transferred to CD–ROM disks. Sofsky had also used the Internet to exchange images of child pornography with other (apparently like-minded) individuals at their computers. There was no claim that Sofsky had ever produced any of the images he received or exchanged with others.

At sentencing, Judge Ross, following the recommendation of the presentence report, determined that the adjusted offense level under the Sentencing Guidelines was 32. In Criminal History Category I, level 32 prescribes a sentence range of 121 to 151 months. Judge Ross imposed a sentence of 121 months to be followed by a three-year term of supervised release. In addition to the standard conditions of supervised release, the Court imposed four special conditions: (1) the defendant must participate in mental health treatment, including a program for sexual disorders, (2) the defendant must permit a search of his premises on reasonable suspicion that contraband or evidence of a violation of a condition of supervision may be found, (3) the defendant may not "access a computer, the Internet, or bulletin board systems at any time, unless approved by the probation officer," and (4) the defendant must not view, purchase, or possess child pornography materials. Only the third condition is challenged on this appeal.

A sentencing court may order a special condition of supervised release that is "reasonably related" to several of the statutory factors governing the selection of sentences, "involves no greater deprivation of liberty than is reasonably necessary" for several statutory purposes of sentencing, and is consistent with Sentencing Commission policy statements. 18 U.S.C.

§ 3583(d). Although the discretion thus conferred is broad, we have cautioned that we will carefully scrutinize unusual and severe conditions.

We previously considered a sentencing component that prohibited access to a computer or the Internet in *United States v. Peterson,* 248 F.3d 79, 82–84 (2d Cir. 2001). The restriction was imposed as a condition of probation for a defendant convicted of larceny because of the defendant's prior state conviction for incest and his accessing of adult pornography on his home computer. Noting that "computers and Internet access have become virtually indispensable in the modern world of communications and information gathering," *id.* at 83, we ruled the condition unreasonable. Appellate courts considering a similar restriction imposed upon defendants convicted of child pornography offenses have reached different conclusions. *Compare United States v. White,* 244 F.3d 1199, 1205–07 (10th Cir. 2001) (invalidating and requiring modification of restriction imposed on defendant who used Internet to receive child pornography), *with United States v. Paul,* 274 F.3d 155, 169 (5th Cir. 2001) (upholding restriction imposed on defendant who produced child pornography and used Internet to distribute it), *and United States v. Crandon,* 173 F.3d 122, 127–28 (3d Cir. 1999) (upholding restriction imposed on defendant who used Internet to contact 14–year–old girl with whom he had sexual relations and photographed such conduct).

We appreciate the Government's point that permitting Sofsky access to a computer and the Internet after serving his ten-year sentence can facilitate continuation of his electronic receipt of child pornography, but we are more persuaded by the observation in *Peterson* that "although a defendant might use the telephone to commit fraud, this would not justify a condition of probation that includes an absolute bar on the use of telephones." *Peterson,* 248 F.3d at 83. The same could be said of a prohibition on the use of the mails imposed on a defendant convicted of mail fraud. A total ban on Internet access prevents use of e-mail, an increasingly widely used form of communication and, as the Tenth Circuit noted, prevents other common-place computer uses such as "doing any research, getting a weather forecast, or reading a newspaper online." *White,* 244 F.3d at 1206. Although the condition prohibiting Sofsky from accessing a computer or the Internet without his probation officer's approval is reasonably related to the purposes of his sentencing, in light of the nature of his offense, we hold that the condition inflicts a greater deprivation on Sofsky's liberty than is reasonably necessary.

The Government contended at oral argument that the restriction must be broad because a restriction limited to accessing pornography would be extremely difficult for the probation officer to enforce without constant monitoring of Sofsky's use of his computer. There are several responses. First, to the extent that even a broad restriction would be enforced by the probation officer, monitoring (presumably unannounced) of Sofsky would be required to check if he was using a computer at all. Second, a more focused restriction, limited to pornography sites and images, can be enforced by unannounced inspections of Sofsky's premises and examination of material stored on his hard drive or removable disks.[12] *Cf. United States v. Knights,* 534 U.S. 112 (2001) (rejecting Fourth Amendment challenge to search, on reasonable suspicion, of probationer's premises). Finally, the Government can check on Sofsky's Internet usage with a sting operation—surreptitiously inviting him to respond to Government placed Internet ads for pornography.

For all the above reasons, the condition of supervised release prohibiting all computer and Internet access is vacated, and the case is remanded for entry of a more restricted condition.

NOTES AND QUESTIONS

1. Are judges well-equipped to determine what kinds of restrictions on computer and Internet use are likely to be effective? Are appellate judges better or worse equipped to resolve such questions than trial judges?

2. If you were a probation officer, how would you respond to the court's guidance in *Sofsky*? According to one newspaper article, probation officers responded by installing monitoring software on several defendants' computers. The software let probation officers access the defendants' computers remotely and obtain records of Web surfing and other online activities. *See* Matt Richtel, *Courts Split on Internet Bans,* N.Y. Times, Jan. 21, 2003. How hard do you think it is for a defendant to circumvent this type of monitoring? Can't the defendant simply purchase another computer?

3. In United States v. Scott, 316 F.3d 733, 736–37 (7th Cir. 2003), Judge Easterbrook offered the following response to the defendant's claim that limitations on Internet access could never be imposed as conditions of supervised release:

> That is not a tenable argument. Computers and the Internet may be used to commit crimes, of which child pornography and fraud are only two examples. Inveterate hackers who have used access to injure others may be ordered to give up the digital world. If full access posed an unacceptable risk of recidivism, yet all controls on access were forbidden, then a judge would have little alternative but to increase the term of imprisonment in order to incapacitate the offender. Few defendants would deem that a beneficial exchange; most would prefer the conditional freedom of supervised release, even with restrictions on using the Internet, to the more regimented life in prison.
>
> This is not to gainsay the point * * * that because the Internet is a medium of communication a total restriction rarely could be justified. The Internet is a vast repository, offering books, newspapers, magazines, and research tools along with smut. A judge who would not forbid [the defendant] to enter a video rental store (which may have an adult-video section) also should not forbid [him] to enter the Internet, even though Disney's web site coexists with others offering filthy pictures or audio files circulated in violation of the copyright laws. A judge who would not

---

12. One of the standard conditions of supervised release imposed on Sofsky requires him to "permit a probation officer to visit him ... at any time at home or elsewhere." Judgment ¶ 11.

> forbid a defendant to send or receive postal mail or use the telephone
> should not forbid that person to send or receive email or to order books at
> Amazon.com. [The defendant] does not have a record of extensive abuse
> of digital communications that could justify an outright ban.

Is forbidding the use of computers like forbidding the use of telephones? Or is
it more like forbidding a person to drive a car, which is a common condition of
probation in drunk driving cases? Or is it more like forbidding a person to
leave his home?

4. For more perspectives on restricting computer use as a condition of
supervised release and probation, see Jessica Habib, Note, *Cyber Crime and
Punishment: Filtering Out Internet Felons*, 14 Fordham Intell. Prop. Media &
Ent. L.J. 1051 (2004); Brian W. McKay, Student Work, *Guardrails on the
Information Superhighway: Supervising Computer Use of the Adjudicated Sex
Offender*, 106 W. Va. L. Rev. 203 (2003); Christopher Wiest, Comment and
Casenote, *The Netsurfing Split: Restrictions Imposed on Internet and Comput-
er Usage by Those Convicted of a Crime Involving a Computer*, 72 U. Cin. L.
Rev. 847 (2003); Doug Hyne, *Examining the Legal Challenges to the Restric-
tion of Computer Access as a Term of Probation or Supervised Release*, 28 New
Eng. J. on Crim. & Civ. Confinement 215 (2002); Christopher M.E. Painter,
Supervised Release and Probation Restrictions in Hacker Cases, U.S.A. Bulle-
tin (March 2001).

5. When should sentencing courts decide on the terms of supervised
release relating to a defendant's computer use? In United States v. Balon, 384
F.3d 38 (2d Cir. 2004), the defendant was sentenced to a five-year prison
term, followed by a period of supervised released. The terms of supervised
release contained a number of restrictions involving computer and Internet
use. In an opinion by Judge Winter, the court held that the defendant's
challenge to the computer and Internet-related aspects of his supervised
release was not yet ripe for review:

> The technology that holds the key to whether the special condition in this
> case involves a greater deprivation of liberty than reasonably necessary is
> constantly and rapidly changing. Because Balon will not begin his term of
> supervised release for three years, it is impossible to evaluate at this time
> whether one method or another, or a combination of methods, will
> occasion a greater deprivation of his liberty than necessary in light of the
> special needs of supervised release.

> We therefore dismiss this portion of the appeal but instruct the district
> court to reconsider * * * the special conditions regarding monitoring of
> Balon's computer at a time closer to Balon's term of supervised release.

Id. at 46–47. Is this a sensible approach? Should the law be changed so that
terms of supervised release are set soon before the supervised released begins,
rather than when the defendant is sentenced following conviction?

CHAPTER 5

THE FOURTH AMENDMENT

■ ■ ■

This chapter considers how the Fourth Amendment governs law enforcement investigations of computer crimes. It analyzes the constitutional limits on the government's ability to gather digital evidence, identify a suspect, and try to establish beyond a reasonable doubt that the defendant has committed the offense. The Fourth Amendment states:

> The right of the people to be secure in their persons, houses, papers, and effects, against unreasonable searches and seizures, shall not be violated, and no Warrants shall issue, but upon probable cause, supported by Oath or affirmation, and particularly describing the place to be searched, and the persons or things to be seized.

The overall framework of Fourth Amendment law is simple to state. The Fourth Amendment prohibits unreasonable searches and seizures. To determine if government conduct violates the Fourth Amendment, one must first identify whether searches or seizures have occurred, and if so, whether they are reasonable or unreasonable. A search or seizure is reasonable if it was authorized by a valid search warrant or if one of the exceptions to the warrant requirement applies. A search warrant is a judicial order authorizing the police to execute a search or seizure; a warrant is valid if it is based on probable cause and particularly describes the property to be searched and the items to be seized. The usual remedy for violations of the Fourth Amendment is suppression of evidence obtained in any subsequent criminal case. While there are many exceptions and caveats to this rule, the basic idea is that the government cannot use the "fruits" of illegal government searches and seizures.

The meaning of the Fourth Amendment is relatively well-established for investigations involving physical evidence. Entering a house or opening a person's private packages constitutes a "search" of that house or package. Taking physical property away "seizes" it. The Fourth Amendment thus requires the police to obtain a warrant or to satisfy an exception to the warrant requirement before they can enter private spaces or take away physical property. The exceptions to the warrant requirement include consent, exigent circumstances, searches incident to a valid arrest, and border searches. All of these exceptions permit investigators to search or seize private property without a warrant.

The central question of this chapter is how these legal doctrines should apply when the government wishes to access digital evidence stored in a computer. In some cases, the searches will occur on-site, without moving the computer itself (at least until after the search). A police officer might come across a computer that he believes contains evidence, and he might want to look through the computer for the evidence. The question is, when can he look through the computer?

In other cases, the searches will occur off-site. The reasons are practical. Analyzing a single computer may take anywhere from a few hours to a few weeks, and often requires specialized tools and expert training. In such cases, it is impractical to require agents to locate computers and search them onsite. Instead, the searches will often occur off-site at a government computer laboratory. The process of searching a computer off-site is often known as the computer forensics process. *See generally* Bill Nelson et al., Guide to Computer Forensics and Investigations (2004). First, the officers will seize the computer from the target's home or possession. They will then bring the computer to the government's computer lab. Next, they use special equipment to generate a "bitstream copy" (also known as an "image") of the storage device onto a government computer. A bitstream copy is different from the kind of copy users normally make when copying individual files from one computer to another. A normal copy duplicates only the identified file, but a bitstream image copies every bit and byte on the target drive in exactly the order it appears on the original. The investigators then conduct their search on the bitstream copy instead of the original. This is necessary to ensure the evidentiary integrity of the original computer. Searching a computer for evidence can alter the evidence it contains, and executing the search on the image preserves the original for use and analysis at trial. The question is, when does the Fourth Amendment allow the government to seize computers, generate images, and search the images for evidence?

The materials in this chapter will consider such questions. It starts with the requirement of government action, and then turns to the meaning of "search" and "seizure." It next turns to exceptions to the warrant requirement; then addresses the law of search warrants; and concludes with how the Fourth Amendment should apply to the Internet.

A. THE REQUIREMENT OF GOVERNMENT ACTION

The Fourth Amendment does not regulate all searches and seizures. As the Supreme Court stated in United States v. Jacobsen, 466 U.S. 109, 113 (1984), the Fourth Amendment is "wholly inapplicable to a search or seizure, even an unreasonable one, effected by a private individual not acting as an agent of the Government or with the participation or knowledge of any governmental official." Where is the line between private searches and government searches?

UNITED STATES v. JARRETT

United States Court of Appeals for the Fourth Circuit, 2003.
338 F.3d 339.

DIANA GRIBBON MOTZ, CIRCUIT JUDGE.

In this case, the Government used information provided by an anonymous computer hacker to initiate a search which produced evidence that William Jarrett violated federal statutes prohibiting the manufacture and receipt of child pornography. The district court suppressed this evidence on the ground that the hacker acted as a Government agent, and so violated the Fourth Amendment, when he procured pornographic files from Jarrett's computer. The Government appeals. Because the Government did not know of, or in any way participate in, the hacker's search of Jarrett's computer at the time of that search, the hacker did not act as a Government agent. Accordingly, we reverse and remand for further proceedings.

I.

The parties do not dispute the underlying facts. Prior to his involvement in the case at hand, the hacker, referred to as Unknownuser, provided information through emails during July 2000 to the FBI and law enforcement agents in Alabama regarding a child pornographer, Dr. Bradley Steiger. In an early email, Unknownuser identified himself only as someone "from Istanbul, Turkey," who could not "afford an overseas phone call and cannot speak English fluently."

Employing the same method that he would later use to hack into Jarrett's computer, Unknownuser obtained access to Steiger's computer via a so-called Trojan Horse program that Unknownuser had attached to a picture he posted to a news group frequented by pornography enthusiasts. When Steiger downloaded the picture to his own computer, he inadvertently downloaded the Trojan Horse program, which then permitted Unknownuser to enter Steiger's computer undetected via the Internet. *See* United States v. Steiger, 318 F.3d 1039, 1044 (11th Cir. 2003). After searching Steiger's hard drive and finding evidence of child pornography, Unknownuser copied certain files and then emailed the information to the law enforcement officials who used it to identify and apprehend Steiger. A jury convicted Steiger of violating various federal statutes prohibiting the sexual exploitation of minors. He was sentenced to 210 months in prison.

Shortly after Steiger was indicted, in late November 2000, FBI Special Agent James Duffy, who served as Legal Attache for the FBI in Turkey, contacted Unknownuser via email and phone. In addition to informing Unknownuser that he would not be prosecuted for his assistance in apprehending Steiger, Duffy requested a meeting and posed a series of questions to Unknownuser, with the hope that Unknownuser would reveal his identity and perhaps agree to testify at Steiger's trial. Although Unknownuser was quite forthcoming in his responses, he refused to meet with Agent Duffy, stating emphatically that he would never allow himself to be identified. Agent Duffy closed this exchange (in an email dated December 4, 2000) by thanking Unknownuser for his assistance and stating that "If you want to bring other information forward, I am available."

Five months later, Agent Duffy contacted Unknownuser via email, informing him of a postponement in the Steiger trial, thanking him again for his assistance, and assuring him that he would not be prosecuted for his actions should he decide to serve as a witness in the Steiger trial. Unknownuser responded, repeating that he had no intention of revealing his identity.

The next contact between Unknownuser and law enforcement did not occur until December 3, 2001, almost seven months later, when Unknownuser sent an unsolicited email to his contact at the Montgomery, Alabama Police Department, Kevin Murphy, informing Murphy that he had "found another child molester from Richmond, VA" and requesting contact information for someone at the FBI dealing with these sorts of crimes. The alleged child molester referred to in the email was William Jarrett.

After contacting the FBI, Murphy informed Unknownuser that the FBI preferred that Unknownuser send the new information to Murphy's email address. On December 4, 2001, Unknownuser sent thirteen email messages to Murphy, including a ten-part series of emails with some forty-five attached files containing the "evidence" that Unknownuser had collected on Jarrett. Murphy forwarded the information to agents at the FBI, who initiated an investigation.

Based on the information provided by Unknownuser, the Government filed a criminal complaint and application for a search warrant against Jarrett on December 13, 2001. After receiving authorization from the district court, the FBI promptly executed the search warrant and arrested Jarrett.

Several days after Jarrett's arrest, on December 16, 2001, Agent Duffy sent Unknownuser an email informing him of Steiger's sentence and thanking Unknownuser for his assistance in the case. At the time, Duffy was unaware of the Jarrett investigation. The next day, Unknownuser replied, informing Duffy of his efforts to identify Jarrett and inquiring why he had heard nothing since he sent the Jarrett files to Murphy on December 4. Unknownuser sent a similar message the following day (December 18) indicating that he had read about Jarrett's arrest in the newspaper and asking Agent Duffy to have Agent Margaret Faulkner—a special agent based in Alabama who had been involved in the Steiger investigation—contact him. On December 19, 2001, Agent Duffy sent an email to Unknownuser thanking him again for his assistance, providing information on the Jarrett investigation and prosecution, and requesting that Unknownuser maintain email contact with Agent Faulkner via her personal email address.

Three weeks later, on January 9, 2002, a grand jury indicted Jarrett on one count of manufacturing child pornography in violation of 18 U.S.C.A. § 2251(a) and seven counts of receiving child pornography in violation of 18 U.S.C.A. § 2252A(a)(2)(A). Jarrett moved to suppress the evidence obtained through the execution of the search warrant on the ground that the Government violated his Fourth Amendment rights in using the information provided by Unknownuser to secure the search warrant. The district court denied the motion. Jarrett then entered a conditional guilty plea to a one-count criminal information charging him with manufacturing child pornography.

Prior to sentencing, however, Jarrett moved to reconsider his earlier motion to suppress on the basis of new evidence—a series of emails exchanged between Unknownuser and FBI agent Faulkner, beginning shortly after Jarrett's arrest and extending for almost two months. The Government did not disclose these emails until after Jarrett had entered his guilty plea.

In the initial email in this series, dated December 19, 2001, Agent Faulkner explicitly thanked Unknownuser for providing the information to law enforcement officials. She then engaged in what can only be characterized as the proverbial "wink and a nod":

> I can not ask you to search out cases such as the ones you have sent to us. That would make you an agent of the Federal Government and make how you obtain your information illegal and we could not use it against the men in the pictures you send. But if you should happen across such pictures as the ones you have sent to us and wish us to look into the matter, please feel free to send them to us. We may have lots of questions and have to email you with the questions. But as long as you are not 'hacking' at our request, we can take the pictures and identify the men and take them to court. We also have no desire to charge you with hacking. You are not a U.S. citizen and are not bound by our laws.

Over the course of the next two months, Agent Faulkner sent at least four additional email messages, which constituted, in the words of the district court, a "pen-pal type correspondence" with Unknownuser. In addition to expressing gratitude and admiration for Unknownuser, Faulkner repeatedly sought to reassure Unknownuser that he was not a target of law enforcement for his hacking activities. For example, in an email dated January 29, 2002, she stated that

> the FACT still stands that you are not a citizen of the United States and are not bound by our laws. Our Federal attorneys have expressed NO desire to charge you with any CRIMINAL offense. You have not hacked into any computer at the request of the FBI or other law enforcement agency. You have not acted as an agent for the FBI or other law enforcement agency. Therefore, the information you have collected can be used in our criminal trials.

In his responses to Agent Faulkner, Unknownuser spoke freely of his "hacking adventures" and suggested in no uncertain terms that he would continue to search for child pornographers using the same methods employed to identify Steiger and Jarrett. As found by the district court, Agent Faulkner, despite her knowledge of Unknownuser's illegal hacking, never instructed Unknownuser that he should cease hacking.

Upon consideration of this series of emails, the district court reversed its earlier decision and suppressed the evidence obtained during the search of Jarrett's residence. At the same time, the court deemed Jarrett's motion to reconsider as a motion to withdraw his guilty plea, which it promptly granted. The court reasoned that the "totality of all the contact between law enforcement and Unknownuser encouraged Unknownuser to continue his behavior and to remain in contact with the FBI." The district court thus concluded that the Government and Unknownuser had "expressed their consent to an agency relationship," thereby rendering any evidence obtained on the basis of Unknownuser's hacking activities inadmissible on the ground that it was procured in violation of Jarrett's Fourth Amendment rights.

II.

The Fourth Amendment protects against unreasonable searches and seizures by Government officials and those private individuals acting as instruments or agents of the Government. *See* U.S. Const. amend. IV; *Coolidge v. New Hampshire,* 403 U.S. 443, 487 (1971). It does not provide protection against searches by private individuals acting in a private capacity. *See United States v. Jacobsen,* 466 U.S. 109, 113 (1984) (holding that the Fourth Amendment is "wholly inapplicable to a search or seizure, even an unreasonable one, effected by a private individual not acting as an agent of the Government or with the participation or knowledge of any governmental official"). Thus, evidence secured by private searches, even if illegal, need not be excluded from a criminal trial.

Determining whether the requisite agency relationship exists "necessarily turns on the degree of the Government's participation in the private party's activities, a question that can only be resolved in light of all the circumstances." *Skinner v. Railway Labor Executives' Ass'n,* 489 U.S. 602, 614–15 (1989). This is a fact-intensive inquiry that is guided by common law agency principles. The defendant bears the burden of proving that an agency relationship exists.

In order to run afoul of the Fourth Amendment, therefore, the Government must do more than passively accept or acquiesce in a private party's search efforts. Rather, there must be some degree of Government participation in the private search. In *Skinner,* for example, the Supreme Court found that private railroads, in performing drug tests on their employees in a manner expressly encouraged and authorized under Government regulations, acted as Government agents sufficient to implicate the Fourth Amendment. As the Court concluded, "specific features of the regulations combine to convince us that the Government did more than adopt a passive position toward the underlying private conduct."

Following the Supreme Court's pronouncements on the matter, the Courts of Appeals have identified two primary factors that should be considered in determining whether a search conducted by a private person constitutes a Government search triggering Fourth Amendment protections. These are: (1) whether the Government knew of and acquiesced in the private search; and (2) whether the private individual intended to assist law enforcement or had some other independent motivation. Although we have never articulated a specific "test," we too have embraced this two-factor approach. * * *

In this case, the Government concedes the existence of the second factor—that Unknownuser's motivation for conducting the illicit searches stemmed solely from his interest in assisting law enforcement authorities. Thus, the only question before us concerns the first factor—did the Government know of and acquiesce in Unknownuser's search in a manner sufficient to transform Unknownuser into an agent of the Government, and so render the search unconstitutional.

In seeking to give content to this factor, we have required evidence of more than mere knowledge and passive acquiescence by the Government before finding an agency relationship.

Viewed in the aggregate, * * * three major lessons emerge from the case law. First, courts should look to the facts and circumstances of each case in determining when a private search is in fact a Government search. Second, before a court will deem a private search a Government search, a defendant must demonstrate that the Government knew of and acquiesced in the private search and that the private individual intended to assist law enforcement authorities. Finally, simple acquiescence by the Government does not suffice to transform a private search into a Government search. Rather, there must be some evidence of Government participation in or affirmative encouragement of the private search before a court will hold it unconstitutional. Passive acceptance by the Government is not enough.

With these principles in mind, we turn to the case at hand.

III.

With respect to fact finding, the district court found the facts as we have recounted them above. The record adequately supports these findings; certainly they are not clearly erroneous.

The district court's conclusions of law, however, present problems. The court concluded that Unknownuser's extensive post-search email exchange with Agent Faulkner, together with the brief exchanges between Unknownuser and Agent Duffy in November and December 2000 (one year prior to the Jarrett search) and May 2001 (seven months prior to the Jarrett search), demonstrated that the Government had an "ongoing relationship" with Unknownuser sufficient to make Unknownuser an agent of the Government. Specifically, the court held that in light of the

Government's collective efforts to praise Unknownuser for his assistance, its repeated requests for further assistance, its assurances that Unknownuser would not be prosecuted for his hacking activities, and its refusal to suggest that Unknownuser should cease hacking, "there was far more than mere knowledge on the government's part."

Although, as the Government conceded at oral argument, the Faulkner email exchange probably does constitute the sort of active Government participation sufficient to create an agency relationship going forward (absent other countervailing facts), the district court erred in relying on this exchange to find that the Government knew of and acquiesced in the Jarrett search. This is so because Unknownuser's email exchange with Faulkner took place after Unknownuser had hacked into Jarrett's computer, after the fruits of Unknownuser's hacking had been made available to the FBI, after Jarrett's home and computer had been searched, and after Jarrett himself had been arrested. Thus, Faulkner's knowledge and acquiescence was entirely post-search. Such after-the-fact conduct cannot serve to transform the prior relationship between Unknownuser and the Government into an agency relationship with respect to the search of Jarrett's computer.

Although the Government operated close to the line in this case, it did not (at least on the evidence before the district court) demonstrate the requisite level of knowledge and acquiescence sufficient to make Unknown user a Government agent when he hacked into Jarrett's computer. When Unknownuser came forward with the Jarrett information, he had not been in contact with the Government for almost seven months, and nothing indicates that the Government had any intention of reestablishing contact with him. The only communications that could possibly be construed as signaling an agency relationship prior to the search of Jarrett's computer (the Duffy communications from November–December 2000 and May 2001) were simply too remote in time and too tenuous in substance to bring the Jarrett search within the scope of an agency relationship.

That the Government did not actively discourage Unknownuser from engaging in illicit hacking does not transform Unknownuser into a Government agent. Although the Government's behavior in this case is discomforting,[5] the Government was under no special obligation to affirmatively discourage Unknownuser from hacking.

At the end of the day, in order to bring Unknownuser within the grasp of an agency relationship, Jarrett would have to show that the Government made more explicit representations and assurances (as in the post-hoc Faulkner emails) that it was interested in furthering its relationship with Unknownuser and availing itself of the fruits of any information that Unknownuser obtained. Although evidence of such "encouragement" would not have to target a particular individual, it would have to signal

---

5. Notwithstanding the Government's assumptions, nothing in the record establishes that Unknownuser is a foreign national and, even if he is, of course, foreign nationals can, as the Government conceded, be prosecuted in the United States for sending and receiving child pornography. Unauthorized hacking also violates United States law.

affirmatively that the Government would be a ready and willing participant in an illegal search.

As the facts in this case make clear, no such relationship existed between Unknownuser and the Government when Unknownuser hacked into Jarrett's computer. Accordingly, we hold that the district court erred when it found that Unknownuser acted as an agent of the Government when he hacked into Jarrett's computer.

NOTES AND QUESTIONS

1. Do you believe that Unknownuser was a resident of Istanbul, Turkey? If Unknownuser had been a local Virginia police officer, would the FBI agents who investigated the case necessarily realize it?

2. Do private searches of computer data create a greater privacy threat than private searches of homes and other physical property? In the physical world, private searches are most often conducted by co-workers, spouses, and roommates. None are particularly likely to report the fruits of their searches to the police. Private searches by strangers are also relatively unlikely to be reported to the police. For example, a burglar is not likely to risk being caught by reporting evidence of crime that he finds inside a victim's home.

Are computer searches different? The anonymity of the Internet may make private searches by perfect strangers significantly more common, and may increase the odds that strangers will report discovered evidence to law enforcement. Any computer user located anywhere in the world can hack in to a person's computer when it is online, and can search the computer for evidence and share what he finds with the police without revealing his identity. Should the private search doctrine be reworked so that the Fourth Amendment regulates computer searches conducted by anonymous hackers? Should the government have the burden of proving that an anonymous hacker was *not* a state actor?

3. A number of reported child pornography convictions followed searches by computer repairmen. In these cases, the defendant brought his personal computer to a local repairman because the computer was malfunctioning. In the course of diagnosing the problem, the repairman looked through the files on the computer, found child pornography, and contacted the police. These cases have held that the repairman's search of the computer and discovery of contraband did not violate the Fourth Amendment because the repairman was a private actor. *See, e.g.,* United States v. Hall, 142 F.3d 988, 993 (7th Cir. 1998).

4. *Reenacting a private search.* According to United States v. Jacobsen, 466 U.S. 109 (1984), government agents who learn of evidence discovered by a private search can reenact the original private search without implicating the Fourth Amendment. The agents cannot "exceed the scope of the private search" without a warrant, *id.* at 115, but they can trace the steps of the prior search with the permission of the private party.

How does this apply to a computer search? If a private party searches a computer and opens a few files, finds evidence of crime, and gives the computer to the police, can the police search the entire computer without a warrant? Or does viewing more than the exact files that were opened by the private party "exceed the scope" of the private search under *Jacobsen?*

B.   DEFINING SEARCHES AND SEIZURES

1.   SEARCHES

A Fourth Amendment "search" occurs when government action violates an individual's "reasonable expectation of privacy." *See* Smith v. Maryland, 442 U.S. 735, 740 (1979). The reasonable expectation of privacy test originated in Justice Harlan's concurrence in Katz v. United States, 389 U.S. 347 (1967). In *Katz*, FBI agents taped a microphone to the top of a public pay phone booth that Katz used to place illegal bets. When Katz entered the phone booth, agents turned on the microphone and recorded his half of the communication. Justice Stewart's majority opinion ruled that the warrantless surveillance of the phone booth was impermissible:

> One who occupies [a public phone booth], shuts the door behind him, and pays the toll that permits him to place a call is surely entitled to assume that the words he utters into the mouthpiece will not be broadcast to the world. To read the Constitution more narrowly is to ignore the vital role that the public telephone has come to play in private communication.
>
> The Government contends, however, that the activities of its agents in this case should not be tested by Fourth Amendment requirements, for the surveillance technique they employed involved no physical penetration of the telephone booth from which the petitioner placed his calls. * * * But the premise that property interests control the right of the Government to search and seize has been discredited. * * * Once this much is acknowledged, and once it is recognized that the Fourth Amendment protects people—and not simply "areas"—against unreasonable searches and seizures, it becomes clear that the reach of that Amendment cannot turn upon the presence or absence of a physical intrusion into any given enclosure.
>
> * * * The Government's activities in electronically listening to and recording the petitioner's words violated the privacy upon which he justifiably relied while using the telephone booth and thus constituted a "search and seizure" within the meaning of the Fourth Amendment. The fact that the electronic device employed to achieve that end did not happen to penetrate the wall of the booth can have no constitutional significance.

Id. at 352–53.

Justice Harlan's concurrence in *Katz* offered a somewhat narrower approach than Justice Stewart's majority opinion:

> As the Court's opinion states, "the Fourth Amendment protects people, not places." The question, however, is what protection it

affords to those people. Generally, as here, the answer to that question requires reference to a "place." My understanding of the rule that has emerged from prior decisions is that there is a twofold requirement, first that a person have exhibited an actual (subjective) expectation of privacy and, second, that the expectation be one that society is prepared to recognize as "reasonable." Thus a man's home is, for most purposes, a place where he expects privacy, but objects, activities, or statements that he exposes to the "plain view" of outsiders are not "protected" because no intention to keep them to himself has been exhibited. On the other hand, conversations in the open would not be protected against being overheard, for the expectation of privacy under the circumstances would be unreasonable.

The critical fact in this case is that "one who occupies [a telephone booth], shuts the door behind him, and pays the toll that permits him to place a call is surely entitled to assume" that his conversation is not being intercepted. The point is not that the booth is "accessible to the public" at other times, but that it is a temporarily private place whose momentary occupants' expectations of freedom from intrusion are recognized as reasonable.

Id. at 361 (Harlan, J., concurring). Justice Harlan's formulation was later adopted by the full Supreme Court. As a result, the *Katz* test is generally said to have two parts: First, a subjective prong, which asks whether the person demonstrated an actual expectation of privacy; and second, an objective prong, which asks whether that expectation was one that society is prepared to recognize as reasonable.

In Rakas v. Illinois, 439 U.S. 128 (1978), then-Justice Rehnquist offered this explanation of when an expectation of privacy is constitutionally "reasonable" or "legitimate":

A legitimate expectation of privacy by definition means more than a subjective expectation of not being discovered. A burglar plying his trade in a summer cabin during the off season may have a thoroughly justified subjective expectation of privacy, but it is not one which the law recognizes as legitimate. His presence * * * is wrongful; his expectation is not one that society is prepared to recognize as reasonable. And it would, of course, be merely tautological to fall back on the notion that those expectations of privacy which are legitimate depend primarily on cases deciding exclusionary-rule issues in criminal cases. Legitimation of expectations of privacy by law must have a source outside of the Fourth Amendment, either by reference to concepts of real or personal property law or to understandings that are recognized and permitted by society.

Id. at 144 n.12.

The *Katz* test is a common source of confusion for law students. The problem is that the Supreme Court has refused to say what makes an expectation of privacy "reasonable." You might be wondering, who is "society," and how are Supreme Court Justices supposed to know what it thinks?

Given these uncertainties, the best way to understand when a person has a reasonable expectation of privacy is to reason by analogy. The Supreme Court has decided many cases involving Fourth Amendment rights in the contents of containers such as letters, packages, boxes, and trunks. The basic rule emerging from these cases is that individuals have a Fourth Amendment reasonable expectation of privacy in the contents of their sealed containers. *See, e.g.*, Robbins v. California, 453 U.S. 420, 427 (1981) (Stewart, J., plurality opinion). The same rule applies across a wide range of different types of containers:

> Even though such a distinction [among different containers] perhaps could evolve in a series of cases in which paper bags, locked trunks, lunch buckets, and orange crates were placed on one side of the line or the other, the central purpose of the Fourth Amendment forecloses such a distinction. For just as the most frail cottage in the kingdom is absolutely entitled to the same guarantees of privacy as the most majestic mansion, so also may a traveler who carries a toothbrush and a few articles of clothing in a paper bag or knotted scarf claim an equal right to conceal his possessions from official inspection as the sophisticated executive with the locked attache case.

United States v. Ross, 456 U.S. 798, 822 (1982). In contrast, "[w]hat a person knowingly exposes to the public, even in his own home or office, is not a subject of Fourth Amendment protection." Katz v. United States, 389 U.S. 347, 351 (1967). The following case considers how these principles apply to searches of computers.

UNITED STATES v. DAVID

United States District Court for the District of Nevada, 1991.
756 F. Supp. 1385.

LAWRENCE R. LEAVITT, UNITED STATES MAGISTRATE JUDGE.

On June 21, 1990, the federal grand jury returned a one-count Indictment charging the defendant, Artem Bautista David, with conspiracy to import more than 20 kilos of heroin into the United States.

An evidentiary hearing was conducted before the undersigned Magistrate Judge on September 12, 1990. The testimony established that in late April, 1990, David flew from Hong Kong to Las Vegas and was taken into custody by Customs agents on a charge of conspiracy to smuggle heroin into the United States. Government counsel engaged in discussions with David's then counsel, John R. Lusk, with a view toward enlisting David's cooperation in exchange for a favorable plea bargain. An agreement was reached whereby David, who would remain in custody under a detention order, would meet periodically with the agents in their office and make full disclosure of his knowledge of drug trafficking activities in an "off the record" proffer. * * * The agreement also provided that at the agents' direction, David would place consensually monitored telephone calls to his criminal associates. The telephone numbers of those associates were kept in David's computer memo book, access to which required the use of a password—"fortune"—which was known only to David.

During one such meeting in early May, 1990, which Lusk attended, David retrieved and disclosed certain information contained in the book. At the time, the agents were sitting across the table from him and were unable to see the password which David used or the information displayed on the book's screen. David did not volunteer the password to the agents, or offer to show them the book.

Jail regulations prohibited David from taking the book back to the jail at night. For the sake of convenience, Lusk permitted the agents to maintain custody of the book at the end of each session. Lusk did not, however, give them permission to access the book. Neither did David. Nor, as noted above, did the assistance agreement itself expressly permit the agents to gain access to the book or, for that matter, to any other property in David's possession.

At the next meeting on May 7, 1990, David met with Customs Special Agent Eric Peterson and DEA Special Agent Don Ware. Lusk did not attend this meeting. According to David's testimony, when he initially accessed the book at this meeting, Agent Peterson got up and stood directly behind him. David was aware that Peterson was looking over his shoulder, but did not feel that he could demand that Peterson move away. David did, however, try to position the book so as to minimize Peterson's view of it.

According to David's testimony, after he made two telephone calls for the agents, Peterson grabbed the book and accused David of deleting certain information. David demanded the book back, but Peterson refused. At the evidentiary hearing, David denied having deleted information from the book. Agent Peterson's version of what occurred at the meeting is a little different. Peterson testified that on May 7, 1990, he first requested the access code from David, but David was unresponsive. Peterson admitted that he then stood behind David and observed David use the password "fortune" to access the book. A little later, while Agent Ware was criticizing David for not cooperating fully during a consensually monitored phone call, Peterson, without requesting David's permission, used the password "fortune" and accessed the book himself. He then reviewed several of its entries. David saw Peterson doing this, but said nothing. Peterson came across an entry which read "1 = 12,000; 2 = 23,000," which, based on his experience as a Customs agent, he knew to be a heroin price list per kilo in Thailand. He then turned off the computer and returned it to David.

The Fourth Amendment provides that the "right of the people to be secure in their persons, houses, papers, and effects, against unreasonable searches and seizures, shall not be violated." The Supreme Court has defined a *search* as an infringement of "an expectation of privacy that society is prepared to consider reasonable." United States v. Jacobsen, 466 U.S. 109, 113 (1984). Hence, a law enforcement officer who looks at something has not engaged in a "search" within the meaning of the Fourth Amendment unless someone else has a right to expect that the thing which is seen will remain private.

In evaluating the factual scenario described above, we begin by identifying those events which may have Fourth Amendment implications. The *first* such event occurred when Agent Peterson deliberately looked over David's shoulder to see the password to the book. David himself voluntarily accessed the book at a time when the agents were in close proximity to him. Agent Peterson was not required to stay seated across the table from David. Nor did David have a reasonable expectation that Peterson would not walk behind him, or remain outside of some imaginary zone of privacy within the enclosed room. It was Peterson's office, and he could move about in it wherever he pleased. The Court therefore finds that under the circumstances David had no reasonable expectation of privacy in the display that appeared on the screen, and accordingly concludes that Peterson's act of looking over David's shoulder to see the password did not constitute a search within the meaning of the Fourth Amendment.

Peterson's act of accessing the book did constitute a search, however, if, under the circumstances, David had a reasonable expectation that when he turned the book off, its contents would remain private. For the purposes of this discussion, the book, in the Court's view, is indistinguishable from any other closed container, and is entitled to the same Fourth Amendment protection. *Robbins v. California,* 453 U.S. 420, 427 (1981); *United States v. Ross,* 456 U.S. 798 (1982). The Court does not question Agent Peterson's testimony that based on David's cooperation agreement with the government, Peterson had a good faith belief that he had the right to access the book. Peterson testified that in his mind the cooperation agreement implied that David would withhold nothing from the agents, including the contents of his memo book. But David's attempt to prevent Peterson from seeing the password, and his deletion of the heroin price list and attempted deletion of the firearms price list, clearly reflect that at the very least David did not *want* to share all of the contents of the book with the agents.

Accordingly, the government should not be allowed to use as evidence the information which Agent Peterson obtained from the book when he accessed it without David's express consent.

Notes and Questions

1. A person ordinarily retains a reasonable expectation of privacy in the contents of his opaque containers when the containers are at home, in his possession, or are stored in a space that he legitimately controls. Opening such a container constitutes a Fourth Amendment search. Under the container analogy followed in *David*, an individual will retain a reasonable expecta-

tion of privacy in the contents of his computers in the same circumstances. When a government agent retrieves contents from the individual's computer, that retrieval is a Fourth Amendment search that ordinarily requires a warrant or a specific exception to the warrant requirement. Of course, if a computer is stored inside a private space such as a home or a car, entering the home or car is a separate search that also needs to be justified under the Fourth Amendment.

2.   Courts have generally concluded that personal computers deserve a high degree of privacy protection under the Fourth Amendment. Consider United States v. Andrus, 483 F.3d 711, 718 (10th Cir. 2007) (internal quotations and citations omitted):

> Courts considering the issue have attempted to analogize computers to other items more commonly seen in Fourth Amendment jurisprudence. Individuals' expectations of privacy in computers have been likened to their expectations of privacy in a suitcase or briefcase. Password-protected files have been compared to a locked footlocker inside the bedroom.

> Given the pervasiveness of computers in American homes, this court must reach some, at least tentative, conclusion about the category into which personal computers fall. A personal computer is often a repository for private information the computer's owner does not intend to share with others.

> For most people, their computers are their most private spaces. People commonly talk about the bedroom as a very private space, yet when they have parties, all the guests-including perfect strangers-are invited to toss their coats on the bed. But if one of those guests is caught exploring the host's computer, that will be his last invitation. Because intimate information is commonly stored on computers, it seems natural that computers should fall into the same category as suitcases, footlockers, or other personal items that command a high degree of privacy.

3.   Is a computer just like any other container for the purposes of the Fourth Amendment? Professor Clancy argues that the container analogy is persuasive:

> Computers are containers. As with all containers, they have the ability to hold physical evidence, including such items as wires, microchips, and hard drives. They also contain electronic evidence, that is, a series of digitally stored 0s and 1s that, when combined with a computer program, yield such items as images, words, and spreadsheets. Accordingly, the traditional standards of the Fourth Amendment regulate obtaining the evidence in containers that happen to be computers.

Thomas K. Clancy, *The Fourth Amendment Aspects of Computer Searches and Seizures: A Perspective and a Primer*, 75 Miss. L.J. 193, 196 (2005). On the other hand, Raphael Winick has suggested that the container analogy may be problematic:

> Analogizing stored computer memory to a closed container presents several problems. The container model may make conceptual sense when discussing small electronic storage devices such as pagers or electronic address books, but the analogy becomes strained when applied to comput-

ers with larger storage capacities. For such systems, an analogy to a massive file cabinet, or even to an entire archive or record center, may be more appropriate.

Raphael Winick, *Searches and Seizures of Computers and Computer Data*, 8 Harv. J.L. & Tech. 75, 82 (1994).

Is this disagreement merely a matter of words rather than substance? A "massive file cabinet" is really just a container of containers. Individuals retain a reasonable expectation of privacy in the contents of their file cabinets just as they do in the contents of their wallets or briefcases.

4. Perhaps the important question is not whether computers can be modeled as containers, but whether computers containing many files should be modeled as single containers or "containers of containers." Note that after the police or a private party have searched a container, the police normally can examine it again without triggering the Fourth Amendment. The first search eliminates a reasonable expectation of privacy in the container, permitting subsequent searches. *See* Illinois v. Andreas, 463 U.S. 765, 771–72 (1983). When a file on a computer has been viewed, however, what exactly has been searched? Is the computer a single container, such that viewing the file searched the entire computer? Is the computer a container of individual files, such that viewing the file searched just that one file?

Courts are divided on this question. In United States v. Barth, 26 F. Supp.2d 929 (W.D. Tex. 1998), the defendant gave his laptop computer to a computer repairman named Kellar. Kellar found contraband images on the computer, and then gave the computer to the Odessa Police Department (OPD). OPD officers searched the rest of the computer without a warrant. The court concluded that the police search of the computer beyond the specific images viewed by Kellar violated the Fourth Amendment: "Because the subsequent search in this case far exceeded Kellar's viewings, Defendant's Fourth Amendment rights were implicated during the OPD's subsequent viewing of his hard drive.... the OPD officers' viewing and copying of its entire contents exceeded the scope of Kellar's initial searches." *Id.* at 937.

A New York state court took a different approach in People v. Emerson, 766 N.Y.S.2d 482 (Sup. Ct. 2003). In *Emerson*, a computer repairman found a number of child pornography images in files located in two folders labeled "xxx" and "MPG." The repairman then brought the computer to the police, and showed them those files and several other files of child pornography located in the same two folders. The court ruled that the repairman was a government actor when he conducted the search in front of the police to help them locate evidence, but that he did not exceed the scope of the initial private search because "the viewing of files on both dates concerned images of child pornography only, and * * * they were files contained in the only two computer file folders, denominated 'xxx' and 'MPG,' accessed during [the repairman's] private search." *Id.* at 487. Had the second search involved different folders, the court suggested, the second search might have exceeded the scope of the initial private search. *See id.* at 487–88.

The Fifth Circuit adopted yet another approach in United States v. Runyan, 275 F.3d 449 (5th Cir. 2001). In *Runyan*, an estranged wife looked through some of her husband's computer disks and found contraband images.

She turned over the entire set of disks to the police, and the police later conducted an extensive search of all of the disks without a warrant. The Fifth Circuit concluded that the police officers did not exceed the scope of the private search when they looked through the disks that the wife had accessed, even though the police viewed files that the wife had not seen. The governmental viewing had merely examined the disks "more thoroughly than did the private parties." *Id.* at 464. In contrast, the police could not search the disks that the wife had not accessed. Viewing files located on those disks exceeded the scope of the private search. *Id.*

Finally, in Commonwealth v. Raboin, 24 Mass.L.Rptr. 278 (Mass. Super. 2008), burglars broke into the defendant's apartment and stole a lockbox. They later opened the lockbox and found 10 DVDs and 13 mini-cassettes inside. All ten DVDs were gold-colored "Maxwell" brand DVD–R's in clear plastic cases with titles written in black marker on the cover. Three of the titles were labeled "My Shit 1," "My Shit 2," and "My Shit 3"; two were each titled "My Porn Pics"; one was labeled "Thumb 1"; two were labeled "FEL 1"; and two were labeled "FEL 2." The 13 mini-cassettes were labeled in similar fashion that suggested that they contained the same materials as the DVDs. The burglars viewed short excerpts of several of the DVDs and found child pornography. They then turned over the DVDs and the mini-cassettes to someone else who then turned over the materials to the police. The police viewed the entirety of all ten of the DVDs and all thirteen mini-cassettes without a warrant.

The Massachusetts Superior Court ruled that under *Runyan*, it was proper to view the entirety of each of the DVDs that had been at least partially observed. *See id.* at *7–*8. The court then ruled that it was also proper to view the DVDs and the mini-cassettes that had not been yet viewed. According to the court, the similar labels on the different DVDs and mini-cassettes created substantial certainty that the DVDs and mini-cassettes that had not been searched contained the same images of child pornography as the DVDs that had been searched before they were turned over to the police. *See id.* at *9–*10.

Which case offers the most persuasive approach? *Barth, Emerson, Runyan,* or *Raboin*? If a government agent views a single file on a hard drive, does that viewing search the file, the folder, or the entire computer? Consider Orin S. Kerr, *Searches and Seizures in a Digital World*, 119 Harv. L. Rev. 531, 556 (2005):

> A single physical storage device can store the private files of thousands of different users. It would be quite odd if looking at one file on a server meant that the entire server had been searched, and that the police could then analyze everything on the server, perhaps belonging to thousands of different people, without any restriction. Furthermore, a single file on a network may actually be stored in several physical boxes. Some computer storage devices may not be stored in any boxes at all. Over time, it should become increasingly clear that the Fourth Amendment should track the information, not the physical box.

See also Clancy, 75 Miss. L.J. at 240 ("[A] computer should be viewed as a physical container with a series of electronic 'containers'—that is, directories, folders, and files that must be each separately opened. Each separate opening is the examination of a new container.'')

5. Does a person retain a reasonable expectation of privacy in the contents of computers that they have stolen, or that they have obtained by fraud? In United States v. Caymen, 404 F.3d 1196 (9th Cir. 2005), a hotel desk clerk obtained the credit card of a hotel customer and used the account number to purchase a computer for his personal use without the customer's permission. The hotel customer complained about the $1,654 bill for a new computer on her credit card, and the investigation was traced back to the desk clerk, Nicolai Caymen. The police searched Caymen's apartment and found the computer in his bedroom. The police then searched the computer for evidence of criminal activity. When the fruits of the search led to criminal charges, Caymen challenged the search of the computer on Fourth Amendment grounds. The Ninth Circuit rejected the challenge on the ground that Caymen did not have a reasonable expectation of privacy in the computer:

> What matters is a reasonable expectation of privacy that society is prepared to accept as reasonable, and one who takes property by theft or fraud cannot reasonably expect to retain possession and exclude others from it once he is caught. Whatever expectation of privacy he might assert is not a legitimate expectation that society is prepared to honor. Because, as the district court found, Caymen obtained the laptop computer by fraud, he had no legitimate expectation of privacy in the contents of the hard drive.

Id. at 1201. Imagine Caymen had given the computer to a friend and did not tell his friend that the computer was obtained by fraud. Would Caymen's friend have a reasonable expectation of privacy in the computer even if Caymen did not?

6. In United States v. Gorshkov, 2001 WL 1024026 (W.D. Wash. 2001), undercover FBI agents lured a suspected hacker to a fake business, Invita, under the pretext of assessing the defendant's abilities as a computer security consultant. The undercover agents asked the suspect to show them his hacking skills using an Invita computer connected to the Internet. Unbeknownst to the suspect, the FBI had installed a monitoring program inside the computer that recorded his password when he logged on to his home account. The software collected the password, and FBI agents later used it to access the suspect's files and establish the suspect's guilt. The district court held that obtaining the suspect's password did not violate his reasonable expectation of privacy:

> The Court finds that Defendant could not have had an actual expectation of privacy in a private computer network belonging to a U.S. company. It was not his computer. When Defendant sat down at the networked computer at the Invita undercover site, he knew that the systems administrator could and likely would monitor his activities. Indeed, the undercover agents told Defendant that they wanted to watch in order to see what he was capable of doing. With the agents present in the room and frequently standing and looking over his shoulder, Defendant sat down at the networked computed and logged on to an account at a computer named "freebsd.tech.net.ru." Therefore, the Defendant had no

expectation of privacy in his actions on the Invita computer. Even if Defendant could assert a subjective expectation of privacy, such an expectation would be unreasonable under these circumstances.

This case is similar to that of United States v. David, 756 F.Supp. 1385 (D. Nev. 1991). In *David*, the Defendant was cooperating with law enforcement and meeting with an agent in the agent's office when he accessed his "computer memo book" in the agent's presence. The agent, looking over David's shoulder, saw the password he entered. The court found that David had no reasonable expectation of privacy because of the agent's presence and monitoring[.]

The circumstances in the present case even more thoroughly refute the notion that the Defendant had a reasonable expectation of privacy in his activities on the Invita computer, because it was not his computer and the entire purpose for his use of it was to demonstrate his hacking acumen for Invita personnel to review. Therefore, under the circumstances of this case, the FBI did not violate the Fourth Amendment by obtaining Defendant's password.

Id. at *2. Is the court's analysis persuasive? Why should looking over the defendant's shoulder remove constitutional protection of information that never appeared on the screen? Should it matter that it was not his computer?

7.   *Hash functions and the Fourth Amendment.* Imagine the police obtain a computer that contains thousands of files, and they want to search through the computer to determine if it has a particular file. One way to do this is through a mathematical process known as a hash function. A hash function is a mathematical program that generates a unique alphanumeric value—sort of a digital fingerprint or "digital DNA"—for each file. To determine if a known file exists on a particular storage device, a computer analyst can run a hash for each of the files on the device and then compare the resulting alphanumeric values to those of known files. As a result, the analyst can learn what files are on the hard drive without actually observing the files.

Does running a hash function to identify whether known files are on a computer constitute a Fourth Amendment search? In United States v. Crist, 627 F.Supp.2d 575 (M.D. Pa. 2008), agents obtained the suspect's computer and ran a hash of the files on the hard drive. Running the hash using a computer forensic program called EnCase revealed a number of known files previously identified as contraband. The court concluded that running the hash was a Fourth Amendment search:

The Government argues that no search occurred in running the EnCase program because the agents didn't look at any files, they simply accessed the computer. The Court rejects this view and finds that the "running of hash values" is a search protected by the Fourth Amendment.... By subjecting the entire computer to a hash value analysis[,] every file, internet history, picture, and "buddy list" became available for Government review. Such examination constitutes a search.

Id. at *9.

8.   *Hashes and child pornography.* Imagine a software tool scans a computer for evidence of child pornography and reports back if it identifies

known contraband images. The police can create a hash of all the files on a particular computer, and they can program software to run an automated search for matches between the hashes of the files on the computer and hashes of known images of child pornography. A positive hit will establish that one of the known images of child pornography is stored on the hard drive. No other information will be revealed. If the police use an automated tool to find images of child pornography on a target's computer, does this amount to a Fourth Amendment search?

The *Crist* case above may suggest the answer is "yes," but consider the Supreme Court's decision in Illinois v. Caballes, 543 U.S. 405 (2005). In *Caballes*, the Supreme Court considered whether using a trained dog to sniff for narcotics constituted a Fourth Amendment search. During a traffic stop, officers dispatched a canine unit to the scene. An officer walked a dog around the trunk of the stopped car, and the dog alerted the officer to the presence of narcotics in the trunk. The officers interpreted the dog's alert as establishing probable cause to believe the trunk contained narcotics. A search of the car led to the discovery of drugs inside the trunk. In an opinion by Justice Stevens, the Court held that the dog sniff was not a search:

> Official conduct that does not compromise any legitimate interest in privacy is not a search subject to the Fourth Amendment. We have held that any interest in possessing contraband cannot be deemed "legitimate," and thus, governmental conduct that only reveals the possession of contraband compromises no legitimate privacy interest. This is because the expectation that certain facts will not come to the attention of the authorities is not the same as an interest in privacy that society is prepared to consider reasonable. * * * Respondent * * * concedes that drug sniffs are designed, and if properly conducted are generally likely, to reveal only the presence of contraband. Although respondent argues that the error rates, particularly the existence of false positives, call into question the premise that drug-detection dogs alert only to contraband, the record contains no evidence or findings that support his argument. Moreover, respondent does not suggest that an erroneous alert, in and of itself, reveals any legitimate private information, and, in this case, the trial judge found that the dog sniff was sufficiently reliable to establish probable cause to conduct a full-blown search of the trunk.

> Accordingly, the use of a well-trained narcotics-detection dog—one that does not expose noncontraband items that otherwise would remain hidden from public view—during a lawful traffic stop, generally does not implicate legitimate privacy interests. In this case, the dog sniff was performed on the exterior of respondent's car while he was lawfully seized for a traffic violation. Any intrusion on respondent's privacy expectations does not rise to the level of a constitutionally cognizable infringement.

Id. at 408–09.

Does *Caballes* apply to retrieving evidence from a computer? Is this analogous to using a trained dog sniffing for narcotics in *Caballes*? Or is *Caballes* distinguishable? *See generally* Richard P. Salgado, *Fourth Amendment Search and the Power of the Hash*, 119 Harv. L. Rev. F. 38, 45–46

(2006). *See also* Michael Adler, Note, *Cyberspace, General Searches, and Digital Contraband: The Fourth Amendment and the Net–Wide Search*, 105 Yale L.J. 1093, 1109–10 (1996).

9. *Data mining and the Fourth Amendment.* Imagine the government collects data, enters it into a database, and then mines the data for information. Analysis of the data in the database reveals important information that the government then uses in criminal cases. Does this datamining trigger the Fourth Amendment?

The usual answer is "no," largely because the information entered into the database normally will not protected by the Fourth Amendment. If information is not protected by the Fourth Amendment, analysis of it inside a database cannot trigger the Fourth Amendment's restrictions. For example, in State v. Sloane, 939 A.2d 796 (N.J. 2008), a defendant tried to challenge a government query of the federal database that contains criminal records known as the National Crime Information Center (NCIC). The query revealed Sloane's past criminal record and warrants out for his arrest. The Supreme Court of New Jersey rejected Sloane's Fourth Amendment challenge on the ground that the information in the NCIC database was not protected:

> An NCIC check is not a search under the federal or state constitutions. Critical to our analysis is the fact that the NCIC database is comprised of matters of public record. Because Sloane had no reasonable expectation of privacy in the public records maintained in NCIC—such as his two outstanding warrants and record of a parole violation—a check of the NCIC database was not a search. . . .

Id. at 803–04.

If the government creates a database containing information protected by the Fourth Amendment, the analysis becomes more complicated and the caselaw becomes very sparse. However, the usual rule of Fourth Amendment law is that if the police observe information protected by the Fourth Amendment, they can view it again without triggering the Fourth Amendment. As the Supreme Court stated in Illinois v. Andreas, 463 U.S. 765, 771–72 (1983), "once the police are lawfully in a position to observe an item firsthand, its owner's privacy interest in that item is lost." As a result, if the police lawfully obtain information protected by the Fourth Amendment and they then observe that information, the owner's privacy interest in the item is lost and the Fourth Amendment should permit the police to then put that information in a database and subject it to further analysis. On the other hand, if the police lawfully obtain computer data stored in a device and have not yet observed the data, so that it maintains its Fourth Amendment protection, any datamining would be subject to the usual Fourth Amendment restrictions: Under the container analogy, retrieving the information will be a Fourth Amendment search.

Do you agree that the Fourth Amendment should be construed to regulate data mining only in these narrow situations? Or should it be interpreted more broadly to impose restrictions on government data mining practices? *See generally* Christopher Slobogin, *Government Data Mining and the Fourth Amendment*, 75 U. Chi. L. Rev. 317 (2008); Joseph T. Thai, *Is Data*

Mining Ever a Search Under Justice Stevens's Fourth Amendment?, 74 Fordham L. Rev. 1731 (2006).

2. SEIZURES

The Supreme Court has defined a "seizure" of property as "some meaningful interference with an individual's possessory interest in [the individual's] property." United States v. Jacobsen, 466 U.S. 109, 113 (1984). Under this definition, a seizure occurs when the police take property away, block a person from being able to control her property in a meaningful way, or interfere with the path of property in transit. For example, if a package is sent through the mail, the police "seize" the package if they go to the mail room and take the package out of the stream of delivery. *See* United States v. Van Leeuwen, 397 U.S. 249 (1970). It is easy to apply these principles to computers in the case of physical storage devices. Under the container analogy, taking a computer away from its owner "seizes" it. This means that if the police want to take a person's computer away, they must ordinarily obtain a warrant to justify the seizure.

The legal question becomes more complicated when computer data is no longer linked to a physical container. For example, imagine that a police officer enters a coffee shop, orders a decaf latte, and sits down at a table. A patron at the table next to him has left his laptop computer on the table while he is away for a few minutes, and the officer sees what appears to be evidence of credit card fraud on the computer's monitor. If the officer writes down the text of what he sees, has he "seized" that data? What if the officer inserts a storage device into an input/output port in the back of the computer and copies the file that appears on the screen? Has he seized the file? Imagine the officer brings more sophisticated equipment and copies the entire computer hard drive. Does that copying seize the entire hard drive? More broadly, if a police officer copies data but does not otherwise interfere with the owner's possessory interest in the physical storage device, is that copying a "seizure"?

The courts have not yet answered such questions. The precedents from earlier technologies are mixed. On one hand, cases like United States v. New York Telephone Co., 434 U.S. 159 (1977), suggest that copying a file seizes it. In *New York Telephone*, the Supreme Court held that Federal Rule of Criminal Procedure 41 authorized the government to apply for a search warrant to install a monitoring device known as a pen register. Rule 41 is the statutory rule that authorizes federal investigators to obtain search warrants "to search for and seize" evidence of criminal activity; a pen register is a device that records the outgoing numbers dialed from a telephone. Although *New York Telephone* involved interpretation of a statutory rule, not the Fourth Amendment, the Court's language is suggestive. The Court ruled that Rule 41 "is broad enough to encompass a 'search' designed to ascertain the use which is being made of a telephone suspected of being employed as a means of facilitating a criminal venture and the 'seizure' of evidence which the 'search' of the telephone produces. * * * Rule 41 is sufficiently broad to include seizures of intangible items such as dial impulses recorded by pen registers as well as tangible items." *Id.* at 169–70.

On the other hand, consider Arizona v. Hicks, 480 U.S. 321 (1987), which points in the opposite direction. In *Hicks*, an officer came across stereo equipment that he believed was stolen. The officer wrote down the serial numbers he observed on the equipment, and he then called in the numbers to the police station to confirm that the equipment was stolen. The Supreme Court held that the act of copying the numbers was not a seizure:

> We agree that the mere recording of the serial numbers did not constitute a seizure. To be sure, that was the first step in a process by which respondent was eventually deprived of the stereo equipment. In and of itself, however, it did not "meaningfully interfere" with respondent's possessory interest in either the serial numbers or the equipment, and therefore did not amount to a seizure.

Id. at 327.

Is copying computer data more like recording a number as in *Hicks* or recording a dialed impulse as in *New York Telephone*? Are these cases reconcilable?

UNITED STATES v. GORSHKOV

United States District Court for the Western District of Washington, 2001.
2001 WL 1024026.

COUGHENOUR, J.

This matter comes before the Court on Defendant's Motion to Suppress Seized Computer Data. Defendant moves this Court for an order suppressing all computer data together with all derivative fruits therefrom seized by federal agents * * * from two computers located in Russia known as "tech.net.ru" and "freebsd.tech.net.ru."

Following an extensive national investigation of a series of computer hacker intrusions into the computer systems of businesses in the United States emanating from Russia, Alexey Ivanov was identified as one of the intruders. Around June, 2000, the FBI set up Invita, a "sting" computer security company in Seattle. On/about November 10, 2000 Mr. Ivanov, along with his "business partner," Defendant Vasiliy Gorshkov, flew from Russia to [the Seattle–Tacoma International Airport].

In Seattle, the two men met with undercover FBI agents at the Invita office. During the meeting and at the behest of the FBI, Defendant Gorshkov used an FBI IBM Thinkpad computer ostensibly to demonstrate his computer hacking and computer security skills and to access his computer system, "tech.net.ru," in Russia. After the meeting and demonstration, both Gorshkov and Ivanov were arrested.

Following the Defendants' arrest, without Defendant Gorshkov's knowledge or consent, the FBI searched and seized the IBM and all key strokes made by the Defendant while he used it, by means of a "sniffer" program which allowed the FBI to track and store the information. The FBI thereby obtained the Defendant's computer user name and password that he had used to access the Russian computer.

Armed with this information the FBI logged onto the subject computer(s) located in Russia. Faced with the possibility that a confederate of the defendant could destroy the files in the Russian computer, the FBI decided to download the file contents of the subject computer(s). This was done without reading same until after a search warrant was obtained. The FBI's downloading and copying of the downloaded data onto CD disk format took until November 21. The warrant was applied for and obtained on December 1, 2000. The delay between the downloading of the data and the procurement of the warrant was due to the slow process of obtaining approval and permission from FBI headquarters and the Department of Justice.

The agents' act of copying the data on the Russian computers was not a seizure under the Fourth Amendment because it did not interfere with Defendant's or anyone else's possessory interest in the data. The data remained intact and unaltered. It remained accessible to Defendant and any co-conspirators or partners with whom he had shared access. The copying of the data had absolutely no impact on his possessory rights.[1] Therefore it was not a seizure under the Fourth Amendment. *See* Arizona v. Hicks, 480 U.S. 321, 324 (1987) (recording of serial number on suspected stolen property was not seizure because it did not "meaningfully interfere" with respondent's possessory interest in either the serial number or the equipment); Bills v. Aseltine, 958 F.2d 697, 707 (6th Cir. 1992) (officer's photographic recording of visual images of scene was not seizure because it did not "meaningfully interfere" with any possessory interest).

Notes and Questions

1. The *Gorshkov* case relies on *Arizona v. Hicks* for the view that copying a computer file is not a seizure. But how should *Hicks* apply to computer data? Is creating a copy of data using electronic means different from manually writing down information that is visually observed? If so, why? Is the difference that the electronic copy is a perfect copy, indistinguishable from the original? Or is the difference that the electronic tool used to copy the data is not a person, and therefore the information has not been exposed to human observation? Or is there no appreciable difference at all?

2. Susan Brenner and Barbara Frederiksen have argued that *Hicks* can be distinguished from cases involving computer files:

---

[1]. Defendant argues that the Government seized the data on the Russian computers because the *tar* command [used to copy the files] block's other users from accessing the data. After hearing the testimony on this subject, the Court is convinced that no authorized user is prevented from accessing the files that are being [copied].

One critical difference between writing down serial numbers in *Hicks* and the act of copying computer files is the nature of the information. The officer did not record information that belonged to Hicks. Serial numbers are not property in the sense that the numbers belong to one person, but are more analogous to license plates or other public records. Serial numbers are assigned by the manufacturer of a product and are used to track and identify that product. Hicks had no interest in these serial numbers because the stereo equipment was stolen from its rightful owners. Hicks had no lawful possessory interest in the equipment or in the serial numbers on the equipment.

Unlike the serial numbers in *Hicks*, the information contained in computer files clearly belongs to the owner of the files.

Susan W. Brenner & Barbara A. Frederiksen, *Computer Searches And Seizures: Some Unresolved Issues*, 8 Mich Telecomm. & Tech. L. Rev. 39, 111–112 (2001–2002).

The usual rule is that observing private communications or property does not seize anything. Observing private facts may constitute a search if it violates an individual's reasonable expectation of privacy, but mere observation is not a seizure. Recall that in the *David* case, Agent Peterson observed David typing his password "fortune" into the computer memo book. The court considered whether this observation was a search, but did not ask whether it was a seizure.

Does copying digital evidence require a different rule? In Katz v. United States, 389 U.S. 347 (1967), the Supreme Court held that "electronically listening to and recording" a defendant's private conversation "constituted a 'search and seizure' within the meaning of the Fourth Amendment." *Katz* was not clear, however, on whether recording the conversation was considered a "search" of the conversation or a "seizure" of it (or both). Which do you think it should be? Also, how would you determine who has a possessory interest in information? Is the key question whether the defendant has a lawful ownership right in the physical property that contains the data, or does some other test provide a better guide?

3.   In United States v. Thomas, 613 F.2d 787 (10th Cir. 1980), a package sent via UPS ripped open during sorting. The opening revealed obscene materials inside the package. UPS employees called the FBI, and an FBI agent made photocopies of the materials before resealing the package. The package was given back to UPS, although it was not delivered because apparently the address was improper. The FBI agents then requested a warrant to seize the package and attached the photocopies to the affidavit. The defendant challenged the FBI's conduct, claiming that photocopying the materials seized them. The Tenth Circuit disagreed: "The materials herein remained in UPS's possession and their delivery was unaffected since they were undeliverable. The materials were searched but not seized." *Id.* at 789.

Similarly, in Bills v. Aseltine, 958 F.2d 697 (6th Cir. 1992), agents took photographs of the plaintiff's home while executing a search warrant there. The plaintiff sued, claiming that taking photographs had "seized" images of his home beyond the scope of the warrant. The Sixth Circuit disagreed, holding that taking photographs did not seize anything because it did not interfere with any possessory interest. *See id.* at 707.

4.   If making a digital copy of data constitutes a seizure, does copying the copy also constitute a seizure? If the police make ten copies of a lawfully obtained file, has the file been seized ten times? Once? Never?

5.   In United States v. Triumph Capital Group, 211 F.R.D. 31 (D. Conn. 2002), an FBI agent made a bitstream copy of a seized hard drive to begin the forensic analysis of its contents. The defendant claimed that creating the copy was a "seizure" not authorized by the warrant. The court offered only the following cursory analysis:

> [The FBI agent] did not seize the entire hard drive when he created the image file, restored it to MOs [magneto-optical disks] for examination purposes or copied blocks of data to MOs and CDs. These were simply preliminary and reasonably necessary steps in the forensic examination, and did not require the magistrate judge's authorization.

Id. at 63–64. Does whether a step is "reasonably necessary" have anything to do with whether the step is a seizure? Or is the court saying that even if the step was a seizure, it wasn't an unreasonable seizure?

C. EXCEPTIONS TO THE WARRANT REQUIREMENT

If government action is a Fourth Amendment search or seizure, its legality hinges on whether the search or seizure is constitutionally "reasonable." Searches and seizures are reasonable if authorized by a valid warrant or an exception to the warrant requirement applies. The following materials consider the various exceptions to the warrant requirement.

1. EXIGENT CIRCUMSTANCES

The exigent circumstances exception permits the government to conduct warrantless searches or seizures when immediately necessary to protect public safety or preserve evidence. *See, e.g.,* Mincey v. Arizona, 437 U.S. 385 (1978). This long-established exception applies when circumstances "would cause a reasonable person to believe that entry ... was necessary to prevent physical harm to the officers or other persons, the destruction of relevant evidence, the escape of the suspect, or some other consequence improperly frustrating legitimate law enforcement efforts." United States v. McConney, 728 F.2d 1195, 1199 (9th Cir. 1984) (en banc).

The Supreme Court has never articulated a clear test for exigent circumstances, and instead has applied a general balancing of interests to determine when and how broadly it applies. As a general matter, interests often include the degree of urgency involved, whether a warrant could have been obtained, the seriousness of the crime investigated, the possibility of danger, the likelihood evidence may be destroyed, and the availability of alternative means of obtaining or securing evidence or protecting public safety. Further, an exigent circumstances search must be "strictly circumscribed by the exigencies which justify its initiation." Terry v. Ohio, 392 U.S. 1, 25–36 (1968).

UNITED STATES v. TROWBRIDGE

United States District Court for the Northern District of Texas, 2007.
2007 WL 4226385.

JANE J. BOYLE, DISTRICT JUDGE.

On January 24, 2007, FBI Special Agents Lynd and Sabol attempted to conduct a "knock and talk" at Jason Trowbridge's Houston, Texas home to obtain information about Guadalupe Martinez, a suspect who had recently been arrested. The agents were also investigating a conspiracy involving Martinez, Trowbridge, Chad Ward, and Stuart Rosoff in which these individuals allegedly exceeded authorized computer access to a commercial database to obtain personal identification information on individuals on telephone partylines, so that the conspirators could harass them by making threatening phone calls, disrupting telephone service and making false 911 calls to elicit response by police, fire and ambulance to residences. In the world of cyber-crime, this activity is known as "swatting."

Agent Lynd testified that there was some urgency to their "knock and talk" with Trowbridge because Martinez had been arrested in the presence of another party line member who told others about his arrest. After traveling to two locations, the agents discovered that they had incorrect information about where Trowbridge lived. At around noon, the agents proceeded to Ward's home and interviewed him. Ward confirmed Trowbridge's address and stated that Trowbridge had a girlfriend who lived with him, that Trowbridge had instructed him to destroy evidence on one occasion, that Trowbridge had seven computers in his home, and that Trowbridge was anti-government and could take care of himself if law enforcement arrived. He also told the agents that Trowbridge had access to a commercial database in his business but did not state whether this database was used at Trowbridge's residence.

The agents proceeded to Trowbridge's town home at about 3:00 p.m to perform their "knock and talk." At this time, they believed that they did not have probable cause to search Trowbridge's residence. The agents observed a car that they believed to be associated with Trowbridge and saw a business card with his name on it inside the car. When the agents knocked on Trowbridge's door, identified themselves, and called out Trowbridge's name, the music inside the home stopped playing. Agent Sabol noticed a cell phone on the balcony and went to the back of the building where he observed two individuals, who did not fit Trowbridge's description, exit the residence and jump over an eight to ten foot fence. When Sabol returned to the front of the home, the cell phone he had previously observed was no longer on the balcony causing him to believe that there might be someone inside the home.

Angela Roberson, Trowbridge's girlfriend who lived with him, eventually answered the door and told the agents that Trowbridge was not home. She agreed to talk to the agents about Martinez and allowed them to come inside. The agents remained on the first floor of the three-level town house during this interview. During the course of the interview, Roberson told the agents that she had exchanged instant messages with Martinez regarding his swatting activities on various computers in the home, that spoof cards had been purchased using computers in the home, and that Trowbridge had computer access to a commercial database at the home. The agents also smelled marijuana and observed drug paraphernalia.

Officer Lynd observed a wireless router that he explained would allow a person within a few hundred yards to access the computers and erase or change them. Officer Lynd testified that if he had access to the computers he could determine whether the allegedly criminal phone calls had been made using spoof cards purchased on Trowbridge's computers. During the interview, the officers noticed three computers downstairs, and Roberson said that there were three upstairs. At the agents' request, Roberson called Trowbridge's cell phone, and the agents heard the phone ring upstairs. Roberson hung up the phone stating that Trowbridge did not answer. At this point, the agents believed that Trowbridge was hiding upstairs but did not know how many people were upstairs, if there were any weapons, or if the individuals who had fled would be returning. Agent Lynd then called and spoke with Trowbridge who said he was not home and that Lynd could make an appointment to speak with him and his attorney. Agent Sabol testified that the design of the multiple level town house would allow someone from upstairs to approach the agents without being discovered.

At some point during the conversation with Roberson, the agents developed probable cause to search the computer hard drives because she identified the computers as being used to have conversations with Martinez and to purchase spoof cards. The agents then spoke with the U.S. Attorney's Offices in Dallas and Houston and determined that exigent circumstances existed to seize the computers. The U.S. Attorney's Office advised them that it would be difficult to get a search warrant in the late afternoon around 4:30 because of Houston traffic.

Agent Lynd testified that in his experience individuals involved in computer crimes had attempted to destroy computer evidence and that Martinez had given a computer away to prevent the agents from obtaining evidence. He also testified that computer evidence is more fragile than drug evidence. It can be destroyed by turning off the computer, smashing it with a hammer, using a magnet, or throwing it into a fire. He stated that software is available to destroy evidence on a computer and that a hard drive is easy to remove and hide. Lynd said that he was sure the evidence would be gone in a few minutes if the agents left.

Both agents testified that they did not believe it would be safe to leave one agent at the residence while the other secured a search warrant.

Officer Lynd based this fear on the fact that Roberson and Trowbridge were concealing Trowbridge's presence upstairs, people had fled the residence, the residence smelled like marijuana, and they could not see what was occurring upstairs. Agent Sabol also knew Trowbridge had been affiliated with an anarchist group. Lynd testified that he was concerned that Ward had called Trowbridge to warn him that the agents were coming.

The agents asked Roberson for a copy of the computers and when she refused informed her that they would seize the computers to prevent the destruction of evidence. At this point Roberson for the first time asked the agents to leave. Trowbridge and Trowbridge's attorney also spoke with the agents on the phone. When Houston police department officers arrived to perform a safety sweep, Roberson told them that Trowbridge was upstairs. The police officers escorted him downstairs. Then additional agents arrived and seized the computers. Trowbridge's attorney also arrived. The agents checked the computers into the evidence control room in Houston, obtained a search warrant, shipped the computers to the Dallas evidence control room, and then delivered them to the North Texas forensic lab. The agents seized only the computers and did not search anything else in the home. They also left two inventories of what was taken from the home.

On June 19, 2007, a grand jury charged Trowbridge with "Conspiracy to Use Access Devices to Modify Telecommunications Instruments and to Access Protected Telecommunications Computers" [in violation of 18 U.S.C. § 371, 18 U.S.C. §§ 1029(a)(9), and 1030(a)(5)(A)(ii)]." Trowbridge moved to suppress all evidence obtained as a result of the January 24, 2007 search of his residence because the search violated his right to be free from unlawful searches and seizures under the Fourth Amendment.

1. Was there an exigency?

A warrantless intrusion into an individual's home is presumptively unreasonable unless the person consents or probable cause and exigent circumstances justify the encroachment. The government bears the burden of proving that an exigency exists. Whether exigent circumstances exist is a question of fact, reversible only if the district court's factual findings are clearly erroneous. We look to the totality of the circumstances surrounding the officers' actions, mindful that our review is more akin to examining a video tape by instant replay than to examining a snapshot.

Exigent circumstances include: (1) reasonable fear for officer's safety; (2) presence of firearms; (3) risk of a criminal suspect escaping; or (4) fear of destruction of evidence. The Court will consider the following factors to determine whether an exigency exists: (1) the degree of urgency involved and amount of time necessary to obtain a warrant; (2) the reasonable belief that contraband is about to be removed; (3) the possibility of danger to the police officers guarding the site of contraband while a search warrant is sought; (4) information indicating that the possessors of the contraband are aware that the police are on their trail; and (5) the ready destructibility of the contraband and the knowledge that efforts to dispose of narcotics and to escape are characteristic behavior of persons engaged in the narcotics traffic.

Applying the first factor to the present case, the degree of urgency and the time required to obtain a warrant, the situation was urgent because the officers believed that Trowbridge was upstairs and could quickly destroy the evidence. Lynd testified that he was sure that the evidence would be gone in a few minutes. The agents also testified that they feared for their safety. With respect to the time it would take to obtain a warrant, the U.S. Attorney's Office told the agents that due to afternoon traffic, it would be difficult to obtain a search warrant that day. As for the second factor, the reasonable belief that contraband will be removed, the officers believed that Trowbridge was hiding upstairs and had access to the computers. They had also been told that Trowbridge had instructed Ward to destroy evidence in the past.

The next factor for the Court to consider is whether it would be dangerous for police officers to guard the site while a search warrant is sought. Both officers credibly testified that they did not believe it would be safe to leave one agent at the residence while the other secured a warrant. Agent Sabol testified about his concern regarding the layout of the town house. He stated that it would be easy for someone to approach the officers without being detected. The officers believed that Roberson and Trowbridge were deceiving them by concealing Trowbridge's presence in the home. Agent Sabol had seen two individuals fleeing the house and was unaware whether they might return or whether there were other individuals or weapons in the home. Ward also told the agents that Trowbridge was anti-government and could take care of himself if law enforcement arrived. The smell of marijuana and the knowledge that Trowbridge was allegedly affiliated with an anarchist group also alarmed the agents. These facts support a finding that it would have been dangerous for one of the officers to guard the residence.

Considering the fourth factor, an indication that the possessors are aware that the police are approaching, Lynd testified that Martinez had recently been arrested and news of this arrest may have been available to party line members. The agents had spoken with Ward, another suspect. They were concerned that he would call Trowbridge to warn him that they were coming. When Roberson called Trowbridge's cell phone, the officers heard the phone ring upstairs. This indicated to the officers that Trowbridge was upstairs and was aware of their presence. The presence of a car that they associated with Trowbridge and the disappearance of the cell phone from the balcony also indicated that Trowbridge might be in the home. In addition, the agents had spoken with Trowbridge on the phone, confirming that he knew of their presence.

Finally, the Court will consider the ready destructibility of the contraband and the knowledge that efforts to dispose of narcotics and to escape are characteristic behaviors of persons engaged in the narcotics traffic. Officer Lynd testified that computer evidence is easier to destroy than drug evidence. Trowbridge argued that even if electronic data may be easily destroyed, one may not assume that the suspect has the means, knowledge, or wherewithal to destroy it. However, the Court found that based on the agents' testimony, there was reason to believe that Trowbridge would destroy the evidence. Ward informed the officers that Trowbridge had instructed him to destroy evidence in the past; therefore, the destruction of computer evidence may be characteristic of his behavior. While this was not a narcotics case, Agent Lynd testified that individuals accused of computer crimes had attempted to destroy evidence in his experience and that Martinez had disposed of computer evidence. In conclusion, the Government has presented sufficient facts to support each factor.

This Court determines, based on the agents' credible testimony and the totality of the circumstances that an exigency existed because of the likelihood that the computer evidence would be destroyed. The Court will now consider whether the agents manufactured the exigent circumstances.

2.   Did the agents manufacture the exigency?

After determining that an exigency existed, the Court must determine whether the police created the exigency. Exigent circumstances may not consist of the likely consequences of the government's own actions or inactions. In determining whether officers create an exigency, this Court focuses on the reasonableness of the officers' investigative tactics leading up to the warrantless entry.

In this case, the Court is convinced that the agents did not have probable cause to search Trowbridge's computers because there was no evidence connecting his computers to the offense they were investigating. Accordingly, it was reasonable for the officers to use the "knock and talk" strategy to further investigate. In addition, Trowbridge and Roberson, not the officers, created the exigency when they attempted to deceive the agents by claiming that Trowbridge was not at home. Based on the agents's testimony, the Court conclude[s] that their investigative tactics were reasonable and did not create the exigency.

Because the Government established an exigency that justified a warrantless seizure of Trowbridge's computers, the Court denies Trowbridge's motion to suppress.

NOTES AND QUESTIONS

1.   The issue in *Trowbridge* was whether the investigators could initially seize Trowbridge's computers, not whether the investigators could then search the computers. The latter issue was not raised because the police obtained a search warrant before they searched the computers that had been

seized. If investigators had not obtained a warrant to search the computers, would exigent circumstances have allowed the investigators to search the computers that had been seized?

This question arose in United States v. David, 756 F. Supp. 1385 (D. Nev. 1991), parts of which appeared earlier in this chapter. At one point, the FBI agent investigating the case saw the defendant deleting files from his computer memo book. The FBI agent, Agent Peterson, quickly seized the computer from David to stop him from deleting evidence of his crimes. Peterson later searched the computer without a warrant. The court held that the seizure was justified but the search was not:

> When destruction of evidence is imminent, a warrantless seizure of that evidence is justified if there is probable cause to believe that the item seized constitutes evidence of criminal activity. Here, Agent Peterson saw David destroying evidence. David's use of the book in retrieving telephone numbers of criminal associates provided ample probable cause that the book contained information relative to criminal activity. Peterson therefore reasonably believed that prompt action was necessary to prevent further destruction of relevant evidence.

> Although Peterson had the authority to seize and hold the book due to the exigency at hand, his authority to examine its contents is a different matter. The seizure of the book affected only David's possessory interests. It did not affect the privacy interests vested in the contents of the book.

> Once he took the book from David the exigency which justified the seizure came to an end. Nevertheless, without seeking a warrant, Peterson conducted a complete search of the book's contents. The seizure of the book did not justify the invasion of privacy involved in the subsequent search.

Id. at 1392–93. In a footnote, the court rejected the government's argument that exigent circumstances justified the search because the computer's batteries might have failed and its memory might have been lost:

> The government argues, lamely, that the exigency continued even after the seizure, because Agent Peterson did not know how much longer the book's batteries would live. It was therefore imperative, according to the government, that Peterson access the book before the batteries died and the information was erased. At the evidentiary hearing, however, no evidence was offered to substantiate this concern. In fact, Peterson testified that he successfully accessed the book at a later time without changing the batteries. The government bears a heavy burden of establishing exigent circumstances. Speculation is insufficient to carry that burden. The government has not met its burden here.

Id. at 1392 n.2.

As these passages from *David* suggest, exigent circumstances to seize a computer are very different from exigent circumstances to search it. Once the computer is secured, it usually will be the case that the exigency is over and a warrant can then be obtained. *See also* Commonwealth v. Kaupp, 899 N.E.2d 809, 814, n.7 (Mass. 2009).

2.   Early cases applying the exigent circumstances doctrine to computer storage devices often involved electronic pagers used in the narcotics trade. Each pager could store a handful of phone numbers that recorded incoming calls. Narcotics investigators would come across a suspect's pager, often immediately after arresting him for narcotics offenses, and would click through the pager and retrieve the phone numbers it contained. Several courts concluded that the search of the pagers was justified by exigent circumstances on the ground that the pagers could only store a few phone numbers. Any new number representing an incoming call would force the pager to delete a previous number, and the previous number could be useful evidence relevant to the offense. *See, e.g.,* United States v. Romero–Garcia, 991 F. Supp. 1223, 1225 (D. Or. 1997), *aff'd on other grounds*, 168 F.3d 502 (9th Cir. 1999). *But see* United States v. Reyes, 922 F. Supp. 818, 835–36 (S.D.N.Y. 1996) (concluding that when investigators found the suspect's pager turned off and turned it on themselves, they could not then rely on the exigent circumstances exception to search the pager because they had created the exigency).

2.   CONSENT

The consent exception is a powerful exception to the warrant requirement. Voluntary consent by a person with a right to consent makes a warrantless search reasonable and therefore constitutional. Whether consent is voluntary is determined by a totality of the circumstances. *See* Schnekloth v. Bustamonte, 412 U.S. 218 (1973).

Consent law raises three basic questions. First, how should courts interpret the scope of consent? Second, when can a third party consent? Third, when can the police reasonably rely on the apparent authority of a third party to consent?

(a) Scope of Consent

UNITED STATES v. AL–MARRI

United States District Court for the Southern District of New York, 2002.
230 F. Supp.2d 535.

MARRERO, DISTRICT JUDGE.

Al–Marri arrived in the United States from Qatar on September 10, 2001 to enroll in a graduate program in computer science at Bradley University in Illinois, from which he had received a bachelor's degree in 1991. In the wake of the September 11 attacks, the Federal Bureau of Investigation received calls reporting that Al–Marri may have been implicated in possible suspicious activity. In response, FBI agents visited Al–Marri twice at his home in Peoria, Illinois.

At the Court's September 5, 2002 evidentiary hearing on the Motion, Nicholas Zambeck and Robert Brown, the two FBI agents who conducted the interviews with Al–Marri and the search of his home and car, testified in person. They stated that during the first visit on October 2, 2001, they asked Al–Marri a series of questions concerning his background, travels, and eventual arrival in the United States. Al–Marri satisfactorily answered the agents' questions and consented to a search of his steamer trunk, which had been mentioned in one of the leads received by the FBI. The agents then ended the interview.

Two months later, at about 4:00 p.m. on December 11, 2001, Zambeck and Brown returned to Al–Marri's home. At the door, Zambeck explained that they had additional questions regarding his date of birth and enrollment at Bradley. It is undisputed that the agents asked permission to enter Al–Marri's home and he agreed, but Al–Marri asked for a few minutes so he could move his wife, who was in an unveiled state and could not be viewed by men, into another part of the house. The agents allowed Al–Marri to do this, and then entered the house.

Once inside, the agents explained that they wanted to conduct the interview back at their office. They contend that Al–Marri agreed to this request. The agents then asked for permission to look around the house, to which they maintain Al–Marri consented. Al–Marri accompanied the agents as they conducted a search of the apartment room by room.

Upon seeing Al–Marri's laptop computer, which was located on a table in the master bedroom and turned on, the agents asked whether they could take it to their office "to take a look at it" because they did not have the skills nor the time to conduct such an examination at the house. According to the agents, Al–Marri agreed to this request, and proceeded to power the computer down. By the agents' account, as he turned the computer off, Al–Marri suggested that the agents carry the computer in his traveling carrying case. Al–Marri retrieved the case from a closet, placed the computer inside and handed it to the agents. On the table, the agents also saw several CDs and diskettes stored inside a container. They testified that they asked Al–Marri if they could take those as well and that Al–Marri agreed. In addition, the agents claimed that Al–Marri gave them permission to search his car, from which they seized additional items of evidence.

The agents then brought Al–Marri back to their office in order to question him further, and arrived at the office at approximately 4:30 p.m. They brought him to an unlocked interview room, offered him a refreshment, and began the interview by requesting that he sign a consent form indicating he had approved the search. Al–Marri declined to sign the form at that point, and asked the agents to set the form aside for the time being. Towards the end of the interview, the conversation grew contentious, and Zambeck reminded Al–Marri of the consequences of lying to an FBI agent. When the interview ended at approximately 10:00 p.m., the agents asked Al–Marri to return the next day to take a polygraph test to verify the information he had provided. Al–Marri agreed, and then was driven home by the agents. Before he left, Al–Marri asked Brown: "Do I get my computer back tonight?" Brown replied: "No, not tonight."

Inspection of Al–Marri's computer and its carrying case, conducted from December 12 to December 23, revealed credit card numbers and other information and resources that, according to the Government charges, could be used to conduct credit card fraud. In examining the laptop, the FBI made several copies of the hard drive, analyzed the data on the computer to identify both current and deleted files, and scrutinized the internet search engine's bookmarks. These examinations revealed several files related to or containing credit card numbers and expiration dates for those numbers, along with comments on whether such numbers were still valid. In addition, the FBI found bookmarks to several web sites that could be used to assist a person conducting credit card fraud.

The evidence taken from Al–Marri's computer, in conjunction with other information gathered by the FBI, led to Al–Marri's arrest on January 28, 2002 under an indictment charging Al–Marri with unauthorized possession of access devices with intent to defraud in violation of 18 U.S.C. § 1029(a)(3).

Al–Marri claims that the scope of the consent did not extend to allowing the Government to seize his computer for inspection of its hard drive.

A warrantless search and seizure is per se unreasonable under the Fourth Amendment—subject only to a few specifically established and well-delineated exceptions. One such exception applies to consensual searches, which have consistently been approved by courts based on the logic that it is "reasonable for the police to conduct a search once they have been permitted to do so." *Florida v. Jimeno,* 500 U.S. 248, 251 (1991).

The issue presented to the Court in regard to the search entails a legal question: [given that] the FBI had consent to search Al–Marri's home, did the extensive search of his computer exceed the scope of such consent? The central requirement of all Fourth Amendment analysis is one of reasonableness. Thus, in measuring the scope of a suspect's consent under the Fourth Amendment, the Supreme Court has imposed a standard of "objective reasonableness—what would the typical reasonable person have understood by the exchange between the officer and the suspect?" *Jimeno,* 500 U.S. at 251.

In the instant case, the agents asked Al–Marri for permission to search the entirety of his home, and Al–Marri agreed to the search. When the agents asked to take his computer back to the FBI office for further examination, Al–Marri agreed to shut the computer down and even helped put the computer in a carrying case for the agents. Al–Marri did not place any explicit limitation on the scope of the search of his home, car or computer, other than to insist that his wife occupy another room in the house to prevent the agents from seeing her in an unveiled state.

Al–Marri would have realized that the examination of his computer would be more than superficial when the agents explained that they did not have the skills nor the time to perform the examination at his home.

Moreover, a graduate student in computer science would clearly understand the technological resources of the FBI and its ability to thoroughly examine his computer. Based on this knowledge, Al–Marri could have provided specific instructions to the FBI about the scope of the search he had permitted, specifically whether there were any files or programs he wanted kept private. He did not offer such guidance. Viewed objectively from the perspective of the agents, it was reasonable for Zambeck and Brown to have understood that this unrestricted grant of access, combined with Al–Marri's expertise in computer technology and his helpful attitude in handing the laptop over, indicated that Al–Marri had no qualms about an extensive search of his computer.

Al–Marri's exchange with Brown at the end of the interview on December 11 also provides insight into Al–Marri's state of mind, and what Brown reasonably could have inferred from Al–Marri's expressions regarding the scope of his consent to search the computer. Viewed objectively, Al–Marri's question "Do I get my computer back tonight?" reasonably indicated that Al–Marri did not know the length of time the FBI would retain the computer, implicitly conveyed Al–Marri's awareness and acceptance of the possibility that the agents' control over it would last beyond "tonight" and extend into an indefinite duration, and suggested that he was not insistent on demanding its immediate return. When he did not respond to Brown's answer "No, not tonight," Al–Marri further demonstrated that he felt no need to put a time limit on the FBI's possession of his laptop. If Al–Marri had any need for use of the computer, or felt any reservation or objection about the FBI's prolonged retention of it, a reasonable person would have expected Al–Marri to ask for the computer to be restored to him within a specified time frame for whatever reason justified a prompt return. Al–Marri's silence on this subject and his failure to raise the issue again the next day persuades this Court that his consent could reasonably have been understood to be open-ended and given without a limitation on time or scope.

Even assuming Al–Marri had not voluntarily handed over his computer to the FBI agents, the Supreme Court has ruled that "a lawful search of a fixed premises generally extends to the entire area where the object of the search could be found." *United States v. Ross,* 456 U.S. 798, 820 (1982). In this case, the object of the search was not made explicit. However, the circumstance that neither Al–Marri nor the agents knew precisely what the object of the search was does not change the nature of the consent.

Here, although the purpose of the FBI's search of Al–Marri's home was not specifically stated, it is clear from the totality of the circumstances that the agents' questioning of Al–Marri related to the investigation of the terrorist attacks of September 11, 2001. Al–Marri, who arrived from Qatar the day before the attacks, had already been interviewed by the same agents on October 2, 2001, exactly three weeks after the attacks. Any reasonable person in Al–Marri's position could not have lived through the events of September 11 and its aftermath and yet not realize that the

FBI's questions of him so soon after—including questions about telephone calls he placed to particular individuals or numbers—related to that investigation, even if such an investigative focus was not expressly conveyed to him.

Consequently, it seems reasonably probable that federal agents involved in an investigation of international terrorist crimes who ask for permission to search a person's home under these circumstances will be understood to be looking for evidence of unlawful conduct. Thus, a reasonable person—and in particular a graduate student in computer science who is fluent in English—would have recognized the agents' request to search his home, car and computer as a search for evidence of possible criminal activities.

NOTES AND QUESTIONS

1. The test for the scope of consent is what a "typical reasonable person" would have understood the consent to have included in light of the specific facts of the case. Would a "typical reasonable person" understand consent to search a place to include consent to search computers located in that place?

Imagine a police officer visits a home in response to a reported burglary. The officer asks the homeowner if he will let the officer "look around for evidence." The homeowner responds, "sure, officer, do whatever you want." Would a reasonable person understand this exchange to permit the officer to search any computers found inside the home? Does it matter whether the officer is searching for evidence of the burglary or evidence of some other crime?

Also consider how this test applies when a suspect consents to a search of a specific computer storage device. Does the consent ordinarily limit the type of evidence the officer may try to find? Does it limit the thoroughness of the search? If a target permits an officer to "look through" his computer, is the officer restricted in terms of what kind of search he can conduct? Or would a "typical reasonable person" understand that permitting an officer to search a computer permits the officer to look for any evidence using any technique?

2. Government agents often ask suspects to sign a written consent form. In some cases, those written consent forms will be drafted by government lawyers and will specifically mention that computers are included in the scope of consent. So long as the officers do not make any oral representations that the search will be more limited, courts generally will conclude that the written consent permits a seizure and subsequent search of computers located in the place to be searched. *See, e.g.,* United States v. Long, 425 F.3d 482, 487 (7th Cir. 2005). In other cases, officers may simply write up a written consent form from a blank piece of paper. The scope of consent will normally be based on what the paper form says. *See, e.g.,* United States v. Luken, 560 F.3d 741, 644–45 (8th Cir. 2009) (handwritten statement in which suspect writes, "I, Jon Luken, give law enforcement the permission to seize & view my Gateway computer" construed to permit extensive computer forensic analysis of computer).

On the other hand, if agents leave the impression that the search will be limited, courts may construe the consent as limited. This is particularly likely if the agents create the reasonable impression that they are looking for one kind of evidence but they then search for another kind of evidence. For example, in United States v. Turner, 169 F.3d 84 (1st Cir. 1999), detectives were investigating a physical assault of a woman named Thomas that had occurred inside her apartment. Thomas's neighbor, a man named Turner, had reported the assault to the police when he had heard it occurring next door. A brief investigation revealed blood stains on the window sill of Turner's apartment, suggesting that the man who committed the assault had escaped by breaking into Turner's apartment. The police then asked Turner if they could look around his apartment to find more clues that may have been left behind. Turner agreed, and he signed a broad consent form allowing the police to search his apartment. An officer searched Turner's computer and found child pornography. The First Circuit held that the search of the computer was beyond the scope of consent:

> We think that an objectively reasonable person assessing in context the exchange between Turner and these detectives would have understood that the police intended to search only in places where an *intruder* hastily might have disposed of any *physical evidence of the Thomas assault* immediately after it occurred; for example, in places where a fleeing suspect might have tossed a knife or bloody clothing. Whereas, in sharp contrast, it obviously would have been impossible to abandon physical evidence of this sort in a personal computer hard drive, and bizarre to suppose—nor has the government suggested—that the suspected intruder stopped to enter incriminating evidence into the Turner computer.

Id. at 88.

3. *Social norms and new technologies.* When a technology is new, it can be difficult to tell how a "typical reasonable person" would interpret a statement permitting a search. The difficulty is demonstrated by United States v. Blas, 1990 WL 265179 (E.D. Wis. 1990), a case involving consent to look at a telephone pager. In 1990, before the widespread use of cell phones, pagers were a useful if rather expensive way to keep in touch with others. Those seeking to contact the pager owner would call the pager telephone number, and the telephone number would appear on the pager device. The pager owner would then find a telephone and call back the initial caller at the number stored in the pager. In 1990, few people carried pagers. They were known to be used mostly by physicians and drug dealers, both members of professions that require constant contact with clients and patients.

The officers in *United States v. Blas* were investigating narcotics traffickers, and they saw a suspect driving a van. They pulled over the van for a traffic violation. During the traffic stop, an officer saw a telephone pager hanging on the suspect's belt. The officer asked the suspect if the pager was his; the suspect replied that it was. The officer then asked, "Can I look at your pager?" The suspect agreed, and he handed the officer the pager. The officer then clicked through the phone numbers stored in the pager and discovered telephone numbers that were valuable to the investigation. After charges were filed, the suspect argued that retrieving the numbers was beyond the scope of consent and that the numbers should be suppressed. The court agreed:

> When the ordinary person asks to look *at* a telephone diary, that person is asking to inspect the physical object. It is commonly understood that the person is asking to see the physical object which includes the pages of numbers contained in the diary. The outside of personal telephone diaries in which numbers are written are commonplace to the general populace and of little interest.

> A pager, on the other hand, while gaining in popularity, is still a device common only amongst certain occupations or professions, albeit drug dealers are included. In any event, when a person asks to look *at* a pager, that person is likely to be interested in what the device is, or how small it is, or what brand of pager it may be. Seldom is the person who asks to look *at* a doctor's pager, for example, asking to look inside at the contents of the pager's memory. Correspondingly, the doctor in responding to the inquiry, does not expect the person to activate the pager, in order to scan its memory bank.

> To the law enforcement officer and the suspected drug dealer, a pager may have more familiarity. However, when a law enforcement officer asks, "is that your pager," or words to that effect, and next asks to look *at* it, the person who was stopped could reasonably think that the officer simply wants to confirm the fact that it is a pager, rather than a weapon.

> Accordingly, this court finds that an individual has the same expectation of privacy in a pager, computer or other electronic data storage and retrieval device as in a closed container, and granting consent to "look at" the container is not a grant of consent to look into the contents of the container.

Id. at *20–21.

Compare *Blas* to a recent case involving a cellular phone. In Lemons v. State, ___ S.W.3d ___, 2009 WL 1314160 (Tex. App. 2009), a police officer named Thornhill learned that Lemons was suspected of having engaged in sexual relations with a 14 year-old girl. Thornhill visited Lemons at work, and he asked Lemons if he had been calling the girl on his cell phone. Shortly after, Thornhill asked Lemons if he could see his cell phone. Lemons handed the phone to Thornhill, and Thornhill pressed the "camera" button to access the part of the telephone that stored photographs. Thornhill found a nude photograph of the girl stored in the phone. The Texas Court of Appeals ruled that Lemons had consented to the search because "it is reasonable to conclude that Appellant's surrender to Thornhill of his cellular telephone in response to Thornhill's open ended request implied Appellant's grant of equally unbridled consent for Thornhill to examine the phone and the information contained therein."

Are *Blas* and *Lemons* consistent? If not, which is correct?

4. *Withdrawn consent and the computer forensics process.* Searching a computer can alter the information it contains. As a result, when the government agents search a computer, they usually make an image of the

computer and then search the image rather than the original. The process protects the evidentiary value of the original computer. If the defendant argues that the government planted data, and that the evidence of crime allegedly found on the computer was not originally there, the government can produce the original computer with the original evidence.

What happens if the government obtains a suspect's consent, makes an image of the government's computer, and then the suspect withdraws his consent? Does the suspect retain control over the image? Or is the image copy now the property of the government, such that the suspect's rights are extinguished and the government can search the computer without limit?

This issue arose in United States v. Megahed, 2009 WL 722481 (M.D. Fla. 2009). Megahed was a college student suspected of making bombs. Agents went to Megahed's home, where he lived with his parents, and they obtained the consent of Megahed's father to remove and then search the family computer that Megahed frequently used. Agents took away the computer, generated an image, and then began searching the image for evidence.

Weeks later, Megahed's father withdrew his consent. Agents continued to search the image, however, eventually finding an Internet history file that incriminated Megahed. At trial, the government wished to use the Internet history file against Megahed. Megahed filed a motion to suppress, arguing that the file was discovered in a search that was beyond the scope of consent because consent had been withdrawn. The court agreed with the government that the Internet history file was admissible:

> Neither the defendant nor [his father] retained a reasonable expectation of privacy in the mirror image copy that the FBI had obtained already with [the father's] consent and had begun already to search. The revocation did not operate retroactively to nullify this history. *See United States v. Ponder,* 444 F.2d 816, 818 (5th Cir.1971) ("A valid consent to a search . . . carries with it the right to examine and photocopy."); *Mason v. Pulliam,* 557 F.2d 426, 429 (5th Cir.1977) (affirming an order that directed the return of original records and documents voluntarily provided to an IRS agent after withdrawal of consent but agreeing that the taxpayer's "withdrawal and reinvocation does not affect the validity of [the agent's] actions prior to the time he received notice that his right to retain Mason's papers was gone. The district court correctly refused to require the return of *copies* made prior to the demand by Mason's attorney."); *United States v. Ward,* 576 F.2d 243, 244–45 (9th Cir. 1978) (adopting the reasoning of *Mason* as to the use of records following revocation but concluding that "any evidence gathered or *copies made* from the records before revocation should not be suppressed.").

Are you persuaded? Does your answer depend on whether you model a computer as a single container or as a container of containers? What result would you reach if the consent was withdrawn before agents conducted an initial search of the image?

5. *A consent brain teaser.* Officer Smith suspects that Fred Rowley is guilty of tax fraud, but he does not have probable cause needed to obtain a warrant to seize Rowley's computer and search it for evidence. Officer Smith visits Rowley at home and explains his suspicions, and Rowley emphatically

denies his guilt. Smith asks Rowley if he would let Smith take his computer away and search it for evidence "just to make sure everything is on the up and up." Rowley doesn't want to arouse the officer's suspicion, so he agrees to let Officer Smith take the computer away and search it for evidence offsite.

The next day, Rowley has second thoughts and calls a lawyer for advice. The lawyer tells Rowley to call Officer Smith immediately and withdraw his consent. When Rowley calls Officer Smith and withdraws his permission to search the computer, Smith explains that he has just finished creating a bitstream copy of Rowley's computer and that he was just about to start searching the copy for evidence of tax fraud. Smith agrees to return the original computer in light of Rowley's withdrawal of consent, but insists that he can search the copy made before Rowley's consent was withdrawn. Officer Smith searches the copy and discovers evidence that Rowley has engaged in a massive tax fraud scheme.

Has Officer Smith violated the Fourth Amendment by searching the copy after Rowley withdrew his consent to search the original? Would Smith violate the Fourth Amendment by retaining the copy, even if he does not search it? When Rowley withdraws his consent, does the Fourth Amendment require Officer Smith to delete the copy? Does it require Smith to give Rowley the government-owned computer that stores the copy?

As you ponder these questions, it may help you to sort through a number of preliminary issues. For example, does consent to take away the computer and search it implicitly permit the officer to generate a copy? Is generating the copy a search, a seizure, or neither? Should the scope of consent that applies to the original also apply to the copy, or is the copy the government's property that Rowley has no rights to control?

If you really want a challenge, consider two variations on the hypothetical. In the first variation, Officer Smith informs Rowley during his visit to Rowley's home that if Rowley consents, Smith will generate a bitstream copy of Rowley's computer and return the original to Rowley. Rowley expressly consents to Smith's creating the copy. When Rowley calls Smith the next day to withdraw his consent, Smith has already generated the copy. Should this change the analysis?

In the second variation, Rowley calls Officer Smith when he is in the middle of generating the bitstream copy. (This is very possible, as the copying process can take several hours to complete.) Can Officer Smith complete the process of generating the copy, or must he unplug the machine as soon as consent is withdrawn? Can he search the portion of the copy that was created before consent was withdrawn?

(b) Third–Party Consent

Criminal investigators often seek consent to search a computer from an individual other than the suspect. In these cases, the government asks a third party to consent to the search for evidence of the suspect's offenses. If the individual who consents has common authority over the property, the consent is valid. United States v. Matlock, 415 U.S. 164, 171

(1974). In *Matlock*, the Supreme Court explained that common authority to establish third-party consent requires:

> mutual use of the property by persons generally having joint access or control for most purposes, so that it is reasonable to recognize that any of the co-inhabitants has the right to permit the inspection in his own right and that the others have assumed the risk that one of their number might permit the common area to be searched.

Id. at 171 n.7. The following case considers how this rule applies to computers.

UNITED STATES v. BUCKNER

United States Court of Appeals for the Fourth Circuit, 2007.
473 F.3d 551.

DIANA GRIBBON MOTZ, CIRCUIT JUDGE.

Frank Gary Buckner appeals from an order denying his motion to suppress evidence gathered from password-protected files on the hard drive of a computer police seized from his home. The officers seized and searched the computer, without a warrant, on the basis of oral consent granted by Buckner's wife, Michelle. On appeal, Buckner contends that although Michelle's consent sufficed to give the officers permission to search the computer itself, her consent could not extend to his password-protected files.

I.

This criminal investigation began when the Grottoes, Virginia police department received a series of complaints regarding online fraud committed by someone using AOL and eBay accounts opened in the name Michelle Buckner. On July 28, 2003, police officers went to the Buckner residence to speak with Michelle, but only Frank Buckner was at home. The officers then left, asking Frank to have Michelle contact them. A short while later, Frank Buckner himself called the police, seeking more information about why they wanted to speak with Michelle. The police responded that they wanted to talk with her about some computer transactions. That evening, Michelle Buckner went to the police station and told officers that she knew nothing about any illegal eBay transactions, but that she did have a home computer leased in her name. She further stated that she only used the home computer occasionally to play solitaire.

The next day, July 29, police returned to the Buckner residence to speak further with Michelle about the online fraud. Frank Buckner was not present. Michelle again cooperated fully, telling the officers "to take whatever they needed" and that she "wanted to be as cooperative as she could be." The computer Michelle had indicated was leased in her name was located on a table in the living room, just inside the front door of the residence. Pursuant to Michelle's oral consent, the officers seized the leased home computer.

At the time the officers seized the computer, it was turned on and running, with the screen visibly lit. The officers did not, at this time, open any files or look at any information on the computer. Instead, with Michelle's blessing, they shut down the computer and took its data-storage components for later forensic analysis. This analysis consisted of "mirroring"—that is, creating a copy of—the hard drive and looking at the computer's files on the mirrored copy.

Ultimately, a grand jury indicted Frank Buckner on twenty counts of wire fraud and twelve counts of mail fraud. At a suppression hearing, Frank Buckner offered the only affirmative evidence on the password issue, testifying that a password was required to use the computer. Buckner stated that he was the only person who could sign on to the computer and the only person who knew the password necessary to view files that he had created. Nothing in the record contradicts this testimony.

In the district court, Buckner challenged both the officers' seizure of the computer and the subsequent search of password-protected files located on the computer's hard drive. On appeal, he challenges only the search.

II.

Although the Fourth Amendment generally prohibits warrantless searches, valid consent to seize and search items provides an exception to the usual warrant requirement. In responding to a defendant's motion to suppress, the Government bears the burden of establishing, by a preponderance of the evidence, that it obtained valid consent to search.

Consent to search is valid if it is (1) knowing and voluntary, and (2) given by one with authority to consent. There is no question in this case that Michelle Buckner's consent was knowing and voluntary; Frank Buckner challenges only her authority to consent. Because the Government has never contended that Michelle had primary ownership of, or sole access to, these files, this case presents an issue of third-party consent.

A third-party has authority to consent to a search of property when she possesses common authority over or other sufficient relationship to the effects sought to be inspected. *United States v. Matlock,* 415 U.S. 164, 171 (1974). "Common authority" in this context is not merely a question of property interest. Rather, it requires evidence of mutual use by one generally having joint access or control for most purposes. *Id.* at 171, n. 7. Such use makes it reasonable to recognize that any of the co-users has the right to permit the inspection in her own right and that the others have assumed the risk that one of their number might permit the common effects to be searched.

We have previously considered whether a computer user has actual authority to consent to a warrantless search of the password-protected files of a co-user. In *Trulock v. Freeh,* 275 F.3d 391 (4th Cir. 2001), when considering whether FBI agents were entitled to qualified immunity in a suit alleging a Fourth Amendment violation, we held that a co-resident of a home and co-user of a computer, who did not know the necessary password for her co-user's password-protected files, lacked the authority to consent to a warrantless search of those files. Borrowing an analogy from *United States v. Block,* 590 F.2d 535, 539 (4th Cir. 1978), we likened these private files to a "locked box" within an area of common authority. Although common authority over a general area confers actual authority to consent to a search of that general area, it does not automatically extend to the interiors of every discrete enclosed space capable of search within the area.

The logic of *Trulock* applies equally here. By using a password, Frank Buckner, like Trulock, affirmatively intended to exclude others from his personal files. For this reason, it cannot be said that Buckner, any more than Trulock, assumed the risk that a joint user of the computer, not privy to password-protected files, would permit others to search his files. Thus, under the *Trulock* rationale, Michelle Buckner did not have actual authority to consent to a search of her husband's password-protected files because she did not share mutual use, general access or common authority over those files.

NOTES AND QUESTIONS

1. Would the result in *Buckner* be different if the defendant had not used passwords? A number of courts have considered consent searches by wives to their husbands' computer files when their husbands used a joint computer to commit crimes without password protecting their files. Courts have concluded that common authority existed to allow consent to search the files. *See, e.g.,* United States v. Mannion, 54 Fed. Appx. 372 (4th Cir. 2002).

2. United States v. Matlock, 415 U.S. 164 (1974), permits a third party to consent if the third-party has "common authority over or other sufficient relationship to the premises or effects sought to be inspected." When the "premises or effects" are computers, should courts focus on common authority over the physical hardware or common authority over specific files? Put another way, should we model the computer from the standpoint of virtual reality or physical reality?

Applying law to computers often raises a choice between modeling facts from a virtual perspective or a physical perspective. The virtual perspective is the perspective of a user who sees the computer as a window to a virtual reality. In contrast, the physical perspective sees the machine as a physical device that sends, receives, and stores zeros and ones.

The *Buckner* court adopts a virtual approach to construing the scope of consent. It assumes the perspective of a computer user, and analogizes password protected files to locked containers. From this perspective, it is natural that different users have different authority to consent to searches of different files or folders on a single computer storage device.

From a physical perspective, however, distinguishing among files or folders may seem quite artificial. When government investigators search computers, they often search them at a physical level instead of a virtual level. From this perspective, the storage device is a magnetic platter or other device with zeros and ones mixed together rather than stored in distinct virtual "folders." Analysts working from a physical perspective may be unable to tell how access to a storage device would appear to a user from a virtual perspective. From the physical perspective, it seems unnatural to say that a user has common authority over some of the data on the device but not others.

If government investigators search computers at a physical level instead of a virtual one, does it make sense for courts to approach the scope of consent from a virtual perspective? Should investigators be required to reconstruct the search from a virtual perspective, and to limit the scope of consent based on what a user would observe?

3. *Consent when the target objects to the search.* In Georgia v. Randolph, 547 U.S. 103 (2006), police officers answered a call reporting a domestic disturbance between a husband and wife. When the police arrived at the home, the wife volunteered to the police that her husband was a cocaine user and that he kept drug-related items inside the home. A police officer asked the husband for his consent to search the home, but he refused. The officer then asked the wife if she would consent to the search, and she readily agreed. The wife brought the officer to an upstairs bedroom where the officer found cocaine.

In a 5–3 decision, the Supreme Court held that the wife's consent to search the home was invalid because the husband was physically present and objected to the search. According to Justice Souter's majority opinion, the "common authority" test of *Matlock* must be interpreted in light of "widely shared social expectations." Individuals in society share a "commonly held understanding about the authority that co-inhabitants may exercise in ways that affect each other's interests," and those commonly held understandings determine the reasonableness of consent and therefore its constitutionality. *Id.* at 111.

In *Randolph*, the Court found the husband's presence and objection to be critical. According to Justice Souter, a common understanding exists that consent is not valid if a co-inhabitant is present and refuses to permit the search. As a result, it was not reasonable for the police to rely on the wife's consent and the warrantless search violated the Fourth Amendment. On the other hand, if the husband had not been present, it would have been reasonable for the police to rely on the wife's consent because there is a commonly held understanding that co-inhabitants can consent to home searches absent an objection.

The Eighth Circuit applied *Randolph* to a computer search in United States v. Hudspeth, 518 F.3d 954 (8th Cir. 2008) (en banc). Hudspeth was discovered in possession of child pornography at work, and he was arrested at work and brought to the police station. The police asked him if he would consent to a search of his home, and he refused. The police then went to Hudspeth's home and asked his wife if she would consent to a seizure and search of her husband's home computer. Mrs. Hudspeth asked what would happen if she refused consent, and the police told her that they would keep an armed officer in the home to prevent destruction of evidence while they obtained a search warrant for the computers. The police did not tell Mrs. Hudspeth that her husband had already denied his consent. Mrs. Hudspeth tried to contact her attorney, but when she could not reach her attorney, she decided to consent to the seizure and search of the computers.

The en banc Eighth Circuit concluded that Mrs. Hudspeth's consent was valid, and that the facts of the case were distinguishable from *Georgia v. Randolph*:

> Unlike *Randolph,* the officers in the present case were not confronted with a "social custom" dilemma, where two physically present co-tenants have contemporaneous competing interests and one consents to a search, while the other objects. Instead, when [the police] asked for Mrs. Hudspeth's consent, Hudspeth was not present because he had been lawfully arrested and jailed based on evidence obtained wholly apart from the evidence sought on the home computer. Thus, this rationale for the narrow holding of *Randolph,* which repeatedly referenced the defendant's physical presence *and* immediate objection, is inapplicable here.

> The *Randolph* opinion repeatedly referred to an "express refusal of consent by a *physically present* resident." The *Randolph* majority candidly admitted "we are drawing a fine line; if a potential defendant with self-interest in objecting is in fact *at the door and objects,* the co-tenant's permission does not suffice for a reasonable search." Hudspeth was not at the door and objecting and does not fall within *Randolph's* "fine line."

Id. at 960–61. Judge Melloy dissented, joined by Judge Wollman and Judge Bye:

> In this case, we are required to decide the issue the Supreme Court left unanswered: Is the express denial of consent by a co-tenant dispositive or is the physical location, i.e., at the front door, controlling? In my view, the *Randolph* Court's primary focus was on legitimate expectations of privacy.

> It seems inconceivable to me that a core value of the Fourth Amendment, the expectation of privacy in one's own home, would be dependent upon a tape measure. The objecting co-tenant in *Randolph* was at the front door. At what point does that co-tenant lose his or her right to object to the search? At the front porch? In the front yard? At the curb? I cannot believe the Supreme Court intended to make one's expectation of privacy dependent upon the happenstance of location.

> I believe that the Supreme Court has made it clear that the government must get a warrant when one co-tenant expressly denies consent to search a shared residence. In this case, that would not have been a significant burden.

Id. at 963–64 (Melloy, J., dissenting).

(c) Apparent Authority

The police may reasonably rely on a third party's claim to have common authority to consent to a search, only to find out later that the third party actually lacked that common authority. Is the search constitutional? In Illinois v. Rodriguez, 497 U.S. 177 (1990), the Supreme Court held that police can rely on a false claim of authority to consent if based on "the facts available to the officer at the moment, ... a man of reasonable caution ... [would believe] that the consenting party had authority" to consent to a search of the premises. *Id.* at 188–89. Under this so-called apparent authority doctrine, courts will not suppress evidence if the police reasonably but incorrectly rely on third-party consent to conduct a search.

UNITED STATES v. ANDRUS

United States Court of Appeals for the Tenth Circuit, 2007.
483 F.3d 711.

MURPHY, CIRCUIT JUDGE.

Defendant–Appellant Ray Andrus was indicted on one count of possession of child pornography, in violation of 18 U.S.C. § 2252(a)(4)(B). Agents of the Bureau of Immigration and Customs Enforcement ("ICE") found pornographic images of children on Andrus' home computer after Andrus' father, Dr. Bailey Andrus, consented to a search of the Andrus home and Andrus' computer. Andrus moved to suppress the inculpatory evidence found on his computer during the search, arguing * * * that Dr. Andrus lacked both actual and apparent authority to consent to a search of the computer.

After the district court's denial of his motion, Andrus pleaded guilty to the charge against him but retained the right to appeal the district court's denial of his suppression motion. He was sentenced to seventy months' imprisonment followed by three years' supervised release. In this appeal, Andrus challenges the district court's denial of his suppression motion.

I. Background

Federal authorities first became interested in Ray Andrus during an investigation of Regpay, a third-party billing and credit card aggregating company that provided subscribers with access to websites containing child pornography. The investigation of Regpay led to an investigation of Regpay subscribers. One of the subscribers providing personal information and a credit card number to Regpay was an individual identifying himself as "Ray Andrus" at "3208 W. 81st Terr., Leawood, KS." The Andrus Regpay subscription was used to access a pornographic website called www.sunshineboys.com. Record checks with the driver's license bureau and post office indicated Ray Andrus, Bailey Andrus, and a third man, Richard Andrus, all used the West 81st Terrace address. The credit card number provided to Regpay was determined to belong to Ray Andrus. The email address provided to Regpay, "bandrus@kc.rr.com," was determined to be associated with Dr. Bailey Andrus.

The federal investigation into the Andrus household began in January 2004 and focused primarily on Ray Andrus. At least one agent conducted surveillance on the Andrus residence and knew Ray Andrus worked at the Shawnee Mission School. Eight months into the investigation, agents believed they did not have enough information to obtain a search warrant for the Andrus residence. They, therefore, attempted to gather more information by doing a "knock and talk" interview with the hope of being able to conduct a consent search. ICE Special Agent Cheatham and Leawood Police Detective Woollen arrived at the Andrus house at approximately 8:45 a.m. on August 27, 2004. ICE Special Agent Kanatzar, a forensic computer expert, accompanied Cheatham and Woollen to the residence, but waited outside in his car for Cheatham's authorization to enter the premises.

Dr. Andrus, age ninety-one, answered the door in his pajamas. Dr. Andrus invited the officers into the residence and, according to the testimony of Cheatham and Woollen, the three sat in Dr. Andrus' living room, where the officers learned that Ray Andrus lived in the center bedroom in the residence. In response to the officers' questions, Dr. Andrus indicated Ray Andrus did not pay rent and lived in the home to help care for his aging parents. Cheatham testified he could see the door to Ray Andrus' bedroom was open and asked Dr. Andrus whether he had access to the bedroom. Dr. Andrus testified he answered "yes" and told the officers he felt free to enter the room when the door was open, but always knocked if the door was closed.

Cheatham asked Dr. Andrus for consent to search the house and any computers in it. Dr. Andrus signed a written consent form indicating his willingness to consent to a premises and computer search. He led Cheatham into Ray Andrus' bedroom to show him where the computer was located. After Dr. Andrus signed the consent form, Cheatham went outside to summon Kanatzar into the residence. Kanatzar went straight into Andrus' bedroom and began assembling his forensic equipment. Kanatzar removed the cover from Andrus' computer and hooked his laptop and other equipment to it. Dr. Andrus testified he was present at the beginning of the search but left the bedroom shortly thereafter. Kanatzar testified it took about ten to fifteen minutes to connect his equipment before he started analyzing the computer.

Kanatzar used EnCase forensic software to examine the contents of the computer's hard drive. The software allowed him direct access to the hard drive without first determining whether a user name or password were needed. He, therefore, did not determine whether the computer was protected by a user name or password prior to previewing the computer's contents. Only later, when he took the computer back to his office for further analysis, did he see Ray Andrus' user profile.[1]

Kanatzar testified he used EnCase to search for .jpg picture files. He explained that clicking on the images he retrieved allowed him to see the pathname for the image, tracing it to particular folders on the computer's

---

1. Kanatzar testified that someone without forensic equipment would need Ray Andrus' user name and password to access files stored within Andrus' user profile.

hard drive. This process revealed folder and file names suggestive of child pornography. Kanatzar estimated it took five minutes to see depictions of child pornography.

Ray Andrus was indicted on one count of knowingly and intentionally possessing pornographic images of minors in violation of 18 U.S.C. § 2252(a)(4)(B). Claiming a Fourth Amendment violation, Andrus moved to suppress the evidence gathered from his residence and his computer.

The district court held an evidentiary hearing at which Detective Woollen, Agent Cheatham, Agent Kanatzar, Agent Smith, Dr. Andrus, and Ray Andrus testified. At the conclusion of the hearing, the court determined Dr. Andrus' consent was voluntary, but concluded Dr. Andrus lacked actual authority to consent to a computer search. The court based its actual authority ruling on its findings that Dr. Andrus did not know how to use the computer, had never used the computer, and did not know the user name that would have allowed him to access the computer.

The district court then proceeded to consider apparent authority. It indicated the resolution of the apparent authority claim in favor of the government was a "close call." The court concluded the agents' belief that Dr. Andrus had authority to consent to a search of the computer was reasonable up until the time they learned there was only one computer in the house. Because Cheatham instructed Kanatzar to suspend the search at that point, there was no Fourth Amendment violation.

On appeal, Andrus contests the district court's apparent authority ruling. He contends that ambiguities in the situation facing the officers at the Andrus residence required the officers to ask further questions concerning Dr. Andrus' authority to consent to a computer search prior to commencing the search.

II. Discussion

Valid third party consent can arise either through the third party's actual authority or the third party's apparent authority. Even where actual authority is lacking, however, a third party has apparent authority to consent to a search when an officer reasonably, even if erroneously, believes the third party possesses authority to consent.

Whether apparent authority exists is an objective, totality-of-the-circumstances inquiry into whether the facts available to the officers at the time they commenced the search would lead a reasonable officer to believe the third party had authority to consent to the search. When the property to be searched is an object or container, the relevant inquiry must address the third party's relationship to the object.

The resolution of this appeal turns on whether the officers' belief in Dr. Andrus' authority was reasonable, despite the lack of any affirmative assertion by Dr. Andrus that he used the computer and despite the existence of a user profile indicating Ray Andrus' intent to exclude other household members from using the computer. For the reasons articulated below, this court concludes the officers' belief in Dr. Andrus' authority was reasonable.

The critical issue in our analysis is whether, under the totality of the circumstances known to Cheatham, Woollen, and Kanatzar, these officers could reasonably have believed Dr. Andrus had authority to consent to a search of the computer. Phrased in the negative, we must ask whether the surrounding circumstances could conceivably be such that a reasonable person would doubt Dr. Andrus' consent and not act upon it without further inquiry. If the circumstances reasonably indicated Dr. Andrus had mutual use of or control over the computer, the officers were under no obligation to ask clarifying questions, even if, as the dissent notes, the burden would have been minimal in this particular case.

We * * * accept the following facts as true: First, the officers knew Dr. Andrus owned the house and lived there with family members. Second, the officers knew Dr. Andrus' house had internet access and that Dr. Andrus paid the Time Warner internet and cable bill. Third, the officers knew the email address bandrus@kc.rr.com had been activated and used to register on a website that provided access to child pornography. Fourth, although the officers knew Ray Andrus lived in the center bedroom, they also knew that Dr. Andrus had access to the room at will. Fifth, the officers saw the computer in plain view on the desk in Andrus' room and it appeared available for use by other household members. Furthermore, the record indicates Dr. Andrus did not say or do anything to indicate his lack of ownership or control over the computer when Cheatham asked for his consent to conduct a computer search. It is uncontested that Dr. Andrus led the officers to the bedroom in which the computer was located, and, even after he saw Kanatzar begin to work on the computer, Dr. Andrus remained silent about any lack of authority he had over the computer. Even if Ray Andrus' computer was protected with a user name and password, there is no indication in the record that the officers knew or had reason to believe such protections were in place.

Andrus argues his computer's password protection indicated his computer was "locked" to third parties, a fact the officers would have known had they asked questions of Dr. Andrus prior to searching the computer. Under our case law, however, officers are not obligated to ask questions unless the circumstances are ambiguous. *United States v. Kimoana,* 383 F.3d 1215, 1222 (10th Cir. 2004). In essence, by suggesting the onus was on the officers to ask about password protection prior to searching the computer, despite the absence of any indication that Dr. Andrus' access to the computer was limited by a password, Andrus necessarily submits there is inherent ambiguity whenever police want to search a household computer and a third party has not affirmatively provided information about his own use of the computer or about password protection.

Andrus' argument presupposes, however, that password protection of home computers is so common that a reasonable officer ought to know password protection is likely. Andrus has neither made this argument directly nor proffered any evidence to demonstrate a high incidence of password protection among home computer users. * * * Without a factual basis on which to proceed, we are unable to address the possibility that passwords create inherent ambiguities.[8]

Viewed under the requisite totality-of-the-circumstances analysis, the facts known to the officers at the time the computer search commenced created an objectively reasonable perception that Dr. Andrus was, at least, *one* user of the computer. That objectively reasonable belief would have been enough to give Dr. Andrus apparent authority to consent to a search.

For the foregoing reasons, this court concludes Dr. Andrus had apparent authority to consent to a search of the computer in Ray Andrus' bedroom. We accordingly affirm the district court's denial of Andrus' motion to suppress.

McKay, CIRCUIT JUDGE, dissenting.

I take issue with the majority's implicit holding that law enforcement may use software deliberately designed to automatically bypass computer password protection based on third-party consent without the need to make a reasonable inquiry regarding the presence of password protection and the third party's access to that password.

The presence of security on Defendant's computer is undisputed. Yet, the majority curiously argues that Defendant's use of password protection is inconsequential because Defendant failed to argue that computer password protection is commonplace. Of course, the decision provides no guidance on what would constitute sufficient proof of the prevalence of password protection, nor does it explain why the court could not take judicial notice that password protection is a standard feature of operating systems.

The development of computer password technology no doubt presents a challenge distinct from that associated with other types of *locked* containers. But this difficulty does not and cannot negate Fourth Amendment protection to computer storage nor render an expectation of computer privacy unreasonable. The unconstrained ability of law enforcement to use forensic software such as the EnCase program to bypass password protection without first determining whether such passwords have been enabled does not "exacerbate" this difficulty; rather, it avoids it altogether, simultaneously and dangerously sidestepping the Fourth Amendment in the process. Indeed, the majority concedes that if such protection were shown to be commonplace, law enforcement's use of forensic software like EnCase "may well be subject to question." But the fact that a computer password "lock" may not be *immediately* visible does not render it unlocked. I appreciate that unlike the locked file cabinet, computers have no handle to pull. But, like the padlocked footlocker, computers do exhibit outward signs of password protection: they display boot password screens,

---

8. If the factual basis were provided, law enforcement's use of forensic software like EnCase, which overrides any password protection without ever indicating whether such protection exists, may well be subject to question. This, however, is not that case.

username/password log-in screens, and/or screen-saver reactivation pass-words.[3]

The fact remains that EnCase's ability to bypass security measures is well known to law enforcement. Here, ICE's forensic computer specialist found Defendant's computer turned off. Without turning it on, he hooked his laptop directly to the hard drive of Defendant's computer and ran the EnCase program. The agents made no effort to ascertain whether such security was enabled prior to initiating the search. The testimony makes clear that such protection was discovered during additional computer analysis conducted at the forensic specialist's office.

The burden on law enforcement to identify ownership of the computer was minimal. A simple question or two would have sufficed. Prior to the computer search, the agents questioned Dr. Andrus about Ray Andrus' status as a renter and Dr. Andrus' ability to enter his 51–year–old son's bedroom in order to determine Dr. Andrus' ability to consent to a search of the room, but the agents did not inquire whether Dr. Andrus used the computer, and if so, whether he had access to his son's password. At the suppression hearing, the agents testified that they were not immediately aware that Defendant's computer was the only one in the house, and they began to doubt Dr. Andrus' authority to consent when they learned this fact. The record reveals that, upon questioning, Dr. Andrus indicated that there was a computer in the house and led the agents to Defendant's room. The forensic specialist was then summoned. It took him approximately fifteen to twenty minutes to set up his equipment, yet, bizarrely, at no point during this period did the agents inquire about the presence of any other computers.

Accordingly, in my view, given the case law indicating the importance of computer password protection, the common knowledge about the prevalence of password usage, and the design of EnCase or similar password bypass mechanisms, the Fourth Amendment and the reasonable inquiry rule, *United States v. Kimoana,* 383 F.3d 1215, 1222 (10th Cir. 2004) (collecting cases), mandate that in consent-based, warrantless computer searches, law enforcement personnel inquire or otherwise check for the presence of password protection and, if a password is present, inquire about the consenter's knowledge of that password and joint access to the computer.

NOTES AND QUESTIONS

1. *The limited scope of* Andrus. Following the publication of the decision above, Andrus petitioned for rehearing before the en banc Tenth Circuit. The en banc court denied rehearing over the dissent of four judges in addition to Judge McKay. When the petition for rehearing was denied, the two judges who were in the majority of the original panel added a rare addendum limiting the panel opinion to its facts:

---

3. I recognize that the ability of users to program automatic log-ins and the capability of operating systems to "memorize" passwords poses potential problems, since these only create the appearance of a restriction without actually blocking access.

The panel majority notes that its opinion is limited to the narrow question of the apparent authority of a homeowner to consent to a search of a computer on premises in the specific factual setting presented, including the undisputed fact that the owner had access to the computer, paid for internet access, and had an e-mail address used to register on a website providing access to the files of interest to law enforcement.

Among the questions not presented in this matter, and for which there is no factual development in the record, are the extent of capability and activation of password protection or user profiles on home computers, the capability of EnCase software to detect the presence of password protection or a user profile, or the degree to which law enforcement confronts password protection or user profiles on home computers.

United States v. Andrus, 499 F.3d 1162, 1162–63 (10th Cir. 2007).

If there had been factual development of these issues, how much should they matter?

2.   The Tenth Circuit's "reasonable inquiry rule" is based on the notion that a police officer presented with an ambiguous situation may not meet his burden of establishing valid third-party consent. If the facts do not establish that a reasonable officer would believe the third party has common authority, apparent authority does not exist. As a result, the officer has the duty to ask the third party about his relationship with the property to be searched so as to establish whether the third party has common authority over it. If the third party answers the questions in a way that would lead a reasonable officer to believe that he has common authority, the officer can rely on the third party's consent. In that sense, the "reasonable inquiry rule" does not impose a duty to ask questions. Rather, it limits the government's ability to rely on third-party authority to search until the government has clarified the third party's authority by making inquiries.

Do you think a reasonable officer in *Andrus* would believe that Andrus the elder had common authority over the files that belonged to Andrus the younger based on what the officers knew, without asking the elder Andrus questions?

3.   Imagine a police officer visits a law school library and observes a law student using a laptop. The officer asks the student if she will consent to a search of the computer. At this point, do you think a reasonable officer would conclude that the student has authority to consent to the search?

Now add in some details. The officer casually looks through the computer and finds evidence of financial fraud. The officer asks the student about the files, and the student truthfully explains that the computer actually belongs to her roommate, who works in finance. She had borrowed her roommate's computer for the day when her own computer crashed, and she has no idea what files are stored on the computer.

Now reconsider the question: Before the search occurred, do you think a reasonable officer would have concluded that the student had authority to consent to the search? Does it matter where on the hard drive the evidence was stored, and whether the files are password-protected?

4. In United States v. James, 353 F.3d 606 (8th Cir. 2003), the defendant was arrested on charges involving sexual misconduct with a minor. From jail, the defendant tried to smuggle out a letter to two friends asking them to contact a third man with instructions to destroy computer discs the defendant had left with him. Specifically, the letter provided instructions that Mr. Michael Laschober should "*destroy* and scratch ALL backup CD discs he has (BROWN envelope I just left) these are old and useless and one has a *virus* tell him to be sure to cut it up too." The letter ended up in the hands of a local prosecutor, and police approached Laschober to determine if he had the defendant's computer discs.

Laschober explained that he had known the defendant since childhood, and that the defendant had left a stack of computer discs with him in an envelope as storage for back-up purposes. The police asked Laschober if they could look at the discs, and Laschober gave them a sealed envelope that contained them. With Laschober's consent, an officer opened the envelope and found ten discs taped together. The top disc had a note attached that indicated the disc contained a dangerous virus as well as confidential and private information. Laschober consented to the police taking away the discs and searching them. Back at the police station, the officers attempted to view the top disc. The officers had some difficulty viewing the images on the disc—the court's opinion does not explain exactly why—but assistance from a computer specialist eventually allowed them to view the images on a special computer. The files on the disc included images of child pornography.

In an opinion by Judge Richard Arnold, the Eighth Circuit ruled that Laschober did not have common authority over the discs:

> We are firmly convinced that Mr. James did not give permission to Mr. Laschober to exercise control over the discs, or to consent to the searching of the discs. Instead, he gave the discs to Mr. Laschober for the sole purpose of storing them (except that, as the police knew, but Mr. Laschober did not, the defendant had given instructions that the discs be destroyed). The discs came to him in sealed envelopes. They were packaged within the envelope in tape. Mr. James never told Mr. Laschober "go ahead and look at these." Instead, he asked only that they be stored (and, as we have noted, that all of them be destroyed). Further, defendant marked the disc in question "confidential" and "private," evidencing a desire that no one, including Mr. Laschober, view the contents of the disc. Similarly important, the disc could not be opened on just any computer. To get access to the disc, a special officer had to use an advanced computer. Taken as a whole, such demonstrations of intended privacy evidence Mr. James's expectation that Mr. Laschober not view the disc's contents.

Id. at 614. The court also held that Laschober did not have apparent authority to consent to searching the disc:

> [The officers] knew that the discs contained in the envelope belonged to defendant and not Mr. Laschober. They knew, once the envelope had been opened, that the top disc said "confidential," "personal," "private." They knew that it took an advanced computer to view the disc's contents. And they had a piece of information that Mr. Laschober did not. They

knew that his actual authority had changed. They knew, because they had intercepted and read the letter * * *, that Mr. Laschober's only authority was to scratch and destroy the discs. This last fact is critical.

It cannot be reasonable to rely on a certain theory of apparent authority, when the police themselves know what the consenting party's actual authority is—in this case, not to store the discs, but to destroy them. The standard of reasonableness is governed by what the law-enforcement officers know, not what the consenting party knows. Here the detectives knew too much about Mr. James's manifested desire to keep others, including Mr. Laschober, from seeing the contents of the disc to rely on Mr. Laschober's authority to consent.

Id. at 615. Is the relevant question the defendant's desire to keep others from seeing the contents of the disc or whether the defendant had given others authority over them? Did James give Laschober authority over the discs by sending a letter asking Laschober to destroy them?

3.   SEARCH INCIDENT TO ARREST

When the police arrest a suspect, they can conduct a "full search" of the arrested person. *See* United States v. Robinson, 414 U.S. 218, 235 (1973). This generally allows the police to search the closed containers that the person is carrying at the time of arrest, including his wallet, address books, and briefcase. *See, e.g.,* United States v. Castro, 596 F.2d 674, 676 (5th Cir. 1979) (search of wallet); United States v. Rodriguez, 995 F.2d 776, 778 (7th Cir. 1993) (search of address book); United States v. Lam Muk Chiu, 522 F.2d 330, 332 (2d Cir. 1975) (search of briefcase).

Does the "search incident to arrest" power allow the government to search the computers and electronic storage devices a person is carrying at the time of their arrest? A law student walking to class may carry a cell phone, an iPod, and a laptop computer. If the student is arrested while walking to class, should the "search incident to arrest" doctrine permit a warrantless search of the student's cell phone? What about the iPod and the laptop? If courts impose limits on what searches can occur incident to a lawful arrest, what kinds of limits should they draw? Should the limits focus on the storage capacity of particular devices? Should courts permit searches that occur at the same time and place as the arrest, but disallow subsequent offsite searches or searches that take too much time?

UNITED STATES v. MURPHY

United States Court of Appeals for the Fourth Circuit, 2009.
552 F.3d 405.

REIDINGER, DISTRICT JUDGE:

Damian Antonio Murphy appeals his conviction for conspiracy to possess with intent to distribute cocaine and hydromorphon.

I.

In the early morning hours of June 6, 2006, Virginia State Trooper Danny Pruett was operating stationary radar along Interstate 81 in Wythe County, Virginia, when he observed a vehicle traveling northbound at a high rate of speed. Radar confirmed that the vehicle was traveling 95 miles per hour. After stopping the vehicle, Trooper Pruett asked the driver for her license and registration. The driver, who was later identified as Marsha Massengill, advised him that she had left her operator's license at home. Massengill told Trooper Pruett that her name was Debbie Arlene Sanchez, and she provided a date of birth. Trooper Pruett observed that Massengill appeared to be nervous and hesitant. The front seat passenger, who was later identified as Damian Murphy, also claimed to have left his license at home. He told Trooper Pruett that his name was Corey Antonio Murphy and provided a date of birth.

[The defendant was arrested during the traffic stop for obstruction of justice, and the police then seized his cell phone.] During the inventory of the items seized from the vehicle, a supervisor advised Trooper Pruett that some of the cell phones contained possible incriminating information, and he instructed Trooper Pruett to log them in as evidence.

The evidence in this case was transferred to Virginia State Police headquarters and subsequently turned over to the custody of a Drug Enforcement Administration (DEA) Task Force Officer, who transported it to the DEA office for processing. The evidence, including Murphy's cell phone, was examined by DEA Special Agent Brian Snedeker on June 29, 2006. Snedeker identified several text messages sent from an individual named Brian Sheppard. In a telephone interview with Snedeker that same day, Sheppard stated that Murphy was his drug supplier.

II.

The Fourth Amendment protects individuals against "unreasonable searches and seizures." U.S. Const. amend. IV. Warrantless searches are per se unreasonable under the Fourth Amendment—subject only to a few specifically established and well-delineated exceptions. One of the well-recognized exceptions to the warrant requirement is a search incident to a lawful arrest. Pursuant to this exception, law enforcement officers following a lawful arrest may search the arrestee's person and the area within his immediate control.

Murphy argues that the warrantless search of the contents of the cell phone was not lawful * * * because there was no evidence of the volatile nature of the cell phone's information.

Citing the "manifest need ... to preserve evidence," this Court has held on at least two prior occasions, albeit in unpublished opinions, that officers may retrieve text messages and other information from cell phones and pagers seized incident to an arrest. *See United States v. Young,* 278 Fed. Appx. 242, 245–46 (4th Cir. 2008) (per curiam) (holding that officers may retrieve text messages from cell phone during search incident to arrest); *United States v. Hunter,* No. 96–4259, 1998 WL 887289, at *3 (4th Cir. Oct.29, 1998) (holding that officers may retrieve telephone numbers from pager during search incident to arrest). Similarly, the Fifth Circuit and Seventh Circuit have held that the need for the preservation of evidence justifies the retrieval of call records and text messages from a cell phone or pager without a warrant during a search incident to arrest. *See United States v. Finley,* 477 F.3d 250, 260 (5th Cir. 2007); *see also United States v. Ortiz,* 84 F.3d 977, 984 (7th Cir. 1996).

Murphy argues that whether a cell phone may be searched without a warrant can be determined only upon the officers ascertaining the cell phone's storage capacity. In so arguing, he concedes that a device with a small storage capacity may be searched without a warrant due to the volatile nature of the information stored, but that a search of a cell phone with a larger storage capacity would implicate a heightened expectation of privacy and thus would require a warrant to be issued before a search could be conducted.

Murphy's argument is problematic for several reasons. First, Murphy has not provided the Court with any standard by which to determine what would constitute a "large" storage capacity as opposed to a "small" storage capacity, as he does not quantify these terms in any meaningful way. Second, Murphy has introduced no evidence that his cell phone had the requisite "large" storage capacity which he contends is subject to a heightened expectation of privacy. Third, even assuming that his cell phone does have a "large" storage capacity, his argument still fails because it is premised on the unwarranted assumption that information stored on a cell phone with a "large" storage capacity would be any less volatile than the information stored on a cell phone with a "small" storage capacity.

Finally, Murphy's argument must be rejected because to require police officers to ascertain the storage capacity of a cell phone before conducting a search would simply be an unworkable and unreasonable rule. It is unlikely that police officers would have any way of knowing whether the text messages and other information stored on a cell phone will be preserved or be automatically deleted simply by looking at the cell phone. Rather, it is very likely that in the time it takes for officers to ascertain a cell phone's particular storage capacity, the information stored therein could be permanently lost. For these reasons, we reject Murphy's argument that the government must ascertain a cell phone's storage capacity in order to justify a warrantless search of that phone incident to arrest.

NOTES AND QUESTIONS

1. If the police can conduct a comprehensive search of a person's wallet or briefcase upon arresting him, is there a principled basis for concluding that they cannot search the electronic storage devices he is carrying at the time of his arrest? The *Murphy* case tries one basis: computers and electronic storage

devices often have a much greater capacity than a wallet or briefcase. Should this make a difference? How much storage should be too much?

2.   Professor Adam Gershowitz has suggested six different ways that the search incident to arrest exception could be applied to computers found on an arrestee's person. First, the law could apply just as it does to physical items. Second, it could allow a search only for evidence relevant to the arrest. Third, courts could defer to state legislative limits on the search incident to arrest port. Fourth, courts could hold that the police can only search applications and programs open at the time of the arrest. Fifth, courts could hold that the government is only allowed to search the computer for a specific number of search steps. Sixth, courts could either limit searches to data inside the computer or else allow searches of data retrievable from the computer and remotely stored. *See* Adam M. Gershowitz, *The iPhone Meets the Fourth Amendment*, 56 UCLA L. Rev. 27 (2008). Which of these approaches is best? Or are there other possibilities that are preferable?

3.   The Fourth Amendment has different rules for the search of evidence found on a person at the time of arrest and the search of evidence near the person at the time of his arrest. Evidence located on a person ordinarily is seized at the time of the arrest, and it can be searched later on while still generally fitting within the search incident to arrest exception. On the other hand, the police can search in the area of the suspect's immediate control only at the time of the arrest. The police cannot go back and search the area that was in the suspect's control (but not on his person) at the time of arrest.

A district court used this difference to limit searches of electronic storage devices incident to arrest in United States v. Park, 2007 WL 1521573 (N.D. Cal. 2007). Park was arrested and his cellular phone was seized. About 90 minutes later, back at the station house, his phone was searched without a warrant. The search of the cell phone revealed stored addresses that were useful to show the defendant's associations. The district court ruled that the evidence discovered in the cell phone must be suppressed:

> For purposes of Fourth Amendment analysis cellular phones should be considered "possessions within an arrestee's immediate control" and not part of "the person." This is so because modern cellular phones have the capacity for storing immense amounts of private information. Unlike pagers or address books, modern cell phones record incoming and outgo-ing calls, and can also contain address books, calendars, voice and text messages, email, video and pictures. Individuals can store highly personal information on their cell phones, and can record their most private thoughts and conversations on their cell phones through email and text, voice and instant messages.

> Any contrary holding could have far-ranging consequences. At the hear-ing, the government asserted that, although the officers here limited their searches to the phones' address books, the officers could have searched any information—such as emails or messages—stored in the cell phones. In addition, in recognition of the fact that the line between cell phones and personal computers has grown increasingly blurry, the government also asserted that officers could lawfully seize and search an arrestee's laptop computer as a warrantless search incident to arrest.

The searches at issue here go far beyond the original rationales for searches incident to arrest, which were to remove weapons to ensure the safety of officers and bystanders, and the need to prevent concealment or destruction of evidence. Officers did not search the phones out of a concern for officer safety, or to prevent the concealment or destruction of evidence.

* * * [A]bsent guidance to the contrary from the Ninth Circuit or the Supreme Court, this Court is unwilling to further extend this doctrine to authorize the warrantless search of the contents of a cellular phone—and to effectively permit the warrantless search of a wide range of electronic storage devices—as a search incident to arrest.

Are you persuaded?

4. BORDER SEARCHES

The Supreme Court has created a special set of Fourth Amendment rules that apply at the international border "or its functional equivalents." United States v. Ortiz, 422 U.S. 891, 896 (1975). The following case considers how such rules apply to searches of computers.

UNITED STATES v. ARNOLD

United States Court of Appeals for the Ninth Circuit, 2008.
533 F.3d 1003.

O'SCANNLAIN, CIRCUIT JUDGE.

We must decide whether customs officers at Los Angeles International Airport may examine the electronic contents of a passenger's laptop computer without reasonable suspicion.

I

On July 17, 2005, forty-three-year-old Michael Arnold arrived at Los Angeles International Airport ("LAX") after a nearly twenty-hour flight from the Philippines. After retrieving his luggage from the baggage claim, Arnold proceeded to customs. U.S. Customs and Border Patrol ("CBP") Officer Laura Peng first saw Arnold while he was in line waiting to go through the checkpoint and selected him for secondary questioning. She asked Arnold where he had traveled, the purpose of his travel, and the length of his trip. Arnold stated that he had been on vacation for three weeks visiting friends in the Philippines.

Peng then inspected Arnold's luggage, which contained his laptop computer, a separate hard drive, a computer memory stick (also called a flash drive or USB drive), and six compact discs. Peng instructed Arnold to turn on the computer so she could see if it was functioning. While the computer was booting up, Peng turned it over to her colleague, CBP Officer John Roberts, and continued to inspect Arnold's luggage.

When the computer had booted up, its desktop displayed numerous icons and folders. Two folders were entitled "Kodak Pictures" and one was entitled "Kodak Memories." Peng and Roberts clicked on the Kodak folders, opened the files, and viewed the photos on Arnold's computer including one that depicted two nude women. Roberts called in supervisors, who in turn called in special agents with the United States Department of Homeland Security, Immigration and Customs Enforcement ("ICE"). The ICE agents questioned Arnold about the contents of his computer and detained him for several hours. They examined the computer equipment and found numerous images depicting what they believed to be child pornography. The officers seized the computer and storage devices but released Arnold.

[After he was charged with child pornography offenses], Arnold filed a motion to suppress arguing that the government conducted the search without reasonable suspicion. The government countered that: (1) reasonable suspicion was not required under the Fourth Amendment because of the border-search doctrine; and (2) if reasonable suspicion were necessary, that it was present in this case.

The district court granted Arnold's motion to suppress finding that: (1) reasonable suspicion was indeed necessary to search the laptop; and (2) the government had failed to meet the burden of showing that the CBP officers had reasonable suspicion to search.

II

Arnold argues that the district court was correct in concluding that reasonable suspicion was required to search his laptop at the border because it is distinguishable from other containers of documents based on its ability to store greater amounts of information and its unique role in modern life.

Arnold argues that "laptop computers are fundamentally different from traditional closed containers," and analogizes them to "homes" and the "human mind." Arnold's analogy of a laptop to a home is based on his conclusion that a laptop's capacity allows for the storage of personal documents in an amount equivalent to that stored in one's home. He argues that a laptop is like the "human mind" because of its ability to record ideas, e-mail, internet chats and web-surfing habits.

Lastly, Arnold argues that application of First Amendment principles requires us to rule contrary to the Fourth Circuit in *United States v. Ickes*, 393 F.3d 501, 506–08 (4th Cir. 2005) (rejecting the argument based on the First Amendment that a higher level of suspicion is needed for searches of "expressive material"), and to promulgate a reasonable suspicion requirement for border searches where the risk is high that expressive material will be exposed.

III

A

Searches of international passengers at American airports are considered border searches because they occur at the "functional equivalent of a border." *Almeida–Sanchez v. United States,* 413 U.S. 266, 273 (1973). It is axiomatic that the United States, as sovereign, has the inherent authority to protect, and a paramount interest in protecting, its territorial integrity. Generally, searches made at the border are reasonable simply by virtue of the fact that they occur at the border.

The Supreme Court has stated that:

> The authority of the United States to search the baggage of arriving international travelers is based on its inherent sovereign authority to protect its territorial integrity. By reason of that authority, it is entitled to require that whoever seeks entry must establish the right to enter and to bring into the country whatever he may carry.

Torres v. Puerto Rico, 442 U.S. 465, 472–73 (1979). In other words, the Government's interest in preventing the entry of unwanted persons and effects is at its zenith at the international border. Therefore, the luggage carried by a traveler entering the country may be searched at random by a customs officer no matter how great the traveler's desire to conceal the contents may be. Furthermore, a traveler who carries a toothbrush and a few articles of clothing in a paper bag or knotted scarf may claim an equal right to conceal his possessions from official inspection as the sophisticated executive with the locked attaché case.

B

Courts have long held that searches of closed containers and their contents can be conducted at the border without particularized suspicion under the Fourth Amendment. Searches of the following specific items have been upheld without particularized suspicion: (1) the contents of a traveler's briefcase and luggage, (2) a traveler's purse, wallet, or pockets, (3) papers found in containers such as pockets, and (4) pictures, films and other graphic materials.

Nevertheless, the Supreme Court has drawn some limits on the border search power. Specifically, the Supreme Court has held that reasonable suspicion is required to search a traveler's "alimentary canal," *United States v. Montoya de Hernandez,* 473 U.S. 531, 541 (1985), because the interests in human dignity and privacy which the Fourth Amendment protects forbid any such intrusion beyond the body's surface on the mere chance that desired evidence might be obtained. However, it has expressly declined to decide what level of suspicion, *if any,* is required for non-routine border searches such as strip, body cavity, or involuntary x-ray searches. Furthermore, the Supreme Court has rejected creating a balancing test based on a "routine" and "non-routine" search framework, and has treated the terms as purely descriptive.

Other than when intrusive searches of *the person* are at issue, the Supreme Court has held open the possibility that some searches of *property* are so destructive as to require particularized suspicion. Indeed, the Supreme Court has left open the question of whether, and under what circumstances, a border search might be deemed "unreasonable" because of the particularly offensive manner in which it is carried out.

C

In any event, the district court's holding that particularized suspicion is required to search a laptop, based on cases involving the search of the person, was erroneous. Its reliance on [cases involving searches of persons] to support its use of a sliding intrusiveness scale to determine when reasonable suspicion is needed to search property at the border is misplaced.

The Supreme Court has stated that "complex balancing tests to determine what is a 'routine' search of a vehicle, as opposed to a more 'intrusive' search of a person, have no place in border searches of vehicles." *United States v. Flores–Montano,* 541 U.S. 149, 152 (2004). Arnold argues that the district court was correct to apply an intrusiveness analysis to a laptop search despite the Supreme Court's holding in *Flores–Montano,* by distinguishing between one's privacy interest in a vehicle compared to a laptop. However, this attempt to distinguish *Flores–Montano* is off the mark. The Supreme Court's analysis determining what protection to give a vehicle was not based on the unique characteristics of vehicles with respect to other property, but was based on the fact that a vehicle, as a piece of property, simply does not implicate the same dignity and privacy concerns as highly intrusive searches of the person.

Furthermore, we have expressly repudiated this type of least restrictive means test in the border search context. Moreover, in both *United States v. Chaudhry,* 424 F.3d 1051, 1054 (9th Cir. 2005) (finding the distinction between "routine" and "non-routine" inapplicable to searches of property) and *Cortez–Rocha,* 394 F.3d at 1122–23, we have recognized that *Flores–Montano* rejected our prior approach of using an intrusiveness analysis to determine the reasonableness of property searches at the international border.

Therefore, we are satisfied that reasonable suspicion is not needed for customs officials to search a laptop or other personal electronic storage devices at the border.

IV

While the Supreme Court left open the possibility of requiring reasonable suspicion for certain border searches of property in *Flores–Montano,* the district court did not base its holding on the two narrow grounds left open by the Supreme Court in that case.

Arnold has never claimed that the government's search of his laptop damaged it in any way; therefore, we need not consider whether "exceptional damage to property" applies. Arnold does raise the "particularly offensive manner" exception to the government's broad border search powers. But, there is nothing in the record to indicate that the manner in which the CBP officers conducted the search was "particularly offensive" in comparison with other lawful border searches. According to Arnold, the CBP officers simply "had me boot the laptop up, and looked at what I had inside."

Whatever "particularly offensive manner" might mean, this search certainly does not meet that test. Arnold has failed to distinguish how the search of his laptop and its electronic contents is logically any different from the suspicionless border searches of travelers' luggage that the Supreme Court and we have allowed.

With respect to these searches, the Supreme Court has refused to draw distinctions between containers of information and contraband with respect to their quality or nature for purposes of determining the appropriate level of Fourth Amendment protection. Arnold's analogy to a search of a home based on a laptop's storage capacity is without merit. The Supreme Court has expressly rejected applying the Fourth Amendment protections afforded to homes to property which is "capable of functioning as a home" simply due to its size, or, distinguishing between "worthy and 'unworthy' containers." *California v. Carney*, 471 U.S. 386, 393–94 (1985).

In *Carney*, the Supreme Court rejected the argument that evidence obtained from a warrantless search of a mobile home should be suppressed because it was "capable of functioning as a home." *Id.* at 387–88. The Supreme Court refused to treat a mobile home differently from other vehicles just because it could be used as a home. The two main reasons that the Court gave in support of its holding, were: (1) that a mobile home is readily movable, and (2) that the expectation of privacy with respect to one's automobile is significantly less than that relating to one's home or office.

Here, beyond the simple fact that one cannot live in a laptop, *Carney* militates against the proposition that a laptop is a home. First, as Arnold himself admits, a laptop goes with the person, and, therefore is readily mobile. Second, one's expectation of privacy at the border is significantly less than that relating to one's home or office.

Moreover, case law does not support a finding that a search which occurs in an otherwise ordinary manner, is "particularly offensive" simply due to the storage capacity of the object being searched. Because there is no basis in the record to support the contention that the manner in which the search occurred was "particularly offensive" in light of other searches allowed by the Supreme Court and our precedents, the district court's judgment cannot be sustained.

NOTES AND QUESTIONS

1. Does the border search exception permit the government to access computers and read their contents, including personal messages, without any prior suspicion? Or does that violate the Fourth Amendment, the First Amendment, or both?

In United States v. Ramsey, 431 U.S. 606 (1977), a postal inspector in New York was investigating a heroin importing conspiracy. In a search for evidence, the inspector opened a first-class international letter mailed from Thailand that was destined for an address in the Washington, D.C., area. The letter contained heroin, leading to criminal charges against the defendants. The defendants challenged the warrantless seizure and search of the envelope, but the Supreme Court rejected the challenge under the border search exception to the Fourth Amendment:

> The border-search exception is grounded in the recognized right of the sovereign to control, subject to substantive limitations imposed by the Constitution, who and what may enter the country. It is clear that there is nothing in the rationale behind the border-search exception which suggests that the mode of entry will be critical. It was conceded at oral argument that customs officials could search, without probable cause and without a warrant, envelopes carried by an entering traveler, whether in his luggage or on his person. Surely no different constitutional standard should apply simply because the envelopes were mailed, not carried. The critical fact is that the envelopes cross the border and enter this country, not that they are brought in by one mode of transportation rather than another. It is their entry into this country from without it that makes a resulting search "reasonable."

> Nor do we agree that, under the circumstances presented by this case, First Amendment considerations dictate a full panoply of Fourth Amendment rights prior to the border search of mailed letters. There is, again, no reason to distinguish between letters mailed into the country, and letters carried on the traveler's person. More fundamentally, however, the existing system of border searches has not been shown to invade protected First Amendment rights, and hence there is no reason to think that the potential presence of correspondence makes the otherwise constitutionally reasonable search "unreasonable."

Id. at 620, 623.

Does *Ramsey* allow the police to read what they discover in the mail that they search at the border? According to United States v. Seljan, 547 F.3d 993 (9th Cir. 2008), the answer is "yes." Seljan sent packages from California to the Philippines via FedEx. Customs inspectors looking for undeclared currency imported in violation of United States currency laws decided to open Seljan's packages at the FedEx routing facility in Oakland, California. The inspectors found letters inside the packages instead of currency, and they then read the letters. Reading the letters revealed that Seljan was planning a trip to the Philippines to engage in illegal sexual contact with minors. That discovery led to charges and a motion to suppress the evidence found in the packages. Specifically, Seljan claimed that the search of his FedEx packages without a warrant or any reasonable suspicion violated his Fourth Amendment rights.

The Ninth Circuit disagreed:

> We agree with Seljan that there was intrusion into his privacy, but the degree of intrusion must be viewed in perspective. Seljan voluntarily gave the package containing the letter to FedEx for delivery to someone in the Philippines, with knowledge that it would have to cross the border and

clear customs. The reasonable expectation of privacy for that package was necessarily tempered.

An envelope containing personal correspondence is not uniquely protected from search at the border. The Supreme Court effectively rejected that contention in *Ramsey* when it reversed a holding of the D.C. Circuit that international letter-class mail could not be opened without a search warrant. As far as the Fourth Amendment is concerned, mailed envelopes are covered by the border search exception, just as envelopes carried on a traveler's person are covered.

Id. at 1002–03. Judge Kozinski vigorously dissented:

The Fourth Amendment guarantees "the right of the people to be secure in their persons, houses, *papers,* and effects. . . ." The reference to papers is not an accident; it's not a scrivener's error. It reflects the Founders' deep concern with safeguarding the privacy of thoughts and ideas—what we might call freedom of conscience—from invasion by the government. Because my colleagues in the majority don't see this right as very important, they authorize the government to read every scrap of paper that crosses our borders, whether in a pocket or purse, a package, suitcase or envelope.

But the Founders were as concerned with invasions of the mind as with those of the body, the home or personal property—which is why they gave papers equal rank in the Fourth Amendment litany. The sum and substance of today's opinion is that we remove papers as an independent sphere of constitutional protection, treating them simply as a species of effects. Because our commission as federal judges does not authorize us to blue-pencil words written by the Founding Fathers, I respectfully dissent.

The majority's reluctance to step between Mr. Seljan and his well-merited punishment is understandable. Seljan's long career of "sexually educating" children is heinous; it's difficult to regret that he will spend the rest of his life in prison. But this result comes at a high price: allowing serious invasions into the privacy of millions of Americans, innocent as well as guilty. The previously narrow border search exception is now a gaping hole. Every envelope containing birthday cards or trade secrets, every e-mail, every diary, every laptop that crosses the border can be opened and its contents read by government agents, without a warrant or even founded suspicion. Worse yet, by treating these seizures as a trivial annoyance rather than a major intrusion into our freedom of thought, my colleagues open the door for police across the United States to read whatever private papers fall into their hands. This is * * * the power the Fourth Amendment was built to shield us against. We sell this birthright very cheaply today.

Id. at 1014, 1019 (Kozinski, J., dissenting).

2. *Off-site border searches and the timing of border searches.* Under *United States v. Arnold*, the government can search computers at the border or its functional equivalent without any suspicion. But does the Fourth Amendment allow the government to seize a computer at the border and then send it to a computer forensic expert for analysis elsewhere? And if the search

occurs at the border, can the officers delay the search or must they search the computer immediately?

These issues arose in United States v. Cotterman, 2009 WL 465028 (D. Ariz. 2009). Federal agents seized Cotterman's computer at the Mexico–Arizona border when Cotterman was attempting to enter the United States. Agents suspected that the computer might contain evidence of a crime, and they wanted to search the computer for that evidence. However, there were no trained computer forensic analyst nearby. The agents let Cotterman enter the United States, and in the meantime they drove the computer to a government forensic analyst in Tucson, Arizona, about 170 miles from the border. The forensic analyst in Tucson put the computer at the front of the line of computers he needed to search. The analyst searched the computer two days later, and he found evidence of crime inside the computer.

The district court held that the search of the computer was outside the border search exception because the computer was searched 170 miles from the border two days after it was seized. The court relied on Ninth Circuit caselaw that has classified two different types of border searches: a search at the border, which requires no suspicion, and an "extended border search," that requires reasonable suspicion. Under Ninth Circuit precedent, as the location and timing of the search becomes removed from the border, the search eventually becomes an "extended border search" and then no border search at all. *See, e.g.,* United States v. Alfonso, 759 F.2d 728, 734 (9th Cir. 1985).

The *Cotterman* court held that by sending the computer to Tucson for analysis, where it was searched two days later, the search was only an extended border search and reasonable suspicion was required:

> In a border search, time and distance do matter. * * * Certainly, 170 miles is too far. Therefore, based on both extended time and distance, the computer forensic search in this case was an extended border search requiring reasonable suspicion of criminal activity before taking the computers away from the port of entry.

The court considered but rejected Cotterman's argument that the time and distance from the original border entry were so substantial that a probable cause warrant was required:

> At some point, the discrepancy in time and distance will become so great that it is no longer an extended border search, thus requiring probable cause and a warrant. Again, there is no bright line test, but an examination of the totality of circumstances, including time, distance and law enforcement efforts is required. For instance, had the forensic examiner in this case placed the Cottermans electronics equipment at the end of the queue, conducting the examination in a month or two, it could be argued the search was so removed in time as to no longer be an extended border search. We need not reach that question here, where the facts show reasonable diligence and speed in conducting the computer forensic examination. Therefore, the Government need only show reasonable suspicion, not probable cause, to justify the search in this case.

Notably, the Ninth Circuit cases concluding that the place and timing of the search are critical involve searches that occurred at the same place as the seizure. It makes sense that the location of the seizure would matter: The idea behind the border search exception is that expectations of privacy vary based on location, so the law adjusts the threshold of cause to correspond to the extent of the experienced intrusion. On the other hand, how much does location matter when a computer is taken from a suspect at the border and searched offsite? Why does it matter that the computer went to the analyst instead of the analyst to the computer given that the owner of the computer was elsewhere?

3. *Pretext searches at the border.* In United States v. Roberts, 86 F. Supp.2d 678 (S.D. Tex. 2000), *aff'd on other grounds*, 274 F.3d 1007 (5th Cir. 2001), investigators suspected that a man named Roberts was carrying a computer containing images of child pornography on a trip from Houston, Texas to Paris, France. The investigators set up a customs inspection station on the jetway at the Houston airport with the sole purpose of harnessing the border search exception. When Roberts arrived at the inspection station, customs agents informed him that they were searching for "currency" and "high technology or other data" to ensure that it was not illegally exported. Of course, the real purpose of the inspection was to search Roberts' computer for child pornography. The agents searched his property and found a laptop computer and six Zip diskettes that together contained thousands of contraband images. The court applied the border search exception and approved the warrantless search because the runway was the "functional equivalent" of the border for an international flight.

Do you think that the agents should have been allowed to use the border exception to justify this search? Note that under Whren v. United States, 517 U.S. 806 (1996), an officer's motive for conducting a search or seizure is irrelevant to its constitutionality.

4. The National Security Agency is widely believed to attempt to collect all international telephone, fax, e-mail, and data transmissions. The program is often referred to by its alleged code name, ECHELON, and is coordinated with the governments of the United Kingdom, Canada, Australia, and New Zealand. *See generally* Lawrence D. Sloan, Note, *ECHELON and the Legal Restraints on Signals Intelligence: A Need for Reevaluation*, 50 Duke L.J. 1467 (2001).

Does ECHELON comply with the Fourth Amendment under the border search exception? What is the "functional equivalent of the border" for an e-mail or other Internet transmission? If the NSA installs a surveillance device at an ISP in the United States, and records all traffic either from abroad or to abroad (or both), does the border search exception permit the surveillance without a warrant?

5. GOVERNMENT WORKPLACE SEARCHES

Many people use computers at work. When a workplace computer is used to commit a crime, the rules that regulate government access to the computer depend on whether the employer is a private company or the government. The Fourth Amendment rules regulating access to private sector workplace computers is similar to the rules regulating access to computers stored in homes, with one major caveat: Employers almost always have common authority to provide third-party consent to a search. *Compare* Chapman v. United States, 365 U.S. 610 (1961) (holding that a landlord lacks authority to consent to search of premises used by his tenant) *with* United States v. Gargiso, 456 F.2d 584 (2d Cir. 1972) (holding that an employer can consent to a search of an employee's locked workspace). When investigators want to seize and analyze a computer in a private workplace, they ordinarily will obtain the employer's authorization and then rely on that consent to seize the computers without a warrant. If the employer does not consent, however, the police ordinarily will obtain a warrant.

Computer searches at government workplaces present a very different situation. In a government workplace, employers are by definition state actors covered by the Fourth Amendment. This sets up a puzzle: If government employers are state actors, does a supervisor violate the Fourth Amendment every time he enters an employee's office without a warrant or the employee's consent? Although they are state actors, government employers normally do not act in a law enforcement capacity at work. Given that, it would be rather odd to require them to obtain a warrant to do their job. Alternatively, it may seem equally troubling to say that government employees have no privacy rights at all in their work-spaces. If that were the case, government employees would forfeit all Fourth Amendment rights upon arriving at work.

The Supreme Court has resolved this tension by creating a somewhat *sui generis* framework for analyzing government employee privacy. The key case is O'Connor v. Ortega, 480 U.S. 709 (1987), which was decided in a plurality opinion by Justice O'Connor combined with a concurrence by Justice Scalia. Under *O'Connor*, Fourth Amendment rights in government workplaces are determined by a two-step framework. First, the court must apply a rather unusual version of the reasonable expectation of privacy test. Unlike the traditional reasonable expectation of privacy test used in homes and private workplaces, the version of the test applied in government workplaces looks to (a) whether the defendant shared his space or property with others; and (b) whether legitimate workplace policies put the defendant on notice that he was denied otherwise existing Fourth Amendment rights. If a government employee shares his space with others, or legitimate workplace policies deny his privacy rights, he cannot have a reasonable expectation of privacy in the workplace.

If a government employee has a reasonable expectation of privacy under this test, the next question is whether the workplace search is "reasonable." In *O'Connor*, the Supreme Court held that this second question should be analyzed under the Supreme Court's "special needs" exception to the warrant requirement. The "special needs" exception permits state actors to dispense with the warrant requirement when acting in a non-law-enforcement capacity, such as the case of a school principal searching student lockers or mandatory drug testing by a government agency. The thinking is that the government interest beyond law enforcement must be balanced with the traditional Fourth Amendment rule, relaxing the warrant requirement when "the burden of obtaining a warrant is likely to frustrate the [non-law-enforcement] governmental purpose behind the search." Camara v. Municipal Court, 387 U.S. 523, 533 (1967). *O'Connor* brought government workplace searches within this category, permitting government employers to conduct reasonable warrantless searches even if the searches violated the employee's reasonable expectation of privacy. The employer must conduct the search for a work-related reason, rather than solely to obtain evidence in a criminal case, and the search must be justified at its inception and permissible in its scope.

LEVENTHAL v. KNAPEK

United States Court of Appeals for the Second Circuit, 2001.
266 F.3d 64.

SOTOMAYOR, CIRCUIT JUDGE:

After receiving anonymous allegations that an employee reasonably suspected to be plaintiff-appellant Gary Leventhal was neglecting his duties in the Accounting Bureau of the New York State Department of Transportation, DOT investigators, without Leventhal's consent, printed out a list of the file names found on Leventhal's office computer. The list of file names contained evidence that certain non-standard software was loaded on Leventhal's computer. This led to additional searches confirming that Leventhal had a personal tax preparation program on his office computer and to disciplinary charges against Leventhal for misconduct. After settling the disciplinary charges, Leventhal sued defendants-appellees, challenging the legality of the searches * * *.

We affirm the district court's grant of summary judgment to defendants * * *. Even though, based on the particular facts of this case, Leventhal had some expectation of privacy in the contents of his computer, the searches were reasonable in light of the DOT's need to investigate the allegations of Leventhal's misconduct as balanced against the modest intrusion caused by the searches.

Background

Leventhal began his career at the DOT in 1974. At the time of the searches in question, Leventhal had risen to the position of Principal Accountant in the Accounting Bureau of the DOT, a grade 27 position. In 1996, and for several previous years, Leventhal maintained a private tax practice while employed at the DOT. He received DOT approval to make up on weekends or after normal work hours any time he missed because of his outside employment. In order to receive approval for this arrangement, Leventhal declared that his outside employment would "not interfere with the complete and proper execution of my duties with the Department of Transportation."

The DOT had a written policy prohibiting theft. The policy broadly defined theft to include:

> improper use of State equipment, material or vehicles. Examples include but are not limited to: conducting personal business on State time; using State equipment, material or vehicles for personal business; improper use of the mail, copiers, fax machines, personal computers, lincs codes or telephones and time spent on non-State business related activities during the workday.

The DOT also had an unwritten rule that only "standard" DOT software could be loaded on DOT computers. Although this rule was never officially promulgated as a DOT policy, Leventhal remarked during his interrogation that "the stated policy" was that employees were not to have personal software on a DOT computer "without permission." Nevertheless, it was known that the staff of the Accounting Bureau had loaded unlicensed copies of "non-standard" software on DOT computers and used the software to perform work-related activities due, at least in part, to the DOT's inability to purchase needed software for its employees. The DOT also had an official policy restricting office Internet access to DOT business.

In July 1996, the DOT circulated a memo from Ann Snow, the Network Administrator for the Budget and Finance Division, which stated that only original, licensed copies of software could be installed on DOT computers. Following the distribution of this memo, however, Leventhal's supervisors discussed their difficulties in complying with the memo because of the department's dependence upon the use of unlicensed software. Leventhal's immediate supervisor at the time, John Chevalier, instructed his subordinates, including Leventhal, that they could continue to use non-standard software for departmental business.

DOT computers were accessible, for certain limited purposes, by those other than their normal users. The computer support staff of the DOT engaged in troubleshooting and the upgrading of individual computers. During these maintenance operations, it was possible for the computer staff to observe whether non-standard DOT software had been loaded on an individual computer. DOT computers were also occasionally accessed without the user's knowledge to retrieve a needed document, sometimes bypassing a password prompt to obtain access. The computer staff of the DOT provided technical support for Leventhal's DOT computer upon his request three or four times between 1994 and 1996, and once, after hours, without his request, in order to change the name of the server.

On October 15, 1996, the New York State Office of the Inspector General referred to the DOT an anonymous letter it had received complaining of abuses at the DOT Accounting Bureau. This letter described specific employees by reference to their salary grades, genders, and job titles, without providing names. The letter made certain allegations concerning a grade 27 employee. Leventhal was the only grade 27 employee in the office at that time and, therefore, the DOT investigators inferred that the grade 27 employee described in the letter was Leventhal. The relevant portion of the letter states:

> The abuse of time and power is so far out of line with the intended functions of the bureau that to cite all specifics would be an endless task. The day to day operation of this bureau is a slap in the face to all good state workers. You have to see this place to believe it. I will cite a few examples. A grade 27 who is late everyday. The majority of his time is spent on non-DOT business related phone calls or talking to other personnel about personal computers. He is only in the office half the time he is either sick or on vacation.

Lawrence Knapek, the Assistant Commissioner of the DOT for the Office of Budget and Finance, met with John Samaniuk, the acting director of the Office of Internal Audit and Investigations, and Gary Cuyler, the chief investigator for that office, to discuss how to respond to the allegations made in the letter. They decided that the Office of Internal Audit and Investigation would conduct an investigation employing "such techniques as reviewing telephone records, reviewing computer records, Internet logs, that kind of thing." A "computer review" was ordered for all of the employees who could be identified from the letter. This involved printing out a list of file names found on these DOT computers to determine whether any contained non-standard software. After business hours on October 25, 1996, the investigators entered Leventhal's office through an open door, turned on his DOT computer, and reviewed the directories of files on the computer's hard drive. There was no power-on password to gain access to Leventhal's computer, but once the machine was turned on, some of the menu selections that appeared were password-protected. In order to perform their search, the investigators may have used a "boot-disk," a disk which allows the computer to start up without encountering the menus normally found there.

Having located the computer directories, the investigators printed out a list of the file names to enable the later identification of the programs loaded on Leventhal's computer without having to open each program. This included a printout of the names of the "hidden" files on Leventhal's computer. These "hidden" directories, the investigators found, contained "Morph," a type of drawing program and "PPU," a program suspected of containing tax software because of file names such as "TAX.FNT," and "CUSTTAX.DBF." On the non-"hidden" directories, the investigators found other non-standard software, including the programs Prodigy, Quicken, and Lotus Suite (although one part of Lotus Suite was standard DOT software at the time). * * *

In February 1997, DOT management and investigators met to examine the results from these searches. Assistant DOT Commissioner Knapek attended the meeting and, aware of Leventhal's private tax practice, was particularly interested in confirming the investigators' suspicion that Leventhal had loaded tax software on his DOT office computer. They decided to conduct a further search of Leventhal's computer to determine with greater certainty whether the "PPU" directory they had discovered during the first search was part of a tax preparation program. Investigators reexamined the computer in Leventhal's office once in February 1997 and twice in April 1997. During these subsequent searches, they copied the "Morph" and "PPU" directories onto a laptop computer, obtained additional printouts of the file directories, and opened a few files to examine their contents. In the first April search, an investigator noticed that some items had been added to the PPU directory since the previous search, indicating recent activity. The PPU directory was later identified as belonging to "Pencil Pushers," a tax preparation program.

On May 2, 1997, shortly after informing Leventhal that he was under investigation and that the computer in his office would be confiscated, the Director of the DOT Employee Relations Bureau observed Leventhal appearing to delete items from his computer directories. Leventhal was then interrogated. He admitted to belonging to a group that had jointly purchased a single copy of the Pencil Pushers software that was then copied onto his computer and the computers of other members of the group. Leventhal also admitted that he had printed out up to five personal income tax returns from the computer in his DOT office.

In September 1997, the DOT brought disciplinary charges against Leventhal under N.Y. Civ. Serv. Law § 75 charging six grounds of misconduct or incompetence. * * * Four days after he settled the DOT disciplinary charges, Leventhal filed this action in United States District Court for the Northern District of New York.

Discussion

The Fourth Amendment protects individuals from unreasonable searches conducted by the Government, even when the Government acts as an employer. The "special needs" of public employers may, however, allow them to dispense with the probable cause and warrant requirements when conducting workplace searches related to investigations of work-related misconduct. *See O'Connor v. Ortega*, 480 U.S. 709, 719–26 (1987) (plurality opinion); *id.* at 732 (Scalia, J. concurring). In these situations, the Fourth Amendment's protection against "unreasonable" searches is enforced by "a careful balancing of governmental and private interests." *New Jersey v. T.L.O.*, 469 U.S. 325, 341 (1985). A public employer's search of an area in which an employee had a reasonable expectation of privacy is "reasonable" when "the measures adopted are reasonably related to the objectives of the search and not excessively intrusive in light of" its purpose. *O'Connor*, 480 U.S. at 726 (plurality opinion).

We begin by inquiring whether the conduct at issue infringed an expectation of privacy that society is prepared to consider reasonable. Without a reasonable expectation of privacy, a workplace search by a public employer will not violate the Fourth Amendment, regardless of the search's nature and scope. The workplace conditions can be such that an employee's expectation of privacy in a certain area is diminished. *See id.* at 717–18 (plurality opinion) (recognizing that offices that are "continually entered by fellow employees and other visitors during the workday for conferences, consultations, and other work-related visits," can be "so open to fellow employees or the public that no expectation of privacy is reasonable."). On the facts of *O'Connor*, the entire Court found a reasonable expectation of privacy with respect to the office desk and file cabinets in which the plaintiff had maintained his personal correspondence, medical files, correspondence from private patients unconnected with his employment, personal financial records, teaching aids and notes, and personal gifts and mementos. *Id.* at 718 (plurality opinion); *id.* at 731 (Scalia, J., concurring). In finding that the plaintiff had a reasonable expectation of privacy, the plurality noted that there was no evidence that the employer had "established a reasonable regulation or policy discouraging employees from storing personal papers and effects in their desks or file cabinets." *Id.* at 719 (plurality opinion).

We hold, based on the particular facts of this case, that Leventhal had a reasonable expectation of privacy in the contents of his office computer. We make this assessment in the context of the employment relation, after considering what access other employees or the public had to Leventhal's office.

Leventhal occupied a private office with a door. He had exclusive use of the desk, filing cabinet, and computer in his office. Leventhal did not share use of his computer with other employees in the Accounting Bureau nor was there evidence that visitors or the public had access to his computer.

We are aware that "public employees' expectations of privacy in their offices, desks, and file cabinets, like similar expectations of employees in the private sector, may be reduced by virtue of actual office practices and procedures, or by legitimate regulation." *Id.* Construing the evidence in favor of Leventhal, as we must in reviewing this grant of summary judgment against him, we do not find that the DOT either had a general practice of routinely conducting searches of office computers or had placed Leventhal on notice that he should have no expectation of privacy in the contents of his office computer.

Viewing the DOT anti-theft policy in the light most favorable to Leventhal, we find that it did not prohibit the mere storage of personal materials in his office computer. Rather, the anti-theft policy prohibited "using" state equipment "for personal business" without defining further these terms. John Samaniuk, acting director of the DOT's Office of Internal Audits and Investigations, testified at Leventhal's disciplinary hearing that an employee would not violate state policies by keeping a personal checkbook in an office drawer, even though it would take up space there. Under the circumstances presented here, we cannot say that the same anti-theft policy prohibited Leventhal from storing personal items in his office computer.

Although the DOT technical support staff had access to all computers in the DOT offices, their maintenance of these computers was normally announced and the one example in the record of an unannounced visit to Leventhal's computer was only to change the name of a server. DOT personnel might also need, at times, to search for a document in an unattended computer, but there was no evidence that these searches were frequent, widespread, or extensive enough to constitute an atmosphere "so open to fellow employees or the public that no expectation of privacy is reasonable." *Id.* at 718 (plurality opinion). This type of infrequent and selective search for maintenance purposes or to retrieve a needed document, justified by reference to the "special needs" of employers to pursue legitimate work-related objectives, does not destroy any underlying expectation of privacy that an employee could otherwise possess in the contents of an office computer.

Even though Leventhal had some expectation of privacy in the contents of his office computer, the investigatory searches by the DOT did not violate his Fourth Amendment rights. An investigatory search for evidence of suspected work-related employee misfeasance will be constitutionally "reasonable" if it is "justified at its inception" and of appropriate scope. *Id.* at 726 (plurality opinion). We agree with the district court that both of these requirements are satisfied here.

[handwritten margin note: reasonable search]

The initial consideration of the search's justification examines whether "there are reasonable grounds for suspecting that the search will turn up evidence that the employee is guilty of work-related misconduct." *O'Connor*, 480 U.S. at 726 (plurality opinion). Here, there were reasonable grounds to believe that the searches would uncover evidence of misconduct. The specific allegations against the grade 27 employee, who was reasonably assumed to be Leventhal, were that (1) he was "late everyday"; (2) he spent "the majority of his time on non-DOT business related phone calls or talking to other personnel about personal computers"; and that (3) "he is only in the office half the time; the other half he is either sick or on vacation." Probable cause is not necessary to conduct a search in this context, a plurality of the Court has explained, because "public employers have a direct and overriding interest in ensuring that the work of the agency is conducted in a proper and efficient manner." *Id.* at 724 (plurality opinion). The individualized suspicion of misconduct in this case justified the DOT's decision to instigate some type of search.

The scope of a search will be appropriate if reasonably related to the objectives of the search and not excessively intrusive in light of the nature of the misconduct. We conclude that the DOT search to identify whether Leventhal was using non-standard DOT software was reasonably related to the DOT's investigation of the allegations of Leventhal's workplace misconduct. Although the anonymous letter did not allege that the grade 27 employee was misusing DOT office computers, it did allege that the grade 27 employee was not attentive to his duties and spent a significant amount of work time discussing personal computers with other employees.

Leventhal argues that a search for non-standard software would be irrelevant to charges of misconduct because the DOT had, de facto, approved of the use of non-standard software needed to conduct DOT business. Even assuming that this were true, the investigation was more broadly aimed at uncovering evidence that Leventhal was using his office computer for non-DOT purposes. The searches accomplished this task by uncovering evidence that Leventhal had loaded a tax preparation program onto his office computer, a program that he later admitted he used to print out personal tax returns in his office.

We also find that the scope of the searches was not excessively intrusive in light of the nature of the misconduct. During the first search, the DOT investigators printed out a list of file names found on Leventhal's office computer. They did not run any program or open any files. The investigators entered Leventhal's office through an open door and found that Leventhal's computer had no power-on password although some menu selections were password protected. The investigators limited their search to viewing and printing file names that were reasonably related to the DOT's need to know whether Leventhal was misusing his office computer. The first search was permissible in scope.

Neither were the three subsequent searches "excessively intrusive." After the first search had established that files named "TAX.FNT" and "CUSTTAX.DBF" were loaded on Leventhal's computer, the investigators reasonably suspected that these files were part of a tax program. When DOT investigators and management met to discuss what they had found in the first search, Assistant Commissioner Knapek expressed a particular interest in confirming whether Leventhal had loaded tax preparation software on his DOT computer, aware that Leventhal had a private tax practice. Investigators reexamined the computer in Leventhal's office once in February 1997 and twice in April 1997. These searches were limited to copying onto a laptop computer the "PPU" directories that they later identified as referring to "Pencil Pushers," a tax preparation program, and the "Morph" directories, pertaining to a graphics program, to printing out additional copies of the file names, and to opening a few files to examine their contents. There is no evidence that the DOT opened and examined any computer files containing individual tax returns that may have been saved on Leventhal's computer, and, therefore, we need not address the permissibility of searching such materials. Considering that the first search yielded evidence upon which it was reasonable to suspect that a more thorough search would turn up additional proof that Leventhal had misused his DOT office computer, the DOT investigators were justified in returning to confirm the nature of the non-standard DOT programs loaded on Leventhal's computer by copying directories, printing file names, and opening selected files.

Because the DOT searches of Leventhal's office computer were not "unreasonable" under the Fourth Amendment, * * * we affirm the district court's grant of summary judgment to defendants.

NOTES AND QUESTIONS

1. *The first step of the* O'Connor *test.* The first step of the *O'Connor* test considers whether the employee shared his space with others and whether legitimate workplace policies put the defendant on notice that no privacy rights should be expected. In *Leventhal v. Knapek*, the court concludes that the workplace policies and practices at the DOT were insufficient to deny Leventhal Fourth Amendment rights. As a result, Leventhal enjoyed Fourth Amendment protection in his computer.

In many other cases, however, government employers have promulgated computer use policies that eliminate Fourth Amendment protection entirely. For example, in United States v. Thorn, 375 F.3d 679 (8th Cir. 2004), an employee of the Missouri Department of Social Services downloaded contraband images to his computer at work. When the employee had obtained computer access two years earlier, he had acknowledged a workplace policy that stated: "Employees *do not* have any personal privacy rights regarding their use of DSS information systems and technology. An employee's use of DSS information systems and technology indicates that the employee understands and *consents* to DSS's right to inspect and audit all such use as described in this policy." The Eighth Circuit held that the policy eliminated the employee's Fourth Amendment rights in his workplace computer. *Id.* at 683–84.

The powerful effect of workplace regulations under the first step of *O'Connor* encourages government employers to install network "banners" or enact Internet use policies. In the case of a banner, the employee is greeted with a privacy notice upon logging in to a workplace computer. In most cases, the notice explains that the user should have no reasonable expectation of privacy in his use of the network. Banners and Internet use policies are generally binding: if a notice says that a government employee has no privacy rights, the employee has no privacy rights. Should government employers be allowed to eliminate Fourth Amendment rights so easily?

2. *The second step of the* O'Connor *test.* At stage two of the *O'Connor* test, the court must determine whether the search was reasonable in its scope and justified by non-law-enforcement needs. *Leventhal v. Knapek* focuses on whether the employer search was reasonable in its scope, and concludes that the search in that case was indeed reasonable. Other cases have focused on the line between law enforcement searches and searches for non-law-enforcement reasons. The line may be difficult to draw because government employers often serve two roles at once. The head of a government office may want to end workplace misconduct and may also control criminal investigators who can build a case against employees who break the rules. In such situations, how should courts distinguish work-related searches from law enforcement searches?

In United States v. Simons, 206 F.3d 392 (4th Cir. 2000), an employee of the Foreign Bureau of Information Services (FBIS), a division of the CIA, used his computer at work to download child pornography. Two employees of the CIA Office of Inspector General, one of whom was a criminal investigator, were sent to search the employee's office for evidence. The Fourth Circuit held that this search fell within the *O'Connor* exception to the warrant requirement even though the dominant purpose of the search was to gather evidence:

> FBIS did not lose its special need for the efficient and proper operation of the workplace, merely because the evidence obtained was evidence of a crime. [The employee]'s violation of FBIS' Internet policy happened also to be a violation of criminal law; this does not mean that FBIS lost the capacity and interests of an employer. *See Gossmeyer v. McDonald,* 128 F.3d 481, 492–93 (7th Cir. 1997) (concluding that presence of law enforcement personnel at search of employee's office by government employer did not preclude application of *O'Connor*); *see also* 4 Wayne R. LaFave, *Search and Seizure* § 10.3(d), at 487–88 (3d ed.1996) (noting that conclusion that warrant requirement does not apply when employer is investigating work-related criminal conduct is consistent with reasoning of *O'Connor*).

Id. at 400.

3. *Computer searches involving probationers.* The special needs doctrine also applies to searches of individuals on probation. *See* Griffin v. Wisconsin, 483 U.S. 868 (1987). For example, in United States v. Lifshitz, 369 F.3d 173 (2d Cir. 2004), the defendant pled guilty to receiving images of child pornography using his computer. The district court imposed a sentence of probation that contained the following restriction, *id.* at 177 n.3:

> The defendant shall consent to the installation of systems that enable the probation officer or designee to monitor and filter computer use, on a regular or random basis, on any computer owned or controlled by the defendant. Upon reasonable suspicion, the probation office may make unannounced examinations of any computer equipment owned or controlled by the defendant, which may result in retrieval and copying of all data from the computer(s) and any internal or external peripherals, and may involve removal of such equipment for the purpose of conducting a more thorough inspection.

The Second Circuit held that the special needs exception permitted conditioning the defendant's probation on his agreement to computer monitoring. The court remanded the case back to the district court, however, on the ground that the district court needed to craft a narrower and more specific condition that would satisfy the reasonableness requirement of the special needs doctrine given the facts of that particular case. *See id.* at 193.

D. SEARCHING AND SEIZING COMPUTERS WITH A WARRANT

Searches and seizures are constitutional when authorized by a valid and properly executed search warrant. A search warrant is a court order signed by a judge that authorizes government agents to enter a place and seize property. The Fourth Amendment's requirement for issuing a search warrant is unusually clear from its text: "no Warrants shall issue, but upon probable cause, supported by Oath or affirmation, and particularly describing the place to be searched, and the persons or things to be seized." The Framers of the Fourth Amendment enacted these restrictions in reaction to the English and early Colonial experience with "general warrants," warrants that gave the King's officials wide discretion to execute searches as they believed necessary to enforce the law. The text of the Fourth Amendment forbids general warrants by ensuring that all warrants must be based on probable cause and must state with specificity where the police will go and what property they will seize.

The requirement that a warrant must be issued "upon probable cause" ordinarily is satisfied by a written affidavit submitted to the issuing judge. The affidavit explains the investigation and articulates the officer's probable cause that evidence of the crime will be located in the place to be searched. The proposed warrant itself is a one-page order containing the judge's authorization to enter the named place to be searched and to seize the property listed in the warrant. If the judge agrees that the affidavit establishes probable cause, and that the place to be searched and property to be seized are "particularly" described, then the judge will sign the warrant. The warrant then becomes a court order permitting the investigator or his agents to execute the search.

Both constitutional and statutory law regulate the process of obtaining and executing search warrants. Probable cause and the particularity requirement are obvious constitutional requirements governing what warrants may issue. The Fourth Amendment also imposes some restrictions on how investigators execute warrants and what property they may seize. Beyond the Fourth Amendment, statutes regulating the warrant process impose a number of nuts-and-bolts restrictions. At the federal level, for example, Federal Rule of Criminal Procedure 41 provides a relatively detailed set of instructions governing how and when warrants must be obtained and executed. Rule 41 requires agents to execute warrants within a period of days after the judge issues the warrant. It also requires agents to leave behind a copy of the warrant when it is executed, as well as to file a "return" of the warrant with the issuing judge listing the property investigators seized. Although the materials in this section will occasionally discuss Rule 41 and associated state statutory restrictions on computer warrants, they focus primarily on constitutional rules under the Fourth Amendment.

Computer searches often involve a two-step process. Agents will first execute the physical search and take away the computers that must be analyzed. They will then execute the electronic search, searching the seized computer for evidence. The bifurcation of the one-step search process into two steps raises a number of difficult questions. For example, should the probable cause required to seize a computer focus on probable cause to believe evidence is located in the physical place where the computer is located, or probable cause that evidence is located in a particular computer? Is the "place to be searched" the physical location of the physical search, the physical location of the electronic search, or the computer itself? What legal restrictions govern the execution of the electronic search stage?

The law governing this area presently is in a state of considerable uncertainty, owing largely to the novelty of the two-step search process. The overarching question is, how can the traditional rules governing warrant searches be applied to the new facts to retain the basic function of existing law? How can the law both deter general warrants and ensure that investigators have the ability to collect digital evidence to protect public safety?

1. PROBABLE CAUSE AND PARTICULARITY

Warrants must be based on probable cause and must particularly describe the property to be searched and the property to be seized. According to the Supreme Court, probable cause is "a fair probability that contraband or evidence of a crime will be found in a particular place." Illinois v. Gates, 462 U.S. 213, 238 (1983). No special rules determine when probable cause exists. The question is whether the affidavit submitted in support of the warrant establishes a fair probability in a practical, common-sense way based on the totality of the circumstances.

The Supreme Court explained the purpose of the particularity requirement in Maryland v. Garrison, 480 U.S. 79, 84 (1987):

> The manifest purpose of this particularity requirement was to prevent general searches. By limiting the authorization to search to the specific areas and things for which there is probable cause to search, the requirement ensures that the search will be carefully tailored to its justifications, and will not take on the character of the wide-ranging exploratory searches the Framers intended to prohibit. Thus, the scope of a lawful search is defined by the object of the search and the places in which there is probable cause to believe that it may be found. Just as probable cause to believe that a stolen lawnmower may be found in a garage will not support a warrant to search an upstairs bedroom, probable cause to believe that undocumented aliens are being transported in a van will not justify a warrantless search of a suitcase.

As this excerpt suggests, the probable cause and particularity requirements work together. A warrant must specify a specific place in which specific evidence of the crime is probably located, and the affidavit must establish probable cause to believe that the evidence is located in the place to be searched.

Importantly, the remedy for violations of these two constitutional requirements is considerably narrower than the rights themselves. In United States v. Leon, 468 U.S. 897 (1984), the Supreme Court held that defects in search warrants should not lead to suppression of evidence if the government investigators have a reasonable good faith belief that the warrant satisfied the Fourth Amendment. The Court reasoned that an officer who has an objectively reasonable belief that the warrant was proper has not committed a wrong that courts must deter:

> It is the magistrate's responsibility to determine whether the officer's allegations establish probable cause and, if so, to issue a warrant comporting in form with the requirements of the Fourth Amendment. In the ordinary case, an officer cannot be expected to question the magistrate's probable-cause determination or his judgment that the form of the warrant is technically sufficient. Once the warrant issues, there is literally nothing more the policeman can do in seeking to comply with the law. Penalizing the officer for the magistrate's error, rather than his own, cannot logically contribute to the deterrence of Fourth Amendment violation. * * * We conclude that the marginal or nonexistent benefits produced by suppressing evidence obtained in objectively reasonable reliance on a subsequently invalidated search warrant cannot justify the substantial costs of exclusion.

Id. at 920. In Malley v. Briggs, 475 U.S. 335, 344 (1986), the Supreme Court held that this "good faith" standard is the same as the qualified immunity standard that the courts have applied in civil suits for Fourth Amendment violations under Harlow v. Fitzgerald, 457 U.S. 800 (1982). This means that whether a Fourth Amendment challenge to a search warrant involves a civil suit or a motion to suppress, the standard is the same: a victim of a search pursuant to a defective warrant can obtain relief only if "it would be clear to a reasonable officer that his conduct was unlawful in the situation he confronted" at the time of the search. Saucier v. Katz, 533 U.S. 194, 202 (2001).

How do these requirements apply to warrants to search and seize computers?

UNITED STATES v. ADJANI

United States Court of Appeals for the Ninth Circuit, 2006.
452 F.3d 1140.

FISHER, CIRCUIT JUDGE:

While executing a search warrant at the home of defendant Christopher Adjani to obtain evidence of his alleged extortion, agents from the Federal Bureau of Investigation seized Adjani's computer and external storage devices, which were later searched at an FBI computer lab. They also seized and subsequently searched a computer belonging to defendant Jana Reinhold, who lived with Adjani, even though she had not at that point been identified as a suspect and was not named as a target in the warrant. Some of the emails found on Reinhold's computer chronicled conversations between her and Adjani that implicated her in the extortion plot. Relying in part on the incriminating emails, the government charged both Adjani and Reinhold with conspiring to commit extortion in violation of 18 U.S.C. § 371 and transmitting a threatening communication with intent to extort in violation of 18 U.S.C. § 875(d).

The defendants brought motions to suppress the emails, arguing that the warrant did not authorize the seizure and search of Reinhold's computer and its contents; but if it did, the warrant was unconstitutionally overbroad or, alternatively, the emails fell outside the scope of the warrant. The district court granted the defendants' motion to suppress the email communications between Reinhold and Adjani, finding that the agents did not have sufficient probable cause to search Reinhold's computer, and that once they discovered information incriminating her, the agents should have obtained an additional search warrant. The government appeals this evidentiary ruling, but only with respect to three emails dated January 12, 2004.

We hold that the government had probable cause to search Reinhold's computer, the warrant satisfied our test for specificity and the seized e-mail communications fell within the scope of the properly issued warrant. Accordingly, we reverse the district court's order suppressing the January 12, 2004 email communications between Reinhold and Adjani.

I. Background

A. *The Extortion Scheme*

Adjani was once employed by Paycom Billing Services Inc. (formerly Epoch), which facilitates payments from Internet users to its client websites. As a payment facilitator, Paycom receives and stores vast amounts of data containing credit card information. On January 8, 2004, a woman (later identified as Reinhold) delivered envelopes to three Paycom partners, Christopher Mallick, Clay Andrews and Joel Hall. Each envelope contained a letter from Adjani advising that he had purchased a copy of Paycom's database containing its clients' sensitive financial information. The letter threatened that Adjani would sell the Paycom database and master client control list if he did not receive $3 million. To prove his threats were real, Adjani included samples of the classified data. He directed the Paycom partners to sign an enclosed agreement attesting to the proposed quid pro quo and fax it back to him by January 12. The letter included Adjani's email address, cadjani@mac.com, and a fax number. Agents later learned that Adjani's email address was billed to Reinhold's account.

Evidence suggested that Adjani left Los Angeles on January 9, 2004, and ultimately ended up in Zurich, Switzerland. From Switzerland, Adjani sent an email on January 12 to Joel Hall to confirm that Hall and the others had received the envelopes. Adjani followed up on this email on January 13 by instructing Hall to contact him through AOL/Mac iChat instant messaging if he wanted to discuss the settlement agreement. With the FBI monitoring, Hall conversed several times with Adjani on the Internet and over the telephone. In spite of Adjani's insistence that he remain overseas, Hall convinced him to come to Los Angeles on January 26 to pick up $2.5 million in exchange for the database.

Adjani returned to Los Angeles on January 22, under FBI surveillance. Reinhold, driving in a car that the FBI had earlier identified as Adjani's, was observed leaving Adjani's residence in Venice, California, picking him up from the airport and returning to his residence. The FBI also observed Reinhold using an Apple computer, the same brand of computer Adjani used to email and chat with Paycom.

B. Obtaining and Executing the Search Warrant

On January 23, 2004, based on the facts recited above and attested to in FBI Agent Cloney's affidavit (which was affixed to the warrant), a federal magistrate judge granted the government an arrest warrant for Adjani and a search warrant covering Adjani's Venice residence, his vehicle, his person and the residence of the individual who had stolen the confidential information from Paycom. The warrant specifically sought "evidence of violations of 18 U.S.C. § 875(d): Transmitting Threatening Communications With Intent to Commit Extortion." Further, the warrant expressly authorized seizure of:

5g. Records, documents and materials containing Paycom's or Epoch's master client control documents, Paycom's or Epoch's email database, or other company information relating to Paycom or Epoch.

5h. Records, documents and materials which reflect communications with Christopher Mallick, Clay Andrews, Joel Hall or other employees or officers of Paycom or Epoch.

5i. Any and all evidence of travel, including hotel bills and receipts, gasoline receipts, plane tickets, bus tickets, train tickets, or any other documents related to travel from January 8, 2004 to the present.

. . . .

5k. Computer, hard drives, computer disks, CD's, and other computer storage devices.

With respect to the computer search, the warrant prescribed the process to be followed: "In searching the data, the computer personnel will examine all of the data contained in the computer equipment and storage devices to view their precise contents and determine whether the data falls within the items to be seized as set forth herein." Additionally, it noted that "in order to search for data that is capable of being read or intercepted by a computer, law enforcement personnel will need to seize and search any computer equipment and storage device capable of being used to commit, further, or store evidence of the offense listed above."

On January 26, 2004, agents observed Reinhold driving Adjani, in a car registered to him, to his meeting with Paycom. While Adjani went into a hotel, Reinhold slipped into the backseat of his car, placing curtains over the windows. At this point, agents proceeded to search Adjani's car. That same day, agents executed the search warrant for Adjani's Venice residence. There they found and seized various computers and hard drives, including Reinhold's computer, which were later sent to an FBI computer lab to be searched. During that search process, the hard drive from Reinhold's computer revealed certain email correspondence between Reinhold and Adjani, implicating Reinhold in the extortion plot and supporting a charge of conspiracy against both of them.

The defendants successfully sought suppression of these seized email communications in the district court. This appeal requires us to determine whether the agents permissibly searched Reinhold's computer; whether the warrant satisfied our specificity standards; and whether the emails seized fell within the scope of the otherwise properly issued warrant.

II. Analysis

A. Probable Cause

The government principally argues that contrary to the district court's finding and the defendants' assertions, the search warrant affidavit established probable cause to search all instrumentalities that might contain "evidence of violations of" 18 U.S.C. § 875(d), including Reinhold's computer and emails. Reinhold counters that the affidavit may have generally established probable cause, but did not do so with respect to her computer, because "in the affidavit, Reinhold was not labeled as a target, suspect, or co-conspirator."

1. Probable cause to issue the warrant

A search warrant is issued upon a showing of probable cause to believe that the legitimate object of a search is located in a particular place, and therefore safeguards an individual's interest in the privacy of his home and possessions against the unjustified intrusion of the police. *Steagald v. United States*, 451 U.S. 204, 213 (1981). As the Supreme Court has explained, the "probable cause standard is a practical, nontechnical conception." *Illinois v. Gates*, 462 U.S. 213, 231 (1983). Furthermore, "probable cause is a fluid concept—turning on the assessment of probabilities in particular factual contexts—not readily, or even usefully, reduced to a neat set of legal rules." *Id.* at 232. The warrant here was supported by probable cause, because the affidavit submitted to the magistrate judge established that "there was a fair probability that contraband or evidence of a crime would be found in" computers at Adjani's residence. *See Gates*, 462 U.S. at 238. The extensive 24–page supporting affidavit described the extortion scheme in detail, including that Adjani possessed a computer-generated database and communicated with Paycom over email, requiring the use of a computer. Furthermore, the agent's affidavit explained the need to search computers, in particular, for evidence of the extortion scheme: "I know that considerable planning is typically performed to construct and consummate an extortion. The plan can be documented in the form of a simple written note or more elaborate information stored on computer equipment."

Probable cause exists if it would be reasonable to seek the evidence in the place indicated in the affidavit. The crime contemplated by the warrant was transmitting a threatening communication with intent to extort. *See* 18 U.S.C. § 875(d). To find evidence of extortion, the government would have probable cause to search for and seize instrumentalities likely to have been used to facilitate the transmission. The magistrate judge could rightfully assume that there was a "fair probability" that such evidence could be contained on computers or storage devices found in Adjani's residence.

2. *Probable cause to search "Reinhold's computer"*

Having held that the affidavit supporting the warrant established probable cause to search for and seize instrumentalities of the extortion (including records, files and computers) in Adjani's residence, we turn to Reinhold's contention that the probable cause for the Adjani warrant did not extend so far as to permit a search of her property. We disagree. The agents, acting pursuant to a valid warrant to look for evidence of a computer-based crime, searched computers found in Adjani's residence and to which he had apparent access. That one of the computers actually belonged to Reinhold did not exempt it from being searched, especially given her association with Adjani and participation (however potentially innocuous) in some of his activities as documented in the agent's supporting affidavit. The officers therefore did not act unreasonably in searching Reinhold's computer as a source of the evidence targeted by the warrant.

Reinhold's argument that there was no probable cause to search her computer, a private and personal piece of property, because the warrant failed to list her as a "target, suspect, or co-conspirator" misunderstands Fourth Amendment jurisprudence. Although individuals undoubtedly have a high expectation of privacy in the files stored on their personal computers, we have never held that agents may establish probable cause to search only those items owned or possessed by the criminal suspect. The law is to the contrary. "The critical element in a reasonable search is not that the owner of the property is suspected of crime but that there is reasonable cause to believe that the specific 'things' to be searched for and seized are located on the property to which entry is sought." *Zurcher v. Stanford Daily*, 436 U.S. 547, 556 (1978).

In *United States v. Hay*, 231 F.3d 630 (9th Cir. 2000), the defendant made an argument similar to Reinhold's, challenging the district court's ruling allowing evidence of child pornography found on his computer to be used against him at trial. Hay claimed that the affidavit submitted by officers to obtain a warrant did not establish probable cause to engage in a search of Hay's computer because "there was no evidence that he fell within a class of persons likely to collect and traffic in child pornography because the affidavit does not indicate that he was a child molester, pedophile, or collector of child pornography and sets forth no evidence that he solicited, sold or transmitted child pornography." *Id.* at 635. We rejected Hay's challenge, holding that "it is well established that a location can be searched for evidence of a crime even if there is no probable cause to arrest the person at the location." *Id.*

Likewise, there was no need here for the agents expressly to claim in the affidavit that they wanted to arrest Reinhold, or even that Reinhold was suspected of any criminal activity. The government needed only to satisfy the magistrate judge that there was probable cause to believe that evidence of the crime in question—here extortion—could be found on computers accessible to Adjani in his home, including as it developed— Reinhold's computer. By setting forth the details of the extortion scheme and the instrumentalities of the crime, augmented by descriptions of Reinhold's involvement with Adjani, the government satisfied its burden. The magistrate judge therefore properly approved the warrant, which in turn encompassed all the computers found at Adjani's residence.

B. *Specificity Requirement*

The defendants argue that if the warrant did authorize a search that properly included Reinhold's computer, the warrant was fatally overbroad, justifying the district court's exclusion of the Reinhold emails. The government counters that the warrant satisfied the particularity standards articulated by this court, so exclusion was improper.

The Fourth Amendment's specificity requirement prevents officers from engaging in general, exploratory searches by limiting their discretion and providing specific guidance as to what can and cannot be searched and seized. However, the level of detail necessary in a warrant is related to the particular circumstances and the nature of the evidence sought. *See United States v. Spilotro*, 800 F.2d 959, 963 (9th Cir. 1986). Warrants which describe generic categories of items are not necessarily invalid if a more precise description of the items subject to seizure is not possible.

In determining whether a warrant is sufficiently particular, we consider one or more of the following factors:

> (1) whether probable cause exists to seize all items of a particular type described in the warrant; (2) whether the warrant sets out objective standards by which executing officers can differentiate items subject to seizure from those which are not; and (3) whether the government was able to describe the items more particularly in light of the information available to it at the time the warrant was issued.

Id. at 963.

Spilotro involved a warrant issued against individuals suspected of loan sharking and gambling activities. The warrant authorized "the seizure of address books, notebooks, notes, documents, records, assets, photographs, and other items and paraphernalia evidencing violations of the multiple criminal statutes listed." *Id*. at 964. It failed, however, to state the "precise identity, type, or contents of the records sought." *Id*. Partly because of this reason, we held that the warrant was not sufficiently specific to pass muster under the Fourth Amendment. More could have been done to tie the documents sought to the crimes alleged by, for example, stating that the police were searching for "records relating to loan sharking and gambling, including pay and collection sheets, lists of loan customers, loan accounts and telephone numbers." *Id.*

In contrast to *Spilotro*, the warrant to search Adjani's residence satisfied our specificity criteria. First, we have already held that there was probable cause to search the computers. As to the second factor, the warrant objectively described the items to be searched and seized with adequate specificity and sufficiently restricted the discretion of agents executing the search. The warrant affidavit began by limiting the search for evidence of a specific crime—transmitting threatening communications with intent to commit extortion. *See id.* ("Reference to a specific illegal activity can, in appropriate cases, provide substantive guidance for the officer's exercise of discretion in executing the warrant."); *see also United States v. Wong*, 334 F.3d 831, 837–38 (9th Cir. 2003) ("The specificity of the items listed in the warrant combined with the language ... directing officers to 'obtain data as it relates to this case' from the computers is sufficiently specific to focus the officer's search."). Further, unlike in *Spilotro*, the Adjani warrant provided the "precise identity" and nature of the items to be seized. For example, paragraph 5h of the warrant instructed agents to search for documents reflecting communications with three individuals or other employees of a specific company. Also, paragraph 5i authorized seizure of "any" evidence of travel but provided a specific, though not exhaustive, list of possible documents that fell within this category and temporally restricted the breadth of the search. Moreover, the extensive statement of probable cause in the affidavit detailed the alleged crime and Adjani's unlawful scheme.

With respect to the final *Spilotro* factor, we conclude that the government described the items to be searched and seized as particularly as could be reasonably expected given the nature of the crime and the evidence it then possessed. The Adjani warrant "described in great detail the items one commonly expects to find on premises used for the criminal activities in question." *Spilotro*, 800 F.2d at 964.

Center Art Galleries–Hawaii, Inc. v. United States, 875 F.2d 747 (9th Cir. 1989), the principal case defendants rely upon in making their overbreadth argument, is distinguishable. In that case, we held that a warrant providing for "the almost unrestricted seizure of items which are 'evidence of violations of federal criminal law' without describing the specific crimes suspected is constitutionally inadequate." *Id.* at 750. In contrast, the government here did describe at some length both the nature of and the means of committing the crime. Further, unlike in *Center Art Galleries*, the affidavit was expressly incorporated into the warrant. *Id.* ("An affidavit can cure the overbreadth of a warrant if the affidavit is 'attached to and incorporated by reference in' the warrant.")

We understand the heightened specificity concerns in the computer context, given the vast amount of data they can store. As the defendants urge, the warrant arguably might have provided for a "less invasive search of Adjani's email 'inbox' and 'outbox' for the addressees specifically cited in the warrant, as opposed to the wholesale search of the contents of all emails purportedly looking for evidence 'reflecting' communications with those individuals." Avoiding that kind of specificity and limitation was not unreasonable under the circumstances here, however. To require such a pinpointed computer search, restricting the search to an email program or to specific search terms, would likely have failed to cast a sufficiently wide net to capture the evidence sought. Moreover, agents are limited by the longstanding principle that a duly issued warrant, even one with a thorough affidavit, may not be used to engage in a general, exploratory search.

Computer files are easy to disguise or rename, and were we to limit the warrant to such a specific search protocol, much evidence could escape discovery simply because of Adjani's (or Reinhold's) labeling of the files documenting Adjani's criminal activity. The government should not be required to trust the suspect's self-labeling when executing a warrant.

C. Scope of the Warrant

Even assuming that the warrant was supported by probable cause and was adequately specific such that a search of Reinhold's computer and emails were permissible, Reinhold argues that the actual emails sought to be introduced into evidence were outside the scope of the warrant. Again, we disagree.

The three seized emails the government seeks to admit clearly fall within the scope of paragraph 5h of the warrant affidavit, authorizing seizure of "records, documents and materials which reflect communications with Christopher Mallick, Clay Andrews, Joel Hall or other employees or officers of Paycom or Epoch," which are relevant evidence of violations of 18 U.S.C. § 875(d). Each email specifically refers to communication with Joel Hall or one of the stated companies (identifying them by name).[8] Reinhold's argument that the term "reflect communications with" should be read narrowly to cover only those emails sent between one of the named Paycom employees and Adjani is nonsensical. The government already had the emails sent between the victims of the extortion and Adjani—obtained from the victims themselves. The purpose of the warrant was to obtain further and corroborating evidence of the extortion scheme and Adjani's criminal intent in communicating with the victims, and the three emails plainly "reflect" the relevant communications specified in paragraph 5h.

To the extent Reinhold argues that the emails were outside the scope of the warrant because they implicated her in the crime and supported a charge of conspiracy to commit extortion (a crime not specifically men-

---

8. The first email, sent from Adjani to Reinhold, states, in relevant part, "I sent Joel the message." The second, a reply from Reinhold, states, "I thought that you were going to wait until after today if they don't respond to send Joel an email?" The third, another email from Reinhold to Adjani, states, "I assume you have read Joel's fax by now. Funny or sucky thing is that I had ran out the door just 3 minutes before he sent that to go to a payphone to call Epoch.... A girl answered and I asked for Joel Hall."

tioned in the warrant), we reject the argument. There is no rule, and Reinhold points to no case law suggesting otherwise, that evidence turned up while officers are rightfully searching a location under a properly issued warrant must be excluded simply because the evidence found may support charges for a related crime (or against a suspect) not expressly contemplated in the warrant.

In *United States v. Beusch*, 596 F.2d 871 (9th Cir. 1979), the defendants argued that certain seized items, including two ledgers and a file, should be excluded because they contained information unrelated to the suspect identified in the warrant. The defendants claimed that the officers impermissibly engaged in a general search by not segregating out those items implicating a third individual in the crime. We rejected this proposition and refused to impose the burden of segregation on the police. In so doing we held,

> All three items admittedly contained information seizable under the terms of the warrant and they therefore met the particularity requirement of the Fourth Amendment. As long as an item appears, at the time of the search, to contain evidence reasonably related to the purposes of the search, there is no reason absent some other Fourth Amendment violation to suppress it. The fact that an item seized happens to contain other incriminating information not covered by the terms of the warrant does not compel its suppression, either in whole or in part. In so holding we are careful to point out that we are discussing single files and single ledgers, i.e., single items which, though theoretically separable, in fact constitute one volume or file folder.

Id. at 877. *Beusch* is analogous to the situation at hand. The agents were rightfully searching Reinhold's computer for evidence of Adjani's crime of extortion. They were looking in Reinhold's email program when they came across information that was both related to the purposes of their search and implicated Reinhold in the crime. That the evidence could now support a new charge against a new (but already identified) person does not compel its suppression. On these facts, we disagree with the district court's conclusion that the officers should have obtained a new search warrant when they came across the incriminating emails. In so concluding, we are careful to note that in this case the evidence discovered was clearly related to the crime referred to in the warrant. We need not decide to what extent the government would be able to introduce evidence discovered that the police knew, at the time of discovery, was not related to the crime cited in the warrant.

III. Conclusion

The Fourth Amendment incorporates a great many specific protections against unreasonable searches and seizures. The contours of these protections in the context of computer searches pose difficult questions. Computers are simultaneously file cabinets (with millions of files) and locked desk drawers; they can be repositories of innocent and deeply personal information, but also of evidence of crimes. The former must be protected, the latter discovered. As society grows ever more reliant on computers as a means of storing data and communicating, courts will be called upon to analyze novel legal issues and develop new rules within our well established Fourth Amendment jurisprudence. The fact of an increasingly technological world is not lost upon us as we consider the proper balance to strike between protecting an individual's right to privacy and ensuring that the government is able to prosecute suspected criminals effectively. In this era of rapid change, we are mindful of Justice Brandeis's worry in *Olmstead v. United States,*

> Ways may some day be developed by which the Government, without removing papers from secret drawers, can reproduce them in court, and by which it will be enabled to expose to a jury the most intimate occurrences of the home. Can it be that the Constitution affords no protection against such invasions of individual security?

277 U.S. 438, 474 (1928) (Brandeis, J., dissenting).

We do not now have occasion to address the myriad complex issues raised in deciding when a court should exclude evidence found on a computer, but are satisfied that the agents in this case acted properly in searching Reinhold's computer and seizing the emails in question here. The district court erred in excluding these emails. Therefore, the district court's ruling on the motion to suppress is reversed, and this matter is remanded for further proceedings consistent with this opinion.

NOTES AND QUESTIONS

1. *Particularity and computer search warrants.* Most computer warrants are executed in two stages. First, the computer hardware is taken away; second, the computers are searched for electronic evidence. The physical search comes first and the electronic search comes second. Should the particularity requirement focus on the physical search stage, the electronic search stage, or both? For example, imagine a warrant states with exquisite particularity exactly what kinds of computer hardware will be seized at the first stage but gives no guidance on the evidence the computer may contain. Alternatively, imagine a warrant names the exact computer file that agents will look for at the second stage, but it doesn't say anything about what computers the agents plan to remove at the place to be searched. Are either of these warrants sufficiently particular?

2. In United States v. Riccardi, 405 F.3d 852 (10th Cir. 2005), police executed a warrant to search for and seize computers in a child pornography investigation. The warrant authorized investigators to search the defendant's home and seize his computer as well as:

> all electronic and magnetic media stored therein, together with all storage devises [sic], internal or external to the computer or computer system, including but not limited to floppy disks, diskettes, hard disks, magnetic tapes, removable media drives, optical media such as CD–ROM, printers, modems, and any other electronic or magnetic devises used as a peripher-

al to the computer or computer system, and all electronic media stored within such devises.

The police executed the warrant, seized the defendant's home computer, and later searched it and found images of child pornography. In an opinion by Judge McConnell, the Tenth Circuit held that the warrant violated the Fourth Amendment because it was not sufficiently particular. According to the Judge McConnell, "warrants for computer searches must affirmatively limit the search to evidence of specific federal crimes or specific types of material." *Id.* at 862.

> The warrant in this case was not limited to any particular files, or to any particular federal crime. * * * By its terms, the warrant thus permitted the officers to search for anything—from child pornography to tax returns to private correspondence. It seemed to authorize precisely the kind of wide-ranging exploratory search that the Framers intended to prohibit.

Id. at 862–63.

Despite this defect, the court admitted the evidence because the officers had relied on the warrant in good faith:

> In determining whether the good-faith exception should apply in a particular case, the inquiry is confined to the objectively ascertainable question whether a reasonably well trained officer would have known that the search was illegal despite the magistrate's authorization. In answering this question, the court should consider all of the circumstances and assume that the executing officers have a reasonable knowledge of what the law prohibits. Even if the court finds the warrant to be facially invalid—as was the case here—it must also review the text of the warrant and the circumstances of the search to ascertain whether the agents might have reasonably presumed it to be valid.

> In this case, upon finding thumbnail files of child pornography on Mr. Riccardi's computer, Agent Finch suspended his search and asked Detective Dickey if they needed a more specific warrant. Detective Dickey consulted with a prosecutor who gave assurances that an additional warrant was not required. Detective Dickey then informed Agent Finch that it would "likely be okay" and that the warrant covered the child pornography found on the computer.

> The district court noted the following factors in support of applying the *Leon* exception: (1) the affidavit limited the search to child pornography; (2) the officers executing the warrant were involved in the investigation throughout, and one of the executing officers actually wrote the affidavit to support the application; (3) Agent Finch stopped to ask if the warrant was sufficient and received assurances from Detective Dickey; (4) the search methodology was limited to finding child pornography; and (5) investigators seized only evidence relevant to the crimes identified in the affidavit.

> These factors, combined with the fact that, at Agent Finch's request, Detective Dickey called the prosecutor for assurances, persuade us that the district court was correct in finding that the *Leon* exception to the exclusionary rule applied and that the evidence obtained from the hard

drive need not have been suppressed. The officers remained within the terms of the warrant as well as the affidavit, and did not conduct a "fishing expedition" beyond the scope of the authorized investigation. They did not search for, or seize, any materials for which probable cause had not been shown. By consulting the prosecutor, they showed their good faith in compliance with constitutional requirements. Nor do we think the defect in the warrant was so flagrant or obvious that the executing officers could not reasonably presume it to be valid.

Id. at 863–64.

Judge McConnell's opinion in *Riccardi* suggests that naming the crimes or types of material sought can limit the scope of the subsequent electronic search. But will such limitations actually limit the scope of the search? Imagine that FBI agents seize a computer and obtain a warrant to search it for "evidence of violations of 18 U.S.C. § 1030." Does that limitation provide real guidance that will limit the scope of the electronic search? Does it stop investigators from conducting a sweeping, comprehensive search of a computer's hard drive? Does naming the crime or material sought limit the search at the initial physical search stage at all?

3.   In Davis v. Gracey, 111 F.3d 1472 (10th Cir. 1997), agents conducting an obscenity investigation obtained a warrant permitting the seizure of "equipment pertaining to the distribution or display of pornographic material in violation of state obscenity laws." Investigators seized two computer servers used to provide digital images and e-mail for about 2,000 subscribers; the servers stored about 150,000 e-mails and about 500 megabytes of software. The owner of the computer and several customers filed a civil suit, claiming that the warrant was insufficiently particular. The Tenth Circuit disagreed:

> The description given in the warrant was sufficient to provide a meaningful limitation on the search, and was far narrower than those we have found lacking sufficient particularity. * * * The warrant here was confined to that equipment pertaining to the distribution or display of pornographic material. This description included only that equipment directly connected to the suspected criminal activity, not a wide range of equipment used for purposes unrelated to the suspected criminal activity. Nor did it encompass all the equipment one might expect to find at a legitimate business. Furthermore, the criminal activity referenced in the warrant was very narrow, providing a ready guide to determine if a given item was one that might be the instrument or evidence of the criminal activity. The warrant was not overbroad.

Id. at 1479.

4.   *Probable cause and digital evidence.* In United States v. Gourde, 440 F.3d 1065 (9th Cir. 2006) (en banc), an undercover FBI agent discovered a website called "Lolitagurls.com." According to the agent, the site contained images of nude and partially-dressed girls, some prepubescent, along with text promising pictures of young girls 12–17 to those who paid the subscription fee of $19.95 per month. The agent purchased a subscription and confirmed that the site hosted hundreds of images of child pornography. The FBI seized the server that hosted the website and obtained the list of e-mail addresses used

by paid subscribers to the site. The FBI then obtained a list of customers associated with these e-mail addresses from Lancelot Security, a credit card processing company that handled credit card processing and access control for Lolitagurls.com.

The FBI later executed warrants at the homes of many of the subscribers. The sole basis for the warrants was the paid subscription with the website. Micah Gourde was a subscriber to Lolitagurls.com for several months, and a search of his home pursuant to a warrant led to the seizure of his computer and the discovery of images of child pornography inside it. Gourde challenged the warrant on the ground that his membership with the website did not establish probable cause to search his home. The en banc Ninth Circuit rejected this argument in an opinion by Judge McKeown:

> Gourde subscribed to Lolitagurls.com for over two months, from November 2001 to January 2002. As a paying member, Gourde had unlimited access to hundreds of illegal images. He clearly had the means to receive and possess images in violation of 18 U.S.C. § 2252. But more importantly, Gourde's status as a member manifested his intention and desire to obtain illegal images.

> Membership is both a small step and a giant leap. To become a member requires what are at first glance little, easy steps. It was easy for Gourde to submit his home address, email address and credit card data, and he consented to have $19.95 deducted from his credit card every month. But these steps, however easy, only could have been intentional and were not insignificant. Gourde could not have become a member by accident or by a mere click of a button. This reality is perhaps easier to see by comparing Gourde to other archetypical visitors to the site. Gourde was not an accidental browser, such as a student who came across the site after "Googling" the term "Lolita" while researching the Internet for a term paper on Nabokov's book. Nor was Gourde someone who took advantage of the free tour but, after viewing the site, balked at taking the active steps necessary to become a member and gain unlimited access to images of child pornography. Gourde is different still from a person who actually mustered the money and nerve to become a member but, the next morning, suffered buyer's remorse or a belated fear of prosecution and cancelled his subscription. Instead, Gourde became a member and never looked back—his membership ended because the FBI shut down the site. The affidavit left little doubt that Gourde had paid to obtain unlimited access to images of child pornography knowingly and willingly, and not involuntary, unwittingly, or even passively. With evidence from Lancelot Security, the FBI linked the email user—"gilbert_95@yahoo. com," a known subscriber to Lolitagurls.com—to Gourde and to his home address in Castle Rock, Washington.

> Having paid for multi-month access to a child pornography site, Gourde was also stuck with the near certainty that his computer would contain evidence of a crime had he received or downloaded images in violation of § 2252. Thanks to the long memory of computers, any evidence of a crime was almost certainly still on his computer, even if he had tried to delete the images. FBI computer experts, cited in the affidavit, stated that "even

if graphic image files have been deleted these files can easily be restored." In other words, his computer would contain at least the digital footprint of the images. It was unlikely that evidence of a crime would have been stale or missing, as less than four months had elapsed between the closing of the Lolitagurls.com website and the execution of the search warrant.

Given this triad of solid facts—the site had illegal images, Gourde intended to have and wanted access to these images, and these images were almost certainly retrievable from his computer if he had ever received or downloaded them—the only inference the magistrate judge needed to make to find probable cause was that there was a "fair probability" Gourde had, in fact, received or downloaded images.

Here, the reasonable inference that Gourde had received or downloaded images easily meets the "fair probability" test. It neither strains logic nor defies common sense to conclude, based on the totality of these circumstances, that someone who paid for access for two months to a website that actually purveyed child pornography probably had viewed or downloaded such images onto his computer. Together these facts form the basis of the totality-of-the-circumstances analysis that informs the probable cause determination. Employing the principles of *Gates*—practicality, common sense, a fluid and nontechnical conception of probable cause, and deference to the magistrate's determination—we conclude that the search warrant was supported by probable cause.

Id. at 1070–71. Judge Kleinfeld dissented:

In my view, the majority errs in concluding that there was probable cause for a search because its inferences depend on unarticulated assumptions that do not make sense. The majority implicitly assumes that a person who likes something probably possesses it, even if possession is against the law.

The importance of this case is considerable because, for most people, their computers are their most private spaces. People commonly talk about the bedroom as a very private space, yet when they have parties, all the guests—including perfect strangers—are invited to toss their coats on the bed. But if one of those guests is caught exploring the host's computer, that will be his last invitation.

There are just too many secrets on people's computers, most legal, some embarrassing, and some potentially tragic in their implications, for loose liberality in allowing search warrants. Emails and history links may show that someone is ordering medication for a disease being kept secret even from family members. Or they may show that someone's child is being counseled by parents for a serious problem that is none of anyone else's business. Or a married mother of three may be carrying on a steamy email correspondence with an old high school boyfriend. Or an otherwise respectable, middle-aged gentleman may be looking at dirty pictures. Just as a conscientious public official may be hounded out of office because a party guest found a homosexual magazine when she went to the bathroom at his house, people's lives may be ruined because of legal but embarrassing materials found on their computers. And, in all but the largest metropolitan areas, it really does not matter whether any formal charges ensue—if the police or other visitors find the material, it will be all over town and hinted at in the newspaper within a few days.

Nor are secrets the only problem. Warrants ordinarily direct seizure, not just search, and computers are often shared by family members. Seizure of a shared family computer may, though unrelated to the law enforcement purpose, effectively confiscate a professor's book, a student's almost completed Ph.D. thesis, or a business's accounts payable and receivable. People cannot get their legitimate work done if their computer is at the police station because of someone else's suspected child pornography downloads. Sex with children is so disgusting to most of us that we may be too liberal in allowing searches when the government investigates child pornography cases. The privacy of people's computers is too important to let it be eroded by sexual disgust.

* * *

The reason [Gourde] could not be assumed to possess child pornography is that possession of child pornography is a very serious crime and the affidavit did not say he had downloaded any. He could use the site to look at child pornography without downloading it, a reasonable assumption in the absence of evidence that he had downloaded images. Common sense suggests that everyone, pervert or not, has the desire to stay out of jail. The ordinary desire to stay out of jail is a factor that must be considered in the totality of circumstances. It would be irrational to assume that an individual is indifferent between subjecting himself to criminal sanctions and avoiding them, when he can attain his object while avoiding them. To commit the crime for which the warrant sought evidence, one has to do something more than look: he must ship, produce, or at the least knowingly possess. The two child pornography statutes at issue do not say that *viewing* child pornography is a crime. Congress could perhaps make it a crime to pay to view such images, but it did not.

Id. at 1077–79. Judge Kleinfeld's argument hinges on a purported distinction between viewing and possessing child pornography. Is Judge Kleinfeld interpreting the law correctly? Does the validity of the warrant in *Gourde* hinge on what it means to "possess" digital images?

More broadly, consider the inferences a court must draw before concluding that membership in a website or online group connected to child pornography creates probable cause to search a member's home for contraband images. Satisfying this burden requires an explicit or implicit assessment of the following questions:

A. How likely is it that the defendant is the one who controlled the account when it was used to join the group?

B. How likely is it that the defendant signed up for the service with the intent to obtain illegal images?

C. How likely is it that the defendant received the images?

D. How likely is it that the defendant initially received the images at home?

E.   How likely is it that the images are currently present in the home? Are judges well-equipped to answer these questions?

5.   Investigators often try to establish probable cause to search a home for evidence of computer crimes by tracing Internet Protocol (IP) addresses. In many cases, the investigators collect evidence by linking IP addresses to accounts and then accounts to physical addresses.

The basic technology of the Internet makes IP addresses an essential tool for tracing Internet activity. Whenever a user connects to the Internet, the service provider that provides the connection will assign the user a series of numbers known as an IP address that serves as the unique identifying address of his computer for that session (and in some cases, for all of that user's sessions). As a general matter, communications sent by or to that user across the Internet will contain that IP address. This means that when investigators know the IP address used in a session of Internet activity that is linked to a crime, they will first identify the service provider known to control the block of IP addresses that includes that specific address.

When investigators know that a particular IP address was used in criminal activity, they can contact the owner/operator of the server that controls the address and try to find out more information. For example, if an IP address belongs to a specific ISP, the ISP system administrator may have business records that indicate what account controlled that address when it was used in criminal activity. If the account is associated with a physical address—in the case of a home user, for example, the home address used for billing purposes—investigators can then focus their suspicion on that physical location.

6.   *Probable cause, wireless networks, and wardriving.* Can investigators reliably trace IP addresses to physical locations when individuals connect to the Internet over a wireless network? Many home users host wireless access points that are left unsecured. Any individual within range of the access point can hop on the Internet using the IP address assigned to the home user.

Unsecured wireless access provides an increasingly popular way to hide criminal activity. One technique is "wardriving," a term for traveling around by car in search of open access points. *See* Brendan I. Koerner, *License to Wardrive*, Legal Affairs, May/June 2005, at 68. A wrongdoer may drive around a neighborhood, find an unsecured wireless access point, and commit crimes ranging from hacking to wire fraud from the comfort of his car parked nearby. When he is done, he can drive away. Weeks or even months later, the police will trace the criminal activity to the account associated with the open wireless network. When they arrive to execute a warrant, however, they will find no evidence. All of the evidence will have vanished from the scene when the criminal drove away weeks before, and the police may end up executing the warrant at the home of an entirely innocent individual. *See* Seth Schiesel, *Growth of Wireless Internet Opens New Path for Thieves*, N.Y. Times, March 19, 2005; Alex Leary, *Wi–Fi Cloaks A New Brand of Intruder*, St. Petersburg Times, July 4, 2005.

The popularity of unsecured wireless networks raises two problems for investigators. The first is practical: How can investigators trace a crime back to its source when the wrongdoer has disguised his identity by using an unsecured wireless access point? The second is legal: How does the possibility that a criminal will have disguised his identity by using another person's wireless access point change what the government must show to establish probable cause to search a home for evidence of crime? When should agents consider the possibility that evidence of a crime that traces back to a home was really the work of a stranger who hopped on to the home's unsecured wireless Internet connection?

7. *Staleness.* One issue that often arises in computer crime cases is the "staleness" of the government's probable cause. Digital evidence may be present one day but erased, deleted, or removed by the next. To establish probable cause, the government must show probable cause to believe evidence of crime exists at the place to be searched at the time the warrant is issued, not just at the time the crime was committed. If too much time has elapsed after the relevant time period of the government's evidence, that evidence may become stale and may no longer satisfy the probable cause standard.

How should courts address staleness concerns in the context of digital evidence? In child pornography cases, several courts have taken judicial notice of the practices of child pornography collectors. Judge Munson offered the following summary in United States v. Lamb, 945 F.Supp. 441 (N.D.N.Y. 1996):

> The observation that images of child pornography are likely to be hoarded by persons interested in those materials in the privacy of their homes is supported by common sense and the cases. Since the materials are illegal to distribute and possess, initial collection is difficult. Having succeeded in obtaining images, collectors are unlikely to quickly destroy them. Because of their illegality and the imprimatur of severe social stigma such images carry, collectors will want to secret them in secure places, like a private residence. This proposition is not novel in either state or federal court: pedophiles, preferential child molesters, and child pornography collectors maintain their materials for significant periods of time.

Id. at 460 (citations omitted). Judge Munson then added an important caveat:

> Of course, before the presumption that pedophiles, preferential child molesters, or child pornography collectors hoard their materials for extended periods can be applied, the judicial officer scrutinizing the warrant application must have sufficient information from which it can be concluded that the target falls within these categories. The Ninth Circuit rejected the application of this presumption in United States v. Weber, 923 F.2d 1338 (9th Cir. 1990). In *Weber*, the facts alleged in the affidavit in support of the warrant were that the suspect made one order solicited by the government for child pornography which was never delivered, and the suspect had been sent advertising material that was described by the customs agent who intercepted it as "apparently child pornography" two years earlier. From this sparse information, the Ninth Circuit ruled that there was insufficient information to determine whether the target of the search was a pedophile, child molester, or child pornography collector. Without such information, the expert opinion that such people maintain large collections of the illegal materials in their

homes was of little value in determining whether evidence of crime would be located at the suspect's home.

Id. at 460–61.

How should courts deal with staleness concerns in other types of computer crime cases? Imagine Sarah uses her personal, home computer to hack into a sensitive government server, and that one year later the police develop reason to believe Sarah was the intruder. The police apply for a warrant to search Sarah's house. What are the chances that Sarah's computer will continue to store evidence of the crime a year after the intrusion? Does evidence stay on a computer forever?

2. THE PHYSICAL SEARCH STAGE

The first stage of executing a warrant to search and seize computers is the physical search stage. At this stage, the government enters the physical place to be searched and removes the computers from the site for subsequent analysis. The key question is, what can the agents seize? Can the agents remove all the computers and search them off-site? What restrictions are there on the seizure of computers and removal to an off-site location for a subsequent electronic search?

UNITED STATES v. HILL

United States Court of Appeals for the Ninth Circuit, 2006.
459 F.3d 966.

FISHER, CIRCUIT JUDGE.

Justin Hill conditionally pled guilty to possession of child pornography subject to his challenge to the admission of evidence that he contends was seized in violation of the Fourth Amendment. We must * * * decide whether it was reasonable under the Fourth Amendment for the police to take all of Hill's computer storage media from his home (they did not find his computer) so they could conduct their search offsite in a police laboratory, rather than carrying out the search onsite and taking only whatever evidence of child pornography they might find.

As we recently discussed in *United States v. Adjani*, 452 F.3d 1140 (9th Cir. 2006), because computers typically contain so much information beyond the scope of the criminal investigation, computer-related searches can raise difficult Fourth Amendment issues different from those encountered when searching paper files. Judge Kozinski, sitting as the district court in this case, thoughtfully addressed some of these issues in a published opinion upholding the validity of the search warrant and its execution. *United States v. Hill*, 322 F. Supp.2d 1081, 1092 (C.D.Cal. 2004). We affirm the district court's ruling in most but not all respects for the reasons Judge Kozinski stated; to the extent we do agree with that reasoning, we adopt it verbatim in this opinion. In sum, we affirm the district court's denial of the defendant's motion to suppress evidence.

I.

A computer technician was repairing defendant's computer when she discovered what she believed to be child pornography. She called Long Beach police, and the detective who took the call obtained a search warrant from a judge of the Long Beach Superior Court. The warrant authorized a search of the computer repair store and seizure of the computer, any work orders relating to the computer, all storage media belonging to either the computer or the individual identifying himself as defendant at the location, and all sexually explicit images depicting minors contained in the storage media. By the time the detective arrived at the store to execute the warrant, defendant had picked up his computer. The detective submitted an affidavit, which included the computer technician's sworn statement describing the images. On the basis of this affidavit, the officer obtained a second warrant, this one directed at defendant's home, authorizing seizure of the same items.

Officers executed the search warrant but did not find the computer in defendant's apartment.[1] In what appeared to be defendant's bedroom, they found and seized computer storage media, specifically: 22 5.25–inch floppy disks, two CD–ROMs, 124 3.5–inch floppy disks and six zip disks. Two of the zip disks were eventually determined to contain images of child pornography; officers also seized other evidence consistent with the warrant. Defendant was subsequently charged with one count of possession of child pornography, in violation of 18 U.S.C. § 2252A(a)(5)(B).

II.

The defendant argues that the search warrant was overbroad because it authorized the officers to seize and remove from his home his computer and storage media without first determining whether they actually contained child pornography.

The warrant here commanded the officers to search for and seize: "1) An IBM 'clone' medium tower personal computer . . . 3) All storage media belonging to either item #1 or the individual identifying himself as defendant at the location. 4) All sexually explicit images depicting minors contained in item #3." Defendant argues the warrant was overbroad because it authorized seizure of storage media whether or not they contained child pornography. He suggests it should have authorized seizure only of media containing child pornography. But it is impossible to tell what a computer storage medium contains just by looking at it. Rather, one has to examine it electronically, using a computer that is running the appropriate operating system, hardware and software. The police had no assurance they would find such a computer at the scene— nor did they, for that matter—or that, if they found one, they could bypass any security measures and operate it.

Defendant suggests that the police could have brought their own laptop computer: Having probable cause to seize only computer storage

---

1. Or anywhere else: The computer was never found.

media that contained certain types of files, the police should have been required to bring with them the equipment necessary to separate the sheep from the goats. Defendant's argument raises an important question about how police must execute seizures pursuant to a warrant. Because seizable materials are seldom found neatly separated from their non-seizable counterparts, how much separating must police do at the scene to avoid taking items that are neither contraband nor evidence of criminal activity?

As always under the Fourth Amendment, the standard is reasonableness. To take an extreme example, if police have probable cause to seize business records, the warrant could not authorize seizure of every piece of paper on the premises on the theory that the police conducting the search might not know how to read.

The court concludes that the police were not required to bring with them equipment capable of reading computer storage media and an officer competent to operate it. Doing so would have posed significant technical problems and made the search more intrusive. To ensure that they could access any electronic storage medium they might find at the scene, police would have needed far more than an ordinary laptop computer. Because computers in common use run a variety of operating systems—various versions or flavors of Windows, Mac OS and Linux, to name only the most common—police would have had to bring with them a computer (or computers) equipped to read not only all of the major media types, but also files encoded by all major operating systems. Because operating systems, media types, file systems and file types are continually evolving, police departments would frequently have to modify their computers to keep them up-to-date. This would not be an insuperable obstacle for larger police departments and federal law enforcement agencies, but it would pose a significant burden on smaller agencies.

Even if the police were to bring with them a properly equipped computer, and someone competent to operate it, using it would pose two significant problems. First, there is a serious risk that the police might damage the storage medium or compromise the integrity of the evidence by attempting to access the data at the scene. As everyone who has accidentally erased a computer file knows, it is fairly easy to make mistakes when operating computer equipment, especially equipment one is not intimately familiar with. The risk that the officer trying to read the suspect's storage medium on the police laptop will make a wrong move and erase what is on the disk is not trivial. Even if the officer executes his task flawlessly, there might be a power failure or equipment malfunction that could affect the contents of the medium being searched. For that reason, experts will make a back-up copy of the medium before they start manipulating its contents. Various other technical problems might arise; without the necessary tools and expertise to deal with them, any effort to read computer files at the scene is fraught with difficulty and risk.

Second, the process of searching the files at the scene can take a long time. To be certain that the medium in question does not contain any seizable material, the officers would have to examine every one of what may be thousands of files on a disk—a process that could take many hours and perhaps days. Taking that much time to conduct the search would not only impose a significant and unjustified burden on police resources, it would also make the search more intrusive. Police would have to be present on the suspect's premises while the search was in progress, and this would necessarily interfere with the suspect's access to his home or business. If the search took hours or days, the intrusion would continue for that entire period, compromising the Fourth Amendment value of making police searches as brief and non-intrusive as possible.

We agree with the district court that under the circumstances here, the warrant was not fatally defective in failing to require an onsite search and isolation of child pornography before removing storage media wholesale. That does not mean, however, that the government has an automatic blank check when seeking or executing warrants in computer-related searches. Although computer technology may in theory justify blanket seizures for the reasons discussed above, the government must still demonstrate to the magistrate factually why such a broad search and seizure authority is reasonable in the case at hand. There may well be situations where the government has no basis for believing that a computer search would involve the kind of technological problems that would make an immediate onsite search and selective removal of relevant evidence impracticable. Thus, there must be some threshold showing before the government may seize the haystack to look for the needle.

Our cases illustrate this principle. In *United States v. Hay*, 231 F.3d 630 (9th Cir. 2000), for example, we held permissible a "generic classification" authorizing seizure of an "entire computer system and virtually every document in the defendant's possession without referencing child pornography or any particular offense conduct" because, although officers knew that a party had sent 19 images of child pornography directly to the defendant's computer, they had no way of knowing where the images were stored. Similarly *United States v. Lacy*, 119 F.3d 742 (9th Cir. 1997), allowed "blanket seizure" of the defendant's entire computer system. We reasoned that no more specific description of the computer equipment sought was possible, because the agents did not know whether the images were stored on the hard drive or on one or more of the defendant's many computer disks.

By contrast, although the warrant in this case authorized a wholesale seizure, the supporting affidavit did not explain why such a seizure was necessary. *See* U.S. Dep't of Justice, Searching and Seizing Computers and Obtaining Electronic Evidence in Criminal Investigations 43, 69 (July 2002) (recommending that "if agents expect that they may need to seize a personal computer and search it off-site to recover the relevant evidence, the affidavit should explain this expectation and its basis to the magistrate judge. The affidavit should inform the court of the practical limitations of conducting an on-site search, and should articulate the plan to remove the entire computer from the site if it becomes necessary.").[11]

We do not approve of issuing warrants authorizing blanket removal of all computer storage media for later examination when there is no affidavit giving a reasonable explanation, such as that provided in *Hay* and *Lacy*, as to why a wholesale seizure is necessary. Without such individualized justification being presented to the magistrate, we cannot be sure that the judge was aware of the officers' intent and the technological limitations meriting the indiscriminate seizure—and thus was intelligently able to exercise the court's oversight function. An explanatory statement in the affidavit also assures us that the officers could not reasonably describe the objects of their search with more specificity. Accordingly, we hold that the warrant here was overbroad in authorizing a blanket seizure in the absence of an explanatory supporting affidavit, which would have documented the informed endorsement of the neutral magistrate.

Nonetheless, * * * we conclude that suppression of the evidence of child pornography found on the defendant's seized zip disks is not an appropriate remedy. The pornographic images from the defendant's zip disks that he sought to exclude as evidence at trial was seized and retained lawfully because described in and therefore taken pursuant to the valid search warrant. As we have discussed above, the officers' wholesale seizure was flawed here because they failed to justify it to the magistrate, not because they acted unreasonably or improperly in executing the warrant. Because the officers were motivated by considerations of practicality rather than by a desire to engage in indiscriminate 'fishing,' we cannot say that the officers so abused the warrant's authority that the otherwise valid warrant was transformed into a general one, thereby requiring all fruits to be suppressed.

Therefore, we hold that the district court properly admitted the evidence of child pornography found on the defendant's computer storage media notwithstanding the lack of a sufficiently detailed supporting affidavit describing the need for wholesale seizure of such media.

III.   Conclusion

We realize that judicial decisions regarding the application of the Fourth Amendment to computer-related searches may be of limited longevity. Technology is rapidly evolving and the concept of what is reasonable for Fourth Amendment purposes will likewise have to evolve. New technology may become readily accessible, for example, to enable more efficient or pinpointed searches of computer data, or to facilitate onsite searches. If so, we may be called upon to reexamine the technological rationales that underpin our Fourth Amendment jurisprudence in this technology-sensitive area of the law.

---

11. In retrospect, it is clear that not all the storage media needed to be seized as evidence of criminal activity; of the 154 disks seized, only two zip disks contained lascivious images of children. There is no evidence or allegation that the officers knew of this result before they searched and seized.

NOTES AND QUESTIONS

1. The Justice Department manual on Searching and Seizing Computers that is cited in *Hill* recommends the following "sample language" that agents can insert into affidavits to explicitly permit the seizure and removal of computers at the physical search stage:

> Based upon my training and experience and information related to me by agents and others involved in the forensic examination of computers, I know that computer data can be stored on a variety of systems and storage devices including hard disk drives, floppy disks, compact disks, magnetic tapes and memory chips. I also know that during the search of the premises it is not always possible to search computer equipment and storage devices for data for a number of reasons, including the following:

> a. Searching computer systems is a highly technical process which requires specific expertise and specialized equipment. * * *

> b. Searching computer systems requires the use of precise, scientific procedures which are designed to maintain the integrity of the evidence and to recover "hidden," erased, compressed, encrypted or password-protected data. * * *

> c. The volume of data stored on many computer systems and storage devices will typically be so large that it will be highly impractical to search for data during the execution of the physical search of the premises. * * *

> d. Computer users can attempt to conceal data within computer equipment and storage devices through a number of methods, including the use of innocuous or misleading filenames and extensions. * * * Therefore, a substantial amount of time is necessary to extract and sort through data that is concealed or encrypted to determine whether it is evidence, contraband or instrumentalities of a crime.

> In light of these concerns, your affiant hereby requests the Court's permission to seize the computer hardware (and associated peripherals) that are believed to contain some or all of the evidence described in the warrant, and to conduct an off-site search of the hardware for the evidence described, if, upon arriving at the scene, the agents executing the search conclude that it would be impractical to search the computer hardware on-site for this evidence.

U.S. Dep't of Justice, *Searching and Seizing Computers and Obtaining Electronic Evidence in Criminal Investigations*, Appendix F (July 2002).

If an agent inserts this form language into an affidavit, does that satisfy *Hill*? If so, how much does the *Hill* court's requirement of an explanation in the affidavit actually matter?

2. Lower courts have concluded that search warrants give the police broad authority to seize computers and search them later offsite. An early example is United States v. Schandl, 947 F.2d 462 (11th Cir. 1991). In *Schandl*, investigators seized paper documents and computer discs at the suspect's home and office as part of an investigation into tax evasion. The

defendant later claimed that the Fourth Amendment required investigators to search through the documents and papers onsite rather than seize them and search them offsite. The Eleventh Circuit rejected the defendant's argument:

> It was inevitable that some irrelevant materials would be seized as agents searched through numerous documents for evidence of tax evasion and failure to file, crimes that are generally only detected through the careful analysis and synthesis of a large number of documents. Indeed, it might have been far more disruptive had the agents made a thorough search of each individual document and computer disc before removing it from Schandl's home and office. To insist on such a practice would substantially increase the time required to conduct the search, thereby aggravating the intrusiveness of the search.

Id. at 465–66.

3. If a warrant does not expressly state that it permits the seizure of computers, should courts nonetheless allow investigators to seize computers they come across during the search if they believe the computers may contain evidence described in the warrant? Imagine investigators execute a search for particular "documents" or "papers," and during the search they come across a computer. Can the investigators seize the computer because it may contain the "documents" or "papers" in electronic form?

Courts have generally allowed the seizure of computers in such circumstances. For example, in People v. Gall, 30 P.3d 145 (Colo. 2001) (en banc), the police were investigating reports that a suspect planned to kill several people at work. Investigators obtained a warrant to search the suspect's home for a number of items, including "[a]ny and all written or printed material which shows an intent to do physical harm or physical damage against any person or building" and "any documents or materials that show the occupier or possessor of the premises." During the search, investigators came across and seized two desktop computers from the living room and five laptop computers found in individual carrying cases on the floor of one of the defendant's closet. The five laptop computers turned out to be stolen, and the defendant was charged with receiving stolen property (among other things). On appeal, the defendant argued that the seizure of the computers was impermissible because it was not authorized by the warrant. A 4–3 majority of the Colorado Supreme Court disagreed, concluding that the warrant could be construed to include the computers:

> In deciding whether items discovered during the execution of a search warrant are within the scope of the warrant, police officers are not obliged to interpret its terms narrowly. They may search the location authorized by the warrant, including any containers at that location that are reasonably likely to contain items described in the warrant. This container rationale is equally applicable to nontraditional, technological "containers" that are reasonably likely to hold information in less tangible forms. Similarly a warrant cannot be expected to anticipate every form an item or repository of information may take, and therefore courts have affirmed the seizure of things that are similar to, or the "functional equivalent" of, items enumerated in a warrant, as well as containers in which they are reasonably likely to be found.

Id. at 153. In dissent, Justice Martinez argued that courts should not permit computers to be seized unless the computers are expressly named in the warrant:

> In my view, the warrant here was insufficient to justify the seizure or search of the computers in this case because the warrant sought writings, not computers. Computers are far more complex and versatile than mere writings and their purpose is significantly different from just a container storing writings. As such, the warrant authorizing the seizure of writings was not sufficiently particularized to include computers. We require a warrant to particularly describe the things to be seized in order to avoid the harm to privacy inherent in the seizure of items that are not the subject of a search. This purpose is not served if computers are seized when writings are sought.

Id. at 160 (Martinez, J., dissenting).

Which side is more persuasive—the majority or the dissent? Should warrants that permit the seizure of writings or documents automatically be construed to permit the seizure of any computer devices that may contain such writings or documents? Should computers be seized in every case? If not, how should courts determine when the seizure of a computer is necessary? How can judges or police officers know when a computer should be seized given that they normally will not know what evidence it contains until it is searched? And how are the answers to these questions changing as more and more devices and tools are becoming computerized?

4. *The Privacy Protection Act and server searches.* Can the government obtain a warrant to search and seize the servers at an ISP to obtain account information relating to one of the ISP's subscribers? Put another way, if there is probable cause to believe an individual account contains evidence of a crime, can investigators obtain a warrant to seize the "haystack" of the ISP's servers just to search for the "needle" of the account?

As a practical matter, investigators will almost never physically seize servers used by a third party such as an ISP. The ISP will have no involvement with the offense, and its employees normally will be willing to share the evidence with law enforcement pursuant to proper court orders. (Almost all ISPs have employees tasked with complying with court orders served by criminal investigators. The next chapter explains the governing statutory law.)

As a matter of Fourth Amendment law, however, such searches are permissible. In Zurcher v. Stanford Daily, 436 U.S. 547 (1978), the Supreme Court held that the Fourth Amendment permitted investigators to execute a search warrant at a newspaper for evidence of crime that the newspaper was believed to have gathered in the course of reporting the news. The Court reasoned that the Fourth Amendment's probable cause and particularity requirement already struck the proper balance, and that no new constitutional rules were needed in a case where the owner of the property searched was an innocent third-party publisher. The same rationale presumably permits searches of ISPs for evidence in individual accounts.

Although such a search may be permissible under the Fourth Amendment, it may violate a federal statute known as the Privacy Protection Act of 1980 (PPA), codified at 42 U.S.C. § 2000aa. The PPA is a complex law, and the details of the statute need not be explored here. In essence, the statute permits innocent third parties to bring a civil cause of action for damages against criminal investigators that search for and seize evidence from them relating to First Amendment activities. The statute was passed in response to *Zurcher*, and would have permitted the newspaper in that case to sue the police for damages. Because servers will often hold evidence relating to First Amendment activities of innocent third parties, searches and seizures of servers may raise difficult questions of civil liability under the PPA. *See, e.g.*, Steve Jackson Games, Inc. v. United States Secret Service, 816 F.Supp. 432 (W.D. Tex. 1993).

3. THE ELECTRONIC SEARCH STAGE

At the electronic search stage, the computer has been brought to a government laboratory and is searched for evidence. The analyst normally begins by making a copy of the storage device. The analyst then searches the copy for evidence. What rules govern searching the copy of the computer for evidence? How invasive can the search be for evidence within the scope of the warrant? And what happens when the agent discovers evidence of crime outside the scope of the warrant, either inadvertently or intentionally? Is that evidence admissible?

UNITED STATES v. KEARNS

United States District Court for the Northern District of Georgia, 2006.
2006 WL 2668538.

JOEL M. FELDMAN, MAGISTRATE JUDGE.

On March 15, 2005, Secret Service Special Agent Dean Glore applied for and received a warrant to search Defendant Steven Kearns' residence at 234 Lindsey Place, Marietta, GA, Defendant's computers, and two of his automobiles, a Hummer SUV and a Corvette.

The March 15, 2005 warrant specifically authorized a search for financial and accounting documents, credit cards, credit applications, documents related to financial transactions, real estate appraisals, and included computers and other electronic media.

Special Agent Glore has personal knowledge of the facts stated in the affidavit, which he ascertained based on conversations with financial institutions, victims, cooperating witnesses, observations of fellow law enforcement agents and officers involved in the investigation, and his training as a Special Agent with the United States Secret Service.

Specifically, on March 1, 2005, Special Agent Glore interviewed Justin Pfaff. Mr. Pfaff informed Special Agent Glore that in October 2004, he gave the Defendant the sum of $25,000 in cash to invest in real estate. In return, the Defendant offered Mr. Pfaff $40,000 if he would purchase real estate located at 765 Brookline Street SW, Atlanta, Georgia. Mr. Pfaff also stated that the Defendant opened an account in January 2005 with the Guitar Center using his identity without his authorization. On January 12, 2005, Mr. Pfaff purchased real property located at 1592 Ezra Church Road, Atlanta, Georgia. Mr. Pfaff did not complete any loan applications for the aforesaid property; and in fact, the Defendant completed all necessary paperwork for the applicable loan.

Mr. Pfaff also informed Special Agent Glore that the Defendant operates his company, Interglobal Investments, out of the residence located at 234 Lindsey Place, Marietta, Georgia, and that the Defendant has several computers in his office at this location.

On March 16, 2005, the agents executed said search warrant and seized from the Defendant's residence at 234 Lindsey Place, Marietta, Georgia, *inter alia,* five computers, a number of computer floppy disks, a digital card, and a black case containing thirty-five computer CDs.

United States Secret Service Special Agent Benedict Murray, assigned to the Electronic Crimes Special Agent Program ("ECSP"), participated in the execution of the search warrant and was the agent assigned to analyze the computers, floppy disks, and CDs seized in the present case.

Special Agent Murray testified that he has been involved in conducting computer searches in at least thirty cases. He further explained that a computer forensic examination involves three stages, to wit: (1) the acquisition stage where the agent copies the suspect information on to a separate hard drive; (2) the authentication stage where the agent verifies that all of the retrieved information is correct; and (3) the retrieval stage where the agent actually tries to retrieve the information he is searching for.

In the instant case, Special Agent Murray imaged (i.e., copied) the contents of the computers' electronic storage media or hard drives and CDs and saved them on a separate hard disk for analysis using the Encase forensic program.

Special Agent Murray first examined the hard drives on the Defendant's computers. After he concluded his examination of the hard drives, Special Agent Murray then began to search, in sequential order, his imaged copies of the thirty-five CDs seized from the Defendant's residence. The first twenty-eight CDs contained business software such as legal forms, legal documents, application forms, and loan forms (i.e., software templates which could be used to create business documents). Special Agent Murray attempted to open every file on these business software disks; however, some of these files could not be opened in their native formats.

The remaining seven CDs contained various types of created files, including document files (.doc), image or picture files (.jpg), and music or audio files (.mp3). In order to determine whether these seven CDs contained information of evidentiary value, Special Agent Murray opened them up in order to briefly review their contents. He explained that his normal procedure in conducting his forensic exams is to open all the files contained on smaller electronic storage media (i.e., a CD).

The first CD of the remaining seven Special Agent Murray examined was CD number 29 titled "Music 12005." This CD contained, *inter alia,* music files, media files, document files, and a word-processing file. Special Agent Murray proceeded to open every file on this CD, which was approximately 104 files, in order to search for files of evidentiary value.

The first file on CD 29 Special Agent Murray opened was a music file titled 01–ll_cool_j_feat_timberland-head_sprung-tas.mp3. He continued to open the remaining files in sequential order. During his search of CD 29, Special Agent Murray came across six files that appeared to constitute child pornography and child erotica, to wit: the third, sixth, fourteenth, seventeenth, twenty-second, and thirtieth files. In between these six files were various other music or media files and one document file. Indeed, the document file titled Adobe Serial Numbers.doc, which was the ninth file on CD 29, contained several software programs of the type relevant in this case.[11] He also made a disk containing the images, but did not re-open the files, nor did he conduct any searches for child pornography on the disks or computers.

In September 2005, the six images of perceived child pornography and child erotica were copied onto another disk and sent to the National Center for Missing and Exploited Children ("NCMEC").[12] NCMEC analyzed the images and sent a report back indicating that at least three of the six images contained child pornography.

On or about November 15, 2005, * * * the Defendant was charged with knowingly receiving child pornography, in violation of Title 18, U.S.C. § 2252A(a)(2)(A).

The Defendant moves to suppress the evidence gained from Special Agent Murray's search of the child pornography files found on CD 29 on the ground that his search of these files was beyond the scope of the warrant authorizing a search for financial, accounting, and real estate fraud-related evidence. Specifically, the Defendant contends that Special Agent Murray conducted an impermissible general search of his computer CDs that exceeded the scope of the March 15, 2005 search warrant; and he further contends that Special Agent Murray made no attempt to address

---

11. Special Agent Murray testified that he was not looking for child pornography at any time while examining the computers and CDs; nor did he direct any searches for child pornography. He stated that he conducted his search pursuant to the warrant (i.e., searching for financial fraud documents). Indeed, he testified that he opened the files on CD 29 not because he believed it might contain child pornography, but rather because it was the next file listed and he was opening all of the files as part of his routine search for the items listed in the search warrant. In addition, he stated that, even if he had not found the images of child pornography, he would have nevertheless still opened all of the files on the CD.

12. Special Agent Murray admitted that, without opening any of the files, he could have taken the files' hash value (i.e., a unique digital fingerprint of a file) and sent it to NCMEC for it to determine whether or not it contains child pornography. However, he also testified that NCMEC does not accept hash values and requires the actual images to be sent for its analysis, in part, because a new image of child pornography may not have a hash value on record with it.

intermingled documents (i.e., documents containing both relevant and irrelevant information) by employing reasonable means available to limit the focus of his search to fraud rather than opening every file on the Defendant's CDs.

It is well-established that the Fourth Amendment requires that a search warrant describe the things to be seized with sufficient particularity to prevent a general exploratory rummaging of a person's belongings. To prevent such rummaging, a warrant must enable the executing officer to ascertain and identify with reasonable certainty those items that the magistrate has authorized him to seize. In some cases, however, it is not immediately apparent whether an item is within the scope of the search warrant; and, in such cases, an agent must briefly examine the item to determine whether it is one that he is authorized to seize.

An agent's conduct in executing a search warrant is governed by the Fourth Amendment's mandate of reasonableness. The resolution of the motion to suppress does not turn on whether Special Agent Murray conducted the most technically advanced search possible, but on whether the search, as conducted was reasonable. Thus, the particularity requirement of the Fourth Amendment must be applied with a practical margin of flexibility, taking into account the nature of the items to be seized and the complexity of the case under investigation. Furthermore, the magnitude of the search is not sufficient to establish a constitutional violation. Instead, the search may be as extensive as reasonably required to locate and seize items described in the warrant. The reasonableness of the search depends upon the complexity of the crime being investigated and the difficulty involved in determining whether certain documents evidence fraud.

Therefore, in some instances, searching officers must be able to examine nearly every document possessed by a suspected criminal, if only to determine whether the documents contain evidence of criminal activity. In applying the standard to a search of a computer, CDs and other electronic media, the agents must be clear as to what it is they are seeking on the computer and search it in a way that avoids searching files of types not authorized by the search warrant. However, a computer search may be as extensive as reasonably required to locate the items described in the warrant. Indeed, as previously mentioned, in some instances, agents are authorized to examine all files located at the specific cite to look for the specified evidence.

So it is not surprising then, that in the course of conducting a lawful search pursuant to a search warrant, law enforcement agents often discover evidence of criminal activity other than that which is the subject of the warrant. If an agent sees, in plain view, evidence of criminal activity other than that for which he is searching, this does not constitute an unreasonable search under the Fourth Amendment.

Here, the March 15, 2005 search warrant explicitly authorized the search and seizure of, *inter alia,* the Defendant's computers, floppy disks, and CDs establishing that probable cause existed that evidence of financial and real estate fraud-related documents would be contained therein. In fact, the Defendant does not contend otherwise. Rather, he asserts that the search of the disks for such information should have stopped short of opening and viewing the contents of the particular files that proved to contain the images of child pornography arguing that Special Agent Murray should have been able to determine what kind of material each computer file contained without having to open the file according to the indication in the file directory of the file type (i.e., whether the file was labeled as a .txt file or .jpg file) or by conducting a file signature analysis match, which would indicate whether a file extension is misidentified. However, contrary to the Defendant's assertion, in executing this search warrant, Special Agent Murray was authorized to cursorily review the files on the computers and CDs to determine if they were of the type covered by the search warrant.

As Special Agent Murray explained, files containing graphical images may be assigned file extensions that are typically assigned to text files and files containing text may be assigned file extensions typically given to graphical image files. Hence, Special Agent Murray could not have determined simply from the file names and extensions that the files on the disks that contained the alleged child pornography did not contain other material relevant to the fraud allegations. He knew from his experience that suspects often intentionally disguise their files by manipulating their file designation.

Even if the sexually suggestive titles would put a reasonable agent on notice that those files contained sexual material, it is reasonable to conclude, as Special Agent Murray did, that these files could have been disguised and still contain evidence of the existence of assets and properties or transactions providing evidence of fraud. Therefore, he could not be certain that files with the .jpg designation did not actually contain items for which he was authorized to search. He could have done that only by opening and inspecting the contents of the files, without regard to the file extensions they bore. Furthermore, even the warrant's authorization of the search for the photographs relating to the fraud (i.e., pictures of homes) allowed Special Agent Murray to open and inspect the contents of the graphical image files on the disks. Indeed, the search for financial fraud evidence in this case was not limited to text files, but also included .pdf and .jpg files.

In fact, Special Agent Murray even found financial or business-related documents that were in a .pdf format that contained .jpgs or pictures. In the course of doing so, he inadvertently discovered evidence of suspected child pornography. Documents not specified by the search warrant may be seized if discovered inadvertently when probable cause to seize exists on its face.

The Defendant heavily relies on the Tenth Circuit's decision in *United States v. Carey,* 172 F.3d 1268 (10th Cir. 1999). However, *Carey* is clearly factually distinguishable and inapposite from the present case. In *Carey,* the police inadvertently discovered child pornography on the defendant's computer while searching for evidence of drug transactions. The officers, however, without obtaining a second warrant, abandoned their search for drug transactions, and proceeded to search for further images of child pornography. Indeed, the officer in *Carey* testified that after he inadvertently found the first image of child pornography, when he thereafter searched the .jpg files, he was specifically looking for child pornography and not drug-related evidence that was the subject of the search warrant. Therefore, the Tenth Circuit held that while the first image of child pornography was inadvertently discovered and not due to be suppressed, the officer had exceeded the scope of the search warrant because when he opened the subsequent .jpg files, he expected to find and was, in fact, looking for child pornography thereby abandoning his search for drug-related evidence and intentionally commencing a search for child pornography not authorized by the existing search warrant.

Of particular importance in this case, in contrast to the facts presented in *Carey,* is that Special Agent Murray testified that he never abandoned his original search nor did he commence a new search for child pornography, but was, rather, continuing his sequential search of CD 29 without regard to file names or designations.

The child pornography seized by Special Agent Murray must have been in plain view during his search for fraud-related evidence. To satisfy the plain view doctrine: (1) the agent must be lawfully in the place where the seized item was in plain view; (2) the item's incriminating nature must have been immediately apparent; and (3) the agent had a lawful right of access to the object itself. *See Horton v. California,* 496 U.S. 128, 136–37 (1990).

Here, pursuant to the valid search warrant, Special Agent Murray determined that the items listed in the search warrant which could be located on computer files could be found in plain text, special text, or graphic files. While searching the graphics files for evidence of fraud, as allowed by the warrant, Special Agent Murray inadvertently discovered what he perceived to be images of child pornography. The incriminating nature of the files was immediately apparent to Special Agent Murray. Since he was lawfully searching for evidence of fraud in the graphics files, that he had legitimately accessed and where the child pornography was located, the evidence was properly seized under the plain view doctrine.

NOTES AND QUESTIONS

1. What rules should the courts impose to regulate the process of retrieving evidence from a computer pursuant to a warrant? Should the police be permitted to take whatever steps are necessary to find the needle in the electronic haystack? In United States v. Ross, 456 U.S. 798, 820–21 (1982), the Supreme Court articulated the following general standards for executing search warrants:

A lawful search of fixed premises generally extends to the entire area in which the object of the search may be found[.] * * * Thus, a warrant that authorizes an officer to search a home for illegal weapons also provides authority to open closets, chests, drawers, and containers in which the weapon might be found. A warrant to open a footlocker to search for marihuana would also authorize the opening of packages found inside. A warrant to search a vehicle would support a search of every part of the vehicle that might contain the object of the search. When a legitimate search is under way, and when its purpose and its limits have been precisely defined, nice distinctions between closets, drawers, and containers, in the case of a home, or between glove compartments, upholstered seats, trunks, and wrapped packages, in the case of a vehicle, must give way to the interest in the prompt and efficient completion of the task at hand.

Is *Kearns* simply a routine application of *Ross*? What, if any, limits should courts impose on how the government executes computer search warrants?

2. The original purpose of the Fourth Amendment was to forbid the use of general warrants. General warrants typically did not name the place to be searched or the property to be seized, and as a result permitted a general rummaging through a suspect's property. The particularity requirement was designed to prevent such general rummaging. By limiting searches to a particular place for particular evidence, the requirement limited the government's powers to conduct dragnet searches.

Does the particularity requirement continue to serve this function in a world of digital evidence? Or do traditional Fourth Amendment rules make computer warrants that are particularized in theory general warrants in practice?

3. The *Kearns* court focuses on the officer's subjective intent. Because the officer was looking for the evidence described in the warrant, the discovery of evidence beyond the scope of the warrant was permitted. If the officer had been looking for other evidence, as in *Carey*, its discovery would have violated the Fourth Amendment.

This subjective approach is in tension with how courts have applied the plain view doctrine in cases involving physical evidence. Under the traditional test, the officer's subjective intent is irrelevant and the standard is an objective one. *See* Horton v. California, 496 U.S. 128, 138–39 (1990) (eliminating the inadvertence requirement from the plain view exception on the ground that the particularity requirement can deter general searches and "evenhanded law enforcement is best achieved by the application of objective standards of conduct, rather than standards that depend upon the subjective state of mind of the officer").

The switch from an objective standard for physical searches adopted by the Supreme Court in *Horton* to a subjective standard for digital evidence searches in *Kearns* and *Carey* arguably reflects a more restrictive approach to the scope of plain view for digital evidence. In a traditional case, officers can intentionally look for evidence beyond the scope of the warrant so long as the search itself is reasonable. In a digital evidence case, they cannot.

Why have courts adopted a more restrictive approach in the context of digital evidence? Is the switch to a subjective approach designed to restore some of the functionality of the particularity requirement? Perhaps the courts are creating less flexible and more privacy-protective rules in the context of searching through computers to make up for the more flexible and less protective rules that courts have allowed for practical reasons to govern computer searches in other cases.

On the merits, do you think that district judges can accurately determine when a police officer was looking for evidence beyond the scope of the warrant? For a criticism of the subjective approach, see Jim Dowell, Note, *Criminal Procedure: Tenth Circuit Erroneously Allows Officers' Intentions to Define Reasonable Searches: United States v. Carey,* 54 Okla. L. Rev. 665, 676 (2001).

4.   Most of the published cases involving the discovery of digital evidence beyond the scope of a warrant involve discovering child pornography. Child pornography offenses are very easy for the government to prove, and the penalties for such offenses are relatively severe. As a result, the discovery of child pornography during a computer search for other evidence may lead prosecutors to call off the initial investigation and bring charges under the child pornography statutes. Does this dynamic help explain why courts have used a subjective test when applying the plain view exception in computer search cases?

5.   Under *Kearns,* a government agent with a search warrant apparently can search anywhere in a computer so long as he looks for material described in the warrant. If the agent comes across evidence unrelated to the crime described in the warrant, the agent can copy the unrelated evidence for use in court. The agent can then continue to search for the evidence named in the warrant, and can continue to copy unrelated evidence he comes across during the search. Alternatively, the agent can use the discovery of the unrelated evidence as the basis for probable cause to obtain a second warrant to search the computer for more of the unrelated evidence. Either way, the unrelated evidence is admissible in court under prevailing Fourth Amendment law.

Do these rules impose sufficient limits on the search of seized computers? If not, should the plain view exception be abolished in computer cases so that any evidence beyond the scope of the warrant cannot be admitted in court?

> The dynamics of computer searches upset the basic assumptions underlying the plain view doctrine. More and more evidence comes into plain view, and the particularity requirement no longer functions effectively as a check on dragnet searches. In this new environment, a tightening of the plain view doctrine may be necessary to ensure that computer warrants that are narrow in theory do not become broad in practice.

> In time, abolishing the plain view exception may best balance the competing needs of privacy and law enforcement in light of developments in computer technology and the digital forensics process. Forensic analysis is an art, not a science; the process is contingent, technical, and difficult to reduce to rules. Eliminating the plain view exception in digital evidence cases would respect law enforcement interests by granting the police every power needed to identify and locate evidence within the scope of a

warrant given the particular context-sensitive needs of the investigation. At the same time, the approach would protect privacy interests by barring the disclosure of any evidence beyond the scope of a valid warrant in most cases. It is an imperfect answer, to be sure, but it may be the best available rule. Although forensic practices may be invasive by technological necessity, a total suppression rule for evidence beyond the scope of a warrant would both remove any incentive for broad searches and neutralize the effect of broad searches that occur. It would regulate invasive practices by imposing use restrictions ex post rather than attempting to control searches ex ante, offering a long-term second-best approach to regulating the computer forensics process. In short, it would allow the police to conduct whatever search they needed to conduct (to ensure recovery) and then limit use of the evidence found (to deter abuses).

Orin S. Kerr, *Searches and Seizures in a Digital World*, 119 Harv. L. Rev. 531, 576–77, 583–84 (2005).

6. The plain view exception allows law enforcement to seize evidence beyond the scope of a warrant only if the incriminating nature of that evidence is "immediately apparent." David Ziff argues that the plain view doctrine plays only a limited role in computer search cases because the incriminating nature of most digital evidence is not immediately apparent. *See* David J.S. Ziff, Note, *Fourth Amendment Limitations on the Execution of Computer Searches Conducted Pursuant to a Warrant*, 105 Colum. L. Rev. 841, 869 (2005):

> [A] file that is not particularly described in the warrant can be seized by officers only if the file's incriminating character becomes immediately apparent before it can be determined that the contents of the file are outside of the scope of the warrant. For the vast majority of computer files, this limitation will shield private information from inspection by officers. For example, suppose an officer is searching the contents of a computer for child pornography and opens a file labeled "letter to grandma.doc." Under the proposed standard, the officer is only allowed to open and view the file to the extent necessary to determine that it is not merely a mislabeled file concealing the object of the warrant. This limitation prohibits the officer from reading the contents of the letter. Any information in the letter, including information relating to other illegal activity, remains private. Even if an individual file appears suspicious to an officer but further investigation beyond what is necessary to determine that the file is outside the scope of the warrant is required to establish probable cause as to its association with criminal activity, the item is not immediately incriminating and cannot be seized pursuant to the plain view doctrine.

Does this argument depend on how broadly the warrant is drafted? Computer warrants can be drafted in very broad ways that require agents to exercise considerable judgment as to whether a particular file is within the scope of the warrant. For example, imagine that the warrant in Ziff's hypothetical were not limited to actual images of child pornography, but instead encompassed "any documents, letters, memos, images, or other information concerning violations of child pornography crimes or child sex offenses." In that case, couldn't the officer read "letter to grandma.doc" to determine whether the letter contained any information relating to child sex offenses or child pornography? And if the letter contained discussions of unrelated crimes, couldn't the officer use the letter to prosecute the defendant for the unrelated crime under the plain view doctrine?

Also note that the "immediately apparent" limitation is only a limit on the seizure of evidence. Agents can view unrelated evidence that they come across in plain view, but can seize the evidence only if its incriminating nature is immediately apparent. This brings us back to a question considered earlier in the chapter: Does copying digital evidence for use in court constitute a Fourth Amendment seizure? If not, does the "immediately apparent" limitation even apply in digital evidence cases?

7. *Search protocols.* One way to limit the invasiveness of computer searches would be to require investigators to follow specific search protocols when a computer is searched. For example, a protocol might explain the search terms the investigators will use to locate evidence, or the specific steps investigators must follow when searching the hard drive. The idea is to restore the function of the particularity requirement for digital evidence by requiring the warrant to be executed in a particular way. *See generally* Raphael Winick, *Searches and Seizures of Computers and Computer Data*, 8 Harv. J. L. & Tech. 75, 106–08 (1994).

A few courts have imposed search protocol requirements to limit the scope of computer searches. For example, in the case of In re Search of 3817 W. West End, 321 F. Supp.2d 953 (N.D. Ill. 2004), investigators had probable cause to believe that a suspect was preparing and retaining fraudulent tax records in her home. Investigators applied for a warrant to search the suspect's home and seize her tax records, whether in paper or electronic form. The magistrate judge agreed that there was probable cause, and also agreed that the computer could be seized. The judge refused to permit investigators to search the computer, however, on the ground that investigators had not agreed to limit their search to a specific set of steps pre-approved by the judge. According to Magistrate Judge Schenkier, approval of a search protocol was necessary before the warrant could be issued:

> The purpose of review of warrant applications by "neutral, disinterested magistrates" is to ensure that the requirements of probable cause and particularity are met. When there are concerns about the particularity of a given search, as is the case here, it is both sensible and constitutionally required to address those concerns at the front end of the process, and to resolve them in a way that avoids the later suppression of evidence. * * * [A]s matters now stand, what the government seeks is a license to roam through everything in the computer without limitation and without standards. Such a request fails to satisfy the particularity requirement of the Fourth Amendment, and the Court therefore will not approve it.

Id. at 962.

Other courts have rejected a search protocol requirement for computer search warrants. For example, in United States v. Hill, 459 F.3d 966 (9th Cir. 2006), a defendant charged with child pornography possession challenged the warrant used to search his computer on the ground that it did not include any search protocols. He claimed that the search should have been limited to certain files that were more likely to be associated with child pornography, such as those with a ".jpg" suffix (which usually identifies files containing images) or those containing the word "sex" or other key words. The Ninth Circuit disagreed, noting that "we look favorably upon the inclusion of a search protocol; but its absence is not fatal." *Id.* at 978. The court concluded that the defendant's proposed search protocol was "unreasonable" in light of investigative realities:

> Computer records are extremely susceptible to tampering, hiding, or destruction, whether deliberate or inadvertent. Images can be hidden in all manner of files, even word processing documents and spreadsheets. Criminals will do all they can to conceal contraband, including the simple expedient of changing the names and extensions of files to disguise their content from the casual observer.

> Forcing police to limit their searches to files that the suspect has labeled in a particular way would be much like saying police may not seize a plastic bag containing a powdery white substance if it is labeled "flour" or "talcum powder." There is no way to know what is in a file without examining its contents, just as there is no sure way of separating talcum from cocaine except by testing it. The ease with which child pornography images can be disguised—whether by renaming sexyteenyboppersxxx.jpg as sundayschoollesson.doc, or something more sophisticated—forecloses defendant's proposed search methodology.

Id. (quoting United States v. Hill, 322 F. Supp.2d 1081, 1090–91 (C.D. Cal. 2004) (Kozinski, J.)).

The decision in *Hill* echoes United States v. Upham, 168 F.3d 532 (1st Cir. 1999). In *Upham*, the police recovered incriminating information by "undeleting" files stored on the defendant's personal computer. This was possible because information stored on a computer often continues to be present when the machine has been reformatted or a file "deleted." The First Circuit held that the warrant permitted investigators to find and recover the deleted files:

> The seizure of unlawful images is within the plain language of the warrant; their recovery, after attempted destruction, is no different than decoding a coded message lawfully seized or pasting together scraps of a torn-up ransom note. The * * * warrant did not prescribe methods of recovery or tests to be performed, but warrants rarely do so. The warrant process is primarily concerned with identifying *what* may be searched or seized—not how—and *whether* there is sufficient cause for the invasion of privacy thus entailed.

Id. at 537. *See also* United States v. Brooks, 427 F.3d 1246, 1251–53 (10th Cir. 2005).

Finally, consider the U.S. Supreme Court's guidance in Dalia v. United States, 441 U.S. 238 (1979). The government obtained a warrant to conduct bugging surveillance, and investigators executed the warrant by covertly entering the place to install the bug. In an opinion by Justice Powell, the

Court rejected the defendant's contention that the warrant had to state that it permitted covert entry:

> Nothing in the language of the Constitution or in this Court's decisions interpreting that language suggests that * * * search warrants also must include a specification of the precise manner in which they are to be executed. On the contrary, it is generally left to the discretion of the executing officers to determine the details of how best to proceed with the performance of a search authorized by warrant—subject of course to the general Fourth Amendment protection against unreasonable searches and seizures.

Id. at 257.

Do computer warrants merit a different approach? Does it depend on whether courts retain the traditional approach to the plain view doctrine in the context of digital evidence? Which is the better way to minimize the intrusiveness of computer searches: imposing ex ante restrictions through search protocols or altering standards ex post by narrowing or eliminating the plain view doctrine? Should courts embrace neither change? Or both?

8.   After the police seize a computer pursuant to a warrant, the computer may be sent to a government forensic laboratory or kept at the police station for later analysis. The process of analyzing a computer can be very time-consuming. As a result, most agencies have a considerable backlog of computers awaiting analysis. Several months may pass before government computer experts begin the search. During that time, the computer's owner must wait for the government to start and then complete its analysis.

Existing statutory rules that regulate the warrant process do not impose many restrictions on when the government must search or return a seized computer. Most statutory warrant rules require the government to execute a search warrant within 7, 10 or 14 days after the warrant is signed. *See, e.g.,* Fed. R. Crim. Pro. 41(e)(2) (stating that a federal search warrant "must command the officer to * * * execute the warrant within a specified time no longer than 14 days"). By forcing investigators to execute the warrant shortly after the magistrate has found probable cause, the time limits ensure that searches are executed before the probable cause has become stale. Courts have held, however, that these limitations apply only to the initial physical search of computers and not to the subsequent electronic search. *See, e.g.,* United States v. Gorrell, 360 F. Supp.2d 48, 54 n.5 (D.D.C. 2004); United States v. Hernandez, 183 F. Supp.2d 468, 480 (D.P.R. 2002) (stating that Rule 41 does not "provide[] for a specific time limit in which a computer may undergo a government forensic examination after it has been seized pursuant to a search warrant").

Some individual magistrate judges have imposed time limits on computer warrants on their own initiative. For example, in United States v. Brunette, 76 F. Supp.2d 30 (D. Me. 1999), a magistrate judge signed a warrant allowing agents to seize the defendant's computers on the condition that the forensic analysis must occur "within 30 days." When agents failed to search the computer during the time window, the court suppressed the evidence discovered on the computer after the 30–day period had elapsed. *Id.* at 42. It is unclear, however, whether existing statutory rules give magistrate judges the authority to condition issuance of warrants on the search of the computer within a specific period of time.

Statutory warrant rules also permit individuals who have had property seized pursuant to a warrant to file a motion in court seeking a return of that property. *See, e.g.,* Fed. R. Crim. Pro. 41(g). The standards for return of property are not uniform among different jurisdictions. At the federal level, however, property ordinarily will be ordered returned only in rare cases. As a general matter, the court must be convinced that the property owner would suffer "irreparable injury" unless the property is returned and the property owner's interest in the property must outweigh the government's interest in continued retention of it. *See, e.g.,* In re the Matter of the Search of Kitty's East, 905 F.2d 1367, 1370–71 (10th Cir. 1990); Ramsden v. United States, 2 F.3d 322, 325–26 (9th Cir. 1993).

Does the Fourth Amendment impose limits on when a seized computer must be searched? Courts have not recognized Fourth Amendment limitations on when the police must search seized documents. Nor have courts imposed Fourth Amendment limitations on when the police must conduct forensic analysis on other types of seized evidence such as guns or DNA samples. In a few recent cases, however, some courts have indicated that computers may be different. In United States v. Grimmett, 2004 WL 3171788 (D. Kan. 2004), police officers seized computers pursuant to a state warrant. Agents searched the computers several weeks later and found the evidence named in the warrant. The defendant claimed that the delay between the seizure and the search (which, all things considered, was actually a relatively brief period) rendered the search unreasonable and the evidence inadmissible as fruits of an unconstitutional search. The court rejected the claim, but did accept the basic idea that the timing of the computer search was governed by a reasonableness analysis:

> The conduct of law enforcement officers in executing a search warrant is governed by the Fourth Amendment's mandate of reasonableness. The Fourth Amendment does not provide a specific time in which a computer may be subjected to a government forensic examination after it has been seized pursuant to a search warrant. The court finds that the Fourth Amendment requires only that the subsequent search of the computer be made within a reasonable time. The court finds that the subsequent search was conducted within a reasonable time since it was concluded within a few weeks of the execution of the warrant.

Id. at *5. *See also* United States v. Syphers, 296 F. Supp.2d 50 (D.N.H. 2003) (finding a seven month delay reasonable).

Do you agree that the Fourth Amendment requires agents to search a seized computer within a reasonable time? If so, how should a court determine whether a particular delay is reasonable? Is a case-by-case inquiry into reasonableness the best way to regulate the timing of computer searches? Should statutory rules require agents to search seized computers within a specific window of time, or to image seized computers and return the original within a particular period? For such a proposal, see Kerr, *Search Warrants in an Era of Digital Evidence*, 75 Miss L.J. at 129–32.

9. When a defendant moves to suppress evidence obtained pursuant to a facially valid warrant, the admissibility of the evidence usually depends on whether the evidence falls within the scope of the warrant. If the evidence is construed to fall beyond the scope of the warrant, the evidence is excluded unless it fits within the "plain view" exception. If the evidence fits within the scope of the warrant, however, it will be admitted unless the warrant was executed in "flagrant disregard" of the warrant's terms.

The "flagrant disregard" standard is very hard for a defense attorney to satisfy. Agents execute a warrant in "flagrant disregard" of its terms only if the search so grossly exceeds what the warrant permits that the authorized search appears to be merely a pretext for a fishing expedition through the target's private property. *See, e.g.,* United States v. Shi Yan Liu, 239 F.3d 138, 140–42 (2d Cir. 2000). Is this burden too high? What kind of search through a computer would be in "flagrant disregard" of the warrant? Should courts regulate computer searches more closely than traditional physical searches, or is the traditional "flagrant disregard" standard appropriate?

4. ENCRYPTION

One special issue that can arise in a computer search is the presence of encryption. Encryption is a way of transforming information into a form that cannot be read without a special code (referred to as a "key") that can return the information into readable form. The readable form is generally known as plaintext; the scrambled form is known as ciphertext. Encryption is a very powerful tool for maintaining privacy in computer data: If a target encrypts evidence of his crime, the government needs to obtain the key to decrypt the ciphertext and view the evidence.

For the most part, the role of encryption is a practical one, not a legal one. If the government seizes ciphertext, it will ordinarily try to use its usual search and seizure powers to seize the key, as well. The government may also try to crack the encryption using "brute force" methods, such as guessing the key. Encryption can raise two interesting and difficult legal questions, however. First, when, if ever, does encryption create a reasonable expectation of privacy? And second, when can the government order a target to divulge his key in light of Fifth Amendment protections?

a. Fourth Amendment Issues

Encryption provides an extraordinarily powerful tool to create privacy in computer data. But can encryption create a reasonable expectation of privacy? The author of these materials has argued that encryption alone cannot create a reasonable expectation of privacy because the Fourth Amendment regulates access to information, not comprehension of data already accessed. A reasonable person can expect privacy in encrypted information, but that privacy derives from technology rather than the Fourth Amendment. *See* Orin S. Kerr, *The Fourth Amendment in Cyberspace: Can Encryption Create a "Reasonable Expectation of Privacy"?*, 33 Conn. L. Rev. 503 (2001).

According to this argument, the government may need a search warrant to obtain a file, but descrambling an encrypted file (transforming ciphertext into plaintext) cannot violate the file owner's reasonable expectation of privacy. This result may seem odd at first, but it parallels precedents involving shredded files and speech in foreign languages. Courts have held that the government can reassemble shredded paper documents and translate materials from a foreign language without implicating the Fourth Amendment. The fact that a reasonable person would expect that shredded documents or speech in a foreign tongue would remain secret does not mean that the government conduct violates a reasonable expectation of privacy.

Is this argument persuasive? Consider the following hypothetical. Renowned criminal Lex Luthor takes out a full page advertisement in *The Daily Planet* containing the following announcement:

> I am planning some colorful entertainment for Metropolis. The following encrypted message explains where and when the fun will take place. To obtain the key that will allow you to decrypt the secret message and learn of my diabolical plans, you must wire $100 million to my Swiss bank account by noon tomorrow. Here is the encrypted message:
>
> J XJMM CMPX VQ UIF UJNFT TRVBSF TVCXBZ TUBUJPO BU OPPO UPNPSSPX CZ MFBWJOH B CPNC JO B QBSLFE DIFWSPMFU UBYJDBC XJUI NPOUBOB MJDFOTF QMBUFT.
>
> Love, *Lex Luthor*

Imagine that an employee of the Metropolis police department sees Luthor's newspaper advertisement during breakfast that morning, and he spends a few minutes trying to decrypt the encoded message. He realizes that the key to Luthor's code is simple: It is the so-called "substitution cipher" that shifts every letter one space (turning A into B, B into C, C into D, etc.). Having generated the key to the encryption, the employee uses the key and unscrambles the message to find the following:

> I WILL BLOW UP THE TIMES SQUARE SUBWAY STATION AT NOON TOMORROW BY LEAVING A BOMB IN A PARKED CHEV-ROLET TAXICAB WITH MONTANA LICENSE PLATES.

The employee calls his supervisors at work and explains Luthor's plans. The police obtain a warrant to search the taxicab, seize a bomb in the trunk just before noon, trace the taxicab back to Luthor, and then charge Luthor with a range of felonies.

Now imagine that Luthor's counsel files a motion to suppress all of the evidence found in the cab. Does the Fourth Amendment require a court to grant Luthor's motion and dismiss the charges against him? It seems intuitively obvious that it does not. But why not? The author of this casebook has argued that decrypting Luthor's message does not implicate the Fourth Amendment because encryption cannot create a reasonable expectation of privacy. Luthor's message was public, and the Fourth Amendment does not regulate efforts to comprehend public information. If encryption did create a reasonable expectation of privacy, he contends, the strange consequence would be that Luthor's motion to suppress must be granted:

> Luthor created a reasonable expectation of privacy in the contents of his message by encrypting the message. By using a "key" to decrypt the message, the police conducted a warrantless search of Luthor's communication in violation of Luthor's Fourth Amendment rights. As a result, the decrypted message must be suppressed, and the evidence found in the taxicab must be suppressed as fruits of the poisonous tree. Lex Luthor must go free.

Id. at 519–20.

Do you agree? Or is it possible to believe that encryption can create Fourth Amendment protection while also agreeing that Luthor's motion to suppress should be denied? Stephen Henderson offers one such argument:

> Luthor's simple substitution cipher is akin to * * * a transparent bag, perhaps a Ziploc. In the words of the Court, "the Fourth Amendment provides protection to the owner of every container that conceals its contents from plain view." A Ziploc bag provides a wonderful seal, but it doesn't conceal its contents from an officer possessing ordinary eyesight. Likewise, a substitution cipher does not conceal a message from an officer possessing ordinary intelligence. In both instances the content is in "plain view."

Stephen E. Henderson, *Nothing New Under the Sun? A Technologically Rational Doctrine of Fourth Amendment Search*, 56 Mercer L. Rev. 507, 534 (2005). Is Professor Henderson applying the plain view doctrine, or something more like the "plain thought" doctrine? Are they the same? How complex must an encryption algorithm be before encrypted data is no longer in plain view?

A number of commentators have stated that encryption triggers Fourth Amendment protection because encryption "locks" information away until a "key" is used to decrypt it. *See, e.g.,* A. Michael Froomkin, *The Metaphor Is the Key: Cryptography, the Clipper Chip, and the Constitution*, 143 U. Pa. L. Rev. 709, 728–35 (1995); Sean J. Edgett, Comment, *Double-clicking on Fourth Amendment Protection: Encryption Creates a Reasonable Expectation of Privacy*, 30 Pepp. L. Rev. 339 (2003). Consider this counterargument:

> The lock that helps trigger a reasonable expectation of privacy in Fourth Amendment cases is a fastener that prevents or limits the movement of two or more surfaces relative to each other. Such a fastener helps create a reasonable expectation of privacy by preventing easy access to the contents of a container. The lock-and-key metaphor in encryption uses a second dictionary definition of "lock" that carries only a passing resemblance to the first one. Encryption

"locks" a communication in the sense that it makes the communication inaccessible by making it incomprehensible. The code that translates ciphertext into plaintext is a "key" because it takes inaccessible ciphertext and helps translate it into understandable plaintext. Using this metaphorical definition of lock-and-key, we might say that a book explaining how the Internet works "provides the key to unlocking the secrets of the Internet." We would not mean that the Internet has a fastener on it that can be unfastened by reading the book; rather, we would mean that the Internet is hard to understand, and that the book can help aid the reader's cognitive understanding. In this sense, the philosophy of Hegel is locked to me, as is Arabic text and my physician's handwriting.

* * * If the government needs a warrant to decrypt an encrypted communication, does it need a warrant before it can read a doctor's messy handwriting or understand Hegel? Does law enforcement need a warrant before it can figure out a criminal's clever scheme, on the ground that the scheme was so subtle that the criminal had a reasonable expectation that it would remain secret? If we decide that the Fourth Amendment can regulate law enforcement efforts to understand what it already has in its possession, it is hard to see where these strange questions can stop. If the Fourth Amendment regulates a state of mind, we have to answer when someone can expect others to think certain thoughts, which depends on who the others are and how much time they would have to think.

Kerr, *The Fourth Amendment in Cyberspace*, 33 Conn. L. Rev. at 522, 523–24. What do you think? Can encryption create a reasonable expectation of privacy?

b.   *Fifth Amendment Issues*

The Fifth Amendment to the United States Constitution states that no person "shall be compelled in any criminal case to be a witness against himself." The Fifth Amendment privilege provides a suspect with a right to decline to provide testimony if that testimony would be incriminating against him. Although Fifth Amendment law is complicated, the privilege is generally triggered when three requirements are met: compulsion, testimony, and incrimination.

Compulsion exists if there is a legal penalty for failure to comply with an act. In that case, the force of law "compels" the action. For example, a subpoena provides compulsion for Fifth Amendment purposes because failure to comply with a valid subpoena can lead to criminal liability for obstruction of justice.

An act is generally testimonial for Fifth Amendment purposes if it requires the individual to divulge the contents of his own mind. Importantly for our purposes, an act of production can be testimonial. If the government orders a person to produce a particular item, under penalty of law, then responding to the order may provide implicit testimony about it that implicates the Fifth Amendment:

The act of production itself may implicitly communicate statements of fact. By producing documents in compliance with a subpoena, the witness would admit that the papers existed, were in his possession or control, and were authentic. Moreover, as was true in this case, when the custodian of documents responds to a subpoena, he may be compelled to take the witness stand and answer questions designed to determine whether he has produced everything demanded by the subpoena. The answers to those questions, as well as the act of production itself, may certainly communicate information about the existence, custody, and authenticity of the documents. Whether the constitutional privilege protects the answers to such questions, or protects the act of production itself, is a question that is distinct from the question whether the unprotected contents of the documents themselves are incriminating.

United States v. Hubbell, 530 U.S. 27, 36–37 (2000).

One exception to this rule is that if the government already knows that a witness possesses a document or knows a particular piece of information exists, and it is therefore a "foregone conclusion," then it is not testimonial to compel a witness to produce the documents or state the fact. *See* Fisher v. United States, 425 U.S. 391, 411 (1976). For example, in United States v. Teeple, 286 F.3d 1047 (8th Cir. 2002), a tax protester who worked as a chiropractor failed to file tax returns for several years. The government issued a subpoena for his financial records, and he asserted his Fifth Amendment privilege. The Fifth Circuit ruled that complying with the subpoena would not be testimonial because Teeple's past conduct had already demonstrated the relevant facts to the government. Specifically, Teeple had made statements at an earlier court hearing that had essentially demonstrated his knowledge and possession of the financial records the government was seeking.

Finally, an act is incriminating if a person has "reasonable ground to apprehend danger to the witness from his being compelled to answer." Brown v. Walker, 161 U.S. 591, 599 (1896). That is, the individual's refusal to comply must be based on "articulated real and appreciable fear" that the information to be disclosed "would be used to incriminate him, or that it would furnish a link in the chain of evidence needed to prosecute him." Hiibel v. Sixth Judicial District Court, 542 U.S. 177, 190 (2004). The notion is that the information disclosed must provide the government with evidence that helps prove a criminal case against the witness.

Imagine the government seizes an encrypted computer belonging to a suspect, and the government wants to compel the suspect to enter in the password and decrypt the computer or the files it contains. Does the Fifth Amendment provide the suspect with a constitutional right not to comply?

IN RE BOUCHER

United States District Court for the District of Vermont, 2007.
2007 WL 4246473.

JEROME J. NIEDERMEIER, UNITED STATES MAGISTRATE JUDGE.

On December 17, 2006, defendant Sebastien Boucher was arrested on a complaint charging him with transportation of child pornography in violation of 18 U.S.C. § 2252A(a)(1). At the time of his arrest government agents seized from him a laptop computer containing child pornography. The government has now determined that the relevant files are encrypted, password-protected, and inaccessible. The grand jury has subpoenaed Boucher to enter a password to allow access to the files on the computer. Boucher has moved to quash the subpoena on the grounds that it violates his Fifth Amendment right against self-incrimination.

Background

On December 17, 2006, Boucher and his father crossed the Canadian border into the United States at Derby Line, Vermont. At the border station, agents directed Boucher's car into secondary inspection. Customs and Border Protection Officer Chris Pike performed the secondary inspection.

Officer Pike found a laptop computer in the back seat of the car. He opened the computer and accessed the files without entering a password. Officer Pike conducted a search of the computer files for any images or videos. He located approximately 40,000 images, some of which appeared to be pornographic based on the names of the files.

Officer Pike asked Boucher whether any of the image files on the laptop contained child pornography. Boucher responded that he was uncertain, and Officer Pike continued investigating the contents of the computer. Officer Pike noticed several file names that appeared to reference child pornography. He then called Special Agent Mark Curtis of Immigration and Customs Enforcement who has experience and training in recognizing child pornography.

When Agent Curtis arrived, he examined the computer and found a file [with a title indicating it was child pornography]. Agent Curtis was unable to open the file to view it. However, Agent Curtis determined that the file had been opened on December 11, 2006. He continued to investigate and found thousands of images of adult pornography and animation depicting adult and child pornography.

Agent Curtis then read Boucher his *Miranda* rights. Boucher waived his rights in writing and agreed to speak to Agent Curtis. Agent Curtis asked Boucher about the file [he had found]. Boucher stated that he downloads many pornographic files from online newsgroups onto a desktop computer at home and then transfers them to his laptop. Boucher also stated that he sometimes unknowingly downloads images that contain child pornography but deletes them when he realizes their contents.

Agent Curtis asked Boucher to show him where the files he download-ed from the newsgroups were located on the laptop. Boucher was allowed access to the laptop and navigated to a part of the hard drive designated as drive Z. Agent Curtis did not see Boucher enter a password to access drive Z. Agent Curtis began searching through drive Z in Boucher's presence though Boucher appeared to be uncomfortable with this.

Agent Curtis located many adult pornographic files and one video [with a name that suggested it was child pornography]. Agent Curtis viewed the video and [confirmed that it was]. He asked Boucher whether he had any similar files on his laptop, and Boucher again stated that he usually deletes files that he discovers to contain child pornography.

Agent Curtis then asked Boucher to leave the room and continued to examine drive Z. He located several images and videos of child pornogra-phy in drive Z. After consulting with the United States Attorney's office, Agent Curtis arrested Boucher. He then seized the laptop, after shutting it down.

On December 29, 2006, Mike Touchette of the Vermont Department of Corrections took custody of the laptop. Touchette created a mirror image of the contents of the laptop. When Touchette began exploring the computer, he could not access drive Z because it was protected by encryption algorithms through the use of the software Pretty Good Privacy ("PGP"), which requires a password to access drive Z. Since shutting down the laptop, the government has been unable to access drive Z to view the images and videos containing child pornography.

Secret Service Agent Matthew Fasvlo, who has experience and train-ing in computer forensics, testified that it is nearly impossible to access these encrypted files without knowing the password. There are no "back doors" or secret entrances to access the files. The only way to get access without the password is to use an automated system which repeatedly guesses passwords. According to the government, the process to unlock drive Z could take years, based on efforts to unlock similarly encrypted files in another case. Despite its best efforts, to date the government has been unable to learn the password to access drive Z.

To gain access to drive Z and the files in question, the grand jury has subpoenaed Boucher directing him to:

> provide all documents, whether in electronic or paper form, reflecting any passwords used or associated with the Alienware Notebook Com-puter, Model D9T, Serial No. NKD900TA5L00859, seized from Sebas-tien Boucher at the Port of Entry at Derby Line, Vermont on December 17, 2006.

Boucher has moved to quash the subpoena as violative of his Fifth Amendment right against self-incrimination. At the hearing the govern-ment suggested that Boucher could enter the password into the computer without the government, the grand jury, or the Court observing or recording the password in any way. The government also suggested that to avoid any Fifth Amendment issue the Court could order that the act of entering the password could not be used against Boucher. The Court must now determine whether compelling Boucher to enter the password into the laptop would violate his Fifth Amendment privilege against self-incrimination.

Discussion

The Fifth Amendment privilege against self-incrimination protects a person against being incriminated by his own compelled testimonial communications. For the privilege to apply, the communication must be compelled, testimonial, and incriminating in nature. Subpoenas require compliance and therefore constitute compulsion. Because the files sought by the government allegedly contain child pornography, the entry of the password would be incriminating. Whether the privilege against self incrimination applies therefore depends on whether the subpoena seeks testimonial communication.

Both parties agree that the *contents* of the laptop do not enjoy Fifth Amendment protection as the contents were voluntarily prepared and are not testimonial. Also, the government concedes that it cannot compel Boucher to disclose the password to the grand jury because the disclosure would be testimonial. The question remains whether entry of the password, giving the government access to drive Z, would be testimonial and therefore privileged.

I.　Entering the Password is Testimonial

Compelling Boucher to enter the password forces him to produce evidence that could be used to incriminate him. Producing the password, as if it were a key to a locked container, forces Boucher to produce the contents of his laptop.

The act of producing even unprivileged evidence can have communicative aspects itself and may be "testimonial" and entitled to Fifth Amendment protection. *United States v. Doe,* 465 U.S. 605, 612 (1984) [hereinafter *Doe I*] ("Although the contents of a document may not be privileged, the act of producing the document may be."). An act is testimonial when the act entails implicit statements of fact, such as admitting that evidence exists, is authentic, or is within a suspect's control. *Doe v. United States,* 487 U.S. 201, 209 (1988) [hereinafter *Doe II*]. The privilege against self-incrimination protects a suspect from being compelled to disclose any knowledge he has, or to speak his guilt. The suspect may not be put in the "cruel trilemma" of choosing between self-accusation, perjury, or contempt.

The government points to *Doe II* in support of its contention that entering the password is non-testimonial and therefore not privileged. In *Doe II,* a suspect was subpoenaed to sign a form requesting his bank records from banks in the Cayman Islands and Bermuda. The suspect asserted his privilege against self-incrimination, arguing that signing the form would be testimonial and incriminating. But the form only spoke in the hypothetical, not referencing specific accounts or banks. The Court held that the form did not acknowledge any accounts and made no statement, implicitly or explicitly, about the existence or control over any accounts. Because signing the form made no statement about the suspect's knowledge, the Court held that the act lacked testimonial significance and the privilege did not apply.

Entering a password into the computer implicitly communicates facts. By entering the password Boucher would be disclosing the fact that he knows the password and has control over the files on drive Z. The procedure is equivalent to asking Boucher, "Do you know the password to the laptop?" If Boucher does know the password, he would be faced with the forbidden trilemma; incriminate himself, lie under oath, or find himself in contempt of court.

Unlike the situation in *Doe II,* Boucher would be compelled to produce his thoughts and the contents of his mind. In *Doe II,* the suspect was compelled to act to obtain access without indicating that he believed himself to have access. Here, when Boucher enters a password he indicates that he believes he has access.

The Supreme Court has held some acts of production are unprivileged such as providing fingerprints, blood samples, or voice recordings. Production of such evidence gives no indication of a person's thoughts or knowledge because it is undeniable that a person possesses his own fingerprints, blood, and voice. Unlike the unprivileged production of such samples, it is not without question that Boucher possesses the password or has access to the files.

In distinguishing testimonial from non-testimonial acts, the Supreme Court has compared revealing the combination to a wall safe to surrendering the key to a strongbox. The combination conveys the contents of one's mind; the key does not and is therefore not testimonial. A password, like a combination, is in the suspect's mind, and is therefore testimonial and beyond the reach of the grand jury subpoena.

II.   Effect of Non–Viewing

The government has offered to restrict the entering of the password so that no one views or records the password. While this would prevent the government from knowing what the password is, it would not change the testimonial significance of the act of entering the password. Boucher would still be implicitly indicating that he knows the password and that he has access to the files. The contents of Boucher's mind would still be displayed, and therefore the testimonial nature does not change merely because no one else will discover the password.

III.   Foregone Conclusion

The government also asserts that the information gained through entry of the password is a "foregone conclusion", therefore no privilege applies. * * * [T]he privilege against self-incrimination does not apply to an act of production if the existence and location of the subpoenaed evidence is known to the government and the production would not "implicitly authenticate" the evidence.

Here, the subpoena can be viewed as either compelling the production of the password itself or compelling the production of the files on drive Z.

If the subpoena is requesting production of the files in drive Z, the foregone conclusion doctrine does not apply. While the government has seen some of the files on drive Z, it has not viewed all or even most of them. While the government may know of the existence and location of the files it has previously viewed, it does not know of the existence of other files on drive Z that may contain incriminating material. By compelling entry of the password the government would be compelling production of all the files on drive Z, both known and unknown. The files the government has not seen could add much to the sum total of the government's information. Therefore, the foregone conclusion doctrine does not apply and the act of production privilege remains.

Since the government is trying to compel the production of the password itself, the foregone conclusion doctrine cannot apply. The password is not a physical thing. If Boucher knows the password, it only exists in his mind. This information is unlike a document, to which the foregone conclusion doctrine usually applies, and unlike any physical evidence the government could already know of. It is pure testimonial production rather than physical evidence having testimonial aspects. Compelling Boucher to produce the password compels him to display the contents of his mind to incriminate himself. The foregone conclusion doctrine does not apply to the production of non-physical evidence, existing only in a suspect's mind where the act of production can be used against him.

For the foregoing reasons, the motion to quash the subpoena is granted.

NOTES AND QUESTIONS

1.   Magistrate Judge Niedermeier's decision in *Boucher* was appealed by the government to the United States District Court. Before the District Court, the government clarified to District Judge William K. Sessions that it was not seeking to have Boucher produce the password. Instead, the government planned to bring Boucher before the grand jury and have him enter in his password without showing the password to the government. Boucher would comply with the subpoena by producing the plaintext version of his computer that would result when he successfully entered in his password.

District Judge Sessions disagreed with Magistrate Judge Niedermeier's application of the foregone conclusion doctrine, and ruled that Boucher had to comply with the subpoena:

The Magistrate Judge determined that the foregone conclusion rationale did not apply, because the government has not viewed most of the files on the Z drive, and therefore does not know whether most of the files on the Z drive contain incriminating material. Second Circuit precedent, however, does not require that the government be aware of the incriminatory *contents* of the files; it requires the government to demonstrate with reasonable particularity that it knows of the existence and location of subpoenaed documents.

Boucher accessed the Z drive of his laptop at the ICE agent's request. The ICE agent viewed the contents of some of the Z drive's files, and ascertained that they may consist of images or videos of child pornography. The Government thus knows of the existence and location of the Z drive and its files. Again providing access to the unencrypted Z drive adds little or nothing to the sum total of the Government's information about the existence and location of files that may contain incriminating information.

Boucher's act of producing an unencrypted version of the Z drive likewise is not necessary to authenticate it. He has already admitted to possession of the computer, and provided the Government with access to the Z drive. The Government has submitted that it can link Boucher with the files on his computer without making use of his production of an unencrypted version of the Z drive, and that it will not use his act of production as evidence of authentication.

Because Boucher has no act of production privilege to refuse to provide the grand jury with an unencrypted version of the Z drive of his computer, his motion to quash the subpoena (as modified by the Government) is denied. Boucher is directed to provide an unencrypted version of the Z drive viewed by the ICE agent.

In re Boucher, 2009 WL 424718 (D. Vt. 2009) (Sessions, District Judge). As of the time of this writing, the case is now on appeal before the United States Court of Appeals for the Second Circuit. How should the Second Circuit rule?

2. Imagine a suspect is ordered to enter in his computer password to decrypt his files, and he responds that he has forgotten it. Or perhaps he simply refuses to comply with an order to disclose his encryption key. What happens next?

Assume for the moment that the court concludes that the witness is falsely claiming to have forgotten, or that he is refusing to comply for reasons other than a valid legal privilege. The Second Circuit has summarized the legal consequences in federal cases as follows:

> Testimonial obduracy by a witness who has been ordered by the court to answer questions may take any of a number of forms. The witness may refuse categorically to answer. Or he may respond in a way that avoids providing information, as, for example, by denying memory of the events under inquiry, denying acquaintance with targets of the inquiry, or denying knowledge of facts sought to be elicited. Or he may purport to state informative facts in response to the questions while in fact testifying falsely.

Any of these three forms of obduracy may be met with the imposition of one or more judicial or governmental sanctions. For example, when the witness has refused to answer questions, he may be adjudged in civil contempt and ordered to answer, or he may be adjudged in criminal contempt and punished for his past failure to answer. In some cases both coercive and punitive sanctions have been imposed.

If the witness has responded falsely to the questions propounded, he may be subject to prosecution for a criminal offense in violation of, *e.g.*, 18 U.S.C. § 1621 (perjury), or 18 U.S.C. § 1623 (false declarations before grand jury or court). If the witness's false testimony has obstructed the court in the performance of its duty, the witness may be met with sanctions for civil contempt or criminal contempt.

The middle category of testimonial obduracy, *i.e.*, the witness's equivocal responses or disclaimers of knowledge or memory, has also been dealt with as contemptuous conduct, warranting sanctions that were coercive, punitive, or both. It has long been the practice of courts viewing such testimony as false and intentionally evasive, and as a sham or subterfuge that purposely avoids giving responsive answers, to ignore the form of the response and treat the witness as having refused to answer.

In re Weiss, 703 F.2d 653, 662–663 (2d Cir. 1983).

If a suspect refuses to comply because he has asserted a valid legal privilege such as the Fifth Amendment, then the court should quash the order to compel the testimony. If a suspect genuinely does not know the information or states truthfully that he has forgotten, then the suspect should not be punished: he then has "just cause" to not comply with the order. 28 U.S.C. § 1826(a) (civil contempt standard). *See also* 18 U.S.C. § 401 (criminal contempt standard). Whether a suspect is being truthful about forgetting the information is a question of fact that normally must be settled by a hearing before the trial judge.

E. THE FOURTH AMENDMENT AND COMPUTER NETWORKS

The materials in this chapter have considered Fourth Amendment limitations on government access to computers and data under their owners' control. In many cases, however, data will not be stored with its owner. Computer users routinely send information over local, national, or even international computer networks. When computer networks are used to commit criminal acts, investigators may wish to collect evidence directly from those networks without approaching the suspect or his home. For example, local police trying to catch a fraud suspect might want to obtain account records and stored e-mail held by the suspect's Internet service provider. FBI agents pursuing a hacker might want to conduct real-time surveillance of his account from inside a victim network. Finally, under-cover police officers trying to catch pedophiles might want to enter an Internet chat room posing as a child. In all of these cases, investigators will attempt to obtain information from a remote network rather than from the suspect's home computer.

This section considers how the Fourth Amendment applies to the collection of computer data sent over or stored on remote computers. To appreciate the difficult questions of Fourth Amendment law raised by network surveillance, it helps to review a few basic features about how computer networks (and specifically, today's Internet protocols) work. Individuals normally connect to networks and the Internet by having an account with a server that is connected to a broader network. For example, a home user may have an Internet service provider that serves as the user's contact point with the network. Every communication sent or received by the user is routed through the user's ISP.

Internet communications are sent across the network by being broken into "packets," individual chunks of data that contain about a page's worth of information. Internet packets are streams of data that act as the computer equivalent of letters between computers. Each packet begins with a IP (Internet protocol) header, a computer-generated envelope that contains the packet's originating and destination address along with information about the type and size of the information the packet carries. The IP header (also referred to as a packet header) is created when the communication is sent, and is used by the network to ensure delivery of the payload. The communication itself becomes the "payload" of the packet, and appears after the header. The header is automatically discarded by the receiving computer when the packet arrives at its destination. The receiving computer then reassembles the various packets into the original file that was sent.

Packet headers are not the only kind of addressing information generated by computers. Sending an e-mail generates an "e-mail header" that contains originating and destination e-mail addresses, as well as a brief history of where and when the e-mail was sent in the course of delivery. Many types of e-mail programs permit you to view the entire e-mail header of e-mails in your inbox; the header is akin to the envelope of a letter, complete with an electronic version of a postmark.

The existence of packet headers, e-mail headers, and other types of Internet communications means that the Fourth Amendment rules that govern network surveillance must consider a very wide range of different communications and surveillance techniques. Information relating to an individual's computer use may include the contents of e-mails, requests for web pages, e-mail headers, IP headers, and many other kinds of information. That information can be monitored in real-time or collected from storage from a wide range of places across the network.

When does a computer user have a reasonable expectation of privacy in such information, such that a particular surveillance technique triggers Fourth Amendment protection?

1. ANALOGIES TO SPEECH, LETTERS, AND TELEPHONE CALLS

Reasoning by analogy is an important tool to help understand how the Fourth Amendment might apply to collecting information from computer networks. The courts have decided many cases applying the Fourth Amendment to earlier communications technologies such as the telephone network and the postal mail network. One way to understand the Fourth Amendment in the context of computer networks is by reasoning from analogy to these earlier technologies. In particular, consider three possible analogies: speech, postal letters, and telephone calls.

The Speech Analogy

Is sending computer data to a remote computer akin to speaking to that computer? When you send e-mail and surf the web, are you telling your ISP to send the information for you and then hearing from your ISP as to what information it received on your behalf? From this perspective, we might model computers as if they were people, and model transmission of information among computers as if it were an open sharing of information among them.

Is this analogy persuasive? If it is, sending data to a remote server likely eliminates a reasonable expectation of privacy in the data. The Supreme Court has consistently held that a person's Fourth Amendment rights are not violated if he reasonably but mistakenly tells another person his secrets and the person then relays that secret to the government.

For example, in Hoffa v. United States, 385 U.S. 293 (1966), James Hoffa admitted criminal activity to a confidant, Partin. Partin turned out to be a paid government informer, and he transmitted the information to the FBI. Hoffa objected, arguing that his Fourth Amendment rights had been violated when Partin shared Hoffa's private information with the police. The Court rejected this argument:

> Neither this Court nor any member of it has ever expressed the view that the Fourth Amendment protects a wrongdoer's misplaced belief that a person to whom he voluntarily confides his wrongdoing will not reveal it. * * * The risk of being overheard by an eavesdropper or betrayed by an informer or deceived as to the identity of one with whom one deals is probably inherent in the conditions of human society. It is the kind of risk we necessarily assume whenever we speak.

Id. at 302–03. Under Hoffa, a person assumes the risk that those within earshot of their speech will hear and understand the speech and will share it with the police. However unlikely it is, the person's Fourth Amendment rights are not violated if it happens.

This is true even if the person does not intend for others overhearing the speech to listen in or understand it. Consider the unpleasant surprise encountered by the Spanish-speaking members of the narcotics conspiracy in United States v. Longoria, 177 F.3d 1179 (10th Cir. 1999). Because the co-conspirators were the only individuals nearby who spoke or understood Spanish, they discussed their criminal activity to each other in Spanish in the presence of outsiders. One such outsider turned out to be a government informant who recorded the defendant's Spanish conversations using audio equipment. The informant did not understand Spanish, but government translators did. They translated the tapes into English and used the translations at trial. The Tenth Circuit rejected the notion that the co-conspirators had a reasonable expectation of privacy because they spoke in a foreign tongue that others present did not comprehend. "[O]ne exposing conversations to others must necessarily assume the risk his statements will be overheard and understood," the court reasoned. "[The defendant] exposed his statements by speaking in a manner clearly audible by the informant. His hope that the informant would not fully understand the contents of the conversation is not an expectation society is prepared to recognize as reasonable." *Id.* at 1182.

Courts have analogized Internet communications to speech in the context of online undercover operations. For example, in State v. Moller, 2002 WL 628634 (Ohio Ct. App. 2002), a police officer entered a chat room for older men posing as a 14 year-old girl. Defendant Moller contacted the officer and the two eventually arranged for Moller to drive 200 miles to meet the "girl" for sexual activities. Following his arrest, Moller argued that the officer's conduct violated his Fourth Amendment rights. The Court disagreed, relying on the rationale of *Hoffa*:

> Like Hoffa, Moller took the risk that the 14 year old he thought he was talking to, and planning to engage in sex with, was not who she seemed to be, but was in reality a police officer. This is a risk that anyone visiting a chat room necessarily takes when communicating with strangers. It is easy for anyone using the Internet to adopt a false persona, whether for purposes of law enforcement, or for other and nefarious purposes. It was unreasonable for Moller to assume that his unsuitable conversations would be kept private. Thus, in our view, his statements made in the chat room to a stranger are not entitled to protection under the Fourth Amendment.

Id. at *5.

The Letter or Package Analogy

Is sending computer data to a remote location like sending a document, letter or package? Existing Fourth Amendment law teaches that individuals who send letters and packages retain a reasonable expectation of privacy in the contents of their sealed containers but not in the exposed exteriors of those containers. Fourth Amendment protections track what is exposed and what is sealed away from view. For example, individuals do not retain a reasonable expectation of privacy in the outside of their letters or packages, or in documents disclosed to others. The police can observe the outside of packages, take pictures of envelopes, read postcards, and analyze disclosed documents all without implicating the Fourth Amendment. On the other hand, opening a sealed letter or package during transit to view its contents is a Fourth Amendment search that implicates the Fourth Amendment rights of the sender and receiver. It requires a warrant or an exception to the warrant requirement.

The Fourth Amendment's protection of postal letters dates back to dicta in Ex Parte Jackson, 96 U.S. (6 Otto) 727 (1877), a decision involving the power of Congress to regulate the postal system. Justice Field wrote the following about the privacy of items sent through the postal system, *id*. at 733:

> Letters and sealed packages * * * in the mail are as fully guarded from examination and inspection, except as to their outward form and weight, as if they were retained by the parties forwarding them in their own domiciles. The constitutional guaranty of the right of the people to be secure in their papers against unreasonable searches and seizures extends to their papers, thus closed against inspection, wherever they may be. Whilst in the mail, they can only be opened and examined under like warrant, issued upon similar oath or affirmation, particularly describing the thing to be seized, as is required when papers are subjected to search in one's own household. No law of Congress can place in the hands of officials connected with the postal service any authority to invade the secrecy of letters and such sealed packages in the mail; and all regulations adopted as to mail matter of this kind must be in subordination to the great principle embodied in the Fourth Amendment of the Constitution.

The basic principle of *Ex Parte Jackson* has been construed fairly broadly. Leaving a sealed package with a trustworthy bailee generally preserves the bailor's Fourth Amendment protections in the package's contents. For example, individuals have been held to retain a reasonable expectation of privacy in the contents of opaque packages when they send packages via private carriers, *see* Walter v. United States, 447 U.S. 649, 651 (1980); when they leave packages with store clerks, *see* United States v. Most, 876 F.2d 191, 197–98 (D.C. Cir. 1989); when they are stored with airport baggage counters, *see* United States v. Barry, 853 F.2d 1479, 1481–83 (8th Cir. 1988); and when they leave packages with their friends for safekeeping, *see* United States v. Presler, 610 F.2d 1206, 1213–14 (4th Cir. 1979). In all of these cases, governmental opening of the sealed package violates the owner's reasonable expectation of privacy.

However, there are two important limits on this principle. First, the sender's reasonable expectation of privacy in a sealed package or letter is eliminated when the package or letter reaches its destination. When the item is delivered and the letter becomes the property of the recipient, governmental access no longer implicates the sender's Fourth Amendment rights. For example, the search of a home that uncovers letters mailed to that address will not implicate the Fourth Amendment rights of the individuals who sent the letters. *See* United States v. King, 55 F.3d 1193, 1196 (6th Cir. 1995).

Second, a person does not have a reasonable expectation of privacy in letters or packages in the course of transit when the carrier has the right to access the contents of the letters or packages. For example, the United States Postal Service has traditionally had a category of mail known as fourth class mail. The postal service retains a right to open letters and packages sent fourth class mail. Courts have held that an individual does not retain a reasonable expectation of privacy in their fourth class mail, as sending a package when the postal service retains a right to open it constitutes consent to opening it that is inconsistent with Fourth Amendment protection. See, e.g., United States v. Huie, 593 F.2d 14, 15 (5th Cir. 1979).

How should these principles apply to computer data sent remotely over a network? Is computer data "sealed"? Do ISPs have a right to "open" it? What is the "destination" of an e-mail or a request for a web page?

The Telephone Analogy

Instead of analogizing computer network communications to speech or letters, we might try to analogize them to telephone calls. The Fourth Amendment framework that governs telephone calls ends up being very similar to the legal framework that governs letters and packages.

The Supreme Court's first decision on how the Fourth Amendment applies to telephone calls was Olmstead v. United States, 277 U.S. 438 (1928). Roy Olmstead was the leader of a massive Prohibition-era conspiracy to import illegal alcohol into the United States. Agents tapped the telephone lines to Olmstead's house and offices and then listened in on the calls to gather evidence against him. The Supreme Court ruled 5–4 that this wiretapping did not constitute a Fourth Amendment search. Writing for the majority, Chief Justice Taft rejected the letter analogy:

> The Fourth Amendment may have proper application to a sealed letter in the mail, because of the constitutional provision for the Postoffice Department and the relations between the government and those who pay to secure protection of their sealed letters. * * * It is plainly within the words of the amendment to say that the unlawful rifling by a government agent of a sealed letter is a search and seizure of the sender's papers or effects. The letter is a paper, an effect, and in the custody of a government that forbids carriage, except under its protection.

> The United States takes no such care of telegraph or telephone messages as of mailed sealed letters. The amendment does not forbid what was done here. There was no searching. There was no seizure. The evidence was secured by the use of the sense of hearing and that only. There was no entry of the houses or offices of the defendants.

By the invention of the telephone 50 years ago, and its application for the purpose of extending communications, one can talk with another at a far distant place.

The language of the amendment cannot be extended and expanded to include telephone wires, reaching to the whole world from the defendant's house or office. The intervening wires are not part of his house or office, any more than are the highways along which they are stretched.

Id. at 464–65. Chief Justice Taft construed telephone calls as more akin to human speech than letters:

The reasonable view is that one who installs in his house a telephone instrument with connecting wires intends to project his voice to those quite outside, and that the wires beyond his house, and messages while passing over them, are not within the protection of the Fourth Amendment. Here those who intercepted the projected voices were not in the house of either party to the conversation.

Id. at 466.

In his famous dissent, Justice Louis Brandeis presented a very different picture of the Fourth Amendment and the role of wiretapping:

When the Fourth and Fifth Amendments were adopted, the form that evil had theretofore taken had been necessarily simple. Force and violence were then the only means known to man by which a government could directly effect self-incrimination. It could compel the individual to testify—a compulsion effected, if need be, by torture. It could secure possession of his papers and other articles incident to his private life—a seizure effected, if need be, by breaking and entry. Protection against such invasion of the sanctities of a man's home and the privacies of life was provided in the Fourth and Fifth Amendments by specific language. But time works changes, brings into existence new conditions and purposes. Subtler and more far-reaching means of invading privacy have become available to the government. Discovery and invention have made it possible for the government, by means far more effective than stretching upon the rack, to obtain disclosure in court of what is whispered in the closet.

Moreover, in the application of a Constitution, our contemplation cannot be only of what has been, but of what may be. The progress of science in furnishing the government with means of espionage is not likely to stop with wire tapping. Ways may some day be developed by which the government, without removing papers from secret drawers, can reproduce them in court, and by which it will be enabled to expose to a jury the most intimate occurrences of the home. Advances in the psychic and related sciences may bring means of exploring unexpressed beliefs, thoughts and emotions. 'That places the liberty of every man in the hands of every petty officer' was said by James Otis of much lesser intrusions than these. To Lord Camden a far slighter intrusion seemed 'subversive of all the comforts of society.' Can it be that the Constitution affords no protection against such invasions of individual security?

In *Ex parte Jackson*, it was held that a sealed letter intrusted to the mail is protected by the amendments. The mail is a public service furnished by the government. The telephone is a public service furnished by its authority. There is, in essence, no difference between the sealed letter and the private telephone message. As Judge Rudkin said below: "True, the one is visible, the other invisible; the one is tangible, the other intangible; the one is sealed, and the other unsealed; but these are distinctions without a difference."

The evil incident to invasion of the privacy of the telephone is far greater than that involved in tampering with the mails. Whenever a telephone line is tapped, the privacy of the persons at both ends of the line is invaded, and all conversations between them upon any subject, and although proper, confidential, and privileged, may be overheard. Moreover, the tapping of one man's telephone line involves the tapping of the telephone of every other person whom he may call, or who may call him. As a means of espionage, writs of assistance and general warrants are but puny instruments of tyranny and oppression when compared with wire tapping.

* * * The makers of our Constitution undertook to secure conditions favorable to the pursuit of happiness. They recognized the significance of man's spiritual nature, of his feelings and of his intellect. They knew that only a part of the pain, pleasure and satisfactions of life are to be found in material things. They sought to protect Americans in their beliefs, their thoughts, their emotions and their sensations. They conferred, as against the government, the right to be let alone— the most comprehensive of rights and the right most valued by civilized men. To protect that right, every unjustifiable intrusion by the government upon the privacy of the individual, whatever the means employed, must be deemed a violation of the Fourth Amendment.

Id. at 473–476, 478–79 (Brandeis, J., dissenting).

The Supreme Court effectively overruled *Olmstead* in two cases, Berger v. New York, 388 U.S. 41 (1967), and Katz v. United States, 389 U.S. 347 (1967). *Berger* invalidated a New York state wiretapping law on the ground that it did not provide sufficient Fourth Amendment safeguards. The majority opinion did not directly hold that the wiretapping violated the rights of the person whose phone was tapped. Instead, the opinion took the opportunity to articulate general Fourth Amendment requirements for wiretapping statutes. Unlike *Berger, Katz* was not a wiretapping case. *Katz* involved a microphone taped to a public phone booth, not the intercept of any calls. However, a passage in the majority opinion announced the end of the *Olmstead* regime:

Although a closely divided Court supposed in *Olmstead* that surveillance without any trespass and without the seizure of any material object fell outside the ambit of the Constitution, we have since departed from the narrow view on which that decision rested. Indeed, we have expressly held that the Fourth Amendment governs not only the seizure of tangible items, but extends as well to the recording of oral statements, over-heard without any technical trespass under local property law. Once this much is acknowledged, and once it is recognized that the Fourth Amendment protects people—and not simply "areas"—against unreasonable searches and seizures, it becomes clear that the reach of that Amendment cannot turn upon the presence or absence of a physical intrusion into any given enclosure.

We conclude that the underpinnings of *Olmstead* * * * have been so eroded by our subsequent decisions that the "trespass" doctrine there enunciated can no longer be regarded as controlling.

Katz, 389 U.S. at 352–53. The combination of *Berger* and *Katz* indicates that wiretapping an individual's telephone calls normally amounts to a Fourth Amendment "search."

Lower courts have held that this rule does not apply in the case of cordless telephones, however. In the 1980s, companies began offering cordless telephones for sale to the public. Cordless telephones work by broadcasting FM radio signals between the base of the phone and the handset. Each phone has two radio transmitters that work at the same time: the base transmits the incoming call signal to the handset, and the handset transmits the outgoing call signal to the base. Before the mid–1990s, cordless phones generally used analog FM signals that were easy to intercept. Government agents would occasionally use widely available FM radio scanners to listen in on the cordless telephone calls of suspects without a warrant. Courts that have addressed this issue have rejected claims of Fourth Amendment protection in the contents of cordless telephone calls. Because cordless-phone intercepting devices merely pick up a signal that has been "broadcast over the radio waves to all who wish to overhear," the interception was held not to violate any reasonable expectation of privacy. McKamey v. Roach, 55 F.3d 1236, 1239–40 (6th Cir. 1995). *See also* Tyler v. Berodt, 877 F.2d 705, 707 (8th Cir. 1989); Price v. Turner, 260 F.3d 1144, 1149 (9th Cir. 2001). Courts reached the same result when the suspect was using a traditional landline telephone and happened to engage in conversation with someone who was using a cordless phone. *See* United States v. McNulty, 47 F.3d 100, 104–106 (4th Cir. 1995).

You may recall from the discussion of letters and packages that the contents of letters or packages are ordinarily protected by the Fourth Amendment, while the outside of the envelopes and packages are not. The Supreme Court created a similar distinction for telephone calls in Smith v. Maryland, 442 U.S. 735 (1979). The police in *Smith* were investigating a robbery, and they had reason to believe that the victim of the robbery was being harassed by the robber through threatening telephone calls. The police suspected that Smith was the robber, and they asked the telephone company to install a device known as a "pen register" on Smith's telephone. In the telephone technology of the 1970s, a pen register was a device that recorded the numbers dialed from a particular telephone line. The pen register did not record the actual contents of the communications, but rather only the telephone numbers dialed to complete the call. The telephone company installed the pen register on Smith's phone line, and it recorded Smith's home telephone line being used to dial the number of the robbery victim.

The Supreme Court concluded in *Smith* that recording the numbers dialed from Smith's phone line was not protected by the Fourth Amendment:

> First, we doubt that people in general entertain any actual expectation of privacy in the numbers they dial. All telephone users realize that they must "convey" phone numbers to the telephone company, since it is through telephone company switching equipment that their calls are completed. All subscribers realize, moreover, that the phone company has facilities for making permanent records of the numbers they dial, for they see a list of their long-distance (toll) calls on their monthly bills. In fact, pen registers and similar devices are routinely used by telephone companies for the purposes of checking billing operations, detecting fraud and preventing violations of law. Electronic equipment is used not only to keep billing records of toll calls, but also to keep a record of all calls dialed from a telephone which is subject to a special rate structure.

> Second, even if petitioner did harbor some subjective expectation that the phone numbers he dialed would remain private, this expectation is not one that society is prepared to recognize as 'reasonable.' This Court consistently has held that a person has no legitimate expectation of privacy in information he voluntarily turns over to third parties. This analysis dictates that petitioner can claim no legitimate expectation of privacy here. When he used his phone, petitioner voluntarily conveyed numerical information to the telephone company and "exposed" that information to its equipment in the ordinary course of business. In so doing, petitioner assumed the risk that the company would reveal to police the numbers he dialed. The switching equipment that processed those numbers is merely the modern counterpart of the operator who, in an earlier day, personally completed calls for the subscriber. Petitioner concedes that if he had placed his calls through an operator, he could claim no legitimate expectation of privacy. We are not inclined to hold that a different constitutional result is required because the telephone company has decided to automate.

> Petitioner argues, however, that automatic switching equipment differs from a live operator in one pertinent respect. An operator, in

theory at least, is capable of remembering every number that is conveyed to him by callers. Electronic equipment, by contrast can "remember" only those numbers it is programmed to record, and telephone companies, in view of their present billing practices, usually do not record local calls. Since petitioner, in calling McDonough, was making a local call, his expectation of privacy as to her number, on this theory, would be "legitimate."

This argument does not withstand scrutiny. The fortuity of whether or not the phone company in fact elects to make a quasi-permanent record of a particular number dialed does not in our view, make any constitutional difference. Regardless of the phone company's election, petitioner voluntarily conveyed to it information that it had facilities for recording and that it was free to record. In these circumstances, petitioner assumed the risk that the information would be divulged to police.

Justice Marshall dissented:

In my view, whether privacy expectations are legitimate within the meaning of *Katz* depends not on the risks an individual can be presumed to accept when imparting information to third parties, but on the risks he should be forced to assume in a free and open society.

The use of pen registers, I believe, constitutes such an extensive intrusion. To hold otherwise ignores the vital role telephonic communication plays in our personal and professional relationships as well as the First and Fourth Amendment interests implicated by unfettered official surveillance. Privacy in placing calls is of value not only to those engaged in criminal activity. The prospect of unregulated governmental monitoring will undoubtedly prove disturbing even to those with nothing illicit to hide. Many individuals, including members of unpopular political organizations or journalists with confidential sources, may legitimately wish to avoid disclosure of their personal contacts. Permitting governmental access to telephone records on less than probable cause may thus impede certain forms of political affiliation and journalistic endeavor that are the hallmark of a truly free society. Particularly given the Government's previous reliance on warrantless telephonic surveillance to trace reporters' sources and monitor protected political activity, I am unwilling to insulate use of pen registers from independent judicial review.

Summarizing the law of how the Fourth Amendment applies to telephone communications, the Fourth Amendment ordinarily protects the contents of calls (with the exception of cordless phone calls) but does not protect the numbers dialed.

2. NON-CONTENT INFORMATION

Information sent over a network can be divided into two types: content information and non-content information. Content information is the communication that a user sends to another user. Non-content information is the information that the network generates to facilitate the transmission and storage of the content information. The following case considers how the Fourth Amendment applies to the surveillance of non-content information sent over a computer network.

UNITED STATES v. FORRESTER

United States Court of Appeals for the Ninth Circuit, 2007.
495 F.3d 1041.

FISHER, CIRCUIT JUDGE:

Defendants-appellants Mark Stephen Forrester and Dennis Louis Alba were charged with various offenses relating to the operation of a large Ecstasy-manufacturing laboratory, and were convicted on all counts following a jury trial. They now appeal their convictions and sentences.

Alba challenges the validity of computer surveillance that enabled the government to learn the to/from addresses of his e-mail messages, the Internet protocol ("IP") addresses of the websites that he visited and the total volume of information transmitted to or from his account. We conclude that this surveillance was analogous to the use of a pen register that the Supreme Court held in *Smith v. Maryland,* 442 U.S. 735 (1979), did not constitute a search for Fourth Amendment purposes.

I. Background

Following a lengthy government investigation, Forrester and Alba were indicted on October 26, 2001, and arraigned shortly thereafter. Forrester was charged with one count of conspiracy to manufacture and distribute 3, 4–methylenedioxymethamphetamine ("Ecstasy"). Alba was also charged with that offense, as well as with engaging in a continuing criminal enterprise, conspiracy to transfer funds outside the United States in promotion of an illegal activity, and conspiracy to conduct financial transactions involving the proceeds of an illegal activity. Both defendants pleaded not guilty to all charges.

During its investigation of Forrester and Alba's Ecstasy-manufacturing operation, the government employed various computer surveillance techniques to monitor Alba's e-mail and Internet activity. The surveillance began in May 2001 after the government applied for and received court permission to install a pen register analogue known as a "mirror port" on Alba's account with PacBell Internet. The mirror port was installed at PacBell's connection facility in San Diego, and enabled the government to learn the to/from addresses of Alba's e-mail messages, the IP addresses of the websites that Alba visited and the total volume of information sent to or from his account. Later, the government obtained a warrant authorizing it to employ imaging and keystroke monitoring techniques, but Alba does not challenge on appeal those techniques' legality or the government's application to use them.

Forrester and Alba were tried by jury. At trial, the government introduced extensive evidence showing that they and their associates built and operated a major Ecstasy laboratory. Witnesses described the lab as "very, very large," and seized documents show that it was intended to produce approximately 440 kilograms of Ecstasy (and $10 million in profit) per month. The government also presented evidence that Alba purchased precursor chemicals for Ecstasy, that Forrester met with a Swedish chemist in Stockholm to learn about manufacturing Ecstasy, that the defendants first tried to construct the lab in two other locations before settling on Escondido, California and that the Escondido lab was located inside an insulated sea/land container and contained an array of devices and chemicals used to make Ecstasy.

The jury convicted Forrester and Alba on all counts. The district court sentenced them each to 360 months in prison and six years of supervised release.

II. Computer Surveillance

Alba contends that the government's surveillance of his e-mail and Internet activity violated the Fourth Amendment * * *.[4] We hold that the surveillance did not constitute a Fourth Amendment search and thus was not unconstitutional.

The Supreme Court held in *Smith v. Maryland,* 442 U.S. 735 (1979), that the use of a pen register (a device that records numbers dialed from a phone line) does not constitute a search for Fourth Amendment purposes. According to the Court, people do not have a subjective expectation of privacy in numbers that they dial because they realize that they must 'convey' phone numbers to the telephone company, since it is through telephone company switching equipment that their calls are completed. Even if there were such a subjective expectation, it would not be one that society is prepared to recognize as reasonable because a person has no legitimate expectation of privacy in information he voluntarily turns over to third parties." Therefore the use of a pen register is not a Fourth Amendment search.

Importantly, the Court distinguished pen registers from more intrusive surveillance techniques on the ground that pen registers do not acquire the *contents* of communications but rather obtain only the addressing information associated with phone calls.

Neither this nor any other circuit has spoken to the constitutionality of computer surveillance techniques that reveal the to/from addresses of e-mail messages, the IP addresses of websites visited and the total amount of data transmitted to or from an account. We conclude that these

---

4. As mentioned earlier, Alba complains only about the initial surveillance through which the government obtained the to/from addresses of his e-mail messages, the IP addresses of the websites that he visited and the total volume of information sent to or from his account. He does not challenge the more intrusive imaging and keystroke monitoring that subsequently took place (though he does argue that the information obtained through those techniques should be suppressed as tainted derivative evidence).

techniques are constitutionally indistinguishable from the use of a pen register that the Court approved in *Smith.*

First, e-mail and Internet users, like the telephone users in *Smith,* rely on third-party equipment in order to engage in communication. *Smith* based its holding that telephone users have no expectation of privacy in the numbers they dial on the users' imputed knowledge that their calls are completed through telephone company switching equipment. Analogously, e-mail and Internet users have no expectation of privacy in the to/from addresses of their messages or the IP addresses of the websites they visit because they should know that these messages are sent and these IP addresses are accessed through the equipment of their Internet service provider and other third parties. Communication by both Internet and telephone requires people to voluntarily turn over information to third parties.

Second, e-mail to/from addresses and IP addresses constitute addressing information and reveal no more about the underlying contents of communication than do phone numbers. When the government learns the phone numbers a person has dialed, it may be able to determine the persons or entities to which the numbers correspond, but it does not know what was said in the actual conversations. Similarly, when the government obtains the to/from addresses of a person's e-mails or the IP addresses of websites visited, it does not find out the contents of the messages or the particular pages on the websites the person viewed. At best, the government may make educated guesses about what was said in the messages or viewed on the websites based on its knowledge of the e-mail to/from addresses and IP addresses—but this is no different from speculation about the contents of a phone conversation on the basis of the identity of the person or entity that was dialed. The distinction between mere addressing and more content-rich information drawn by the Court in *Smith* and *Katz v. United States,* 389 U.S. 347 (1967), is thus preserved, because the computer surveillance techniques at issue here enable only the discovery of addressing information.[6]

The government's surveillance of e-mail addresses also may be technologically sophisticated, but it is conceptually indistinguishable from government surveillance of physical mail. In a line of cases dating back to the nineteenth century, the Supreme Court has held that the government cannot engage in a warrantless search of the contents of sealed mail, but can observe whatever information people put on the outside of mail, because that information is voluntarily transmitted to third parties. E-

---

6. Surveillance techniques that enable the government to determine not only the IP addresses that a person accesses but also the uniform resource locators ("URL") of the pages visited might be more constitutionally problematic. A URL, unlike an IP address, identifies the particular document within a website that a person views and thus reveals much more information about the person's Internet activity. For instance, a surveillance technique that captures IP addresses would show only that a person visited the New York Times' website at http:// www.nytimes.com, whereas a technique that captures URLs would also divulge the particular articles the person viewed. *See In re Application of the United States of America,* 396 F. Supp.2d 45, 49 (2005) ("[I]f the user then enters a search phrase [in the Google search engine], that search phrase would appear in the URL after the first forward slash. This would reveal content. . . .").

mail, like physical mail, has an outside address "visible" to the third-party carriers that transmit it to its intended location, and also a package of content that the sender presumes will be read only by the intended recipient. The privacy interests in these two forms of communication are identical. The contents may deserve Fourth Amendment protection, but the address and size of the package do not.

Finally, the pen register in *Smith* was able to disclose not only the phone numbers dialed but also the number of calls made. There is no difference of constitutional magnitude between this aspect of the pen register and the government's monitoring here of the total volume of data transmitted to or from Alba's account. Devices that obtain addressing information also inevitably reveal the amount of information coming and going, and do not thereby breach the line between mere addressing and more content-rich information.

We therefore hold that the computer surveillance techniques that Alba challenges are not Fourth Amendment searches. However, our holding extends only to these particular techniques and does not imply that more intrusive techniques or techniques that reveal more content information are also constitutionally identical to the use of a pen register.

NOTES AND QUESTIONS

1. Do you agree that IP addresses are similar to the numbers dialed for a telephone call and the outside of traditional mail? Or is collecting IP addresses more invasive?

2. Footnote 6 of the *Forrester* case suggests that URLs might provide a difficult case of distinguishing content and non-content. In your view, does a URL pointing to a particular story reveal content or non-content information? How about a URL that contains search terms, such as you might see when you submit a query to a search engine? What exactly is the constitutional line between content and non-content information?

3. Network surveillance can be divided into prospective surveillance and retrospective surveillance. Prospective surveillance refers to "real time" monitoring while communications are in transit. For example, wiretapping is prospective; it catches communications crossing the point being tapped. In contrast, retrospective surveillance refers to the collection of stored records generated by the network without government interference. For example, the telephone company may keep records of calls for billing purposes, and may keep a file for each account describing how that account was used. Government agents may approach the telephone service provider and ask (or order) it to divulge account records in its possession relating to a particular account.

As you might expect, the basic Fourth Amendment rules for the retrospective surveillance of a communication are the same as the rules for the prospective surveillance of that communication. For example, government agents can obtain account records relating to the past usage of a telephone account from the telephone company without implicating the telephone customer's Fourth Amendment rights. The same rule applies to other kinds of account records. *See, e.g.,* In re Grand Jury Proceedings, 827 F.2d 301, 302–03 (8th Cir. 1987) (Western Union account records). The one possible difference between how the Fourth Amendment treats prospective and retrospective surveillance was suggested in Berger v. New York, 388 U.S. 41 (1967). In *Berger,* the Court suggested that prospective surveillance raises heightened Fourth Amendment concerns because real-time wiretapping can permit a more invasive search over a long period of time as compared to a traditional search. *See id.* at 57. *See also id.* at 65 (Douglas, J., concurring). As a general rule, however, the Fourth Amendment rules for retrospective and prospective surveillance are the same.

4. *Fourth Amendment protection for basic subscriber information.* In United States v. Hambrick, 225 F.3d 656 (4th Cir. 2000), investigators served an invalid subpoena on MindSpring, a large commercial ISP, for basic subscriber information about a particular account. When compliance with the subpoena helped yield evidence of criminal activity, the account holder challenged the disclosure of his basic subscriber information on the ground that the invalidity of the subpoena rendered its use unconstitutional. The merits of this argument hinged on whether Hambrick had Fourth Amendment rights in the data to challenge its disclosure. The Fourth Circuit held that Hambrick had no reasonable expectation of privacy in his basic subscriber information:

> The subpoena at issue in this case requested that MindSpring produce "any records pertaining to the billing and/or user records documenting the subject using your services on March 14th, 1998 at 1210HRS (EST) using the Internet Protocol Number 207.69.169.92." This information was requested in order to determine the identity of the individual using [a particular] screen name * * * as this screen name is tied to the user's identity in all of MindSpring's business records. The information the government received from MindSpring consisted of Hambrick's subscriber information, which included his name; billing address; home, work, and fax phone numbers; and other billing information. When Hambrick entered into a service agreement with MindSpring, he knowingly revealed this information to MindSpring and its employees. The records that the government obtained from MindSpring had been available to MindSpring employees in the normal course of business. Once the government received this information, it was not later utilized to read Hambrick's e-mails or to attain any other content information.

> While under certain circumstances, a person may have an expectation of privacy in content information, a person does not have an interest in the account information given to the ISP in order to establish the e-mail account, which is non-content information. Disclosure of this non-content information to a third party destroys the privacy expectation that might have existed previously. In this case, the government never utilized the non-content information retrieved from MindSpring to attain additional content information, such as the substance of Hambrick's e-mails. In this case, as in *Miller,* there is no legitimate expectation of privacy in information voluntarily conveyed to a third party and exposed to their employees in the ordinary course of business. The information subject to

the motion to suppress is merely third-party business records, and therefore, Hambrick's Fourth Amendment claim cannot succeed.

Id. at *4.

How broadly should this principle extend? Should it apply only to basic subscriber information? To all non-content information? To both content and non-content information?

Imagine the faulty subpoena had ordered MindSpring to collect and disclose the following information about Hambrick's account, and that MindSpring had complied with the subpoena. In which of these cases does Hambrick have a reasonable expectation of privacy in the data such that compliance with the invalid subpoena violates Hambrick's Fourth Amendment rights?

A. Login records indicating when Hambrick was online during the month preceding March 14, 1998, the date of Hambrick's criminal activity.

B. A list of all IP addresses assigned to Hambrick's account from January 1, 1998 to March 14, 1998, assuming that Mindspring assigned a new IP address to the account when the account owner logged in (so-called "dynamic" addressing).

C. Retrospective records, if any exist, of the URLs of any websites Hambrick visited using the account on March 14, 1998.

D. Prospective records listing all of the URLs of any websites that Hambrick will visit during the week following the receipt of the subpoena.

E. Records of the e-mail headers of any e-mails stored in Hambrick's account on the day the subpoena is received.

F. Prospective records of the e-mail headers from any e-mails that will arrive in Hambrick's account for the month after the subpoena is received.

G. The contents of any opened e-mail stored in Hambrick's inbox on the date the subpoena is received.

H. The contents of any outgoing e-mail stored in Hambrick's account on the date the subpoena is received.

I. The entire contents of Hambrick's account on the date the subpoena is received.

J. Prospective surveillance of every communication sent or received through Hambrick's account for a six-month period starting the day the subpoena is received.

5. In Kyllo v. United States, 533 U.S. 27 (2001), the Supreme Court held that the warrantless use of an infrared camera directed at a home violates the Fourth Amendment by disclosing previously unknowable facts about the home, such as the temperature inside a room:

While it may be difficult to refine *Katz* when the search of areas such as telephone booths, automobiles, or even the curtilage and uncovered portions of residences are at issue, in the case of the search of the interior of homes—the prototypical and hence most commonly litigated area of protected privacy—there is a ready criterion, with roots deep in the common law, of the minimal expectation of privacy that *exists*, and that is acknowledged to be *reasonable*. To withdraw protection of this minimum expectation would be to permit police technology to erode the privacy guaranteed by the Fourth Amendment. We think that obtaining by sense-enhancing technology any information regarding the interior of the home that could not otherwise have been obtained without physical intrusion into a constitutionally protected area, constitutes a search—at least where (as here) the technology in question is not in general public use. This assures preservation of that degree of privacy against government that existed when the Fourth Amendment was adopted.

Id. at 28. The Internet did not exist when the Fourth Amendment was adopted. Does *Kyllo* have any application to computers and the Internet? Should the Fourth Amendment match the privacy we experience online to the privacy we experience in the physical world, and thus to the privacy the Framers experienced in their homes?

3.   CONTENT INFORMATION

The next case considers what Fourth Amendment rules should apply to government access to the contents of communications, such as e-mails and text messages.

QUON v. ARCH WIRELESS OPERATING CO.

United States Court of Appeals for the Ninth Circuit, 2008.
529 F.3d 892.

Wardlaw, Circuit Judge:

This case arises from the Ontario Police Department's review of text messages sent and received by Jeff Quon, a Sergeant and member of the City of Ontario's SWAT team.

I.

On October 24, 2001, Arch Wireless contracted to provide wireless text-messaging services for the City of Ontario. The City received twenty two-way alphanumeric pagers, which it distributed to its employees, including Ontario Police Department ("OPD" or "Department") Sergeants Quon and Trujillo, in late 2001 or early 2002.

A text message originating from an Arch Wireless two-way alphanumeric text-messaging pager is sent to another two-way text-messaging pager as follows: The message leaves the originating pager via a radio frequency transmission. That transmission is received by any one of many receiving stations, which are owned by Arch Wireless. Depending on the location of the receiving station, the message is then entered into the Arch Wireless computer network either by wire transmission or via satellite by another radio frequency transmission. Once in the Arch Wireless computer network, the message is sent to the Arch Wireless computer server. Once in the server, a copy of the message is archived. The message is also stored in the server system, for a period of up to 72 hours, until the recipient pager is ready to receive delivery of the text message. The recipient pager is ready to receive delivery of a message when it is both activated and located in an Arch Wireless service area.

Once the recipient pager is able to receive delivery of the text message, the Arch Wireless server retrieves the stored message and sends it, via wire or radio frequency transmission, to the transmitting station closest to the recipient pager. The transmitting stations are owned by Arch Wireless. The message is then sent from the transmitting station, via a radio frequency transmission, to the recipient pager where it can be read by the user of the recipient pager.

The City had no official policy directed to text-messaging by use of the pagers. However, the City did have a general "Computer Usage, Internet and E-mail Policy" applicable to all employees. The Policy stated that "the use of City-owned computers and all associated equipment, software, programs, networks, Internet, e-mail and other systems operating on these computers is limited to City of Ontario related business. The use of these tools for personal benefit is a significant violation of City of Ontario Policy."

Although the City had no official policy expressly governing use of the pagers, the City did have an informal policy governing their use. Under the City's contract with Arch Wireless, each pager was allotted 25,000 characters, after which the City was required to pay overage charges. Lieutenant Duke was in charge of the purchasing contract and responsible for procuring payment for overages. He stated that "the practice was, if there was overage, that the employee would pay for the overage that the City had. We would usually call the employee and say, 'Hey, look, you're over X amount of characters. It comes out to X amount of dollars. Can you write me a check for your overage?' "

[Plaintiff Sergeant Jeff] Quon went over the monthly character limit three or four times and paid the City for the overages. Each time, Lieutenant Duke would come and tell him that he owed X amount of dollars because he went over his allotted characters. Each of those times, Quon paid the City for the overages.

In August 2002, Quon and another officer again exceeded the 25,000 character limit. Lieutenant Duke then let it be known at a meeting that he was "tired of being a bill collector with guys going over the allotted amount of characters on their text pagers." In response, Chief Scharf ordered Lieutenant Duke to request the transcripts of those pagers for auditing purposes. Chief Scharf asked Lieutenant Duke to determine if the messages were exclusively work related, thereby requiring an increase in the number of characters officers were permitted, which had occurred in the past, or if they were using the pagers for personal matters. One of the officers whose transcripts he requested was plaintiff Jeff Quon.

City officials were not able to access the text messages themselves. Instead, the City e-mailed Jackie Deavers, a major account support specialist for Arch Wireless, requesting the transcripts. According to Deavers:

> I checked the phone numbers on the transcripts against the e-mail that I had gotten, and I looked into the system to make sure they were actually pagers that belonged to the City of Ontario, and they were. So I took the transcripts and put them in a manila envelope and brought them to the City.

Deavers stated that she did not determine whether private messages were being released, though she acknowledged that, upon reviewing approximately four lines of the transcript, she had realized that the messages were sexually explicit. She also stated that she would only deliver messages to the "contact" on the account, and that she would not deliver messages to the "user" unless he was also the contact on the account. In this case, the "contact" was the City.

After receiving the transcripts, Lieutenant Duke conducted an initial audit and reported the results to Chief Scharf. * * * The transcripts revealed that Quon had exceeded his monthly allotted characters by 15,158 characters, and that many of these messages were personal in nature and were often sexually explicit. These messages were directed to and received from, among others, the other Appellants.

II.

Appellants assert that they are entitled to summary judgment on their Fourth Amendment claim against the City, the Department, and Scharf * * * [because] they had a reasonable expectation of privacy in the text messages.

The extent to which the Fourth Amendment provides protection for the contents of electronic communications in the Internet age is an open question. The recently minted standard of electronic communication via e-mails, text messages, and other means opens a new frontier in Fourth Amendment jurisprudence that has been little explored. Here, we must first answer the threshold question: Do users of text messaging services such as those provided by Arch Wireless have a reasonable expectation of privacy in their text messages stored on the service provider's network? We hold that they do.

In *Katz v. United States,* 389 U.S. 347 (1967), the government placed an electronic listening device on a public telephone booth, which allowed the government to listen to the telephone user's conversation. The Supreme Court held that listening to the conversation through the electronic device violated the user's reasonable expectation of privacy. In so holding, the Court reasoned, "One who occupies a phone booth, shuts the door behind him, and pays the toll that permits him to place a call is surely entitled to assume that the words he utters into the mouthpiece will not be broadcast to the world. To read the Constitution more narrowly is to ignore the vital role that the public telephone has come to play in private communication." *Id.* at 352. Therefore, "the Government's activities in electronically listening to and recording the petitioner's words violated the privacy upon which he justifiably relied while using the telephone booth and thus constituted a 'search and seizure' within the meaning of the Fourth Amendment." *Id.* at 353.

On the other hand, the Court has also held that the government's use of a pen register—a device that records the phone numbers one dials—does not violate the Fourth Amendment. This is because people "realize that they must 'convey' phone numbers to the telephone company, since it is through telephone company switching equipment that their calls are completed." *Smith v. Maryland,* 442 U.S. 735 (1979). The Court distinguished *Katz* by noting that "a pen register differs significantly from the listening device employed in *Katz,* for pen registers do not acquire the *contents* of communications." *Id.* at 741.

This distinction also applies to written communications, such as letters. It is well-settled that, since 1878, the Fourth Amendment's protection against 'unreasonable searches and seizures' protects a citizen against the warrantless opening of sealed letters and packages addressed to him in order to examine the contents. However, as with the phone numbers they dial, individuals do not enjoy a reasonable expectation of privacy in what they write on the outside of an envelope.

Our Internet jurisprudence is instructive. In *United States v. Forrester,* 512 F.3d 500, 510 (9th Cir. 2008), we held that e-mail users have no expectation of privacy in the to/from addresses of their messages because they should know that this information is provided to and used by Internet service providers for the specific purpose of directing the routing of information. Thus, we have extended the pen register and outside-of-envelope rationales to the "to/from" line of e-mails. But we have not ruled on whether persons have a reasonable expectation of privacy in the content of e-mails. Like the Supreme Court in *Smith,* in *Forrester* we explicitly noted that e-mail to/from addresses ... constitute addressing information and do not necessarily reveal any more about the underlying contents of communication than do phone numbers. Thus, we concluded that the privacy interests in these two forms of communication letters and e-mails are identical, and that, while the contents may deserve Fourth Amendment protection, the address and size of the package do not.

We see no meaningful difference between the e-mails at issue in *Forrester* and the text messages at issue here. Both are sent from user to user via a service provider that stores the messages on its servers. Similarly, as in *Forrester,* we also see no meaningful distinction between text messages and letters. As with letters and e-mails, it is not reasonable to expect privacy in the information used to "address" a text message, such as the dialing of a phone number to send a message. However, users do have a reasonable expectation of privacy in the content of their text messages vis-a-vis the service provider. That Arch Wireless may have been able to access the contents of the messages for its own purposes is irrelevant.

We do not endorse a monolithic view of text message users' reasonable expectation of privacy, as this is necessarily a context-sensitive inquiry. Absent an agreement to the contrary, Trujillo, Florio, and Jerilyn Quon had no reasonable expectation that Jeff Quon would maintain the private nature of their text messages, or vice versa. Had Jeff Quon voluntarily permitted the Department to review his text messages, the remaining Appellants would have no claims. Nevertheless, the OPD surreptitiously reviewed messages that all parties reasonably believed were free from third-party review. As a matter of law, Trujillo, Florio, and Jerilyn Quon had a reasonable expectation that the Department would not review their messages absent consent from either a sender or recipient of the text messages.

NOTES AND QUESTIONS

1. Is a text message like the contents of a landline phone call or a first-class letter, both of which are protected by the Fourth Amendment? Or is it more like the contents of a cordless phone call or a fourth-class package, neither of which are protected by the Fourth Amendment?

2. *Contents posted on the World Wide Web, both without password protection and with it.* Imagine a person posts a photograph on the Web. Does the Fourth Amendment protect access to it?

If the photograph is available for all to see, the answer is "no." In United States v. Gines–Perez, 214 F. Supp.2d 205 (D.P.R. 2002), the defendant managed a computer store and was also a suspect in a major heroin smuggling investigation. He had begun to set up a website for the computer store, and had posted a group portrait of all of the store's employees that included his own image. The officers who were investigating the smuggling operation found the picture and distributed it among themselves to help them recognize the defendant. The photograph helped the police identify the car the defendant was driving, which led to the discovery of 1.4 kilos of heroin and $5,000 in cash in the car. The defendant argued unsuccessfully that he had a subjective and objectively reasonable expectation of privacy in the photograph he posted on the web:

> The Court is convinced that placing information on the information superhighway necessarily makes said matter accessible to the public, no matter how many protectionist measures may be taken, or even when a web page is "under construction." While it is true that there is no case law on point regarding this issue, it strikes the Court as obvious that a claim to privacy is unavailable to someone who places information on an indisputably, public medium, such as the Internet, without taking any measures to protect the information.

> The defense may claim that the web site in controversy was not intended to be "public" or "commercial" in nature. But it is not the intention of the person who uses the Internet to communicate information which is

important; it is the medium in which he or she places the information and the nature of the materials placed on the web which are important. A person who places information on the information superhighway clearly subjects said information to being accessed by every conceivable interested party. Simply expressed, if privacy is sought, then public communication mediums such as the Internet are not adequate forums without protective measures.

The Court finds that this society is simply not prepared to recognize as "reasonable" a claim that a picture on the Internet is "private" in nature, such that the Government cannot access it. In fact, the Court believes that our society would recognize the opposite; that a person who places a photograph on the Internet precisely intends to forsake and renounce all privacy rights to such imagery, particularly under circumstances such as here, where the Defendant did not employ protective measures or devices that would have controlled access to the Web page or the photograph itself.

Id. at 225.

On the other hand, at least one court has reached a different result when the website was protected by a password. In United States v. D'Andrea, 497 F. Supp.2d 117 (D. Mass. 2007), a government agent received a tip that a suspect had stored files containing evidence of crime in a password-protected account on a Sprint PCS website. The tipster told the government the password, and the government agent used the password to view the files. The district court ruled that the password protection created a reasonable expectation of privacy, and that using the password to view the files therefore was a Fourth Amendment search:

While a service provider has a need to access information regarding the identity of a site holder and the volume and extent of her usage, it has no legitimate reason to inspect the actual contents of the site, anymore than the postal service has a legitimate interest in reading the contents of first class mail, or a telephone company has a legitimate interest in listening to a customer's conversations. Reliance on protections such as individual computer accounts, password protection, and perhaps encryption of data should be no less reasonable than reliance upon locks, bolts, and burglar alarms, even though each form of protection is penetrable.

Id. at 121 (citing and quoting Wayne R. LaFave, 1 *Search and Seizure* § 2.6 at 721 (4th ed. 2006).

3. *Post-cut-through dialed digits.* Telephone users are often prompted to enter in numbers after a call has been connected. For example, a person might enter in a password to access a voicemail account or might enter the last four digits of her Social Security number to verify identification. Such numbers are known as "post-cut-through dialed digits." (The awkward name derives from the fact that the "cut through" is the moment a call is placed. Digits entered after the "cut through" are therefore "post-cut-through dialed digits.") Are these post-cut-through dialed digits protected by the Fourth Amendment? Consider the argument that they are:

While individuals may not have a reasonable expectation of privacy in the numbers that they dial to connect a phone call, the content they communicate over a phone line in the form of PCTDD is different. Technology has transformed the way Americans use phone lines. Now, instead of a human operator, individuals are asked to relay information to a machine by way of PCTDD in order to process requests and obtain information. When this communication includes content, it is the functional equivalent of voice communication and is protected by *Katz* and its progeny as such. Moreover, the information that is often transmitted via PCTDD is often sensitive and personal. Bank account numbers, pin numbers and passwords, prescription identification numbers, social security numbers, credit card numbers, and so on, all encompass the kind of information that an individual wants and reasonably expects to be kept private.

In re Applications of the United States, 515 F. Supp.2d 325, 336 (E.D.N.Y. 2007) (Azrack, Magistrate Judge).

4. *Remote access to files stored on a personal computer connected to a network.* Imagine a person uses his personal computer to connect to a computer network, and by making the network connection enables others on the network to observe the files stored on the personal computer. If a government agent views the contents of the person's personal computer using the network, does that remote viewing violate a reasonable expectation of privacy?

Consider two precedents. In United States v. Heckenkamp, 482 F.3d 1142 (9th. Cir. 2007), a student at the University of Wisconsin used the university's computer network to hack into computers from his dorm room. A system administrator of the university network knew the student's username and password, and he accessed the student's computer remotely to confirm that it was the suspect's computer that was responsible. The court held that the student had a reasonable expectation of privacy in the contents of his personal computer even though it was connected to the network:

> The salient question is whether the defendant's objectively reasonable expectation of privacy in his computer was eliminated when he attached it to the university network. We conclude under the facts of this case that the act of attaching his computer to the network did not extinguish his legitimate, objectively reasonable privacy expectations.

> A person's reasonable expectation of privacy may be diminished in transmissions over the Internet or e-mail that have already arrived at the recipient. However, the mere act of accessing a network does not in itself extinguish privacy expectations, nor does the fact that others may have occasional access to the computer.

> * * * [W]e must reject the government's contention that [the student] had no objectively reasonable expectation of privacy in his personal computer, which was protected by a screen-saver password, located in his dormitory room, and subject to no policy allowing the university actively to monitor or audit his computer usage.

Id. at 1146–47.

Contrast *Heckenkamp* with United States v. Ganoe, 538 F.3d 1117 (9th Cir. 2008). In *Ganoe,* an undercover agent used the file-sharing program LimeWire to find a movie containing child pornography. LimeWire allows users to share various files with other users who have downloaded the free LimeWire software. Ganoe had installed LimeWire on his home computer, and he used the program to find music files. Unbeknownst to him, however, the software was configured to reveal several movies of child pornography located on his home computer. An undercover agent using LimeWire to look for child pornography found it stored on Ganoe's computer, leading to charges against Ganoe.

The Ninth Circuit held that the undercover agent's use of LimeWire to search Ganoe's computer did not violate Ganoe's Fourth Amendment rights:

> Although as a general matter an individual has an objectively reasonable expectation of privacy in his personal computer, we fail to see how this expectation can survive Ganoe's decision to install and use file-sharing software, thereby opening his computer to anyone else with the same freely available program. The crux of Ganoe's argument is that he simply did not know that others would be able to access files stored on his own computer. But he knew he had file-sharing software on his computer; indeed, he admitted that he used it—he says to get music. Moreover, he was explicitly warned before completing the installation that the folder into which files are downloaded would be shared with other users in the peer-to-peer network. Ganoe thus opened up his download folder to the world, including [the undercover agent]. To argue that Ganoe lacked the technical savvy or good sense to configure LimeWire to prevent access to his pornography files is like saying that he did not know enough to close his drapes. Having failed to demonstrate an expectation of privacy that society is prepared to accept as reasonable, Ganoe cannot invoke the protections of the Fourth Amendment.

Id. at 1127.

Is the analogy to closing the drapes persuasive? Everyone knows how to close the drapes. Does everyone know how to configure a computer program to avoid inadvertently exposing files? How much computer savvy should courts assume when identifying when an expectation of privacy is reasonable?

5. *Should banners or Terms of Service define Fourth Amendment rights?* In Freedman v. America Online, 412 F. Supp.2d 174 (D. Conn. 2005), the plaintiff used an AOL account with a pseudonymous screenname to send a threatening e-mail to two supporters of a political opponent. The recipients of the e-mail filed a report with the local police, and the police filled out a search warrant form ordering AOL to disclose basic subscriber information for that account. The police neglected to have the warrant signed by a judge, however, and ended up faxing the unsigned warrant to AOL. AOL in turn disclosed the plaintiff's identity to the police. The plaintiff later sued AOL, claiming that its disclosure of his identity pursuant to an invalid warrant violated his Fourth Amendment rights. The plaintiff argued that the terms of AOL's privacy policy created Fourth Amendment protections. The court rejected the plaintiff's argument on at least the partial ground that AOL's privacy policy could be read to allow the disclosure: "AOL's promise was not absolute, as it had

expressly informed Plaintiff that it may, in limited circumstances, reveal his subscriber information." *Id.* at 183.

Should the terms of AOL's privacy policy make a difference? Why should they be relevant?

6. In contrast with letters and phone calls, Internet communications blend content and non-content information in a single stream of zeros and ones. The Internet works by combining content and non-content information into packets and sending them across networks. Computers that process the data can identify the zeros and ones that are content information only because distinctive patterns of zeros and ones indicate what data should be treated as contents and what data should be treated as non-content addressing information.

If computer communications blend content and non-content information together, does it make sense that the Fourth Amendment should provide a different level of protection for contents and addressing information? Does it make sense that some zeros and ones in a stream of data receive Fourth Amendment protection while others do not? If it doesn't make sense to treat content and non-content information differently, which standard should apply? Should the Fourth Amendment protect the entire stream of data or none of it?

7. *The role of statutory privacy laws.* Congress has passed a comprehensive statutory regime to protect the privacy of Internet communications. As a result, the rules governing Internet surveillance tend to be primarily statutory, not constitutional. How should the existence of statutory privacy laws impact interpretations of the Fourth Amendment?

Courts have suggested different answers to this question. Some courts have hinted that statutory protections might strengthen the case for Fourth Amendment protection. According to this rationale, the existence of statutory protection makes an expectation of privacy more reasonable. For example, in the case of In re John Doe Proceeding, 680 N.W.2d 792 (Wis. 2004), the Dane County, Wisconsin, District Attorney opened a criminal investigation to investigate public corruption in the Wisconsin state government. The DA issued a subpoena to the state Legislative Technology Services Bureau (LTSB), a public agency in the Wisconsin government that stores back-up tapes of the contents of the servers used by the Wisconsin state government. Under Wisconsin law, the LTSB generates back-up tapes of the state legislature's 54 servers, and stores copies of those back-up tapes on what appears to be a permanent basis.

The Supreme Court of Wisconsin agreed that the subpoena was overbroad in violation of the Fourth Amendment. In the course of reaching this conclusion, the Court discussed whether the data stored on the back-up tapes was protected by a reasonable expectation of privacy:

> Technology clearly has changed the ways in which we work and communicate with others. The federal government recognized that changing technology required changing laws, and to address those changes, it passed the Electronic Communications Privacy Act of 1986. The ECPA extended the privacy protections that have been given voice communica-

tions to electronic communications such as e-mail. This is a strong expression of society's expectation of privacy in electronic communications.

Legislators use electronic technology to compose budgets, to prepare position papers, and to draft legislation; they communicate with each other, with their staff members and with their constituents via e-mail and instant messaging. According to the LTSB, the legislative e-mail system processes more than 60,000 transactions each day. Electronic assists to communication is the way in which the legislature does its work, and all of the data created is stored on the backup tapes at the LTSB.

These circumstances—the way in which the legislature now does business; that the LTSB was created to serve legislators on "both sides of the aisle;" and the statutory directive of Wis. Stat. § 13.96 that requires that all data stored by the LTSB shall be kept confidential—support an objectively reasonable expectation of privacy by legislators in the data on the backup tapes. Therefore, we conclude that society has recognized a reasonable expectation of privacy in the electronically stored information on the backup tapes.

Id. at 806. Do you agree that statutory protections help make an expectation of privacy reasonable? If statutory protections are weaker than the potential constitutional protections, which they generally are, doesn't the fact that Congress opted for less protection undercut the argument that statutory law reflects a societal consensus that an expectation of privacy is reasonable? Or does the statutory half loaf make the full loaf "reasonable"?

Other courts have reached different conclusions. Some courts have suggested that the existence of statutory privacy laws should actually *discourage* broad readings of the Fourth Amendment in new technologies. In United States v. McNulty, 47 F.3d 100 (4th Cir. 1995), the Fourth Circuit rejected a claim that the interception of a cordless phone call violated the Fourth Amendment. Judge Wilkinson's opinion suggested that the presence of the statutory Wiretap Act (also known as "Title III") bolstered the case against Fourth Amendment protections:

In the fast-developing area of communications technology, courts should be cautious not to wield the amorphous "reasonable expectation of privacy" standard in a manner that nullifies the balance between privacy rights and law enforcement needs struck by Congress in Title III. Decisionmaking in this area demands a comprehension of complex technologies. Such understanding, however, requires precisely the type of expertise that courts are institutionally ill-equipped to acquire and to apply. As new technologies continue to appear in the marketplace and outpace existing surveillance law, the primary job of evaluating their impact on privacy rights and of updating the law must remain with the branch of government designed to make such policy choices, the legislature.

Id. at 105–06.

Should statutory protections lead courts to be expansive in their application of the Fourth Amendment to the Internet, or should it lead courts to be cautious? Do we need courts to determine when an expectation of privacy is "reasonable" if Congress is actively involved? *See generally* Orin S. Kerr, *The Fourth Amendment and New Technologies: Constitutional Myths and the Case for Caution*, 102 Mich. L. Rev. 801 (2004); Daniel Solove, *Fourth Amendment Codification and Professor Kerr's Misguided Call for Judicial Deference*, 74 Fordham L. Rev. 747 (2005).

8. Assuming individuals can have a reasonable expectation of privacy in the contents of their remotely stored files, what legal framework determines the reasonableness of collecting and searching through that data pursuant to a search warrant? Imagine a suspect has an account with an ISP, and government investigators obtain a search warrant permitting the seizure of the account files. Do the agents have to execute the warrant themselves, or can they just fax the warrant to the ISP and ask its employees to collect the files and send them to the agents? What standards determine whether the warrant is sufficiently particular? If agents fax a warrant to the ISP and receive a computer disk containing the files in response, what constitutional rules must agents follow when searching through the disk?

Three cases shed light on these questions.

United States v. Bach, 310 F.3d 1063 (8th Cir. 2002), establishes that investigators can fax warrants to system administrators and have the system administrators execute the warrants on the government's behalf. In *Bach*, the government applied for and received a search warrant to obtain copies of materials in the defendant's Yahoo! e-mail account. The investigators faxed a copy of the warrant to Yahoo!, and employees at Yahoo! searched the servers, identified the materials named in the warrant, and sent the materials to the investigators. The defendant argued that this procedure was constitutionally "unreasonable" because the Fourth Amendment traditionally requires warrants to be executed by the police rather than by private individuals. The Eighth Circuit held that the execution of the warrant by Yahoo! employees was constitutionally "reasonable" in light of the totality of the circumstances:

> We consider several factors in this case to determine whether the search and seizure of Bach's e-mail from Yahoo!'s server by Yahoo! technicians violated Bach's Fourth Amendment rights, including the fact that no warrant was physically "served," no persons or premises were searched in the traditional sense, and there was no confrontation between Yahoo! technicians and Bach. Other factors crucial to our decision include: (1) the actual physical presence of an officer would not have aided the search (in fact may have hindered it); (2) the technical expertise of Yahoo!'s technicians far outweighs that of the officers; (3) the items "seized" were located on Yahoo!'s property; (4) there was a warrant signed by a judge authorizing the search; and (5) the officers complied with the provisions of the Electronic Communications Privacy Act, 18 U.S.C. § 2701. All of these factors weigh in favor of the government and we therefore find that the search was constitutional under the Fourth Amendment's reasonableness standard.

Id. at 1067–68.

United States v. Lamb, 945 F.Supp. 441 (N.D.N.Y. 1996), considered how the particularity requirement applies to a search warrant for the contents of Internet accounts. In *Lamb*, investigators obtained a search warrant for 78 individual AOL accounts used by suspects that had traded images of child pornography using AOL services. The warrant requested all e-mails sent to or received by all 78 accounts as well as all stored files held by AOL relating to the 78 accounts. Judge Munson ruled that even this very broad warrant was sufficiently particular.

> Although the language does not limit investigators to seizing image files only or image files of child pornography only, the actual content of a computer file usually cannot be determined until it is opened with the appropriate application software on a computer. The agents who were tasked to obtain account records related to seventy-eight individuals were not obligated to identify the contents of computer files on AOL's premises. Because there was probable cause to believe that stored files in the accounts of the suspects contained evidence of the crime, *viz.* the depictions of child pornography themselves, the warrant properly authorized the search and seizure of these particular items.

Id. at 458–59. In a footnote, the court added that "it is unreasonable to require the executing officers to identify which files actually contain child pornography and which do not in AOL's Virginia headquarters. That task may be more properly performed by a government computer technician at an FBI lab or office." *Id.* at 458, n.10.

Assuming it makes sense for AOL to send the entire contents of the account to the FBI and for FBI agents to search the files themselves, do you agree that the warrant in *Lamb* is sufficiently particular?

Finally, United States v. Maxwell, 45 M.J. 406 (C.A.A.F. 1996), applied the plain view doctrine to a search of an Internet account. In *Maxwell*, federal investigators informed employees at AOL that they planned to apply for a search warrant to obtain all e-mail associated with a list of AOL screennames. AOL employees collected the e-mails and waited for the warrant to arrive. When the warrant arrived, AOL employees released the e-mails to the investigators without scrutinizing the warrant. The employees failed to realize that the warrant actually obtained was substantially narrower than the one the agents had expected to obtain. The original list had included the screenname "Zirloc," but the signed warrant did not include this screenname on the list of accounts that could be seized. Investigators searched through Zirloc's e-mails, and learned that Zirloc was an Air Force member who questioned his sexual orientation. In litigation, the government defended the government search through Zirloc's files under the plain view exception. The Court of Appeals for the Armed Forces rejected this argument:

> The Supreme Court has recognized that if police are legitimately in a place where a citizen has a right of privacy, the police may seize contraband or other evidence of crime that is in "plain view." We decline, however, to hold the search of the "Zirloc" files was valid under a plain-view analysis. Because the warrant did not authorize the search of these files, the view was obtained as a result of the improper governmental "opening" of the files and not as a result of seeing what was legitimately in "plain view." The search here exceeded the scope of the search warrant; thus the "plain-view" exception does not apply.

Id. at 422.

9. Subpoenas are legal orders that compel the recipient either to testify or else to produce materials in the recipient's possession. Whereas a search warrant authorizes the government to search property directly, a government subpoena compels the recipient to give property in his possession to the government within a specific period of time.

The law governing subpoenas is very different from the law governing search warrants. Most importantly, subpoenas do not require probable cause. As a general matter, the government can issue a grand jury subpoena when the evidence to be obtained is believed to be relevant to an investigation and compliance with the subpoena is not oppressive or overly burdensome. Warrants and subpoenas also differ in how and when they can be challenged in court. The recipient of a subpoena can challenge it (moving to "quash" the subpoena) before complying with it. In contrast, warrants can only be challenged after the warrant is executed.

Subpoenas for evidence are primarily useful when a third party has evidence in its possession. Criminal suspects normally have a Fifth Amendment privilege not to comply with subpoenas for evidence, which means that the government normally cannot use a subpoena to collect evidence directly from suspects. In contrast, the Fifth Amendment privilege does not permit a third party to refuse to disclose evidence in its possession. *See* Fisher v. United States, 425 U.S. 391, 397 (1976) (holding that Fifth Amendment privilege does not immunize third-party agent from complying with subpoena directed to suspect's information in the agent's possession). Third parties can be subpoenaed and required to produce the property of others that happens to be in their possession, usually without notice to the person whose property is to be disclosed.

The role of subpoenas has obvious importance in the context of computer networks. Third parties such as ISPs and their system administrators often possess private information relating to hundreds or even thousands of individual users. If that information is not protected by a reasonable expectation of privacy, then individual users cannot challenge the subpoenas. The disclosure to a third party eliminates Fourth Amendment protection, so the court need not reach the standard that would apply if the record did retain Fourth Amendment protection. But imagine a government agent subpoenas user information from an ISP that *is* protected by the Fourth Amendment. What standard should govern? If the user challenges the subpoena, should the subpoena be upheld so long as it is relevant and compliance is not overly burdensome? Or should the subpoena be upheld only if it is based on probable cause? *See, e.g.,* United States v. Barr, 605 F. Supp. 114 (S.D.N.Y. 1985); Patricia L. Bellia, *Surveillance Law Through Cyberlaw's Lens*, 72 Geo. Wash. L. Rev. 1375, 1410–13 (2004).

Chapter 6

Statutory Privacy Protections

■ ■ ■

In the stand-alone computer environment, Fourth Amendment protections are the primary privacy protections that regulate government access to data. In a network environment, Fourth Amendment protections are supplemented by an important set of statutory privacy laws. This chapter covers the three federal statutory privacy laws that regulate access to computer network communications in criminal investigations. The three laws are the Wiretap Act, 18 U.S.C. §§ 2510–22; the Pen Register statute, 18 U.S.C. §§ 3121–27; and the Stored Communications Act, 18 U.S.C. §§ 2701–11.

Most computer crime investigations begin in a network environment. A computer misuse investigation might begin when a system administrator realizes that his server has been attacked; a threat investigation might begin with the victim's receipt of an e-mail containing the threat; a child pornography case might begin when an undercover investigator is contacted in a chat room. In all these cases, the first question is the same: Who is responsible for the criminal conduct? Investigators generally try to answer this question by collecting evidence from the network to trace the criminal conduct back to its source. A successful investigation might trace communications back to an Internet account being used from the suspect's home; a search of the suspect's home might then yield evidence establishing guilt beyond a reasonable doubt.

The major purpose of the statutory privacy laws is to regulate efforts by criminal investigators to collect evidence that can help them identify who is responsible for criminal conduct online. The Wiretap Act regulates efforts to collect evidence by intercepting the contents of Internet communications in real time; the Pen Register statute regulates collecting evidence by obtaining non-content information in real time; and the Stored Communications Act regulates access to stored content and non-content records held by ISPs.

Brief History of Statutory Privacy Laws

To understand the statutory privacy laws that regulate digital evidence collection, a page of history is worth a volume of logic. That history begins with the telephone network in the period following the Supreme

Court's decision in Olmstead v. United States, 277 U.S. 438 (1928). *Olmstead* held that the Fourth Amendment did not regulate telephone wiretapping. The opinion for the Court expressly invited Congress to enact statutory prohibitions on wiretapping practices: "Congress may, of course, protect the secrecy of telephone messages by making them, when intercepted, inadmissible in evidence in federal criminal trials, by direct legislation." *Id.* at 465–66.

Congress responded in 1934 with the New Deal legislation known as the Communications Act. A provision of the Communications Act codified at 47 U.S.C. § 605 became the first federal wiretapping statute (with the exception of a temporary statute passed during World War I and repealed shortly after the war). In its original form, § 605 stated that "no person not being authorized by the sender shall intercept any communication and divulge or publish the existence, contents, substance, purport, effect, or meaning of such intercepted communication to any person." In Nardone v. United States, 302 U.S. 379, 384 (1937), the Supreme Court held that the remedy for violating this statute was suppression of any evidence unlawfully obtained.

It soon became clear that the Communications Act of 1934 was poorly suited to regulate telephone wiretapping. First, the statute did not provide an exception when the government had obtained a warrant. Second, the statute prohibited only the combination of "intercepting" and "divulging or publishing," which the Justice Department interpreted as permitting wiretapping so long as the information was never used in court. The combination made the statute both under-inclusive and over-inclusive: the FBI could wiretap without restriction so long as it didn't use the evidence in court, but the government could not obtain a warrant permitting admission of wiretapping evidence in court even in the most compelling case. Finally, the law only regulated the admissibility of wiretapping evidence in federal court. It had no application when state investigators sought to introduce wiretapping evidence in state court. *See* Schwartz v. Texas, 344 U.S. 199 (1952).

Congress revisited the law regulating telephone wiretapping in the late 1960s. Congress's goal was to replace the unsatisfactory Communications Act and regulate two distinct privacy-invading practices: bugging, the use of secret recording devices in a room or physical space; and wiretapping, the interception of private telephone calls. The statutory design was heavily influenced by the Supreme Court's pair of decisions in 1967 that explained the constitutional limitations on such practices. The first case, Berger v. New York, 388 U.S. 41 (1967), articulated constitutional requirements for wiretapping. The second case, Katz v. United States, 389 U.S. 347 (1967), articulated constitutional limits on bugging.

The law that Congress passed to regulate wiretapping is generally known either as the Wiretap Act or Title III,[1] and is codified at 18 U.S.C.

---

1. The Wiretap Act is often called "Title III" because the statute was passed as the third part (or "title") of the massive Omnibus Crime Control and Safe Streets Act of 1968, Pub. L. No. 90–351 (1968).

§§ 2510–22. The statute regulates both government actors and private parties, and it imposes strict limitations on the use of devices to intercept "oral communications" (that is, use of a bugging device to listen in on private conversations) or "wire communications" (that is, use of a wire-tapping device to tap a telephone and listen in on private telephone conversations). It also allows the government to obtain court orders permitting interception when investigators have probable cause and can satisfy a number of additional requirements. The heightened requirements of Title III beyond the usual search warrant requirement have led some to describe Title III intercept orders as "super warrants."

The Wiretap Act effectively and comprehensively regulated government access to the contents of traditional telephone calls. In the 1980s, however, it became clear that additional privacy laws were necessary. This was true for two reasons. First, the Supreme Court's decision in Smith v. Maryland, 442 U.S. 735 (1979), indicated that the Fourth Amendment did not provide robust privacy protection in the network context. *Smith* made clear that the Fourth Amendment did not regulate the use of pen registers, and the opinion left uncertain how or even whether the Fourth Amendment would apply to computer networks. Second, the Wiretap Act was not equipped to protect computer network communications. The Wiretap Act applied only to "oral communications" and "wire communications," both of which were limited to communications containing the human voice. Further, the Wiretap Act applied only to the acquisition of communications "in transit," such as real-time wiretapping, and did not apply to accessing stored communications. This made sense for the traditional telephone network, as calls were never stored (or at least only rarely, as voicemail was in its infancy at the time). In contrast, computer communications were stored routinely, either in temporary storage pending transmission or after a communication had been delivered. *See* Office of Tech. Assessment, Federal Government Information Technology: Electronic Surveillance and Civil Liberties (1985).

In 1986, Congress passed the Electronic Communications Privacy Act, Pub. L. No. 99–508 (1986) ("ECPA"), to correct the gaps in existing legislation and respond to the new computer network technologies. ECPA included three basic parts. The first part expanded the Wiretap Act to include a new category of protected communications, "electronic communications," which broadly includes computer communications. The second part created a new statute to regulate access to stored electronic communications known as the Stored Communications Act, codified at 18 U.S.C. §§ 2701–11. Finally, the third part created a new statute, generally known as the Pen Register Statute, 18 U.S.C. §§ 3121–27, that responds to *Smith v. Maryland* and regulates the use of pen registers.[2]

In 1986, when ECPA was passed, Congress did not know how courts might apply the Fourth Amendment to computers. As a result, the

---

2. Somewhat confusingly, cases and authorities refer to these statutes either by their individual names or as ECPA, the Act in which they were passed. These materials will refer to the individual names and refer to ECPA only to mean the 1986 Act as a whole.

statutory privacy laws put in place by ECPA attempted to create what amounts to a statutory version of the Fourth Amendment for computer networks. In recent years, courts have begun to fill in some previously unanswered questions about how the Fourth Amendment might apply. It is therefore important to see the protections offered by the Fourth Amendment and ECPA together: The Fourth Amendment protections form a base that provides protections in some cases and not others, and the statutory protections provide additional protections beyond the constitutional baseline.

The Basic Structure of the Statutory Privacy Laws

The basic framework created by ECPA remains in place today. The framework is premised on two major distinctions: the distinction between prospective surveillance and retrospective surveillance, and the distinction between the contents of communications and non-content information.

Prospective surveillance refers to obtaining communications still in the course of transmission, typically by installing a monitoring device at a particular point in the network and scanning the traffic as it passes by that point. The monitoring is prospective because the communication has not yet reached the place where the surveillance device is installed. For example, a traditional wiretapping device taps into the conversation while it is happening; any communication sent over the line will be tapped. Similarly, an Internet wiretapping program such as a "packet sniffer" scans packets of Internet traffic at a particular place in the network where the program is directed to function.

In contrast, retrospective surveillance refers to access to stored communications that may be kept in the ordinary course of business by a third-party provider. For example, if an FBI agent issues a subpoena ordering an ISP to disclose basic subscriber information about a particular Internet account, that access is a type of retrospective surveillance. The ISP will have generated that record at some time in the past in the ordinary course of its business; the subpoena seeks the disclosure of a stored record that already has been created.

The basic distinction between the contents of communications and non-content information was introduced in the previous chapter. Contents of communications are the substance of the message communicated from sender to receiver, while non-content information refers to the information used to deliver the communications from senders to receivers and other network-generated information about the communication. In the case of a telephone call, for example, a basic difference exists between the contents of the call itself (the conversation) and mere information about the call (such as the phone numbers of the two parties and the duration of the call).

The three privacy statutes reflect these two distinctions. The Wiretap Act and the Pen Register statute regulate prospective surveillance, and the Stored Communications Act regulates retrospective surveillance. Within the category of prospective surveillance, the Wiretap Act handles access to the contents of communications, and the Pen Register regulates access to non-content information. The basic framework looks like this:

	Prospective	**Retrospective**
Contents	Wiretap Act 18 U.S.C. §§ 2510–22	Stored Communications Act 18 U.S.C. §§ 2701–11
Non-content	Pen Register Statute 18 U.S.C. §§ 3121–27	Stored Communications Act 18 U.S.C. §§ 2701–11

Remedies and A Note About Studying the Statutory Privacy Laws

One very unusual feature of the statutory privacy laws is the remedial scheme for statutory violations. The Fourth Amendment is enforced with an exclusionary rule, but the statutory privacy laws do not include a statutory suppression remedy in the computer context. Violations of the Wiretap Act, Pen Register statute, and Stored Communications Act can lead to criminal liability, as noted on pages 185–187. Violations of the Wiretap Act and the Stored Communications Act can also lead to civil liability, including attorney's fees awards and the possibility of punitive damages. However, suppression of evidence unlawfully obtained is not an available remedy in most computer-related cases. The only statutory suppression remedy is for violations of the Wiretap Act involving the interception of human voice communications. *See* 18 U.S.C. § 2515. Because computer communications normally do not include the human voice, no statutory suppression remedy exists for their unlawful interception.

The limited statutory suppression remedy dates back to 1986, when Congress first enacted ECPA. The rationale at the time was that computer communications implicated lesser privacy concerns than telephone calls and speech involving the human voice, so that the suppression remedy imposed by the Wiretap Act for violations relating to telephone calls did not need to be extended to cases involving computers. *See* Michael S. Leib, *E-mail and the Wiretap Laws: Why Congress Should Add Electronic Communication to Title III's Statutory Exclusionary Rule and Expressly Reject a "Good Faith" Exception*, 34 Harv. J. on Legis. 393 (1997).

It seems likely that Congress eventually will revisit this judgment. In 1986, it may have been rational to distinguish between voice transmissions and computer communications. Today it is not. Nonetheless, the law currently lacks a statutory suppression remedy for communications other than voice transmissions.

The narrow scope of the statutory exclusionary rule creates a special challenge for students attempting to understand the statutory privacy laws. Because no suppression remedy exists in most cases, defense lawyers in computer crime cases ordinarily have no incentive to file statutory challenges to government surveillance practices. The absence of challenges means that few judicial opinions explain how the statutory laws apply to computer technologies. *See generally* Orin S. Kerr, *Lifting the 'Fog' of Internet Surveillance: How a Suppression Remedy Would Change Comput-*

er Crime Law, 54 Hastings L.J. 805 (2003). Learning how the statutes work requires careful study of statutory text and legislative history, drawing analogies from decisions involving telephone surveillance, and careful scrutiny of existing civil cases.

A. THE WIRETAP ACT

The Wiretap Act, 18 U.S.C. §§ 2510–22, is the first and probably the most important of the statutory privacy laws. It prohibits the real-time interception of telephone calls and computer communications unless an exception applies or investigators have a "super warrant" interception order. The statute applies whenever a surveillance device has been installed that acquires the contents of communications during transit. The exceptions to the statute articulate specific contexts in which the surveillance can occur without a court order.

The materials begin by exploring the basic framework of the statute and its prohibition on intercepting communications in transit. They then turn to the three most important exceptions to the statute: the consent exception, the provider exception, and the computer trespasser exception.

1. THE BASIC STRUCTURE

The basic structure of the Wiretap Act is surprisingly simple. The statute envisions that an individual is exchanging communications with another person or machine. The statute makes it a crime for someone who is not a party to the communication to use an intercepting device to intentionally access the private communications in "real time."

The following case shows how the framework works in practice. Although it is based on Florida law, the case interprets portions of the Florida statute that are identical to the federal Wiretap Act.

O'BRIEN v. O'BRIEN

District Court of Appeal of Florida, Fifth District, 2005.
899 So.2d 1133.

SAWAYA, C.J.

Emanating from a rather contentious divorce proceeding is an issue we must resolve regarding application of certain provisions of the Security of Communications Act found in Chapter 934, Florida Statutes (2003). Specifically, we must determine whether the trial court properly concluded that pursuant to section 934.03(1), certain communications were inadmissible because they were illegally intercepted by the Wife who, unbeknownst to the Husband, had installed a spyware program on a computer used by the Husband that copied and stored electronic communications between the Husband and another woman.

When marital discord erupted between the Husband and the Wife, the Wife secretly installed a spyware program called Spector on the Husband's computer. It is undisputed that the Husband engaged in private on-line chats with another woman while playing Yahoo Dominoes on his computer. The Spector spyware secretly took snapshots of what appeared on the computer screen, and the frequency of these snapshots allowed Spector to capture and record all chat conversations, instant messages, e-mails sent and received, and the websites visited by the user of the computer. When the Husband discovered the Wife's clandestine attempt to monitor and record his conversations with his Dominoes partner, the Husband uninstalled the Spector software and filed a Motion for Temporary Injunction, which was subsequently granted, to prevent the Wife from disclosing the communications. Thereafter, the Husband requested and received a permanent injunction to prevent the Wife's disclosure of the communications and to prevent her from engaging in this activity in the future. The latter motion also requested that the trial court preclude introduction of the communications into evidence in the divorce proceeding. This request was also granted. The trial court, without considering the communications, entered a final judgment of dissolution of marriage. The Wife moved for rehearing, which was subsequently denied.

The Wife appeals the order granting the permanent injunction, the final judgment, and the order denying the Wife's motion for rehearing on the narrow issue of whether the trial court erred in refusing to admit evidence of the Husband's computer activities obtained through the spyware the Wife secretly installed on the computer. The Wife argues that the electronic communications do not fall under the umbra of the Act because these communications were retrieved from storage and, therefore, are not "intercepted communications" as defined by the Act. In opposition, the Husband contends that the Spector spyware installed on the computer acquired his electronic communications real-time as they were in transmission and, therefore, are intercepts illegally obtained under the Act.

The trial court found that the electronic communications were illegally obtained in violation of section 934.03(1)(a)–(e), and so we begin our analysis with the pertinent provisions of that statute, which subjects any person to criminal penalties who * * *:

> Intentionally intercepts, endeavors to intercept, or procures any other person to intercept or endeavor to intercept any wire, oral, or electronic communication;

§ 934.03(1)(a), Fla. Stat. (2003). Enactment of these prohibitions connotes a policy decision by the Florida legislature to allow each party to a conversation to have an expectation of privacy from interception by another party to the conversation. The purpose of the Act is to protect every person's right to privacy and to prevent the pernicious effect on all citizens who would otherwise feel insecure from intrusion into their private conversations and communications.

The clear intent of the Legislature in enacting section 934.03 was to make it illegal for a person to intercept wire, oral, or electronic communications. It is beyond doubt that what the trial court excluded from evidence are "electronic communications." The core of the issue lies in whether the electronic communications were intercepted. The term "intercept" is defined by the Act as "the aural or other acquisition of the contents of any wire, electronic, or oral communication through the use of any electronic, mechanical, or other device." § 934.02(3). We discern that there is a rather fine distinction between what is transmitted as an electronic communication subject to interception and the storage of what has been previously communicated. It is here that we tread upon new ground. Because we have found no precedent rendered by the Florida courts that considers this distinction, and in light of the fact that the Act was modeled after the Federal Wiretap Act, we advert to decisions by the federal courts that have addressed this issue for guidance.

The federal courts have consistently held that electronic communications, in order to be intercepted, must be acquired contemporaneously with transmission and that electronic communications are not intercepted within the meaning of the Federal Wiretap Act if they are retrieved from storage. *See Fraser v. Nationwide Mut. Ins. Co.*, 352 F.3d 107 (3d Cir. 2003); *Theofel v. Farey–Jones*, 359 F.3d 1066 (9th Cir. 2004); *United States v. Steiger*, 318 F.3d 1039 (11th Cir. 2003); *Konop v. Hawaiian Airlines, Inc.*, 302 F.3d 868 (9th Cir. 2002). * * * [T]he particular facts and circumstances of the instant case reveal that the electronic communications were intercepted contemporaneously with transmission.

The Spector spyware program that the Wife surreptitiously installed on the computer used by the Husband intercepted and copied the electronic communications as they were transmitted. We believe that particular method constitutes interception within the meaning of the Florida Act, and the decision in *Steiger* supports this conclusion. In *Steiger*, an individual was able to hack into the defendant's computer via a Trojan horse virus that allowed the hacker access to pornographic materials stored on the hard drive. The hacker was successful in transferring the pornographic material from that computer to the hacker's computer. The court held that because the Trojan horse virus simply copied information that had previously been stored on the computer's hard drive, the capture of the electronic communication was not an interception within the meaning of the Federal Wiretap Act. The court did indicate, however, that interception could occur if the virus or software intercepted the communication as it was being transmitted and copied it. The court stated:

> There is only a narrow window during which an E-mail interception may occur—the seconds or milli-seconds before which a newly composed message is saved to any temporary location following a send command. Therefore, unless some type of automatic routing software is used (for example, a duplicate of all of an employee's messages are automatically sent to the employee's boss), interception of E-mail within the prohibition of the Wiretap Act is virtually impossible.

Steiger, 318 F.3d at 1050 (quoting Jarrod J. White, *E–Mail@Work.com: Employer Monitoring of Employee E–Mail*, 48 Ala. L. Rev. 1079, 1083

(1997)). Hence, a valid distinction exists between a spyware program similar to that in *Steiger*, which simply breaks into a computer and retrieves information already stored on the hard drive, and a spyware program similar to the one installed by the Wife in the instant case, which copies the communication as it is transmitted and routes the copy to a storage file in the computer.

The Wife argues that the communications were in fact stored before acquisition because once the text image became visible on the screen, the communication was no longer in transit and, therefore, not subject to intercept. We disagree. We do not believe that this evanescent time period is sufficient to transform acquisition of the communications from a contemporaneous interception to retrieval from electronic storage. We conclude that because the spyware installed by the Wife intercepted the electronic communication contemporaneously with transmission, copied it, and routed the copy to a file in the computer's hard drive, the electronic communications were intercepted in violation of the Florida Act.

We must next determine whether the improperly intercepted electronic communications may be excluded from evidence under the Act. The exclusionary provisions of the Act are found in section 934.06, Florida Statutes (2003), which provides that "whenever any wire or oral communication has been intercepted, no part of the contents of such communication and no evidence derived therefrom may be received in evidence." Conspicuously absent from the provisions of this statute is any reference to electronic communications. The federal courts, which interpreted an identical statute contained in the Federal Wiretap Act, have held that because provision is not made for exclusion of intercepted electronic communications, Congress intended that such communications not be excluded under the Federal Wiretap Act. We agree with this reasoning and conclude that the intercepted electronic communications in the instant case are not excludable under the Act. But this does not end the inquiry.

Although not specifically excludable under the Act, it is illegal and punishable as a crime under the Act to intercept electronic communications. § 934.03, Fla. Stat. (2003). The trial court found that the electronic communications were illegally intercepted in violation of the Act and ordered that they not be admitted in evidence. Generally, the admission of evidence is a matter within the sound discretion of the trial court. Because the evidence was illegally obtained, we conclude that the trial court did not abuse its discretion in refusing to admit it.

We affirm the orders and the final judgment under review in the instant case.

NOTES AND QUESTIONS

1. The *O'Brien* case interprets a Florida state law that mirrors the federal Wiretap Act, 18 U.S.C. §§ 2510–22. At this point it may be helpful to turn to the statutory materials reprinted in the Appendix and carefully read

the Wiretap Act to get an idea of its structure. Key terms used in the statute are defined in 18 U.S.C. § 2510, and § 2511(1) contains the basic prohibitions against intercepting oral, wire, and electronic communications. Section 2511(2) lists the most important exceptions to the statute, including the provider exception, § 2511(2)(a)(i), the consent exception, § 2511(2)(c)–(d), and the computer trespasser exception, § 2511(2)(i). Sections 2515 and 2518 create a statutory suppression remedy for violations involving oral and wire communications (although not violations involving electronic communications), and § 2516 lays out the requirements the government must follow to obtain Title III intercept "super warrants."

Notably, several sections of the statute are not directly relevant to our goal of understanding how the Wiretap Act works in computer crime cases. Just to give you a flavor of what you're missing, though, here is a rundown: 18 U.S.C. § 2512 prohibits possessing or distributing wiretapping devices in some circumstances; § 2513 involves the forfeiture of such devices; § 2514 has been repealed; § 2517 concerns the use and disclosure of the fruits of wiretapping; § 2519 requires the filing of annual reports on government wiretapping practices; § 2520 permits civil damages for unlawful wiretapping; § 2521 permits injunctions in civil cases; and § 2522 involves compliance with the Communications Assistance for Law Enforcement Act. It's all good stuff, but not material you need to worry about for this course.

2. *Oral, wire, and electronic communications.* The Wiretap Act covers three distinct types of communications: wire communications, electronic communications, and oral communications. Wire communications are communications that contain the human voice and that are sent over a wire. 18 U.S.C. § 2510(1); 18 U.S.C. § 2510(18). Oral communications are "in person" recordings of the human voice that can be picked up by a bugging device or microphone when the person recorded has a reasonable expectation of privacy. 18 U.S.C. § 2510(2). Electronic communications are communications that do not contain the human voice. 18 U.S.C. § 2510(12).

For our purposes, the two most important categories are wire communications and electronic communications. To simplify matters, telephone calls count as wire communications and almost all computer transmissions count as electronic communications. Computer communications can be wire communications in narrow situations; the most obvious examples are services that transfer the human voice using Internet protocols (so-called voice-over-Internet–Protocol, or VOIP). VOIP communications are "aural transfers" under 18 U.S.C. § 2510(18), as they contain the human voice at the point of origin and reception. This makes such communications "wire communications" under 18 U.S.C. § 2510(1).

3. *Prospective and retrospective surveillance.* The Wiretap Act only applies when a surveillance device is used to "intercept" a communication. 18 U.S.C. § 2510(4) defines intercept as "the aural or other acquisition of the contents of any wire, electronic, or oral communication through the use of any electronic, mechanical, or other device." As the *O'Brien* opinion indicates, the word "acquisition" generally has been understood to mean acquisition contemporaneously with transmission rather than when the communication has

been stored. This explains why the Wiretap Act regulates prospective surveillance and not retrospective surveillance.

At the same time, the line between prospective surveillance and retrospective surveillance can become fuzzy. To see why, consider the facts of United States v. Councilman, 418 F.3d 67 (1st Cir. 2005) (en banc). Councilman was the Vice–President of Interloc, Inc., a book listing service that provided e-mail accounts for its customers. Councilman instructed an Interloc employee to design and install a computer program to scan all incoming e-mail sent to its customers at Interloc that originated from the bookseller Amazon.com. The program scanned incoming mail in the instant before delivery in the customer's inbox. The court explained the technology as follows:

> Data transmitted across the Internet are broken down into small "packets" that are forwarded from one computer to another until they reach their destination, where they are reconstituted. Each service on the Internet—e.g., e-mail, the World Wide Web, or instant messaging—has its own protocol for using packets of data to transmit information from one place to another. The e-mail protocol is known as Simple Mail Transfer Protocol ("SMTP").

> After a user composes a message in an e-mail client program, a program called a mail transfer agent ("MTA") formats that message and sends it to another program that "packetizes" it and sends the packets out to the Internet. Computers on the network then pass the packets from one to another; each computer along the route stores the packets in memory, retrieves the addresses of their final destinations, and then determines where to send them next. At various points the packets are reassembled to form the original e-mail message, copied, and then repacketized for the next leg of the journey. Sometimes messages cannot be transferred immediately and must be saved for later delivery. Even when delivery is immediate, intermediate computers often retain backup copies, which they delete later. This method of transmission is commonly called "store and forward" delivery.

> Once all the packets reach the recipient's mail server, they are reassembled to form the e-mail message. A mail delivery agent ("MDA") accepts the message from the MTA, determines which user should receive the message, and performs the actual delivery by placing the message in that user's mailbox. One popular MDA is "procmail," which is controlled by short programs or scripts called "recipe files." These recipe files can be used in various ways. For example, a procmail recipe can instruct the MDA to deposit mail addressed to one address into another user's mailbox (e.g., to send mail addressed to "help" to the tech support department), to reject mail from certain addresses, or to make copies of certain messages.

> Once the MDA has deposited a message into the recipient's mailbox, the recipient simply needs to use an e-mail client program to retrieve and read the message. While the journey from sender to recipient may seem rather involved, it usually takes just a few seconds, with each intermediate step taking well under a second.

* * * Councilman directed Interloc employees to intercept and copy all incoming communications to subscriber dealers from Amazon.com, an Internet retailer that sells books and other products. Interloc's systems administrator modified the server's procmail recipe so that, before delivering any message from Amazon.com to the recipient's mailbox, procmail would copy the message and place the copy in a separate mailbox that Councilman could access. Thus, procmail would intercept and copy all incoming messages from Amazon.com before they were delivered to the recipient's mailbox, and therefore, before the intended recipient could read the message. This diversion intercepted thousands of messages, and Councilman and other Interloc employees routinely read the e-mail messages sent to Interloc subscribers in the hope of gaining a commercial advantage.

Id. at 69–71. The First Circuit did not decide whether the use of the device "intercepted" the e-mails in question under the Wiretap Act, although the court suggested in dicta that it probably did. *Id.* at 80.

Do you think the use of the procmail recipe intercepted the customer e-mails in *Councilman*? If so, why? Is it because the e-mail was not yet delivered? Because it was collected in real-time? Because it was the functional equivalent of a wiretap, and the details of the technology shouldn't matter? Imagine that Councilman had instructed the system administrator to check the inboxes of customers with Interloc accounts once a week, and to read any e-mails from Amazon. Would checking the e-mail accounts and reading the e-mails constitute an "intercept" of those e-mails? Does it depend on whether the e-mails had been accessed by their recipients and had been read by them already? Does the situation change if the system administrator checks the e-mail inboxes once a day? How about once an hour? How about every minute, or every ten seconds? *See also* United States v. Szymuszkiewicz, 2009 WL 1873657 (E.D.Wis. 2009) (autoforward of all e-mails in account intercepted messages because it obtained them "in an ongoing, prospective fashion.").

4. *Contents and non-content information.* The Wiretap Act applies only to the acquisition of "contents." Contents are defined somewhat awkwardly based on what they include, rather than what they are. According to 18 U.S.C. § 2510(8), " 'contents', when used with respect to any wire, oral, or electronic communication, includes any information concerning the substance, purport, or meaning of that communication." The phrase "substance, purport, or meaning" derives largely from language originally used in the first wiretapping prohibition in the Communications Act of 1934. The 1934 statute stated that "no person not being authorized by the sender shall intercept any communication and divulge or publish the existence, contents, substance, purport, effect, or meaning of such intercepted communication to any person." The existing definition of "contents" retains the inclusion of "substance, purport, or meaning," but drops the "existence" and "effect" of the communication.

The scope of "contents" under the Wiretap Act is clear in some cases. It includes e-mail messages and the subject lines of e-mails. *See* In re Application of United States for an Order Authorizing Use of A Pen Register, 396 F. Supp.2d 45, 48 (D. Mass. 2005) (stating that e-mail subject lines are contents).

It presumably includes the text of any attachments to e-mails, such as document files. As we will see when we study the Pen Register statute, it also excludes "dialing, routing, addressing, or signaling information," which presumably refers to IP headers and e-mail headers (other than subject lines). *See* 18 U.S.C. § 3127(3)–(4).

Other cases are less clear. Consider the status of "Uniform Resource Locators," also known as URLs, the address lines commonly used to retrieve information on the World Wide Web. Do you think a URL entered into a web browser contains contents?

Does it depend on the URL? For example, does the URL "http://www.cnn.com" contain contents? How about this URL:

> http://www.cnn.com/2005/US/12/11/wikipedia.ap/index.html

Or how about this one:

> http://www.google.com/search?hl=en&lr=&q=Ì+must+kill+the+queen

Do any of these URLs contain contents? Note that typing the first URL into a functioning browser will direct a visitor to the CNN.com homepage; entering the second will direct the user to a particular story; and entering the third will run a Google query and return matches for the quotation "I must kill the queen." *See generally* The Naked Gun (Paramount Pictures 1988).

Consider Orin S. Kerr, *Internet Surveillance Law After the USA Patriot Act: The Big Brother That Isn't*, 97 Nw. U. L. Rev. 607, 646, 646 n.190 (2003):

> When an Internet user surfs the web, he sends commands to his computer directing it to send commands to the host computer, asking the host to send back packets of data that will be assembled by his computer into a web page. We can look at the user's command in two ways: either the command is the "content" of the communication between the user and his computer or it is merely "addressing information" that the user entered into his computer to tell the computer where it should go and what it should do, much like the pen register information in *Smith v. Maryland*.

> This is a difficulty latent in *Smith* that has not yet fully been appreciated. In *Smith*, the Court analogized dialing a phone number to contacting an operator and asking the operator to connect the call. Because disclosing the number to an operator would eliminate the speaker's reasonable expectation of privacy in the information, so did disclosing the information to the phone company's computer. So far, so good. The difficulty is that if a speaker calls the operator and places that request, then that request constitutes the contents of the communication between the speaker and the operator. The contents of the conversation between the speaker and the operator becomes the addressing information for the ensuing conversation between the speaker and the person he wishes to call. As a result, it is difficult in the abstract to say whether that initial communication should be considered addressing information or contents.

See also In re Pharmatrak Privacy Litigation, 329 F.3d 9, 18 (1st Cir. 2003) (stating that the Wiretap Act's definition of contents "encompasses personally identifiable information such as a party's name, date of birth, and medical condition" entered into a web site and then included as a URL term); *In re Application*, 396 F. Supp.2d at 49 (suggesting in dicta that search terms in URLs are contents, as they reveal the "substance" and meaning" of the user's search for information).

Imagine a computer hacker attempts to take over a remote server, and that the FBI is monitoring the hacker and intercepts the hacker's communications. Are those communications "contents," such that intercepting them implicates the Wiretap Act? *See* United States Telecom Ass'n v. FCC, 227 F.3d 450, 462 (D.C. Cir. 2000) ("Post-cut-through dialed digits [dialed on a telephone, such as with voicemail systems] can also represent call content. For example, subjects calling automated banking services enter account numbers. When calling voicemail systems, they enter passwords. When calling pagers, they dial digits that convey actual messages. And when calling pharmacies to renew prescriptions, they enter prescription numbers."); In re Applications of the United States, 515 F. Supp.2d 325 (E.D.N.Y. 2007) (holding that post-cut-through dialed digits are contents). *See also* Matthew J. Tokson, *The Content/Envelope Distinction in Internet Law*, 50 Wm. & Mary L. Rev. 2105 (2009).

5. *Packet sniffers and "Carnivore."* Many different kinds of tools can be used to intercept computer and Internet communications. One popular type of tool is known as a "packet sniffer." A packet sniffer scans the packets of network traffic passing by a particular point in the network, and it then copies the parts of the traffic that match whatever characteristics the sniffer has been programmed to copy. *See generally* David McPhie, *Almost Private: Pen Registers, Packet Sniffers, and Privacy at the Margin*, 2005 Stan. Tech. L. Rev. 1.

Packets themselves are actually just streams of zeros and ones of data, and specific patterns of zeros and ones represent specific alphanumeric symbols. For example, a packet sniffer looking for the e-mail address "bob@aol.com," will scan for the following sequence: 01100010011011110110000100100000001100001. If this particular sequence appears, the sniffer can then begin to record a particular number of digits representing the remainder of the packet. The fruits of the sniffer can then be copied to a file, and a user can access the file at a later time and reconstruct the packets into readable form.

Whether a packet sniffer intercepts the contents of communications depends on how it is programmed. A sniffer program must be programmed to scan for and record particular sequences of traffic. If a sniffer is programmed in a way such that the zeros and ones collected include parts of communications that are "contents," then the use of the sniffer implicates the Wiretap Act. On the other hand, if the sniffer is programmed such that it does not copy any data streams that represent contents, then the sniffer will not implicate the Wiretap Act.

In the late 1990s, a great deal of media attention focused on the FBI's "Carnivore" surveillance tool. Carnivore, later renamed "DCS–1000," was a packet sniffer with an unusually sophisticated filter designed specifically to comply with court orders. The Carnivore system presented the user with a graphic user interface set for "content" or "non-content" monitoring, and adjusted the filter automatically. The FBI developed Carnivore in the late 1990s because commercial packet sniffer software available at that time lacked a sophisticated filter, and the commercial software could accidentally collect some content information when the sniffer was programmed to intercept only non-content information. By 2003, improvements in commercial packet sniffer design led to a phase-out of Carnivore/DCS–1000.

For more on Carnivore, see Illinois Institute of Technology Research Institute, Independent Review of Carnivore System—Final Report (2000); Griffin S. Dunham, Note, *Carnivore, The FBI's E–Mail Surveillance System: Devouring Criminals, Not Privacy*, 54 Fed. Comm. L.J. 543 (2002).

6. *The beginning and end of the Wiretap Act.* In the case of a traditional telephone call, the beginning and end point of the Wiretap Act's protection is very clear. The Act applies from handset to handset. Information becomes a "wire communication" when the human voice is transferred into a signal, and ceases to be a wire communication when the signal is transferred back to a human voice. In the case of computer communications such as e-mails, however, the picture is more complicated. Computer data does not change form when that data is an "electronic communication," creating interesting issues about where and when the statute's protection begins and where and when it ends.

Consider an example. Suppose Jane turns on her computer at 9 am and begins to type up an e-mail that she plans to send to her boss Catherine. Jane completes the e-mail at 9:30 am, but decides not to send it immediately. Instead, she saves the e-mail as a draft. At 2 pm, Jane pulls up the draft, looks it over for a few minutes, and sends it. The e-mail arrives at Catherine's ISP at 2:15 pm. Catherine logs in to her e-mail account at 3:00 pm, downloads the file unopened to her laptop at 3:15 pm, and then reads the file from her laptop at 3:30 pm. Now imagine that the government believes that the e-mail from Jane to Catherine contains evidence of a crime, and that investigators want to obtain a copy. Does the Wiretap Act apply to efforts to obtain the email at 9:30 am? 2 pm? 3 pm? At any other time?

Two different sources of law regulate this question. First, the definition of intercept requires that the collection of evidence must be contemporaneous with transmission. Second, the Wiretap Act defines "electronic communication" in relevant part as *"any transfer of signs, signals, writing, images, sounds, data, or intelligence of any nature transmitted in whole or in part by a wire, radio, electromagnetic, photoelectronic or photooptical system that affects interstate or foreign commerce"*. 18 U.S.C. § 2510(12) (emphasis added). This definition suggests that the Wiretap Act begins when data is first transferred over an interstate system, and that it ends when data reaches its destination and is no longer being transferred over an interstate system. A communication typed into a desktop computer that is not connected to the Internet should not be subject to the Wiretap Act, as the communication is not a transfer (at least yet).

Goldman v. United States, 316 U.S. 129 (1942), may provide additional insight. *Goldman* interpreted 47 U.S.C. § 605 of the 1934 Communications Act, the predecessor to the Wiretap Act that shares a number of principles with it. The *Goldman* defendants were attorneys engaged in a conspiracy relating to a bankruptcy scheme. Federal agents entered the room next door to one attorney's office, and used a type of microphone placed against the wall to amplify the sound from the adjacent room and record the defendant's speech while he was talking on the telephone. The defendant claimed that the use of the microphone from the next room had "intercepted" the "communication" of his telephone call. The Supreme Court disagreed:

> What is protected is the message itself throughout the course of its transmission by the instrumentality or agency of transmission. Words written by a person and intended ultimately to be carried as so written to a telegraph office do not constitute a communication within the terms of the Act until they are handed to an agent of the telegraph company. Words spoken in a room in the presence of another into a telephone receiver do not constitute a communication by wire within the meaning of the section. Letters deposited in the Post Office are protected from examination by federal statute, but it could not rightly be claimed that the office carbon of such letter, or indeed the letter itself before it has left the office of the sender, comes within the protection of the statute.

Id. at 133–34.

Did the *O'Brien* court apply these principles correctly? What is the electronic equivalent of handing a message to an agent of the telegraph company? In the case of e-mail, is it pressing "send"?

7. *Remedies.* The *O'Brien* court comes up with a rather creative way to impose a suppression remedy. The statute itself imposes no such remedy, and a federal court in analogous circumstances would not suppress the evidence. As a matter of policy, is a suppression remedy appropriate in this case? Note that the *O'Brien* case is a civil dispute: the Wife monitored the Husband, and she wanted to use the evidence against him in a divorce proceeding.

Should the Wiretap Act include a statutory suppression remedy, either for government violations, for private violations, or for both?

8. A number of provisions in the Wiretap Act seem rather odd today because they are artifacts from the telephone era of the 1950s and 1960s. For example, the definition of "intercept" in 18 U.S.C. § 2510(4) requires that a communication must be obtained "through the use of any electronic, mechanical, or other device." Section 2510(5) in turn broadly defines "electronic, mechanical, or other device" to mean "any device or apparatus which can be used to intercept a wire, oral, or electronic communication," with two notable exceptions:

> (a) any telephone or telegraph instrument, equipment or facility, or any component thereof,
>
> > (i) furnished to the subscriber or user by a provider of wire or electronic communication service in the ordinary course of its business and being used by the subscriber or user in the ordinary course of its business or furnished by such subscriber or user for connection to the facilities of such service and used in the ordinary course of its business; or

(ii) being used by a provider of wire or electronic communication service in the ordinary course of its business, or by an investigative or law enforcement officer in the ordinary course of his duties;

(b) a hearing aid or similar device being used to correct subnormal hearing to not better than normal.

This requirement and the two exceptions were designed to deal with the specific dynamics of the telephone. The requirement of a device made sense in the telephone-only era, when an eavesdropper could listen in to a call by being in the next room or hiding nearby. Excluding hearing aids was important before telephones had volume controls; hearing-impaired telephone users had to purchase amplifiers and attach them to the handset to increase volume.

The exclusion of telephones used "in the ordinary course of business" that appears in 18 U.S.C. § 2510(5)(a)(i) is generally known as the extension telephone exception. This exception was designed to permit businesses to use an "extension telephone" to monitor the performance of their employees when they spoke on the phone to customers. The exception establishes that when a phone company furnishes an employer with an extension telephone for a legitimate work-related purpose, employer monitoring of employees using the extension phone for legitimate work-related purposes does not violate the Wiretap Act. *See* Briggs v. American Air Filter Co., 630 F.2d 414, 418 (5th Cir. 1980).

Finally, the exemption of monitoring by police officers in 18 U.S.C. § 2510(5)(a)(ii) that involves the use of "any telephone" by "an investigative or law enforcement officer in the ordinary course of his duties" is easily misunderstood. Although the language appears broad, it has been interpreted to permit routine monitoring of calls to and from police stations and little else. *See, e.g.*, Amati v. City of Woodstock, 176 F.3d 952, 955 (7th Cir. 1999).

9.   The Wiretap Act permits agents to intercept communications pursuant to a court order. *See* 18 U.S.C. §§ 2516, 2518. Obtaining a Title III "super warrant" order is quite burdensome, however, as the requirements extend far beyond probable cause and involve a great deal of paperwork. The Justice Department explains:

High-level Justice Department approval is required for federal Title III applications, by statute in the case of wire communications, and by Justice Department policy in the case of electronic communications (except for numeric pagers). When authorized by the Justice Department and signed by a United States District Court or Court of Appeals judge, a Title III order permits law enforcement to intercept communications for up to thirty days. *See* § 2518.

18 U.S.C. §§ 2516–2518 imposes several formidable requirements that must be satisfied before investigators can obtain a Title III order. Most importantly, the application for the order must show probable cause to believe that the interception will reveal evidence of a predicate felony offense listed in § 2516. *See* § 2518(3)(a)–(b). For federal agents, the predicate felony offense must be one of the crimes specifically enumerated in § 2516(1)(a)–(r) to intercept wire communications, or any federal

felony to intercept electronic communications. *See* 18 U.S.C. § 2516(3). The predicate crimes for state investigations are listed in 18 U.S.C. § 2516(2). The application for a Title III order also (1) must show that normal investigative procedures have been tried and failed, or that they reasonably appear to be unlikely to succeed or to be too dangerous, *see* § 2518(1)(c); (2) must establish probable cause that the communication facility is being used in a crime; and (3) must show that the surveillance will be conducted in a way that minimizes the interception of communications that do not provide evidence of a crime.

U.S. Department of Justice, Searching and Seizing Computers (2002), available at http://www.cybercrime.gov/s & smanual2002.htm#_IVD3a_.

The difficulty of obtaining a Title III order results in such orders being obtained only rarely. This is particularly true in computer-related cases. In as typical year, only a handful of Title III orders are obtained to monitor only electronic communications. The overwhelming majority of wiretap orders in the United States are obtained to tap telephones in narcotics cases. *See, e.g.,* Administrative Office of the U.S. Courts, 2008 Wiretap Report (2008).

The very low number of Title III orders in computer cases should direct our attention to the three main exceptions applicable in computer wiretapping cases: the consent exception, § 2511(2)(c)–(d), the provider exception, § 2511(2)(a)(i), and the computer trespasser exception, § 2511(2)(i). In the great majority of cases, monitoring occurs pursuant to one of these three exceptions.

2. THE CONSENT EXCEPTION

Like the Fourth Amendment, the Wiretap Act has a consent exception. 18 U.S.C. § 2511(2)(c) and (d) state:

(c) It shall not be unlawful under this chapter for a person acting under color of law to intercept a wire, oral, or electronic communication, where such person is a party to the communication or one of the parties to the communication has given prior consent to such interception.

(d) It shall not be unlawful under this chapter for a person not acting under color of law to intercept a wire, oral, or electronic communication where such person is a party to the communication or where one of the parties to the communication has given prior consent to such interception unless such communication is intercepted for the purpose of committing any criminal or tortious act in violation of the Constitution or laws of the United States or of any State.

This exception permits "a party to the communication" to give "prior consent" to interception. If a party to the communication consents to the interception, the interception does not violate the Wiretap Act. For example, an undercover government agent can record a conversation between himself and a suspect or permit others to record the call. Similarly, if a private person records his own telephone conversations with others, his consent authorizes the interception unless the commission of a criminal, tortious, or other injurious act was a determinative factor in the person's motivation for intercepting the communication. *See* United States v. Cassiere, 4 F.3d 1006, 1021 (1st Cir. 1993).

GRIGGS–RYAN v. SMITH

United States Court of Appeals for the First Circuit, 1990.
904 F.2d 112.

SELYA, CIRCUIT JUDGE.

Reaching out to touch someone, plaintiff-appellant Gerald Griggs–Ryan filed two related civil actions in the United States District Court for the District of Maine. Suing his landlady, Beulah Smith, plaintiff alleged that she unlawfully intercepted and disclosed the contents of a telephone conversation in which he participated.

I.

Plaintiff was a tenant at a campground which Smith operated in Wells. The individual units did not have telephones, but lodgers were allowed to use the landlady's telephone. During the summer of 1987, Smith was plagued by obscene calls. On the police department's advice, she began to record incoming calls through her answering machine. Because she suspected that plaintiff's friend, Paul Jackson, was responsible for the offensive overtures, Smith informed plaintiff on a number of occasions that all calls to her home were being recorded. She hoped, of course, that plaintiff would relay the message to Jackson.

On September 14, 1987, Smith answered the telephone in her bedroom. The caller identified himself as "Richard Kierstead" and asked to speak with plaintiff. Smith held the line open to maintain the connection while her daughter went to fetch plaintiff. When Griggs–Ryan picked up the office extension, Smith started to cradle her instrument. Overhearing the caller say, "Hi, it's Paul, she thinks it's Kierstead," and believing the voice to be Paul Jackson's, Smith changed her mind. She did not hang up but instead listened to and recorded the ensuing discussion.

As a result of the eavesdropping, Smith came to suspect that the overheard conversation concerned a drug transaction. She immediately contacted the authorities. At police headquarters, she played the tape for defendant Connelly. Sharing Smith's suspicions, the detective revealed the conversation's contents to the district attorney and to a local magistrate. The magistrate issued a warrant to search plaintiff's abode and the Wells police executed it, seizing marijuana. Griggs–Ryan was arrested and charged with trafficking.

A suppression hearing was held in the state superior court. Smith testified about what she told Griggs–Ryan concerning her recording practice. The judge found that plaintiff was "unaware" that Smith was listening to, or recording, the September 14 conversation, and ruled that

Smith's interception of the conversation was therefore inadmissible under Maine law. On September 28, 1989, the judge suppressed the fruits of the search.

In the meantime, plaintiff had begun the instant suits in federal court. For their part, defendants argued that plaintiff, by electing to talk to Jackson after Smith's warning that all incoming calls were being recorded, effectively acquiesced in the interception.

The district court concluded that the landlady's actions were not proscribed by federal law because Smith informed Plaintiff on more than one occasion that she was recording all incoming calls and that there was no evidence that Smith qualified her statements to Plaintiff on the matter. Thus, the district court held that Plaintiff's receiving of a telephone call inside of Smith's home, when considered in light of the warning he received, manifests implied consent sufficient to trigger the prior consent exception to Title III.

II.

Although plaintiff repeatedly declaims that wire communications are "protected absolutely from illegal interception," that rallying cry—like most sloganeering—overstates the proposition. Title III was intended to prohibit all interceptions except those specifically provided for in the Act. Congress, in its wisdom, chose to insert a myriad of exceptions and restrictive definitions into Title III, purposely leaving certain wire communications unprotected. Accordingly, there is little to be gained by pejorative declamations; the question is simply whether a particular intercept runs afoul of the statute's imperatives.

18 U.S.C. § 2511(2)(d) outlines a Title III exclusion applicable where one of the parties to the communication has given prior consent to such interception. We agree with the Second Circuit that "Congress intended the consent requirement to be construed broadly." United States v. Amen, 831 F.2d 373, 378 (2d Cir. 1987). In this spirit, we—and other courts— have held that Title III affords safe harbor not only for persons who intercept calls with the explicit consent of a conversant but also for those who do so after receiving implied consent. See United States v. Willoughby, 860 F.2d 15, 19 (2d Cir. 1988); Watkins v. L.M. Berry & Co., 704 F.2d 577, 581 (11th Cir. 1983); Campiti v. Walonis, 611 F.2d 387, 393 (1st Cir. 1979). Acknowledging the doctrinal vitality of implied consent, however, does not address its parameters—nor can we suggest any pat, all-purpose definition. In the Title III milieu as in other settings, consent inheres where a person's behavior manifests acquiescence or a comparable voluntary diminution of his or her otherwise protected rights.

Of course, implied consent is not constructive consent. Rather, implied consent is "consent in fact" which is inferred from surrounding circumstances indicating that the party knowingly agreed to the surveillance. Thus, implied consent—or the absence of it—may be deduced from the circumstances prevailing in a given situation. The circumstances relevant to an implication of consent will vary from case to case, but the compendium will ordinarily include language or acts which tend to prove (or disprove) that a party knows of, or assents to, encroachments on the routine expectation that conversations are private. And the ultimate determination must proceed in light of the prophylactic purpose of Title III—a purpose which suggests that consent should not casually be inferred.

The salient facts are these. Prior to September 14, Griggs–Ryan had been repeatedly informed that all incoming calls were being monitored. Smith's affidavit in this respect stands uncontradicted and unimpeached:

> On several occasions during the course of the summer I spoke to Mr. Ryan and informed him that all incoming telephone calls to my home were being tape recorded. I had made it quite clear to Mr. Ryan by virtue of these several conversations that all of the incoming telephone calls to my home on my phones were being tape recorded.

There is no evidence that Smith, whatever her actual practice might have been, ever informed plaintiff that she would cease monitoring a call once she determined that it was not harassing. Indeed, the only record evidence speaking directly to this question is Smith's testimony at the state court suppression hearing, where the following colloquy occurred:

> Q. When you told Mr. Ryan that you were taping every phone call, did you tell him that you have stopped taping once you identified who the caller was?
>
> A. No.

* * * [W]e take as undisputed that (1) plaintiff was told unequivocally that all incoming calls would be recorded, and (2) Smith did not qualify the warning by telling him that she planned to listen only until she could ascertain whether the call was offensive.

It remains only for us to link applicable law to undisputed fact. The district court ruled that plaintiff, in taking the call from Jackson and conversing with him on Smith's telephone, impliedly consented to the interception. We think that this ruling was inevitable. Plaintiff had been unmistakably warned on a number of occasions that all incoming calls were being monitored. In light of so sweeping a warning, he continued to receive calls and talk unguardedly on Smith's personal line without the slightest hint of coercion or exigent circumstance. Plaintiff was free to use some other instrument; or since outgoing calls were not recorded, to return calls on Smith's telephone and thus avoid any unwanted eavesdropping. Given the circumstances prevailing, it seems altogether clear that plaintiff knowingly agreed to the surveillance. His consent, albeit not explicit, was manifest. No more was required.

Smith's conduct on September 14 fell squarely within the parameters of what she had repeatedly told plaintiff to expect, and thus, fell squarely within the bounds of plaintiff's consent. Having persisted in using Smith's telephone to converse with callers in the face of unambiguous, unqualified notice that every incoming call would be monitored, plaintiff's consent necessarily encompassed every portion of every call he accepted on his landlady's line.

Plaintiff's final fizgig, centering on the upshot of the state court suppression hearing, is equally unimpressive. It is true that the state court found plaintiff "unaware" that the call in question was being recorded. Even assuming, however, that the finding has evidentiary significance in a federal civil case involving persons not parties to the state criminal proceedings—a matter on which we do not opine—it is beside the present point. Whether a person is cognizant that a particular call is being recorded does not answer, or fully respond to, the question of whether the scope of consent previously granted was sufficiently expansive to cover a generalized practice of recording.

Because plaintiff unqualifiedly consented to Smith's interception of all incoming calls, the latter's conduct was "not unlawful" within the meaning of 18 U.S.C. § 2511(2)(d). Consequently, no cause of action could be maintained against Smith under Title III.

NOTES AND QUESTIONS

1. In what sense did Griggs–Ryan consent to Smith's monitoring? He had been told a few times in the months leading up to the call that Smith was recording calls made to her phone. But there was no evidence that he knew this particular call was recorded. Is the key question whether Griggs–Ryan proceeded after receiving notice, or whether he actually consented to being taped? Which court was right: the state court that ruled Griggs–Ryan had not consented, or the federal court that ruled he had?

Which is the better approach as a matter of policy? Should notice of monitoring be sufficient even if the person monitored did not realize the call was being monitored?

2. Compare *Griggs–Ryan* with Deal v. Spears, 980 F.2d 1153 (8th Cir. 1992). In *Spears*, owners of a packaging store suspected that an employee was involved in an earlier burglary of the store. The employee often spent much of her day flirting on the store telephone with her boyfriend, and the store owners asked the employee to cut down on her personal calls and warned that they might start recording her calls to curtail abuses. The owners later decided to record all calls to and from the store in an effort to catch the employee making an unguarded admission of her involvement in the burglary. When the monitoring recorded the employee admitting petty wrongdoing at the store, the store owners fired her. The employee then brought a wiretapping suit against the store owners. Held: The owners' warning that they "might" begin to monitor calls was insufficient to generate consent under the Wiretap Act. *See id.* at 1157.

3. Does a telephone or Internet user impliedly consent to monitoring if she did not receive notice but should have known that the communications would be monitored? Cases suggest that the answer is "no." For example, in United States v. Lanoue, 71 F.3d 966 (1st Cir. 1995), the defendant was a

prisoner who was monitored while making calls from a detention center that did not notify prisoners of monitoring. The First Circuit articulated the following standard to determine whether consent exists absent sufficient formal notice:

> Deficient notice will almost always defeat a claim of implied consent. Keeping in mind that implied consent is not constructive consent but 'consent in fact,' consent might be implied in spite of deficient notice, but only in a rare case where the court can conclude with assurance from surrounding circumstances that the party knowingly agreed to the surveillance. We emphasize that consent should not casually be inferred, particularly in a case of deficient notice. The surrounding circumstances must convincingly show that the party knew about and consented to the interception in spite of the lack of formal notice or deficient formal notice.

Id. at 981. Similarly, in Jandak v. Village of Brookfield, 520 F.Supp. 815, 820 n. 5 (N.D. Ill. 1981), a police officer placed a personal call from the police station to another person. The call was secretly recorded, and the court rejected the notion that one of the parties consented because they should have known that a call from the police station would be recorded:

> [C]onsent may be implied in fact, from surrounding circumstances indicating that the party knowingly agreed to the surveillance. Defendants here are asking that the consent be implied in law, if the party reasonably should have known. This goes far beyond the language of the statute, or any indications in the legislative history, and the court declines to so expansively read the exception.

4. Computer owners sometimes install network banners to generate users' consent and permit monitoring. A banner is a message that greets computer users when they log on to a network; a typical banner informs users that their communications on the network may be monitored. After a user sees the banner and has knowledge of the monitoring, the computer can be monitored without violating the Wiretap Act under the consent theory of *Griggs–Ryan v. Smith.*

Banners are routinely used in government workplaces to regulate rights on government networks. In the context of government employment, computer network banners perform two functions at once. They generate consent to monitoring for purposes of Title III, and they also constitute a legitimate workplace policy that eliminates Fourth Amendment privacy rights in the network under O'Connor v. Ortega, 480 U.S. 709 (1987).

How clear must the wording of a banner be to generate a computer user's consent to monitoring? Should the banner require users to "click through" the notice? Is it sufficient if the notice of monitoring can be found somewhere in the Terms of Service or an employee manual? What if the computer user does not see the banner or does not understand it? What if the user is trying to avoid the banner and bypasses it to avoid actual notice?

5. *Problem.* A commercial ISP called Overcast requires its new subscribers to agree to Terms of Service as a condition of service. One of the terms states: "Overcast may wish to intercept your communications. By registering for an account with Overcast, you agree to allow Overcast to monitor your

communications." A new subscriber named Hoover J. Edgar signs up with Overcast, and clicks "I Agree" to start his service contract. Like almost all subscribers, however, Edgar does not actually read the Terms of Service and has no idea what terms he has agreed to follow. Five years later, the FBI is conducting a terrorism investigation and suspects that Edgar may be involved with a terrorist plot. An FBI agent approaches an Overcast employee and asks Overcast to intercept all of Edgar's e-mails and send them to the FBI. Overcast agrees, relying on the Terms of Service, and begins to intercept Edgar's e-mails.

Does this monitoring violate the Wiretap Act, or is it permitted under the consent exception?

6. *Computers, victims, and intermediaries as parties to the communication.* In the case of telephone calls, a "party to the communication" is usually easy to identify. Any human participant in a telephone conversation is a party to the communication. The simple framework of a two-way communication between two parties may be more difficult to apply in the case of a computer network.

> When a hacker launches an attack against a computer network, for example, he may route the attack through a handful of compromised computer systems before directing the attack at a final victim. At the victim's computer, the hacker may direct the attack at a user's network account, at the system administrator's "root" account, or at common files. Finding a "person" who is a "party to the communication"—other than the hacker himself, of course—can be a difficult (if not entirely metaphysical) task.

U.S. Department of Justice, Searching and Seizing Computers (2002), available at www.cybercrime.gov/s & smanual2002.htm#_IVD3b_.

Can a computer be a party to the communication that can consent to monitoring under the Wiretap Act? Is the owner or system administrator a party to the communication? Recall the early case of United States v. Seidlitz, 589 F.2d 152 (4th Cir. 1978), first introduced in Chapter 2. Seidlitz used a stolen account to break into computers owned and operated by OSI. Employees at OSI monitored Seidlitz's unauthorized use of the OSI computer and used that monitoring to trace the attack back to Seidlitz. At trial, Seidlitz argued that the evidence of his conduct could not be used against him because the monitoring violated the Wiretap Act. The case was decided before the passage of ECPA, and the Fourth Circuit properly rejected the claim on the ground that the computer communication was not a "wire communication" protected by the 1968 statute. The Court then suggested this secondary rationale for its holding:

> Title III specifically authorizes the interception of a wire communication by a party to the communication or by a person acting with the consent of a party to the communication. 18 U.S.C. § 2511(2)(c), (d). In our opinion OSI, which leased, housed, programmed, and maintained the computers and subscribed to the relevant telephone numbers, was for all intents and purposes a party to the communications initiated by the defendant, since in a very real sense the company used the computers solely as a medium for imparting to customers, via telephone lines, its own expertise. Insofar

as OSI installed on its line a computer which was capable of recording the messages exchanged in the course of responding to a remote user's requests, we consider this case analogous to those which recognize that a party may, consistent with Title III, use a device to capture and record both sides of his telephone conversation with another party.

Id. at 158. Do you agree that OSI was a party to the communication in the *Seidlitz* case? If not, can OSI monitor intrusions into its network? As a matter of policy, what rights should the victim of a computer intrusion have to monitor attacks against it? *See also* United States v. Mullins, 992 F.2d 1472, 1478 (9th Cir. 1993) (suggesting in passing that the consent exception authorizes monitoring of computer system misuse because the owner of the victimized computer system is a party to the communication).

If you agree that OSI was a party to the communication in the *Seidlitz* case, do you reach the same conclusion with respect to intermediary computers that may be involved in computer intrusion cases? The question is very important in computer hacking investigations:

> When the government investigates a computer hacking incident, investigators generally start at the victim that has reported the crime and trace back the attack to its origin. To avoid detection, hackers will not mount their attacks directly from their ISPs. Rather, they will route communications through a few victim computers along the way to throw the government off the trail. This can effectively disguise their location because computers only reveal the immediate source from which a user sent a communication. If a user routes a command from A to B to C to D, the computer at D will only know that the command came from C, and will not know that the command actually originated from A. To identify the intruder, the government must trace the communication step by step from D to C to B to A.
>
> The rules that govern this tracing process depend heavily on whether the computers that the hacker has victimized count as parties to the communication under the Wiretap Act. Consider an example. Imagine that a computer hacker in New York plans to attack sensitive Defense Department computers in California, and starts off by accessing the Internet through his ISP in New Jersey. Rather than hack directly into the Defense Department computers in California, the hacker first breaks into a computer at a small company in Nebraska, and from that site in Nebraska he hacks into another computer belonging to a high school in Arizona. Finally, from the computer in Arizona he launches a computer attack against Defense Department computers in California that contain potentially sensitive information relating to national security. Defense Department criminal investigators then begin an investigation into the attacks.

Orin S. Kerr, *Internet Surveillance Law After the USA Patriot Act: The Big Brother That Isn't*, 97 Nw. U. L. Rev. 607, 662–63 (2003). Do you think that the Defense Department computer in California is a party to the communication? How about the ISP in New Jersey? The small company in Nebraska? The high school in Arizona? Consider the stakes from the standpoint of privacy, focusing on whether the police would be able to monitor the hacker's activities at the school in Arizona with the consent of the school:

> [W]hether the police can conduct the monitoring with the school's consent depends on whether the school is a "party" to the hacker's communication. If the school is a party, the school can consent to law enforcement monitoring; if it is not a party, the school cannot consent to the monitoring without violating the Wiretap Act.
>
> Whether the school constitutes a party under the Wiretap Act then hinges upon how the hacker's attack is modeled. On one hand, if the hacker sent a communication to the school with instructions for the school's computer to launch attacks against the California victims, then the school itself is a party to the communication and can consent to the government's monitoring. This approach reflects a broad theory of the "party to the communication" exception. On the other hand, if we say that the hacker himself sent the communication to the California victim but merely routed the communication through the school, then the school is not a party and cannot consent. This approach applies a narrow conception of the "party to the communication" exception.
>
> What complicates this picture is that labeling the school a party to the communication may sound logical here because the school is a victim of crime, but ultimately would eviscerate the privacy protections of the Wiretap Act. Internet communications almost never travel directly from their point of origin to their destination: most travel from hop to hop as they traverse the network. If each hop is a party to the communication, as the broader approach to the exception would dictate, then any provider can monitor any communication within its network or can consent to monitoring by others.

Id. at 664–65.

If you write an e-mail to your best friend, is your ISP a party to the communication? Is your friend's ISP a party to the communication? Or are you and your friend the only parties to the communication?

A somewhat related issue came up in a case brought under 47 U.S.C. § 605, the predecessor to the Wiretap statute. In United States v. Dote, 371 F.2d 176 (7th Cir. 1966), the Illinois Bell Telephone company tipped off IRS agents that a particular telephone was being used in an illegal gambling ring. Acting at the request of IRS investigators, the company installed a pen register on the phone. The pen register led IRS investigators to the members of the gambling enterprise, who were then arrested and convicted of tax evasion. They appealed their convictions on the ground that the pen register violated 47 U.S.C. § 605. (Although the pen register did not collect contents, § 605 applied both to content and non-content information at that time.) The government defended its use of the pen register on the ground that the dial pulses of the numbers dialed from the telephone were communications to the phone company. In the parlance of the modern Wiretap Act, the government's claim was that the phone company could consent to monitoring because it was a party to the communication of the numbers dialed. The Seventh Circuit disagreed:

We see no reason to indulge in a game of words, * * * [on] whether the telephone company as a legal entity is sufficiently embodied in the wires and devices of its system to be an intended recipient of the dial pulse signal. * * * [N]o person was the intended recipient of the dial pulses, but rather the communications system through which the pulses were to be relayed as a signal to activate the telephone of the intended recipient of a telephone call. * * * The dial telephone system does not generally require human intervention to connect two telephones. The telephone company was not therefore the intended recipient of the signal. The 'intended recipient' was the telephone of another subscriber, which would ring to notify the subscriber of a call. Ultimately, the intended human recipient of the signal was the subscriber called.

Id. at 180.

7. *All-party consent statutes.* The federal Wiretap Act is a one-party consent statute. That is, the consent of any one party to the communication permits monitoring of every other party. In contrast, some state wiretap statutes require every party to consent before the state consent exception applies. In the case of a telephone call, for example, each person on the call must authorize the monitoring.

How does an all-party consent approach apply to monitoring computer communications? In Commonwealth v. Proetto, 771 A.2d 823 (Pa. Super. Ct. 2001), *aff'd*, 837 A.2d 1163 (Pa. 2003), the defendant engaged in chat and e-mail communications with an undercover police officer who was posing as a young girl. The police officer recorded all of the communications, and print-outs of the exchanges were admitted at trial. Pennsylvania's state wiretap statute requires the consent of all parties, and the defendant argued that the officer had intercepted his communications unlawfully because the defendant had not consented to the officer recording his chat and e-mail exchanges. The Pennsylvania Superior Court rejected the claim, finding the defendant's consent implicit in his use of the technology:

This situation is unlike one in which a party is engaging in a conversation over the telephone. While engaging in a conversation over the telephone, a party would have no reason to believe that the other party was taping the conversation. Any reasonably intelligent person, savvy enough to be using the Internet, however, would be aware of the fact that messages are received in a recorded format, by their very nature, and can be download-ed or printed by the party receiving the message. By the very act of sending a communication over the Internet, the party expressly consents to the recording of the message.

See id. at 830. Is this reasoning persuasive? Does an Internet user expressly (or impliedly) permit intended recipients of his communications to make copies of his communications?

3. THE PROVIDER EXCEPTION

The next exception to the Wiretap Act is the provider exception, 18 U.S.C. § 2511(2)(a)(i). The provider exception is particularly important in computer misuse cases, as it allows reasonable monitoring of computer misuse. The exception states in relevant part:

an officer, employee, or agent of a provider of wire or electronic communication service, whose facilities are used in the transmission of a wire or electronic communication, [can] intercept, disclose, or use that communication in the normal course of his employment while engaged in any activity which is a necessary incident to the rendition of his service or to the protection of the rights or property of the provider of that service.

The provider exception recognizes that providers of network services may have legitimate business reasons to tap communications within their networks. Networks can be misused or abused, and providers may need to monitor the misuse to identify the wrongdoer and stop the misconduct. The provider exception thus gives providers a limited right to monitor communications to protect their property. The basic standard is reasonableness. *See* United States v. Harvey, 540 F.2d 1345, 1350 (8th Cir. 1976). Providers are permitted to conduct reasonable monitoring to protect their rights or property and can disclose the fruits of what they obtain to the government. However, they cannot take the monitoring or disclosure too far.

UNITED STATES v. AULER

United States Court of Appeals for the Seventh Circuit, 1976.
539 F.2d 642.

FAIRCHILD, CHIEF JUDGE.

In this appeal we are once again asked to consider the scope of the authority of a common carrier to intercept and disclose wire communications, 18 U.S.C. § 2511(2)(a)(i). The appellant, Raymond Auler, was convicted for violating the Wire Fraud Statute, 18 U.S.C. § 1343, and sentenced to six months imprisonment.

I

During June 1973, a security supervisor for the Wisconsin Telephone Company, Bernard G. Schlimgen, attached a 2600 cycle detecting device to the telephone line serving Auler's residence in Milwaukee. Schlimgen believed that there was in use a device known as a "blue box" to fraudulently place toll-free long distance calls. The blue box is used to electronically bypass the telephone company's billing equipment. After engaging a wide area telephone service system (WATS), the blue box emits a 2600 cycle tone which allows the user to remain within the toll system after the WATS line has been disconnected. Subsequently, the user "key pulses" through the blue box a series of multifrequency tones, comparable to those normally generated by a long distance call. The telephone company's billing equipment only records the original toll-free call; consequently, the user is not charged for the call made with the blue box.

The 2600 cycle detector indicated that an out of state call was made by use of the blue box technique. Schlimgen informed Roger Davis, then a Special Agent for the F.B.I., of this suspected violation of the Wire Fraud

Statute. Davis obtained a warrant, and accompanied by Schlimgen, searched Auler's residence. They did not find a blue box, but learned from Auler's daughter that Auler had been present earlier, but was moving to Wisconsin Dells.

On June 21, 1973, Schlimgen contacted Gary Mattila, a security agent for the General Telephone Company, the company which provides telephone service for the Wisconsin Dells area, concerning Auler's alleged use of the blue box. Mattila discovered that Auler had two telephone listings at a Wisconsin Dells residence. He further learned from another Wisconsin Telephone Company security agent that Auler was a suspected blue box user. This information was obtained by examining a computer printout list of all the toll-free calls placed in that area. On the basis of these reports, Mattila ordered on July 13, and 17, 1973 the installation of a 2600 cycle detector placed on both of Auler's Wisconsin Dells telephone lines.

After the detection of numerous 2600 cycle tones, Mattila, on July 27, 1973, ordered the attachment of magnetic tape recording devices to Auler's lines to monitor all multifrequency tones and conversations originating from Auler's residence. This taping was discontinued on one line on July 29, and on the other on July 30. General Telephone's logs indicate that the magnetic recorders also taped traffic over Auler's lines on August 2 through 3, and August 9 through 13.

On July 30 and 31, Mattila advised F.B.I. Agent Hunter that General Telephone had conducted an investigation regarding Raymond Auler, and that based on this investigation Auler was suspected of using a blue box. Hunter obtained a warrant on August 3 to search Auler's residence. Accompanied by Mattila, Hunter executed the warrant on August 10. Immediately preceding the search Mattila had been in contact with General Telephone agents who were monitoring Auler's lines. These agents informed Mattila that they had detected a 2600 cycle tone and had recorded Auler completing a call. During the search Hunter found and seized a blue box and other equipment. Auler was subsequently tried on stipulated facts and found guilty. Prior to trial Auler had unsuccessfully sought to suppress any evidence that was the product of General Telephone's interception of his telephone lines.

II

Section 2511(2)(a)(i) provides a telephone company with the power to protect its property through limited monitoring of the lines of suspected illegal users and the subsequent immunity to disclose necessary information to law enforcement agencies.

This authority of the telephone company to intercept and disclose wire communications is not unlimited. It may only intercept a communication which is a necessary incident to the rendition of service or for the protection of the company's rights or property. * * * Therefore, we think that any surveillance of a suspected blue box user must be restricted to a determination of (1) whether a blue box is being used; (2) the multifrequency tones of the number "dialed" by the blue box; (3) whether the call was completed; (4) the duration of the call; and (5) the identity of the caller. This information can be obtained through a 2600 cycle detector, or similar device, and a tape recording of the salutations at the beginning of the conversation. Therefore, section 2511(2)(a)(i) must reasonably be read to permit the telephone company to divulge, at least, the existence of the illegal calls and the fact that they were completed (the salutations) to law enforcement authorities. These authorized disclosures could properly be used to obtain a search warrant and would be admissible as evidence.

Auler points out that General Telephone's surveillance of his conversations extended beyond the scope of permissible interception just outlined. At oral argument, the Government conceded that during the approximately two week period of surveillance, General Telephone monitored and committed to tape all calls, whether made illicitly with a blue box or in compliance with the subscription agreement. This intrusive interception provided General Telephone with far more information than it needed to protect its interests.

However, General Telephone only disclosed to the F.B.I. the limited evidence which section 2511(2)(a)(i) reasonably permits. This consisted of edited tape recordings containing tones identified as those transmitted by a blue box, dialing signals, and salutations of the appellant. The interception of the material recorded on these tapes may be viewed apart from those more intrusive acts of surveillance which are not immunized by section 2511(2)(a)(i). The reasonable and necessary interceptions and disclosures need not be suppressed as the "fruits" of illegal surveillance. Neither the statute nor the Fourth Amendment, which does not prohibit unreasonable searches by private individuals, require lawful interceptions and disclosures to be excluded as evidence; only evidence obtained through surveillance beyond the authorization of section 2511(2)(a)(i) * * * must be suppressed. General Telephone provided no evidence stemming from excessive interception to the F.B.I., and the Government offered none at trial.[10] The edited tapes offered at trial were properly admitted. We do assume for the purpose of this discussion that General Telephone conducted excessive and therefore illegal surveillance. Any consequences to General Telephone in the context of the civil and criminal penalties imposed by [the Wiretap Act] would be the subject of an action to which General Telephone would be a party.

III

The appellant further argues that even if section 2511(2)(a)(i) permits limited telephone company surveillance, he is entitled to the protection provided by the Fourth Amendment. Auler asserts that the search warrant, executed by the F.B.I. was obtained as a result of illegal surveillance directed by Government agents. The tape recordings and the evidence

---

10. Evidence which is obtained through an unreasonably broad surveillance cannot be legally disclosed to the government, regardless whether it is offered at trial.

secured as a result of the search of Auler's Wisconsin Dells residence should, he claims, therefore have been suppressed.

Auler relies on the principles that Government agents, state or federal, who engage in electronic eavesdropping must comply with the constitutional requirements of a reasonable search, *Katz v. United States,* 389 U.S. 347, 359 (1967), and that evidence, tangible or testimonial, which is seized without adherence to these constitutional safeguards must be excluded. *Weeks v. United States*, 232 U.S. 383, 391–92 (1914); *Wong Sun v. United States*, 371 U.S. 471, 485 (1963). Before we can apply these principles to the case before us, the appellant must demonstrate that the Government was directly or indirectly engaged in gathering the alleged illegal surveillance.

The district court found that the F.B.I. neither initiated nor directed the surveillance conducted by General Telephone. Our own search of the record supports this conclusion. Nor do we find that the F.B.I. participated in or tacitly approved of the interceptions made by General Telephone to the degree that they became a government search. Finally, we cannot agree with the circuitous reasoning that would label the surveillance permitted by section 2511(2)(a)(i) as governmental action, thereby requiring a warrant.

Auler further contends that the intimate collaboration between F.B.I. Agent Hunter and General Telephone employees Mattila and Nelson constituted a government wiretap, resulting in an illegally executed search warrant. The facts stipulated by both parties do indicate that on August 10, 1973 Nelson informed Mattila that the blue box was being used and that Auler had identified himself during the illegal call. Mattila received this information while he was in the company of Agent Hunter; both men were stationed outside Auler's residence. Upon receipt of this surveillance Hunter and Mattila executed the search warrant and found the blue box.

We are aware, as was the Government at oral argument, that Government agents must not rely on telephone company employees to act on their behalf without complying with the requirements of the Fourth Amendment. In no situation may the Government direct the telephone company to intercept wire communications in order to circumvent the warrant requirements of a reasonable search. The Government may not use their ears for what it cannot do. On the morning of August 10, 1973 General Telephone was engaged in surveillance permitted by section 2511(2)(a)(i). The interceptions recorded by Nelson were part of the continuing effort by General Telephone to gather evidence concerning Auler's illegal use of the telephone lines. The disclosure of this continuing illegal conduct was in furtherance of General Telephone's attempt to protect its equipment.

Based on information supplied by General Telephone, Agent Hunter had secured a valid search warrant. He had asked Mattila to accompany him to identify any illegal equipment found during the course of the search. Mattila's disclosure, just prior to execution of the warrant, that the blue box was being used, was a disclosure of information lawfully acquired through surveillance necessary to protect company rights and property. The surveillance had been conducted independently of any governmental direction. The search warrant had been obtained on the basis of legally intercepted and disclosed information. Consequently, the final disclosure by Mattila cannot transform authorized conduct into an illegal Government search. The trial record and the district court's analysis of these facts can bear no other interpretation.

For the reasons set forth above, the judgment appealed from is affirmed.

NOTES AND QUESTIONS

1. Imagine a system administrator has reason to believe that a computer hacker has intruded into his network from a particular IP address using a particular destination port.[3] The system administrator wants to take the following steps:

    A.   Record every command from that IP address to that destination port for one week.

    B.   Record every command from that IP address to any port for one week.

    C.   Record every command to that port regardless of IP address for one week.

    D.   Record every command into the network at every IP address and every port for 24 hours.

    E.   Install intrusion detection software that will automatically record future intrusions that match known attack patterns common among computer hackers.

Which of these steps fall within the provider exception? Does it depend on the IP address, or how much traffic the network receives on that particular port? Does it depend on the intrusion detection software and how it is configured? Does it depend on what kind of communications the hacker routes through the victim network? What if the hacker sets up a private Internet chat channel from inside the network—can the system administrator monitor the Internet chat communications to identify the hacker?

2. Unlike other Wiretap Act exceptions, the provider exception regulates both the interception and the disclosure of communications. If a provider wants to monitor communications and disclose them to the government under the provider exception, both steps must be independently justified. In contrast, exceptions such as the consent exception focus entirely on interception; when a communication has been intercepted permissibly under the consent

---

   3. Ports enable computers to classify different types of Internet traffic. Every computer server connected to the Internet makes its functions available to those connecting to the server by using specific numbered ports. Different port numbers translate into different services available on that server. For example, World Wide Web traffic typically is sent at port 80, and ftp (file transfer protocol) commands are sent at port 21. Most Internet packets are assigned a port number, and the port number tells the receiving computer what to do with the traffic when it arrives.

exception, the Wiretap Act places no additional restrictions on its use or disclosure.

3. How broadly should courts interpret the "rights or property" of a provider? Are rights or property limited to delivering communications and protecting the network from attack, or do they extend to the broader purposes of the network and the interests of its owner?

Suppose a university provides Internet services to its undergraduate students living in on-campus dormitories. Can the university justify wiretapping student accounts under the provider exception to protect the safety of its students? May it do so to ensure that the students are not downloading copyrighted materials without permission? Can it monitor accounts to make sure no students are taking drugs? Is the university's interest limited to providing network services, or does it extend to taking care of students?

4. Does the existence of the provider exception shed new light on whether an intermediary computer should be a "party to the communication" for the purposes of the consent exception? The provider exception permits victims of unauthorized access to monitor unauthorized behavior to protect their "rights or property," 18 U.S.C. § 2511(2)(a)(i). In other words, victims can conduct monitoring without being parties to the communication under the consent exception. Does this suggest that a narrow approach to identifying a "party to the communication" is preferable to a broader approach?

5. *Fourth Amendment redux.* The *Auler* decision provides a helpful reminder of how statutory and constitutional issues can apply simultaneously in wiretapping investigations. Most network providers are private actors, and therefore are bound by the Wiretap Act but not the Fourth Amendment. As they collect evidence of wrongdoing, however, providers may wish to contact law enforcement investigators either to ask them for help or to forward on incriminating evidence. At some point, the private providers may become state actors under the Fourth Amendment.

Monitoring under the provider exception may raise interesting Fourth Amendment issues if a provider crosses the line and becomes a state actor. For example, does a computer hacker have a reasonable expectation of privacy against the monitoring of his communications inside the victim network? In Rakas v. Illinois, 439 U.S. 128, 143 n.12 (1978), the Supreme Court stated that: "[a] burglar plying his trade in a summer cabin during the off season may have a thoroughly justified subjective expectation of privacy, but it is not one which the law recognizes as 'legitimate.' His presence, * * * is wrongful; his expectation is not one that society is prepared to recognize as 'reasonable.'" For Fourth Amendment purposes, is a hacker just an electronic burglar?

Consider the dicta relevant to this issue in United States v. Seidlitz, 589 F.2d 152 (4th Cir. 1978). Recall that Seidlitz hacked into OSI, and employees at OSI installed a surveillance tool known as the Milten Spy to recorded the intrusion. After rejecting the defendant's argument that the monitoring violated his statutory privacy rights, the Fourth Circuit added this interesting aside:

[W]e discern a certain speciousness which infects all of the illegal surveillance contentions made by the defendant with respect to the evidence which was obtained through use of the Milten Spy. Unlike the typical telephone user who employs the telephone merely as a convenience to converse with other persons over distances, Seidlitz used the telephone to tamper with and manipulate a machine which was owned by others, located on their premises, and obviously not intended for his use. * * * In this sense the use by the witnesses below of the term "intruder" to describe an unauthorized user of the computers is aptly applied to the defendant, since by telephonic signal he in fact intruded or trespassed upon the physical property of OSI as effectively as if he had broken into the Rockville facility and instructed the computers from one of the terminals directly wired to the machines. Under these circumstances, having been 'caught with his hand in the cookie jar', we seriously doubt that he is entitled to raise either statutory or constitutional objections to the evidence.

Id. at 160.

McCLELLAND v. McGRATH

United States District Court for the Northern District of Illinois, 1998.
31 F. Supp.2d 616.

ASPEN, CHIEF JUDGE.

At first glance, it might seem the very definition of chutzpah for Michael McClelland to sue the City of Chicago and several of its police officers for asking a phone company to intercept a call he made on a cloned cellular phone. The user of a cloned cellular phone—a phone which has been rigged to imitate a legitimate cellular phone—is stealing from the phone company, and phone companies routinely investigate such theft.

The complication in this case is that the officers were investigating a kidnapping, not cellular service theft. Adalberto Valdavia had been abducted, and the officers asked Ameritech, the local telephone service provider, to trace the ransom calls. Ameritech determined that the calls were being made on a cellular line dedicated to Cellular One, and Cellular One informed Ameritech, who informed the officers, that the ransom calls had indeed been made on a cellular telephone and that other calls on the same line had been made almost simultaneously in another part of the state, where the cellular subscriber was located. From this Cellular One concluded that the ransom calls were being made on a cloned phone, and Cellular One indicated that it was able to monitor any conversations involving the cloned phone and to isolate its approximate location. The officers asked Cellular One to relay any information from those calls which might assist them in finding the kidnapper, and Cellular One agreed.

Late that afternoon, someone used the cloned phone to call a lifeguard station and informed the station that he would not be able to come to work that day. Cellular One intercepted the call and relayed the information to Ameritech, who informed the officers, who dispatched other officers to the lifeguard station. (No judge ever approved this intercept.) The officers learned that the caller was Michael McClelland, whom they arrested after securing Valdavia's release. McClelland was incarcerated pending trial on aggravated kidnapping charges, but for reasons unknown to us, his prosecution was terminated.

McClelland learned of the interception during his prosecution, and he filed a complaint with this Court alleging that the officers' failure to obtain judicial authorization for the interception constituted a violation of Title III of the Omnibus Crime Control and Safe Streets Act of 1968, which is codified at 18 U.S.C. §§ 2510–2520 and is popularly known as the "Wiretap Act." The defendants moved to dismiss the complaint on the ground that the Wiretap Act contains an exemption for interceptions by an employee of a phone company who intercepts, discloses, or uses that communication in the normal course of his employment while engaged in any activity which is a necessary incident to the protection of the rights or property of the provider of that service. They argued that since Cellular One intercepted the call and since Cellular one intercepts communications on cloned phones as a necessary incident to the protection of its rights or property, the interception of the call and the subsequent use of its contents was lawful * * *.

The defendants are of course correct that Cellular One is entitled to "intercept, disclose, and use," in the words of § 2511(2)(a)(ii), communications and their contents in order to protect its rights or property. McClelland does not dispute this point—in fact he did not even sue Cellular One. And obviously he would not have had a gripe with the officers had Cellular One intercepted his cloned phone calls on its own and then turned to the officers for assistance.

What the officers do not seem to understand, however, is that *they* are not free to ask or direct Cellular One to intercept *any* phone calls or disclose their contents, at least not without complying with the judicial authorization provisions of the Wiretap Act, *regardless* of whether Cellular One would have been entitled to intercept those calls on its own initiative. This is why the courts in [other cases] go to such lengths to determine whether the phone companies in those cases were acting at the request or direction of police officers.

This case is different, for here a jury could reasonably find that Cellular One was acting as an "instrument or agent" of the government. The officers, after being informed by Cellular One that it could monitor calls made on the cloned phone, asked that Cellular One relay the contents of those calls to them. This shows both that Cellular One acted at the government's request and (ergo) that the government knew of and agreed to Cellular One's actions, two important factors in the "instrument or agent" analysis. In addition, it seems clear that Cellular One was motivated by its desire to help the officers rather than to protect its own property, another important "instrument or agent" factor, *see id.,* as the content of the communication they passed along to the officers—that the caller wouldn't be at work that day—is irrelevant to a cloned phone investigation but is very useful to a kidnapping investigation. *Cf. United States v. Auler,* 539 F.2d 642, 646 (7th Cir. 1976) (telephone companies which intercept calls pursuant to § 2511(2)(a)(i) may forward to the police no more of the content of those calls than is necessary to protect telephone company rights).

It is easy to think that McClelland, the accused kidnapper and confessed cellular service thief, has no right to sue the officers whose jobs required that they find the kidnapper with all possible speed. But anyone who cannot shake this intuition would be wise to recall the sage words of Justices Holmes and Brandeis in an early wiretap case. The former thought it a lesser evil "that some criminals should escape than the government should play an ignoble part," and the latter wrote that "In a government of laws, existence of the government will be imperiled if it fails to observe the law scrupulously," since if "the government becomes a lawbreaker, it breeds contempt for law; it invites every man to become a law unto himself; it invites anarchy." *Olmstead v. United States,* 277 U.S. 438, 469, 485 (1928) (Holmes, J., and Brandeis, J., dissenting). They dissented that day, but their view has prevailed.

NOTES AND QUESTIONS

1. Imagine the facts had been different: Upon being contacted by the police, the provider decided to listen in on the call in an effort to combat cloned phone usage rather than to help the police find the kidnapper. Would the outcome of the case be different? What if the provider had decided on its own to monitor the calls to find the kidnapper, and it was never asked to do so by the police? Should the provider's intent matter? Should it matter whether the provider or the police came up with the idea of monitoring?

2. Did McClelland have Fourth Amendment rights in his telephone call? If not, does it make sense that he should have statutory rights against monitoring? Note that Wiretap Act protections do not hinge on judgments as to whether a particular telephone call implicates greater or lesser legitimate privacy interests. Every call receives full privacy protection, regardless of context.

3. Imagine that you set up a monitoring system on your home personal computer that records every communication sent from and received by your computer. You leave your computer logged on to an Internet connection 24 hours a day. One day, a burglar breaks into your apartment when you are away; after rifling through your valuables, the burglar decides to take a break and surf the web. He opens a web browser on your computer and visits a few blogs such as "How Appealing" and "The Volokh Conspiracy." He then gathers up your valuables, puts them in a large sack, and departs. The next day, you return to your apartment and find that your valuables are missing.

Does your use of the monitoring system to record all of the burglar's communications violate the Wiretap Act? Can the burglar sue you under the

Wiretap Act for violating his privacy? If not, what exception applies? *Hint:* Look carefully at the elements of 18 U.S.C. § 2511(1)(a).

4. Consider the practical impact of the *McGrath* case on computer intrusion investigations. Such investigations generally require investigators to track back the attack from the victim through intermediary computers and back to the intruder. If a hacker starts at computer *A*, routes communications through computer *B* and then attacks computer *C*, investigators must start at *C* and trace the attack back to *B* and then back to *A*.

What legal rules regulate this process? Imagine you are an FBI agent, and a system administrator at computer *C* contacts you and tells you that network *C* has been hacked. The sysadmin informs you that he has installed a "sniffer" device that is monitoring the intruder. The sysadmin seeks your advice: he wants to know how he should monitor the intruder to make sure that he has collected the evidence needed to prosecute the intruder when he is caught. After reading *McClelland v. McGrath*, what should you tell him?

Assume that you decline to give the system administrator advice on how to monitor the hacker. Instead, you tell the sysadmin that he is free to disclose the fruits of his wiretapping to you to the extent necessary to protect his "rights or property." (Note that such a limit isn't necessary if the victim is a "party to the communication," but is necessary otherwise under the provider exception.) The sysadmin tells you that the attacks are coming from a specific IP address hosted by computer *B*. You contact the system administrator at computer *B* and ask if he knows that his network is hosting an intruder. The sysadmin at *B* expresses surprise, but volunteers to help monitor the hacker; he indicates that he wants to be a "good citizen" and help the FBI catch the bad guy. Can you accept the offer of help under *McClelland v. McGrath*?

Assume you accept the offer of help, and the sysadmin at *B* starts monitoring the hacker's communications. The hacker is detected attacking through computer *A*, and the sysadmin calls you to tell you that the attacks are originating at *A*. Does this disclosure violate the Wiretap Act?

4. THE COMPUTER TRESPASSER EXCEPTION

The computer trespasser exception, 18 U.S.C. § 2511(2)(i), is the narrowest of the three exceptions to the Wiretap Act covered in this chapter. The consent exception applies in a very wide range of cases, and the provider exception ordinarily is used by providers outside of government investigations. In contrast, the computer trespasser exception deals with a very narrow and specific problem common in 18 U.S.C. § 1030 investigations.

At a general level, the trespasser exception responds to differences between the telephone network and the Internet. The Wiretap Act was originally designed to regulate telephone network privacy, and reflects the assumption that every telephone call deserves privacy. This is a fair assumption in the case of the telephone network: even cases such as *Auler* and *McClelland* involved interceptions of private calls. But computer communications reflect a much broader array of contents than telephone communications. Whereas telephone calls consist only of person-to-person speech, Internet communications include the full diversity of what users do online. Most of those communications deserve privacy, but some presumably do not. In particular, it seems plausible that computer users committing unauthorized accesses should not have privacy rights in their unauthorized behavior. The trespasser exception amends the Wiretap Act to ensure that the statute better reflects the full diversity of computer communications.

At a more specific level, the trespasser exception was designed to deal specifically with the dynamics of 18 U.S.C. § 1030 investigations. In particular, it deals with the critical question of authority to conduct monitoring in computer intrusion cases when the primary interest in monitoring comes from the government instead of the victim provider. In a sense, the exception responds to *McClelland v. McGrath*. Whereas *McGrath* held that the officers could not "hijack" provider monitoring, the trespasser exception permits such hijacking in a specific set of circumstances.

The exception provides:

It shall not be unlawful under this chapter for a person acting under color of law to intercept the wire or electronic communications of a computer trespasser transmitted to, through, or from the protected computer, if—

(I) the owner or operator of the protected computer authorizes the interception of the computer trespasser's communications on the protected computer;

(II) the person acting under color of law is lawfully engaged in an investigation;

(III) the person acting under color of law has reasonable grounds to believe that the contents of the computer trespasser's communications will be relevant to the investigation; and

(IV) such interception does not acquire communications other than those transmitted to or from the computer trespasser.

18 U.S.C. § 2511(2)(i). The phrase "computer trespasser" is defined in § 2510(21):

"computer trespasser"—

(A) means a person who accesses a protected computer without authorization and thus has no reasonable expectation of privacy in any communication transmitted to, through, or from the protected computer; and

(B) does not include a person known by the owner or operator of the protected computer to have an existing contractual relationship with the owner or operator of the protected computer for access to all or part of the protected computer.

Putting the two pieces together reveals how the trespasser exception works. For the exception to apply, an investigator must already be conducting an investigation, § 2511(2)(i)(II), and must have reasonable grounds to believe that intercepting an intruder's communication will further that investigation, § 2511(2)(i)(III), § 2510(21). The trespasser exception permits investigators to intercept the intruder's communications with the provider's consent, § 2511(2)(i)(II), although the exception does not justify any other monitoring, § 2511(2)(i)(IV). So long as the government is already conducting an investigation, the government can intercept the hacker's communications with the victim provider's permission.

The computer trespasser exception was enacted in 2001 as Section 217 of the USA Patriot Act. After the enactment of the Patriot Act, the Justice Department released the following guidance to the exception.

UNITED STATES DEPARTMENT OF JUSTICE— FIELD GUIDANCE ON NEW AUTHORITIES THAT RELATE TO COMPUTER CRIME AND ELECTRONIC EVIDENCE ENACTED IN THE USA PATRIOT ACT OF 2001

(2001), available at www.usdoj.gov/criminal/cybercrime/PatriotAct.htm.

Although the wiretap statute allows computer owners to monitor the activity on their machines to protect their rights and property, until Section 217 of the Act was enacted it was unclear whether computer owners could obtain the assistance of law enforcement in conducting such monitoring. This lack of clarity prevented law enforcement from assisting victims to take the natural and reasonable steps in their own defense that would be entirely legal in the physical world. In the physical world, burglary victims may invite the police into their homes to help them catch burglars in the act of committing their crimes. The wiretap statute should not block investigators from responding to similar requests in the computer context simply because the means of committing the burglary happen to fall within the definition of a "wire or electronic communication" according to the wiretap statute. Indeed, because providers often lack the expertise, equipment, or financial resources required to monitor attacks themselves, they commonly have no effective way to exercise their rights to protect themselves from unauthorized attackers. This anomaly in the law created * * * a bizarre result, in which a computer hacker's undeserved statutory privacy right trumps the legitimate privacy rights of the hacker's victims.

To correct this problem, the amendments in Section 217 of the Act allow victims of computer attacks to authorize persons "acting under color of law" to monitor trespassers on their computer systems. Under new section 2511(2)(i), law enforcement may intercept the communications of a computer trespasser transmitted to, through, or from a protected computer. Before monitoring can occur, however, four requirements must be met.

First, section 2511(2)(i)(I) requires that the owner or operator of the protected computer must authorize the interception of the trespasser's communications. Second, section 2511(2)(i)(II) requires that the person who intercepts the communication be lawfully engaged in an ongoing investigation. Both criminal and intelligence investigations qualify, but the authority to intercept ceases at the conclusion of the investigation.

Third, section 2511(2)(i)(III) requires that the person acting under color of law have reasonable grounds to believe that the contents of the communication to be intercepted will be relevant to the ongoing investigation. Fourth, section 2511(2)(i)(IV) requires that investigators intercept only the communications sent or received by trespassers. Thus, this section would only apply where the configuration of the computer system allows the interception of communications to and from the trespasser, and not the interception of non-consenting users authorized to use the computer.

Finally, section 217 of the Act amends section 2510 of title 18 to create a definition of "computer trespasser." Such trespassers include any person who accesses a protected computer without authorization. In addition, the definition explicitly excludes any person "known by the owner or operator of the protected computer to have an existing contractual relationship with the owner or operator for access to all or part of the computer." 18 U.S.C. § 2510(21). For example, certain Internet service providers do not allow their customers to send bulk unsolicited e-mails (or "spam"). Customers who send spam would be in violation of the provider's terms of service, but would not qualify as trespassers—both because they are authorized users and because they have an existing contractual relationship with the provider.

NOTES AND QUESTIONS

1. *"A person acting under color of law."* The trespasser exception contemplates interceptions by persons "acting under color of law." The phrase "under color of law" has a long history, and ordinarily has been construed as equivalent to "state action" under the Fourteenth Amendment:

> Private persons, jointly engaged with state officials in the prohibited action, are acting 'under color' of law * * *. To act 'under color' of law does not require that the accused be an officer of the State. It is enough that he is a willful participant in joint activity with the State or its agents.

United States v. Price, 383 U.S. 787, 794 (1966).

Presumably, then, the trespasser exception permits monitoring either by government investigators or private individuals acting on their behalf. Note, however, that under §§ 2511(2)(i)(II)–(III) the person acting under color of law must be lawfully engaged in an investigation and must have reasonable grounds to believe that the contents of the intercepted communications must be relevant to that investigation. In a case where investigators ask a provider to monitor a hacker on the government's behalf, who is the "person acting under color of law" that must have these reasonable grounds: the investigators, or the owner/operator of the network?

2. The trespasser exception requires the owner or operator of the protected computer to authorize the interception of trespasser communications. *See* 18 U.S.C. § 2511(2)(i)(I). What does it mean to "authorize" an interception? Is authorization different from consent under the consent exception?

3. *Defining "computer trespasser."* The definition of computer trespasser in § 2510(21) recalls materials covered in Chapter 2, and specifically the meaning of "access without authorization" and "exceeds authorized access" for the purposes of 18 U.S.C. § 1030. Under § 2510(21)(A), a computer trespasser is a person who has accessed a computer "without authorization."

The text of § 2510(21)(A) adds that such a person "thus has no reasonable expectation of privacy in any communication transmitted to, through, or from the protected computer." This is a rather puzzling addition. Congress does not normally add commentary explaining when it believes a person has Fourth Amendment protection, and the addition does not appear to have any other effect.

18 U.S.C. § 2510(21)(B) was added in response to concern about an early draft of the Patriot Act. Critics feared that uncertainty over the meaning of "without authorization" in 18 U.S.C. § 1030 would let the computer trespasser exception authorize the government to monitor Internet users who violated Terms of Service or Terms of Use. Section 2510(21)(B) clarifies that mere contractual breach cannot make a person a "computer trespasser."

Can you reconcile the definition of "computer trespasser" with the meaning of "access without authorization" and "exceeds authorized access" in § 1030? Does the definition of computer trespasser include those who breach code-based restrictions, but not those who circumvent contractual restrictions? Does the trespasser exception shed light on the meaning of § 1030?

4. The trespasser exception has interesting consequences for the scope of the consent exception, and in particular who can be a "party to a communication":

> Before the Patriot Act, it was unclear whether a pass-through intermediary computer could consent to monitoring, but at least two courts of appeals had suggested that they might. Such a reading would eviscerate the privacy protection offered by the Wiretap Act. The trespasser exception is the best argument against such a reading: the exception only makes sense if mere pass-through computers are not parties to communications. Otherwise, the trespasser exception would merely cover ground already covered by the consent exception. The existence of the trespasser exception sends a strong signal to the courts: to give effect to the trespasser exception, courts should construe the consent exception narrowly.

Orin S. Kerr, *Internet Surveillance Law After the USA Patriot Act: The Big Brother That Isn't*, 97 Nw. U. L. Rev. 607, 670 (2003). Does the trespasser exception also suggest that hacker commands ordinarily will constitute "contents" of communications under 18 U.S.C. § 2510(8)?

5.   Let's return to a hypothetical we considered in the materials on the provider exception. This time, however, we can consider the role of the computer trespasser exception.

Suppose you are an FBI agent, and a system administrator at computer C contacts you and tells you that network C has been hacked. The sysadmin informs you that he has installed a "sniffer" device that is monitoring the intruder. The sysadmin seeks your advice: he wants to know how he should monitor the intruder to make sure that he has collected the evidence needed to prosecute the intruder when he is caught. What can you tell him?

Assume you tell the sysadmin to intercept all of the hacker's communications. The sysadmin does so, and the next day he intercepts communications indicating that the attacks are coming from a specific IP address hosted by computer B. You contact the system administrator at computer B and ask if he knows that his network is hosting an intruder. The sysadmin at B expresses surprise, but volunteers to help monitor the hacker; he indicates that he wants to be a "good citizen" and help the FBI catch the bad guy. Can you accept the offer of help?

Assume you accept the offer of help, and the sysadmin at B starts monitoring the hacker's communications. The hacker is detected attacking through computer A, and the sysadmin calls you to tell you that the attacks are originating at A. Does this disclosure violate the Wiretap Act?

6.   *Honey pots and the Wiretap Act.* Computer security professionals occasionally set up "honey pot" computer networks to test security efforts and understand hacker techniques. A "honey pot" is a decoy network connected to the Internet. To an intruder, the network looks like any other network. In truth, the network is a fake; it is set up with the sole purpose of being a target for anonymous attackers. When hackers try to break in, as some inevitably will, every aspect of the intrusion will be monitored, recorded, and later analyzed.

Does the use of honey pots by a computer security professional violate the Wiretap Act? Can you justify monitoring intrusions into the honey pot under the consent exception? Under the provider exception? Under the trespasser exception? Does the legal picture change if a criminal investigator wishes to set up a honey pot to identify intruders?

7.   Are the Wiretap Act's exceptions too broad? Too narrow? Just right? Given that the Act was originally drafted for the telephone, does it still work well in the context of Internet crime investigations? Or is the difference between monitoring phone calls and monitoring Internet communications too great for the same statute to regulate both contexts?

B.   THE PEN REGISTER STATUTE

The Pen Registers and Trap and Trace Devices statute, commonly known as the Pen Register statute, is codified at 18 U.S.C. §§ 3121–27. At a very general level, the Pen Register statute can be understood as a non-content cousin of the Wiretap Act. Because it deals only with non-content information, however, the Pen Register statute generally receives substantially less attention than the Wiretap Act. Its prohibitions are weaker, its exceptions are broader, and penalties for violating the statute are modest.

The statute's history explains its rather odd structure. The Pen Register statute was designed as a legislative response to *Smith v. Maryland*, 442 U.S. 735 (1979). As enacted in 1986, the statute prohibited the installation of pen registers and trap and trace devices without a court order unless a statutory exception applied. In the technological era of the 1960s and 1970s, pen registers were devices that could be installed to record the numbers dialed from a telephone line, and "trap and trace" devices could be used to record the incoming numbers dialed into a phone line. (They were called "trap and trace" devices because collecting incoming numbers originally required the telephone company to trace the phone line using a tool known as a "terminating trap." *See* In re United States, 610 F.2d 1148, 1151 (3d Cir. 1979)). When first passed in 1986, the Pen Register statute regulated the use of the tools that were used to collect "to" and "from" information for telephone calls, namely pen registers and trap and trace devices.

The structure of the Pen Register statute makes sense in light of this history. Section 3121 contains the basic prohibition on the use of a pen register or trap and trace device, subject to exceptions in § 3121(b); § 3122 tells investigators how to apply for court orders authorizing the use of such devices; § 3123 instructs judges on what the orders should look like and what they should say; and § 3124 tells network providers how to comply with the orders. Finally, § 3125 concerns emergency court orders, § 3126 is a reporting requirement, and § 3127 contains definitions of key terms.

The trick to understanding the modern Pen Register statute is the definition of "pen register" and "trap and trace device" in §§ 3127(3)–(4). Section 216 of the USA Patriot Act replaced the telephone-focused language of the 1986 Act with more general language that covers non-content addressing information for both telephone calls and Internet communications. Specifically, a pen register is defined as "a device or process which records or decodes dialing, routing, addressing, or signaling information transmitted by an instrument or facility from which a wire or electronic communication is transmitted, provided, however, that such information shall not include the contents of any communication." 18 U.S.C. § 3127(3). A trap and trace device is defined as "a device or process which captures the incoming electronic or other impulses which identify the originating number or other dialing, routing, addressing, and signaling information reasonably likely to identify the source of a wire or electronic communication, provided, however, that such information shall not include the contents of any communication." 18 U.S.C. § 3127(4).

Putting the new definitions into the old statutory text yields a statute that regulates the collection of non-content "dialing, routing, addressing, or signaling information" for both telephone calls and Internet communications. For example, if investigators or providers install a sniffer device that collects only non-content addressing information such as IP headers, the sniffer device acts as both a pen register (when it collects "from" information) and a trap and trace device (when it collects "to" information). Because Internet communications normally combine "to" and "from" information, the two sides usually work together; the surveillance device becomes a "pen/trap," and the court order permitting the surveillance is often referred to as a "pen/trap order."

In practice, issues involving the Pen Register statute often arise at the same time as issues involving the Wiretap Act. Which statute applies depends on the filter setting of the particular surveillance tool. For example, a sniffer device that collects contents is a wiretap device implicating the Wiretap statute; a sniffer device that only collects non-content addressing information is a pen/trap that implicates the Pen Register statute. A sniffer device that collects both content and non-content information acts as both a wiretap device and a pen/trap, and must be used in compliance with both statutes.

Although the Pen Register statute is a non-content cousin of the Wiretap Act, Congress chose to regulate non-content acquisition very differently than content acquisition. The following case explores some of the differences between the Wiretap Act and the Pen Register statute.

IN RE APPLICATION OF THE UNITED STATES OF AMERICA

United States District Court for the Middle District of Florida, 1994.
846 F.Supp. 1555.

Merryday, District Judge.

The magistrate judge has twice denied the United States' application for an order authorizing the installation and use of a pen register and trap and trace device. The latter of the two applications, a somewhat supplemented edition of the earlier application, states in part that:

> Applicant certifies that the Federal Bureau of Investigation, United States Customs Service, County Sheriff's Office and * * * * Police Department are conducting a criminal investigation of * * * * *, owner/operator of * * * * *, located in * * * * *, Florida; employees of * * * * * located at * * * * *, and others known and unknown, in connection with possible violations of, inter alia, Title 21, United States Code, Sections 846 and 841(a)(1), occurring within the Middle District of Florida and elsewhere; that it is believed that the subjects of the investigation are using telephone number (* * *) * * *-* * * *, listed in the name of * * * * * and located at * * * * *, in furtherance of the subject offenses; and that the information likely to be obtained from the pen register and trap and trace device, that is, a caller ID device, is relevant to the ongoing criminal investigation being conducted by the aforementioned law enforcement agencies in

that it is believed that this information will concern the aforementioned offenses.

This Court has jurisdiction to issue an order authorizing the installation and use of the requested pen register and trap and trace device in that the actual pen register equipment and trap and trace device which will be used to monitor telephone number (* * *) * * *-* * * * [and] will be installed and used at the * * * * * County Sheriff's Office located in * * * * * County, within the Middle District of Florida.

Applicant knows that there are incoming telephone calls to telephone number (* * *) * * *-* * * * and believes the identification of the calling telephone facility will be relevant to the ongoing criminal investigation and that this information will concern the aforementioned offenses.[2]

The magistrate judge premised his denial on the failure of the United States to advance a factual demonstration that the pen register is likely to disclose information relevant to an ongoing criminal investigation that has a nexus to the Middle District of Florida. The magistrate judge determined that the statute governing the installation and use of pen registers requires a demonstration of qualifying facts sufficient to establish the correctness of both the United States' assertion of this court's jurisdiction and the pen register's purpose and probable results, i.e., the discovery of information beneficial to an investigation with a nexus to the Middle District of Florida. Asserting energetically that the pen register statute envisions only perfunctory judicial involvement, the United States appeals to the district court. The magistrate judge's order is reversed because the application of the United States satisfies the requirements of the applicable statute.

II.

In 1986, Congress enacted 18 U.S.C. §§ 3121–27, which governs pen registers. Section 3121(a) provides, with a few irrelevant exceptions, that "no person may install or use a pen register or a trap and trace device without first obtaining a court order under section 3123 of this title or under the Foreign Intelligence Surveillance Act of 1978 (50 U.S.C. 1801, *et seq.*)." Pursuant to Section 3121(c), the penalty for violation of the statute is imprisonment for not more than one year, a fine, or both.

Section 3122(a) authorizes an attorney for the United States to apply for an order, "in writing, under oath or equivalent affirmation, to a court of competent jurisdiction." First, Section 3122(b)(1) requires the application to include both the identity of the applying attorney and the identity of the law enforcement agency conducting the investigation. Second, Section 3122(b)(2) requires the application to include a certification by the

---

2. Because the original of this order is filed *in camera* and relates to an ongoing criminal investigation, any revealing and identifying words are replaced by asterisks.

attorney "that the information likely to be obtained is relevant to an ongoing criminal investigation being conducted by that agency."

Section 3123(a) states that, after a complying application:

> [T]he court shall enter an ex parte order authorizing the installation and use of a pen register or a trap and trace device within the jurisdiction of the court if the court finds that the attorney for the Government ... has certified to the court that the information likely to be obtained by such installation and use is relevant to an ongoing criminal investigation.

Section 3124 requires that providers of telephone services and other persons, if the court so orders, must assist with the installation of the pen register. Section 3124(e) provides to any cooperating person a complete defense against either civil or criminal liability, if the person relies in good faith on a court order authorizing the pen register.

A review of these provisions demonstrates that Congress, absent Fourth Amendment concerns, intended to require an identified and presumably responsible official to attest the facts supporting the pen register application. The salient purpose of requiring the application to the court for an order is to affix personal responsibility for the veracity of the application (i.e., to ensure that the attesting United States Attorney is readily identifiable and legally qualified) and to confirm that the United States Attorney has sworn that the required investigation is in progress. Section 3122(b) requires only identification and certification by the official applying for the order. Section 3123(a) requires only confirmation by the court that identification and certification have occurred. No provision appears for independent judicial inquiry into the veracity of the attested facts. As a form of deterrence and as a guarantee of compliance, the statute provides instead for a term of imprisonment and a fine as punishment for a violation.

Requiring identification and certification, but nothing further, admittedly extends only minimal protection to whatever privacy expectations attend the dialing of a telephone number. On the other hand, prompt availability of pen registers usefully expedites law enforcement with no countervailing loss, the Supreme Court instructs, of the Fourth Amendment's protections against search and seizure. In other words, the statute's structure balances the need for accountability, the legitimate interest of law enforcement in advancing a criminal investigation, and the residual privacy interest of the public.

III.

A comparison of the statute governing wiretaps, 18 U.S.C. §§ 2510–21, with the statute governing pen registers demonstrates that Congress intended only minimal safeguards against the unwarranted use of a pen register. The procedure for obtaining authorization for a pen register is summary in nature and the requisite disclosure is perfunctory. In contrast, the wiretap statute provides formidable procedural protections and requires extensive and detailed information in the application. Perhaps most pertinent to this order is the presence of the following provision in Section 2518(2) of the wiretap statute:

> The judge may require the applicant to furnish additional testimony or documentary evidence in support of the application.

No similar provision for additional judicial inquiry appears in the pen register statute, indicating that Congress intended no focused judicial scrutiny of an application for a pen register (at least at the time of the application). The legislative history of the pen register statute contains a similar signal:

> To issue an order [authorizing a pen register], the court must first be satisfied that the information sought is relevant to an ongoing criminal investigation. This provision does not envision an independent judicial review of whether the application meets the relevance standard, rather the court needs only to review the completeness of the certification submitted.

S. Rep. No. 541, 99th Cong., 2d Sess. 47, *reprinted in* 1986 U.S.C.C.A.N. 3555, 3601.

Under Section 2518(1)(b) of the wiretap statute, an application must contain "a full and complete statement of the facts and circumstances relied upon by the applicant to justify his belief that an order should be issued," including details of the offense, the sites of the interception devices, the type of communication subject to interception, and the identity of the person whose communications are subject to interception. Section 2518(1)(c) requires that a wiretap application include "a full and complete statement as to whether or not other investigative procedures have been tried and failed or why they reasonably appear to be unlikely to succeed if tried or to be too dangerous." Section 2518(d) requires a prediction of the duration of the wiretap and Section 2518(e) requires a statement of the circumstances of any previous wiretap applications involving the same person or place. Section 2518(f) provides that, if the application extends a previous authorization, the application must contain "a statement setting forth the results thus far obtained from the interception, or a reasonable explanation of the failure to obtain such results."

By comparison, an application for a pen register includes only the identification and certification required by Section 3122(b). No requirement exists for a pen register applicant to unsuccessfully attempt other investigative techniques or to explain the failure to attempt other investigative techniques. Section 3123(c)(2) permits a pen register applicant to obtain an extension of an authorizing order by providing the same identification and certification required by the initial application. The statute excludes any requirement that an applicant for an extension set forth either the results previously obtained or an explanation for the failure to obtain results.

Other comparisons are similarly instructive. To authorize a wiretap, the court must find (1) probable cause to believe that an individual has committed, is committing, or imminently will commit an offense listed in the statute, (2) probable cause to believe that the intercepted communications will relate to the alleged offense, (3) probable cause to believe (with limited exceptions) that the communications facilities subject to the wiretap are being used in connection with the offense, and (4) that other investigative procedures have failed, are likely to fail, or will be too dangerous. To authorize a pen register, the court need not find any of these facts. The pen register statute contains no requirement for a finding of "probable cause," "reasonable suspicion," or the like.

Section 2518(6) of the wiretap statute permits the court to require periodic reports by the intercepting authorities of the progress of the wiretap. Sections 2518(8)(a) and (d) of the wiretap statute require that the intercepted communications be recorded and maintained both under seal and unedited and that an inventory of the intercepted communications be provided to the subjects after termination of the wiretap. Section 2518(9) of the wiretap statute bars the use of intercepted communications at trial without advance notice. Neither these provisions nor approximations of them appear in the pen register statute.

Section 2518(10)(a) of the wiretap statute provides for suppression of evidence obtained by wiretap [of wire communications] if the evidence was obtained in violation of the statute. The pen register statute contains no exclusionary remedy, and *United States v. Thompson*, 936 F.2d 1249 (11th Cir. 1991), declines to create a common law rule of exclusion.

As punishment for an unlawfully obtained wiretap, Section 2511(4)(a) of the wiretap statute provides a maximum penalty of imprisonment for five years and a fine. As noted already, Section 3121(c) provides that the maximum penalty for violation of the pen register statute is imprisonment for one year and a fine. Section 2520 of the wiretap statute also authorizes recovery of civil damages, including statutory damages of up to $10,000, punitive damages, equitable relief, and recovery of costs and attorney fees. The pen register statute contains no provision for recovery of civil damages.

The breadth and intricacy of the wiretap statute illustrate that Congress, when electing to do so, conceived and implemented formidable safeguards, including extensive judicial review, for the protection of electronic communications. Congress elected to provide only minimal regulation of the use of pen registers. Absent recognized constitutional considerations, the court should create and implement by decisional law no more extensive restrictions on the use of pen registers than Congress has provided explicitly in the governing statute after consideration in gross of all the pertinent factors, not the least of which is privacy.

IV.

No judicial imprimatur on pen registers is required, permitted, or implied under the pen register statute. The court is not asked to "approve" the application for a pen register in the sense that the court would vouch initially for the propriety of the use of a wiretap. Congress asks the court only to confirm that the approved safety measures are observed— that is, primarily, that the responsible persons are identified and accountable if any malfeasance or misprision comes to light and that the nature of that misconduct is readily provable. Undoubtedly, Congress knew that providing to a court false information about the nature of an investigation is an offense which, especially if committed by a United States Attorney, is due for a most unforgiving penalty.

Far from compromising the judiciary, the statutory procedure removes the court from unnecessary entanglement in decisions properly residing in the first instance in law enforcement and prosecuting authorities, yet subject to judicial inquiry at the end of the day. The judiciary is not the daily supervisor of the prosecutor. The judiciary should maintain a sanitary distance from law enforcement. The more the court is insinuated unduly into an *ex parte* inquiry conducted *in camera*, the more the independence of the judiciary is compromised. Serious Fourth Amendment concerns commend, in fact compel, a routinely undesirable, *ex parte* inquiry before the authorization of an arrest, a search, or a wiretap. But this is not so for the authorization of a mere pen register, which presents no privacy issue that rises to Fourth Amendment severity. On behalf of judicial independence, the court is better kept safely apart from the investigatory function unless some constitutional matter (or statutory, if Congress so declares) warrants intrusion. Only in this way is independence and integrity maintained.

The matter of judicial integrity and independence serves, on balance, to separate my conclusion from the magistrate judge's conclusion. He concludes that authorizing a pen register based on no more than the certification of a United States Attorney and without judicial scrutiny breeds suspicion and implies a compromise of independence. I conclude that undue entanglement with the prosecutor, if not required by constitutional matters, breeds suspicion and implies compromise. *Ex parte* and *in camera* hearings, I conclude, amplify those unsavory appearances, if they exist at all.

I conclude that the independence and integrity of the judiciary is best served by preserving, free of any undue entanglement and until a later stage, the oversight function of the court. This is the general rule. Exceptions appear for an arrest, a search, a wiretap, and for certain aspects of the grand jury's proceedings. However, at each stage for which an exception appears, the constitution appears also. Similarly, if no constitutional or statutory command appears, the courts must conform to the sharply constrained role assigned in pen register cases. To attempt after *Smith v. Maryland*, 442 U.S. 735 (1979), to raise a privacy consideration to sufficient dignity to overcome a direct Congressional limitation is to risk a form of judicial behavior likely to taint integrity more tellingly than the taint, if any, attendant to a mere application for a pen register.

V.

In the present case, the magistrate judge rejected the pen register application because the United States, in his view, failed to show that the pen register is "within the jurisdiction of the court" as required by Section 3123(a). The magistrate judge raised this concern because the pen register, which will be located in this district, will monitor a telephone located in the Southern District of Florida. The magistrate judge required "a factual demonstration that the pen register is likely to disclose information relevant to an ongoing criminal investigation that has a nexus to the Middle District of Florida." He determined that the United States failed to show the qualifying facts.

The court finds that the United States has met the requirements of the statute. The application contains the identification and certification required by Section 3122(b). In the certification, an assistant United States Attorney reports that local law enforcement agencies within this district and federal law enforcement agencies, acting in concert, are conducting within this district and within the Southern District an investigation of possible criminal offenses occurring within this district and elsewhere. Part of this investigation is prospectively a pen register installed in a county within the Middle District of Florida. This certification amply demonstrates that the pen register is "within the jurisdiction of the court." No further factual showing is necessary.

The order of the magistrate judge denying the application for a pen register is reversed. The application of the United States is granted.

NOTES AND QUESTIONS

1. Should the threshold for obtaining a pen register order be raised? If so, what should the new standard be? Should the law require reasonable suspicion? Should it require judicial review of the facts instead of certification by the applicant?

2. As amended by the Patriot Act, the Pen Register statute regulates the acquisition of "dialing, routing, addressing, or signaling information" relating to wire and electronic communications. But what exactly is "dialing, routing, addressing, or signaling information," a.k.a. DRAS? DRAS clearly includes IP addresses, as well as non-content information relating to e-mails. *See* In re Application of the United States, 396 F. Supp.2d 45, 48 (D. Mass. 2005) (IP addresses); In re Application of the United States, 416 F. Supp.2d 13 (D.D.C. 2006) (non-content information relating to e-mails).

But is all non-content information DRAS by default? Or does a category of information exist beyond contents and DRAS that is not covered either by the Wiretap Act or the Pen Register statute? If there is such a category, what treatment should it receive under the statutory privacy laws?

3. *Post-cut-through dialed digits.* In the case of In re Applications of the United States, 515 F. Supp.2d 325 (E.D.N.Y. 2007), federal investigators sought court orders allowing the collection of all dialed digits entered from a telephone line used by a particular suspect. The orders sought in the applica-

tions would have allowed the government both to record the numbers dialed to place the call as well as to record any numbers entered after the call was placed. Such numbers are known as "post-cut-through dialed digits," as they refer to digits entered after the "cut through," that is, the placing of the call. Examples include PIN numbers, account numbers, numbers entered in to navigate the maze of computerized help desks, and the like.

The applications were filed before Magistrate Judge Joan Azrack, who granted the application as to the numbers dialed to place the call but denied the application as to the post-cut-through dialed digits. According to Judge Azrack, digits entered after a call were very likely contents protected by the Fourth Amendment. As a result, the doctrine of constitutional avoidance counseled against interpreting the Pen Register statute as allowing the collection of such information:

> The doctrine of constitutional avoidance is a tool for choosing between competing plausible interpretations of a statutory text, resting on the reasonable presumption that Congress did not intend [an] alternative [that could] raise serious constitutional doubts. This canon is a means of giving effect to congressional intent, not of subverting it. In the instant case, the doctrine is particularly compelling. The Supreme Court has long held that the Fourth Amendment bars the Government from obtaining the contents of communication without a showing of probable cause. Because the Government's reading of the Pen/Trap Statute would violate this long-standing principle, the instant application must be denied.

Id. at 335.

4. When a cellular telephone is turned on, the phone sends out regular communications to nearby cell towers letting the towers know that the phone is nearby. Such communications are an essential part of the cellular phone network; phones must be located before the network can route calls to them. If the phone company records the information, it will generate a log of the rough physical location of the phone when it is turned on. Criminal investigators sometimes seek access to such records in real time; because most people keep their cell phones with them, the telephone location information (called "cell site" data) can be used as a type of tracking device.

Can the government obtain a Pen Register order requiring the phone company to record cell-site information and give the log to the government? Does "dialing, routing, addressing, and signaling information" include cell-site data? Magistrate Judge Stephen Smith has concluded that the answer is "no":

> First, the Patriot Act's expansion of pen/trap definitions was intended only to reach electronic communications such as e-mail. The added term "dialing, routing, addressing, and signaling information," while not defined in the statute, was touted by the bill's proponents as a way to update the pen/trap statute to cover Internet traffic. *See* 147 Cong. Rec. S11006–07 (Oct. 25, 2001) (statement of Sen. Leahy); 147 Cong. Rec. H7197 (Oct. 23, 2001) (statement of Rep. Conyers). Nothing in the admittedly abbreviated legislative history of the Patriot Act suggests that this new definition would extend the reach of the Pen/Trap Statute to cell phone tracking. Contemporary summaries of the Patriot Act prepared by

knowledgeable commentators, including the DOJ itself, make no mention of expanding pen/traps to capture cell site data. Surely, even amidst the other important features of that broad-ranging statute, such an important change in electronic surveillance law would have been noticed by *someone*.

Nor is it certain that the new definition actually encompasses the cell site data now sought by the government. The traditional pen register was triggered only when the user dialed a telephone number; no information was recorded by the device unless the user attempted to make a call. The Patriot Act clarified that a pen register could also record "routing, addressing, and signaling information," as well as numbers dialed. But the expanded definition also indicates that this "routing, addressing, and signaling" information is generated by, and incidental to, the transmission of "a wire or electronic communication." 18 U.S.C. § 3127(3). In other words, today's pen register must still be tied to an actual or attempted phone call. As we have already seen, much cell site data is transmitted even when the user is not making or receiving a call, *i.e.*, when no wire or electronic communication is transmitted. In short, neither the text nor the legislative history of the Patriot Act offer much support for the government's contention that the cell site data it seeks is covered by the new pen/trap definitions.

In re Application for Pen Register and Trap/Trace Device with Cell Site Location Authority, 396 F. Supp.2d 747, 761–62 (S.D. Tex. 2005). Are these arguments persuasive? In response to the latter argument, isn't the telephone's signal identifying itself to the cell tower an electronic communication?

If cell-site information is not DRAS, and it clearly is not content, then what is it?

5. Does the difference between contents and DRAS justify the very different protections of the Wiretap Act and the Pen Register statute? Daniel Solove contends that content and non-content addressing information raise equally strong privacy concerns and should be protected under the same statutory scheme:

> [T]he distinction between content and envelope information does not correlate well to the distinction between sensitive and innocuous information. Envelope information can be quite sensitive; content information can be quite innocuous. Admittedly, in many cases, people do not care very much about maintaining privacy over the identities of their friends and associates. But it is also true that in many cases, the contents of communications are not very revealing. Many e-mails are short messages which do not reveal any deep secrets, and even Kerr would agree that this should not lessen their protection under the law. This is because content information has the potential to be quite sensitive—but this is also the case with envelope information.

Daniel J. Solove, *Reconstructing Electronic Surveillance Law*, 72 Geo. Wash. L. Rev. 1264, 1288 (2004).

Do you agree? Should Congress come up with a new way to distinguish high-privacy communications from low-privacy communications? If so, what distinction would you propose? Should there be two categories, three categories, or more? *See generally* Susan Freiwald, *Online Surveillance: Remembering the Lessons of the Wiretap Act*, 56 Ala. L. Rev. 9, 69–74 (2004).

6. The Pen Register statute regulates prospective surveillance but not retrospective surveillance. The textual hook for this conclusion is the exclusion found in the definition of "pen register" in 18 U.S.C. § 3127(3). According to the definition, the term "pen register" does not include:

> any device or process used by a provider or customer of a wire or electronic communication service for billing, or recording as an incident to billing, for communications services provided by such provider or any device or process used by a provider or customer of a wire communication service for cost accounting or other like purposes in the ordinary course of its business.

Although this language is not a model of clarity, it has the effect of excluding retrospective surveillance from the scope of the Pen Register statute. If the government seeks records that were already made in the past and are stored by the provider, those records must have been made "in the ordinary course" of the provider's business for "cost accounting or other like purposes."

7. *Exceptions to the Pen Register statute.* The exceptions to the Pen Register statute appear in 18 U.S.C. § 3121(b):

> The prohibition of subsection (a) does not apply with respect to the use of a pen register or a trap and trace device by a provider of electronic or wire communication service—
>
> (1) relating to the operation, maintenance, and testing of a wire or electronic communication service or to the protection of the rights or property of such provider, or to the protection of users of that service from abuse of service or unlawful use of service; or
>
> (2) to record the fact that a wire or electronic communication was initiated or completed in order to protect such provider, another provider furnishing service toward the completion of the wire communication, or a user of that service, from fraudulent, unlawful or abusive use of service; or
>
> (3) where the consent of the user of that service has been obtained.

These exceptions are best understood in reference to the analogous exceptions of the Wiretap Act. Starting at the bottom, the consent exception in § 3121(b)(3) appears to mirror the Wiretap Act's consent exception in 18 U.S.C. § 2511(2)(c)–(d). Presumably the same standards apply. The consent exception in the Pen Register statute has a particularly important commonsense application: It makes sure that caller ID services are not illegal. *See, e.g.,* Wisconsin Professional Police Ass'n v. Public Service Commission, 555 N.W.2d 179 (Wisc. App. 1996).

The exceptions in § 3121(b)(1)–(2) appear to create an expanded version of the Wiretap Act's provider exception, 18 U.S.C. § 2511(2)(a)(i). The Pen Register statute's version starts with the common "rights or property" language, and then adds protection of users from abuse of service or unlawful service as well as protection of providers from fraudulent, unlawful, or abusive service. No cases explain how far these exceptions extend beyond the provider exception of the Wiretap Act, but it seems likely that courts would give such language the expansive reading the text suggests.

Although the statute is not explicit on this point, monitoring justified under the trespasser exception of the Wiretap Act for content data apparently would fall within 18 U.S.C. §§ 3121(b)(1)–(2) for non-content information. The trespasser exception requires that the trespasser must have engaged in access without authorization, and such access will always be unlawful and an abuse of the computer service under 18 U.S.C. §§ 3121(b)(1)–(2).

8.   United States v. Freeman, 524 F.2d 337 (7th Cir. 1975), also suggests that exceptions to the Pen Register statute should be construed broadly. In *Freeman*, the telephone company was investigating blue box fraud and installed a Hekimian Dialed Number Recorder (DNR) on the suspect telephone line. The DNR was a type of pen register; it registered outgoing calls made on a paper tape, and transcribed the time of a call, the date, and the number called. When the DNR would signal that a fraudulent phone call had been placed, the phone company would connect a wiretapping device that would record the first two minutes of the phone call. The government then used the device to convict the defendant Freeman of wire fraud.

On appeal, Freeman challenged the wiretapping of his phone calls, but the Seventh Circuit held that the wiretapping was in compliance with the provider exception, 18 U.S.C. § 2511(2)(a)(i). Freeman next challenged the use of the DNR under 47 U.S.C. § 605, a predecessor statute to the Wiretap Act that also covered some non-content information. The Seventh Circuit rejected the argument on policy grounds:

> An affirmative answer to this question would lead to an anomalous, if not absurd, result. To arrive at such an answer we would have to conclude that the paper taping operation, a lesser intrusion of privacy, compels suppression while the conversation recording, a greater intrusion, does not.

Freeman, 524 F.2d at 341. If the same reasoning applies to the Pen Register statute, its exceptions presumably are at least as broad as analogous exceptions to the Wiretap Act.

9.   *Problem.* Sam is the system administrator of a computer network at a small college. One day, a student named Kelly contacts him and reports that she suspects that someone has been breaking into her school web-based e-mail account. Kelly believes that her ex-boyfriend Charles may be the perpetrator, and that Charles guessed her password and is reading her mail. Sam agrees to help. The next day, he writes a software program that logs whenever anyone accesses Kelly's e-mail account: the software automatically records the time and IP address of the login. He then writes a program to record every IP address assigned to Charles' account. Over the course of the next 48 hours, Sam's program records 9 different logins to Kelly's account. In three of the cases, the IP address of the login matches the IP address used by Charles's account, indicating that Charles has in fact logged into Kelly's account.

Has Sam violated the Pen Register statute? Would he violate the Pen Register statute if he next began monitoring all non-content information sent to or from Charles's account? If he switched to full-content monitoring, would that surveillance violate the Wiretap Act?

10. Does the Pen Register statute permit wide-scale monitoring, or must the monitoring be limited to a single user or account? Imagine the FBI receives an anonymous tip that an ISP subscriber with the last name "Smith" is a narcotics dealer who frequently e-mails his sources in Mexico to arrange for more deliveries. Can the FBI obtain a pen register order requiring the ISP to monitor all of the e-mails sent from all of the accounts owned by customers named Smith, and to collect the e-mail addresses and mail headers (minus the subject lines) for all of those e-mails? Can the FBI obtain a pen register order compelling the ISP to collect the e-mail headers (minus subject lines) for every e-mail sent by a customer named Smith to one of the major ISPs in Mexico? *See* 18 U.S.C. §§ 3122–23.

11. *Intended and inadvertent collection.* When evaluating the legality of any prospective network surveillance, the first question should be whether the surveillance targets the collection of "contents" or "dialing, routing, addressing, or signaling information." If the surveillance targets contents, the Wiretap Act applies and the monitoring requires a Title III order or an applicable exception from 18 U.S.C. § 2511(2). If not, the Pen Register statute applies and the monitoring requires a Pen/Trap order or an exception from 18 U.S.C. § 3121(b).

What happens if surveillance targets DRAS, but due to technological limitations inadvertently collects contents? The inadvertent collection will not violate the Wiretap Act, as the Wiretap Act prohibits only intentional interception of contents. *See* 18 U.S.C. § 2511(1)(a). *See also* 18 U.S.C. § 3121(c) (requiring that pen register orders be implemented using technologies "reasonably available" to the government that "restrict[ ] the recording or decoding of electronic or other impulses to the dialing, routing, addressing, and signaling information utilized in the processing and transmitting of wire or electronic communications so as not to include the contents of any wire or electronic communications").

C. THE STORED COMMUNICATIONS ACT

The third and final statutory privacy law is the Stored Communications Act ("SCA"), codified at 18 U.S.C. §§ 2701–11. The SCA regulates the retrospective surveillance of telephone and Internet communications. More specifically, the SCA governs interactions between government investigators and system administrators in the case of stored content and non-content records.

The SCA shares common themes with the Wiretap Act and Pen Register statute, but it is also very different in two important ways. First, the SCA deals with retrospective surveillance instead of prospective surveillance. In other words, the SCA applies when investigators seek information already in a provider's possession rather than communications in transit. Second, the SCA is considerably more limited in its scope. Whereas the Wiretap Act and the Pen Register statute apply broadly to accessing communications in transit, the SCA only regulates records relating to legitimate customers and subscribers of two specific types of providers.

The heart of the SCA is found in § 2702 and § 2703. The former regulates voluntary disclosure and the latter regulates compelled disclosure. The other important sections for our purposes are the delayed notice provisions found in § 2705, the remedies limitation of § 2708, and the definitions of § 2711.[4]

1. THE BASIC STRUCTURE[5]

The SCA offers network account holders a range of statutory privacy rights against access to stored account information held by network service providers. The statute creates a set of Fourth Amendment-like privacy protections by statute, regulating the relationship between government investigators and service providers in possession of users' private information. It does this in two ways. First, the statute creates limits on the government's ability to compel providers to disclose information in their possession about their customers and subscribers. Although the Fourth Amendment may require no more than a subpoena to obtain e-mails, the statute confers greater privacy protection. Second, the statute places limits on the ability of ISPs to voluntarily disclose information about their customers and subscribers to the government. Although the private search doctrine of the Fourth Amendment allows private providers to make such disclosures, the SCA imposes limitations on the circumstances in which such a disclosure can occur.

Entities Regulated by the Stored Communications Act

The focal point of the SCA is the set of network service providers regulated by the statute. The statute creates rights held by "customers" and "subscribers" of network service providers in both content and non-content information held by two particular types of providers. To know whether and how the SCA protects the privacy of a particular communication, you must start by classifying the provider to see whether it falls within the scope of the providers regulated by the statute—and if it does, which category of provider applies. If the provider fits within the two categories, the SCA protects the communication; otherwise, only Fourth Amendment protections apply.

The SCA provides privacy protection to communications held by two types of providers. As the 1986 Senate Report on the SCA explains, computer network account holders at that time generally used third-party network service providers in two ways. First, account holders used their

---

4. Other sections of the Act are less important for our purposes. Section 2701 is a rarely used criminal provision, covered briefly in Chapter 2. Section 2704 is almost never used; § 2706 involves reimbursement of costs for provider monitoring; § 2707 permits a civil remedy for violations; § 2709 involves intelligence national security letters; and § 2710 regulates video rental privacy.

5. This discussion is adapted from Orin S. Kerr, *A User's Guide to the Stored Communications Act, and A Legislator's Guide to Amending It,* 72 Geo. Wash. L. Rev. 1208, 1212–23 (2004).

accounts to send and receive communications such as e-mail. The use of computer networks to communicate prompted privacy concerns because in the course of sending and retrieving messages, it was common for computers to copy the messages and store them temporarily pending delivery. The copies that these providers of "electronic communication service" created and placed in temporary "electronic storage" in the course of transmission sometimes stayed on a provider's computer for several months.

The second reason account holders used network service providers was to outsource computing tasks. For example, users paid to have remote computers store extra files or process large amounts of data. (This was in the era before spreadsheet programs, so users generally needed to outsource tasks to perform what by today's standards are simple number-crunching jobs.) When users hired such commercial "remote computing services" to perform tasks for them, they would send a copy of their private information to a third-party computing service, which retained the data for storage or processing. Remote computing services raised privacy concerns because the service providers often retained these copies of their customers' files for long periods of time.

The SCA adopts these two distinctions, freezing into the law the understandings of computer network use as of 1986. The text regulates two types of providers: providers of electronic communication service ("ECS") and providers of remote computing service ("RCS"). The statute defines ECS as "any service which provides to users thereof the ability to send or receive wire or electronic communications," and it defines "electronic storage" as "any temporary, intermediate storage of a wire or electronic communication incidental to the electronic transmission thereof," 18 U.S.C. § 2510(17)(A), plus any backup copies of files in such temporary storage. RCS is defined as "the provision to the public of computer storage or processing services by means of an electronic communications system." 18 U.S.C. § 2711(2). An "electronic communications system" is in turn defined as "any wire, radio, electromagnetic, photooptical or photoelectronic facilities for the transmission of electronic communications, and any computer facilities or related electronic equipment for the electronic storage of such communications." 18 U.S.C. § 2510(14).

The narrow scope of the SCA has two important implications. First, there are many problems of Internet privacy that the SCA does not address. The SCA is not a catch-all statute designed to protect the privacy of stored Internet communications; instead it is narrowly tailored to provide a set of Fourth Amendment-like protections for computer networks.

The second implication of the two distinctions adopted by the SCA is that we need to distinguish between providers of ECS, providers of RCS, and providers that provide neither ECS nor RCS. These distinctions are important because, as we will see shortly, the scope of privacy protections hinges on such distinctions. The distinction between providers of ECS and

RCS is made somewhat confusing by the fact that most network service providers are multifunctional. They can act as providers of ECS in some contexts, providers of RCS in other contexts, and as neither in some contexts as well. In light of this, it is essential to recognize the functional nature of the definitions of ECS and RCS. The classifications of ECS and RCS are context sensitive: the key is the provider's role with respect to a particular copy of a particular communication, rather than the provider's status in the abstract. A provider can act as an RCS with respect to some communications, an ECS with respect to other communications, and neither an RCS nor an ECS with respect to other communications.

What does this mean in practice? Some cases are easy. For example, when an e-mail sits unopened on an ISP's server, the ISP is acting as a provider of ECS with respect to that e-mail. On the other hand, if I author a document and send it via ftp to a commercial long-term storage site for safekeeping, the storage site is acting as a provider of RCS with respect to that file. There are closer cases, however, and some of these closer cases are important ones. In particular, the proper treatment of opened e-mail is currently unclear. The traditional understanding has been that a copy of opened e-mail sitting on a server is protected by the RCS rules, not the ECS rules. The thinking is that when an e-mail customer leaves a copy of an already-accessed e-mail stored on a server, that copy is no longer "incident to transmission" nor a backup copy of a file that is incident to transmission: rather, it is just in remote storage like any other file held by an RCS.

An example can help explain how the rules fit together under this traditional understanding. Imagine that I send an e-mail to my friend Jane who has an account at a commercial ISP. When the message first arrives at the ISP, the ISP acts a provider of ECS with respect to the e-mail. The e-mail is in "electronic storage" awaiting Jane's retrieval of the message. Once Jane retrieves my e-mail, she can either delete the message from the ISP's server or leave the message stored on the ISP's server for safekeeping. If Jane chooses to store the e-mail with the ISP, the ISP now acts as a provider of RCS (and not ECS) with respect to that copy of the e-mail so long as the ISP is available to the public. The role of the ISP has changed from a transmitter of the e-mail to a storage facility available to the public, from an ECS to an RCS. If the ISP is not available to the public, then the ISP provides neither ECS nor RCS, and the remotely stored e-mail now is protected only under the Fourth Amendment. If Jane downloads a copy of the e-mail onto her personal computer, the ISP acts as neither a provider of ECS nor RCS with respect to the downloaded copy regardless of whether the ISP is available to the public. The ISP is not holding the downloaded copy either incident to transmission or for storage; in fact, the ISP does not hold that copy at all. As a result, only Fourth Amendment privacy protections apply.

Although this is the traditional understanding of how the ECS/RCS distinction applies to e-mail, a recent decision by the Ninth Circuit has taken a very different approach. In Theofel v. Farey–Jones, 359 F.3d 1066

(9th Cir. 2004), the Ninth Circuit concluded that all e-mails held by a server are protected under the ECS rules until "the underlying message has expired in the normal course," regardless of whether the e-mail has been accessed. This appears to be a fact-sensitive test: under *Theofel*, a server acts as a provider of ECS with respect to a message until both the user and the ISP no longer need the e-mail message.

The Privacy Protections of the Stored Communications Act

The privacy protections contained in 18 U.S.C. §§ 2702 and 2703 provide the heart of the SCA. Section 2703 provides the rules that the government must follow when it seeks to compel a provider to disclose information. Section 2702 provides the rules that govern whether a provider can disclose information to the government voluntarily.

A. Compelled Disclosure Rules in 18 U.S.C. § 2703

Section 2703 mandates different standards the government must satisfy to compel different types of communications. To compel a provider of ECS to disclose contents of communications in its possession that are in temporary "electronic storage" for 180 days or less, the government must obtain a search warrant. To compel a provider of ECS to disclose contents in electronic storage for greater than 180 days or to compel a provider of RCS to disclose contents, the government has three options. First, the government can obtain a search warrant. Alternatively, investigators can use less process than a warrant, as long as they combine that process with prior notice. Specifically, the government can use either a subpoena or a "specific and articulable facts" court order pursuant to 18 U.S.C. § 2703(d), combined with prior notice to the "subscriber or customer" (which can be delayed in some circumstances). The court order found in § 2703(d), often referred to as a "2703(d)" order or simply a "d" order, is something like a mix between a subpoena and a search warrant. To obtain the order, the government must provide "specific and articulable facts showing that there are reasonable grounds to believe" that the information to be compelled is "relevant and material to an ongoing criminal investigation." If the judge finds that the factual showing has been made, the judge signs the order. The order is then served like an ordinary subpoena; investigators bring or fax the order to the ISP, and the ISP complies by turning over the information to the investigators.

The rules governing compelled disclosure also cover non-content records, such as logs maintained by a network server. The rules are the same for providers of ECS and RCS and give the government several ways to compel non-content records. First, the government can obtain a 2703(d) order to compel such records. Alternatively, the government can obtain a search warrant instead. Investigators can also compel the disclosure of non-content records if they obtain the consent of the customer or subscriber to such disclosure, and in the rare case that involves telemarketing fraud, they can obtain non-content records merely by submitting a formal written request to the provider. Finally, the SCA has special rules for compelling a subset of non-content records that Congress has deemed less private than other records. These records are sometimes known as "basic subscriber information" because they mostly involve information about the subscriber's identity. The government can obtain the basic subscriber information with a mere subpoena according to 18 U.S.C. § 2703(c)(2).

One interesting aspect of § 2703 is that it generally allows the government to obtain greater process when lesser process will do. If a provision of § 2703 allows government agents to compel information with a subpoena, it also allows them to obtain that information with a 2703(d) order; if it allows agents to obtain information with a 2703(d) order, then a search warrant is also acceptable. Why might the government want this option? The main reason is efficiency. Investigators may decide that they need to compel several types of information, some of which can be obtained with lesser process and some of which requires greater process. The "greater includes the lesser" rule in § 2703 allows the government to obtain only one court order—whatever process is greatest—and compel all of the information in one order all at once.

B. Voluntary Disclosure Rules in 18 U.S.C. § 2702

The rules regulating voluntary disclosure by providers of RCS and ECS appear in 18 U.S.C. § 2702. Importantly, § 2702 imposes restrictions only on providers of ECS and RCS that provide services "to the public." Nonpublic providers can voluntarily disclose information freely without violating the SCA. Among providers to the public, providers are also free to disclose non-content information to nongovernment entities. For example, a company can disclose records about how its customers used its services to a marketing company. In contrast, § 2702(a) generally bans disclosure of contents by public providers, as well as the disclosure of non-content records to any government entities. The statute then provides specific exceptions in which voluntary disclosure is allowed.

For mostly historical reasons that are of little importance today, § 2702 has slightly different exceptions depending on whether the information to be voluntarily disclosed consists of content or non-content information.

Of the eight exceptions in § 2702(b), numbers one through four are common sense exceptions: a provider can divulge contents if it needs to do so in order to deliver the communication (§ 2702(b)(1), (4)), if otherwise authorized by law (§ 2702(b)(2)), or if the person whose rights are at stake consents (§ 2702(b)(3)). The remaining exceptions deal with specific circumstances in which an individual's privacy rights give way to other competing interests. A provider can disclose contents when disclosure is necessary given a dangerous emergency (§ 2702(b)(8)); when the provider inadvertently discovers the evidence and it relates to a crime

(§ 2702(b)(7)); when such disclosure is needed to protect the provider, such as from unauthorized use of the network (§ 2702(b)(5)); and when a provider discovers images of child pornography that the provider must disclose to the police by federal law (§ 2702(b)(6)).

The exceptions for the disclosure of non-content records in § 2702(c) are similar, but not quite identical, to those for contents.

Putting the Pieces Together

Although the rules found in § 2702 and § 2703 can seem maddeningly complicated at first, they prove surprisingly straightforward in practice. The rules for compelled disclosure operate like an upside-down pyramid. Because the SCA's rules allow greater process to include the lesser, different levels of process can compel different groups of information. The higher up the pyramid you go, the more information the government can obtain.

At the lowest threshold, only a simple subpoena is needed to compel basic subscriber information. Higher up the pyramid, a 2703(d) order compels all non-content records. A simple subpoena combined with prior notice compels three categories of information: basic subscriber information, plus any opened e-mails or other permanently held files (covered by the RCS rules), plus any contents in temporary "electronic storage" such as unretrieved e-mails in storage for more than 180 days. A 2703(d) order plus prior notice is sufficient to compel all non-content records, plus any opened e-mails or other permanently held files (covered by the RCS rules), plus any contents in temporary "electronic storage" such as unretrieved e-mails in storage for more than 180 days. Put another way, a 2703(d) order plus prior notice compels everything except contents in temporary "electronic storage" 180 days or less. Finally, a search warrant is needed to compel everything stored in an account.

The rules governing voluntary disclosure by providers are even simpler in practice. Nonpublic providers can disclose without restriction. Providers of ECS or RCS to the public ordinarily cannot disclose either content or non-content information. Disclosure is allowed only when an exception applies: in the case of contents, the facts must fit within one of the eight exceptions found in § 2702(b); in the case of non-content records, the facts must fit within one of the six exceptions found in § 2702(c).

This chart summarizes the basic rules of the SCA under both the traditional understanding and *Theofel v. Farey–Jones*. The first two columns on the left-hand side represent the categories of information under both the traditional understanding and *Theofel*. The columns in the center cover the voluntary disclosure rules for those categories, and the columns on the right-hand side cover the compelled disclosure rules.

Traditional Understanding	*Theofel v. Farey–Jones*	Voluntary Disclosure Allowed?		Mechanisms to Compel Disclosure	
		Public Provider	Non–Public Provider	Public Provider	Non–Public Provider
Unopened e-mail in storage 180 days or less	"Unexpired" e-mail in storage 180 days or less	No, unless § 2702(b) exception applies [§ 2702(a)(1)]	Yes [§ 2702(a)(1)]	Search warrant [§ 2703(a)]	Search warrant [§ 2703(a)]
Unopened e-mail in storage more than 180 days	"Unexpired" e-mail in storage more than 180 days	No, unless § 2702(b) exception applies [§ 2702(a)(1)]	Yes [§ 2702(a)(1)]	Subpoena with notice; 2703(d) order with notice; or search warrant [§ 2703(a,b)]	Subpoena with notice; 2703(d) order with notice; or search warrant [§ 2703(a,b)]
Opened e-mail, other content files being remotely stored or processed	Files not covered above being remotely stored or processed	No, unless § 2702(b) exception applies [§ 2702(a)(2)]	Yes [§ 2702(a)(2)]	Subpoena with notice; 2703(d) order with notice; or search warrant [§ 2703(b)]	SCA doesn't apply [§ 2711(2)]
Most non-content records	Most non-content records	No, unless § 2702(c) exception applies [§ 2702(a)(3)]	Yes [§ 2702(a)(3)]	2703(d) order or search warrant [§ 2703(c)(1)]	2703(d) order or search warrant § 2703(c)(1)]
Basic subscriber information, session logs, IP addresses	Basic subscriber information, session logs, IP addresses	No, unless § 2702(c) exception applies [§ 2702(a)(3)]	Yes [§ 2702(a)(3)]	Subpoena; 2703(d) order; or search warrant [§ 2703(c)(2)]	Subpoena; 2703(d) order; or search warrant [§ 2703(c)(2)]

Notes and Questions

1. Although the SCA is significantly more complicated than the Wiretap Act and the Pen Register statute, it borrows a number of their terms. The SCA borrows the terms "wire communication," "electronic communication," "provider," "consent," "necessarily incident to the rendition of the service or to the protection of the rights or property of the provider," and "contents" from § 2510 of the Wiretap Act. *See* 18 U.S.C. § 2711(1). The SCA also borrows the term "court of competent jurisdiction" from § 3127 of the Pen Register statute. *See* 18 U.S.C. § 2711(3).

2. The most difficult aspect of the SCA is the scope of the two types of covered providers, providers of electronic communications service (ECS) and remote computing service (RCS). Before you spend time trying to master the difference, keep in mind that the meaning of these terms will matter only in two discrete ways. First, a threshold decision must be made in every SCA case as to whether the provider is a covered provider under the statute. Second, the difference between ECS and RCS becomes important primarily to determine the scope of protection for opened e-mails. The next few notes take a closer look at these two issues.

3. *Providers not covered by the SCA.* Computer network operators can be exempt from the SCA if they provide neither ECS nor RCS. Consider the facts of In re Jetblue Airways Corp. Privacy Litigation, 379 F. Supp.2d 299 (E.D.N.Y. 2005). A nationwide class of airline customers sued the airline JetBlue under the SCA for disclosing customer data. The airline had disclosed data from the JetBlue Passenger Reservation System computer to a company that had contracted with the government to explore data mining techniques. The plaintiffs claimed that the disclosure of customer data violated the voluntary disclosure provisions of 18 U.S.C. § 2702. The district court correct-

ly held that JetBlue did not violate the SCA because it was not a provider covered by the statute. First, JetBlue did not provide ECS:

> The term "electronic communication service," as defined, refers to a service that provides users with capacity to transmit electronic communications. Although JetBlue operates a website that receives and transmits data to and from its customers, it is undisputed that it is not the provider of the electronic communication service that allows such data to be transmitted over the Internet. Rather, JetBlue is more appropriately characterized as a provider of air travel services and a consumer of electronic communication services. The website that it operates, like a telephone, enables the company to communicate with its customers in the regular course of business. Mere operation of the website, however, does not transform JetBlue into a provider of internet access, just as the use of a telephone to accept telephone reservations does not transform the company into a provider of telephone service. Thus, a company such as JetBlue does not become an "electronic communication service" provider simply because it maintains a website that allows for the transmission of electronic communications between itself and its customers.

> This reading of the statute finds substantial support in the case law. Although the Second Circuit has not yet had occasion to construe the term "electronic communication service," a number of courts in this and other circuits have done so, some in cases factually similar to this case. The weight of this persuasive authority holds that companies that provide traditional products and services over the Internet, as opposed to Internet access itself, are not "electronic communication service" providers within the meaning of the ECPA.

Id. at 307. Next, the court held that JetBlue was not a provider of RCS:

> Plaintiffs have also failed to establish that JetBlue is a remote computing service. Plaintiffs simply make the allegation without providing any legal or factual support for such a claim. As discussed, the term "remote computing service" is defined in the ECPA as "the provision to the public of computer storage or processing services by means of an electronic communication system." 18 U.S.C. § 2711(2). The statute's legislative history explains that such services exist to provide sophisticated and convenient data processing services to subscribers and customers, such as hospitals and banks, from remote facilities. *See* S. Rep. No. 99–541 (1986), *reprinted in* 1986 U.S.C.C.A.N. 3555, 3564. By supplying the necessary equipment, remote computing services alleviate the need for users of computer technology to process data in-house. Customers or subscribers may enter into time-sharing arrangements with the remote computing service, or data processing may be accomplished by the service provider on the basis of information supplied by the subscriber or customer. Although plaintiffs allege that JetBlue operates a website and computer servers, no facts alleged indicate that JetBlue provides either computer processing services or computer storage to the public. As such, under the plain meaning of the statute, JetBlue is not a remote computing service.

Id. at 310.

4. A court reached a similar result to that in the *JetBlue* litigation in United States v. Standefer, 2007 WL 2301760 (S.D. Cal. 2007), a case involving subpoenas issued to compel account records from a payment pro-

cessing service called "e-gold." E-gold is akin to the popular site Paypal: It allows individuals to make online purchases and send payments. In *Standefer*, account records obtained in the investigation revealed evidence of crime. The defendant challenged the evidence collection on the ground that the subpoenas to e-gold violated the Stored Communications Act. The District Court rejected the challenge on the ground that e-gold was not regulated by the Stored Communications Act. First, the court concluded that the site did not provide ECS:

> The Court concludes that e-gold is not a service which *provides* users the ability to send or receive electronic communications, rather e-gold is a service which *utilizes* the ability to send or receive electronic communications to permit the instant transfer of gold ownership between its users. Therefore, the Government was not required by [the SCA] to utilize a warrant to obtain the requested information from e-gold.

Id. at *4. The court next held that e-gold did not provide RCS:

> The Court concludes that e-gold provides neither computer storage nor processing services, as those terms are used in § 2711(2), to the public. A client of e-gold does not outsource tasks, but rather uses e-gold to transfer gold ownership to other users. Neither does an e-gold customer use e-gold to simply store electronic data.

Id. at *5.

5. *The surprisingly difficult case of opened e-mails*. Courts are presently divided on how the ECS/RCS distinction applies to opened e-mails. The source of the difficulty is the complex definition of "electronic storage" in 18 U.S.C. § 2510(17). This definition is critical because contents in "electronic storage" are the only types of contents held by providers of ECS. In other words, only contents in "electronic storage" receive ECS protections. As a result, the meaning of "electronic storage" defines whether particular contents receive ECS protections or RCS protections.

18 U.S.C. § 2510(17) defines "electronic storage" as:

(A) any temporary, intermediate storage of a wire or electronic communication incidental to the electronic transmission thereof; and

(B) any storage of such communication by an electronic communication service for purposes of backup protection of such communication[.]

Note that this is a counterintuitive definition. It refers only to a particular type of electronic storage rather than all electronic storage. Specifically, § 2510(17)(A) reflects the very specific function of ECS providers: servers may make temporary copies of e-mails in the course of transmission, and § 2510(17)(A) protects those temporary copies made pending transmission of communications. For example, unopened e-mail in a user's in-box is in "electronic storage," as it is awaiting the user's retrieval of the message.

The difficult question is how to interpret the text of the backup provision, § 2510(17)(B). Consider two possibilities. First, the backup provision may refer to backups made by the provider for the provider's purposes. It is common for system administrators to make backup copies of their files in the event of a system malfunction, and § 2510(17)(B) may simply ensure that the copies of e-mails generated as part of the backup process receive the same protections as originals.

An example shows the role of § 2510(17)(B) under this interpretation. Imagine an ISP makes backup copies of its entire server every night, and criminal investigators want a copy of an unopened e-mail in a particular customer's account. A day after the e-mail arrives, the ISP will have two copies of the opened e-mail, not one: it will have both the original copy in the account and the backup copy. Unlike the original, however, the backup copy is not a "temporary" or "intermediate" copy in storage "incidental" to transmission. It is a permanent copy made by the provider in the event of a system malfunction. Without § 2510(17)(B), the backup copy would not receive the same treatment as the original. Under this interpretation, the backup provision of the definition makes clear that the same legal rules govern access to the original and the backup copy.

Alternatively, the backup provision may refer to copies stored by the user for the user's purposes. After reading an e-mail, users often leave the e-mail on the ISP's server. At that point, the e-mail is no longer stored "incidental to the electronic transmission" of the communication. Users may think of their opened e-mails left with their ISP as "backups" of their messages. Under this approach, the purpose of § 2510(17)(B) is to ensure that opened and unopened e-mails receive the same protection. Opening an e-mail takes an e-mail from electronic storage in § 2510(17)(A) to electronic storage in § 2510(17)(B).

The difference between these two interpretations may seem very technical, but it has tremendous practical importance. Although there are no statistics on this question, it seems likely that most e-mail stored with ISPs is opened e-mail. Under the first approach, opened e-mails are no longer covered by the ECS rules because they are not in "electronic storage." Under the second approach, in contrast, opened e-mails are still in "electronic storage."

So which interpretation is correct? Right now, the answer is frustratingly unclear. The Justice Department and several district courts have endorsed the first approach. *See, e.g,* DOJ Search and Seizure Manual (2002), available at http://www.usdoj.gov/criminal/cybercrime/s & smanual2002.htm#_IIIB_; Fraser v. Nationwide Mut. Ins., 135 F. Supp.2d 623 (E.D. Pa. 2001), *aff'd on other grounds*, 352 F.3d 107 (3d. Cir. 2003); In re DoubleClick, Inc. Privacy Litig., 154 F. Supp.2d 497, 511–12 (S.D.N.Y.2001). *See also* H.R. Rep. No. 99–647, at 64–65 (1986) (suggesting that opened e-mail should be covered by provisions relating to RCS rather than ECS).

In contrast, the Ninth Circuit endorsed the second approach in a case arising from rather unusual facts. *See* Theofel v. Farey–Jones, 359 F.3d 1066 (9th Cir. 2004). *Theofel* involved an abusive tactic in a civil discovery dispute. The defendants sent an overly broad subpoena to the plaintiffs' ISP; the subpoena asked for all of the plaintiffs' e-mails. The ISP responded to the subpoena by providing the defendants with all of the e-mails from the plaintiffs' accounts. Compliance with the subpoena presumably violated § 2703, but the plaintiffs did not sue under that statute. Instead, the plaintiffs sued under 18 U.S.C. § 2701, on the theory that issuing the overly broad subpoena had "accessed" the ISP "without authorization."

Surprisingly, Judge Kozinski agreed. Writing for the panel, Judge Kozinski held that the plaintiff's use of the overbroad subpoena to get information was an unauthorized access, the legal equivalent of hacking into the ISP. *See id.* at 1073–74. (Aside: Do you agree with this interpretation?) Notably, however, § 2701 applies only to contents in electronic storage held by providers of ECS. As a result, Judge Kozinski needed to conclude that the e-mails disclosed—most of which, presumably, had been opened and read—were in "electronic storage."

Judge Kozinski held that the e-mails in the accounts were in electronic storage regardless of whether they had been opened. According to Kozinski, the opened e-mails in the accounts were covered by the backup provisions of 18 U.S.C. § 2510(17)(B):

> An obvious purpose for storing a message on an ISP's server after delivery is to provide a second copy of the message in the event that the user needs to download it again—if, for example, the message is accidentally erased from the user's own computer. The ISP copy of the message functions as a "backup" for the user. Notably, nothing in the Act requires that the backup protection be for the benefit of the ISP rather than the user. Storage under these circumstances thus literally falls within the statutory definition. * * *

> The United States, as *amicus curiae*, disputes our interpretation. It first argues that, because subsection (B) refers to "any storage of such communication," it applies only to backup copies of messages that are themselves in temporary, intermediate storage under subsection (A). The text of the statute, however, does not support this reading. Subsection (A) identifies a type of communication ("a wire or electronic communication") and a type of storage ("temporary, intermediate storage ... incidental to the electronic transmission thereof"). The phrase "such communication" in subsection (B) does not, as a matter of grammar, reference attributes of the type of storage defined in subsection (A). The government's argument would be correct if subsection (B) referred to "a communication in such storage," or if subsection (A) referred to a communication in temporary, intermediate storage rather than temporary, intermediate storage of a communication. However, as the statute is written, "such communication" is nothing more than shorthand for "a wire or electronic communication."

> The government's contrary interpretation * * * drains subsection (B) of independent content because virtually any backup of a subsection (A) message will itself qualify as a message in temporary, intermediate storage. The government counters that the statute requires only that the underlying message be temporary, not the backup. But the lifespan of a backup is necessarily tied to that of the underlying message. Where the underlying message has expired in the normal course, any copy is no longer performing any backup function. An ISP that kept permanent copies of temporary messages could not fairly be described as "backing up" those messages.

Id. at 1075–76.

Which interpretation do you think is most consistent with the text of the statute? Which interpretation is better from the standpoint of policy?

6. Companies that provide text messaging services sometimes store copies of sent text messages that are generated in the course of transmission. If the government seeks copies of the text messages, which legal framework applies? Are the text messages held in electronic storage by providers of ECS, or are they remotely stored files held as a provider of RCS? In Quon v. Arch Wireless Operating Co., 529 F.3d 892 (9th Cir. 2008), the Ninth Circuit concluded that the text messages are contents in electronic storage held by providers of ECS, not remotely stored files held as a provider of RCS:

> We turn to the plain language of the SCA, including its common-sense definitions, to properly categorize Arch Wireless. An ECS is defined as "any service which provides to users thereof the ability to send or receive wire or electronic communications." 18 U.S.C. § 2510(15). On its face, this describes the text-messaging pager services that Arch Wireless provided. Arch Wireless provided a "service" that enabled Quon and the other Appellants to "send or receive . . . electronic communications," i.e., text messages. Contrast that definition with that for an RCS, which "means the provision to the public of computer storage or processing services by means of an electronic communications system." Id. § 2711(2). Arch Wireless did not provide to the City "computer storage"; nor did it provide "processing services." By archiving the text messages on its server, Arch Wireless certainly was "storing" the messages. However, Congress contemplated this exact function could be performed by an ECS as well, stating that an ECS would provide (A) temporary storage incidental to the communication; and (B) storage for backup protection. Id. § 2510(17).

> In the Senate Report [on the SCA], Congress made clear what it meant by "storage and processing of information." It provided the following example of storage: "physicians and hospitals maintain medical files in offsite data banks." Congress appeared to view "storage" as a virtual filing cabinet, which is not the function Arch Wireless contracted to provide here. The Senate Report also provided an example of "processing of information": "businesses of all sizes transmit their records to remote computers to obtain sophisticated data processing services." In light of the Report's elaboration upon what Congress intended by the term "Remote Computer Services," it is clear that, before the advent of advanced computer processing programs such as Microsoft Excel, businesses had to farm out sophisticated processing to a service that would process the information. Neither of these examples describes the service that Arch Wireless provided to the City.

Id. at 901–02.

On the other hand, the district court in Flagg v. City of Detroit, 252 F.R.D. 346 (E.D. Mich. 2008), reached a different result in a case involving old text messages stored by a provider long after the account had been terminated. In Flagg, the City of Detroit had contracted with SkyTel to provide text pagers to a number of the City's employees. Although the contract with the City had terminated four years earlier, SkyTel continued to store thousands of old text messages belonging to the City. District Judge Rosen ruled that SkyTel was a provider of RCS rather than ECS with respect to the text messages that SkyTel was continuing to store:

> In light of the SCA's functional, context-specific definitions of an ECS and an RCS, it is not dispositive that SkyTel indisputably did provide an ECS to the City of Detroit in the past, or that it presumably kept text messages in "electronic storage" at times in connection with the ECS that it provided. Rather, the ECS/RCS inquiry in this case turns upon the characterization of the service that SkyTel *presently* provides to the City, pursuant to which the company is being called upon to retrieve text messages from an archive of communications sent and received by City employees in years past using SkyTel text messaging devices. The resolution of this issue, in turn, depends upon whether SkyTel has maintained this archive "for purposes of backup protection," 18 U.S.C. § 2510(17)(B), so that its contents may be deemed to be held in "electronic storage" by an ECS, 18 U.S.C. § 2702(a)(1), or whether this archive is more properly viewed as "computer storage" offered by an RCS, 18 U.S.C. § 2711(2).
>
> SkyTel is no longer providing, and has long since ceased to provide, a text messaging service to the City of Detroit—the City, by its own admission, discontinued this service in 2004, and the text messaging devices issued by SkyTel are no longer in use. Consequently, any archive of text messages that SkyTel continues to maintain on the City's behalf constitutes the *only* available record of these communications, and cannot possibly serve as a "backup" copy of communications stored elsewhere. * * * The service provided by SkyTel may properly be characterized as a "virtual filing cabinet" of communications sent and received by City employees. The Court finds, therefore, that the archive maintained by SkyTel constitutes "computer storage," and that the company's maintenance of this archive on behalf of the City is a "remote computing service" as defined under the SCA.

Id. at 362–63.

2. COMPELLED DISCLOSURE UNDER § 2703

Section 2703 contains the rules that govern compelled disclosure of stored records. Section 2703(a) covers the requirements for compelling contents from a provider of ECS; § 2703(b) addresses requirements for compelling contents from providers of RCS; and § 2703(c) turns to the rules that regulate non-content records.

UNITED STATES v. KENNEDY

United States District Court for the District of Kansas, 2000.
81 F. Supp.2d 1103.

BELOT, DISTRICT JUDGE.

On August 25, 1999, Defendant Michael R. Kennedy was indicted for the intentional receipt of child pornography in violation of 18 U.S.C.

§ 2252(a)(2) and forfeiture under 18 U.S.C. § 2253. An evidentiary hearing was held December 2, 1999. For the following reasons, defendant's motion to suppress is denied.

Facts

On July 2, 1999, Steven Idelman was working as a customer support specialist for Road Runner, a high speed Internet service provider. At approximately 9:00 p.m., Idelman received an anonymous phone call from a still-unidentified male ("the caller"). The caller told Idelman that he was at a friend's house, scanning other computers through the Internet and had viewed images of child pornography on a computer the caller believed to be serviced by Road Runner. The caller told Idelman the IP address of the computer from which the images were viewed, 24.94.200.54, and the directory and file names in which the images were located.[4] The caller did not say that he was a law enforcement officer or that he was directed to view the computer's files by any law enforcement officer. The caller did not ask Idelman to call the police.

Shortly after the anonymous call, Idelman went to a computer and accessed the IP address given to him by the caller. His purpose was to determine if what the caller told him was correct. He located the computer with the IP address 24.94.200.54 and the directory tree and files mentioned by the caller. Idelman viewed two images located within those files. One of the images depicted two boys, whom Idelman estimated to be approximately eight or nine years old, posed in a sexual nature. Idelman then sent an e-mail to his supervisor, Anna Madden, describing the anonymous phone call and the results of his search of the computer with IP address 24.94.200.54.

On July 6, 1999, Kerry Jones, a network engineer for Road Runner, received an e-mail from Anna Madden asking him to research the owner of the Road Runner account connecting to the computer with the IP address 24.94.200.54. Jones was able to determine that the account was assigned to Rosemary D. Kennedy. Mr. Jones was able to determine that the account was assigned to the same IP address on July 2, 1999. Believing that the customer service agreement between Road Runner and the account holder authorized him to search a computer's files for offensive material, Jones then viewed the files on the computer's hard drive.[7] The files depicted images of boys, whom Jones estimated to be approximately 10 to 13 years old, engaged in sexual activity. Jones then printed out an image of the computer's directory tree in which the files with offensive material were located.

That same day, after consulting with Road Runner's corporate attorney, Scott Petrie, the manager of Road Runner, made the decision to

---

4. The caller was able to view the computer's files because the computer with IP address 24.94.200.54 had its print and file sharing mechanism turned on, allowing other computers to view its files over the Internet.

7. Jones was able to do so because the computer's print and file sharing mechanism was still turned on.

contact law enforcement authorities. Kerry Jones contacted the Exploited Children's Unit of the Wichita Police Department, but his phone call was not returned. Road Runner then contacted Special Agent Leslie Earl of the FBI. Special Agent Earl was informed by Road Runner that the FBI would need to obtain a court order for it to be able to supply the FBI with any subscriber information.

The United States Attorney's Office then applied to a United States magistrate judge for an order directing Road Runner to disclose subscriber information related to IP address 24.94.200.54. In the application, the Assistant United States Attorney stated that:

> the Federal Bureau of Investigation is conducting a criminal investigation in connection with possible violation(s) of Tile 18, United States Code, Sections 2252 and 2252A; it is believed that the subject of the investigation used Road Runner's IP address 24.94.200.54 on July 2, 1999, at 11:48 p.m. in furtherance of the subject offenses; and that the information sought to be obtained is relevant to a legitimate law enforcement inquiry in that it is believed that this information will assist in the investigation relating to the aforementioned offenses.

The magistrate judge issued an order, which was presented to Road Runner personnel, who provided the FBI with the following information:

> The subscriber whose computer used I.P. address 24.94.200.54 on July 2, 1999, at 11:49 p.m. was Rosemay (sic) D. Kennedy of 9120 Harvest Court, Wichita, Kansas, telephone 316–722–6593. Two users were listed for that account: RKENNEDY@KSCable.COM and KENNEDYM@KSCable.Com. The account had been active since June 7, 1999.

Special Agent Earl next went to the house located at 9120 Harvest Court in Wichita, Kansas. He observed a Chrysler Sebring parked in the driveway. A records check with the Kansas Department of Motor Vehicles revealed that the car was registered to Michael R. Kennedy. Special Agent Earl then called the phone number given to the government by Road Runner. A person identifying himself as Michael Kennedy answered the phone.

In initiating the phone call, Special Agent Earl asked Kennedy if he was satisfied with his Road Runner cable modem Internet service.

> Kennedy confirmed that his address was 9120 Harvest Court, Wichita, Kansas, and he confirmed that he was the primary user of the Road Runner cable modem Internet service. Kennedy said he was satisfied with the service and especially liked the speed and quality of the e-mail service. Kennedy estimated he spent an average of two to three hours per night online. Kennedy noted that he always left his system on and connected to the Internet. Kennedy said he used his Internet access only for pleasure and his computer and modem were located in his home.

Kennedy said his computer system was a Gateway 450 megahertz Pentium II with a 17 gigabyte hard drive. When asked if he had any concerns about the Road Runner service Kennedy said he thought the company should warn customers about the possibility of someone else trying to enter their computers through the Internet. Kennedy said he held Internet accounts through Netcom and AOL in the past. Kennedy left those services because they were too slow and he could not use e-mail and Usenet news groups the way he wanted to. Kennedy noted that it took too long for him to download mail with pictures attached on those other services.

Affidavit in Support of Search Warrant at 14–15, Doc. 14, Ex. A. The government applied for and obtained a search warrant for property and evidence located at 9120 Harvest Court.

Analysis

18 U.S.C. §§ 2701 *et seq.* regulates the disclosure of electronic communications and subscriber information. Section 2703(c)(1)(B) states that "[a] provider of electronic communication service ... shall disclose a record or other information pertaining to a subscriber to or customer of such service ... to a governmental entity only when the governmental entity ... (ii) obtains a court order for such disclosure under subsection (d) of this section." Subsection (d) sets forth the requirements of such a court order:

A court order for disclosure under subsection (b) or (c) ... shall issue only if the governmental entity offers *specific and articulable facts* showing that there are reasonable grounds to believe that the contents of a wire or electronic communication, or the records or other information sought, are relevant and material to an ongoing criminal investigation.

18 U.S.C. § 2703(d) (emphasis added).

Defendant argues the government's application did not state specific and articulable facts, but mere conclusions. The government responds that at the time of the application, it did not know the identity of the subscriber, whether the subscriber was the person using the computer to store illegal material and how much child pornography was held by the computer. The government argues that the information it had at the time was minimal and the purpose of obtaining the order was to investigate the subscriber information completely.

The government's argument does not address the issue as to conclusory versus specific and articulable facts in regard to the information it *did* have. The government's application merely listed that the subscriber information connected to IP address 24.94.200.54 would possibly relate to an on-going criminal investigation.[8] In accordance with 18 U.S.C.

---

8. It appears as though the government's application would have satisfied the statute's requirements prior to the 1994 amendments to the ECPA. As the statute was originally enacted, the government's application for the court order sufficed by showing there was reason to believe

§ 2703(d), the government should have articulated more specific facts such as how the government obtained the information it did have at the time and how this information lead the agents to believe that the attainment of the subscriber information of this particular IP address would assist in the investigation. The government's application for a section 2703(d) order did not meet the requirements of the statute.

Nonetheless, the government correctly points out that even if Road Runner divulged defendant's subscriber information pursuant to a court order based on an inadequate government application, suppression is not a remedy contemplated under the ECPA. The statute specifically allows for civil damages and criminal punishment for violations of the ECPA, *see* 18 U.S.C. §§ 2707, 2701(b), but speaks nothing about the suppression of information in a court proceeding. Instead, Congress clearly intended for suppression not to be an option for a defendant whose electronic communications have been intercepted in violation of the ECPA. The statute specifically states that "[t]he remedies and sanctions described in this chapter are the only judicial remedies and sanctions for nonconstitutional violations of this chapter." 18 U.S.C. § 2708.

NOTES AND QUESTIONS

1. The prosecutor in the *Kennedy* case applied for the wrong order and then obtained it in the wrong way. The prosecutor applied for an § 2703(d) order under 18 U.S.C. § 2703(c)(1)(B), and requested "subscriber information" from the ISP. However, the prosecutor could have obtained that information from the ISP using a mere subpoena, without establishing "specific and articulable facts," under 18 U.S.C. § 2703(c)(2). The prosecutor then erred a second time by not establishing the "specific and articulable facts" required by § 2703(d).

2. *Compelling non-content records.* The SCA has two sets of rules for compelling non-content records from covered providers. Basic subscriber information listed in 18 U.S.C. § 2703(c)(2) can be compelled with a subpoena. Compelling other non-content records requires a § 2703(d) order. As noted in the *Kennedy* case, the § 2703(d) standard requires "specific and articulable facts showing that there are reasonable grounds to believe" that

---

the information sought was "relevant to a legitimate law enforcement inquiry." Electronic Communications Privacy Act, Pub. L. No. 99–508 § 201. In the early 1990's, a task force, assembled by Senator Patrick Leahy "questioned whether current restrictions on government access to transactional records generated in the course of electronic communications were adequate." H.R. Rep. No. 103–827, at 12 (1994), *reprinted in* 1994 U.S.C.A.A.N. 3489, 3492. In response, the statute was amended to its current version. *See* Communications Assistance for Law Enforcement Act, Pub. L. No. 103–414 § 207(2). The House Report reflects that

this section imposes an intermediate standard to protect on-line transactional records. It is a standard higher than a subpoena, but not a probable cause warrant. The intent of raising the standard for access to transactional data is to guard against "fishing expeditions" by law enforcement. Under the intermediate standard, the court must find, *based on law enforcement's showing of facts, that there are specific and articulable grounds to believe that the records are relevant and material to an ongoing criminal investigation.*

H.R. Rep. No. 103–827, at 31–32 (1994), *reprinted in* 1994 U.S.C.A.A.N. 3489, 3511–12 (emphasis added).

the information sought is "relevant and material to an ongoing criminal investigation."

Congress borrowed the "specific and articulable facts" language from Fourth Amendment law, and specifically the temporary stop standard articulated in Terry v. Ohio, 392 U.S. 1, 21 (1968) ("[I]n justifying the particular intrusion the police officer must be able to point to specific and articulable facts which, taken together with rational inferences from those facts, reasonably warrant that intrusion."). Did the government have enough information to make such a showing in *Kennedy*?

3. The two-tiered approach to compelling non-content records was enacted as part of the Communications Assistance for Law Enforcement Act of 1994, Pub. L. No. 103–414 (1994) ("CALEA"). A Senate Report issued during work on S. 2375, a bill introduced on the way to the passage of CALEA, justified the change on the following grounds:

> In the 8 years since the enactment of ECPA, society's patterns of using electronic communications technology have changed dramatically. Millions of people now have electronic mail addresses. Business, nonprofit organizations and political groups conduct their work over the Internet. Individuals maintain a wide range of relationships on-line. Transactional records documenting these activities and associations are generated by service providers. For those who increasingly use these services, this transactional data reveals a great deal about their private lives, all of it compiled in one place.

> Therefore, S. 2375 includes provisions, which FBI Director Freeh supported in his testimony, that add protections to the exercise of the Government's current surveillance authority. Specifically, the bill * * * [e]liminates the use of subpoenas to obtain E-mail addresses and other similar transactional data from electronic communications service providers. Currently, the Government can obtain transactional logs containing a person's entire on-line profile merely upon presentation of an administrative subpoena issued by an investigator without any judicial intervention. Under S. 2375, a court order would be required.

S. Rep. No. 103–402, at 17–18 (1994).

4. Note that the SCA requires "specific and articulable facts" for the retrospective surveillance of non-content transactional information, but the Pen Register statute only requires a certification of relevance for prospective surveillance of such information. In other words, government investigators can obtain non-content transactional information more easily prospectively than retrospectively. Does this make sense? Should the standards for prospective surveillance be lower than retrospective surveillance?

5. *Compelling content records.* The SCA's rules for compelling contents are also two-tiered. The top tier, required when the government seeks to compel contents from an ECS in electronic storage for 180 days or fewer, requires a probable cause search warrant. *See* 18 U.S.C. § 2703(a). The second tier, required when the government seeks to compel contents from an ECS in storage greater than 180 days or when it seeks to compel contents from an RCS, requires either a subpoena with prior notice, a § 2703(d) order

with prior notice, or a search warrant. *See* 18 U.S.C. § 2703(b). Of course, what exactly this covers hinges on how you interpret the ECS/RCS distinction, as noted earlier in the discussion of *Theofel*.

6. Is the SCA's two-tiered approach to compelling contents desirable as a matter of policy? Should opened e-mail be treated differently than unopened e-mail? Should files stored with a remote storage facility be treated differently than unopened e-mails? Should unopened e-mail in storage for more than 180 days be treated differently than "fresh" e-mail, on the theory that the former has been "abandoned" and should be protected less? Should privacy protections for e-mail hinge on whether the e-mails have "expired in the normal course"? Alternatively, should Congress create a broad warrant requirement for all contents, regardless of the circumstances?

7. Note that the SCA requires a standard search warrant for retrospective access to stored unopened e-mails, but the Wiretap Act requires a "super warrant" order for prospective interception of e-mail. In other words, government investigators can obtain content information more easily retrospectively than prospectively. Do you think this is appropriate? Or do you agree with Judge Boochever that "an electronic communication in storage is no more or less private than an electronic communication in transmission," and that "distinguishing between the two for purposes of protection from interception is irrational"? Konop v. Hawaiian Airlines, 236 F.3d 1035 (9th Cir. 2001), *withdrawn*, 262 F.3d 972 (9th Cir. 2001), *reargued*, 302 F.3d 868 (9th Cir. 2002), *cert. denied*, 537 U.S. 1193 (2003).

If the standards for retrospective and prospective content surveillance should be the same, which standard should Congress adopt? Should Congress use the standard search warrant requirement now used for retrospective surveillance or the "super warrant" standard currently reserved for prospective surveillance?

8. When investigators obtain court orders under 18 U.S.C. § 2703, the language of the court orders generally tracks the language of the statute. For example, a 2703(d) order might require the disclosure of contents in "electronic storage" for greater than 180 days, plus any contents held by the provider in its capacity as an RCS, plus any non-content records. The ISP must then comply, implicitly interpreting the requirements of the SCA along the way. If an ISP hands over information that exceeds the limits of the statute, is the ISP liable? Or are the investigators liable?

9. Does 18 U.S.C. § 2703(b) violate the Fourth Amendment by allowing the government to compel contents of communications with less process than a probable cause warrant? Section 2703(b) allows the government to obtain contents with a subpoena or a 2703(d) order if the contents are stored by a provider of ECS for more than 180 days or if the contents are held by an RCS. Do you think the Fourth Amendment allows this? *See generally* Patricia L. Bellia & Susan Freiwald, *Fourth Amendment Protection for Stored E-mail*, 2008 U. Chi. Legal F. 121; Orin S. Kerr, *Applying the Fourth Amendment to the Internet: A General Approach*, 62 Stan. L. Rev. (forthcoming 2010).

10. *Notice requirements*. The statutory privacy laws put in place by ECPA require notice to the person monitored only in two contexts. First, the Wiretap Act requires that, within 90 days after an intercept order has expired,

the persons named in the wiretap order and other parties to communications intercepted by the order "as the judge may determine in his discretion that is in the interest of justice" must receive notice of the dates and period of the monitoring. *See* 18 U.S.C. § 2518(8)(d).

Second, the SCA requires "prior notice from the governmental entity to the subscriber or customer" when investigators seek to compel contents of stored communications from covered providers with legal process lesser than a search warrant. 18 U.S.C. § 2703(b)(1)(B). Notably, however, the notice provisions of § 2703 are subject to the delayed notice provisions of § 2705. The delayed notice provisions permit a delay of notice up to 90 days "if there is reason to believe" that notice would trigger an "adverse result," defined as: "(A) endangering the life or physical safety of an individual; (B) flight from prosecution; (C) destruction of or tampering with evidence; (D) intimidation of potential witnesses; or (E) otherwise seriously jeopardizing an investigation or unduly delaying a trial." 18 U.S.C. § 2705(a)(2). The government may also obtain extensions beyond the initial delay period.

Are these notice provisions sufficient? How hard do you think it is to persuade a judge that there is "reason to believe" that notice might lead to an "adverse result"? How do the statutory notice requirements compare to notice requirements of the Fourth Amendment? *See generally* Brian D. Kaiser, Note, *Government Access to Transactional Information and the Lack of Subscriber Notice*, 8 B.U. J. Sci. & Tech. L. 648 (2002).

11. *Pre-disclosure challenges under § 2704.* 18 U.S.C. § 2704 permits the government to invite a pre-disclosure legal challenge to the compulsion of content with less process than a warrant. Under the statute, the government can order the ISP to make a backup of the contents to be disclosed, to provide notice to the customer or subscriber of the pending disclosure, and then to wait for 14 days. If the customer or subscriber does not challenge the order in that window, the provider can disclose the contents to the government. If the subscriber wishes to challenge the order, the provider will hold the backup copy and wait for the court to rule on the subscriber's motion to quash. Importantly, § 2704 is not mandatory. 18 U.S.C. § 2704(a)(1) states that the government "may" invite this challenge, not that it "must." Perhaps unsurprisingly, investigators and prosecutors invariably decline the invitation. Should § 2704 be amended to require such challenges when the government seeks contents without a search warrant?

12. *Preservation requests.* 18 U.S.C. § 2703(f) permits investigators to notify providers that they plan to seek a court order requiring the disclosure of particular records. Providers must then "take all necessary steps" to preserve those records. 18 U.S.C. § 2703(f)(1). As the Justice Department explains:

> Some providers retain records for months, others for hours, and others not at all. As a practical matter, this means that evidence may be destroyed or lost before law enforcement can obtain the appropriate legal order compelling disclosure. For example, agents may learn of a child pornography case on Day 1, begin work on a search warrant on Day 2, obtain the warrant on Day 5, and then learn that the network service provider deleted the records in the ordinary course of business on Day 3.

To minimize this risk, ECPA permits the government to direct providers to "freeze" stored records and communications pursuant to 18 U.S.C. § 2703(f).

Searching and Seizing Computers (2002), available at www.cybercrime.gov/s & smanual2002.htm#_IIIG1_.

Importantly, the authority under § 2703(f) has no prospective effect. Providers must preserve records already generated in the ordinary course of business, but the authority does not permit investigators to request prospective monitoring.

13.   Assume that an ISP retains the following information relating to an Internet account:

   A.   name, address, home phone number, and credit card number

   B.   login records for the last 30 days

   C.   records of IP addresses assigned to that account for 20 days

   D.   e-mail addresses associated with that account

   E.   "buddy list" of other accounts belonging to friends of the subscriber

   F.   opened e-mails received a year ago

   G.   unopened e-mails received a year ago

   H.   opened e-mails received the previous day

   I.   unopened e-mails received the previous day

   J.   copies of all outgoing e-mails for the last year

What legal process must the government use under the SCA to compel the ISP to disclose these records? In which cases does the answer hinge on whether you adopt the Justice Department's or the Ninth Circuit's approach to the ECS/RCS distinction?

14.   Can attorneys for a criminal defendant obtain § 2703(d) orders in the course of trial preparation? In United States v. Amawi, 552 F. Supp.2d 679 (N.D. Ohio 2008), the Office of the Federal Public Defender in the Northern District of Ohio sought to obtain such an order. The court rejected the application on the ground that the Office of the Federal Public Defender was not a "government entity":

> 18 U.S.C. § 2703(d) ... permits disclosure by a provider to a "government entity" upon court order. Defendant claims that, as part of the United States Courts, the Office of the Federal Public Defender is a "government entity" which can seek a court order compelling production of electronic communications.

> The government contends, and its contention is well taken, that the Office of the Federal Public Defender is not a "government entity" within the meaning of § 2703. "Government entity" is defined in 18 U.S.C. § 2711(4), as "a department or agency of the United States or any State or political subdivision thereof." The judiciary is not a department or agency of the United States; thus, the judiciary and its components,

including the Federal Public Defender, cannot obtain a court order under
§ 2703(d).

Id. at 680.

3.   VOLUNTARY DISCLOSURE UNDER § 2702

The SCA's rules that regulate voluntary disclosure by providers
appear in 18 U.S.C. § 2702. The first important question under § 2702 is
whether the provider provides services "to the public." If the provider
does not provide services to the public, disclosure is allowed. If the services
are provided to the public, the next question is whether voluntary disclosure is allowed pursuant to one of the exceptions found in § 2702(b)–(c).
The following two cases consider these two issues in turn.

ANDERSEN CONSULTING LLP v. UOP

United States District Court for the Northern District of Illinois, 1998.
991 F.Supp. 1041.

BUCKLO, DISTRICT JUDGE.

Plaintiff, Andersen Consulting LLP, brought an eight count complaint
against the defendants, UOP and its counsel, the law firm of Bickel &
Brewer. Andersen alleges that the defendants knowingly divulged, or
caused to be divulged, the contents of Andersen's e-mail messages in
violation of the Electronic Communications Privacy Act, 18 U.S.C. § 2701
et seq. For the reasons set forth below, the defendants' motion to dismiss
is granted.

UOP hired Andersen to perform a systems integration project in 1992.
During the project, Andersen employees had access to and used UOP's
internal e-mail system to communicate with each other, with UOP, and
with third parties.

Dissatisfied with Andersen's performance, UOP terminated the project in December 1993. Subsequently UOP hired Bickel and Brewer and
brought suit in Connecticut state court charging Andersen with breach of
contract, negligence, and fraud. Andersen countersued in two different
suits for defamation.

While these three cases were pending, UOP and Bickel and Brewer
divulged the contents of Andersen's e-mail messages on UOP's e-mail
system to the *Wall Street Journal.* The *Journal* published an article on
June 19, 1997 titled "E–Mail Trail Could Haunt Consultant in Court."
The article excerpted some of Andersen's e-mail messages made during
the course of its assignment at UOP. This disclosure of the e-mail
messages and their subsequent publication is the basis of this suit.

18 U.S.C. § 2702(a)(1) states that "a person or entity providing an
electronic communication service to the public shall not knowingly divulge
to any person or entity the contents of a communication while in electronic storage by that service." Andersen claims that the defendants violated

this section by knowingly divulging the contents of its e-mail message to the Wall Street Journal.

To be liable for the disclosure of Andersen's e-mail messages, UOP must fall under the purview of the Act: UOP must provide "electronic communication service to the public." 18 U.S.C. § 2702(a)(1). The statute defines "electronic communication service" as "any service which provides to users thereof the ability to send or receive wire or electronic communications." 18 U.S.C. § 2510(15). The statute does not define "public." The word "public," however, is unambiguous. Public means the "aggregate of the citizens" or "everybody" or "the people at large" or "the community at large." *Black's Law Dictionary* 1227 (6th ed. 1990). Thus, the statute covers any entity that provides electronic communication service (e.g., e-mail) to the community at large.

Andersen attempts to render the phrase "to the public" superfluous by arguing that the statutory language indicates that the term "public" means something other than the community at large. It claims that if Congress wanted public to mean the community at large, it would have used the term "general public." However, the fact that Congress used both "public" and "general public" in the same statute does not lead to the conclusion that Congress intended public to have any other meaning than its commonly understood meaning. *Compare* 18 U.S.C. § 2511(2)(g) (using the term "general public") *with* §§ 2511(2)(a)(i), (3)(a), (3)(b), (4)(c)(ii) (using the term "public").

Andersen argues that the legislative history indicates that a provider of electronic communication services is subject to Section 2702 even if that provider maintains the system primarily for its own use and does not provide services to the general public. This legislative history argument is misguided. A court's starting point to determine the intent of Congress is the language of the statute itself. If the language is clear and unambiguous, the court must give effect to the plain meaning of the statute. Since the meaning of "public" is clear, there is no need to resort to legislative history.

Even if the language was somehow ambiguous, the legislative history does not support Andersen's interpretation. The legislative history indicates that there is a distinction between public and proprietary. In describing "electronic mail," the legislative history stated that "electronic mail systems may be available for public use or may be proprietary, such as systems operated by private companies for internal correspondence." S. Rep. No. 99–541, at 8 (1986), *reprinted in* 1986 U.S.C.C.A.N. 3555, 3562. Thus, Andersen must show that UOP's electronic mail system was available for public use.

In its complaint, Andersen alleges that UOP "is a general partnership which licenses process technologies and supplies catalysts, specialty chemicals, and other products to the petroleum refining, petrochemical, and gas processing industries." Complaint ¶ 3. UOP is not in the business of providing electronic communication services. It does, however, have an e-mail system for internal communication as e-mail is a necessary tool for almost any business today. *See State Wide Photocopy v. Tokai Fin. Servs., Inc.,* 909 F. Supp. 137, 145 (S.D.N.Y.1995) (finding that defendant was in the business of financing and that the mere use of fax machines and computers, as necessary tools of business, did not make it an electronic communication service provider).

UOP hired Andersen to provide services in connection with the integration of certain computer systems. As part of the project, "UOP provided an electronic communication service for Andersen to use. That electronic communication service could be used, and was used by Andersen and UOP personnel, to electronically communicate with (*i.e.,* send e-mail messages to, and receive e-mail messages from) other Andersen personnel, UOP personnel, third-party vendors and other third-parties both in and outside of Illinois." Complaint ¶ 10.

Based on these allegations, Andersen claims that UOP provides an electronic communication service to the public. However, giving Andersen access to its e-mail system is not equivalent to providing e-mail to the public. Andersen was hired by UOP to do a project and as such, was given access to UOP's e-mail system similar to UOP employees. Andersen was not any member of the community at large, but a hired contractor. Further, the fact that Andersen could communicate to third-parties over the internet and that third-parties could communicate with it did not mean that UOP provided an electronic communication service to the public. UOP's internal e-mail system is separate from the internet. UOP must purchase internet access from an electronic communication service provider like any other consumer; it does not independently provide internet services.

NOTES AND QUESTIONS

1. Why doesn't the SCA impose any restrictions on voluntary disclosure by non-public providers? Here is some speculation:

Nonpublic accounts may exist more for the benefit of providers than for the benefit of users. For example, companies often provide e-mail accounts to employees for work-related purposes; the U.S. military often provides accounts to service members for official government business. These nonpublic providers generally have a legitimate interest in controlling and accessing the accounts they provide to users. Plus, their users tend to recognize that the providers will view those provider interests as more important than the privacy interests of users.

In contrast, an individual who contracts with a commercial ISP available to the public usually does so solely for his own benefit. The account belongs to the user, not the provider. As a result, the user may understandably rely more heavily on the privacy of the commercial account from the public provider rather than another account with a nonpublic provider. Many Internet users have experienced this dynamic. When an e-mail exchange using a work account turns to private matters, it is common for a user to move the discussion to a commercial account. "I don't want my boss to read this," a user might note, "I'll e-mail you from my personal account later." The law recognizes this distinction by drawing a line between accounts held with public and nonpublic providers. In practice, the public/nonpublic line often acts as a proxy for the distinction between a user's private account and one assigned to him by his employer.

A related explanation for this distinction is that private providers with a relationship to their users may approach their users' privacy differently than would commercial providers available to the public. To a commercial ISP, a particular customer is a source of revenue, no more and no less. In contrast, nonpublic providers may have a long-term, multifaceted relationship with their users, giving nonpublic providers unique incentives to protect the privacy of their users. The law may wish to protect privacy more heavily in the case of public providers because there is less incentive for public providers to protect their users' privacy. Alternatively, the law may take a more hands-off approach with respect to nonpublic providers in recognition of the different relationships that nonpublic providers may have with their users.

Orin S. Kerr, *A User's Guide to the Stored Communications Act, and A Legislator's Guide to Amending It*, 72 Geo. Wash. L. Rev. 1208, 1226–27 (2004).

Assuming this explanation is right as a descriptive matter, is the argument persuasive as a normative matter? Should § 2702 be amended to restrict disclosures by all providers? If an account exists for the provider's purposes rather than the user's, won't the provider obtain the user's consent to disclosure? Why not set a pro-privacy default and permit providers to contract around it?

2. Every law school issues e-mail accounts to students and faculty members, and many students and faculty members use those accounts as primary e-mail addresses. Does a university provide e-mail "to the public"? Can a university disclose the contents of student e-mail accounts without restriction under the SCA? Does it matter whether the university is a state university or a private institution? Note that the disclosure may be prohibited by other laws, such as the Family Educational Rights and Privacy Act, codified at 20 U.S.C. § 1232g.

JAYNE v. SPRINT PCS

United States District Court for the Eastern District of California, 2009.
2009 WL 426117.

GREGORY G. HOLLOWS, UNITED STATES MAGISTRATE JUDGE.

Plaintiff, a state prisoner proceeding pro se, seeks relief pursuant to 42 U.S.C. § 1983.

[According to the plaintiff's complaint,] a Miss Shanda Kessler went to the Anderson police to file a restraining order against plaintiff. [According to the complaint, Anderson police] coerced Kessler into saying plaintiff had held her against her will for six hours.

These officers then sent an exigent circumstances request/demand to plaintiff's cell phone provider, saying that plaintiff was wanted for kidnapping and that the cell phone service was to provide plaintiff's cell phone records and GPS location. Plaintiff asserts that this request/demand was made "without a warrant or real cause," and claims that defendant Sprint PCS provided the cell phone records to the Anderson police "based on this false and illegal pretense."

Defendant Sprint identifies itself as a wireless communications company having customers in every state, including California, and acknowledges that plaintiff was one such customer. Further, Sprint accepts as true plaintiff's allegation that Sprint provided plaintiff's cell phone records to defendants upon a demand/request by [the Anderson police] predicated on exigent circumstances.[4] Nor does Sprint, which disclaims any knowledge of plaintiff's interaction with law enforcement, in any manner contest plaintiff's version of the facts with regard to the legitimacy of the basis for the defendants' request.

What this defendant does assert, however, is that plaintiff "has alleged precisely the facts that establish by law that Sprint has no liability for the disclosure of his phone records in response to an emergency request from law enforcement." Sprint contends that under the Stored Communications Act at 18 U.S.C. § 2702(c)(4), service providers are permitted to disclose telephone records so long as they have a good faith belief that there is an emergency requiring authorization. Defendant Sprint seeks dismissal from this action with prejudice.

Sprint argues that the SCA, pursuant to 18 U.S.C. § 2702(c)(4), allows service providers to disclose telephone records if the provider has a good faith belief that an emergency exists requiring disclosure.

To his opposition, plaintiff attaches as Exhibit A, an unauthenticated copy of a document entitled "Mandatory Information for Exigent Circumstance Requests," which appears to be a Sprint PCS form, which indicates that the Anderson Police Department sought plaintiff's phone records from Sprint and set forth the alleged exigent circumstances therein. In reply, Sprint does not challenge the accuracy or authenticity of the form.

Under 18 U.S.C. § 2702(c)(4), a provider of an electronic communication service "may divulge a record or other information pertaining to a subscriber to or customer of such service (not including the contents of communications covered by subsection (a)(1) or (a)(2))-":

> to a governmental entity, if the provider, in good faith, believes that an emergency involving danger of death or serious physical injury to any person requires disclosure without delay of information relating to the emergency.

---

4. In fact, defendant Sprint expressly affirms that it provided "the records requested in reliance on the certification from Anderson Police that the records were necessary because of an exigent situation involving danger of death or serious physical injury to any person."

Defendant Sprint, a cell phone provider, identifies itself as a provider of an electronic communication service. Congress passed the Stored Communications Act in 1986 as part of the Electronic Communications Privacy Act. The SCA was enacted because the advent of the Internet presented a host of potential privacy breaches that the Fourth Amendment does not address. Generally, the SCA prevents "providers" of communication services from divulging private communications to certain entities and/or individuals.

From the papers submitted by the United States Attorney, it is clear that the disclosure without a court order by the provider in the instant case was due to the fact that the government was investigating a kidnapping which included a demand for ransom. This is precisely the type of emergency situation which involves immediate danger of death or serious physical injury to a person. A year after the passage of the Patriot Act, Congress, in the Homeland Security Act of 2002, Pub L. 107–296, § 225(h)(1) amended 18 U.S.C. § 2703(e) to provide that:

> No cause of action shall lie in any court against any provider of wire or electronic communication service, its officers, employees, agents, or other specified persons for providing information, facilities, or assistance in accordance with the terms of a court order, warrant, subpoena, *statutory authorization* . . .

Thus, a provider who discloses records or other information pursuant to the authorization contained in 18 U.S.C. § 2702(c)(4) in emergency circumstances has the same protection from lawsuits as a provider who discloses the records pursuant to a court order.

In his opposition, plaintiff contends that the Anderson police acted in a conspiracy to illegally obtain evidence by misstating the facts on a Sprint PCS form claiming plaintiff was wanted for kidnapping. Plaintiff further challenges the legality of the form such that it could have been sufficient to permit Sprint to divulge his personal information, including call logs, GPS locations, and social security number "without legal oversight or a warrant."

Sprint is correct that plaintiff's allegations regarding any claimed conspiracy by law enforcement is irrelevant to plaintiff's claim against Sprint. To the extent that Sprint's actions came within the provision of 18 U.S.C. § 2702(c)(4), on the face of it, under § 2703(e), Sprint should be dismissed with prejudice as a defendant.

NOTES AND QUESTIONS

1. Disclosure of customer-related records by public providers is forbidden under § 2702 unless one of the statutory exceptions applies. The exceptions appear in § 2702(b) for contents and § 2702(c) for non-content records. Some of the § 2702 exceptions mirror analogous exceptions in the Wiretap Act. For example, the SCA has a consent exception, *see* § 2702(b)(3) (contents), § 2702(c)(2) (non-content records), and also has a provider exception,

see § 2702(b)(5) (contents), § 2702(c)(3) (non-content records). Presumably these exceptions have the same meaning in the context of the SCA that they have in the context of the Wiretap Act.

2.   The *Jayne* case applies the emergency exception in § 2702 that is somewhat analogous to the exigent circumstances exception to the Fourth Amendment's warrant requirement. The emergency exception permits disclosure "to a governmental entity, if the provider, in good faith, believes that an emergency involving danger of death or serious physical injury to any person requires disclosure without delay of [communications or information] relating to the emergency." 18 U.S.C. § 2702(b)(8) (contents), § 2702(c)(4) (non-content records).

Do you think Sprint had a good faith belief that an emergency involving danger of death or serious bodily injury required disclosure without delay of Jayne's records? Is Sprint entitled to rely on the representation of law enforcement officers that an emergency exists? In other words, does receipt of the "exigent circumstances request/demand" resolve Sprint of all liability? Or must Sprint inquire as to the basis of the government's belief?

3.   *The NSA Call Records Program.* In 2006, the *USA Today* revealed the existence of a classified program of the National Security Agency (NSA) that involved collecting the customer call records of the largest telephone companies, AT & T, Verizon and BellSouth. *See* Leslie Caulie, *NSA Has Massive Database of Americans' Phone Calls*, USA Today, May 11, 2006. The NSA approached the telephone companies shortly after the September 11, 2001 attacks and asked the companies to disclose their call records to the NSA. According to *USA Today*, "the agency made an urgent pitch: National security is at risk, and we need your help to protect the country from attacks." *Id.* The NSA reportedly told the companies that the call records would be very helpful to track terrorists in the United States and to prevent another terrorist attack. The companies then disclosed many millions of call records to the NSA.

Did the phone companies' disclosures violate § 2702(c)(4)? Was the disclosure lawful on the ground that the phone companies had a good faith belief that an "emergency involving danger of death or serious physical injury to any person required disclosure without delay of information relating to the emergency"?

4.   Section 2702(b)(7) contains an exception for contents that is roughly analogous to the Fourth Amendment's plain view exception. It states that the disclosure of contents is permitted "to a law enforcement agency ... if the contents (i) were inadvertently obtained by the service provider; and (ii) appear to pertain to the commission of a crime." 18 U.S.C. § 2702(b)(7). This exception permits a system administer to disclose evidence of crime to law enforcement if he happens to come across such evidence in the course of his usual duties.

5.   Perhaps the most unique exceptions in § 2702 are the reporting requirements in § 2702(b)(6) and § 2702(c)(5) involving reports to the National Center for Missing and Exploited Children mandated by 47 U.S.C. § 13032. 47 U.S.C. § 13032 imposes a reporting requirement on public

providers of ECS and RCS for evidence relating to child exploitation and child pornography crimes:

> Whoever, while engaged in providing an electronic communication service or a remote computing service to the public, through a facility or means of interstate or foreign commerce, obtains knowledge of facts or circumstances from which a violation of section 2251, 2251A, 2252, 2252A, 2252B, or 2260 of Title 18, involving child pornography (as defined in section 2256 of that title), or a violation of section 1466A of that title, is apparent, shall, as soon as reasonably possible, make a report of such facts or circumstances to the Cyber Tip Line at the National Center for Missing and Exploited Children, which shall forward that report to a law enforcement agency or agencies designated by the Attorney General.

47 U.S.C. § 13032(b)(1).

6. Section 2702 does not prohibit the disclosure of non-content records when the disclosure is to a non-governmental entity. *See* 18 U.S.C. § 2702(a)(3). This provision allows providers to sell non-content user data to marketers without triggering liability under the SCA.

7. *Who can consent to voluntary disclosure under § 2702?* The voluntary disclosure provisions of § 2702 assign the right to consent to disclosure based on the nature of the service and whether the disclosure involves contents or non-content information. In the case of contents held by an ECS, the right to consent is held by "the originator or an addressee or intended recipient of such communication." In the case of contents held by an RCS, the right to consent is held by the "subscriber." In the case of non-content information, the right to consent is held by "the customer or subscriber." 18 U.S.C. § 2702(b)(3) (contents), § 2702(c)(2) (non-content records).

In some cases, it can be tricky to identify exactly who has the right to consent. Consider Flagg v. City of Detroit, 252 F.R.D. 346 (E.D. Mich. 2008), a civil discovery dispute involving text messages sent between Detroit Mayor Kwame Kilpatrick and his former Chief of Staff Christine Beatty on their city-issued SkyTel pagers. The plaintiff, Flagg, attempted to obtain the messages directly from the City of Detroit, even though the files were stored with the provider, SkyTel. Whether the messages were discoverable from the City ended up hinging on who had the right to control consent to disclose the messages pursuant to § 2702.

The City argued that SkyTel was acting as a provider of ECS. As a result, the City had no control over the messages: the rights to consent were held by Kilpatrick and Beatty as "the originator or an addressee or intended recipient of such communication." Flagg responded that the City had the right to control access to the messages because SkyTel was a provider of RCS, not ECS. As a result, the proper question was not who was the "originator" or "addressee" but rather who was the account "subscriber." Both Flagg and the City agreed that the City was the "subscriber" because it had purchased the pagers and provided them to Kilpatrick and Beatty.

The district court held that given the specific facts of the case, SkyTel was acting as a provider of RCS. The City had the right to consent and to control access to the text messages under § 2702 and the messages were therefore discoverable from the City. *Id.* at 363. The court added that even if SkyTel was acting as a provider of ECS, Kilpatrick and Beatty had likely consented to the disclosure pursuant to workplace monitoring rules in effect at their office. Even if they had the right to control their access to the messages, they had impliedly waived that right and consented to the disclosure. *Id.* at 365–66.

8. The SCA presupposes a sharp line between compelled disclosure (covered by § 2703) and voluntary disclosure (covered by § 2702). However, the line can be hazy in practice. For example, a police officer might ask a provider if he is interested in disclosing voluntarily; the sysadmin might agree only because he feels compelled to do so. Alternatively, a sysadmin may want to disclose voluntarily, but may ask for a subpoena to be served so the ISP's lawyers have some legal process for their records. Should such cases be analyzed under § 2702, § 2703, or both?

The line between § 2702 and § 2703 was a central issue in Freedman v. America Online, 303 F. Supp.2d 121 (D. Conn. 2004). In *Freedman,* two police officers were investigating a threatening AOL e-mail, and they wanted to know who had sent the e-mail. The officers filled out a state warrant application seeking the identity of the subscriber and faxed it to AOL without the warrant being signed by a judge. AOL complied with the warrant form and disclosed the plaintiff's identity. The plaintiff sued, contending that the use of an unsigned warrant violated § 2703. The officers first contended that they had not violated § 2703 because they had merely requested disclosure, not actually required it. The court disagreed:

> Defendants' argument that they merely requested but did not require AOL to disclose the information is disingenuous and does not absolve them from liability under the ECPA. The ECPA imposes an obligation on governmental entities to follow specific legal processes when seeking such information. 18 U.S.C. § 2703(c). Congress designed such procedures to both (1) protect personal privacy against unwarranted government searches and (2) preserve the legitimate needs of law enforcement. To conclude that Defendants did not act improperly upon merely requesting such information without following the ECPA procedural safeguards ignores the fact that a request accompanied by a court form has substantial resemblance to a compulsory court order. The deficiency would have excused AOL from complying. In what was submitted Young and Bensey clearly intended that AOL supply the information sought. That AOL responded was nothing less than what was intended and cannot be found to be otherwise. To hold that AOL was less than expected, i.e. required to respond, would erode Congress's intended protection in the ECPA and would undermine personal privacy rights. In soliciting the information from AOL, Defendants knew, or should have known, that AOL was requested to violate the ECPA. Even if AOL acted without lawful authority in disclosing the information, this does not absolve Defendants from unlawfully requesting or soliciting AOL's disclosure. Putting the burden and obligation on *both* the government and ISPs is consistent with Congress's intent to protect personal privacy. Violation by one does not excuse the other.

Id. at 127. The officers next claimed that AOL's disclosure did not violate the SCA because AOL may have disclosed the information of their own accord. The officers speculated that AOL employees may have realized that the threat under investigation was an emergency, and that they had acted voluntarily under § 2702(c)(4). Once again, the court disagreed:

> The government may not circumvent the legal process specified in the ECPA pursuant to the "emergency" exception on such a speculative basis. This is not a situation where, on its own initiative, AOL voluntarily disclosed Plaintiff's subscriber information to the government. Instead, the government's request, submitted with an invalid warrant, triggered AOL's response, six days later. The Court declines to speculate whether it would ever be appropriate, under exigent circumstances when it would not be feasible to get a signed warrant or comply with other legal process, for the government to notify the ISP of an emergency and receive subscriber information without conforming with the ECPA.

Id. at 128. Do you think such emergency disclosures should fall under § 2702 or § 2703?

9. In McVeigh v. Cohen, 983 F.Supp. 215 (D.D.C. 1998), a Navy Lieutenant who was a member of the JAG Corps was investigating the sexual orientation of a Naval serviceman named McVeigh under the policy commonly known as "Don't Ask, Don't Tell." An AOL profile for the screenname "boysrch" indicated that the account holder for "boysrch" was gay, and the Lieutenant had reason to believe that McVeigh owned the "boysrch" account. The Lieutenant asked another serviceman to contact AOL and determine if the AOL screenname belonged to McVeigh. The serviceman called AOL's customer service number and falsely claimed to be a third party in receipt of a fax sheet who needed confirmation that the AOL profile belonged to McVeigh. The AOL representative fell for the serviceman's ruse and affirmatively identified McVeigh as the owner of "boysrch."

Did AOL's disclosure violate the SCA? If so, what section was violated, and who violated it?

10. Imagine that a public ISP is hacked, and a system administrator at the ISP conducts warrantless monitoring of the intrusions under exceptions to the Wiretap Act and Pen Register statute. The ISP wishes to disclose the evidence to the FBI for criminal prosecution. Assuming that the monitoring and disclosure comply with the Pen Register statute and the Wiretap Act, does the disclosure automatically satisfy the SCA?

The proper answer is "no," although as a practical matter the SCA will bar disclosures in such cases only very rarely. The SCA will permit the disclosure in the great majority of cases for three possible reasons.

The first reason is that the disclosure prohibitions in § 2702 only regulate records that "pertain[ ] to a subscriber to or customer of such service." 18 U.S.C. § 2702(a)(3). That is, the SCA only limits the disclosure of information and communications belonging or referring to individual legitimate subscribers. In the case of a computer intrusion, the records an ISP might wish to disclose usually won't pertain to a legitimate subscriber, and thus § 2702 does not bar the disclosure. Hackers may have some rights against monitoring under the Wiretap Act and the Pen Register statute, but they have no rights against disclosure under § 2702 of the Stored Communications Act.

Second, if the ISP wishes to disclose records relating to a customer who is not implicated in the unlawful activity, the ISP can disclose the materials with the customer's consent. *See* 18 U.S.C. § 2702(b)(3) (contents), § 2702(c)(2) (non-content records). For example, if a hacker guesses Sarah's password and uses her account to engage in criminal activity, Sarah can consent to the disclosure of her account information to law enforcement.

Finally, § 2702 permits disclosure that is "necessarily incident . . . to the rights or property" of the ISP, which will often permit the disclosure. *See* 18 U.S.C. § 2702(b)(5) (contents), § 2702(c)(5) (non-content records).

11. *Problem.* An anonymous person puts up a website purporting to be authored by you. The website contains a number of false and misleading statements about you. You contact the service provider that hosts the site, and you ask the representative to tell you the name and contact information for the subscriber who set up and posted the site. Does 18 U.S.C. § 2702 apply, and if so, how? Can the service provider disclose the information to you voluntarily? What can you do to compel the host to disclose the information? As a matter of policy, what law should govern such situations?

12. The Stored Communications Act does not include a statutory suppression remedy. *See* 18 U.S.C. §§ 2707–08. What remedy should Congress impose for violations of 18 U.S.C. § 2702? When the provider errs instead of the government, is an exclusionary rule appropriate? If the only remedy is civil liability, who should be liable: the government or the providers? Should the answer be the same for § 2702 and § 2703 violations?

D. PROBLEMS

In each of the following problems, consider whether the investigation violated any of the statutory privacy laws or the Fourth Amendment.

PROBLEM ONE

You are a law student at Kennedy University. You find out that someone is using your Gmail e-mail account without your permission and is sending out all sorts of e-mails in your name. You suspect that this "someone" is fellow law student Fred Rowley, your arch enemy, who uses an e-mail account frowley@law.kennedy.edu.

You contact the FBI for help. An FBI agent calls both Gmail and the computer center at Kennedy University asking for their help to catch Fred. Both are eager to help. The contact at Gmail agrees to send the FBI all of the stored e-mails and account records relating to your account, and the system administrator at Kennedy University agrees to do the same with Fred's stored e-mails and account records.

The system administrator at Kennedy University also agrees to monitor Rowley's account prospectively, albeit in a limited way. He writes a program that logs the IP address of every login to Rowley's account and sends the results to the FBI every few days to keep the FBI informed of Rowley's whereabouts.

When all the e-mails and records are in, however, it turns out that Rowley is not the individual who is using your account.

PROBLEM TWO

John Jefferson is a system administrator for an online auction site, www.better-than-ebay.com. One day, Jefferson notices that the server is acting strangely, and he suspects that the site may have been accessed by an intruder. Jefferson pulls up the server logs and quickly sees that yes, a hacker coming in from the IP address 152.163.159.233 had connected to the network a few hours earlier. Jefferson knows that this IP address is controlled by the ISP MindThink, and concludes that someone using a MindThink account hacked into his network.

Jefferson is terribly worried. He decides that he will try to catch the intruder in the act the next time and watch his every move. Jefferson installs a sniffer on his network and configures it to record all incoming information originating from any IP address belonging to MindThink. Whenever any MindThink user connects to www.better-than-ebay.com, the sniffer will record everything.

Over the course of the next few days, the sniffer collects a tremendous amount of data unrelated to the hacking, including thousands of requests for webpages and hundreds of messages sent to www.better-than-ebay.com by MindThink subscribers who are legitimate users of the auction site. The sniffer also picks up the hacker re-entering the auction site server. The sniffer records the commands that the hacker entered, enabling Jefferson to reconstruct that the hacker broke in to the network, looked around, and then read opened and unopened e-mail of the auction site employees who have work e-mail accounts stored on the auction site server.

Jefferson contacts the FBI, and speaks with FBI Special Agent Mary Markley. Jefferson tells Markley what happened and volunteers to send Markley copies of all of the documents he has collected. Markley agrees and opens a criminal investigation into the computer intrusion incident. Jefferson sends Markley copies of all of the logs, the entire output of the sniffer, and the employee e-mails stored on the server belonging to www.better-than-ebay.com.

PROBLEM THREE

FBI Special Agent Free Louis is undercover in an America Online chatroom called "helikesthemyoung," using the screenname "britney14f." An individual in the chat room who uses the screenname "FunTimeinCA" sends an instant message to "britney14f" asking if she "likes to party with older men."

Special Agent Louis suspects that the person who controls "FunTimeinCA" is a pedophile in possession of child pornography. To confirm his suspicions, Louis serves a subpoena on AOL ordering AOL to disclose a) the name and billing address on file associated with the screenname "FunTimein-CA," b) any additional screennames associated with the account, and c) any images of child pornography stored as an attachment in any e-mail sent from or to that account that is stored with AOL.

An AOL employee receives the subpoena and attempts to comply with it. First, he accesses AOL's computer and prints out a page containing all of the basic subscriber information listed in 18 U.S.C. § 2703(c)(2) relating to the "FunTimeinCA" account. The page includes the alternative screennames associated with the "FunTimeinCA" account.

The AOL employee then looks through the stored e-mail in the account. The AOL employee finds nine images of what appear to be child pornography. He sends a fax to Special Agent Louis containing the page of basic subscriber information and the nine images.

CHAPTER 7

JURISDICTION

■ ■ ■

Traditional crimes usually occur in a single jurisdiction. The evidence is collected locally, and charges are brought under state criminal codes. Computer crimes are different. The borderless Internet makes jurisdictional issues routine. In most computer crime cases, the defendant, intermediaries, and the victim are located in different states—and sometimes in different countries. The Internet is borderless but the law is not, resulting in complex questions of both substantive and procedural law.

This chapter considers the jurisdictional questions that arise frequently in computer crime cases. The first part of the chapter considers the role of federal law. Does the borderless nature of the Internet make all computer crime law federal computer crime law? What are the limits on federal power to regulate computer crimes?

The second part turns to the role of the states in the enforcement of computer crime law. What powers do states have to prohibit interstate computer crimes? How are state authorities governing the collection of digital evidence different from analogous federal authorities? How can state investigators collect digital evidence located beyond state borders?

The third part of the chapter turns to international computer crimes. When is an international computer crime a violation of United States law? Procedurally, what laws govern the collection of evidence outside the United States needed for computer crime prosecutions inside the United States? What laws govern the collection of evidence inside the United States for prosecutions abroad?

As you read these materials, consider the role of uniformity. The borderless Internet exerts strong pressures toward uniform computer crime laws. Uniform laws simplify both the investigation and prosecution of criminal activity. Is uniformity desirable? What are the alternatives?

A. FEDERAL POWER

This book has focused largely on federal law; the materials in this section will help explain why. Congress has almost limitless power to regulate computer crimes, and statutory jurisdictional hurdles usually are easy to meet. This section considers the limits of federal criminal law in domestic computer crime investigations. It analyzes three questions: First, what constitutional limits exist on the ability of Congress to punish computer crimes in the United States? Second, what evidence is required to establish statutory jurisdictional hooks, such as interstate commerce requirements? Third, what procedural limits exist on how federal investigators can gather digital evidence located in different states?

1. CONSTITUTIONAL LIMITS

Most federal computer crimes have been enacted under the Congressional power "[t]o regulate Commerce ... among the several States" granted by Article I, Section 8, Clause 3 of the United States Constitution. The Supreme Court has construed the Commerce Clause power very broadly. United States v. Lopez, 514 U.S. 549, 558–59 (1995), explains the three basic types of conduct that can be regulated under the Commerce Clause:

> First, Congress may regulate the use of the channels of interstate commerce. Second, Congress is empowered to regulate and protect the instrumentalities of interstate commerce, or persons or things in interstate commerce, even though the threat may come only from intrastate activities. Finally, Congress's commerce authority includes the power to regulate those activities having a substantial relation to interstate commerce, i.e., those activities that substantially affect interstate commerce.

Federal statutes that regulate the telephone network and the Internet are generally covered by the first and second categories, as interstate communications networks are considered both channels and instrumentalities of interstate commerce. As the Eleventh Circuit emphasized in United States v. Hornaday, 392 F.3d 1306, 1311 (11th Cir. 2004):

> The Internet is an instrumentality of interstate commerce. Congress clearly has the power to regulate the Internet, as it does other instrumentalities and channels of interstate commerce, and to prohibit its use for harmful or immoral purposes regardless of whether those purposes would have a primarily intrastate impact.

See also United States v. Gilbert, 181 F.3d 152 (1st Cir. 1999) (holding that the telephone network is an instrumentality of interstate commerce, even when a specific call in question is intrastate); United States v. Carnes, 309 F.3d 950 (6th Cir. 2002) (upholding the Wiretap Act as a valid regulation of interstate commerce because "telecommunications are both channels and instrumentalities of interstate commerce"); United States v. Mitra, 405 F.3d 492, 496 (7th Cir. 2005) ("Section 1030 is within the national power as applied to computer-based channel-switching communications systems."). Such broad readings of the Commerce Clause give Congress broad and unquestioned authority to regulate interstate computer networks and the Internet.

The harder questions arise in cases that involve stand-alone computers. For example, the child pornography laws prohibit producing or possessing child pornography images within one state when the images are "produced using materials that have been mailed, or shipped or transported" in interstate commerce. 18 U.S.C. § 2252(a)(4)(B), § 2252A(a)(5)(B), and § 2251(a). The law does not require that the images have been transported in interstate commerce, or that they have been distributed or received over the Internet. Rather, it generally prohibits the storage of images on the ground that the materials used to produce the images have themselves been transported in interstate commerce. Is this prohibition within the scope of Congressional power?

UNITED STATES v. JERONIMO–BAUTISTA

United States Court of Appeals for the Tenth Circuit, 2005.
425 F.3d 1266.

Seymour, Circuit Judge.

Virgilio Jeronimo–Bautista was indicted, in part, for coercing a minor to engage in sexually explicit conduct "for the purpose of producing visual depictions of such conduct using materials that have been transported in interstate and foreign commerce," in violation of 18 U.S.C. § 2251(a). The district court dismissed the charge, concluding that as applied to Mr. Jeronimo–Bautista, § 2251(a) exceeded Congress's authority under the Commerce Clause. The government appeals, and we reverse.

I

While Mr. Jeronimo–Bautista asserts he is actually innocent, for the purposes of our review * * * we make all factual inferences in favor of the government, assuming it could prove the facts alleged against Mr. Jeronimo–Bautista at a trial. Accordingly, for the purposes of this appeal only, we assume the following facts.

On January 29, 2004, Mr. Jeronimo–Bautista and two other men, while in the company of a thirteen year-old girl, entered a vacant residence in Magna, Utah. At some point the girl became unconscious, possibly after ingesting an intoxicating substance. After she lost consciousness, the three men removed her clothing, sexually assaulted her, and took photographs of their actions. The camera used to take the photographs was not manufactured in the state of Utah.

One of the men took the film to a one-hour photo lab for processing. In the course of developing the film, staff at the lab noticed images that appeared to depict the sexual assault of a minor female. The manager of the lab called the police, who viewed the photographs and then initiated an investigation resulting in the arrest and indictment of Mr. Jeronimo–Bautista. As noted by the district court, it was undisputed that Mr. Jeronimo–Bautista was a citizen of Mexico and resided in the State of Utah. The victim was born in Utah and was not transported across state lines in connection with the acts charged in the indictment. Moreover, the photos were never disseminated, were not stored or transmitted electronically via the Internet, the United States Postal Service, nor by any other method across state lines or internationally.

The indictment charged that Mr. Jeronimo–Bautista, along with the two other men, did knowingly employ, use, persuade, induce, entice, and coerce a minor to engage in sexually explicit conduct for the purpose of producing visual depictions of such conduct, which visual depictions were produced using materials that have been mailed, shipped, and transported in interstate and foreign commerce, and did aid and abet each other therein, thereby violating § 2251(a) (production of child pornography) and 18 U.S.C. § 2 (aiding and abetting). Mr. Jeronimo–Bautista moved to dismiss the indictment on the ground that the district court did not have subject matter jurisdiction over the acts charged against him, contending § 2251(a) violated the Commerce Clause as applied to him. The district court agreed, concluding that Mr. Jeronimo–Bautista's charged activity "was not of a type demonstrated to be substantially connected or related to interstate commerce." This case is now before us on the government's appeal.

II

The United States Constitution grants to Congress the power to regulate Commerce among the several States. U.S. Const. art I, § 8, cl. 3. As relevant here, "Congress's commerce authority includes the power to regulate those activities having a substantial relation to interstate commerce, i.e., those activities that substantially affect interstate commerce." *United States v. Lopez*, 514 U.S. 549, 558–59 (1995). Hence we must determine whether Mr. Jeronimo–Bautista's local production of pornographic images of a child substantially affects interstate commerce.

In addressing Mr. Jeronimo–Bautista's as applied challenge to the statute, the district court noted the four factors delineated by the Supreme Court in *United States v. Morrison*, 529 U.S. 598 (2000), and in *Lopez* for consideration in addressing the constitutionality of a statute based upon Commerce Clause authority. The court accurately described those factors as (1) whether the prohibited activity is commercial or economic in nature; (2) whether the statute's reach was limited by an express jurisdictional element; (3) whether Congress made findings about the effects of the prohibited conduct on interstate commerce; and (4) whether there exists a link between the prohibited conduct and the effect on interstate commerce.

Working its way through the *Lopez/Morrison* factors, the district court first rejected the argument that Mr. Jeronimo–Bautista's activity was economic in nature and, in doing so, rejected the assertion that Mr. Jeronimo–Bautista's intrastate activities could, in the aggregate, affect interstate commerce. Second, the court determined § 2251(a)'s express jurisdictional element failed to place any meaningful restrictions on federal jurisdiction and failed to establish the link between the violation and interstate commerce. Third, the court was not convinced the existence of

Congressional findings regarding the child pornography industry was sufficient, by itself, to sustain the constitutionality of Commerce Clause legislation as applied to the facts of this case. Finally, referring back to its determination that Mr. Jeronimo–Bautista's activity could not be deemed economic in nature, the court also rejected the use of an aggregation theory to support the argument that there existed something more than only a tenuous link between Mr. Jeronimo–Bautista's prohibited activity and interstate commerce. The court dismissed the indictment against Mr. Jeronimo–Bautista on the grounds that as applied to the specific facts of his case, § 2251(a) violated the Commerce Clause.

Pending this appeal, the Supreme Court decided *Gonzales v. Raich*, 545 U.S. 1 (2005), in which it rejected an as applied challenge to the Controlled Substances Act (CSA), 21 U.S.C. § 801 *et seq.*, and held that Congress could regulate the purely local production, possession, and use of marijuana for personal medical purposes. As we discuss in more detail below, the Court's reasoning in *Raich*, coupled with the standard four factor *Lopez/Morrison* analysis, supports our conclusion that the district court erred in concluding § 2251(a) violates the Commerce Clause as applied to Mr. Jeronimo–Bautista.

We begin by examining the findings accompanying the comprehensive scheme developed by Congress to eliminate the production, possession, and dissemination of child pornography. When Congress first passed the Protection of Children Against Sexual Exploitation Act of 1977, it noted "that child pornography has become a highly organized, multimillion dollar industry that operates on a nationwide scale and that the sale and distribution of such pornographic materials are carried on to a substantial extent through the mails and other instrumentalities of interstate and foreign commerce." S. Rep. No. 95–438, at 5 (1977), *reprinted in* 1978 U.S.C.C.A.N. 40, 42–43. Findings supporting the 1977 Act also noted that

> since the production, distribution and sale of child pornography is often a clandestine operation, it is extremely difficult to determine its full extent. At present, however, a wide variety of child pornography is available in most areas of the country. Moreover, because of the vast potential profits involved, it would appear that this sordid enterprise is growing at a rapid rate.

Id. at 43.

Amendments to the Act in 1984 eliminated the requirement that the production, receipt, transportation, or distribution of child pornography be for a pecuniary profit. The purpose of this amendment was to eliminate an enforcement gap in the statute: "Many of the individuals who distribute materials covered by the statute do so by gift or exchange without any commercial motive and thus remain outside the coverage of this provision." H.R. Rep. No. 98–536, at 2 (1983), *reprinted in* 1984 U.S.C.C.A.N. 492, 493. Likewise, in 1984, in support of § 2251, Congress echoed its findings supporting the original 1977 legislation, stating in part that "child pornography has developed into a highly organized, multi-million-dollar industry which operates on a nationwide scale." H.R. 3635, 98th Cong. (2nd Sess. 1984).

In 1996, Congress further amended the Act regarding the electronic creation of child pornography. The findings supporting those amendments noted that "the existence of child pornographic images inflames the desires of child molesters, pedophiles, and child pornographers who prey on children, thereby increasing the creation and distribution of child pornography." S. Rep. No. 104–358, at 2 (1996). Congress also stated that "prohibiting the possession and viewing of child pornography will encourage the possessors of such material to rid themselves of or destroy the material, thereby helping to protect the victims of child pornography and to eliminate the market for the sexual exploitative use of children." *Id.* at 3. Finally, in a 1998 amendment to the Act, a jurisdictional element was added to cover child pornography created "using materials that have been mailed, shipped, or transported in interstate or foreign commerce by any means." § 2251(a). This addition reflected Congress's concern about federal law enforcement's current inability to prosecute 'a number of cases where the defendant produced the child pornography but did not intend to transport the images in interstate commerce.

In reviewing this history, we acknowledge that Congress may not have engaged in specific fact finding regarding how the intrastate production of child pornography substantially affects the larger interstate pornography market. But the Supreme Court noted in *Raich*, 545 U.S. at 21, that it has "never required Congress to make particularized findings in order to legislate." Moreover, we agree with our colleagues on the First Circuit that Congress's explicit findings regarding the extensive national market in child pornography and the need to diminish that national market support the contention that prohibiting the production of child pornography at the local level helps to further the Congressional goal.

The decision in *Raich* also supports the conclusion that Mr. Jeronimo–Bautista's production of the images in this case is economic in nature. "Economics refers to the production, distribution, and consumption of commodities." *Raich*, 545 U.S. at 25. The Court held that the Controlled Substances Act "is a statute that regulates the production, distribution, and consumption of commodities for which there is an established, and lucrative, interstate market. Prohibiting the intrastate possession or manufacture of an article of commerce is a rational (and commonly utilized) means of regulating commerce in that product." *Id.* at 26. The same reasoning is applicable to the intrastate production of child pornography. Like the CSA, the child pornography statutes regulate the production, distribution, and consumption of commodities for which there is an established, and lucrative, interstate market. Congress's prohibition against the intrastate possession or manufacture of child pornography is a rational (and commonly utilized) means of regulating commerce in that product.

In holding that a sufficient link existed between the local production and use of marijuana and its effect on interstate commerce, the Court in *Raich* relied extensively on *Wickard v. Filburn*, 317 U.S. 111 (1942). In *Wickard*, the Court upheld the Agriculture Adjustment Act of 1938, 52 Stat. 31, which permitted congressional regulation of a farmer's wholly intrastate production and consumption of wheat on his farm. *Wickard* "establishes that Congress can regulate purely intrastate activity that is not itself 'commercial,' in that it is not produced for sale, if it concludes that failure to regulate that class of activity would undercut the regulation of the interstate market in that commodity." *Raich*, 545 U.S. at 18. The Court noted that

> in *Wickard*, we had no difficulty concluding that Congress had a rational basis for believing that, when viewed in the aggregate, leaving home-consumed wheat outside the regulatory scheme would have a substantial influence on price and market conditions. Here too, Congress had a rational basis for concluding that leaving home-consumed marijuana outside federal control would similarly affect price and market conditions.

Id. at 19. It viewed its task as not to determine whether respondents' activities, taken in the aggregate, substantially affect interstate commerce in fact, but only whether a 'rational basis' exists for so concluding.

Dismissing arguments that regulation of locally cultivated and possessed marijuana was beyond the "outer limits" of Congress's Commerce Clause authority, the Court observed:

> one need not have a degree in economics to understand why a nationwide exemption for the vast quantity of marijuana (or other drugs) locally cultivated for personal use (which presumably would include use by friends, neighbors, and family members) may have a substantial impact on the interstate market for this extraordinarily popular substance. The congressional judgment that an exemption for such a significant segment of the total market would undermine the orderly enforcement of the entire regulatory scheme is entitled to a strong presumption of validity.

Id. Finally, noting the "findings in the CSA and the undisputed magnitude of the commercial market for marijuana, the decisions in *Wickard v. Filburn* and the later cases endorsing its reasoning," the Court concluded Congress could regulate the "intrastate, noncommercial cultivation, possession and use of marijuana." *Id.* at 32–33.

This reasoning applies to the child pornography statute at issue here. Under the aggregation theory espoused in *Wickard* and in *Raich*, the intrastate production of child pornography could, in the aggregate, have a substantial effect on the interstate market for such materials. In *Raich*, the respondents were "cultivating, for home consumption, a fungible commodity for which there was an established, albeit illegal, interstate market." *Id.* at 18. Child pornography is equally fungible and there is no question an established market exists for its sale and exchange. The Court in *Raich* reasoned that where there is a high demand in the interstate market for a product, the exemption from regulation of materials produced intrastate "tends to frustrate the federal interest in eliminating commercial transactions in the interstate market in their entirety." *Id.* at 19. For the same reasons, § 2251(a) is squarely within Congress's commerce power because production of the commodity meant for home consumption, be it wheat, marijuana, or child pornography has a substantial effect on supply and demand in the national market for the commodity.

Mr. Jeronimo–Bautista is challenging the statute's constitutionality as applied to him. The Court in *Raich* held the plaintiffs' as applied challenges to the CSA failed because the Court had no difficulty concluding that Congress acted rationally in determining that the intrastate, noncommercial, cultivation, possession, and use of marijuana for personal medical uses, whether viewed individually or in the aggregate, did not compel an exemption from the CSA. * * * So too in Mr. Jeronimo–Bautista's case. Congress's decision to deem illegal Mr. Jeronimo–Bautista's local production of child pornography represents a rational determination that such local activities constitute an essential part of the interstate market for child pornography that is well within Congress's power to regulate.

NOTES AND QUESTIONS

1. Can you distinguish the market in marijuana at issue in *Gonzales v. Raich* from the market for child pornography images at issue in this case?

2. Federal child pornography laws prohibit producing or possessing child pornography images within one state when the images are "produced using materials that have been mailed, or shipped or transported" in interstate commerce. 18 U.S.C. § 2252(a)(4)(B), § 2252A(a)(5)(B), and § 2251(a). Is this jurisdictional hook constitutionally required? Under *Gonzales v. Raich*, as interpreted in *Jeronimo–Bautista*, could Congress remove this requirement and simply prohibit possessing images of child pornography?

3. Is any computer crime beyond the Commerce Clause power? Can you envision any criminal activity involving any kind of computer that cannot be regulated by the federal government?

2. SUBSTANTIVE STATUTORY LIMITS

As the preceding materials suggest, Congress has virtually plenary authority to punish computer-related activity in the United States. Most statutes do not go this far. Federal computer crime statutes often impose some kind of statutory interstate requirement that the government must satisfy in each prosecution.

UNITED STATES v. KAMMERSELL

United States Court of Appeals for the Tenth Circuit, 1999.
196 F.3d 1137.

PAUL KELLY, JR., CIRCUIT JUDGE.

Defendant–Appellant Matthew Joseph Kammersell entered a conditional guilty plea to a charge of transmitting a threatening communication in interstate commerce, in violation of 18 U.S.C. § 875(c). Upon recommendation of the magistrate judge, the district court rejected Mr. Kammersell's contention that federal jurisdiction did not exist because both he and the recipient of the threat were located in the same state when the transmission occurred. He was sentenced to four months imprisonment, and twenty-four months supervised release. Our jurisdiction arises under 28 U.S.C. § 1291 and we affirm.

Background

The facts in this case are undisputed. On January 16, 1997, Mr. Kammersell, then nineteen years old, logged on to the Internet service provider America OnLine from his home computer in Riverdale, Utah. Mr. Kammersell's girlfriend was employed at AOL's service center in Ogden, Utah. He sent a bomb threat to her computer terminal via instant message, hoping that the threat would enable her to leave work early so they could go on a date.

When he sent the bomb threat, it was automatically transmitted through interstate telephone lines from his computer in Utah to the AOL server in Virginia and then back to Utah to his girlfriend's terminal at the Ogden service center. Every message sent via AOL automatically goes from the state of origin to AOL's main server in Virginia before going on to its final destination. This pattern of transmission is the same whether the communication is an electronic mail message or an instant message.

Mr. Kammersell does not contest that the threat traveled out of Utah to Virginia before returning to Utah. Nor does he contest that his message constituted a sufficient "threat" to trigger § 875(c). His only claim is that the jurisdictional element of § 875(c) cannot be met if based solely on the route of the transmission, where the sender and recipient are both in the same state.

Discussion

The district court's refusal to dismiss the case on jurisdictional grounds was based upon its interpretation of § 875(c), therefore, its conclusion is reviewed de novo. Section 875(c) provides:

> Whoever transmits in interstate or foreign commerce any communication containing any threat to kidnap any person or any threat to injure the person of another, shall be fined under this title or imprisoned not more than five years, or both.

This provision was enacted in 1934, and its last significant amendment was in 1939. At that time, the telegraph was still the primary mode of interstate communication.

Mr. Kammersell argues that the statute must be interpreted in light of the sweeping changes in technology over the past 60 years and with reference to Congressional intent. The government urges the court to adhere to the plain meaning of the statute; because Mr. Kamersell's threat was transmitted from Utah to Virginia to Utah, it was "transmitted in interstate commerce." Because so many local telephone calls and locally-sent Internet messages are routed out of state, under the government's interpretation, federal jurisdiction would exist to cover almost any communication made by telephone or modem, no matter how much it would otherwise appear to be intrastate in nature. Mr. Kammersell argues that such an interpretation will immeasurably broaden federal criminal jurisdiction without any discussion by Congress of the matter, and it would be wrong to view sixty years of Congressional inaction on the statute as clear intent.

This may be a compelling argument that Congress should re-examine the statute, but it cannot remove Mr. Kammersell from the reach of the current statute. A federal court must give effect to the will of Congress, and where its will has been expressed in reasonably plain terms, that language must ordinarily be regarded as conclusive. As long as the statutory scheme is coherent and consistent, there generally is no need for a court to inquire beyond the plain language of the statute. A threat that was unquestionably transmitted over interstate telephone lines falls within the literal scope of the statute and gives rise to federal jurisdiction.

Mr. Kammersell argues that the threat should not be considered as transmitted interstate because only the recipient could have viewed this instant message. An instant message can only be sent if the recipient is online at the time of transmission, whereas an e-mail may be held in a holding center until it is retrieved. According to Mr. Kammersell, this distinction is crucial because it means that no one outside of the State of Utah could have seen the threat. The distinction, even if correct, is immaterial. No requirement exists under § 875(c) that the threat actually be received or seen by anyone out of state. The gravamen of the crime is the threat itself.

The "instant message" distinction does enable Kammersell to distinguish the primary case upon which the Government relies, but in the end this does not help him either. Because this is a case of first impression, both sides must rely on analogies. The Government relies upon *United States v. Kelner,* 534 F.2d 1020 (2d Cir. 1976). There, the defendant was convicted under § 875(c) for threatening to assassinate Yasser Arafat during a television interview that was broadcast over three states. Both the defendant and Arafat were in New York at the time the threat was made. Like Mr. Kammersell, Kelner argued that the nexus of his activity was predominantly local, and that the statute should not be read literally to reach into spheres of primarily local concern. In upholding Kelner's conviction, the court noted:

> However much we might agree as a matter of principle that the congressional reach should not be overextended or that prosecutorial discretion might be exercised more frequently to permit essentially local crimes to be prosecuted locally, we do not feel that Congress is powerless to regulate matters in commerce when the interstate features of the activity represent a relatively small, or in a sense unimportant, portion of the overall criminal scheme. Our problem is not whether the nexus of the activity is "local" or "interstate"; rather, under the standards which we are to apply, so long as the crime involves a necessary interstate element, the statute must be treated as valid.

Id at 1024. While *Kelner* can be distinguished on the ground that it involved a transmission that was seen by people in more than one state, the Second Circuit's logic remains just as cogent when applied to the current case.

Finally, Mr. Kammersell contends that, based on the spirit of the Supreme Court's decision in *United States v. Lopez,* 514 U.S. 549 (1995), federal jurisdiction is inappropriate in this case. "*Lopez* stands for the proposition that Congress may not limitlessly expand the federal criminal jurisdiction based on the commerce clause," and "after *Lopez* the constitutionality of assertions of federal jurisdiction over what are essentially local crimes must be closely scrutinized." Aplt. Br. at 34. Yet, we cannot overlook plain language in favor of the "spirit" of *Lopez,* particularly given the difference between the deficient statute in *Lopez,* 18 U.S.C. § 922(q)(1)(A), and § 875(c). The deficient statute in *Lopez* did not require an interstate jurisdictional nexus. *See Lopez,* 514 U.S. at 561 (noting that statute does not contain a requirement that would ensure that the firearm possession in question would affect interstate commerce). Because § 875(c) requires the use of a channel of interstate commerce, it is not subject to the same limiting interpretation as *Lopez.*

NOTES AND QUESTIONS

1.   The federal interstate threat statute is phrased in general terms. It covers "any communication" transmitted in interstate or foreign commerce. Under *Kammersell,* this means that the scope of the statute depends on the technical details of the network. If AOL configured its networks so that the instant message stayed inside Utah, the federal statute apparently would not apply. But AOL's technical decision to route all IMs through Virginia seems to ensure that all IMs are covered by the federal statute (except those from one person in Virginia to another person in Virginia). Does this make sense? Should the communication's physical path make a difference?

2.   Should it matter whether Matthew Kammersell knew that the instant message he sent traveled out of Utah in the course of delivery? According to

one news report, Kammersell was a former employee of AOL. The prosecutor in the case argued that Kammersell presumably knew that his threat traveled to Virginia and back in the course of delivery. *See* Sheila R. McCann, '*Net Threat A Federal Offense?; Prosecutors Argue It Crossed State Lines*, Salt Lake Trib. Oct. 14, 1997, at A1. In other cases, however, the defendant may have no idea that his communication is going to travel interstate. Should the defendant's awareness of the interstate nexus make a difference?

The general rule is that when a federal criminal statute is based on the Commerce Clause power, knowledge of an interstate nexus is not required as matter of statutory law. *See* United States v. Darby, 37 F.3d 1059, 1067 (4th Cir. 1994); United States v. Blackmon, 839 F.2d 900, 907 (2d Cir. 1988). Cases involving telephone calls illustrate the principle. In United States v. Francis, 975 F.Supp. 288 (S.D.N.Y. 1997), *rev'd on other grounds*, 164 F.3d 120 (2d Cir. 1999), the defendant placed several telephone calls from Santa Cruz, California, to San Francisco, California. The victim did not pick up the call, and the defendant left threatening messages for the victim on his voicemail. Unbeknownst to the defendant, the defendant had implemented a "call forwarding" feature on his telephone, and the messages were automatically routed to New York instead of to San Francisco. The district court held that the calls satisfied the jurisdictional nexus because they had been sent from California and were received in New York. *See id.* at 291–92.

An unpublished decision, United States v. Veliz, 2004 WL 964005 (S.D.N.Y. 2004), reflects a similar dynamic. Veliz called Arreaga's cell phone from New York and threatened to kill him. Although Arreaga's cell phone was registered to a New York-area number, Arreaga answered the call when he was in Palm Beach, Florida. The Court refused to dismiss the indictment on jurisdictional grounds, noting that the call had originated in New York and had been received in Florida.

3.   Assuming Kammersell's conduct fell within the federal threat statute, we are still left with the interesting question of why he was prosecuted. The full text of the bomb threat is unknown, as is the reaction of AOL to the threat. One news clip on Kammersell's arrest makes the threat seem fairly innocuous. According to that report, the threat included the following:

> You should really check out those new keyboards, if you know what I mean, . . . We are sick of your censorship and bad service. You can kiss your assess [sic] goodbye.

High–Tech Bomb Scare, Salt Lake Trib, March 8, 1997, at B2.

Following his conviction and sentencing to four months in prison, Kammersell was interviewed by a reporter and had the following comment:

> I do recognize what I did was wrong . . . I just think this is going too far for a prank. It's like putting me in front of a firing squad for throwing an apple.

Ray Rivera, *Cyber–Prank Earns Prison Term*, Salt Lake Trib., October 16, 1998, at D6. Why do you think Kammersell was prosecuted?

UNITED STATES v. LEWIS

United States Court of Appeals for the First Circuit, 2009.
554 F.3d 208.

Howard, Circuit Judge.

A jury convicted Andrew Lewis of one count of receipt of child pornography in violation of 18 U.S.C. § 2252(a)(2), in connection with ten videos found on his home computer. Lewis now argues that the evidence was insufficient to convict him, pointing in particular to the "interstate commerce" element of the crime and claiming that the government presented no evidence to satisfy this element.

I. Facts

Andrew Lewis came to the attention of federal law enforcement in connection with some "inappropriate" images discovered on a computer on the grounds of the Salem Maritime National Historic Site, where Lewis worked as a United States Park Ranger. He was later indicted for receipt of child pornography in connection with other videos he admitted downloading to his computer at home.

Forensic analysis of Lewis's home computer revealed that the videos had likely been downloaded using Lewis's Comcast Internet connection and a peer-to-peer file-sharing application called LimeWire. The government presented expert testimony about Lewis's computer and the software; the expert witness conceded on cross-examination that it is possible a given file transfer made using LimeWire might have been conducted entirely within the borders of one state.

The government sought, and Lewis objected to, a jury instruction that stated, "If you find that the video images were transmitted or received over the Internet, that is sufficient to find that the images moved or traveled in interstate or foreign commerce." The district court agreed with the government and gave a substantially similar instruction: "An image has been shipped or transported in interstate commerce if it has been transmitted over the Internet." Lewis objected both before and after the instruction was given.

The jury asked one question of the district court during its deliberations: "If a file is transported exclusively within a single state on the Internet, is that considered interstate commerce?" After consultation, and over further objection by Lewis, the district court answered the question in the affirmative. A little more than one hour later, the jury returned its guilty verdict.

II. Discussion

It is undisputed that Lewis knowingly possessed video files of child pornography, and that he procured those files using his computer, the Internet and LimeWire. The sole question is whether the government met its burden to prove that the videos had been "shipped or transported in interstate or foreign commerce."

The government introduced evidence, and Lewis did not contest, that he downloaded the images using the Internet. Lewis, however, contends that § 2252(a)(2) requires the actual shipment or communications of the images across state lines. And, he continues, the mere fact that he used the Internet is insufficient to prove the images crossed state lines.

The government first challenges Lewis's operating assumption—that § 2252(a)(2) requires actual shipment or communication of the images across state lines. The government makes two distinct arguments. First, it argues that no actual crossing of a state or national border is necessary— the statute should be read, the government says, to require only transmission or shipment in the "stream" or "flow" of commerce. Second, the government argues that even if the statute incorporates a general requirement of actual interstate movement, transmission or shipment by computer should be considered differently than other kinds of shipment or transmission. In that medium, the government argues, the jurisdictional requirement of the statute should be relaxed. We find neither argument convincing.

In making its first argument—that the statute does not require proof of actual shipment or communication across a border—the government contends that Congress intended to reach purely intrastate transmission of child pornography that used a channel or instrumentality of interstate commerce. But this is not what the statute says. "Congress uses different modifiers to the word 'commerce' in the design and enactment of its statutes." *Circuit City Stores v. Adams*, 532 U.S. 105, 115 (2001). "The word 'involving,' like 'affecting,' signals an intent to exercise Congress's commerce power to the full. Unlike those phrases, however, the general words 'in commerce' and the specific phrase 'engaged in commerce' are understood to have a more limited reach." *Id.*

The interstate commerce requirement at issue here is like that of many other criminal statutes. *See, e.g.*, 18 U.S.C. § 1343 ("Whoever ... transmits or causes to be transmitted by means of wire, radio, or television communication in interstate or foreign commerce [the relevant materials shall be guilty of a crime].""); *Id.* § 2314 (subjecting to criminal liability "[w]hoever transports, transmits, or transfers in interstate or foreign commerce" the items subject to the statute). These provisions, too, have long been held to require actual crossing of a state or national border. *See, e.g., United States v. Cassiere*, 4 F.3d 1006, 1011 (1st Cir. 1993) (elements of § 1343 include "the use of interstate wire communications"); First Circuit Pattern Jury Instructions, § 4.20 (actual interstate movement required for § 2314). The government, then, cannot excise completely the requirement that the child pornography cross a state or national border. To hold otherwise would do violence to the plain language of the statute and fly in the face of practice, including that of the government itself, with regard to this and a host of similarly worded statutes.

The government's second argument attempts to create a distinction between items that are "shipped or transported" using a computer, and those that are "shipped or transported" using other means. While we concede that it is possible Congress meant to make purely intrastate transmission by computer of these materials into a federal crime, by the plain language of the statute, it did not do so. We are therefore constrained from altering the statute based on our assumptions about what Congress wanted.

Having concluded that § 2252(a)(2) *does* require that the government prove actual interstate transmission or shipment of the images, we turn to the government's next argument—that it proved interstate transmission occurred in this case because the prosecution introduced evidence that Lewis used the Internet. In support of this argument the government cites *United States v. Carroll*, 105 F.3d 740 (1st Cir. 1997). After close review of *Carroll*, we agree with the government that Lewis' sufficiency claim must fail.

In *Carroll*, we addressed whether there was sufficient evidence to convict the defendant of violating 18 U.S.C. § 2251(a) which criminalizes the production of child pornography, "if such person knows or has reason to know that such visual depiction will be transported in interstate or foreign commerce by any means, including by computer." We cited three different ways the government had satisfied the interstate transmission element of the statute. One of them was by presenting evidence that the defendant planned to use the photographs he took as illustrations for a "dating service" site on the Internet. We wrote, "transmission of photographs by means of the Internet is tantamount to moving photographs across state lines and thus constitutes transportation in interstate commerce."

We conclude that the government proved the images traveled interstate when it introduced evidence that Lewis received images that were transmitted over the Internet.

Lewis argues that, unlike in this case, in *Carroll* there was other, "substantial evidence" of interstate movement. True, we identified other grounds for our holding in *Carroll*. For example, we noted that the defendant told an individual that he intended to take film across state lines. Nevertheless, that alternative grounds existed for our holding fails to detract from our express conclusion that the use of the Internet in that case was enough, standing alone, to satisfy the jurisdictional element.

For the sake of completeness, we should note that Congress recently amended the child pornography statutes, including the one before us, to expand the jurisdictional coverage. It did so by replacing all instances of "in interstate" with "in or affecting interstate" commerce. Effective Child Pornography Prosecution Act of 2007, Pub.L. No. 110–358, § 103. The legislative history indicates that Congress was unhappy with circuit court decisions narrowly construing the prior statute and wanted to put issues like ours to rest. *See* 153 Cong. Rec. H13591–92 (daily ed. Nov. 13, 2007) (statement of Rep. Conyers); *id.* at H13592 (statement of Rep. Goodlatte). Despite these recent developments, this case is governed by the statute as written at the time of Lewis's conduct, and our interpretation rests only on the law as it stood at that time.

NOTES AND QUESTIONS

1. Is use of the Internet really "tantamount" to interstate commerce? What if a person happens to use the Internet in a way that did not actually involve the crossing of state lines? For example, a person in Los Angeles could log on to his ISP in San Francisco and then visit a website in San Diego. Is this merely *intra*state transmission, or is it interstate transmission? Alternatively, does the low likelihood of this happening, paired with the difficulty of reconstructing the path of an Internet communication, justify the *Lewis/Carroll* rule that use of the Internet is "tantamount" to having communications cross state lines?

Notably, the Tenth Circuit has expressly disagreed with the view that transmission over the Internet automatically satisfies the requirement of interstate commerce. The Tenth Circuit recognized the low chances that an Internet communication did not cross state lines, but concluded that the Government must still satisfy its burden that this did in fact occur. United States v. Schaefer, 501 F.3d 1197, 1205 (10th Cir. 2007) ("We decline to assume that Internet use automatically equates with a movement across state lines. With respect to such interstate movement, the government must introduce sufficient evidence to satisfy its burden of proof.").

2. *The Effective Child Pornography Prosecution Act of 2007.* The last paragraph of *Lewis* notes that Congress amended the federal child pornography statutes in 2007 to eliminate the statutory jurisdictional threshold as part of the Effective Child Pornography Prosecution Act of 2007, Pub. L. No. 110–358. Congress resolved the disagreement between cases like *Lewis* and cases like *Schaefer* by taking an even more expansive view of federal power. In particular, the 2007 Act replaced the jurisdictional requirement "in interstate or foreign commerce" with the new requirement "using any means or facility of interstate or foreign commerce or in or affecting interstate or foreign commerce."

When Congress uses the phrase "affecting interstate commerce," that is generally understood to express Congress's intent to regulate as far as the Commerce Clause will allow. *See* Russell v. United States, 471 U.S. 858, 859 (1985) (noting that prohibition regulating conduct "affecting interstate or foreign commerce" expresses "an intent by Congress to exercise its full power under the Commerce Clause"); Scarborough v. United States, 431 U.S. 563, 571 (1977) ("Congress is aware of the distinction between legislation limited to activities 'in commerce' and an assertion of its full Commerce Clause power so as to cover all activity substantially affecting interstate commerce."). When Congress uses the jurisdictional hook of "affecting interstate commerce," or its close cousin "affecting interstate or foreign commerce," the scope of the jurisdictional hook is defined by constitutional limitations on the Commerce Clause.

After the Effective Child Pornography Prosecution Act of 2007, and considering cases like Gonzales v. Raich, 545 U.S. 1 (2005), and United States v. Jeronimo–Bautista, 425 F.3d 1266 (10th Cir. 2005), are there now *any* jurisdictional limits on the federal child pornography laws?

3. *Jurisdictional hurdles in 18 U.S.C. § 1030 cases.* The 2007 amendment of the child pornography laws is part of a broader trend. In recent years, Congress has tended to minimize or even eliminate the interstate jurisdictional requirements in computer crime statutes.

Consider the amendments to the meaning of the term "protected computer" in 18 U.S.C. § 1030. From 1996 to 2001, the meaning of the term "protected computer" included a computer "which is used in interstate or foreign commerce or communication." In 2001, as part of the USA Patriot Act, Congress expanded that definition. The 2001 version stated that a "protected computer" includes a computer

> which is used in interstate or foreign commerce or communication, *including a computer located outside the United States that is used in a manner that affects interstate or foreign commerce or communication of the United States.*

18 U.S.C. § 1030(e)(2)(B) (2001) (with language added in 2001 in italics). In 2008, Section 207 of the Vice President Protection Act expanded this definition to the scope of Congress's commerce power. The new version states that a "protected computer" is a computer

> which is used in *or affecting* interstate or foreign commerce or communication, including a computer located outside the United States that is used in a manner that affects interstate or foreign commerce or communication of the United States.

18 U.S.C. § 1030(e)(2)(B) (2001) (with language added in 2008 in italics). The new language is somewhat awkward, but the use of the phrase "affecting" appears to express Congress's intent to extend the scope of 18 U.S.C. § 1030 to any computer that could be regulated under the Commerce Clause. In other words, a "protected computer" is *any* computer that can be regulated by Congress's power to regulate interstate commerce as a matter of constitutional law.

4. As a matter of normative policy, what limits should Congress impose on the scope of federal computer crimes? Should Congress regulate all computer crimes, no matter how local, and then permit the proper division of federal and state power to be drawn as a matter of prosecutorial discretion? Or should Congress carve out a category of local computer crimes that are beyond the reach of federal law enforcement authorities?

5. A number of federal crimes regulate conduct within "the special maritime and territorial jurisdiction of the United States." *See, e.g.*, 18 U.S.C. § 2252(a)(3)(A), § 2252(a)(4)(A). This phrase is defined in 18 U.S.C. § 7, and it mostly refers to places owned by the United States government such as United States military bases and federal parks.

The meaning of "special maritime and territorial jurisdiction" has particular importance under the Assimilative Crimes Act, 18 U.S.C. § 13. The Assimilative Crimes Act makes it a federal crime to violate a state criminal law within "the special maritime and territorial jurisdiction of the United States." As the name of the Act suggests, the statute assimilates state law, in effect federalizing the law of the home state. Here is the relevant text:

> Whoever within or upon any of the places now existing or hereafter reserved or acquired as provided in [18 U.S.C. § 7] * * * is guilty of any act or omission which, although not made punishable by any enactment of Congress, would be punishable if committed or omitted within the jurisdiction of the State, Territory, Possession, or District in which such place is situated, by the laws thereof in force at the time of such act or omission, shall be guilty of a like offense and subject to a like punishment.

18 U.S.C. § 13(a).

The Assimilative Crimes Act can be used in computer crime cases when a state's computer crime laws are broader than federal law. For example, if a person on a United States military base commits a computer-related offense that violates state law, the person can be charged in federal court under the federal Assimilated Crimes Act based on the state law violation. *Cf.* United States v. Smith, 47 M.J. 588 (N.M. Ct. Crim. App. 1997) (charging defendant on a military base in North Carolina with violations of the Assimilative Crimes Act for showing another person images of child pornography in violation of North Carolina state law).

3. PROCEDURAL STATUTORY LIMITS

Statutory limits on the scope of federal power can also impact the investigatory powers of federal agents. This can occur in two ways. First, the scope of statutory prohibitions can exclude some intrastate conduct by federal officials. Second, statutory limits can determine where federal officials must obtain court orders needed to collect digital evidence.

A) Statutory Privacy Laws

Although the Fourth Amendment regulates federal investigators at all times, statutory laws that contain an interstate commerce requirement can have a more limited scope. When a federal statute regulates criminal investigations and includes an interstate requirement, intrastate conduct by federal officials may not trigger the statute's prohibitions.

The interstate requirements of statutory privacy laws have arisen in a number of cases involving the Wiretap Act. In United States v. Scarfo, 180 F. Supp.2d 572 (D.N.J. 2001), FBI investigators secretly placed a Key Logger System (KLS) inside the defendant's computer. To avoid implicating the Wiretap Act, the KLS was programmed to record the defendant's keystrokes only when the computer was not connected to the Internet. After the KLS recorded the defendant's passphrase, leading to proof of the defendant's criminal activity, the defendant argued that the evidence could not be used against him because it was obtained without a wiretap order. The Court rejected the defendant's argument on the ground that the design of the KLS placed it outside the scope of the Wiretap Act:

[T]he Court finds that the KLS technique * * * did not intercept any wire communications and therefore did not violate the wiretap statute, Title III, 18 U.S.C. § 2510. I am satisfied the KLS did not operate during any period of time in which the computer's modem was activated.

* * * Recognizing that Scarfo's computer had a modem and thus was capable of transmitting electronic communications via the modem, the F.B.I. configured the KLS to avoid intercepting electronic communications typed on the keyboard and simultaneously transmitted in real time via the communication ports. * * * Hence, when the modem was operating, the KLS did not record keystrokes. It was designed to prohibit the capture of keyboard keystrokes whenever the modem operated. Since Scarfo's computer possessed no other means of communicating with another computer save for the modem, the KLS did not intercept any wire communications. Accordingly, the Defendants' motion to suppress evidence for violation of Title III is denied.

Id. at 581–82.[1]

The jurisdictional scope of the Wiretap Act also arose in United States v. Ropp, 347 F. Supp.2d 831 (C.D. Cal. 2004). Ropp installed a keystroke monitoring device called a "KeyKatcher" on the workplace computer of Karen Beck. The KeyKatcher was connected to the cable between Beck's keyboard and computer, and recorded all of Beck's keystrokes, including messages typed as part of e-mails she sent. Ropp was indicted for violating the Wiretap Act, but Judge Feess dismissed the indictment on the ground that the keystroke monitoring device had merely recorded impulses inside Beck's computer:

[T]he Court concludes that the communication in question is not an "electronic communication" within the meaning of the statute because it is not transmitted by a system that affects interstate or foreign commerce. The "system" involved consists of the local computer's hardware—the Central Processing Unit, hard drive and peripherals (including the keyboard)—and one or more software programs including the computer's operating system (most likely some version of Microsoft Windows although other possibilities exist), and either an e-mail or other communications program being used to compose messages. Although this system is connected to a larger system—the network—which affects interstate or foreign commerce, the transmission in issue did not involve that system. The network connection is irrelevant to the transmissions, which could have been made on a stand-alone computer that had no link at all to the internet or any other external network. Thus, although defendant engaged in a

---

1. Note that the defendant's argument also should have failed because Title III does not include a suppression remedy for the interception of electronic communications.

gross invasion of privacy by his installation of the KeyKatcher on Ms. Beck's computer, his conduct did not violate the Wiretap Act.

Id. at 837–38.

Ropp suggests that the government would not need a Wiretap order to install a similar device; a standard probable cause warrant under the Fourth Amendment would suffice. On the other hand, was *Ropp* correctly decided? The definition of "electronic communication" covers "any transfer * * * transmitted in whole or in part by a wire, radio, electromagnetic, photoelectronic or photooptical system that affects interstate or foreign commerce." 18 U.S.C. § 2510(12). If a computer is connected to a network, isn't the "system" the network as a whole rather than the individual computer?

B) National Versus Local Orders

A second limit on the scope of federal power concerns the enforcement of federal orders that cross state or district lines. When federal investigators wish to obtain a court order, must they obtain the order in the district where the evidence is stored? Or can they obtain an order in one state permitting the collection of evidence in another state?

Most federal statutes permit the federal government to obtain a court order in one state or district for evidence in another state or district. For example, federal subpoenas are nationwide in scope. *See generally* Weinberg v. United States, 126 F.2d 1004, 1008 (2d Cir. 1942) (citing American Lithographic Co. v. Werckmeister, 221 U.S. 603 (1911)). As a result, a federal prosecutor in state *A* can serve a subpoena on an ISP in state *B*, and the ISP must comply with the out-of-state federal subpoena.

Court orders obtained under the Pen Register statute and 18 U.S.C. § 2703(d) of the Stored Communications Act also are nationwide in scope. 18 U.S.C. § 3121(a) of the Pen Register statute states that pen/trap orders "authoriz[e] the installation and use of a pen register or trap and trace device anywhere within the United States." Similarly, the text of § 2703(d) provides that "any court that is a court of competent jurisdiction" may issue the order, and 18 U.S.C. § 2711(3) establishes that this includes "any Federal court * * * without geographic limitation."

Federal search warrants present a somewhat different picture. Search warrants for physical evidence ordinarily must be obtained in the district where the physical evidence is located. Some exceptions exist. Federal Rule of Criminal Procedure 41(b) states:

> (1) a magistrate judge with authority in the district—or if none is reasonably available, a judge of a state court of record in the district—has authority to issue a warrant to search for and seize a person or property located within the district;

> (2) a magistrate judge with authority in the district has authority to issue a warrant for a person or property outside the district if the person or property is located within the district when the warrant is

issued but might move or be moved outside the district before the warrant is executed;

(3) a magistrate judge—in an investigation of domestic terrorism or international terrorism—with authority in any district in which activities related to the terrorism may have occurred has authority to issue a warrant for a person or property within or outside that district;

(4) a magistrate judge with authority in the district has authority to issue a warrant to install within the district a tracking device; the warrant may authorize use of the device to track the movement of a person or property located within the district, outside the district, or both; and

(5) a magistrate judge having authority in any district where activities related to the crime may have occurred, or in the District of Columbia, may issue a warrant for property that is located outside the jurisdiction of any state or district, but within any of the following:

(A) a United States territory, possession, or commonwealth;

(B) the premises—no matter who owns them—of a United States diplomatic or consular mission in a foreign state, including any appurtenant building, part of a building, or land used for the mission's purposes; or

(C) a residence and any appurtenant land owned or leased by the United States and used by United States personnel assigned to a United States diplomatic or consular mission in a foreign state.

See Fed. R. Crim. Pro. 41(b) (as amended 2009).

Search warrants for electronic evidence obtained to satisfy 18 U.S.C. § 2703(a) can be nationwide in scope. Prior to the passage of the USA Patriot Act in 2001, Section 2703(a) required warrants to be obtained in the district where the evidence was located. Section 220 of the USA Patriot Act, titled "Nationwide Service of Search Warrants for Electronic Evidence," amended 18 U.S.C. § 2703(a) to specify that search warrants obtained to satisfy that section must be obtained "using the procedures described in the Federal Rules of Criminal Procedure by a court with jurisdiction over the offense." The Justice Department intended this amendment to permit nationwide warrants obtained under 18 U.S.C. § 2703(a). Any court with an open investigation into the offense has "jurisdiction over the offense," and federal courts in those districts should be able to issue § 2703(a) warrants "using the procedures described" in Rule 41.

Finally, Title III intercept orders obtained under 18 U.S.C. § 2518 can be obtained in the state where the tap is placed or where the investigators who will review the collected evidence are located. While the statute authorizes a district judge to approve "interception within the territorial jurisdiction of the court in which the judge is sitting," 18 U.S.C.

§ 2518(3), courts have held that the situs of an interception is where it is first heard and understood by human ears. *See, e.g.,* United States v. Rodriguez, 968 F.2d 130, 136 (2d Cir. 1992). As a result, use of a monitoring device in state *A* that pipes data to officials located in state *B* is an intercept in state *B* for purposes of the statute, and officers can obtain a Wiretap order in state *B* even though the device is installed in state *A*.

B. STATE POWER

Congress has virtually plenary power to regulate computer-related crimes, and most federal court orders can be obtained with nationwide effect. State powers are quite different. State officials face considerable substantive and procedural barriers to the successful investigation and prosecution of computer crimes. The materials that follow start with substantive law, and in particular the limits imposed on state efforts to regulate interstate computer crimes imposed by the so-called "dormant" Commerce Clause. The materials then turn to procedural laws, and study the procedural hurdles faced by state computer crime investigators. As you read these materials, keep this question in mind: What role can states play in the enforcement of computer crime laws?

1. SUBSTANTIVE LIMITS

AMERICAN LIBRARY ASSOCIATION v. PATAKI

United States District Court for the Southern District of New York, 1997.
969 F.Supp. 160.

PRESKA, DISTRICT JUDGE.

The plaintiffs in the present case filed this action challenging New York Penal Law § 235.21(3). Plaintiffs contend that the Act is unconstitutional * * * because it unduly burdens interstate commerce in violation of the Commerce Clause. For the reasons that follow, the motion for a preliminary injunction is granted.

The Act in question amended N.Y. Penal Law § 235.21 by adding a new subdivision. The amendment makes it a crime for an individual:

> Knowing the character and content of the communication which, in whole or in part, depicts actual or simulated nudity, sexual conduct or sado-masochistic abuse, and which is harmful to minors, to intentionally use any computer communication system allowing the input, output, examination or transfer, of computer data or computer programs from one computer to another, to initiate or engage in such communication with a person who is a minor.

Violation of the Act is a Class E felony, punishable by one to four years of incarceration. The Act applies to both commercial and non-commercial disseminations of material.

Section 235.20(6) defines "harmful to minors" as:

that quality of any description or representation, in whatever form, of nudity, sexual conduct, sexual excitement, or sado-masochistic abuse, when it:

(a) Considered as a whole, appeals to the prurient interest in sex of minors; and

(b) Is patently offensive to prevailing standards in the adult community as a whole with respect to what is suitable material for minors; and

(c) Considered as a whole, lacks serious literary, artistic, political and scientific value for minors.

N.Y. Penal Law § 235.20(6). The statute provides six defenses to liability. First, Section 235.15(1) provides the following affirmative defense to prosecution under § 235.21(3):

In any prosecution for obscenity, or disseminating indecent material to minors in the second degree in violation of subdivision three of section 235.21 of this article, it is an affirmative defense that the persons to whom the allegedly obscene or indecent material was disseminated, or the audience to an allegedly obscene performance, consisted of persons or institutions having scientific, educational, governmental or other similar justification for possessing, disseminating or viewing the same.

The statute further provides four regular defenses to prosecution:

(a) The defendant made a reasonable effort to ascertain the true age of the minor and was unable to do so as a result of the actions taken by the minor; or

(b) The defendant has taken, in good faith, reasonable, effective and appropriate actions under the circumstances to restrict or prevent access by minors to materials specified in such subdivision, which may involve any appropriate measures to restrict minors from access to such communications, including any method which is feasible under available technology; or

(c) The defendant has restricted access to such materials by requiring use of a verified credit card, debit account, adult access code or adult personal identification number; or

(d) The defendant has in good faith established a mechanism such that the labeling, segregation or other mechanism enables such material to be automatically blocked or screened by software or other capabilities reasonably available to responsible adults wishing to effect such blocking or screening and the defendant has not otherwise solicited minors not subject to such screening or blocking capabilities to access that material or circumvent any such screening or blocking.

N.Y. Penal Law § 235.23(3). And, finally, Section 235.24 provides that no individual shall be held liable:

> solely for providing access or connection to or from a facility, system, or network not under that person's control, including transmission, downloading, intermediate storage, access software, or other related capabilities that are incidental to providing such access or connection that do not include the creation of the content of the communication.

N.Y. Penal Law § 235.24.

The borderless world of the Internet raises profound questions concerning the relationship among the several states and the relationship of the federal government to each state, questions that go to the heart of "our federalism."

The unique nature of the Internet highlights the likelihood that a single actor might be subject to haphazard, uncoordinated, and even outright inconsistent regulation by states that the actor never intended to reach and possibly was unaware were being accessed. Typically, states' jurisdictional limits are related to geography; geography, however, is a virtually meaningless construct on the Internet. The menace of inconsistent state regulation invites analysis under the Commerce Clause of the Constitution, because that clause represented the framers' reaction to overreaching by the individual states that might jeopardize the growth of the nation—and in particular, the national infrastructure of communications and trade—as a whole.

The Commerce Clause is more than an affirmative grant of power to Congress. As long ago as 1824, Justice Johnson in his concurring opinion in *Gibbons v. Ogden,* 9 Wheat. 1, 231–32 (1824), recognized that the Commerce Clause has a negative sweep as well. In what commentators have come to term its negative or "dormant" aspect, the Commerce Clause restricts the individual states' interference with the flow of interstate commerce in two ways. The Clause prohibits discrimination aimed directly at interstate commerce, and bars state regulations that, although facially nondiscriminatory, unduly burden interstate commerce. Moreover, courts have long held that state regulation of those aspects of commerce that by their unique nature demand cohesive national treatment is offensive to the Commerce Clause.

Thus, as will be discussed in more detail below, the New York Act is concerned with interstate commerce and contravenes the Commerce Clause for three reasons. First, the Act represents an unconstitutional projection of New York law into conduct that occurs wholly outside New York. Second, the Act is invalid because although protecting children from indecent material is a legitimate and indisputably worthy subject of state legislation, the burdens on interstate commerce resulting from the Act clearly exceed any local benefit derived from it. Finally, the Internet is one of those areas of commerce that must be marked off as a national preserve to protect users from inconsistent legislation that, taken to its most extreme, could paralyze development of the Internet altogether. Thus, the

Commerce Clause ordains that only Congress can legislate in this area, subject, of course, to whatever limitations other provisions of the Constitution (such as the First Amendment) may require.

A. The Act Concerns Interstate Commerce

At oral argument, the defendants advanced the theory that the Act is aimed solely at intrastate conduct. This argument is unsupportable in light of the text of the statute itself, its legislative history, and the reality of Internet communications. The section in question contains no such limitation; it reads:

A person is guilty of disseminating indecent material to minors in the second degree when: * * *

(3) Knowing the character and content of the communication which, in whole or in part, depicts actual or simulated nudity, sexual conduct or sado-masochistic abuse, and which is harmful to minors, he intentionally uses any computer communication system allowing the input, output, examination or transfer, of computer data or computer programs from one computer to another, to initiate or engage in such communication with a person who is a minor.

N.Y. Penal Law § 235.21(3). Section 235.20, which contains the definitions applicable to the challenged portion of the Act, does not import any restriction that the criminal communication must take place entirely within the State of New York. By its terms, the Act applies to any communication, intrastate or interstate, that fits within the prohibition and over which New York has the capacity to exercise criminal jurisdiction.

The conclusion that the Act must apply to interstate as well as intrastate communications receives perhaps its strongest support from the nature of the Internet itself. The Internet is wholly insensitive to geographic distinctions. In almost every case, users of the Internet neither know nor care about the physical location of the Internet resources they access. Internet protocols were designed to ignore rather than document geographic location; while computers on the network do have "addresses," they are logical addresses on the network rather than geographic addresses in real space.

Moreover, no aspect of the Internet can feasibly be closed off to users from another state. An internet user who posts a Web page cannot prevent New Yorkers or Oklahomans or Iowans from accessing that page and will not even know from what state visitors to that site hail. Nor can a participant in a chat room prevent other participants from a particular state from joining the conversation. Someone who uses a mail exploder is similarly unaware of the precise contours of the mailing list that will ultimately determine the recipients of his or her message, because users can add or remove their names from a mailing list automatically. Thus, a person could choose a list believed not to include any New Yorkers, but an after-added New Yorker would still receive the message.

The New York Act, therefore, cannot effectively be limited to purely intrastate communications over the Internet because no such communications exist. No user could reliably restrict her communications only to New York recipients. Moreover, no user could avoid liability under the New York Act simply by directing his or her communications elsewhere, given that there is no feasible way to preclude New Yorkers from accessing a Web site, receiving a mail exploder message or a newsgroup posting, or participating in a chat room. Similarly, a user has no way to ensure that an e-mail does not pass through New York even if the ultimate recipient is not located there, or that a message never leaves New York even if both sender and recipient are located there.

The courts have long recognized that railroads, trucks, and highways are themselves "instruments of commerce," because they serve as conduits for the transport of products and services. The Internet is more than a means of communication; it also serves as a conduit for transporting digitized goods, including software, data, music, graphics, and videos which can be downloaded from the provider's site to the Internet user's computer.

The inescapable conclusion is that the Internet represents an instrument of interstate commerce, albeit an innovative one; the novelty of the technology should not obscure the fact that regulation of the Internet impels traditional Commerce Clause considerations. The New York Act is therefore closely concerned with interstate commerce, and scrutiny of the Act under the Commerce Clause is entirely appropriate. As discussed in the following sections, the Act cannot survive such scrutiny, because it places an undue burden on interstate traffic, whether that traffic be in goods, services, or ideas.

B. New York Has Overreached by Enacting a Law That Seeks to Regulate Conduct Occurring Outside its Borders

The interdiction against direct interference with interstate commerce by state legislative overreaching is apparent in a number of the Supreme Court's decisions. In *Baldwin v. G.A.F. Seelig, Inc.,* 294 U.S. 511, 521 (1935), for example, Justice Cardozo authored an opinion enjoining enforcement of a law that prohibited a dealer from selling within New York milk purchased from the producer in Vermont at less than the minimum price fixed for milk produced in New York. Justice Cardozo sternly admonished, "New York has no power to project its legislation into Vermont by regulating the price to be paid in that state for milk," finding that "such a power, if exerted, would set a barrier to traffic between one state and another as effective as if customs duties, equal to the price differential, had been laid upon the thing transported." *Id.*

In the present case, a number of witnesses testified to the chill that they felt as a result of the enactment of the New York statute; these witnesses refrained from engaging in particular types of interstate commerce. In particular, I note the testimony of Rudolf Kinsky, an artist with a virtual studio on Art on the Net's Website. Mr. Kinsky testified that he removed several images from his virtual studio because he feared prosecution under the New York Act. As described above, no Web siteholder is able to close his site to New Yorkers. Thus, even if Mr. Kinsky were located in California and wanted to display his work to a prospective purchaser in Oregon, he could not employ his virtual studio to do so without risking prosecution under the New York law.

The nature of the Internet makes it impossible to restrict the effects of the New York Act to conduct occurring within New York. An Internet user may not intend that a message be accessible to New Yorkers, but lacks the ability to prevent New Yorkers from visiting a particular Website or viewing a particular newsgroup posting or receiving a particular mail exploder. Thus, conduct that may be legal in the state in which the user acts can subject the user to prosecution in New York and thus subordinate the user's home state's policy—perhaps favoring freedom of expression over a more protective stance—to New York's local concerns. New York has deliberately imposed its legislation on the Internet and, by doing so, projected its law into other states whose citizens use the Net. This encroachment upon the authority which the Constitution specifically confers upon the federal government and upon the sovereignty of New York's sister states is per se violative of the Commerce Clause.

C. The Burdens the Act Imposes on Interstate Commerce Exceed Any Local Benefit

Even if the Act were not a per se violation of the Commerce Clause by virtue of its extraterritorial effects, the Act would nonetheless be an invalid indirect regulation of interstate commerce, because the burdens it imposes on interstate commerce are excessive in relation to the local benefits it confers. The Supreme Court set forth the balancing test applicable to indirect regulations of interstate commerce in *Pike v. Bruce Church,* 397 U.S. 137, 142 (1970). *Pike* requires a two-fold inquiry. The first level of examination is directed at the legitimacy of the state's interest. The next, and more difficult, determination weighs the burden on interstate commerce in light of the local benefit derived from the statute.

In the present case, I accept that the protection of children against pedophilia is a quintessentially legitimate state objective—a proposition with which I believe even the plaintiffs have expressed no quarrel. The defendants spent considerable time in their Memorandum and at argument asserting the legitimacy of the state's interest. Even with the fullest recognition that the protection of children from sexual exploitation is an indisputably valid state goal, however, the present statute cannot survive even the lesser scrutiny to which indirect regulations of interstate commerce are subject under the Constitution. * * *

The local benefits likely to result from the New York Act are not overwhelming. The Act can have no effect on communications originating outside the United States. Further, in the present case, New York's prosecution of parties from out of state who have allegedly violated the Act, but whose only contact with New York occurs via the Internet, is beset with practical difficulties, even if New York is able to exercise criminal jurisdiction over such parties. The prospect of New York bounty hunters dragging pedophiles from the other 49 states into New York is not consistent with traditional concepts of comity.

The Act is, of course, not the only law in New York's statute books designed to protect children against sexual exploitation. The State is able to protect children through vigorous enforcement of the existing laws criminalizing obscenity and child pornography. Moreover, plaintiffs do not challenge the sections of the statute that criminalize the sale of obscene materials to children, over the Internet or otherwise, and prohibit adults from luring children into sexual contact by communicating with them via the Internet. *See* N.Y. Penal Law § 235.21(1); N.Y. Penal Law § 235.22(2). The local benefit to be derived from the challenged section of the statute is therefore confined to that narrow class of cases that does not fit within the parameters of any other law. The efficacy of the statute is further limited, as discussed above, to those cases which New York is realistically able to prosecute.

Balanced against the limited local benefits resulting from the Act is an extreme burden on interstate commerce. The New York Act casts its net worldwide; moreover, the chilling effect that it produces is bound to exceed the actual cases that are likely to be prosecuted, as Internet users will steer clear of the Act by significant margin. At oral argument, the State asserted that only a small percentage of Internet communications are "harmful to minors" and would fall within the proscriptions of the statute; therefore, the State argued, the burden on interstate commerce is small. On the record before me, I conclude that the range of Internet communications potentially affected by the Act is far broader than the State suggests. I note that in the past, various communities within the United States have found works including *I Know Why the Caged Bird Sings* by Maya Angelou, *Funhouse* by Dean Koontz, *The Adventures of Huckleberry Finn* by Mark Twain, and *The Color Purple* by Alice Walker to be indecent.

D. The Act Unconstitutionally Subjects Interstate Use of the Internet to Inconsistent Regulations

Finally, a third mode of Commerce Clause analysis further confirms that the plaintiffs are likely to succeed on the merits of their claim that the New York Act is unconstitutional. The courts have long recognized that certain types of commerce demand consistent treatment and are therefore susceptible to regulation only on a national level. The Internet represents one of those areas; effective regulation will require national, and more likely global, cooperation. Regulation by any single state can only result in chaos, because at least some states will likely enact laws subjecting Internet users to conflicting obligations. Without the limitation's imposed by the Commerce Clause, these inconsistent regulatory schemes could paralyze the development of the Internet altogether.

The Internet * * * requires a cohesive national scheme of regulation so that users are reasonably able to determine their obligations. Regulation on a local level, by contrast, will leave users lost in a welter of inconsistent laws, imposed by different states with different priorities. New York is not the only state to enact a law purporting to regulate the content of communications on the Internet. Already Oklahoma and Georgia have enacted laws designed to protect minors from indecent communications over the Internet; as might be expected, the states have selected different methods to accomplish their aims. Georgia has made it a crime to communicate anonymously over the Internet, while Oklahoma, like New York, has prohibited the online transmission of material deemed harmful to minors. *See* Ga. Code Ann. § 16–19–93.1 (1996); Okla. Stat. tit. 21, § 1040.76 (1996).

Moreover, the regulation of communications that may be "harmful to minors" taking place over the Internet poses particular difficulties. New York has defined "harmful to minors" as including:

> that quality of any description or representation, in whatever form, of nudity, sexual conduct, sexual excitement, or sado-masochistic abuse, when it:
>
> (a) Considered as a whole, appeals to the prurient interest in sex of minors; and
>
> (b) Is patently offensive to prevailing standards in the adult community as a whole with respect to what is suitable material for minors; and
>
> (c) Considered as a whole, lacks serious literary, artistic, political and scientific value for minors.

N.Y. Penal Law § 235.20(6). Courts have long recognized, however, that there is no single "prevailing community standard" in the United States. Thus, even were all 50 states to enact laws that were verbatim copies of the New York Act, Internet users would still be subject to discordant responsibilities.

As discussed at length above, an Internet user cannot foreclose access to her work from certain states or send differing versions of her communication to different jurisdictions. In this sense, the Internet user is in a worse position than the truck driver or train engineer who can steer around Illinois or Arizona, or change the mudguard or train configuration at the state line; the Internet user has no ability to bypass any particular state. The user must thus comply with the regulation imposed by the state with the most stringent standard or forego Internet communication of the message that might or might not subject her to prosecution.

Further development of the Internet requires that users be able to predict the results of their Internet use with some degree of assurance. Haphazard and uncoordinated state regulation can only frustrate the growth of cyberspace. The need for uniformity in this unique sphere of commerce requires that New York's law be stricken as a violation of the Commerce Clause.

NOTES AND QUESTIONS

1. Other courts have agreed with the approach of the *Pataki* decision, and have enjoined similar statutes enacted in other states. *See, e.g.*, American Booksellers Foundation v. Dean, 342 F.3d 96 (2d Cir. 2003) (enjoining a Vermont law); American Civil Liberties Union v. Johnson, 194 F.3d 1149 (10th Cir. 1999) (enjoining a New Mexico law); PSINet, Inc. v. Chapman, 362 F.3d 227 (4th Cir. 2004) (Virginia statute).

2. Does the dormant Commerce Clause require exclusively federal regulation of the Internet? Consider American Booksellers Foundation v. Dean, 342 F.3d 96, 103–04 (2d Cir. 2003), commenting on a Vermont statute similar to the one struck down in *Pataki*:

> Even if a website is never visited by people in Vermont, it is available to them in a way that a beer purchase in New York or Massachusetts is plainly not. Vermont's interest in out-of-state internet activity is thus more significant than a state's interest in the price of out-of-state beer sales. However, internet regulation of the sort at issue here still runs afoul of the dormant Commerce Clause because the Clause protects against inconsistent legislation arising from the projection of one state regulatory regime into the jurisdiction of another State. Thus, at the same time that the internet's geographic reach increases Vermont's interest in regulating out-of-state conduct, it makes state regulation impracticable. We think it likely that the internet will soon be seen as falling within the class of subjects that are protected from State regulation because they imperatively demand a single uniform rule.

For a critical perspective on this "common wisdom," and an argument that the dormant Commerce Clause permits vigorous state regulation of the Internet, see Jack L. Goldsmith & Alan O. Sykes, *The Internet and the Dormant Commerce Clause*, 110 Yale L.J. 785 (2001).

3. *Online solicitation*. In People v. Hsu, 99 Cal.Rptr.2d 184 (Cal. App. 2000), a man in California e-mailed pornographic pictures to a 14 year-old boy in California in an effort to convince the boy to meet him for sexual activities. The defendant was charged with violating California Penal Code § 288.2(b), which prohibits knowingly sending "harmful matter" to a minor with the intent of seducing that minor. A state court rejected the defendant's argument that the statute violated the dormant Commerce Clause:

> Under the *Pike* test, section 288.2, subdivision (b) does not violate the commerce clause. Statutes affecting public safety carry a strong presumption of validity, and the definition and enforcement of criminal laws lie primarily with states. States have a compelling interest in protecting minors from harm generally and certainly from being seduced to engage in sexual activities. Conversely, it is difficult to conceive of any legitimate commerce that would be burdened by penalizing the transmission of harmful sexual material to known minors in order to seduce them. To the extent section 288.2, subdivision (b) may affect interstate commerce, its

effect is incidental at best and far outweighed by the state's abiding interest in preventing harm to minors.

Id. at 983–84. The court distinguished *Pataki* as follows, *id.* at 984–85:

> The knowledge and intent elements missing from the New York statute but present in section 288.2, subdivision (b) significantly distinguish the two statutes. The New York statute broadly banned the communication of harmful material to minors via the Internet. The scope of section 288.2, subdivision (b) is much narrower. Only when the material is disseminated to a *known* minor with the *intent* to arouse the prurient interest of the sender and/or minor and with the *intent* to seduce the minor does the dissemination become a criminal act. The proscription against Internet use for these specifically defined and limited purposes does not burden interstate commerce by subjecting Internet users to inconsistent regulations. As *Pataki* itself observed,* * * New York could realistically prosecute violations of New York Penal Law section 235.22(2), which, like section 288.2, subdivision (b), prohibits adults from luring minors into sexual contact via Internet communication of harmful material, without violating the commerce clause.

> When section 288.2, subdivision (b) is harmonized with the entire California penal scheme, it does not effectively regulate activities beyond California. California prosecutes only those criminal acts that occur wholly or partially within the state. Statutes must be construed in the light of the general principle that, ordinarily, a state does not impose punishment for acts done outside its territory. Section 288.2, subdivision (b) makes no reference to place of performance, so courts must assume the Legislature did not intend to regulate conduct taking place outside the state. Given the historical and statutory limitations on California's ability to prosecute, section 288.2, subdivision (b) cannot be enforced beyond what is jurisdictionally allowed. Consequently, such enforcement would not burden interstate commerce.

4. *State anti-spam statutes.* Several states prohibit the distribution of spam, unsolicited commercial e-mail. Most states have upheld such statutes against Commerce Clause challenges. For example, in State v. Heckel, 24 P.3d 404 (Wash. 2001), the Washington Supreme Court upheld a state law that prohibited using false or misleading subject lines in commercial e-mail sent in or to residents of Washington. The Court held that the truthfulness requirement satisfied the *Pike* balancing test, as it protected ISPs and consumers without placing any burden on commerce.

The permissible scope of state anti-spam statutes is also limited by the preemption provision in the federal anti-spam statute, the Controlling the Assault of Non–Solicited Pornography and Marketing (CAN–SPAM) Act of 2003, Pub. L. No. 108–187 (2003). Section 8(b)(1) of the Act states:

> This Act supersedes any statute, regulation, or rule of a State or political subdivision of a State that expressly regulates the use of electronic mail to send commercial messages, except to the extent that any such statute, regulation, or rule prohibits falsity or deception in any portion of a commercial electronic mail message or information attached thereto.

15 U.S.C.A. § 7707(b)(1). For a discussion of how this provision applies to state anti-spam statutes, see Roger Allan Ford, *Preemption of State Spam Laws By The Federal CAN–SPAM Act*, 72 U. Chi. L. Rev. 355, 370–79 (2005).

5. In 2002, Pennsylvania enacted the Internet Child Pornography Act, codified at 18 Pa. Cons. Stat. §§ 7621–30, in an effort to block the availability of Internet child pornography in Pennsylvania. The statute permits law enforcement officials in Pennsylvania to seek an ex parte court order ordering an ISP located anywhere in the United States to "remove or disable items residing on or accessible through" an ISP's service upon a showing of probable cause that the item constitutes child pornography and is available in Pennsylvania. The apparent thinking behind the statute is that states have no power to block the distribution of out-of-state child pornography, but they may be able to require ISPs to block such information and thus make it unavailable from inside the state. When challenged in court, however, a district court invalidated the Pennsylvania law on dormant Commerce Clause grounds (among other rationales):

> The burdens imposed by the Act are clearly excessive in relation to the local benefits. Defendant claims the Act is justified by reducing the sexual abuse of children. However, as discussed, defendant did not produce any evidence that the Act effectuates this goal. To the contrary, there have been no prosecutions of child pornographers and the evidence shows that individuals interested in obtaining or providing child pornography can evade blocking efforts using a number of different methods.

> Moreover, there is evidence that this Act places a substantial burden on interstate commerce. Defendant argues that the Act only burdens child pornography, which is not a legitimate form of commerce. To the contrary, the evidence demonstrates that implementation of the Act has impacted a number of entities involved in the commerce of the Internet— ISPs, web publishers, and users of the Internet. To comply with the Act, ISPs have used two types of filtering—IP filtering and DNS filtering—to disable access to alleged child pornography. This filtering resulted in the suppression of 376 web sites containing child pornography, certainly a local benefit. However, the filtering used by the ISPs also resulted in the suppression of in excess of 1,190,000 web sites not targeted by defendant and, as demonstrated at trial, a number of these web sites, probably most of them, do not contain child pornography. The overblocking harms web publishers which seek wide distribution for their web sites and Internet users who want access to the broadest range of content possible. For example, as a result of a block implemented by AOL in response to an Informal Notice, Ms. Goldwater, a self employed documentary film maker, was unable to access a web site selling movie posters.

> This Act [also] has the practical effect of exporting Pennsylvania's domestic policies. As an example, a WorldCom witness testified that a customer in Minnesota would not be able to access a web site hosted in Georgia if an IP Address was blocked by a Pennsylvania order. The Act is even more burdensome than the legislation examined in *Pataki* because Pennsylvania has suppressed speech that was not targeted by the Act. Thus, a

Minnesotan would be prevented from accessing a Georgia web site that is not even alleged to contain child pornography.

Center For Democracy & Technology v. Pappert, 337 F. Supp.2d 606, 661–63 (E.D. Pa. 2004). Should the result be the same if the Pennsylvania law only applies to ISPs based in Pennsylvania? Would such a law be effective? For a critique of the Pennsylvania law, see Jonathan Zittrain, *Internet Points of Control*, 44 B.C. L. Rev. 653, 674–88 (2003).

6.   In Hageseth v. Superior Court, 59 Cal.Rptr.3d 385 (Cal. App. 2007), a Colorado doctor who participated in an online pharmacy issued an online prescription to a patient in California. The doctor was then charged criminally in California state court with practicing medicine without a license. The doctor claimed that he couldn't be charged with a California crime because his crime had occurred in cyberspace, not in California real space. The court disagreed, finding that under traditional principles of extraterritorial application of criminal law the state of California could reach the doctor's conduct:

> Petitioner does not make the bold claim that cyberspace is or should be beyond the reach of the criminal law, but he does insist that the People's assertion of extraterritorial jurisdiction over his Internet conduct is unreasonable because (1) he and others are not on notice of the unlawfulness of such conduct, and (2) the assertion of jurisdiction would not deter others from his allegedly unlawful conduct[.]

> The claim that petitioner and others like him who prescribe medications over the Internet lack notice of the unlawfulness of that conduct is unacceptable. California's proscription of the unlicensed practice of medicine is neither an obscure nor an unusual state prohibition of which ignorance can reasonably be claimed, and certainly not by persons like petitioner who are licensed health care providers. Nor can such persons reasonably claim ignorance of the fact that authorization of a prescription pharmaceutical constitutes the practice of medicine.

> Given the absence at this time of any significant national or international effort to deter the widespread and growing use of the Internet to sell drugs without a prescription made on the basis of a good faith hands-on medical examination by a physician licensed in the state in which the patient resides (or without any prescription at all), the denial of state jurisdiction to punish the practice would provide the unscrupulous physicians who engage in it even greater freedom to do so than they already possess. Moreover, while state efforts to identify and obtain personal jurisdiction over such physicians are now often frustrated by Internet technology, technological innovations, network engineering, and Internet intermediaries are making it easier to identify and locate those whose unlawful acts take place in cyberspace and to enforce the law. The prospect of other technological developments counsels judicial caution in accepting technology-based arguments against the assertion of jurisdiction, as that would eliminate incentives for technology developers to innovate in ways that would facilitate law enforcement and support public values.

Id. at 1423–24.

2. PROCEDURAL LIMITS

State investigators confront a number of procedural hurdles to the collection of digital evidence that their federal counterparts do not encounter. Like federal investigators, state officers are bound by the Fourth Amendment and federal privacy laws. Unlike federal investigators, however, state investigators are also bound by four additional limits:

(1) federal privacy laws that expressly regulate the states,

(2) state statutory laws that extend beyond federal statutory laws,

(3) state constitutional protections that extend beyond the federal Fourth Amendment, and

(4) limits on the ability of state subpoena and search warrant authorities to demand evidence out-of-state.

Let's start with the first case, federal privacy laws that expressly regulate the states. Each of the federal statutory privacy laws has special rules that apply to state investigations, and that determine when and how state officials can obtain court orders. For example, the Wiretap Act places significant federal limits on state wiretapping laws. 18 U.S.C. § 2516(2) provides that state investigators can only obtain wiretapping orders "when such interception may provide or has provided evidence of the commission of the offense of murder, kidnapping, gambling, robbery, bribery, extortion, or dealing in narcotic drugs, marihuana or other dangerous drugs, or other crime dangerous to life, limb, or property, and punishable by imprisonment for more than one year." Further, a state investigator can only obtain a wiretapping order if the state legislature has decided to enact a wiretapping statute. If the state has chosen not to pass a wiretapping law, state investigators cannot obtain wiretap orders. *But see* 18 U.S.C. § 2703(d) (explaining when state courts can issue SCA orders); 18 U.S.C. § 3122(a)(2) (permitting state courts to issue pen register orders).

Second, state statutory privacy laws can impose greater restrictions than federal law. Such restrictions are binding only on state investigators: Under the Supremacy Clause, federal officials acting in the course of their official duties are not bound by state statutory privacy laws. However, states may choose to limit state investigators more than federal law requires. States may impose higher thresholds than federal law, or may carve out narrower exceptions. For example, a number of states require the consent of all parties to satisfy the consent exception of state wiretap statutes. If state undercover investigators wish to record telephone calls or Internet communications, state law may require the consent of the monitored parties even if federal law does not. For a useful summary of the state statutes that regulate wiretapping, pen registers, and access to stored communications, see Charles H. Kennedy & Peter P. Swire, *State Wiretaps and Electronic Surveillance After September 11*, 54 Hastings L.J. 971, 987–1162 (2003).

Even if a state enacts statutory surveillance laws that match federal standards, state courts are free to construe state constitutions in ways that impose greater restrictions than those imposed by the Fourth Amendment.

STATE v. REID

Supreme Court of New Jersey, 2008.
945 A.2d 26.

CHIEF JUSTICE RABNER delivered the opinion of the Court.

Modern technology has raised a number of questions that are intertwined in this case: To what extent can private individuals "surf" the "Web" anonymously? Do Internet subscribers have a reasonable expectation of privacy in their identity while accessing Internet websites? And under what circumstances may the State learn the actual identity of Internet users?

In this case, defendant Shirley Reid allegedly logged onto an Internet website from her home computer. The site belonged to a company that supplied material to her employer's business. While on the supplier's website, Reid allegedly changed her employer's password and shipping address to a non-existent address.

Whenever an individual logs onto an Internet website, that user's identity is revealed only in the form of a unique multi-digit number (an "IP address") assigned by the user's Internet Service Provider ("ISP"). A website may collect that number, but only a service provider can translate it into the name of an actual user or subscriber.

Here, the supplier's website captured a ten-digit IP address, and the supplier told Reid's employer what had occurred. The employer, in turn, reported the IP address to local authorities. They issued a deficient municipal subpoena to Comcast, the service provider, and Comcast revealed that the IP address was assigned to Shirley Reid.

Reid is now under indictment for second-degree computer theft. She successfully moved to suppress the subscriber information obtained via the municipal subpoena.

We now hold that citizens have a reasonable expectation of privacy, protected by Article I, Paragraph 7, of the New Jersey Constitution, in the subscriber information they provide to Internet service providers-just as New Jersey citizens have a privacy interest in their bank records stored by banks and telephone billing records kept by phone companies. Law enforcement officials can satisfy that constitutional protection and obtain subscriber information by serving a grand jury subpoena on an ISP without notice to the subscriber.

Because the police used a deficient municipal subpoena to obtain protected subscriber information in this case, defendant's motion to suppress was properly granted. However, records of the protected subscriber information existed independently of the faulty process the police used, and the conduct of the police did not affect that information. As a result, the State may seek to reacquire the subscriber information with a proper grand jury subpoena.

I.

On August 27, 2004, Timothy Wilson, the owner of Jersey Diesel, reported to the Lower Township Police Department that someone had used a computer to change his company's shipping address and password for its suppliers. The shipping address was changed to a non-existent address.

In response to a question by the police, Wilson explained that Shirley Reid, an employee who had been on disability leave, could have made the changes. Reid returned to work on the morning of August 24, had an argument with Wilson about her temporary light duty assignment, and left. According to Wilson, Reid was the only employee who knew the company's computer password and ID.

Wilson learned of the changes through one of his suppliers, Donaldson Company, Inc. Both the password and shipping address for Jersey Diesel had been changed on Donaldson's website on August 24, 2004. According to an information technology specialist at Donaldson, someone accessed their website and used Jersey Diesel's username and password to sign on at 9:57 a.m. The individual changed the password and Jersey Diesel's shipping address and then completed the requests at 10:07 a.m.

Donaldson's website captured the user's IP address, 68.32.145.220, which was registered to Comcast. When Wilson contacted Comcast and asked for subscriber information associated with that address—so that he could identify the person who made the unauthorized changes-Comcast declined to respond without a subpoena.

On September 7, 2004, a subpoena *duces tecum* issued by the Lower Township Municipal Court was served on Comcast. The subpoena sought "any and all information pertaining to IP Address information belonging to IP address: 68.32.145.220, which occurred on 08/24/04 between 8:00 a.m. and 11:00 a.m. EST." The subpoena was captioned "Timothy C. Wilson, Plaintiff, vs. Shirley Reid, Defendant," although no such case was pending.

Comcast responded on September 16, 2004 and identified Reid as the subscriber of the IP address. In addition, Comcast provided the following information: Reid's address, telephone number, type of service provided, IP assignment (dynamic), account number, e-mail address, and method of payment.

An arrest warrant was issued on September 29, 2004, and Reid was arrested ten days later. On February 22, 2005, the Cape May County Grand Jury returned an indictment charging Reid with second-degree computer theft, in violation of *N.J.S.A.* 2C:20–25(b).

Reid moved to suppress the evidence obtained via the municipal court subpoena. On September 22, 2005, the trial court granted Reid's motion. The court identified various flaws with the municipal court subpoena and noted that the procedure followed by the police was "unauthorized in its entirety." The court also concluded that Reid had an expectation of privacy in her Internet subscriber information on file with Comcast. Therefore, the trial court held that the subpoena violated Reid's "right to be free from unreasonable searches and seizures" and was unconstitutional.

II.

We first consider the existence of a New Jersey citizen's privacy interest in Internet subscriber information.

Both the Fourth Amendment to the United States Constitution and Article I, Paragraph 7, of the New Jersey Constitution protect, in nearly identical language, the right of the people to be secure against unreasonable searches and seizures.

Federal case law interpreting the Fourth Amendment has found no expectation of privacy in Internet subscriber information. *See Guest v. Leis,* 255 F.3d 325, 336 (6th Cir. 2001); *Freedman v. America Online, Inc.,* 412 F. Supp.2d 174, 181 (D. Conn. 2005); *United States v. Kennedy,* 81 F. Supp.2d 1103, 1110 (D. Kans. 2000); *United States v. Hambrick,* 55 F.Supp.2d 504, 508–09 (W.D. Va. 1999), *aff'd,* 225 F.3d 656 (4th Cir. 2000). Those decisions draw on settled federal law that a person has no reasonable expectation of privacy in information exposed to third parties, like a telephone company or bank. *See Smith v. Maryland,* 442 U.S. 735, 742 (1979) (finding no privacy interest in telephone numbers dialed). The logic of those precedents extends to subscriber information revealed to an ISP.

Our inquiry does not end there because despite the congruity of the language, the search and seizure protections in the federal and New Jersey Constitutions are not always coterminous. Indeed, on multiple occasions this Court has held that the New Jersey Constitution affords our citizens greater protection against unreasonable searches and seizures than the Fourth Amendment.

During the past twenty-five years, a series of New Jersey cases has expanded the privacy rights enjoyed by citizens of this state. In 1982, this Court concluded in *State v. Hunt,* 91 N.J. 338, 347 (1982), that telephone toll billing records are "part of the privacy package." In language that resonates today on the subject of computers, the Court observed that the telephone has become an essential instrument in carrying on our personal affairs. Moreover, a list of telephone numbers dialed in the privacy of one's home could reveal the identities of the persons and the places called, and thus reveal the most intimate details of a person's life. Finding that Article I, Paragraph 7, of the New Jersey Constitution provides more protection than federal law affords, this Court concluded that a person "is entitled to assume that the numbers he dials in the privacy of his home will be recorded solely for the telephone company's business purposes. The Court rejected the underpinnings of federal case law by explaining that

> [i]t is unrealistic to say that the cloak of privacy has been shed because the telephone company and some of its employees are aware of this information. . . . This disclosure has been necessitated because of the nature of the instrumentality, but more significantly the disclosure has been made for a limited business purpose and not for release to other persons for other reasons.

More recently, in *State v. McAllister*, 184 N.J. 17, 32–33 (2005), this Court held that the New Jersey Constitution provides bank account holders a reasonable expectation of privacy in their bank records. As in *Hunt*, the Court noted that bank accounts have become an indispensable part of modern commerce for our citizens. Like long distance billing records, bank records reveal a great deal about the personal affairs, opinions, habits, and associations of depositors. The Court also noted that, although bank customers voluntarily provide information to banks, "they do so with the understanding that it will remain confidential." The disclosure is done to facilitate financial transactions, not to enable banks to broadcast the affairs of their customers.

B.

ISP records share much in common with long distance billing information and bank records. All are integrally connected to essential activities of today's society. Indeed, it is hard to overstate how important computers and the Internet have become to everyday, modern life. Citizens routinely access the Web for all manner of daily activities: to gather information, explore ideas, read, study, shop, and more.

Individuals need an ISP address in order to access the Internet. However, when users surf the Web from the privacy of their homes, they have reason to expect that their actions are confidential. Many are unaware that a numerical IP address can be captured by the websites they visit. More sophisticated users understand that that unique string of numbers, standing alone, reveals little if anything to the outside world. Only an Internet service provider can translate an IP address into a user's name.

In addition, while decoded IP addresses do not reveal the content of Internet communications, subscriber information alone can tell a great deal about a person. With a complete listing of IP addresses, one can track a person's Internet usage. "The government can learn the names of stores at which a person shops, the political organizations a person finds interesting, a person's fantasies, her health concerns, and so on." Daniel Solove, *The Future of Internet Surveillance Law*, 72 Geo. Wash. L. Rev. 1264, 1287 (2004). Such information can reveal intimate details about one's personal affairs in the same way disclosure of telephone billing records does. Although the contents of Internet communications may be even more revealing, both types of information implicate privacy interests.

It is well-settled under New Jersey law that disclosure to a third-party provider, as an essential step to obtaining service altogether, does not upend the privacy interest at stake. In the world of the Internet, the nature of the technology requires individuals to obtain an IP address to access the Web. Users make disclosures to ISPs for the limited goal of using that technology and not to promote the release of personal information to others. Under our precedents, users are entitled to expect confidentiality under these circumstances.

One additional point bears mention about the right to privacy in ISP subscriber information: the reasonableness of the privacy interest may change as technology evolves. A *reasonable* expectation of privacy is required to establish a protected privacy interest. Internet users today enjoy relatively complete IP address anonymity when surfing the Web. Given the current state of technology, the dynamic, temporarily assigned, numerical IP address cannot be matched to an individual user without the help of an ISP. Therefore, we accept as reasonable the expectation that one's identity will not be discovered through a string of numbers left behind on a website.

The availability of IP Address Locator Websites has not altered that expectation because they reveal the name and address of service providers but not individual users. Should that reality change over time, the reasonableness of the expectation of privacy in Internet subscriber information might change as well. For example, if one day new software allowed individuals to type IP addresses into a "reverse directory" and identify the name of a user—as is possible with reverse telephone directories—today's ruling might need to be reexamined.

C.

We turn next to the type of protection ISP subscriber information should receive in the face of legitimate investigative needs.

Recent case law informs our discussion. In *McAllister,* this Court concluded that issuance of a grand jury subpoena to obtain bank records, upon a showing of relevance, satisfies the constitutional protection against improper government intrusion. The Court further found that notice to the account holder was not constitutionally required. The same principles apply here.

In *McAllister,* the Court rejected arguments similar to those advanced in this case. In declining to adopt a heightened standard of probable cause to support the issuance of a grand jury subpoena, the Court found guidance in the words of Chief Justice Weintraub, writing in *In re Addonizio,* 53 N.J. 107 (1968). His explanation rings true today:

> A grand jury's power to investigate would be feeble indeed if the grand jury had to know at the outset everything needed to arrest a man or to invade his home. Nor would it serve the public interest to

stay a probe until the grand jury reveals what it has or what it seeks. Such disclosures could defeat the inquiry and impede the apprehension of the culprit. This is one of the reasons why the law cloaks the grand jury investigation with secrecy.

More recently, in *State v. Domicz,* 188 N.J. 285, 297 (2006), this Court determined that acquiring electric utility records with a grand jury subpoena was proper under our Constitution. The Court noted that "whatever privacy interest attached" to utility records, obtaining them through the use of a grand jury subpoena satisfies Article I, Paragraph 7, of the State Constitution.

Utility records expose less information about a person's private life than either bank records or subscriber information. But we see no material difference between bank records and ISP subscriber information and decline to treat them differently. They reveal comparably detailed information about one's private affairs and are entitled to comparable protection under our law. In both cases, a grand jury subpoena based on a relevancy standard is sufficient to meet constitutional concerns.

The police in this case used a defective municipal subpoena to obtain Reid's ISP subscriber information from Comcast. We turn now to the consequences that flow from this violation of her rights.

Suppression under the circumstances present here does not mean that the evidence is lost in its entirety. Comcast's records existed independently of the faulty process the police followed. And unlike a confession coerced from a defendant in violation of her constitutional rights, the record does not suggest that police conduct in this case in any way affected the records Comcast kept. As a result, the records can be reliably reproduced and lawfully reacquired through a proper grand jury subpoena.

This outcome is readily apparent if viewed in the context of a motion to quash. Had Comcast sought to quash the municipal court subpoena, the trial court would have granted that relief for the same reasons it gave at the motion to suppress. At that point, nothing would have prevented the police from seeking the subscriber information from Comcast a second time, this time armed with an appropriate grand jury subpoena.

Therefore, the State may attempt to reacquire Comcast's records with a proper grand jury subpoena limited to seeking subscriber information for the IP address in question.

To recap, the trial court properly suppressed the subscriber information obtained, and the State may not proceed with the pending indictment absent proof that the indictment has a sufficient basis without relying on the suppressed evidence. Alternatively, the State may move to dismiss the pending indictment, re-serve a proper grand jury subpoena on Comcast, and seek a new indictment.

NOTES AND QUESTIONS

1. The *Reid* court applies the New Jersey Constitution's privacy protections very differently than courts apply the federal Fourth Amendment. The *Reid* court extends state privacy protections broadly, but then makes a decision as to how much privacy protection is needed. The federal Fourth Amendment is different. Constitutional protections do not extend as far. Once information is protected, however, it is generally protected by a full warrant requirement.

How might the rationale of *Reid* apply to other kinds of digital evidence? How much authority do the police need to install an Internet pen/trap device? To obtain logs from an ISP? To conduct real time monitoring of Internet accounts? Given the flexible nature of the New Jersey constitution, as applied in *Reid*, do you know the New Jersey rules until the New Jersey Supreme Court announces them?

2. According to Stephen Henderson, New Jersey is one of eleven states in which courts have rejected the third-party disclosure principle underlying *Smith v. Maryland* as a matter of state constitutional law. In those eleven states, state investigators must obtain a probable cause search warrant to install a pen register. In contrast, courts in eighteen states either have explicitly adopted *Smith v. Maryland* as a matter of state constitutional law or else have strongly suggested they would do so if the question were directly raised. The remaining states have not addressed the question. *See* Stephen E. Henderson, *Learning From All Fifty States: How to Apply the Fourth Amendment and its State Analogs to Protect Third Party Information From Unreasonable Search*, 55 Cath. U. L. Rev. 373, 395–412 (2006).

Computer crime investigations often cross state lines, which means that police in one state may need to collect digital evidence located in another state. What powers do state investigators have to obtain digital evidence located outside state borders?

STATE v. SIGNORE

Superior Court of Connecticut, 2001.
31 Conn. L. Rptr. 91.

KAVANEWSKY, J.

The defendant has filed a motion to suppress "tangible evidence," more particularly evidence obtained from America Online following the production of a search and seizure warrant to it for account or subscriber information relating to the defendant.

* * * [T]he Greenwich police applied for a search and seizure warrant for AOL account information relating to the defendant. A court found probable cause and signed the warrant. The Greenwich police then faxed the warrant to AOL headquarters in Dulles, Virginia. They obtained the requested information.

The sole issue now before the court is whether, on federal and state constitutional grounds, evidence obtained as the result of the AOL search and seizure warrant, and any derivative evidence, should be suppressed. The defendant contends that the Court had no jurisdiction over the property outside of this state, and the Greenwich Police officers had no authority to act outside of the Town of Greenwich.

The court believes that the authority of the Greenwich police to carry out the search and seizure order derives from the provisions of 18 U.S.C. § 2701 et seq.

The language of 18 U.S.C. § 2703 is plain and unambiguous. It requires that the service provider disclose the subject information only when the governmental entity "obtains" the warrant. While it may not be entirely self-executing, any question as to how service of the warrant may be made can be considered against the backdrop of Connecticut's own legislation concerning search and seizure warrants.

The case of State v. Stevens, 224 Conn. 730 (1993), while not on point, is at least instructive. There, a Connecticut police officer performed field sobriety tests and gathered consensual blood samples from a defendant at a hospital in Rhode Island to which she had been transported by emergency medical personnel for treatment of her injuries following a car accident and her arrest. The defendant challenged the admission of evidence of the sobriety tests and * * * the analysis of the blood samples. She claimed that the officer had no authority to act as a police officer outside his territorial jurisdiction for purposes of that statute. The Supreme Court rejected that claim. "Although bereft of some of his statutory and common law authority outside of Connecticut and the municipality that employed him, the officer did not cease to be a Connecticut police officer for purposes of § 14–227b(b)." *Stevens*, 224 Conn. at 742–43. "In similar circumstances, courts of other states have held that the fact that evidence had been gathered outside an officer's territorial jurisdiction does not require suppression of the evidence." *Id.* at 741.

The defendant's motion to suppress seeks, in practice and effect, to apply the exclusionary rule to the information obtained under the AOL warrant. The facts of this case do not justify this sanction. The exclusionary rule is a judicially created remedy for protecting citizens' Fourth Amendment rights from overzealous law enforcement officials. The law enforcement officials here, having obtained a warrant supported by a neutral and detached Magistrate's determination of probable cause, can hardly be accused of overzealous behavior. The circumstances do not warrant application of the exclusionary rule.

NOTES AND QUESTIONS

1. In *Signore*, the police faxed a Connecticut state warrant to AOL in Virginia. AOL complied with the warrant and sent the information back to Connecticut under 18 U.S.C. § 2703. But was AOL required to respond? The

text of § 2703 states that a "governmental entity" may require a provider to disclose evidence "only pursuant to a warrant issued using the procedures described in the Federal Rules of Criminal Procedure by a court with jurisdiction over the offense under investigation or equivalent State warrant." This language has generally been understood as a limit on when ISPs can disclose evidence rather than an affirmative requirement that ISPs must comply with all federal and state warrants.

2. When a state court order attempts to compel the collection of evidence outside the state, individuals and officials outside the state may opt to comply with the order. However, the fact that state authorities can *allow* extraterritorial enforcement does not mean that they can *compel* it. As a general rule, state court orders issued in one state are not enforceable outside the state. A state subpoena or warrant issued in state *A* for evidence in state *B* does not have binding force in state *B*. *See, e.g.*, Ex parte Dillon, 29 S.W.2d 236, 238 (Mo. Ct. App. 1930) (holding that Full Faith and Credit clause does not require states to recognize court orders from other states); National Institute of Justice, Electronic Crime Needs Assessment for State and Local Law Enforcement 25 (2001).

3. If you are a criminal investigator in one state, and you need digital evidence located in another state, how can you ensure that you can collect the out-of-state evidence? One way for a state to collect out-of-state evidence is to persuade law enforcement officials in the other state to open an investigation and obtain court orders locally. Some state law enforcement offices set aside resources to provide this service for investigators in sister states as a matter of comity. A good example is the sheriff's office in Loudoun County, Virginia, home to the ISP America Online. In 2000, AOL had 23 million customers. State criminal investigators sought warrants to compel AOL to disclose account information several hundred times per year. To assist state officials outside Virginia, the sheriff's office assigned Detective Ron Horak the task of opening Virginia investigations and obtaining Virginia warrants to serve on AOL. When contacted by state investigators from outside Virginia, Horak would open a local investigation, obtain the local warrant, serve it on AOL, and then forward the information sent to him from AOL to the investigators outside Virginia. *See* Maria Glod, *Loudoun's AOL Detective Finds Clues in E–Mail*, Wash. Post, Aug. 28, 2000, at A1.

If you are a state computer crime investigator, can you rely on such arrangements to collect evidence outside your state? What if you need evidence from a small ISP in Rhode Island rather than AOL?

4. In response to the perceived inadequacy of relying on voluntary assistance to enforce court orders extraterritorially, a few states have passed laws requiring ISPs to comply with out-of-state legal process. Terry Berg explains:

> In order to address the problem of gathering evidence from out-of-state service providers, some states have adopted, or are considering adopting, a state statute requiring ISP's doing business within the state to accept and comply with the legal process from other state courts, and further requiring the resident agent of any out-of-state ISP registered to do business within the state to comply with process from forum state courts

upon service of the resident agent. This approach is relatively new and remains untested in the courts, but it clearly addresses lowering the hurdles that state courts currently face when needing to obtain records from an out-of-state service provider.

Terrence Berg, *WWW.WILDWEST.GOV: The Impact of the Internet on State Power to Enforce the Law*, 2000 BYU L. Rev. 1305, 1355.

An example of such a law is Cal. Penal Code 1524.2. Under this law, ISPs incorporated in California must comply with out-of-state warrants:

> A California corporation that provides electronic communication services or remote computing services to the general public, when served with a warrant issued by another state to produce records that would reveal the identity of the customers using those services, data stored by, or on behalf of, the customer, the customer's usage of those services, the recipient or destination of communications sent to or from those customers, or the content of those communications, shall produce those records as if that warrant had been issued by a California court.

Cal. Penal Code § 1524.2(c). Further, ISPs that do business in California must comply with California state warrants:

> The following provisions shall apply to any search warrant issued pursuant to this chapter allowing a search for records that are in the actual or constructive possession of a foreign corporation that provides electronic communication services or remote computing services to the general public, where those records would reveal the identity of the customers using those services, data stored by, or on behalf of, the customer, the customer's usage of those services, the recipient or destination of communications sent to or from those customers, or the content of those communications.

> * * * When properly served with a search warrant issued by the California court, a foreign corporation subject to this section shall provide to the applicant, all records sought pursuant to that warrant within five business days of receipt, including those records maintained or located outside this state.

Cal. Penal Code § 1524.2(b)–(b)(1).

5. A government-funded research report on state and local cybercrime law summarized the problem of extraterritorial evidence collection in the following way:

> Currently there is no formal legal mechanism to allow for the enforcement of State subpoenas in other States. Cooperation can be achieved when one State attorney general's office voluntarily assists a sister State authority in either serving an out-of-State subpoena or seeking an in-State court order to enforce the out-of-State subpoena. However, the reliability and consistency of this procedure is not uniform, and the ability to secure enforcement of an out-of-State subpoena on a recalcitrant party is questionable at best.

> To enhance the authority of State and local law enforcement to investigate cybercrimes that are too small to justify the investment of Federal

resources but nevertheless require interstate process, more effective tools are required for enforcing State subpoenas in other jurisdictions. There are at least two possible models for creating these tools. One model is to develop an interstate compact that would establish procedures for signatory States to follow in enforcing out-of-State subpoenas. The Uniform Act to Secure the Attendance of Witnesses from Without a State in Criminal Proceedings is a comparable legal regime that has been adopted in the 50 States, the District of Columbia, Puerto Rico, and the Virgin Islands.

A second model involves a Federal statute empowering the Federal courts to issue "full faith and credit" orders enforcing out-of-State criminal subpoenas. This alternative might avoid the complexities of developing and adopting an interstate agreement, but it could possibly raise federalism concerns. Whichever type of approach is pursued, action is necessary in this area to ensure that victims of Internet crime have an effective recourse to which they can turn for protection and enforcement.

National Institute of Justice, Electronic Crime Needs Assessment for State and Local Law Enforcement 25–26 (2001).

Professor Brenner has discussed one important effort to draft a federal statute. Susan W. Brenner, *Need for Reciprocal Enforcement of Warrants and Subpoenas in Cybercrime Cases*, 37 Prosecutor 29, 30 (2003). The National Institute of Justice's Electronic Crime Partnership Initiative prepared the following draft statute:

18 U.S. Code § ___

(a) Full Faith and Credit—Any production order issued that is consistent with subsection (b) of this section by the court of another State (the issuing State) shall be accorded full faith and credit by the court of another State (the enforcing State) and enforced as if it were the order of the enforcing state.

(b) Production Order—A production order issued by a State court is consistent with this subsection if—(1) The order is pursuant to the investigation or prosecution of a crime of the issuing state; (2) The order was issued in accordance with the law of the issuing state; and (3) Such court had jurisdiction over the criminal investigation or prosecution under the law of the issuing state.

(c) "Production Order" means any order, warrant, or subpoena for the production of records, issued by a court of competent jurisdiction.

(d) "Records" includes those items in whatever form created or stored.

Should Congress enact such a statute?

6. How important is it for state computer crime investigators to have the legal tools necessary to collect digital evidence nationwide? Is voluntary compliance adequate? Are model state statutes needed? Or is a federal statute the best solution? If a federal solution is needed, should the federal statute focus specifically on ISPs and computer crime cases or should it be more general in scope? Alternatively, is it appropriate in our federal system that state investigators cannot compel evidence nationwide?

C. INTERNATIONAL COMPUTER CRIMES

Computer crimes can cross national boundaries just as easily as they can cross state lines. As a result, federal investigators routinely face international jurisdictional issues analogous to those confronted by state investigators. Investigators might want to prosecute a defendant for committing a computer crime that originated domestically but targeted computers outside its borders, or they might want to punish a crime originating abroad that targets a computer inside the United States. Evidence might need to be collected outside the United States for an otherwise domestic investigation. Foreign governments face the same questions from the other side, as well: law enforcement officials from other countries may wish to punish computer crimes originating in the United States directed at computers in their home countries, or they may need to collect evidence in the United States to help domestic investigations. The following materials consider the law regulating international computer crime cases.

1. UNITED STATES SUBSTANTIVE LAW

Do computer crime laws in the United States apply to conduct either originating from outside the United States or targeting computers located outside the United States?

UNITED STATES v. IVANOV

United States District Court for the District of Connecticut, 2001.
175 F. Supp.2d 367.

THOMPSON, DISTRICT JUDGE.

Defendant Aleksey Vladimirovich Ivanov has been indicted, in a superseding indictment, on charges of conspiracy, computer fraud and related activity, extortion and possession of unauthorized access devices. Ivanov has moved to dismiss the indictment on the grounds that the court lacks subject matter jurisdiction. Ivanov argues that because it is alleged that he was physically located in Russia when the offenses were committed, he cannot be charged with violations of United States law. For the reasons set forth below, the defendant's motion is being denied.

I. Background

Online Information Bureau, Inc. ("OIB"), the alleged victim in this case, is a Connecticut corporation based in Vernon, Connecticut. It is an "e-commerce" business which assists retail and Internet merchants by, among other things, hosting their websites and processing their credit card data and other financial transactions. In this capacity, OIB acts as a financial transaction "clearinghouse," by aggregating and assisting in the debiting or crediting of funds against each account for thousands of retail and Internet purchasers and vendors. In doing so, OIB collects and maintains customer credit card information, merchant account numbers, and related financial data from credit card companies and other financial institutions.

The government alleges that Ivanov hacked into OIB's computer system and obtained the key passwords to control OIB's entire network. The government contends that in late January and early February 2000, OIB received from Ivanov a series of unsolicited e-mails indicating that the defendant had obtained the "root" passwords for certain computer systems operated by OIB. A "root" password grants its user access to and control over an entire computer system, including the ability to manipulate, extract, and delete any and all data. Such passwords are generally reserved for use by the system administrator only.

The government claims that Ivanov then threatened OIB with the destruction of its computer systems (including its merchant account database) and demanded approximately $10,000 for his assistance in making those systems secure. It claims, for example, that on February 3, 2000, after his initial solicitations had been rebuffed, Ivanov sent the following e-mail to an employee of OIB:

> [name redacted], now imagine please Somebody hack you network (and not notify you about this), he download Atomic software with more than 300 merchants, transfer money, and after this did 'rm-rf/' and after this you company be ruined. I don't want this, and because this I notify you about possible hack in you network, if you want you can hire me and im allways be check security in you network. What you think about this?[1]

The government contends that Ivanov's extortionate communications originated from an e-mail account at Lightrealm.com, an Internet Service Provider based in Kirkland, Washington. It contends that while he was in Russia, Ivanov gained access to the Lightrealm computer network and that he used that system to communicate with OIB, also while he was in Russia. Thus, each e-mail sent by Ivanov was allegedly transmitted from a Lightrealm.com computer in Kirkland, Washington through the Internet to an OIB computer in Vernon, Connecticut, where the e-mail was opened by an OIB employee.

The parties agree that the defendant was physically located in Russia (or one of the other former Soviet Bloc countries) when, it is alleged, he committed the offenses set forth in the superseding indictment.

The superseding indictment comprises eight counts. Count One charges that beginning in or about December 1999, or earlier, the defendant and others conspired to commit the substantive offenses charged in Counts Two through Eight of the indictment, in violation of 18 U.S.C. § 371. Count Two charges that the defendant, knowingly and with intent to defraud, accessed protected computers owned by OIB and by means of this conduct furthered a fraud and obtained something of value, in

---

1. An individual with "root access" who inputs the UNIX command "rm-rf/" will delete all files on the network server, including all operating system software.

violation of 18 U.S.C. §§ 2, 1030(a)(4) and 1030(c)(3)(A). Count Three charges that the defendant intentionally accessed protected computers owned by OIB and thereby obtained information, which conduct involved interstate and foreign communications and was engaged in for purposes of financial gain and in furtherance of a criminal act, in violation of 18 U.S.C. §§ 2, 1030(a)(2)(c) and 1030(c)(2)(B).

Count Six charges that the defendant transmitted in interstate and foreign commerce communications containing a threat to cause damage to protected computers owned by OIB, in violation of 18 U.S.C. §§ 1030(a)(7) and 1030(c)(3)(A). Count Seven charges that the defendant obstructed, delayed and affected commerce, and attempted to obstruct, delay and affect commerce, by means of extortion by attempting to obtain property from OIB with OIB's consent, inducing such consent by means of threats to damage OIB and its business unless OIB paid the defendant money and hired the defendant as a security consultant, in violation of 18 U.S.C. § 1951(a). Count Eight charges that the defendant, knowingly and with intent to defraud, possessed unauthorized access devices, which conduct affected interstate and foreign commerce, in violation of 18 U.S.C. § 1029(a)(3).

II. Discussion

The defendant and the government agree that when Ivanov allegedly engaged in the conduct charged in the superseding indictment, he was physically present in Russia and using a computer there at all relevant times. Ivanov contends that for this reason, charging him under the Hobbs Act, 18 U.S.C. § 1951, under the Computer Fraud and Abuse Act, 18 U.S.C. § 1030, and under the access device statute, 18 U.S.C. § 1029, would in each case require extraterritorial application of that law and such application is impermissible. The court concludes that it has jurisdiction, first, because the intended and actual detrimental effects of Ivanov's actions in Russia occurred within the United States, and second, because each of the statutes under which Ivanov was charged with a substantive offense was intended by Congress to apply extraterritorially.

A. The Intended and Actual Detrimental Effects of the Charged Offenses Occurred Within the United States

As noted by the court in *United States v. Muench,* 694 F.2d 28 (2d Cir. 1982), the intent to cause effects within the United States makes it reasonable to apply to persons outside United States territory a statute which is not expressly extraterritorial in scope. It has long been a commonplace of criminal liability that a person may be charged in the place where the evil results, though he is beyond the jurisdiction when he starts the train of events of which that evil is the fruit. The Government may punish a defendant in the same manner as if he were present in the jurisdiction when the detrimental effects occurred.

The Supreme Court has quoted with approval the following language from Moore's International Law Digest:

The principle that a man, who outside of a country willfully puts in motion a force to take effect in it, is answerable at the place where the evil is done, is recognized in the criminal jurisprudence of all countries. And the methods which modern invention has furnished for the performance of criminal acts in that manner has made this principle one of constantly growing importance and of increasing frequency of application.

Moreover, the court noted in *Marc Rich & Co. v. United States,* 707 F.2d 663 (2d Cir. 1983) that:

It is certain that the courts of many countries, even of countries which have given their criminal legislation a strictly territorial character, interpret criminal law in the sense that offences, the authors of which at the moment of commission are in the territory of another State, are nevertheless to be regarded as having been committed in the national territory, if one of the constituent elements of the offence, and more especially its effects, have taken place there.

Id. at 666.

Here, all of the intended and actual detrimental effects of the substantive offenses Ivanov is charged with in the indictment occurred within the United States. In Counts Two and Three, the defendant is charged with accessing OIB's computers. Those computers were located in Vernon, Connecticut. The fact that the computers were accessed by means of a complex process initiated and controlled from a remote location does not alter the fact that the accessing of the computers, i.e. part of the detrimental effect prohibited by the statute, occurred at the place where the computers were physically located, namely OIB's place of business in Vernon, Connecticut.

Count Two charges further that Ivanov obtained something of value when he accessed OIB's computers, that "something of value" being the data obtained from OIB's computers. In order for Ivanov to violate § 1030(a)(4), it was necessary that he do more than merely access OIB's computers and view the data. *See United States v. Czubinski,* 106 F.3d 1069, 1078 (1st Cir. 1997) ("Merely viewing information cannot be deemed the same as obtaining something of value for purposes of this statute. This section should apply to those who steal information through unauthorized access."). The indictment charges that Ivanov did more than merely gain unauthorized access and view the data. Ivanov allegedly obtained root access to the OIB computers located in Vernon, Connecticut. Once Ivanov had root access to the computers, he was able to control the data, e.g., credit card numbers and merchant account numbers, stored in the OIB computers; Ivanov could copy, sell, transfer, alter, or destroy that data. That data is intangible property of OIB. In determining where, in the case of intangibles, possession resides, the measure of control exercised is the deciding factor.

At the point Ivanov gained root access to OIB's computers, he had complete control over that data, and consequently, had possession of it.

That data was in OIB's computers. Since Ivanov possessed that data while it was in OIB's computers in Vernon, Connecticut, the court concludes that he obtained it, for purposes of § 1030(a)(4), in Vernon, Connecticut. The fact that Ivanov is charged with obtaining OIB's valuable data by means of a complex process initiated and controlled from a remote location, and that he subsequently moved that data to a computer located in Russia, does not alter the fact that at the point when Ivanov first possessed that data, it was on OIB's computers in Vernon, Connecticut.

Count Three charges further that when he accessed OIB's computers, Ivanov obtained information from protected computers. The analysis as to the location at which Ivanov obtained the information referenced in this count is the same as the analysis as to the location at which he obtained the "something of value" referenced in Count Two. Thus, as to both Counts Two and Three, it is charged that the balance of the detrimental effect prohibited by the pertinent statute, i.e., Ivanov's obtaining something of value or obtaining information, also occurred within the United States.

Count Six charges that Ivanov transmitted a threat to cause damage to protected computers. The detrimental effect prohibited by § 1030(a)(7), namely the receipt by an individual or entity of a threat to cause damage to a protected computer, occurred in Vernon, Connecticut because that is where OIB was located, where it received the threat, and where the protected computers were located. The analysis is the same as to Count Seven, the charge under the Hobbs Act.

Count Eight charges that Ivanov knowingly and with intent to defraud possessed over ten thousand unauthorized access devices, i.e., credit card numbers and merchant account numbers. For the reasons discussed above, although it is charged that Ivanov later transferred this intangible property to Russia, he first possessed it while it was on OIB's computers in Vernon, Connecticut. Had he not possessed it here, he would not have been able to transfer it to his computer in Russia. Thus, the detrimental effect prohibited by the statute occurred within the United States.

Finally, Count One charges that Ivanov and others conspired to commit each of the substantive offenses charged in the indictment. The Second Circuit has stated that "the jurisdictional element should be viewed for purposes of the conspiracy count exactly as we view it for purposes of the substantive offense." *United States v. Blackmon*, 839 F.2d 900, 910 (2d Cir. 1988). Federal jurisdiction over a conspiracy charge is established by proof that the accused planned to commit a substantive offense which, if attainable, would have violated a federal statute, and that at least one overt act has been committed in furtherance of the conspiracy. Here, Ivanov is charged with planning to commit substantive offenses in violation of federal statutes, and it is charged that at least one overt act was committed in furtherance of the conspiracy. As discussed above, the court has jurisdiction over the underlying substantive charges. Therefore, the court has jurisdiction over the conspiracy charge, at a minimum, to the extent it relates to Counts Two, Three, Six, Seven or Eight.

Accordingly, the court concludes that it has subject matter jurisdiction over each of the charges against Ivanov, whether or not the statutes under which the substantive offenses are charged are intended by Congress to apply extraterritorially, because the intended and actual detrimental effects of the substantive offenses Ivanov is charged with in the indictment occurred within the United States.

B. Intended Extraterritorial Application

The defendant's motion should also be denied because, as to each of the statutes under which the defendant has been indicted for a substantive offense, there is clear evidence that the statute was intended by Congress to apply extraterritorially. This fact is evidenced by both the plain language and the legislative history of each of these statutes.

There is a presumption that Congress intends its acts to apply only within the United States, and not extraterritorially. However, this presumption against extraterritoriality may be overcome by showing clear evidence of congressional intent to apply a statute beyond our borders. Congress has the authority to enforce its laws beyond the territorial boundaries of the United States. Whether Congress has in fact exercised that authority in a particular case is a matter of statutory construction.

The Computer Fraud and Abuse Act was amended in 1996 by Pub. L. No. 104–294, 110 Stat. 3491, 3508. The 1996 amendments made several changes that are relevant to the issue of extraterritoriality, including a change in the definition of "protected computer" so that it included any computer "which is used in interstate *or foreign* commerce or communication." 18 U.S.C. § 1030(e)(2)(B) (emphasis added). The 1996 amendments also added subsections (a)(2)(c) and (a)(7), which explicitly address "interstate or foreign commerce," and subsection (e)(9), which added to the definition of "government entity" the clause "any foreign country, and any state, province, municipality or other political subdivision of a foreign country."

The plain language of the statute, as amended, is clear. Congress intended the CFAA to apply to computers used "in interstate or foreign commerce or communication." The defendant argues that this language is ambiguous. The court disagrees. The Supreme Court has often stated that "a statute ought, upon the whole, to be so construed that, if it can be prevented, no clause, sentence, or word shall be superfluous, void, or insignificant." *Regions Hosp. v. Shalala*, 522 U.S. 448, 467 (1998). In order for the word "foreign" to have meaning, and not be superfluous, it must mean something other than "interstate." In other words, "foreign" in this context must mean international. Thus, Congress has clearly manifested its intent to apply § 1030 to computers used either in interstate or in foreign commerce.

The legislative history of the CFAA supports this reading of the plain language of the statute. The Senate Judiciary Committee issued a report explaining its reasons for adopting the 1996 amendments. S. Rep. No. 357, 104th Congr., 2d Sess. (1996). In that report, the Committee specifically noted its concern that the statute as it existed prior to the 1996 amendments did not cover "computers used in foreign communications or commerce, despite the fact that hackers are often foreign-based." *Id.* at 4. The Committee cited two specific cases in which foreign-based hackers had infiltrated computer systems in the United States, as examples of the kind of situation the amendments were intended to address:

> For example, the 1994 intrusion into the Rome Laboratory at Grifess Air Force Base in New York, was perpetrated by a 16 year-old hacker in the United Kingdom. More recently, in March 1996, the Justice Department tracked down a young Argentinean man who had broken into Harvard University's computers from Buenos Aires and used those computers as a staging ground to hack into many other computer sites, including the Defense Department and NASA.

Id. at 4–5. Congress has the power to apply its statutes extraterritorially, and in the case of 18 U.S.C. § 1030, it has clearly manifested its intention to do so.

NOTES AND QUESTIONS

1. As a matter of policy, should it be a federal crime for a person located abroad to hack into or damage a computer located in the United States? Why not let officials in the other country handle the case? Is it likely that Russian authorities would prosecute Ivanov for his unauthorized access into United States computers?

2. Should it be a federal crime for a person located in the United States to hack into or damage a computer located in a foreign country? Imagine that a person in the United States dislikes the government of China, and he decides to launch a denial-of-service attack against computers owned by the Chinese government located in China. Does the attack violate United States law? As a matter of policy, should it?

3. *The scope of § 1030 and international investigations.* The USA Patriot Act of 2001 amended the definition of "protected computer" in 18 U.S.C. § 1030(e)(2) so that it now explicitly includes computers located outside of the United States. Before the Patriot Act, the term "protected computer" was defined (as in the *Ivanov* case) as including a computer "which is used in interstate or foreign commerce or communication." 18 U.S.C. § 1030(e)(2) (1996). The Patriot Act added the phrase "including a computer located outside the United States that is used in a manner that affects interstate or foreign commerce or communication of the United States." The Justice Department has offered the following explanation for the amendment:

> Because of the interdependency and availability of global computer networks, hackers from within the United States are increasingly targeting systems located entirely outside of this country. The statute did not

explicitly allow for prosecution of such hackers. In addition, individuals in foreign countries frequently route communications through the United States, even as they hack from one foreign country to another. In such cases, their hope may be that the lack of any U.S. victim would either prevent or discourage U.S. law enforcement agencies from assisting in any foreign investigation or prosecution.

Section 814 of the Act amends the definition of "protected computer" to make clear that this term includes computers outside of the United States so long as they affect "interstate or foreign commerce or communication of the United States." 18 U.S.C. § 1030(e)(2)(B). By clarifying the fact that a domestic offense exists, the United States can now use speedier domestic procedures to join in international hacker investigations. As these crimes often involve investigators and victims in more than one country, fostering international law enforcement cooperation is essential.

In addition, the amendment creates the option, where appropriate, of prosecuting such criminals in the United States. Since the U.S. is urging other countries to ensure that they can vindicate the interests of U.S. victims for computer crimes that originate in their nations, this provision will allow the U.S. to provide reciprocal coverage.

Computer Crime and Intellectual Property Section (CCIPS), Field Guidance on New Authorities that Relate to Computer Crime and Electronic Evidence Enacted in the USA Patriot Act of 2001 (2001), *available at* www.cybercrime.gov/PatriotAct.htm.

Note that the Justice Department mostly justifies the expansion of 18 U.S.C. § 1030 based on its impact on international investigations. According to DOJ, "the United States can now use speedier domestic procedures to join in international hacker investigations." When an international computer crime does not violate U.S. law, officials must follow fairly complicated and time-consuming evidence-collecting procedures (described later in this chapter). On the other hand, if an international computer crime violates 18 U.S.C. § 1030, U.S. law enforcement officials can open a *domestic* investigation into the violation. They can then use statutes such as the Electronic Communications Privacy Act to collect digital evidence in the United States and forward their findings on to counterparts abroad. As a result, a change in the substantive law of 18 U.S.C. § 1030 can have important procedural implications for international computer crime cases.

We observed a similar dynamic in the context of state criminal investigations that cross state lines. Recall that if investigators in state *A* need electronic evidence in state *B*, law enforcement officials in state *B* can open an investigation in that state, obtain the evidence, and then send it to officials in state *A*. Opening a second investigation in the jurisdiction where the evidence is located circumvents the hurdle of extraterritorial evidence collection, at least if the officials in the second jurisdiction are willing to help. The Patriot Act's amendment to § 1030(e)(2)(B) permits United States officials to perform the same role for foreign authorities investigating international computer crimes.

Is this a good idea? One commentator has argued that this expansion of 18 U.S.C. § 1030 goes too far:

Where the affect on U.S. computer networks is slight—to the point of non-existence—the U.S. should not impose its law on the activity.

The new statute requires no threshold of damage or even effect on U.S. computers to trigger U.S. sovereignty. The vast majority of Internet traffic travels through the United States, with more than half of the traffic traveling through Northern Virginia alone. The mere fact that packets relating to the criminal activity travel through the United States should not be enough to trigger U.S. jurisdiction, even though such traffic would "affect" international commerce, albeit infinitesimally.

Mark Rasch, *Ashcroft's Global Internet Power–Grab* (Nov. 25, 2001), http://www.security focus.com/columnists/39. Should Congress change the law back to the 1996 version?

4.   In May 2000, the Internet was hit by an e-mail-based computer virus known as the "I Love You" virus. The virus was believed to have been sent by Onel A. de Guzman, a 23 year-old computer programmer from the Philippines. The virus quickly infected millions of machines. Although the precise way in which the virus was unleashed remains unknown, let's assume that it began when de Guzman sent an e-mail using an account in the Philippines to various individuals with e-mail accounts in the Philippines. The virus then spread outside the Philippines and infected computers all around the world.

Assuming these facts are accurate, did Onel de Guzman violate 18 U.S.C. § 1030? Does the answer depend on whether the definition of "protected computer" is the 1996 definition or the current definition enacted by the Patriot Act? Does the answer depend on de Guzman's *mens rea* with respect to whether the virus would damage computers located in the United States?

5.   Ellen S. Podgor, *International Computer Fraud: A Paradigm for Limiting National Jurisdiction*, 35 U.C. Davis L. Rev. 267, 269–70, 317 (2002):

Should the United States acquire jurisdiction of all criminal activity when the medium for the crime involves the use of a computer, and the activity has an effect in this country? U.S. law enforcement should tread carefully in imposing its jurisdiction throughout the world. It is one thing to lead the charge in prosecuting international computer fraud crimes; it is another, however, to take charge. Until sufficient international measures are operational, it is important for the United States to remind itself that it is not the world's police, prosecutor and court.

Do you agree? Why is this important?

6.   *Internet gambling and international law.* Recall that in United States v. Cohen, 260 F.3d 68 (2d Cir. 2001), discussed in Chapter 3, the defendant was convicted in New York for operating an Internet sports betting site from Antigua. Given that the computer was operated from Antigua, what was the basis for prosecuting Cohen in New York?

More broadly, can the United States government prevent foreign gambling sites from being available inside the United States without making them unavailable outside the United States? If the United States wants to ban such sites, but other countries do not, which side should win? And who should decide? The World Trade Organization considered a case brought by Antigua and Barbuda alleging that the United States ban on Internet gambling violated the General Agreement on Trade Services (GATS). *See* Jonathan Schwartz, Essay, *Click the Mouse and Bet the House: The United States' Internet Gambling Restrictions Before the World Trade Organization*, 2005 U. Ill. J.L. Tech. & Pol'y 125. Is the WTO the proper forum for resolving the legality of Internet gambling?

2. UNITED STATES PROCEDURAL LAW

When a computer crime occurs entirely in the United States, federal investigators must comply with the Fourth Amendment, the Wiretap Act, the Pen Register Statute, and the Stored Communications Act. But what laws govern investigations when the collection of evidence occurs in part or in whole outside the United States?

The case of statutory law is relatively easy. Several courts have held that the Wiretap Act applies only to interception inside the United States. Any interception of wire or electronic communications outside the United States is not covered by the Act. *See, e.g.,* United States v. Cotroni, 527 F.2d 708, 711 (2d Cir. 1975). As a district court has explained:

Congress intended Title III to protect the integrity of United States communications systems against unauthorized interceptions taking place in the United States. If Congress had meant to require law enforcement agencies to satisfy Title III for interceptions conducted outside the United States, it would have provided some mechanism by which agents could obtain such approval. Congress did not do so.

United States v. Angulo–Hurtado, 165 F. Supp.2d 1363, 1369 (N.D. Ga. 2001).

Although courts have not addressed the question, it seems likely that the Stored Communications Act and the Pen Register statute have the same territorial limit. Both statutes share common roots with the Wiretap Act, as well as many statutory terms, so it seems probable that they share the Wiretap Act's territorial scope. As a result, acquisition of digital evidence outside the United States does not require compliance with the statutory surveillance laws.

Fourth Amendment limits on the acquisition of digital evidence outside the United States are much more complicated. Existing caselaw remains sparse, but the framework appears to hinge on two key questions: first, who is being monitored, and second, who is doing the monitoring. The next case introduces the framework.

UNITED STATES v. BARONA
United States Court of Appeals for the Ninth Circuit, 1995.
56 F.3d 1087.

WALLACE, CHIEF JUDGE.

Following extensive investigation, including wiretaps in foreign countries, the appellants were indicted and convicted of drug-related crimes.

I

The issues we discuss arose in the context of a criminal prosecution of six individuals for an ongoing conspiracy to distribute cocaine. Mario Ernesto Villabona–Alvarado and Brian Bennett organized and supervised the operation. Cocaine from Colombia entered the United States through a source named "Oscar." The cocaine was then delivered by Maria Barona and Luz Janneth Martinez to Michael McCarver and Michael Harris for further distribution.

Several events led to the identification of this conspiracy and its participants. Between 1985 and 1987, the Drug Enforcement Administration and the Los Angeles Police Department conducted a money-laundering investigation code-named "Operation Pisces." The result of this investigation was the arrest of Leonardo Gomez in Villabona's residence. Then in December 1987, Villabona and Bennett traveled to Copenhagen, Denmark, and registered at the Savoy Hotel. On December 7, 1987, Villabona, his wife (Helle Nielsen), and Bennett traveled to Aalborg, Denmark, to stay with Nielsen's parents. While in Aalborg, Villabona placed calls from the Nielsen residence and from a public telephone. On December 8, 1987, Villabona and Bennett returned to Copenhagen and stayed at the Hotel Sara–Dan. From Copenhagen, Villabona and Bennett flew to Milan, Italy, and registered at the Hilton International Hotel on December 9, 1987. In late March 1988, Villabona returned to Aalborg, Denmark, and again used the same public telephone. In each of these locations, the telephone calls made by Villabona were monitored by the Danish (or in one case, Italian) authorities. Tapes of these wiretaps were played for the jury and were relied on at least in part to convict Villabona, Bennett, Martinez, Barona, Harris, and McCarver.

Between March and November 1988, Bennett asked Stanley McCarns to transport 502 kilograms of cocaine from Los Angeles to Detroit and to return with millions of dollars. Stanley McCarns then arranged for Willie Childress and his cousin, James McCarns, to transport the cocaine. Childress and James McCarns were stopped en route on November 6, 1988, and a Missouri state trooper seized the cocaine. On November 11, 1988, domestic wiretaps commenced on two cellular telephones used by Villabona. These taps also resulted in the interception of several incriminating conversations.

II

The district court ruled on the motion to suppress the Denmark wiretap evidence as follows:

> The Court agrees with the Defense, that other than the Milan Wiretap, that these were wiretaps which were engaged in as a joint venture by the United States and Denmark. The Court finds that the order issued by the Danish Court was lawful and in accordance with their law. The Court finds that the United States authorities reasonably relied upon the representations of the Danish officials with

respect to the wiretaps, and therefore they were acting—in the Court's opinion—in good faith.

The question of whether the wiretaps were a joint venture requires the district court to scrutinize the attendant facts. Therefore, we will not disturb such a finding unless it is clearly erroneous. We review de novo, however, the finding that the wiretaps were conducted in accordance with foreign law, *United States v. Peterson,* 812 F.2d 486, 490 (9th Cir. 1987), as well as the question of whether United States agents reasonably relied in good faith upon the foreign officials' representations that the wiretaps were legal under foreign law.

A.

When determining the validity of a foreign wiretap, we start with two general and undisputed propositions. The first is that Title III of the Omnibus Crime Control and Safe Streets Act of 1968, 18 U.S.C. §§ 2510–21, "has no extraterritorial force." *Peterson,* 812 F.2d at 492. Our analysis, then, is guided only by the applicable principles of constitutional law. The second proposition is that neither our Fourth Amendment nor the judicially created exclusionary rule applies to acts of foreign officials.

Two very limited exceptions apply. One exception, clearly inapplicable here, occurs if the circumstances of the foreign search and seizure are so extreme that they shock the judicial conscience, so that a federal appellate court in the exercise of its supervisory powers can require exclusion of the evidence. This type of exclusion is not based on our Fourth Amendment jurisprudence, but rather on the recognition that we may employ our supervisory powers when absolutely necessary to preserve the integrity of the criminal justice system. The wiretaps at issue cannot be said to shock the conscience. Even when no authorization for a foreign wiretap was secured in violation of the foreign law itself, we have not excluded the evidence under this rationale, nor should we. Here, the foreign courts were involved and purported to authorize the wiretaps. The conduct here, therefore, does not come close to requiring the invocation of this exception.

The second exception to the inapplicability of the exclusionary rule applies when United States agents' participation in the investigation is so substantial that the action is a joint venture between United States and foreign officials. If a joint venture is found to have existed, the law of the foreign country must be consulted at the outset as part of the determination whether or not the search was reasonable. If foreign law was not complied with, the good faith exception to the exclusionary rule becomes part of the analysis. The good faith exception is grounded in the realization that the exclusionary rule does not function as a deterrent in cases in which the law enforcement officers acted on a reasonable belief that their conduct was legal.

It is this exception that the appellants invoke, asking us to conclude (1) that the United States and foreign officials were engaged in a joint venture, (2) that a violation of foreign law occurred making the search unreasonable, and (3) that the United States did not rely in good faith upon the foreign officials' representations that their law was being complied with.

B.

Because this exception is based solely on the Fourth Amendment, the appellants must first show that they are among the class of persons that the Fourth Amendment was meant to protect. In this case, three appellants, Martinez, Barona, and Villabona, are not United States citizens.

The Supreme Court has said, with regard to foreign searches involving aliens with "no voluntary connection" to the United States, that the Fourth Amendment is simply inapplicable. *See United States v. Verdugo–Urquidez,* 494 U.S. 259, 274–75 (1990). *Verdugo* reversed a decision of this circuit in which the panel majority found the Fourth Amendment applicable to a search of a Mexican citizen's Mexicali residence. *See United States v. Verdugo–Urquidez,* 856 F.2d 1214 (9th Cir. 1988), *rev'd,* 494 U.S. 259 (1990). The Supreme Court rejected this court's "global view of the Fourth Amendment's applicability which would plunge us into a sea of uncertainty as to what might be reasonable in the way of searches and seizures conducted abroad." *Verdugo,* 494 U.S. at 274.

Unlike the Due Process Clause of the Fifth Amendment, which protects all "persons," the Fourth Amendment protects only "the People of the United States." *Id.* at 265 (explaining that the term "people" used in the Fourth Amendment was a term of art employed in selected parts of the Constitution to refer to "the People of the United States"). This term "refers to a class of persons who are part of a national community or who have otherwise developed sufficient connection with this country to be considered part of that community." *Id.* The Fourth Amendment therefore protects a much narrower class of individuals than the Fifth Amendment.

Because our constitutional theory is premised in large measure on the conception that our Constitution is a "social contract," *Verdugo–Urquidez,* 856 F.2d at 1231–33, the scope of an alien's rights depends intimately on the extent to which he has chosen to shoulder the burdens that citizens must bear. Not until an alien has assumed the complete range of obligations that we impose on the citizenry may he be considered one of 'the people of the United States' entitled to the full panoply of rights guaranteed by our Constitution.

The term "People of the United States" includes "American citizens at home and abroad" and lawful resident aliens within the borders of the United States "who are victims of actions taken *in the United States* by American officials." *Verdugo–Urquidez,* 856 F.2d at 1234 (Wallace, J., dissenting) (emphasis in original). It is yet to be decided, however, whether a resident alien has undertaken sufficient obligations of citizenship or has otherwise developed sufficient connection with this country to be considered one of "the People of the United States" even when he or she steps outside the territorial borders of the United States.

It is not clear, therefore, that Villabona or the other non-citizen defendants in this case are entitled to receive any Fourth Amendment protection whatsoever. Any entitlement that they may have to invoke the Fourth Amendment in the context of an *extraterritorial* search is by no means clear. We could hold, therefore, that Barona, Martinez, and Villabona have failed to demonstrate that, at the time of the extraterritorial search, they were "People of the United States" entitled to receive the full panoply of rights guaranteed by our Constitution. We choose, however, not to reach the question because even if they were entitled to invoke the Fourth Amendment, their effort would be unsuccessful.

C.

Bennett, Harris, and McCarver are all United States citizens, and thus can invoke the protection of the Fourth Amendment generally. Our cases establishing the exception as to when the Fourth Amendment can be invoked in an extraterritorial search control our analysis.

First, the district court did not clearly err in finding that the four Danish wiretaps at issue were "joint ventures." In *Peterson,* we gave weight to the fact that the DEA "was involved daily in translating and decoding intercepted transmissions as well as advising the foreign authorities of their relevance." 812 F.2d at 490. Similarly here, the American Embassy was interested in the movement of Villabona and Bennett, American agents requested the wiretaps, information obtained was immediately forwarded to them, and throughout the surveillance a Spanish to English interpreter was provided by the United States.

Because there was a joint venture, we must decide whether the search was reasonable. In determining whether the search was reasonable, we must first consult the law of the relevant foreign countries. The relevant provisions of Danish law are: (1) section 191 of the Danish Criminal Code (Code) and (2) sections 780–791 of the Danish Administration of Justice Act (Justice Act).

Justice Act § 781(1) authorizes the intervention of secret communications, including the wiretapping of telephonic communications, if: (1) "weighty reasons" exist to assume messages are being conveyed via the medium in question, (2) the intervention is of decisive importance to the investigation, and (3) the investigation concerns an offense punishable by six or more years or is one of several other specifically enumerated offenses. Under Code § 191(1), the drug offenses at issue here are punishable by six or more years, thus satisfying section 781(1)(3).

In addition to these three requirements under Justice Act § 781(1), Danish law is somewhat more strict when it comes to monitoring conversations by use of a listening device or "bug" rather than by the tapping of telephone lines. Justice Act § 781(4) allows the use of such devices to intercept communications only if the suspected offense involves "danger to the lives or welfare of human beings or considerable social assets." This latter section was relevant to the Danish Court in two of the surveillances because the government sought to use both a listening device and wiretaps. The section is not relevant to us, however, because it appears that no surveillance evidence, other than wiretap evidence, was used at trial. Even if such evidence were admitted, however, section 781(4) was followed.

Justice Act § 783 outlines procedures to acquire a wiretap, section 784 provides for an attorney to be appointed for the target party, and section 788 provides for notification of the wiretap to the target party, unless the court omits or postpones such notification under section 788(4). After carefully reviewing the record, we are satisfied that Danish law was followed.

The first monitoring of communications occurred at the Savoy Hotel, Copenhagen, from December 4 to 7, 1987. The Danish police monitored communications both by tapping the hotel telephone lines, and by installing an electronic listening device in Villabona's room. In accordance with Danish law, the court held a hearing on December 5, 1987, at 10:00 a.m. to determine whether the wiretap and electronic eavesdropping, begun on December 4, 1987, was to be maintained. Justice Act § 783(3) allows police to make the necessary intervention subject to court approval within 24 hours. The Danish court gave its approval based on information that Villabona, Nielsen (who is not a party in this appeal), and Bennett (the occupants of the room) were suspected of violations of Code § 191, that they had transferred large amounts of money to Danish bank accounts, and that within a few days they had spent thousands of dollars on telephone calls. The Danish court concluded: "According to the available information, including, especially the transfers of money and the extent of the telephone bills, definite reasons exist to believe that the said telephone is being used to give information to, or from, a person suspected of violation of Penal Code § 191." These findings satisfied Justice Act §§ 781(1), (3), and the Danish court satisfied Justice Act § 781(2) by determining that the monitoring was of definite importance to the investigation. The targeted parties had been appointed counsel according to Justice Act § 784(1)(1)–(3). The court authorized the monitoring until December 11, 1987.

The second wiretaps were of the Nielsen residence and the public telephone, Aalborg, from December 7 to 9, 1987. On December 7, 1987, the court was notified that Villabona, Bennett, and Nielsen had made plans to travel to Aalborg. The Danish police then requested permission to monitor the telephone at Nielsen's residence in Aalborg, as well as authorization to install an electronic eavesdropping device in any hotel rooms they might move to, and to monitor any telephone calls from any such hotel rooms. The court granted the requested authorization until December 11, 1987.

After investigators observed Villabona making calls from the public telephone in Aalborg, Danish officials requested that the public telephone calls also be monitored. The Aalborg court allowed the monitoring of the public telephone calls until December 11, 1987. Again, the provisions of the Justice Act were followed. On December 18, 1987, the court, in accordance with Justice Act § 788 found that Nielsen and the owner of the public telephone "should not be informed about the phone bugging undertaken, as disclosure would be damaging to the investigation of the case."

The third wiretap involved the Hotel Sara–Dan, Copenhagen, from December 8 to 9, 1987. On December 9, 1987, the Copenhagen Municipal Court was told that on December 8 a tap was placed on a telephone at the Hotel Sara–Dan. Villabona and Bennett had returned from Aalborg to Copenhagen so that they could fly to Milan on December 9, 1987. The court, in accordance with Justice Act § 781, found that "definite reasons" existed to believe that the monitored communications contained information concerning suspected violations of Penal Code § 191, and that the monitoring "must be considered of decisive importance for the investigation." The monitoring stopped on December 9 because Villabona, Bennett, and Nielsen left the hotel. As in the previous episodes, the court waived the "duty to notify" the targets in accordance with Justice Act § 788(4).

The fourth tap involved the Nielsen residence and the public telephone, Aalborg, from March 28 to April 16, 1988. The Aalborg court was informed that Villabona and Nielsen were to return to Aalborg on March 28. Permission to tap the telephone at Nielsen's residence and the public telephone were sought. The Aalborg court found that based on Villabona's and Nielsen's last visit and telephone use, the tap was justified under the Justice Act. The tap was to expire on April 22, 1988, "with the provision that monitoring must be discontinued immediately if the defendants move."

A fifth wiretap occurred in Milan, Italy. On December 9, 1987, Villabona and Bennett arrived in Milan from Copenhagen. The day before, the Danish police notified a United States special agent of this planned trip. He, in turn, telephoned a United States special agent in Milan and requested physical surveillance. The latter agent contacted Major Rabiti of the Guardia Di Finanza and requested a watch on Villabona and Bennett. Rabiti obtained authorization to wiretap their hotel room.

The district court found that this wiretap was not the product of a joint venture between United States and Italian authorities. That a United States agent told Rabiti about Villabona and Bennett did not create a "joint venture" between the United States and Italy regarding this wiretap. We hold that the district court did not clearly err when it found no joint investigation surrounding the Milan wiretap, and, therefore, that Fourth Amendment principles do not apply. Because the wiretap was conducted by foreign officials without substantial United States involvement, the results are admissible.

In summary, the finding that the Milan wiretap was not a joint venture is not clearly erroneous. The finding that the Danish wiretaps were conducted pursuant to a joint venture is also not clearly erroneous, but Danish law was complied with for each Danish wiretap. None of the evidence from the wiretaps is therefore subject to exclusion under the Fourth Amendment.

REINHARDT, CIRCUIT JUDGE, dissenting.

Here, in a few, short, deceptively simple paragraphs, the majority has taken another substantial step toward the elimination of what was once a firmly established constitutional right—the right of American citizens to be free from unreasonable searches conducted by their own government.

This time, the majority holds that for all practical purposes the Fourth Amendment's protections do not extend beyond our borders, and that the only limitations on searches of Americans abroad are those imposed by foreign governments, *even when our government initiates and participates in the search*. Oddly, the majority reaches this erroneous and unfortunate result by first acknowledging what it must—that the Fourth Amendment *is* applicable to such searches. However, it then strips this important principle of all significance by holding that we must look exclusively to *foreign law* when determining whether the search violates the Fourth Amendment. According to the majority, our government's decision to initiate the search of an American citizen satisfies the requirements of that once powerful Amendment so long as the foreign officials who conduct the search comply with their own laws. Thus, the majority opinion stands for the paradoxical rule that the Fourth Amendment applies to searches of American citizens in which United States agents play a substantial role but that probable cause, the most basic requirement of the Fourth Amendment, does not—except in the unlikely circumstance that the foreign land in which the search is conducted happens to have the identical requirements that our Constitution imposes.

The practical consequences of the majority's opinion can be simply stated. Without the probable cause requirement, the Fourth Amendment is without any real force. Searches of American citizens abroad can be instigated at the will of government agents. Any American traveling outside our nation's boundaries on vacation, business, or just visiting his family, is now fair game for wiretapping, surreptitious searches, and other invasions of privacy *whenever* members of the CIA, the DEA, the FBI, or who knows how many other alphabet law enforcement agencies, so desire.

Put simply, what the majority holds is that the only Fourth Amendment protections United States citizens who travel abroad enjoy vis-a-vis the United States government are those safeguards, if any, afforded by the laws of the foreign nations they visit. Under the majority's holding, the Fourth Amendment's requirements are wholly redundant since they provide nothing more than is already provided by foreign law. In fact, under the majority's rule, the Fourth Amendment provides even less protection than foreign law since, according to the principal case on which the majority relies, the Constitution does not even require foreign officials to comply with their own law; all that is required is that American officials have a good faith belief that they did so. Thus, even though the majority concedes that the Fourth Amendment applies to joint-venture searches like the one before us, it holds that when Americans enter Iraq, Iran, Singapore, Kuwait, China, or other similarly inclined foreign lands, they can be treated by the United States government exactly the way those foreign nations treat their own citizens—at least for Fourth Amendment purposes.

NOTES AND QUESTIONS

1. *The first question: Who is being monitored?* As the *Barona* case explains, the threshold Fourth Amendment question in a case involving extraterritorial evidence collection is the identity of the person subject to surveillance.

The key case is United States v. Verdugo–Urquidez, 494 U.S. 259 (1990), which considered a search of Mexican residences belonging to a suspected drug kingpin who was a citizen of Mexico. The defendant was arrested in Mexico by Mexico authorities, and he was turned over to the United States to face criminal charges in the United States. United States agents arranged a search of the defendant's home as part of a joint operation between United States and Mexico law enforcement agencies. A search of Verdugo–Urquidez's residence in Mexicali, Mexico, uncovered a "tally sheet" that investigators believed reflected quantities of marijuana smuggled into the United States. When charges were filed against Verdugo–Urquidez in the United States, his attorney moved to suppress the tally sheet on the ground that the search of the defendant's Mexicali home violated the Fourth Amendment.

In a majority opinion by Chief Justice Rehnquist, the Supreme Court concluded that the defendant had no Fourth Amendment rights because he lacked sufficient voluntary contacts with the United States to be among "the People" covered by the Fourth Amendment:

> What we know of the history of the drafting of the Fourth Amendment * * * suggests that its purpose was to restrict searches and seizures which might be conducted by the United States in domestic matters. * * * The available historical data show * * * that the purpose of the Fourth Amendment was to protect the people of the United States against arbitrary action by their own Government; it was never suggested that the provision was intended to restrain the actions of the Federal Government against aliens outside of the United States territory.

> We think that the text of the Fourth Amendment, its history, and our cases discussing the application of the Constitution to aliens and extraterritorially require rejection of respondent's claim. At the time of the search, he was a citizen and resident of Mexico with no voluntary attachment to the United States, and the place searched was located in Mexico. Under these circumstances, the Fourth Amendment has no application.

> For better or for worse, we live in a world of nation-states in which our Government must be able to function effectively in the company of sovereign nations. Some who violate our laws may live outside our

borders under a regime quite different from that which obtains in this country. Situations threatening to important American interests may arise half-way around the globe, situations which in the view of the political branches of our Government require an American response with armed force. If there are to be restrictions on searches and seizures which occur incident to such American action, they must be imposed by the political branches through diplomatic understanding, treaty, or legislation.

Id. at 266, 274–75.

Justice Kennedy provided the fifth vote for the *Verdugo–Urquidez* majority opinion, but he also wrote a concurring opinion suggesting a different approach. Justice Kennedy rejected Chief Justice Rehnquist's focus on the original meaning of "the People," and instead focused on the practical difficulty of applying a warrant requirement overseas:

> I cannot place any weight on the reference to "the people" in the Fourth Amendment as a source of restricting its protections. With respect, I submit these words do not detract from its force or its reach. Given the history of our Nation's concern over warrantless and unreasonable searches, explicit recognition of "the right of the people" to Fourth Amendment protection may be interpreted to underscore the importance of the right, rather than to restrict the category of persons who may assert it. The restrictions that the United States must observe with reference to aliens beyond its territory or jurisdiction depend, as a consequence, on general principles of interpretation, not on an inquiry as to who formed the Constitution or a construction that some rights are mentioned as being those of "the people."

> The conditions and considerations of this case would make adherence to the Fourth Amendment's warrant requirement impracticable and anomalous. * * * [T]he Constitution does not require United States agents to obtain a warrant when searching the foreign home of a nonresident alien. If the search had occurred in a residence within the United States, I have little doubt that the full protections of the Fourth Amendment would apply. But that is not this case. The absence of local judges or magistrates available to issue warrants, the differing and perhaps unascertainable conceptions of reasonableness and privacy that prevail abroad, and the need to cooperate with foreign officials all indicate that the Fourth Amendment's warrant requirement should not apply in Mexico as it does in this country. For this reason, in addition to the other persuasive justifications stated by the Court, I agree that no violation of the Fourth Amendment has occurred in the case before us.

Id. at 276, 278 (Kennedy, J., concurring). Justice Brennan dissented, joined by Justice Marshall:

> The majority ignores * * * the most obvious connection between Verdugo–Urquidez and the United States: he was investigated and is being prosecuted for violations of United States law and may well spend the rest of his life in a United States prison. The "sufficient connection" is supplied not by Verdugo–Urquidez, but by the Government. Respondent is entitled to the protections of the Fourth Amendment because our

Government, by investigating him and attempting to hold him accountable under United States criminal laws, has treated him as a member of our community for purposes of enforcing our laws. He has become, quite literally, one of the governed. Fundamental fairness and the ideals underlying our Bill of Rights compel the conclusion that when we impose societal obligations such as the obligation to comply with our criminal laws, on foreign nationals, we in turn are obliged to respect certain correlative rights, among them the Fourth Amendment.

Id. at 283–84 (Brennan, J., dissenting).

The *Barona* majority opinion suggests that Barona, Martinez, and Villabona might have no Fourth Amendment rights under *Verdugo–Urquidez.* Do you agree? What facts would you want to know to answer this question?

2. *The second question: Who is doing the monitoring?* Assuming that a defendant has Fourth Amendment rights under *Verdugo–Urquidez,* the next question considers who is doing the monitoring. There are three categories to consider: investigations conducted by foreign governments; joint investigations by U.S. officials and foreign government investigators; and investigations conducted exclusively by U.S. officials. The following notes consider these three categories.

3. *Investigations conducted by foreign governments.* As the *Barona* case indicates, the Fourth Amendment does not apply to investigations by foreign governments. This makes sense: The Fourth Amendment does not regulate conduct by private actors, and officials from foreign governments are the equivalent of private actors from a constitutional standpoint. At the same time, some courts have suggested that there are limits on the admissibility of evidence from searches and seizures by foreign governments. The *Barona* case articulates the standard that has been recited a number of times in the Ninth Circuit: the test is whether the search and seizure by the foreign government "shocks the judicial conscience." If it does, the court can require exclusion of the evidence "in the exercise of its supervisory powers." *But see* United States v. Mount, 757 F.2d 1315, 1320 (D.C. Cir. 1985) (Bork, J., concurring) (arguing that lower courts lack supervisory powers to impose an exclusionary rule for searches by foreign governments).

4. *Joint investigations.* The Fourth Amendment does apply to searches and seizures undertaken as part of a joint investigation by U.S. officials and foreign government investigators. The governing law here is rather murky, as the Supreme Court has never directly addressed the relevant legal standard. In the Ninth Circuit, however, the general Fourth Amendment command is reasonableness; specifically, it is reasonableness measured by reference to the law in the country where the search occurred. If investigators in the United States ask French investigators to wiretap an e-mail account in France, for example, the constitutional reasonableness of the surveillance is measured by reference to French law. This standard requires judges to apply foreign law and determine if the monitoring was legal where it occurred. If it was legal, the thinking goes, it was constitutionally reasonable. *See* United States v. Peterson, 812 F.2d 486, 490 (9th Cir. 1987) (Kennedy, J.).

This standard incorporates a good faith exception. So long as United States officials reasonably rely on representations of foreign officials that searches comply with foreign law, the evidence will not be suppressed. As then-Judge, now-Justice Anthony Kennedy explained in *Peterson*, 812 F.2d at 492:

> The good faith exception is grounded in the realization that the exclusionary rule does not function as a deterrent in cases in which the law enforcement officers acted on a reasonable belief that their conduct was legal. It is true, as appellants note, that *Leon* speaks only in terms of good faith reliance on a facially valid search warrant. That is not dispositive, however. We conclude that the reasoning applies as well to reliance on foreign law enforcement officers' representations that there has been compliance with their own law. American law enforcement officers were not in an advantageous position to judge whether the search was lawful, as would have been the case in a domestic setting. Holding them to a strict liability standard for failings of their foreign associates would be even more incongruous than holding law enforcement officials to a strict liability standard as to the adequacy of domestic warrants. We conclude that the good faith exception to the exclusionary rule announced in *Leon* applies to the foreign search.

> We do not suggest that objectively unreasonable reliance on foreign law officers can cloak the search with immunity from the exclusionary rule. That said, permitting reasonable reliance on representations about foreign law is a rational accommodation to the exigencies of foreign investigations.

5. *Searches and seizures conducted exclusively by the United States government.* The Fourth Amendment also applies to searches abroad conducted exclusively by United States officials. Few cases reveal how the law applies in this situation, as United States officials normally will work with governments abroad in criminal cases. In such instances, the cooperation will trigger the "joint investigation" standards. For the most part, international searches conducted exclusively by the United States abroad will occur in national security cases rather than in criminal cases. The Fourth Amendment issues will be litigated only in the rare event that the national security investigation eventually leads to criminal charges in the United States.

A significant case in which this occurred was In re Terrorist Bombings of U.S. Embassies in East Africa, 552 F.3d 157 (2d Cir. 2008). This case involved surveillance of a United States citizen, Wadih El–Hage, when he was located in Kenya and was operating as part of an Al Qaeda terrorist cell. The United States listened in on El–Hage's telephone calls without a warrant and without cooperating with Kenyan officials. When El–Hage was later brought to the United States and charged with involvement in the bombings of United States Embassies in Africa, he moved to suppress on the ground that the warrantless surveillance had violated his Fourth Amendment rights.

In an opinion by Judge Cabranes, the Second Circuit held that the Warrant Clause of the Fourth Amendment has no application to searches and seizures outside the United States. Thus, searches and seizures outside the United States did not require the United States to obtain a warrant:

> First, there is nothing in our history or our precedents suggesting that U.S. officials must first obtain a warrant before conducting an overseas

search. El–Hage has pointed to no authority—and we are aware of none—directly supporting the proposition that warrants are necessary for searches conducted abroad by U.S. law enforcement officers or local agents acting in collaboration with them; nor has El–Hage identified any instances in our history where a foreign search was conducted pursuant to an American search warrant. This dearth of authority is not surprising in light of the history of the Fourth Amendment and its Warrant Clause as well as the history of international affairs.

Second, nothing in the history of the foreign relations of the United States would require that U.S. officials obtain warrants from foreign magistrates before conducting searches overseas or, indeed, to suppose that all other states have search and investigation rules akin to our own. * * * The American procedure of issuing search warrants on a showing of probable cause simply does not extend throughout the globe and, pursuant to the Supreme Court's instructions, the Constitution does not condition our government's investigative powers on the practices of foreign legal regimes quite different from that which obtains in this country.

Third, if U.S. judicial officers were to issue search warrants intended to have extraterritorial effect, such warrants would have dubious legal significance, if any, in a foreign nation. A warrant issued by a U.S. court would neither empower a U.S. agent to conduct a search nor would it necessarily compel the intended target to comply. It would be a nullity, or in the words of the Supreme Court, "a dead letter."

Fourth and finally, it is by no means clear that U.S. judicial officers could be authorized to issue warrants for overseas searches, although we need not resolve that issue here.

Id. at 169–71. According to the Second Circuit, the constitutionality of a search or seizure overseas should be governed by a "totality of the circumstances" reasonableness standard, balancing "the degree to which it intrudes upon an individual's privacy" and "the degree to which it is needed for the promotion of legitimate governmental interests." *Id.* at 172.[1]

Are the legal rules that govern foreign searches exclusively by the United States Government consistent with the legal rules that govern foreign searches by joint investigations? Imagine the United States and Belgium cooperate to wiretap a United States citizen located in Belgium. Belgian law requires a warrant to conduct the monitoring, which means that a proper Belgian warrant is needed to satisfy the Fourth Amendment. On the other hand, if the United States decides to ignore the Belgian authorities and wiretap the account on its own, then no warrant needs to be obtained.

Are these rules inconsistent? Note that there is a way to reconcile the two sets of law. If you assume that a Belgian warrant is not actually a "warrant" for Fourth Amendment purposes, then the requirement of obtaining a Belgian warrant in the joint investigation is not formally a warrant requirement.

---

1. How the court applied the reasonableness standard is covered in the next chapter at pages 662–63.

Rather, obtaining the Belgian warrant is necessary only to make the search "reasonable" even though a United States warrant is not necessary.

6. *Rule 41 and Searches Outside the United States.* In 2008, Federal Rule of Criminal Procedure 41 was amended to allow investigators to obtain a United States warrant to conduct a search outside the United States in a few limited situations. According to the new Rule 41(b)(5),

> a magistrate judge having authority in any district where activities related to the crime may have occurred, or in the District of Columbia, may issue a warrant for property that is located outside the jurisdiction of any state or district, but within any of the following: (A) a United States territory, possession, or commonwealth; (B) the premises—no matter who owns them—of a United States diplomatic or consular mission in a foreign state, including any appurtenant building, part of a building, or land used for the mission's purposes; or (C) a residence and any appurtenant land owned or leased by the United States and used by United States personnel assigned to a United States diplomatic or consular mission in a foreign state.

Rule 41(b)(5). The 2008 Federal Rules of Criminal Procedure Advisory Committee Notes explain the provision as follows:

> Rule 41(b)(5) authorizes a magistrate judge to issue a search warrant for property located within certain delineated parts of United States jurisdiction that are outside of any State or any federal judicial district. The locations covered by the rule include United States territories, possessions, and commonwealths not within a federal judicial district as well as certain premises associated with United States diplomatic and consular missions. These are locations in which the United States has a legally cognizable interest or in which it exerts lawful authority and control.
> * * *
> Rule 41(b)(5) provides the authority to issue warrants for the seizure of property in the designated locations when law enforcement officials are required or find it desirable to obtain such warrants. The Committee takes no position on the question whether the Constitution requires a warrant for searches covered by the rule, or whether any international agreements, treaties, or laws of a foreign nation might be applicable.

As the 2008 Amendments show, Rule 41 can be amended to provide authority for investigators to obtain a warrant to conduct searches outside the United States, even beyond the limited category provided. As a matter of policy, should such warrants be allowed? Should they be required?

7. In the *Barona* case, Judge Wallace and Judge Reinhardt disagree on the Fourth Amendment framework that should apply to "joint investigations" outside the United States. Judge Wallace measures reasonableness based on compliance with the law where the search occurs, whereas Judge Reinhardt apparently would analyze joint searches outside the United States using the same Fourth Amendment rules that apply inside the United States to searches conducted exclusively by United States investigators.

Which approach makes more sense? Let's break down the possibilities. If the Fourth Amendment and foreign search and seizure law happen to be identical, then it makes no difference which approach is followed. If foreign law is more privacy-protective than the Fourth Amendment, however, Judge Wallace's approach will hold investigators to a higher standard than will Judge Reinhardt's standard. For example, if surveillance law in Freedonia does not have a consent exception, a joint investigation that listens in on a telephone call of a United States citizen vacationing in Freedonia with the other party's consent would violate the Fourth Amendment even if the same surveillance technique would not violate the Fourth Amendment if it occurred inside the United States. On the other hand, if foreign law is less protective than the Fourth Amendment, Judge Wallace's approach will hold investigators to a lower standard than Judge Reinhardt's standard. For example, if surveillance law in Freedonia lets the police obtain a wiretap order based only on reasonable suspicion (that is, without probable cause), a joint investigation that taps a phone in Freedonia would not violate the Fourth Amendment even if the same technique would violate the Fourth Amendment if it occurred inside the United States.

Does it make sense that the Fourth Amendment rights of United States citizens fluctuates based on the domestic law of the country where they are physically present? Does your answer depend on whether foreign law only determines the reasonableness of searches, as compared to compliance with the Fourth Amendment more broadly? The difference may be important. For example, suppose the Freedonia Constitution requires a probable cause search warrant to install a pen register. Does this mean that the warrantless use of a pen register in Freedonia to monitor a United States citizen violates the Fourth Amendment? Or does *Smith v. Maryland* apply to the question of what is a search, with the *Barona* inquiry into foreign law used only to determine whether a search or seizure is reasonable?

Finally, consider how Judge Reinhardt's approach might work (or not work) in practice. If United States investigators must follow the same Fourth Amendment rules abroad that they follow in the United States, they may need to obtain court orders or follow procedures that local law does not have or even flatly forbids. For example, one pillar of Fourth Amendment law is that warrants must be issued by a detached and neutral magistrate. *See* Johnson v. United States, 333 U.S. 10, 13–14 (1948). Foreign judges may not qualify under this standard, as not every country follows the tripartite scheme of separation of powers found in the United States. Does this mean that foreign search warrants may not satisfy the Fourth Amendment, even if they require probable cause and particularity? If so, how can United States investigators collect evidence without violating the Fourth Amendment?

8. *Foreign law and the exclusionary rule.* In his *Barona* dissent, Judge Reinhardt claims that "[u]nder the majority's holding, the Fourth Amendment's requirements are wholly redundant since they provide nothing more than is already provided by foreign law." Is this accurate? Fourth Amendment protection adds something critically important: the remedy of a constitutional exclusionary rule. The exclusionary rule is very rare outside the United States, and where it applies it is optional rather than mandatory. *See* Craig M. Bradley, *The Emerging International Consensus as to Criminal Procedure Rule*, 14 Mich. J. Int'l L. 171, 174 (1993).

9. *Cross-border searches.* In United States v. Gorshkov, 2001 WL 1024026 (W.D. Wash. 2001), a computer hacker from Russia who had hacked into several United States computers was lured to the United States by an FBI undercover operation. The hacker believed that he was interviewing for a computer security job at an American company called "Invita." Working from Invita's office, he used his username and password to access an Internet account in Russia. FBI agents copied the username and password, and they later used them to remotely access and download the defendant's files stored on the Russian server. The district court held that accessing and downloading the file did not violate the Fourth Amendment under *Verdugo–Urquidez*:

> The use of the password to access the Russian computers and download the data did not constitute a Fourth Amendment violation. The Fourth Amendment does not apply to the agents' extraterritorial access to computers in Russia and their copying of data contained thereon. * * * [T]he Russian computers are not protected by the Fourth Amendment because they are property of a non-resident and located outside the territory of the United States. Under *United States v. Verdugo–Urquidez*, 494 U.S. 259 (1990), the Fourth Amendment does not apply to a search or seizure of a non-resident alien's property outside the territory of the United States. In this case, the computers accessed by the agents were located in Russia, as was the data contained on those computers that the agents copied. Until the copied data was transmitted to the United States, it was outside the territory of this country and not subject to the protections of the Fourth Amendment.
>
> Defendant attempts to distinguish *Verdugo* by first noting that the defendant in that case was found not to have significant contacts with the United States because he involuntarily entered the country after his arrest, while in this case Defendant Gorshkov voluntarily entered the country. The Court finds, however, that a single entry into the United States that is made for a criminal purpose is hardly the sort of voluntary association with this country that should qualify Defendant as part of our national community for purposes of the Fourth Amendment. Defendant also attempts to distinguish *Verdugo* by noting that the search in *Verdugo* was effected by a joint effort made lawfully pursuant to Mexican law, with the consent and authorization of Mexican officials, while in this case the search was done by FBI fiat. Nothing in the opinion, however, indicates that the reach of the Fourth Amendment turns on this issue. Therefore, the search of the Russian computers was not protected by the Fourth Amendment.

Id. at *3. Is this argument persuasive? Did the defendant really enter the United States "for a criminal purpose"? Wasn't his purpose to obtain legitimate employment as a computer security consultant?

More broadly, what legal framework should govern so-called "cross-border searches," remote searches from one country of data located in another country?

Assume FBI agents are conducting an investigation of a United States citizen located abroad. What Fourth Amendment rules regulate access to that person's remotely stored files? Should the location of the person under investigation make any difference? Should the legality of such searches consider the law where the data is located?

What factors are relevant to determining a "reasonable expectation of privacy" abroad? If an FBI agent in the United States accesses an account in France belonging to an American citizen, should the FBI agent need to obtain a warrant? Where can he obtain the warrant—in the United States or in France? What if the FBI agent is located in France?

For more on cross-border searches, see Stewart M. Young, Comment, *Verdugo in Cyberspace: Boundaries of Fourth Amendment Rights for Foreign Nationals in Cybercrime Cases*, 10 Mich. Telecomm. & Tech. L. Rev. 139 (2003); Jack L. Goldsmith, *The Internet and the Legitimacy of Remote Cross–Border Searches*, 2001 U. Chi. Legal. F. 103; Patricia L. Bellia, *Chasing Bits Across Borders*, 2001 U. Chi. Legal. F. 35.

3. MUTUAL LEGAL ASSISTANCE AND INTERNATIONAL TREATIES

In most computer crime cases, digital evidence located abroad is collected by agents of foreign governments under laws that govern mutual legal assistance. These laws regulate both the collection of evidence in the United States by United States officials at the behest of foreign governments and the collection of evidence outside of the United States by foreign governments at the behest of the United States.

There are two primary methods of obtaining legal assistance from foreign governments. The first method is through letters rogatory, and the second method is through procedures described in mutual legal assistance treaties.

PREPARATION OF LETTERS ROGATORY

United States Department of State.
http://travel.state.gov/law/info/judicial/judicial_683.html.

Letters rogatory are the customary method of obtaining judicial assistance from abroad in the absence of a treaty or executive agreement. Letters rogatory are requests from courts in one country to the judiciary of a foreign country requesting the performance of an act which, if done without the sanction of the foreign court, could constitute a violation of that country's sovereignty. Letters rogatory may be used in countries where multi-lateral or bilateral treaties on judicial assistance are not in force to effect service of process or to obtain evidence if permitted by the laws of the foreign country.

Execution of letters rogatory may take a year or more worldwide. Letters rogatory are customarily transmitted via the diplomatic channel, a time-consuming means of transmission. The time involved may be shortened by transmitting a copy of the request through local legal counsel if permitted in the foreign country.

Letters Rogatory Checklist [for U.S. Officials Seeking to Issue Letters Rogatory]: First, review the country specific judicial assistance information on the Department of State internet page. Then review U.S. state or federal law on the subject. After you prepare your draft, consider whether a judge in a foreign country speaking another language will understand what you are requesting. You will then need to secure the signature of a judge in the United States on your Letters rogatory. Next, obtain any necessary authentications specified in the Department of State country specific information.

If the language of the country where the letters rogatory are to be presented is not English, you will need to obtain a certified translation of the letters rogatory and any supporting documents and prepare the entire package in duplicate for transmittal to the U.S. Department of State.

Essential elements of letters rogatory:

- A statement that a request for international judicial assistance is being made in the interests of justice;

- A brief synopsis of the case, including identification of the parties and the nature of the claim and relief sought to enable the foreign court to understand the issues involved;

- The type of case [e.g. civil, criminal, administrative];

- The nature of the assistance required [compel testimony or production of evidence; service of process];

- Name, address and other identifiers, such as corporate title, of the person abroad to be served or from whom evidence is to be compelled, documents to be served;

- A list of questions to be asked, where applicable, generally in the form of written interrogatories;

- A list of documents or other evidence to be produced;

- A statement from the requesting court expressing a willingness to provide similar assistance to judicial authorities of the receiving state;

- Statement that the requesting court or counsel is willing to reimburse the judicial authorities of the receiving state for costs incurred in executing the requesting court's letters rogatory.

Signature and Authentication: Letters rogatory must be signed by a judge. The clerk should not sign on behalf of the judge. For most countries, the seal of the court and signature of the judge is sufficient. Many countries will not accept letters rogatory issued by an Administrative Law Judge. In administrative cases, it is possible to obtain letters rogatory issued by a federal district court under the All Writs Act, 28 U.S.C. 1651.

Translation: The letters rogatory and any accompanying documents must be translated into the official language of the foreign country. The translator should execute an affidavit as to the validity of the translation before a notary.

Transmittal of Letters Rogatory by Department of State to the Foreign Authorities through Diplomatic Channel: Letters rogatory generally are transmitted to foreign judicial authorities through the diplomatic channel. The diplomatic channel is a route by which the documents are sent to the foreign court. The normal process is as follows:

Letters rogatory transmitted by court or counsel to Department of State;

Letters rogatory transmitted by Department of State to U.S. Embassy;

Letters rogatory transmitted to Ministry of Foreign Affairs by U.S. Embassy;

Letters rogatory transmitted to Ministry of Justice by Ministry of Foreign Affairs;

Letters rogatory transmitted to Foreign Court by Ministry of Justice.

Execution of Letters Rogatory by the Foreign Court: The foreign court will execute letters rogatory in accordance with the laws and regulations of the foreign country. In compelling evidence, for example, many foreign courts do not permit foreign attorneys to participate in their court proceedings. Not all foreign countries utilize the services of court reporters or routinely provide verbatim transcripts. Sometimes the presiding judge will dictate his or her recollection of the witness' responses.

Return of Executed Letters Rogatory: When letters rogatory are executed by the foreign authorities, they are generally returned to the Department of State via the diplomatic channel and the Office of American Citizens Services will send them to the requesting court in the United States via certified mail. Requesting counsel is also notified. At the request of the court, the executed letter rogatory and proof of service/evidence produced can be returned directly to requesting counsel. If transmittal by commercial express delivery service is preferred, please include your account number in the covering letter.

Authority: The issuance of letters rogatory by federal courts is provided for under Rule 28(b) Fed. R. Civ. P. and Rule 4(f)(2)(B), Fed. R. Civ. P. Letters rogatory have also been issued under the All Writs Act, 28 U.S.C. 1651. 28 U.S.C. 1781 and 28 U.S.C. 1782 describe the transmittal of letters rogatory through the Department of State and through the district courts; 28 U.S.C. 1696 provides for the use of letters rogatory for service of process pursuant to a request by a foreign tribunal.

EXAMPLE - LETTERS ROGATORY

NAME OF COURT REQUESTING JUDICIAL ASSISTANCE

NAME OF PLAINTIFF

DOCKET NUMBER

V.

NAME OF DEFENDANT

REQUEST FOR INTERNATIONAL JUDICIAL ASSISTANCE (LETTER ROGATORY)

(Name of the requesting court) presents its compliments to the appropriate judicial authority of (name of receiving state), and requests international judicial assistance to (obtain evidence/effect service of process) to be used in a (civil, criminal, administrative) proceeding before this court in the above captioned matter. A (trial/hearing) on this matter is scheduled at present for (date) in (city, state, country).

This court requests the assistance described herein as necessary in the interests of justice. The assistance requested is that the appropriate judicial authority of (name of receiving state) (compel the appearance of the below named individuals to give evidence/produce documents) (effect service of process upon the below named individuals).

(NAMES OF WITNESSES/PERSONS TO BE SERVED)

(NATIONALITY OF WITNESSES/PERSONS TO BE SERVED)

(ADDRESS OF WITNESSES/PERSONS TO BE SERVED)

(DESCRIPTION OF DOCUMENTS OR OTHER EVIDENCE TO BE PRODUCED)

FACTS

(The facts of the case pending before the requesting court should be stated briefly here, including a list of those laws of the sending state which govern the matter pending before the court in the receiving state.)

QUESTIONS

(If the request is for evidence, the questions for the witnesses should be listed here).

(List any special rights of witnesses pursuant to the laws of the requesting state here).

(List any special methods or procedures to be followed).

(Include request for notification of time and place for examination of witnesses/documents before the court in the receiving state here).

RECIPROCITY

The requesting court should include a statement expressing a willingness to provide similar assistance to judicial authorities of the receiving state.

REIMBURSEMENT FOR COSTS

The requesting court should include a statement expressing a willingness to reimburse the judicial authorities of the receiving state for costs incurred in executing the requesting court's letters rogatory.

SIGNATURE OF REQUESTING JUDGE

NAME OF REQUESTING COURT

NOTES AND QUESTIONS

1. *Letters rogatory by state officials.* State law enforcement officials can obtain letters rogatory to collect evidence abroad much like federal officials can. *See* Susan W. Brenner & Joseph J. Schwerha IV, *Transnational Evidence Gathering and Local Prosecution of International Cybercrime*, 20 J. Marshall J. Computer & Info. L. 347, 384–85 (2002).

2. *Letters rogatory by the defense.* After a defendant is charged, counsel for the defendant can obtain letters rogatory for use at trial. The defendant must ask the trial court for the authority to issue the letter, and must satisfy any other legal requirements for the request. *See, e.g.,* United States v. Korogodsky, 4 F. Supp.2d 262 (S.D.N.Y. 1998). *See also* Ellen S. Podgor, Understanding International Criminal Law 89 (2004).

The more effective and efficient alternative to letters rogatory are mutual legal assistance treaties (MLATs) negotiated between and among different countries. When countries negotiate and sign an MLAT, they agree in advance as to what kinds of assistance will be provided. When an MLAT has been signed, requests for information are obligatory as a matter of international law. The request for assistance cannot be refused if it complies with the treaty. In contrast, letters rogatory are followed entirely for reasons of comity: governments have no legal obligation to comply with them. MLATs are also preferable because they specify the form and procedure in which information will be obtained and transmitted, allowing each country to specify what is necessary for the admission of evidence in its courts.

The following case demonstrates how international cooperation through an MLAT can work, as well as the Fourth Amendment issues that it may raise.

UNITED STATES v. VILAR

United States District Court for the Southern District of New York, 2007.
2007 WL 1075041.

KARAS, J.

Defendants Alberto William Vilar and Gary Alan Tanaka are charged with an alleged fraud scheme involving investors' funds. The Superseding Indictment, filed on August 15, 2006, charges Defendants with conspiracy to commit securities, mail, wire, and investment advisor fraud and money laundering. They are also charged in separate substantive counts with securities fraud, investment advisor fraud, mail fraud, two counts of wire fraud, and four counts of money laundering.

Each Defendant has filed a Motion to Suppress the fruits of [a search of the offices of a business "Amerindo U.K."] conducted at the Government's request, pursuant to a Mutual Legal Assistance Treaty and two

U.K. search warrants, in the United Kingdom on October 13 and 14, 2005. The motions to suppress the U.K. search are denied.

I.

Detective Sergeant Shaw is a 23–year veteran of the Metropolitan Police in London, England, who has spent much of his law enforcement career investigating white collar crime. At the time of the contested search, Detective Sergeant Shaw was assigned to the International Assistance Unit. Among other things, this Unit processes foreign evidence requests made of the United Kingdom through a Mutual Legal Assistance Treaty ("MLAT"). It is pursuant to such a treaty, for example, that a foreign government agency can request that United Kingdom law enforcement officials conduct a search of a business premises. According to Detective Sergeant Shaw, any such request must come from the proper authority and otherwise comport with the terms of the particular MLAT. Among other such terms, the U.K.'s MLATs require that the requested search be part of an investigation of conduct that is a crime under British law. A MLAT request to search a premises is first reviewed by the United Kingdom Central Authority ("UKCA"), which vets the request to determine if it comports with the MLAT and British law.

If the request is satisfactory, it then is assigned to the appropriate U.K. law enforcement agency. Detective Sergeant Shaw testified that when he receives a MLAT request to conduct a search from the UKCA, he first reviews the request to determine if the request, in his view, is based on sufficient information to justify a warrant. In his experience, he has rejected many requests for a search at this stage of the process. If, however, the request appears to be substantiated, Detective Sergeant Shaw then conducts a background inquiry by, for example, investigating the target premises. Once Detective Sergeant Shaw determines that the request is in order and completes his own inquiry, Detective Sergeant Shaw then awaits a "direction" from the Home Office specifically authorizing him to conduct the search.

From there, U.K. law requires Detective Sergeant Shaw to submit his search warrant request to a senior police officer unconnected to the investigation. This is yet another stage where the request can be rejected. If, however, the senior officer approves the search request, then Detective Sergeant Shaw formally applies for the search warrant through the "clerk of the Court," a court staff person who advises his view of the validity of the warrant. According to Detective Sergeant Shaw, it is not uncommon for the court clerk to recommend rejecting a search warrant request. If, however, the clerk recommends approval of the warrant, the clerk will initial the request and make arrangements for the Detective Sergeant to formally apply for the warrant before the duty judge.

Detective Sergeant Shaw testified that he was the Metropolitan Police official who was assigned the American government's request to conduct a search of Amerindo U.K.'s premises. According to Detective Sergeant Shaw, he received a telephone call from the UKCA in July 2005 regarding an urgent request from American law enforcement officials to search the business premises of Amerindo, U.K. Following the procedure he had described, Detective Sergeant Shaw reviewed the MLAT request to determine if there was a valid basis to apply for a search warrant of Amerindo's business premises. In his words, he believed the request to be "comprehensive and sound."

The search warrant application consisted of a template application that Detective Sergeant Shaw filled in, a typed rider that came directly from the MLAT request, and the information in support of the warrant application which Shaw typed himself. . . . Upon arriving at Bow Street Magistrate's Court, Detective Sergeant Shaw handed the application to Mrs. Elizabeth Franey, a senior legal adviser at the court with approximately twenty years of experience . . . . . Approximately five hours later, Detective Sergeant Shaw returned to the Bow Street Magistrate's Court hoping to be able to make his application to a judge. Mrs. Franey informed him that she had reviewed the application and passed it to a judge, thereby indicating her approval of the application. Then Detective Sergeant Shaw made his application to the senior district judge at the court, Timothy Workman, who was the "duty judge" that day. Judge Workman is the most senior district judge in England and Whales, with the power to issue Schedule I orders and warrants.

Judge Workman asked Detective Sergeant Shaw a series of questions including questions about the nature of the premises, whether the search would extend beyond Amerindo U.K.'s eight crates, the anticipated length of the search, the nature of the property where the materials had previously been located, and whether that property had been shared. . . . Judge Workman then stated that he was satisfied with the application, which was kept at the court, and signed the warrant. Detective Sergeant Shaw believed he was then in possession of a lawfully-obtained, lawfully-issued warrant. After obtaining the warrant, Detective Sergeant Shaw met with the American authorities, including Inspector Fraterrigo. At that meeting, Detective Sergeant Shaw explained that the warrant had been granted, and consequently that the Americans had not wasted their trip over. They then discussed their respective roles during the execution of the search. Detective Sergeant Shaw explained that the Americans were entitled to assist in the search, but that they remained under British supervision and that the ultimate decision regarding whether to seize particular items would rest with the British authorities.

The warrant signed by Judge Workman was executed on Thursday, October 13, 2005.

II.

While the Second Circuit has not addressed this issue, other courts have held that a foreign search is reasonable if it meets the requirement s of the law of the nation in which the search is executed, as long as those requirements do not permit conscious-shocking conduct. As such, Defendants' claims that the U.K. search was unreasonable under American standards because, for example, it was a general warrant that permitted seizure of virtually all Amerindo U.K. records or because it was not based on a finding of probable cause, are not dispositive. Indeed, Defendants cite to no authority to support this novel position.

As an alternative, Defendants spend a great deal of energy attempting to explain why the [U.K.] search contravened British law, but to no avail.[35] The crux of Defendants' claim is that because it was likely that the Amerindo U.K. materials at Cadogan Tate would include legally privileged and "special procedure material," Detective Sergeant Shaw should have obtained a "Schedule 1" order or warrant, instead of the "Section 8" warrant he twice obtained from British judges. The provision invoked by Detective Sergeant Shaw can be summarized as follows:

Section 8 of the Police and Criminal Evidence Act 1984 ["PACE"] empowers magistrates to issue search warrants at the request of the police if certain conditions have been fulfilled. These conditions fall into two categories. The first category, in section 8(1), concerns the nature of the material sought. Generally speaking, the material has to relate to a serious arrestable offence and has to be likely to assist the investigation or to constitute relevant evidence. The second category, in section 8(2), describes the circumstances in which resort to a warrant is justified. They are: either that it is impractical to contact the person in charge of the premises, or that such person is unlikely to allow access without a warrant, or that alerting such person in advance may frustrate the investigation. A search warrant is issued ex parte on the basis of information provided by the police on oath.

[*Very detailed analysis of United Kingdom search and seizure law omitted. The court ultimately concludes that UK law was followed, and if it was not followed, any errors were in good faith.*]

Applying these principles to this case, the Court rejects the claim by Defendants that the search of the Cadogan Tate facility violated U.K. law, or otherwise was unreasonable.

NOTES AND QUESTIONS

1. The *Vilar* case shows how the MLAT process impacts the scope of Fourth Amendment protection. Mutual legal assistance turns the investiga-

---

35. Each side elected to fight the battle over U.K. law with expert opinion. Defendants relied on a thoughtful "Report by English Counsel Instructed on Behalf of Mr. Tanaka." This report, prepared by English Barrister Clare Sibson, is a synopsis of U.K. law on searches. One obvious and admitted limitation of this report, however, is that Ms. Sibson had not been made aware of the facts of the matter concerning Mr. Tanaka in New York. Therefore, among other things, Ms. Sibson offers no opinion about the legality of the warrants issued in connection with the Cadogan Tate search, nor does she say anything about the propriety of the statements Detective Sergeant Shaw made in support of the warrant applications. The Government countered by offering the testimony of Detective Sergeant Shaw. This testimony was helpful in the sense that it was based on the actual events of this case, but of course is limited by the fact that Detective Sergeant Shaw is neither a solicitor nor a barrister. That said, Detective Sergeant Shaw impressed the Court with his grasp of U.K. search and seizure law.

Though foreign law once was treated as an issue of fact, it now is viewed as a question of law and may be determined through the use of any relevant source, including expert testimony.

tion into a "joint investigation" for Fourth amendment purposes, triggering the *Barona* standard and raising the issue of whether the investigators complied with foreign law.

2.   A second way a defendant can attempt to suppress evidence obtained through MLATs is by raising an evidentiary challenge. Specifically, a defendant can argue that the evidence obtained via mutual legal assistance does not satisfy the authenticity standards of the Federal Rules of Evidence. *See, e.g.,* United States v. Phillips, 1979 WL 1505 (M.D. Fla. 1979).

MICHAEL A. SUSSMANN—THE CRITICAL CHALLENGES FROM INTERNATIONAL HIGH–TECH AND COMPUTER–RELATED CRIME AT THE MILLENNIUM

9 Duke J. Comp. & Int'l L. 451, 453–84 (1999).

Imagine this scene out of tomorrow's headlines: A hacker, going on-line through the Internet, breaks into computers that the Federal Aviation Administration uses for air traffic control. He disrupts a regional air traffic network, and the disruption causes the crash of a DC–10 in the Rocky Mountains, killing all aboard. The FAA and the FBI know there has been a hacker intrusion, originating through the Internet, but nothing else. Since anyone can access the Internet from anywhere in the world, the FBI has no idea where the hacker may be located. Moreover, they do not know the motive of the attack or the identity of the attackers. Is it a terrorist group, targeting the United States and likely to strike again at any time, or is it a fourteen-year-old hacker whose prank has spun tragically out of control?

Let us follow this scenario a bit further. Within thirty minutes of the plane crash, the FBI tracks the source of the attack to an Internet Service Provider in Germany. Assuming the worst, another attack could occur at any time, and hundreds of planes in flight over the United States are at risk. The next investigative step is to determine whether the ISP in Germany is a mere conduit, or whether the attack actually originated with a subscriber to that service. In either case, the FBI needs the assistance of the German ISP to help identify the source of the attack, but it is now 3:00 a.m. in Germany.

- Does the FBI dare wait until morning in Europe to seek formal legal assistance from Germany or permission from the German government to continue its investigation within their borders?

- Does the Department of Justice authorize the FBI's computer experts to conduct a search, without German consent, on the German ISP from their terminals in Washington?

- Does the FBI agent need a U.S. court order to access private information overseas? What would be the reach of such an order?

- If the FBI agent plows forward and accesses information from computers in Germany, will the German government be sympathetic to the U.S. plight, will the violation of German sovereignty be condemned, or both?

● What are the diplomatic and foreign policy implications of the United States remotely (and without advance notice) conducting a search that may intrude into German sovereignty?

The legal and policy implications of possible "transborder searches," such as the one contemplated in this scenario, are quickly becoming a concern for law enforcement agencies around the globe as they grapple with new challenges posed by networked communications and new technologies. Traditional investigative procedures—and particularly the often cumbersome procedures that govern investigations at the international level—may not be adequate to meet the need in computer crime cases for immediate law enforcement action reaching beyond national borders. The globalization of criminal activity has created vexing problems that, in some cases, defy simple solutions.

Needed: Sufficient Laws to Punish Computer Crimes

When Country A criminalizes certain conduct and Country B does not, a bridge for cooperation in solving a crime committed in Country A may not be possible. The United States has entered into bilateral treaties of extradition with over 100 countries. These treaties are either "list treaties," containing a list of offenses for which extradition is available, or they require dual criminality (i.e., require that the conduct under investigation is a crime in both the requesting and requested countries and is punishable by at least one year in prison). With regard to treaties for international legal assistance such as those involving the issuance of subpoenas, interviewing of witnesses, or production of documents, some treaties permit assistance as long as the conduct under investigation is a crime in the requesting state. The United States strongly favors this approach. Other treaties permit assistance only if dual criminality exits and if the offense is extraditable. Therefore, if one country does not criminalize computer misuse (or provide for sufficient punishment), extradition and the collection of certain evidence may be prohibited. Consider the following two examples.

In 1992, hackers from Switzerland attacked the San Diego Supercomputer Center. The United States sought help from the Swiss, but the investigation was stymied due to lack of dual criminality (i.e., the two nations did not have similar laws banning the conduct), which became an impediment to official cooperation. Eventually, local police in Zurich did render informal assistance, and they prepared a list of questions for U.S. authorities to answer, transmitted through official channels, so the case could be properly pursued. After the United States answered those questions, but before follow-up questions could be answered through official channels, the hacking stopped, the trail went cold, and the case had to be closed.

Several years later a similar problem arose, when the United States found itself unable to reach a criminal in order to bring him to justice. From August 1995 until February 1996, the Naval Criminal Investigative Service and the FBI investigated a hacker who was stealing password files and altering log files in military, university, and other private computer systems. Many of these systems contained sensitive research on satellites, radiation, and energy-related engineering. U.S. authorities tracked the hacker to Argentina and notified a local Argentine telecommunications carrier. The carrier contacted local law enforcement, which began its own investigation. Subsequently, an Argentine judge authorized the search of the hacker's apartment and the seizure of his computer equipment based on potential violations of Argentine law. Unfortunately, the treaty between Argentina and the United States did not authorize the extradition of individuals for "computer crimes" (although it does for more traditional crimes). The U.S. Attorney's Office in Boston charged the perpetrator with several criminal violations, but it was unclear whether or not the case would ever be resolved due to the absence of uniformity between U.S. and Argentine laws. Fortunately, the hacker agreed to a plea bargain wherein he waived extradition and agreed to plead guilty in the United States.

These cases demonstrate how inadequate laws can allow criminals to go unpunished in one country, while they thwart the efforts of other countries to vindicate the rights of the state and protect its citizens. While the United States has amended its criminal code to specifically penalize a wide variety of computer crimes, other countries have been slower to do so. At a meeting of senior law enforcement officials from the G–8 countries in January 1997, Attorney General Reno stated:

> [U]ntil recently, computer crime has not received the emphasis that other international crimes have engendered. Even now, not all affected nations recognize the threat it poses to public safety or the need for international cooperation to effectively respond to the problem. Consequently, many countries have weak laws, or no laws, against computer hacking—a major obstacle to solving and to prosecuting computer crimes.

The solution to this problem is simple to state: countries need to reach a consensus as to which computer and technology-related activities should be criminalized, and then commit to taking appropriate domestic actions. But it is not as easy to implement. An international consensus concerning the activities that universally should be criminalized may take time to develop. Meanwhile, individual countries that lack this kind of legislation will each have to pass new laws, an often cumbersome and time-consuming process. In the United States, for example, action by both the Congress and the President is required for new legislation.

Needed: Experts Available on a Twenty–Four Hour Basis

A unique feature of high-tech and computer-related crime is that it requires immediate action to locate and identify perpetrators. Due to a general lack of historical communications data, the trail of a criminal may be impossible to trace once a communication link is terminated. This lack of data is due, in part, to the fact that businesses no longer bill their customers by individual telephone call or Internet connection but, instead, by bulk billing (e.g., a single rate for one month of usage). When bulk billing is employed, there is no longer a business need to record the transmission information (i.e., connection times or source and destination) for individual connections; therefore, traffic data may not be available at a later date. Thus, investigators and prosecutors with expertise in this field must be available twenty-four hours a day, at home and by pager, so that appropriate steps can be taken in a fast-breaking high-tech case.

Needed: Effective Means for Obtaining Evidence Internationally

Even if all countries have adequate computer crime laws, possess dedicated, well-trained and well-equipped experts who are available twenty-four hours a day, and have the ability to locate and identify criminals who use networked communications, there remains a significant hurdle to overcome. How does law enforcement collect electronic evidence that may be scattered across several different countries, can be deleted or altered with one click of a mouse, may be encrypted, and will ultimately need to be authenticated in another country's court? Again, these are areas where the challenges have been recognized but solutions either may not be apparent or may be difficult to implement.

1. *Protected Seizures or "Quick Freeze/Quick Thaw."* One characteristic of electronic evidence is that it can be altered, transferred or destroyed almost instantaneously, and from remote locations, often with little more than a single keystroke. These changes to evidence may result from a criminal trying to cover his tracks, or a system administrator routinely clearing old e-mails or other data from a company's servers. Whatever the case, critical evidence can be lost—long before an international request for assistance is ever transmitted. Traditional methods of obtaining evidence from foreign governments can include lengthy delays, as foreign legal processes, translations, and diplomacy slowly proceed. Old modalities may not always be practical when considering new technologies.

Therefore, when electronic evidence is sought, there may be a need for mechanisms such as a "preservation of evidence request" or "protected seizure," which would work as follows. Where there is a particularized concern about the loss of electronic evidence, a country would make an informal international request that the data immediately be preserved. This could be accomplished in a number of ways, from having a telecommunications carrier or ISP copy and store a customer's data, to actually seizing a criminal's computer and securing, but not searching, it for a short period of time. Once data is protected from loss, expedited processes would provide the foreign country with formal documentation to authorize the issuance of a domestic search warrant or similar process.

2. *Transborder Search and Seizure.* Since paper documents must be within close proximity to be of use, they are usually located in the same country as the person being investigated. By contrast, electronic documents are often stored remotely on computers, sometimes thousands of miles away from their author. This may be done because of the structure of a particular business (where data is maintained at company headquarters) or the architecture of the network. At other times, data may be purposely stored in another country to keep it beyond the reach of law enforcement.

A transborder search occurs when a law enforcement agent in his or her own country accesses a computer in another country to obtain electronic evidence, perhaps in furtherance of the execution of a domestic warrant. * * * Because searches made under exigent circumstances (including those where it is believed evidence will be destroyed if not seized) and inadvertent searches across borders are likely to occur, it may be wise for countries to consider developing rules and/or guidelines to govern a transborder search (e.g., regarding notice to the searched country).

Governments have three potential solutions at this juncture. First, governments could decide to forego the development of principles, allowing each country to decide for itself whether transborder searches constitute an acceptable law enforcement practice. Second, governments could limit transborder searches to cases where production of the data could otherwise be compelled through legal processes. This approach expedites the gathering of certain critical evidence while allowing data outside the traditional reach of a country to remain so. The third solution involves creating principles permitting law enforcement agents to conduct transborder searches under clearly defined circumstances that are more broad than those above. Support for this approach may rest on a consensus that the need for effective law enforcement outweighs concerns over protecting data stored in a particular country.

What Is Being Done by Multi-lateral Organizations?

To date, three multilateral organizations (i.e., groups with multiple-nation membership) are doing the bulk of the international policy work on high-tech and computer-related crime: the Council of Europe, the European Union and its related institutions, and the G–8. To a lesser degree, some work in this area has been done by the Organization for Economic Cooperation and Development, and the United Nations.

Of the three main groups, the G–8 has been particularly effective in making progress on several fronts. While the EU and COE have large European memberships, the G–8 has broader representation, with members from Europe, Russia, North America, and Japan. Because networked communications traverse every continent, and because leading communications and computer technology is developed in areas besides Europe (such as Asia and North America), regional efforts to solve universal crime problems will inevitably be either slower or less effective than similar efforts by policy-making bodies with a broad geographic base.

The heads of state of the G–8 countries meet annually. At their 1998 Summit, they adopted a comprehensive plan to fight high-tech and computer-related crime. While the COE started addressing computer crime at the technical level in 1988, its heads of state have only met twice since 1949 when the COE was created, and have never addressed computer crime. While EU heads of state called for a study of the subject and development of relevant policies, the heads of state from its member countries have not settled on a specific plan of action to combat computer crime. Finally, unlike the COE and EU, the G–8 is neither governed by international convention nor constrained by a convention-created bureaucracy. It can therefore move faster and address new and emerging areas as the will of its leaders dictates.

A. The Council of Europe

The Council of Europe is an international organization based in Strasbourg, France. It was established by ten Western European countries in the wake of the Second World War, with the signing of its founding treaty, known as the Statute of the Council of Europe, in 1949. Today, it has a pan-European membership of forty countries, which include the Baltic states, Russia and Turkey. It defines its main role as strengthening democracy, human rights, and the rule of law throughout its member states. In the area of criminal law, twenty conventions and over eighty recommendations have been adopted, as well as a number of reports on crime issues.

In 1989, the Committee of Ministers adopted a recommendation and report on computer-related crime, Recommendation No. R. (89) 9. The recommendation called on member states to consider computer crimes when either reviewing or proposing domestic legislation, and the report contained guidelines in this area for legislators. In 1995, the Committee adopted Recommendation No. R. (95) 13, which provided procedures for implementing Recommendation (89) 9, and contained principles "concerning problems of criminal procedure law connected with information technology" on such topics as search and seizure, technical surveillance, electronic evidence, encryption, and international cooperation.

In February 1997, a Committee of Experts on Crime in Cyber-space (PC–CY) was formed to examine computer crime and related problems in criminal procedure law. Its work is aimed at drafting a binding legal instrument (i.e., a "Cybercrime Convention") which defines cybercrime offenses, and addresses such topics as jurisdiction, international cooperation, search and seizure, data protection, and liability of ISPs. * * * After approval by the Committee of Ministers, the Convention will be open for signature by COE members and non-member states which participated in its drafting.

B. The European Union

The European Union has its roots in three organizations formed in the 1950s by Belgium, West Germany, France, Italy, Luxembourg, and the

Netherlands: the European Coal and Steel Community (ECSC); the European Atomic Energy Community (Euratom); and the European Economic Community (EEC). These three communities are still at the heart of the EU, and the treaties which founded them have since been revised and extended. The Treaty on European Union, generally called the Maastricht Treaty, gives a single legal framework to the three European Communities.

The EU now has fifteen member states, and its own flag, anthem and currency (the Euro). The EU's objective is to "promote economic and social progress which is balanced and sustainable, assert the European identity on the international scene, and introduce a European citizenship for the nationals of the Member States."

In the area of high-tech crime, the EU has issued several texts. In 1995, it promulgated a directive which established certain rights and protections for citizens concerning electronically processed data. For example, the directive establishes the right of a citizen to know what electronic data a corporation maintains on that person, and provides protection against personal data being transferred to a non-EU country if that country has inadequate privacy protections. Member states are required to establish mechanisms to enforce these rights. In 1997, the EU issued a directive designed to ensure privacy relating to telecommunications data. That directive requires telecommunications carriers to delete traffic data at the end of each transmission (with exceptions for billing purposes and for law enforcement and national security needs). In light of these Directives, it is imperative that government policy decisions concerning electronic commerce and privacy be made in concert with decisions concerning public safety.

In 1997, the European Council endorsed an action plan to combat organized crime, and assembled a Multidisciplinary Group on Organized Crime (MDG) to implement the action plan. Recommendation Five of the action plan calls for a study on high-tech crime, and development of a policy addressing public safety which provides law enforcement and judicial authorities with the means to prevent and combat the misuse of new technologies. Since its inception, the MDG has adopted the study of Dr. Ulrich Sieber on legal aspects of computer related crime, and it is exploring what role Europol might play in combating computer crime.

C.　The G–8

1. Background. The present G–8 (or "Group of Eight") leading industrialized democracies originated in 1975 at an Economic Summit convened by President Valery Giscard d'Estaing of France and attended by leaders from Germany, Japan, the United Kingdom and the United States. President Giscard and Chancellor Schmidt of Germany wanted to establish an informal forum for world leaders to discuss world economic issues. Italy and Canada joined this original "Group of Five" in 1976–77 and the configuration became known as the Group of Seven, or "G–7." G–7 meetings followed a limited agenda of economic issues, and were intended to provide an informal consultation forum. In the 1980s, these annual meetings became more formalized, with an agreed statement, or communique, issued by the leaders at the conclusion of each summit. Leaders such as President Reagan, French President Mitterand, German Chancellor Kohl, and British Prime Minister Thatcher brought increasingly broader agendas to the table. At the end of the cold war, as democratic and economic reform got underway in Russia, Russian leaders were gradually integrated into the G–7. In 1998, the group's name was formally changed to the "G–8," and the first full G–8 Summit was held in Birmingham in June of that year.

In its current configuration, the G–8's membership includes the majority of the world's most powerful democracies—countries that are global leaders economically, technologically, legally, and politically. This small but powerful membership gives the G–8 certain advantages over more bureaucratic or cumbersome multilateral organizations.

2. Focus on High-tech Crime. After the 1995 Summit in Halifax, Nova Scotia, a group of experts was brought together to look for better ways to fight international crime. In 1996 this group (which became known as the "Lyon Group") produced forty recommendations to combat international crime that were endorsed by the G–8 heads of state at the Lyon Summit in June 1996. Recommendation Sixteen, in part, called for countries to "review their laws in order to ensure that abuses of modern technology that are deserving of criminal sanctions are criminalized and that problems with respect to jurisdiction, enforcement powers, investigation, training, crime prevention and international cooperation in respect of such abuses are effectively addressed."

To implement Recommendation Sixteen and otherwise enhance the abilities of law enforcement in combating high-tech and computer-related crime, a subgroup of the Lyon Group was formed in January 1997 ("G–8 Subgroup on High-tech Crime"), and it held its first five meetings during that year. In December 1997, Attorney General Reno hosted the first-ever meeting of her counterparts from the G–8 countries, and the meeting centered on computer crime. At the conclusion of the meeting, the Ministers adopted ten Principles and a ten-point Action Plan to combat high-tech crime, and issued a Communique. At the 1998 G–8 Summit in Birmingham, England, the Heads of State endorsed and agreed to implement their Ministers' Principles and Action Plan. Essentially an international template for fighting high-tech crime, the Principles and Action Plan have been adopted by President Clinton, British Prime Minister Tony Blair, French President Jacques Chirac, Russian President Boris Yeltsin, and the other G–8 leaders. This is quite significant. It is the first time a group of powerful world leaders have jointly adopted a detailed plan for fighting computer crime. Additionally, instead of referring the plan back to member countries for individual action, a subgroup of G–8 experts meets regularly to work cooperatively toward implementation of the Action Plan.

3.   *High-tech Crime Subgroup*. As of May 1999, the G–8 Subgroup on High-tech Crime had met fourteen times. Its focus has been on enhancing the abilities of law enforcement to investigate and prosecute high-tech and computer-related crime. The Subgroup's progress and accomplishments include * * * high-tech points of contact. In March 1998, a network of high-tech points of contact for law enforcement in each of the G–8 countries was established. These contacts are available twenty-four hours a day to respond to urgent requests for assistance in international high-tech crime investigations or cases involving electronic evidence. Recruitment and education efforts are currently underway to expand this network to include many more Internet-connected countries. The hope is that in the near future, international investigations in this area will not be delayed because of the inability to locate the proper computer crime expert or because of differences in time zones.

NOTES AND QUESTIONS

1.   Recall the case of the "I Love You" virus allegedly sent by a student from the Philippines in 2000. The student was not charged with a crime after authorities in the Philippines concluded that his conduct was not criminal under domestic law. The Philippines did not have a computer misuse statute at the time. The fact that the student's conduct was not criminal according to local law meant that he could not be extradited to the United States to face prosecution under 18 U.S.C. § 1030.

How should United States policymakers respond to such situations? Should they: (a) resign themselves to the fact that they cannot prosecute all international computer crimes, (b) encourage other countries to enact computer crime statutes that resemble U.S. computer crime laws, or (c) try to negotiate extradition treaties that do not require mutual criminality?

2.   A study of computer crime laws conducted after the "I Love You" virus case found that only about 20% of countries have adequate computer crime laws. Many countries have no computer crime laws at all. *See* McConnell International, Cyber Crime . . . and Punishment? Archaic Laws Threaten Global Information (2000).

3.   *Uniformity versus diversity and the problem of reciprocity.* In recent years, the United States government has encouraged other countries to synchronize their substantive and procedural computer crime laws to avoid problems such as the one that surfaced in the "I Love You" virus case. Is this inevitable? Is it desirable? Should the entire world adopt a single model approach to computer crime laws, or are local differences desirable? How much of the substantive criminal law covered in Chapters 2 and 3 is normatively desirable at the global level? How much of the procedural law covered in Chapters 5 and 6 is normatively desirable at the global level?

Is it possible to resolve the tension between the need for uniform laws to enforce computer crime statutes and the need for regional variation based on local preferences? Consider the case of child pornography. Imagine the government of Freedonia decides that it should be legal to possess or distribute images of child pornography in Freedonia, including on servers located in

Freedonia that are connected to the Internet. Will such a decision have a significant impact on the enforcement of child pornography laws worldwide? Can an individual simply post images from Freedonia and escape liability (or at least capture)? Does the popularity of Internet gambling sites based in countries like Antigua provide empirical support for the answer?

Alternatively, consider foreign criminal laws prohibiting racist speech, the sale of Nazi memorabilia, or the distribution of virtual child pornography. In the United States, First Amendment protection renders such laws unenforceable. Should the United States be allowed to "opt out" of assisting other countries in their efforts to prosecute violations of these laws? Is there an argument that the United States should be able to opt out of helping foreign governments with investigations that violate the First Amendment, but that Freedonia should not be allowed to opt out of assisting other countries with child pornography prosecutions?

For more on the process of synchronizing computer crime laws, see Abraham D. Sofaer & Seymour E. Goodman, Eds., The Transnational Dimension of Cyber Crime and Terrorism (2001).

4. *The Council of Europe Convention on Cybercrime.* The most important effort to synchronize computer crime laws to date is the Council of Europe Convention on Cybercrime. The Convention articulates a set of principles that member states agree to adopt in their domestic law. The United States is not a member of the Council of Europe, but representatives of the United States Department of Justice, State, and Commerce were "observers" and active participants in the negotiating and drafting of the convention. The United States was one of the thirty countries that signed the convention in 2001, and the United States Senate ratified the convention in 2006. Here are the key portions of the text:

COUNCIL OF EUROPE—CONVENTION ON CYBERCRIME

http://conventions.coe.int/Treaty/en/Treaties/Html/185.htm (2001).

Section 1—Substantive criminal law

Article 2—Illegal access

Each Party shall adopt such legislative and other measures as may be necessary to establish as criminal offences under its domestic law, when committed intentionally, the access to the whole or any part of a computer system without right. A Party may require that the offence be committed by infringing security measures, with the intent of obtaining computer data or other dishonest intent, or in relation to a computer system that is connected to another computer system.

Article 3—Illegal interception

Each Party shall adopt such legislative and other measures as may be necessary to establish as criminal offences under its domestic law, when committed intentionally, the interception without right, made by technical means, of non-public transmissions of computer data to, from or within a computer system, including electromagnetic emissions from a computer system carrying such computer data. A Party may require that the offence be committed with dishonest intent, or in relation to a computer system that is connected to another computer system.

Article 4—Data interference

1. Each Party shall adopt such legislative and other measures as may be necessary to establish as criminal offences under its domestic law, when committed intentionally, the damaging, deletion, deterioration, alteration or suppression of computer data without right.

2. A Party may reserve the right to require that the conduct described in paragraph 1 result in serious harm.

Article 7—Computer-related forgery

Each Party shall adopt such legislative and other measures as may be necessary to establish as criminal offences under its domestic law, when committed intentionally and without right, the input, alteration, deletion, or suppression of computer data, resulting in inauthentic data with the intent that it be considered or acted upon for legal purposes as if it were authentic, regardless whether or not the data is directly readable and intelligible. A Party may require an intent to defraud, or similar dishonest intent, before criminal liability attaches.

Article 8—Computer-related fraud

Each Party shall adopt such legislative and other measures as may be necessary to establish as criminal offences under its domestic law, when committed intentionally and without right, the causing of a loss of property to another by:

    a.   any input, alteration, deletion or suppression of computer data,

    b.   any interference with the functioning of a computer system,

with fraudulent or dishonest intent of procuring, without right, an economic benefit for oneself or for another.

Article 9—Offences related to child pornography

Each Party shall adopt such legislative and other measures as may be necessary to establish as criminal offences under its domestic law, when committed intentionally and without right, the following conduct:

    a.   producing child pornography for the purpose of its distribution through a computer system;

    b.   offering or making available child pornography through a computer system;

    c.   distributing or transmitting child pornography through a computer system;

    d.   procuring child pornography through a computer system for oneself or for another;

e. possessing child pornography in a computer system or on a computer-data storage medium.

Article 10—Offences related to infringements of copyright and related rights

Each Party shall adopt such legislative and other measures as may be necessary to establish as criminal offences under its domestic law the infringement of copyright, as defined under the law of that Party pursuant to the obligations it has undertaken under the Paris Act of 24 July 1971 of the Bern Convention for the Protection of Literary and Artistic Works, the Agreement on Trade–Related Aspects of Intellectual Property Rights and the WIPO Copyright Treaty, with the exception of any moral rights conferred by such Conventions, where such acts are committed wilfully, on a commercial scale and by means of a computer system.

Section 2–Procedural law

Article 14—Scope of procedural provisions

Each Party shall adopt such legislative and other measures as may be necessary to establish the powers and procedures provided for in this Section for the purpose of specific criminal investigations or proceedings.

Article 15—Conditions and safeguards

Each Party shall ensure that the establishment, implementation and application of the powers and procedures provided for in this Section are subject to conditions and safeguards provided for under its domestic law, which shall provide for the adequate protection of human rights and liberties, including rights arising pursuant to obligations it has undertaken under the 1950 Council of Europe Convention for the Protection of Human Rights and Fundamental Freedoms, the 1966 United Nations International Covenant on Civil and Political Rights, and other applicable international human rights instruments, and which shall incorporate the principle of proportionality.

Article 16—Expedited preservation of stored computer data

Each Party shall adopt such legislative and other measures as may be necessary to enable its competent authorities to order or similarly obtain the expeditious preservation of specified computer data, including traffic data, that has been stored by means of a computer system, in particular where there are grounds to believe that the computer data is particularly vulnerable to loss or modification.

Article 18—Production order

1. Each Party shall adopt such legislative and other measures as may be necessary to empower its competent authorities to order:

     a. a person in its territory to submit specified computer data in that person's possession or control, which is stored in a computer system or a computer-data storage medium; and

b. a service provider offering its services in the territory of the Party to submit subscriber information relating to such services in that service provider's possession or control;

3. For the purpose of this article, "subscriber information" means any information, contained in the form of computer data or any other form, that is held by a service provider, relating to subscribers of its services, other than traffic or content data, by which can be established:

a. the type of the communication service used, the technical provisions taken thereto and the period of service;

b. the subscriber's identity, postal or geographic address, telephone and other access number, billing and payment information, available on the basis of the service agreement or arrangement;

c. any other information on the site of the installation of communication equipment available on the basis of the service agreement or arrangement.

Article 19—Search and seizure of stored computer data

1. Each Party shall adopt such legislative and other measures as may be necessary to empower its competent authorities to search or similarly access:

a. a computer system or part of it and computer data stored therein; and

b. computer-data storage medium in which computer data may be stored in its territory.

2. Each Party shall adopt such legislative and other measures as may be necessary to ensure that where its authorities search or similarly access a specific computer system or part of it, pursuant to paragraph 1(a), and have grounds to believe that the data sought is stored in another computer system or part of it in its territory, and such data is lawfully accessible from or available to the initial system, such authorities shall be able to expeditiously extend the search or similar accessing to the other system.

3. Each Party shall adopt such legislative and other measures as may be necessary to empower its competent authorities to seize or similarly secure computer data accessed according to paragraphs 1 or 2. These measures shall include the power to:

a. seize or similarly secure a computer system or part of it or a computer-data storage medium;

b. make and retain a copy of those computer data;

c. maintain the integrity of the relevant stored computer data; and

d. render inaccessible or remove those computer data in the accessed computer system.

Article 20—Real-time collection of traffic data

Each Party shall adopt such legislative and other measures as may be necessary to empower its competent authorities to:

a. collect or record through application of technical means on the territory of that Party, and

b. compel a service provider, within its existing technical capability, to:

> i. collect or record through application of technical means on the territory of that Party, or ii. co-operate and assist the competent authorities in the collection or recording of, traffic data, in real-time, associated with specified communications in its territory transmitted by means of a computer system.

Article 21—Interception of content data

Each Party shall adopt such legislative and other measures as may be necessary, in relation to a range of serious offences to be determined by domestic law, to empower its competent authorities to:

a. collect or record through application of technical means on the territory of that Party, and

b. compel a service provider, within its existing technical capability, to:

> i. collect or record through application of technical means on the territory of that Party, or ii. co-operate and assist the competent authorities in the collection or recording of, content data, in real-time, of specified communications in its territory transmitted by means of a computer system.

Chapter III–International co-operation

Article 23—General principles relating to international co-operation

The Parties shall co-operate with each other, in accordance with the provisions of this chapter, and through the application of relevant international instruments on international co-operation in criminal matters, arrangements agreed on the basis of uniform or reciprocal legislation, and domestic laws, to the widest extent possible for the purposes of investigations or proceedings concerning criminal offences related to computer systems and data, or for the collection of evidence in electronic form of a criminal offence.

Article 24—Extradition

1. This article applies to extradition between Parties for the criminal offences established in accordance with Articles 2 through 11 of this Convention, provided that they are punishable under the laws of both Parties concerned by deprivation of liberty for a maximum period of at least one year, or by a more severe penalty.

2. The criminal offences described in paragraph 1 of this article shall be deemed to be included as extraditable offences in any extradition treaty existing between or among the Parties. The Parties undertake to include such offences as extraditable offences in any extradition treaty to be concluded between or among them.

Article 25—General principles relating to mutual assistance

The Parties shall afford one another mutual assistance to the widest extent possible for the purpose of investigations or proceedings concerning criminal offences related to computer systems and data, or for the collection of evidence in electronic form of a criminal offence.

Article 27—Procedures pertaining to mutual assistance requests in the absence of applicable international agreements

Where there is no mutual assistance treaty or arrangement on the basis of uniform or reciprocal legislation in force between the requesting and requested Parties, the provisions of paragraphs 2 through 9 of this article shall apply. The provisions of this article shall not apply where such treaty, arrangement or legislation exists, unless the Parties concerned agree to apply any or all of the remainder of this article in lieu thereof.

Article 31—Mutual assistance regarding accessing of stored computer data

A Party may request another Party to search or similarly access, seize or similarly secure, and disclose data stored by means of a computer system located within the territory of the requested Party.

Article 32—Trans-border access to stored computer data with consent or where publicly available

A Party may, without the authorisation of another Party:

a. access publicly available (open source) stored computer data, regardless of where the data is located geographically; or

b. access or receive, through a computer system in its territory, stored computer data located in another Party, if the Party obtains the lawful and voluntary consent of the person who has the lawful authority to disclose the data to the Party through that computer system.

Article 33—Mutual assistance regarding the real-time collection of traffic data

1. The Parties shall provide mutual assistance to each other in the real-time collection of traffic data associated with specified communications in their territory transmitted by means of a computer system. Subject to the provisions of paragraph 2, this assistance shall be governed by the conditions and procedures provided for under domestic law.

2. Each Party shall provide such assistance at least with respect to criminal offences for which real-time collection of traffic data would be available in a similar domestic case.

Article 34—Mutual assistance regarding the interception of content data

The Parties shall provide mutual assistance to each other in the real-time collection or recording of content data of specified communications transmitted by means of a computer system to the extent permitted under their applicable treaties and domestic laws.

Article 35—24/7 Network

Each Party shall designate a point of contact available on a twenty-four hour, seven-day-a-week basis, in order to ensure the provision of immediate assistance for the purpose of investigations or proceedings concerning criminal offences related to computer systems and data, or for the collection of evidence in electronic form of a criminal offence. Such assistance shall include facilitating, or, if permitted by its domestic law and practice, directly carrying out the following measures:

a. the provision of technical advice;

b. the preservation of data pursuant to Articles 29 and 30;

c. the collection of evidence, the provision of legal information, and locating of suspects.

NOTES AND QUESTIONS

1. Are any provisions of the COE convention inconsistent with United States law? Or are the terms of the convention a restatement of the basic elements of United States computer crime law? *See generally* Richard W. Downing, *Shoring up the Weakest Link: What Lawmakers Around the World Need to Consider in Developing Comprehensive Laws to Combat Cybercrime*, 43 Colum. J. Transnat'l L. 705 (2005).

2. *The additional protocol on "racist and xenophobic" acts.* In 2002, at the request of the French government, the Council of Europe added an additional protocol "concerning the criminalisation of acts of a racist and xenophobic nature committed through computer systems." The protocol requires each country that signs it to criminalize a number of acts, including: distributing racist and xenophobic material to the public through a computer system; sending an Internet threat solely because of a person's race, national origin or religion; insulting a person through a computer communication on the basis of the person's race, national origin or religion; and denying, grossly minimizing, or justifying atrocities or crimes against humanity. *See generally* Christopher D. Van Blarcum, Note, *Internet Hate Speech: The European Framework and the Emerging American Haven*, 62 Wash. & Lee L. Rev. 781, 787–802 (2005).

A number of countries have signed the additional protocol, which acts as a separate agreement in addition to the cybercrime convention. Of course, the

United States has not signed the protocol. Government officials have indicated that the United States cannot agree to the protocol because its provisions would violate the First Amendment. *See* Declan McCullagh, *U.S. Won't Support Net "Hate Speech" Ban*, C–Net News, Nov. 15, 2002. As a result, the requirements of the additional protocol have no effect on United States policy.

3.   The COE cybercrime convention has been controversial less for what it does than for what it does not do. Privacy advocates and civil liberties groups note that the convention focuses on law enforcement powers but does not address privacy protections beyond the general statement in Article 15. The convention empowers governments without limiting how they might exercise those new powers. Consider the perspective offered by one group, the Center for Democracy and Technology:

> The treaty is fundamentally imbalanced: it includes very detailed and sweeping powers of computer search and seizure and government surveillance of voice, email and data communications, but no correspondingly detailed standards to protect privacy and limit government use of such powers, despite the fact that privacy is the #1 concern of Internet users worldwide who see an increase, not a decrease, in the surveillance capabilities of governments brought on by the digital revolution.

> While the treaty's express terms do not require companies to modify their equipment or business practices, the treaty must be viewed as part of the ongoing government efforts nationally and internationally to require telephone companies, Internet service providers, web site operators, and computer hardware and software manufacturers to design their systems, their record-keeping procedures and their very business models to guarantee the practical effectiveness of such surveillance authorities.

Comments of the Center for Democracy and Technology on the Council of Europe Draft "Convention on Cyber-crime," *available at* http://www.cdt.org/international/cybercrime/010206cdt.shtml.

Should the COE convention mandate privacy protections as well as law enforcement powers? If so, what should those protections look like? Should the convention require every country to impose a probable cause warrant requirement for wiretapping or government access to stored e-mail? Should the requirements track current United States law, or should they be more (or less) protective? Does an international consensus exist on standards for Internet privacy law? If not, who should decide what the standard will be?

4.   Another criticism of the COE convention is that its requirements are too general. The convention's broad language requires general categories of legislation instead of specific statutes. Are general categories sufficient to achieve the uniformity that the convention's drafters had in mind? If one country enacts a narrow statute and another enacts a broad one, will the laws be sufficiently uniform to facilitate international evidence collection and extradition? Should the convention itself contain the precise statutory text of the criminal prohibitions and procedural laws that signatories must enact? For such a suggestion, see Shannon Hopkins, *Cybercrime Convention: A*

Positive Beginning to a Long Road Ahead, 2 J. High Tech. L. 101, 104–07 (2003).

Imagine COE countries decided to adopt this suggestion. What would the model law look like? Suppose the COE convention were amended so that every country was required to copy United States computer crime law as it exists today in every detail. Would this be a good idea? Is existing United States law an appropriate model?

Of course, it is highly unlikely that the United States could persuade COE member countries to adopt existing United States law as a universal model. Different countries have very different traditions, legal systems, and constitutional requirements. If it were possible to reach an agreement on the specific text for a uniform set of computer crime laws, it seems likely that the language chosen would involve a major re-writing of existing United States law. United States negotiators would have some influence over this process, but would be only one voice among many.

Further, such an agreement would block individual countries from attempting to improve their own computer crime statutes unilaterally. To change United States computer crime law without violating the convention, United States officials would be required to renegotiate the cybercrime convention first. The new language agreed to by the members of the Council of Europe would then be submitted for Senate approval, requiring a vote on the very specific language negotiated abroad. Is this desirable?

Finally, some variation in the law is inevitable because different courts will construe the same language differently. Imagine every country adopted a uniform computer crime law that prohibited "access without authorization," "unreasonable searches and seizures," and "interception of the contents of communications without the consent of a party." What are the chances that the United States Supreme Court, the French Cour de Cassation, and the German Bundesgerichtsh would interpret these phrases in exactly (or even roughly) the same way?

4. FOREIGN COMPUTER CRIME LAW

Although the materials in this book focus on United States computer crime law, the preceding materials point out the role of foreign computer crime laws even for domestic investigations. For example, if a defendant located in a foreign country damages a computer in the United States, and the United States wishes to bring a criminal prosecution, the outcome may hinge on (a) whether the offense is a substantive criminal offense under the law of the country where the defendant is located (for extradition purposes), and (b) whether the other country has procedural laws in place allowing investigators in that country to investigate the crime and share the evidence with investigators in the United States. The next case considers the interpretation of a computer misuse law in the United Kingdom for purposes of an extradition proceeding brought at the request of the United States.

REX v. BOW STREET MAGISTRATES' COURT

House of Lords, [1999] 4 All ER 1.

LORD HOBHOUSE OF WOODBOROUGH

My Lords,

On 18 March 1997, Mr. Allison was arrested upon a provisional warrant issued under the Extradition Act 1989 at the request of the Government of the United States. It alleged that he had between 1 January 1996 and 18 June 1996 within the jurisdiction of the United States of America conspired with Joan Ojomo and others (1) to secure unauthorised access to the American Express computer system with intent to commit theft, (2) to secure unauthorised access to the American Express computer system with intent to commit forgery, and (3) to cause unauthorised modification to the contents of the American Express computer system.

On 11 June 1997 the Bow Street Magistrate committed Mr. Allison on the third charge but declined to commit him on the first and second of the proposed charges. Mr. Allison brought *Habeas Corpus* proceedings challenging the view that any of the offences alleged were "extradition crimes" under the Act of 1989 and the United States of America (Extradition) Order 1976, SI 1976 No. 2144. The Government brought judicial review proceedings challenging the decision in law of the magistrate that the evidence did not disclose a *prima facie* case that there had been a conspiracy to commit offences falling within section 2 of the Computer Misuse Act 1990 as alleged in the first and second charges in the warrant.

Joan Ojomo was an employee of American Express. She was assigned to the credit section of the Company's office in Plantation, Florida, as a credit analyst. In her daily work it was possible for her to access all customers' accounts but she was only authorised to access those accounts that were assigned to her. However she accessed various other accounts and files which had not been assigned to her and which she had not been given authority to work on. Having accessed those accounts and files without authority, she gave confidential information obtained from those accounts and files to, among others, Mr. Allison. The information she gave to him and to others was then used to encode other credit cards and supply PIN numbers which could then be fraudulently used to obtain large sums of money from automatic teller machines.

The evidence concerning Joan Ojomo's authority to access the material data showed that she did not have authority to access the data she used for this purpose. At no time did she have any blanket authorisation to access any account or file not specifically assigned to her to work on. Any access by her to an account which she was not authorised to be working on would be considered a breach of company policy and ethics and would be considered an unauthorised access by the Company. The computer records showed that she accessed 189 accounts that did not fall within the scope of her duties. Her accessing of these accounts was unauthorised.

Using these methods, she and her fellow conspirators defrauded American Express of approximately $1,000,000. Mr. Allison was arrested with forged American Express cards in his possession and was photographed using one such card to obtain money from an automatic teller machine in London.

The proposed charges against Mr. Allison therefore involved his alleged conspiracy with Joan Ojomo for her to secure unauthorised access to data on the American Express computer with the intent to commit the further offences of forging cards and stealing from that Company. It is Joan Ojomo's alleged lack of authority which is an essential element in the offences charged.

The [Extradition] Act of 1989 was enacted following reports of the English and Scottish Law Commissions recommending revisions of the law of extradition. The Act consolidated the previous law with amendments to give effect to those recommendations. The Extradition Act 1870 was among those repealed by the Act of 1989. The Act of 1870 included a definition of "extradition crime" as meaning "a crime which, if committed in England, would be one of the crimes described in the first schedule" to the Act. The schedule, as would be expected having regard to its date, consisted of a relatively short list. Between 1870 and 1989 the list was extensively added to by later Acts. But none of these statutes included a reference to computer crime such as that made criminal by the Computer Misuse Act 1990.

The relevant Order in Council governing extradition to the United States of America * * * gives effect to and schedules the Extradition Treaty between the respective Governments of the United Kingdom and the United States. Article III of the Treaty provides:

(1) Extradition shall be granted for an act or omission the facts of which disclose an offence within any of the descriptions listed in the Schedule annexed to this Treaty, which is an integral part of the Treaty, or any other offence, if:

> (a) the offence is punishable under the laws of both Parties by imprisonment or other form of detention for more than one year or by the death penalty;

> (b) the offence is extraditable under the relevant law, being the law of the United Kingdom or other territory to which this Treaty applies by virtue of sub-paragraph (1)(a) of Article II; and

> (c) the offence constitutes a felony under the law of the United States of America.

(2) Extradition shall also be granted for any attempt or conspiracy to commit an offence within paragraph (1) of this Article if such attempt or conspiracy is one for which extradition may be granted under the

laws of both Parties and is punishable under the laws of both Parties by imprisonment or other form of detention for more than one year or by the death penalty.

The schedule annexed to the Treaty does not include any reference to computer crime. Therefore if an offence under the Computer Misuse Act 1990 is to come within the terms of the Treaty it will have to be as some "other offence." There is no dispute in the present case that an offence under § 2 of the Act of 1990 comes within (1)(a) being punishable by imprisonment for more than one year. Similarly it is not disputed that the conduct charged would constitute felonies under the law of the United States, (1)(c). The question which has been raised by Mr. Allison on his *Habeas Corpus* application is whether the offences alleged are extraditable under the law of the United Kingdom, (1)(b), and therefore as conspiracies come within paragraph (2) of the Article.

In September 1989 there was no provision of the law of the United Kingdom which made computer crime extraditable; indeed, there was no such provision which made it (as such) criminal at all. At that time such conduct fell outside the scope of the criminal law of the United Kingdom and accordingly outside the scope of the Extradition Treaty.

The Treaty and the Order in Council have not been amended. The provision which has been relied upon by the Government of the United States as bringing offences under the Computer Misuse Act 1990 within the terms of the Treaty is § 15 of that Act which provides—

The offences to which an Order in Council under § 2 of the Extradition Act 1870 can apply shall include—(a) offences under § 2 or 3 above; (b) any conspiracy to commit such an offence; and (c) any attempt to commit an offence under § 3 above.

The Computer Misuse Act 1990 does not purport to alter the Treaty or the Order nor does it need to; they include not only the offences listed in the schedule annexed to the Treaty but also "any other offence." All that is needed is some provision of the law of the United Kingdom which provides, supplementing the provisions of the 1989 and earlier Acts, that computer crime shall both become an offence and be extraditable under the law of the United Kingdom; the 1990 Act contains provisions that meet this need.

Sections 1 and 2 of the [Computer Misuse Act of 1990] provide:

1(1) A person is guilty of an offence if—

    (a) he causes a computer to perform any function with intent to secure access to any program or data held in any computer;

    (b) the access he intends to secure is unauthorised; and

    (c) he knows at the time when he causes the computer to perform the function that that is the case.

(2) The intent a person has to have to commit an offence under this section need not be directed at—

(a) any particular program or data;

(b) a program or data of any particular kind; or

(c) a program or data held in any particular computer....

2(1) A person is guilty of an offence under this section if he commits an offence under section 1 above ("the unauthorised access offence") with intent (a) to commit an offence to which this section applies; or (b) to facilitate the commission of such an offence (whether by himself or by any other person).

Section 2 is thus dependent on § 1.

On the evidence before the magistrate, the conduct of Joan Ojomo came fairly and squarely within the provisions of § 1(1). She intentionally caused a computer to give her access to data which she knew she was not authorised to access. The reason why the magistrate did not commit Mr. Allison on charges 1 and 2 was that he felt constrained by the provisions of § 17 * * *. The relevant subsections of § 17 reads—

(1) The following provisions of this section apply for the interpretation of this Act.

(2) A person secures access to any program or data held in a computer if by causing a computer to perform any function he—

(a) alters or erases the program or data;

(b) copies or moves it to any storage medium other than that in which it is held or to a different location in the storage medium in which it is held;

(c) uses it; or

(d) has it output from the computer in which it is held (whether by having it displayed or in any other manner); and references to access to a program or data (and to an intent to secure such access) shall be read accordingly.

(5) Access of any kind by any person to any program or data held in a computer is unauthorised if—(a) he is not himself entitled to control access of the kind in question to the program or data; and (b) he does not have consent to access by him of the kind in question to the program or data from any person who is so entitled.

Section 17 is an interpretation section. Subsection (2) defines what is meant by access and securing access to any programme or data. It lists four ways in which this may occur or be achieved. Its purpose is clearly to give a specific meaning to the phrase "to secure access." Subsection (5) is to be read with subsection (2). It deals with the relationship between the widened definition of securing access and the scope of the authority which the relevant person may hold. That is why the subsection refers to "access of any kind" and "access of the kind in question." Authority to view data may not extend to authority to copy or alter that data. The refinement of the concept of access requires a refinement of the concept of authorisation. The authorisation must be authority to secure access of the kind in question. As part of this refinement, the subsection lays down two cumulative requirements of lack of authority. The first is the requirement that the relevant person be not the person entitled to control the relevant kind of access. The word "control" in this context clearly means authorise and forbid. If the relevant person is so entitled, then it would be unrealistic to treat his access as being unauthorised. The second is that the relevant person does not have the consent to secure the relevant kind of access from a person entitled to control, *i.e.* authorise, that access.

Subsection (5) therefore has a plain meaning subsidiary to the other provisions of the Act. It simply identifies the two ways in which authority may be acquired—by being oneself the person entitled to authorise and by being a person who has been authorised by a person entitled to authorise. It also makes clear that the authority must relate not simply to the data or programme but also to the actual kind of access secured.

My Lords, what I have already said serves to identify the points upon which the Divisional Court fell into error. The certified question refers to "authority to access data of the kind in question". The use of the phrase "data of the kind in question" seems to derive from a simple mis-reading of § 17(5) and a confusion between kinds of access and kinds of data. Nor is § 1 of the Act concerned with authority to access kinds of data. It is concerned with authority to access the actual data involved. Because § 1(1) creates an offence which can be committed as a result of having an intent to secure unauthorised access without in fact actually succeeding in accessing any data, § 1(2) does not require that the relevant intent relate to any specific data. But that does not mean that access to the data in question does not have to be authorised.

* * * [The lower court judge] treats the phrase "entitlement to control" as if it related to the control of the computer as opposed to the entitlement to authorise operators access to programs and data. He adopts the extraneous idea of an authorised level of access without considering whether, on the facts of the case, it corresponds to the relevant person's authority to access the data in fact accessed. He confines § 1 of the Act to the "hacking" of computer systems as opposed to the use of a computer to secure unauthorised access to programs or data. Upon a misreading of § 17(5), he fails to give effect to the plain words of § 1. The meaning of the statute is clear and unambiguous. But it is right that I should briefly say something about the argument based upon the Working Party Paper and Report of the Law Commission which (together with the Report of the Scottish Law Commission) led to the passing of the Act of 1990. * * * The Respondent quoted passages from the Paper and the Report to the effect:

> It should be made clear that 'unauthorised' refers to the obtaining of access to a computer system. Our preliminary view is that it would be undesirable for a hacking offence to extend to an authorised user who is using the computer system for an unauthorised purpose.

> If an employee deliberately seeks to enter part of his employer's system from which he is clearly debarred his conduct is of the same

type as the outside hacker, and our proposed offence will apply to him as much as it applies to the outside hacker.

If the hacking offence is to be aimed at protecting the integrity of the computer (and our view is that it should), then there is no justification for exempting employees who threaten that integrity.

Read as a whole, the Report makes it clear that the term "hacking" is used conveniently to refer to all forms of unauthorised access whether by insiders or outsiders and that the problem of misuse by insiders is as serious as that by outsiders. The offence should cover a person who causes the computer to perform a function when he "should know that *that* access is unauthorised." An employee should only be guilty of an offence if his employer has clearly defined the limits of the employee's authority to access a program or data.

The consideration of the mischief which the Act was designed to meet confirms and does not contradict the clear meaning of § 1 of the Act and the equally clear purpose of § 17(2) and (5).

The decision of the Divisional Court in the present case was erroneous and the appeal fell to be allowed.

N<small>OTES AND</small> Q<small>UESTIONS</small>

1. This case involves one piece of an international fraud scheme.[2] Two American Express employees, Joan Ojomo and Blessing Egbarin, obtained secret information from American Express computers in violation of American Express workplace rules. The information permitted individuals to create counterfeit credit cards or file fraudulent applications for new cards. Ojomo sold the information to a number of street dealers both inside and outside the United States. American Express suffered millions of dollars in losses from the scheme.

In 1996, Ojomo and 12 co-conspirators were indicted in the United States. Ojomo pled guilty and agreed to assist the government in its efforts to prosecute the remaining co-conspirators. Defendant Allison was indicted in the United States but was found in the United Kingdom. Although at least two other defendants in the case were charged in the United Kingdom under UK law, the United States government sought Allison's extradition so Allison could face charges in the United States.

2. How different is the computer misuse statute in the United Kingdom from 18 U.S.C. § 1030 in the United States? Is the legal issue raised in the case you just read one that also arises under § 1030? If the issues are similar, is that because the nature of computer misuse demands that courts in different countries confront the same questions? Or is it because the two statutes use the same basic principles?

3. According to a 2002 study performed by Judge Stein Schjolberg of Norway, 44 countries have enacted some form of "unauthorized access"

---

2. This summary draws from the briefs and decisions in two related cases, United Kingdom v. United States, 238 F.3d 1312 (11th Cir. 2001) and United States v. Ojomo, 149 F.3d 1195 (11th Cir. 1998) (unpublished).

statutes modeled after 18 U.S.C. § 1030. *See* Stein Schjolberg, Unauthorized Access to Computer Systems: Penal Legislation in 44 Countries 2 (2002).

4. *Alternatives to extradition: The Ardita case.* In one unusual case in the mid–1990s, an Argentinian computer hacker named Julio Ardita hacked into about two hundred government and university computers in the United States from his location in Argentina. United States investigators traced the attack back to Buenos Aires, and Ardita was located with the help of Argentine authorities. The United States government sought extradition, but Ardita persuaded an Argentinian count that extradition was improper because his offense was not illegal under the law of Argentina (and thus the dual criminality requirement was not met).

The case did not end there, however. Although Ardita did not face the threat of extradition to the United States from Argentina, he faced a risk of extradition if he traveled to a country that had an extradition treaty with the United States in which his acts would have violated the domestic law of that country. Rather than face that risk, Ardita reached an agreement with United States officials: he agreed to waive extradition and plead guilty to reduced charges in the United States. Ardita was fined $5,000 and sentenced to three years of probation. *See* Russell G. Smith, Peter Grabosky, & Gregor Urbas, Cyber Criminals on Trial 56 (2004).

5. The materials in this chapter suggest that the legal issues raised by computer-related crime are not merely questions for the legal system in the United States. Most industrialized countries are facing the same issues, and all are being called on to adjust their domestic regimes of criminal law and criminal procedure in response to the new dynamics of computer crimes.

In light of the materials you have read in this book, do you think governments face a major challenge? Does computer crime require a fundamental rethinking of domestic and international approaches to criminal investigations and prosecutions? Will computer crimes "change everything"? Or do the new crimes simply require a slight tweaking of the old principles, or even no adjustment at all?

Are computers and the Internet the kind of transformative technologies that are likely to have a profound effect on criminal law doctrine? Some legal historians have argued that the invention of the railroad had a profound effect on tort law principles a century ago. Will computers and the Internet have a similar impact on criminal law and procedure in the next century?

CHAPTER 8

NATIONAL SECURITY

■ ■ ■

On the morning of September 11, 2001, members of the Al Qaeda terrorist network hijacked four planes and crashed them into the World Trade Center towers, the Pentagon, and a field in southwest Pennsylvania. The attacks caused approximately 3,000 American deaths. Following the attacks, American intelligence agencies quickly mobilized efforts to uncover any additional terrorist plots. The monitoring included surveillance of e-mail and other Internet transactions on a massive scale, both in the United States and abroad. Although terrorist plots would obviously violate criminal law, the surveillance efforts were not designed to collect evidence that could prove a criminal case beyond a reasonable doubt. Rather, the purpose of the surveillance was to collect information that could thwart a future terrorist attack.

The wide-scale Internet surveillance that followed the September 11th attacks is one example of national security intelligence surveillance. The purpose of such surveillance is to gather information about threats to the United States and the status of foreign governments with the hope that United States government officials can use the information to protect the United States and further its interests in world affairs. Essentially all governments engage in such surveillance, and United States intelligence efforts are particularly vast. The United States intelligence budget is classified, but just one agency, the National Security Agency, has been estimated to employ about 38,000 individuals full time. *See* James Bamford, Body of Secrets 482 (2001).

National security surveillance plays no role in most computer crime cases, but it can play an essential role in a few particularly important investigations. A great deal of intelligence surveillance involves e-mail and other Internet communications, and individuals subject to intelligence monitoring eventually may be charged criminally. In such cases, digital evidence collected under national security authorities may be essential to the government's case.

The use of digital evidence collected for national security reasons raises three important questions. First, how does the Fourth Amendment apply to the collection of digital evidence for national security purposes? Second, how does the Foreign Intelligence Surveillance Act (FISA) regulate the collection of digital evidence for such purposes? And third, when can digital evidence collected under FISA be admitted in criminal prosecutions?

A. THE FOURTH AMENDMENT

In the decades before Katz v. United States, 389 U.S. 347 (1967), government officials conducted warrantless wiretapping for national security purposes with little or no legal restriction. The Fourth Amendment did not apply to wiretapping under Olmstead v. United States, 277 U.S. 438 (1928). The Communications Act of 1934 prohibited "intercepting" and "disclosing" wire communications, but the Justice Department construed this to prohibit only the combination of wiretapping and publicly disclosing the fruits of the monitoring. Because national security wiretapping did not require public disclosure, government agents could tap telephone and telegraph lines unhindered by statutory or constitutional regulation.

Katz changed the legal picture considerably, although it settled very little. The *Katz* court certainly was aware of the special constitutional questions raised by national security monitoring. However, Justice Stewart's majority opinion expressly declined to take a position on these issues. *See Katz,* 389 U.S. at 358 n.23 ("Whether safeguards other than prior authorization by a magistrate would satisfy the Fourth Amendment in a situation involving the national security is a question not presented by this case."). Justice White's solo concurrence was more explicit, and expressed the following opinion:

> Wiretapping to protect the security of the Nation has been authorized by successive Presidents. The present Administration would apparently save national security cases from restrictions against wiretapping. We should not require the warrant procedure and the magistrate's judgment if the President of the United States or his chief legal officer, the Attorney General, has considered the requirements of national security and authorized electronic surveillance as reasonable.

Id. at 363 (White, J., concurring).

Congress took a hands-off approach to national security surveillance when it passed the Wiretap Act in 1968, a year after *Katz*. In the original version of the Wiretap Act, Congress carved out an exception to the statute for national security monitoring. When the President deemed it necessary to use his constitutional power to conduct national security monitoring, such monitoring was exempt from the statutory prohibition of the Wiretap Act. *See* 18 U.S.C. § 2511(3) (1968). This approach left open the constitutional question of the President's authority to conduct such monitoring in light of the *Katz*-era Fourth Amendment. The following case was the first (and so far, the only) Supreme Court case to help answer this question.

UNITED STATES v. UNITED STATES DISTRICT COURT

Supreme Court of the United States, 1972.
407 U.S. 297.

MR. JUSTICE POWELL delivered the opinion of the Court.

The issue before us is an important one for the people of our country and their Government. It involves the delicate question of the President's power, acting through the Attorney General, to authorize electronic surveillance in internal security matters without prior judicial approval. Successive Presidents for more than one-quarter of a century have authorized such surveillance in varying degrees, without guidance from the Congress or a definitive decision of this Court. This case brings the issue here for the first time. Its resolution is a matter of national concern, requiring sensitivity both to the Government's right to protect itself from unlawful subversion and attack and to the citizen's right to be secure in his privacy against unreasonable Government intrusion.

This case arises from a criminal proceeding in the United States District Court for the Eastern District of Michigan, in which the United States charged three defendants with conspiracy to destroy Government property in violation of 18 U.S.C. § 371. One of the defendants, Plamondon, was charged with the dynamite bombing of an office of the Central Intelligence Agency in Ann Arbor, Michigan.

During pretrial proceedings, the defendants moved to compel the United States to disclose certain electronic surveillance information and to conduct a hearing to determine whether this information "tainted" the evidence on which the indictment was based or which the Government intended to offer at trial. In response, the Government filed an affidavit of the Attorney General, acknowledging that its agents had overheard conversations in which Plamondon had participated. The affidavit also stated that the Attorney General approved the wiretaps "to gather intelligence information deemed necessary to protect the nation from attempts of domestic organizations to attack and subvert the existing structure of the Government." The logs of the surveillance were filed in a sealed exhibit for *in camera* inspection by the District Court.

On the basis of the Attorney General's affidavit and the sealed exhibit, the Government asserted that the surveillance was lawful, though conducted without prior judicial approval, as a reasonable exercise of the President's power (exercised through the Attorney General) to protect the national security. The District Court held that the surveillance violated the Fourth Amendment, and ordered the Government to make full disclosure to Plamondon of his overheard conversations.

The Government then filed in the Court of Appeals for the Sixth Circuit a petition for a writ of mandamus to set aside the District Court order, which was stayed pending final disposition of the case. After concluding that it had jurisdiction, that court held that the surveillance was unlawful and that the District Court had properly required disclosure of the overheard conversations. We granted certiorari.

I

Title III of the Omnibus Crime Control and Safe Streets Act, 18 U.S.C. §§ 2510–20, authorizes the use of electronic surveillance for classes of crimes carefully specified in 18 U.S.C. § 2516. Such surveillance is subject to prior court order. Section 2518 sets forth the detailed and particularized application necessary to obtain such an order as well as carefully circumscribed conditions for its use. The Act represents a comprehensive attempt by Congress to promote more effective control of crime while protecting the privacy of individual thought and expression. Much of Title III was drawn to meet the constitutional requirements for electronic surveillance enunciated by this Court in Berger v. New York, 388 U.S. 41 (1967), and Katz v. United States, 389 U.S. 347 (1967).

Together with the elaborate surveillance requirements in Title III, there is the following proviso, 18 U.S.C. § 2511(3):

> Nothing contained in this chapter or in section 605 of the Communications Act of 1934 shall limit the constitutional power of the President to take such measures as he deems necessary to protect the Nation against actual or potential attack or other hostile acts of a foreign power, to obtain foreign intelligence information deemed essential to the security of the United States, or to protect national security information against foreign intelligence activities. *Nor shall anything contained in this chapter be deemed to limit the constitutional power of the President to take such measures as he deems necessary to protect the United States against the overthrow of the Government by force or other unlawful means, or against any other clear and present danger to the structure or existence of the Government.* The contents of any wire or oral communication intercepted by authority of the President in the exercise of the foregoing powers may be received in evidence in any trial hearing, or other proceeding only where such interception was reasonable, and shall not be otherwise used or disclosed except as is necessary to implement that power. (Emphasis supplied.)

The Government relies on § 2511(3). It argues that "in excepting national security surveillances from the Act's warrant requirement Congress recognized the President's authority to conduct such surveillances without prior judicial approval." Brief for United States 7, 28. The section thus is viewed as a recognition or affirmance of a constitutional authority in the President to conduct warrantless domestic security surveillance such as that involved in this case.

We think the language of § 2511(3), as well as the legislative history of the statute, refutes this interpretation. The relevant language is that: "Nothing contained in this chapter ... shall limit the constitutional power of the President to take such measures as he deems necessary to protect" against the dangers specified. At most, this is an implicit recognition that the President does have certain powers in the specified areas. Few would doubt this, as the section refers—among other things—to protection "against actual or potential attack or other hostile acts of a foreign power." But so far as the use of the President's electronic surveillance power is concerned, the language is essentially neutral.

Section 2511(3) certainly confers no power, as the language is wholly inappropriate for such a purpose. It merely provides that the Act shall not be interpreted to limit or disturb such power as the President may have under the Constitution. In short, Congress simply left presidential powers where it found them.

* * * [N]othing in § 2511(3) was intended to *expand* or to *contract* or to *define* whatever presidential surveillance powers existed in matters affecting the national security. If we could accept the Government's characterization of § 2511(3) as a congressionally prescribed exception to the general requirement of a warrant, it would be necessary to consider the question of whether the surveillance in this case came within the exception and, if so, whether the statutory exception was itself constitutionally valid. But viewing § 2511(3) as a congressional disclaimer and expression of neutrality, we hold that the statute is not the measure of the executive authority asserted in this case. Rather, we must look to the constitutional powers of the President.

II

It is important at the outset to emphasize the limited nature of the question before the Court. This case raises no constitutional challenge to electronic surveillance as specifically authorized by Title III of the Omnibus Crime Control and Safe Streets Act of 1968. Nor is there any question or doubt as to the necessity of obtaining a warrant in the surveillance of crimes unrelated to the national security interest. Katz v. United States, 389 U.S. 347 (1967); Berger v. New York, 388 U.S. 41 (1967). Further, the instant case requires no judgment on the scope of the President's surveillance power with respect to the activities of foreign powers, within or without this country. The Attorney General's affidavit in this case states that the surveillances were "deemed necessary to protect the nation from attempts of *domestic organizations* to attack and subvert the existing structure of Government" (emphasis supplied). There is no evidence of any involvement, directly or indirectly, of a foreign power.[1]

Our present inquiry, though important, is therefore a narrow one. * * * The determination of this question requires the essential Fourth Amendment inquiry into the "reasonableness" of the search and seizure

---

1. Although we attempt no precise definition, we use the term "domestic organization" in this opinion to mean a group or organization (whether formally or informally constituted) composed of citizens of the United States and which has no significant connection with a foreign power, its agents or agencies. No doubt there are cases where it will be difficult to distinguish between "domestic" and "foreign" unlawful activities directed against the Government of the United States where there is collaboration in varying degrees between domestic groups or organizations and agents or agencies of foreign powers. But this is not such a case.

in question, and the way in which that "reasonableness" derives content and meaning through reference to the warrant clause.

We begin the inquiry by noting that the President of the United States has the fundamental duty, under Art. II, § 1, of the Constitution, to "preserve, protect and defend the Constitution of the United States." Implicit in that duty is the power to protect our Government against those who would subvert or overthrow it by unlawful means. In the discharge of this duty, the President—through the Attorney General—may find it necessary to employ electronic surveillance to obtain intelligence information on the plans of those who plot unlawful acts against the Government. The use of such surveillance in internal security cases has been sanctioned more or less continuously by various Presidents and Attorneys General since July 1946. Herbert Brownell, Attorney General under President Eisenhower, urged the use of electronic surveillance both in internal and international security matters on the grounds that those acting against the Government

> "turn to the telephone to carry on their intrigue. The success of their plans frequently rests upon piecing together shreds of information received from many sources and many nests. The participants in the conspiracy are often dispersed and stationed in various strategic positions in government and industry throughout the country."[11]

Though the Government and respondents debate their seriousness and magnitude, threats and acts of sabotage against the Government exist in sufficient number to justify investigative powers with respect to them. The covertness and complexity of potential unlawful conduct against the Government and the necessary dependency of many conspirators upon the telephone make electronic surveillance an effective investigatory instrument in certain circumstances. The marked acceleration in technological developments and sophistication in their use have resulted in new techniques for the planning, commission, and concealment of criminal activities. It would be contrary to the public interest for Government to deny to itself the prudent and lawful employment of those very techniques which are employed against the Government and its law-abiding citizens.

It has been said that the most basic function of any government is to provide for the security of the individual and of his property. And unless Government safeguards its own capacity to function and to preserve the security of its people, society itself could become so disordered that all rights and liberties would be endangered.

But a recognition of these elementary truths does not make the employment by Government of electronic surveillance a welcome development—even when employed with restraint and under judicial supervision. There is, understandably, a deep-seated uneasiness and apprehension that this capability will be used to intrude upon cherished privacy of law-abiding citizens. We look to the Bill of Rights to safeguard this privacy. Though physical entry of the home is the chief evil against which the

---

11. Brownell, The Public Security and Wire Tapping, 39 Cornell L.Q. 195, 202 (1954).

wording of the Fourth Amendment is directed, its broader spirit now shields private speech from unreasonable surveillance. Our decision in *Katz* refused to lock the Fourth Amendment into instances of actual physical trespass. Rather, the Amendment governs "not only the seizure of tangible items, but extends as well to the recording of oral statements without any 'technical trespass under local property law.' " *Katz, supra,* 389 U.S. at 353. That decision implicitly recognized that the broad and unsuspected governmental incursions into conversational privacy which electronic surveillance entails necessitate the application of Fourth Amendment safeguards.

National security cases, moreover, often reflect a convergence of First and Fourth Amendment values not present in cases of "ordinary" crime. Though the investigative duty of the executive may be stronger in such cases, so also is there greater jeopardy to constitutionally protected speech. * * * History abundantly documents the tendency of Government—however benevolent and benign its motives—to view with suspicion those who most fervently dispute its policies. Fourth Amendment protections become the more necessary when the targets of official surveillance may be those suspected of unorthodoxy in their political beliefs. The danger to political dissent is acute where the Government attempts to act under so vague a concept as the power to protect "domestic security." Given the difficulty of defining the domestic security interest, the danger of abuse in acting to protect that interest becomes apparent. * * * The price of lawful public dissent must not be a dread of subjection to an unchecked surveillance power. Nor must the fear of unauthorized official eavesdropping deter vigorous citizen dissent and discussion of Government action in private conversation. For private dissent, no less than open public discourse, is essential to our free society.

III

As the Fourth Amendment is not absolute in its terms, our task is to examine and balance the basic values at stake in this case: the duty of Government to protect the domestic security, and the potential danger posed by unreasonable surveillance to individual privacy and free expression. If the legitimate need of Government to safeguard domestic security requires the use of electronic surveillance, the question is whether the needs of citizens for privacy and free expression may not be better protected by requiring a warrant before such surveillance is undertaken. We must also ask whether a warrant requirement would unduly frustrate the efforts of Government to protect itself from acts of subversion and overthrow directed against it.

Over two centuries ago, Lord Mansfield held that common-law principles prohibited warrants that ordered the arrest of unnamed individuals who the *officer* might conclude were guilty of seditious libel. "It is not fit," said Mansfield, "that the receiving or judging of the information should be left to the discretion of the officer. The magistrate ought to judge; and should give certain directions to the officer." Leach v. Three of the King's Messengers, 19 How. St. Tr. 1001, 1027 (1765).

Lord Mansfield's formulation touches the very heart of the Fourth Amendment directive: that, where practical, a governmental search and seizure should represent both the efforts of the officer to gather evidence of wrongful acts and the judgment of the magistrate that the collected evidence is sufficient to justify invasion of a citizen's private premises or conversation. Inherent in the concept of a warrant is its issuance by a "neutral and detached magistrate." * * * The Fourth Amendment does not contemplate the executive officers of Government as neutral and disinterested magistrates. Their duty and responsibility are to enforce the laws, to investigate, and to prosecute. But those charged with this investigative and prosecutorial duty should not be the sole judges of when to utilize constitutionally sensitive means in pursuing their tasks. The historical judgment, which the Fourth Amendment accepts, is that unreviewed executive discretion may yield too readily to pressures to obtain incriminating evidence and overlook potential invasions of privacy and protected speech.

It is true that there have been some exceptions to the warrant requirement. But those exceptions are few in number and carefully delineated; in general, they serve the legitimate needs of law enforcement officers to protect their own well-being and preserve evidence from destruction. Even while carving out those exceptions, the Court has reaffirmed the principle that the police must, whenever practicable, obtain advance judicial approval of searches and seizures through the warrant procedure.

The Government argues that the special circumstances applicable to domestic security surveillances necessitate a further exception to the warrant requirement. It is urged that the requirement of prior judicial review would obstruct the President in the discharge of his constitutional duty to protect domestic security. We are told further that these surveillances are directed primarily to the collecting and maintaining of intelligence with respect to subversive forces, and are not an attempt to gather evidence for specific criminal prosecutions. It is said that this type of surveillance should not be subject to traditional warrant requirements which were established to govern investigation of criminal activity, not ongoing intelligence gathering.

The Government further insists that courts as a practical matter would have neither the knowledge nor the techniques necessary to determine whether there was probable cause to believe that surveillance was necessary to protect national security. These security problems, the Government contends, involve a large number of complex and subtle factors beyond the competence of courts to evaluate.

* * * There is, no doubt, pragmatic force to the Government's position.* * * But we do not think a case has been made for the requested departure from Fourth Amendment standards. The circumstances de-

scribed do not justify complete exemption of domestic security surveillance from prior judicial scrutiny. Official surveillance, whether its purpose be criminal investigation or ongoing intelligence gathering, risks infringement of constitutionally protected privacy of speech. Security surveillances are especially sensitive because of the inherent vagueness of the domestic security concept, the necessarily broad and continuing nature of intelligence gathering, and the temptation to utilize such surveillances to oversee political dissent. We recognize, as we have before, the constitutional basis of the President's domestic security role, but we think it must be exercised in a manner compatible with the Fourth Amendment. In this case we hold that this requires an appropriate prior warrant procedure.

We cannot accept the Government's argument that internal security matters are too subtle and complex for judicial evaluation. Courts regularly deal with the most difficult issues of our society. There is no reason to believe that federal judges will be insensitive to or uncomprehending of the issues involved in domestic security cases. Certainly courts can recognize that domestic security surveillance involves different considerations from the surveillance of "ordinary crime." If the threat is too subtle or complex for our senior law enforcement officers to convey its significance to a court, one may question whether there is probable cause for surveillance.

Thus, we conclude that the Government's concerns do not justify departure in this case from the customary Fourth Amendment requirement of judicial approval prior to initiation of a search or surveillance. Although some added burden will be imposed upon the Attorney General, this inconvenience is justified in a free society to protect constitutional values. Nor do we think the Government's domestic surveillance powers will be impaired to any significant degree. A prior warrant establishes presumptive validity of the surveillance and will minimize the burden of justification in post-surveillance judicial review. By no means of least importance will be the reassurance of the public generally that indiscriminate wiretapping and bugging of law-abiding citizens cannot occur.

IV

We emphasize, before concluding this opinion, the scope of our decision. As stated at the outset, this case involves only the domestic aspects of national security. We have not addressed, and express no opinion as to, the issues which may be involved with respect to activities of foreign powers or their agents. Nor does our decision rest on the language of § 2511(3) or any other section of Title III of the Omnibus Crime Control and Safe Streets Act of 1968. That Act does not attempt to define or delineate the powers of the President to meet domestic threats to the national security.

Moreover, we do not hold that the same type of standards and procedures prescribed by Title III are necessarily applicable to this case. We recognize that domestic security surveillance may involve different policy and practical considerations from the surveillance of "ordinary crime." The gathering of security intelligence is often long range and involves the interrelation of various sources and types of information. The exact targets of such surveillance may be more difficult to identify than in surveillance operations against many types of crime specified in Title III. Often, too, the emphasis of domestic intelligence gathering is on the prevention of unlawful activity or the enhancement of the Government's preparedness for some possible future crisis or emergency. Thus, the focus of domestic surveillance may be less precise than that directed against more conventional types of crime.

Given those potential distinctions between Title III criminal surveillances and those involving the domestic security, Congress may wish to consider protective standards for the latter which differ from those already prescribed for specified crimes in Title III. Different standards may be compatible with the Fourth Amendment if they are reasonable both in relation to the legitimate need of Government for intelligence information and the protected rights of our citizens. For the warrant application may vary according to the governmental interest to be enforced and the nature of citizen rights deserving protection. As the Court said in Camara v. Municipal Court, 387 U.S. 523, 534–535 (1967):

> In cases in which the Fourth Amendment requires that a warrant to search be obtained, 'probable cause' is the standard by which a particular decision to search is tested against the constitutional mandate of reasonableness. In determining whether a particular inspection is reasonable—and thus in determining whether there is probable cause to issue a warrant for that inspection—the need for the inspection must be weighed in terms of these reasonable goals of code enforcement.

It may be that Congress, for example, would judge that the application and affidavit showing probable cause need not follow the exact requirements of § 2518 but should allege other circumstances more appropriate to domestic security cases; that the request for prior court authorization could, in sensitive cases, be made to any member of a specially designated court (*e.g.*, the District Court for the District of Columbia or the Court of Appeals for the District of Columbia Circuit); and that the time and reporting requirements need not be so strict as those in § 2518.

The above paragraph does not, of course, attempt to guide the congressional judgment but rather to delineate the present scope of our own opinion. We do not attempt to detail the precise standards for domestic security warrants any more than our decision in *Katz* sought to set the refined requirements for the specified criminal surveillances which now constitute Title III. We do hold, however, that prior judicial approval is required for the type of domestic security surveillance involved in this case and that such approval may be made in accordance with such reasonable standards as the Congress may prescribe.

NOTES AND QUESTIONS

1. *United States v. United States District Court* is generally known as "the *Keith* case" because the district court judge in the case was Judge Damon Keith. The case has an unusual procedural history that explains its unusual name. The defendants were accused of bombing a CIA office in Michigan, and they claimed that the government had conducted warrantless interception of their telephone calls in violation of the Fourth Amendment. The government agreed that it had monitored the defendants, but argued that the warrantless monitoring was legal.

At the trial level, Judge Keith agreed with the defendants that the monitoring violated the Fourth Amendment. Under Alderman v. United States, 394 U.S. 165 (1969), the proper procedure for addressing the scope of the taint from illegal wiretapping was disclosure to the defendants of all of the wiretapping evidence against them so they could litigate the scope of the suppression remedy under the "fruit of the poisonous tree" doctrine. Judge Keith applied *Alderman*, ordered the government to turn over the wiretapping evidence to the defense, and announced that he would hold a suppression hearing to determine the scope of the remedy. *See* United States v. Sinclair, 321 F.Supp. 1074 (E.D. Mich. 1971).

The government then filed a petition for a writ of mandamus in the court of appeals seeking to overturn Judge Keith's order. The legality of the government's surveillance was the central issue in the *Keith* case because *Alderman*'s disclosure requirement applied only if the wiretapping was illegal. If the monitoring was lawful, there was no need for a hearing to determine the scope of the suppression remedy and no need for the government to turn over the evidence to the defense.

The unusual case name derives from the government's choice of writ. The government's petition was styled as a petition for a writ of mandamus, which is a request for an order from the higher court ordering the lower court to take a specific action. For historical reasons, such petitions are styled as lawsuits by the petitioner against the lower court. In the *Keith* case, the United States government wanted the Supreme Court to order Judge Keith of the United States District Court to rescind the disclosure order. Thus the strange case title, *United States v. United States District Court*.

2. Justice Powell's opinion in the *Keith* case is quintessentially pragmatic. Justice Powell views the constitutional question as a balance between government and individual interests in the context of domestic security surveillance cases. The key language appears at the beginning of Part III:

> Our task is to examine and balance the basic values at stake in this case: the duty of Government to protect the domestic security, and the potential danger posed by unreasonable surveillance to individual privacy and free expression. If the legitimate need of Government to safeguard domestic security requires the use of electronic surveillance, the question is whether the needs of citizens for privacy and free expression may not be better protected by requiring a warrant before such surveillance is undertaken. We must also ask whether a warrant requirement would

unduly frustrate the efforts of Government to protect itself from acts of subversion and overthrow directed against it.

Justice Powell concludes that the balance favors a warrant requirement: in his view, the requirement would better protect the needs of citizens and would not unduly frustrate the efforts of the government.

At the same time, the warrant requirement Justice Powell has in mind is no ordinary warrant requirement. Part IV of the opinion explains that Congress is free to enact a new type of warrant procedure and a new type of warrant that is tailored to the needs of domestic security investigations. The new procedures simply need to be "reasonable both in relation to the legitimate need of Government for intelligence information and the protected rights of our citizens." Once again, the standard is reasonableness. Putting Part III and Part IV of the *Keith* opinion together, a warrant is required in domestic security cases because some kind of reasonable warrant requirement would be a reasonable limitation on government surveillance practices.

3. *Domestic security versus foreign intelligence.* The *Keith* opinion considers legal standards for domestic security surveillance, but it explicitly excludes foreign intelligence surveillance. What's the difference?

Although the opinion does not elaborate extensively on the two categories, it seems that domestic security surveillance refers to the monitoring of threats to the nation from United States citizens operating in the United States, while foreign intelligence surveillance refers to gathering intelligence concerning foreign nations, governments, and their agents. The two categories may not seem intuitive today. The idea that the Nation would face threats to its existence from its own citizenry may seem puzzling, as does the notion that foreign threats are limited to threats from foreign governments and their agents. At the time of the *Keith* case, however, these two categories seemed more natural. Domestic intelligence referred to monitoring of American citizens who were believed to be communists, fascists, or members of radical groups committed to overthrowing the United States government. Foreign intelligence referred to the monitoring of foreign governments and their agents, such as Soviet spies and employees of foreign embassies.

Today the most important goal of national security monitoring is to identify and disrupt terror attacks planned by groups such as the Al Qaeda network. Does monitoring designed to disrupt such attacks count as foreign intelligence, domestic intelligence, or something else? *See* 50 U.S.C. § 1801(a)(4) (defining "foreign power" to include "a group engaged in international terrorism or activities in preparation therefor").

4. *Fourth Amendment standards for foreign intelligence surveillance.* The Supreme Court has never addressed whether and when foreign intelligence surveillance requires a search warrant, or what kind of warrant it may require. However, the Court's opinions in related areas narrow the inquiry. For example, a great deal of foreign intelligence surveillance does not trigger Fourth Amendment protections under United States v. Verdugo–Urquidez, 494 U.S. 259 (1990). *See* pages 607–609. Under *Verdugo*, foreign nationals located outside the United States normally have no Fourth Amendment rights. *Verdugo* thus permits a great deal of monitoring by United States intelligence authorities abroad.

Second, the border search exception to the Fourth Amendment as interpreted in cases like United States v. Ramsey, 431 U.S. 606 (1977), probably permits intelligence agencies to monitor computer traffic entering and exiting the United States. *See* pages 360–61. Finally, in both the domestic and foreign intelligence surveillance context, Fourth Amendment protections exist only to the extent a user has a reasonable expectation of privacy in remote data.

Let's assume that none of these doctrines eliminate Fourth Amendment protection, and that a computer user normally has a reasonable expectation of privacy in the contents of his communications online. According to the *Keith* case, the government normally must obtain a warrant to monitor that individual's communications if the government is engaging in domestic intelligence surveillance. But does the warrant requirement apply if the government is conducting *foreign* intelligence surveillance?

Two court of appeals cases shed light on this question. United States v. Butenko, 494 F.2d 593 (3d Cir. 1974) (en banc), involved the prosecution of a Soviet national and an American citizen for transmitting defense information to the Soviet Union. The Soviet national, Igor Ivanov, sought disclosure of the fruits of warrantless wiretapping against him on the ground that the monitoring was illegal. In an opinion by Judge Adams, the Third Circuit concluded that the Fourth Amendment did not require a warrant before the government conducted foreign intelligence surveillance:

> [F]oreign intelligence gathering is a clandestine and highly unstructured activity, and the need for electronic surveillance often cannot be anticipated in advance. Certainly occasions arise when officers, acting under the President's authority, are seeking foreign intelligence information, where exigent circumstances would excuse a warrant. To demand that such officers be so sensitive to the nuances of complex situations that they must interrupt their activities and rush to the nearest available magistrate to seek a warrant would seriously fetter the Executive in the performance of his foreign affairs duties.

Id. at 605. According to the Third Circuit, the Fourth Amendment merely requires that foreign intelligence surveillance be reasonable:

> The government interest here—to acquire the information necessary to exercise an informed judgment in foreign affairs—is surely weighty. Moreover, officers conceivably undertake certain electronic surveillance with no suspicion that a criminal activity may be discovered. Thus, a demand that they show that before engaging in such surveillance they had a reasonable belief that criminal activity would be unearthed would be to ignore the overriding object of the intrusions. Since the primary purpose of these searches is to secure foreign intelligence information, a judge, when reviewing a particular search must, above all, be assured that this was in fact its primary purpose and that the accumulation of evidence of criminal activity was incidental. If the court, for example, finds that members of a domestic political organization were the subjects of wiretaps or that the agents were looking for evidence of criminal conduct unrelated to the foreign affairs needs of a President, then he would undoubtedly hold the surveillances to be illegal and take appropriate measures.

Id. at 606.

The Fourth Circuit reached a similar conclusion in United States v. Truong Dinh Hung, 629 F.2d 908 (4th Cir. 1980). A Vietnamese citizen was convicted of espionage for passing classified diplomatic cables and sensitive strategic plans to the government of the Socialist Republic of Vietnam. The defendant's home telephone was tapped for 268 consecutive days without a warrant, and the evidence was used against him at trial. The defendant challenged the surveillance under the Fourth Amendment, but the Fourth Circuit held that the monitoring was legal:

> [T]he needs of the executive are so compelling in the area of foreign intelligence, unlike the area of domestic security, that a uniform warrant requirement would, following *Keith*, "unduly frustrate" the President in carrying out his foreign affairs responsibilities. First of all, attempts to counter foreign threats to the national security require the utmost stealth, speed, and secrecy. A warrant requirement would add a procedural hurdle that would reduce the flexibility of executive foreign intelligence initiatives, in some cases delay executive response to foreign intelligence threats, and increase the chance of leaks regarding sensitive executive operations.

> More importantly, the executive possesses unparalleled expertise to make the decision whether to conduct foreign intelligence surveillance, whereas the judiciary is largely inexperienced in making the delicate and complex decisions that lie behind foreign intelligence surveillance. The executive branch, containing the State Department, the intelligence agencies, and the military, is constantly aware of the nation's security needs and the magnitude of external threats posed by a panoply of foreign nations and organizations. On the other hand, while the courts possess expertise in making the probable cause determination involved in surveillance of suspected criminals, the courts are unschooled in diplomacy and military affairs, a mastery of which would be essential to passing upon an executive branch request that a foreign intelligence wiretap be authorized. Few, if any, district courts would be truly competent to judge the importance of particular information to the security of the United States or the "probable cause" to demonstrate that the government in fact needs to recover that information from one particular source.

> Perhaps most crucially, the executive branch not only has superior expertise in the area of foreign intelligence, it is also constitutionally designated as the pre-eminent authority in foreign affairs. The President and his deputies are charged by the constitution with the conduct of the foreign policy of the United States in times of war and peace. Just as the separation of powers in *Keith* forced the executive to recognize a judicial role when the President conducts domestic security surveillance, so the separation of powers requires us to acknowledge the principal responsibility of the President for foreign affairs and concomitantly for foreign intelligence surveillance.

Id. at 913–14. The Court limited this holding to contexts in which two requirements were met. "First, the government should be relieved of seeking a warrant only when the object of the search or the surveillance is a foreign power, its agent or collaborators." *Id.* at 915. Second, "the executive should be excused from securing a warrant only when the surveillance is conducted primarily for foreign intelligence reasons." *Id.* The court explained:

> [O]nce surveillance becomes primarily a criminal investigation, the courts are entirely competent to make the usual probable cause determination, and * * * individual privacy interests come to the fore and government foreign policy concerns recede when the government is primarily attempting to form the basis for a criminal prosecution. We thus reject the government's assertion that, if surveillance is to any degree directed at gathering foreign intelligence, the executive may ignore the warrant requirement of the Fourth Amendment.

Id. In those contexts, warrantless surveillance was permissible so long as it was "reasonable."

5. *The Fourth Amendment and extraterritorial national security searches.* In the case of In re Terrorist Bombings of U.S. Embassies in East Africa, 552 F.3d 157 (2d Cir. 2008), the Second Circuit concluded that the constitutionality of warrantless wiretapping that targeted a U.S. citizen in Kenya should be evaluated under a general reasonableness standard. In that case, the government learned of five phone numbers being used by active members of Al Qaeda. One such number happened to belong to El–Hage, who was an American citizen. His home telephone was monitored without a warrant for about one year. The Second Circuit concluded that the warrantless wiretapping of El–Hage's telephone in Kenya was reasonable and therefore constitutional under the circumstances:

> It cannot be denied that El–Hage suffered, while abroad, a significant invasion of privacy by virtue of the government's year-long surveillance of his telephonic communications. The Supreme Court has recognized that, like a physical search, electronic monitoring intrudes on "the innermost secrets of one's home or office" and that "few threats to liberty exist which are greater than that posed by the use of eavesdropping devices." *Berger v. New York,* 388 U.S. 41, 63 (1967). For its part, the government does not contradict El–Hage's claims that the surveillance was broad and loosely minimized. Instead, the government sets forth a variety of reasons justifying the breadth of the surveillance. These justifications, regardless of their merit, do not lessen the intrusion El–Hage suffered while abroad, and we accord this intrusion substantial weight in our balancing analysis.

> Turning to the government's interest, we encounter again the self-evident need to investigate threats to national security presented by foreign terrorist organizations. When U.S. intelligence learned that five telephone lines were being used by suspected al Qaeda operatives, the need to monitor communications traveling on those lines was paramount, and we are loath to discount—much less disparage—the government's decision to do so.

> Our balancing of these compelling, and competing, interests turns on whether the scope of the intrusion here was justified by the government's surveillance needs. We conclude that it was, for at least the following four reasons.

First, complex, wide-ranging, and decentralized organizations, such as al Qaeda, warrant sustained and intense monitoring in order to understand their features and identify their members.

Second, foreign intelligence gathering of the sort considered here must delve into the superficially mundane because it is not always readily apparent what information is relevant.

Third, members of covert terrorist organizations, as with other sophisticated criminal enterprises, often communicate in code, or at least through ambiguous language. Hence, more extensive and careful monitoring of these communications may be necessary.

Fourth, because the monitored conversations were conducted in foreign languages, the task of determining relevance and identifying coded language was further complicated.

Because the surveillance of suspected al Qaeda operatives must be sustained and thorough in order to be effective, we cannot conclude that the scope of the government's electronic surveillance was overbroad. While the intrusion on El–Hage's privacy was great, the need for the government to so intrude was even greater. Accordingly, the electronic surveillance was reasonable under the Fourth Amendment.

Id. at 175–76.

6.   In 2005, *The New York Times* disclosed that the National Security Agency was tapping telecommunications switches in the United States to intercept international telephone calls and Internet communications without first obtaining a warrant. The alleged program focuses mostly on communications among individuals outside the United States that happen to be routed inside the United States in the course of delivery, but includes some communications between United States citizens and permanent residents in the United States and others outside the United States. *See generally* James Risen, State of War 39–60 (2006). According to one report, the program works by generating copies of millions and millions of e-mails and telephone calls being sent through individual communications switches—mostly communications among those inside the United States—and scanning the communications for particular e-mail addresses or keywords believed to relate to members of Al Qaeda or allied organizations. Communications that register with the filters are then reviewed by individuals at the NSA for further action. *See* James Bamford, *Big Brother is Listening*, The Atlantic Monthly, April 2006, at 65–70.

The Justice Department has defended the constitutionality of this program under the "special needs" exception to the Fourth Amendment, which is arguably the same doctrinal box applied in the *Keith* case. Here is the argument:

With respect to the individual privacy interests at stake, there can be no doubt that, as a general matter, interception of telephone communications implicates a significant privacy interest of the individual whose conversation is intercepted. The Supreme Court has made clear at least since Katz v. United States, 389 U.S. 347 (1967), that individuals have a substantial and constitutionally protected reasonable expectation of privacy that their telephone conversations will not be subject to governmental eavesdropping. Although the individual privacy interests at stake may be substantial, it is well recognized that a variety of governmental interests—including routine law enforcement and foreign-intelligence gathering—can overcome those interests.

On the other side of the scale here, the Government's interest in engaging in the NSA activities is the most compelling interest possible— securing the Nation from foreign attack in the midst of an armed conflict. One attack already has taken thousands of lives and placed the Nation in state of armed conflict. Defending the Nation from attack is perhaps the most important function of the federal Government—and one of the few express obligations of the federal Government enshrined in the Constitution. As the Supreme Court has declared, "[i]t is 'obvious and unarguable' that no governmental interest is more compelling than the security of the Nation." Haig v. Agee, 453 U.S. 280, 307 (1981). The Government's overwhelming interest in detecting and thwarting further al Qaeda attacks is easily sufficient to make reasonable the intrusion into privacy involved in intercepting one-end foreign communications where there is "a reasonable basis to conclude that one party to the communication is a member of al Qaeda, affiliated with al Qaeda, or a member of an organization affiliated with al Qaeda."

Of course, because the magnitude of the Government's interest here depends in part upon the threat posed by al Qaeda, it might be possible for the weight that interest carries in the balance to change over time. It is thus significant for the reasonableness of the NSA activities that the President has established a system under which he authorizes the surveillance only for a limited period, typically for 45 days. This process of reauthorization ensures a periodic review to evaluate whether the threat from al Qaeda remains sufficiently strong that the Government's interest in protecting the Nation and its citizens from foreign attack continues to outweigh the individual privacy interests at stake.

United States Department of Justice, Legal Authorities Supporting the Activities of the National Security Agency Described by the President 39–40 (Jan. 19, 2006).

Is this defense persuasive? Does it depend on the magnitude of the Al Qaeda threat, or on the technical details of the surveillance program?

7. *Reasonable warrants under the USA Patriot Act.* The *Keith* case establishes that warrants are required for domestic security surveillance, and advises that such warrants must be "reasonable both in relation to the legitimate need of Government for intelligence information and the protected rights of our citizens." What does this mean? What types of warrants can Congress authorize in intelligence cases that will satisfy this test?

This issue arose in In re Sealed Case, 310 F.3d 717 (Foreign Intel. Surv. Ct. Rev. 2002), which considered the constitutionality of amendments to the Foreign Intelligence Surveillance Act (FISA) put in place by the USA Patriot Act of 2001. Before the Patriot Act, FISA conditioned the issuance of national security warrants on the absence of intent to collect evidence for possible criminal prosecution. Specifically, FISA required investigators seeking a national security warrant to establish probable cause that the person monitored was an agent of a foreign power and that "the purpose of the surveillance is to obtain foreign intelligence information."

The Patriot Act changed the standard to permit intelligence officials to share information collected under FISA with criminal investigators. The new standard requires the government to establish probable cause that the person monitored is the agent of a foreign power, and that "a significant purpose" of surveillance is to obtain foreign intelligence information. 50 U.S.C. § 1804(a)(7)(B). It also adds a provision allowing "Federal officers who conduct electronic surveillance to acquire foreign intelligence information" to "consult with Federal law enforcement officers to coordinate efforts to investigate or protect against" attack or other grave hostile acts, sabotage or international terrorism, or clandestine intelligence activities, by foreign powers or their agents. 50 U.S.C. § 1806(k)(1).

The Foreign Intelligence Surveillance Court of Review, a special court of three federal appellate judges, ruled that this statutory framework satisfies the *Keith* reasonableness standard:

> FISA's general programmatic purpose, to protect the nation against terrorists and espionage threats directed by foreign powers, has from its outset been distinguishable from "ordinary crime control." After the events of September 11, 2001, though, it is hard to imagine greater emergencies facing Americans than those experienced on that date.

> Although * * * the threat to society is not dispositive in determining whether a search or seizure is reasonable, it certainly remains a crucial factor. Our case may well involve the most serious threat our country faces. Even without taking into account the President's inherent constitutional authority to conduct warrantless foreign intelligence surveillance, we think the procedures and government showings required under FISA, if they do not meet the minimum Fourth Amendment warrant standards, certainly come close. We, therefore, believe firmly, applying the balancing test drawn from *Keith,* that FISA as amended is constitutional because the surveillances it authorizes are reasonable.

In re Sealed Case, 310 F.3d at 746.

B.   THE FOREIGN INTELLIGENCE SURVEILLANCE ACT

The *Keith* case pointed to the need for statutory regulation of national security surveillance. That need became particularly clear in the mid 1970s during hearings into intelligence collection abuses held by the United States Senate Select Committee to Study Governmental Operations with Respect to Intelligence Activities, presided over by Senator Frank Church. The so-called "Church Committee" published 14 reports in 1975 and 1976 detailing the intelligence practices of several government agencies, and the reports led to calls for a new statute to regulate intelligence surveillance. *See generally* Peter P. Swire, *The System of Foreign Intelligence Surveillance Law*, 72 Geo. Wash. L. Rev. 1306, 1315–20 (2004).

Congress responded by enacting the Foreign Intelligence Surveillance Act (FISA), Pub. L. 95–511 (1978). FISA replaced the reservation clause of 18 U.S.C. § 2511(3) (1968), and imposed direct regulation of Executive Branch intelligence activities. *See* 18 U.S.C. § 2511(2)(f). Under FISA, if the government seeks evidence of domestic security violations, it must follow the usual criminal law authorities. If the President wishes to conduct foreign intelligence surveillance, the President must comply with the requirements of the FISA statute, which acts as a cousin of the criminal-law statutory privacy laws covered in Chapter 6.

FISA requires the Executive Branch to apply for and obtain court orders to conduct foreign intelligence surveillance from the Foreign Intelligence Surveillance Court. Eleven United States District Court judges are appointed to the court by the Chief Justice of the United States. *See* 50 U.S.C. § 1803. When the government needs a FISA order signed, it submits an application to one of the eleven judges assigned to the Court.

FISA's Equivalent of the Wiretap Act

The FISA equivalent of the Wiretap Act is codified at 50 U.S.C. §§ 1801–11. In lieu of regulating the interception of contents of wire and electronic communications, FISA regulates engaging in "electronic surveillance." "Electronic surveillance" is defined in a fairly complicated way by 50 U.S.C. § 1801(f):

(1) the acquisition by an electronic, mechanical, or other surveillance device of the contents of any wire or radio communication sent by or intended to be received by a particular, known United States person who is in the United States, if the contents are acquired by intentionally targeting that United States person, under circumstances in which a person has a reasonable expectation of privacy and a warrant would be required for law enforcement purposes;

(2) the acquisition by an electronic, mechanical, or other surveillance device of the contents of any wire communication to or from a person in the United States, without the consent of any party thereto, if such acquisition occurs in the United States, but does not include the acquisition of those communications of computer trespassers that would be permissible under section 2511(2)(i) of Title 18;

(3) the intentional acquisition by an electronic, mechanical, or other surveillance device of the contents of any radio communication, under circumstances in which a person has a reasonable expectation of privacy and a warrant would be required for law enforcement purposes, and if both the sender and all intended recipients are located within the United States; or

(4) the installation or use of an electronic, mechanical, or other surveillance device in the United States for monitoring to acquire information, other than from a wire or radio communication, under circumstances in which a person has a reasonable expectation of

privacy and a warrant would be required for law enforcement purposes.

It is important to note that FISA's version of the Wiretap Act contains definitions that differ from the same terms used in the Wiretap Act. For example, "contents" are defined more broadly in FISA than in the Wiretap Act. According to 50 U.S.C. § 1801(n), "contents" as used in FISA "includes any information concerning the identity of the parties to such communication or the existence, substance, purport, or meaning of that communication." Similarly, "wire communication" in FISA does not mean a call containing the human voice, but rather means "any communication while it is being carried by a wire, cable, or other like connection furnished or operated by any person engaged as a common carrier in providing or operating such facilities for the transmission of interstate or foreign communications." *Id.* § 1801(*l*). FISA also occasionally hinges rules on whether the subject of monitoring is a "United States person," which essentially means a United States citizen or permanent resident alien. *See id.* § 1801(i).

FISA prohibits intentionally conducting electronic surveillance "except as authorized by statute," *id.* § 1809(a)(1), and provides a statutory authority for obtaining FISA wiretap orders. *See* 50 U.S.C. § 1804. The government's application to the FISC must be personally reviewed by the Attorney General, and must include the following, *id.* § 1804(a):

(1) the identity of the Federal officer making the application;

(2) the authority conferred on the Attorney General by the President of the United States and the approval of the Attorney General to make the application;

(3) the identity, if known, or a description of the target of the electronic surveillance;

(4) a statement of the facts and circumstances relied upon by the applicant to justify his belief that—

(A) the target of the electronic surveillance is a foreign power or an agent of a foreign power; and

(B) each of the facilities or places at which the electronic surveillance is directed is being used, or is about to be used, by a foreign power or an agent of a foreign power;

(5) a statement of the proposed minimization procedures;

(6) a detailed description of the nature of the information sought and the type of communications or activities to be subjected to the surveillance;

(7) a certification or certifications by the Assistant to the President for National Security Affairs or an executive branch official or officials designated by the President from among those executive officers employed in the area of national security or defense and appointed by the President with the advice and consent of the Senate—

    (A) that the certifying official deems the information sought to be foreign intelligence information;

    (B) that a significant purpose of the surveillance is to obtain foreign intelligence information;

    (C) that such information cannot reasonably be obtained by normal investigative techniques;

    (D) that designates the type of foreign intelligence information being sought according to the categories described in section 1801 (e) of this title; and

    (E) including a statement of the basis for the certification that— (i) the information sought is the type of foreign intelligence information designated; and (ii) such information cannot reasonably be obtained by normal investigative techniques;

(8) a statement of the means by which the surveillance will be effected and a statement whether physical entry is required to effect the surveillance;

(9) a statement of the facts concerning all previous applications that have been made to any judge under this subchapter involving any of the persons, facilities, or places specified in the application, and the action taken on each previous application;

(10) a statement of the period of time for which the electronic surveillance is required to be maintained, and if the nature of the intelligence gathering is such that the approval of the use of electronic surveillance under this subchapter should not automatically terminate when the described type of information has first been obtained, a description of facts supporting the belief that additional information of the same type will be obtained thereafter; and

(11) whenever more than one electronic, mechanical or other surveillance device is to be used with respect to a particular proposed electronic surveillance, the coverage of the devices involved and what minimization procedures apply to information acquired by each device.

The reviewing judge must then issue the order if the statutory requirements are met and "there is probable cause to believe that … the target of the electronic surveillance is a foreign power or an agent of a foreign power," provided that "no United States person may be considered a foreign power or an agent of a foreign power solely upon the basis of activities protected by the first amendment to the Constitution of the United States." 50 U.S.C. § 1805(a)(3).

FISA's Equivalent of the Pen Register Statute

The FISA equivalent of the Pen Register statute is codified at 50 U.S.C. §§ 1841–46. Pen registers and trap and trace devices are defined under FISA using the definitions in the Pen Register statute. *See* 50

U.S.C. § 1841(2). FISA states that a pen/trap order can be obtained if investigators submit:

> a certification by the applicant that the information likely to be obtained is foreign intelligence information not concerning a United States person or is relevant to an ongoing investigation to protect against international terrorism or clandestine intelligence activities, provided that such investigation of a United States person is not conducted solely upon the basis of activities protected by the first amendment to the Constitution.

50 U.S.C. § 1842(c)(2).

FISA's Equivalent of the Stored Communications Act

FISA's equivalent of the Stored Communications Act is found among several different statutes. When FBI investigators seek to compel non-content information from ISPs for intelligence cases, they use 18 U.S.C. § 2709. Section 2709 is a "National Security Letter" provision in the SCA itself. The National Security Letter provision in § 2709 is something like an administrative subpoena authority, as it does not require an order signed by a judge or issued by a court. Instead, high-ranking FBI officials can request information from ISPs via written letters. According to § 2709, a "wire or electronic communication service provider shall comply with a request for subscriber information and toll billing records information, or electronic communication transactional records in its custody or possession" made by appropriate authorities within the FBI. 18 U.S.C. § 2709(a). The records sought must be "relevant to an authorized investigation to protect against international terrorism or clandestine intelligence activities, provided that such an investigation of a United States person is not conducted solely on the basis of activities protected by the first amendment to the Constitution of the United States." *Id.* § 2709(b).

Intelligence investigators normally compel the contents of communications held by ISPs using the authorities in 50 U.S.C. §§ 1821–29. These provisions regulate "physical searches," defined as "any physical intrusion within the United States into premises or property (including examination of the interior of property by technical means) that is intended to result in a seizure, reproduction, inspection, or alteration of information, material, or property, under circumstances in which a person has a reasonable expectation of privacy and a warrant would be required for law enforcement purposes." 50 U.S.C. § 1821(5). Although the scope of this authority is somewhat unclear in the case of Internet investigations, it seems that intelligence investigators generally have interpreted this provision as the required statutory framework that applies to the compelled disclosure of contents of communications from ISPs. The statute requires the government to establish probable cause that:

(A) the target of the physical search is a foreign power or an agent of a foreign power, except that no United States person may be considered an agent of a foreign power solely upon the basis of activities protected by the first amendment to the Constitution of the United States; and

(B) the premises or property to be searched is owned, used, possessed by, or is in transit to or from an agent of a foreign power or a foreign power[.]

50 U.S.C. § 1824(a)(3). In the case of Internet communications, the "premises or property" presumably would be the account and its contents rather than the physical ISP.

Intelligence investigators also can compel information from ISPs using Section 215 orders. *See* 50 U.S.C. §§ 1861–62. Section 215 orders are the national security equivalent of grand jury subpoenas, and are so-named because the authority was expanded under Section 215 of the USA Patriot Act. The Section 215 authority has been the subject of particular controversy in recent years in light of concerns that the authority might be used at libraries to compel library records. The Section 215 authority permits high-level FBI officials to apply for a FISA order requiring the recipient to produce "any tangible things (including books, records, papers, documents, and other items) for an investigation to obtain foreign intelligence information not concerning a United States person or to protect against international terrorism or clandestine intelligence activities, provided that such investigation of a United States person is not conducted solely upon the basis of activities protected by the first amendment to the Constitution." 50 U.S.C. § 1861(a)(1). As amended in 2006, the statute requires the government's application to establish:

reasonable grounds to believe that the tangible things sought are relevant to an authorized investigation * * * to obtain foreign intelligence information not concerning a United States person or to protect against international terrorism or clandestine intelligence activities, such things being presumptively relevant to an authorized investigation if the applicant shows in the statement of the facts that they pertain to—

(i) a foreign power or an agent of a foreign power;

(ii) the activities of a suspected agent of a foreign power who is the subject of such authorized investigation; or

(iii) an individual in contact with, or known to, a suspected agent of a foreign power who is the subject of such authorized investigation[.]

Id. § 1861(b)(2)(A).

The scope of Section 215 orders remains unclear. There is some evidence that the FBI interprets Section 215 orders as permitting only the disclosure of non-content transactional information. The former chief of the FBI's National Security Law Unit has stated: "Given that § 215 was clearly part of a set of parallel revisions to all FBI counterintelligence authorities for access to transactional information (national security letters, pen register/trap and trace, and business records), it seems reasonable to conclude that Congress saw § 215 as applying only to transactional information that is not subject to constitutional protections." Michael J. Woods, *Counterintelligence and Access to Transactional Records: A Practical History of USA Patriot Act Section 215*, 1 J. Nat'l Security L. & Pol'y 37, 59 (2005). To the extent that this interpretation is correct, Section 215 is a general parallel authority to the specific authority in 18 U.S.C. § 2709.

Voluntary disclosure by ISPs in national security cases is governed by 18 U.S.C. § 2702, just as in criminal investigations. Note that the emergency disclosure provisions in § 2702 are phrased in general terms: they permit disclosure to "a governmental entity," not just to law enforcement officials. 18 U.S.C. §§ 2702(b)(8), 2702(c)(4).

NOTES AND QUESTIONS

1. How do the surveillance standards for foreign intelligence investigations compare to the standards for criminal investigations? Are they lower? Higher? Or are they just different? Consider the Foreign Intelligence Surveillance Court of Review's comparison of the wiretapping authorities in Title III and FISA:

> With limited exceptions not at issue here, both Title III and FISA require prior judicial scrutiny of an application for an order authorizing electronic surveillance.

> The statutes differ to some extent in their probable cause showings. Title III allows a court to enter an ex parte order authorizing electronic surveillance if it determines on the basis of the facts submitted in the government's application that there is probable cause for belief that an individual is committing, has committed, or is about to commit a specified predicate offense. FISA by contrast requires a showing of probable cause that the target is a foreign power or an agent of a foreign power. * * * FISA applies only to certain carefully delineated, and particularly serious, foreign threats to national security.

> Turning then to the first of the particularity requirements, while Title III requires probable cause to believe that particular communications concerning the specified crime will be obtained through the interception, FISA instead requires an official to designate the type of foreign intelligence information being sought, and to certify that the information sought is foreign intelligence information. When the target is a U.S. person, the FISA judge reviews the certification for clear error, but this standard of review is not, of course, comparable to a probable cause finding by the judge. Nevertheless, FISA provides additional protections to ensure that only pertinent information is sought. The certification must be made by a national security officer—typically the FBI Director— and must be approved by the Attorney General or the Attorney General's Deputy. Congress recognized that this certification would assure written accountability within the Executive Branch and provide an internal check on Executive Branch arbitrariness.

With respect to the second element of particularity, although Title III generally requires probable cause to believe that the facilities subject to surveillance are being used or are about to be used in connection with the commission of a crime or are leased to, listed in the name of, or used by the individual committing the crime, FISA requires probable cause to believe that each of the facilities or places at which the surveillance is directed is being used, or is about to be used, by a foreign power or agent. In cases where the targeted facilities are not leased to, listed in the name of, or used by the individual committing the crime, Title III requires the government to show a nexus between the facilities and communications regarding the criminal offense. The government does not have to show, however, anything about the target of the surveillance; it is enough that "an individual"—not necessarily the target—is committing a crime. On the other hand, FISA requires probable cause to believe the target is an agent of a foreign power (that is, the individual committing a foreign intelligence crime) who uses or is about to use the targeted facility. Simply put, FISA requires less of a nexus between the facility and the pertinent communications than Title III, but more of a nexus between the target and the pertinent communications.

* * * Both statutes have a "necessity" provision, which requires the court to find that the information sought is not available through normal investigative procedures. Although the court's clearly erroneous review under FISA is more limited than under Title III, this greater deference must be viewed in light of FISA's additional requirement that the certification of necessity come from an upper level Executive Branch official. The statutes also have duration provisions; Title III orders may last up to 30 days, while FISA orders may last up to 90 days for U.S. persons. This difference is based on the nature of national security surveillance, which is "often long range and involves the interrelation of various sources and types of information." *Keith*, 407 U.S. at 322. Moreover, the longer surveillance period is balanced by continuing FISA court oversight of minimization procedures during that period. And where Title III requires minimization of what is acquired, as we have discussed, for U.S. persons, FISA requires minimization of what is acquired, retained, and disseminated. The FISA court notes, however, that in practice FISA surveillance devices are normally left on continuously, and the minimization occurs in the process of indexing and logging the pertinent communications. The reasonableness of this approach depends on the facts and circumstances of each case. Less minimization in the acquisition stage may well be justified to the extent the intercepted communications are ambiguous in nature or apparently involve guarded or coded language, or the investigation is focusing on what is thought to be a widespread conspiracy where more extensive surveillance may be justified in an attempt to determine the precise scope of the enterprise. Given the targets of FISA surveillance, it will often be the case that intercepted communications will be in code or a foreign language for which there is no contemporaneously available translator, and the activities of foreign agents will involve multiple actors and complex plots.

Based on the foregoing, it should be evident that while Title III contains some protections that are not in FISA, in many significant respects the two statutes are equivalent, and in some, FISA contains additional protections.

In re Sealed Case, 310 F.3d 717, 738–41 (Foreign Intel. Surv. Ct. of Rev. 2002). Do you agree? How do the standards compare when investigators seek to install a pen register or to compel content or non-content information stored with ISPs?

Some commentators argue that FISA standards are considerably lower than ECPA standards used in criminal investigations, and have expressed concern that criminal investigators may use the lower standards under FISA to conduct investigations with far fewer checks and balances than exist in the criminal law context. They argue that criminal investigators can use FISA authorities to conduct surveillance even in cases where the investigators do not have a *bona fide* purpose to collect foreign intelligence information. The ACLU has offered the following perspective:

> Under [FISA as modified by] the Patriot Act, the FBI can secretly conduct a physical search or wiretap on American citizens to obtain evidence of crime without proving probable cause, as the Fourth Amendment explicitly requires.
>
> A 1978 law called the Foreign Intelligence Surveillance Act created an exception to the Fourth Amendment's requirement for probable cause when the purpose of a wiretap or search was to gather foreign intelligence. The rationale was that since the search was not conducted for the purpose of gathering evidence to put someone on trial, the standards could be loosened. In a stark demonstration of why it can be dangerous to create exceptions to fundamental rights, however, the Patriot Act expanded this once-narrow exception to cover wiretaps and searches that *do* collect evidence for regular domestic criminal cases. FISA previously allowed searches only if the primary purpose was to gather foreign intelligence. But the Patriot Act changes the law to allow searches when "a significant purpose" is intelligence. That lets the government circumvent the Constitution's probable cause requirement even when its main goal is ordinary law enforcement.

Surveillance Under the USA PATRIOT Act (Apr. 3, 2003), *available at* http://www.aclu.org/safefree/general/17326res20030403.html.

Is the ACLU's description accurate? How likely is it that criminal investigators will obtain court orders under FISA instead of obtaining orders under the Wiretap Act, the Pen Register statute, and the Stored Communications Act?

2. *Surveillance of individuals reasonably believed to be outside the United States.* The United States intelligence agencies may wish to monitor individuals believed to be outside the United States who are believed to be agents of foreign powers. The statutory rules that regulate such monitoring depend on the target's relationship to the United States and where the monitoring will occur. If the person is a United States citizen or permanent U.S. resident believed to be an agent of a foreign power, and the U.S.

Government is seeking foreign intelligence information, the Executive branch must obtain a warrant based on "probable cause to believe that the target is (i) a person reasonably believed to be located outside the United States; and (ii) a foreign power, an agent of a foreign power, or an officer or employee of a foreign power;" 50 U.S.C. § 1881b(c)(1)(B). If that person is not a U.S. citizen or permanent U.S. resident, and the monitoring is occurring from monitoring sites located outside the United States, then the monitoring is not regulated by FISA.

On the other hand, many communications of non-citizens and non-residents located outside the United States are routed through the United States in the course of transmission. The United States government may wish to monitor those communications. The FISA Amendments Act of 2008, Pub. L. 110–261, creates a procedure for such monitoring. As explained in 50 U.S.C. § 1881a(a), "the Attorney General and the Director of National Intelligence may authorize jointly, for a period of up to 1 year from the effective date of the authorization, the targeting of persons reasonably believed to be located outside the United States to acquire foreign intelligence information."

A certification is then filed before the Foreign Intelligence Surveillance Court as to the nature of the monitoring, as well as to the fact that the planned monitoring will comply with statutory requirements. The FISC then evaluates the certification to determine if it complies with the law, and in particular whether "the procedures are reasonably designed to ensure that an acquisition authorized under subsection (a) is limited to targeting persons reasonably believed to be located outside the United States ... and prevent the intentional acquisition of any communication as to which the sender and all intended recipients are known at the time of the acquisition to be located in the United States." 50 U.S.C. § 1881a(i)(2)(B).

3. *Is the FISA Court a "rubber stamp"?* The Justice Department publishes a very brief report every year indicating the number of applications the FISA Court received and the number of applications that were approved (in whole or in part) under FISA's authorities relating to wiretapping and physical searches. Consider the statistics for the number of applications and approvals from 1998 to 2008:

Year	Applications	Approvals
2008	2,083	2,081
2007	2,371	2,368
2006	2,175	2,176
2005	2,074	2,072
2004	1,758	1,754
2003	1,727	1,724
2002	1,228	1,228
2001	932	932
2000	1,005	1,005
1999	886	886
1998	796	796

The third column indicates the number of approvals in the calendar year; the middle column adds the number of approvals with the number of denied applications. Note that the chart does not reflect the number of applications that were filed but then withdrawn in response to judicial questioning or judicial objection.

Do these numbers suggest that the FISA Court acts as a "rubber stamp" that approves almost every application? Or do you think the Justice Department is overly cautious, submitting an application for wiretapping or physical searches to the FISA Court judges only when the legal standard clearly has been met? How do the answers to these questions influence your understanding of whether the FISA regime is effective?

C. USE OF FISA EVIDENCE IN CRIMINAL CASES

Evidence collected under FISA can be used in criminal cases subject to the Fourth Amendment's exclusionary rule and the procedures and statutory suppression remedies found in 50 U.S.C. § 1806 (electronic surveillance), § 1825 (physical searches), and § 1845 (pen/trap). The procedures are designed to permit judicial review without the disclosure of sensitive national security information.

The statutory procedures are essentially the same under the different authorities. The government must first notify the court and the defendant that it seeks to use evidence either collected under FISA or derived from such evidence. *See* 50 U.S.C. § 1806(c). The defendant can then file a motion to suppress electronic surveillance or its fruits on the ground that (1) the information was unlawfully acquired; or (2) the surveillance was not made in conformity with an order of authorization or approval. *See id.* § 1806(e). Next, the Attorney General ordinarily will file an affidavit under oath taking the position that disclosure of how the evidence was obtained or an adversary hearing addressing that question would harm the national security of the United States. *See id.* § 1806(f). If such an application is filed, the district court must:

> review in camera and ex parte the application, order, and such other materials relating to the surveillance as may be necessary to determine whether the surveillance of the aggrieved person was lawfully authorized and conducted. In making this determination, the court may disclose to the aggrieved person, under appropriate security procedures and protective orders, portions of the application, order, or other materials relating to the surveillance only where such disclosure is necessary to make an accurate determination of the legality of the surveillance.

Id. If the court concludes that disclosure of materials relating to the surveillance is not necessary for the court to make an accurate determination of the legality of the surveillance, the court will not disclose the materials to the defendant. Instead, the court will make the determination in chambers without an adversary hearing.

UNITED STATES v. SQUILLACOTE

United States Court of Appeals for the Fourth Circuit, 2000.
221 F.3d 542.

TRAXLER, CIRCUIT JUDGE.

Appellants Theresa Squillacote and her husband Kurt Stand appeal from their convictions on various espionage-related charges. We affirm.

I.

Viewed in the light most favorable to the government, the evidence presented at trial established the following. Kurt Stand's parents fled to the United States from Germany during Hitler's reign. After the war, his family maintained contact with friends in the German Democratic Republic ("East Germany"). When Stand was approximately 18, his father introduced him to Lothar Ziemer, an officer with the Ministerium fur Staatssicherheit ("MfS"), East Germany's intelligence agency. The "HVA" was the foreign intelligence arm of the MfS, and Ziemer was in charge of Section 3 of the HVA's Department XI. The "primary mission" of Department XI was the operational reconnaissance of North America. Its purpose was to "acquire data of significance to the German Democratic Republic that could not be acquired by legal means." In the early 1970s, Stand began working for Ziemer as an HVA agent.

Stand's HVA activities consisted primarily of recruiting other agents. In 1976, Stand invited James Michael Clark, a college friend, to travel with him to Germany. Stand introduced Clark to an HVA operative, who introduced him to Ziemer. Ziemer invited Clark to join his organization, which he described as performing intelligence work on behalf of East Germany and other socialist countries, as well as "liberation movements" in Asia, Latin America, and Africa. Clark agreed. Sometime between 1979 and 1981, Stand brought his wife Theresa Squillacote into the fold, and she too became what Ziemer described as an "informal collaborator." At some point, Squillacote's relationship with Ziemer became more than professional, and they had an affair that lasted until 1996.

The HVA devoted substantial resources to the training of Stand, Squillacote, and Clark. They traveled to many countries, including East Germany and Mexico, to meet with their "handlers." They received training on detecting and avoiding surveillance, receiving and decoding messages sent by shortwave radio from Cuba, mailing and receiving packages through the use of "accommodation" addresses, using codewords and phrases, using a miniature camera to photograph documents, and removing classified markings from documents. HVA records indicate that the three conspirators were together paid more than $40,000 between 1985 and 1989, primarily as reimbursement for travel expenses.

As part of his "operational plan" devised with Ziemer, Clark moved to Washington, D.C., and obtained a master's degree in Russian. For a time

Clark worked for a private company in a position that required him to obtain a security clearance. He later obtained a position with the United States Army, in its environmental law division, which also required a security clearance. Clark had friends who worked for the State Department, and through them he obtained numerous classified documents that he turned over to the HVA.

Squillacote and Stand also moved to Washington, D.C., and she went to law school at the HVA's suggestion. Squillacote first followed in her father's footsteps by becoming an attorney for the National Labor Relations Board. When she realized that she had taken a career path that was not "in the best direction," she began trying to move her professional work more in line with the commitments that she had made. To that end, Squillacote used her father's connections to obtain an unprecedented temporary detail from the NLRB to the House Armed Services Committee. In 1991, Squillacote obtained a permanent job as an attorney in the Department of Defense, eventually becoming the Director of Legislative Affairs in the Office of the Undersecretary of Defense (Acquisition Reform), a position that required a security clearance and provided access to valuable information. During her tenure with the federal government, Squillacote applied for numerous government jobs, including positions with the Central Intelligence Agency, the National Security Agency, United States Army, Navy, and Air Force, and the Departments of State, Commerce, Energy, and Treasury. Apparently it was not until she began working for the Department of Defense that Squillacote gained access to the kind of information sought by her handlers. However, by that time, East Germany had collapsed.

After the fall of the Berlin Wall, Ziemer began working with the KGB, the Soviet Union's intelligence agency. Ziemer maintained his relationships with Stand, Squillacote, and Clark during this time, and they, too, became involved with the KGB. Stand, Squillacote, and Clark each traveled overseas to meet with Ziemer during the period after the collapse of East Germany. Ziemer instructed the conspirators to purchase Casio digital diaries with interchangeable memory cards. The conspirators, Ziemer, and their KGB contacts communicated with each other by exchanging memory cards.

In April 1992, Ziemer and another former HVA official were arrested and ultimately convicted for their post-unification intelligence activities with the KGB. Stand, Squillacote, and Clark became understandably concerned about their personal safety after Ziemer's arrest. They knew that "western services" were looking for two men and one woman operating out of Washington, D.C., and that the western services were aware of code names they had used. However, they believed that Ziemer and other former HVA officials would not compromise their identities. When Ziemer was released from prison in September 1992, Stand, Squillacote, and Clark re-established a system of communication with him, one purpose of which was to keep everyone informed about any threats to their safety.

From the beginning of their involvement with the HVA, Stand, Squillacote, and Clark operated independently of each other and generally were unaware of the others' activities. After Ziemer's arrest in 1992, however, the three began talking in detail about their activities and precautions needed to maintain their security. They began discussing the possibility of future intelligence work, perhaps for Vietnam or Cuba. Squillacote also talked to Clark about her interest in South Africa's Communist Party.

In 1994, Squillacote, as part of her search for "another connection," went to Amsterdam to speak to David Truong, whom she had met in college. Truong, who had been convicted of espionage on behalf of North Vietnam, was intrigued, but took no further action.

In 1995, Squillacote went to great lengths to obtain a post office box under the name of "Lisa Martin." In June 1995, Squillacote, as Lisa Martin, sent a letter to Ronnie Kasrils, the Deputy Defense Minister of South Africa. Kasrils was a Communist party official, and had received training in East Germany, the Soviet Union, and Cuba. The letter, which took Squillacote months to write, was primarily devoted to Squillacote's explanation for the collapse of socialism that began with the fall of the Berlin Wall, and her views on how the communist movement should proceed in the future. The letter was an attempt by Squillacote to make a connection with Kasrils, whom Squillacote hoped would "read between the lines." Stand and Clark were aware of the letter, but Clark apparently doubted its effectiveness.

In February 1996, Squillacote received a Christmas card from Kasrils addressed to L. Martin. In the card, Kasrils thanked "Lisa" for "the best letter" he had received in 1995. Stand and Squillacote were thrilled they received the note, and they began to think that perhaps a connection could be made. In September 1996, Squillacote found another letter from Kasrils in her Lisa Martin post office box. The letter stated that "you may have the interest and vision to assist in our struggle," and invited Squillacote to a meeting in New York City with a representative of "our special components."

Squillacote and Stand, however, were unaware that, for many years, they had been the subjects of an intense FBI investigation. As part of its investigation, the FBI in January 1996 obtained authorization to conduct clandestine electronic surveillance, which included the monitoring of all conversations in the Appellants' home, as well as calls made to and from their home and Squillacote's office. Through its investigation, the FBI had learned of Squillacote's letter to Kasrils and the Appellants' response to the February 1996 note from Kasrils. The September 1996 Kasrils letter in fact was written by the FBI as part of a "false flag" operation intended to uncover information about the prior espionage activities of Stand, Squillacote, and Clark.

When designing the false flag operation, the FBI's Behavioral Analysis Program Team prepared a report to examine the personality of

Squillacote, and based on this examination, to provide suggestions that could be used * * * to obtain evidence regarding the subject's espionage activity. The report (the "BAP report") was based on information the FBI had learned during its extensive investigation and surveillance of the Appellants.

The BAP report traced Squillacote's family background, including the suicide of her older sister and her mother's history of depression. The report stated that Squillacote was suffering from depression and listed the anti-depressant medications she was taking. The primary focus of the BAP report, however, was Squillacote's emotional makeup and how to tailor the approach to her emotional characteristics. * * * The BAP report also made very specific recommendations about how the false flag operation should be designed:

> The following scenario has been developed upon an analysis of the subject's personality, and includes suggestions designed to exploit her narcissistic and histrionic characteristics. It is believed that Squillacote will be susceptible to an approach through her mail drop based on her recent rejection by her long-term German handler, and her thrill at receiving a Christmas card from the South African official.

J.A. 2064.

The false flag letter received by Squillacote in September 1996 served its intended purpose. Unaware of any FBI involvement, Squillacote and Stand were thrilled about the letter, and Squillacote began enthusiastically making plans for a trip to New York City to meet the South African emissary.

In October 1996, Squillacote met with an undercover FBI agent posing as a South African intelligence officer. She had face-to-face meetings with the agent a total of four times, including one meeting where she brought Stand and her two children. Several letters were also exchanged, including a letter that Squillacote wrote at the request of the undercover agent describing her previous activities with Ziemer. In these meetings and letters, Squillacote expressed her enthusiasm for her new South African connection and her hope for a productive collaboration.

Throughout her association with the undercover agent, Squillacote discussed the possibility of bringing Ziemer and other former East German contacts into the operation. In December 1996, she contacted Ziemer to see if he was interested in the operation. According to Squillacote, Ziemer's response was "yes, yes, yes, yes, yes!"

At the second meeting with the undercover agent on January 5, 1997, Squillacote presented the agent with four classified documents she had obtained from the Department of Defense. Although the agent had never requested any documents or classified information from Squillacote, she explained that one day when she and her secretary were alone in her office, she decided to "score what she could score."

Squillacote and Stand were convicted of conspiracy to transmit information relating to the national defense, *see* 18 U.S.C. § 794(a) and (c); attempted transmission of national defense information, *see* 18 U.S.C. § 794(a); and obtaining national defense information, *see* 18 U.S.C. § 793(b).

II.

The government conducted 550 consecutive days of clandestine surveillance of the Appellants, surveillance that was authorized under the Foreign Intelligence Surveillance Act of 1978, 50 U.S.C. § 1801–1811. FISA was enacted to put to rest a troubling constitutional issue regarding the President's "inherent power to conduct warrantless electronic surveillance in order to gather foreign intelligence in the interests of national security," *ACLU Found. of Southern California v. Barr*, 952 F.2d 457, 460 (D.C. Cir. 1991), a question that had not been definitively answered by the Supreme Court. FISA thus created a secure framework by which the Executive Branch may conduct legitimate electronic surveillance for foreign intelligence purposes within the context of this Nation's commitment to privacy and individual rights.

Prior to trial, the Appellants sought to suppress the fruits of the FISA surveillance. They attacked the validity of the surveillance on several grounds, all of which were rejected by the district court. On appeal, however, the Appellants press only one FISA-related issue: They contend that the surveillance was improper because there was no probable cause to believe that Squillacote or Stand were agents of a foreign power. We disagree.

Under FISA, an agent of a foreign power is any person who "knowingly engages in clandestine intelligence gathering activities for or on behalf of a foreign power, which activities involve or may involve a violation of the criminal statutes of the United States." 50 U.S.C. § 1801(b)(2)(A). One who knowingly aids and abets another engaging in such clandestine intelligence activities, or one who knowingly conspires with another to engage in the clandestine intelligence activities, is also considered an agent of a foreign power. *See* 50 U.S.C. § 1801(b)(2)(D). A "United States person" may not be determined to be an agent of a foreign power "solely upon the basis of activities protected by the first amendment to the Constitution of the United States." 50 U.S.C. § 1805(a)(3)(A).

FISA provides that the district court must review *in camera* and *ex parte* the FISA application and other materials necessary to rule upon a defendant's suppression motion "if the Attorney General files an affidavit under oath that disclosure or an adversary hearing would harm the national security of the United States." 50 U.S.C. § 1806(f). Because the Attorney General filed such an affidavit in this case, the district court reviewed the applications and other materials *in camera*, and the documents were not disclosed to counsel for the Appellants. *See* 50 U.S.C. § 1806(f) (The district court "may disclose to the aggrieved person, under appropriate security procedures and protective orders, portions of the application, order, or other materials relating to the surveillance only where such disclosure is necessary to make an accurate determination of the legality of the surveillance.'').

After reviewing the applications, the district court concluded that each of the more than 20 FISA applications established probable cause to believe that the Appellants were agents of a foreign power. We have reviewed de novo the relevant materials, and likewise conclude that each FISA application established probable cause to believe that Squillacote and Stand were agents of a foreign power at the time the applications were granted, notwithstanding the fact that East Germany was no longer in existence when the applications were granted. *See* 50 U.S.C. § 1801(a) (defining "foreign power"); 50 U.S.C. § 1801(b) (defining "agent of a foreign power"). We are also satisfied that the Appellants were not targeted solely because of any protected First Amendment activities in which they may have engaged. Given the sensitive nature of the information upon which we have relied in making this determination and the Attorney General's conclusion that disclosure of the underlying information would harm the national security, it would be improper to elaborate further.

NOTES AND QUESTIONS

1. The FISA Court issued more than 20 orders permitting 550 days of consecutive monitoring. On one hand, the facts described in the opinion clearly indicate that the appellants were agents of a foreign power at some point. On the other hand, the opinion does not tell us enough to establish probable cause that the appellants were agents of a foreign power each time the orders were granted. As a result, the opinion does not establish that the evidence used against the appellants was collected using properly obtained FISA orders. Instead, the court recites public facts and the relevant legal standard, and then announces that the court is satisfied that the legal standards were met and that "it would be improper to elaborate further."

Is this a satisfying resolution of the appellants' case? Are you confident that the court was correct? On the other hand, what are the alternatives? If the basis for the court's conclusion involves national security secrets, disclosing that basis would disclose the secret. Are there alternatives to this approach that can better balance interests in judicial review with interests in secrecy? Or is this the best that can be done?

2. *The Classified Information Procedures Act.* Shortly after the passage of FISA, Congress enacted the Classified Information Procedures Act (CIPA), Pub. L. 96–456 (1980), codified at 18 U.S.C. app. §§ 1–16. CIPA regulates the discovery and use of classified information in criminal trials. The statute authorizes judges to control the disclosure of classified information using *ex parte, in camera* proceedings. Under CIPA, the presiding judge serves a gatekeeping function, hearing all claims concerning the discovery of and disclosure of classified information pre-trial. The gatekeeping serves a number of functions, including limiting a defendant's ability to avoid prosecution by threatening to disclose secrets if prosecuted (a practice known as "greymail").

See generally Saul M. Pilchen & Benjamin B. Klubes, *Using the Classified Information Procedures Act in Criminal Cases: A Primer for Defense Counsel,* 31 Am. Crim. L. Rev. 191 (1994).

The requirements of CIPA arose in United States v. Scarfo, 180 F. Supp.2d 572 (D.N.J. 2001), a case involving a Key Logger System installed on a mob boss's computer to collect his passphrase and decrypt his seized files. When Scarfo sought discovery of the details of the Key Logger System (KLS) to argue his motion to suppress, the United States objected on the ground that the workings of the KLS were classified. Judge Politan resolved the discovery dispute under CIPA as follows:

> In light of the government's grave concern over the national security implications such a revelation might raise, the Court permitted the United States to submit any additional evidence which would provide particular and specific reasons how and why disclosure of the KLS would jeopardize both ongoing and future domestic criminal investigations and national security interests.
>
> The United States responded by filing a request for modification of this Court's August 7, 2001, Letter Opinion and Order so as to comply with the procedures set forth in the Classified Information Procedures Act, Title 18, United States Code, Appendix III, § 1 et seq. ("CIPA"). * * * Defendant Scarfo objected to the government's request, alleging that the United States did not make a sufficient showing that the information concerning the KLS had been properly classified.
>
> In response to Scarfo's objection, the United States submitted the affidavit of Neil J. Gallagher, Assistant Director, Federal Bureau of Investigation, dated September 6, 2001. In his affidavit, Mr. Gallagher stated that the characteristics and/or functional components of the KLS were previously classified and marked "SECRET" at or around November 1997.
>
> The Court heard oral argument on September 7, 2001, to explore whether the government may invoke CIPA and, specifically, whether the government had classified the KLS. Although the defense conceded that the KLS was classified for purposes of CIPA, the Court reserved on that question and ordered the government to provide written submissions to the Court. The government then filed an *ex parte, in camera* motion for the Court's inspection of the classified material.
>
> On September 26, 2001, the Court held an *in camera, ex parte hearing* with several high-ranking officials from the United States Attorney General's office and the F.B.I. Because of the sensitive nature of the material presented, all CIPA regulations were followed and only those persons with top-secret clearance were permitted to attend. Pursuant to CIPA's regulations, the United States presented the Court with detailed and top-secret, classified information regarding the KLS, including how it operates in connection with a modem. The government also demonstrated to the Court how the KLS affects national security.
>
> After reviewing the classified material, I issued a Protective Order pursuant [to] CIPA on October 2, 2001, wherein I found that the government could properly invoke CIPA and that the government made a sufficient

showing to warrant the issuance of an order protecting against disclosure of the classified information. The October 2, 2001, Protective Order also directed that the government's proposed unclassified summary of information relating to the KLS under Section 4 of CIPA would be sufficient to allow the defense to effectively argue the motion to suppress. Accordingly, the Protective Order permitted the government to provide Scarfo with the unclassified summary statement in lieu of the classified information regarding the KLS. Pursuant to Section 6(d) of CIPA, the Court also sealed the transcript of the September 26th ex parte, in camera hearing and the government's supporting Affidavits. The government filed with the Court and served on Scarfo the unclassified summary on October 5, 2001, in the form of an October 4, 2001, Affidavit of Randall S. Murch, Supervisory Special Agent of the Federal Bureau of Investigation, Laboratory Division (the "Murch Affidavit").

Pursuant to CIPA, the United States requested a hearing in order to block the disclosure of supposedly classified information concerning the KLS technique. The Court held an *in camera, ex parte* hearing on September 26, 2001, to assess the classified nature of the KLS and the sufficiency of the unclassified summary proposed by the government. Prior to the September 26th *in camera, ex parte* hearing, and as expressed during the September 7th hearing, the Court was not satisfied that the KLS was properly classified as defined by CIPA. Nor was the Court at the time content with the United States' conclusory and generalized expressions of concern that revelation of the KLS would compromise the national security of the United States.

However, as a result of the September 26th *in camera, ex parte hearing*, the Court is now satisfied that the KLS was in fact classified as defined by CIPA. The Court also concludes that under Section 4 and 6(c) of CIPA the government met its burden in showing that the information sought by the Defendants constitutes classified information touching upon national security concerns as defined in CIPA. Moreover, it is the opinion of the Court that as a result of the September 26th hearing, the government presented to the Court's satisfaction proof that disclosure of the classified KLS information would cause identifiable damage to the national security of the United States. The Court is precluded from discussing this information in detail since it remains classified.

Further, upon comparing the specific classified information sought and the government's proposed unclassified summary, the Court finds that the United States met its burden in showing that the summary in the form of the Murch Affidavit would provide Scarfo with substantially the same ability to make his defense as would disclosure of the specific classified information regarding the KLS technique. The Murch Affidavit explains, to a reasonable and sufficient degree of specificity without disclosing the highly sensitive and classified information, the operating features of the KLS. The Murch Affidavit is more than sufficient and has provided ample information for the Defendants to litigate this motion. Therefore, no further discovery with regard to the KLS technique is necessary.

Id. at 575–76, 580–81. For more on CIPA, see Richard P. Salgado, Note, *Government Secrets, Fair Trials, and the Classified Information Procedures Act*, 98 Yale L.J. 427 (1988); Brian Z. Tamanaha, *A Critical Review of the Classified Information Procedures Act*, 13 Am. J. Crim. L. 277 (1986).

3. *Information warfare.* If the law of intelligence surveillance is the national security analog of criminal procedure, the law of information warfare is the national security analog of computer misuse law. United States government networks can come under attack by agents of foreign governments engaging in "information warfare." Such attacks raise a number of questions. For example, when should a computer intrusion be treated as an act of war instead of as a simple criminal act? What rights do United States government officials have to launch counterattacks to defend the United States? *See, e.g.,* Richard W. Aldrich, *How Do You Know You Are at War in the Information Age?*, 22 Hous. J. Int'l L. 223, 224–26 (2000): Michael N. Schmitt, *Computer Network Attack and the Use of Force in International Law: Thoughts on a Normative Framework*, 37 Colum. J. Transnat'l L. 885 (1999); Eric Talbot Jensen, *Computer Attacks on Critical National Infrastructure: A Use of Force Invoking the Right of Self–Defense*, 38 Stan. J. Int'l L. 207 (2002). *Cf.* 18 U.S.C. § 1030(f) ("This section does not prohibit any lawfully authorized investigative, protective, or intelligence activity of a law enforcement agency of the United States, a State, or a political subdivision of a State, or of an intelligence agency of the United States.").

APPENDIX

STATUTORY SUPPLEMENT

■ ■ ■

18 U.S.C. § 2. PRINCIPALS

(a) Whoever commits an offense against the United States or aids, abets, counsels, commands, induces or procures its commission, is punishable as a principal.

(b) Whoever willfully causes an act to be done which if directly performed by him or another would be an offense against the United States, is punishable as a principal.

18 U.S.C. § 641. PUBLIC MONEY, PROPERTY OR RECORDS

Whoever embezzles, steals, purloins, or knowingly converts to his use or the use of another, or without authority, sells, conveys or disposes of any record, voucher, money, or thing of value of the United States or of any department or agency thereof, or any property made or being made under contract for the United States or any department or agency thereof; or

Whoever receives, conceals, or retains the same with intent to convert it to his use or gain, knowing it to have been embezzled, stolen, purloined or converted—

> Shall be fined under this title or imprisoned not more than ten years, or both; but if the value of such property in the aggregate, combining amounts from all the counts for which the defendant is convicted in a single case, does not exceed the sum of $1,000, he shall be fined under this title or imprisoned not more than one year, or both.

The word "value" means face, par, or market value, or cost price, either wholesale or retail, whichever is greater.

18 U.S.C. § 875. INTERSTATE COMMUNICATIONS

(a) Whoever transmits in interstate or foreign commerce any communication containing any demand or request for a ransom or reward for the release of any kidnapped person, shall be fined under this title or imprisoned not more than twenty years, or both.

685

(b) Whoever, with intent to extort from any person, firm, association, or corporation, any money or other thing of value, transmits in interstate or foreign commerce any communication containing any threat to kidnap any person or any threat to injure the person of another, shall be fined under this title or imprisoned not more than twenty years, or both.

(c) Whoever transmits in interstate or foreign commerce any communication containing any threat to kidnap any person or any threat to injure the person of another, shall be fined under this title or imprisoned not more than five years, or both.

(d) Whoever, with intent to extort from any person, firm, association, or corporation, any money or other thing of value, transmits in interstate or foreign commerce any communication containing any threat to injure the property or reputation of the addressee or of another or the reputation of a deceased person or any threat to accuse the addressee or any other person of a crime, shall be fined under this title or imprisoned not more than two years, or both.

18 U.S.C. § 1028. FRAUD AND RELATED ACTIVITY IN CONNECTION WITH IDENTIFICATION DOCUMENTS, AUTHENTICATION FEATURES, AND INFORMATION

(a) Whoever, in a circumstance described in subsection (c) of this section—

(1) knowingly and without lawful authority produces an identification document, authentication feature, or a false identification document;

(2) knowingly transfers an identification document, authentication feature, or a false identification document knowing that such document or feature was stolen or produced without lawful authority;

(3) knowingly possesses with intent to use unlawfully or transfer unlawfully five or more identification documents (other than those issued lawfully for the use of the possessor), authentication features, or false identification documents;

(4) knowingly possesses an identification document (other than one issued lawfully for the use of the possessor), authentication feature, or a false identification document, with the intent such document or feature be used to defraud the United States;

(5) knowingly produces, transfers, or possesses a document-making implement or authentication feature with the intent such document-making implement or authentication feature will be used in the production of a false identification document or another document-making implement or authentication feature which will be so used;

(6) knowingly possesses an identification document or authentication feature that is or appears to be an identification document or authentication feature of the United States or a sponsoring entity of an event designated as a special event of national significance which is

stolen or produced without lawful authority knowing that such document or feature was stolen or produced without such authority;

(7) knowingly transfers, possesses, or uses, without lawful authority, a means of identification of another person with the intent to commit, or to aid or abet, or in connection with, any unlawful activity that constitutes a violation of Federal law, or that constitutes a felony under any applicable State or local law; or

(8) knowingly traffics in false or actual authentication features for use in false identification documents, document-making implements, or means of identification; shall be punished * * *.

* * *

(c) The circumstance referred to in subsection (a) of this section is that—

(1) the identification document, authentication feature, or false identification document is or appears to be issued by or under the authority of the United States or a sponsoring entity of an event designated as a special event of national significance or the document-making implement is designed or suited for making such an identification document, authentication feature, or false identification document;

(2) the offense is an offense under subsection (a) (4) of this section; or

(3) either—

(A) the production, transfer, possession, or use prohibited by this section is in or affects interstate or foreign commerce, including the transfer of a document by electronic means; or

(B) the means of identification, identification document, false identification document, or document-making implement is transported in the mail in the course of the production, transfer, possession, or use prohibited by this section.

(d) In this section and section 1028A—

(1) the term "authentication feature" means any hologram, watermark, certification, symbol, code, image, sequence of numbers or letters, or other feature that either individually or in combination with another feature is used by the issuing authority on an identification document, document-making implement, or means of identification to determine if the document is counterfeit, altered, or otherwise falsified;

(2) the term "document-making implement" means any implement, impression, template, computer file, computer disc, electronic device, or computer hardware or software, that is specifically configured or primarily used for making an identification document, a false identification document, or another document-making implement;

(3) the term "identification document" means a document made or issued by or under the authority of the United States Government, a State, political subdivision of a State, a sponsoring entity of an event designated as a special event of national significance, a foreign government, political subdivision of a foreign government, an international governmental or an international quasi-governmental organization which, when completed with information concerning a particular individual, is of a type intended or commonly accepted for the purpose of identification of individuals;

(4) the term "false identification document" means a document of a type intended or commonly accepted for the purposes of identification of individuals that—

(A) is not issued by or under the authority of a governmental entity or was issued under the authority of a governmental entity but was subsequently altered for purposes of deceit; and

(B) appears to be issued by or under the authority of the United States Government, a State, a political subdivision of a State, a sponsoring entity of an event designated by the President as a special event of national significance, a foreign government, a political subdivision of a foreign government, or an international governmental or quasi-governmental organization;

(5) the term "false authentication feature" means an authentication feature that—

(A) is genuine in origin, but, without the authorization of the issuing authority, has been tampered with or altered for purposes of deceit;

(B) is genuine, but has been distributed, or is intended for distribution, without the authorization of the issuing authority and not in connection with a lawfully made identification document, document-making implement, or means of identification to which such authentication feature is intended to be affixed or embedded by the respective issuing authority; or

(C) appears to be genuine, but is not;

(6) the term "issuing authority"—

(A) means any governmental entity or agency that is authorized to issue identification documents, means of identification, or authentication features; and

(B) includes the United States Government, a State, a political subdivision of a State, a sponsoring entity of an event designated by the President as a special event of national significance, a foreign government, a political subdivision of a foreign government, or an international government or quasi-governmental organization;

(7) the term "means of identification" means any name or number that may be used, alone or in conjunction with any other information, to identify a specific individual, including any—

(A) name, social security number, date of birth, official State or government issued driver's license or identification number, alien registration number, government passport number, employer or taxpayer identification number;

(B) unique biometric data, such as fingerprint, voice print, retina or iris image, or other unique physical representation;

(C) unique electronic identification number, address, or routing code; or

(D) telecommunication identifying information or access device (as defined in section 1029(e));

(8) the term "personal identification card" means an identification document issued by a State or local government solely for the purpose of identification;

(9) the term "produce" includes alter, authenticate, or assemble;

(10) the term "transfer" includes selecting an identification document, false identification document, or document-making implement and placing or directing the placement of such identification document, false identification document, or document-making implement on an online location where it is available to others;

(11) the term "State" includes any State of the United States, the District of Columbia, the Commonwealth of Puerto Rico, and any other commonwealth, possession, or territory of the United States; and

(12) the term "traffic" means—

(A) to transport, transfer, or otherwise dispose of, to another, as consideration for anything of value; or

(B) to make or obtain control of with intent to so transport, transfer, or otherwise dispose of.

(e) This section does not prohibit any lawfully authorized investigative, protective, or intelligence activity of a law enforcement agency of the United States, a State, or a political subdivision of a State, or of an intelligence agency of the United States, or any activity authorized under chapter 224 of this title.

(f) **Attempt and conspiracy.**—Any person who attempts or conspires to commit any offense under this section shall be subject to the same penalties as those prescribed for the offense, the commission of which was the object of the attempt or conspiracy.

18 U.S.C. § 1028A. AGGRAVATED IDENTITY THEFT

(a) **Offenses.**

(1) **In general.** Whoever, during and in relation to any felony violation enumerated in subsection (c), knowingly transfers, possesses, or uses, without lawful authority, a means of identification of another person shall, in addition to the punishment provided for such felony, be sentenced to a term of imprisonment of 2 years.

(2) **Terrorism offense.** Whoever, during and in relation to any felony violation enumerated in section 2332b(g)(5)(B), knowingly transfers, possesses, or uses, without lawful authority, a means of identification of another person or a false identification document shall, in addition to the punishment provided for such felony, be sentenced to a term of imprisonment of 5 years.

* * *

(c) **Definition.** For purposes of this section, the term "felony violation enumerated in subsection (c)" means any offense that is a felony violation of—

(1) section 641 (relating to theft of public money, property, or records), section 656 (relating to theft, embezzlement, or misapplication by bank officer or employee), or section 664 (relating to theft from employee benefit plans);

(2) section 911 (relating to false personation of citizenship);

(3) section 922(a)(6) (relating to false statements in connection with the acquisition of a firearm);

(4) any provision contained in this chapter (relating to fraud and false statements), other than this section or section 1028(a)(7);

(5) any provision contained in chapter 63 (relating to mail, bank, and wire fraud);

(6) any provision contained in chapter 69 (relating to nationality and citizenship);

(7) any provision contained in chapter 75 (relating to passports and visas);

(8) section 523 of the Gramm–Leach–Bliley Act (15 U.S.C. 6823) (relating to obtaining customer information by false pretenses);

(9) section 243 or 266 of the Immigration and Nationality Act (8 U.S.C. 1253 and 1306) (relating to willfully failing to leave the United States after deportation and creating a counterfeit alien registration card);

(10) any provision contained in chapter 8 of title II of the Immigration and Nationality Act (8 U.S.C. 1321 et seq.) (relating to various immigration offenses); or

(11) section 208, 811, 1107(b), 1128B(a), or 1632 of the Social Security Act (42 U.S.C. 408, 1011, 1307(b), 1320a–7b(a), and 1383a) (relating to false statements relating to programs under the Act).

18 U.S.C. § 1029. Fraud and Related Activity in Connection with Access Devices

(a) Whoever—

(1) knowingly and with intent to defraud produces, uses, or traffics in one or more counterfeit access devices;

(2) knowingly and with intent to defraud traffics in or uses one or more unauthorized access devices during any one-year period, and by such conduct obtains anything of value aggregating $1,000 or more during that period;

(3) knowingly and with intent to defraud possesses fifteen or more devices which are counterfeit or unauthorized access devices;

(4) knowingly, and with intent to defraud, produces, traffics in, has control or custody of, or possesses device-making equipment;

(5) knowingly and with intent to defraud effects transactions, with 1 or more access devices issued to another person or persons, to receive payment or any other thing of value during any 1–year period the aggregate value of which is equal to or greater than $1,000;

(6) without the authorization of the issuer of the access device, knowingly and with intent to defraud solicits a person for the purpose of—

(A) offering an access device; or

(B) selling information regarding or an application to obtain an access device;

(7) knowingly and with intent to defraud uses, produces, traffics in, has control or custody of, or possesses a telecommunications instrument that has been modified or altered to obtain unauthorized use of telecommunications services;

(8) knowingly and with intent to defraud uses, produces, traffics in, has control or custody of, or possesses a scanning receiver;

(9) knowingly uses, produces, traffics in, has control or custody of, or possesses hardware or software, knowing it has been configured to insert or modify telecommunication identifying information associated with or contained in a telecommunications instrument so that such instrument may be used to obtain telecommunications service without authorization; or

(10) without the authorization of the credit card system member or its agent, knowingly and with intent to defraud causes or arranges for another person to present to the member or its agent, for payment, 1 or more evidences or records of transactions made by an access device;

shall, if the offense affects interstate or foreign commerce, be punished as provided in subsection (c) of this section.

(b) (1) Whoever attempts to commit an offense under subsection (a) of this section shall be subject to the same penalties as those prescribed for the offense attempted.

(2) Whoever is a party to a conspiracy of two or more persons to commit an offense under subsection (a) of this section, if any of the parties engages in any conduct in furtherance of such offense, shall be fined an amount not greater than the amount provided as the maximum fine for such offense under subsection (c) of this section or imprisoned not longer than one-half the period provided as the maximum imprisonment for such offense under subsection (c) of this section, or both.

* * *

(e) As used in this section—

(1) the term "access device" means any card, plate, code, account number, electronic serial number, mobile identification number, personal identification number, or other telecommunications service, equipment, or instrument identifier, or other means of account access that can be used, alone or in conjunction with another access device, to obtain money, goods, services, or any other thing of value, or that can be used to initiate a transfer of funds (other than a transfer originated solely by paper instrument);

(2) the term "counterfeit access device" means any access device that is counterfeit, fictitious, altered, or forged, or an identifiable component of an access device or a counterfeit access device;

(3) the term "unauthorized access device" means any access device that is lost, stolen, expired, revoked, canceled, or obtained with intent to defraud;

(4) the term "produce" includes design, alter, authenticate, duplicate, or assemble;

(5) the term "traffic" means transfer, or otherwise dispose of, to another, or obtain control of with intent to transfer or dispose of;

(6) the term "device-making equipment" means any equipment, mechanism, or impression designed or primarily used for making an access device or a counterfeit access device;

(7) The term "credit card system member" means a financial institution or other entity that is a member of a credit card system, including an entity, whether affiliated with or identical to the credit card issuer, that is the sole member of a credit card system;

(8) the term "scanning receiver" means a device or apparatus that can be used to intercept a wire or electronic communication in violation of chapter 119 or to intercept an electronic serial number, mobile identification number, or other identifier of any telecommunications service, equipment, or instrument;

(9) the term "telecommunications service" has the meaning given in such term in section 3 of title I of the Communications Act of 1934 (47 U.S.C. § 153);

(10) the term "facilities-based carrier" means an entity that owns communications transmission facilities, is responsible for the operation and maintenance of those facilities, and holds an operating license issued by the Federal Communications Commission under the authority of title III of the Communications Act of 1934; and

(11) the term "telecommunication identifying information" means electronic serial number or any other number or signal that identifies a specific telecommunications instrument or account, or a specific communication transmitted from a telecommunications instrument.

(f) This section does not prohibit any lawfully authorized investigative, protective, or intelligence activity of a law enforcement agency of the United States, a State, or a political subdivision of a State, or of an intelligence agency of the United States, or any activity authorized under chapter 224 of this title. For purposes of this subsection, the term "State" includes a State of the United States, the District of Columbia, and any commonwealth, territory, or possession of the United States.

(g) (1) It is not a violation of subsection (a)(9) for an officer, employee, or agent of, or a person engaged in business with, a facilities-based carrier, to engage in conduct (other than trafficking) otherwise prohibited by that subsection for the purpose of protecting the property or legal rights of that carrier, unless such conduct is for the purpose of obtaining telecommunications service provided by another facilities-based carrier without the authorization of such carrier.

(2) In a prosecution for a violation of subsection (a)(9), (other than a violation consisting of producing or trafficking) it is an affirmative defense (which the defendant must establish by a preponderance of the evidence) that the conduct charged was engaged in for research or development in connection with a lawful purpose.

(h) Any person who, outside the jurisdiction of the United States, engages in any act that, if committed within the jurisdiction of the United States, would constitute an offense under subsection (a) or (b) of this section, shall be subject to the fines, penalties, imprisonment, and forfeiture provided in this title if—

(1) the offense involves an access device issued, owned, managed, or controlled by a financial institution, account issuer, credit card system member, or other entity within the jurisdiction of the United States; and

(2) the person transports, delivers, conveys, transfers to or through, or otherwise stores, secrets, or holds within the jurisdiction of the United States, any article used to assist in the commission of

the offense or the proceeds of such offense or property derived therefrom.

18 U.S.C. § 1030.   FRAUD AND RELATED ACTIVITY IN CONNECTION WITH COMPUTERS

(a) Whoever—

(1) having knowingly accessed a computer without authorization or exceeding authorized access, and by means of such conduct having obtained information that has been determined by the United States Government pursuant to an Executive order or statute to require protection against unauthorized disclosure for reasons of national defense or foreign relations, or any restricted data, as defined in paragraph y. of section 11 of the Atomic Energy Act of 1954, with reason to believe that such information so obtained could be used to the injury of the United States, or to the advantage of any foreign nation willfully communicates, delivers, transmits, or causes to be communicated, delivered, or transmitted, or attempts to communicate, deliver, transmit or cause to be communicated, delivered, or transmitted the same to any person not entitled to receive it, or willfully retains the same and fails to deliver it to the officer or employee of the United States entitled to receive it;

(2) intentionally accesses a computer without authorization or exceeds authorized access, and thereby obtains—

(A) information contained in a financial record of a financial institution, or of a card issuer as defined in section 1602(n) of title 15, or contained in a file of a consumer reporting agency on a consumer, as such terms are defined in the Fair Credit Reporting Act (15 U.S.C. 1681 et seq.);

(B) information from any department or agency of the United States; or

(C) information from any protected computer;

(3) intentionally, without authorization to access any nonpublic computer of a department or agency of the United States, accesses such a computer of that department or agency that is exclusively for the use of the Government of the United States or, in the case of a computer not exclusively for such use, is used by or for the Government of the United States and such conduct affects that use by or for the Government of the United States;

(4) knowingly and with intent to defraud, accesses a protected computer without authorization, or exceeds authorized access, and by means of such conduct furthers the intended fraud and obtains anything of value, unless the object of the fraud and the thing obtained consists only of the use of the computer and the value of such use is not more than $5,000 in any 1–year period;

(5) (A) knowingly causes the transmission of a program, information, code, or command, and as a result of such conduct, intentionally causes damage without authorization, to a protected computer;

(B) intentionally accesses a protected computer without authorization, and as a result of such conduct, recklessly causes damage; or

(C) intentionally accesses a protected computer without authorization, and as a result of such conduct, causes damage and loss.

(6) knowingly and with intent to defraud traffics (as defined in section 1029) in any password or similar information through which a computer may be accessed without authorization, if—

(A) such trafficking affects interstate or foreign commerce; or

(B) such computer is used by or for the Government of the United States;

(7) with intent to extort from any person any money or other thing of value, transmits in interstate or foreign commerce any communication containing any—

(A) threat to cause damage to a protected computer;

(B) threat to obtain information from a protected computer without authorization or in excess of authorization or to impair the confidentiality of information obtained from a protected computer without authorization or by exceeding authorized access; or

(C) demand or request for money or other thing of value in relation to damage to a protected computer, where such damage was caused to facilitate the extortion;

shall be punished as provided in subsection (c) of this section.

(b) Whoever conspires to commit or attempts to commit an offense under subsection (a) of this section shall be punished as provided in subsection (c) of this section.

(c) The punishment for an offense under subsection (a) or (b) of this section is—

(1) (A) a fine under this title or imprisonment for not more than ten years, or both, in the case of an offense under subsection (a)(1) of this section which does not occur after a conviction for another offense under this section, or an attempt to commit an offense punishable under this subparagraph; and

(B) a fine under this title or imprisonment for not more than twenty years, or both, in the case of an offense under subsection (a)(1) of this section which occurs after a conviction for another offense under this section, or an attempt to commit an offense punishable under this subparagraph;

(2) (A) except as provided in subparagraph (B), a fine under this title or imprisonment for not more than one year, or both, in the case of an offense under subsection (a)(2), (a)(3), or (a)(6) of this section which does not occur after a conviction for another offense under this section, or an attempt to commit an offense punishable under this subparagraph;

(B) a fine under this title or imprisonment for not more than 5 years, or both, in the case of an offense under subsection (a)(2), or an attempt to commit an offense punishable under this subparagraph, if—

(i) the offense was committed for purposes of commercial advantage or private financial gain;

(ii) the offense was committed in furtherance of any criminal or tortious act in violation of the Constitution or laws of the United States or of any State; or

(iii) the value of the information obtained exceeds $5,000; and

(C) a fine under this title or imprisonment for not more than ten years, or both, in the case of an offense under subsection (a)(2), (a)(3) or (a)(6) of this section which occurs after a conviction for another offense under this section, or an attempt to commit an offense punishable under this subparagraph;

(3) (A) a fine under this title or imprisonment for not more than five years, or both, in the case of an offense under subsection (a)(4) or (a)(7) of this section which does not occur after a conviction for another offense under this section, or an attempt to commit an offense punishable under this subparagraph; and

(B) a fine under this title or imprisonment for not more than ten years, or both, in the case of an offense under subsection (a)(4) or (a)(7) of this section which occurs after a conviction for another offense under this section, or an attempt to commit an offense punishable under this subparagraph;

(4) (A) except as provided in subparagraphs (E) and (F), a fine under this title, imprisonment for not more than 5 years, or both, in the case of—

(i) an offense under subsection (a)(5)(B), which does not occur after a conviction for another offense under this section, if the offense caused (or, in the case of an attempted offense, would, if completed, have caused)—

(I) loss to 1 or more persons during any 1–year period (and, for purposes of an investigation, prosecution, or other proceeding brought by the United States only, loss resulting from a related course of conduct affecting 1 or more other protected computers) aggregating at least \$5,000 in value;

(II) the modification or impairment, or potential modification or impairment, of the medical examination, diagnosis, treatment, or care of 1 or more individuals;

(III) physical injury to any person;

(IV) a threat to public health or safety;

(V) damage affecting a computer used by or for an entity of the United States Government in furtherance of the administration of justice, national defense, or national security; or

(VI) damage affecting 10 or more protected computers during any 1–year period; or

(ii) an attempt to commit an offense punishable under this subparagraph;

(B) except as provided in subparagraphs (E) and (F), a fine under this title, imprisonment for not more than 10 years, or both, in the case of—

(i) an offense under subsection (a)(5)(A), which does not occur after a conviction for another offense under this section, if the offense caused (or, in the case of an attempted offense, would, if completed, have caused) a harm provided in subclauses (I) through (VI) of subparagraph (A)(i); or

(ii) an attempt to commit an offense punishable under this subparagraph;

(C) except as provided in subparagraphs (E) and (F), a fine under this title, imprisonment for not more than 20 years, or both, in the case of—

(i) an offense or an attempt to commit an offense under subparagraphs (A) or (B) of subsection (a)(5) that occurs after a conviction for another offense under this section; or

(ii) an attempt to commit an offense punishable under this subparagraph;

(D) a fine under this title, imprisonment for not more than 10 years, or both, in the case of—

(i) an offense or an attempt to commit an offense under subsection (a)(5)(C) that occurs after a conviction for another offense under this section; or

(ii) an attempt to commit an offense punishable under this subparagraph;

(E) if the offender attempts to cause or knowingly or recklessly causes serious bodily injury from conduct in violation of subsection (a)(5)(A), a fine under this title, imprisonment for not more than 20 years, or both;

(F) if the offender attempts to cause or knowingly or recklessly causes death from conduct in violation of subsection (a)(5)(A), a fine under this title, imprisonment for any term of years or for life, or both; or

(G) a fine under this title, imprisonment for not more than 1 year, or both, for—

(i) any other offense under subsection (a)(5); or

(ii) an attempt to commit an offense punishable under this subparagraph.

(d) (1) The United States Secret Service shall, in addition to any other agency having such authority, have the authority to investigate offenses under this section.

(2) The Federal Bureau of Investigation shall have primary authority to investigate offenses under subsection (a)(1) for any cases involving espionage, foreign counterintelligence, information protected against unauthorized disclosure for reasons of national defense or foreign relations, or Restricted Data (as that term is defined in section 11y of the Atomic Energy Act of 1954 (42 U.S.C. 2014(y)), except for offenses affecting the duties of the United States Secret Service pursuant to section 3056(a) of this title.

(3) Such authority shall be exercised in accordance with an agreement which shall be entered into by the Secretary of the Treasury and the Attorney General.

(e) As used in this section—

(1) the term "computer" means an electronic, magnetic, optical, electrochemical, or other high speed data processing device performing logical, arithmetic, or storage functions, and includes any data storage facility or communications facility directly related to or operating in conjunction with such device, but such term does not include an automated typewriter or typesetter, a portable hand held calculator, or other similar device;

(2) the term "protected computer" means a computer—

(A) exclusively for the use of a financial institution or the United States Government, or, in the case of a computer not exclusively for such use, used by or for a financial institution or the United States Government and the conduct constituting the offense affects that use by or for the financial institution or the Government; or

(B) which is used in or affecting interstate or foreign commerce or communication, including a computer located outside the United States that is used in a manner that affects interstate or foreign commerce or communication of the United States;

(3) the term "State" includes the District of Columbia, the Commonwealth of Puerto Rico, and any other commonwealth, possession or territory of the United States;

(4) the term "financial institution" means—

(A) an institution, with deposits insured by the Federal Deposit Insurance Corporation;

(B) the Federal Reserve or a member of the Federal Reserve including any Federal Reserve Bank;

(C) a credit union with accounts insured by the National Credit Union Administration;

(D) a member of the Federal home loan bank system and any home loan bank;

(E) any institution of the Farm Credit System under the Farm Credit Act of 1971;

(F) a broker-dealer registered with the Securities and Exchange Commission pursuant to section 15 of the Securities Exchange Act of 1934;

(G) the Securities Investor Protection Corporation;

(H) a branch or agency of a foreign bank (as such terms are defined in paragraphs (1) and (3) of section 1(b) of the International Banking Act of 1978); and

(I) an organization operating under section 25 or section 25(a) of the Federal Reserve Act;

(5) the term "financial record" means information derived from any record held by a financial institution pertaining to a customer's relationship with the financial institution;

(6) the term "exceeds authorized access" means to access a computer with authorization and to use such access to obtain or alter information in the computer that the accesser is not entitled so to obtain or alter;

(7) the term "department of the United States" means the legislative or judicial branch of the Government or one of the executive departments enumerated in section 101 of title 5;

(8) the term "damage" means any impairment to the integrity or availability of data, a program, a system, or information;

(9) the term "government entity" includes the Government of the United States, any State or political subdivision of the United States, any foreign country, and any state, province, municipality, or other political subdivision of a foreign country;

(10) the term "conviction" shall include a conviction under the law of any State for a crime punishable by imprisonment for more than 1 year, an element of which is unauthorized access, or exceeding authorized access, to a computer;

(11) the term "loss" means any reasonable cost to any victim, including the cost of responding to an offense, conducting a damage assessment, and restoring the data, program, system, or information to its condition prior to the offense, and any revenue lost, cost incurred, or other consequential damages incurred because of interruption of service; and

(12) the term "person" means any individual, firm, corporation, educational institution, financial institution, governmental entity, or legal or other entity.

(f) This section does not prohibit any lawfully authorized investigative, protective, or intelligence activity of a law enforcement agency of the United States, a State, or a political subdivision of a State, or of an intelligence agency of the United States.

(g) Any person who suffers damage or loss by reason of a violation of this section may maintain a civil action against the violator to obtain compensatory damages and injunctive relief or other equitable relief. A civil action for a violation of this section may be brought only if the conduct involves 1 of the factors set forth in subclauses (I), (II), (III), (IV), or (V) of subsection (c)(4)(A)(i). Damages for a violation involving only conduct described in subsection (c)(4)(A)(i)(I) are limited to economic damages. No action may be brought under this subsection unless such action is begun within 2 years of the date of the act complained of or the date of the discovery of the damage. No action may be brought under this subsection for the negligent design or manufacture of computer hardware, computer software, or firmware.

(h) The Attorney General and the Secretary of the Treasury shall report to the Congress annually, during the first 3 years following the date of the enactment of this subsection, concerning investigations and prosecutions under subsection (a)(5).

(i) (1) The court, in imposing sentence on any person convicted of a violation of this section, or convicted of conspiracy to violate this section, shall order, in addition to any other sentence imposed and irrespective of any provision of State law, that such person forfeit to the United States—

(A) such person's interest in any personal property that was used or intended to be used to commit or to facilitate the commission of such violation; and

(B) any property, real or personal, constituting or derived from, any proceeds that such person obtained, directly or indirectly, as a result of such violation.

(2) The criminal forfeiture of property under this subsection, any seizure and disposition thereof, and any judicial proceeding in relation thereto, shall be governed by the provisions of section 413 of the Comprehensive Drug Abuse Prevention and Control Act of 1970 (21 U.S.C. 853), except subsection (d) of that section.

(j) For purposes of subsection (i), the following shall be subject to forfeiture to the United States and no property right shall exist in them:

(1) Any personal property used or intended to be used to commit or to facilitate the commission of any violation of this section, or a conspiracy to violate this section.

(2) Any property, real or personal, which constitutes or is derived from proceeds traceable to any violation of this section, or a conspiracy to violate this section.

18 U.S.C. § 1084. TRANSMISSION OF WAGERING INFORMATION; PENALTIES

(a) Whoever being engaged in the business of betting or wagering knowingly uses a wire communication facility for the transmission in interstate or foreign commerce of bets or wagers or information assisting in the placing of bets or wagers on any sporting event or contest, or for the transmission of a wire communication which entitles the recipient to receive money or credit as a result of bets or wagers, or for information assisting in the placing of bets or wagers, shall be fined under this title or imprisoned not more than two years, or both.

(b) Nothing in this section shall be construed to prevent the transmission in interstate or foreign commerce of information for use in news reporting of sporting events or contests, or for the transmission of information assisting in the placing of bets or wagers on a sporting event or contest from a State or foreign country where betting on that sporting event or contest is legal into a State or foreign country in which such betting is legal.

(c) Nothing contained in this section shall create immunity from criminal prosecution under any laws of any State.

(d) When any common carrier, subject to the jurisdiction of the Federal Communications Commission, is notified in writing by a Federal, State, or local law enforcement agency, acting within its jurisdiction, that any facility furnished by it is being used or will be used for the purpose of transmitting or receiving gambling information in interstate or foreign commerce in violation of Federal, State or local law, it shall discontinue or refuse, the leasing, furnishing, or maintaining of such facility, after reasonable notice to the subscriber, but no damages, penalty or forfeiture, civil or criminal, shall be found against any common carrier for any act done in compliance with any notice received from a law enforcement agency. Nothing in this section shall be deemed to prejudice the right of any person affected thereby to secure an appropriate determination, as otherwise provided by law, in a Federal court or in a State or local tribunal or agency, that such facility should not be discontinued or removed, or should be restored.

(e) As used in this section, the term "State" means a State of the United States, the District of Columbia, the Commonwealth of Puerto Rico, or a commonwealth, territory or possession of the United States.

18 U.S.C. § 1343. Fraud by Wire, Radio. or Television

Whoever, having devised or intending to devise any scheme or artifice to defraud, or for obtaining money or property by means of false or fraudulent pretenses, representations, or promises, transmits or causes to be transmitted by means of wire, radio, or television communication in interstate or foreign commerce, any writings, signs, signals, pictures, or sounds for the purpose of executing such scheme or artifice, shall be fined under this title or imprisoned not more than 20 years, or both. If the violation occurs in relation to, or involving any benefit authorized, transported, transmitted, transferred, disbursed, or paid in connection with, a presidentially declared major disaster or emergency (as those terms are defined in section 102 of the Robert T. Stafford Disaster Relief and Emergency Assistance Act (42 U.S.C. 5122)), or affects a financial institution, such person shall be fined not more than $1,000,000 or imprisoned not more than 30 years, or both.

18 U.S.C. § 1462. Importation or Transportation of Obscene Matters

Whoever brings into the United States, or any place subject to the jurisdiction thereof, or knowingly uses any express company or other common carrier or interactive computer service (as defined in section 230(e)(2) of the Communications Act of 1934), for carriage in interstate or foreign commerce—

(a) any obscene, lewd, lascivious, or filthy book, pamphlet, picture, motion-picture film, paper, letter, writing, print, or other matter of indecent character; or

(b) any obscene, lewd, lascivious, or filthy phonograph recording, electrical transcription, or other article or thing capable of producing sound; or

(c) any drug, medicine, article, or thing designed, adapted, or intended for producing abortion, or for any indecent or immoral use; or any written or printed card, letter, circular, book, pamphlet, advertisement, or notice of any kind giving information, directly or indirectly, where, how, or of whom, or by what means any of such mentioned articles, matters, or things may be obtained or made; or

Whoever knowingly takes or receives, from such express company or other common carrier or interactive computer service (as defined in section 230(e)(2) of the Communications Act of 1934) any matter or thing the carriage or importation of which is herein made unlawful—

Shall be fined under this title or imprisoned not more than five years, or both, for the first such offense and shall be fined under this title or imprisoned not more than ten years, or both, for each such offense thereafter.

18 U.S.C. § 1465. Production and Transportation of Obscene Matters for Sale or Distribution

Whoever knowingly produces with the intent to transport, distribute, or transmit in interstate or foreign commerce, or whoever knowingly transports or travels in, or uses a facility or means of, interstate or foreign commerce or an interactive computer service (as defined in section 230(e)(2) of the Communications Act of 1934) in or affecting such commerce, for the purpose of sale or distribution of any obscene, lewd, lascivious, or filthy book, pamphlet, picture, film, paper, letter, writing, print, silhouette, drawing, figure, image, cast, phonograph recording, electrical transcription or other article capable of producing sound or any other matter of indecent or immoral character, shall be fined under this title or imprisoned not more than five years, or both.

The transportation as aforesaid of two or more copies of any publication or two or more of any article of the character described above, or a combined total of five such publications and articles, shall create a presumption that such publications or articles are intended for sale or distribution, but such presumption shall be rebuttable.

18 U.S.C. § 1831. Economic Espionage

(a) **In general.**—Whoever, intending or knowing that the offense will benefit any foreign government, foreign instrumentality, or foreign agent, knowingly—

(1) steals, or without authorization appropriates, takes, carries away, or conceals, or by fraud, artifice, or deception obtains a trade secret;

(2) without authorization copies, duplicates, sketches, draws, photographs, downloads, uploads, alters, destroys, photocopies, replicates, transmits, delivers, sends, mails, communicates, or conveys a trade secret;

(3) receives, buys, or possesses a trade secret, knowing the same to have been stolen or appropriated, obtained, or converted without authorization;

(4) attempts to commit any offense described in any of paragraphs (1) through (3); or

(5) conspires with one or more other persons to commit any offense described in any of paragraphs (1) through (3), and one or more of such persons do any act to effect the object of the conspiracy,

shall, except as provided in subsection (b), be fined not more than $500,000 or imprisoned not more than 15 years, or both.

(b) **Organizations.**—Any organization that commits any offense described in subsection (a) shall be fined not more than $10,000,000.

18 U.S.C. § 1832. THEFT OF TRADE SECRETS

(a) Whoever, with intent to convert a trade secret, that is related to or included in a product that is produced for or placed in interstate or foreign commerce, to the economic benefit of anyone other than the owner thereof, and intending or knowing that the offense will, injure any owner of that trade secret, knowingly—

(1) steals, or without authorization appropriates, takes, carries away, or conceals, or by fraud, artifice, or deception obtains such information;

(2) without authorization copies, duplicates, sketches, draws, photographs, downloads, uploads, alters, destroys, photocopies, replicates, transmits, delivers, sends, mails, communicates, or conveys such information;

(3) receives, buys, or possesses such information, knowing the same to have been stolen or appropriated, obtained, or converted without authorization;

(4) attempts to commit any offense described in paragraphs (1) through (3); or

(5) conspires with one or more other persons to commit any offense described in paragraphs (1) through (3), and one or more of such persons do any act to effect the object of the conspiracy,

shall, except as provided in subsection (b), be fined under this title or imprisoned not more than 10 years, or both.

(b) Any organization that commits any offense described in subsection (a) shall be fined not more than $5,000,000.

18 U.S.C. § 1839. DEFINITIONS

As used in this chapter—

(1) the term "foreign instrumentality" means any agency, bureau, ministry, component, institution, association, or any legal, commercial, or business organization, corporation, firm, or entity that is substantially owned, controlled, sponsored, commanded, managed, or dominated by a foreign government;

(2) the term "foreign agent" means any officer, employee, proxy, servant, delegate, or representative of a foreign government;

(3) the term "trade secret" means all forms and types of financial, business, scientific, technical, economic, or engineering information, including patterns, plans, compilations, program devices, formulas, designs, prototypes, methods, techniques, processes, procedures, programs, or codes, whether tangible or intangible, and whether or how stored, compiled, or memorialized physically, electronically, graphically, photographically, or in writing if—

(A) the owner thereof has taken reasonable measures to keep such information secret; and

(B) the information derives independent economic value, actual or potential, from not being generally known to, and not being readily ascertainable through proper means by, the public; and

(4) the term "owner", with respect to a trade secret, means the person or entity in whom or in which rightful legal or equitable title to, or license in, the trade secret is reposed.

18 U.S.C. § 2251. SEXUAL EXPLOITATION OF CHILDREN

(a) Any person who employs, uses, persuades, induces, entices, or coerces any minor to engage in, or who has a minor assist any other person to engage in, or who transports any minor in or affecting interstate or foreign commerce, or in any Territory or Possession of the United States, with the intent that such minor engage in, any sexually explicit conduct for the purpose of producing any visual depiction of such conduct or for the purpose of transmitting a live visual depiction of such conduct, shall be punished as provided under subsection (e), if such person knows or has reason to know that such visual depiction will be transported or transmitted using any means or facility of interstate or foreign commerce or in or affecting interstate or foreign commerce or mailed, if that visual depiction was produced or transmitted using materials that have been mailed, shipped, or transported in or affecting interstate or foreign commerce by any means, including by computer, or if such visual depiction has actually been transported or transmitted using any means or facility of interstate or foreign commerce or in or affecting interstate or foreign commerce or mailed.

(b) Any parent, legal guardian, or person having custody or control of a minor who knowingly permits such minor to engage in, or to assist any other person to engage in, sexually explicit conduct for the purpose of producing any visual depiction of such conduct or for the purpose of transmitting a live visual depiction of such conduct shall be punished as provided under subsection (e) of this section, if such parent, legal guardian, or person knows or has reason to know that such visual depiction will be transported or transmitted using any means or facility of interstate or foreign commerce or in or affecting interstate or foreign commerce or mailed, if that visual depiction was produced or transmitted using materials that have been mailed, shipped, or transported in or affecting interstate or foreign commerce by any means, including by computer, or if such visual depiction has actually been transported or transmitted using any means or facility of interstate or foreign commerce or in or affecting interstate or foreign commerce or mailed.

(c) (1) Any person who, in a circumstance described in paragraph (2), employs, uses, persuades, induces, entices, or coerces any minor to engage in, or who has a minor assist any other person to engage in, any sexually explicit conduct outside of the United States, its territories or possessions, for the purpose of producing any visual depiction of such conduct, shall be punished as provided under subsection (e).

(2) The circumstance referred to in paragraph (1) is that—

    (A) the person intends such visual depiction to be transported to the United States, its territories or possessions, by any means, including by using any means or facility of interstate or foreign commerce or mail; or

    (B) the person transports such visual depiction to the United States, its territories or possessions, by any means, including by using any means or facility of interstate or foreign commerce or mail.

(d) (1) Any person who, in a circumstance described in paragraph (2), knowingly makes, prints, or publishes, or causes to be made, printed, or published, any notice or advertisement seeking or offering—

    (A) to receive, exchange, buy, produce, display, distribute, or reproduce, any visual depiction, if the production of such visual depiction involves the use of a minor engaging in sexually explicit conduct and such visual depiction is of such conduct; or

    (B) participation in any act of sexually explicit conduct by or with any minor for the purpose of producing a visual depiction of such conduct:

shall be punished as provided under subsection (e).

(2) The circumstance referred to in paragraph (1) is that—

    (A) such person knows or has reason to know that such notice or advertisement will be transported using any means or facility of interstate or foreign commerce or in or affecting interstate or foreign commerce by any means including by computer or mailed; or

    (B) such notice or advertisement is transported using any means or facility of interstate or foreign commerce or in or affecting interstate or foreign commerce by any means including by computer or mailed.

(e) Any individual who violates, or attempts or conspires to violate, this section shall be fined under this title and imprisoned not less than 15 years nor more than 30 years, but if such person has one prior conviction under this chapter, section 1591, chapter 71, chapter 109A, or chapter 117, or under section 920 of title 10 (article 120 of the Uniform Code of Military Justice), or under the laws of any State relating to aggravated sexual abuse, sexual abuse, abusive sexual contact involving a minor or ward, or sex trafficking of children, or the production, possession, receipt, mailing, sale, distribution, shipment, or transportation of child pornography, such person shall be fined under this title and imprisoned for not less than 25 years nor more than 50 years, but if such person has 2 or more prior convictions under this chapter, chapter 71, chapter 109A, or chapter 117, or under section 920 of title 10 (article 120 of the Uniform Code of Military Justice), or under the laws of any State relating to the sexual exploitation of children, such person shall be fined under this title and imprisoned not less than 35 years nor more than life. Any organization that violates, or attempts or conspires to violate, this section shall be fined under this title. Whoever, in the course of an offense under this section, engages in conduct that results in the death of a person, shall be punished by death or imprisoned for not less than 30 years or for life.

18 U.S.C. § 2252.　Certain Activities Relating to Material Involving the Sexual Exploitation of Minors

(a) Any person who—

(1) knowingly transports or ships using any means or facility of interstate or foreign commerce or in or affecting interstate or foreign commerce by any means including by computer or mails, any visual depiction, if—

(A) the producing of such visual depiction involves the use of a minor engaging in sexually explicit conduct; and

(B) such visual depiction is of such conduct;

(2) knowingly receives, or distributes, any visual depiction using any means or facility of interstate or foreign commerce or that has been mailed, or has been shipped or transported in or affecting interstate or foreign commerce, or which contains materials which have been mailed or so shipped or transported, by any means including by computer, or knowingly reproduces any visual depiction for distribution using any means or facility of interstate or foreign commerce or in or affecting interstate or foreign commerce or through the mails, if—

(A) the producing of such visual depiction involves the use of a minor engaging in sexually explicit conduct; and

(B) such visual depiction is of such conduct;

(3) either—

(A) in the special maritime and territorial jurisdiction of the United States, or on any land or building owned by, leased to, or otherwise used by or under the control of the Government of the United States, or in the Indian country as defined in section 1151 of this title, knowingly sells or possesses with intent to sell any visual depiction; or

(B) knowingly sells or possesses with intent to sell any visual depiction that has been mailed, shipped, or transported using any means or facility of interstate or foreign commerce, or has been shipped or transported in or affecting interstate or foreign commerce, or which was produced using materials which have been mailed or so shipped or transported using any means or facility of interstate or foreign commerce, including by computer, if—

(i) the producing of such visual depiction involves the use of a minor engaging in sexually explicit conduct; and

(ii) such visual depiction is of such conduct; or

(4) either—

(A) in the special maritime and territorial jurisdiction of the United States, or on any land or building owned by, leased to, or otherwise used by or under the control of the Government of the United States, or in the Indian country as defined in section 1151 of this title, knowingly possesses, or knowingly accesses with intent to view, 1 or more books, magazines, periodicals, films, video tapes, or other matter which contain any visual depiction; or

(B) knowingly possesses, or knowingly accesses with intent to view, 1 or more books, magazines, periodicals, films, video tapes, or other matter which contain any visual depiction that has been mailed, or has been shipped or transported using any means or facility of interstate or foreign commerce or in or affecting interstate or foreign commerce, or which was produced using materials which have been mailed or so shipped or transported, by any means including by computer, if—

(i) the producing of such visual depiction involves the use of a minor engaging in sexually explicit conduct; and

(ii) such visual depiction is of such conduct;

shall be punished as provided in subsection (b) of this section.

(b) (1) Whoever violates, or attempts or conspires to violate, paragraph (1), (2), or (3) of subsection (a) shall be fined under this title and imprisoned not less than 5 years and not more than 20 years, but if such person has a prior conviction under this chapter, section 1591, chapter 71, chapter 109A, chapter 117, or under section 920 of title 10 (article 120 of the Uniform Code of Military Justice), or under the laws of any State relating to aggravated sexual abuse, sexual abuse, or abusive sexual conduct involving a minor or ward, or the production, possession, receipt, mailing, sale, distribution, shipment, or transportation of child pornography, or sex trafficking of children, such person shall be fined under this title and imprisoned for not less than 15 years nor more than 40 years.

(2) Whoever violates, or attempts or conspires to violate, paragraph (4) of subsection (a) shall be fined under this title or imprisoned not more than 10 years, or both, but if such person has a prior conviction under this chapter, chapter 71, chapter 109A, or chapter 117, or under section 920 of Title 10 (article 120 of the Uniform Code of Military Justice), or under the laws of any State relating to aggravated sexual abuse, sexual abuse, or abusive sexual conduct involving a minor or ward, or the production, possession, receipt, mailing, sale, distribution, shipment, or transportation of child pornography, such person shall be fined under this title and imprisoned for not less than 10 years nor more than 20 years.

(c) Affirmative defense.—It shall be an affirmative defense to a charge of violating paragraph (4) of subsection (a) that the defendant—

(1) possessed less than three matters containing any visual depiction proscribed by that paragraph; and

(2) promptly and in good faith, and without retaining or allowing any person, other than a law enforcement agency, to access any visual depiction or copy thereof—

(A) took reasonable steps to destroy each such visual depiction; or

(B) reported the matter to a law enforcement agency and afforded that agency access to each such visual depiction.

18 U.S.C. § 2252A. CERTAIN ACTIVITIES RELATING TO MATERIAL CONSTITUTING OR CONTAINING CHILD PORNOGRAPHY

(a) Any person who—

(1) knowingly mails, or transports or ships using any means or facility of interstate or foreign commerce or in or affecting interstate or foreign commerce by any means, including by computer, any child pornography;

(2) knowingly receives or distributes—

(A) any child pornography that has been mailed, or using any means or facility of interstate or foreign commerce shipped or transported in or affecting interstate or foreign commerce by any means, including by computer; or

(B) any material that contains child pornography that has been mailed, or using any means or facility of interstate or foreign commerce shipped or transported in or affecting interstate or foreign commerce by any means, including by computer;

(3) knowingly—

(A) reproduces any child pornography for distribution through the mails, or using any means or facility of interstate or foreign commerce or in or affecting interstate or foreign commerce by any means, including by computer; or

(B) advertises, promotes, presents, distributes, or solicits through the mails, or using any means or facility of interstate or foreign commerce or in or affecting interstate or foreign commerce by any means, including by computer, any material or purported material in a manner that reflects the belief, or that is intended to cause another to believe, that the material or purported material is, or contains—

(i) an obscene visual depiction of a minor engaging in sexually explicit conduct; or

(ii) a visual depiction of an actual minor engaging in sexually explicit conduct;

(4) either—

(A) in the special maritime and territorial jurisdiction of the United States, or on any land or building owned by, leased to, or otherwise used by or under the control of the United States Government, or in the Indian country (as defined in section 1151), knowingly sells or possesses with the intent to sell any child pornography; or

(B) knowingly sells or possesses with the intent to sell any child pornography that has been mailed, or shipped or transported using any means or facility of interstate or foreign commerce or in or affecting interstate or foreign commerce by any means, including by computer, or that was produced using materials that have been mailed, or shipped or transported in or affecting interstate or foreign commerce by any means, including by computer;

(5) either—

(A) in the special maritime and territorial jurisdiction of the United States, or on any land or building owned by, leased to, or otherwise used by or under the control of the United States Government, or in the Indian country (as defined in section 1151), knowingly possesses, or knowingly accesses with intent to view, any book, magazine, periodical, film, videotape, computer disk, or any other material that contains an image of child pornography; or

(B) knowingly possesses, or knowingly accesses with intent to view, any book, magazine, periodical, film, videotape, computer disk, or any other material that contains an image of child pornography that has been mailed, or shipped or transported using any means or facility of interstate or foreign commerce or in or affecting interstate or foreign commerce by any means, including by computer, or that was produced using materials that have been mailed, or shipped or transported in or affecting interstate or foreign commerce by any means, including by computer;

(6) knowingly distributes, offers, sends, or provides to a minor any visual depiction, including any photograph, film, video, picture, or computer generated image or picture, whether made or produced by electronic, mechanical, or other means, where such visual depiction is, or appears to be, of a minor engaging in sexually explicit conduct—

(A) that has been mailed, shipped, or transported using any means or facility of interstate or foreign commerce or in or affecting interstate or foreign commerce by any means, including by computer;

(B) that was produced using materials that have been mailed, shipped, or transported in or affecting interstate or foreign commerce by any means, including by computer; or

(C) which distribution, offer, sending, or provision is accomplished using the mails or any means or facility of interstate or foreign commerce, for purposes of inducing or persuading a minor to participate in any activity that is illegal; or

(7) knowingly produces with intent to distribute, or distributes, by any means, including a computer, in or affecting interstate or foreign commerce, child pornography that is an adapted or modified depiction of an identifiable minor.

shall be punished as provided in subsection (b).

(b) (1) Whoever violates, or attempts or conspires to violate, paragraph (1), (2), (3), (4), or (6) of subsection (a) shall be fined under this title and imprisoned not less than 5 years and not more than 20 years, but, if such person has a prior conviction under this chapter, section 1591, chapter 71, chapter 109A, chapter 117, or under section 920 of title 10 (article 120 of the Uniform Code of Military Justice), or under the laws of any State relating to aggravated sexual abuse, sexual abuse, or abusive sexual conduct involving a minor or ward, or the production, possession, receipt, mailing, sale, distribution, shipment, or transportation of child pornography, or sex trafficking of children, such person shall be fined under this title and imprisoned for not less than 15 years nor more than 40 years.

(2) Whoever violates, or attempts or conspires to violate, subsection (a)(5) shall be fined under this title or imprisoned not more than 10 years, or both, but, if such person has a prior conviction under this chapter, chapter 71, chapter 109A, or chapter 117, or under section 920 of title 10 (article 120 of the Uniform Code of Military Justice), or under the laws of any State relating to aggravated sexual abuse, sexual abuse, or abusive sexual conduct involving a minor or ward, or the production, possession, receipt, mailing, sale, distribution, shipment, or transportation of child pornography, such person shall be fined under this title and imprisoned for not less than 10 years nor more than 20 years.

(3) Whoever violates, or attempts or conspires to violate, subsection (a)(7) shall be fined under this title or imprisoned not more than 15 years, or both.

(c) It shall be an affirmative defense to a charge of violating paragraph (1), (2), (3)(A), (4), or (5) of subsection (a) that—

(1) (A) the alleged child pornography was produced using an actual person or persons engaging in sexually explicit conduct; and

(B) each such person was an adult at the time the material was produced; or

(2) the alleged child pornography was not produced using any actual minor or minors.

No affirmative defense under subsection (c)(2) shall be available in any prosecution that involves child pornography as described in section 2256(8)(C). A defendant may not assert an affirmative defense to a charge of violating paragraph (1), (2), (3)(A), (4), or (5) of subsection (a) unless, within the time provided for filing pretrial motions or at such time prior to trial as the judge may direct, but in no event later than 10 days before the commencement of the trial, the defendant provides the court and the United States with notice of the intent to assert such defense and the substance of any expert or other specialized testimony or evidence upon which the defendant intends to rely. If the defendant fails to comply with this subsection, the court shall, absent a finding of extraordinary circumstances that prevented timely compliance, prohibit the defendant from asserting such defense to a charge of violating paragraph (1), (2), (3)(A), (4), or (5) of subsection (a) or presenting any evidence for which the defendant has failed to provide proper and timely notice.

(d) **Affirmative defense.** It shall be an affirmative defense to a charge of violating subsection (a)(5) that the defendant—

(1) possessed less than three images of child pornography; and

(2) promptly and in good faith, and without retaining or allowing any person, other than a law enforcement agency, to access any image or copy thereof—

(A) took reasonable steps to destroy each such image; or

(B) reported the matter to a law enforcement agency and afforded that agency access to each such image.

(e) **Admissibility of evidence.** On motion of the government, in any prosecution under this chapter or section 1466A, except for good cause shown, the name, address, social security number, or other nonphysical identifying information, other than the age or approximate age, of any minor who is depicted in any child pornography shall not be admissible and may be redacted from any otherwise admissible evidence, and the jury shall be instructed, upon request of the United States, that it can draw no inference from the absence of such evidence in deciding whether the child pornography depicts an actual minor.

(f) **Civil remedies.**—

(1) *In general.* Any person aggrieved by reason of the conduct prohibited under subsection (a) or (b) or section 1466A may commence a civil action for the relief set forth in paragraph (2).

(2) *Relief.* In any action commenced in accordance with paragraph (1), the court may award appropriate relief, including—

(A) temporary, preliminary, or permanent injunctive relief;

(B) compensatory and punitive damages; and

(C) the costs of the civil action and reasonable fees for attorneys and expert witnesses.

(g) **Child exploitation enterprises.**

(1) Whoever engages in a child exploitation enterprise shall be fined under this title and imprisoned for any term of years not less than 20 or for life.

(2) A person engages in a child exploitation enterprise for the purposes of this section if the person violates section 1591, section 1201 if the victim is a minor, or chapter 109A (involving a minor victim), 110 (except for sections 2257 and 2257A), or 117 (involving a minor victim), as a part of a series of felony violations constituting three or more separate incidents and involving more than one victim, and commits those offenses in concert with three or more other persons.

18 U.S.C. § 2256.   Definitions for Chapter

For the purposes of this chapter, the term—

(1) "minor" means any person under the age of eighteen years;

(2) (A) Except as provided in subparagraph (B), "sexually explicit conduct" means actual or simulated—

> (i) sexual intercourse, including genital-genital, oral-genital, anal-genital, or oral-anal, whether between persons of the same or opposite sex;
>
> (ii) bestiality;
>
> (iii) masturbation;
>
> (iv) sadistic or masochistic abuse; or
>
> (v) lascivious exhibition of the genitals or pubic area of any person;

(B) For purposes of subsection 8(B) of this section, "sexually explicit conduct" means—

> (i) graphic sexual intercourse, including genital-genital, oral-genital, anal-genital, or oral-anal, whether between persons of the same or opposite sex, or lascivious simulated sexual intercourse where the genitals, breast, or pubic area of any person is exhibited;
>
> (ii) graphic or lascivious simulated;
>
>> (I) bestiality;
>>
>> (II) masturbation; or
>>
>> (III) sadistic or masochistic abuse; or
>
> (iii) graphic or simulated lascivious exhibition of the genitals or pubic area of any person;

(3) "producing" means producing, directing, manufacturing, issuing, publishing, or advertising;

(4) "organization" means a person other than an individual;

(5) "visual depiction" includes undeveloped film and videotape, data stored on computer disk or by electronic means which is capable of conversion into a visual image, and data which is capable of conversion into a visual image that has been transmitted by any means, whether or not stored in a permanent format;

(6) "computer" has the meaning given that term in section 1030 of this title;

(7) "custody or control" includes temporary supervision over or responsibility for a minor whether legally or illegally obtained;

(8) "child pornography" means any visual depiction, including any photograph, film, video, picture, or computer or computer-generated image or picture, whether made or produced by electronic, mechanical, or other means, of sexually explicit conduct, where—

(A) the production of such visual depiction involves the use of a minor engaging in sexually explicit conduct;

(B) such visual depiction is a digital image, computer image, or computer-generated image that is, or is indistinguishable from, that of a minor engaging in sexually explicit conduct; or

(C) such visual depiction has been created, adapted, or modified to appear that an identifiable minor is engaging in sexually explicit conduct.

(9) "identifiable minor"—

(A) means a person—

(i) (I) who was a minor at the time the visual depiction was created, adapted, or modified; or

(II) whose image as a minor was used in creating, adapting, or modifying the visual depiction; and

(ii) who is recognizable as an actual person by the person's face, likeness, or other distinguishing characteristic, such as a unique birthmark or other recognizable feature; and

(B) shall not be construed to require proof of the actual identity of the identifiable minor.

(10) "graphic", when used with respect to a depiction of sexually explicit conduct, means that a viewer can observe any part of the genitals or pubic area of any depicted person or animal during any part of the time that the sexually explicit conduct is being depicted; and

(11) the term "indistinguishable" used with respect to a depiction, means virtually indistinguishable, in that the depiction is such that an ordinary person viewing the depiction would conclude that the depiction is of an actual minor engaged in sexually explicit conduct. This definition does not apply to depictions that are drawings, cartoons, sculptures, or paintings depicting minors or adults.

18 U.S.C. § 2258A. REPORTING REQUIREMENTS OF ELECTRONIC COMMUNICATION SERVICE PROVIDERS AND REMOTE COMPUTING SERVICE PROVIDERS

(a) **Duty to report.**

(1) **In general.** Whoever, while engaged in providing an electronic communication service or a remote computing service to the public through a facility or means of interstate or foreign commerce, obtains actual knowledge of any facts or circumstances described in paragraph (2) shall, as soon as reasonably possible—

(A) provide to the CyberTipline of the National Center for Missing and Exploited Children, or any successor to the Cyber-Tipline operated by such center, the mailing address, telephone number, facsimile number, electronic mail address of, and individual point of contact for, such electronic communication service provider or remote computing service provider; and

(B) make a report of such facts or circumstances to the CyberTipline, or any successor to the CyberTipline operated by such center.

(2) **Facts or circumstances.** The facts or circumstances described in this paragraph are any facts or circumstances from which there is an apparent violation of—

(A) section 2251, 2251A, 2252, 2252A, 2252B, or 2260 that involves child pornography; or

(B) section 1466A.

(b) **Contents of report.** To the extent the information is within the custody or control of an electronic communication service provider or a remote computing service provider, the facts and circumstances included in each report under subsection (a)(1) may include the following information:

(1) **Information about the involved individual.** Information relating to the identity of any individual who appears to have violated a Federal law described in subsection (a)(2), which may, to the extent reasonably practicable, include the electronic mail address, Internet Protocol address, uniform resource locator, or any other identifying information, including self-reported identifying information.

(2) **Historical reference.** Information relating to when and how a customer or subscriber of an electronic communication service or a remote computing service uploaded, transmitted, or received apparent child pornography or when and how apparent child pornography was reported to, or discovered by the electronic communication service provider or remote computing service provider, including a date and time stamp and time zone.

(3) **Geographic location information.**

(A) *In general.* Information relating to the geographic location of the involved individual or website, which may include the Internet Protocol address or verified billing address, or, if not reasonably available, at least 1 form of geographic identifying information, including area code or zip code.

(B) *Inclusion.* The information described in subparagraph (A) may also include any geographic information provided to the electronic communication service or remote computing service by the customer or subscriber.

(4) **Images of apparent child pornography.** Any image of apparent child pornography relating to the incident such report is regarding.

(5) **Complete communication.** The complete communication containing any image of apparent child pornography, including—

(A) any data or information regarding the transmission of the communication; and

(B) any images, data, or other digital files contained in, or attached to, the communication.

(c) **Forwarding of report to law enforcement.**

(1) **In general.** The National Center for Missing and Exploited Children shall forward each report made under subsection (a)(1) to any appropriate law enforcement agency designated by the Attorney General under subsection (d)(2).

(2) **State and local law enforcement.** The National Center for Missing and Exploited Children may forward any report made under subsection (a)(1) to an appropriate law enforcement official of a State or political subdivision of a State for the purpose of enforcing State criminal law.

(3) **Foreign law enforcement.**

(A) *In general.* The National Center for Missing and Exploited Children may forward any report made under subsection (a)(1) to any appropriate foreign law enforcement agency designated by the Attorney General under subsection (d)(3), subject to the conditions established by the Attorney General under subsection (d)(3).

(B) *Transmittal to designated Federal agencies.* If the National Center for Missing and Exploited Children forwards a report to a foreign law enforcement agency under subparagraph (A), the National Center for Missing and Exploited Children shall concurrently provide a copy of the report and the identity of the foreign law enforcement agency to—

(i) the Attorney General; or

(ii) the Federal law enforcement agency or agencies designated by the Attorney General under subsection (d)(2).

(d) **Attorney general responsibilities.**

(1) **In general.** The Attorney General shall enforce this section.

(2) **Designation of Federal agencies.** The Attorney General shall designate promptly the Federal law enforcement agency or agencies to which a report shall be forwarded under subsection (c)(1).

(3) **Designation of foreign agencies.** The Attorney General shall promptly—

(A) in consultation with the Secretary of State, designate the foreign law enforcement agencies to which a report may be forwarded under subsection (c)(3);

(B) establish the conditions under which such a report may be forwarded to such agencies; and

(C) develop a process for foreign law enforcement agencies to request assistance from Federal law enforcement agencies in obtaining evidence related to a report referred under subsection (c)(3).

(4) **Reporting designated foreign agencies.** The Attorney General shall maintain and make available to the Department of State, the National Center for Missing and Exploited Children, electronic communication service providers, remote computing service providers, the Committee on the Judiciary of the Senate, and the Committee on the Judiciary of the House of Representatives a list of the foreign law enforcement agencies designated under paragraph (3).

(5) **Sense of Congress regarding designation of foreign agencies.** It is the sense of Congress that—

(A) combating the international manufacturing, possession, and trade in online child pornography requires cooperation with competent, qualified, and appropriately trained foreign law enforcement agencies; and

(B) the Attorney General, in cooperation with the Secretary of State, should make a substantial effort to expand the list of foreign agencies designated under paragraph (3).

(6) **Notification to providers.** If an electronic communication service provider or remote computing service provider notifies the National Center for Missing and Exploited Children that the electronic communication service provider or remote computing service provider is making a report under this section as the result of a request by a foreign law enforcement agency, the National Center for Missing and Exploited Children shall—

(A) if the Center forwards the report to the requesting foreign law enforcement agency or another agency in the same country designated by the Attorney General under paragraph (3), notify the electronic communication service provider or remote computing service provider of—

(i) the identity of the foreign law enforcement agency to which the report was forwarded; and

(ii) the date on which the report was forwarded; or

(B) notify the electronic communication service provider or remote computing service provider if the Center declines to forward the report because the Center, in consultation with the Attorney General, determines that no law enforcement agency in the foreign country has been designated by the Attorney General under paragraph (3).

(e) **Failure to report.** An electronic communication service provider or remote computing service provider that knowingly and willfully fails to make a report required under subsection (a)(1) shall be fined—

(1) in the case of an initial knowing and willful failure to make a report, not more than $150,000; and

(2) in the case of any second or subsequent knowing and willful failure to make a report, not more than $300,000.

(f) **Protection of privacy.** Nothing in this section shall be construed to require an electronic communication service provider or a remote computing service provider to—

(1) monitor any user, subscriber, or customer of that provider;

(2) monitor the content of any communication of any person described in paragraph (1); or

(3) affirmatively seek facts or circumstances described in sections (a) and (b).

(g) **Conditions of disclosure information contained within report.**

(1) **In general.** Except as provided in paragraph (2), a law enforcement agency that receives a report under subsection (c) shall not disclose any information contained in that report.

(2) **Permitted disclosures by law enforcement.**

(A) *In general.* A law enforcement agency may disclose information in a report received under subsection (c)—

(i) to an attorney for the government for use in the performance of the official duties of that attorney;

(ii) to such officers and employees of that law enforcement agency, as may be necessary in the performance of their investigative and recordkeeping functions;

(iii) to such other government personnel (including personnel of a State or subdivision of a State) as are determined to be necessary by an attorney for the government to assist the attorney in the performance of the official duties of the attorney in enforcing Federal criminal law;

(iv) if the report discloses a violation of State criminal law, to an appropriate official of a State or subdivision of a State for the purpose of enforcing such State law;

(v) to a defendant in a criminal case or the attorney for that defendant, subject to the terms and limitations under section 3509(m) or a similar State law, to the extent the information relates to a criminal charge pending against that defendant;

(vi) subject to subparagraph (B), to an electronic communication service provider or remote computing provider if necessary to facilitate response to legal process issued in connection to a criminal investigation, prosecution, or post-conviction remedy relating to that report; and

(vii) as ordered by a court upon a showing of good cause and pursuant to any protective orders or other conditions that the court may impose.

(B) *Limitations.*

(i) *Limitations on further disclosure.* The electronic communication service provider or remote computing service provider shall be prohibited from disclosing the contents of a report provided under subparagraph (A)(vi) to any person, except as necessary to respond to the legal process.

(ii) *Effect.* Nothing in subparagraph (A)(vi) authorizes a law enforcement agency to provide child pornography images to an electronic communications service provider or a remote computing service.

(3) Permitted disclosures by the National Center for Missing and Exploited Children.—The National Center for Missing and Exploited Children may disclose information received in a report under subsection (a) only—

(A) to any Federal law enforcement agency designated by the Attorney General under subsection (d)(2);

(B) to any State, local, or tribal law enforcement agency involved in the investigation of child pornography, child exploitation, kidnapping, or enticement crimes;

(C) to any foreign law enforcement agency designated by the Attorney General under subsection (d)(3); and

(D) to an electronic communication service provider or remote computing service provider as described in section 2258C.

(h) **Preservation.**

(1) **In general.** For the purposes of this section, the notification to an electronic communication service provider or a remote computing service provider by the CyberTipline of receipt of a report under subsection (a)(1) shall be treated as a request to preserve, as if such request was made pursuant to section 2703(f).

(2) **Preservation of report.** Pursuant to paragraph (1), an electronic communication service provider or a remote computing

service shall preserve the contents of the report provided pursuant to subsection (b) for 90 days after such notification by the CyberTipline.

(3) **Preservation of commingled images.** Pursuant to paragraph (1), an electronic communication service provider or a remote computing service shall preserve any images, data, or other digital files that are commingled or interspersed among the images of apparent child pornography within a particular communication or user-created folder or directory.

(4) **Protection of preserved materials.** An electronic communications service or remote computing service preserving materials under this section shall maintain the materials in a secure location and take appropriate steps to limit access by agents or employees of the service to the materials to that access necessary to comply with the requirements of this subsection.

(5) **Authorities and duties not affected.** Nothing in this section shall be construed as replacing, amending, or otherwise interfering with the authorities and duties under section 2703.

18 U.S.C. § 2261A. Stalking

Whoever—

(1) travels in interstate or foreign commerce or within the special maritime and territorial jurisdiction of the United States, or enters or leaves Indian country, with the intent to kill, injure, harass, or place under surveillance with intent to kill, injure, harass, or intimidate another person, and in the course of, or as a result of, such travel places that person in reasonable fear of the death of, or serious bodily injury to, or causes substantial emotional distress to that person, a member of the immediate family (as defined in section 115) of that person, or the spouse or intimate partner of that person; or

(2) with the intent—

(A) to kill, injure, harass, or place under surveillance with intent to kill, injure, harass, or intimidate, or cause substantial emotional distress to a person in another State or tribal jurisdiction or within the special maritime and territorial jurisdiction of the United States; or

(B) to place a person in another State or tribal jurisdiction, or within the special maritime and territorial jurisdiction of the United States, in reasonable fear of the death of, or serious bodily injury to—

(i) that person;

(ii) a member of the immediate family (as defined in section 115 of that person; or

(iii) a spouse or intimate partner of that person;

uses the mail, any interactive computer service, or any facility of interstate or foreign commerce to engage in a course of conduct that causes substantial emotional distress to that person or places that person in reasonable fear of the death of, or serious bodily injury to, any of the persons described in clauses (i) through (iii) of subparagraph (B);

shall be punished as provided in section 2261(b) of this title.

18 U.S.C. § 2314. Transportation of Stolen Goods, Securities, Moneys, Fraudulent State Tax Stamps, or Articles Used in Counterfeiting

Whoever transports, transmits, or transfers in interstate or foreign commerce any goods, wares, merchandise, securities or money, of the value of $5,000 or more, knowing the same to have been stolen, converted or taken by fraud; or

Whoever, having devised or intending to devise any scheme or artifice to defraud, or for obtaining money or property by means of false or fraudulent pretenses, representations, or promises, transports or causes to be transported, or induces any person or persons to travel in, or to be transported in interstate or foreign commerce in the execution or concealment of a scheme or artifice to defraud that person or those persons of money or property having a value of $5,000 or more; or

Whoever, with unlawful or fraudulent intent, transports in interstate or foreign commerce any falsely made, forged, altered, or counterfeited securities or tax stamps, knowing the same to have been falsely made, forged, altered, or counterfeited; or

Whoever, with unlawful or fraudulent intent, transports in interstate or foreign commerce any traveler's check bearing a forged countersignature; or

Whoever, with unlawful or fraudulent intent, transports in interstate or foreign commerce, any tool, implement, or thing used or fitted to be used in falsely making, forging, altering, or counterfeiting any security or tax stamps, or any part thereof—

Shall be fined under this title or imprisoned not more than ten years, or both.

This section shall not apply to any falsely made, forged, altered, counterfeited or spurious representation of an obligation or other security of the United States, or of an obligation, bond, certificate, security, treasury note, bill, promise to pay or bank note issued by any foreign government. This section also shall not apply to any falsely made, forged, altered, counterfeited, or spurious representation of any bank note or bill issued by a bank or corporation of any foreign country which is intended by the laws or usage of such country to circulate as money.

18 U.S.C. § 2319. Criminal Infringement of a Copyright

(a) Any person who violates section 506(a) (relating to criminal offenses) of title 17 shall be punished as provided in subsections (b), (c), and (d) and such penalties shall be in addition to any other provisions of title 17 or any other law.

(b) Any person who commits an offense under section 506(a)(1)(A) of title 17—

(1) shall be imprisoned not more than 5 years, or fined in the amount set forth in this title, or both, if the offense consists of the reproduction or distribution, including by electronic means, during any 180–day period, of at least 10 copies or phonorecords, of 1 or more copyrighted works, which have a total retail value of more than $2,500;

(2) shall be imprisoned not more than 10 years, or fined in the amount set forth in this title, or both, if the offense is a felony and is a second or subsequent offense under subsection (a); and

(3) shall be imprisoned not more than 1 year, or fined in the amount set forth in this title, or both, in any other case.

(c) Any person who commits an offense under section 506(a)(1)(B) of title 17—

(1) shall be imprisoned not more than 3 years, or fined in the amount set forth in this title, or both, if the offense consists of the reproduction or distribution of 10 or more copies or phonorecords of 1 or more copyrighted works, which have a total retail value of $2,500 or more;

(2) shall be imprisoned not more than 6 years, or fined in the amount set forth in this title, or both, if the offense is a felony and is a second or subsequent offense under subsection (a); and

(3) shall be imprisoned not more than 1 year, or fined in the amount set forth in this title, or both, if the offense consists of the reproduction or distribution of 1 or more copies or phonorecords of 1 or more copyrighted works, which have a total retail value of more than $1,000.

(d) Any person who commits an offense under section 506(a)(1)(C) of title 17—

(1) shall be imprisoned not more than 3 years, fined under this title, or both;

(2) shall be imprisoned not more than 5 years, fined under this title, or both, if the offense was committed for purposes of commercial advantage or private financial gain;

(3) shall be imprisoned not more than 6 years, fined under this title, or both, if the offense is a felony and is a second or subsequent offense under subsection (a); and

(4) shall be imprisoned not more than 10 years, fined under this title, or both, if the offense is a felony and is a second or subsequent offense under paragraph (2).

(e) (1) During preparation of the presentence report pursuant to Rule 32(c) of the Federal Rules of Criminal Procedure, victims of the offense shall be permitted to submit, and the probation officer shall receive, a victim impact statement that identifies the victim of the offense and the extent and scope of the injury and loss suffered by the victim, including the estimated economic impact of the offense on that victim.

(2) Persons permitted to submit victim impact statements shall include—

(A) producers and sellers of legitimate works affected by conduct involved in the offense;

(B) holders of intellectual property rights in such works; and

(C) the legal representatives of such producers, sellers, and holders.

(f) As used in this section—

(1) the terms "phonorecord" and "copies" have, respectively, the meanings set forth in section 101 (relating to definitions) of title 17;

(2) the terms "reproduction" and "distribution" refer to the exclusive rights of a copyright owner under clauses (1) and (3) respectively of section 106 (relating to exclusive rights in copyrighted works), as limited by sections 107 through 122, of title 17;

(3) the term "financial gain" has the meaning given the term in section 101 of title 17; and

(4) the term "work being prepared for commercial distribution" has the meaning given the term in section 506(a) of title 17.

17 U.S.C. § 506. CRIMINAL OFFENSES

(a) Criminal infringement.

(1) *In general.* Any person who willfully infringes a copyright shall be punished as provided under section 2319 of title 18, if the infringement was committed—

(A) for purposes of commercial advantage or private financial gain;

(B) by the reproduction or distribution, including by electronic means, during any 180–day period, of 1 or more copies or phonorecords of 1 or more copyrighted works, which have a total retail value of more than $1,000; or

(C) by the distribution of a work being prepared for commercial distribution, by making it available on a computer network accessible to members of the public, if such person knew or should have known that the work was intended for commercial distribution.

(2) *Evidence.* For purposes of this subsection, evidence of reproduction or distribution of a copyrighted work, by itself, shall not be sufficient to establish willful infringement of a copyright.

(3) *Definition.* In this subsection, the term "work being prepared for commercial distribution" means—

(A) a computer program, a musical work, a motion picture or other audiovisual work, or a sound recording, if, at the time of unauthorized distribution—

(i) the copyright owner has a reasonable expectation of commercial distribution; and

(ii) the copies or phonorecords of the work have not been commercially distributed; or

(B) a motion picture, if, at the time of unauthorized distribution, the motion picture—

(i) has been made available for viewing in a motion picture exhibition facility; and

(ii) has not been made available in copies for sale to the general public in the United States in a format intended to permit viewing outside a motion picture exhibition facility.

(b) **Forfeiture, destruction, and restitution.** Forfeiture, destruction, and restitution relating to this section shall be subject to section 2323 of title 18, to the extent provided in that section, in addition to any other similar remedies provided by law.

(c) **Fraudulent Copyright Notice.** Any person who, with fraudulent intent, places on any article a notice of copyright or words of the same purport that such person knows to be false, or who, with fraudulent intent, publicly distributes or imports for public distribution any article bearing such notice or words that such person knows to be false, shall be fined not more than $2,500.

(d) **Fraudulent Removal of Copyright Notice.** Any person who, with fraudulent intent, removes or alters any notice of copyright appearing on a copy of a copyrighted work shall be fined not more than $2,500.

(e) **False Representation.** Any person who knowingly makes a false representation of a material fact in the application for copyright registration provided for by section 409, or in any written statement filed in connection with the application, shall be fined not more than $2,500.

(f) **Rights of Attribution and Integrity.** Nothing in this section applies to infringement of the rights conferred by section 106A(a).

18 U.S.C. § 2422. COERCION AND ENTICEMENT

(a) Whoever knowingly persuades, induces, entices, or coerces any individual to travel in interstate or foreign commerce, or in any Territory or Possession of the United States, to engage in prostitution, or in any sexual activity for which any person can be charged with a criminal offense, or attempts to do so, shall be fined under this title or imprisoned not more than 20 years, or both.

(b) Whoever, using the mail or any facility or means of interstate or foreign commerce, or within the special maritime and territorial jurisdiction of the United States knowingly persuades, induces, entices, or coerces any individual who has not attained the age of 18 years, to engage in prostitution or any sexual activity for which any person can be charged with a criminal offense, or attempts to do so, shall be fined under this title and imprisoned not less than 10 years or for life.

18 U.S.C. § 2423.   TRANSPORTATION OF MINORS

(a) **Transportation with intent to engage in criminal sexual activity.** A person who knowingly transports an individual who has not attained the age of 18 years in interstate or foreign commerce, or in any commonwealth, territory or possession of the United States, with intent that the individual engage in prostitution, or in any sexual activity for which any person can be charged with a criminal offense, shall be fined under this title and imprisoned not less than 10 years or for life.

(b) **Travel with intent to engage in illicit sexual conduct.** A person who travels in interstate commerce or travels into the United States, or a United States citizen or an alien admitted for permanent residence in the United States who travels in foreign commerce, for the purpose of engaging in any illicit sexual conduct with another person shall be fined under this title or imprisoned not more than 30 years, or both.

(c) **Engaging in illicit sexual conduct in foreign places.** Any United States citizen or alien admitted for permanent residence who travels in foreign commerce, and engages in any illicit sexual conduct with another person shall be fined under this title or imprisoned not more than 30 years, or both.

(d) **Ancillary offenses.** Whoever, for the purpose of commercial advantage or private financial gain, arranges, induces, procures, or facilitates the travel of a person knowing that such a person is traveling in interstate commerce or foreign commerce for the purpose of engaging in illicit sexual conduct shall be fined under this title, imprisoned not more than 30 years, or both.

(e) **Attempt and conspiracy.** Whoever attempts or conspires to violate subsection (a), (b), (c), or (d) shall be punishable in the same manner as a completed violation of that subsection.

(f) **Definition.** As used in this section, the term "illicit sexual conduct" means (1) a sexual act (as defined in section 2246) with a person under 18 years of age that would be in violation of chapter 109A if the sexual act occurred in the special maritime and territorial jurisdiction of the United States; or (2) any commercial sex act (as defined in section 1591) with a person under 18 years of age.

(g) **Defense.** In a prosecution under this section based on illicit sexual conduct as defined in subsection (f)(2), it is a defense, which the defendant must establish by a preponderance of the evidence, that the defendant reasonably believed that the person with whom the defendant engaged in the commercial sex act had attained the age of 18 years.

18 U.S.C. § 2510. DEFINITIONS

As used in this chapter—

(1) "wire communication" means any aural transfer made in whole or in part through the use of facilities for the transmission of communications by the aid of wire, cable, or other like connection between the point of origin and the point of reception (including the use of such connection in a switching station) furnished or operated by any person engaged in providing or operating such facilities for the transmission of interstate or foreign communications or communications affecting interstate or foreign commerce;

(2) "oral communication" means any oral communication uttered by a person exhibiting an expectation that such communication is not subject to interception under circumstances justifying such expectation, but such term does not include any electronic communication;

(3) "State" means any State of the United States, the District of Columbia, the Commonwealth of Puerto Rico, and any territory or possession of the United States;

(4) "intercept" means the aural or other acquisition of the contents of any wire, electronic, or oral communication through the use of any electronic, mechanical, or other device.

(5) "electronic, mechanical, or other device" means any device or apparatus which can be used to intercept a wire, oral, or electronic communication other than—

> (a) any telephone or telegraph instrument, equipment or facility, or any component thereof, (i) furnished to the subscriber or user by a provider of wire or electronic communication service in the ordinary course of its business and being used by the subscriber or user in the ordinary course of its business or furnished by such subscriber or user for connection to the facilities of such service and used in the ordinary course of its business; or (ii) being used by a provider of wire or electronic communication service in the ordinary course of its business, or by an investigative or law enforcement officer in the ordinary course of his duties;

> (b) a hearing aid or similar device being used to correct subnormal hearing to not better than normal;

(6) "person" means any employee, or agent of the United States or any State or political subdivision thereof, and any individual, partnership, association, joint stock company, trust, or corporation;

(7) "Investigative or law enforcement officer" means any officer of the United States or of a State or political subdivision thereof, who is empowered by law to conduct investigations of or to make arrests for offenses enumerated in this chapter, and any attorney authorized by law to prosecute or participate in the prosecution of such offenses;

(8) "contents", when used with respect to any wire, oral, or electronic communication, includes any information concerning the substance, purport, or meaning of that communication;

(9) "Judge of competent jurisdiction" means—

 (a) a judge of a United States district court or a United States court of appeals; and

 (b) a judge of any court of general criminal jurisdiction of a State who is authorized by a statute of that State to enter orders authorizing interceptions of wire, oral, or electronic communications;

(10) "communication common carrier" has the meaning given that term in section 3 of the Communications Act of 1934;

(11) "aggrieved person" means a person who was a party to any intercepted wire, oral, or electronic communication or a person against whom the interception was directed;

(12) "electronic communication" means any transfer of signs, signals, writing, images, sounds, data, or intelligence of any nature transmitted in whole or in part by a wire, radio, electromagnetic, photoelectronic or photooptical system that affects interstate or foreign commerce, but does not include—

 (A) any wire or oral communication;

 (B) any communication made through a tone-only paging device;

 (C) any communication from a tracking device (as defined in section 3117 of this title); or

 (D) electronic funds transfer information stored by a financial institution in a communications system used for the electronic storage and transfer of funds;

(13) "user" means any person or entity who—

 (A) uses an electronic communication service; and

 (B) is duly authorized by the provider of such service to engage in such use;

(14) "electronic communications system" means any wire, radio, electromagnetic, photooptical or photoelectronic facilities for the transmission of wire or electronic communications, and any computer facilities or related electronic equipment for the electronic storage of such communications;

(15) "electronic communication service" means any service which provides to users thereof the ability to send or receive wire or electronic communications;

(16) "readily accessible to the general public" means, with respect to a radio communication, that such communication is not—

(A) scrambled or encrypted;

(B) transmitted using modulation techniques whose essential parameters have been withheld from the public with the intention of preserving the privacy of such communication;

(C) carried on a subcarrier or other signal subsidiary to a radio transmission;

(D) transmitted over a communication system provided by a common carrier, unless the communication is a tone only paging system communication; or

(E) transmitted on frequencies allocated under part 25, subpart D, E, or F of part 74, or part 94 of the Rules of the Federal Communications Commission, unless, in the case of a communication transmitted on a frequency allocated under part 74 that is not exclusively allocated to broadcast auxiliary services, the communication is a two-way voice communication by radio;

(17) "electronic storage" means—

(A) any temporary, intermediate storage of a wire or electronic communication incidental to the electronic transmission thereof; and

(B) any storage of such communication by an electronic communication service for purposes of backup protection of such communication;

(18) "aural transfer" means a transfer containing the human voice at any point between and including the point of origin and the point of reception;

(19) "foreign intelligence information", for purposes of section 2517(6) of this title, means—

(A) information, whether or not concerning a United States person, that relates to the ability of the United States to protect against—

(i) actual or potential attack or other grave hostile acts of a foreign power or an agent of a foreign power;

(ii) sabotage or international terrorism by a foreign power or an agent of a foreign power; or

(iii) clandestine intelligence activities by an intelligence service or network of a foreign power or by an agent of a foreign power; or

(B) information, whether or not concerning a United States person, with respect to a foreign power or foreign territory that relates to—

(i) the national defense or the security of the United States; or

(ii) the conduct of the foreign affairs of the United States;

(20) "protected computer" has the meaning set forth in section 1030; and

(21) "computer trespasser"—

(A) means a person who accesses a protected computer without authorization and thus has no reasonable expectation of privacy in any communication transmitted to, through, or from the protected computer; and

(B) does not include a person known by the owner or operator of the protected computer to have an existing contractual relationship with the owner or operator of the protected computer for access to all or part of the protected computer.

18 U.S.C. § 2511. INTERCEPTION AND DISCLOSURE OF WIRE, ORAL, OR ELECTRONIC COMMUNICATIONS PROHIBITED

(1) Except as otherwise specifically provided in this chapter any person who—

(a) intentionally intercepts, endeavors to intercept, or procures any other person to intercept or endeavor to intercept, any wire, oral, or electronic communication;

(b) intentionally uses, endeavors to use, or procures any other person to use or endeavor to use any electronic, mechanical, or other device to intercept any oral communication when—

(i) such device is affixed to, or otherwise transmits a signal through, a wire, cable, or other like connection used in wire communication; or

(ii) such device transmits communications by radio, or interferes with the transmission of such communication; or

(iii) such person knows, or has reason to know, that such device or any component thereof has been sent through the mail or transported in interstate or foreign commerce; or

(iv) such use or endeavor to use (A) takes place on the premises of any business or other commercial establishment the operations of which affect interstate or foreign commerce; or (B) obtains or is for the purpose of obtaining information relating to the operations of any business or other commercial establishment the operations of which affect interstate or foreign commerce; or

(v) such person acts in the District of Columbia, the Commonwealth of Puerto Rico, or any territory or possession of the United States;

(c) intentionally discloses, or endeavors to disclose, to any other person the contents of any wire, oral, or electronic communication, knowing or having reason to know that the information was obtained through the interception of a wire, oral, or electronic communication in violation of this subsection;

(d) intentionally uses, or endeavors to use, the contents of any wire, oral, or electronic communication, knowing or having reason to know that the information was obtained through the interception of a wire, oral, or electronic communication in violation of this subsection; or

(e) (i) intentionally discloses, or endeavors to disclose, to any other person the contents of any wire, oral, or electronic communication, intercepted by means authorized by sections 2511(2)(a)(ii), 2511(2)(b)–(c), 2511(2)(e), 2516, and 2518 of this chapter, (ii) knowing or having reason to know that the information was obtained through the interception of such a communication in connection with a criminal investigation, (iii) having obtained or received the information in connection with a criminal investigation, and (iv) with intent to improperly obstruct, impede, or interfere with a duly authorized criminal investigation,

shall be punished as provided in subsection (4) or shall be subject to suit as provided in subsection (5).

(2) (a) (i) It shall not be unlawful under this chapter for an operator of a switchboard, or an officer, employee, or agent of a provider of wire or electronic communication service, whose facilities are used in the transmission of a wire or electronic communication, to intercept, disclose, or use that communication in the normal course of his employment while engaged in any activity which is a necessary incident to the rendition of his service or to the protection of the rights or property of the provider of that service, except that a provider of wire communication service to the public shall not utilize service observing or random monitoring except for mechanical or service quality control checks.

(ii) Notwithstanding any other law, providers of wire or electronic communication service, their officers, employees, and agents, landlords, custodians, or other persons, are authorized to provide information, facilities, or technical assistance to persons authorized by law to intercept wire, oral, or electronic communications or to conduct electronic surveillance, as defined in section 101 of the Foreign Intelligence Surveillance Act of 1978, if such provider, its officers, employees, or agents, landlord, custodian, or other specified person, has been provided with—

(A) a court order directing such assistance or a court order pursuant to section 704 of the Foreign Intelligence Surveillance Act of 1978 signed by the authorizing judge, or

(B) a certification in writing by a person specified in section 2518(7) of this title or the Attorney General of the United States that no warrant or court order is required by law, that all statutory requirements have been met, and that the specified assistance is required,

setting forth period of time during which the provision of the information, facilities, or technical assistance is authorized and specifying the information, facilities, or technical assistance required. No provider of wire or electronic communication service, officer, employee, or agent thereof, or landlord, custodian, or other specified person shall disclose the existence of any interception or surveillance or the device used to accomplish the interception or surveillance with respect to which the person has been furnished a court order or certification under this chapter, except as may otherwise be required by legal process and then only after prior notification to the Attorney General or to the principal prosecuting attorney of a State or any political subdivision of a State, as may be appropriate. Any such disclosure, shall render such person liable for the civil damages provided for in section 2520. No cause of action shall lie in any court against any provider of wire or electronic communication service, its officers, employees, or agents, landlord, custodian, or other specified person for providing information, facilities, or assistance in accordance with the terms of a court order, statutory authorization, or certification under this chapter.

(iii) If a certification under subparagraph (ii)(B) for assistance to obtain foreign intelligence information is based on statutory authority, the certification shall identify the specific statutory provision and shall certify that the statutory requirements have been met.

(b) It shall not be unlawful under this chapter for an officer, employee, or agent of the Federal Communications Commission, in the normal course of his employment and in discharge of the monitoring responsibilities exercised by the Commission in the enforcement of chapter 5 of title 47 of the United States Code, to intercept a wire or electronic communication, or oral communication transmitted by radio, or to disclose or use the information thereby obtained.

(c) It shall not be unlawful under this chapter for a person acting under color of law to intercept a wire, oral, or electronic communication, where such person is a party to the communication or one of the parties to the communication has given prior consent to such interception.

(d) It shall not be unlawful under this chapter for a person not acting under color of law to intercept a wire, oral, or electronic communication where such person is a party to the communication or where one of the parties to the communication has given prior consent to such interception unless such communication is intercepted for the purpose of committing any criminal or tortious act in violation of the Constitution or laws of the United States or of any State.

(e) Notwithstanding any other provision of this title or section 705 or 706 of the Communications Act of 1934, it shall not be unlawful for an officer, employee, or agent of the United States in the normal course of his official duty to conduct electronic surveillance, as defined in section 101 of the Foreign Intelligence Surveillance Act of 1978, as authorized by that Act.

(f) Nothing contained in this chapter or chapter 121 or 206 of this title, or section 705 of the Communications Act of 1934, shall be deemed to affect the acquisition by the United States Government of foreign intelligence information from international or foreign communications, or foreign intelligence activities conducted in accordance with otherwise applicable Federal law involving a foreign electronic communications system, utilizing a means other than electronic surveillance as defined in section 101 of the Foreign Intelligence Surveillance Act of 1978, and procedures in this chapter or chapter 121 and the Foreign Intelligence Surveillance Act of 1978 shall be the exclusive means by which electronic surveillance, as defined in section 101 of such Act, and the interception of domestic wire, oral, and electronic communications may be conducted.

(g) It shall not be unlawful under this chapter or chapter 121 of this title for any person—

(i) to intercept or access an electronic communication made through an electronic communication system that is configured so that such electronic communication is readily accessible to the general public;

(ii) to intercept any radio communication which is transmitted—

(I) by any station for the use of the general public, or that relates to ships, aircraft, vehicles, or persons in distress;

(II) by any governmental, law enforcement, civil defense, private land mobile, or public safety communications system, including police and fire, readily accessible to the general public;

(III) by a station operating on an authorized frequency within the bands allocated to the amateur, citizens band, or general mobile radio services; or

(IV) by any marine or aeronautical communications system;

(iii) to engage in any conduct which—

(I) is prohibited by section 633 of the Communications Act of 1934; or

(II) is excepted from the application of section 705(a) of the Communications Act of 1934 by section 705(b) of that Act;

(iv) to intercept any wire or electronic communication the transmission of which is causing harmful interference to any lawfully operating station or consumer electronic equipment, to the extent necessary to identify the source of such interference; or

(v) for other users of the same frequency to intercept any radio communication made through a system that utilizes frequencies monitored by individuals engaged in the provision or the use of such system, if such communication is not scrambled or encrypted.

(h) It shall not be unlawful under this chapter—

(i) to use a pen register or a trap and trace device (as those terms are defined for the purposes of chapter 206 (relating to pen registers and trap and trace devices) of this title); or

(ii) for a provider of electronic communication service to record the fact that a wire or electronic communication was initiated or completed in order to protect such provider, another provider furnishing service toward the completion of the wire or electronic communication, or a user of that service, from fraudulent, unlawful or abusive use of such service.

(i) It shall not be unlawful under this chapter for a person acting under color of law to intercept the wire or electronic communications of a computer trespasser transmitted to, through, or from the protected computer, if—

(I) the owner or operator of the protected computer authorizes the interception of the computer trespasser's communications on the protected computer;

(II) the person acting under color of law is lawfully engaged in an investigation;

(III) the person acting under color of law has reasonable grounds to believe that the contents of the computer trespasser's communications will be relevant to the investigation; and

(IV) such interception does not acquire communications other than those transmitted to or from the computer trespasser.

(3) (a) Except as provided in paragraph (b) of this subsection, a person or entity providing an electronic communication service to the public shall not intentionally divulge the contents of any communication (other than one to such person or entity, or an agent thereof) while in transmission on that service to any person or entity other than an addressee or intended recipient of such communication or an agent of such addressee or intended recipient.

(b) A person or entity providing electronic communication service to the public may divulge the contents of any such communication—

(i) as otherwise authorized in section 2511(2)(a) or 2517 of this title;

(ii) with the lawful consent of the originator or any addressee or intended recipient of such communication;

(iii) to a person employed or authorized, or whose facilities are used, to forward such communication to its destination; or

(iv) which were inadvertently obtained by the service provider and which appear to pertain to the commission of a crime, if such divulgence is made to a law enforcement agency.

(4) (a) Except as provided in paragraph (b) of this subsection or in subsection (5), whoever violates subsection (1) of this section shall be fined under this title or imprisoned not more than five years, or both.

(b) Conduct otherwise an offense under this subsection that consists of or relates to the interception of a satellite transmission that is not encrypted or scrambled and that is transmitted—

(i) to a broadcasting station for purposes of retransmission to the general public; or

(ii) as an audio subcarrier intended for redistribution to facilities open to the public, but not including data transmissions or telephone calls,

is not an offense under this subsection unless the conduct is for the purposes of direct or indirect commercial advantage or private financial gain.

(5) (a) (i) If the communication is—

(A) a private satellite video communication that is not scrambled or encrypted and the conduct in violation of this chapter is the private viewing of that communication and is not for a tortious or illegal purpose or for purposes of direct or indirect commercial advantage or private commercial gain; or

(B) a radio communication that is transmitted on frequencies allocated under subpart D of part 74 of the rules of the Federal Communications Commission that is not scrambled or encrypted and the conduct in violation of this chapter is not for a tortious or illegal purpose or for purposes of direct or indirect commercial advantage or private commercial gain,

then the person who engages in such conduct shall be subject to suit by the Federal Government in a court of competent jurisdiction.

(ii) In an action under this subsection—

(A) if the violation of this chapter is a first offense for the person under paragraph (a) of subsection (4) and such person has not been found liable in a civil action under section 2520 of this title, the Federal Government shall be entitled to appropriate injunctive relief; and

(B) if the violation of this chapter is a second or subsequent offense under paragraph (a) of subsection (4) or such person has been found liable in any prior civil action under section 2520, the person shall be subject to a mandatory $500 civil fine.

(b) The court may use any means within its authority to enforce an injunction issued under paragraph (ii)(A), and shall impose a civil fine of not less than $500 for each violation of such an injunction.

18 U.S.C. § 2512. MANUFACTURE, DISTRIBUTION, POSSESSION, AND ADVERTISING OF WIRE, ORAL, OR ELECTRONIC COMMUNICATION INTERCEPTING DEVICES PROHIBITED

(1) Except as otherwise specifically provided in this chapter, any person who intentionally—

(a) sends through the mail, or sends or carries in interstate or foreign commerce, any electronic, mechanical, or other device, knowing or having reason to know that the design of such device renders it primarily useful for the purpose of the surreptitious interception of wire, oral, or electronic communications;

(b) manufactures, assembles, possesses, or sells any electronic, mechanical, or other device, knowing or having reason to know that the design of such device renders it primarily useful for the purpose of the surreptitious interception of wire, oral, or electronic communications, and that such device or any component thereof has been or will be sent through the mail or transported in interstate or foreign commerce; or

(c) places in any newspaper, magazine, handbill, or other publication or disseminates by electronic means any advertisement of—

(i) any electronic, mechanical, or other device knowing the content of the advertisement and knowing or having reason to know that the design of such device renders it primarily useful for the purpose of the surreptitious interception of wire, oral, or electronic communications; or

(ii) any other electronic, mechanical, or other device, where such advertisement promotes the use of such device for the purpose of the surreptitious interception of wire, oral, or electronic communications,

knowing the content of the advertisement and knowing or having reason to know that such advertisement will be sent through the mail or transported in interstate or foreign commerce, shall be fined under this title or imprisoned not more than five years, or both.

(2) It shall not be unlawful under this section for—

(a) a provider of wire or electronic communication service or an officer, agent, or employee of, or a person under contract with, such a provider, in the normal course of the business of providing that wire or electronic communication service, or

(b) an officer, agent, or employee of, or a person under contract with, the United States, a State, or a political subdivision thereof, in the normal course of the activities of the United States, a State, or a political subdivision thereof,

to send through the mail, send or carry in interstate or foreign commerce, or manufacture, assemble, possess, or sell any electronic, mechanical, or other device knowing or having reason to know that the design of such device renders it primarily useful for the purpose of the surreptitious interception of wire, oral, or electronic communications.

(3) It shall not be unlawful under this section to advertise for sale a device described in subsection (1) of this section if the advertisement is mailed, sent, or carried in interstate or foreign commerce solely to a domestic provider of wire or electronic communication service or to an agency of the United States, a State, or a political subdivision thereof which is duly authorized to use such device.

18 U.S.C. § 2513. CONFISCATION OF WIRE, ORAL, OR ELECTRONIC COMMUNICATION INTERCEPTING DEVICES

Any electronic, mechanical, or other device used, sent, carried, manufactured, assembled, possessed, sold, or advertised in violation of section 2511 or section 2512 of this chapter may be seized and forfeited to the United States. All provisions of law relating to (1) the seizure, summary and judicial forfeiture, and condemnation of vessels, vehicles, merchandise, and baggage for violations of the customs laws contained in title 19 of the United States Code, (2) the disposition of such vessels, vehicles, merchandise, and baggage or the proceeds from the sale thereof, (3) the remission or mitigation of such forfeiture, (4) the compromise of claims, and (5) the award of compensation to informers in respect of such forfeitures, shall apply to seizures and forfeitures incurred, or alleged to have been incurred, under the provisions of this section, insofar as applicable and not inconsistent with the provisions of this section; except that such duties as are imposed upon the collector of customs or any other person with respect to the seizure and forfeiture of vessels, vehicles, merchandise, and baggage under the provisions of the customs laws contained in title 19 of the United States Code shall be performed with respect to seizure and forfeiture of electronic, mechanical, or other intercepting devices under this section by such officers, agents, or other persons as may be authorized or designated for that purpose by the Attorney General.

18 U.S.C. § 2515. PROHIBITION OF USE AS EVIDENCE OF INTERCEPTED WIRE OR ORAL COMMUNICATIONS

Whenever any wire or oral communication has been intercepted, no part of the contents of such communication and no evidence derived therefrom may be received in evidence in any trial, hearing, or other proceeding in or before any court, grand jury, department, officer, agency, regulatory body, legislative committee, or other authority of the United States, a State, or a political subdivision thereof if the disclosure of that information would be in violation of this chapter.

18 U.S.C. § 2516. AUTHORIZATION FOR INTERCEPTION OF WIRE, ORAL, OR ELECTRONIC COMMUNICATIONS

(1) The Attorney General, Deputy Attorney General, Associate Attorney General, or any Assistant Attorney General, any acting Assistant Attorney General, or any Deputy Assistant Attorney General or acting Deputy Assistant Attorney General in the Criminal Division or National Security Division specially designated by the Attorney General, may authorize an application to a Federal judge of competent jurisdiction for, and such judge may grant in conformity with section 2518 of this chapter an order authorizing or approving the interception of wire or oral communications by the Federal Bureau of Investigation, or a Federal agency having responsibility for the investigation of the offense as to which the application is made, when such interception may provide or has provided evidence of—

(a) any offense punishable by death or by imprisonment for more than one year under sections 2122 and 2274 through 2277 of title 42 of the United States Code (relating to the enforcement of the Atomic Energy Act of 1954), section 2284 of title 42 of the United States Code (relating to sabotage of nuclear facilities or fuel), or under the following chapters of this title: chapter 10 (relating to biological weapons), chapter 37 (relating to espionage), chapter 55 (relating to kidnapping), chapter 90 (relating to protection of trade secrets), chapter 105 (relating to sabotage), chapter 115 (relating to treason), chapter 102 (relating to riots), chapter 65 (relating to malicious mischief), chapter 111 (relating to destruction of vessels), or chapter 81 (relating to piracy);

(b) a violation of section 186 or section 501(c) of title 29, United States Code (dealing with restrictions on payments and loans to labor organizations), or any offense which involves murder, kidnapping, robbery, or extortion, and which is punishable under this title;

(c) any offense which is punishable under the following sections of this title: section 37 (relating to violence at international airports), section 43 (relating to animal enterprise terrorism), section 81 (arson within special maritime and territorial jurisdiction), section 201 (bribery of public officials and witnesses), section 215 (relating to bribery of bank officials), section 224 (bribery in sporting contests), subsection (d), (e), (f), (g), (h), or (i) of section 844 (unlawful use of explosives), section 1032 (relating to concealment of assets), section 1084 (transmission of wagering information), section 751 (relating to escape), section 832 (relating to nuclear and weapons of mass destruction threats), section 842 (relating to explosive materials), section 930 (relating to possession of weapons in Federal facilities), section 1014 (relating to loans and credit applications generally; renewals and discounts), section 1114 (relating to officers and employees of the United States), section 1116 (relating to protection of foreign officials), sections 1503, 1512, and 1513 (influencing or injuring an officer, juror, or witness generally), section 1510 (obstruction of criminal investigations), section 1511 (obstruction of State or local law enforcement), section 1591 (sex trafficking of children by force, fraud, or coercion), section 1751 (Presidential and Presidential staff assassination, kidnapping, and assault), section 1951 (interference with commerce by threats or violence), section 1952 (interstate and foreign travel or transportation in aid of racketeering enterprises), section 1958 (relating to use of interstate commerce facilities in the commission of murder for hire), section 1959 (relating to violent crimes in aid of racketeering activity), section 1954 (offer, acceptance, or solicitation to influence operations of employee benefit plan), section 1955 (prohibition of business enterprises of gambling), section 1956 (laundering of monetary instruments), section 1957 (relating to engaging in monetary transactions in property derived from specified unlawful activity), section 659 (theft from interstate shipment), section 664 (embezzlement from pension and welfare funds), section 1343 (fraud by wire, radio, or television), section 1344 (relating to bank fraud), section 1992 (relating to terrorist attacks against mass transportation), sections 2251 and 2252 (sexual exploitation of children), section 2251A (selling or buying of children), section 2252A (relating to material constituting or containing child pornography), section 1466A (relating to child obscenity), section 2260 (production of sexually explicit depictions of a minor for importation into the United States), sections 2421, 2422, 2423, and 2425 (relating to transportation for illegal sexual activity and related crimes), sections 2312, 2313, 2314, and 2315 (interstate transportation of stolen property), section 2321 (relating to trafficking in certain motor vehicles or motor vehicle parts), section 2340A (relating to torture), section 1203 (relating to hostage taking), section 1029 (relating to fraud and related activity in connection with access devices), section 3146 (relating to penalty for failure to appear), section 3521(b)(3) (relating to witness relocation and assistance), section 32 (relating to destruction of aircraft or aircraft facilities), section 38 (relating to aircraft parts fraud), section 1963 (violations with respect to racketeer influenced and corrupt organizations), section 115 (relating to threatening or retaliating against a Federal official), section 1341 (relating to mail fraud), a felony violation of section 1030 (relating to computer fraud and abuse), section 351 (violations with respect to congressional, Cabinet, or Supreme Court assassinations, kidnapping, and assault), section 831 (relating to prohibited transactions involving nuclear materials), section 33 (relating to destruction of motor vehicles or motor vehicle facilities), section 175 (relating to biological weapons), section 175c (relating to variola virus), section 956 (conspiracy to harm persons or property overseas), a felony violation of section 1028 (relating to production of false identification documentation), section 1425 (relating to the procurement of citizenship or nationalization unlawfully), section 1426 (relating to the reproduction of naturalization or citizenship papers), section 1427 (relating to the sale of naturalization or citizenship papers), section 1541 (relating to passport issuance without authority), section 1542 (relating to false statements in passport applications), section 1543 (relating to forgery or false use of passports), section 1544 (relating to misuse of passports), or section 1546 (relating to fraud and misuse of visas, permits, and other documents);

(d) any offense involving counterfeiting punishable under section 471, 472, or 473 of this title;

(e) any offense involving fraud connected with a case under title 11 or the manufacture, importation, receiving, concealment, buying, selling, or otherwise dealing in narcotic drugs, marihuana, or other dangerous drugs, punishable under any law of the United States;

(f) any offense including extortionate credit transactions under sections 892, 893, or 894 of this title;

(g) a violation of section 5322 of title 31, United States Code (dealing with the reporting of currency transactions), or section 5324 of title 31, United States Code (relating to structuring transactions to evade reporting requirement prohibited);

(h) any felony violation of sections 2511 and 2512 (relating to interception and disclosure of certain communications and to certain intercepting devices) of this title;

(i) any felony violation of chapter 71 (relating to obscenity) of this title;

(j) any violation of section 60123(b) (relating to destruction of a natural gas pipeline), section 46502 (relating to aircraft piracy), the second sentence of section 46504 (relating to assault on a flight crew with dangerous weapon), or section 46505(b)(3) or (c) (relating to explosive or incendiary devices, or endangerment of human life, by means of weapons on aircraft) of title 49;

(k) any criminal violation of section 2778 of title 22 (relating to the Arms Export Control Act);

(*l*) the location of any fugitive from justice from an offense described in this section;

(m) a violation of section 274, 277, or 278 of the Immigration and Nationality Act (8 U.S.C. 1324, 1327, or 1328) (relating to the smuggling of aliens);

(n) any felony violation of sections 922 and 924 of title 18, United States Code (relating to firearms);

(o) any violation of section 5861 of the Internal Revenue Code of 1986 (relating to firearms);

(p) a felony violation of section 1028 (relating to production of false identification documents), section 1542 (relating to false statements in passport applications), section 1546 (relating to fraud and misuse of visas, permits, and other documents), section 1028A (relating to aggravated identity theft) of this title or a violation of section 274, 277, or 278 of the Immigration and Nationality Act (relating to the smuggling of aliens); or

(q) any criminal violation of section 229 (relating to chemical weapons) or sections 2332, 2332a, 2332b, 2332d, 2332f, 2332g, 2332h, 2339, 2339A, 2339B, 2339C, or 2339D of this title (relating to terrorism);

(r) any criminal violation of section 1 (relating to illegal restraints of trade or commerce), 2 (relating to illegal monopolizing of trade or commerce), or 3 (relating to illegal restraints of trade or commerce in territories or the District of Columbia) of the Sherman Act (15 U.S.C. 1, 2, 3); or

(s) any conspiracy to commit any offense described in any subparagraph of this paragraph.

(2) The principal prosecuting attorney of any State, or the principal prosecuting attorney of any political subdivision thereof, if such attorney is authorized by a statute of that State to make application to a State court judge of competent jurisdiction for an order authorizing or approving the interception of wire, oral, or electronic communications, may apply to such judge for, and such judge may grant in conformity with section 2518 of this chapter and with the applicable State statute an order authorizing, or approving the interception of wire, oral, or electronic communications by investigative or law enforcement officers having responsibility for the investigation of the offense as to which the application is made, when such interception may provide or has provided evidence of the commission of the offense of murder, kidnapping, gambling, robbery, bribery, extortion, or dealing in narcotic drugs, marihuana or other dangerous drugs, or other crime dangerous to life, limb, or property, and punishable by imprisonment for more than one year, designated in any applicable State statute authorizing such interception, or any conspiracy to commit any of the foregoing offenses.

(3) Any attorney for the Government (as such term is defined for the purposes of the Federal Rules of Criminal Procedure) may authorize an application to a Federal judge of competent jurisdiction for, and such judge

may grant, in conformity with section 2518 of this title, an order authorizing or approving the interception of electronic communications by an investigative or law enforcement officer having responsibility for the investigation of the offense as to which the application is made, when such interception may provide or has provided evidence of any Federal felony.

18 U.S.C. § 2517. Authorization for Disclosure and Use of Intercepted Wire, Oral, or Electronic Communications

(1) Any investigative or law enforcement officer who, by any means authorized by this chapter, has obtained knowledge of the contents of any wire, oral, or electronic communication, or evidence derived therefrom, may disclose such contents to another investigative or law enforcement officer to the extent that such disclosure is appropriate to the proper performance of the official duties of the officer making or receiving the disclosure.

(2) Any investigative or law enforcement officer who, by any means authorized by this chapter, has obtained knowledge of the contents of any wire, oral, or electronic communication or evidence derived therefrom may use such contents to the extent such use is appropriate to the proper performance of his official duties.

(3) Any person who has received, by any means authorized by this chapter, any information concerning a wire, oral, or electronic communication, or evidence derived therefrom intercepted in accordance with the provisions of this chapter may disclose the contents of that communication or such derivative evidence while giving testimony under oath or affirmation in any proceeding held under the authority of the United States or of any State or political subdivision thereof.

(4) No otherwise privileged wire, oral, or electronic communication intercepted in accordance with, or in violation of, the provisions of this chapter shall lose its privileged character.

(5) When an investigative or law enforcement officer, while engaged in intercepting wire, oral, or electronic communications in the manner authorized herein, intercepts wire, oral, or electronic communications relating to offenses other than those specified in the order of authorization or approval, the contents thereof, and evidence derived therefrom, may be disclosed or used as provided in subsections (1) and (2) of this section. Such contents and any evidence derived therefrom may be used under subsection (3) of this section when authorized or approved by a judge of competent jurisdiction where such judge finds on subsequent application that the contents were otherwise intercepted in accordance with the provisions of this chapter. Such application shall be made as soon as practicable.

(6) Any investigative or law enforcement officer, or attorney for the Government, who by any means authorized by this chapter, has obtained knowledge of the contents of any wire, oral, or electronic communication, or evidence derived therefrom, may disclose such contents to any other

Federal law enforcement, intelligence, protective, immigration, national defense, or national security official to the extent that such contents include foreign intelligence or counterintelligence (as defined in section 3 of the National Security Act of 1947 (50 U.S.C. 401a)), or foreign intelligence information (as defined in subsection (19) of section 2510 of this title), to assist the official who is to receive that information in the performance of his official duties. Any Federal official who receives information pursuant to this provision may use that information only as necessary in the conduct of that person's official duties subject to any limitations on the unauthorized disclosure of such information.

(7) Any investigative or law enforcement officer, or other Federal official in carrying out official duties as such Federal official, who by any means authorized by this chapter, has obtained knowledge of the contents of any wire, oral, or electronic communication, or evidence derived therefrom, may disclose such contents or derivative evidence to a foreign investigative or law enforcement officer to the extent that such disclosure is appropriate to the proper performance of the official duties of the officer making or receiving the disclosure, and foreign investigative or law enforcement officers may use or disclose such contents or derivative evidence to the extent such use or disclosure is appropriate to the proper performance of their official duties.

(8) Any investigative or law enforcement officer, or other Federal official in carrying out official duties as such Federal official, who by any means authorized by this chapter, has obtained knowledge of the contents of any wire, oral, or electronic communication, or evidence derived therefrom, may disclose such contents or derivative evidence to any appropriate Federal, State, local, or foreign government official to the extent that such contents or derivative evidence reveals a threat of actual or potential attack or other grave hostile acts of a foreign power or an agent of a foreign power, domestic or international sabotage, domestic or international terrorism, or clandestine intelligence gathering activities by an intelligence service or network of a foreign power or by an agent of a foreign power, within the United States or elsewhere, for the purpose of preventing or responding to such a threat. Any official who receives information pursuant to this provision may use that information only as necessary in the conduct of that person's official duties subject to any limitations on the unauthorized disclosure of such information, and any State, local, or foreign official who receives information pursuant to this provision may use that information only consistent with such guidelines as the Attorney General and Director of Central Intelligence shall jointly issue.

18 U.S.C. § 2518. PROCEDURE FOR INTERCEPTION OF WIRE, ORAL, OR ELECTRONIC COMMUNICATIONS

(1) Each application for an order authorizing or approving the interception of a wire, oral, or electronic communication under this chapter shall be made in writing upon oath or affirmation to a judge of competent

jurisdiction and shall state the applicant's authority to make such application. Each application shall include the following information:

(a) the identity of the investigative or law enforcement officer making the application, and the officer authorizing the application;

(b) a full and complete statement of the facts and circumstances relied upon by the applicant, to justify his belief that an order should be issued, including (i) details as to the particular offense that has been, is being, or is about to be committed, (ii) except as provided in subsection (11), a particular description of the nature and location of the facilities from which or the place where the communication is to be intercepted, (iii) a particular description of the type of communications sought to be intercepted, (iv) the identity of the person, if known, committing the offense and whose communications are to be intercepted;

(c) a full and complete statement as to whether or not other investigative procedures have been tried and failed or why they reasonably appear to be unlikely to succeed if tried or to be too dangerous;

(d) a statement of the period of time for which the interception is required to be maintained. If the nature of the investigation is such that the authorization for interception should not automatically terminate when the described type of communication has been first obtained, a particular description of facts establishing probable cause to believe that additional communications of the same type will occur thereafter;

(e) a full and complete statement of the facts concerning all previous applications known to the individual authorizing and making the application, made to any judge for authorization to intercept, or for approval of interceptions of, wire, oral, or electronic communications involving any of the same persons, facilities or places specified in the application, and the action taken by the judge on each such application; and

(f) where the application is for the extension of an order, a statement setting forth the results thus far obtained from the interception, or a reasonable explanation of the failure to obtain such results.

(2) The judge may require the applicant to furnish additional testimony or documentary evidence in support of the application.

(3) Upon such application the judge may enter an ex parte order, as requested or as modified, authorizing or approving interception of wire, oral, or electronic communications within the territorial jurisdiction of the court in which the judge is sitting (and outside that jurisdiction but within the United States in the case of a mobile interception device authorized by a Federal court within such jurisdiction), if the judge determines on the basis of the facts submitted by the applicant that—

(a) there is probable cause for belief that an individual is committing, has committed, or is about to commit a particular offense enumerated in section 2516 of this chapter;

(b) there is probable cause for belief that particular communications concerning that offense will be obtained through such interception;

(c) normal investigative procedures have been tried and have failed or reasonably appear to be unlikely to succeed if tried or to be too dangerous;

(d) except as provided in subsection (11), there is probable cause for belief that the facilities from which, or the place where, the wire, oral, or electronic communications are to be intercepted are being used, or are about to be used, in connection with the commission of such offense, or are leased to, listed in the name of, or commonly used by such person.

(4) Each order authorizing or approving the interception of any wire, oral, or electronic communication under this chapter shall specify—

(a) the identity of the person, if known, whose communications are to be intercepted;

(b) the nature and location of the communications facilities as to which, or the place where, authority to intercept is granted;

(c) a particular description of the type of communication sought to be intercepted, and a statement of the particular offense to which it relates;

(d) the identity of the agency authorized to intercept the communications, and of the person authorizing the application; and

(e) the period of time during which such interception is authorized, including a statement as to whether or not the interception shall automatically terminate when the described communication has been first obtained.

An order authorizing the interception of a wire, oral, or electronic communication under this chapter shall, upon request of the applicant, direct that a provider of wire or electronic communication service, landlord, custodian or other person shall furnish the applicant forthwith all information, facilities, and technical assistance necessary to accomplish the interception unobtrusively and with a minimum of interference with the services that such service provider, landlord, custodian, or person is according the person whose communications are to be intercepted. Any provider of wire or electronic communication service, landlord, custodian or other person furnishing such facilities or technical assistance shall be compensated therefor by the applicant for reasonable expenses incurred in providing such facilities or assistance. Pursuant to section 2522 of this chapter, an order may also be issued to enforce the assistance capability and capacity requirements under the Communications Assistance for Law Enforcement Act.

(5) No order entered under this section may authorize or approve the interception of any wire, oral, or electronic communication for any period longer than is necessary to achieve the objective of the authorization, nor in any event longer than thirty days. Such thirty-day period begins on the earlier of the day on which the investigative or law enforcement officer first begins to conduct an interception under the order or ten days after the order is entered. Extensions of an order may be granted, but only upon application for an extension made in accordance with subsection (1) of this section and the court making the findings required by subsection (3) of this section. The period of extension shall be no longer than the authorizing judge deems necessary to achieve the purposes for which it was granted and in no event for longer than thirty days. Every order and extension thereof shall contain a provision that the authorization to intercept shall be executed as soon as practicable, shall be conducted in such a way as to minimize the interception of communications not otherwise subject to interception under this chapter, and must terminate upon attainment of the authorized objective, or in any event in thirty days. In the event the intercepted communication is in a code or foreign language, and an expert in that foreign language or code is not reasonably available during the interception period, minimization may be accomplished as soon as practicable after such interception. An interception under this chapter may be conducted in whole or in part by Government personnel, or by an individual operating under a contract with the Government, acting under the supervision of an investigative or law enforcement officer authorized to conduct the interception.

(6) Whenever an order authorizing interception is entered pursuant to this chapter, the order may require reports to be made to the judge who issued the order showing what progress has been made toward achievement of the authorized objective and the need for continued interception. Such reports shall be made at such intervals as the judge may require.

(7) Notwithstanding any other provision of this chapter, any investigative or law enforcement officer, specially designated by the Attorney General, the Deputy Attorney General, the Associate Attorney General, or by the principal prosecuting attorney of any State or subdivision thereof acting pursuant to a statute of that State, who reasonably determines that—

    (a) an emergency situation exists that involves—

        (i) immediate danger of death or serious physical injury to any person,

        (ii) conspiratorial activities threatening the national security interest, or

        (iii) conspiratorial activities characteristic of organized crime, that requires a wire, oral, or electronic communication to be intercepted before an order authorizing such interception can, with due diligence, be obtained, and

(b) there are grounds upon which an order could be entered under this chapter to authorize such interception,

may intercept such wire, oral, or electronic communication if an application for an order approving the interception is made in accordance with this section within forty-eight hours after the interception has occurred, or begins to occur. In the absence of an order, such interception shall immediately terminate when the communication sought is obtained or when the application for the order is denied, whichever is earlier. In the event such application for approval is denied, or in any other case where the interception is terminated without an order having been issued, the contents of any wire, oral, or electronic communication intercepted shall be treated as having been obtained in violation of this chapter, and an inventory shall be served as provided for in subsection (d) of this section on the person named in the application.

(8) (a) The contents of any wire, oral, or electronic communication intercepted by any means authorized by this chapter shall, if possible, be recorded on tape or wire or other comparable device. The recording of the contents of any wire, oral, or electronic communication under this subsection shall be done in such a way as will protect the recording from editing or other alterations. Immediately upon the expiration of the period of the order, or extensions thereof, such recordings shall be made available to the judge issuing such order and sealed under his directions. Custody of the recordings shall be wherever the judge orders. They shall not be destroyed except upon an order of the issuing or denying judge and in any event shall be kept for ten years. Duplicate recordings may be made for use or disclosure pursuant to the provisions of subsections (1) and (2) of section 2517 of this chapter for investigations. The presence of the seal provided for by this subsection, or a satisfactory explanation for the absence thereof, shall be a prerequisite for the use or disclosure of the contents of any wire, oral, or electronic communication or evidence derived therefrom under subsection (3) of section 2517.

(b) Applications made and orders granted under this chapter shall be sealed by the judge. Custody of the applications and orders shall be wherever the judge directs. Such applications and orders shall be disclosed only upon a showing of good cause before a judge of competent jurisdiction and shall not be destroyed except on order of the issuing or denying judge, and in any event shall be kept for ten years.

(c) Any violation of the provisions of this subsection may be punished as contempt of the issuing or denying judge.

(d) Within a reasonable time but not later than ninety days after the filing of an application for an order of approval under section 2518(7)(b) which is denied or the termination of the period of an order or extensions thereof, the issuing or denying judge shall cause to be served, on the persons named in the order or the application, and such other parties to intercepted communications as the judge may determine in his discretion that is in the interest of justice, an inventory which shall include notice of—

(1) the fact of the entry of the order or the application;

(2) the date of the entry and the period of authorized, approved or disapproved interception, or the denial of the application; and

(3) the fact that during the period wire, oral, or electronic communications were or were not intercepted.

The judge, upon the filing of a motion, may in his discretion make available to such person or his counsel for inspection such portions of the intercepted communications, applications and orders as the judge determines to be in the interest of justice. On an ex parte showing of good cause to a judge of competent jurisdiction the serving of the inventory required by this subsection may be postponed.

(9) The contents of any wire, oral, or electronic communication intercepted pursuant to this chapter or evidence derived therefrom shall not be received in evidence or otherwise disclosed in any trial, hearing, or other proceeding in a Federal or State court unless each party, not less than ten days before the trial, hearing, or proceeding, has been furnished with a copy of the court order, and accompanying application, under which the interception was authorized or approved. This ten-day period may be waived by the judge if he finds that it was not possible to furnish the party with the above information ten days before the trial, hearing, or proceeding and that the party will not be prejudiced by the delay in receiving such information.

(10) (a) Any aggrieved person in any trial, hearing, or proceeding in or before any court, department, officer, agency, regulatory body, or other authority of the United States, a State, or a political subdivision thereof, may move to suppress the contents of any wire or oral communication intercepted pursuant to this chapter, or evidence derived therefrom, on the grounds that—

(i) the communication was unlawfully intercepted;

(ii) the order of authorization or approval under which it was intercepted is insufficient on its face; or

(iii) the interception was not made in conformity with the order of authorization or approval.

Such motion shall be made before the trial, hearing, or proceeding unless there was no opportunity to make such motion or the person was not aware of the grounds of the motion. If the motion is granted, the contents of the intercepted wire or oral communication, or evidence derived therefrom, shall be treated as having been obtained in violation of this chapter. The judge, upon the filing of such motion by the aggrieved person, may in his discretion make available to the aggrieved person or his counsel for inspection such portions of the intercepted communication or evidence derived therefrom as the judge determines to be in the interests of justice.

(b) In addition to any other right to appeal, the United States shall have the right to appeal from an order granting a motion to suppress made under paragraph (a) of this subsection, or the denial of an application for an order of approval, if the United States attorney shall certify to the judge or other official granting such motion or denying such application that the appeal is not taken for purposes of delay. Such appeal shall be taken within thirty days after the date the order was entered and shall be diligently prosecuted.

(c) The remedies and sanctions described in this chapter with respect to the interception of electronic communications are the only judicial remedies and sanctions for nonconstitutional violations of this chapter involving such communications.

(11) The requirements of subsections (1)(b)(ii) and (3)(d) of this section relating to the specification of the facilities from which, or the place where, the communication is to be intercepted do not apply if—

(a) in the case of an application with respect to the interception of an oral communication—

(i) the application is by a Federal investigative or law enforcement officer and is approved by the Attorney General, the Deputy Attorney General, the Associate Attorney General, an Assistant Attorney General, or an acting Assistant Attorney General;

(ii) the application contains a full and complete statement as to why such specification is not practical and identifies the person committing the offense and whose communications are to be intercepted; and

(iii) the judge finds that such specification is not practical; and

(b) in the case of an application with respect to a wire or electronic communication—

(i) the application is by a Federal investigative or law enforcement officer and is approved by the Attorney General, the Deputy Attorney General, the Associate Attorney General, an Assistant Attorney General, or an acting Assistant Attorney General;

(ii) the application identifies the person believed to be committing the offense and whose communications are to be intercepted and the applicant makes a showing that there is probable cause to believe that the person's actions could have the effect of thwarting interception from a specified facility;

(iii) the judge finds that such showing has been adequately made; and

(iv) the order authorizing or approving the interception is limited to interception only for such time as it is reasonable to presume that the person identified in the application is or was reasonably proximate to the instrument through which such communication will be or was transmitted.

(12) An interception of a communication under an order with respect to which the requirements of subsections (1)(b)(ii) and (3)(d) of this section do not apply by reason of subsection (11)(a) shall not begin until the place where the communication is to be intercepted is ascertained by the person implementing the interception order. A provider of wire or electronic communications service that has received an order as provided for in subsection (11)(b) may move the court to modify or quash the order on the ground that its assistance with respect to the interception cannot be performed in a timely or reasonable fashion. The court, upon notice to the government, shall decide such a motion expeditiously.

18 U.S.C. § 2519. REPORTS CONCERNING INTERCEPTED WIRE, ORAL, OR ELECTRONIC COMMUNICATIONS

(1) Within thirty days after the expiration of an order (or each extension thereof) entered under section 2518, or the denial of an order approving an interception, the issuing or denying judge shall report to the Administrative Office of the United States Courts—

(a) the fact that an order or extension was applied for;

(b) the kind of order or extension applied for (including whether or not the order was an order with respect to which the requirements of sections 2518(1)(b)(ii) and 2518(3)(d) of this title did not apply by reason of section 2518(11) of this title);

(c) the fact that the order or extension was granted as applied for, was modified, or was denied;

(d) the period of interceptions authorized by the order, and the number and duration of any extensions of the order;

(e) the offense specified in the order or application, or extension of an order;

(f) the identity of the applying investigative or law enforcement officer and agency making the application and the person authorizing the application; and

(g) the nature of the facilities from which or the place where communications were to be intercepted.

(2) In January of each year the Attorney General, an Assistant Attorney General specially designated by the Attorney General, or the

principal prosecuting attorney of a State, or the principal prosecuting attorney for any political subdivision of a State, shall report to the Administrative Office of the United States Courts—

(a) the information required by paragraphs (a) through (g) of subsection (1) of this section with respect to each application for an order or extension made during the preceding calendar year;

(b) a general description of the interceptions made under such order or extension, including (i) the approximate nature and frequency of incriminating communications intercepted, (ii) the approximate nature and frequency of other communications intercepted, (iii) the approximate number of persons whose communications were intercepted, (iv) the number of orders in which encryption was encountered and whether such encryption prevented law enforcement from obtaining the plain text of communications intercepted pursuant to such order, and (v) the approximate nature, amount, and cost of the manpower and other resources used in the interceptions;

(c) the number of arrests resulting from interceptions made under such order or extension, and the offenses for which arrests were made;

(d) the number of trials resulting from such interceptions;

(e) the number of motions to suppress made with respect to such interceptions, and the number granted or denied;

(f) the number of convictions resulting from such interceptions and the offenses for which the convictions were obtained and a general assessment of the importance of the interceptions; and

(g) the information required by paragraphs (b) through (f) of this subsection with respect to orders or extensions obtained in a preceding calendar year.

(3) In April of each year the Director of the Administrative Office of the United States Courts shall transmit to the Congress a full and complete report concerning the number of applications for orders authorizing or approving the interception of wire, oral, or electronic communications pursuant to this chapter and the number of orders and extensions granted or denied pursuant to this chapter during the preceding calendar year. Such report shall include a summary and analysis of the data required to be filed with the Administrative Office by subsections (1) and (2) of this section. The Director of the Administrative Office of the United States Courts is authorized to issue binding regulations dealing with the content and form of the reports required to be filed by subsections (1) and (2) of this section.

18 U.S.C. § 2520.   RECOVERY OF CIVIL DAMAGES AUTHORIZED

(a) **In general.** Except as provided in section 2511(2)(a)(ii), any person whose wire, oral, or electronic communication is intercepted, disclosed, or intentionally used in violation of this chapter may in a civil action recover from the person or entity, other than the United States, which engaged in that violation such relief as may be appropriate.

(b) **Relief.** In an action under this section, appropriate relief includes—

(1) such preliminary and other equitable or declaratory relief as may be appropriate;

(2) damages under subsection (c) and punitive damages in appropriate cases; and

(3) a reasonable attorney's fee and other litigation costs reasonably incurred.

(c) **Computation of damages.**

(1) In an action under this section, if the conduct in violation of this chapter is the private viewing of a private satellite video communication that is not scrambled or encrypted or if the communication is a radio communication that is transmitted on frequencies allocated under subpart D of part 74 of the rules of the Federal Communications Commission that is not scrambled or encrypted and the conduct is not for a tortious or illegal purpose or for purposes of direct or indirect commercial advantage or private commercial gain, then the court shall assess damages as follows:

(A) If the person who engaged in that conduct has not previously been enjoined under section 2511(5) and has not been found liable in a prior civil action under this section, the court shall assess the greater of the sum of actual damages suffered by the plaintiff, or statutory damages of not less than $50 and not more than $500.

(B) If, on one prior occasion, the person who engaged in that conduct has been enjoined under section 2511(5) or has been found liable in a civil action under this section, the court shall assess the greater of the sum of actual damages suffered by the plaintiff, or statutory damages of not less than $100 and not more than $1000.

(2) In any other action under this section, the court may assess as damages whichever is the greater of—

(A) the sum of the actual damages suffered by the plaintiff and any profits made by the violator as a result of the violation; or

(B) statutory damages of whichever is the greater of $100 a day for each day of violation or $10,000.

(d) **Defense.** A good faith reliance on—

(1) a court warrant or order, a grand jury subpoena, a legislative authorization, or a statutory authorization;

(2) a request of an investigative or law enforcement officer under section 2518(7) of this title; or

(3) a good faith determination that section 2511(3) or 2511(2)(i) of this title permitted the conduct complained of;

is a complete defense against any civil or criminal action brought under this chapter or any other law.

(e) **Limitation.** A civil action under this section may not be commenced later than two years after the date upon which the claimant first has a reasonable opportunity to discover the violation.

(f) **Administrative discipline.** If a court or appropriate department or agency determines that the United States or any of its departments or agencies has violated any provision of this chapter, and the court or appropriate department or agency finds that the circumstances surrounding the violation raise serious questions about whether or not an officer or employee of the United States acted willfully or intentionally with respect to the violation, the department or agency shall, upon receipt of a true and correct copy of the decision and findings of the court or appropriate department or agency promptly initiate a proceeding to determine whether disciplinary action against the officer or employee is warranted. If the head of the department or agency involved determines that disciplinary action is not warranted, he or she shall notify the Inspector General with jurisdiction over the department or agency concerned and shall provide the Inspector General with the reasons for such determination.

(g) **Improper disclosure is violation.** Any willful disclosure or use by an investigative or law enforcement officer or governmental entity of information beyond the extent permitted by section 2517 is a violation of this chapter for purposes of section 2520(a).

18 U.S.C. § 2521. INJUNCTION AGAINST ILLEGAL INTERCEPTION

Whenever it shall appear that any person is engaged or is about to engage in any act which constitutes or will constitute a felony violation of this chapter, the Attorney General may initiate a civil action in a district court of the United States to enjoin such violation. The court shall proceed as soon as practicable to the hearing and determination of such an action, and may, at any time before final determination, enter such a restraining order or prohibition, or take such other action, as is warranted to prevent a continuing and substantial injury to the United States or to any person or class of persons for whose protection the action is brought. A proceeding under this section is governed by the Federal Rules of Civil Procedure, except that, if an indictment has been returned against the respondent, discovery is governed by the Federal Rules of Criminal Procedure.

18 U.S.C. § 2522. ENFORCEMENT OF THE COMMUNICATIONS ASSISTANCE FOR LAW ENFORCEMENT ACT

(a) **Enforcement by court issuing surveillance order.** If a court authorizing an interception under this chapter, a State statute, or the

Foreign Intelligence Surveillance Act of 1978 (50 U.S.C. 1801 et seq.) or authorizing use of a pen register or a trap and trace device under chapter 206 or a State statute finds that a telecommunications carrier has failed to comply with the requirements of the Communications Assistance for Law Enforcement Act, the court may, in accordance with section 108 of such Act, direct that the carrier comply forthwith and may direct that a provider of support services to the carrier or the manufacturer of the carrier's transmission or switching equipment furnish forthwith modifications necessary for the carrier to comply.

(b) **Enforcement upon application by Attorney General.** The Attorney General may, in a civil action in the appropriate United States district court, obtain an order, in accordance with section 108 of the Communications Assistance for Law Enforcement Act, directing that a telecommunications carrier, a manufacturer of telecommunications transmission or switching equipment, or a provider of telecommunications support services comply with such Act.

(c) **Civil penalty.—**

(1) *In general.* A court issuing an order under this section against a telecommunications carrier, a manufacturer of telecommunications transmission or switching equipment, or a provider of telecommunications support services may impose a civil penalty of up to $10,000 per day for each day in violation after the issuance of the order or after such future date as the court may specify.

(2) *Considerations.* In determining whether to impose a civil penalty and in determining its amount, the court shall take into account—

(A) the nature, circumstances, and extent of the violation;

(B) the violator's ability to pay, the violator's good faith efforts to comply in a timely manner, any effect on the violator's ability to continue to do business, the degree of culpability, and the length of any delay in undertaking efforts to comply; and

(C) such other matters as justice may require.

(d) **Definitions.** As used in this section, the terms defined in section 102 of the Communications Assistance for Law Enforcement Act have the meanings provided, respectively, in such section.

18 U.S.C. § 2701. UNLAWFUL ACCESS TO STORED COMMUNICATIONS

(a) **Offense.** Except as provided in subsection (c) of this section whoever—

(1) intentionally accesses without authorization a facility through which an electronic communication service is provided; or

(2) intentionally exceeds an authorization to access that facility;

and thereby obtains, alters, or prevents authorized access to a wire or electronic communication while it is in electronic storage in such system shall be punished as provided in subsection (b) of this section.

(b) **Punishment.** The punishment for an offense under subsection (a) of this section is—

(1) if the offense is committed for purposes of commercial advantage, malicious destruction or damage, or private commercial gain, or in furtherance of any criminal or tortious act in violation of the Constitution or laws of the United States or any State—

(A) a fine under this title or imprisonment for not more than 5 years, or both, in the case of a first offense under this subparagraph; and

(B) a fine under this title or imprisonment for not more than 10 years, or both, for any subsequent offense under this subparagraph; and

(2) in any other case—

(A) a fine under this title or imprisonment for not more than 1 year or both, in the case of a first offense under this paragraph; and

(B) a fine under this title or imprisonment for not more than 5 years, or both, in the case of an offense under this subparagraph that occurs after a conviction of another offense under this section.

(c) **Exceptions.** Subsection (a) of this section does not apply with respect to conduct authorized—

(1) by the person or entity providing a wire or electronic communications service;

(2) by a user of that service with respect to a communication of or intended for that user; or

(3) in section 2703, 2704 or 2518 of this title.

18 U.S.C. § 2702. VOLUNTARY DISCLOSURE OF CUSTOMER COMMUNICATIONS OR RECORDS

(a) **Prohibitions.** Except as provided in subsection (b) or (c)—

(1) a person or entity providing an electronic communication service to the public shall not knowingly divulge to any person or entity the contents of a communication while in electronic storage by that service; and

(2) a person or entity providing remote computing service to the public shall not knowingly divulge to any person or entity the contents of any communication which is carried or maintained on that service—

(A) on behalf of, and received by means of electronic transmission from (or created by means of computer processing of communications received by means of electronic transmission from), a subscriber or customer of such service;

(B) solely for the purpose of providing storage or computer processing services to such subscriber or customer, if the provider is not authorized to access the contents of any such communications for purposes of providing any services other than storage or computer processing; and

(3) a provider of remote computing service or electronic communication service to the public shall not knowingly divulge a record or other information pertaining to a subscriber to or customer of such service (not including the contents of communications covered by paragraph (1) or (2)) to any governmental entity.

(b) **Exceptions for disclosure of communications.** A provider described in subsection (a) may divulge the contents of a communication—

(1) to an addressee or intended recipient of such communication or an agent of such addressee or intended recipient;

(2) as otherwise authorized in section 2517, 2511(2)(a), or 2703 of this title;

(3) with the lawful consent of the originator or an addressee or intended recipient of such communication, or the subscriber in the case of remote computing service;

(4) to a person employed or authorized or whose facilities are used to forward such communication to its destination;

(5) as may be necessarily incident to the rendition of the service or to the protection of the rights or property of the provider of that service;

(6) to the National Center for Missing and Exploited Children, in connection with a report submitted thereto under section 2258A;

(7) to a law enforcement agency—

(A) if the contents—

(i) were inadvertently obtained by the service provider; and

(ii) appear to pertain to the commission of a crime; or

(8) to a governmental entity, if the provider, in good faith, believes that an emergency involving danger of death or serious physical injury to any person requires disclosure without delay of communications relating to the emergency.

(c) **Exceptions for disclosure of customer records.** A provider described in subsection (a) may divulge a record or other information pertaining to a subscriber to or customer of such service (not including the contents of communications covered by subsection (a)(1) or (a)(2))—

(1) as otherwise authorized in section 2703;

(2) with the lawful consent of the customer or subscriber;

(3) as may be necessarily incident to the rendition of the service or to the protection of the rights or property of the provider of that service;

(4) to a governmental entity, if the provider, in good faith, believes that an emergency involving danger of death or serious physical injury to any person requires disclosure without delay of information relating to the emergency;

(5) to the National Center for Missing and Exploited Children, in connection with a report submitted thereto under section 2258A; or

(6) to any person other than a governmental entity.

(d) **Reporting of emergency disclosures.** On an annual basis, the Attorney General shall submit to the Committee on the Judiciary of the House of Representatives and the Committee on the Judiciary of the Senate a report containing—

(1) the number of accounts from which the Department of Justice has received voluntary disclosures under subsection (b)(8); and

(2) a summary of the basis for disclosure in those instances where—

(A) voluntary disclosures under subsection (b)(8) were made to the Department of Justice; and

(B) the investigation pertaining to those disclosures was closed without the filing of criminal charges.

18 U.S.C. § 2703. REQUIRED DISCLOSURE OF CUSTOMER COMMUNICATIONS OR RECORDS

(a) **Contents of wire or electronic communications in electronic storage.** A governmental entity may require the disclosure by a provider of electronic communication service of the contents of a wire or electronic communication, that is in electronic storage in an electronic communications system for one hundred and eighty days or less, only pursuant to a warrant issued using the procedures described in the Federal Rules of Criminal Procedure by a court with jurisdiction over the offense under investigation or equivalent State warrant. A governmental entity may require the disclosure by a provider of electronic communications services of the contents of a wire or electronic communication that has been in electronic storage in an electronic communications system for more than one hundred and eighty days by the means available under subsection (b) of this section.

(b) **Contents of wire or electronic communications in a remote computing service.**

(1) A governmental entity may require a provider of remote computing service to disclose the contents of any wire or electronic

communication to which this paragraph is made applicable by paragraph (2) of this subsection—

> (A) without required notice to the subscriber or customer, if the governmental entity obtains a warrant issued using the procedures described in the Federal Rules of Criminal Procedure by a court with jurisdiction over the offense under investigation or equivalent State warrant; or

> (B) with prior notice from the governmental entity to the subscriber or customer if the governmental entity—

>> (i) uses an administrative subpoena authorized by a Federal or State statute or a Federal or State grand jury or trial subpoena; or

>> (ii) obtains a court order for such disclosure under subsection (d) of this section;

except that delayed notice may be given pursuant to section 2705 of this title.

(2) Paragraph (1) is applicable with respect to any wire or electronic communication that is held or maintained on that service—

> (A) on behalf of, and received by means of electronic transmission from (or created by means of computer processing of communications received by means of electronic transmission from), a subscriber or customer of such remote computing service; and

> (B) solely for the purpose of providing storage or computer processing services to such subscriber or customer, if the provider is not authorized to access the contents of any such communications for purposes of providing any services other than storage or computer processing.

(c) Records concerning electronic communication service or remote computing service.

(1) A governmental entity may require a provider of electronic communication service or remote computing service to disclose a record or other information pertaining to a subscriber to or customer of such service (not including the contents of communications) only when the governmental entity—

> (A) obtains a warrant issued using the procedures described in the Federal Rules of Criminal Procedure by a court with jurisdiction over the offense under investigation or equivalent State warrant;

> (B) obtains a court order for such disclosure under subsection (d) of this section;

> (C) has the consent of the subscriber or customer to such disclosure;

(D) submits a formal written request relevant to a law enforcement investigation concerning telemarketing fraud for the name, address, and place of business of a subscriber or customer of such provider, which subscriber or customer is engaged in telemarketing (as such term is defined in section 2325 of this title); or

(E) seeks information under paragraph (2).

(2) A provider of electronic communication service or remote computing service shall disclose to a governmental entity the—

(A) name;

(B) address;

(C) local and long distance telephone connection records, or records of session times and durations;

(D) length of service (including start date) and types of service utilized;

(E) telephone or instrument number or other subscriber number or identity, including any temporarily assigned network address; and

(F) means and source of payment for such service (including any credit card or bank account number),

of a subscriber to or customer of such service when the governmental entity uses an administrative subpoena authorized by a Federal or State statute or a Federal or State grand jury or trial subpoena or any means available under paragraph (1).

(3) A governmental entity receiving records or information under this subsection is not required to provide notice to a subscriber or customer.

(d) **Requirements for court order.** A court order for disclosure under subsection (b) or (c) may be issued by any court that is a court of competent jurisdiction and shall issue only if the governmental entity offers specific and articulable facts showing that there are reasonable grounds to believe that the contents of a wire or electronic communication, or the records or other information sought, are relevant and material to an ongoing criminal investigation. In the case of a State governmental authority, such a court order shall not issue if prohibited by the law of such State. A court issuing an order pursuant to this section, on a motion made promptly by the service provider, may quash or modify such order, if the information or records requested are unusually voluminous in nature or compliance with such order otherwise would cause an undue burden on such provider.

(e) **No cause of action against a provider disclosing information under this chapter.** No cause of action shall lie in any court against any provider of wire or electronic communication service, its officers, employees, agents, or other specified persons for providing information, facilities, or assistance in accordance with the terms of a court order, warrant, subpoena, statutory authorization, or certification under this chapter.

(f) **Requirement to preserve evidence.**

(1) *In general.* A provider of wire or electronic communication services or a remote computing service, upon the request of a governmental entity, shall take all necessary steps to preserve records and other evidence in its possession pending the issuance of a court order or other process.

(2) Period of retention. Records referred to in paragraph (1) shall be retained for a period of 90 days, which shall be extended for an additional 90–day period upon a renewed request by the governmental entity.

(g) **Presence of officer not required.** Notwithstanding section 3105 of this title, the presence of an officer shall not be required for service or execution of a search warrant issued in accordance with this chapter requiring disclosure by a provider of electronic communications service or remote computing service of the contents of communications or records or other information pertaining to a subscriber to or customer of such service.

18 U.S.C. § 2704.　BACKUP PRESERVATION

(a) **Backup preservation.**

(1) A governmental entity acting under section 2703(b)(2) may include in its subpoena or court order a requirement that the service provider to whom the request is directed create a backup copy of the contents of the electronic communications sought in order to preserve those communications. Without notifying the subscriber or customer of such subpoena or court order, such service provider shall create such backup copy as soon as practicable consistent with its regular business practices and shall confirm to the governmental entity that such backup copy has been made. Such backup copy shall be created within two business days after receipt by the service provider of the subpoena or court order.

(2) Notice to the subscriber or customer shall be made by the governmental entity within three days after receipt of such confirmation, unless such notice is delayed pursuant to section 2705(a).

(3) The service provider shall not destroy such backup copy until the later of—

(A) the delivery of the information; or

(B) the resolution of any proceedings (including appeals of any proceeding) concerning the government's subpoena or court order.

(4) The service provider shall release such backup copy to the requesting governmental entity no sooner than fourteen days after the governmental entity's notice to the subscriber or customer if such service provider—

(A) has not received notice from the subscriber or customer that the subscriber or customer has challenged the governmental entity's request; and

(B) has not initiated proceedings to challenge the request of the governmental entity.

(5) A governmental entity may seek to require the creation of a backup copy under subsection (a)(1) of this section if in its sole discretion such entity determines that there is reason to believe that notification under section 2703 of this title of the existence of the subpoena or court order may result in destruction of or tampering with evidence. This determination is not subject to challenge by the subscriber or customer or service provider.

(b) **Customer challenges.**

(1) Within fourteen days after notice by the governmental entity to the subscriber or customer under subsection (a)(2) of this section, such subscriber or customer may file a motion to quash such subpoena or vacate such court order, with copies served upon the governmental entity and with written notice of such challenge to the service provider. A motion to vacate a court order shall be filed in the court which issued such order. A motion to quash a subpoena shall be filed in the appropriate United States district court or State court. Such motion or application shall contain an affidavit or sworn statement—

(A) stating that the applicant is a customer or subscriber to the service from which the contents of electronic communications maintained for him have been sought; and

(B) stating the applicant's reasons for believing that the records sought are not relevant to a legitimate law enforcement inquiry or that there has not been substantial compliance with the provisions of this chapter in some other respect.

(2) Service shall be made under this section upon a governmental entity by delivering or mailing by registered or certified mail a copy of the papers to the person, office, or department specified in the notice which the customer has received pursuant to this chapter. For the purposes of this section, the term "delivery" has the meaning given that term in the Federal Rules of Civil Procedure.

(3) If the court finds that the customer has complied with paragraphs (1) and (2) of this subsection, the court shall order the governmental entity to file a sworn response, which may be filed in camera if the governmental entity includes in its response the reasons which make in camera review appropriate. If the court is unable to determine the motion or application on the basis of the parties' initial

allegations and response, the court may conduct such additional proceedings as it deems appropriate. All such proceedings shall be completed and the motion or application decided as soon as practicable after the filing of the governmental entity's response.

(4) If the court finds that the applicant is not the subscriber or customer for whom the communications sought by the governmental entity are maintained, or that there is a reason to believe that the law enforcement inquiry is legitimate and that the communications sought are relevant to that inquiry, it shall deny the motion or application and order such process enforced. If the court finds that the applicant is the subscriber or customer for whom the communications sought by the governmental entity are maintained, and that there is not a reason to believe that the communications sought are relevant to a legitimate law enforcement inquiry, or that there has not been substantial compliance with the provisions of this chapter, it shall order the process quashed.

(5) A court order denying a motion or application under this section shall not be deemed a final order and no interlocutory appeal may be taken therefrom by the customer.

18 U.S.C. § 2705.　Delayed Notice

(a) Delay of notification.

(1) A governmental entity acting under section 2703(b) of this title may—

(A) where a court order is sought, include in the application a request, which the court shall grant, for an order delaying the notification required under section 2703(b) of this title for a period not to exceed ninety days, if the court determines that there is reason to believe that notification of the existence of the court order may have an adverse result described in paragraph (2) of this subsection; or

(B) where an administrative subpoena authorized by a Federal or State statute or a Federal or State grand jury subpoena is obtained, delay the notification required under section 2703(b) of this title for a period not to exceed ninety days upon the execution of a written certification of a supervisory official that there is reason to believe that notification of the existence of the subpoena may have an adverse result described in paragraph (2) of this subsection.

(2) An adverse result for the purposes of paragraph (1) of this subsection is—

(A) endangering the life or physical safety of an individual;

(B) flight from prosecution;

(C) destruction of or tampering with evidence;

(D) intimidation of potential witnesses; or

(E) otherwise seriously jeopardizing an investigation or unduly delaying a trial.

(3) The governmental entity shall maintain a true copy of certification under paragraph (1)(B).

(4) Extensions of the delay of notification provided in section 2703 of up to ninety days each may be granted by the court upon application, or by certification by a governmental entity, but only in accordance with subsection (b) of this section.

(5) Upon expiration of the period of delay of notification under paragraph (1) or (4) of this subsection, the governmental entity shall serve upon, or deliver by registered or first-class mail to, the customer or subscriber a copy of the process or request together with notice that—

(A) states with reasonable specificity the nature of the law enforcement inquiry; and

(B) informs such customer or subscriber—

(i) that information maintained for such customer or subscriber by the service provider named in such process or request was supplied to or requested by that governmental authority and the date on which the supplying or request took place;

(ii) that notification of such customer or subscriber was delayed;

(iii) what governmental entity or court made the certification or determination pursuant to which that delay was made; and

(iv) which provision of this chapter allowed such delay.

(6) As used in this subsection, the term "supervisory official" means the investigative agent in charge or assistant investigative agent in charge or an equivalent of an investigating agency's headquarters or regional office, or the chief prosecuting attorney or the first assistant prosecuting attorney or an equivalent of a prosecuting attorney's headquarters or regional office.

(b) **Preclusion of notice to subject of governmental access.** A governmental entity acting under section 2703, when it is not required to notify the subscriber or customer under section 2703(b)(1), or to the extent that it may delay such notice pursuant to subsection (a) of this section, may apply to a court for an order commanding a provider of electronic communications service or remote computing service to whom a warrant, subpoena, or court order is directed, for such period as the court deems appropriate, not to notify any other person of the existence of the warrant, subpoena, or court order. The court shall enter such an order if it determines that there is reason to believe that notification of the existence of the warrant, subpoena, or court order will result in—

(1) endangering the life or physical safety of an individual;

(2) flight from prosecution;

(3) destruction of or tampering with evidence;

(4) intimidation of potential witnesses; or

(5) otherwise seriously jeopardizing an investigation or unduly delaying a trial.

18 U.S.C. § 2706. COST REIMBURSEMENT

(a) **Payment.** Except as otherwise provided in subsection (c), a governmental entity obtaining the contents of communications, records, or other information under section 2702, 2703, or 2704 of this title shall pay to the person or entity assembling or providing such information a fee for reimbursement for such costs as are reasonably necessary and which have been directly incurred in searching for, assembling, reproducing, or otherwise providing such information. Such reimbursable costs shall include any costs due to necessary disruption of normal operations of any electronic communication service or remote computing service in which such information may be stored.

(b) **Amount.** The amount of the fee provided by subsection (a) shall be as mutually agreed by the governmental entity and the person or entity providing the information, or, in the absence of agreement, shall be as determined by the court which issued the order for production of such information (or the court before which a criminal prosecution relating to such information would be brought, if no court order was issued for production of the information).

(c) **Exception.** The requirement of subsection (a) of this section does not apply with respect to records or other information maintained by a communications common carrier that relate to telephone toll records and telephone listings obtained under section 2703 of this title. The court may, however, order a payment as described in subsection (a) if the court determines the information required is unusually voluminous in nature or otherwise caused an undue burden on the provider.

18 U.S.C. § 2707. CIVIL ACTION

(a) **Cause of action.** Except as provided in section 2703(e), any provider of electronic communication service, subscriber, or other person aggrieved by any violation of this chapter in which the conduct constituting the violation is engaged in with a knowing or intentional state of mind may, in a civil action, recover from the person or entity, other than the United States, which engaged in that violation such relief as may be appropriate.

(b) **Relief.** In a civil action under this section, appropriate relief includes—

(1) such preliminary and other equitable or declaratory relief as may be appropriate;

(2) damages under subsection (c); and

(3) a reasonable attorney's fee and other litigation costs reasonably incurred.

(c) **Damages.** The court may assess as damages in a civil action under this section the sum of the actual damages suffered by the plaintiff and any profits made by the violator as a result of the violation, but in no case shall a person entitled to recover receive less than the sum of $1,000. If the violation is willful or intentional, the court may assess punitive damages. In the case of a successful action to enforce liability under this section, the court may assess the costs of the action, together with reasonable attorney fees determined by the court.

(d) **Administrative discipline.** If a court or appropriate department or agency determines that the United States or any of its departments or agencies has violated any provision of this chapter, and the court or appropriate department or agency finds that the circumstances surrounding the violation raise serious questions about whether or not an officer or employee of the United States acted willfully or intentionally with respect to the violation, the department or agency shall, upon receipt of a true and correct copy of the decision and findings of the court or appropriate department or agency promptly initiate a proceeding to determine whether disciplinary action against the officer or employee is warranted. If the head of the department or agency involved determines that disciplinary action is not warranted, he or she shall notify the Inspector General with jurisdiction over the department or agency concerned and shall provide the Inspector General with the reasons for such determination.

(e) **Defense.** A good faith reliance on—

(1) a court warrant or order, a grand jury subpoena, a legislative authorization, or a statutory authorization (including a request of a governmental entity under section 2703(f) of this title);

(2) a request of an investigative or law enforcement officer under section 2518(7) of this title; or

(3) a good faith determination that section 2511(3) of this title permitted the conduct complained of;

is a complete defense to any civil or criminal action brought under this chapter or any other law.

(f) **Limitation.** A civil action under this section may not be commenced later than two years after the date upon which the claimant first discovered or had a reasonable opportunity to discover the violation.

(g) **Improper disclosure.** Any willful disclosure of a 'record', as that term is defined in section 552a(a) of title 5, United States Code, obtained by an investigative or law enforcement officer, or a governmental entity, pursuant to section 2703 of this title, or from a device installed pursuant to section 3123 or 3125 of this title, that is not a disclosure made in the proper performance of the official functions of the officer or governmental entity making the disclosure, is a violation of this chapter. This provision shall not apply to information previously lawfully disclosed (prior to the commencement of any civil or administrative proceeding under this chapter) to the public by a Federal, State, or local governmental entity or by the plaintiff in a civil action under this chapter.

18 U.S.C. § 2708. Exclusivity of Remedies

The remedies and sanctions described in this chapter are the only judicial remedies and sanctions for nonconstitutional violations of this chapter.

18 U.S.C. § 2711. Definitions for Chapter

As used in this chapter—

(1) the terms defined in section 2510 of this title have, respectively, the definitions given such terms in that section;

(2) the term "remote computing service" means the provision to the public of computer storage or processing services by means of an electronic communications system;

(3) the term "court of competent jurisdiction" has the meaning assigned by section 3127, and includes any Federal court within that definition, without geographic limitation; and

(4) the term "governmental entity" means a department or agency of the United States or any State or political subdivision thereof.

18 U.S.C. § 3121. General Prohibition on Pen Register and Trap and Trace Device Use; Exception

(a) **In general.** Except as provided in this section, no person may install or use a pen register or a trap and trace device without first obtaining a court order under section 3123 of this title or under the Foreign Intelligence Surveillance Act of 1978 (50 U.S.C. 1801 et seq.).

(b) **Exception.** The prohibition of subsection (a) does not apply with respect to the use of a pen register or a trap and trace device by a provider of electronic or wire communication service—

(1) relating to the operation, maintenance, and testing of a wire or electronic communication service or to the protection of the rights or property of such provider, or to the protection of users of that service from abuse of service or unlawful use of service; or

(2) to record the fact that a wire or electronic communication was initiated or completed in order to protect such provider, another provider furnishing service toward the completion of the wire communication, or a user of that service, from fraudulent, unlawful or abusive use of service; or

(3) where the consent of the user of that service has been obtained.

(c) **Limitation.** A government agency authorized to install and use a pen register or trap and trace device under this chapter or under State law shall use technology reasonably available to it that restricts the recording or decoding of electronic or other impulses to the dialing, routing, addressing, and signaling information utilized in the processing and transmitting of wire or electronic communications so as not to include the contents of any wire or electronic communications.

(d) **Penalty.** Whoever knowingly violates subsection (a) shall be fined under this title or imprisoned not more than one year, or both.

18 U.S.C. § 3122. APPLICATION FOR AN ORDER FOR A PEN REGISTER OR A TRAP AND TRACE DEVICE

(a) **Application.**

(1) An attorney for the Government may make application for an order or an extension of an order under section 3123 of this title authorizing or approving the installation and use of a pen register or a trap and trace device under this chapter, in writing under oath or equivalent affirmation, to a court of competent jurisdiction.

(2) Unless prohibited by State law, a State investigative or law enforcement officer may make application for an order or an extension of an order under section 3123 of this title authorizing or approving the installation and use of a pen register or a trap and trace device under this chapter, in writing under oath or equivalent affirmation, to a court of competent jurisdiction of such State.

(b) **Contents of application.** An application under subsection (a) of this section shall include—

(1) the identity of the attorney for the Government or the State law enforcement or investigative officer making the application and the identity of the law enforcement agency conducting the investigation; and

(2) a certification by the applicant that the information likely to be obtained is relevant to an ongoing criminal investigation being conducted by that agency.

18 U.S.C. § 3123. ISSUANCE OF AN ORDER FOR A PEN REGISTER OR A TRAP AND TRACE DEVICE

(a) **In general.**

(1) *Attorney for the Government.* Upon an application made under section 3122(a)(1), the court shall enter an ex parte order authorizing the installation and use of a pen register or trap and trace device anywhere within the United States, if the court finds that the attorney for the Government has certified to the court that the information likely to be obtained by such installation and use is

relevant to an ongoing criminal investigation. The order, upon service of that order, shall apply to any person or entity providing wire or electronic communication service in the United States whose assistance may facilitate the execution of the order. Whenever such an order is served on any person or entity not specifically named in the order, upon request of such person or entity, the attorney for the Government or law enforcement or investigative officer that is serving the order shall provide written or electronic certification that the order applies to the person or entity being served.

(2) *State investigative or law enforcement officer.* Upon an application made under section 3122(a)(2), the court shall enter an ex parte order authorizing the installation and use of a pen register or trap and trace device within the jurisdiction of the court, if the court finds that the State law enforcement or investigative officer has certified to the court that the information likely to be obtained by such installation and use is relevant to an ongoing criminal investigation.

(3) (A) Where the law enforcement agency implementing an ex parte order under this subsection seeks to do so by installing and using its own pen register or trap and trace device on a packet-switched data network of a provider of electronic communication service to the public, the agency shall ensure that a record will be maintained which will identify—

> (i) any officer or officers who installed the device and any officer or officers who accessed the device to obtain information from the network;

> (ii) the date and time the device was installed, the date and time the device was uninstalled, and the date, time, and duration of each time the device is accessed to obtain information;

> (iii) the configuration of the device at the time of its installation and any subsequent modification thereof; and

> (iv) any information which has been collected by the device.

To the extent that the pen register or trap and trace device can be set automatically to record this information electronically, the record shall be maintained electronically throughout the installation and use of such device.

> (B) The record maintained under subparagraph (A) shall be provided ex parte and under seal to the court which entered the ex parte order authorizing the installation and use of the device within 30 days after termination of the order (including any extensions thereof).

(b) **Contents of order.** An order issued under this section—

(1) shall specify—

    (A) the identity, if known, of the person to whom is leased or in whose name is listed the telephone line or other facility to which the pen register or trap and trace device is to be attached or applied;

    (B) the identity, if known, of the person who is the subject of the criminal investigation;

    (C) the attributes of the communications to which the order applies, including the number or other identifier and, if known, the location of the telephone line or other facility to which the pen register or trap and trace device is to be attached or applied, and, in the case of an order authorizing installation and use of a trap and trace device under subsection (a)(2), the geographic limits of the order; and''.

    (D) a statement of the offense to which the information likely to be obtained by the pen register or trap and trace device relates; and

(2) shall direct, upon the request of the applicant, the furnishing of information, facilities, and technical assistance necessary to accomplish the installation of the pen register or trap and trace device under section 3124 of this title.

(c) **Time period and extensions.**

    (1) An order issued under this section shall authorize the installation and use of a pen register or a trap and trace device for a period not to exceed sixty days.

    (2) Extensions of such an order may be granted, but only upon an application for an order under section 3122 of this title and upon the judicial finding required by subsection (a) of this section. The period of extension shall be for a period not to exceed sixty days.

(d) **Nondisclosure of existence of pen register or a trap and trace device.** An order authorizing or approving the installation and use of a pen register or a trap and trace device shall direct that

    (1) the order be sealed until otherwise ordered by the court; and

    (2) the person owning or leasing the line or other facility to which the pen register or a trap and trace device is attached, or applied, or who is obligated by the order to provide assistance to the applicant, not disclose the existence of the pen register or trap and trace device or the existence of the investigation to the listed subscriber, or to any other person, unless or until otherwise ordered by the court.

18 U.S.C. § 3124. ASSISTANCE IN INSTALLATION AND USE OF A PEN REGISTER OR A TRAP AND TRACE DEVICE

(a) **Pen registers.** Upon the request of an attorney for the Government or an officer of a law enforcement agency authorized to install and use a pen register under this chapter, a provider of wire or electronic communication service, landlord, custodian, or other person shall furnish such investigative or law enforcement officer forthwith all information, facilities, and technical assistance necessary to accomplish the installation of the pen register unobtrusively and with a minimum of interference with the services that the person so ordered by the court accords the party with respect to whom the installation and use is to take place, if such assistance is directed by a court order as provided in section 3123(b)(2) of this title.

(b) **Trap and trace device.** Upon the request of an attorney for the Government or an officer of a law enforcement agency authorized to receive the results of a trap and trace device under this chapter, a provider of a wire or electronic communication service, landlord, custodian, or other person shall install such device forthwith on the appropriate line or other facility and shall furnish such investigative or law enforcement officer all additional information, facilities and technical assistance including installation and operation of the device unobtrusively and with a minimum of interference with the services that the person so ordered by the court accords the party with respect to whom the installation and use is to take place, if such installation and assistance is directed by a court order as provided in section 3123(b)(2) of this title. Unless otherwise ordered by the court, the results of the trap and trace device shall be furnished, pursuant to section 3123(b) or section 3125 of this title, to the officer of a law enforcement agency, designated in the court order, at reasonable intervals during regular business hours for the duration of the order.

(c) **Compensation.** A provider of a wire or electronic communication service, landlord, custodian, or other person who furnishes facilities or technical assistance pursuant to this section shall be reasonably compensated for such reasonable expenses incurred in providing such facilities and assistance.

(d) **No cause of action against a provider disclosing information under this chapter.** No cause of action shall lie in any court against any provider of a wire or electronic communication service, its officers, employees, agents, or other specified persons for providing information, facilities, or assistance in accordance with a court order under this chapter or request pursuant to section 3125 of this title.

(e) **Defense.** A good faith reliance on a court order under this chapter, a request pursuant to section 3125 of this title, a legislative authorization, or a statutory authorization is a complete defense against any civil or criminal action brought under this chapter or any other law.

(f) **Communications assistance enforcement orders.** Pursuant to section 2522, an order may be issued to enforce the assistance capability and capacity requirements under the Communications Assistance for Law Enforcement Act.

18 U.S.C. § 3125. EMERGENCY PEN REGISTER AND TRAP AND TRACE DEVICE INSTALLATION

(a) Notwithstanding any other provision of this chapter, any investigative or law enforcement officer, specially designated by the Attorney General, the Deputy Attorney General, the Associate Attorney General, any Assistant Attorney General, any acting Assistant Attorney General, or any Deputy Assistant Attorney General, or by the principal prosecuting attorney of any State or subdivision thereof acting pursuant to a statute of that State, who reasonably determines that—

(1) an emergency situation exists that involves—

(A) immediate danger of death or serious bodily injury to any person;

(B) conspiratorial activities characteristic of organized crime;

(C) an immediate threat to a national security interest; or

(D) an ongoing attack on a protected computer (as defined in section 1030) that constitutes a crime punishable by a term of imprisonment greater than one year;

that requires the installation and use of a pen register or a trap and trace device before an order authorizing such installation and use can, with due diligence, be obtained, and

(2) there are grounds upon which an order could be entered under this chapter to authorize such installation and use;

may have installed and use a pen register or trap and trace device if, within forty-eight hours after the installation has occurred, or begins to occur, an order approving the installation or use is issued in accordance with section 3123 of this title.

(b) In the absence of an authorizing order, such use shall immediately terminate when the information sought is obtained, when the application for the order is denied or when forty-eight hours have lapsed since the installation of the pen register or trap and trace device, whichever is earlier.

(c) The knowing installation or use by any investigative or law enforcement officer of a pen register or trap and trace device pursuant to subsection (a) without application for the authorizing order within forty-eight hours of the installation shall constitute a violation of this chapter.

(d) A provider of a wire or electronic service, landlord, custodian, or other person who furnished facilities or technical assistance pursuant to this section shall be reasonably compensated for such reasonable expenses incurred in providing such facilities and assistance.

18 U.S.C. § 3126. REPORTS CONCERNING PEN REGISTERS AND TRAP AND TRACE DEVICES

The Attorney General shall annually report to Congress on the number of pen register orders and orders for trap and trace devices applied for by law enforcement agencies of the Department of Justice, which report shall include information concerning—

(1) the period of interceptions authorized by the order, and the number and duration of any extensions of the order;

(2) the offense specified in the order or application, or extension of an order;

(3) the number of investigations involved;

(4) the number and nature of the facilities affected; and

(5) the identity, including district, of the applying investigative or law enforcement agency making the application and the person authorizing the order.

18 U.S.C. § 3127. DEFINITIONS FOR CHAPTER

As used in this chapter—

(1) the terms "wire communication", "electronic communication", "electronic communication service", and "contents" have the meanings set forth for such terms in section 2510 of this title;

(2) the term "court of competent jurisdiction" means—

(A) any district court of the United States (including a magistrate judge of such a court) or any United States court of appeals having jurisdiction over the offense being investigated; or

(B) a court of general criminal jurisdiction of a State authorized by the law of that State to enter orders authorizing the use of a pen register or a trap and trace device;

(3) the term "pen register" means a device or process which records or decodes dialing, routing, addressing, or signaling information transmitted by an instrument or facility from which a wire or electronic communication is transmitted, provided, however, that such information shall not include the contents of any communication, but such term does not include any device or process used by a provider or customer of a wire or electronic communication service for billing, or recording as an incident to billing, for communications services provided by such provider or any device or process used by a provider or customer of a wire communication service for cost accounting or other like purposes in the ordinary course of its business;

(4) the term "trap and trace device" means a device or process which captures the incoming electronic or other impulses which identify the originating number or other dialing, routing, addressing, and signaling information reasonably likely to identify the source of a wire or electronic communication, provided, however, that such information shall not include the contents of any communication;

(5) the term "attorney for the Government" has the meaning given such term for the purposes of the Federal Rules of Criminal Procedure; and

(6) the term "State" means a State, the District of Columbia, Puerto Rico, and any other possession or territory of the United States.

47 U.S.C. § 223. OBSCENE OR HARASSING TELEPHONE CALLS IN THE DISTRICT OF COLUMBIA OR IN INTERSTATE OR FOREIGN COMMUNICATIONS

(a) **Prohibited acts generally.** Whoever—

(1) in interstate or foreign communications—

(A) by means of a telecommunications device knowingly—

(i) makes, creates, or solicits, and

(ii) initiates the transmission of,

any comment, request, suggestion, proposal, image, or other communication which is obscene or child pornography, with intent to annoy, abuse, threaten, or harass another person;

(B) by means of a telecommunications device knowingly—

(i) makes, creates, or solicits, and

(ii) initiates the transmission of,

any comment, request, suggestion, proposal, image, or other communication which is obscene or child pornography, knowing that the recipient of the communication is under 18 years of age, regardless of whether the maker of such communication placed the call or initiated the communication;

(C) makes a telephone call or utilizes a telecommunications device, whether or not conversation or communication ensues, without disclosing his identity and with intent to annoy, abuse, threaten, or harass any person at the called number or who receives the communications;

(D) makes or causes the telephone of another repeatedly or continuously to ring, with intent to harass any person at the called number; or

(E) makes repeated telephone calls or repeatedly initiates communication with a telecommunications device, during which conversation or communication ensues, solely to harass any person at the called number or who receives the communication; or

(2) knowingly permits any telecommunications facility under his control to be used for any activity prohibited by paragraph (1) with the intent that it be used for such activity,

shall be fined under Title 18 or imprisoned not more than two years, or both.

(b) **Prohibited acts for commercial purposes; defense to prosecution.**

(1) Whoever knowingly—

(A) within the United States, by means of telephone, makes (directly or by recording device) any obscene communication for commercial purposes to any person, regardless of whether the maker of such communication placed the call; or

(B) permits any telephone facility under such person's control to be used for an activity prohibited by subparagraph (A),

shall be fined in accordance with Title 18 or imprisoned not more than two years, or both.

(2) Whoever knowingly—

(A) within the United States, by means of telephone, makes (directly or by recording device) any indecent communication for commercial purposes which is available to any person under 18 years of age or to any other person without that person's consent, regardless of whether the maker of such communication placed the call; or

(B) permits any telephone facility under such person's control to be used for an activity prohibited by subparagraph (A), shall be fined not more than $50,000 or imprisoned not more than six months, or both.

(3) It is a defense to prosecution under paragraph (2) of this subsection that the defendant restricted access to the prohibited communication to persons 18 years of age or older in accordance with subsection (c) of this section and with such procedures as the Commission may prescribe by regulation.

(4) In addition to the penalties under paragraph (1), whoever, within the United States, intentionally violates paragraph (1) or (2) shall be subject to a fine of not more than $50,000 for each violation. For purposes of this paragraph, each day of violation shall constitute a separate violation.

(5) (A) In addition to the penalties under paragraphs (1), (2), and (5), whoever, within the United States, violates paragraph (1) or (2) shall be subject to a civil fine of not more than $50,000 for each violation. For purposes of this paragraph, each day of violation shall constitute a separate violation.

(B) A fine under this paragraph may be assessed either—

(i) by a court, pursuant to civil action by the Commission or any attorney employed by the Commission who is designated by the Commission for such purposes, or

(ii) by the Commission after appropriate administrative proceedings.

(6) The Attorney General may bring a suit in the appropriate district court of the United States to enjoin any act or practice which violates paragraph (1) or (2). An injunction may be granted in accordance with the Federal Rules of Civil Procedure.

(c) **Restriction on access to subscribers by common carriers; judicial remedies respecting restrictions.**

(1) A common carrier within the District of Columbia or within any State, or in interstate or foreign commerce, shall not, to the extent technically feasible, provide access to a communication specified in subsection (b) of this section from the telephone of any subscriber who has not previously requested in writing the carrier to provide access to such communication if the carrier collects from subscribers an identifiable charge for such communication that the carrier remits, in whole or in part, to the provider of such communication.

(2) Except as provided in paragraph (3), no cause of action may be brought in any court or administrative agency against any common carrier, or any of its affiliates, including their officers, directors, employees, agents, or authorized representatives on account of—

(A) any action which the carrier demonstrates was taken in good faith to restrict access pursuant to paragraph (1) of this subsection; or

(B) any access permitted—

(i) in good faith reliance upon the lack of any representation by a provider of communications that communications provided by that provider are communications specified in subsection (b) of this section, or

(ii) because a specific representation by the provider did not allow the carrier, acting in good faith, a sufficient period to restrict access to communications described in subsection (b) of this section.

(3) Notwithstanding paragraph (2) of this subsection, a provider of communications services to which subscribers are denied access pursuant to paragraph (1) of this subsection may bring an action for a declaratory judgment or similar action in a court. Any such action shall be limited to the question of whether the communications which the provider seeks to provide fall within the category of communications to which the carrier will provide access only to subscribers who have previously requested such access.

(d) **Sending or displaying offensive material to persons under 18.** Whoever—

(1) in interstate or foreign communications knowingly—

(A) uses an interactive computer service to send to a specific person or persons under 18 years of age, or

(B) uses any interactive computer service to display in a manner available to a person under 18 years of age,

any comment, request, suggestion, proposal, image, or other communication that, is obscene or child pornography, regardless of whether the user of such service placed the call or initiated the communication; or

(2) knowingly permits any telecommunications facility under such person's control to be used for an activity prohibited by paragraph (1) with the intent that it be used for such activity,

shall be fined under Title 18 or imprisoned not more than two years, or both.

(e) **Defenses.** In addition to any other defenses available by law:

(1) No person shall be held to have violated subsection (a) or (d) of this section solely for providing access or connection to or from a facility, system, or network not under that person's control, including transmission, downloading, intermediate storage, access software, or other related capabilities that are incidental to providing such access or connection that does not include the creation of the content of the communication.

(2) The defenses provided by paragraph (1) of this subsection shall not be applicable to a person who is a conspirator with an entity actively involved in the creation or knowing distribution of communications that violate this section, or who knowingly advertises the availability of such communications.

(3) The defenses provided in paragraph (1) of this subsection shall not be applicable to a person who provides access or connection to a facility, system, or network engaged in the violation of this section that is owned or controlled by such person.

(4) No employer shall be held liable under this section for the actions of an employee or agent unless the employee's or agent's conduct is within the scope of his or her employment or agency and the employer (A) having knowledge of such conduct, authorizes or ratifies such conduct, or (B) recklessly disregards such conduct.

(5) It is a defense to a prosecution under subsection (a)(1)(B) or (d) of this section, or under subsection (a)(2) of this section with respect to the use of a facility for an activity under subsection (a)(1)(B) of this section that a person—

(A) has taken, in good faith, reasonable, effective, and appropriate actions under the circumstances to restrict or prevent access by minors to a communication specified in such subsections, which may involve any appropriate measures to restrict minors from such communications, including any method which is feasible under available technology; or

(B) has restricted access to such communication by requiring use of a verified credit card, debit account, adult access code, or adult personal identification number.

(6) The Commission may describe measures which are reasonable, effective, and appropriate to restrict access to prohibited commu-

nications under subsection (d) of this section. Nothing in this section authorizes the Commission to enforce, or is intended to provide the Commission with the authority to approve, sanction, or permit, the use of such measures. The Commission shall have no enforcement authority over the failure to utilize such measures. The Commission shall not endorse specific products relating to such measures. The use of such measures shall be admitted as evidence of good faith efforts for purposes of paragraph (5) in any action arising under subsection (d) of this section. Nothing in this section shall be construed to treat interactive computer services as common carriers or telecommunications carriers.

(f) **Violations of law required; commercial entities, nonprofit libraries, or institutions of higher education.**

(1) No cause of action may be brought in any court or administrative agency against any person on account of any activity that is not in violation of any law punishable by criminal or civil penalty, and that the person has taken in good faith to implement a defense authorized under this section or otherwise to restrict or prevent the transmission of, or access to, a communication specified in this section.

(2) No State or local government may impose any liability for commercial activities or actions by commercial entities, nonprofit libraries, or institutions of higher education in connection with an activity or action described in subsection (a)(2) or (d) of this section that is inconsistent with the treatment of those activities or actions under this section: *Provided, however,* That nothing herein shall preclude any State or local government from enacting and enforcing complementary oversight, liability, and regulatory systems, procedures, and requirements, so long as such systems, procedures, and requirements govern only intrastate services and do not result in the imposition of inconsistent rights, duties or obligations on the provision of interstate services. Nothing in this subsection shall preclude any State or local government from governing conduct not covered by this section.

(g) **Application and enforcement of other Federal law.** Nothing in subsection (a), (d), (e), or (f) of this section or in the defenses to prosecution under subsection (a) or (d) of this section shall be construed to affect or limit the application or enforcement of any other Federal law.

(h) **Definitions.** For purposes of this section—

(1) The use of the term "telecommunications device" in this section—

(A) shall not impose new obligations on broadcasting station licensees and cable operators covered by obscenity and indecency provisions elsewhere in this chapter;

(B) does not include an interactive computer service; and

(C) in the case of subparagraph (C) of subsection (a)(1), includes any device or software that can be used to originate telecommunications or other types of communications that are transmitted, in whole or in part, by the Internet (as such term is defined in section 1104 of the Internet Tax Freedom Act (47 U.S.C. 151 note)).

(2) The term "interactive computer service" has the meaning provided in section 230(f)(2) of this title.

(3) The term "access software" means software (including client or server software) or enabling tools that do not create or provide the content of the communication but that allow a user to do any one or more of the following:

(A) filter, screen, allow, or disallow content;

(B) pick, choose, analyze, or digest content; or

(C) transmit, receive, display, forward, cache, search, subset, organize, reorganize, or translate content.

(4) The term "institution of higher education" has the meaning provided in section 1001 of Title 20.

(5) The term "library" means a library eligible for participation in State-based plans for funds under title III of the Library Services and Construction Act (20 U.S.C. 355e et seq.).

FEDERAL RULE OF CRIMINAL PROCEDURE 41

SEARCH AND SEIZURE

(a) **Scope and Definitions.**

(1) *Scope.* This rule does not modify any statute regulating search or seizure, or the issuance and execution of a search warrant in special circumstances.

(2) *Definitions.* The following definitions apply under this rule:

(A) "Property" includes documents, books, papers, any other tangible objects, and information.

(B) "Daytime" means the hours between 6:00 a.m. and 10:00 p.m. according to local time.

(C) "Federal law enforcement officer" means a government agent (other than an attorney for the government) who is engaged in enforcing the criminal laws and is within any category of officers authorized by the Attorney General to request a search warrant.

(D) "Domestic terrorism" and "international terrorism" have the meanings set out in 18 U.S.C. § 2331.

(E) "Tracking device" has the meaning set out in 18 U.S.C. § 3117(b).

(b) **Authority to Issue a Warrant.** At the request of a federal law enforcement officer or an attorney for the government:

(1) a magistrate judge with authority in the district—or if none is reasonably available, a judge of a state court of record in the district—has authority to issue a warrant to search for and seize a person or property located within the district;

(2) a magistrate judge with authority in the district has authority to issue a warrant for a person or property outside the district if the person or property is located within the district when the warrant is issued but might move or be moved outside the district before the warrant is executed;

(3) a magistrate judge—in an investigation of domestic terrorism or international terrorism—with authority in any district in which activities related to the terrorism may have occurred has authority to issue a warrant for a person or property within or outside that district;

(4) a magistrate judge with authority in the district has authority to issue a warrant to install within the district a tracking device; the warrant may authorize use of the device to track the movement of a person or property located within the district, outside the district, or both; and

(5) a magistrate judge having authority in any district where activities related to the crime may have occurred, or in the District of Columbia, may issue a warrant for property that is located outside the jurisdiction of any state or district, but within any of the following:

(A) a United States territory, possession, or commonwealth;

(B) the premises—no matter who owns them—of a United States diplomatic or consular mission in a foreign state, including any appurtenant building, part of a building, or land used for the mission's purposes; or

(C) a residence and any appurtenant land owned or leased by the United States and used by United States personnel assigned to a United States diplomatic or consular mission in a foreign state.

(c) **Persons or Property Subject to Search or Seizure.** A warrant may be issued for any of the following:

(1) evidence of a crime;

(2) contraband, fruits of crime, or other items illegally possessed;

(3) property designed for use, intended for use, or used in committing a crime; or

(4) a person to be arrested or a person who is unlawfully restrained.

(d) **Obtaining a Warrant.**

(1) *In General.* After receiving an affidavit or other information, a magistrate judge—or if authorized by Rule 41(b), a judge of a state court of record—must issue the warrant if there is probable cause to search for and seize a person or property or to install and use a tracking device.

(2) *Requesting a Warrant in the Presence of a Judge.*

(A) *Warrant on an Affidavit.* When a federal law enforcement officer or an attorney for the government presents an affidavit in support of a warrant, the judge may require the affiant to appear personally and may examine under oath the affiant and any witness the affiant produces.

(B) *Warrant on Sworn Testimony.* The judge may wholly or partially dispense with a written affidavit and base a warrant on sworn testimony if doing so is reasonable under the circumstances.

(C) *Recording Testimony.* Testimony taken in support of a warrant must be recorded by a court reporter or by a suitable recording device, and the judge must file the transcript or recording with the clerk, along with any affidavit.

(3) *Requesting a Warrant by Telephonic or Other Means.*

(A) *In General.* A magistrate judge may issue a warrant based on information communicated by telephone or other reliable electronic means.

(B) *Recording Testimony.* Upon learning that an applicant is requesting a warrant under Rule 41(d)(3)(A), a magistrate judge must:

(i) place under oath the applicant and any person on whose testimony the application is based; and

(ii) make a verbatim record of the conversation with a suitable recording device, if available, or by a court reporter, or in writing.

(C) *Certifying Testimony.* The magistrate judge must have any recording or court reporter's notes transcribed, certify the transcription's accuracy, and file a copy of the record and the transcription with the clerk. Any written verbatim record must be signed by the magistrate judge and filed with the clerk.

(D) *Suppression Limited.* Absent a finding of bad faith, evidence obtained from a warrant issued under Rule 41(d)(3)(A) is not subject to suppression on the ground that issuing the warrant in that manner was unreasonable under the circumstances.

(e) **Issuing the Warrant.**

(1) *In General.* The magistrate judge or a judge of a state court of record must issue the warrant to an officer authorized to execute it.

(2) *Contents of the Warrant.*

(A) *Warrant to Search for and Seize a Person or Property.* Except for a tracking-device warrant, the warrant must identify the person or property to be searched, identify any person or property to be seized, and designate the magistrate judge to whom it must be returned. The warrant must command the officer to:

    (i) execute the warrant within a specified time no longer than 14 days;

    (ii) execute the warrant during the daytime, unless the judge for good cause expressly authorizes execution at another time; and

    (iii) return the warrant to the magistrate judge designated in the warrant.

(B) *Warrant Seeking Electronically Stored Information.* A warrant under Rule 41(e)(2)(A) may authorize the seizure of electronic storage media or the seizure or copying of electronically stored information. Unless otherwise specified, the warrant authorizes a later review of the media or information consistent with the warrant. The time for executing the warrant in Rule 41(e)(2)(A) and (f)(1)(A) refers to the seizure or on-site copying of the media or information, and not to any later off-site copying or review.

(C) *Warrant for a Tracking Device.* A tracking-device warrant must identify the person or property to be tracked, designate the magistrate judge to whom it must be returned, and specify a reasonable length of time that the device may be used. The time must not exceed 45 days from the date the warrant was issued. The court may, for good cause, grant one or more extensions for a reasonable period not to exceed 45 days each. The warrant must command the officer to:

    (i) complete any installation authorized by the warrant within a specified time no longer than 10 calendar days;

    (ii) perform any installation authorized by the warrant during the daytime, unless the judge for good cause expressly authorizes installation at another time; and

    (iii) return the warrant to the judge designated in the warrant.

(3) *Warrant by Telephonic or Other Means.* If a magistrate judge decides to proceed under Rule 41(d)(3)(A), the following additional procedures apply:

(A) *Preparing a Proposed Duplicate Original Warrant.* The applicant must prepare a "proposed duplicate original warrant" and must read or otherwise transmit the contents of that document verbatim to the magistrate judge.

(B) *Preparing an Original Warrant.* If the applicant reads the contents of the proposed duplicate original warrant, the magistrate judge must enter those contents into an original warrant. If the applicant transmits the contents by reliable electronic means, that transmission may serve as the original warrant.

(C) *Modification.* The magistrate judge may modify the original warrant. The judge must transmit any modified warrant to the applicant by reliable electronic means under Rule 41(e)(3)(D) or direct the applicant to modify the proposed duplicate original warrant accordingly.

(D) *Signing the Warrant.* Upon determining to issue the warrant, the magistrate judge must immediately sign the original warrant, enter on its face the exact date and time it is issued, and transmit it by reliable electronic means to the applicant or direct the applicant to sign the judge's name on the duplicate original warrant.

(f) **Executing and Returning the Warrant.**

(1) *Warrant to Search for and Seize a Person or Property.*

(A) *Noting the Time.* The officer executing the warrant must enter on it the exact date and time it was executed.

(B) *Inventory.* An officer present during the execution of the warrant must prepare and verify an inventory of any property seized. The officer must do so in the presence of another officer and the person from whom, or from whose premises, the property was taken. If either one is not present, the officer must prepare and verify the inventory in the presence of at least one other credible person. In a case involving the seizure of electronic storage media or the seizure or copying of electronically stored information, the inventory may be limited to describing the physical storage media that were seized or copied. The officer may retain a copy of the electronically stored information that was seized or copied.

(C) *Receipt.* The officer executing the warrant must give a copy of the warrant and a receipt for the property taken to the person from whom, or from whose premises, the property was taken or leave a copy of the warrant and receipt at the place where the officer took the property.

(D) *Return.* The officer executing the warrant must promptly return it—together with a copy of the inventory—to the magistrate judge designated on the warrant. The judge must, on request, give a copy of the inventory to the person from whom, or from whose premises, the property was taken and to the applicant for the warrant.

(2) *Warrant for a Tracking Device.*

(A) *Noting the Time.* The officer executing a tracking-device warrant must enter on it the exact date and time the device was installed and the period during which it was used.

(B) *Return.* Within 10 calendar days after the use of the tracking device has ended, the officer executing the warrant must return it to the judge designated in the warrant.

(C) *Service.* Within 10 calendar days after the use of the tracking device has ended, the officer executing a tracking-device warrant must serve a copy of the warrant on the person who was tracked or whose property was tracked. Service may be accomplished by delivering a copy to the person who, or whose property, was tracked; or by leaving a copy at the person's residence or usual place of abode with an individual of suitable age and discretion who resides at that location and by mailing a copy to the person's last known address. Upon request of the government, the judge may delay notice as provided in Rule 41(f)(3).

(3) *Delayed Notice.* Upon the government's request, a magistrate judge—or if authorized by Rule 41(b), a judge of a state court of record—may delay any notice required by this rule if the delay is authorized by statute.

(g) **Motion to Return Property.** A person aggrieved by an unlawful search and seizure of property or by the deprivation of property may move for the property's return. The motion must be filed in the district where the property was seized. The court must receive evidence on any factual issue necessary to decide the motion. If it grants the motion, the court must return the property to the movant, but may impose reasonable conditions to protect access to the property and its use in later proceedings.

(h) **Motion to Suppress.** A defendant may move to suppress evidence in the court where the trial will occur, as Rule 12 provides.

(i) **Forwarding Papers to the Clerk.** The magistrate judge to whom the warrant is returned must attach to the warrant a copy of the return, of the inventory, and of all other related papers and must deliver them to the clerk in the district where the property was seized.

INDEX

References are to Pages

†